The History of Irish Tennis

Tom Higgins (b. Longford 6th February 1948) was educated at St. Michael's National School, Longford, Cistercian College, Roscrea, and Terenure College, Dublin. He qualified as a civil engineer at University College, Galway where he received his master's degree in the field of water pollution control. He is a Fellow of the Institution of Engineers of Ireland and the Chartered Institution of Water and Environmental Management. He now lectures at the Institute of Technology, Sligo.

His initial interest in tennis, at the age of about 8, was at the nearby County Longford Lawn Tennis Club where his father, sister and six brothers also played. He was later a member of Glasnevin LTC, a founding member of Ashbourne TC and Sligo TC, and honorary life president of the latter. He has been involved in several sports as a player, administrator and coach. He is a former president of Ashbourne Rugby Football Club, and of the Connacht Branch of the Badminton Union of Ireland. Apart from tennis, his particular sporting interests are rugby, athletics, badminton and golf. Other interests include travel, photography, chess, family history, art and philately.

Tom met his wife Ursula (Broderick) at a tennis tournament in Longford. They now have three grown up daughters who have all played tennis and badminton. He has written many articles on engineering and sport matters over the years. This is his first book and has taken over seven years of research and writing to bring to a conclusion.

List of Sponsors

The writer acknowledges gratefully the generosity of the sponsors who have contributed significantly to the publication of *The History of Irish Tennis.*

David & Neil McCann

Institute of Technology, Sligo

John & Susan Magnier
Coolmore Stud

McNaughton Paper Ireland Ltd.

Gerry Duggan

Damien Torsney
The Crofton Group

Sir Anthony O'Reilly
Independent News & Media

Envirocare Pollution Control Ltd.

Personal Contributor

The History of Irish Tennis

Volume 1

Tom Higgins
Sligo Tennis Club

The History of Irish Tennis (in 3 volumes)
First Published in Ireland in 2006
Tom Higgins
Sligo Tennis Club
Ireland.
Copyright © the author.

ISBN number   0-948879-04-4

Printed by Turner's Printing Company Limited, Earl Street, Longford, Ireland.
Original sketches by Stephanie Paxton, Sligo, Des O'Brien, Kenilworth, Fitzwilliam, Cardiff Castle & Dyvours LTCs and John Tormey, St. Mel's & Shankill LTCs.
Jacket Designs by Tom Higgins and Noel Strange.

Dedicated to Ursula

We are what we remember.

(source unknown)

Contents

Foreword
by
Seamus McCusker
President Tennis Ireland (2003-2004)   *i*

Acknowledgements   *ii*

Introduction   *v*

Volume I

Volume II

Volume III

Foreword

This book is the first one of its kind to record the history of tennis in Ireland and has been a labour of love for Tom. In his research he has unearthed many interesting and fascinating facts about the game.

What started out as a history of the North West has developed into a major work embracing the whole of Ireland and culminating in this magnificent chronicle of the game we love and play. It contains club histories, information about club and national players, anecdotes about personalities and much, much more.

It is a book that will be invaluable in years to come as a major source for all curious to know and learn how the game originated and developed in Ireland and I heartily recommend it to everyone.

Seamus McCusker
President Tennis Ireland (2003-2004)

Acknowledgements

In putting together this story of Irish tennis I have learned, among other things, that records are not as extensive as one might have thought. I was reminded of a story I heard a number of years ago. When an elderly badminton player in this country died his extensive collection of files on the sport was binned, his wife not being a follower of the sport. Fortunately, this is not always the case. Here an attempt is made to put together the extensive story of Irish tennis. Some of the best information came from individuals who did keep records, including newspaper cuttings and photographs. Added to this are organisations, minute books and libraries. Large numbers of photographs were encouragingly loaned and are included. Sincere apologies to those whose photographs were accidentally omitted, or just could not be fitted in.

Primary sources of material included Tennis Ireland, the National Library in Dublin, the All-England Croquet & Lawn Tennis Club library, individual club histories and Fitzwilliam Lawn Tennis Club. Many thanks to the staff at Tennis Ireland, and, in particular, Des Allen (Chief Executive Officer) for their support in so many ways. One of the world experts on tennis history, Alan Little the honorary librarian at the Wimbledon Lawn Tennis Museum, was enthusiastic and helpful and managed to unearth some elusive pieces of information. I would like to include in my thanks Jim Foran (librarian, Institute of Technology, Sligo). Club histories, small and large, were to prove invaluable sources and were directed my way by Mary Rose Lyons (Naas Lawn Tennis Club), Ivar Boden (Queen's Club, London), Gerry Clarke (Veteran's LTCI), Pat Crowe (Carrickmines Croquet & Lawn Tennis Club), Pauline Daly (Lattin LTC), George Hehir (Limerick Lawn TC), Mara O'Reilly (Enniskillen Lawn Tennis Club), James Cahill (Clontarf Lawn Tennis Club), Jill Meghen (De Visci Lawn Tennis Club), Jerry Cahir (Fergus Lawn Tennis Club), Paddy Murphy (St. Anne's-Waterford Tennis Club), Dermot Quinn (Sutton Lawn Tennis Club), Bryan O'Neill , Kevin Kenna and Judy O'Shea (Monkstown LTC), Valerie O'Toole (Grove Lawn Tennis Club), James Brewster (Brookfield LTC), Mary Briscoe (Elm Park), Sally Dawson & others (Donnybrook Lawn Tennis Club), Brenda Cooper & Donal Deering (Kilkenny County & City LTC), Glenageary LTC, Maura O'Riordan (Sandycove Tennis & Squash Club), Fiona Parker (Galway LTC) and the late Declan Lynagh (Boyle Community Tennis Club). Deliberately left to last is Fitzwilliam Lawn Tennis Club. Apart from providing copies of the two histories of the club (1927 and 1977), the staff and members of 'Fitz' could not have done more in supplying information directly, access to many books, photographs etc. Among them must be mentioned Jimmy McDonagh (Director of Tennis & Squash), Albert Tee (former honorary secretary & chairman of tennis), Hugh Hamilton (former honorary secretary), Gar Holohan (former honorary secretary & president), Doctor Harry Barniville (former president), David Fassbender (former president), Peter Gilligan (president 2002-2004), Terry Jermyn (general manager), Rosalind Dignam (administrator) as well as many other members and employees. I am especially indebted to Joe Hackett. From the outset, Joe, a former Davis Cup player and Centenary President at Fitzwilliam Lawn Tennis Club, has had a great enthusiasm for this project. He has an extensive knowledge on the game and its history and was able to guide me towards new sources of information. He could readily and reliably recall many facts on important aspects of the Irish and international game. Without his assistance this book would be very much the poorer.

During the last few years many hundreds of letters were written and phone calls made. There were some disappointments on the way but this was more than made up for by the eagerness of so many to contribute. One such person is Doreen Muskett from Belfast who went out of her way to put together a history of the Belfast YMCA Lawn Tennis Club. In a similar manner, passion for tennis and its history came from Lyn Jamison (President, Ulster Branch). Lyn your efforts, in so many ways, and your interest has been a great boost. That visit you arranged to the Boat Club and the meeting with Ken Reid, Cecil Pedlow and Peter Jackson was a highlight. Peter, your 100-year-old suitcase proved to be a goldmine. Another rich source of data was the two little 'black books' of Alan Haughton and his father Ben, two Davis Cup players. It was a pleasure meeting Alan at the Sunday's Well club, and to be trusted with the records going back as far as 1908. He is one of the most highly respected gentlemen of Irish tennis. Janine Walsh (Strawberry Hill, London) a former member of Sligo TC was more than generous with her time and eagerness in researching hidden data from the Wimbledon library. I wish her every success in her own research towards a doctorate on ladies' tennis. Sports follower and researcher, Tom Hunt from Mullingar, was one of the non-tennis players to be of great help, uncovering hidden information from years past. The enthusiasm and encouragement of Paul Rouse (RTE) and William Murphy of the Humanities Institute of Ireland was most welcome. Not forgotten either is Geoff Oakley from Birr who, on missing the post, drove to Mullingar, got on the train to Sligo, and personally delivered a number of valuable items and photographs.

Since 1978, when Sligo Tennis Club was founded, I have had the privilege to meet, organise, and play tennis with so many enthusiastic players. Not to be forgotten are the badminton, table tennis and squash players, as well as golfers, in the club. Through keen members, and some £50 to start with, we have managed to build a fine club. Thanks to all, officers and ordinary members alike. In relation to the development of the club and the preparation of this book a number of members must be mentioned for their special support and contributions. Two I would like to pick out. Hugh Hanly, our first chairman, who when work brought him to Ballina, was to be equally willing to promote the game there. Another, fellow engineer and Midlander, John Burke, whose support and keenness to talk tennis (and this book) at any time over many years is much appreciated. Many thanks also to the following members who have contributed in various ways to this endeavour: Ed Blake and family, Lilian Brennan, Billy Burke, Michael Burke and family, Des Butler, Maura Butler, Helen Coleman and family, Kay Curley, John Dolan, the late Bob English, Marie Farrell, Marie Forkan, Ted Gallagher, Marcelline Gordon, Padraic Hackett & family, Pat Harte, Catherine Holohan, Keith Hopkins, the late Brendan Kenny, John Kielty, Meg Leahy, Edel McDermott, Patsy McElhinney, Emmet McGarry, Vincent and Agatha McGee, Kevin McGloin and family, Michael McGowan, John McHugh, Michael McHugh, Joe O'Brien, Orla O'Mahony, Seamus

O'Toole and family, Rachel Rhatigan, Olivia Seery, Ted Smith, Marina Swann, Gerry Walsh, Louie Walsh and Michael Whelan.

Important sources of information were the Tennis Ireland/Irish Lawn Tennis Association Minutes' and Yearbooks. A pivotal contributor to the latter was Gerry More O'Ferrall who filled in many gaps in information. The Connacht Branch Minutes' book was most welcome too. Other gems included "A History of Munster Tennis" by the late Bill Tayler and the Munster Tennis News compiled by Tim Conway. ILTA Yearbooks prior to the mid-1970s were extremely difficult to find. Some Ulster Yearbooks from Peter Jackson were used in expanding the information for that province back as far as the 1950's. Recent Tennis Ireland magazines as well as the Irish Racquets Review were worthwhile sources in relation to recent years. Frank Egan (Fitzwillliam LTC) was very generous in providing significant material from his family files. Many thanks to colleagues Marie Claude Ward and Martine Lucas who assisted with securing data from Nice LTC on George Lyttleton Rogers, and their valued translations. From Presidents of the national organisation down to ordinary members in the smallest of clubs a broad range of views, mini-histories, anecdotes, memoirs, lists of officers, lists of champions, brochures, prints, sketches, photographs, books and newspaper cuttings were made available, and added significantly to the book. Without these contributions, the dusts of time would have permanently buried a great sporting heritage. Contributors included Derek Arthurs (Windsor LTC, now in Australia), Frank Aiken (Ardee LTC), Eileen Andrews (Coleraine), Badminton Union of Ireland (Baldoyle, Dublin), Julie Anne Bailie (nee Thornton), Paul Barber (Birr), Scott Barron (Dublin), Peter Bayliss (CIYMC LTC), Dr. Harry (Carrickmines Croquet & LTC and Fitzwilliam LTC), Dr. Geraldine Barniville (Birr LTC, Carrickmines Croquet & LTC and Fitzwilliam LTC), Mrs. D. E. Biscomb (Belfast), Ivar Boden (Queen's Club, London), Pat Boran (Dublin), Bowyer family (USA), Larry Brassil (Blackrock, County Dublin), Pat Bree (Westport TC), James Brewster (Brookfield LTC), Mary Briscoe (Elm Park), Gareth Brophy (Ardee LTC), Gerard Browne (Ennis LT & Badminton Club), Terry Browne (Dublin), Vincent Browne (Merville & Fitzwilliam LTCs), the late Willie Browne (Longford LTC & Elm Park), Mary Bryan (Carrickmines Croquet & LTC), Nancy Buchanan (Burt TC), Ken Burbage (Hawarden LTC), Tommy Burke (Dublin), Seamus Butler (Longford TC), Larry Byrne (Dublin), June Ann Byrne (Carrickmines Croquet & LTC), Michael Byrne (Dublin Lawn Tennis Council), Ursula Cafferty Kane (Mullingar), Jerry Cahir (Fergus LTC), Nicholas Campbell (Carrick on Shannon TC), Maria Casey (Castlebar TC), Owen Casey (Dublin), Pat Casey (Limerick Lawn TC) Gretta Charlton (Horley, England), Gerry Clarke (Fitzwilliam & Templeogue LTCs), Peter Clarke (Donnybrook LTC), Giulio Clerici (Italy), Bob Collins (Boston Globe), Philip Comyn (Mallow LTC), Franklin Connellan (Longford TC), Seamus Connellan (Carlow), Nan Conner (Argideen Vale LTC), Gretta Conway (Ballisodare), Tim Conway (Munster Branch), Denis Costello (Kent LTA), Anne Coughlan (Tullamore LTC), the late Michael Creighton (Mullingar TC), Dymphna Cronin (Strandhill TC), Tommy Crooks (Windsor LTC), Ed Curran (Belfast Telegraph), Ronald Davis (Anglesea LTC), Sally Dawson (Donnybrook LTC), Cees de Bondt (Netherlands), Maura Deegan (Munster Branch), Jimmy Deenihan (TD), Donal Deering (Kilkenny County & City LTC), Manuel di Lucia (Kilkee), Eamon de Valera (Fitzwilliam LTC), Maire Dixon (Belmullet TC), Eugene Dooley (Athlone TC), Yvonne Doyle (River Racquets Club/Fitzwilliam LTC), Eileen Dundee (St. Patrick's TC), Michael Dunne (Dublin), Tony Ensor (Wexford), Gordon Exshaw (Sunday's Well), George Fairbrother (Limerick), Harry Farrell (Longford Leader), Mixie Farrell (Roscommon), Jim Fenwick (Dublin), Stella Fitzgerald (Longford LTC), Gerry Fitzpatrick (Elm Park), Michael Fleming (Carrick on Shannon), Jo Flinn (Donnybrook LTC), Joe Flood (Deerpark TC), Alec Foley (Sligo), the late Mrs. Estelle Foley (County Sligo LTC), Vincent Frawley (Ballina TC), Eddie French (Carrickmines Croquet & LTC), Franks Furney (Mallow LTC), Gaelic Athletic Association, Ann Garavan (Castlebar TC), John Garavan (Castlebar TC), Roy Garland (Belfast), Frank Gearty (Longford TC), Padraic Gearty (Longford TC), Roger Geraghty (Director of Development, Tennis Ireland), Robin Gibney (Elm Park/Fitzwilliam LTC), Heiner Gillmeister (University of Bonn), Norah Glynn (Westwood Sports & Leisure Club), Jim Good (Sunday's Well/Argideen Vale LTC), Sir Josslyn Gore-Booth (Lissadell), the late Vivian Gotto (Windsor LTC), Aileen Gough (Claremorris TC), Alan Graham (Donegal), Seamus Granahan (Castlebar TC), John Griffin (Enniskillen LTC), Bernadette Griffith (Donnnybrook LTC), Gerry Halpenny (Dublin), Mrs. Bridget Hamilton (UK), Paul Hamilton (Sligo), Richard Hamilton (Glenageary LTC), George Hamilton (Greystones), Hugh Hamilton (Fitzwilliam LTC), Mrs. Hamilton (Enniskerry), Sally Harte (Merville LTC), Carrie Harvey (Letterkenny), Marie Harvey (Lansdowne LTC), Phil Heveron (Enniskillen LTC), Mavis Hogg (Hawarden LTC), Angela Horn (Coach), the late John Horn (player/coach), Mrs. Anne Indunii (Worthing), the late Claire Jennings (Sligo), Maeve Jennings (Ballina TC), David Keenahan (Gonzaga College, Dublin), Anna Kelly (Wilton LTC), Greg Kelly (Castlepollard LTC), Cyril Kemp (Fitzwilliam LTC), Michael Kennedy (Sligo), the late Bobby Keogh (Templeogue LTC), Des Keogh (Dublin), Anna Kelly (Wilton LTC), Brendan Kelly (Fitzwilliam LTC), Noreen Kelly (Mount Crozier LTC), Michael Kilcoyne (Sligo), Gary Kilduff (Dublin), Mrs. Emer Kilgallon (Sligo), Harriett Killoran (Ballyfarnon LTC), Sheila Kilkelly (Castlebar TC), Jimmy Kinehan (St. Mary's LTC), Tadgh Lambe (Limerick Lawn TC), Father Billy Langan (Carmelite Fathers), Peter Langford (Fitzwilliam LTC), Lady Langrishe, Roy Leary (Lisnaskea LTC), Helen Lennon (Dublin), Aine Leonard (Navan), Monsieur Bernard Leydet (Nice LTC), Kelly Liggan (Marbella), Kay Lonergan (Parks Tennis Ireland), Fiona Long (Limerick Lawn TC), Hadassah Lord (Coleraine), Peter Lowther (Lansdowne & Fitzwilliam LTCs), Richard Lyons (Sligo), Malachy Mahon (Irvinestown TC), Karoly Mazak (Budapest, Hungary), Mona McElroy (Sligo), Eleanor McFadden (Dublin), the late Jim McGarry (Collooney, County Sligo), Eddie McGettrick (Ballymote LTC), George McGill (Limerick Lawn TC), Willie McGowan (Donegal), Anne McGranaghan (Stranorlar), James McGuire (Royal Irish Academy), Elizabeth McKean (Donegal), Victor McKean (Donegal), Pauline McManus (Drumshanbo LTC), David Miley, (International Tennis Federation, London), the late John Miley (Grove LTC), Peter Minnis (Ward Park LTC), Seamus Mulherin (Rushbrooke LT & Croquet Club), Carmel Mullen (Ballymote), Niamh Murphy (Athlone), Matt Murphy (Texas), Paddy Murphy (St. Anne's-Waterford LTC), Anne-Marie Mullen (Ballymote), Doreen Muskett (Belfast), Jim Nestor (Sligo), Ted Neville (Irish Real Tennis Association), Niland family (Limerick Lawn TC), Derek Noblett (Belfast), Karen Nugent (Dublin), Colin O'Brien (Malahide LTC), my niece Ailish O'Brien (Limerick), the late Des O'Brien (Scotland), John O'Brien (Limerick, Lansdowne & Fitzwilliam LTCs), Ann O'Connor (Leinster Branch), Mary O'Connor (Clane TC), Anthea & Redmond O'Donogue (Rushbrooke Croquet & LTC and St.

Anne's-Waterford LTC), Tony O'Donoghue (Limerick LTC), Peadar O'Dowd (Galway LTC), Linda O'Gara (Woodville LTC), Ogmore (Lansdowne LTC), Gary O' Lochlainn (Galway LTC), Tom O'Loughlin (Parks Tennis), Aoife O'Neill (Lansdowne LTC), Berrie O'Neill (Percy French Association, County Down), Marie O'Neill (Swinford TC), Elsa O'Riain (FED Cup player), John O'Riordan (Carndonagh TC), Frank Peard (Lansdowne LTC), Sue Peard (Lucan), Mrs. Pearse (Roscommon), Frank van Rensselaer Phelps (Pennsylvania, USA), Nigel Pratt (County Wicklow), Brendan Quinn (Sutton LTC), Dermot Quinn (Sutton LTC), Jennifer Quinn (Carlow), Pat Rafferty (The Pavilion, Balla & St. Mel's LTCs), Olywn Raftery (Galway LTC), Peter Read (Roscrea), Jim Shanahan (Dictionary of Irish Biography), Sheela Reeves-Smyth (Tullow, County Carlow), Terence Reeves-Smith (Belfast), Mrs. V. Rowan (Omagh LTC), Caitriona Ruane (Castlebar TC), Jean Russell (St. Anne's-Waterford TC), Bill Ryan (Castlepollard LTC), Maureen Ryan (St. Anne's-Waterford TC), St. Columba's College (Dublin), Tim Scannell (Navan), Dr. Barney Sherry (Foxford & Fitzwilliam LTCs), Rachel Sherry (Dublin), the late Seamus Sherry (Foxford LTC), Colm Smith (Glasnevin LTC), Eamon Smith (Cork), George Stevenson (Ulster Branch), the late Nora Taylor (Enniskillen & Omagh LTCs), Tom Tebbutt (Ontario, Canada), Tom Tierney (Templeogue), Donal Tinney (County Library, Sligo), Hugh Tinney (Fitzwilliam LTC), John Tormey (St. Mel's & Shankill LTCs), Rosaleen Treacy (Belleek Tennis Club), Florrie Turner (County Longford LTC), Alice Tunney (Donnybrook LTC), John Walsh (Sundays Well Boating & LTC), Lucy Warner-Ryan (Limerick Lawn TC), Billy Watson (Letterkenny), Norman & Joan Watt (Raphoe LTC), Dr. Trevor West (TCD), Percy J. Winder S J (Clongowes Wood College), Kevin Winter (Australian Veterans' Association), Dick Wood-Martin (YMCA LTC), Ken Wright (Photographer, Castlebar) and Mark Young (Tennis Hall of Fame, Rhode Island, USA). If any contributors are not acknowledged then my sincere apologies.

One of the gems that came my way during the preparation of this book was an 1896 Rules Book for Longford Tennis Club. It was printed by Turner's Printing of Longford. Appropriately, it is the same company that have printed this book. I am extremely grateful to all the staff there for their patience and skill in taking on this work. I would particularly like to thank Derick Turner for his advice and encouragement throughout, and Noel Strange for his technical expertise. Original sketches by Stephanie Paxton (Sligo), Des O'Brien (Kenilworth, Fitzwilliam, Cardiff Castle 7 Dyvours LTCs) and John Tormey (St. Mel's & Shankill LTCs) are valued inputs to this book. The National Gallery of Ireland was most helpful in identifying and providing a copy of a William Orphen sketch. On the computing side there are a number of my colleagues at the Institute of Technology, Sligo, who have been more than helpful. I must pick out John Hession in particular who, though under extreme pressure himself, assisted me in so many ways. Thanks John. Aengus Sheerin, Jim Sheridan, Gerladine McGovern and Sharon Ginning, as well as my daughters Trudy, Olga and Sonya, were among the others to come to my assistance. In a similar vein, many thanks to Michael Vickers and Compupac for their generous assistance with hard and soft ware.

Advice on books and allied matters came from many quarters. Particular thanks to John McTiernan, Michael Keohane and Frank Kelly. Not to be forgotten are the many newspapers that have included items in connection with the book's research. The County libraries in Sligo, Offaly, Leitrim, Longford and Westmeath have willingly helped with unearthing some of the older pieces on tennis long forgotten. Without willing workers sport would not survive. Many thousands of players have in the past and, no doubt, will in the future, benefit from the enjoyment obtained from the sport of tennis. Thanks to those workers whose efforts I hope are adequately included here. A limit had to be set on the extent of this book, an effort that grew and grew, fed by material coming from all directions. Where credits have accidentally been omitted my sincere apologies. Advice and assistance in various forms, in relation to the book promotion and launches, has been freely given, and was most welcome. Included here must be mentioned Leo Gray (Sligo Champion) and Adrian Eames (RTE Sport). The book production required some financial support in order to ensure the printing costs were matches up with sales and without the cover price being excessive. Apart from a personal donation (from a person who wishes to remain anonymous), invaluable contributions came from David & Neil McCann (Fyffes), The Institute of Technology, Sligo, John & Susan Magnier (Coolmore Stud), Gerry Duggan, Dublin Lawn Tennis Council, Envirocare Pollution Control, Damien Torsney (The Crofton Group), McNaughton Paper Ireland Ltd., Envirocare Pollution Control Ltd., and Sir Anthony O' Reilly (Independent News & Media).

I have left some of my key thanks to last. Firstly to Seamus McCusker, an Irvinestown LTC man who came to the sport late and was President of Tennis Ireland from 2003 to 2004. Many thanks Seamus for you kind words and encouragement and your assistance on the proof reading side. Not one of the proofreaders asked declined to help. From them came suggestions for amendments, which were included. Apart from Seamus, other proofreaders to be thanked are John Burke, Maura Butler, Donal Crowley, John Dolan, Joan Grennan, Seamus & Toni Kenneally, Geraldine Lowry, Francie Mahon, Brendan McCormack, Phyllis McFadden, Agatha McGee, Maura McMorland, Rachel Rhatigan, David & Marina Swann, Elma Walsh, Lesley Walsh, Louie Walsh, Sarah Walsh and Emer Ward, all present or former members of Sligo Tennis Club. Added to this list are Dr. harry Barniville (Fitzwilliam LTC), Gerry Clarke (Templeogue LTC), Joe Earley (civil engineering colleague), Joe Hackett (Fitzwilliam LTC), Alan Haughton (Sunday's Well Boating & LTC), Lyn Jamison (Portadown Tennis Club), Frank Peard (Lansdowne LTC), Kathryn Ryan (civil engineering colleague), and last, but by no means least, Ursula, Trudy, Paul and Niall Higgins. Growing up, my own father, Syl, encouraged us all in a wide range of sports including playing at the nearby Longford Tennis Club. My brothers, Pat, Brian, Paul, Declan and Niall for their games on court and the stories they remembered. My three daughters, Trudy, Olga and Sonya, who grew up with Sligo Tennis Club and helped me in so many ways, probably most frequently by taking all those phone messages. Finally, Ursula, for playing in that Longford Open Week so many years ago and, apart from the many sports days in between, just being there for me time after time.

Tom Higgins
Sligo Tennis Club
Summer 2006

Introduction

The game of tennis – at one time referred to as lawn tennis, in the day when green grass was the predominant playing surface – is now one of the most international of sports. While the game is still played on grass, the playing surfaces vary considerably with climate and national preferences. Clay, tarmacadam, wood, concrete, cow dung and artificial grass are among the variants to be found. The introduction of lawn tennis on to the many croquet lawns of Ireland came shortly after the 1874 patenting and sale of lawn tennis sets, for 5 guineas each, by England's Major Walter Clopton Wingfield (initially he called the game *Sphairistike,* after the Greek word for ball game). Though initially considered an alternative pastime, lawn tennis spread widely and quickly, particularly where there was an English influence. We now know, however, that for several previous centuries there had been a range of ball and bat games played. 'Tennis', or 'real tennis' as it became known, was being played in France by the end of the 12th century. Tennis Court Lane can be found on John Speed's 1610 map of Dublin. A 'fives' court was laid at Trinity College, Dublin in 1694 and a real tennis court in 1741. A 1626 painting of Prince Frederick Henry, Prince of Orange, shows him playing an outdoor game of tennis over a net. The outdoor game in England seems to have been started by Major Harry Gem and Spaniard Juan Batista Augurio Pereira, at the latter's home on Ampton Road, Edgbaston, Birmingham. From about 1869, these keen 'rackets' players had been experimenting with the outdoor game. They first called it 'pelota' and then 'lawn rackets'. However, the influence of Wingfield's tennis sets, and then the All-England Croquet Club, who changed their name in 1877 to the All-England Croquet and Lawn Tennis Club, were fundamental in kindling the game. The support in Ireland for the 'new' pastime/sport was significant in its success in the early decades.

Wimbledon watched on television in over 150 countries each summer - is one of the four 'Grand Slam' events in the sport of tennis, the others being the Australian, French and US Opens. The term *Grand Slam* was first used by American journalist John Kiernan in 1933. He was describing Australian Jack Crawford's attempt that year to add the US championships to the Australian, French and All-England singles championships. He was foiled in a five-set match by Fred Perry of England. The feat has been achieved by Don Budge (USA in 1938), Maureen Connolly (USA in 1953), Rod Laver (Australia in 1962 and 1969), Margaret Smith Court (Australia in 1970) and Steffi Graf (Germany in 1988). Kiernan selected the four titles as they were the biggest at the time, and were the main international championships held in the only four countries that had won the Davis Cup.

In 1988 Steffi Graf added the Olympic title making her the only winner of the *Golden Grand Slam*. The first modern Olympic Games were held in Athens in 1896. Dubliner John Pius Boland became the winner of the gold medal in both singles and doubles.

The first Wimbledon championships were held in 1877. A few weeks later the first Open championships was held in Ireland. This was not in Dublin but at the Limerick Lawn Tennis Club. The All-England Championships commenced on the 10th July. According to John Barrett (2001) the event *had been organised to raise funds for the repair of the broken pony roller that was essential to the upkeep of the croquet lawns-some of which had been turned over to lawn tennis in 1875 in response to the interest among members in the new game.* In the early years only men's singles was played. In Limerick, from the 26th to the 28th July, the 'Grand Lawn Tennis Tournament' consisted of four events, men's open singles, ladies' open singles, men's open doubles and men's handicap singles. When the Irish Championships took off in 1879 the men of Fitzwilliam included ladies' singles and mixed doubles.

We have had a number of Wimbledon champions in this country but less known is the fact Mabel Cahill from Ballyraggett, County Kilkenny, won the singles, doubles and mixed at the United States Championships in 1891 and 1892. She became the first player in world tennis to win three titles in a single year at any of the four 'grand slam' championships. In 1890 all three Wimbledon titles were won by Irish players. Lena Rice (New Inn, County Tipperary) and Willoughby Hamilton winning the singles and the top pairing in the world at the time, Joshua Pim and Frank Stoker, the doubles.

In Lance Tingay's 1983 book *The Guinness Book of Tennis Facts and Feats* we come across another Irish player of note. Tingay includes James Cecil Parke, from Clones, County Monaghan, as the best 'all-rounder' in lawn tennis (his female equivalent being Lottie Dod). Discovering this unknown Irish player was a significant reason why this book, originally a club history, ended up being expanded to cover the game on this island as a whole. Parke's exploits included the sports of chess, cricket, athletics, golf and rugby. On the tennis front his wins included eight Irish singles championships. He did reach the Wimbledon semi-final (1910 & 1913) in singles and the men's doubles All-Comer's final (1911, 1912 & 1913). He was mixed doubles champion twice (1912, 1914). However, it was in the Davis Cup that he made world headlines. He was on the Great Britain team that travelled to Melbourne to wrest the cup from the Australasian team that had held it from 1907 to 1911. He won both his singles but his win over the great Norman Brookes (*The Wizard*) entered him in tennis folklore. The media summarised his part in the Cup victory, *Ireland with a little help from England win the Davis Cup.* He again won his two singles in the 1913 final, held at Wimbledon. This time it was the *The Californian Comet,* Maurice McLoughlin, (US champion in 1912 and 1913 and the first notable exponent of the cannon-ball service) that Parke beat. The match went all the way 7/5 in the fifth set. However, the home team lost the other three matches.

The greatest years of Irish tennis were in the 19th century. Lena Rice, Joshua Pim, Harold Mahony and Willoughby Hamilton were all singles champions at the Irish and All-England championships (Wimbledon). An early start to the Golden era of Irish tennis was in 1889. Louisa Martin won the first of her nine singles titles in Dublin and, at the same championships, Hamilton gained revenge for his five set final loss to Ernest Renshaw (England) the previous year. Tennis historians will know that William Renshaw (twin to Ernest) was probably the best player in the 1880s, winning three Irish and seven Wimbledon singles titles. Ernest was no slouch either, with four singles wins at Fitz-William Square and one at Worple Road. In 1889 Hamilton beat both twins in winning the Irish championship, with a three-set victory over Willie in final. According to William Orphen (1925), Hamilton *after the last stroke hit a ball over the houses that surround Fitz-William Square-a great "belt" to give a ball surely!*. In 1890 Hamilton became the first of four Irish wins in the men's singles at Wimbledon. Especially satisfactory was to beat Willie Renshaw in what was his eighth final, and the only one he was to lose.

Times move on and the 'Golden Era' of Irish tennis has passed. For many reason, it may be a long time before the sport will achieve the sporting headlines it once enjoyed. This is no reason to neglect the games' glorious past in Ireland. In fact, seeing was has been achieved should give us the energy and enthusiasm to achieve dreams. This book documents the efforts of our individuals and teams, playing internally and abroad, and attempts to identify the key administrators, coaches and referees. No doubt, if Alf Walsh or Harry Maunsell – honorary secretaries of the Irish Lawn Tennis Association covering the period 1920 to 1971 - had spare time and energy to fully document the sport of lawn tennis in this country, this book would be more comprehensive. They were exceptional among amateur officials and used every spare moment in promoting the game. Such was their input to tennis that it is unlikely that they had the time to seriously consider putting a history together. Prior to their time must be noted the efforts of the energetic Arthur Coutenay, a man who became the first president of the ILTA. Mavis Hogg and Charlie Brennan are among the more recent luminaries. Both received the Raymund Egan Award for services to Irish tennis, and awards from the European Tennis Association. Mavis received an MBE fro her services to tennis in Northern Ireland. Among other awards are the Maunsell trophies, given to the top Irish man and woman each year. Of more recent vintage are the Eagle Star national club awards.

The book evolved from a club story. What started out – over seven years ago – as a series of articles on the clubs and people associated with tennis in the Sligo area later expanded, in two stages. Firstly, to include the northwest, and then, having realised there was no history covering the sport for the whole of Ireland, to the present publication. Over this lengthy period, when there were often not enough hours in the day, there were many satisfying moments. Apart from unearthing so many interesting facts, it has been a pleasure to come in contact with a wide range of tennis aficionados. Perhaps, above all, what kept me going was the fact that there were so many people who were delighted that the book was being written.

A straightforward history would have left out much of the content now enclosed. However, the game has been so widely played in Ireland and, with so many vignettes from the smallest to the largest of clubs, it was deliberately decided to include as much as was possible, even though the book proved to be significantly greater in size than planned. It evolved! In the later stages of the elephant-like gestation it was decided to split the book into three volumes. The main reason for this was the fact that binding in one volume was not possible. One benefit in having this division is the fact that each volume, though over 500 pages each, will be more easily read. There is the temptation that having a flick through the three volumes, they might be left down as a nice book to have. I do encourage the readers to look beyond the photographs and personalities of immediate interest. I think much can be enjoyed, and learned by doing so about a game so many have played over the decades and in so many differing circumstances.

Ireland's team tennis goes back to 1881 when we lost 2/1 to England, the match being played at the time of the Irish Championships. The following year we beat the visitors 5/4. Apart from England, our next international opponents were Germany. We lost 4/11 in Berlin in 1909 but beat them 12/3 when they came to Dublin the following year.Our first Davis Cup encounter as an Irish team was in 1923, we were beaten 4/1 by France. Identified in this book are over 500 senior tennis international matches, held between 1881 and 2006. Junior internationals add to this considerable number of challenges. In recent decades veteran tennis has taken off, here and abroad. On the 1st July 2005 we had 17 players on the world veteran ranking lists. The best Irish player was Lesley O'Halloran with a very respectable ranking of 15 in the over 40 category. Senior rankings only became official in Ireland in 1932. The twin giants George Lyttleton Rogers and Norma Stoker were deemed the best players in Ireland at the end of that season. Rogers beat many of the world's top players when he was at his best. There was no official ranking at that time. With the ATP and WTA systems now in place we can be clearer on how our players are positioned on the world tennis ladder. Our best male and female rankings in recent years (ATP and WTA respectively) were Owen Casey at 220 in 1993 and Kelly Liggan at 181 in 2003. American born Anne Mall who has now declared for Ireland was 139 in 1994. In the under 18 categories (ITF) Stephen Nugent was 110 in 1998 and Claire Curran was 93 in 1995. Every sport attempts to attain the highest levels possible for the elite stars and teams. In tennis, Ireland is ranked (April 2006) 57 of 90 nations that play in the FED cup, the international ladies' team event. In the Davis Cup for men we are 70 of the 139 nations with a ranking. Belgium, a country with double our population, but four times as many tennis players, has rankings of 5 and 21 for the women's and men's team respectively. Croatia, with a similar population to Irelands has probably less tennis players but is ranked 12 and 1 respectively in the FED and Davis Cup listing of nations. On the 1st May 2006, Ireland had four players in the top 900 on the ATPs world ranking for men, and two in the top 700 on the WTAs world ranking for women. The top man was Peter Clarke at 426 and top lady Kelly Liggan at 249.

Included in Volume 1 is a brief overview of sport in Ireland, including reference to our all-rounders. The evolution of the game includes an attempt to link the many racquet sports that have been played throughout the world. Of special note here is the playing of the Tivoli Cup on the strand of Kilkee, County Clare, a unique mixture of tennis and squash. The game of 'real' tennis was considered by one source to have first been named by an Irishman, to distinguish it from lawn tennis. The game of tennis has grown in Ireland in various phases with over 700 clubs founded since 1877. Many have fallen by the way side. Hardcourts of the tarmacadam variety were encouraged in the 1930s in order to extend the tennis-playing season. Today grass is a rare playing surface with all-weather surfaces dominating. Indoor tennis has grown, but in a relatively small way.

The game has always been a social one. This fact has been recorded time and again, the tennis club often being the sole social centre in a small community. Many marriages made their first steps at the tennis 'dance' or 'hop' or 'disco'. Tennis for the young has increased dramatically, children as young as six or seven taking the initial steps into a game for life. At the other end of the scale, veteran tennis seems to have grown exponentially. While at one time it was the parents who introduced the game to the rest of the family, now many grandparents are actively involved. A small chapter deals with the progress of the game in the secondary schools and universities. The former continue to play an important role in promoting the sport among the young. National schools' tennis and Parks tennis play equally important roles.

Where man is active, so too are the scribes. In 1877 probably the longest poem ever on the sport of tennis was written about the tournament at the fledgling Monkstown Lawn Tennis Club in Dublin. Percy French, a man who played in the Irish Championships, was a keen player who penned many lines on the game. A small chapter deals with a range of such writings, one more recent is the entertaining tennis story by Pat Boran on the game in Portlaoise in the 1970s.

The Tennis Clubs of Ireland form a significant chapter in Volume 1. It was not possible to detail the history of every club. Readily available club histories were the basis for many entries here. What was difficult to identify were details on clubs that are no longer extant. Tennis Ireland became the modern title for the national organisation in 1990. It was called the Irish Lawn Tennis Association (ILTA) when founded in 1908. The Dublin Lawn tennis Council (DLTC), the organisers of probably the biggest tennis leagues in any country, predates the ILTA by six years. The DLTC leagues originally catered for summer tennis for ladies and men. Today, they cater for many graded leagues for junior, senior and veteran players. Winter and Floodlit leagues are part of their successful programme. Not dissimilar are the leagues run by the Belfast and District council. Not to be forgotten are the many voluntary committee members on the national organisation, as well as the provincial councils/branches. Most of these individuals are involved in promoting the sport within their own clubs. Tennis Ireland has now a salaried staff to bear much of the work load.

Volume 2 has two distinct elements, the competitions and the people. It was impossible to track down all the results one would like to include here as a record of the game in Ireland. However, some important tables have been prepared, including senior interprovincial results, the South, East, West and Ulster Championships, the County Dublin Championships and the Irish Open Championships. The Irish Open is a key championship that has attracted the best players in the world for many decades. Since the professional ('Open') era kick-started at the end of the 1960s it has been difficult to bring the best players to Ireland. Finance is a major obstacle. However it, and many other tournaments, have survived. A number of these date back to the 1880s.

Profiles of over 1,100 people are included in the book. Some are brief. Much research has enabled details on long-forgotten heroes to be published in a way I hope brings them to life again. Volume 3 starts off with a few small, apparently random, sub-chapters. These include transport, where we find the story of the four Dublin men who, during the Second World War, decided the best way to get to Cork was with two tandem bicycles. Having played the tournament in Cork, they cycled back to Dublin, via additional tennis in Wicklow. Changes in fashions and equipment, never mind costs, have been dramatic in over a century and a quarter of Irish tennis. These are discussed in this chapter.

Lastly, the players and people of the north-west are dealt with in chapter 8. As already mentioned, the book commenced its life in this region and much of the original script has been retained. Preserving this integrity may not be the ideal path for a history covering the whole of Ireland. Practical and loyalty factors lead to this approach.

Many expansive books have proportionally lengthy introductions. This can be useful. However, rather than attempt to concisely introduce all elements of the book, the briefer version above provides a useful taste. The reader will probably flit from chapter to chapter. In the end, while an attempt is made here to cover all angles of the Irish game, I recognise that it would take another five years to be as complete and as accurate as one would desire. If the reader can learn more about the sport and its past through this book, then, like the writer, her or she can consolidate their passion for tennis, or begin to love the game in a wholly different manner. If this is achieved then it will have been worth the effort.

Tom Higgins

Chapter 1
The Sporting Irish

1.1   *Our Many and Varied Sports*

Ireland (the rugby team) *are proof that sport can rise above religion*
and politics and assist in breaking down the barriers peacefully.
(John Beattie, former Scottish international in 1990)

Without elaborating the subject, it is well recorded that sports and pastimes have been around for thousands of years, and in a range of guises. This book will look at tennis, and related sports, in some detail. However, it is worth considering, even briefly, how we find ourselves today and how we came to be here, in a sporting context. Lawn tennis is just over one and a quarter centuries old. Ball games of various types go back thousands of years. As far back as 1169 we find that the last official Aenach Tailteann Games took place. Before that sports have been recorded in various parts of the world. Of particular interest are the Olympic Games. It is known with certainty that in July 776 BC a man called Coroibos, a cook, won a foot race in ancient Greece. However, it is thought that the ancient Games date from about 1370 BC. These games are of particular interest to the Irish reader, in that when Baron de Coubertin instigated the modern Olympics in 1896, many new sports were included. Lawn Tennis was part of those games that started on the 6th April of that year. The gold medal winner, in singles and doubles, was Dublin man John Pius Boland. He became the first Irishman to win a medal in the modern Olympics. More about him later!

We can look at how various sports, and how they developed, in this country. Much of their progress has taken place in the last century or so. They form a large blend of activities, skilled and not so skilled, sedentary and fast moving, aesthetic and of the rough and tumble variety, demanding strength and/or a delicate touch. They all provide, for the participant, and often the observer, various degrees of pleasure and satisfaction. In addition they usually have health promoting properties, of mind and/or body. They are a form of social intercourse. Unfortunately, they have sometimes been socially divisive. For the true sports person they have so many benefits that they could not imagine having a life without them. Apart from the odd injury, which prevents participation for a period, they are to be celebrated. There are sports suitable for five year old. At the other end of the scale when we hear of people in their nineties enjoying bridge, playing tennis or golf, we can immediately see what so many may be missing. The reader of this book is unlikely to belong to the latter category.

In the 19th century sports took off in the 'developed' world. Ireland was to have so many new sports, some considered non-native and only associated with the gentry class. In this new century we can now look back, enjoy the past stories and successes and hope future generations participate in as many sports as possible, without being limited by a lack of means or by social barriers.

One hundred years may not seem long in the life of a nation. However, in little over a hundred years, sport has become a major element of people's lives. In all parts of Ireland survival during and after the famine was a prerogative. Gradually, sport played a more significant role in a wider population. Until the

foundation of the GAA (Gaelic Athletic Association) in 1884, sport among the general populace was sporadic, despite the fact that hurling and other activities, such as *cathu clogh* (stone throwing), running, jumping and wrestling were commonly enjoyed. *Cad*, a ball game common among Celtic peoples, appeared to have originated over 1000 years ago. It was probably the origin of Gaelic football, soccer and rugby.

The gentry and military had gradually brought in a range of other sports, such as hockey, golf, tennis, badminton, rugby, snooker and polo. According to one source, *Handball is an obvious relative of racquet games such as real-tennis, tennis and squash.* To this could be added racquetball. Over 3 million play racquetball in the USA (where it started in 1972). In Britain, where it introduced as recently as 1975, play was initially on squash courts. The Racquetball Association of Ireland was founded in 1979. The table on the next presents some of the facts in relation to a range of sports played in Ireland.

While the 19th century saw the introduction of tennis (as well as golf, rugby, hockey etc.) from foreign shores, there can be no doubt that the formation of the GAA was the catalyst for organised sport on a large scale throughout the whole country. This one body grew rapidly. Within one year there were some three hundred clubs in the country. There is no doubt that sport developed at various paces depending upon the location and the people involved. The success of the GAA had a nationalist flavour and a need to express an Irish identity after many years of foreign influence. Unfortunately, politics, religion and social standing often got in the way.

While this is not a social history lesson we can learn from the past connections between sport and society. Sport can be valued for its own sake, and the qualities it brings to our lives. There is no doubt that many sports, for many years, were sectarian in their operation. Soccer in Ireland is a good example where all persuasions have been involved for a lengthy period of time, and with the minimum of social division. The GAA ban, once a serious barrier to social 'inclusiveness', has now gone and, ones hopes, that the freedom to play the sport one prefers will permeate to all corners. Certainly, the latter half of the 20th century indicates that this is possible.

A couple of interesting pen pictures might be considered when trying to understand the development of Irish sport. An Ulsterman man in Dublin, after a big rugby win in the European Cup, asks a Dublin sports journalist: *What do you think of a 32 county Ulster?* (or words to that effect). John Beattie, Scottish rugby international, in 1990 wrote that *if the truth be told the Irish team are the one outfit that could persuade me that sport and politics do not mix.* He added, *Ireland* (the rugby team) *are proof that sport can rise above religion and politics and assist in breaking down the*

Some Irish Sporting Facts

c. 2000 BC	**Handball**	The oldest of sports. Many sports evolved from playing with a ball using the hands or feet. (see chapter 2). Irish handball has been known to have been played prior to 1527. There was a ball alley in Ballymote, County Sligo, as early as 1837. In 1887, a match between Ireland and the USA was played in New York. An alley was built at Summerhill College, Sligo in 1899. Comhairle Liathroid Laimhe na hEireann was founded in 1924.
c. 1150	**Tennis**	A chain of events, starting, it appears in the French monasteries in the 12th century, lead to the modern game of (lawn) tennis. Varieties included real tennis and court tennis (see chapter 2). Real tennis was played in Dublin in 1609, though the use of the term 'real' came much later. The earliest lawn tennis clubs in Ireland were Dublin University, Monkstown, Limerick Lawn, Lansdowne and Fitzwilliam. The ILTA (Irish Lawn Tennis Association) was founded in 1908 and replaced by Tennis Ireland in 1990.
c. 1250	**Cricket**	The earliest evidence of cricket was from a drawing in about 1250 with two men playing with a bat and ball. Played in Guilford, Surrey in 1550. First recorded cricket match in Ireland in 1792. Played in the Catholic school, Clongowes Wood College, in a crude form in 1820. In about 1832 the first Irish club (Phoenix) was formed. In 1923 the Irish Cricket Union (ICU) established.
1277	**Hockey**	There is evidence that it was played in Lincolnshire in 1277. The first club with a continuous history is Teddington, formed in 1871. The Irish Hockey Union was formed in 1893. Early clubs included the Sligo Excelsior and Lissadell cricket clubs.
1457	**Golf**	Golf was played in Scotland in 1457 but there is some evidence that it may have been played earlier, in some form, in places as diverse as China, Denmark and Holland. The first club formed was in 1744. First played in Ireland at the Curragh in 1852. The GUI was formed in 1891.
1823	**Rugby**	First played at Rugby School in November 1823 when football rules were breached. The second oldest club in the world was formed at Trinity College Dublin in 1855. The IRFU was established in 1874. The Sligo RFC was founded in about 1895.
1830s.	**Croquet**	This sport has been defined as a country house game first played in Ireland when it originally called *crokey*. The Croquet Association of Ireland was formed in 1900. In 1948, St. Tiernan's Lawn Tennis and Croquet Club was founded in Crossmolina.
1850	**Squash**	Appears to have first being played at Harrow school in 1850 as a substitute for rackets. The first championships were in the USA in 1906. Irish women's Open first held in 1930. The ASRA and AWSRA were replaced by Irish Squash in 1993.
1860	**Badminton**	Shuttles were played with for centuries and hit with bats in a game called battledore. At Badminton House in 1860 a net was included. It was at Poona in 1873 that the first regulated version of the game was played. The Badminton Union of Ireland (BUI) was formed on the 25th November 1899. The first Irish Open Championships were in 1902. The inaugural winner of the men's event was Blaney Hamilton. He and his brother Willoughby won the men's doubles. The later was Wimbledon tennis champion in 1890.
1863	**Soccer**	While football , in various versions, has been played in many places for centuries, the Football Association (FA) was only founded in 1863. The Irish Football Association (IFA) was formed in 1880. Sligo Rovers was founded in 1908. The FAI (Football Association of Ireland) was formed in 1921. The Irish Ladies Football Association was formed in 1973.
1872	**Athletics**	The Dublin University Football Club Foot Races Committee was established in 1857. The first official sports meetings were organised by the university. These 'Trinity Races' were a *closed shop*. When the GAA was formed in 1884, athletics was equally as important as hurling and football. The Amateur Athletic Union of Eire (AAUE) and the National Athletic and Cycling Association of Ireland (NACAI) merged to form Bord Luthchleas na hEireann (BLE) in 1967. More recently Athletics Ireland became the governing body based in the Republic.
1884	**GAA games**	The Gaelic Athletic Association (GAA) was founded in Thurles in 1884 with aims that included *the preservation and promotion of Gaelic Games and pastimes.* Hurling was an ancient sport, some records go back to 1272 BC. By 1889 there were 25 affiliated clubs in the county of Sligo alone. The ladies camogie association was formed in 1904 and the ladies football in 1974.
1896	**Olympics**	The modern Olympics were first held in Greece in 1896. Among the medallists was Dubliner John Pius Boland who won gold in both the singles and doubles. Tennis went through a period of not be held at these games (see chapter 5). In 1900, at the Paris games, cricket and croquet were held. Golf and lacrosse were part of the 1904 games in St. Louis. In 1908, in London, the sports of rackets, polo, motorboating, rugby union and jeu de la paume were included. Apart from (lawn) tennis, these other sports have long been discontinued.
1890s	**Table Tennis**	Called Whiff-Whaff, Gossima and Ping Pong at various stages, table tennis has been a popular pastime and competitive sport throughout the world.

barriers peacefully. It appears that Michael Cusack, in 1884, saw the formation of the GAA *predominantly directed towards the revitalisation of Irish sports for Irish people.* A laudable concept! According to Edmund van Esbeck (Irish Rugby, 1874-1999) *the fraternity that existed between the various 'gaelic' and 'non-gaelic' groups can be gauged from the sporting backgrounds of two of the founders of the Gaelic Athletic Association.* It appears that George St. J. McCarthy played rugby for Trinity College Dublin and Ireland and that Michael Cusack was a keen rugby and cricket player. Maurice Davin, the first president of the GAA, was one of a great sporting family from Carrick on Suir. He was six foot in height, weighted 15 stone and had a chest size of 47 inches. He was one of the most versatile of Irish sportsmen in history. Apart from his many athletic achievements he also played cricket, hurling, football and rowed. He was a great swimmer and once swam 12 miles of the river Suir from Clonmel to Carrick for a wager. His brother Pat held six world athletic records at one stage as well been involved in the sports of boxing, cricket, rowing, cross-country running, hurling, football and steeplechasing. These were true sporting heroes, often forgotten.

The discussion on sport, religion, culture and politics, and how they inter-react, could go on forever. The intermingling of facts and ideas at the inaugural Sports History Conference in 2005, and the second annual event in February 2006, were timely in terms of our societies' maturity. Organised by Paul Rouse and William Murphy, they blended many sides of the sports into a uniform context. Despite many variations, each sport, and the people associated with them, continue to contribute to society in many ways.

In this new century we might simply go back to the dictionary definition of sport: *an athletic activity* or *any game or pastime.* We can learn from the development of sport, and attempt to ignore factors that interfere with their enjoyment. They can be but good for the individual and a community, large or small. Depending on the sport they can be enjoyed by young and old, the very fit and not so fit, including the handicapped. When sportsmen, and those handling funds for sporting endeavour, sit down to discuss developments, coaching etc. it is sport that should be the main focus. Does the sport, and the facilities in schools and clubs, meet the needs of those that enjoy those sports? If we can answer yes to the latter then we will have learned new lessons and be better off.

While the GAA may have been one of the biggest sporting organisations in Ireland, and still is, we have a large number of organisations now in place and catering for all tastes. The list in the following table is no doubt not a complete one. Picking up a few publications we can identify the range. The 2000 Edition of the *Local Ireland Almanac* lists forty sports and their organisation. The late, international athlete, Noel Carroll, was author of *Sport in Ireland* in 1979.

He identifies, and gives nice details, on some sixty sports. Not included is racquetball, a sport that was only taking off in Ireland with the formation of the Racquetball Association of Ireland in 1979. The *Seven-Up Book of Irish Sport* was published in Olympic Year 1984 and edited by Malachy Logan of The Irish Times. It includes a series of stories and results for 1983 in a limited number of sports. A small little book, *The Sporting Irish,* by Leo Bowes (with no apparent publication date that this reader could find) has a most enjoyable series of 55 stories covering a period of over 100 years. The sport of "strandpulling" is included in one of the essays. Lastly, in the Republic of Ireland's *Targeting Sporting Change in Ireland,* published by the Department of Education in 1997, we find no less than 68 sports which have received grants in the period 1994 to 1996. Among the unusual ones is baton twirling.

In a further table many of the key dates in Irish sport are identified. These are, in the main, the years in which organisations were set up. It is not a complete listing but does clearly show the importance of the last two decades of the 19th century. In that relatively short time span the sports of athletics, Gaelic games, soccer, rugby, golf, tennis, yachting, badminton, hockey and rowing became organised national sports for the first time. Additional sports, such as cycling, croquet, horse racing and cricket, were active on a countrywide scale and would later have national bodies looking after their interests. Never before or since has such an upsurge taken place. Participation in many has grown throughout the 20th century in Ireland. Local interests were dominant before transport became widely available. The spectator interest has grown since the arrival of television to Ireland in the late 1950's and early 1960's. Publications are now available in the form of magazines catering for particular sporting interests. They may be weekly, monthly and/or annually.

The press has always been a good indicator of activity. As far back as 1881 a new Dublin newspaper, titled *Sport,* was on sale for one penny each Saturday. The issue of the 27th August 1881 (volume 1 number 36) had a front page of advertisements for such diverse items as furniture, cutlery, Indian teas, washing wringing & mangling machines, tobacco and table lamps which burnt petroleum oil. The Horse Show was advertised, as were the Carlow Amateur Athletic Sports, fishing tackle and Howe bicycles and tricycles. John Lawerence of 63 Grafton Street were advertised as being Cricket & tennis outfitters and were the *Special Agent for Ayre's Celebrated Bats. £3 Set includes four Cedar-handle racquets.* By the May 31st 1890 issue the cycling adverts were dominant. That issue had a front page with sporting advertisements which included those for cricket & tennis suits, footballs, field glasses (for the racecourse), betting (with Mr. Alfred Crook of Boulogne-sur Mer) and Donegal tweeds (for hunting, shooting, fishing or walking).

The History of Irish Tennis

Irish Sports Exposure

Sport	Articles in local press (1875-2000)+	The Sporting Irish	Sport in Ireland (1979)	Results in 7 Up book (1983)	Sports Receiving Grants (1994-1996)++	Local Ireland Almanac 2000
adventure sports					X	
aerobics/keep fit	X	X			X	
aeromodelling			X			
archery			X		X	
athletics	X	X	X	X	X	X
badminton	X		X		X	X
ballooning			X			
baseball & softball					X	
basketball	X		X	X	X	X
baton twirling					X	
billiards			X		X	X
blind sports					X	X
bowling			X		X	X
boxing	X	X	X	X	X	X
bridge	X					
camogie		X	X		X	X
canoeing			X		X	X
caving (speleology)			X		X	
cerebral palsy sport					X	
chess	X	X				
coarsing	X					
community games	X		X		X	
cricket		X	X	X	X	
croquet					X	X
cumann luthchleas gael					X	
cycling	X	X	X	X	X	
darts	X					X
deaf sports					X	
draughts	X					
eventing			X	X	X	X
fencing			X		X	X
fishing	X	X	X		X	
flying			X			
gaelic football	X	X	X	X	X	X
gliding			X			
golf	X	X	X	X	X	X
greyhound racing			X	X		X
gymnastics	X	X	X		X	
handball	X	X	X		X	
hang gliding			X		X	
hill walking/mountaineering	X		X		X	
hockey	X	X	X	X	X	X
horse racing	X	X	X	X	X	X
horseshoe pitching					X	

Sport	Articles in local press (1875-2000)+	The Sporting Irish	Sport in Ireland (1979)	Results in 7 Up book (1983)	Sports Receiving Grants (1994-1996)++	Local Ireland Almanac 2000
hunting	X		X		X	X
hurling	X	X	X	X	X	X
martial arts/judo	X		X		X	
motor sports	X	X	X	X	X	X
netball			X		X	X
olympic handball					X	
orienteering	X		X		X	X
parachuting			X		X	
pitch & putt	X		X		X	X
polo			X			
pony trekking			X			
pool	X					
racquetball	X				X	X
road bowls			X		X	
rounders			X			
rowing	X	X	X		X	X
rugby	X	X	X	X	X	X
shooting	X	X	X		X	
show jumping	X		X	X	X	
skiing (snow)			X			
snooker			X		X	X
soccer	X	X	X	X	X	X
special olympics					X	X
squash			X		X	X
steeplechasing		X	X			
strandpulling		X				
sub-aqua/scuba diving	X		X			
surfing	X				X	X
swimming	X	X	X	X	X	X
table-tennis	X		X		X	
taekwondo						X
tennis (lawn)	X	X	X	X	X	X
ten-pin bowling			X		X	
triathlon					X	
tug-o-war	X				X	X
volleyball			X		X	X
water polo		X			X	
water skiing					X	
wheelchair sports			X	X	X	
weight lifting		X	X		X	
women's gaelic football					X	X
wrestling			X		X	X
yachting/sailing	X		X		X	X

(two newspapers/12 issues/25 year gaps/see script for details)+
(Department of Education Report-Republic of Ireland)++

The History of Irish Tennis

Some Important Dates in Irish Sport

1169	The last official Aenach Tailteann Games took place.
1527	The Statutes of Galway forbade hurling and other sports "except alone football".
1609	**Real tennis** first played in Ireland in Thomas Street, Dublin.
1694	A **Fives** court built at Trinity College, Dublin.
1720	Poet Mathew Concanen records his native Swords beating Lusk at football.
1792	First recorded cricket match in Ireland took place in the Phoenix Park, Dublin.
1834	Croquet parties held at Castlebellingham, County Louth.
2nd September 1836	Inaugural meeting of the Pembroke (Boat) Club at Radley's Hotel, College Green.
1852	First recorded playing of golf in Ireland, at The Curragh.
28th February 1857	First sports (athletics) meeting at Trinity College, Dublin.
1862	The Board of Trinity College, Dublin, agree to construct a **Rackets** court.
18th January 1873	Establishment of the Irish Champions Athletic Club (I.C.A.C.).
14th December 1874	The Irish Rugby Football Union (originally the Irish Football Union) founded.
1875	The Royal Yachting Association founded.
10th May 1876	First **lacrosse** match (exhibition) played in Ireland at North of Ireland Cricket Club.
c. 1876	A **lacrosse** club formed at Trinity College, followed by founding of Irish Lacrosse Union.
1877	**First lawn tennis clubs established**-Lansdowne*, Dublin University, Limerick Lawn, Monkstown & Fitzwillian
2nd August 1877	Ireland's **first open lawn tennis tournament** commences on grounds of County Limerick Cricket Club
1st January 1878	Rules for the Irish Amateur Athletic Association (I.A.A.A.) come into force.
1879	Dublin University 'Laws of Hurley' published in the Handbook of Cricket in Ireland
4th June 1879	The **first Lawn Tennis Championships of Ireland** commences, organised by Fitzwilliam Lawn Tennis Club
1880	The Irish Football Association founded.
Summer 1884	The Caledonian Games held at Lansdowne Road attracts 20,000.
1st November 1884	Foundation of the Gaelic Athletic Association (G.A.A.) at Hayes' Hotel, Thurles.
January 1886	The Cross Country Association of Ireland founded.
25th November 1899	The **Badminton** Union of Ireland founded.
1890	The Real Tennis World Championships held at Earlsfort Terrace court, Dublin.
13th May 1891	First women's golf competition held in Ireland at Killymoon Golf Club.
1891	The Golfing Union of Ireland (GUI) founded.
1893	Irish Hockey Union formed.
1893	The Irish Ladies Golf Union (ILGU) founded.
2nd October 1894	The Irish Ladies Hockey Union founded at Alexandra College, Earlsfort Terrace, Dublin.
1896	John Pius Boland wins two gold medals for lawn tennis at the first modern Olympic Games.
1899	The Irish Amateur Rowing founded.
1900	Croquet Association of Ireland founded.
1901	Motorsport Ireland founded.
1902	Motor Cycle Union of Ireland founded.
1902	**First Irish Open Badminton** Championships.
1903	**First Badminton International** in world. England beat Ireland 5/2 in Dublin.
1904	Cumann Camogaiochta na nGael founded.
1904	The Irish Bowling Association founded.
27th April 1908	The **Irish Lawn Tennis Association** founded.
1911	The Irish Amateur Boxing Association founded.
1923	The Irish Cricket Union founded.
1924	The first Tailteann Games held in Dublin.
1924	Establishment of the Irish Amateur **Handball** Association.
1930	The first Irish Women's Open **Squash** Championships held.
1931	Equestrian Federation of Ireland founded.
1932	First **Squash Rackets** Championship of Ireland.
1935	Inaugural Tivoli Cup for **Squash Racquets (Kilkee variety)** competition.
1936	First record of Irish women playing a cricket match.
1937	**Irish Table Tennis Association** formed.
1938	The Leinster Women's Cricket Union founded.
1939	The Earl of Iveagh leaves the world famous black marble real tennis court to the nation.
19th July 1940	The girls of County Longford are reported as playing **handball**.
1945	The Irish Basketball Association (IBA) founded.
1946	The Irish Sailing Association founded.
1947	The Northern Women's Cricket Union founded.
1947	The Irish Amateur Wrestling Association founded.
1949	Northern Ireland Netball Association founded.
1953	The Irish Federation of Sea Anglers founded.
1958	Bord na gCon founded.
1959	Republic of Ireland Billiards and Snooker Association founded.
1960	The Pitch and Putt Union of Ireland founded.
1960	The Irish Canoe Union founded.
1967	The AAUE and NACAI merge to form Bord Luthchleas na hEireann, the organising body for Irish athletics.
1967	Irish Surfing Association formed.
1967	The Irish Tug of War Association formed.
1968	The Volleyball Association of Ireland formed.
1970	Irish Orienteering Association founded.
1973	The Irish Ladies Football Association founded.
1974	Cumann Peil Gael na Mban founded.
1978	Special Olympics Ireland founded.
1978	The Taekwondo Association of Northern Ireland formed.
1979	Irish National Darts Organisation founded.
1979	Founding of The **Racquetball Association of Ireland**.
1982	The Irish Women's Cricket Union founded.
1988	Irish Cycling Federation founded
1989	The Northern Ireland Blind Sports founded.
1989	Irish Blind Sports organisation founded.
1990	**Tennis Ireland** becomes new name for the **Irish Lawn Tennis Association**
1993	**Irish Squash** founded
1994	Irish Horseracing Authority formed.
1995	**Ulster Squash** founded.
1998	The Irish **Real Tennis** Association formed.
1999	Irish swimming comes under newly founded organisation, Swim Ireland.
4th July 2000	The new County Mayo Cricket club take on the White City 'All-Stars' at The Mall, Castlebar.

* Some data suggests Lansdowne LTC was even earlier

The History of Irish Tennis

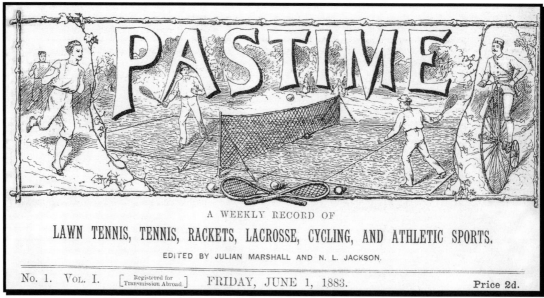

The First Issue of Pastime, Volume 1, Number 1, Friday, June 1, 1883.

Pastime, which was to be good source for tennis information, was first published in England on Friday June 1, 1883 and priced two pence. It was weekly paper too. The sketch below is from its first issue. Interestingly the front page article was titled *TENNIS: A Dip into the Future.* It is a discussion on the past 'slow' development of tennis and its likely future. It is an amusing article and includes reference to a prophet of the 19th century who said man would be "toothless, hairless, slow-limbed, incapable of extended locomotion". The writer points out that "Some of our best Tennis-players are already becoming bald. Of some, again, their dentists might relate a sad tale of insufficient dentition; it may be feared even that others are growing slower-limbed and less capable of extended locomotion". He also suggests that because of "The diminution in the stock of wood available" that the racket of the future "may be of metal throughout, frame and strings being alike composed of iron or steel". Court lighting was also suggested with electricity now available. The reader today might not recognise the terms of "dedans", "chase" and "grille". The simple reason being that the game being discussed was not tennis as we know it but rather the ancient variety, the one which had been played for hundreds of years. (see chapter 2). Lawn tennis was discussed in page two where we find that Ernest de Sylly Hami Browne of Dublin is winning his matches during 'The Bath Week'. Worthy of mention in this issue was a listing of open tennis tournaments. Irish ones were to be held at the **Kilkenny County & City LTC** (from June 18th), the South of Ireland Championships at Limerick County (from July 16th) and the tournament at the **Waterford Croquet & LTC** (from August 6th). The Irish Championships were also reported, they had been concluded the previous Saturday. In an attempt to identify the growth in sports interest since 1850, a local paper in County Sligo and one in County Leitrim were scanned. Two issues of the *Sligo Champion* and the *Leitrim Observer* were selected in the middle of the month of January and the same in June for 25-year intervals, up to 2000. The top 10 'references' of the 40 sports that were reported on in some fashion were as follows:

Number of References*	Sport
22	Gaelic football
18	Athletics
17	Golf
16	Soccer
10	Cycling
10	Swimming
9	Bridge
8	Tennis
8	Community Games
7	Basketball
7	Horse racing
7	Hurling

*Sporting references in two provincial newspapers between 1850 and 2000. Data based upon a January and a June week at 25-year intervals.

In preparing the graph on the following page some 14 issues of both papers were scanned i.e. 7 years x 2 weeks per year. The total number of sports items was 208 i.e. an average of just over 7 per issue. The number of references are plotted as annual totals (i.e. for 4 issues). We can see that there was a spectacular growth, from a zero base in 1850, especially in the latter half of the 20th century. The average number of items in 1975 was just over 20 per issue and reflects the significant interest in sport among the publishers and readers. The total sports coverage for the eight issues selected for 1875 and 1900 was 18 items, (athletics (2), cycling (6), fishing (1), golf (1), horse racing (2), shooting (4) and yachting/sailing (2). Sport has always been a normal spare time activity for man. When the 'modern' game of lawn tennis took off in the late 19th century it should not have been any surprise. The time was right among the leisured classes in England, and by association, in Ireland. There were to be certain sports linked to those of means. Lawn tennis required a 'lawned' area and the croquet houses of Ireland were many. The new game was to have a number of advantages.

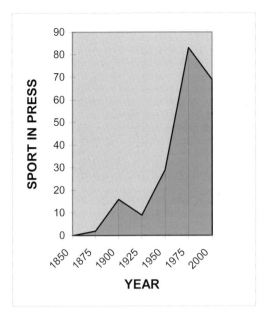

Total number of sports items in 4 local newspaper issues (2 Sligo Champion/2 Leitrim Observer).

The following piece was written by H.W.W. Wilberforce in 1895 in his introduction to a book entitled simply *Lawn Tennis*. The sub-title was *With a Chapter for Ladies* by Mrs. Hillyard, formerly Blanche Bingley, who at the time the book was published, had won three Wimbledon and two Irish singles titles, and would win more. Wilberforce was a barrister-at-law and secretary to the All-England LTC (1888-1891). He was "four-handed champion" (i.e. doubles) with the Honorable P.Bowes-Lyon in 1887. They won that final in three sets and took the Renshaws to five sets the final year. He also reached the semi-finals at the Championships in 1886. He was in a position, therefore, to offer many opinions on the game as he saw it at that time. In his introductory chapter he says the following:

To that anomalous individual, the thoughtful observer the success of lawn tennis, unprecedented alike in extent and rapidity, cannot have been a matter of surprise. "A priori" it is just the game to fill a want in human nature, or at any rate in the nature of English men and women. Croquet was all very well in its way, but it gave no exercise; its social advantages are equally shared by lawn tennis; and it fostered (for this reason principally it fell) the ascendancy of the curate.

Cricket, on the other hand, requires more time than many people can give to a pastime, it takes a larger number of players, and even the best men can never be sure whether it will be his lot to spend the day in the most violent exertion or in lounging in the pavilion. To my mind this element of uncertainty is most unpleasant: there are times when one is possessed with a frantic desire for running about, and then it is very trying to have to sit still and watch the activity of others; equally annoying it is to be called on to go out and field in the hot sun just when one wants to "sport with Amaryllis in the shade". However, whether these feelings are shared by others or not, the result has been that not only are England, Ireland, and in a less degree Scotland, white with lines of lawn-tennis courts, but in all the colonies, in America, in the south of France-everywhere, in short, where two or three Englishmen are gathered together, the game flourishes and tournaments abound.

Finally, a note of celebration. On the 21st June 2003 all eyes were on the Special Olympics which opened in Croagh Park, Dublin. A sporting showpiece for all! Those participating probably obtained more joy and satisfaction than the more advantaged have ever obtained. The lesson! No matter what your standard etc. enjoy sport as a life enhancing activity.

Three contrasting Irish sports with lengthy heritages are cricket, lawn tennis and croquet (the latter thought to have been first played in this country).

Above, the students at Clongowes Wood College (circa 1930), County Kildare, playing cricket and tennis. To the left, croquet players from Clontarf Lawn Tennis Club, Dublin, in 1972.

The History of Irish Tennis

1.2 Who Plays Tennis?

He lived life to the full, as it should be played, to the full to the end.
(Sheila Reeves Smith, in 2001, concerning her late husband, Patrick)

In sifting through a range of tennis records one can come across, usually by accident, a well-known public personality and find that they have been a tennis aficionado in the past, or are still playing the game. As this book attempts to cover all angles on the sport in Ireland, a few lines on our varied players will not go amiss.

Taken at the California Tennis Club, San Francisco, in about 1940 were Matt Murphy Senior and Junior. The Dad was Irish Consul at the time. The son would become an enthusiastic Irish Davis Cup player in 1950.

Our first President, Douglas Hyde, was a keen tennis player, in addition to participating in hunting, boating and boxing. He spent much of his younger day playing at **Boyle LTC**. Details are included in chapter 8. Maeve Markievicz, daughter of Countess Markievitz (nee Gore-Booth) the 'rebel' and patriot, was a keen player at the exclusive **County Sligo TC** in the late 1910s at a time when her mother was in the news as a national personality. In the Sligo Open tournament of 1919, for example, Maeve played off –15 in the ladies handicap singles, and reached the semi-finals. This was the first Sligo 'Open' after the Great War. In the doubles she played with Miss Eithne L'Estrange and won that event beating the Fitzgerald sisters 3/6 7/5 6/4 in the final. One suspects that her mother must also have played the game at Lissadell, the family home of the Gore-Booths. Fanciful perhaps, maybe William Butler Yeats played there while on his visits.

A writer that we can confirm as having played tennis was Samuel Beckett. On his families grass court at home in Dublin he played with his older brother Frank and his father. He and Frank won junior tournaments at **Carrickmines Croquet & LTC**. He also played golf and, in the annual world cricket almanac, he is noted as the only "first-class" cricketer who was also a Nobel Prize winner.

In 1925 Matt Murphy was sent to New York as the first Consul representing the new Irish Free State. A keen player, who subsequently opened the first Irish Consulate in San Francisco (1933) and then the first legation in South America (Buenos Aires, 1947). Tennis went with him. His wife played and Matt junior was promised $5 for the first set he could take off his dad. This took him several years to achieve. However, Matt junior was keen and eventually was ranked in the USA, Argentina and became number 2 in Ireland as well as representing us in the Davis Cup.

Politicians

Before World War 2, Garrett Fitzgerald, the Fine Gael politician and former taoiseach, recalls that there was a tennis court in the field in front of the family home at Bray. *During the summer there were tennis parties on many weekends, although the court was also used for croquet occasionally! (the clock golf was played on a different lawn). However I never played myself. Any attempt to do so failed because of my extreme clumsiness and inability to connect the ball and racquet.* Senator Edward (*Ned*) McGuire was probably better known in his younger days as an international tennis player than a public representative. He played his first Davis Cup match back in 1926.

A reasonably successful tennis player was Padraic Flynn (Fianna Fail TD and former European Commissioner). He, and his brother, were keen and capable members of the **Castlebar TC.** In 1962, Padraic, playing with a Miss Rochford, won the Connacht hardcourt mixed championships. In the final they beat Bobby Keogh and Ann Mahony 4/6 7/5 6/3. To add to his interest he also coached younger players. Daughter Beverley, who became a TD herself, was keen on sport having played basketball, volleyball, golf and squash. She also participated in athletics where sprinting and the high jump were her specialties. Tennis was a sport she was keen on and took up the game at seven years of age at **Castlebar TC.** She admired Borg, Everett and Connors as players. Her need for a racquet was highlighted on the Marion Finucane radio programme a couple of years ago. She went straight to her father who happened to be having a clinic (political) at the time. There were plenty of locals in the waiting room seeking his attentions. This did not deter the young Beverley and she waited in the room along with the others. Dad, spotting her, asked in his direct and forceful fashion: *What are you doing here?* (or words to that effect).

Joe O'Malley, the noted political commentator was a very useful tennis player when growing up in Limerick. This photograph was taken at Limerick Lawn Tennis Club in about 1958. Dick Quin is with his charges that were challenging the best at the Irish Championships at Fitzwilliam LTC. From left: Joe O'Malley, Redmond O'Hanlon, Maeve O'Malley, John O'Brien and Michael Hickey. The latter two boys became international players of note.

She explained, in an equally determined fashion, her need for a racquet and money to buy same. Needless to say she achieved her objective fairly quickly. Was this a political lesson in achieving a target?

Politician John Bruton, a keen tennis fan for many years and a playing members at Lansdowne LTC.

Another family to take to tennis were the O'Malleys of Limerick. Des O'Malley (Progressive Democrat founder) can clearly remember the day, in 1952, when Maureen Connolly visited the **Limerick LTC**. An astute club member knew she was at Shannon airport, on her way back to the USA having won her first Wimbledon and Irish championships, and invited her to visit the club. Des was one of a large number of youngsters to have a group photograph taken with Little Mo. Des would not consider himself as being a good tennis player; rugby, and later golf, were more his forte. He did say that his brother Joe was a useful player. Former Fine Gael leader and Taoiseach, John Bruton, took up the game in about 1955, playing at the **North Kildare LTC.** He also played at Clongowes Wood College and, in recent years, has been seen playing at **Lansdowne LTC** and **Dunboyne LTC.** He has no major wins to his credit but is a sure and certain follower: *I enjoy the game every time I play.* No doubt the game is a great tonic away from the pressures of political life. In his younger days he also played rugby, *badly* for the North Kildare RFC. Senator Maurice Manning took up the game at 10 years of age on the courts of **Bagnelstown LTC.** Later he played on a club team and was also a member of the UCD tennis club while a student there. His other sporting interests include swimming and golf. Alan Shatter is another politician with a wide sporting interest. He took up the game at the age of ten, playing for the **Maccabi** club in Dublin. He attended the High School and later Trinity College. He is currently a member of **Riverview Racquets Club** at Clonskeagh. He is pleased with *any win I can manage* and plays like *Donald Duck.* One is not sure how the Disney character would play tennis. One suspects this rangy sportsman is not that bad. Apart from an interest in chess and draughts, he has played rugby, table tennis and soccer and was a useful athlete. He was athletics school captain and later a member of the TCD athletics team and Crusaders AC, the quarter and half mile being his specialties.

Jimmy Deenihan, the Fine Gael politician, was involved in the highlighting women's sport through a special conference in 2004. This Listowel man won five all-Ireland football medals with Kerry between 1975 and 1981. He was appointed to the Senate in 1982 and was elected to the Dail in 1987. In 2002 he became the Opposition Spokesperson for Arts, Sport and Tourism. He has many sporting interests including tennis and jests that the Fine Gael leader John Bruton dropped him from the 'front bench' only after Jimmy beat John in a tennis match at **Lansdowne LTC**.

John Pius Boland (1870-1958) was a member of the noted confectionery family (Boland's Bakery). Apart from being a barrister and writer, he was a noted nationalist politician. His sporting claim to fame was the tennis gold medals, singles and doubles, he won at the inaugural modern Olympics at Athens in 1896.

One last politician seen with racquet in hand is former Taoiseach, Albert Reynolds. He has sons who were particularly useful when playing at **County Longford LTC,** evidence on his own expertise is limited but he was seen on court at the opening of the **Riverview Racquets Club.** In June 2002, across the water, the British Prime Minister, Tony Blair, was good enough to play on the show court at the Queen's Club after the final of Stella Artois. This was a men's doubles charity affair, he is a useful exponent of the game. Recently elected TD, Doctor Jimmy Devins, has been known to play tennis as a recreational sport but, with politics taking up so much time, he has hardly any spare hours left to even play in his fourball (golf) at Rosses Point on a regular basis, never mind tennis. His wife Mary, a judge, is more than useful at the sport and does play regularly. Their children have all played from time to time.

Entertainers

One of Ireland's greatest all round entertainers in his day was Percy French. He was a member of **Boyle LTC** and played as a student at Trinity College, Dublin. His writings on tennis are discussed in chapter 3 and his own story in chapter 8. It is not known whether Count John McCormack, the world famous tenor, played tennis in Athlone but he was certainly a member of the **County Kildare Club** (now **Naas LTC**). Another Irish tenor of international note, Frank Patterson, was a keen tennis player. In 2000, he died at the age of 62. *From an early age he was a keen and accomplished sportsman. He played hurling for Marfield, home of the legendary Tipperary hurler Theo English. He was also a leading light of Hillview Tennis Club and the King Willow Cricket Club. He continued to play tennis throughout his life and became a single-figure golfer. He was a member of Lake Isle Golf Club of New York and Milltown Golf Club, Dublin* (Irish Times, 17th June 2000). A fellow singer who travelled through the US and Canada in 1966 was baritone Brendan Kelly from Strandhill, County Sligo. Brendan not alone won the Connacht boy's tennis championship but represented the province in both veteran's tennis and squash.

Frank Patterson-professional singer-was also adept at hurling, tennis and golf.

We all know of Cliff Richard's singing at Wimbledon, during rain breaks. Many will not know that soccer supporter Elton John (full name Reginald Kenneth White) was also fond of the game of tennis. In fact, during a game in the South of France (Nice), he was called off the court. His doctor was on the phone telling him he needed a pacemaker. That stopped the day's play. Ireland's showband star, Waterford's showband singer Brendan Bowyer, has now a family of tennis players. His wife Maeve (Brennan), originally from Galway and children Brendan, Clodagh and Aisling have all excelled at the sport (see chapter 3.5).

Westlife, that popular pop group of the present day, has a hidden tennis player on the team. Sligo's Mark Feehily, was an exceptional tennis (and badminton) player as a youngster. Presumably he can go back to the game any time his busy recording and concert schedule permits. Television holiday presenter, Craig Doyle is a useful player and just might make a good opponent if you just happen to meet him on one of his worldwide trips. Ask.

Talk of recordings reminds me of Lyric FM's Des Keogh. A man of many parts, Des has always been a more than useful tennis player. In his early days he was a member of **Birr LTC**. He was good enough as a teenager to win his school's championship for four years in a row. He also reached the semi-finals of the Leinster under 15 boys' championship in about 1950.

A one-time regular on the airwaves was Bunny Carr. A founder of Carr Communications, he was also, if my information is correct a volleyer of the fluffy covered ball and a member of **Sutton LTC**. Now, we all know who Limerick's Terry Wogan is. It came as a surprise to this writer that he also played tennis, in addition to his Pro-Celebrity golf matches. In addition, he has written, amusingly on the sport, (see Chapter 3.7). RTE broadcasters Pat Kenny and Ryan Tubridy are said to be tennis players. Under the category of entertainer one could include Berrie O'Neill. This interesting man, born 4th May 1930 at Eyrecourt, east County Galway, took up tennis at the age of ten at the local rectory. He attended Wilson's Hospital school

in County Westmeath and then Mountjoy School in Dublin. There was no serious tennis at either school. In his working life he was a bank manager and lived in many parts of the country. In the 1950s, while in Dublin, he became a member of the Aer Lingus Club at Brighton Square and of the **Leinster Stratford LTC**. Tennis was only a social sport for Berrie. However, he played and was successful at other sports. He was a member of Wanderers RFC (1948-1958) and captain of Corinthian's Hockey Club (1960). Moving to Belfast, he became captain of the Belfast YMCA Hockey Club (1961/1962). This team won the All-Ireland Senior Hockey Cup in 1961.

From 1950 to 1960 Berrie became a squash-playing member of the Banker's Club in Dublin. He played on the Leinster squash team for several seasons in the late 1950s. Between 1962 and 1972 he played squash at the CIYMS in Belfast. This club won the Ulster Senior League in 1970. At number 1 on the team was another all-rounder, Cecil Pedlow, the Irish international, and Lions, rugby player and Ulster tennis player who was Irish Boy's Open Champion in 1952. On the tennis front, even though he enjoyed the sport, Berrie's successes were more limiting. He does recall winning the handicap men's doubles at the **Leinster-Stratford LTC** in the mid-1950s. Some *members thought my sliced forehand was unsporting as the ball did not bounce on sticky grass courts.* He was a great admirer of Cyril Kemp, Ireland's number 1 player in the 1940s.

The 1955 Birr Open Championships. Des Keogh (on left), the noted presenter and entertainer, won the singles, beating J. C. Dawson 6/2 8/6 in the final. He and Miss J. Kennedy beat Des Houlihan and Miss O'Meara 6/4 3/6 11/9 in the mixed final. In the men's doubles he and Des (beside him) beat J. C. Dawson & W. J. Dalton 6/3 6/2.

TV and radio personality Bunny Carr was Tennis Captain at Sutton LTC in 1950.

Mark Feehily of Westlife, learned the sports of tennis and badminton at Sligo Tennis Club.

Today, Berrie is retired but has a very significant connection with a tennis player of old. He has been involved with *The Percy French Society* since it was founded in 1983. A bit like Berrie, Percy was a multi-talented individual who played tennis. Percy wrote widely on the sport (see chapter 3.7) and even played in the Irish Championships (see chapter 8). Berrie is one of the chief organisers of this North Down group and is the compiler of *The Jarvey*. Issue 70 of this regular Newsletter was circulated in January 2004. In issue 69 he refers to the many parodies of Percy and noted that he was a keen member of **Fitzwilliam LTC**. *One of them "The Tennis Tournament-A Lay of Modern Dublin" is based on the historical epic style of Lord Macauley with his "Lays of Ancient Rome" except that in the irreverent imagination of Percy French they are from "Lays of Ancient Hens" written*

by "Lord What-you-may-call-eh?" Some other tennis parodies, "Fitzwilliam Square" and "How Hiawatha Won the Cup", are clearly based on the work of Henry Wadsworth Longfellow as Percy French is impressed by the parade of world tennis champions that once used come to Dublin after the Wimbledon Tournament-the equivalent of the Borgs and McEnroes of the modern era:

Let me hymn those mighty heroes,
Let me sing their deeds sublime,
Let me send their names resounding
Down the ringing grooves of time.

Like Percy French, Berrie O'Neill is a bit of all-rounder - work, sport and entertainment all being amalgamated into a collage for living. This formula for a contented and satisfying life is one we can all learn from in our own way.

Businessmen, professionals et al.

The list of businessmen taking to the court as a form of exercise is lengthy. These include Jim Flannery (MD, Claims Management International), Duncan Styles (MD, QMS), Ralf Lissek (Executive Director of the German-Irish Chamber of Industry and Commerce), Galen Bales (Founder and Vice-President of Point Information Systems), Des Thornton (Finance Director, Hewlett-Packard), John Lowe (Founder and MD of Providence Finance Services Limited), Nell Stewart-Liberty (publisher of *Social & Personal)* and Jerome Kennedy (Partner, KPMG). Paul Kilduff, the Vice-President of Merrill Lynch Capital Markets Bank is also an author of financial thrillers. His main form of exercise is tennis and was captain of the **Sandycove LTC** veterans (35+) team in 2001.

Redmond O'Donoghue, the successful CEO of Waterford-Wedgewood, has been successful on the tennis-playing front too.

Redmond O'Donoghue (Chief Executive of Waterford-Wedgewood) has been an exceptionally useful player for many years. In a business column in the *Irish Times* (7th March 2002) he professed to be

Dr. Chris Horan (left) the chairman of Iona Technologies and of The Irish Management Institute is also a useful tennis player. Here he discusses his sponsorship of the National Veteran's Championships with his father John (centre), the former Wimbledon junior champion and professional coach, and Gerry Clarke, the organiser of veteran's tennis in Ireland.

part of the "glass half-full" school. Perhaps this attitude is why he has been so successful in his chosen career, as well as at tennis from an early age. In 1977, when **Fitzwilliam LTC** was celebrating their centenary, an eight-sided team tournament was arranged. This included four provincial teams. Redmond was captain of the Munster side and, twenty-five years later, is remembered as providing one of the great entertaining speeches at the post-tennis festivities.

Bob Essner, chairman, chief executive & president of Wyeth, is a keen amateur photographer and also *enjoys a game of tennis. Oliver Hughes,* the 46-year-old owner of Lillies Bordello nightclub and the Porterhouse pub and brewery group, is also a barrister. He plays indoor football and tennis as his active leisure pursuits. In 2005, Martin Rafferty, retired as chairman of the United Drug company. He is keen on all sports and has been a competitive tennis player for years. In recent times he played for the Connacht veterans'team. The busy 58-year-old John Fitzgerald was born in Limerick and has been the Dublin City Manager for a number of years. His hobbies include walking and tennis.

Richard Nesbitt, a barrister and director of Arnotts, the Dublin retail company where his great grandfather worked in 1867, is a keen tennis player. In addition, he swims, cycles and enjoys skiing, windsurfing, hill walking and travel. Carl McCann, the 50-year-old chairman of Fyffes, the fruit importers, is in a business

that is in the blood. His father Neil, and grandfather, Charles trace the family interest back to the beginning of the 20th century. Carl *likes tennis* but, at present, his four young children occupy most of his free time. His father Neil has played the game of tennis for many years.

Exceptionally successful, property developer Paddy Kelly was born in Clonmore, near Portlaoise, in 1944. He is *A keen dancer, he also did a lot of running with the Belfield Bachelors. A good tennis player, he is currently working hard on his golf handicap (The Irish Times, 26th November 2004).*

In February 2005 Ian Cairnduff died at the age of 69. He could be considered an all-rounder. Apart from being a successful accountant and businessman, this Dublin man of many fine qualities, was possibly best known for his rugby with Old Wesley and as president of the Leinster Branch IRFU. He boxed while at school in St. Andrews and was also interested in athletics. On the tennis front he became a member of **Fitzwilliam LTC** and its honorary secretary in 1983.

According to the *Sunday Independent* (30th March 2003), Gavin O'Reilly, the chief operating officer of Independent News & Media plc, has hobbies, which include a *poor game of tennis.* The other hobby listed is that of *chauffeuring his two daughters around.* Aengus Fanning, the well-known editor of the *Sunday Independent* is a keen cricket fan. However, there is tennis in the family. His mother Clara Adelaide Connell was of Northern Presbyterian stock and worked for the *Belfast Telegraph*. His father, Arnold Patrick *(Paddy)*, grew up in Birr, County Offaly, and as an adult moved to Ulster where he taught science and mathematics. Clara and Paddy met though their love of tennis and badminton. In order to marry, Clara converted to Catholicism. He secured a teaching post in Tralee and they moved there in the early 1930s. Clara died at the age of 98 in July 2004.

Doctor Chris Horn, Chairman of Iona Technologies, and recently elected Chairman of the Irish Management Institute, plays tennis, and why wouldn't he. His parents are the noted Angela, and the late John Horn. Both qualified and practised as professional coaches. In recent times Chris's firm has been generously associated with sponsorship of the annual National Veterans' Championships held each autumn at **Lansdowne LTC.**

Peter Cowan, director of dental affairs, Royal College of Surgeons in Ireland, said in the Irish Times (March 2005) that his father, father, grandfather and great-great uncles were all dentists. He used to be a drummer in a rock. *My other passion is for tennis, which I have played (rather better than my drumming experiences) all my life. It would have been an experience to play on the circuit if I had been good enough. For me, a serious game of tennis is my stress reliever provided the backhand volley is working well.*

Professor Des McHale, of the Department of Mathematics at University College, Cork, learned to play tennis at **Castlebar Tennis Club.** He was not all brains and proved to be a useful player representing both Galway and Keele Universities (the latter while studying for his PhD). He also represented Connacht, playing on the Under 21 team. He has written a series of five WIT books with some tennis thrown in. Dr. Sean McDonagh, another mathematician, and former head of the Institute of Technology in Dundalk was a keen player though not in the same league.

Edward William Delany *(Lany)* Bacon died on the 9th February 2005, at the age of 80. This Dublin man was a brilliant barrister who became known as a brilliant wordsmith, the drafter of Irish legislation for over 50 years. This gregarious character had many interest including the theatre, the French language. He enjoyed squash and water-skiing. He played tennis and cycled right up to the end. An eclectic personality if ever there was one.

Sportspersons

George McVeagh, Solicitor General for Ireland in 1950, captained the Davis Cup team to play in Warsaw that same year. He excelled at many sports. Mendel Stein, born into the Jewish community who arrived in Ireland in the late 19th century, died in recent years in his eighties. He was known as the "Eye" optician but was a keen sportsman in the background. He was involved in setting up the Apollo gym in 1945 and was an active member of the Dublin Maccabi Sports Club and **Fitzwilliam LTC.** Lieutenant-Colonel Herbert Purcell, MBE, was born in Dublin in 1910 and had a varied military career having joined the RAF in 1915. He was a successful rugby player at Belvedere

College, Dublin, and ultimately be a sporting all-rounder being successful at rowing, polo and *was a well-known and very good tennis player, being a member of Carrickmines, Fitzwilliam and Monkstown clubs.* Professor Aidan Moran and restaurateur, Patrick Guibaud, take to the courts as a primary form of fresh air activity.

Two of our current top professional golfers, Paul McGinley and Padraic Harrington, are known to potter around at tennis. Both were made honorary members at **Templeogue LTC** following their world cup win at Kiawah Island in 1997. It might be noted that the great Jack Nicklaus and the current world star, Ernie Els were both useful tennis players. Who says you can mix tennis and golf?

Michael Fleming a civil engineering, originally from County Wicklow, became County Engineer in Sligo and Leitrim before retiring in 1982. As an engineer he was involved in designing the layout at the golf course at Ballyliffin in County Donegal. As a sportsman he has been successful at rugby (on the winning Blackrock SCT in the 1930s), a golfer, a fisherman, a gunman and an interprovincial badminton and tennis player. This photograph was taken following a sportsman of the year award (for badminton) in 1970.

Mr. Justice Seamus Egan died in January 2004 at the age of 85. He was born in Tuam, County Galway, and when the family moved to Dublin he attended Synge Street and Blackrock College. He studied law at UCD and the Kings Inns before joining the Western Circuit as a barrister in 1945. He was a keen tennis player and played both tennis and table tennis for Connacht. He met his wife, Ada Leady at the **Anglesea LTC** in Dublin. He became a lifelong member of **Fitzwilliam LTC** and was also a keen playing member at Milltown Golf Club. Also to pass on in recent times was Archbishop Michael Courtney who originally hailed from Nenagh, County Tipperary. He attended

Clongowes Wood College where his love of sport was extensive. He was tragically killed in Burundi on the 29th December 2003 at the age of 58. He had been Apostolic Nuncio in that country at the time of his death. His sporting interests included rugby (he was captain of the school team), swimming, snow and water skiing, sailing and lawn tennis. James White (16th September 1913-June 2nd 2003) was an art critic and headed the National Gallery of Ireland. In 1937 he was a founder member of the Irish Ballet Club. In an RTE interview he explained that: *Through ballet, I saw the meaning of painting as a background to movement and music.* He attended Belvedere College in Dublin where, apart from his developing interest in art, he played both the sports of rugby and tennis. He later played a considerable amount of golf at Portmarnock Golf Club.

John O'Shea, known originally as a newspaper reporter, and, latterly, as the driving force behind GOAL (the international charity), is also an exceptional tennis player (see chapter 6). On the 8th March 2002, John Daly, in his BBC chat show, had well known northern personality, Stephen Watson, on his show. He announced that one of Stephen's claims to fame was that he had played against Ille Nastase, presumably in a charity game. Stephen, not a 'real' tennis player, would admit that Ille pointed out that he played like a woman, and should be wearing a skirt. I'm sure a good coach would sort out his game in quick order. Fintan Drury attended Blackrock College in Dublin and has been associated with sports all his life. In 2004 he was in the news through his job as a professional football agent. In his mid 40s he is also chairman of Paddy Power Bookmakers and Platinum One and is a director of Anglo Irish. He said in a *Sunday Independent* interview (January 9th 2005) that his hobbies were: *Spending time with his family, playing golf and tennis and supporting Manchester United.*

Peter Jackson (left) the Dunlop representative and also a Davis Cup player has a 'rally' with Mary Peters, the Olympic Gold medallist (athletics). Mary's niece Shannon (Peters) travelled from Australia to win the Irish Open Ladies' Singles Championship in 1990. Also in photo are Sam Jameson and Irish international Susan Minford.

Ulick O'Connor is known for his writings. However, at one time he was lauded for his skills at boxing and the polevault, among other things. He has written the history of the first 100 years of **Fitzwilliam LTC**,

mentioned here in a number of chapters. In 2003 he wrote "The Ulick O'Connor Diaries, 1970-1981". In the *Sunday Independent* (19th October 2003) Victoria Mary Clarke reviewed the book, a man she calls *The Ultimate Renaissance man, Ulick O'Connor has been a sportsman, poet, playwright, biographer and barrister......*She adds that *The diaries are punctuated with sporting interludes, including tennis with Desmond Guinness at Castletown, judging the Trinity College Races, cricket with the Georgian Society and sparring with Charlie Nash in Derry.* An interesting Irish character, certainly one with a love for a wide range of sports!

In the chapter of all-rounders we identify many sports people who are all-rounders of the highest calibre. Some are obvious, such as rugby internationals Tony O'Reilly and Tony Ensor. Kevin Flynn, who earned 22 Irish caps between 1959 and 1973, had been a long-standing member of Templeogue tennis club when asked, in about 1977, to train the Irish Davis Cup squad. He found that they were not as fit as they might be. Other all-rounders who have played tennis include athletes Sophie Pierce-Evans (also known as Lady Mary Heath, the flying adventurer), Ronnie Delaney, Maeve Kyle and even Kathrina McKiernan has had a go. Squash players such as Willie Hosey, John Kielty and Ben Cranwell are all useful tennis players. The story goes that Willie, as a fifteen year old, was out playing tennis when the local team were a man short for an important squash match. He duly obliged, won his match comfortably, and an international squash player was born. Of course, he didn't lick it off the grass. His father was a noted sportsman before him in Carlow. Players to succeed at squash after tennis include Michael Hickey, Geraldine Barniville, Dorothy Armstrong, Ross Niland and, recently, his sister Gina Niland

Two noted hurlers are among the broad band of tennis players. The great Tipperary hurler, Nicky English, was a promising tennis player at the Tipperary County club. At 18 he decided to concentrate of hurling as his primary sport. Former Tipperary hurling goalkeeper, John O' Donogue, kept up playing tennis was still doing so in recent years. Enda Colleran (1942-2004) was the charismatic Galway footballer and captain of the team that won three all-Ireland football championships in the 1960s. When the ban was lifted this teacher by profession played rugby with Corinthians RFC in Galway. He played many other sports including golf and tennis (becoming a Connacht verteran interprovincial player)

The Devlin sisters (Sue and Judy), *Curly* Mack, Frank Peard, J.J. Fitzgibbon, Audrey Kinkead and Mary Dinan were all known for their badminton activity on the international stage. The first four were also tennis players of international standing. Des O'Brien, Betty Henderson (nee Kyle), Maeve Kyle, Jennifer O'Brien, Sandra O'Gorman, George McVeagh, Fiona Ruttle and Rita Rutherfoord were all noted hockey *and* tennis players. In 1932 Bob Tisdall won the Olympic Gold medal for Ireland in Los Angeles. His event was the 400 metres hurdles. He was a natural athlete. He ran in world record time but as he knocked over one of the hurdles it could not be ratified. The Hollywood filmstars of that time, which included Douglas Fairbanks, Jean Harlow and Mary Pickford, selected the 25-year-old Bob as the most physically perfect specimen of the 1,456 competitors at the Games. While Bob always considered his home as being Nenagh, County Tipperary, he lived much of his life in Australia. In 2000, at the age of 93, Bob jogged through Sydney for 500 yards with the Olympic torch. He swam regularly, took up golf and also played tennis. Always a thorough gentleman, Bob, who was born on the 16th May 1907, died at the age of 97, in July 2004. An interesting list of tennis players is those who also played rugby. It is a fact that, historically, schools that have rugby as the main winter sport would, more often than not, have tennis (or possibly cricket) as a main summer sport. Joe Hackett, the Davis Cup, player was known to have said that if he had to choose only one sport that it would have been rugby. He was a Leinster Interprovincal rugby player in his day.

1959-Patrick Reeves-Smyth lining the court at home with daughter Anne supervising.

Those sometimes hidden band of sportswriters were in fact also more than expert at the sport itself. Included among them are the late Vera McWeeney of the Irish Times. In 1940 she won the Irish Close doubles championships with Norma Stoker. Played at **Elm Park**, they beat Barbara Good and Norah Conway 6/1 6/1 in the final. Vera was ranked number four in Ireland at the end of the 1937 season. Colm Smith, now retired, was a class 1 tennis player at **Glasnevin LTC** and featured in doubles with John Murray on the Leinster senior team in the 1960s. Not alone did he attend many Wimbledon championships, on behalf of the Irish Independent, but played tennis whenever he got a chance. One year he had to fly back to Dublin on the mid-Sunday of the championships to play a league match, under an assumed name. He was an excellent reporter on other sports, which included rugby and golf.

Pat Reeves-Smyth

The following story of tennis was sent to me by a keen tennis fan, Sheila Reeves Smyth. For the best part of a century her family have played all over Ireland and abroad. Tennis was in her blood from an early date. Her husband, Patrick Reeves Smyth, was born on the 8th June 1918 in Dublin but died of cancer in 1979. He attended Belvedere College in Dublin and later Downside in England. His tennis was played on their two grass courts at home in Ashbrook and then as a club member of Carrickmines and Fitzwilliam. He also played hockey for Three Rock Rovers and Rathoath and as an interprovincial for Leinster. In addition, he enjoyed cricket and was an amateur horse rider. Billy Dawson was a contemporary of his; as boys they played singles 'all day long'. As teenagers they won the County Wicklow Open Men's Doubles in 1933. Fifteen years later, playing with D. C. Coome, Pat was a winner of the Open Men's Doubles event at Tipperary. In the same year (1945) he won a mixed handicap event at Fitzwilliam with a Miss B. Talbot and at Carrickmines six years later with a Miss S. Reeves.

Sheila and Patrick had six children who played the game (Terence, Carola, Anne, Alice, Nigel and Justina). Sheila was born in 1926 and has many happy memories recollected in this moving piece penned in June 2001.

Tennis has been in the family a long time judging by some of the trophies on my side-board here in Hardymount, County Carlow, where I now live. My father, Thomas Somerville Reeves, from West Cork won the men's singles in Cairo in 1918 and my mother, Olive Kingsford, whose family come from Wicklow, won the ladies in Gibraltar in 1919 having worked in the Censorship office there during the war.

We had a court growing up in Hampshire and our parents used to play tennis with us as small children, my brother Terence, sister Alice and myself. When I went to boarding school at Rookesbury Park, Wickham, there were some beautiful courts among the rhododendrons, always seemingly in flower, where I used to love playing altho' I was frequently sent off the court for being too noisy! Later, at St. Swithuns, Winchester, I played for my house and reached the top of the junior ladder just before war broke out. 'Bagging' one of the courts with racquet and balls and a quick sprint after supper would ensure a game each evening till bed-time.

Returning to Ireland after serving in the W.R.N.S. we lived at Wilton House overlooking __Fitzwilliam Lawn Tennis Club__. Here we would watch such players as Joe Hackett and Cyril Kemp from the windows. During the Open Week at Fitzwilliam we would often hear the name 'Patrick Reeves Smyth' called out over the loudspeaker- This intrigued us because of the similarity of the name! (was he late for his matches, perhaps!?)- We soon moved to Blackcastle, Navan where there was a dilapidated hard court. My brother had been killed during the last week of the war in Germany and my sister had gone to live in Kenya so it wasn't much fun and tennis was confined to parties at the Rectory.

I met Patrick in 1949 and all was to change. He played a lot of tennis at Ashbrook, Castleknock where he lived-hockey all winter and was a keen amateur rider. He introduced me to the tournaments. It was good way to see each other. Organisation was difficult as I had no phone but I __did__ have a car so we used to meet half-way. My tennis wasn't up to scratch so Patrick sent me off to a coach in __Elm Park__-I also cut out all Little Mo'' articles in the Irish Times on how to improve ones game. He also suggested I join __North Kildare__ (the courts were along the road and the ball would frequently fly onto the road!) where I played Number 2 with Felicity Kinahan.

We also joined __Carrickmines Tennis Club__ where John and Myra Stokes had just re-instated the club. (My father had been a member there years previously while a doctor in Leopardstown Hospital and recalled the time the I.R.A. raided and they all hid under the tables in the club house!).What fun the club tournaments used to be! The highlight of the year, it seemed. Round this time Rory Fawcett asked me to play with him in the Fitzwilliam Open. It was to be my most nerve-wrecking experience playing the Fitches from South Africa on the centre court. They later went on to win the tournament but we did manage to get a few games. (The mixed winners in 1949 were E. E. Fannin (Davis Cup player) and Miss J. Fitch; the latter also won the Irish Open Ladies doubles title). That same year I got into the finals of the Plate playing Maeve Lanigan on a hard court in the finals.

We did the round of tournaments that year and the next. __Mullingar__ (we always seemed to be late having been swimming in Loch Owel on the way down), __Ardee__, __Dundalk__ (where Larry Steen and James McArdle reigned supreme), __Birr__, __Cavan__ (John Blaney and Cyril Odlum battled it out in the finals and __Bray__ with its beautiful wooden club house. I played here one year with James Comyn Q.C.. He was Patrick's best friend, had been a half-blue for squash at Oxford-the match went on for hours and hours I remember! __Carlow__, __Rushbrooke__, even Dundee in Scotland, __Enniscorthy__, __Fitzwilliam__, __Lansdowne__ and __Carrickmines__.

The matches always took place in the evenings after office hours at the country tournaments-Cavan was different- There we all stayed at the Farnham Arms or sometimes we would be asked to stay with Doe and Vincent Maxwell at Tullyvin. Matches could start early-too early-and one would be yanked out of bed at some ungodly hour of the morning! Patrick was riding a lot too and would sometimes dash off after a round of tennis to ride in a bumper, chase or hurdle only to play the next round on his return having driven half-way across Ireland and back!

We were married in 1951 and moved to Flemington, Ratoath where Patrick lovingly tended the grass court. We continued the round of tournaments and had lots of tennis parties – Dorothy and Patrick Leonard from Jenkinstown - Hope and Jack Furney from Wexford - Mimes O'Reilly from Roseboro', Naas – Winnie and

Billie Moore from Mooretown, Ardee (they had two grass courts) – Frank and Nori Plunkett-Dillon, Ludford Park, Dundrum – Peter and Dorothy de Stacpoole, Tobertynan – All had grass courts and we in turn would be asked back to tennis and always supper afterwards. Terence, my first born, would always come too-in his cari-cot or, later, play pen where he would sit in ear-shot! Life became complicated when there were six!

After happy years in Flemington we moved to Ashbrook and never a day went by in the summer when we didn't change into our whites and play, the children likewise-Patrick wouldn't allow colours on the court. It was hard sometimes my mustering up enough energy having been with the children all day! He even chose holiday venues with courts. Tobago and in 1978, Gran Canaria, where we packed our racquets and played. Patrick died in early 1979 of dreadful painful cancer, but he lived life to the full, as it should be played, to the full to the end. Days of wine and roses don't last forever and things are different now.

Pseudonyms

Not all players would admit to playing tennis. It may have been a game for the elite or the perceived 'snobs', certainly not the ordinary people. Perhaps it was considered a game for sissies.

In the 19th century tennis *was* a pastime for the elite. Over a lengthy period of time this changed. In the early days playing sport in public was not socially acceptable in certain families. Ladies were particularly shunned or reluctant to enter competition, part of the reason why the entries in the Irish and English Championships were so low. The spirit of tennis did not stop many of them. The use of pseudonyms was the answer. This practice was not just an Irish one.

In 1894, the inaugural tournament was a huge success at Bad Homborg in Germany. Heiner Gillmeister (1997) points out participants included Count Voss, the Grand Duchess Anastasia, and her brother, the Russian Grand Duke Mikhail Mikhailovich. Anastasia was critized for participating by the Empress Friedrich-even though she entered under the name of "Mrs. W." The liberally-minded Baron von Fichard was of the opposite view and wrote:

We will not fail to point out the praiseworthy example given by Her Royal Highness, the Grand Duchess of Meckenbuurg-Schwerin, by engaging in the tournament, to Germany's womanhood. If, in order to liberate the latter from the trammels of a narrow-minded prejudice which excluded German women and girls from health-improving games, a special effort is needed: here indeed it was made by the high-minded lady, to whom we most thankfully pay homage.

Irishmen, Harold Mahony and Dr. Joshua Pim, two of the greats of that era, played at Bad Homborg in 1898. This was in the German Championships. They met in the final, Mahony taking the title. Pim played under the name "Mr. J. Wilson". He would also use a pseudonym in 1903 when selected to play for the Davis Cup team travelling to the USA. In 1899,

The History of Irish Tennis

Charlotte Cooper of England won the German Championship, beating "Frau Hartwig" in the final. The latter was in fact the German number one lady, Countess Clara von der Schulenburg. Her husband's first name was Hartwig. As Gillmeister points out, it is not known why she did this. In earlier and later tournaments she was to use her full name. Another German aristocrat, the Count of Mecklenburg, and a pupil of the Irish coach Burke, used the name "Wenden" in the German Championships in the late 1890s.

Gillmeister had the following comment to make on the adoption of pseudonyms. It was *a necessity at the time for society people who, for reasons of propriety, did not want their names made public in connection with sports: members of the high aristocracy, physicians, officials, military men without a leave of absence or pupils playing truant. Sometimes, it was a downright abuse, as in the case of that ubiquitous and distinguished player "A.N. Other" who, around the turn of the century, frequently graced continental courts with his presence and on one occasion even entered for the Championship of Germany. This pseudonym served two purposes. It either helped to eliminate byes, or functioned as a disguise for a top player, or a player who was not sure whether he could come, and who thus was at liberty to arrive at the venue long after the list of entries had been closed. It was, so to speak, the Victorian Wild Card. On one occasion there were no fewer than three A.N. Others in a single draw.*

Before we leave Germany a few other entries identified by Gillmeister in their tennis tournaments are worth a mention. Two ladies appeared as "T. Ennis" and G. Olf". Among the men were "Dr. Zobeltier" (literally "Dr. Sable Beast) and "W. Uchtig" ("M. Assive") playing in singles and "T. Ruber" and "B. Lick" ("B. Leary" and "E. Eyed") as a pair in the doubles. This was in the early days of the 20th century.

In the first Irish Championships in 1879 the ultimate winner was "St. Leger". He also won the first recorded South of Ireland Championships the previous year; the results for 1877 have been lost in time. His full name became Vere Thomas St. Leger Goold and was ultimately to die in the infamous prison on Devil's Island, having committed a gruesome murder. This story is detailed elsewhere in the book. At Fitzwilliam Square in 1879 there was also a Mr. "B. Philips" from **County Carlow LTC** and a Mr. "H. Arthur" from the host club, **Fitzwilliam LTC.** "Phillips" and "St. Leger" reached the semi-final of the men's doubles championships that year.

In 1882, we find a Mr. J. "Jeffery" and a Captain "De Courcey" entered in the singles. The former failed to turn up and the latter, from the Fitzwilliam Club, was beaten by Mr. O. R. Coote of **Castlerea LTC**, one of the earliest references to tennis in that county. In the 1883 mixed we find a Mr. H. "Gordon", a Miss "Black" and Mrs. "Wordsworth" and in the men's singles a new name, a Mr. M. "Randal" of the **Fitzwilliam LTC.** In 1884 new names included in the men's singles were Mr. W. T. "Bernard" of **Wilton**

LTC and Mr. H. "Evelyn" of **Fitzwilliam LTC.** "Bernard" played with Mr. W. "Russell" of **Wilton LTC** in the doubles. It is interesting to note that, at that time, pairs entered in the doubles must be from the same club. That year there was a Veteran's Cup (over 40) held in conjunction with the Irish Championships. Mr. J. "Granville" lost in the second round. Unlike the Championships singles, the event was the best of three sets in each match.

Reports from other early Irish tournaments showed few if any secretive tendencies, but the same could not be said about the All-England events at Wimbledon. We find only one among the singles finalists. It was that "St. Leger" again. From the Waterford area, he was our first Irish Champion in 1879. He reached the Wimbledon All-Comers final the same year, losing to John Hartley. As Frank Hadow did not 'defend' this was effectively the Championship final. At SW19, other lesser lights did appear under various names in the men's singles such as F. "Harold", W. H. "D'Esterre", "Castor", "Pollux", E. "Cotton", J. J. "Stone", E. "Stanley", A. "Raleigh", S. "Herbert", T. "Jones", J. "Robinson", R. "Trebor", H. "Wilson", E. A. "Ess", F. "Karl", H. M. "Robin", R. "James" and finally, in 1921, J. "Sydney".

Among the Wimbledon ladies singles players there were some interesting names including "Hungerford" (1896). "Ireland" appeared in the draw in 1898 but gave a walk over to Ireland's Louise Martin. She met her also in the first round in 1900 and lost 6/0 6/2.

Today, it is not a matter of hiding ones identity, but quite the opposite. Every full-time player has sponsors and the more they are in the news the better. The names now given to players, other than those chosen by their parents, are all part of the good publicity for the game. Some are complimentary, others not so. When we hear mention of the *Ice Maiden*, the *Super Brat, Bobo* or *Boom Boom* the keen follower will know we are referring to Chris Evert, John McEnroe, Slobodan Zivojinovic and Boris Becker respectively.

Tennis Personae

Like all sports, tennis has had its characters. They come in a range of guises. There are the obvious ones that one can spot a mile away and, at the other end of the scale, those that gradually come to the surface when the night's festivities are well under way. The latter may have needed some fuel of a specific composition to start their engines. They may socialise until dawn, and be the last to leave. Then there are many grey shades in between. The characters may be on court, such as the Dublin player who used to whistle while playing in competitive matches. Others, such as Jim Fitzgibbon, were extremely witty and a joy to be in his company. Then there are those personalities that achieve the highest of office. These are the men and women deserving of the highest praise. They can guide a committee, or club, and do so with a good humour that is infectious. These gifted individuals can make anyone do nearly anything.

Some time ago a few Ulster Davis Cup players were chatting about days gone by. They agreed that record breaking Nora Taylor of **Enniskillen LTC** and then

Omagh LTC fitted into one of these 'personae'. She started playing tennis in the 1920s and was still playing nearly 80 years later. She featured all over Ireland and was a useful player. Few committees could turn down her request for a good partner in the mixed and, on court, she was as wily as they come. However, the wee lads from Ulster, all about twenty years her junior, recall that she would, when the tennis was over, 'drink and dance you off the floor'. A spirited lady if ever there was one.

Norah Taylor in 1948

Peter Jackson, that intrepid Davis Cup player from Belfast, could readily fit into the character slot. For many years he was a sports representative for Dunlop. He readily moved from the world of golf to tennis and elsewhere, all in a day's work. He could, and still does, chat like nobody's business and would entertain any audience with 'true' stories. One of his tales refers to another 'character', NA Palmer. This man was known as NA, everywhere in Ulster. His first name was in fact Norman. It was thought that NA first came to Ulster from England. It was said, "he was shell shocked from a war". Peter postulates (jokingly) that it might have been The Boer War. He was, NA that is, an "incredible wee man, slim man, with varicose veins". His initial point of contact was Vivian Gotto, then one of Ulster's best. This was the 1950s. He persuaded Vivian that he was not a bad player, in fact was quite good and thus gained himself a useful partner for the first tournament he entered. Viv was a bit concerned that he (an international player) would be out of his depth. In fact it was not long before NA was found out.

NA was keen. Between trips/jobs as a toy salesman he played tournaments, everywhere. Peter can recall seeing him on the road, with suitcase under his arm full of toys at 7 a.m. NA would, however, be back for his match at 10 o'clock. The thing was that he was not very good and all players were afraid to meet him in the first round, just in case they might lose and be forever teased by their club mates and probably everyone else at the tournament. Rumours abounded about players who gave up the game when beaten by NA. In one case, again a rumour, a player beaten by NA was off for a swim when NA pulled him back from the water-he thought the player was going to commit suicide. The last laugh was on Peter. He was a great all-round sportsman. However, squash was not his forte. He was beaten regularly, and remembers being "destroyed" by a useful lady player, Louise Cousden. In his club, **Windsor LTC**, he was a travelling sub. When he did play he was regularly beaten. In a crowded dressing room he asked was there an NA Palmer in squash i.e. a player he could beat and thus gain some confidence in his game. As quick as anything, Ken Reid, pipes up: "Peter you **are** the NA Palmer of squash".

The Hamiltons

Finally, a mention must be given to the great Hamilton sporting family. Willoughby was the Wimbledon champion in 1890. He was known as the 'Ghost'. He also won the first Open Men's doubles badminton championship, with one of his brothers, Blaney Balfour, known as 'Bud'. Blaney was Irish Open Badminton championship in that year of 1902. Bud was capped for Ireland at hockey and cricket, as did the eldest brother, William Drummond ('Drum'). Drum played in the Irish tennis championships but was not nearly as good as the 'Ghost'. The latter's nephew, also Willoughby, was known as the 'Rat' Hamilton. It is not known how that name arrived but he was said to have signed his cheques Rat Hamilton. He was top of the world badminton rankings in the 1930s. The sports careers of Arthur and Mavis are also dealt with later.

People arrive at tennis in many ways, through nearby clubs, through schools, through family etc. It is the profession for many. However it is the amateurs that are in the majority. The latter may have very successful lives in other spheres. An attempt has been made here to recognise the eclectic nature of the sport and its people. Included are only a few of the 'well-known' people who have enjoyed the sport. Some names are a surprise. All long-term players will recognise why so many love the sport. Can more be encouraged to lift up a racquet?

In 1985, Dr. Theodor Saretsky published the compiled and annotated writings of Sigmund Freud on the topic of tennis. Freud wrote widely on the connection between tennis and sex. The following 1923 quotation may partly explain why so many people enjoy tennis.

> "All the cultural achievements of which man is so proud, all his spiritual values and the like, are merely sublimations of basic instinctual drives, sex and tennis being the most fundamental."

Now we know why so many love tennis for so long. Or do we?

The History of Irish Tennis

1.3   Tennis All-Rounders

Vitality was the quality above all the others with which he was endowed, that made George McVeagh into one of Ireland's games players. (Irish Times, 12th June 1968)

The era of all-round sports people appears to have vanished. In the days when professional sport was looked down on many superb amateurs came to the fore. These were the well off who devoted much time to their 'pastimes'. They were dedicated amateurs who could afford the luxury of sport whenever they wished. In the USA for example, the wealthy Roosevelt family produced many good tennis players taking one singles and four doubles titles in the US Open. If we look at tennis success in the early days it was more often than not the wealthy that succeeded. Mind you, some of the slightly less well off gentry did prosper on the courts.

Less than one hundred years ago golf professionals were not allowed enter the clubhouse. In some cases this was a fairly recent state of affairs. Further back we find the lord of the manor employing professional cricketers as part of *his* team. Gambling was an accepted part of the upper classes. In tennis, the first big professional tournaments appeared to have begun in the early 1930's with *open* tennis eventually arriving, following an ILTF special general meeting in Paris on the 30th March 1968. In the modern era, it will be difficult to find all-rounders of international standing. Yes, you will find professional tennis players who have a golf handicap of less than ten e.g. Ivan Lendl, Todd Woodforde. Difficult to find players who might, for example, have been Davis Cup players as well as featuring on a Ryder or Walker Cup. Mind you there are professional golfers who were useful tennis players but had to make choices. Two examples come to mind, South African Ernie Els and Jack Nicklaus from the USA.

Zelie Godfrey won the Irish Close Ladies Doubles and Mixed Doubles lawn tennis titles in 1941 (at Sunday's Well). In 1964, as Mrs. Fallon, she was playing in her 13th consecutive home international golf series and was crowned Irish Close Champion at Portrush.

At home we know many sportsmen and women who move to golf and do quite well at it. One example was Munster's Zelia Godfrey. She was Irish Girls Open Champion in 1934. She won very many mixed titles with Alan Haughton who was a couple of years older. In 1938, they played in the senior tournament at

Blackrock (Cork) losing 6/8 3/6 to J.V.M. Howe and Betty Harman in the second round. Their first significant title was the Munster Hardcourt Championships in 1939. In the final they met and beat Teddy Daly (the number 2 man in Munster) and his sister Frances, the 'best in Cork' at the time, 6/8 6/4 6/2. In 1941 they beat the same pair in the final of the Irish Close Championships at Sunday's Well. The score was a particularly close one, at least in the first set (9/7 0/6 6/3). Zelia also won the Irish Close Ladies Doubles title that year, playing with Frances. In 1944, she had married a golfer and had become Mrs. Fallon (later Mrs. Gaynor). With Alan, they would won the Blackrock tournament, played at Sunday's Well,. In the final they beat Frank Mockler and Mrs. Lister 1/6 7/5 6/3. Golf shortly took over and she would duly become a member of Douglas Golf Club. By 1961 she had won an impressive 5 Munster titles. What was even more impressive was the fact that she secured her first Irish cap so quickly. This was in 1952. She played on every home international team until 1965, then again in 1968, 1970 and, as captain, in 1972. 1964 was particularly impressive when she won the Irish Close title (beating Pat O' Sullivan of Tramore GC at the 37th hole at Portrush) and was picked for the Great Britain & Ireland team. What was the loss to the sport of tennis was a great gain for Irish golf.

Dickie Lloyd and Harry Read, Ireland's first specialised rugby half-backs (1910-1913). Read (on right) played cricket, tennis and croquet for Ireland.

High standards and professional sport now require concentrated dedication, other sports being a leisure activity. For the record, George Kerr who began life as a ball boy was, according to Treacy (1927), appointed an assistant professional at Fitzwilliam LTC in 1883. *He became the greatest of the early professional Lawn Tennis Players, and six years later was allowed to go to America, where he played and defeated Thomas Pettit, in a series of matches for the professional championship of the world. A return match was played in Fitzwilliam Square, to which the club gave ample financial support, and Kerr was again successful. I divert.*

The love of sport in Ireland appears to be an in-built genetic trait. It is probably the physical energetic challenge and ensuing excitement. Add to that, the big social advantage of meeting people through a common love. A boss of mine one time illustrated this importance. Socialising with an Englishman the night before an important meeting he attempted to find a common ground for conversation. Politics might be sensitive and Gaelic Games would definitely not be appropriate. He brought up matters such as the recent FA Cup final, the rugby internationals and even Wimbledon. No bites or nibbles. Next he tried to break through the social barrier with cricket; I think the Ashes had recently been played for. This proved to be

the magic elixir that broke through a difficult barrier. Subsequently, the Irishman and the Englishman were on the best of friendly terms. Though from County Leitrim, he had many all round sporting interests. Cricket happened to be one of them. (Again for the record, one might be surprised to learn that in 19th century Ireland there were cricket matches taking place all over Leitrim.) The following morning they greeted each other like long lost friends. The power of sport! Among the ladies, hockey, squash and badminton seems to be common winter sports linked to tennis. One would probably find a full Irish hockey side over the years with players of a national tennis standing too. This can definitely be said of rugby. There is no doubt that the rugby playing schools, usually with their own tennis courts, have produced players of international standing in both sports. As a curiosity, and a talking point, I have tried to pick an Irish rugby team of former internationals but composed of tennis players. Some are duel internationals, other of a varied tennis standard. It was with great difficulty that a pack of tennis playing forwards was found. The number of rugby caps, and the relevant years, are given in brackets:

Tony Ensor
[22](1973-1978)
Wanderers RFC
UCD, Lansdowne, Enniscorthy LTCs

Jim Parke
[20] (1903-1909)
Monkstown RFC
TCD, Clones and Northern LTCs

Cecil Pedlow
[30] (1953-1963)
Queen's & CIYMS RFCs
Lurgan, Queen's, Windsor Belfast Boat Club LTCs.

Kevin Flynn
[22] (1959-1973)
Wanderers RFC
Templeogue LTC

Tony O'Reilly
[29] (1955-1970)
Old Belvedere and
Leicester RFCs,
Fitzwilliam LTC

John P. Murray
[1](1963)
UCD RFC, UCD LTC

Harry M. Read
[13](1910-1913)
TCD & Roscrea RFC's
Roscrea LTC, TCD LTC

Ernest W. Stoker
[2](1888)
Wanderers RFC

Ken Kennedy
[45] (1965-1975)
QUB, London Irish RFC's

Claude Carroll
[1] (1930)
Bective RFC

H. J. Millar
[4] (1904-1905)
Monkstown RFC
Monkstown LTC

Frank O. Stoker
[5] (1886-1889)
Wanderers RFC
Lansdowne LTC

Des O'Brien
[20] (1948-1952)
London Irish,Cardiff,Old Belvedere RFC's
Kenilworth, Fitzwilliam, Cardiff Castle,
& Dyvours LTCs

Dave O' Loughlin
[6] (1938-1939)
UCC,Garryowen RFC's

Mick Doyle
[20] (1965-1968)
Blackrock College,UCD,
Cambridge Univ.& Edin.
Wanderers RFC.
Naas LTC

Substitutes: **Daniel J. Ross** [5](1884-1886) *Belfast Academy RFC*; **Kevin O'Flanagan** [1](1947) *London Irish RFC;* **Mick O'Flanagan** [1](1948) *Lansdowne RFC, Templeogue LTC:* **Alastair McKibbin** [14](1977-19800 *Queen's Univ., London Irish RFC's,* **M. J. Carpendale** [4](1886-1888), *Monkstown RFC.,* **John J. Blaney** [1] *(1950) UCD & Wanderers RFCs, Fitzwilliam LTC,* **Robbie McGrath** [16] *(1977-1984) Wanderers RFC , Sutton LTC* and **Paul Dean** [33](*1981-1989) St. Mary's College RFC.*

Manager: Declan Kidney.   **Referee: Ray Williams**   **Touch Judge: Bryan O'Neill**

The History of Irish Tennis

Hackett Wins Duel Of Rugby Out-Halves

IN conditions which were anything but conducive to good Lawn Tennis, the East of Ireland championships were continued at Londonbridge Road, yesterday. The unfortunate "powers that be" would almost certainly have ruled out play in the interests of the courts as well as the competitors but for the fact that they were so very far behind.

Foothold was a precarious business and practically all the competitors were sliding and skidding around the place, but the results were in all cases representative of true form.

J. D. Hackett, firm favourite to win the Men's title, dropped a set to H. Crowe, but was fairly well on top in the third session, keeping a good length and advancing to the net at the appropriate moments.

This battle of rugby out-halves provided plenty of entertainment, with Crowe steady from the back of the court and Hackett the more decisive at the net.

After winning the first set 6/3, G. D. Fitzpatrick had to survive many anxious moments before getting the better of I. McG. Boden in a prolonged second set which went to twenty-two games. Boden actually had two set points, but though his sliced backhand won him many points he was never quite at home on the soft surface.

Men's Singles — Second Round — J. D. Hackett bt H. Crowe, 6/4, 5/7, 6/3; B. Carroll w.o. J. S. Hewitt scr.; B. Barry bt. H. G. Viani 2/6, 7/5, 6/4; J. P. McHale bt. J. P. Buckley 6/1, 6/0; D. J. Mulligan bt. V. E. Cross 7/9, 6/0, 6/3; J. D. Fitzpatrick bt. I. McG. Boden 6/3, 12/10; T. P. Byrne bt. W. J. Pentz 6/3, 6/0; J. J. Fitzgibbon bt R. W Tunney 6/2, 6/2; J. Horne bt J. A. Clarke 8/6, 6/2; D. Pratt bt. T. Courtney, 6/1, 6/2.

Ladies' Singles—Second Round—Mrs. J. J. Fitzgibbon bt. Miss J. Mullan 6/2, 6/0; Miss R. Maguire bt. Miss S. Milimo 6/4, 6/4; Miss H. Bretland bt. Mrs. F. B. Lillis 3/6, 7/5, 10/8; Miss N. Sheehan bt. Miss L. McGuire 6/1, 6/0.

Irish Independent 9 June 1955

Harry Read represented Ireland at rugby and cricket and was of an international standing at tennis. He and Dickie Lloyd were the selected half back pairing for thirteen consecutive internationals (1919-1913). At Trinity College they set a record cricket 'stand' of 323 runs. It is not known whether Lloyd ever played tennis or not. As a schoolboy, Lloyd was a member of the Portora Royal School XV that provided all the Ulster schools backline and beat Leinster by a record 72-0, *still believed by many to be the best school team ever seen in Irish rugby* (Van Esbeck, 1999).

If we take squash players we find such luminaries as Geraldine Barniville, Eleanor McFadden and Helen Lennon who were Federation Cup players before taking up the game of squash seriously. Currently, Gina Niland, who has had an extensive tennis career, is trying her hand at the game. Among the men, George McVeagh, Cyril Kemp, Guy Jackson, Michael Hickey, Peter Ledbetter and Ross Niland have played both sports at international level. Davis Cup player Derek Arthurs earned six squash caps and was an Ulster interprovincial badminton player. Others, such as Des O'Brien, Ivar Boden and Willie Hosey, have been squash internationals and more than useful tennis players. It was at rugby that Des O'Brien made the greatest impact in that famous back row after the war. While also a hockey international, he would love to have attempted to qualify for Wimbledon.

Harry Read was multi-talented and played four sports for Ireland. He was captain of teams at school and at Trinity College. Top two photos are the school rugby and cricket teams (seated middle in lower photograph). In golfing mode he obviously had a good swing, probably at his local Roscrea G.C..

The History of Irish Tennis

Rugby Players In Lively Tennis Duel

By B. S. NOLAN

WELL-KNOWN Rugby players, H. Crowe, the U.C.D. out-half, and J. Horne, the Bective Rangers scrum-half, were opposed in the men's singles in the East of Ireland tennis championships at Londonbridge Road yesterday, and, after an absorbing battle, victory went to Horne in the third set.

Crowe started well, striking his backhand fluently and serving with pace and accuracy to win the first set for the loss of two games. Horne gradually assumed mastery after this, however, and, using the court cleverly, he was a deserved winner.

The Munster challenger, F. O. Furney, made further progress, using his long reach to good effect to dispose of the Trinity player, D. Pratt. Using his two-handed backhand skilfully, Pratt captured the first set and held his own for a long time in the second. Once Furney took this in the tenth game, however, the initiative switched to him, and, striking the ball with admirable confidence, he was well on top in the final set.

G. D. Fitzpatrick was given plenty to do by G. Sweetman, who matched his better-known opponent from the back of the court, but Fitzpatrick's ability to raid the net and bring off the occasional coup told in the end.

MEN'S SINGLES — Third Round — B. Kilcoyne bt. P. Nolan, 6-4, 6-3; J. J. FitzGibbon bt. G. Sullivan, 6-1, 6-2; F. O. Furney bt. D. Pratt, 2-6, 6-4, 6-2; G. D. FitzPatrick bt. R. Sweetman, 6-4, 6-4; P. J. Horne bt. H. Crowe, 2-6, 6-3, 6-3; G. D. Foynes bt. B. Citron, 8-6, 2-6, 6-3; I. McG. Boden w.o., W. Hopley scr.

LADIES' SINGLES—First Round—Miss I. Peard bt. Mrs. J. O'Kelly, 6-3, 7-5. Second Round—Miss B. Lindsay bt. Miss F. Kinahan, 6-3, 6-3; Mrs. J. H. Morton bt. Mrs. Peard, 6-1, 6-1; Mrs. L. Cawthorn bt. Miss C. O'Connor, 6-1, 6-1; Miss H. Boyd bt. Miss P. Callaghan, 6-4, 6-3. Third Round—Miss J. A. FitzPatrick bt. Miss B. Moran, 6-4, 6-0.

MEN'S DOUBLES—First Round—R. F. Egan and J. J. FitzGibbon bt. R. Feeley and P. Nolan, 6-1, 6-1; G. D. Foynes and F. O. Furney w.o., P. Quinn and M. Walsh scr.

MIXED DOUBLES—First Round—R. F. Egan and Mrs. Egan bt. R. Sweetman and Mrs. J. O'Kelly, 6-0, 6-3. Second Round —J. J. FitzGibbon and Mrs. FitzGibbon bt. B. Connolly and Miss B. McCrae, 6-0, 6-0; F. J. Timoney and Miss M. Doran bt. D. Cotter and Miss M. Kennedy, 6-2, 4-6, 6-3; I. McG. Boden and Miss J. A. FitzPatrick bt. B. Citron and Miss H. Boyd, 6-2, 6-2; R. Feeley and Mrs. P. Cawthorn bt. J. K. Downey and Miss B. Lindsay, 6-4, 6-4; F. O. Furney and Mrs. F. B. Lillis bt. A. R. Gillespie and Miss J. Morris, 6-2, 6-4.

Irish Independent 10th June 1954

While working in Wales, Des represented that country in hockey and was a reserve on their tennis team. While he played 20 times for the Irish rugby team (1948-1952) and 10 times for the Irish squash team (1952-1965), he never did get picked on the Irish tennis side and would be the first to admit that he had not done enough to merit such a selection.

The late Willie Brown (Elm Park) excelled at whatever he set him mind on. He was particularly known for his expertise on the soccer pitch and was the last true amateur to play for the Republic of Ireland in the 1960s (see Chapter 8.2). North of Ireland soccer international of note, and Arsenal FC player, Sammy Nelson was an excellent junior tennis player before devoting his life to soccer.

Doctor Geraldine Barniville (nee Houlihan) having become one of Ireland's most successful tennis players took up squash and proceeded to accumulate a very large number of titles and international caps in this sport too.

Wille Browne (centre) of Bohemians FC was the last Irish amateur to play for the Republic of Ireland. He played many other sports including GAA football, hockey, badminton, golf, cricket and was a tennis interprovincial.

The History of Irish Tennis

Probably one of the best back rows that the Irish rugby team have ever had. Left to right are Bill McKay, Des O' Brien & Jim McCarthy. They played together 14 times and only lost three matches. Their wins included the two triple crown years, 1948 and 1949. Des O'Brien, despite being an international in the sports of rugby, hockey and squash, had one regret- that he did not get to play at Wimbledon. He played his early tennis at Kenilworth Square, Dublin. Much of his later tennis was played in Wales where he represented South Wales. On one of his visits home he played in the County Dublin Championships at Carrickmines where he reached the final of the singles.

Dorothy Armstrong (right) was Nestle All-Ireland girl's tennis winner in 1964 and won the Lawn Tennis Championship of Ulster (1972). She turned to squash in the 1970s and became Irish Close champion (1975 & 1979) and earned about 70 international caps. On left is Fran Marshall of England.

The Guinness Book of Tennis Facts and Feats has Jim Parke the best male tennis-playing all-rounder ever.

IRISH RACQUETS REVIEW
EIR 1.00 incl VAT (90p Sterling Area)
Vol. 1 No. 7 1990
BADMINTON - SQUASH - TENNIS

Women's World's Squash Championships
Dick O'Rafferty's Coaching Column
Eoin Collins - "Open" King

Helen Lennon was, not alone a Federation Cup player, a Class 1 badminton player, interprovincial squash player, a 14 handicap golfer but is also a coach. She has captained the FED Cup team and the Irish Squash team. Above she is with the latter team in 1990.. Fron left: Rebecca Best, Barry Whitlock (coach), Helen Lennon (manager), Marjorie Croke, Brian Connolly (sponsor, Langdon Ltd., agents for Le Coq Sportif) and Jill McHaughey.

Ivar Boden, also an all-rounder, did play at Wimbledon, but did not quite make the Davis Cup team, there were many useful players around in the post-war era. Joe Hackett and Viv Gotto were tennis internationals but also made a name in other sports, both have played squash for Leinster and Ulster, respectively. There are many, perhaps less known, squash players who have been more than useful tennis players too. Counted among them might be Tadgh Lambe of Tullamore who coaches both sports.

We do not often hear of racquetball players but Dublin's Martyn Evans, originally from Birmingham, an international in this sport, is perhaps one of the most prolific all-rounders of the modern era. He has played League of Ireland soccer with Waterford 'B', a cricket trialist for Warwickshire, a maximum break of 83 in snooker, a keen golfer off 15 and going down, a premier squash player for **Fitzwilliam LTC**, a Leinster badminton interprovincial and good enough to play in the Irish Open Tennis Championships. In *Irish Rackets Review (1989),* Philip Quinn had the following to say about him:

With his ample frame and Mexican moustache, Martyn doesn't look like a candidate for the front cover of "Sports Illustrated" but place a racquet, bat, club or cue in his hands and he is deadly. Just listen to what his sporting rivals say about him . Tennis- "He's the most powerful serve and volley I've ever faced."

(Greg Allen). Badminton –"He can smash anyone in this country off the court." (Aidan Murray). Golf – "If he could control his slice, he'd be off six in no time." (Pat Marron).

In 1986, there was an Irish Racquet Sports Championship held at the UCD facilities in Belfield. The winner was many times squash international, Willie Hosey, also a dab hand at tennis. Second was Davis Cup player Jim McArdle, also a squash interprovincial. Martyn Evans was third. He would later say that he would love to have another go. His favourite to win such a repeat event would be David Borton, who plays squash and badminton to a very high standard. It is surprising that no one has taken up the mantle of a national racquet sports championship. This could be an annual sporting accolade to be prized and maintain the multi-faced nature of Irish sport. In addition to tennis, squash and badminton, there is no reason why racquetball and table tennis could not be included. Martyn would compare the demands of the three big racquet sports as follows: *Badminton is the hardest by far, squash is second and tennis is a poor third. I've played them all and believe me badminton takes more out of you than you might think.*

In conversation, a number of years ago, if my memory has not failed, with a talented all-rounder, it was agreed that to reach a high standard, with appropriate skills, given a reasonable natural ability, then it would take about three years for squash, five for badminton and eight for tennis. There are obviously many exceptions to this, and the ratios might well be argued are 2, 3 and 5.

Badminton has a long history and it is not surprising that there are significant links between the two sports. Like tennis, Ireland was at the forefront of the development of badminton. For many, they would have their season. Badminton taking over in September, and depending upon weather, tennis could come into it's own in April. The Badminton Union of Ireland was formed in 1899, nine years before the ILTA. There have been many badminton players who did well at tennis, and visa versa. Kitty Mc Kane (with an Irish connection) and Mrs. Lambert Chambers have won All-England badminton and tennis titles. The badminton "All-England" titles have the same reverence paid to them by the best players in the world (most now from the Far-East) in the same way as Wimbledon is sanctified by the tennis players.

Without labouring the matter, Frank Devlin, the man whose name is given to the "Devlin Era" of badminton history (the 1920s), had two daughters, Judy and Sue, who would mop up world titles. Both were also ranked among the best tennis players in the USA, when they lived there. Sue married Frank Peard, one of Ireland's best for nearly half a century. He was good enough to play in Wimbledon but decided to concentrate on badminton. Jim (JJ) Fitzgibbon is probably best known for his badminton, yet he was ranked number 3 tennis player in Ireland in 1951. Mary Dinan was an all-rounder of note having in her pocket an All-Ireland camogie medal, a Leinster Junior Cup (team) for golf and 58 caps for badminton. She also played hockey and tennis.

Mary Dinan was to win an All Ireland camogie medal for Wexford. She has 58 badminton caps but also was successful at tennis, golf and hockey.

Derek Arthurs from Belfast excelled at many sports but was particularly noted as a Davis Cup player. He moved to Australia in 1966 where he continued his interest in racquet sports. He won many tennis titles including a world veteran doubles title (60+) in 2001 with Bob Howes. He has six Irish caps for squash. At badminton, he represented Ulster and later South Australia. Derek's son Wayne was on the winning Australian Davis Cup team in 2004.

Frances Dwyer (nee Daly) from Cork played for the Irish hockey team for 30 consecutive matches in the 1930s. In tennis she was ranked number 6 in Ireland in 1936 and 1941.

1982-Cecil Pedlow collecting squash trophy.

Limerick born all-rounders Mary Bryan (nee O'Sullivan) and Michael Hickey reached the Irish Open Mixed lawn tennis final in 1964. They lost 7/5 6/3 to Britain's Jaroslav Drobny and Christine Truman. Mary won the Irish under 15 title in 1951 and under 18 title in 1954. She won the Irish Close Tennis singles title in 1954 and 1955. Her first Irish tennis ranking was equal third in 1955. Her highest ranking was number 2 in 1968. She became one of the best badminton players in the world and has won nine Irish Open titles (3 singles and 6 doubles) between 1956 and 1972. Michael's first Irish tennis ranking was joint sixth in 1960, he was number one for at least seven seasons. Michael has won the Irish Close, South of Ireland, Irish Hardcourt, Leinster Open and County Dublin tennis championships. He has played Davis Cup 21 times and has had 18 Irish caps for squash (1965-1972). He was also a good rugby player and a scratch golfer, at Castletroy G.C.. Mary has been a member of Claremont, UCD, Bective, Lansdowne and Carrickmines tennis clubs while Michael grew up playing at Limerick Lawn and later was a member of Fitzwilliam.

The History of Irish Tennis

This photograph of Tony O'Reilly (left) and Cecil Pedlow was taken at the Riviera Hotel, Johannesburg, just before a friendly game of tennis, during the 1955 Lions rugby tour. As a teenager at Belvedere College Dublin, Tony O'Reilly was one of the top Irish juniors. In 1952 Cecil Pedlow became Irish Open Boy's Champion. The former concentrated on rugby while the Ulster man, in addition to rugby, played representative tennis and squash for many years.

The History of Irish Tennis

The Devlin sisters (Judy left, Sue on right) were to win six All-England doubles badminton titles between 1954 and 1966. When they lived in the USA they were ranked among the top doubles tennis players in that country.

Ranked among the top badminton players in the world, in singles and doubles, Mary Bryan (nee O'Sullivan) would be an international tennis player too, ranked number 3 in Ireland in the early 1960s behind that great duo of Eleanor O'Neill and Geraldine Barniville.

A forgotten all-rounder was Johnnie McCallum. In his book, *Sixty Years of Irish Badminton (1995),* Frank Peard, deservedly, allocates a chapter to Major J. D. M. McCallum CBE, DSO. He was one of the great 'characters' of Irish badminton. He must be included as an all-rounder. He played for the Irish badminton team 8 times. He had a trial for the Irish rugby team and was wicket-keeper for the 1910 Irish cricket team. His major claim to fame, to use a pun, accidentally, was as an administrator. Apart from being the honorary secretary of the Northern Branch of the Badminton Union of Ireland (BUI) for 52 years, he was to make the top of world badminton and become president of the International Badminton Federation (IBF). What about his tennis? Little is known. He did play in the Ulster Open Championships in 1927 at 43 years of age. He was in the main draw but lost in the first round to C. C. Gotto, who was subsequently beaten by finalist R. Pedlow (Ulster interpro player that year). Now they are two surnames we recognise from a later era in Ulster and Irish tennis (the 1950's). In the men's doubles that year, McCallum, playing with H. Bindon Blood, reached the Ulster doubles semi-finals, losing to the eventual winners J. Mathie and J. T. Turner. Gordon (*Curly*) Mack was a 'brilliant' badminton player and would win 8 All-England titles in his time. He reached the semi-final of the Jubilee Championship of Ireland Doubles in 1927 and would be a Davis Cup player three years later. The all-round Hamilton family are dealt with later.

Parke and Dod

By the end of his sports career Jim Parke would have achieved so much that he is in the *Guinness Book of Tennis Facts and Figures* as arguably the **best all-rounder in lawn tennis**. The book, compiled by Lance Tingay has Lottie Dod as **probably the best woman all-rounder.** Those who know their tennis will recognise the fact that it was this Cheshire girl that won Wimbledon at the age of 15 in 1887. She won this title the four other years she competed, the last being in 1893. She lost only one set (out of 19 played) and 37 games (out of 151 played). She won three Irish Championship titles, singles in 1887, ladies' doubles in 1892 and mixed doubles in 1887. She was a hockey international in 1899 and 1900, both matches were against Ireland. She won the British Women's Golf Championship at Troon in 1904. She beat the great Irish lady golfer of that era, Irish champion May Hezlet, by one hole. In the 1908 Olympic Games Lottie won a silver medal in archery. While Lottie Dod has become a name permanently positioned in tennis legend, not so Jim Parke. That is unless you examine his achievements in detail.

Most players on this Terenure College 1966 junior tennis teams excelled at other sports, particularly rugby. Back row (l. to r.): Peter Dunne, Conor Sparks & Declan Herbert. Sitting (l. to r.): Robin Considine, Pat Mahony and John Cronin.

In tennis, he was Irish singles champion eight times between 1904 and 1913, the men's doubles five times between 1909 and 1913 and the mixed twice, in 1909 and 1912. He played Davis Cup in 1908, 1909, 1912, 1913, 1914 and 1920. His tennis playing in 1912 was such as to be nominated by an American tennis magazine as the best player in the world that year. When he virtually won the Davis Cup on his own, and whom he beat, we can see why this was the case. He did win the Wimbledon mixed title (1912 & 1914) and

Dubliner Bobby Keogh excelled at tennis, athletics and rugby

Monkstown Rugby Football Clubs and was capped twenty times for Ireland, three times as captain. His first was against Wales at the age of 21 while at university. He played in the centre and was a regular goal kicker and try scorer. At golf he was a scratch player and he appears to have earned two caps for Ireland. He was a noted sprinter and a first class cricketer. Olympic medallist, Ronnie Delaney, has been a successful tennis-playing member of **Carrickmines Croquet & LTC** for many years. Full time tennis coach and veterans international, Billy Bolster, was noted as an international athlete in his earlier days. Among the ladies on has to go back to an outstanding lady athlete of the 1920's. At a time when ladies were not encouraged to play sports, Sophie Pierce-Evans was a bit of an all rounder with tennis as part of her portfolio. This woman from Knockaderry, County Limerick, held several world athletics records. Noel Henry highlights this outstanding woman in his book *From Sophie to Sonia: A history of women's athletics* (1998), well worth a read. Other lady athletes to play tennis include Maeve Kyle, Betty Kyle, Katrina McKiernan and Niamh Richardson.

a silver medal at the Olympic Games in 1908 for doubles. He played rugby for Dublin University and

George McVeagh (right) one of Ireland's most successful all-rounders. He played Davis Cup (1933 to 1948) was Irish squash champion between 1935 and 1938 (with 1 cap in 1937). He also played international cricket (20 caps, the first in 1926) and hockey (24 consecutive matches between, the first in 1932).

Guy Jackson — Irish Sportsman

By PAUL MacWEENEY

When the Davis Cup was resumed in 1946 after the war there were large gaps to be filled on the Irish team. The two men who had put up a number of sterling performances during the 1930s, George Lyttleton Rogers and George McVeagh, were no longer available, yet Cyril Kemp and Raymund Egan had given the powerful Swedes a tough battle in Stockholm, a 5-0 margin being an unjust reflection of their efforts. The following year another strong side, Yugoslavia, had paid a successful visit to Fitzwilliam and it was then becoming clear that firmer support for Kemp would be essential if we were to find the winning formula again.

The draw for the 1948 Davis Cup was more favourable, for Luxembourg were not likely to be formidable opposition and therefore made the ideal platform for Guy Jackson's debut. At 26 years of age he was sufficiently mature not to be overawed by the occasion and he had had plenty of tournament experience behind him. Straight away he settled down in the tense atmosphere of international competition and he and Kemp were convincing in their removal of the Luxembourgers but still it was difficult to assess his potential until a sterner test was forthcoming.

That was provided by Denmark in the next round, for in Kurt Neilsen and Torben Ulrich they had two of the best young players in Europe. On the first day any doubts concerning Jackson's quality were dispelled, for only after a tremendous battle did he go down to Neilsen 6-4 in the final set. That gave the Danes a 2-0 lead for after suffering a painful injury in the first set, Kemp had lost to Ulrich. The doubles put Ireland back into contention, for Jackson and Kemp combined so smoothly as to achieve the unlikely victory over Neilsen and Ulrich in a five-setter of high quality. On the last day Neilsen gave Denmark their margin at Kemp's ex-

pense but Jackson rounded off a personal triumph by defeating Ulrich, again in a cliff-hanging five-setter—no Irish player had ever made a more impressive start to a Davis Cup career which, in his case, was to extend over 12 years.

There was to be a long and frustrating gap before we could celebrate another win in the world team event, for not until 1956 were Finland mastered at Fitzwilliam, but Jackson continued to hold his own in distinguished company. He beat the second string Chilean at Fitzwilliam in 1949 and a year later put up an outstanding performance in defeating one of Europe's top men, van Swol of Holland, in Amsterdam. He and Joe Hackett developed into a notable doubles partnership, a straight sets win over a talented German pair at Fitzwilliam being a highlight, and considering the fact that he was the most amateur of players in an otherwise semi-professional field he retained a remarkably high standard throughout his career.

He had a long string of successes to his credit in the international series against England, Scotland and Wales and dominated the home scene for a number of years. Without commanding the service power of the leading group of world players his placing of the delivery was shrewd and adequately difficult to handle but the basis of his game was the strength and consistency of his ground shots on both wings. With an unusually short back swing he punched the ball with a low trajectory and was a master in disguising direction, any opponent who came in after anything less than a full-length return found himself passed at the net time after time. He himself built up a useful volleying technique and as his length was consistent he became expert at tucking away the low volley but was less effective overhead.

His court manners were perfect, for in a game so dependent on outisde factors such as a linesman's decision on a crucial point I never saw him throw a tantrum or in any way attempt to influence a call. In all aspects of his life he had the faculty of deep concentration, so to allow extraneous matters to intrude would be to break that concentration.

Guy was one of that dying race of sportsmen, an all-rounder of great ability. He had shown talent at hockey as a youngster at Marlborough College and after gaining a double Blue at Oxford — tennis as well as hockey — he joined Three Rock Rovers. In the face of powerful competition he was chosen for his country in 1959 and his third international honour was secured at squash, a game he took up late in his sporting life and mainly for the short, sharp exercise it provided. However in any of his games his talent was bound to emerge, so he fully earned his selection for his country, and apart from the world number one Jonah Barrington, he was the only Irish player to beat an English opponent. Before he went on court that day at Fitzwilliam I had a bet with him as to how many points he would get against Neville Hooper ; perhaps that was an extra spur, but at the end I had to land out a good deal more than I could have anticipated !

Guy always took the closest and most practical interest in Fitzwilliam's affairs and a most fitting honour was paid to him in his election as vice-President this year. He would have occupied the presidential chair during the first full year in the new headquarters had not fate decreed otherwise.

Irish Lawn Tennis Championship Programme 1972

Croquet playing by members of Clontarf LTC (1972).

Some Irish Tennis Playing All-Rounders

Percy French (1854-1920) — Tennis, Cycling, Croquet, Cricket, Golf, Gaelic football.

Daniel Ross (c.1861-1951) — Tennis, **Rugby** (4 caps 1880s**), Lacrosse** (c.1879**),** Cricket, Golf, **Polo** (c.1910), Billiards, Horseriding, Swimming, Fishing.

Willoughby (*Ghost*) Hamilton (1864-1943) — **Tennis** (Wimbledon Champ.1890**), Soccer** (1895), **Badminton.**

Frank Owen Stoker (1866-1938) — **Tennis** (Wimbledon doubles winner, 1890), **Rugby** (5 caps, 1886+)

Blaney Hamilton (1872-1946) — Tennis, **Hockey** (1 cap), **Cricket** (19 caps), **Badminton** (First Open Champion in 1902.

James Cecil Parke (1881-1946) — **Tennis** (Davis Cup winning team 1912), **Golf** (2 caps) **Rugby** (20 caps), Athletics, Cricket.

Johnnie McCallum (1883-1967) — Tennis, **Badminton** (8 caps, 1913-1926), **Cricket** (1 cap),Rugby.

Harry M. Read (b.c.1890) — Tennis, **Rugby** (13 caps, 1910-1913), **Cricket**, Golf.

Sophie Pierce-Evans (1896-1939) — Tennis, **Athletics** (1922-1926), Golf, Horseriding**.**

Louis Meldon (1886-1956) — **Tennis** (Davis Cup, 1923-1927), **Cricket**

Gordon (*Curly*) Mack (1900-1949) — **Tennis** (Davis Cup, 1930), **Badminton** (8 All-England titles)

Arthur Hamilton (b. 1905) — Tennis, **Badminton,** Squash (First Irish Open Champion,1932).

George McVeagh (1906-1968) — **Tennis,** (Davis Cup 1933-1948), **Hockey, Cricket, Squash**, Billiards.

Willoughby (*Rat*) Hamilton (1907-1971) — Tennis, **Badminton** (20 major titles).

Mavis Macnaughton (nee Hamilton) (1911-1958) — **Badminton** (1 Open and 5 Close singles titles), Tennis

Kevin O'Flanagan (b.c.1917) — Tennis, **Rugby** (1 cap),**Soccer**(10 caps), golf, athletics

Cyril Kemp (b. c. 1918) — **Tennis** (Davis Cup,1946-1952), **Squash** (12 caps, 1938-1951), **Table Tennis.**

Des O'Brien (1919-2005) — Tennis, **Rugby** (20 caps including 2 triple crowns), **Squash** (10 caps), **Hockey**.

Rita Rutherfoord (b. c.1920) — Tennis (President Donnybrook LTC 1979-1981), **Hockey** (1950+), **Lacrosse** (1947+)

Frank Peard (b.1920) — **Tennis** (Wimbledon in 1946), **Badminton**

Vivian Gotto (b. 1921) — **Tennis** (Davis Cup,'53-'61), Squash (Ulster interprovincial), Soccer, Table-Tennis, Badminton.

Guy Jackson (1922-1972) — **Tennis** (Davis Cup, 1948-1964), **Squash** (1952-1954), **Hockey** (1959).

Jim Fitzgibbon (b. c. 1922) — **Tennis** (Davis Cup, 1952), **Badminton.**

Joe Hackett (b. 1925) — **Tennis** (Davis Cup 1950-1961), Rugby (interpro.), Squash (interpro.)

Maeve Kyle (nee Shankley) (b. 1928) — Tennis (TCD colours), **Athletics** (Olympian 1956, 1960), Sailing, **Hockey** (58 caps, including triple crown in 1950).

Betty Henderson (nee Kyle) (b. c.1929) — Tennis, **Hockey** (1948+), Lacrosse, Netball, Cricket.

Sue Peard (nee Devlin) (b. 1931) — Tennis (Ranked in USA), **Badminton** (Six All-England doubles titles), **lacrosse**, hockey & basketball.

Cecil Pedlow (b. 1934) — Tennis (Ulster interprovincial), **Rugby** (30 caps, first in 1953)

Peter Hedley Jackson (b. 1934) — **Tennis** (18 Davis Cup caps, over 50 international caps), Rugby (Ulster Junior team), Athletics, Golf, Cricket, Table Tennis.

Delany Ronnie (b. 1935) — Tennis, **Athletics** (Olympic 1500 m champion, 1956)

Browne Willie (1936-2004) — Tennis (Leinster interprovincial), **Soccer** (International 1957-1964), Cricket, Badminton, Hockey, Golf, Gaelic football.

Mary Bryan (nee O'Sullivan) (b. 1936) — **Tennis, Badminton** (Extensive titles in both sports)

Derek Arthurs (b. 1940) — **Tennis** (Davis Cup 1962-1966), **Squash** (6 caps**),** Badminton (interpro), Cricket.

Michael Hickey (b. c. 1940) — **Tennis** (21 Davis Cup appearances), **Squash** (18 caps), Golf, Rugby.

Eleanor O'Neill (nee McFadden) (b. c. 1940) — **Tennis** (Federation Cup), Squash (interprovincial).

Dr. Geraldine Barniville (nee Houlihan)(b.1942) — **Tennis** (Federation Cup), **Squash**, Cycling, Hockey (interprovincial)

Mary Dinan (nee Sinnott) (b.c.1942) — Tennis, **Badminton** (58 caps), Golf (Leinster Junior Cup winner), Hockey, Camogie (All Ireland title with Wexford).

Norah Glynn (nee Mageen) (b. 1945) — **Tennis** (International Veterans), **Netball** (British World Cup Squad), Squash, Basketball.

Helen Lennon (b.1946) — **Tennis** (First Federation Cup, 1974), Badminton, Golf, Squash (interpro.)

Billy Bolster (b. c.1946) — **Tennis** (International Veterans), **Athletics.**

Jim McArdle (b. 1950) — **Tennis** (25 caps, six Davis Cups), Squash (Leinster interprovincial).

Tony Ensor (b. c.1950) — Tennis (Schools interprovincial), **Rugby** (22 caps, first 1973)

Maria Bolster (b. c. 1952) — **Tennis** (Federation Cup), **Basketball**

Martyn Evans (b. c.1953) — Tennis, **Racquetball**, Squash, Badminton, Soccer, Snooker, Golf, Cricket.

Hosey Willie (b. c.1960) — Tennis, **Squash**

Sandra O'Gorman (b. c.1968) — Tennis, **Hockey** (World Cup 1994)

Jennifer O'Brien (b. c. 1970) — **Tennis** (Federation Cup, 1989), **Hockey** (Leinster schools team)

Niamh Richardson (nee Murphy) (b. c. 1970) — Tennis , Camogie (County player), **Athletics.**

Ross Niland (b. 1974) — **Tennis, Squash** (under 14), Soccer, Gaelic football.

*Where sport is in **bold** the player has been an international.   + Year of first international cap.

Chapter 2
The Evolution of Tennis

2   *The Evolution of Tennis*

Who would have thought that tennis, dragged into existence from a hotchpotch of early versions of 'lawn tennis' with five-foot nets, hourglass-shaped courts and two-inch balls in 1874, would develop into the sleek, fast, sexy and wealthy sport it is today?

(Richard Jago, 1998)

The readers of this book will all be aware of the difference between lawn tennis and tennis. Or will they? The normal response would be that one is played on grass, the other on a range of surfaces. Both are the same game, with the same equipment and rules, the surface being the only difference. To older players who have enjoyed the dying sport of tennis played on grass, it was **the only surface**. The other versions were forced upon us by a wet climate, and a desire to play twelve months of the year. Many younger players have only seen grass courts on television, courtesy of the Wimbledon Championships. What a pleasure they have missed.

However, there has always been some confusion on the origins and development of the sport. One hears of *Real* and *Royal* tennis. What do these forms of tennis mean? Are there links between tennis, squash, racquetball and badminton? Are there other, less known, sports connected in any way? The more widely read will have heard of the French origins and the term *Jeu de paume.* Why is this linked to the international, widely played and televised game of tennis?

Even the spelling of the word tennis has many variations. Where does the word come from? This writer used to think that the spelling of *racquet* always had a 'q' in it and that the spelling with a 'k' was an Americanized version. This chapter will try and answer these queries. It should be remembered that games or pastimes may have been practiced in limited regions for many years, recognition coming much later. A point is reached where they become more organised, clubs sprout up and a fixed set of rules are established. Ruling bodies may define the game in different ways. When the game becomes truly international then that body unifies the sport and defines the rules to be applied in challenges between countries.

This chapter will attempt to clarify the fuzz in people's minds, if it exists. Despite all the historical research, there will be questions that do not have an exact answer. The reason is simply that, in most cases, when the sport was first conceived there was no committee around, no secretary and no minutes' book. Rules, and variations of them, travelled by word of mouth. It should be possible to define exactly the origins of more recently established sports. Many sports have had a commercial origin. I think a great example is the Frisbee. This is the plastic disc that floats through the air and is thrown between two or more people. There are now serious Frisbee league competitions in sunny climes such as Sydney and California. The sport consists of teams of five or six on a pitch and is quick, requiring agility and skill. There is even a world championship. This beach 'product' of the 1970s is now a team sport. The various beach bats and balls we see used throughout the Mediterranean as an alternative to tanning and swimming may well follow this route.

Handball has been around for thousands of years, it developed into pastimes or sports with gloves, then bats and then rackets. The shuttlecock was just a ball with feathers for improved flight. It had a parallel development. The names 'badminton' and 'lawn tennis' came into sporting use virtually at the same time (in *the summer of 1873* and in *March 1874* respectively, accordingly to documented sources). Squash rackets came into being some twenty years earlier, a side product of the 16th century rackets. Racquetball, on the other hand is a late 20th century innovation combining handball and squash.

One could devote an entire book to the history and development of 'racket' sports. It would reflect a series of gradually developments such as ball to shuttle and bat to strung racket. Such changes include the use of open courts versus walled courts. Many were pure children's pastimes, such as battledore. With the industrial revolution and the age of leisure for all, clubs formed, national and international organisations followed. Improved transport and communications had a significant bearing on the speed of development. In the latter half of the 20th century television has made several sports, such as tennis, truly a peoples game.

Different world regions have different priorities, for historical, financial and social reasons. Many will have forgotten that Fred Perry was once world table tennis champion in 1929. This was some five years before winning Wimbledon. China now leads the way in table tennis but how many Chinese tennis players have we heard of. In the latter half of the 20th century Sweden have produced world-class players in table tennis and badminton, but particularly noteworthy numbers in the sports of golf and tennis. Why? A simple answer might be a national determination to make the best of their youth and put money and time into sports development. There is a realisation that in this age of plenty, the effort is worthwhile. One suspects most countries could learn from this example of cause and effect on a national scale.

While Lene Koppen was once the pride of Danish badminton, it is in countries such as Malaysia that fans are fanatical. They turn up in many thousands for national championships. The Khan's of Pakistan, and Jonah Barrington, have made squash a well-known sport. One sportsperson suggested that until we have a world number one from the USA it will never gain Olympic status. Is this a modern commercial fact or is it a view that could be changed. In other words can racket sports thrive without a major commercial/television influence? I think they can.

In England, the question of why they have not been producing Wimbledon champions of late is continually asked. In Ireland we might ask the same question, perhaps with a lesser degree of expectancy based upon pure numbers alone. Team sports such as soccer, rugby, Gaelic football and hurling are all thriving. The golden era of Irish tennis is gone. We do need national heroes. Out of apparently nowhere Sean Kelly and Stephen Roche put cycling on the map. Our golfers have won the Dunhill Cup several times since its inauguration in 1985. Golf is now a peoples sport with a big television following. Can tennis do the same? We love sport in Ireland. There is no reason why not. We must reflect on the past, good and bad, learn from countries such as Sweden, see that funding is not limited, create a new ethos and image. The frustrated administrators will think we have tried it all before. New angles, a bit of lateral thinking is called for. Look what Sean Collins managed to achieve in bringing the top lady players to Dublin in December 2002. The lovers of the game have to influence the young. They know that the sport is skilled, a great social outlet and a game for life and world travel. Can we convince enough people to take up the game, pass on our enthusiasm and skills? I think the answer is yes.

Tennis

Starting with the Oxford Dictionary definition we find that tennis means *either of two ball games for 2 or four players, played with rackets over a net with a soft ball on an open court (**lawn tennis**) or with a hard ball in a walled court (**real tennis**, in the USA called **court tennis**).* One might add the fact that **real tennis** is also referred to as **royal tennis**, particularly in Australia. Real is in fact the Spanish for royal. One assumes, therefore, that the game that was earlier played in the courts of Paris, was initially royal tennis and later became real tennis on gaining popularity by royal society in England.

Normally, the person who indicates that they are going for a game of tennis is talking about lawn tennis. The word lawn has been obviously dropped from common usage as the majority of lawn tennis courts no longer have a grass surface. In July 1977, the International Lawn Tennis Federation, the world ruling body for the sport, recognised this change and dropped 'lawn' from its title. There are still many clubs proud to have, and care for, the original grass variety. May they long continue to do so!

King James I (on the throne of England between 1603 and 1625) suggested to his son a range of exercises that included **tennise.** Around the same period of time, Shakespeare (1564-1616) in *Much Ado About Nothing* refers to **stuffed tennis balls** and, in Henry V, there is the classic line '**Tennis balls,** my liege'. The French verb **tenir** means to hold, to take it, to keep and to play. Its imperative form is **tenetz**. Ian McAulay (1986) indicates that one theory on the word was that the French monks playing the original game (jeu de paume) would cry **tenez** (attention!) when about to serve. According to Lance Tingay (1983) the antiquity of tennis may be emphasised by recording the 24 variant spellings it has had over the centuries (I have added in an additional one, tenis).

Teneis	Tenes	Tenetz
Teneys	Tenez	Tenice
Tenis	Tenise	Tenisse
Tennes	Tenisz	Tennies
Tennis	Tennice	Tennys
Tennyse	Tennise	Tenyce
Tenys	Tennysse	Tenyys
Tinneis	Tenyse	Tinnis
Tynes	Tinnies	

The following table includes a small selection of tennis terms from several countries. Closer to home we have the Scotch Gaelic and the Irish Gaelic terms, old languages and peoples not normally associated with tennis. In the 1980s, Cospoir, The National Sports Council (Republic of Ireland), produced a booklet solely dealing with Lawn Tennis terms. This included some 207 individual words or phrases. In 2005 TG4, the Irish language television channel covered Wimbledon very successfully. Some terms used during the transmission included eacht (ace), imreoir dolamhach (ambidextrous player), culbhuile (backhand shot), buaiteoir (winner), botun (fault), naid (love) and smiste (smash). When reading, enjoy the various terms by saying them out loud. For example, flugtskud, the Danish word for volley, suggests a missile. Make your own judgements. In the ancient world there were various forms of handball and some suggest the true roots of tennis are a lot older than the French source. There is an Egyptian town on the Nile called **Tinnis** (in Arabic) thus adding to the speculation on the origin of the name.

English	Tennis	Tennis Court	Tennis Racket	Volley
Danish	Tennis	Tennisbane	Tennisketsjer	Flugtskud
French	Tennis	Terrain de tennis (or Court de tennis)	Raquette	Volee
Gaelic (Ireland)	Leadóg	Cuirte Leadóige	Raicead Leadóige	Eitleóg
Gaelic (Scotland)	Cluich-cneutaig		Callaid	Ladach
German	Tennis	Tennisplatz	Tennis-Schlager	Flugball
Hungarian	Tenisz	Teniszpálya	Teniszütö	Röpte
Italian	Tennis	Campo da tennis	Racchetta da tennis	Pallavolo
Spanish	Tenis	Caucha de tenis (or Pista de tenis)	Raqueta de tenis	Volea (or Voleo)

Racket

The word **racket** leads to some confusion. In the Collier's Dictionary it is described as *An implement for striking a ball, as in the game of tennis*. It mentions an alternative spelling as being **racquet** and two origins of the word being **racquette**, from the French and **raha** from the Arabic. Elsewhere the spelling of the latter is found to be **rahat**. The Arabic translation means 'palm of the hand'. We know that 'jeu de paume' is sport played in the French monasteries of the 11th century. At that stage it was a handball game over a net. According to Masters (2000), legend has it that a wandering minstrel brought the game to the French Royal Court. In later years gloves were used and eventually short bats. By 1500 the **racket** was no longer made of wood but had a head that was strung with sheep gut.

In the 14th century **racket** was a game played with dice (The Oxford English Dictionary, 1991). In the 16th century, we find the phrase *Striking and receaving the balle with a racquet* (NEWTON *Health Magazine, 1574*). In 1603, we find *The Gods perdie doe reckon and racket us men as their tennis balles* (FLORIO *Montaigne*). In a 1690 record, the following phrase was found (LOCKE *Hum.Und.*): *A Tennis-Ball, whether in motion by the stroke of a Racket, or lying still at rest*. American and English dictionary sources use both common spellings of the word, racket and racquet. Perhaps an early English speaker preferred to use 'k', as opposed to the more clearly French form with 'q'. You choose your preference. The following are a few variations:

Racchetta (It.)	Rackat	Racket
Rackette	Racquet	Rakat
Rakcat	Raket (Du.)	Rakete (G.)
Rakette (G.)	Rakkett	Rakkettis
Raquet	Raqueta (Pg.)	Raquette

Apart from the ancient game of **rackets** (also spelt **racquets**) there are also the more modern sports of **racketball** (UK) and **racquetball** (USA and Ireland). Squash is also called **squash racquets** or **squash rackets**, the latter spelling being the more popular. How should you spell that implement used in tennis. A scan of some 22 advertisements and articles on the sport indicate a fairly random use of 'k' and 'q'. On the **racket** side was *The Field* reporting on Wimbledon in 1878, Hely's advert in 1932, and noted players Naratilova (1983) and Newcombe (1983). Percy French used the **racquet** version in his tennis writings in 1889. So did James Cecil Parke, when

writing about his career in 1927. Slazenger's and Ayre's were supplying **racquets**, according to The Sligo Independent in 1910. In the US magazine, *World Tennis* in September 1984, the use was evenly divided. In the same year the ITF Rules on the sport use the 'k' version. The final score was **Racket 16 Racquet 6**. Most probably the French spelling of the word (**raquette**) was the first to introduce the 'q', the Spanish held on to it (**raqueta**) and the English first used the phonetic version (**racket**).

A Modern signpost at Chartres in northern France identifies the location of a Jeu de Paume court in operation between the 16th and 18th centuries.

Balls Games

Ball games are at the core of many modern sports. The simple throwing or kicking of a ball, or even propelling it with ones head, are mans way of passing time. A variety of such games have been found in all parts of the world, some associated with religious ceremonies. Up to the time rubber was developed and used in balls they were most often made of strips of leather, stuffed with hair, feather or cloth.

Handball games were recorded as early as 2000BC in both Egypt and Mexico. Alexander the Great (450 BC) is thought to have spread a handball game throughout the Roman Empire. In France, the monks played a handball game, which became known as *jeu de paume* (game of the palm). Later, *la longue paume* appeared. It was an open space form of jeu de paume. It is not known whether at this stage the hand had been replaced by the bat, or not. It is thought that from France jeu de paume spread to northern Spain where *pelota* has its origins. Pelota means ball in Spanish. Earliest records for this sport seem to be the 16th century.

In Galway, in 1527, the Town Statues forbade the playing of ball games against the walls of the town (O'Connor, 2000). Spain, at that time had trading links with Galway and perhaps some Spanish visitors brought balls and associated games with them, or visa versa. One may never know. King James I of Scotland was playing handball (against a wall) in 1427. Perhaps this was another parallel development that lead to the game of *fives* (a handball game with three or four walls) and its organised forms, at Eton, Rugby and Winchester. Trinity College, Dublin, built a fives court in 1694. Others have been identified in Wexford and Clare. While the *Irish handballers* started out using one wall it was perhaps the influence of fives that saw the game ultimately develop into a four-walled game. The Irish did bring their game abroad to places such as Australia, South Africa and North America. By 1883 it was established in the USA where it has thrived since, modifications of rules etc. creeping in over the years. The first international match was between the USA and Ireland in 1887. World championships commenced in 1964. An interesting aside is the fact that the great lawn tennis player, Jim Parke, used to practice his strokes in a ball alley when no courts were readily available.

Olympic handball has a slightly different genesis in that it was basically a game of soccer played with nets but the ball is thrown rather than kicked. It was first played in about 1895. It first became an organised sport in Germany and an Olympic event in Berlin in 1936. *Fistball* was invented as recently as 1989 in Estonia. Using a tennis ball, the game uses heads, hands and feet and is played in squash courts.

Shuttle Games

Shuttles were originally balls with feathers attached to improve flight. They were probably simple throwing pastimes and records indicate their use in about 1000 BC. At one time they were projected by the feet in China. It was significantly later that *shuttlecock* was played in England (before 1390) and with bats. By the 17th century it was popular in several European countries when it was called *battledore* (the name given to the bat or racket used) or *jeu de volant.* Battledore was known to be a volleying game, played indoors and outdoors in England, with small headed bat having a parchment, animal skin or strung face. One assumes jeu de volant was the French name for the same pastime. No net was involved. *Featherball* was a court game using a strung (short-handled) racquet in France in or before 1638. It is known that this sport, using chicken feathers and a soft ball, was also played at that time in Denmark, Germany and Sweden. This was probably the pastime later called jeu de volant and battledore.

*There have been many links between badminton and tennis in Ireland. This Leinster badminton team (c. 1952) contains at least three players (underlined) who played in Irish Close or Open Tennis Championship finals. Back row (l. to r.) **Jim Fitzgibbon**, Chick Doyle, Des Lacey & **Frank Peard.** Front row (l. to r.) Dorrie Donaldson, **Barbara Good,** Dymphna Bevan and Jean Sharkey.*

The modern game of *badminton* is said to have been first 'regulated' in 1873, in India, when it was called *Poona*, the town where the rules were formulated. According to an anonymous author (in 1883) of *Lawn Tennis, Croquet, Racquets etc.,* "....badminton was introduced into England by the Duke of Beaufort in the summer of 1874" (at the family home, Badminton House). The writer also describes it as "Lawn Tennis played with shuttlecocks instead of balls". A *short badminton* version was introduced into England, for very young players, in about 1990. Ireland was the second country in the world to have a national badminton association (1899). The game is essentially the same as it was over one hundred years ago. The shuttle has always had a cork tip but the shortage of suitable feathers lead to the development of longer lasting plastic shuttles. *Short badminton* is the most recent 'new' game, designed for the very young in about 1990 in England. Before the sports of tennis and badminton became full-time and professional, it was very common, from the end of the 19th century to about 1960, to see the top players concentrate on badminton in Ireland (and elsewhere) for the winter and tennis during the summer. One of the sporting Irish Hamiltons, Willoughby (1864-1943), won Wimbledon in 1890 and twelve years later won the Irish Open Mixed Doubles title in badminton. Dublin's *Curly* Mack won the All-England Badminton championships in 1924 which, theoretically, made him the best player in the world at the time, and five years later won the Irish Open Men's Doubles tennis championships followed by a place on the Davis Cup panel in 1930. Ian Maconachie won the All-England mixed title in 1937. In 1939, after many years of trying, Tom Boyle and Jim Rankin of Ulster won the All-England Men's Doubles title. In the 1940s and 1950s, Irishmen JJ Fitzgibbon and Frank Peard were among those who excelled at both sports. In *The Badminton Story* (Adams, 1980) the following note was made about this pair: *By 1951 Ireland had acquired a world class doubles pair in the tigerishly quick Frank Peard and the wily Jim Fitzgibbon.* Also excelling in both at that time were Mary Nichols (later Mrs. Fitzgibbon), Barbara Good and Norah Conway. Of course one should not forget both of Frank Devlin's daughters, Judy and Sue, the top ladies doubles pairing in the world for many years and ranked among the best tennis doubles pairs when in the USA. Sue married Frank Peard and two of their children, Pam and Chippy, were to be among Ireland's best badminton players towards the end of the 20th century. Mary Bryan (nee O'Sullivan) would follow in the late 1950s. By the 1980s few top players excelled at both sports though many were twin exponents at club level, and still are. Mrs. Betty Uber, of Uber Cup fame, was one of the top lady badminton players in the world in the 1930s. She was an international in both sports and compared them as follows. While a tennis player might cover more mileage during a match the badminton player would have the more strenuous and exhausting match "since it requires so very much more strength and effort to play overhead shots continuously than it does to play ground strokes".

Dubliner's Frank Devlin and G.S.B. (Curly) Mack (far side) won six All-England doubles titles (badminton) as a pair between 1923 and 1931. In addition, they won seven singles titles at the championships in the same period. Mack was one of Ireland's top lawn tennis players. The Devlin daughters (Judy & Sue) went on to win six All-England ladies doubles titles between 1954 and 1966. When living in the USA they were ranked as one of the top doubles pairings at tennis.

Irish Badminton Singles Champions *(*known tennis players)*				
	Open		**National** (Year refers to start of season)	
Year	**Men's**	**Ladies**	**Men's**	**Ladies**
1902-04	Blaney Hamilton* (Irl.)	no competition	no competition	no competition
1905-06	H.N. Marrett (England)	no competition	no competition	no competition
1907-09	A.M. Cave* (Ireland)	no competition	no competition	no competition
1910	F. Chesterton (England)	no competition	no competition	no competition
1911	George Thomas* (Eng.)	no competition	R.H. Lambert	Miss H. Pigot
1912	George Thomas* (Eng.)	no competition		Mrs. R.H. Plews*
1913	George Thomas* (Eng.)	no competition	F.A. Kennedy	Miss E.F. Stewart
1914	George Thomas* (Eng.)	no competition		
1919	no competition	no competition	G.S.B.(*Curly)* Mack*	Mrs. Beattie
1920	George Thomas* (Eng.)	no competition		Miss E.F. Stewart
1921	George Thomas* (Eng.)	no competition	G.S.B.(*Curly)* Mack*	no competition
1922	G.A. Sautter (England)	no competition	F.A. Kennedy	Miss D. Pilkington
1923	G.S.B.(*Curly)* Mack (Irl.)	no competition		Miss D. Pilkington
1924	Frank Devlin (Ireland)*	Mrs. R. J. Horsley (Eng.)	G.S.B.(*Curly)* Mack*	Miss D. Pilkington
1925	G.S.B.(*Curly)* Mack (Irl.)	Mrs. R.C. Tragett (Eng.)	no competition	no competition
1926	Frank Devlin (Ireland)*	Mrs. R.C. Tragett (Eng.)	Willoughby Hamilton*	Mrs. T.D. Good*
1927	George Thomas* (Eng.)	Miss D. Pilkington* (Ire.)	no competition	no competition
1928	A.E. Harbot (England)	Mrs. F.G. Barrett (Eng.)	no competition	no competition
1929	Willoughby Hamilton*(Ir.)	Miss D. Good* (Ireland)	no competition	no competition
1930	Willoughby Hamilton*(Ir.)	Betty Uber *(England)	no competition	no competition
1931	Willoughby Hamilton*(Ir.)	Mrs. R.J. Horsley (Eng.)	Arthur Hamilton*	Mavis Hamilton*
1932	R. M. White (England)	Betty Uber* (England)r	Arthur Hamilton*	Mavis Hamilton*
1933	Willoughby Hamilton*(Ir.)	Miss O. Wilson (Ireland)	Willoughby Hamilton*	Mavis Hamilton*
1934	R.M. White (England)	Miss T. Kingsbury (Eng.)	Willoughby Hamilton*	Mavis MacNaughton*
1935	Jim Rankin (Ireland)	Mrs. R.J. Teague (Eng.)	R. Hanna	Mavis MacNaughton*
1936	Ralph Nichols (England)	Miss T. Kingsbury (Eng.)	Geoff Trapnell*	Norma Stoker*
1937	Jim Rankin (Ireland)	Miss E.A.R. Anderson	no competition	no competition
1938	Tom Boyle (Ireland)	Miss D.M.C. Young (Eng.)	no competition	no competition
1939	A.S. Samuel (Malaya)	Mavis MacNaughton* (Ir.)	no competition	no competition
1947	Noel Radford (England)	Miss Q.M. Allen (England)	Dennis Green	Barbara Good*
1948	Noel Radford (England)	Miss Q.M. Allen (England)	J.J. (Jim) Fitzgibbon*	Barbara Good*
1949	Ong Po Lim (Malaya)	Miss Q.M. Allen (England)	Frank Peard*	Miss B. Curran
1950	Frank Peard* (Ireland)	Mrs. A.M. Horner (Scot.)	Frank Peard*	Mrs. B.I. Donaldson
1951	Eddy Choong (Malaya)	Elizabeth O' Beirne (Eng.)	Frank Peard*	Jean Lawless
1952	Eddy Choong (Malaya)	Jean Lawless (Ireland)	Frank Peard*	Miss S. Moore
1953	Eddy Choong (Malaya)	Iris Cooley (England)	J.P. (*Chick)* Doyle	Miss E. Abraham
1954	Jeff Robson (N. Zealand)*	Heather Robson* (N. Z.)	J.P. (*Chick)* Doyle	Miss E. Abraham
1955	A.D. Jordon (England)	Iris Cooley (England)	J.P. (*Chick)* Doyle	Yvonne Kelly*
1956	J.P. (*Chick)* Doyle (Irl.)	Mary O' Sullivan* (Irl.)	J.P. (*Chick)* Doyle	Yvonne Kelly*
1957	Eddy Choong (Malaya)	Mrs. W.C.E. Rogers	J.P. (*Chick)* Doyle	Yvonne Kelly*
1958	Oon Chong Jin (Malaya)	Yvonne Kelly *(Ireland)	J.P. (*Chick)* Doyle	Mary O' Sullivan*
1959	C.T. Coates (England)	Miss H.M. Ward (England)	J.P. (*Chick)* Doyle	Mary O' Sullivan*
1960	R. S. Mc Coig (Scotland)	Mary O' Sullivan* (Irl.)	J.P. (*Chick)* Doyle	Yvonne Kelly*
1961	C.T. Coates (England)	Miss U.H. Smith (England)	Winston Wilkinson	Mary O' Sullivan*
1962	C. Wattanasin (Thailand)	Miss U.H. Smith (England)	R. Harris	Mary O' Sullivan*
1963	C.J. Beacom (England)	Miss U.H. Smith (England)	R. Harris	Mary O' Sullivan*
1964	R.S. Mc Coig (Scotland)	Judy Hashman* (USA)	R. Harris	Yvonne Kelly*
1965	R.H. Purser (New Zealand)	Miss A.M. Bairstow (Eng.)	R. Harris	Mary Bryan*
1966	Lee Kin Tat (Singapore)	Mary Bryan* (Ireland)	J.J. McCloy	Yvonne Kelly*
1967	A. Parsons (South Africa))	Miss A.M. Bairstow (Eng.)	R. Harris	Mary Bryan*
1968	Lee Kin Tat (Singapore)	Mary Bryan* (Ireland)	P. Moore	Mary Bryan*
1969	A.J. Sharp (England)	Gillian Perrin (England)	R. Harris	Maureen Mockford
1970	R.S. Mc Coig (Scotland)	Yvonne Kelly (Ireland)	M. Morrow	Mary Bryan*
1971	Derek Talbot (England)	Miss M. Beck (England)	P. Moore	Mary Bryan*
1972	Colin Bell (Ireland)	Yvonne Kelly (Ireland)	Colin Bell	Barbara Beckett
1973	Colin Bell (Ireland)	Barbara Beckett (Ireland)	John Taylor*	Barbara Beckett
1974	R.S. Mc Coig	Miss D. Tyghe (Scotland)	John Taylor*	Barbara Beckett
1975	P. Ridder (Netherlands)	Miss J. van Beasekom (N)	Adriene Bell	Barbara Beckett
1976	M. Wilks ((England)	Barbara Beckett (Ireland)	John Scott	Barbara Beckett
1977	T. Goode (England)	Pamela Hamilton (Scot.)	Colin Bell	Dorothy Cunningham
1978	R. Purser (N. Zealand)	Dorothy Cunningham (Irl.)	Bill Thompson	Barbara Beckett
1979	B. Wallwork (England)	Miss S. Ledbetter (Eng.)	Colin Bell	Barbara Beckett
1980	Dan Travers (Scotland)	Miss E. Thoresen (Nor.)	John Taylor*	Lynn Mc Crave
1981	Andy Goode (England)	Helen Troke (England)	Bill Thompson*	Diane Underwood
1982	Mark Elliott (England)	Barbara Beckett (Ireland)		
'84-'86			Pat Marron	
1987	Alec White (Scotland)	Sara Halsall (England)		
1988	Alec White (Scotland)	Anne Gibson (Scotland)		

The History of Irish Tennis

Racket/Bat Games

When one considers the development of rackets in various sports what must be included are bats (sometimes called paddles). The original game of **jue de paume** (12th century France) used hands and later gloves. It had a field version called **la longue paume** at a later stage. Moving from the monasteries to the castles and cities of France bats were introduced. By 1500 the tennis racket had a head that was strung with sheep gut. Because of the lightness of the shuttle, heads covered in parchment were still used as late as 1845.

The handles got longer and the quality of the rackets improved in the 19th century when leisure time was more widespread. In that century squash, lawn tennis and badminton became well organised as sports. While most racquets had oval like shapes, the royal (real) racket was to become lobsided, suiting the intricacies of the sport. Materials for tennis racquets developed throughout the 20th century with 'titanium' and 'carbon' among the materials replacing wood. Before **lawn tennis** established itself there were a number of games in the same ilk. Details have been lost in time. We do know about **sphairistike**, as invented by Major Clopton Wingfield, but we know little of **lawn rackets, field tennis** and **bandy.**

We do know that **real tennis** (England) was the game of **jeu de paume** (France) in the form that used a bat or racket. Today, the exact same sport is called **royal tennis** in Australia and **court tennis** in the USA. In England, a number of players have moved over from lawn tennis to real tennis. Rob Fahey (the Australian whose antecedants travelled out from Ireland) is the 2000 world champion. He plays about forty matches a year, his longest ever took four hours (1993). Seemingly, some of the great (lawn) tennis champions have tried the game. *Pat Cash was pretty good* but he was rather less than complimentary about Mats Wilander, his top-spin was not suitable for the game of real tennis. The game was until recent times dominated by men however there is now a Ladies Real Tennis Association and this historical exclusion has disappeared. (It might be noted that Prince Edward has now taken up the sport, thus keeping up the royal tradition).

Because of size and cost, most clubs have only one court. It is not, therefore, a social game. In January 2000 Middlesex University built a new court, cost £1.5 million sterling. The real tennis fans refer to the outdoor tennis players as "lawners". There have been real tennis courts in several parts of Ireland including Galway, Waterford, Kilkenny and Dublin. In 1885, Sir Edward Guinness, of the Dublin brewing firm, built a real tennis court in Dublin. In 1939, his son, Rupert (2nd Earl of Iveagh) generously donated his residence, Iveagh House (now the Department of Foreign Affairs), the Iveagh Gardens (open to the public) and the Tennis Court to the nation. He wrote to the Taoiseach Eamon de Valera saying *I am loath to think of the tennis court being destroyed, as I think it is unique in its way and might be appreciated by players in Dublin.*

An Irish Real Tennis Association (IRTA) was formed a few years ago with objectives which included renewing an interest in the game and the preservation of this court. The following letter in the *Irish Times* (25th May 2000) highlights the game and its history in Ireland.

REAL TENNIS COURT

A Chara, — In the last week of May 1890, 110 years ago, two athletes in their prime stepped into a marble-clad court in Dublin to play for the the oldest world championship in sport, that of Real Tennis.

The court which had been built five years earlier by Sir Edward Guinness at his city residence , 80/81 St Stephen's Green (now Iveagh House, the Dept of Foreign Affairs), was chosen as a nuetral venue between Pettitt (Boston) and Saunders (London), who played to packed galleries on the Monday, Wednesday and Friday,when the former retained his title in a match which is still regarded as one of the classic encounters.

Ireland can boast of few world championship venues, and the necessary facilities and associated costs in attracting such events make them an increasingly rare proposition in any sport.

The Dublin court, famed over all others because of its exotic construction, was given as a gift to Ireland in 1939 by the then Earl of Iveagh, himself an athlete of some renown having won the Henley Diamond Sculling title. Players at the court offered to run the facility as a club without burden to the State. The offer was rejected, the internal playing features dismantled and play had to cease, since when no ball has been cut (sic) in 60 years.

What a pity that in this time of Celtic affluence, much talk of heritage and stated Government policy to promote participation in sport, that it is left to voluntary enthusiasts to battle the same Government's plan to convert the court building to a recital hall, and just as a purpose-built one is due to be vacated by UCD next door!

Real Tennis is enjoying a decade-long worldwide resurgence — what a loss to Ireland's sportspeople that they cannot partake in their native court. Who's to say that we could not produce our own world champion just like the present holder, Robert Fahey of Australia, who's great-great-grandfather left Co Galway after the Famine. Those were poorer times. Can we not now respect and seek to enjoy the richness of our fortunate inheritance? — Is mise,

TED NEVILLE,
Secretary,
Irish Real Tennis Association,
Carrigaline Road,
Douglas,
Co Cork.

The other branch of **royal tennis** sees **rackets,** a 15th century ancestor of **squash (squash rackets).** An interesting comment from Spencer Gore, shortly after becoming the first winner of the Wimbledon championships (1877) was as follows:

> *Lawn tennis will never rank among our great games, and anybody who has played cricket or rackets will soon be choked off by the monotony of the sport.*

Not an auspicious start to what was to become of the world's great racquet sports. Perhaps **rackets** has been underestimated. **Squash** started life in England in about 1850 and by the 1890s we see that **squash tennis** was played first in the USA. **Racquetball** or **racquet ball** has been described as a game resembling **paddle ball.** A more vivid description would be the four walled game of handball (Irish or American) played with a small racquet. Its origins are in the USA in the late 1960s. It became popular in Ireland in the 1970s and a national association was formed in 1979.

In the 20th century developments of various types occurred in the USA. They brought us **paddle tennis** (1921) followed by **platform tennis.** In 1984, J.P. Dunleavy, author of the bestseller *The Ginger Man*, wrote a book titled **De Alfonce Tennis.** Its subtitle was *The Superlative Game of Eccentric Champions.* It is a detailed account of a sport that started on board a motor launch in the 1930s. It was deemed to have a predecessor in **bangokok**, *now only played by the most ancient but still astonishingly physically fit of old fogies.* It has all the accoutrements of an organised rackets sport, from the court to the racket to the clothing to be worn. Is it a well-conceived skit, has it a little or an extensive connection to real or imagined events? Many questions need answering, but for a bit or diversion I recommend this book for some light relief. Never before has so much detail been ascribed to a sport which is 'not very well known'. It is a sport with much imagination, including some great terms such as a *Chalura, En Croissant, Nurt* and a Zeke. In the Preface he explains the origins of the book:

Upon Squash, Badminton, Lacrosse, Basketball, Handball and even Chess players, among others, who oft times stood in the wings silently watching and then would follow me off court to ask in awe as to what the game was one was playing, and then consequent upon imprecations from its handful of devoted practitioners, I finally was prevailed upon to write the present Manual, in order that this venerable and long nearly secretly played sport could reach out from its small rarefied confines to spread its playing pleasure to the rest of the world.

At the time of writing the author has not been able to contact Mr. Dunleavy, who has lived in the Mullingar area for some years, and to obtain first hand views on the sport. However, perhaps you the reader might obtain a copy and have a read yourself. He details *everything*. Sweat bands, for example, for tournament match play, should be pure cotton in hue, navy blue with care being taken that they are not *too tight to the point of restricting the blood flow in the wrists.* He spends two pages describing 'underfittings' for ladies and gentlemen; particularly impressive is his know-how on solving the bouncing bosum problem. He lets the cat out of the bag when, in the copyright statement, he refers to merchandising in the 'megagalactic cosmos' and transmission by pigeon. In an absorbable frame of mind this book is well worth a read and perhaps might ultimately lead to someone eventually making it an Olympic sport.

Table tennis still uses wooden bats as do the sports of paddle and platform tennis. In England, in the latter half of the 19th century, **gossima** and **whiff whaff** were names applied to the table version of tennis. By 1902, the trade name of **ping-pong**, lead to the formation of the Ping-Pong Association. The English **Table Tennis** Association was formed on the 24th April 1921, the first country to have one.

One of the more modern games, and unique to Ireland, is that of **squash racquets.** This is not the name regularly attributed to squash, the indoor game. It is, however, an outdoor game, developed, and, apparently, only played at the seaside resort of Kilkee, County Clare. Further details follow.

On the 30th April 1988, a fairly unique gathering of racket players took place at Sligo Tennis Club. It was a National Racquet Sports seminar organised by the home club with a view to discussing common factors among the sports of lawn tennis, squash, table-tennis, badminton and racquetball. The organising and coaching of the sports was a key feature. In a similar manner to other clubs with several sports options, there are many who play two and three racquet sports at Sligo Tennis Club. The Minister of Finance at the time, Sligo's Ray McSharry, opened the proceedings and recognised the value of sports and the role of administrators and coaches.

A good attendance and list of speakers included John Taylor, an international badminton player, who also plays squash and tennis, and who was present in his role as the Chief Executive of the ILTA. The second tennis speaker was Jerry Sheehan. He was a former junior international player, was President of the Leinster Council (ILTA) (1988-1989) and specifically a member of the ILTA Coaching Committee at the time of the conference. Olympian Ronnie Delaney, a tennis player at Carrickmines Croquet & Lawn Tennis, was returning to Sligo (having opened the new clubhouse in 1985) and spoke as a member of COSPOIR, the national sports body.

Des Butler (left), President of Sligo Tennis Club, with the Minister for Finance, Ray Mc Sharry, at the National Racquets Sports Seminar organised by the club.

Jerry Sheehan (right) President Leinster Council ILTA with David Taylor and Catherine Holohan (Sligo TC members) at National Racquet Sports Seminar.

John Taylor (right) Chief Executive of the ILTA in contemplative discussion with Senior Coaches Alan Strong (centre) (ITTA) and Winston Wilkinson (BUI) at the Sligo Seminar (30.4.1988).

Ronnie Delaney (Chairman, COSPOIR), was the guest speaker at the National Racquet Sports Seminar. Seen here with co-ordinator, Tom Higgins (Sligo TC).

The following page list the various names associated with 'tennis' games and their links. At the end there is a table that identifies the various basic features of the sports e.g the use of bats and racquets versus those that are handball games. Where we see the term *paume* (French) and *mano* (Spanish) these refer to the handball games. *Jeu* and *juego* are the words used for game. One subtle distinction is the difference between *jeu de paume* and *jeu de la paume*. The first refers to the court where the ball or tennis game took/takes place, while the second refers to the game itself. *Jeu Carre* for example is a version of tennis where the gallery element in the old style indoor courts was left out. For those keen to follow up on this topic, I suggest, once again, without hesitation, a read of Heiner Gillmeister's *Tennis: A Cultural History*. He refers to a vast range of sources.

The flow diagram at the end of the chapter is an attempt to link the various sports having a tennis connection. In simple terms we have many ancient foot and hand ball games, including balls with feathers implanted (i.e. shuttles). Some of these evolved into pure ball games played today including varieties found in the low-countries, Central and South America, the Canary Islands and Ireland. The evidence appears to be that the range of tennis games emerged from the handball games of the monasteries and people of France. Apart from the modern day (lawn) tennis, we find many descendants of the ancient (pre 1200) jeu de la paume. However, the use of a bat or racquet appears to have first reared its head in the middle of the 16th century, while the word tennis is to be found in the middle of the 12th century.

Squash, racquetball, squash racquets (found only at Kilkee, County Clare) are some of the combinations of handball games where walls are used. Pelota is the Spanish for ball and is used in pure ball games but also games that have a 'racket' component such as Jai Alai. In the flow diagram we find a Frisbee game, DDC, because of the court nature of the game, obviously no ball being used. Gillmeister links the ancient games, not unsurprisingly when you think about it, to sports

such as billiards and cricket. You are possibly now confused. Read on and, if a conscientious student of the matter, it will all eventually fit together – even though there will be some strands of the evolution that might never be fully documented.

Badminton

There are several unknowns about the origins of the sport (Adams, 1980). It is played with a strung racquet and a shuttle made with a cork tip and feathers (plastic being also used instead of feathers**). Battledore, shuttlecock, featherball and jeu de volant** are some of the names for predecessor sports. The seventh Duke of Beaufort, who lived at Badminton House, had eleven children. It is thought they perhaps got fed up with Battledore and strung a string across a room to introduce a court element to the game. In 1860 Isaac Spratt (a London toy dealer) published *Badminton Battledore-a new game*. This is probably the first organised form of this game, even though it was perhaps though of as a children's activity at the time.

Outdoor badminton at the Devlin home in Dublin prior to the first World War. Frank in sunhat is kneeling down on right hand side.

Sport	Year	Country	Indoors	Outdoors	Hands	Feet	Head	Ball	Shuttle	Disc/'tamis'/Slab	Bat/Paddle/Racket	Net/Cord	Walls/Roofs	Table	Wheelchair
Handball/Mexican Handball	c.2000BC	Egypt/other	X	X	X			X					X		
Battledore/Shuttlecock	pre 1000BC	China etc.		X		X			X		X				
Pila Trigonalis	pre 100	Italy			X	X		X							
Jeu de Paume(original)	pre 1200	France			X	X						X	X		
La Longue Paume(aka "Alla Distesa")	pre 1200	France			X	X		X				X	X		
Jeu de Bonde	pre 1300	France			X	X		X							
Jeu de la Paume	pre 1300	France/Belgium													
Jeu de Tamis/Jeu de Pelote a Main	c.1300	France/Belgium			X	X		X							
Keatsen (Kaatsen)	Mid Ages	Holland/Belgium			X	X	X	X							
Parkspel	Mid Ages	Goland (Sweden)			X	X	X	X							
Saterlandic ballgame	Mid Ages	Germany			X	X	X	X							
Jeu a dedans		France			X	X		X							
Jeu Carre	1539			X				X				X	X	X	
Basque Pelota		France/Spain	X	X				X					X		
Bote Luzea/Lachoa		Spain			X	X		X		X					
Juego de las Chaza	16th century	Columbia/Ecuador			X	X		X							
Jou de Paumo		Provence			X	X		X		X					
Juego de la Pelota/Pelotamano	pre 1600	Canaries			X	X		X		X					
La Mano Desnuda					X	X		X							
Pelota Mixteca	16th century	Mexico			X	X		X		X					
Baggataway	pre 1492	North America		X				X			X				
Jeu de la Crosse		France		X				X			X	X			
Jeu de la Paume(today)***	pre 1496	France	X					X			X	X	X		
Court/Real/Royal Tennis**	pre 1496	France	X					X			X	X	X		
Irish Handball	pre 1527	Ireland	X	X	X			X					X		
Rackets	pre 1529	England	X	(X)				X			X		X		
Lacrosse		Canada		X				X			X				
La jeu Royal de la paume	pre 1632	France	X					X			X	X	X		
Featherball	pre 1638	France	X					X			X	?			
Fives	pre 1694	England?	X	X	X			X					X		
Bandy	pre 1699	England		X				X			X	?			
Jeu de Volant	pre 1700	France	X						X		X?	X			
Field Tennis	pre 1800	England		X				X				X			
Hard Racquets	1822	England	X					X			X		X		
Eton Fives	pre 1825	England	X	X	X			X					X		
Basque Pelota	pre 1844	Spain		X				X			X		X		
Rugby Fives	1850	England	X	X	X			X					X		
Squash/Squash Racquets	c.1850	England	X					X			X		X		
Winchester Fives	c.1850	England	X	X	X			X					X		
Basque Pelota Vasca	c.1860	Spain	X					X			X		X		
Poona	1873	India		X					X		X	X			
Badminton	1874	England	X	X					X		X	X			
Spairistike/Lawn Tennis**	1874	England	X	X				X			X	X			
American Handball	c.1883	USA	X	X	X			X					X		
Badminton Battledore	1860	England	X						X		X	X			
Gossima/Whiff-Whaff	c.1890	England	X	X				X			X	X		X	
Squash Tennis	c.1890	USA	X					X			X		X		
Table Tennis	1890's	England	X					X			X	X		X	
Olympic Handball	c.1895	Germany	X	X	X			X							
Lawn Rackets	19th century	England?		X				X			X	X			
Jai Alai	c.1900	Cuba	X	X				X			X		X		
Ping Pong	c.1900	USA?	X	X				X			X	X			
Paddle Tennis	1921	USA	X					X			X	X			
Platform Paddle Tennis	1928	USA		X				X			X	X			
Swimming Pool Badminton	1930's	USA	X					X			X				
Squash Racquets (Kilkee)	1934	Ireland		X				X			X		X		
Bangokok/De Alfonce Tennis*	c.1938	at sea		X				X			X	X			
Tennequoits/Deck Tennis	pre 1942	at sea					X			ring		X			
Padder Tennis	1950	England	X					X			X	X			
Batinton	1963	Austalia	X						X		X	X			
Racquetball	c.1969	USA	X					X			X		X		
Beach Tennis	1970's	Europe?		X				X			X				
Short Tennis	1970's	Sweden	X					X				X			
Swingball	1970's	?		X				X			X				
Double Disc Court	c.1975	Australia		X	X					X					
Wheelchair Tennis	1976	USA	X	X				X			X	X			X
Padel Tenis	c.1979	Argentina?		X				X			X	X			
Fistball	1989	Estonia	X		X	X	X	X					X		
Short Badminton	c.1990	England	X						X		X	X			
Paddleball	20th century	USA?	X	X				X			X	X			
Platform Tennis	20th century	USA		X				X			X	X			

*Also called tennis without prefix   ***French name for Court(USA), Royal(Australia) or Real(UK) tennis

Some 'Racket' Sport Origins and Other Details

The 1924 Irish team that was beaten 5/4 by England. Major McCallum (seated left) was also a keen, and useful, tennis player-like many badminton players of that era.

Action from the Irish-Scottish match held in Sligo on the 15th February 1989. The ladies doubles pairing was Holly Lane (smashing) playing in attack formation with Ann O' Sullivan.

Like her father Frank, Judy Hashman (nee Devlin) reached the top of world badminton, both won the All-England Badminton Championships several times. Judy and sister Sue (Peard) were among the top tennis doubles pairings when they lived in the USA.

Teenager John Taylor (1966) became Ireland's top badminton player and later Chief Executive for the Irish Lawn Tennis Association.

Kitty (left) and Margaret McKane from London won the All-England badminton doubles title in 1921. Kitty not did Kitty win the singles (1920-1923) but won the All-England tennis singles (Wimbledon) too (1924 & 1926). She was at one time engaged to an Irishman but ended up marrying Leslie Godfree on a tennis trip to South Africa in 1926. She won the County Dublin Championships at Carrickmines in 1924.

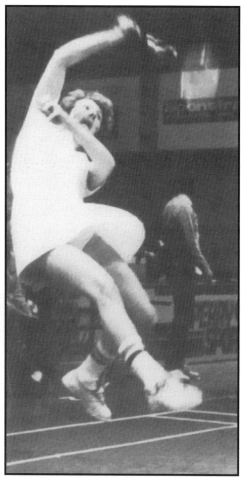

Mary Dinan-One of Ireland's top all-rounders has many international caps for badminton. Tennis, golf and camogie are among her others sporting interests.

The modern game was an organised outdoor sport played in India in 1867 or earlier. It was played in England by returning British army officers in 1869. In 1874 the Duke of Beaufort introduced the sport at the family home, Badminton House (thus the name). The first rules were framed at **Poona** (India) in 1873. The first All-England Championships were held in 1899. It is the national sport of Denmark. Played indoors in Ireland, badminton courts are now regularly used for the sport of **short tennis**. There is also a sport of **short badminton,** for the very young beginner. Badminton became the most watched TV sport on its first introduction to the Olympic Games, in Barcelona in 1992. An offshoot of badminton was a game called **batinton** invented by an Australian in 1963.

The Badminton Union of Ireland was founded on the 25th November 1899 with four clubs. These were Dalkey, Dundrum, Sandford and Wicklow who met at 4 Foster Place, Dublin. Today there are about 600 clubs affiliated to the association. It is the second oldest national organisation in the world. The first Irish Championships were played in 1902, showing a profit of £22. The winner of the singles appears to have been Willoughby James Hamilton, the Wimbledon tennis champion of 1890. He also won the mixed, with a Mrs. Goff and the men's doubles with his brother Blaney (or so it appears). Both were

international cricket and tennis players. Badminton's equivalent of the Davis Cup is the Thomas Cup and in the first ever match in the competition Ireland played Denmark. That was in 1948. The Women's World team championship, for the Uber Cup, started eight years later. One source indicates that the oldest organised club in the world was the New York Badminton Club, founded in 1878.

Badminton Stars Game Display In Tennis Tests

By VERA McWEENEY

THERE were some good matches in the Singles in the Leinster Tennis Championships which were continued at Templeogue yesterday, one of the best being the encounter between Miss Y. Kelly, the badminton international, and the junior interprovincial Miss Geraldine Houlihan.

Miss Houlihan won in straight sets but not without a struggle. Miss Kelly scored numerous points with her strong service but found these cancelled by her ration of at least one double fault per game. Miss Houlihan, too, was guilty of this offence but not to the same extent. Once the ball was in play, however, there were some long and exciting rallies

LIVELY EXCHANGES

Miss Houlihan was not at all afraid to come to the net, and as Miss Kelly prefers to volley there were some lively exchanges. Miss Houlihan got off to a good start, winning the first two games for the loss of only three points, but thereafter she had to work for her games.

Miss Kelly discovered early on that her opponent was vulnerable to a high lob, and she alternated deep back-hand drives with high tosses which disconcerted Miss Houlihan. The younger girl, however, abandoned her efforts to smash these and, waiting for them to bounce, she angled them away with her powerful forehand, and with this weapon neutralised, Miss Kelly's threat was removed.

J. P. Buckley was far too accurate and severe for the Templeogue club junior, J. C. Kelly, who served well and hit some really

good forearm drives in winning three games in the second set.

There was a most interesting men's singles in the late evening between two former Irish junior champions, G. Rice (1944) and J. O'Connell (1953). The 9 years difference between these two was nullified by Rice's canny placements, and it was only supreme stamina which eventually brought O'Connell through.

O'Connell, who had played a first-round singles in the morning, seemed all the better for this pipe-opener, for he has seldom played better. He got an early lead in the first set and just kept ahead to take it 6-3, and in the second set every game went to deuce and vantage with O'Connell just having the slight edge on the vital points.

CLOSE SET

J. Drury Byrne had a close second set against D. P. Foley. Drury Byrne looked all set to coast to an easy victory when he won the first set 6-0 but Foley fought every inch of the way in the second set and had he managed to level at 5-all might have taken it to a third, but he failed to hold his own service at the crucial moment and the match was over.

MEN'S SINGLES—1st Round—J. P. Buckley bt. J. C. Kelly, 6-0, 6-3; J. J. Fitzgibbon w.o.; R. Fearon scr.; J. G. O'Brien bt J. C. Bruton, 7-5, 6-4; T. Buggy bt J. McDonnell, 6-1, 9-7; M. Davila bt T. Griffin, 6-2, 6-3; R. Behan bt T. McCurtain, 6-3, 6-2; H. O'Neill w.o., M. O'Connell scr.; M. Hickey bt P. Reynolds, 6-2, 6-3; J. O'Connell bt L. Maher, 6-2, 6-1.

Second Round—R. Feely bt B. Barry, 6-4, 6-2; J. O'Connell bt G. Rice, 6-3, 6-2; J. Drury Byrne bt D. P. Foley 6-0, 6-4.

LADIES' SINGLES—2nd Round—Miss N. Butler bt Miss E. Ward, 6-1, 6-1; Mrs. J. Russell bt Miss M. Ryan, 6-3, 6-0, Miss P. Dillon bt Miss E. Foley, 6-0, 6-0; Miss J. Plews bt. Miss S. Duffy, 6-2, 6-0; Miss P. Doyle bt Miss A. Dempsey, 6-6, 6-2; Miss G. Houlihan bt Miss Y. Kelly, 6-2, 6-3.

MEN'S DOUBLES — 1st Round — R. Donovan and E. Carmody bt. K. Ruttledge and E. Byrne, 6-2, 5-7, 6-2; F. O'Mahony and P. Delaney bt. G. Rice and D. Moroney 6-1, 6-2.

LADIES' DOUBLES—Second Round—Miss Houlihan and Miss Burke bt Misses R. and L. Maguire, 6-2, 6-2; Third Round — Misses O'Neill and Hogan bt Misses R. Duffner and A. Huet, 6-2, 6-4.

Irish Independent 5th August 1959

Apart from Frank Peard, the Devlin sisters and Mary Bryan there were other Irish Open Badminton Champions who were more than useful tennis players. These include (with badminton titles in brackets): Curly Mack (MS 1923,1925; MD 1922-1925, 1927,1931; MxD 1924,1925,1927); Willoughby Hamilton jnr. (MS 1929-1931,1933; MD 1934); Jim Rankin (MS 1935, 1937; MD 1933, 1935-1937,1939,1947; MxD 1933,1937); Tom Boyle (MS 1938, MD 1933,1939,1947; Mx D 1938,1939); Mavis Macnaughton (nee Hamilton) (LS 1939; LD 1937, 1939; Mx D 1933); Norma Stoker (LD 1937, 1938), Norah Conway (LD 1948) and Barbara Good (LD 1948).

A modern Irish badminton team. Ireland recorded an historic first time victory in the Helvetia Cup held in Sandefjord, Norway. Back row (left to right) Bill Thompson, Peter Ferguson, Clifford Mc Ilwaine, Colin Bell and Frazer Evans. Front (left to right): Lennox Robinson (coach), Mary Dinan, Wendy Orr, Diane Underwood and Joe Kinkead (manager). John Taylor would later be Chief Executive of the ILTA.

Baggataway

Old name (North America) for **lacrosse.**

Bandy

Bandy appears to have two sporting connotations. The first is a game, similar to ice hockey, played at one time in Scandinavia, the Baltic States and Mongolia. The second is obscure but a 1699 quotation in The Oxford English Dictionary is "to bandie at **tennis**". It means *to throw or strike (a ball) to and fro, as in the games of tennis or bandy.* The dictionary further adds that it was *A particular way of playing at **tennis**, the nature of which is not now known.*

Basque Pelota Vasca

See **Pelota**

Batinton

In the December 1st edition of *Lawn Tennis and Badminton in 1963* a new game of batinton was brought to the attention of the international public. It was invented by Australian Pat Hanna of Melbourne and was first on public display at the Outdoor Life Exhibition at Olympia the previous year. The entire cost of equipment to play the game came to a total of £5 and it was sponsored by the Central Council of Physical recreation and was taken up by various youth organisations. The game consists of two or four players playing with hard plastic bats and a shuttlecock. The bat is about one-third the size of a badminton racquet. The net height is five feet and the court space required is only 36 feet by 12 feet. While table tennis scoring can be used the game has rules that are also applicable to badminton and tennis. Like other similar sports it is only when they have widespread use and competition that the rules are ultimately standardised.

The game of batinton introduced in the early 1960s.

Battledore

The sport of badminton evolved from the ancient games of **battledore** and **shuttlecock**. Battledore (also called **shuttlecock**) was a simple pastime with two small bats and a shuttlecock, hit back and forward as many times as possible without letting it hit the ground. It has been played by adults and children for at least two thousand years, in ancient Greece, China, Japan, India and Siam. Feet were sometimes used instead of a bat. By the seventeenth century it was popular among peasants and the leisured classes in Europe.

Beach tennis can be a great form of exercise.

Beach Tennis

Since the 1970s, on many beaches world wide, one can see a range of beach tennis games played. Bats are usually short and made from wood or plastic. Some form of rubber ball is used, it may be hollow or solid. Usually it is between two people on a small strip of sand. There are no known rules and the object of the pastime is to keep the ball in play for as long as possible. Sometimes a 'normal' tennis court is marked out on a flat piece of sand and tennis racquets are used.

Court Tennis

USA name for **tennis, real tennis** or **royal tennis.**

De Alfonce Tennis

In 1984 J.P. Donleavy, an Irish American, living in Mullingar for many years, published an intriguing book with the title *De Alfonce Tennis: The Superlative Game of Eccentric Champions. Its History, Accoutrements, Rules, Conduct and Regimen.* The writing and presentation makes one wonder was this a real or imagined sport! Either way, it is so well considered, it is worthy of mention. The sport with suitable racquets, ball nets etc. all is played on board a ship, later transferred to land, was 'invented' in the late 1930s. The early version was called 'Bangokok'.

Deck Tennis

Deck Tennis is associated with an informal game played on the deck of a ship. It is also known as "Tennequoits"

as it can be considered a combination of tennis and quoits. A typical court is 30 to 40 feet long and up to 15 feet wide. A three foot high net is strung across the middle. The court is divided into four equal segments. Players throw the quoit (flat ring) with the object of it landing on the ground before being caught. Scoring is the same as in lawn tennis. The game can be indoors. In Elizabeth Bowen's *Bowen's Court* (1942) she described the family life passing through the family home at Doneraile, County Cork over the centuries. An 1876 family diary recorded playing croquet during fine weather. On the 27th July of that year sixty visitors to the garden party, including six clergymen, played the game. Two weeks earlier the family attended a cricket match at Doneraile. No mention of lawn tennis. In the late 1940s swimming and walking were summer activites and in wet weather *we played deck tennis or French cricket in the Long Room.*

Large shuttles can be used in beach or garden games

Double Disc Court (DDC)

DDC is one of a number of sports in the Frisbee (or flying disc) family. It is a little like **tennis** using two frisbees on a continuous basis. It is for teams of two. The teams stand in square courts on about 13m, separated by a distance of 17m. A game is usually to 15 or 21 and points are scored if a team drop a disc, throw it out or are caught touching both discs simultaneously (2 points). The Frisbee sports have been organised since the 1960s and are played competitively in many countries worldwide, being particularly strong in Australia. The origin of the name Frisbee has been disputed though most agree it came from The Frisbie Baking Company (Bridgeport, Connecticut) where college students found that empty Frisbie tins made superb missiles. The plastic commercial version was made in 1948 (under the name Pluto Platter) but was first commercial sold as Frisbee in 1957. Arthur (*Spud*) Melin [1924-2002] was born in Los Angeles was the co-inventor of the Hula-Hoop and manufacturer of the Frisbee, the Hacky Sack, the Superball and a long inventory of wheezes. At one point he patented a two-handed tennis racket with an adjustable handle. In Ireland the leading club is Pookas in Dublin. They participate competitively in what is known as Ultimate Frisbee, defined as a *mix of football, netball and basketball,* and entered two teams in the World Championships in Germany in 2000.

Eton Fives

Eton Fives is a handball game, played in a three-sided court. The game uses a hard ball made of rubber and cork and slightly larger than a golf ball. It is played by two teams with two players each. Courts vary in dimensions and detail but the complicated design is based upon a bay formed by the buttresses at the base of the chapel steps at Eton College, England. It was played at Eton in 1825. In 1765 a handball game was played against the church wall at Barbary, Somerset and in 1773 a court existed at Lord Weymouth's School (now Warminster School). It is played in countries as far a field as Switzerland, Malaya, Australia, Argentina and Nigeria. The Eton Fives Association is based in Sevenoaks, Kent. A **fives** court was built in Trinity College, Dublin in 1694.

Featherball

This sport is directly related to badminton and battledore. It was played as early as 1638 in France and also became popular in Denmark, Germany and Sweden. It was usually played with a soft ball made from chicken feathers and with short handled, small-headed strung racquets. In 1650 Queen Kristina of Sweden built a featherball court in Stockholm, the building is now a church.

Field Tennis

This sport was played in England up to about 1800. It was an open-air version of **real tennis** and a forerunner to **lawn tennis** though not directly. Nothing known about its rules and the extent it was played.

Fistball

This sport originated in Estonia in 1989 by university students. Not unlike squash rules, the sport uses a standard tennis ball. The ball can, however, be struck with the feet, fists or head. It is still evolving and is promoted by the Handball Association of Finland.

Fives

A form of **handball** once played widely in England and at a few locations in Dublin such as Trinity College. See **Eton Fives.**

Frontenis

Game played in a *fronton.* See **Pelota**

Gossima

An old, shortly lived, name for **table tennis.**

Handball

Those that watch the Olympics will come across the sport of handball, a game where the ball is thrown into goals. Most forms of handball, however, require the use of open hand or closed fist and utilize one or more walls against which the ball is hit. The sport is usually for two or four players. Many ancient forms exist and it is thought a form of handball was played in Mexico about 3,000 years ago. One record suggests a ball game with the hand was played in Egypt as long ago as 2000 BC. Alexander the Great was credited with spreading it throughout the Roman Empire. In the 15th century King James I of Scotland was said to be a keen player. It was played in Ireland as early as 1700. Irishman, Phil Casey was said to have built the first court in the USA (in New York) in about 1883.

The first connection with **tennis** was the French game of **Jeu de Paume**, basically handball over a net. This was the early forerunner of **lawn tennis**. By the time it reached Paris bats, and then racquets, were used. The long history of handball in Ireland was formalised with the establishment of the Irish Amateur Handball Association in 1924 and under the auspices of the GAA. There was a semi-professional Irish Handball Union but it died out in the 1930s. Today there are approximately 180 clubs with over 7000 members in Comhairle Liathroid Laimhe na hEireann. In 2000 Duxie Walsh of Kilkenny won a phenomenal 88th All Ireland **handball** title.

Duxie Walsh of Kilkenny, the most prolific handballer in the History of the Game in Ireland, receiving his championship cup from the President of Ireland, Mary McAleese.

Hard Racquets

The name sometimes given to **racquets** to distinguish it from **squash racquets**. See **rackets.**

Jai Alai

The name given to **pelota** when it arrived in Cuba, in about 1900.

Handball in Ireland in the 19th century. From "Illustrated Sporting and Dramatic News", 16th February 1884.

Jeu a Dedans

This is a version of the French game of Jeu de paume, dedans referring to a goal that had to be defended. This was at a time before a net was introduced.

Jeu de Bonde

This is a medieval French name for tennis and referred to in the medieval play, 'Miracle de Nostre-Dame' which was written in about 1300. Jeu de bonde is 'the bouncing ball game'. Gillmeister suggests it used a sieve or some slanting surface to start the game and that its name is certainly older than the *famous jeu de paume.*

Jeu de Paume

This sport is the antecedent of all racquet sports. The translation of **jeu de paume** is game of the palm. It started as a game played around the cloisters of monasteries in France (and Italy, according to one source). At one stage it became so popular that the Pope banned the monks from playing it. It spread from cloister to castle and then to the cities. After a time gloves were used then gradually wooden bats were introduced. Later, crude racquets covered with parchment were in vogue and, by the Tudor era in England, strings made from animal gut were in use. In the early days a sagging rope or line was used. The early balls were made of leather or goatskin, and stuffed with materials such as hemp and hair. As can be seen from the chart the racquet games of today can be linked to this sport that was played perhaps 900 years ago. The term **jeu de paume** is still used (in France) in relation to the sport known elsewhere as **real** (GB)**, royal** (Australia) or **court tennis** (USA)**.** In 1612 we find the term **Le jeu Royal de la paume** as an indoor game with sloping net, ball and bats.

Jeu de Tamis

This is a variation of tennis which was recorded as early as 1498 in the area of Boulogne-sur-Mer in north-western France. A 'tamais' or 'sas' was a sieve. It was also recorded as being played in Belgium in 1598. The game is one of many off-shoots of the medieval **jeu de la paume**. In this case a portable three-legged (corn) sieve is used as a substitute for the slanting roof and the ball is projected off the tamis to start the game. As sketch from Louvain's Pig's College (c. 1649) show a three-sided match in progress.

The game has survived in the south of Belgium, among the Walloons and the Flemings, where it is known as **jeu de pelote a main** and **kaatsen** respectively. Variations of the game have worked their way south and across to Mexico. In Provence the server ('boundaire') uses as his trampoline for the ball (instead of a sieve), a stone or iron platform. It was here called **jo de paumo**. Heiner Gillmeister says that the game must *have reached Upper Italy by the end of the sixteenth century at the latest.* He adds that *On its way to the Iberian peninsula, the 'jeu de tamis' left its traces in the oldest varieties of Basque pelota,' bote luzea' and 'lachoa'.......In the highly spectacular Basque pelota game 'jai alai', the fact that the ball has to be bounced onto the floor before the service may well be a reminder of serving it on to some slanting surface in the days of yore.*

In the Canaries, particularly Lanzarote, there is reference, in 1616, to the ball playing area called the **juego de la pelota**. The game now goes by the name of **pelotamano.** The Spaniards obviously brought the game across the Atlantic for we find a not dissimilar game called **pelota mixteca.** In parts of Southern Columbia we find a variation called either simply **pelota** or **juego de la chaza.**

Jeu de Volant

Name given to **battledore** when it became popular in Europe in the seventeenth century (see **badminton** and **battledore**).

Juego de la Chaza

A game found in South America that seems to have come across the Atlantic with the Spaniards. See **Jeu de Tamis.**

Lacrosse

The games origin was in North American, pre 1492, where the Indians called it **baggataway.** (Much earlier, there were Mayan and Aztec ball courts dedicated to religion rather than sport.) Religious ceremonies were followed by inter-tribe sports from which baggataway was developed. The French game of **jeu de la crosse** combined with **baggataway** gave us the game known as **lacrosse.** Lacrosse is a ten-aside field game where the ball is advanced along a pitch with a **racketlike** implement called a *crosse* in order to score between the opposition's goal posts. As early as 1810 it was in fact referred to as a racket. Longest throw recorded was 163 yards by Barney Quinn (sounds Irish?) in Ottawa on the 10th September 1892. In 1867 the game was introduced to Britain by a team of Caughnawaga Indians who played a match for Queen Victoria.

La Longue Paume

A variation of **jeu de paume** was **la longue paume.** This appears to have been similar in concept to the more widely known **jeu de paume** but played in an open space without any constricting walls. Two teams of two or more would play in a defined flat area with a marked line or cord dividing the sides. The suggestion of lawn tennis is definitely here.

La Mano Desnuda

This is the Basque pelota game of relatively modern vintage. The translation of **la mano desnuda** is literally the naked hand.

Lawn Rackets

An early name for **lawn tennis**, probably short lived when Major Clopton Wingfield's patented sport of **Sphairistike** or **lawn tennis** became popular.

Lawn Tennis

The game of **jeu de paume** was popular as a handball game for many centuries in France. It became **real tennis** (also called **royal** and **court tennis**). It is still called **jeu de paume** in France. Over a period of time it became popular among royalty in France and then in England and Scotland. Henry VIII nominated himself as World Champion and built courts everywhere, including four in Whitehall. Two English kings banned **real tennis**, it distracted from archery practice. The Tudors and Elizabeth I loved the sport. In the Victorian era inventions were popular. The first lawn mower was patented in 1830 and the Shanks horse drawn version was a hit at the Great Exhibition in 1851, where Napoleon III bought one. There was even an impractical steam powered lawn mower by 1893. Bowling and, more particularly, croquet were popular lawn games. Major Wingfield's **Sphairistike** was the true start of lawn tennis (see below) in 1874.

> On the 25th February 1875 the All England Croquet Club agreed a motion *That one ground be set apart for Lawn Tennis and Badminton during the ensuing season.* On the 3rd March 1875 the MCC (Marylebone Cricket Club) organised a meeting of interested parties and an agreed set of rules for the sport were issued on the 29th May.

In the same year the Staten Island Cricket and Baseball Club laid down a lawn tennis court, the first in the USA.

The first playing of the sport in Ireland does not seem to have been recorded. It is suspected that it was brought to our shores by the gentry who would have seen it played during their London visits. It was probably organised by gentleman with military backgrounds in many areas. In Limerick, for example, the Limerick Chronicle of the 17th July 1877 announced the forthcoming lawn tennis tournament. It was to commence on the 2nd August on the grounds of the County Limerick Cricket Club. By then the game was played in several parts of the country and the tournament was *successful to the highest degree with an unprecedented number of entries both of ladies and gentlemen.* Earlier that year (14th April) the name of the All England Croquet Club was changed to the *All England Croquet and Lawn Tennis Club.* Their first championships started on the 9th July, just 24 days before the Limerick tournament. In November, some ten men met and formed the Dublin Lawn Tennis Club. By the 6th of December a grounds had been leased in Upper Pembroke Street (just off Fitzwilliam Square) and it was agreed to name the new club the Fitzwilliam Lawn Tennis Club. The Championship of Ireland followed in 1879 when the first competition started on Wednesday 4th June after a 48-hour rain delay. The US, French and Australian Championships were to follow in 1881, 1891 and 1905 respectively.

The Davis Cup (the International Lawn tennis Championship) was started in 1900 with two teams, the USA and Britain. By 1969, there were 51 teams competing and by 1998 the number of nations involved was 131. Ireland's first representative was Joshua Pim in 1903 (then on a British team). As a country in their own right, Ireland played their first match against India in Dublin in 1923, winning 3/2.

The Federation Cup for women was inaugurated in 1963. Ireland's first entry was in 1964. The first full match between any two nations was in 1892. Held in Dublin, Ireland beat England 5/4. The match consisted of all men's doubles. The Irish Lawn tennis Association was formed in 1908 and became Tennis Ireland in January 1990. It currently has about 220 registered clubs and nearly 100,000 registered members.

Mexican Handball

See **Handball**.

Olympic Handball

Similar to indoor football with hands used instead of feet. First played in about 1895. The sport was first played at the Olympics in 1936.

Padder Tennis

In 1950, a meeting of sports enthusiasts in London launched Padder Tennis. A similar game had been played on board English ships in the 1930s without taking off. This new version, using large five-ply wooden bats and a tennis ball (instead of a soft ball). The game was played using lawn tennis rules on a court with dimensions of 39 feet by 18 feet and a net 2 feet 3 inches high at the centre. It could be played on any permanent surface, indoors or outdoors. The first president of the Padder tennis association was Sir Stanley Rous (secretary of the Football Association. Sets for four players, including net, were marketed by Slazengers Ltd. at £7.12.6.

Dan Maskell and Miss M. Frith at an exhibition of the new game of Padder in 1950 (Lawn Tennis & Badminton, 1950).

It was launched with the support of Dan Maskell, a man then considered a top coach. He was involved in a series of exhibition matches at the time. It could probably be considered the forerunner to 'short tennis'. In the November 15 issue (1950) of *Lawn Tennis & Badminton* it was described as follows: *Padder tennis provides an excellent form of vigorous exercise for all ages in a limited space and is excellent training for young children who find the dimensions of a lawn tennis court too much for their physical powers. Complementary to lawn tennis rather than a competitor, the game must appeal to schools, boys' clubs, youth centres and the like with limited space,*

and one of its biggest assets is of course that it is cheap and easy to install.

The Padder set as promoted by Slazengers in 1950.

Padder Tennis Finals

The finals of the Dublin Inter-Playground Padder Tennis Tournament, organised by the Civics Institute of Ireland, were played at the Mountjoy Square Playground yesterday.

The results were: Boys' Singles—Paddy Noonan. Hill St. Girls' Singles—Maura Foran. Mountjoy Square. Boys' Doubles—D Dennis and K. Martin. Mountjoy Square. Girls' Doubles—M. Foran and K. Sullivan. Mountjoy Square.

Irish Independent 23rd August 1956

Paddleball

A range of sports using paddles or bats. It might be a beach game (**beach tennis**) or the more organised **paddles tennis,** as first played in the USA in 1921.

Paddle Tennis

Paddle tennis was invented by the Reverend Frank Peer Beal, in New York in 1921. He installed the first court in his church gymnasium. It is much the same rules as lawn tennis but played with a laminated plywood bat (maximum length 17 inches). The net is 2 foot six inches high at the centre. The full court size is 44 feet long by 20 feet wide. The ball used is about the same size as a lawn tennis ball and made of light sponge rubber. The American Paddle Tennis Association (now the US Paddle Tennis Association) was formed in 1923.

Padel Tenis

Padel Tenis is similar in concept to the Paddle tennis invented in 1921. Its origins appear to have been in South America in the late 1970s. The walled court is 20m x 10m and the net identical to that in lawn tennis. A paddle is used instead of a tennis racquet, normal tennis balls and scoring are used. The sport is now widespread in South America, particularly in Argentina, and in Spain, France and Italy.

Pelota

Pelota is also called **pilota, pelote Basque** and **pelota vasca**. The name **pelotamano** has also been used. The sport of **pelota** has several different variations. According to one source it originated in Italy where it was called **longue paume**. Another source puts its origins as being that of **jeu de paume** in France. It developed from a form of handball and then used a flat wooden bat. In the north of Spain the sport was called **pelota vasca** or **Basque pelota vasca.** It was well established in Spain by 1600, the word pelota being the Spanish for ball. In 1900 it was introduced to Cuba and was called **jai alai** ('merry festival'). The game is popular is places as diverse as Mexico, Spain, Egypt, Cuba and the USA. It uses a three-walled court called a *fronton* that can be up to 200 feet in length (other versions have used single and two walled courts). Games played in a *fronton* include **frontenis, pelote** and **paleta.** (McWhirter, 1977) **Pelota vasca** uses a ball harder and heavier than a golf ball and thrown by a cesta (introduced about 1860) which is a 0.76 m curved wicker scoop, strapped to one arm. Speeds of up to 260 km/h are obtained making it the fastest of ball games. The *Federacion Internacional de Pelota Vasca* was founded in 1925. An excellent real-tennis web site (www.real-tennis-nl) discusses the 16th century tennis playing princes in various Italian states. Duke Emanuele Filberto of Savoy (d. 1580) played *pillotta* matches of more than three hours. The state of Parma had its main castle, *Palazzo della Pilotta,* named after the ballgame.

Pelota Mixteca

A game found in parts of Mexico with obvious Sapnish origins. See **Pelota** and **Jeu de Tamis**.

Pila Trigonalis

An ancient Roman ball game, described in a Latin poem 'Laus Pisonis' and one where three players formed a triangle throwing the ball to one another and attempting to catch one another out.

Ping Pong

Ping pong was an early trade name for **table tennis**, first used in about 1900, probably in the USA. Still used.

Platform Paddle Tennis

This outdoor version of Paddle Tennis was invented by Fessenden S. Blanchard and James K. Cogswell from Scarsdale, New York in 1928. The platform may be permanent or portable, and can be placed on top of a lawn tennis court during the winter months. It is almost exclusively a doubles sport.

Platform Tennis

This is an unusual game played on a raised platform about a quarter the size of a tennis court.

Poona

Poona was the 'original' name for **badminton**. It was at Poona (India) that the first set of rules was formulated. It was a game for up to five people on either side of the net and was played outdoors.

Racketball

See **Racquetball**

Rackets

The game of **rackets**, also spelt **racquets,** is a game played in a four-walled court. The court is larger than a **squash** court and the ball is harder. It may be played with two or four players. The court is generally 18m long by 9 m wide (another source mentions the dimensions 60 feet x 30 feet x 30 feet high ceiling). The rackets are about 27 to 30 inches in length with a small round head (7 to 8 inches in diameter). The ball used is 1 inch in diameter and has a renewable tape covering. The game is played to 15 points or 'aces' and matches are the best of three or five sets for singles and the best of seven for doubles or tournament play. It was once thought to have originated in Fleet Prison in England in the middle of the 18th century. From there it spread to taverns and other public houses. The most common opinion is that its origin was in **real tennis,** which is of a much earlier vintage, and in fact rackets has been traced back to 1529.

In 1872, J. R. Atkins published *The Book of Racquets.* In this he says that *both games* (rackets and real tennis*) have so much in common that it is impossible to separate them historically; for practical purposes we must regard them as identical.* In 1822, it was introduced into Harrow School (England) and then became respectable. Here it was played within four walls. In 1862 the Board of Trinity College, Dublin, agreed to the construction of a **rackets** court for the students.

The Queen's Club in London was opened in 1887 and became the headquarters for the game. The rules of the game were drawn up for the first time in 1890 by rackets player Major Spens and tennis historian Julian Marsh. The Tennis, Rackets and Fives Association was formed in 1907. It is still based at the Queens club. The game has been played in the USA, Canada, Argentina, India and Malta. In the 20th century, it could be said that **squash** became its popular son. In

Ireland, according to Ted Neville, the Honorary Secretary of the Irish Real Tennis Association, the surviving Rackets courts in Ireland which are all converted or in disuse are at R.I.A.C., Dublin; Trinity College (library); the Kildare Street Club (a National Library store), Aras an Uachtarain (a gym), the Curragh Military camp (squash courts) and at Carton House. A recent cutting from the *Irish Times* (5th February 2003) suggests the game was played in rural Ireland near 200 years ago.

Racquetball

The sport of **racquetball** (also spelt **racquet ball and racketball**) appears to have originated in the USA in the late 1960s. It appears that a former tennis player, needing some extra exercise, cut down the handle of an old tennis racquet and went into a handball court with racquet and a tennis ball and set about keeping fit. It has been described as being similar to **paddle ball** and also a cross between **handball** and **tennis.** It is played in a four-walled court similar in size to a handball court, and uses a short handled string racket that has an attached cord around the wrist. The court dimensions are 20 feet wide x 40 feet long x 20 feet high with a 12-foot back wall. The ceiling is flat and becomes a fifth wall during play.

Kathleen Cadden, Ballydoogan, winner of the RAI singles title at the Arklow Championships in the late 1980s.

The rubber ball is smaller than a tennis ball and bigger than a squash ball. It became most popular in the USA and Ireland where handball already had a following. It came to Ireland in 1978. The Racquetball Association of Ireland was founded in 1979 and there are about 40 clubs affiliated to it. Ireland first took part in the World Championships in 1981 when they were held in Santa Clara, California. Irish players have won many medals, individual and team, at various world championships. There is a professional circuit. About 60 countries are affiliated to the international federation.

Racquets

See **rackets.**

Real Tennis

This game is a direct descendent of the French game **Jeu de la Paume.** It was well established there by the end of the 12th century. In 1530 Francis 1 of France built a court in the Louvre palace. At this stage short racquets rather than hands were used to propel the ball. It was popular until the French revolution. In 1789, the National Assembly of France, in defiance of Louis XVI, assembled in the court at Versaille, swearing never to disperse until France had a constitution- the famous *Tennis Court Oath.* During the sixteenth century there were over 1000 courts in Paris alone. It was a Royal favourite and spread to England and elsewhere. While still called **tennis**, it became known as **real tennis** (mainly Britain) or **royal tennis** (mainly Australia) and, in the USA, **court tennis.** The court is an enclosed area of about 92 feet by 32 feet. (No two courts are alike and in the USA the court is about 110 feet by 38 feet). The racquet is not dissimilar to a tennis racquet but has a lob-sided head, giving 'cut' to the ball. The ball is solid and there are a number of unusual features in the court itself. Henry VIII had one built at Hampton Court Palace in 1529 and is still there today. Apparently, because of his size he had one of the servants throw the ball up for him to commence play. It is understood that this is how the term *service* entered the game of tennis. Many of the terms used in the sport allude to the French origins. The scoring of 15, 30 and 40 in lawn tennis originated with this sport too. The following quotations say something about the attraction of the sport

Running, jumping and hitting chess (The Times)

A fascinating spectator sport, the complexity and quirkiness of real tennis are the attraction to those who play it. (Ian Macaulay, 1986)

When I saw the real tennis court for the first time I was fascinated-I couldn't believe my eyes. I went on court without any idea of the rules and that was it, I was hooked. (Alex Warren-Piper, 1987)

The oldest existing court in the world is in Paris (built in 1496). The Amateur Championship of the British Isles was instituted in 1780. Today, there is resurgence in the game and there are perhaps several thousand players worldwide. About 45 courts are currently in use in France, Great Britain, Australia and the USA. The Queens Club in London, noted for its lawn tennis facilities and tournaments, is an important centre for

The History of Irish Tennis

this sport. It is noted that a 1610 map of Dublin includes "Tennis Court Lane" in the inner city.

.....at the Guinness (Iveagh) Court, Earlsfort Terrace (St. Stephen's Green) Dublin, in the last week of May 1890. Pettitt (Boston) retains his title against Saunders (London). Sir Edward Guinness congratulates the winner. Among his personal guests is Lord Wimborne of Dorset on whose court the Dublin court is modelled. (sourced by Mr Brian Rich from 'The Graphic' magazine)

The 1890 World title match between Pettit and Saunders as depicted by "Graphic Magazine".

Charles Saunders (England) failed against Tom Pettit of the USA in the 1890 Real tennis title challenge. (Courtesy National Tennis Club, Newport, Rhode Island).

Tom Pettit (USA) Real Tennis World Champion held off Charles Saunders (England) challenge at Earlsfort Terrace, Dublin in 1890. (Courtesy National Tennis Club, Newport, Rhode Island).

Sir Edward Cecil Guinness constructed the Real Tennis Court at Earlsfort Terrace, Dublin, in 1885.(courtesy of Guinness Archives).

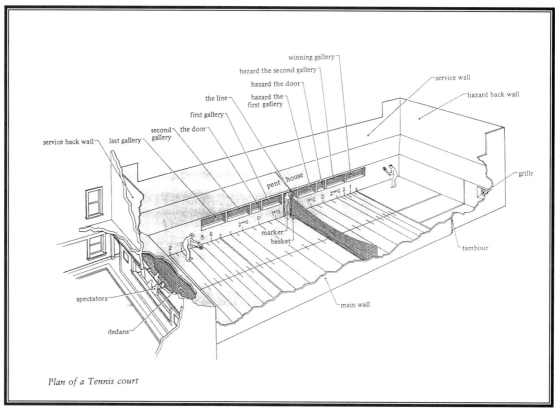

Plan of a Tennis court

A typical "real tennis" court (courtesy of Irish Real Tennis Association). Real Tennis in its present form has been played for over 400 years. Currently it is played on 42 courts worldwide. Courts have been recorded in Ireland in Dublin, Kilkenny, Galway and Waterford. The game supports fifty professionals world-wide. The world champion for much of the last decade is Australian Rob Fahey, a man of Irish extraction. The Earlsfort Terrace Court is unique for several reasons. It is the only one left in Ireland and the only one in the world constructed of marble. It is the only one given by an individual to a nation. It is one of only six courts in the world to have hosted the world championship challenge in the last 150 years.

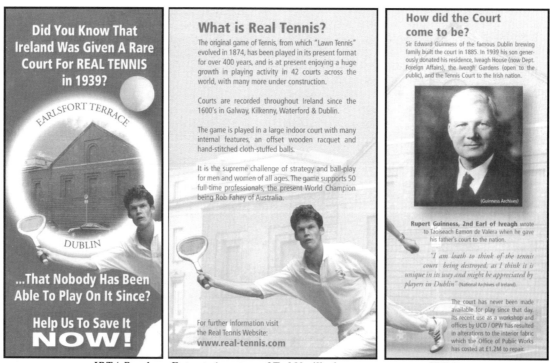

IRTA Brochure Extracts (courtesy of Ted Neville, honorary secretary, IRTA).
Player in action is Richard Henman, brother of Davis Cup player Tim.

In 1939, Rupert Guinness, the Earl of Iveagh, presented his world-famed black marble court (at Earlsfort Terrace, Dublin 1) to the Irish nation as a gift. Despite his written wishes, the court was immediately shut down and internal playing features dismantled. In 1998 The Irish Real Tennis Association was formed to prevent it being permanently converted and to have it re-opened for its intended purpose. The game was first played in Ireland in 1609 in a court in Thomas Street, Dublin.

According to *The Bold Collegians* (West 1991) a court was constructed at Trinity College, Dublin in 1741. In additional, the book mentions that the only court still in Ireland was on Lambay Island. As the Earlsfort Terrace Court had been 'reconstructed' it was not mentioned. It might be noted that the World championships were held in the Earlsfort Terrace Court in 1890.

Another Irish connection is that the best player in the world in recent years has been Australia's Robert Fahey. The likeable and irreverent player has been nicknamed the *Tasmanian Devil* due to his freewheeling style. Up to December 2001 he had won seven consecutive Grand Slams. These as the same ones as recognised for lawn tennis i.e. the Australian, French, British and US Open Championships. By 2003 he had won the world championships for 10 years in a row. It might be noted also that he was formerly the number one lawn tennis player in Tasmania. His great-great-grandfather was born in Loughrea in 1832 and emigrated to Australia in 1855.

Royal Tennis

Another name used, mainly in Australia, for **tennis, court tennis** or **real tennis.**

Rugby Fives

A variation of Eton Fives, this handball game dates from about 1850. The Rugby Fives Association was formed in London in 1927 and the court standardised in 1931.

Short Badminton

A variation of badminton introduced in England (c.1990) for young children being introduced to the sport.

Short Tennis

This sport is one used to introduce young children to the sport of lawn tennis. Light plastic or badminton racquets can be used. The ball is larger than a tennis ball and made of sponge. It can be played on a badminton court with a net at a height of 0.8m in the centre and 0.85m high at the posts. Scoring is usually on a first to 11 points basis. It originated in Sweden in the 1970s and was first organised in Ireland in 1981. Court sizes are 13.4 m x 6.1m (44 feet x 20 feet), the same size as a badminton court.

Shuttlecock

Shuttlecock was another name for **battledore** and an antecedant of **badminton**. (see above). Was played in England as early as 1390 and much earlier in Ancient Greece and several Asian countries.

Sphairistike

In the summer of 1859 Major Harry Gem (solicitor) and Augurio Pereira (merchant)(also spelt Perara in some sources), both keen **rackets** players, experimented with an outdoor version. This was on the Pereira's lawn at Fairlight, Ampton Road, Edgbaston, Birmingham. In 1872 they, together with Dr.Frederick Haynes and Dr. Arthur Tomkins, founded the Leamington Lawn Tennis Club, the world's first lawn tennis club. At Rhysnant Hall, Montgomeryshire, Major Walter Clopton Wingfield was also trying out such an outdoor game. He saw the business potential and on the 23rd February 1874 patented a game called **Sphairistike** (from the Greek meaning ball game). He successfully marketed the game as *Sphairistike or Lawn Tennis,* selling rackets, balls and a net in a box for five guineas. In the first year over 1000 boxed-sets were purchased. The court initially played on was hourglass in shape (Gem's was rectangular), similar to the badminton courts of the era. The term **lawn tennis** was to quickly become the dominant name.

The original cover for the Spairistike boxed sets.

Squash

Squash is a modification of the old game of **rackets**. It is also called **squash racquets** and **squash rackets**. It probably originated at Harrow, England, in the middle of the 19th century. By the 1920s it had become more popular than its parent game **rackets**. The racquet is just over two feet in length and has a strung head significantly smaller than a tennis racquet. It is played in a four-walled court and with a pneumatic rubber ball nearly two inches in diameter. In the USA doubles squash is popular but in Ireland it is primary a game for two people. Irish Squash is the present governing body and was formed in 1993 and is located in Dublin. It has about 111 clubs affiliated to it. Its sister organisation, Ulster squash, was founded in 1995 and is based in Belfast with about 49 clubs affiliated to it.

Jonah Barrington, recognised as one of the great squash players, was not always on top of the world. Brown & Brown (1983), in *The Book of Sports Lists,* include the following jobs he had before taking up the

Men's Irish Open Squash Championships

Year	Winner	Runner-Up	Year	Winner	Runner-Up
1931	Arthur Hamilton*		1963	Donald Pratt*	Barton Kilcoyne*
1932	R.W. Beadle (Eng.)		1964	Donald Pratt*	M. Grundy (Eng.)
1933	R.W.S. Greene	George Mc Veagh*	1965	Donald Pratt*	Barton Kilcoyne*
1934	George McVeagh*	Bruce Cairn-Duff	1966	Jonah Barrington	Azam Khan (Pak.)
1935	George McVeagh*	Sir Basil Goulding*	1967	Jonah Barrington	Donald Pratt*
1936	George McVeagh*	Sir Basil Goulding*	1968	Donald Pratt*	BIll Barr
1937	R.A. McNeile	Willie Sandys*	1969	Jonah Barrington	Donald Pratt*
1938	S.G.S. Pawle (Eng)	Willie Sandys*	1970	Bill Barr	R.Chalmers
1939	Sir Basil Goulding*	R.A. Mc Neile	1971	Donald Pratt*	R. Weir
1940	Paul McWeeney*	Tim O' Driscoll	1972	Geoff Hunt (Aus.)	Jonah Barrington
1941	Paul McWeeney*	Tim O' Driscoll	1973	Geoff Hunt (Aus.)	W.C.Nancarrow(Aus.)
1942	Tim O' Driscoll	George McVeagh*	1974	G. Alauddin (Pak.)	H. Jahan (Pak.)
1943	Cyril Kemp*	J. J. O' Keeffe	1975	Geoff Hunt (Aus.)	Q. Zaman (Pak.)
1944	J. J. O' Keeffe	Tommy Hogan	1976	Geoff Hunt (Aus.)	Jonah Barrington
1945	J. J. O' Keeffe	Cyril Kemp*	1977	Q. Zaman (Pak.)	Geoff Hunt 9Aus.)
1946	Shane Jameson	Paul Mc Weeney*	1978	P. Kenyon (Eng.)	F. Donnelly 9Aus.)
1947	Shane Jameson	D.N. Sell	1979	Jonah Barrington	J. Khan (Pak.)
1948	David Sell	Des O' Brien*	1980	H. Jahan (Pak.)	B. Brownlee (N.Z.)
1949	A. G. Aitchison (Scot.)	D.N. Sell	1981	J. Khan (Pak.)	H. Jahan (Pak.)
1950	Joe McHale*	Seamus Monahan*	1982	J. Khan (Pak.)	Q. Zaman (Pak.)
1951	Joe McHale*	Seamus Monahan*scr.	1983	Willie Hosey*	J. Barrett
1952	W. R. Howson (Eng.)	Hugh O' Donoghue	1984	G. Briars (Eng.)	R. Norman (Aus.)
1953	Hugh O' Donoghue	C. Zarb (Malta)	1985	R. Norman (N.Z.)	S. Davenport (N.Z.)
1954	Hugh O' Donoghue	Lee Lyons*	1986	G. Briars (Eng.)	S. Davenport (N.Z.)
1955	Patrick Knox-Peebles	Lee Lyons*	1987	Jansher Khan (Pak.)	G. Briars (Eng.)
1956	Hugh O' Donohue*	Donald Pratt*	'88-'90	Not held	
1957	Donald Pratt*	Barton Kilcoyne*	1991	C. Robertson (Aus.)	P. Whitlock (Eng.)
1958	Donald Pratt*	Barton Kilcoyne*	'92-'99	Not held	
1959	Donald Pratt*	Barton Kilcoyne*	2000	Peter Nichol (Scot.)	JonathanPower (Can)
1960	Barton Kilcoyne*	Donald Pratt*	2005	Ong Beng Hee (Mas.)	Laurens Jan Anjema (H.)
1961	Donald Pratt*	P. Heaney	2006	Borja Golan (Spain)	Davide Bianchetti (It.)
1962	Donald Pratt*	John Copeland		*Known tennis players1994	

Irish Women's Closed Champions
Dorothy Boyd Cup

1973	Barbara Sanderson
1974	Irene Hewitt
1975	Dorothy Armstrong
1976-1977	Irene Hewitt
1978	Geraldine Barniville
1979	Dorothy Armstrong
1980	Irene Hewitt
1981	Geraldine Barniville
1982	Marjorie Burke
1983-1987	Mary Byrne
1988-1993	Rebecca O'Callaghan (nee Best)
1994-1996	Aisling McArdle
1997-1999	Madeline Perry
2000	Eleanor Lapthorne
2001-2002	Madeline Perry

Irish Open Ladies' Squash

2002	Vanessa Atkinson (Holland)
2003	Vanessa Atkinson (Holland) beat Jenny Tranfield (England) 10/8 9/1 9/3
2005 & 2006	Madeline Perry (Ireland)

Top Irish squash player Willie Hosey from Carlow started out as a very useful young tennis player.

The History of Irish Tennis

In 2001 the Fitzwilliam Lawn Tennis Club ladies' squash team came third in the European club championships. From left: Aisling McArdle, Claire O'Brien, Aisling Blake and Louise Finnegan.

game: teacher in Spain, grounds man, coalman in Cornwall, cottage painter in Devon, carpet cleaner in London, schoolmaster in York, milkman in Earls Court, dishwasher and nude model. Barrington attended Trinity College Dublin and was deemed to have been a good soccer and tennis player in the 1950s. He won the squash world championships (i.e. the British Open) six times between 1966 and 1972 and was largely responsible for popularising the game worldwide.

Barrington was born in England to an Irish family, attended Headford School in Kells, and represented Ireland on court, undoubtedly leading to its subsequent growth in popularity in Ireland. Another noted Trinity squash player was Donald Pratt who won the Irish Championships ten times. His uncle was the great all-rounder, George McVeagh. Both played for Ireland and were active members of **Fitzwilliam LTC,** the venue for the Irish Open Men's Championships.

Squash Rackets

An alternative name for **squash** and **squash racquets.** According to Brown & Brown (1983) the following is the origin of the sport we now call squash.

At the end of the nineteenth century there were too many boys at Harrow School who wished to play rackets, so a new game was devised for the juniors, with a larger and softer ball and a smaller and cheaper court. This became known as squash rackets.

Squash Racquets

An alternative name for **squash** and **squash rackets.** It also refers to a game that was first instituted as a competitive sport in the early 1930s in Kilkee, County Clare. After the Irish famine of the 19th century a work scheme saw the construction of the massive sea wall separating the village from the beach. It was built in about 1850. During the First World War handball was played against this extensive wall. When the tide is out the level sand provides a base for the game. Sometime between 1918 and 1934 'squash racquets' was introduced by simply using a racquet instead of playing by hand. Captain J. Wallace presented the Tivoli Cup which is played for each July. It is a mixed doubles format, though men's singles are also played, with a court marked out on the sand opposite the four smoothed and painted wall sections.

The main tournament each summer was for the Tivoli Cup in July with an additional tournament also held in August. Currently local Manuel di Lucia and other locals are keen to revive the game. Each court is about 40 feet wide with a rectangle market out from the wall, the court length being about 70 feet. The balls used are of a black rubber variety, slightly smaller than but *like a tennis ball without the fluff.* Scoring is the first to 21. At 20 all, the best of five points (i.e. first to 3) is played. The lady always serves first to the lady and the man to the man. The serve could go over the end line twice before losing ones serve. Serves to the side were out. Like badminton, the servers could only win points. 'Butting' the ball to the base of the wall, like handball and squash, would win many points as only one hop was allowed before the opposition must get it back.

Kilkee is a holiday resort and many people from the city of Limerick would spend their holidays at the resort. The Harris family were among them and all four brothers, Jimmy, Dickie, Ivan and Billy have all won the event on different occasions. The late Richard (Dickie) Harris, the film star, has won the title on a record of four consecutive occasions. On the 3rd May 2001 he was in Kilkee to present a replica Tivoli Cup to the town as an enticement to have the sport played once again. The last championships were held in 1993. The original cup is completely full with names of the winners. Richard Harris was delighted to replace it with an identical one.

Many notable personalities have played the game. One winner, to become a famous tennis player, was Michael Hickey. He and Mrs. Stanley Walshe won the event in 1956. Dickie Harris won it with Phillis Woods, Rita Ringrose, Betty Ryan and Mrs. Godsil in the years 1948 to 1951. Local Paul Costello has the distinction of being the winner on seven different occasions between 1961 and 1974. He had five different partners in that those winning years. In 1962 and 1963 he met his brother John, with partner, in the final only to lose both. In 1955, Richard Harris presented the Harris Cup for juveniles, a mixed doubles event also. It was his brother Billy who was the first winner. Johnny McDonnell of Limerick has won this cup three times (1963, 1964 and 1966).

A 2001 view of two of the four "Squash Racquets" Court Walls at Kilkee, Co. Clare (photo Eilish O'Brien).

Tivoli Cup Winners

1935	Brother Finbarr/M.D. O' Sullivan
1936	S.Walsh/Joan Wallace
1937	J. De Courcey/Mrs. Rentoul
1938	J.W. Stokes/M. O' Sullivan
1939	St. J. Murphy/E.A. Grieve
1940	St. J. Murphy/B. Mc Carthy
1941	St. J. Murphy/Pauline Woods
1942	M. Shinkwin/Moira Mc Dermot
1943	Jimmy Harris/Deirdre Lloyd
1944	Jimmy Harris/Rosaleen Marion
1945	B. Mc Green/Mrs. J.Dolan
1946	Ivan Harris/Gwen Wallace
1947	Niall Quaid/Carmel Holmes
1948	Dickie Harris/Phillis Woods
1949	Dickie Harris/Rita Ringrose
1950	Dickie Harris/Betty Ryan
1951	Dickie Harris/Mrs. Godsil
1952	Billy Quaid/Betty Cross
1953	Niall Quadi/Nuala Byrnes
1954	Paddy Dundon/Elaine Murphy
1955	Billy Quaid Grace Lloyd
1956	Michael Hickey/Mrs. Stanley Walshe
1957	Noel Ryan/E.Foley
1958	Billy Harris/Betsy Twoomey
1959	Noel Ryan/Evelyn O' Meara
1960	Joe Costello/Ann Mc Mahon
1961	Paul Costello/Helen Nolan
1962	John Costello/Ann Counihan
1963	John Costello/Helen breen
1964	Joe Keane/Helen Nolan
1965	Paul Costell/geraldine Kirby
1966	Paul Costello/Nell Fennell
1967	Paul Costello/Betty Maxwell
1968	Joe Keane/Helen Nolan
1969	Tom Nolan/Nuala Mc Donagh
1970	Gus O' Neill/Nuala Byrne
1971	Joe Keane/Nuala Mc Donagh
1972	Paul Costello/Betty Maxwell
1973	Paul Costello/Vivienne Gabbett
1974	Paul Costello/Vivienne Gabbett

1976	Tom Prendergast/Margaret Hogan
1977	Peter Finnegan/Marjorie Hayes
1978	Dennis Twoomey/Veronica Hickey
1979	Michael Cleary/Susan Holmes
1980	Michael Hickey/Bernadette Hayes
1981	Harry Hodkinson/Kate Roche
1982	Michael Cleary/Hilary Clein
1983	Michael Cleary/Adeamer Wood
1984	Andrew Cleary/Caroline Munnelly
1985	David Curtin/Sarah Mc Garry
1986	John Nolan/Sarah Barry
1987	John Nolan/Imelda Murphy
1993	Mary O'Byrne/Declan Forde

Richard Harris with the Tivoli Cup. He won this unique event for a record of four consecutive years (1948 to 1951). In May 2001 he presented a new Tivoli Cup to the people of Kilkee.

Squash Tennis

This game is essentially the same as **squash** with a racquet similar to a **lawn tennis** racquet and using a ball not dissimilar to a tennis ball but slightly smaller. The ball makes the game quicker than squash. It was first played in the USA in the early 1890s and is still played in that country to a limited extent.

Sticke

This sport involves was not unlike lawn tennis in an enclosed court. It was played outdoors with a hard floor and wooden wall and a short tennis net. It was played with a tennis racket and a coverless tennis ball. It appears that the first court constructed was that at the Queen's, London, as an experiment in the first decade of the 20th century. It was opened by a game between Eustace Miles and R.E. 'Tip' Foster, the latter captained England at cricket and soccer and was also a squash player.

Sticke was described variously as *by no means a bad game: in fact if one had nothing better to do it would be a godsend* and It was good fun for people getting too old for squash. According to Roy McKelvie in *the Queen's Club Story* their court was once used for a duel with pistols and wax bullets.

Swimming Pool Badminton

Swimming pool badminton was a recreational game played in the United States during the 1930s. It is not known if it was played or developed in any other country.

Swingball

This is a proprietary game involving a (tennis) ball attached to a pole by a string. It is hit with a bat (or tennis racquet). It was introduced on the market in the 1970s and is still manufactured. Suitable for even the smallest back garden.

Table Tennis

In the 17th century Prince James, Duke of York, was recorded as playing on a court with a racket described later as being similar to a strung **table tennis** racket. Many early racket sports use wooden bats that were abandoned when animal gut came into use in the form of stringing. According to Brown & Brown (1983) it was James Cribb of Croydon, London, who first invented table tennis. It appears, as a winter diversion, in about 1890, the game started when a pile of books were placed across a large dining room table to form the net. Table tennis was played as a miniature form of lawn tennis.

The Sticke Court at the Queen's Club, London, circa 1910.(from The Queen's Club Story 1886-1986)

Paddle Tenis has become popular since it was first established in the late 1970s. It is played in several South American countries, France, Italy, Germany (?) and Spain. The above court is at the Maspalomas Tenis Club, Gran Canaria. The court has walls, a shorter court than 'lawn' tennis but with an identical net. Normal tennis balls are used but a 'bat' (paddle) is used instead of a tennis racquet. Scoring is similar to tennis.

The Game of Swimming Pool Badminton became popular in the USA in the 1930s (The Sunday Times)

In the United States of America, in about 1900, the game of table tennis was played using a celluloid ball, and with hollow vellum 'battledores' (light racquets). The racquet with a crude frame, covered with a drumhead skin, made the distinctive sound which lead to the 'trade-mark' name Ping-Pong. Previously it had been called **whiff-whaff** and **gossima** when a web-covered ball was being used. The original Ping Pong Association broke up in about 1905. There was a revival in about 1920 followed by the formation of the Table Tennis Association in 1921. The International Table Tennis Federation was founded in 1926. Despite its popularity worldwide it was only first played as an Olympic Sport in Seoul in 1988. It is the national sport of China who dominated the medals in the Sydney Olympics. The 2002 world champions were Wang Liqin and Wang Nan, both from China.

An interesting connection with lawn tennis was Bjorn Borg's first racquet. His father had won a local table-tennis competition and Bjorn persuaded him to choose the tennis racquet as his prize. Later the younger Borg began to treat the racquet as his own. The rest is history.

The Irish Table Tennis Association was formed in 1937. Cyril Kemp, the Davis Cup player, was one of Ireland's best, and an international player at table tennis. During the 1970s Tommy Caffrey and Jimmy Langan had each by-passed the 200 mark in international appearances. In the late 1970s the number one Irish player was only 14 years of age.

12-years-old Boy Wins Men's Title

TWELVE - YEARS - OLD Thomas Caffrey (Balbriggan) became the youngest Leinster Junior Table Tennis title-holder ever, when in the final of the Men's Singles Championship, at the Abbey Lecture Hall, last night, he defeated Tony Timmins (Dun Laoghaire), 21-17, 21-19.

Young Caffrey also had the distinction of coming through the finals "proper"—four matches in all—without losing a game. For a boy of his age, his concentration was quite remarkable, and the manner in which he varied his strokes and retrieved shots from almost impossible angles, stamps him as a player of great promise.

Irish Independent (17th February 1956) report on the boy who became Ireland's number 1 senior player and the most capped (151) Irish international in any sport in this country.

Tennequoits

Alternative name used for **Deck Tennis.**

Tennis

Tennis is the generic name for a range of racquet sports. Though debatable, the name is thought to come from the French word **Tenez** meaning to hold or take heed, a word they would call out before serving.

Wheelchair Table Tennis

This sport is a straight-forward version of table tennis with the participants using wheelchairs.

Wheelchair Tennis

Wheelchair table-tennis competition run in parallel with standard events.

The game of **lawn tennis** played from **wheelchairs.** The game had its beginning in 1976 in California when a man called Brad Parks first started playing while in a wheel chair. It has been an organised sport since the 1980s. It is now played in over 100 nations and is one of the most popular disabled sports. In 1998 the Insternational Wheelchair Tennis Federation was fully integrated within the International Tennis Federation (ITF). There is now a World Team Cup and official world rankings. Jayant Mistry the world's number 8 in 2000, plays every week, and in about twenty tournaments each year.

Many would be surprised to learn that there are quite a number of professional wheelchair players. In 1998 a new charity was named after the late Dan Maskell with the aim of giving disadvantaged children the opportunity to enjoy tennis. Invacare and NEC have been major sponsors of the sport worldwide. In the same year it was introduced into the Paralympics as a demonstration sport. From 1992 at Barcelona it has become a full medal sport. In 1999 the Irish Wheelchair team became runners-up at a tournament in Bratislava and qualified for the Invacare World Team Cup in New York. In the summer heat of New York the team came 22nd out of 32 competing. They had 2/1 wins over Puerto Rico and Slovakia but lost (3/) to Canada, Hungary and Spain.

At the Stadium Court, Flushing Meadow, New York, during the Invacare World Team Cup were Aubrey Bingham, Jim Watt and Jason Black.

The Department of Physical Education at Baylor University (Texas, USA) has studied the benefits of various sports. They described badminton as one of the finest *conditioning game activities available.* The following table comparing tennis and badminton will of interest to exponents of both sports.

	Tennis	Badminton
Time duration	3 h 18m	1h 16m
Ball/shuttle in play	18 minutes	37 minutes
Match intensity	9%	48%
Shots	1004	1972
Shots per rally	3.4	13.5
Distance covered	2 miles	4 miles

(It is not known how "match intensity" was defined or measured, the other parameters are clear.)

At the World Team Cup in New York in 1999 were (from left) Aubrey Bingham, Jim Watt & Ivor Jess.

Whiff-Whaff

An old, shortly lived, name for **table tennis.**

Winchester Fives

A variation of the **Eton Fives** handball games. Also related to the **Rugby Fives** game.

*****

Indoor tennis at the official opening of the court at Sligo TC in 1985. The visiting pair of Ronnie Delaney (top, serving) (Carrickmines Croquet & LTC) and Donal Dempsey (Galway LTC) took on locals Bob English (serving) and Tom Higgins. In July 2005 Tennis Ireland opened the national indoor centre at Glasnevin, Dublin.

London newspaper sketch of 'rackets' action in the late 1880s, a sport with similarities to handball and squash.

In the first ever international badminton match, England beat Ireland 5/2 in Dublin. Most of these players probably played tennis during the summer months. The English team included George Thomas who reached the Irish Championship lawn tennis singles finals in 1912, 1913, 1914 & 1920. Thomas did win the mixed, in 1920 with that great American doubles expert, Elizabeth Ryan.

On the 20ᵗʰ April 1988 a National Racquet Sports Seminar was organised and held at Sligo Tennis Club. Among the top administrators and coaches speaking were (back, from left) Winston Wilkinson (Senior Coach, BUI), Alan Strong (Senior Coach, ITTA), David Taylor (Chief Executive, ILTA), Des Butler (President, Sligo TC), Tim O' Sullivan (President, ISRA), Tom Higgins (co-ordinator) and Jerry Sheehan (Coaching Committee, ILTA). Front row (from left): John Mc Guigan (former president, BUI), Audrey Kinkead (Honorary Secretary, BUI), Bob English (President, Connacht Council, ILTA), Pat Forkan (Vice-President, Sligo TC), Robbie McNabb (Chairman, table tennis session) and Prue Hamilton (European Squash Racquets Federation).

A. M. Cave who was Irish Open badminton champion in the years 1906-1909 was also a very successful lawn tennis player.

The great Frank Devlin in badminton action. This world-class badminton player also played interprovincial tennis.

A sixteenth century predecessor to lawn tennis

Judy (left) and Sue Peard won six All-England badminton doubles titles together between 1954 and 1966. They were ranked among the top lawn tennis doubles pairings in the USA at one time.

The History of
IrishTennis

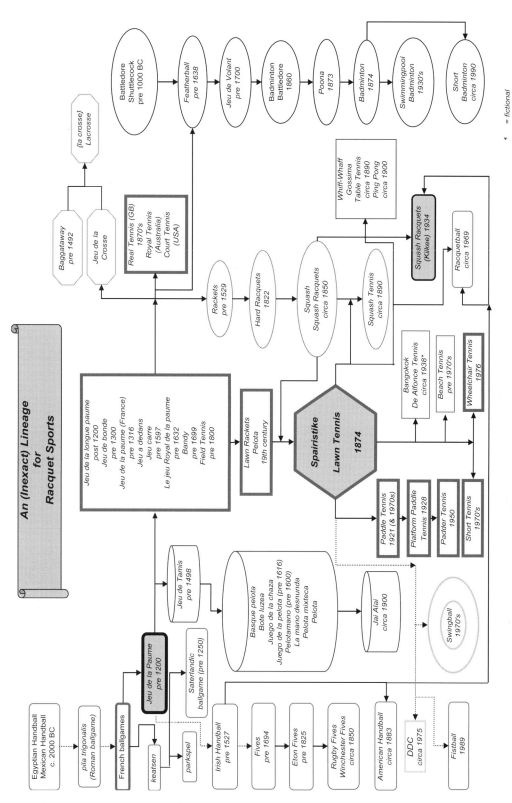

An (Inexact) Lineage for Racquet Sports

* = *fictional*

.... = *tentative connection*

Battledore Shuttlecock pre 1000 BC

Featherball pre 1638

Jeu de Volant pre 1700

Badminton Battledore 1860

Poona 1873

Badminton 1874

Swimmingpool Badminton 1930's

Short Badminton circa 1990

{la crosse} Lacrosse

Baggataway pre 1492

Jeu de la Crosse

Real Tennis (GB) 1870's Royal Tennis (Australia) Court Tennis (USA)

Rackets pre 1529

Hard Racquets 1822

Squash Squash Racquets circa 1850

Squash Tennis circa 1890

Whiff-Whaff Gossima Table Tennis circa 1890 Ping Pong circa 1900

Squash Racquets (Kilkee) 1934

Racquetball circa 1969

Jeu de la longue paume post 1200
Jeu de bonde pre 1300
Jeu de la paume (France) pre 1316
Jeu a dedans pre 1597
Le Jeu Royal de la paume pre 1632
Bandy pre 1699
Field Tennis pre 1800

Lawn Rackets Pelota 19th century

Spairistike Lawn Tennis 1874

Bangokok De Alfonce Tennis circa 1938*

Beach Tennis pre 1970's

Wheelchair Tennis 1976

Paddle Tennis 1921 (& 1970s)

Platform Paddle Tennis 1928

Padder Tennis 1950

Short Tennis 1970's

Jeu de Tamis pre 1498

Basque pelota Bote luzea Juego de la chaza Juego de la pelota (pre 1616) Pelotamano (pre 1600) La mano desnunda Pelota mixteca Pelota

Jai Alai circa 1900

Swingball 1970's

Jeu de la Paume pre 1200

Saterlandic ballgame (pre 1250)

Egyptian Handball Mexican Handball c. 2000 BC

pila trigonalis (Roman ballgame)

French ballgames

keatsen

parkspel

Irish Handball pre 1527

Fives pre 1694

Eton Fives pre 1825

Rugby Fives Winchester Fives circa 1850

American Handball circa 1883

DDC circa 1975

Fistball 1989

Cumann Leadóige na h-Éireann

IRISH
REAL TENNIS
ASSOCIATION

The IRTA was formed to promote
the game of real-tennis in Ireland.

International
Badminton:
Ireland
v
Scotland
(1989).

Freddie South (Munster) was Irish
Close tennis champion, an
international badminton player and an
interprovincial hockey player (see
chapter 6).

The History of Irish Tennis

Sligo Open Table Tennis (c. 1988)

The County Sligo badminton team won the all-Ireland junior cup for the first time in 1969.
The majority of the team were all tennis players during the summer months. Back (l. to r.):
Michael Fleming, W. Murphy, Tommy Fallon (manager), Jarlath Whelan & Joss
Galbraith. Front (l. to r.): Grace McDonagh, Madge Fleming, the Mayor of Sligo
Councillor John Fallon, Miss Watson & Joan Hamilton.

Badminton international John Taylor
in action (1980s).

R. PYKE.

(Drawn by

1930s cartoon of top Ulster badminton
and tennis player Major McCallum

Geoff Hunt from Australia won the Irish Open
Squash Championships at Fitzwilliam LTC in
1973, 1974, 1977 and 1977. He was world
number 1 from 1975 to 1980.

Chapter 3

Tennis as a Social Development

3.1 The Growth of Irish Tennis

*There weren't many Catholics in the club and I got the impression people in
the trade were frowned upon.*(Edward McGuire, Davis Cup player 1926 to 1935)

Joining clubs was, and still is, important for all social classes. In Ireland, we like to consider ourselves as relatively classless. To a great extent this is true today. However, in the 19th century, with the game in its infancy, this was certainly not the case. Grass courts were first built at the gentry' houses, and when participating numbers became significant, clubs were formed. By 1900 there were 300 clubs affiliated to the Lawn Tennis Association, a relatively small number of the 50 or so Irish clubs were among that number. The popularity of the sport grew significantly in the first half of the 20th century, despite the interruption of two world wars. At least two significant factors came in to play.

With the development of suburban housing, private courts were now built more frequently in people's gardens. In the twenty years or so following the Treaty of 1921, there was a new 'freedom' in the 26 counties. It was a breaking free from previous social and cultural binds. The Catholic sector in the community now felt free to participate in tennis clubs as a legitimate form of recreation. This is not surprising when we bear in mind it was an ideal sport for both sexes. Quite often the leaders of these clubs were the local (Catholic) clergy. Schools tennis also took off. North of the border no such freedom occurred. The existing sports clubs remained sectarian in their nature. There were sports played by Protestants such as hockey, cricket, rugby, golf, tennis and badminton. Catholics were strongly allied to the Gaelic games of football, hurling and handball. In a variety of ways cycling, athletics and soccer were common.

**Tea time at Roscrea Lawn Tennis Club-Circa 1920.
The sport was originally a social pastime, the social
element is still important in todays professional era.**

Most clubs have had humble beginnings. The numbers playing were initially small and facilities limited. Others, particularly in the cities and large towns, grew quickly where there was already a significant interest and a population of significance. Perhaps demand exceeded supply. In the early days, when there was a nearby garrison, cricket was extremely popular among young men. Tennis was the new game, it provided an excellent opportunity to mix socially and play sport in the company of suitable young ladies. At first tennis was, like snooker and croquet, more a pastime than a seriously competitive sport. The Leitrim Advertiser

(31st May 1900) put the game of a century ago in perspective:

LAWN-TENNIS is a favourite pastime in Carrick-on-Shannon amongst the "upper circle" during the present, delightfully warm evenings. The tennis-court on The Liberty is thronged with votaries of the game, whilst a number of ladies and gentlemen are comforted by looking on from the recumbent seats beneath the shady trees. Alas! Pastimes and games seem to be a thing of the past in Mohill.

Tennis Parties

Developments in Mullingar were not untypical of the early days of the sport. In The Westmeath Guardian of the 8th July 1887, an interesting article under the pseudonym "Patrick O' Shaughnessy" appeared. Titled "TENNIS PARTIES", it may today appear to be a bit quaint, or possibly a bit of a skit. I suspect not and it was a reasonably factual account of a relatively new sport in the area. The following are some extracts:

Now that tennis is so much the rage, and Miss Lottie Dod and the brothers Renshaw is in every one's mouth, I think that perhaps a few words on the subject of tennis Parties, from one who has a good deal of experience in that line, may not be out of place.

If I was asked "what game is most interesting to those who play, and most uninteresting to those who look on?" I should reply "by all means tennis". Perhaps I may give a short sketch of a tennis-party on a small scale, to which I was invited the other day. After a long and dusty drive we arrived at the place I shall call Millmount House. We alighted from our carriage and strolled towards the gay scene, where King tennis was holding his court; (having first shaken out our xxxxx and grasped our parasols with a more imposing air, if possible, than before). As we were not of the tennis worshippers, and did not play, we could not expect to be hailed with the delight a "swagger" player would have been, if he was a lord or a threadbare curate it would have been all the same. Society is above making those differences now-a-days; yet, our hostess welcomed us with a beaming smile. One would have thought from her manner that she had been pining for our arrival the whole afternoon and was only saved from fainting, or fit of hysterics or some other of the numerous resources ladies have at their disposal on those occasions, by seeing our carriage arrive up the avenue. Of course I was asked to play.

Before we proceed, a few notes on the above. Lottie (Charlotte) Dod at the time this article was written was just fifteen years of age and had, a few weeks earlier, won the first of her five Wimbledon titles as well as her only Irish title. The Renshaw twins, also from England, won eight Wimbledon singles titles between them. In 1887, Ernest won the first of his three Irish titles. The Mullingar society players were probably among the audience at the **Fitzwilliam LTC** for *The Lawn Tennis Championships of Ireland*, an event not to be missed. The railway line was a bonus for players at the time and the more successful of the early clubs (including Mullingar) had reasonable access to such transport.

The Tennis Worshippers sound like some modern groupies or intensely keen players. In fact, this is the title of one of Percy French's rhymes of the time. It includes the lines:

> *And men and maiden must repair*
> *To thy green sward Fitzwilliam Square*
> *And worship at the verdant fane*
> *Where good King tennis reigns again*
> *And where the monarchs of the sport*
> *In summer hold their court.*

The full version is recalled in the chapter on tennis writings.

In 1888, commencing on the 1st August, the first tournament took place in County Westmeath. This was in the private grounds of R. Smyth, Esq., Gaybrook, a gentry householder living about four miles south east of Mullingar town. Due to wet weather the three-day event took ten days to complete. The total entry included fifteen men and fourteen ladies as follows:

Gentlemen	Ladies
E. V. Levinge	Miss Percy
A. Annesley	Mrs. Annesley
T. Carson	Miss Hodson
H. W. Lloyd	Miss Preston
F. Thornhill	Miss Bellingham
Captain Welman	Miss Swift
V. Annesley	Miss Seymour
J. W. Murray	Miss Hunter
S. D. Chatterton	Miss Wilson
Captain W. Fetherston	Miss Lloyd
P. O'Reilly	Miss Thornhill
F. J. H. Bell	Miss Somers
V. Annesley	Miss M. Lemon
R. Lyons	Miss Lemon
A. E. Joyce	

The results of the tournament finals were as follows (all handicap) Ladies and Gentleman's Doubles, S. D. Chatterton and Miss Wilson beat T. Carson and Miss Hodson 11/9 6/4; Gentleman's Doubles, S. D. Chatterton and T. Carson beat A. & V. Annesley 6/1 6/1 6/4; Ladies Singles, Miss Wilson beat Miss Percy 6/0 6/1; Gentlemen's Singles, V. Annesley beat P. O'Reilly 7/5 6/1. Some interesting prizes were presented to the winners, a handkerchief sachet, a photo framed writing case, 2 handsome knives, a gauze painted fan and a very handsome ornamental clock. The band of the Royal Irish Rifles was present and *added much to the enjoyment of those assembled.*

On the 22nd and 25th August (1888) a self –selected County Westmeath team took on a County Longford team at the home of Mr. & Mrs. T. N. Edgeworth, located at Mount Murray, a gentry holding at the

north-western corner of Lough Owel. The location is about two miles from the old Clonhugh Railway Station. The Longford team won by 7 matches to 4. This is the first evidence of tennis played in that county, the County Longford Club in Longford town being formed some eight years later. This was obviously one of the first inter-county match to have taken place in Ireland.

1950s-Tennis was always a game to aid mixing among young and old.

In many areas of the country it was the proliferation of the game at private courts that lead to the need for clubs. On the 5th May 1892 the game was thriving in Mullingar and the first general meeting of Mullingar Lawn Tennis Club was held at the Bank of Ireland in the town. The elected committee were *Col. Goodwyn (East Lancashire Regt.), Major O'Brien, R. M.; M. F. Barnes, Esq.; Col. Cooper, D. L.; J. R. B. Jennings, Esq.; Charles Kelly, Esq.; H. C. Levinge, Esq., D. L.; V. Lucas, Esq.; J. W. Murray, Esq.; E. E. Mason, Esq.; P. O'Reilly, Esq.D. L.; Col. Smyth.* The honorary treasurer was R. Macbeth, Esq. and the honorary secretary, H. W. Lloyd, Esq. Obviously, there had been significant activity before this meeting as there were 130 members already in the club. In late June, the new club grounds at Annebrook were open for play when *members of the local gentry were present, thereby showing that great interest is taken in the game, and wishes were manifest that the boon thrown out to the county at large would be taken advantage of and appreciated. The band of the East Lancashire Regiment were present.*

At Home

A regular feature of clubs at the time were the "At Home" days. These appeared to have been both a social and tennis-playing day when all members would attend, a great 'spread' would be laid on and entertainment was just as important as the tennis. The term was retained for many years to come. At the Clontarf club (founded 1887) an 'At Home' at the turn of the century was one where *the all male committee organised a croquet competition for the Ladies- to keep them entertained while the men got on with the serious business of drinking and Tennis.* In Mullingar's case, they held such a day every second Thursday. The first such day was on the 30th June 1892 and the local paper published a listing of those present. These included a General as well as several Colonels, Doctors and Reverends, their wives and daughters (tennis players and of an eligible age, one presumes). The bands musical programme was also published. A military band (from the nearby Connacht Rangers barracks) regularly gave an extensive presentation at the **Boyle LTC** club in the 1880s and 1890s.

"County" Clubs

The term 'county' had distinct connotations other than a geographical boundary. The Oxford dictionary defines it as *the families of high social level long established in a county.* It was such county people that formed the bulk of many clubs in Ireland. It was not surprising that the main club in a county took on this title. The Mullingar club became the County Westmeath Lawn Tennis Club and was known right up until its demise in the 1960s as the *County* Club. Members of such clubs were definitely the elite and with a penchant for leisure time. Apart from socialising, they were involved in such sports/pastimes as croquet, cricket, fox hunting, sailing, rugby, golf and tennis.

Other counties to have *county* tennis clubs included Cavan (1895), Longford (1920), Sligo (1881), Limerick (1877), Wicklow (1894), Meath (pre-1911) and Kildare (1881). The present Athenry Tennis Club was originally the **County Galway LTC** and was regularly represented on the ILTA from the founding year of 1908. **Banagher TC** was formerly **King's County West LTC** (pre 1909) and the earlier of the two clubs in Birr was called **King's County and Ormond LTC** (pre 1908). The club in Kilkenny was one of the earliest in the country (1879) and is still called the **Kilkenny County & City LTC**. Some confusion exists over the **County Clare LTC**; it appears to have been called the **Killaloe/Ballina LTC** and then the **Bridge LTC** Perhaps there are two different clubs involved. Alternatively it might have been the original club in Ennis itself.

Elite Members

The elite of society in the 19th century were usually the well educated and were either minor or major landowners. The local surgeon, and military men of high rank, could be added to this list. The opening chapter of The Fitzwilliam Story (1877-1977) reveals a slightly different emphasis in Dublin City. The founders of the club were Anglo-Irish and Protestant, drawn mainly from the Dublin professional classes. *There would always be a sprinkling of gentry among the members.* There were ten regiments in Dublin at the time and a special effort was made to attract officers to the club. (In 1879 army officers were given a preferential £1 annual subscription and in 1903, when Colonel A.H. Courtenay was their first President, a bulk subscription of £5 *per regiment* was offered).

In 1879, the **Limerick County Lawn Tennis Club** held the Grand Lawn Tennis Tournament, played on the Limerick County Cricket Ground. With Lord John Thomas William Massy (6th Baron in the peerage of Ireland) as club President, and Charles Heaton Armstrong as Honorary Secretary and Treasurer) there was a full committee of twenty (all men). This included one major, one colonel and three captains. For the record the first open tournament was held two years earlier. Many interesting pieces of information can be gleaned from George Hehir's booklet on *The First Decade: Limerick Lawn Tennis Club (1877-1886).* The tournaments of the time were attended by the band of the 82nd regiment. The local press were out in force and published the list of the more important attendees at the tournament and the associated ball. During the 1878 event the Grand Ball was held in the Royal George Hotel on the 27th September. At the ball were the Earl and Countess of Limerick, Lord and Lady Emly, Lord and Lady Massy, Lord and Lady Fermoy, Lord and Lady Muskerry, Lord Clarina, Lord and Lady Monteagle and Sir Croker Barrington. This was certainly an impressive list of the cream of Irish society at the time. He also includes the following in relation to Lord Massy's title: *It may evoke a wry chuckle to note that the present holder of the title is a greengrocer in Leicester. Sic transit etc.*

Billy Jackson uses the old tennis ball in playing with dog at Cavehill LTC in the mid-1950s.

George noted that E.H.M. Elliott was probably the most influential of the first committee at Limerick. His research uncovered the fact that, in April 1877, Edward Hay Mackensie Elliott, an officer in the 82nd Regiment, was posted to Limerick. *It is not unreasonable to surmise that this young man had been infected with the prevailing London passion for Lawn tennis and that he had brought this enthusiasm for the new game with him to Limerick. Indeed, a perusal of early committee lists and tournament competitors makes it clear that officers from the regiment in Limerick played an important role in organising and competing in all the early tournaments.*

Multi-Sports Club

Colonel Thomas John de Burgh (1851-1931), the founder of the County Kildare Club (now Naas LTC) in 1881.

In 1870s cricket was thriving in the active Naas and County Kildare Cricket Club. Colonel Thomas John de Burgh became the primary instigator in developing tennis in Naas. In August 1880, he outlined a proposal to form the County Kildare Club, which would include the existing cricket club with the added sports of football (rugby), archery, lawn tennis, pigeon shooting and polo. (Lacrosse, athletics, trap and pearifle shooting, soccer, pitch & putt and hockey were to be part of club activities in later years). The annual subscription of £2 was proposed. The club officially came into being on the 1st January 1881. Years later it became the **Naas LTC**. An interesting aspect of the present club is the fact that three generations of de Burgh's were associated with the club. The founder in 1881 was Colonel Thomas John de Burgh while his son, Captain Hubert Henry de Burgh and grandson, Major John Hugh de Burgh were also to be members (the latter was elected the President in 1971, and from 1975 to the present. This must be a fairly unique lineage in any clubs history.

Catholics Can Play Too

As the military emphasis changed from the time of the 'Treaty', so too did the membership of the tennis clubs throughout the country. Businessmen and other, non-gentry classes, became acceptable in urban and rural clubs. Before 1900 few Catholics would have had the opportunity to play the sport. When the opportunity came, the Catholics of post Treaty Ireland had no hesitation in setting up new clubs or joining existing ones. In the 1930s and 1940s many new clubs, with a Catholic base, as opposed to the earlier Protestant one, sprung up in the most diverse locations. Cavan, Boyle, Longford, Mullingar, Belturbet, Athlone and Tralee were all small or medium sized towns where one would expect to find only one club. Tralee is unusual in that it had two clubs, the **Tralee Green LTC** and the **Tralee Sports Field LTC**, by 1911. Few clubs, if any, had rules on religion but there were definitely class or social issues.

In 1921, Edward McGuire, a Jesuit educated Clongownian (1915-1919), was invited to join the **Fitzwilliam LTC** having first been successful at the **Mount Temple LTC**. He said later *There weren't many Catholics in the club* (i.e. Fitzwilliam) *and I had the impression people in the trade were frowned upon.* Ulick O'Connor (1977) had some interesting points to make concerning life at that time. *In 1922 the social and political pattern in Dublin changed....The British garrison was evacuated and Dublin Castle, seat of the colonial administration, handed over to the new rulers. The tricolour replaced the Union Jack. The pillar boxes were painted green instead of red. ....One can imagine the reaction of some Fitzwilliam members as they walked over from their clubs in the Green and noted that Fitzwilliam Place had become "Plas Mac-Liam".*

In the 1913 edition of *The Clongownian* there is a great article by Val Miley (Irish Open Champion in 1920) on "Lawn Tennis as a Game for Schools". One of the oldest Catholic schools in Ireland Clongowes Wood College in County Kildare was a great promoter of the sport of tennis. Apart from Edward McGuire, who became a senator and a Davis Cup player (1926-1935) and Captain (1938), there were other excellent players developed at Clongowes, which included Houlihans from Birr, the Mocklers from Cork, the Scroope brothers and a forgotten Daniel Ross. The latter was born in Belfast he attended Clongowes Wood College from 1876 to 1879. *He played rugby, cricket, golf, lacrosse, polo, tennis, billiards, and all very well indeed* according to an entry in the 1952 edition of the school magazine (he died in 1951). He was on the Irish team for cricket, rugby, polo and lacrosse. Val Miley, who argued strongly in favour of tennis at school level (including playing the game during the winter months), is an antecedent to David Miley a well-known tennis coach of today.

Back to Mullingar! The annual meeting of the club (AGM) was held on the 27th April 1893 in the pavilion under the chairmanship of Colonel Cooper, D. L.. The grounds were to be open for play on Monday 1st May followed by a "club day" on Thursday the 4th. On the same day the committee for the ensuing season was to be elected. Perhaps a day when most members were present was considered a better option. The club had now 150 members and the names of seven candidates for admission were handed in *to be balloted for.*

The promotion of tennis at schools has been and will always be an important foundation for the game at senior level. Above, the 1958 girl's team at the Prior School, Lifford. Back (l. to r.) Jeanna Fairman, Pearl Barclay, Alex Raffan (headmaster), Irene Patterson & Ruth McClure. Front (l. to r.) Olive Roulston, Frankie McCreary, Audrey Elliott, Mina Patterson, Harriet Craig & Angela Ewing.

Joining Up

Joining a private club can now be a problem, never mind in the 19th century. If we look at sports clubs today we see two distinct threads. Virtually any football club is delighted when new members turn up at the beginning of the season. They put on their boots and are virtually immediately rushed out onto the training pitch. A committee member will usually obtain a name and address, and phone number fairly promptly, particularly if a player looks anyway useful. A follow on question will elucidate where the new member played before, and at what level. The new member may moved to the area recently, have seen a notice in the local press or perhaps a shop window on the first training day of the season. Equally as likely he may be working with an existing member who persuades him to join. Also possible is the fact that he may have just left school and is keen to continue his sport as an adult. With very few exceptions that new player arriving is made more than welcome, no application forms are required and his subscription will be obtained later. The playing and social life of a football club is a priority. New blood is vital for the new season. We are considering here the amateur games of football. Professional rugby and soccer are different matters. They will likely require contracts and surprise arrivals at relevant clubs are not usual. With the formation of the Gaelic Players Association on (GPA) we may in future have a significant third group of professional footballers on the island.

At one stage there was a very distinct exception to the welcome i.e. the membership ban, from GAA clubs. The biggest sporting organisation in Ireland, with over 2,500 clubs, has a most interesting history. Understanding the 'ethos' and approach of this thriving organisation is worth the effort. In simple terms, there were rugby players, cricketers and Protestants all involved in its establishment in 1884 when *The Gaelic Athletic Association (G.A.A.) was founded on November 1st 1884, by a group of spirited Irishmen who had the foresight to realise the importance of establishing a national organisation to revive and nurture traditional, indigenous pastimes,* (GAA website, 2000). At the time athletics was the main focus though the football and hurling activities mushroomed very quickly.

While the political aspect of the organisation is not as it was prior to 1921, the cultural issue is still there. The anti-English ban on the GAA's own members playing cricket, rugby and soccer were contentious issues up until the 'lifting of the Ban'. The controversial Rule 27 was removed in 1971. Apart from Antrim and Sligo all other county conventions voted for its removal. Why were equally foreign games such as badminton, tennis and golf not banned? I have been unable to find an official answer and realise the issues are complex. In simple terms the answer is probably that these, and other minor sports, were of no threat.

Balloting

The standard procedure of "balloting in" members to the **Westmeath Lawn Tennis Club** in 1893 was probably fairly typical in all clubs of the time. In many clubs today a list of prospective new members will still be presented to the committee. Golf clubs post a list with proposers and seconders on their notice boards. Today, a refusal to take a new member on, in the majority of sports clubs, has nothing to do with social factors but availability.

The term "black balled" did have a distinct use in tennis clubs in the past. The following extract from the 1881 rules of the **County Kildare Club** (formulated at a general meeting on the 18th February of that year) details the procedure for admitting new members:

> *3. No person shall be admitted as a Member of the Club after the 1st May 1881, except by Ballot. The names of the candidates are to be proposed by one member and seconded by another, from their personal knowledge of the candidates. Persons balloted for, but not elected, may be proposed again, but not more than twice in one year. The ballot to take place on the Club grounds, between the hours of 11am and 6pm on any day on which an advertised cricket match shall take place. Ten or more members voting, to constitute a ballot. The candidate shall be put up for ballot not sooner than one week after he has been proposed, and has had his name posted in the Pavilion. One black ball in 5 to exclude.*

This was the first year tennis was played at the now named **Naas LTC**. This democratic procedure was an open one. Nearly fifty years later, in 1928, this rule was essentially the same with the day of a ballot to be one when *a Tennis Tournament, Football, Hockey or Cricket Match shall take place*. The one-week between proposal and ballot was extended to two and the candidates name and address was to be placed in a *conspicuous* place in the Pavilion.

A similar and interesting rule appears in the 1914 *Rules of the Mallow Lawn Tennis and Croquet Club* as follows:

The names of intending Members, their proposers and seconders, must be sent to the Hon.Sec., and posted by him in the Pavilion six clear days before ballot, which shall take place on Tuesdays only, and between the hours of 3 and 5pm. One black bean in five to exclude; ten votes to comprise a ballot. No voting by proxy. Officers of the Army, Navy, their wives and families may join without ballot or entrance fee. Officers of the Regiment stationed at Buttevant may join the Club on a payment by the Mess of £5, and shall be entitled to appoint one of their number to the committee, in addition to the seven Members thereof elected annually.

Rule III goes on to add the following: *Proposers and seconders are liable for subscriptions for those whom they introduce*. A lesson here perhaps for treasurers having difficulty collecting annual membership fees?

The first General Meeting of **Donnybrook LTC** was held on Monday 10th April 1893 and a set of rules, drawn up by the provisional committee was read. At that meeting it was decided to allow all ladies and gentlemen (who had sent in their names) as members up to this date, without an entrance fee. Eighteen further candidates were proposed for membership, *the ballot to take place in the Pavilion between 4 and 6 o'clock on Wednesday the 26th inst.*

At **Fitzwilliam LTC** the rules (in recent times) required the candidates to be known by the proposers and seconders for 3 years and with four letters of support. In many clubs it was a matter of the names being submitted to the committee for approval. In towns and villages someone on the committee would usually indicate their knowledge of the candidate. The Galway LTC application form for 1988 is welcoming. *Applicants may use the facilities having applied for membership and paid the appropriate membership fee, but only become members when approved at a meeting of the board of directors.*

Mid-1950s at Portrush championships. Players relaxing and awaiting their own turn to play. In the photograph are top players Cecil Pedlow (back, second from right) and Peter Jackson (front middle).

Self-Determination

Padraig Griffin, a long time promoter of athletics in Ireland, published an excellent book in 1990. The title *The Politics of Irish Athletics 1850-1990* says it all. If one is to develop a reasonable understanding of the development of native Irish sports then I highly recommend both this book and Marcus de Burca's *The GAA. A History* published in 1980. Maurice Davin, from Tipperary, was to become the first President of the GAA. He and his two brothers dominated Irish athletics in the 1870s. He was internationally famous with victories over leading British athletes. The playing of foreign games was, initially, not the major issue. As de Burca pointed out:

Like Cusack, he had also sampled English games-in his case, cricket and rugby; like Nally (the great Mayo athlete of the time) he was an all-rounder, his interests extending to rowing, boxing and even coursing. At the founding of the GAA in Thurles (3pm Saturday 1st November, 1884) *Davin in a short statement pointed out the incongruity of Irishmen permitting Englishmen to organise Irish sport, emphasised that this had lead to the decline of native pastimes and called for a body to draft rules to aid in their revival and to open athletics to the poor* (De Burca, 1980). There was a cry here for self-determination. At the time, most Irishmen would not have been acceptable entrants at athletic events. Looking at tennis, for it's first thirty years the island was treated as a 'county'

21ˢᵗ June 2002-Elm Park members attending the Dublin Lawn Tennis Council Centenary dinner.

under the umbrella of the Lawn Tennis Association in London. It took until 1908 for the Irish Lawn tennis Association to be formed and until 1923 before we had our own Davis Cup team.

Foreign Games

Charles Stewart Parnell, Michael Davitt and Archbishop T.W. Croke were all invited to become patrons of the newly formed GAA. Michael Cusack, the Honorary Secretary of the new organisation, sent out the invitations. All accepted in December 1884, with a lengthy reply from the Archbishop of Cashel. It reflects the underlying annoyance with English dominance. Tennis is included among the *foreign and fantastic field sports* but he had a distinct urge to support the new organisation and it's objectives. His letter is worth quoting in full:

My Dear Sir- I beg to acknowledge the receipt of your communication inviting me to become a patron of the 'Gaelic Athletic Association', of which you are, it appears, the hon. secretary. I accede to your request with the utmost pleasure.

One of the most painful, let me assure you, and, at the same time, one of the most frequently recurring reflections that, as an Irishman, I am compelled to make in connection with the present aspect of things in this country, is derived from the ugly and irritating fact that we are daily importing from England not only her manufactured goods, which we cannot help doing, since she has practically strangled our own manufacturing appliances, but, together with her fashions, her accent, her vicious literature, her music, her dances, and her manifold mannerisms, her games also and her pastimes, to the utter discredit of our own grand national sports, and to the sore humiliation, as I believe, of every genuine son and daughter of the old land.

Ball-playing, hurling, football kicking, according to Irish rules,' casting', leaping in various ways, wrestling, handy-grips, top-pegging, leap-frog, rounders, tip-in-the-hat, and all such favourite exercises and amusements amongst men and boys, may now be said to be not only dead and buried, but in several localities to be entirely forgotten and unknown. And what have we got in their stead? We have got such foreign and fantastic field sports as lawn-tennis, polo, croquet, cricket, and the like-very excellent, I believe, and health-giving exercises in their way, still not racy of the soil, but rather alien, on the contrary, to it, as area, indeed, for the most part the men and women who first imported and still continue to patronise them.

And, unfortunately, it is not our national sports alone that are held in dishonour, and dying out, but even our most suggestive national celebrations are being gradually effaced and extinguished, one after another, as well. Who hears now of snap-apple night, or bonfire night? They are things of the past, too vulgar to be spoken of, except in ridicule, by the degenerate dandies of the day. No doubt, there is something rather pleasing to the eye in the 'get-up' of a modern young man who, arrayed in light attire, with parti-coloured cap on and racket in hand, in making his way, with or without a companion, to the tennis ground. But, for my part, I should vastly prefer to behold, or think of, the youthful athletes whom I used to see in my early days at fair and pattern, bereft of shoes and coat, and thus prepared to play at hand-ball, to fly over any number of horses, to throw the 'sledge' or 'winding-stone', and to test each other's mettle and activity by the trying ordeal of 'three leaps', or a 'hop, step, and a jump'.

Indeed, if we continue travelling for the next score of years in the same direction that we have been going in for some time past, condemning the sports that were practiced but our forefathers, effacing our national

The 1928 Open at Enniskillen LTC.

features as though we were ashamed of them, and putting on, with England's stuffs and broadcloths, her 'masher' habits and such effeminate follies as she may recommend, we had better at once, and publicly, adjure our nationality, clap hands for joy at the sight of the Union Jack, and place 'England's bloody red evultingly above 'the green'.

Deprecating, as I do, any such dire and disgraceful consummation, and seeing in your society of athletes something altogether opposed to it, I shall be happy to do all I can, and authorise you now formally to place my name on the roll of your patrons.

In conclusion, I earnestly hope that our national journals will not distain, in future, to give suitable notices of those Irish sports and pastimes which your society means to patronise and promote, and that the masters and pupils of our Irish colleges, will not henceforth exclude from their athletic programmes such manly exercises as I have referred to and commemorated. I remain, my dear sir, your faithful servant,
T.W. Croke, Archbishop of Cashel.

Leisure Time

At the time, leisure activity was increasing in the 'developed' world and an increasing number of the less well off in Ireland had an urge to participate as spectators and participants. Without dwelling excessively on the matter there were equivalent 'cultural' changes taking place in England. Neil Wigglesworth's *The Evolution of English Sport* (1996) is worth a read by the interested sport's historian. The word 'class' appears regularly in the text, as one might expect. The following quotations summarise the developments taking place:

As the mercantile class of the eighteenth century evolved into the middle class of the nineteenth with a million more families entering that socio-economic group, opportunities for leisure grew with the increasing prosperity and free time, particularly in the south-east of the country where such growth was disproportionately high. Sporting activity provided this new group with opportunities for exercise, excitement, conspicuous consumption and social advancement, and during the century middle-class

participation grew in hunting, shooting, fishing and the major ball games, as well as in bowls, croquet, lawn tennis, golf and boating.

At the same time there was a move towards the provision of recreational facilities for the less prosperous at club, municipal and works level as philanthropists of various persuasions sponsored or subsidised different sports.

The Fitzwilliam Cycling Club 'At Home' in 1897.

In England, with Queen Victoria at the helm, the feeling of dominance was widespread. Despite the problems associated with gambling, professionalism and drunkenness, sporting activity increased dramatically. There too, was the problem of play on Sundays. Soccer and cricket were widely followed by the masses. To gain a respectable image, clubs changed their names and the word 'amateur' was added to their titles in order to underline their bone fides. Women and sport is another social issue with developments occurring in this era. They became acceptable participants in sports such as archery, croquet, hunting and tennis. By 1890 the Cycling Touring Club of England had some 60,000 members, 20,000 of whom were women.

Ulster Move

As we start a new century, sporting separation (by social, religious and political divides) is now changing rapidly. **Irvinestown TC** is one of the clubs to be positive on this matter. Founded in 1991, it has, in its short ten years, a membership of nearly 300, uniformly representing both sides of the community. Among its many successes was the honour bestowed on Seamus McCusker. He was the club's president from 1991 to 1994 and subsequently elected as president of the Ulster Branch in 1998 and 1999. Probably the first Catholic to be honoured with this post he has, in his own quiet way, made a giant leap forward in sports integration in the province. In 2003 he became president of Tennis Ireland. He sees the value of sport for young and old. He has an interest in all sports. Many would be surprised to learn that he was in his forties when he took up tennis and, even more surprising, that he played minor, under 21 and senior football with County Fermanagh.

Tennis is a social game for these lady members at Tramore LTC (circa 2003).

Tennis throughout Ireland is still a 'minority' sport. In Ulster we all hope that sport will become a unifying factor. Tennis can play a role here in view of its international appeal and it's suitability for the young and for both sexes. We could look at the list of Irish tennis clubs over the years and find clubs with a religious theme. These are more connected with the base upon which the club was founded rather than a deliberate religious statement. The Belfast Jewish Institution, **First Dromore Presbyterian Church LTC**, Church of Ireland (Cork) and St. Mel's tennis clubs are such examples. Equally, clubs have been connected with other sports. Some examples are the **Armagh Archery LTC**, **Castlerock Golf Club TC**, **St. Tiernan's LT & Croquet Club**, **Civil Service Hockey & TC**, **Muckamore Cricket & LTC**, **Larne Bowling and LTC**, **Ennis LT and Badminton Club**, **Sandycove Tennis and Squash Club**, **Sunday's Well Boating and LTC**, **Stackallen LT & Pitch and Putt Club** and **Riverview Racquet and Fitness Club**.

Croquet

The sport most frequently associated with tennis in the past was croquet. This was due to the fact that both were played on a similar surface with croquet lawns being adapted for the new sport of lawn tennis. It might be of interest to know that in 1870 the All England Croquet Club was formed. Five years later the sports of badminton and tennis were included and, in 1877, the name was changed to The All England Croquet and Lawn Tennis Club. Some Irish clubs to have croquet in their title at one time or another are listed below.

Ballycastle Lawn Tennis and Croquet Club (1908)
Carrickmines Croquet and Lawn Tennis Club (1902)
St. Tiernan's Lawn Tennis and Croquet Club (1948)
Garden Vale Lawn Tennis and Croquet Club (<1911)
Glanmire Lawn Tennis and Croquet Club (<1908)
Greystones Lawn Tennis and Croquet Club (<1908)
Malahide Lawn Tennis and Croquet Club (1879)
Muskerry Lawn Tennis and Croquet Club (<1881)
Nenagh Lawn Tennis and Croquet Club (1880)
Rushbrooke Lawn Tennis and Croquet Club (1884)

A club may have been formed as a result of a cohesive employment, educational or community sector. Some examples are **Aer Lingus TC**, **Du Pont LTC**, **Boyle Community Association TC**, **Dublin City University TC**, **Electricity Supply Board LTC**, **Royal Victoria Hospital LTC**, **Queen's University Staff LTC** and the **Hospital LTC** in Letterkenny. An early club was the **Railway and Steam Packet Union LTC**. As was the **Cork Garrison LTC**. One presumes the present **Collins Barracks LTC** is it's descendent. There was a club at the Curragh Camp prior to 1911. Virtually all early military establishment had sports connections.

The croquet lawn today at Rushbrooke Lawn Tennis and Croquet Club. The club runs tennis, croquet & lawn bowls competitions.

An "American Tournament" at Fitzwilliam Lawn Tennis Club in early 1992.

The vast majority of clubs are keen to take in new members. Some have waiting lists and a very few are 'exclusive'. In general, there are enough clubs in the country to satisfy the needs of those interested. A popular social club, such as **Mount Pleasant LTC**, provides more than just the sport of tennis and is situated in a populated area of Dublin. You may have to wait a few months, but you will be more than welcomed when a place is vacated.

Competitive clubs in urban settings will open doors for good quality players. Just as **Fitzwilliam LTC** were happy to invite Edward McGuire to join in 1921. So too did **Templeogue LTC** in 1979. They welcomed the very promising young Castlebar player Caitriona Ruane into the club under the Junior Scholarship Scheme. This meant free membership for two years for a player who would have a lot of travelling and tennis expenses.

Some shots from the archives of Fitzwilliam Lawn Tennis Club

Squash players (?)

Jim Fitzgibbon gives an entertaining speech.

Matt Doyle (centre) the former Irish number 1 and an important member of the Davis Cup campaigns in the 1980s.

Des Ryan and Joe Hackett (right) have seen it all.

International Comparisons

The spread of tennis in Ireland, and the extent the game is and has been played, is a multi-faceted issue. The 'pastime' eventually became one of the most international of professional sports. Along with golf, it is probably the most televised of individual sports. Ireland has been at the forefront of the games promotion, with much early success on courts at the US, Australian and All-England Championships. The annual question the LTA ask in relation to a lack of home champions, is one we might look at too.

It is not an objective of this book to thoroughly analyse, with a view to future promotion of the game in this country. Many of the facts are presented, and some suggestions made, in various chapters. Discussed elsewhere in the book, are the issues of schools tennis, participation in the Davis and Fed cups, and the importance of clubs, the Parks scheme etc.. Here a brief look at some known facts on up to 62 tennis-playing countries is presented. Most of the information has been sourced in the European Tennis Association handbook. Other facts came from a range of sources. It is probably impossible to be complete, on a world-wide basis. Nevertheless, one can see some patterns.

Ireland's standing in the world of tennis *was* a high one for various reasons. Firstly, being one of the 'early' tennis powers. Secondly, close links with the LTA, England and tournaments there have been good for our game. Our personalities on international committees and organisations have, in the past, continue to have, an influence to this day. Some of our noted players are elected members of the All-England club at Wimbledon. Two Irishmen have been chairmen of the prestigious Queens club in London. Sadly only one Irish player, Mabel Cahill, has yet been elected to the International Hall of Fame in the USA. A notable absentee is Dr. Joshua Pim from Dublin, a man during the 'Golden Era' of Irish tennis was the number one player in the world.

Some tennis facts on 49 countries are presented in the table that follows. In the case of 13 countries only playing numbers were available. In the graph playing populations are shown, with every second country named.

Populations, court numbers etc. all change with time. What is missing are facts on public or state courts, as well as those in schools. These are essential to the development of the game in many countries where the 'club' ethos is not a strong one. One must be, therefore, careful is coming to any strong conclusions. Why should Croatia, with 143 clubs and about 3,000 registered players, be more successful than Ireland, with about 220 clubs, and 41,000 registered players?

Of the four Grand Slams, Irish players identify most with Wimbledon. There are several reasons for this including locality, history and the event all the top world players recognise as *the* one to win. In terms of singles wins at these championships the nationality and numbers of wins are as follows:

Wimbledon Titles (1877-2006)		
Country	Men's Singles	Ladies' Singles
USA	33	49
GB	31	35
Australia	21	5
France	7	7
Sweden	7	0
Germany	4	8
Ireland	4	1
New Zealand	4	0
Switzerland	4	1
Netherlands	1	0
Spain	1	1
Czechoslovakia	1	1
Croatia	1	0
Egypt	1	0
Brazil	0	3
Russia	0	1

If we divide the current known playing population by the total singles wins we see some interesting 'win ratios'. Playing populations for New Zealand, Egypt and Brazil were not known and the ratio could not be computed. The poorest ratio is Spain, with two wins for 1.6 million players. The 'clay court' factor must have a bearing here. Next poorest come the USA and Germany. The best ratio is Croatia with 1 win for a playing population of under 3000 players. Ireland comes second best with 5 wins i.e. a win for each 8200 players. Brazil and New Zealand are probably high too. Great Britain, despite a large number of wins in the early days of the sport, has only one win in 43,970 players. The calculations are probably pedantic in nature due to the large changes that have taken place in the sport. More relevant to the future of the game in this country is our standing on current facts and related actions. On balance we are about half way down the limited league of 62 countries identified here. We are 22nd in terms of population and 29th in the number of players. With less than one person in 100 playing we come 29th. The best ratio is Australia where one in nearly every ten people play the sport. The poorest is Albania with a total of only 135 players identified. Mind you they have only 15 tennis courts in the whole country. Of the 49 countries with fuller details, Ireland comes 27th in terms of court numbers. Germany has over 50,000 tennis courts and tops the list, we have less than 1000 and come 27th of the 49. There is one message here. In terms of clubs we have 220 and are 31st. This is a bit deceptive as many countries have many public court facilities, not associated with a club. In terms of players per court we are again languishing at 28th. If the figures are correct then Spain has over 300 players per court and tops the list with Croatia having less than 2 players per court i.e. 2988 licensed players and 1780 courts. These ratios are obviously flawed in some way. Has Spain exaggerated its number of players and/or Croatia exaggerated its court numbers? The numbers of licensed players and casual ones are enumerated in different nations in various ways. For the record Ireland has 44 registered players per court. Issues such as diversions, funds, government policy, coaching and hunger are some of those requiring attention if we are to upgrade the game in Ireland.

Country	Population (millions)	Number of players	% of population	Number of Clubs	Players per Club	Number of Courts	Players per Court
Albania	3.5	135	0.004	5	27.0	15	9.0
Andorra	0.06	670	1.117	5	134.0	26	25.8
Armenia	3	1,060	0.035	2	530.0	45	23.6
Austria	7.5	604,118	8.055	1,815	332.8	6,354	95.1
Azerbaijan	7.87	1112	0.014	16	69.5	39	28.5
Belarus	10.5	30,000	0.286	25	1200.0	140	214.3
Belgium	10	187,000	1.870	950	196.8	5,700	32.8
Bosnia-Herzegovina	3.35	1,085	0.032	22	49.3	74	14.7
Bulgaria	8.5	17,100	0.201	60	285.0	499	34.3
Croatia	4.855	2,988	0.062	143	20.9	1780	1.7
Cyprus	0.7	5,500	0.786	13	423.1	240	22.9
Czech Republic	10.5	267,497	2.548	841	318.1	4850	55.2
Denmark	5.3	80,133	1.512	361	222.0	1,760	45.5
Estonia	1.5	5,230	0.349	32	163.4	212	24.7
Finland	5.1	117,982	2.313	249	473.8	1,950	60.5
France	58	1,039,013	1.791	9,432	110.2	33,056	31.4
Georgia	5.3	1,690	0.032	12	140.8	108	15.6
Germany	82.024	2,155,765	2.628	10,305	209.2	51,313	42.0
Great Britain	56	2,902,045	5.182	2,360	1229.7	34,910	83.1
Greece	11	67,500	0.614	220	306.8	768	87.9
Hungary	11	122,300	1.112	330	370.6	3,300	37.1
Iceland	0.275	3,800	1.382	8	475.0	40	95.0
Ireland	5	41,000	0.820	220	186.4	930	44.1
Israel	5	45,000	0.900	200	225.0	1,503	29.9
Italy	57.25	2,081,875	3.636	3,708	561.5	13,457	154.7
Latvia	2.5	2,456	0.098	28	87.7	244	10.1
Liechtenstein	0.03	2,540	8.467	8	317.5	49	51.8
Lithuania	3.7	560	0.015	34	16.5	110	5.1
Luxembourg	0.435	16,005	3.679	56	285.8	300	53.4
Macedonia	2	680	0.034	15	45.3	84	8.1
Malta	0.36	1,330	0.369	20	66.5	55	24.2
Moldova	4.315	1,223	0.028	12	101.9	55	22.2
Monaco	0.03	1,877	6.257	4	469.3	23	81.6
Netherlands	15	727,000	4.847	1,800	403.9	11,800	61.6
Norway	4.1	20,000	0.488	170	117.6	725	27.6
Poland	40	153,500	0.384	360	426.4	1,550	99.0
Portugal	11	130,916	1.190	351	373.0	2,050	63.9
Romania	23	22,900	0.100	245	93.5	817	28.0
Russia	180	25,750	0.014	150	171.7	3,335	7.7
San Marino	0	800	3.077	4	200.0	18	44.4
Slovak Republic	5.2	16,550	0.318	160	103.4	883	18.7
Slovenia	2.1	22,050	1.050	100	220.5	2,200	10.0
Spain	39	1,620,884	4.156	1,081	1499.4	5,097	318.0
Sweden	9	361,000	4.011	690	523.2	4,500	80.2
Switzerland	7	247,127	3.530	964	256.4	3,323	74.4
Turkey	65	9,500	0.015	53	179.2	535	17.8
Ukraine	50.6	61,114	0.121	25	2444.6	713	85.7
Yugoslavia	11	12,310	0.112	130	94.7	969	12.7
Australia	17.632	1,657,447	9.400	2,500	663.0	20,000	82.9
Chile	14.36	315,981	2.200				
Argentina	30.925	340,178	1.100				
Canada	30.439	1,217,548	4.000				
Japan	126.522	3,036,534	2.400				
Mexico	88.533	885,331	1.000				
Singapore	38.247	141,514	0.370				
South Africa	36.171	651,083	1.800				
South Korea	47.588	618,639	1.300				
Taiwan	20.071	802,852	4.000				
USA	266.239	14,110,692	5.300				
Colombia	33	10,000	0.030				
Qatar	0.45	3,800	0.844				
China	1,199	502,800	0.042				

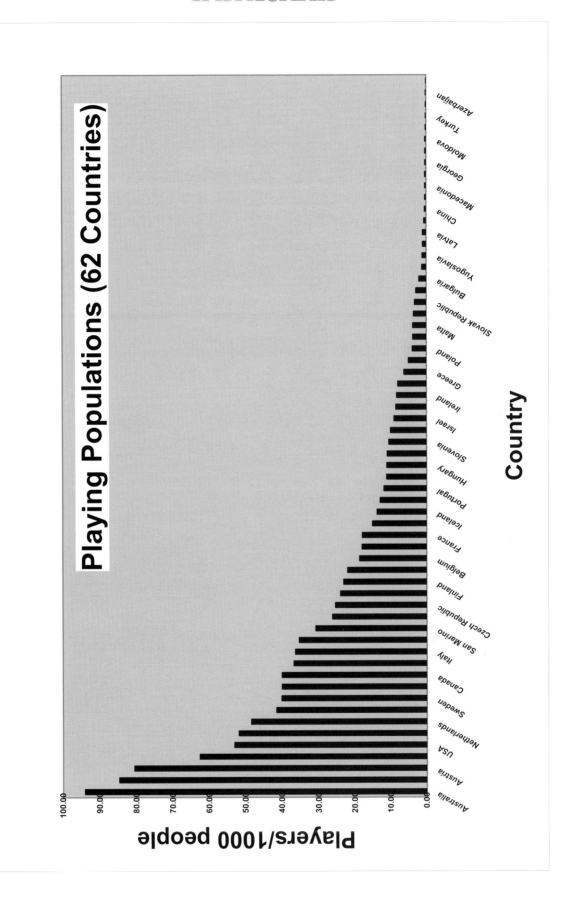

Playing Populations (62 Countries)

Interprovincial Ladies (c. 1953). From left: Meta Foley [Munster], Gladys McCoy [Ulster], Maeve Jennings [C], June Ann Byrne [L], Eileen Kirkpatrick [U] and Eithne Flattery [C].

3.2　　　　　　　　*Women and Sport*

In blissful ignorance the gents had put the "Men Only" sign on their membership form.
(Newspaper article, John Burke, 1957)

Women at Home

In the 19th century it was expected, even with women who were well off, to be tied to the family home. They had few rights in law. In 1882 The Married Women's Property Act (UK) was an early step to self-determination. In that they could buy and own their own properties and keep their own earnings. Between 1851 and 1901 the population of Britain rose from 22 to 38 millions. Allied to this there was plenty of work for dockers and seamen with the many new commercial markets opening in Africa and South America. After the recovery from the 'famine' in Ireland, the same thriving activity was to take place here, though at a different pace. The middle classes in these islands had more money, could employ more servants and could devote more time to leisure activity.

In 1871 there were about 1.5 million people, mainly women, employed "in service" in Britain. There too, like Ireland, there was tremendous poverty with a life of just survival for many families. In the late 19th century there was a high death rate due to tuberculosis and there was a high proportion of females, many widows, engaged in 'distribution' i.e. were involved in selling fruit, vegetables, fish etc. One report at that time found in many cases children were also trading to a significant extent. *Typical of such households was a twelve year old girl who sold matches earning 3/- a week to supplement her widowed mother's earnings of 5/- as a dealer.* (Mary E. Daly, 1985).

It is worth noting that the percentage of women in 'society' was relatively small and that it was many years later that equal rights, throughout the whole population, were obtained. This matter is still ongoing over a century later. The fact that sport for women took off at all was a bit of a minor miracle.

Hidden Tennis

The Fitzwilliam club were lauded when they held the first Ladies Championship in 1879, five years ahead of Wimbledon. Even for the gentry' class, to participate and play in a competitive sport for ladies was a bit adventurous. To allow for this reluctance and, to *keep the matches as private as possible*, the first Ladies' Single Championship was held at the Fitzwilliam Club and not at Fitzwilliam Square. Access was by member's voucher. The seclusion lead to a great demand for tickets.

The mixed doubles was a different matter; it was played in the square with the men's singles and doubles. *The Field* report (in 1880) commented as follows: *Of course the ladies' competitions suffer very much from the unwillingness of the fair sex to play in public, though this is partly met by the club setting apart their private ground for the ladies' singles to take place in, and to this (as last year) admission is only obtained by member's voucher.*

Gilbert Webb in the **Glenageary LTC** Centenary Brochure told one amusing tale in 1987. He was referring to a time in the early 1920s when women's tennis in the club was coming to the fore and the ladies team won Class II of the Dublin leagues. However, home matters often came first. He reports:

There were, of course, minor problems common to all clubs like when the eminent lady member, who was successful in remaining in all three events up to three days before the day of the finals, announced that she could not play at all the next day "because her sewing woman was "coming".

In the same brochure, Norah Conway, one of the top players in Ireland in the 1930s and 1940s, and in fact ranked number four in Ireland in 1949 and 1950, recalls her younger days when women were useful for providing teas:

With regard to the position of men and women in the Club-we always felt the men seized the best courts! The women were regarded as useful for providing tea, and they went to great trouble for the "At Homes". The "AT Home" day was a great social occasion and we all went to it dressed in our best to watch the finals. A few visitors were invited.

Separate Pavilions

The **Northern LTC** was formed at Old Trafford in Manchester in the autumn of 1881. Ladies were not eligible as members but *were admissible under the same rule as strangers (viz.: names to be entered in a book and not to be allowed to play if courts were required by members), but without limit as to the numbers of times of introduction and without charge for playing.* (G.C.B., 1937). Interestingly, the club decided, in 1884, *to erect a new pavilion, beyond the bar, for the use of the ladies, at a cost of £60*, even though the rules would not be changed to allow them in as members until 1893. This is not a dissimilar situation to that at Sunday's Well in Cork where the ladies changing rooms was a building at the end of the courts well away from main clubhouse. In Cork, this was still in use in the 1960s. In addition, some long term members can recall that drinks from the bar were handed out to the ladies through the window. In other words until the 1950s at least, it appears that it was run as a men's club with limitation on women's rights.

The 1887 Lawn Tennis Supplement to the Irish Cyclist and Athlete. This extract includes reference to the top Irish ladies of that time, Miss Butler, Miss Stanuell and Miss Martin. However, England's Lottie Dod who was 15 at the time, won both the Irish and Wimbledon titles that year. Lou Martin won the Irish title 9 times between 1889 and 1903. Florence Stanuell from Mallow won the title in 1893.

Back at Old Trafford there is no doubt that it was only a limited number of ladies that wished to take up the sport. The era of women's freedom from the home was a long time off. The club had at least 250 male members and a maximum of 50 ladies. A few years later the number of ladies increased dramatically.

Tournament Success

The Northern Tournament, run in Liverpool and Manchester, became a very big event quite quickly and was nearly a second home for the top Irish players of the late 19th century and early 20th century. The Ladies' Singles Championship, introduced in 1882, two years after the men's, was noteworthy in that their southern rivals (Wimbledon) did not do so until 1884. In 1882, May Langrishe from Kilkenny won this championship, the ladies doubles with her sister Beatrice (deemed to be the first ever major ladies' doubles championship in the world), and the mixed with the great English player Willie Renshaw.

In the early years Irish players dominated the Northern Championships. Notable among the ladies' was Louisa Martin who won the ladies' singles seven times in all before the Great War. She had won the Championship Cup outright in 1903. Among other wins at the

'Northern' tournament, Louisa took the mixed titles in 1901 and 1902 with Englishman Sidney Smith. During the 1890s it was Irishman Harold Mahony, with Englishwoman, Chattie Cooper, that made mixed headlines.

The pair may be regarded as the inventors of the modern mixed game, with both players volleying, instead of the lady playing from the base line, and the man waiting his chance of an intervention at the net. The success of this formation was clearly shown by the fact that they won the Mixed (carrying the title of the All-England Championship) each year from 1894 to 1898, inclusive.

Mahony and Cooper also won the Irish Championship in 1895 and 1896.

Revolution

In 1897 Millicent Fawcett founded the National Union of Women's Suffrage, an organisaiton that sought to have votes for women. Progress was slow. Emmeline Pankhurst, with her daughters Christabel and Sylvia, set up the Women's Social and Political Union in 1903. At a political meeting in Manchester in 1905, Christabel and Annie Kenney asked Liberal politicians Winston

Churchill and Sir Edward Grey if they believed women should have the right to vote. Neither men replied. Eventually the ladies were arrested for causing an obstruction and a technical assault on a police officer. They refused to pay a fine and were imprisoned. Later Emmiline Pankhurst would say in her autobiography that

This was the beginning of a campaign the like of which was never known in England, or for that matter in any other country....we interrupted a great many meetings....and we were violently thrown out and insulted. Often we were painfully bruised and hurt.

In June 1913 suffragette Emily Wilding Davidson was killed when she threw herself in front of the King's horse Anmer at the English Derby. This highlighted the movement even further. Educated women were rightly determined to have their say in society. It was a time when women realised their true potential. Constance Markievicz was presented at the court of Queen Victoria and was referred to as 'the new Irish beauty'. She did study art, but the normal comfortable way of life for a lady of her time and disposition was not for her. In 1908 she became active in Irish politics and later an Irish revolutionary of note.

In similar ways Pankhurst and Markievicz were rebelling against the status quo. On a more mundane front a more gradual revolution was also taking place on the tennis court. In 1910 Mrs. Lambert Chambers wrote *Lawn Tennis for Ladies*, recently republished by Kessingers. Dorothea Lambert Chambers (nee Douglass) was Wimbledon singles champion seven times between 1903 and 1914. In 1919 - the Great War had stopped play for four years – as holder she fought a valiant defence of her title in the challenge round. She was beaten by France's Suzanne Lenglen 10/8 4/6 9/7. Dorothea was 40 years of age, her opponent had just turned 20. The match was second longest ever in a ladies' singles final or challenge round at the championships. Dorothea's last match at Wimbledon, her 115th, was in doubles in 1927. She was nearly 49 years old at the time. In addition to her tennis successes this lady also won two All-England badminton titles (ladies' doubles in 1903 and mixed doubles in 1904). She became a professional tennis coach in 1928.

Her writings covered many facets of the game. She stated that *athletics have done much for the health and mind of the modern girl*. She noted that objections on the past generations to games for girls included *(1) that they are injurious to health; (2) that they impair the womanliness of woman; (3) that they mar her appearance. There may be something to be said for these contentions, but to my mind the 'props' materially outweigh the 'cons'.* She quoted an old doctor friend who said that in his youth the great plague of his life was the *hysterical female.* Mrs. Chambers in 1910 thought that these types of women were now rare. She added:

The woman of the present generation is calm, collected, and free from emotional outbursts, and I believe outdoor exercise is the chief cause.

She develops her argument on sport for women very well and it is no surprise that this lady played competitive tennis for so long. Her further thoughts are equally applicable nearly 100 years later:

Exercise in the open air, and exercise of a thorough and engrossing character, carried out with cheerful and stimulating surroundings, with scientific methods, rational aims, and absorbing character. Surely this is the foundation of health culture.

Mrs. Chambers extolled the virtues of competitive play, the need to study opponents and to practice. On dress for tennis she noted that 'first-class' players knew how to be comfortable and least hampered by their clothing. *But the less experienced are wont to appear in a "garden-party" trailing skirt, trimmed hat and dressy blouse-a most unbusiness-like costume for the game.* She recommended that plain skirts should be used and be about four or five inches above the ground. Within a decade Suzanne Lenglen would further, and dramatically, revolutionise women's tennis. Apart from the use of make up and the 'star' appeal she encouraged her new fashions were dramatic. Max Roberstson (1974) described her influence thus:

Lenglen appeared in a flimsy, one-piece cotton 'frock'. The skirt was pleated from the waist but it reached only to mid-claf. More-over, it was worn without petticoats or corsets and its short sleeves showed her bare elbows. In contrast to the starched layers and general bulk of the other players' clothing the effect was staggering.

The Great War interrupted normal living between 1914 and 1918, women ended up doing 'men's work' as part of the war effort. Women got the vote. This was followed by the 'roaring 20s' when women were free to express themselves in ways never previously acceptable. Today the revolution continues, 'equal' prize money is on offer in three of the Grand Slam tennis events, Wimbledon however has not yet changed.

Fire at Cavehill

In a 1957 article in a national paper, reporter John Burke, had an interesting piece in the sports section. In connection with **Cavehill LTC**, he discussed the tennis playing sisters, Eileen & Joan Wallace, the outstanding player in the club, Peter Jackson, the upcoming inaugural Belfast Hard Court Championships, rain interrupted play, and the day the club was attacked. This was obviously many years earlier, and it is difficult to verify its accuracy. No names are mentioned, and it is a good story!

Back in the good old days when men were very much men and woman's place was exclusively in the home, a moustachioed bunch of the boys who five years earlier had formed Cavehill Bowling Club decided to expand and include tennis. Everything seemed fine and dandy. But, alas, there was a snag. For this was a time when the good womenfolk were beginning to spread their wings, when the more rebellious of the sex were determined there was more to life than washing the dishes and darning socks.

In blissful ignorance, the gents had put the "Men Only" sign on their membership form. The outraged females were livid-but patience triumphed for two years. They, no doubt believing that this was another snub for their movement to be recognised, an ardent band of Belfast suffragettes decided to act.

So one night a throng of them took themselves up the Cavehill slopes complete with paraffin and matches-and methodically burnt the place to the ground. (It is interesting to note that the club to-day caters for men-and women!).

Sheila O' Flanagan's hero, Billie Jean King, in action at the Irish Championships. She won the Irish Open as an amateur in 1963 and as a professional in 1969.

Billie Jean herself has said, at a young age, that she "wanted to be the best in the world". Many players, including her, were not from wealthy families. She genuinely felt that women tennis player's were considered as second-class citizens. At the time, in the USA, women couldn't apply for a credit card in their own right; they needed a man's signature. The Italian Open, for example in the late 1960s, had prize money of $3,500 for the winner of the men's singles while the winner of the ladies event received something like $600. As Sheila said, money in tennis gave women options to their lifestyles. Billie Jean King became the first woman to earn $100,000 in a single season. Her winnings on the professional-circuit in 1971 were $117,000. Today that is small money but at the time it was the greatest amount ever earned by any sportswoman in one season, and it was a target others could aspire to.

Open tennis arrived in the late 1960s. There was no longer the great need to distinguish between professional and amateur players. The Grand Slams were now open to all. An interesting comment of Billie Jean's relates to the typical American view on this. She pointed out that in the USA, anyone who was an 'amateur' was not really very good at the sport while being a 'professional' means you 'are good'. No doubt, the professional era helped with marketing the game in the USA and elsewhere.

On the 20th September 1973, the American Billie Jean King in a celebrated US challenge beat Bobby Riggs, defined as a misogynist, in straight sets (6/4 6/3 6/3). The game was watched by a record (for tennis) crowd of 30,492 in the Houston Astrodome and an estimated 50 million on television around the world. This was one of the few times in which women played men in competition. Sheila O' Flanagan remembers this well. She got excited about the match and thought, "of course she'll win". The $100,000 winner takes all purse was certainly an incentive. The fact that she did win made a big impression on Sheila and her friends-Billie Jean was certainly her hero. Subsequently, another admirer of the American, Elton John, wrote and released a song in her

Dressing up for the "At Home" at Donnybrook LTC in July 1930-the important social and tournament day of the year.

"My Hero"

On Irish radio (RTE) Kevin Rafter interviewed Sheila O'Flanagan in the summer of 2003 about times passed. Sheila had a successful career in banking and then, based in Dublin, started her first novel at the age of thirty-five. It was published in 1997. She has had many since including the number one best seller, "My Favourite Goodbye". In her spare time she plays competitive badminton. She talked about her 'hero', Billie Jean King. As a young girl in the 1960s and 1970s, the Irish girl followed the tennis activity of the young American. She was impressed the way Billie Jean challenged the system when asking for equal money at a mixed tournament in the USA. The ladies missed this tournament in protest and played in the Virginia Slims event, the event later becoming one of the premier events on the Women's tour.

honour- "Philadelphia Freedom". John Barrett (1999) had the following to say on this remarkable lady.

Born 22/11/43. Perhaps the most important single figure in the history of women's tennis, as player, stateswoman, innovator and entrepreneur (usually with lawyer husband, Larry King, whom she married in 1965), she has worked tirelessly to gain recognition and respect for *the women's game. One of the founders of the women's pro tour in 1970, twice President of the Women's Tennis Association, and the prime mover behind Team Tennis, she has been involved in most aspects of the game. As a player her natural exuberance and bubbling personality suited her attacking serve-and-volley game and made her a fearsome opponent.*

Top Irish ladies' in the 1930s, Norma Stoker and Vera Mahony (right). Vera (later McWeeney) became a stalwart of Irish ladies hockey and a significant sportswriter for the Irish Times. Norma won five Open Ladies' Doubles Championships (1930-1940)

Barniville boosts the ladies' claim

DOCTOR Geraldine Barniville, a mother of three, won the unique mixed singles tennis championship when the finals of the Players Number 6 Dun Laoghaire Open were decided at Clarinda Park yesterday.

And her win over Munster interprovincial player John O'Shea must surely add weight to the idea of women playing in men's tennis.

But Geraldine, who powered her way to a 6-4, 4-6, 6-1 win, does not think it will make any difference with the I.L.T.A. "It's hard to change their rules," she quipped. "There should, nonetheless, be more and more of these tournaments to give the women a chance to match their skills against top men players," she added.

O'Shea's fate seemed ominous early on when he dropped the first two games. He broke back service to get on terms but his game from mid-court to the net was generally erratic.

FINALS

Details, Mixed singles — Mrs. G. Barniville bt. J. O'Shea, 6-4, 4-6, 6-1.

Men's singles—J. O'Brien bt. J. Casey, 6-4, 6-3.

Women's singles—A. Keegan bt. C. O'Neill, 6-2, 6-1.

Mens Doubles Final—H. Sheridan and J. Mulvey beat H. Barniville and K. Fitzgibbon, 6-4, 10-8.

Women's Doubles Semi-final—Miss M. Burns and Mrs. H. Johnstone beat Misses A. and F. Keegan, 6-4, 8-10, 6-2.

Final—N. Glenn and C. O'Neill beat Burns and Johnstone, 6-3, 6-3.

1974 newspaper report

Irish Challenge

In 1974, Ireland came up with its own challenge. The ILTF had a rule that prevented women playing against men in singles competition. The competition, at Clarinda Park Dun Laoghaire, overcame this problem by making it an invitation event. Prior to the match some of the top Irish ladies were asked their views on the subject (*Evening Press 19th April 1974*):

Niamh Glenn
I wouldn't like to see tennis turning into a competition between the sexes. I think I'd feel a bit sorry for any man who lost a match to a woman because he might feel it demoralising. Mixed games are great because they bring up the standard of women's tennis by offering stiff competition and I think most men would be glad to improve women's games, but I'd prefer to play in a women's tournament any day.

Paula Mullen
I don't see this tournament as equality for women. I think it's an entertaining idea that will promote tennis in a light-hearted way rather than a viscous battle of the sexes. Unless women find some way of becoming physically as strong as men they can never equal male tennis players, Billie Jean King beat Bobby Riggs because he was old-58. I don't feel bad about the fact that Fitzwilliam don't admit women-men built the club so it's up to them to admit who they like. From their own point of view, though, I think it would improve the club if it had a mixed membership.

Geraldine Barniville
Tennis is such a traditional old game that in general the administrators are ultra-conservative. There's no denying that men are better tennis players than women because they're stronger, but that doesn't mean that an averagely good man can't be beaten by a good woman player on the basis of skill. Tennis tends to be dragged down by 100-year-old traditions. I think it's a disgrace that a club like Fitzwilliam should be confined to men. Women would be willing to pay anything to join but they haven't a hope.

All the points made by these ladies are pertinent. It is noted that in the intervening years, **Fitzwilliam LTC** have changed, radically and for the better, with the introduction of women into the club. Three results of the above competition, at the Players No. 6 tournament, were published in the *Irish Times* on the 23rd April. J.J. Fitzgibbon, the former international player and Irish number 3 in 1951, beat Ann Keegan the Irish number 5 in 1975, 6/4 6/3. He was *far too wily* according to Vera McWeeney's report. Colm Smith, the sports writer, but a Class I League member of **Glasnevin LTC**, had some trouble in beat Margaret Byrne one of the top ladies that year, 6/4 7/5. Niamh Glenn, the Irish number 4 in 1972, had a win over Carrickmines player Ronnie Delaney (the former Olympic athlete) 6/4 6/2. Ronnie was no lightweight but Niamh *hit the ball very hard and* (with) *acute angles.*

Serving Hard et al.

When playing football of any sort, hard tackles, legal and illegal, are expected in sports that were historically played only by men. The fact that more and more women are playing all codes of football has brought the fairer sex into games that their grandmothers would rarely watch, never mind participate in. In parallel, though not necessarily directly related, is the fact that young women are using more bad language than ever before. There are no doubt sociological explanations for both of these changes.

In the game of tennis there was a day that the gentle sport, and it really was so at one time, was frowned upon as being not suitable for young ladies. This barrier was well and truly crossed long before the end of the 19th century. Mixed tennis was definitely a social sport, and still is. The problem persists however; at most levels of the game, as to how hard a man should serve to a woman. Good female players are delighted in having a hard rally and have no problems in receiving hard services. Weaker ladies' probably shy away from mixed if they thought the opposing man was likely to send too many missiles in their direction.

A gentleman on court would certainly not blast the ball at a weak lady at every opportunity. But not all men are gentlemen. On the other hand serving easy to a lady can be a losing tactic, if she has that ability to get everything back, and to a location on court of her choosing. Thus the dilemma that will possibly be with us always.

In the period before the First World War, Irishman James Parke won the mixed title at Wimbledon. However, in one competitive semi-final, at Wimbledon in 1913, he hit his lady partner, Mrs. Ethel Larcombe, in the eye and they had to concede the match. Edward McGuire, a Davis Cup player in the 1920s and 1930s made the following note in his memoirs:

There has always been tension in competitive tennis, but the social atmosphere in which the game was played limited displays of bad manners and the uttering of rude words to an absolute minimum. Eustace Fannin, a Davis Cup player for Ireland of my time, was known to express his chagrin by saying, "Bother". This was an era, furthermore, in which "social" tennis-popularly known as Vicarage Party tennis-was played to provide a focal point for nice people to come together for tea in restful gardens. It was customary to call "Service" when one was about to serve. Serving hard to the ladies was ungentlemanly and just was not "done". It was usual to say "Sorry" when one missed a shot or poached into a partner's court.

Competitive lady tennis players at Elm Park in 1987 (left to right) Maebh McEvoy, Julie Russell June-Anne Byrne and Patricia O'Gorman.

Poaching in an interesting phenomenon. Some men, and women, poach all day long in 'level' matches, if they think they are better than their partner, or just don't think. In mixed it is rare for the female partner to poach, unless all concerned are aware that she is by far the stronger player and she must play this part if a few point or games are to be won. Some players just do not realise that they are poaching; such is their focus on their own game. This is at its worst in mixed doubles if the man takes over completely and his partner is kept out of the game. On the other hand, a competitive lady has no problem with a man poaching where this regularly results in winning points. A lady from **Ennis LTC** recalls a nice story of the big prize she won. Her male partner had obviously hit the vast majority of balls from their side of the court. This was an instance where poaching was appreciated by the 'weaker' sex. One must conclude that each case must be treated on its merits. Edward McGuire recalled an interesting mixed match

when the 'the Nastase of his day', the rude Ludy Von Salm of Austria was playing with a Mrs. Barry. This appears to have been around the 1920s. The lady was quite possibly Irish, as there was at least one Barry lady of note on the tennis circuit at that time.

I once saw Von Salm playing in a mixed doubles final at Montreux Festival. His partner was a <u>habitué</u> of tournaments in France and Switzerland, a Mrs. Barry, who practised the steady, baseline game then in fashion. Mrs. Barry's lobbing was untypically short on this occasion and Von Salm, dodging around at the net, was being peppered with smashes from the male half of the opposing team. After one potentially crippling near-miss, he turned to Mrs. Barry and cried out, "Forty years playing tennis and you can't lob yet!" He did not qualify for gentleman of the year.

Tennis Notables

There were many lady tennis players who left a mark on the game in Ireland and abroad. Among these are players such as Geraldine Houlihan and Eleanor McFadden who were out on there own in this country, mainly in the 1960s. In the 1980s and 1990s Lesley O'Halloran had an extensive period in the top ranks with Gina Niland creating an even more impressive record. Yvonne Doyle was to impress in the 1990s but her winning of the Irish Championship in 2001 was an important milestone, it had been 50 years since a home-grown player (Betty Lombard in 1951) had captured this event.

Louisa Martin-Winner of a record nine Irish Singles Championships (1889-1903).

We should not forget Siobhan Nicholson. She took the title in 1987, when beating Margaret Redfearn of South Africa. In 1962 her parents, Martin and Susan, emigrated from Dangan, Tuam, County Galway, and brother Miceal, immigrated to England. Joseph, her second brother, and Siobhan were born in Wimbledon. Her father was an athlete and also a hurler. Siobhan's first tournament here was when she won the Irish under 14 title at **Fitzwilliam LTC** in 1980. She first played for Ireland in the Queen Sofia Cup (U18) in Belgium in July

The History of Irish Tennis

1982. Siobhan considers herself Irish and was proud to win the Irish Open and well as five Closed titles. Also added to that are two Indoor titles at Riverview. Probably her biggest disappointment was in 1992 when Gina Niland and herself qualified represent Ireland in doubles at the Barcelona Olympics. The Irish Olympic Council would not sanction their entry-interestingly, the top men's pairing of Owen Casey and Eoin Collins also qualified and did play there successfully.

May Langrishe-winner of the first Ladies' singles title in Ireland and at the 'Northern' in England.

Mary Fitzgibbon (nee Nichols) and husband Jim were had the unusual success when taking the Irish mixed title in 1951, the only Irish married couple to do so. Sister and brother combinations also to win this event were the Haughton's (Ben and Marjorie) in 1923 and the Wallis's (C. S. and Hilda) in 1924). Overall, Hilda was our top lady from the mid-1920s to the mid-1930s, winning four Irish singles championships in that time. The record number of singles titles goes to Louisa Martin, winning this title nine times between 1896 and 1903. She was probably the most unfortunate of Irish ladies' not to have won Wimbledon. She reached three All-Comer's finals, only to be beaten by Chattie Sterry (nee Cooper), a lady she had beaten in two of her ten Irish finals. May Langrishe, from the Kilkenny tennis-playing family, won three Irish singles titles, including the first in 1879. She also won the first 'Northern' singles and doubles, with one of her sisters, in 1882. This ladies doubles, at the "Wimbledon of the North", has been considered the first major ladies' doubles championship to be held anywhere in the world of tennis.

Helena Rice from New Inn became Ireland's only lady Wimbledon champion. She thus became one of Ireland's first female sportswomen of note. This was in 1890. It was noted in latter years that the entry of five ladies was a record low entry. However, her tussles with the top English lady of that era, and the best in the world, Blanche Hillyard (nee Bingley) suggest that there was little between 'Lena' and herself. Blanche beat her 4/6 8/6 6/4 in the Wimbledon final in 1889, Lena had three

match points (she was 40/15 and 5/3 up in the second set). At the Irish Championships Blanche beat her 7/5 7/5 in the semi-final. At the 1889 Wimbledon she made a bit of additional history. She became the first woman to officiate at a Championship match-she took a "line" in the semi-final match between Willie Renshaw, who was on his way to a seventh singles titles, and Herbert Lawford, the champion of 1887. Lena's competitive tennis playing career spanned less than three years but, nevertheless, left an impact.

Lena Rice-The only Irish lady to win Wimbledon

Hilda Wallis-Four times Irish Open Champion

Betty Lombard
Irish Open Champion
1942 1943&1951

Siobhan Nicholson
Irish Open Champion
1987

Yvonne Doyle
Irish Open Champion
2001

The History of Irish Tennis

Tennis has been active in many Irish towns for over 100 years. This is the Carlow ladies' team in the late 1930s. At that time the club had six grass courts and about 80 members, 40 of whom were ladies. Back (l. to r.): Miss V. Montgomery, Miss K. Ryan & Miss B. Murray. Front (l. to r.): Miss E. Good, Mrs. T. Keogh, Miss M. Jackson & Miss M. Ryan.

Sutton Lawn Tennis Club. Ladies' Night 2002-Entertaining the members were (from left): Enda Annelynck, Catherine O'Neill, Linda Foley, Clodagh Whelan, Elizabeth Guinan, Collette Sheridan, Agnes Grahan, Mary O'Donoghue and Margaret O'Donnell.

3.3   *The Social Scene*

To the innocent (and there are not many of them around) it seemed as though every
active (and indeed a few inactive) tennis players turned up to reveal or disguise their
kitchen skills.   (Longford Leader,
                                    19th April 1996)

Sport has always had a social dimension. Sport may be connected to ones schooling, lifestyle, religion and our type of employment. In was noted in one small rural tennis club that the secretary had difficulty in getting players out for a team. They were farmers whose work came first. In towns and cities, time allocation to the sport is fitted into the weekly schedule. In fact some players were known, during the summer months, to be at the court at 6am with a view to getting tennis in before work.

Here we look at some aspects of the sport not normally dealt with. It has proved to be important to young people in their development, as well as a linkage in different generations within the family unit. Many clubs were the focal point in villages and towns. Its big advantage, in the past and today, is that the sport is equally suitable for both sexes and for many age groups. The fact that it was a socially exclusive pastime/sport at one time is recognised. This factor gradually became less important as more clubs developed and the relative price of a racquet reduced considerably. The television age proved to be a boost to the sport in terms of exposure and the feeling that it could be played as readily as any other sport. Time and space only allow a speckled glance at the subject. However, the few examples illustrated here do help to expose a forgotten past. The modern reader can absorb and just wonder.

Society Gathering

On Friday evening a most successful dance took place in the Court-house. The rooms were beautifully decorated with water lilies and quantities of tennis racquets, tied with the club colours-blue, red, brown and gold-which was most effective. (The Sligo Independent, August 11th, 1883, reporting on the annual Sligo Open prize giving night).

It was a real society gathering. The success of the teas reflects the highest credit upon Mrs. L'Estrange, Mrs. Cook, Mrs. A. M. Lyons, Miss La Touche, and Miss Wood-Martin, each lady being most kind and indefatigable in looking after the wants of those present in this connection. (The 1921 report on the same tournament).

Sir William Orphen, apart from his painting and sketches, some of which were on tennis topics, wrote on days of old in *Stories of Old Ireland & Myself"(1925),* where he gave us a range of insights into Dublin social life and related matters. He put the Irish Championships into context as follows:

The Fitz-William Lawn tennis Tournament Week in Dublin then was as important socially as the Horse Show Week. All the hotels were full of English visitors, all the houses were full of guests. Henry Wilson (Field-marshal Sir Henry Wilson) and his brother used to come over and stay with Mrs. George Orr Wilson at her place near Blackrock. I remember well how, when they appeared on the platform of the little railway station in the mornings to take the train to Dublin, a sort of hush spread over the little crowd waiting to be taken to the city to their daily tasks. Such perfect figures, such perfect clothes, spats to wonder at, boots to dream of! Sir Henry always with a raincoat thrown over one shoulder, always with his yellow-gloved hands clasped behind him.

It wasn't just in Dublin that tennis was an important vehicle for social interchange. *A very pleasant function took place at the Cafe Cairo on Tuesday night last, when the Merville Lawn Tennis Club celebrated the close of its season by a Cinderella dance, at which opportunity was taken to distribute the cups and medals won during the session. ....The music was supplied by O'Hara's Syncopated Orchestra and gave complete satisfaction* (Sligo Champion, 7th November 1925).

At the head of affairs was our popular friend, Mr. H. R. Wood-Martin, a gentleman of the first order. His smiling countenance is always a pleasure to look upon, and were it not for his presence I fear the tournament would be lacking in many respects. Long may his secretaryship continue. (The "Observer", reporting on the 1926 Open at Ardaghowen).

Mixed Doubles at Glenageary LTC (Circa 1940s)

We would cross the Curlews as the sun rose.......at the end of the Longford Open Week (Sligo player returning home, late 1950s)

"Let's hear it for Alison! Applause for our favourite songbird!" The tennis-players responded to his call with a frantic bout of handclapping, with screams of adulation. The people at the bar were not sure that they wanted to be distracted by a tennis player, but

when they saw Alison's legs they decided that it would be worth their while. Anthony stumbled into her as he made his way from the toilet. Alison saw a chance of forging a bond with him, whether of triumph or disgrace." Come on, Anthony! Come and sing with me!" (Ronan Sheehan's 1977 novel *Tennis Players*).

BARBEQUE NIGHT A GREAT SUCCESS: The tennis club was the centre (of) Longford sporting, culinary and sartorial worlds last Friday night when the Club celebrated with unrestrained relish the imminent departure to the USA of Cheryl Stephany! Mike has decided to send her back to the states for a short course in self-assertiveness!! It was a night {or early morning} to remember. To the innocent {and there are not many of them around} it seemed as though every active {and indeed a few inactive} tennis players turned up to reveal or disguise their kitchen skills. (Longford Leader, 19th April 1996).

Apart from the novel by Ronan Sheenan the above pen pictures are a small representation of the thousands of true stories that can be told about tennis people and their clubs. Even the novel, dealing with junior tournaments down the country is, one suspects, based somewhat on true experiences. Everyone who has played the game for any period of time has a few encounters worth recording. They may be outrageous or mundane but to the player they had meaning.

Birr tennis players-1940s

Club AGMs

Small clubs have their distinct advantages and disadvantages. We can define such a club as having one or two courts. They, in fact, may have no courts, relying on the local school or hospital for their play area. Membership will be variable from season to season; by the AGM they will have some thirty or so paid up adults and perhaps a similar number or fewer juniors. Each May the annual general meeting is called to organise the coming summers programme. If they are lucky fifteen players will turn up. In a bad year this could be as few as the dedicated five or six diehards. In such cases a new date for the AGM is called and contacts with existing members made on a personal basis. While the small notice in the local paper has some effect, attractive posters in the local bar, supermarket etc. will bring results. The meeting eventually takes off

with the minutes of the previous year's meeting followed by the reports of the secretary and treasurer. The secretary will read a two or three page summary of what happened or, in some cases, why decisions made could not be translated into action. The treasurer, often a local bank official, expected to be ideal in terms of his (or her) honesty and accounting skills, will present the facts. *We started the year with a credit of £15.25 and finished with £35.75, a profit of £20.50 was made.* The chairman thanks both and, I'm not too sure why, congratulates the treasurer on making a profit. Applause from the members!

Fitzwilliam Lawn Tennis Club-1920s Function

If there was a deficit, he will have made arrangements with the bank (where he works, naturally) to have an overdraft facility. However, some members will have honest queries. Did we really need a new net? This might be the question from an occasional player- certainly not from a keen player who knows the value of a net with no holes. *Where do all the affiliation fees go?,* and, *Did the Smith family not pay their subscription last year?,* may be the typical queries needing an answer.

What is important at these AGMs is that the club is, once again, at the starting blocks. The hassle the secretary or captain had in arranging friendly or competition matches, a coach for a week-end or entries for the a club tournament are now in the past. Apart from the treasurer, everyone will have forgotten that he/she will have spent all July and August chasing up the last subscriptions. Funny, it is always the same people who hold on to their money as long as possible. In many cases they are better off than Joe Coughlan who paid up the night of the last AGM. The treasurer swears he will not do the job again. After a bit of moral arm-twisting he agrees to do it for one more year. (In the back of his mind he knows that by this time next year he will probably be transferred and he might as well have another go).

Thanks are made at this stage to all who have helped in any way. It may be the local rector or priest who enabled the club to secure courts for the summer. The issue of insurance raises its head again. It may be the ladies committee who organised the teas after the home matches. In truth this 'committee' is probably an ad hoc one lead by the secretary with the assistance of three or four keen lady members. Some may have retired from playing but like to be involved in this social occasion. The smaller and more isolated the club the more important these teas become. The meeting will be told that last year they ran a raffle, which made £85 and went a long way towards keeping the club in the black. On the deficit side some £50 was presented to the local Vincent de Paul or other worthy charity. People know that they are fortunate to be healthy and playing tennis. This is rarely queried.

Fund Raising

The main source of funds for a club is the annual subscriptions. In general, the subscription matched the facilities on offer and was index linked (in a haphazard sort of way). Demand also plays a part. In a large city, a club with a waiting list can ask for more. In a small town charges are kept to the minimum. The same may apply in a medium sized town today; there are many more distractions and the social aspect of a tennis club has not the attraction it once had.

In 1877 the annual subscription in the **Fitzwilliam LTC** was £3. By 1996, with a vastly improved club, the annual subscription was £710 in addition to the joining fee of £1200. In the County Kildare Club (now Naas) it was £2 in 1881. Move forward to 1938 and we find that Ballyfarnon TC, a new and small club, were happy to charge 4/-6 for adults and 2/-6 for juniors under 16. The established Sligo YMCA club were charging their members £1-12-6 in 1959. The present Sligo Tennis Club set an annual rate of £4 in their first season in 1978. A discussion on the cost of tennis is dealt with elsewhere in the book.

Raising money, either in small or large amounts, requires the same endeavour. A target, a mechanism, and sufficient willing bodies. Raffle tickets at a suitable social will bring in small amounts. Sponsors for tournaments will help defray costs and possibly provide a surplus. One may have one large sponsor (such as Carlsberg, Dunlop, Pamela Scott or a bank) or a large number of local business people contributing smaller amounts.

Carroll's, the cigarette manufacturer, was associated with the national Carroll's Doubles event while Nestle, the food manufacturer, have contributed much towards promoting junior tennis at home and abroad.

1963-Elm Park members take a trip to the seaside at Ballybunion, County Kerry. Front (l. to r.) Damien Hand, Valerie O'Connor, Peter Murnaghan, Miriam O'Connor & Des Halley. Back includes Maurice Rafter, Myles Stanistreet, John Murnaghan & Jim Kerr.

In smaller tournaments, one or several local businesses (and possibly members themselves) will present prizes. Any surplus will be associated with the entry fee. In official events, the capitation fee must be paid to the national body, Tennis Ireland (formerly the Irish Lawn Tennis Association). This can amount to perhaps 25% of the entry fee. There was usually little objection to this payment as it went to support the national, regional teams etc. However, down the country, the national body had little influence or interaction. This has now changed and there is an increased realisation that tennis does have an active life outside the major cities.

Many non-tennis players would have considered the game as one for the well to do. It might even have been thought of as a sissy's sport at one time. But the big excuse for not trying the game was cost. Apart from the annual subscription, a racquet, shoes, t-shirt and shirt or shorts were necessary. Ordinary socks would do. This was too much money for many to even consider. (Little did they realise that the game was much more than just a sport.). The AGM always gave due consideration to the year's subscription. More often than not a family and junior fee was established as well as that for adults.

Juniors

Many youngsters, with little or no initial interest, followed their big brother or sister to the club; a family subscription had been paid. Twelve months later they were hooked. The balancing act at the AGM was to keep the subscription as low as possible and yet survive. The simple philosophy for this is that there was rarely an excess of members; newcomers to the area must also be encouraged to join. While this logic was right for several years it meant that a new net required additional funds from elsewhere. The good committee will have brought their members with them and, in time, ways of raising money for court re-surfacing, or even a new court, could be found. Quite often change was seen as a catch twenty-two with no way forward in sight.

The lucky club might have had a committee of eight; this includes five good workers. With such a number it is possible to increase membership numbers, organise juniors and generally expand the club's activities. A problem eventually arises, that of adequate court time in the evenings. This was always a sign that the club was succeeding, even though a rule banning juniors after 7pm had to be introduced.

1950s at Birr

Equally lucky were the clubs where there were two or three members running the show since Methuselah (he was a Hebrew patriarch, said to have lived for 969 years). In other words no one can remember these *institutions* not being involved in the club. In rare cases it was an individual with a strong personality with a willing committee ready to follow instructions. Sometimes they became autocrats who were rarely challenged. Eventually they either died in office (when the complainers would say how great they were for the club), left town (when there would be a sigh of relief followed by *what do we do now?)* or were challenged. This usually happened quite innocently when new members arrived in the club and made perfectly innocent suggestions at the AGM. What they did not realise was that the 'boss' had strong views of a contradictory nature.

In any decade a tennis club can be easily associated with the few who have been prepared to make an effort. The club will survive with a reasonably small, but keen, membership.

Unfortunately, changing times, a raised ground rent, a court being converted into a car park and/or the departure from town of key officers are reasons why a club dies. (e.g. The YMCA club (Sligo) folded due to the lack of £400 in 1961.) Many such clubs can be revived.

1960s-Alf Walsh (far right), the honorary secretary of the Irish Lawn Tennis Association) at tennis function in Belfast.

Decisions That Work

In the larger clubs the problems are similar in terms of the years programme, the need for willing workers and a successful budget. A decision to build two new tennis courts or a modern clubhouse has major implications on funds available. While the small club may be short of a few pounds at the end of the year the bigger club has to ensure that any moves *actually* work.

Once a decision is made then a strong commitment by both the officers and members must be followed up by action. Every club can afford talkers but it cannot afford to be without the willing workers. The bigger the club the more likely that such willing workers can be found. Unfortunately, it is in these circumstances that many will sit back thinking that others will do it all. Apart from finances, a dose of enthusiasm, planning and effort will produce fruits and, at the same time, show others the way.

A club with only one senior team, and a small number of juniors to supervise and coach, has a major advantage on its side. The time required to ensure all goes well is fairly small. If a tournament is cancelled due to bad weather then it can be easily re-scheduled for next week. In large clubs demand for court and a timetabled summer are essential. Flexibility is more difficult. Diplomacy between sub committees is required.

Warming up for the Sligo Tennis Club Anniversary Ball at the Sligo Park Hotel in 1999 were (from left) Siobhan McDermott, Francie Mahon, Annette Stephens, Patsy McElhinney, Bridie McElhinney & Mrs. McDermott.

Small clubs are integrated bodies and are like one family with a common love for tennis. This is rarely the case in bigger clubs where one finds the best players stick together, the novices likewise. This is a natural series of conglomerations but all must be deliberately integrated (from time to time) if long term dissensions are not to occur. The principle must also apply when more than one sport are housed in the same club.

Social Value

Where clubs have not survived then a community has lost a sporting and social asset. Ballymote tennis club, for example, thrived for about eighty years; revival attempts have been made in the 1990s but with no permanency.

Significant numbers of small clubs in Ireland lasted for twenty or thirty years and died. They can be revived. Newcomers to the area with a passion for the game can see through many obstacles and motivate others.

A tennis club is not just a location to play and be coached in a sport but a social challenge worth facing. Friends will be made with those of a similar ilk and with many who one would otherwise rarely meet. Apart from a few cases when religious limitations, allied to the clubs founding fathers, one can find a complete cross-culture of society in the vast majority of clubs. This was not always the case (a matter discussed elsewhere in the book). How many clubs, sporting or otherwise, can cater for the needs of seven and seventy year olds, all enjoying and participating in equal measure? A question, with no answer required, and has been asked in many

tennis playing families was/is "What would we do without the tennis club?" This question verifies the thesis that these clubs have a great social value. Eighty years ago one might find it difficult to find juniors in clubs, and their introduction lead to painful discussions and decisions. Thankfully this changed dramatically and today, in many cases, it is the juniors that came along first and the parents joined later.

Social Class

For many years it was social 'class' rather than religion that dictated who could become a member of a club. One member of a Protestant family was asked why they did not become members of the 'County' LTC, one of two tennis clubs in an Irish town. The clear answer was that they would not have been acceptable- they were in trade. This distinction seems to have been fairly widespread and only weakened when numbers and viability of a club was threatened.

In the re-union booklet brought out by the former tennis players of Ennis there is a little story that illustrates the feeling of the time. Ennis, as detailed elsewhere, had the old County Clare Lawn Tennis Club, founded in the 19th century.

The Fergus LTC was set up in about 1935 and was open to all. Eventually, the two clubs combined. However, the following little anecdote occurred when both clubs were fully active. It was 1940. Noel Cassidy was a teenager at the time but it was a memory not to be forgotten.

> The 'County' club *could be described as a strictly private club with membership reserved for the chosen few. It ran a very successful open week annually up to 1940. In that year the Men's Singles Championship was won by Sean Casey, UCD, son of Garda Superintendent Pat Casey, Cusack Road, Ennis. It was said at the time that smelling salts had to be administered to those in the Royal Box who were shocked that a commoner had swiped the Crown Jewels. It was a mighty victory for the proletariat.*

In Ireland, the school you went to often decide the sports and social life you were likely to enjoy as an adult. While a diocesan Catholic college were more likely to promote Gaelic football, hurling and handball, a Grammar school was likely to promote rugby and hockey as their main team sports. A Mercy convent today might have camogie as the main sport but are just as likely to promote hockey or basketball.

Tennis was often passed over as a minority sport. Cricket, on the other hand is found in the long established, and expensive boarding schools, both Catholic and Protestant. Many would be surprised to hear that St. Mel's College, Longford, the diocesan college for Ardagh and Clonmacnoise, a nursery for Gaelic footballers, had cricket as its main sport in the early years of the twentieth century (Mc Gee, 1996).

Thankfully, tennis and badminton have eased themselves out a social scene belonging to the 19th century. Apart from the long running issue of women members at **Fitzwilliam LTC**, now resolved, there have been no other social revolutions required. One can readily state that the love of racquet sports, and a naturally broadening of their bases, has merged together many people of different creeds and social standings. Squash and racquetball have developed late in Ireland and have no social connotations; table tennis could always be found in a small room in a church hall but, equally, in any schools spare room- like darts, bridge and other *minor* sports they have thrived, quietly and without any fuss.

Competition

In Leinster, the Town's Cup has long drawn together smaller clubs in an annual event. There is also the Belfast and District League. All provinces have their senior, junior and school cup events. For over forty years there has been a hidden northwest league in Donegal-Derry region run by the unheralded, outside the area, Billy Watson. In recent times, another cross border league has drawn together Omagh, Sligo and Enniskillen.

In numerical strength, the vast Dublin population has seen a large increase in club numbers and demand. The Dublin Lawn tennis Council have provided the city region with one of the biggest tennis leagues anywhere in the world. It can proudly look back over a 100 years of growth. The wise are now travelling, in greater numbers, further a field where they are assured of a great social weekend.

In the early part of the 20th century few travelled any significant distance. Economics, poor roads and the lack of motorised transport were the main limitations. The railways were the great movers of people. Wandering Australians were found playing tournaments in Enniskillen. Luminaries, such as Joe Hackett and Gerry Clarke, are still remembered in Sligo as participants in the West of Ireland over fifty years ago. Who said people forget.

Open weeks were, and still are, a big attraction. Some would travel to these events, possibly over sixty miles away, for six or seven days in the same week. It must be remembered that the roads and cars were not as efficient as they are to day. The local committee would be surprised if the keen players did not return. The reason was simple. They were always made welcome, were indeed special to the event and, invariably reached the latter stages of a tournament. What this amounted to was low key, but competitive tennis. The socialising afterwards, and the feel good factor, resulted in repeat entries.

Memories of past times and summer tennis are usually filled with sunshine. It was only the rare hassle that arose. A player who travelled some distance, only to be told that they must come back the following evening for their first round match, was rightly annoyed at the time.

Will the adults of tomorrow have fond memories of their youth and the sport of tennis? It is up to the players and the organisers to ensure that the special ethos of the game is maintained.

Tennis is a sport that is played in a gentlemanly or ladylike way, depending upon the participants involved. It can be competitive or easygoing. Acing your opponent or volleying past the number two seed is a satisfaction hard to define. One can lose 6/2 6/2 against a good player in a tournament but yet enjoy their company socially. Doubles, and mixed in particular, provides maximum interaction. This is club tennis at its best. Many long time relationships have started at the tennis club.

Celebration at Lansdowne Lawn Tennis Club

New Members

The unselfish time injected into a club by the backbone members must not be forgotten. Better and more experienced members *must* help the juniors, novices, new members and in the running of club affairs. Only in this way can a long term and successful club ethos be achieved. Today, there is a tendency to be selfish. Socially, most will look after their own corner first. While it might be acceptable to arrange a playing time best suited to oneself, it is definitely not acceptable to completely ignore a less talented player. They too have paid their annual subscription or tournament entry fee. Consideration for the young or less talented will always pay dividends for the long-term health of that club.

John McEnroe (USA) gives that long stare at the line during his 1992 match versus Pat Cash (Australia) at the 1992 Wimbledon championships. The American won in five sets.

In smaller clubs *any* new players should feel that they are welcome. Simple common sense! If the player is particularly good, then there are many low level conversations of a complementary nature. The league team is suddenly gone up a few notches in terms of potential success. There is possibly one player, who had been hanging on to the number four spot on the team for the last few years, who suddenly realises that their time is up. Mind you, if there are only two courts and the popular playing time is 7 to 8pm on a summers evening, some might be ruffled if it is the new members that seem to be taking over their slot. Such competition for play should be seen as a healthy sign.

Members in larger clubs will hardly notice the ten new members who joined in the month of May. In fact, they will become part of the club without having any effect on the playing time whatsoever. The danger here is apathy. If they are not welcomed in some fashion, and made at home, they may have disappeared by the following season. One lost member, for any reason, can be inhibitory to others joining. The opposite is also true. A new member, junior or senior, who is made feel at home from day one, will not only be a long term member but will readily support club activities. Ultimately, he or she may become part of the club's organising wing.

Such happy members are worth ten new members in due course, never mind the knock on financial benefits to the club. Perhaps clubs should all have a *Welcoming Officer* as an official post, rather than relying on the already busy secretary or captain.

"Manners"

Being a good player has its kudos. It must be accompanied by appropriate behaviour on and off court. Sean Sorensen, the Cork lad who was a Davis Cup player between 1976 and 1986, was, not alone an excellent tennis player but, I'm told, *he was a lovely lad.* This is an important addendum in terms of a tennis person. Even lesser players will gain attention provided he/she has the minimum requirement of good behaviour. There are exceptions. Ilie Nastase was a good player, with the looks and charm, but would argue with umpires on a regular basis. Once, playing the French Open doubles with Ion Tiriac he decided, in mid-rally, to chat up a blonde in the front row. His comment on return to the court (phone number scribbled on his hand) was *There will be another point along in a minute, but there may never be another blonde like that.* He would, undoubtedly, be acceptable company for all off court and probably would be delighted to have a drink with the umpire afterwards.

Sounds to me like Ilie could be Irish. John McEnroe has Irish blood but would not be buying a drink for the umpire. He had the talent, but his aggressiveness was excessive for most. One could admire his intensity and skill and his love for the game but it's a pity, at least from the public's point of view, that he missed out on some social skills. Brownie points lost.

Wimbledon 1992-John McEnroe ignoring the young Irish autograph hunter.

In his 2002 autobiography "Serious" one can see the game from his perspective without necessarily agreeing with all he has to say. While admitting that his behaviour got away from him, he immediately states that he thought *tennis had had enough of manners. To me, 'manners' meant sleeping linesmen at Wimbledon, and bowing and curtsying to rich people with hereditary titles who didn't pay any taxes. Manners meant tennis clubs that demanded you wear white clothes, and cost too much money to join, and excluded blacks and Jews and God knows who else. Manners meant the hush-hush atmosphere at tennis matches, where excitement of any kind was frowned upon.*

He goes on to contrast this with noisy South American Davis Cup matches. McEnroe was not the first player to lose his cool on court. He provided tennis entertainment when at his peak in the 1980s. He put bums on seats and could be considered to be partly responsible for the upgrading of tennis administration. In 100 years time will we have fully automated tennis matches with machines alone in charge? Will players even shake hands after a match? Who knows? Will "manners" have disappeared altogether? McEnroe may be thanked, or criticised!

Tennis Families

The sport, like many I suppose, has ongoing links between children, their parents and grandparents. Lance Tingay (1983) suggested that lawn tennis skill has a genetic factor. *A more obvious cause is environmental.* No matter what the reasons, there have always been successful members within the same family unit. In the early day the Renshaw twins (William and Ernest) ruled the roost. For ten years, between 1881 and 1890, one or other was in the Wimbledon singles final, they won eight of the titles. In addition, they won seven Irish Open titles between 1880 and 1892. (It was Willie's seven wins at Wimbledon that Pete Sampras equalled in 2000). It might be noted for historical purposes that the only player to beat Willie in a Wimbledon final was in fact Willoughby J. Hamilton, a member of Fitzwilliam LTC.

The Irish team that played against England in Buxton in 1921 contained no less than three brothers. Ireland lost the match by the narrow margin of 8 matches to 7. From left: Harry Read, Charles Scroope, Gervase Scroope, Cecil Campbell, Simon Scroope & E. D'Arcy McCrea.

Ireland's Langrishe sisters, Beatrice and May, travelled far and wide to play tennis in the 19th century. According to the Guinness Book of Tennis Facts and Feats (1983) they were the first winners of any ladies doubles title when they won the Northern Lawn Tennis Championships in Manchester in 1882. More notable, perhaps, was the fact that May, at the age of 14, won the first Irish Open Championships, the first ladies singles title anywhere in the world. That was in 1879, five years before Wimbledon held such an event. A third sister, Adela Constance, and brother, Hercules, also competed in tournament tennis.

There are many cases of sons following fathers onto national teams, the Krishnan's from India, the Mottrams from Great Britain and a few mothers and daughters, such as May and Dorothy Bundy from the USA. Famous brothers include the McEnroes, Lloyds, Jensens, Blacks and the Armitrajs. Who can forget the Gullikson twins, Tim and Tom? Sisters will never be the same after Wimbledon 2000, Serena versus Venus in the semi-finals, Serena supporting Venus in the final, and both together winning the doubles.

We can jump back in time to 1884, the first ladies singles at Wimbledon. Maud Watson beats her sister Lilian 6/8 6/3 6/3 in the final. An amazing family run was the period 1881 to 1906. In those twenty-six years three sets of brothers dominated Wimbledon. The Renshaw twins won six doubles titles, the Baddeley twins (Wilfred and Herbert) four, plus runners up twice, followed by the ten consecutive finals of the Doherty brothers, Reggie and Laurie. They won eight. It might be added that of the five doubles titles not won in this period by these sets of brothers two were won by Irishmen, Joshua Pim and Frank Stoker (1890 and 1893). In the same era, the Irish Open at Fitzwilliam saw a similar pattern. Renshaws (4 wins), Baddeleys (2 wins) and Dohertys (5 wins). Just for good measure Pim and Stoker won five. The Dohertys won the US Open twice (1902, 1903) and the South African Open once (1909).

Returning to the Irish scene we can find some notable family feats worth mentioning. Recently we saw Conor Niland join his sister Gina in the ranks of senior international tennis. The Miley family have a long tennis pedigree. International Val Miley was Fitzwilliam's club champion in 1912 and 1913. His brother John (Jack) was of a similar standard. David Miley was on his school's (Clongowes) tennis team in 1936 and another David Miley was a tour player in 1980s and a professional tennis coach. The Munster Mockler family have many tennis players of note over the years. Peter was senior Munster player in the 1960s and 1970s. The 1967 Davis Cup team included Peter Mockler, Peter Jackson and the luminaries, Michael Hickey and Vivian Gotto. Frank Mockler was President of the ILTA in 1955. Frank's brother Eamon was a surgeon in the Royal Navy and won their singles championships in 1936 at Wimbledon.

Perhaps unique in international tennis terms were the Scroope brothers. Charlie and Simon were both Davis Cup players in the period 1923 to 1931. They were joined by Gervase in the annual Ireland-England international in Buxton in 1921. For the record Ireland lost 8 matches to 7, Charlie and Simon being responsible for four of the Irish points (two singles and two doubles wins).

At a more local, mainly club, level family tennis has been always an important feature. The Kirkwood's of Boyle LTC were most active about 100 years ago. In the Castlebar club, founded in 1937, one finds the Garavans, Kilkellys, Milletts, Ruanes and Flynns in the last thirty years. The old County Sligo LTC (founded in 1881) had the landed Wynne and Wood-Martin families, the Lyons's, MacDowels and Phibbs's. (Ever hear of the famous legal firm of Argue and Phibbs?.) The old Irvinestown club had many Magee's playing and the modern club, established in 1991, has large numbers of McCuskers and Maguires, the latter being a well-established Fermanagh name.

In the old Merville club there were many excellent tennis players in the 1940s and 1950s. Among them was the Burke family and the Flattery sisters, Maeve being ranked number 7 in Ireland in 1952. Galway tennis club has had many tennis families over the years. Not least among them are the Dempseys. Donal senior is a coach, noted player and former President of the ILTA. Daughter Emer, and Donal junior, are Connacht interprovincials. Salthill's Pat and David Ryan were useful players in the 1960s; Pat is now the proud mother of some of Munster's best, Ross, Conor and Gina Niland. Loughrea's Jim Pringle, apart from being the dad to Irish ranked James Pringle is weekly coaching some future Louth tennis stars.

One could look in every Irish club and find a tennis dynasty. In days long past there tended to be a stability among membership in a region. Bankers were moved around but most employment, where available, was fairly fixed. Today, job mobility sees tennis players on the move in bigger numbers. It is one sport that travels and is certainly provides an opening to making new friends for all members of a family.

Summary

The tennis club may have been an exclusive social venue in the past. It may have represented a no go area for the young or the not so well off. This, thankfully, has changed as society has matured. The 'relative' price of a tennis racquet has reduced considerably. To quote long time Sligo businessman and tennis player, Ted Smith, *At one time a tennis racquet would be two weeks wages of a shop assistant. Today it is one third or one half of the week's wage.*

Most clubs in rural Ireland aspire to a permanent clubhouse and flood lit courts, permitting year round play. One can genuinely regret the loss of grass courts but celebrate the expansions that have taken place. People will make friends for life, both on and off court. The sport provides a solid foundation for social inter-action by young and old and between the sexes. Lengthy matches between members, or on the 'box', can be talking points for weeks. The excellent tournament, the brilliant visitor, the late night disco, the planning of a trip to Wimbledon, the tennis camp, the bald tennis balls that Johnny Smith always produces, the reaction from Mary when Michael Corcoran served into the back of his wife's head, all provide talking points. When did you ever hear a player not looking forward to his next game? Tennis has all the social needs to enjoy life to the full. If you think otherwise then you have missed out on the experiences which will become most fondly caressed memories.

In 2000 two pairs of brothers featured on this winning veterans (55+) league team from St. Mary's LTC, Dublin. Back (l. to r.) Jack Delaney, Simon Gordan & Barry Leonard. Front (l. to r.) Des Delaney, Frank Cinnamond & Dave Leonard.

The 1953 Irish Championships at Fitzwilliam Lawn Tennis Club. Miss D. Pratt and her brother Donald (right) lost out in the first round mixed to Naresh Kumar (India) and Shirley Bloomer (GB). Donald went on to become one of Ireland's top squash players, winning an exceptional 52 caps between 1952 and 1972. he won the Irish Open Squash Championship on ten occasions.

Galway LTC 2000. Three members of the Niland family from Limerick featured on the Munster team in the interprovincials. From left: Ray (won 2 of 3 doubles), Conor (won 2 out of 2 singles) and Gina (won 3 out of 3 singles).

3.3.1   *Dancing and Romancing*

*Most of us gravitated to the tennis club because that was
where all the good-looking women congregated.* John Gallagher (Fergus LTC booklet, 2000)

Before discos there were the 'tennis hops' and before them the annual 'tennis dance'. These are/were special social functions in a club. It was here that a young man might approach a young lady that he has taken to. It may be the clumsy groping infatuation of a teenager, a valid state of development for a young person, or a more serious approach with long-term implications. A suitable partner to bring home to ones parents might have been the thinking in years past. Today it might just be a suitable partner. Percy French might have been one of the first to meet his future wife at a tennis function. Certainly, he was not the last.

A male or female might have had their eye on a player during an open week. It might have been the good tennis, looks or some indefinable quality. Whatever the attraction, the 'dance', 'hop' or 'disco' at the end of the week was a chance to get closer, perhaps making a date for the 'pictures' (multiplex cinema today). A fellow might see a future mixed doubles partner on court, getting closer would be necessary. Does she have any similar feelings? Today it is often just as likely that the girl will do the chasing, again with the same intentions. For tennis players, the sport is part of the game of life. Witness the large number of young, and not so young, males following Anna Kournikova at Wimbledon. You can rest assured it is not just her tennis that they are observing. It is the whole package. If she did not play tennis I suspect her admirers would be considerably fewer. The girls/women today will admit to following more than the ball during a men's tennis match. Looks, long legs, a small tight 'butt' (they did not exist by the way in times past!!), well-groomed hair etc. can all keep the observer from recording the score. However, a bad tempered player loses brownie points rapidly.

Without question the sport of tennis has provided many occasions to meet members of the opposite sex. If the truth were known, the vast majority of the early players saw the game as a social pastime more than a sporting event. The emphasis, looking into the distant past, has been on the international players. We may have heard of a few of those who made a name in the game. Others have been forgotten, apart from their curious descendants. Nonetheless, there are many alive today who can thank tennis for an opportunity of meeting a boy or girl, man or woman, in a pleasant sporting environment. Even the most dedicated player must have capitulated to the charms of an admirer following a winning match.

Case Studies

Let's go back to about 1950. **The County Longford Lawn Tennis Club** was then in grass court heaven. Summers were always warm, and the line of evergreen
trees could be guaranteed to produce millions of midges along the northern boundary of the club.

Cricket was played in the field behind these trees; Longford rugby club now has its home there. Midway along the southern boundary was the typical clubhouse of the early/mid twentieth century, built of wood and galvanised iron. Each side the hedge stretched and two or three garden seats provided accommodation for the audience. It was perhaps on one of these a group of teenage girls gathered, in increasing excitement.

Two visiting young men, about twenty years of age, were on court playing with their local hosts. All were on holidays from 'uni'. The visitors were not only tanned; one was particularly good looking and both good tennis players. The locals did not get a second glance as the girls took in every stroke and movement of the visitors' play. What made it even more exciting was the fact that both were foreigners, one an Australian, and one from South Africa. These were definitely unusual and exotic visitors meriting some attention. Fifty years ago it was unlikely that many Longford girls had ever seen the like. Waiting patiently until the game was over; there was a rising hope of possibly meeting either, particularly the better looking of the two. One can perhaps imagine the chatter and the speculation. The match ended, the young men, not appearing to take notice of the audience, went into the small building to change in the 8' x 10' dressing room. Eventually they arrived out. Utter deflation! The hopes of a few were dashed in an instant. Expectation was squashed. The "looker" was dressed in a black suit and a white collar. He was a student priest, and definitely out of bounds.

In the late 1950s could be found some of the best players in the land playing at Ballycastle. They had come for the annual County Antrim Championships on the excellent 10 grass courts (with two stand-by hard courts). International Peter Jackson was one such player. The old Jamison family had been there for many years. Their granddaughter Marjorie was visiting for the summer and played a more social game. She was about 19 at the time. Romance blossomed and they were married a few years later (1962).

An equally successful encounter ensued in about 1980. Young civil engineer Billy Mulvaney, recently returned from work abroad, was keen on some activity and especially one that might involve meeting girls. Friend, John McManus, a keen tennis player, suggested joining the local tennis club in Sligo. The only available gear available included old football shorts, certainly not white, a black tee shirt, matching black socks, and shoes that were more runners than footwear designed for the tennis court. The only racquet he could find was nearly as old as himself. Fortune favoured the brave. Billy entered the mixed doubles in the organised tournament and was picked with the tall and attractive Mary O'Connor. She was a keen and useful player. Apart from winning the club ladies doubles championship (in 1979), Mary was part of the club's successful ladies team a few years later. Billy's appearance was not a barrier to what became a successful married pair and, just a few years later, with their own tennis court. There are stories such as these abounding in the game of tennis. Look around your club, how many can you count?

Billy and Mary Mulvaney as romantic as ever over twenty years after first meeting at a mixed doubles tournament.

Back in the 1940s we would see two of the top Irish players develop a most successful relationship. JJ Fitzgibbon, of sports shop fame, was a noted badminton player, certainly one of the best of his era. He played tennis too and through the game met Mary Nichols. Mary was the Irish Girls Open Champion in 1938, 1939 and 1940. By 1942 she was ranked number 2 in Ireland having won the Irish Open Championship title the previous year. Both played at Wimbledon at various stages, such was their standard. To make a long story short, they married in 1949. He was ranked number 3 in Ireland in 1951; she was number 1 in 1950 and number 2 in 1952. Naturally, they played a lot together and won the Irish Open Mixed Championships in 1951. To the best of my knowledge no other Irish husband and wife pairing have won this title since it was first played for in 1879.

The tennis element of **Muckamore Cricket and Lawn Tennis Club** started in 1908 and was a great success. Socially it proved a great boost for the club. In their Centenary Booklet (1974) we find the following:

Before the First World War, opportunities for young people to meet socially were limited to an extent which is hardly credible today. So the role of the tennis club was enormously important. It was accepted as a place in which young men and women with broadly similar backgrounds could develop friendships, although perhaps Mama might count the number of times the ball disappeared into the rhododendrons and question the joint recovery time. Many's the "And they lived happily ever after" marriages began with a meeting at the tennis club,

not just in the early days but also up to the present. To list them might be invidious.

On the romantic front, Kathleen (*Kitty*) Mc Kane is worth mentioning here. Even though English she had distinct Irish connections. For a start, one of her grandparents was Irish. In modern parlance she would be eligible for the national side. Kitty was born on the 7th May 1896. Her sporting interest was fostered while attending St. Leonard's School in St. Andrews (Scotland) from 1909 to 1914. In this girl's school all were encouraged to participate in sports which included, in apparent order of importance, cricket, hockey, lacrosse, tennis, golf and Eton Fives (see chapter 2).

Kitty later won many titles at tennis including, the Wimbledon singles in 1924 and 1926. In 1925, she was runner-up in the US Open to Helen Wills. The match was a three-setter. In the same competition she had earlier beaten two other top Americans, Elizabeth Ryan and Molla Mallory. It was at badminton that she was perhaps first noticed when winning the All-England singles title four times between 1920 and 1924. With her older sister, Margaret (born April 1895), they won two badminton All-England ladies doubles titles in 1921 and 1924. Margaret won the singles title in 1925.

According to *The Badminton Story* by Bernard Adams (1980) Kitty was engaged to marry Dublin man J. F. (Frank) Devlin in February 1924. They made a *devastating mixed doubles combination* and won the All-England as a pair in 1924 and 1925. For the information of non-badminton followers, Frank was the best player in the World in the 1920s winning 18 titles at these championships between 1922 and 1931. His badminton doubles partner was 'Curly' Mack, another Dubliner. Curly later became a Davis Cup player.

Kitty was selected to tour South Africa with an English tennis team from October 1925 to February 1926. She had known Leslie Godfree for some time; he was one of the top players in England at the time. Before leaving South Africa they married quietly on the 18th January and, to avoid the news reaching home via the press, announced their marriage to the rest of the team on the boat when they were returning. A few months later the Godfrees became the first, and only, married couple to win the Wimbledon tennis mixed title, winning 6/3 6/4 against Howard Kinsey and Miss Mary Kendall Browne of the United States. In her own life story, written by Geoffrey Green and published in 1987 (*Kitty Godfree- Lady of a Golden Age*), she recalls another Irish connection. During her many tournament wins she had accumulated some £80 worth of vouchers. With them she bought a diamond ring and, through an Irish boyfriend in the jewellery business, managed to have it converted into cash and buy her real dream. This was a two-seater green open-topped car in which she drove to and from the Irish Open in 1924. For fear of problems with the LTA she only admitted this extravagance to her family some sixty years later.

They still know how to enjoy themselves.
The Fergus LTC reunion at Ennis in July 2000.

There are so many tennis romances but few to come forward with details. A few other Irish ones include Harry Barniville and Geraldine Houlihan. Brian Lawlor and Lucy Meehan had a romantic connection while the UCD team visited the USA in 1976. At Rushbrooke, Redmond O' Donoghue, a useful player, was to meet local organiser Anthea O' Donoghue. They were married a few years later after many mixed matches together. John Garavan met his future wife Ann when she arrived from Dublin for the Open tournament at Castlebar Tennis Club in the later 1950s. John and Angela Horn met through tennis in England, moved to Ireland and fell in love with live here; both were to become honorary Irish persons. John O' Shea and Judy Gallagher did well at Junior Fitzwilliam in 1962. They have now great tennis records at **Monkstown LTC** with children Lisa and Stephen now setting new standards for the family.

On the international front we are all aware of Kim Clijsters (Belgium) and her links with Lleyton Hewitt of Australia, both among the best in the world. Further back in time we have had the marriage of the great Bjorn Borg (Sweden) to Mariana Simonescue of Romania. It was not to last. Most will remember that English heartthrob John Lloyd married US top player Chris Evert in 1979. They divorced in 1987. Top world players Steffi Graf and Andrea Agassi have now married and, while he continues on the world stage, she looks on from the sideline. I'm sure the reader could add many pairs to this brief one.

Back in the 19th century Percy French was to include tennis among his many writings. He knew the social connotations of the game. As he said in writing about

The Irish Championships in *A Fitzwilliam Square Tennis Tournament:*

In the spring the maiden comes in the latest fashions dressed,
In the spring the young man's fancy gets himself a brighter vest;
Any my spirit leaps before me to behold the coming scene,
With the Nation's Tennis players grappling in the central green.

Following an early visit to Fitzwilliam Lawn Tennis Club he penned the following:

'*Everyone her is tennis mad. Tennis teas, Tennis At Homes and Tennis Dances are quite the order of the day; in fact no one has a thought beyond or above them.*

'*Last Thursday a very successful at Home was given by the members of the Fitzwilliam Lawn Tennis Club at the club grounds in Wilton Place. The sun shone delightfully, while the band of the Scottish Highlanders was a great addition.*

He translated many nursery rhymes into tennis ones with his collaborator Richard Orphen adding the appropriate sketches.

Dancing

To add to social intercourse, tennis has always had parties, with dance bands, balls of the ballroom variety, "hooly's", "hops" and, most recently discos. The dance band might even be of the orchestral variety or, in the 1950s and 1960s, a showband on big occasions. In 2000, Vincent Power told their story, warts and all. The title, *Send 'Em Home 'Sweatin*, tells it all. Those that can remember the Miami, the Dixies, the Clipper Carlton et al. will enjoy this book.

An "at home" was another variety of entertainment when a day's tennis was linked to food and social interchange. The more isolated a club was, the more meaningful the tennis dance or party. Where a clubhouse was too small a special event might be held in a local hotel or a marquee erected for the occasion. A few examples might enable the reader to picture the scenes of many locations and changing times. In doing so we might note that the big event was normally once or twice a year, and was looked forward to by all attending. It was as an exclusive affair in the first fifty years of Irish tennis and, in many areas, became a community event in the 1930s and 1940s. It provided an opportunity for members, and others, to meet members of the opposite sex. It was possibly the one chance a young man or woman could home in on a potential date to the cinema. The importance of the event, the likely size of the turn out and availability of suitable venues dictated what music would be provided. On very special occasions it might be an all dress affair i.e. black tie for the gentlemen and expensive new hairstyles and long dresses for the ladies.

Edward McGuire (1901-1992) fondly recalled his dancing days in the 1920s when compiling his memoirs. *I was a very enthusiastic dancer, having acquired a certain proficiency which helped to make me popular with attractive female tennis fans. I was a regular attender at the famous Leggett Byrne academy in Dublin which catered for followers of the Victor Sylvester style of dancing, so much in vogue in the 1920s. I shall always remember with pleasure the parties on the nights when Davis Cup ties were concluded: dining and dancing in Berlin, Copenhagen, Stockholm and Vienna. Being treated as a notable personality was a very pleasant experience indeed.*

Even today, fifty years later, I meet old ladies who tell me how much they enjoyed watching me and my contemporaries in Fitzwilliam. Twice in recent years, when being admitted to Dublin hospitals for surgeries, I have been greeted by the Mother Superior who, in the presence of the nurses about to minister to me, recalled watching me with pleasure from the side-lines of the tennis court. The nurses were suitably impressed and my erstwhile glory made me a V.I.P. patient.

There were, however, some causes of over-enthusiasm. On Davis Cup duty in Germany one year at the famous Roth Weiss Club in Grunervvald, Berlin, I attracted the attention of a German princess. She introduced herself one afternoon after a practice session. I accepted her invitation to her parents' home and afterwards took her out to dinner a few times. Every day she sat alongside the court during our team practice. At first it was quite fun to talk to her and have her to tea together with the other boys, but after a few days her presence became tiresome and a bore. I was beginning to feel trapped. She came

to the final night's tennis dinner and I found it difficult to manage to dance with any of the other women present.

Some famous tennis-playing married couples at Carrickmines Croquet and Lawn Tennis Club

Peter Ledbetter and Paula Mullen

Jim Buckley and Sonja Murphy

Raymund Egan and Pam O'Reilly

Even when I returned to Dublin, her persistence continued. On arriving home with my wife from a dance at three in the morning, I discovered a letter on the hall table, a coat of arms on the envelope. It was from the German princess, telling me that she proposed to attend the forthcoming Irish tennis championships. I telephoned Berlin the next day and it was as much as I could do to persuade her not to come. I succeeded, but that was not the last I heard from her. Towards the end of the Second World War I received a letter telling me things were very bad in Berlin and would I be kind enough to send a parcel of coffee which would be greatly appreciated. I never heard from her again.

The Tennis Ball

Let's look at some of the social activity at a few clubs. The oldest club in the country appears to be **Limerick Lawn Tennis Club** (founded in 1877). Local member and historian George Hehir has been very active and the following is a short extract from his writings that sets the scene in the early days:

Most of the original committee members would, for reasons of business or pleasure, have been frequent visitors to London and would have been familiar with the social trends there.

For some unstated reason the first tournament was postponed for a week and actually took place on Thursday, Friday and Saturday, 2nd, 3rd and 4th August 1877. The report of the tournament, which appeared in the social rather than the sporting columns of the Limerick Chronicle on the Saturday evening, stated that it had been "successful to the highest degree" and had attracted an "unprecedented number of entries, both of Ladies and Gentlemen". We are told that "The attendance also was unusually large, being composed of the 'elite' of the county and city." Finally we learn that the Band of the 82nd Regiment had been present on the Friday and Saturday and had "rendered some fine selections of music........"

In its early days, Lawn tennis was almost entirely the preserve of the wealthy classes. It was fashionable to hold Tennis Parties in the grounds of one's estate and because of the large amount of these estates contiguous to Limerick, together with the influence of regularly changed Army regiments, it is not surprising that the game took off so successfully here........

An indication of the social status which the new game had quickly acquired can be garnered from the prominent reportage which was given to what became, from 1878 on, the social highlight of the tournament week, The Grand Ball, which was usually held in the Royal George Hotel. In the edition of the paper following the event, the Limerick Chronicle usually published a list of the principal attenders and these lists read like a 'who's who' of Limerick and, indeed, Munster society. For instance, heading the list in 1878 were The Earl and Countess of Limerick, Lord and Lady Emly, Lord and Lady Massy, Lord and Lady Fermoy, Lord and Lady Muskerry, Lord Clarina, Lord and Lady Monteagle and Sir Croker Barrington.

This attendance is impressive; it is unlikely that any tennis ball anywhere in this country, or elsewhere, had such an impressive list of lords and ladies. Perhaps an exception might have been The All-England Championships! The tennis competition attracted the best players in Ireland and England. To even matches out, the committee in 1883 introduced a rule that in future all winners of the Wimbledon or Fitzwilliam championships would receive a handicap of minus 15.

At **Fitzwilliam LTC**, the hosts of the Irish Championships since 1879, Master (later Colonel) A. H. Courtenay, was organiser in chief. He became a member in 1879, was Honorary Secretary from 1886 to 1896 and then President from 1896 until 1927. Under his leadership, *everything was carried out in the most perfect style; hospitality was unbounded, and Fitzwilliam Week quickly developed into one of the chief social events of the Dublin year* (Treacy, 1927).

Annual Fitzwilliam LTC function (1920s)

Apart from the attendance of high quality players from home and abroad, there were a large number of dances held during the week at which all attended. During the "season" young ladies from all quarters attended the many social events. Visitors to the city stayed in the Shelbourne Hotel or in some of the big Georgian houses around Fitzwilliam or Merrion Square. *In the mornings, the young ladies would sleep on after their late night but in the afternoon would be up, watching anxiously at the windows for the mounted orderlies who came riding through the streets, delivering invitations to the Castle balls and parties* (O'Connor, 1977). As Percy French was to point out in one of his parodies:

> *Gay were the College Races,*
> *The Lansdowne Sports were gay;*
> *But the great Fitzwilliam Tournament*
> *Is now our whitest day.*

Merville LTC commenced their Annual Cinderella Dances in 1925 to link in with the end of the season and the presentation of prizes. Late nights were guaranteed and the event was held at the Café Cairo or Lyons Café. In 1925 *the music was supplied by O'Hara's Syncopated Orchestra and, in 1929, they still played: first-class music being supplied by Mr.P. O'Hara's Syncopated Orchestra.*

In 1941 George Hamilton immigrated from

Ballisodare to England. He is now (2001) retired in County Wicklow. His memories are vivid. Kathleen Clifford tried to teach him to do the Old-Time Waltz at the tennis club (**Woodville LTC** in Ballisodare, County Sligo) during the summer of 1941.

I worked near Cheltenham, within a week or two I strolled into the ballroom there, where one of the BBC bands was playing. I felt a bit intimidated by the size of the ballroom and the orchestra in their dress suits, my previous experience of a palatial dance hall having been confined to the Plaza in Strandhill. I think Pat O'Hara who played there had a trumpet and a drummer and he himself swung every tune on a home-made fiddle.

The Band struck up the "Blue Danube" and I could hear Kathleen Clifford say "One, two, three, One two three....". Indeed, it was this thought, which inspired me to advance towards an English damsel, and in my best Carrickbanagher/Knockbeg accent "May I have the pleasure of this dance?" She rose and faced me. Her left hand found my right one and we twirled away, turning and reversing. Our feet moved in unison and the maple floor seemed to spring with each step to this well-known waltz.

I felt as if I were floating on air. My enchantment was short lived. A Slow-Foxtrot was announced and after my success in the Waltz, I was now convinced that my feet were the masters of the music and not its slaves. Brimming with confidence, I searched for the best-looking girl in the room and steered her to the edge of the floor. As I lead off with my right foot she did likewise-tragedy straightaway! We tripped and I nobly apologised for what was her mistake. From that moment my feet just would not obey the music. We staggered half-way around the floor then she let go of me and stepping backward she scowled "Did you 'dance' or 'play about'?" Those were her exact words and I have never forgotten them. I was alone in the middle of the floor-as she raced away I am sure I heard "To Hell or to Connaught with you". Dancers were going slow, slow, slow, quick, quick, slow, all round me. Trying to avoid collisions, I eventually reached the side of the floor cursing all women. Just in time I remembered those sweet souls in the Ballisodare Tennis pavilion who taught me how to waltz as Johann Strauss intended. I felt very homesick. Perhaps it was the hurt to my pride on foreign soil. Fifteen years later a Dublin friend asked me to come with him on a blind date. He called for me with his girlfriend and her friend. As I opened the rere door of the car, the introduction was made "George, this Kathleen". It was none other than Kathleen Clifford, the world's best Old-Time Waltz instructor.

Hidden away in the far west is the town of Belmullet. It now has an excellent golf course, attracting visitors to this most scenic of regions. Distances, and a poor road structure, meant that entertainment had to be self-sufficient. According to Maire Dixon (nee Coleman) the founding of the tennis club was ***the greatest social happening in this Mayo town ever.*** This was in the 1940s. She can recall her first dance at the age of sixteen; it was the Tennis Dance in

James's Hall, a major (if not *the major*) social event of the year.

Cavehill LTC social function (Circa 1960)

The Hop

The tennis *hop* is remembered fondly by many tennis players over the age of, say, forty. Those younger will think in terms of discos. One gentleman of the 1960s, not a tennis player, was eligible to attend the local hop. If you were in with the local boys then an invitation to the summer hop, or hops, was on the cards. The local committee might let you in if you were 'respectable' and known. Times were relatively innocent but the 'sexual revolution' was on the way. They probably said the same thing in the 1920s.

TENNIS DANCE.
TOWN HALL, SLIGO,
Tuesday, 28th July, 1925.
TICKETS:
Gentlemen, 7s 6d; Ladies, .5s; Double, 10s.
Dancing 10 p.m. to 6 a.m.
Dublin Band.   Running Buffet.
Tickets from A. C. Cook, A. M. Lyons, H. R. Wood-Martin, W. T. Phibbs, A. P. Jackson.

In conjunction with the annual open (now the West of Ireland) the County Sligo Lawn Tennis Club held several social functions. The 1925 'Tennis Dance' was a lively affair with dancing until "6 a. m.". (Advert in the local paper on 25th July 1925).

Anyway, the attraction of such events was that one was likely to meet 'nice' girls; certainly all the local attractive ones would be there. One is sure the girls, in their conclaves, had the same notion about the local boys. Males would not normally be privy to such views. All would have their "best gear" on for the night. How far one could go dress wise was related to the fashions of the time. In the early days of the Beatles long hair would have been frowned upon. Eventually, a few years later, even the tennis players would have long hair, later in a ponytail, and would be allowed in. We are talking about the boy's hair by the way. In the previous era, the Elvis hairstyle and the winkle pickers would have got the bums rush but, invariably, would be later accepted. In the case of the

This 1898 photograph was taken at the Bad Homborg tournament in Germany. Irishman, Harold Mahony (with racquet) was known to be a ladies' man. He beat Joshua Pim in the final (also Irish).

1963- Young players relaxing courtside at Co. Longford LTC. The group includes Eamon Dinneen, Dennis Crotty, Paddy Quinn, Patrick Quinn, Geraldine Connolly, Frances Crotty & Una Connellan.

Merville LTC (1940s)
Left:(l. to r.): Patsy Nash, Dalton McElroy and Maeve Flattery.

Right: Gerry Westby (on left) leads the musicans.

1997 tournament organisers at Enniskillen LTC were (from left) Mara O'Reilly, Dympna Slowey, Mary Fee and Mary Davidson.

Young members relaxing at the Fergus Lawn Tennis Club in Ennis in the 1950s.

girls, the 'frocks' of the 1950s would be replaced by Twiggy's mini-skirts.

An interesting view of one such attendee was as follows. His town had its tennis clubs and hops, mainly attended by boys and girls from the local convent and the Catholic boys' school. However, not twenty miles away, was a tennis club whose hop had a different clientele. There, the girls were not from convent schools. These would be particularly desirable, so I hear from the horse's mouth. It was thought that such girls were not subject to the same moral rigours inculcated in the convent girls. That is, they were more likely to provide opportunities for that French kiss. In addition, petting or fondling was likely to progress further. That was the theory. Can you the reader verify this difference or was it just an innocent myth? Teenagers of the 1960s stand up and own up!

At Home

The "At Home" was a feature of many clubs for so many years. In the days of home entertaining in polite society this term 'At Home' meant that on a specific day of the week, and between certain hours, the host or hostess, would be in their own home. Visitors would call and leave as they pleased. There would therefore be a circuit of places to call to during the week. The Oxford English Dictionary (1989) notes the terms use as far back as 1483 (or even earlier). An interesting reference in *the Etiquette of Good Society* (1880) says *In the country a bride's first appearance in church is taken as a sign that she is 'At home'.*

In the minutes book of the **Clontarf LTC** we find a number of social events enumerated. The 1894 minutes book records that it was decided that "whiskey be added to the list of drinks authorised to be supplied only to adult members of the Club and to be sold at the rate of 3d per half glass". For the "At Home" Mrs. White of Tivoli was invited to present the prizes and a Military Band was engaged. The following year's "At Home" saw a Miss Vernon presenting the prizes and a 'smoking concert' was arranged to help clear the building debt to Brooks Thomas. In 1896 (the "At Home" again) Mrs. Stuart looked after the teas, Mrs. Graham distributed the prizes and music was provided by the West Kent Regiment. Clontarf had a great variety of music for their special days: 1897: the Band of the R.I.C.; 1898: the Band of the Bedforshire Regiment; 1899: the Argyll and Sutherlanders band; 1900: the Band of the 21st Lancers and in 1904 the Band of the 6th Enniskillen Dragoons. There were many more. The Wiltshire Regiment (The Buffs) provided music for the "At Home" on the 29th July 1911 when the Gents Championship was contested between S. E. Polden and E. S. Lowe the honorary secretary. A marquee was hired in 1919 and in 1920. In 1922 dancing was again sanctioned during the winter (*good for raising money*).

This enterprising club had a profit of £23-15-6 in 1935, selling raffle tickets at 6d each. The prize was a sea cruise on the SS Montrose leaving for South Africa on Saturday the 28th September. In 1936 we see that, because of the advice of Mr. Lavery K. C. to the ILTA, tickets had to be issued to those wishing to invite friends to Tennis Dances. On the 7th July 1937 the club held its Jubilee day. During the afternoon music was provided by St. George's Brass Band. *At 9pm our Jubilee Dance commenced in a marquee 75' x 30' and continued until 2 a.m. Music was supplied by Charlie Nutty's Band, and the supper was ably served in the Pavilion by the Ladies Committee.*

A resolution to hold Sunday dances was defeated at an EGM in 1943. There were obvious cut backs in all sorts of ways during the war years. The *At Home* was still held with some members undertaking to provide butter, the Ladies were asked to contribute one or two teaspoonfuls of tea each. A policeman was hired to keep an eye on things.

Club "At Homes"

TANEY

Championships — Singles — W. J. Clayton bt. R. Orr, 6-3; 7-5. Miss G. Carson bt Miss C. Taylor, 7-9, 6-0 9-7. Junior—J. Howe bt A Gregory, 6-2 6-3.

Handicap winners—A. R. Taylor and R. Patterson; Miss H. Robertson and Miss D. Orr; J. Paul and Miss J Ruddock.

SANDYFORD

Championships—Singles — J. Duff bt. R. O'Connell, 6-4, 8-6; Miss B. Little bt. Miss B. Duff, 6-3, 6-3.

Handicap winners — H. McLoughlin and W. Cullinane; Misses B. Little and B. Duff, R. O'Connell and Miss B Duff.

GARDA

CHAMPIONSHIPS—Singles—N. Mountaine bt. P. J. Sheerin 8-6, 8-10, 3-6, 6-4, 6-4. Miss K. Butler bt Miss M. Timmons 3-6, 6-4, 6-4. Doubles — N. Mountaine and S. Cunningham bt. T. Dixon and M. Sexton 6-2 4-6, 6-4. Miss K. Timmons and Miss A. Whelan bt. Miss J. Kinsella and Miss M. McGloughlin 9-7, 5-7, 6-0.

SANDYCOVE

CHAMPIONSHIPS—Singles—S. Cullen bt. S. Breen, 8-6, 6-4; Mrs. E. Foley bt. Miss I. Breen, 6-4, 4-6, 6-2. Doubles—S. Cullen and F. Martin bt. J. O'Shea and B. Henderson, 6-3, 6-4.

TRITONVILLE

CHAMPIONSHIPS—Singles—J. Smyth bt. R. Beckett, 6-3, 8-6 6-3; Miss E. Anderson bt. Miss M. Hade, 6-3, 6-3. Doubles — Beckett and S. Conneff bt. Smyth and J. Johnston, 6-3. 6-1, 9-7. Misses M. Odlum and S. Moffett bt. Misses M Rippengale and J. Callan, 5-7, 6-3, 6-2. Smyth and Miss Anderson bt. J. Jorgensen and Miss Odlum, 6-3, 7-5.

13th September 1959

"At Home's"

LEINSTER—STRATFORD

CHAMPIONSHIPS—Singles—W. Pappin beat C. Trinder 9-7, 6-4, 6-3; Mrs. H. Squires beat Miss V. Kelly 6-1, 8-6. Doubles—L. Belford and W. Pasley beat Trinder and Pappin 4-6, 6-1, 6-4, 7-5. Mrs. W Pappin and Mrs. Squires beat Misses Kelly and Margetson 6-1, 6-3. W. Pasley and Mrs. H. Squires beat C. Trinder and Miss R. Allison 7-9, 6-0, 6-3.

THORNDALE

CHAMPIONSHIPS — Singles — K. Bray beat B. Leech 2-6, 6-2, 7-5, 6-3; Miss P. Reynolds beat Miss E. Leech 8-6, 6-4. Doubles—J. Bray and B. Leech beat J. Byrne and C. Nordell 6-4, 7-5. Misses U. Harris and M. O'Connor beat Misses B. Young and D. Lawless 0-6, 6-4, 6-4.

LANSDOWNE

CHAMPIONSHIPS—Singles—M. Hickey beat J. O'Brien 6-4, 6-3; Miss M. O'Sullivan beat Miss H. Bretland 6-2, 6-3. Doubles—Hickey and U. Lyons beat J. De Courcy and M. Bruton, 6-3, 8-6; Misses B. Lombard and D. McNamara beat Misses A. Huet and J. Shields 6-0, retired; A. Burns and Miss J. Kennedy beat C. O'Brien and Miss H. Bretland, 6-3, 4-6, 6-2.

MONKSTOWN

Championships—Singles, E. Cahill bt. A Davy, 6-2, 6-3. Mrs N O'Doherty bt. Mrs. F. Blair, 6-4, 6-2. Doubles—E. Cahill and A. Davy bt. E. McGettrick and D. Hughes, 6-3, 6-4. Mrs. N O'Doherty and Mrs F Blair bt Misses S. Coleary and G. McGuinness 6-3, 5-7, 6-2 Davy and Mrs. Blair bt. D. Balfe and Miss A. Delahunt, 6-4, 6-4.

CLAREMONT

Championships — Singles — M. F. Davitt bt. T. Buggy 6-4, 6-4, 6-1; Miss V. H. Gillespie bt. Mrs. P. Clarke, 7-5, 6-2. Doubles—D. P. Foley and T. Buggy bt. A. R. Gillespie and C. F. Davitt, 6-4, 3-6, 7-5, 6-2; Miss V. H. Gillespie and Miss V. McMullen w.o. Miss B. Thompson and Mrs. P. Clarke scr.; A. R. Gillespie and Miss Gillespie bt. T. Buggy and Miss H. Browne, 6-4, 6-3.

BLACKROCK

Championships — Singles — P. Galligan bt. M. O'Riordan, 6-4, 6-2, 6-2; Miss J. Martin bt. Miss K. Perry, 6-1, 6-1; Galligan and D. Jones bt. O'Riordan and J. Lawler, 6-4, 6-3, 6-2; Misses June and Jacqueline Martin bt. Miss D. O'Brien and Miss A. Kennedy, 8-6, 11-9; O'Riordan and Miss C. Fenlon bt. C. Ryan and Jacqueline Martin, 2-6, 6-2, 7-5.

LONGFORD GARDENS

Championship — Singles—G. J. O'Shaughnessy bt. F. Garvey, 9-7, 6-2, 6-2. Miss M. Smithwick bt. Miss A. Patten, 6-1, 6-1. Doubles—O'Shaughnessy and A. E. Timmons bt. F. Garvey and P. J. Lyons, 6-2, 6-2. P. J. Lyons and Miss M. Smithwick bt. Timmons and Miss Z. Smalldridge 6-0, 6-1

L. C. C.

CHAMPIONSHIPS — Singles: W. Browne bt. J. Lombard, 6-2, 8-6, 6-2. Miss R. Maher bt. Miss M. Cahill. 6-3, 6-3. Doubles—J. Lombard and C. Kevany bt. W. Browne and S. O'Brien, 6-4, 1-6, 4-6, 6-2, 6-2. Misses M. Cahill and N. Mullen bt. Miss N. Kelly and Mrs. K. Kevany, 6-2 6-4; W. Browne and Miss Cahill bt. S. O'Brien and Miss I. Murphy 6-2, 9-11, 6-2.

FAIRVIEW G.Y.M.S.

CHAMPIONSHIPS—Singles—J Carey beat C. Dunne 6-4, 6-4, 4-6, 6-1; Miss M. Murphy beat Miss L. Ambrose 6-4, 6-4. Doubles—Miss M. McLoughlin and L. Murray beat Miss T. Booth and E. Mulligan 7-5, 6-3; T. Pidgeon and B. Murphy beat B. Hampson and B. Fitzsimmons 7-5, 6-4.

GLASNEVIN

CHAMPIONSHIPS—Singles—J. O'Sullivan bt. W. Lawlor 6-1, 3-6, 6-2, 9-7; Miss F. Keegan bt. Miss J. Mahony 6-2, 6-1. Doubles—Misses F. Keegan and J. Mahony bt. Misses G. Avaldi and M. O'Mahony 6-3, 6-2.

6th September 1959

At the Sligo Tennis Club's 21st Anniversary Ball in 1999 were (from left) Ursula Higgins, Olivia Kenny, Dr. Donal Smyth and Michael Whelan.

The accompaniment of the May's string band. In 1907, however, the annual dance was abandoned as only 43 people were willing to take the floor but five years later they were in party mood again and cavorted at the Café Cairo. The first club 'At home' and club tournament was held in 1894. For many years this was the club's big annual event. Astounding as it may seem, in 1895 some *600 people attended* the day's events. A marquee (50 feet by 30 feet) was erected.

Guests were invited from other clubs. The press were also invited. A noteworthy attendee at the 1927 'At Home' was William Butler Yeats.

The army bands no longer play at tennis club tournaments, "at homes" or otherwise. The equivalent of the "at home" is probably the finals of the club championships- "finals day" which will be followed by a presentation and function. Dressing up to watch tennis in one's best finery is not usual. Any dressing up will be for the club function. The principle is the same, the format just appears different.

"Anyone for Ennis?"

The **Fergus LTC** held a re-union in July 2000 with many memories relived by the large attendance. An excellent booklet was prepared for the event with a series of anecdotes included. Tom Mannion, a prominent member in the 1950s, recalled the hops and allied matters in his contribution.

These were held at the old club house every Saturday night with an entrance fee of one shilling and three pence in the early days but later increased to one and six. The increase gave rise to controversy from some of our members who objected to the "exorbitant" increase which resulted in some members intentionally arriving late and paying the original entrance fee, claiming that they had missed over an hour's dancing. To ensure that the new charge was implemented in its entirety, yours truly, as treasurer at the time, used to call to individuals after the weekend to collect the extra three pence. Music for the socials was provided by the McMahon brothers and Miko Ball. I acted as MC for the hops during which we used to have many fun dance variations such as "Statue Dance", "Mistletoe Dance" and the "Excuse Me Dance".

Frank (Diver) McNamara was always in charge of the mineral bar which consisted of crates of minerals outside the corner shed.

Tom then mentions the two fundraising dances held each year, in the Hydro Hotel in Kilkee and the Old Thomond Hotel in Lisdoonvarna. They also had an annual black tie dinner dance at the Old Ground Hotel in Ennis. He recalls a 21st birthday as follows. It paints a picture:

A prominent member of our club at the time, and a great accordion player, had his 21st birthday party in his parents' home in Co. Limerick. The Daffy Brothers, Andy and Allen, provided a Vauxall car, which in some strange way was capable of carrying

Dublin tennis "at home's"

ANGLESEA
CHAMPIONSHIPS—Singles—R Shortall beat T. McGirr, 7-5, 6-3, 4-6, 6-3; Miss V. Barry beat Miss N. Butler, 6-4, 8-6. Doubles—T. J. Ryan and S. Egan beat W. Dwyer and H. Vickery 6-3, 8-6, 6-4

BECTIVE
CHAMPIONSHIPS—Singles—J. O'Connell beat B. McHugh, 6-4, 6-4, 6-1; Miss M. Kearns beat Miss Gough, 2-6, 6-2, 6-3.

GLENAGEARY
CHAMPIONSHIPS — Singles — S. K. McComas bt. J. H. De Lacey 6-3, 6-8, 7-5; Mrs. O. Briggs bt. Mrs. J. Marks 6-4, 2-6, 6-3. Doubles — McComas and B. Watchorn bt. De Lacey and H. D. Legge 6-4, 6-2; Miss C. Robinson and Mrs. B. Murray bt. Mrs. Briggs and Miss N. Buchanan 6-2, 8-6. Mixed—De Lacey and Miss Buchanan bt. McComas and Mrs. Briggs 6-2, 6-4.

GLENANNE
CHAMPIONSHIPS—Junior Boys'—T Murphy bt. D. O'Doherty, 6-1, 6-0 Girls'—N. Dunne bt. E. Meehan, 6-3, 6-1. Juvenile Boys — E. O'Doherty bt. J O'Connor, 6-2, 3-6, 6-3. Girls' —M Quirke bt. T. Rowsome, 6-0, 6-4 HANDICAPS—Juveniles — J. O'Connor bt. J. Meehan 6-4, 6-4; N. Lawson bt T. Rowsome 6-3, 6-3. Mixed—O'Connor and Miss C. Merren bt. V. O'Toole and Miss Y. Fox 6-4, 6-4

MOUNT TEMPLE
CHAMPIONSHIPS — Singles — G. D. Fitzpatrick bt B Barry, 6-0, 6-1; Mrs. J. C. Dawson bt. Mrs. K. Dunne, 6-4, 2-6, 7-5. Mixed H'cap Doubles—G. McNamara and Miss M. Ryan bt. H. Cummins and Mrs. K. Dunne, 6-4, 6-1.

23rd August 1959

In December 1943 **Clontarf Lawn Tennis Club** held a masked fancy dress ball, there was no admission unless properly attired and masks were to be worn until midnight. 1948 saw some complaints when members were drinking in the kitchen during club dances. It was also noted in the centenary book that, in the very early days of the club, the all male committee organised a croquet competition for the ladies during the 'At Home' in order *to keep them entertained while the men got on with the serious business of drinking and Tennis.*

At **Donnybrook LTC**, *Club dances went in and out of popularity. One of the first was held in November 1894 in the Pillar Room where 260 people waltzed to*

11 passengers (yes 11) who duly made the trip. On the return journey at 6 a.m. we got a puncture at Ballycasey Cross, but had no spare. The accordion was taken out and we danced a half-set on the Junction Road which was witnessed and photographed by American visitors, who probably thought we were all mad, but we weren't really……just enjoying ourselves.

Jerry Cahir had also many vivid pictures to paint. Memories from the 1940s into the 1960s:

Apart from the cut and trust of the rivalry of tennis matches, tournaments and championships the club's Victorian wooden pavilion was the gathering place on balmy summer evenings for the weekly "hops" when boy met girl and learned and applied the art of dancing to old time waltzes, quick steps, fox trots and the very popular jiving and rock and roll.

We greatly admired the teddy boys with their sleek oil brushed-back hairstyles, drainpipe trousers and chunky suede shoes, few of us had the courage to join

their ranks. Courting, shifting and doing a line were the in words of this romance era and drugs (referred to as medicine) were only taken when prescribed by doctors and dispensed by chemists for their sick children.

Many a romance flourished to a longer commitment. However, this was balanced by the many vocations to the priesthood and convents. Whereas many took over family businesses and stayed in town, many left for other parts of Ireland, Britain and Europe, the USA and as far away as the West Indies, Hong Kong and other exotic places where they carved out successful careers in the public service, industry, politics, the professions (medical, legal, accountancy, science, dentistry etc.)

Sometimes the social gatherings of the club spilled over into house teenage parties. There was so much competition in this area that venues often clashed and loyalties were strained in having to make choices. I remember gangs of us, male and female, setting off on long cycles and enjoying picnics. High nellies were much in vogue among the females, as their modesty had to be protected as demanded by the dress code of the period……….I remember the famous camping holiday in Kilkee and that wonderful leaking tent which was our home and castle as we entertained our female contemporaries to alfresco food and drink.

The Hangers On

John Gallagher was one of the non-playing tennis followers at the club in Ennis. While he may have been involved in other sports, he appreciated the value of the tennis club. He too appreciated the gathering of the tennis followers at the big re-union in 2000.

Many of us were engaged in different sports – golf, swimming, GAA etc., but gravitated to the tennis club because that was where most of the good-looking women congregated. It seems funny now, after forty

years,that I can't remember a rainy day. I can remember fine days sitting on the grass or on the steps watching Diver foostering around the place and keeping a friendly eye on all of us.

The Saturday hops were the highlight of the week. It was there that I first started stumbling towards dancing, taught by Mary Quinn. I'm delighted now to be able to say thank you to her. I can remember the heat, the frantic gyrations and the envy at Tom Mannion as he swept around. Sometimes, when he dropped his partner on his knee, I have to admit that I wished she might have broken it!

It was an age of innocence in which hearts were lifted and broken with a casualness that bore no malice. It was a time when a bottle of orange indicated strong interest and holding hands a definite commitment.

As hangers on we were never made to feel awkward or unwelcome and I would like to thank the tennis members for that. I am grateful; also that Jerry Cahir decided to include us in this get-together.

Before leaving the social side of Ennis of long ago, an interesting piece was penned by D. Travers, described as the Dirty-minded Ard na Greine Boy. Was the name a pseudonym; was he in fact a tennis player? His memory was clear on girls, Woodbines and related matters. A story that might have been told by many others, perhaps not with the same detail. If the clergy of the time only knew what young minds were up to perhaps there might have been a ban on tennis clubs!

The tennis club in the 50s was one of the few places where young people of both genders could meet ("sexes" would seem to be an inappropriate term for those times). For the opportunistic (or predatory!) among us, it offered glimpses of the other sex not easily available to us by any other means. Other lesser opportunities were a bit of pushing and shoving of Convent of Mercy girls off the footpath on the way home from school, or the possibility of some mingling for a bit of "ecumenical" activity in the Pro-Cathedral gallery during confraternity!

But these were a much lesser form of pastime. The tennis club offered visions of youthful beauty at play. This meant opportunities for the inactive and prurient to get a glimpse above a knee of blue knickers and sometimes (oh joy) a bit of elastic!

Later at the hop, the self-same would coyly but alluringly enrobed in seersucker or waffle cotton topped with an alice-band. Those of us who watched and prayed might be consoled by a shared Woodbine and the occasional swig of a fortified glass of Hassetts or Downs & Howard red lemonade.

There is no question that sporting activity of the mixed variety has always been an opportunity for the natural mixing of the sexes. Victorian fathers saw this when tennis became the new pastime. The game of tennis was a bit more active than croquet, yet it was suitable for young ladies. Quickly, the young ladies took it on board despite the fact that it was to be several decades before women's tennis was taken seriously. The court, the tennis parties, the mixed doubles and the tea and cakes would all ideally congeal. Romance regularly followed. Many things in life have changed but that basic connection between tennis and an opportunity for social interchange has thankfully remained.

Fans

Sports fans are not a new phenomenon. Most sports attract fellow-competitors, followers of the sport, cameramen and television, reporters and 'fans'. Part and parcel of modern sport is the fact that it is a spectator event that requires exposure. The publicity and sponsorship are sometimes more important than the result itself. Certainly, in the era of widespread professional sport, income to the sport is important. The sports men and women are today very aware of their crucial role in promoting their sport through interviews, fan clubs, signing autographs etc.

In the 1920s one of the biggest tennis events ever was the match between superstars Susan Lenglen and Helen Wills in the south of France. The Burke brothers were the primary promoters of this match between the top two ladies' in the world. It became a tennis match all tennis fans wished to attend. Some details are given elsewhere in this book. Tennis stars have had their fans for many decades. 'Henman Hill' at Wimbledon has probably many tennis admirers who have never held a tennis racquet in their lives. [Renamed Murray Field in 2005]. Their presence is part of the continuing attraction of a game with a public who can understand the scoring, get involved and enjoy the occasion. Some tennis players, like stars of the cinema and the pop world, attract large numbers of fans. Evonne Goolagong, Bjorn Borg, Pat Rafter, Gabriela Sabatini, Anna Kournikova and Roger Federer are some of the players in recent decades with more than their share of followers. Have we ever had Irish players with 'star' status? The answer is yes. In the early days of the sport Irishmen, such as Joshua Pim and Harold Mahony, who were champions at Wimbledon had their fans.

In the 1920s Edward McGuire was one of our top tennis players and had his share of admirers. In his memoirs he records the following on the matter of fans.

Like all prominent athletes, I was the subject of attention from the female sex, young and old. Tennis, of course, is a highly individual sport, where one is like and actor on a theatre stage performing before an audience. Schoolgirls were keen to get my autograph, but this could be quite onerous at times. They swarmed around with autograph albums or pieces of paper immediately after I had finished a hard match, and with my hand sweating and shaking it was difficult to perform more than a scribbled imitation of my well-formed signature, in which I took some.....pride. After a Davis Cup fixture in Fitzwilliam I might have to sign for seventy or more schoolgirls, who were brought en masse to the International games dressed in their navy blue uniforms and light blue hats. It was hard work....but very flattering, and I would not have missed it for anything. My first experience of what would now be called a fan came in 1924. I was single and living with my parents in Cambridge House and had just been selected for Ireland's Davis Cup team. Four or five times a week, the telephone would ring at seven o'clock in the evening and a most attractive female voice proceeded to tell me how much she was interested in me and my tennis. She never revealed who she was, but if she was as charming as her voice, she must have been worth getting to know. Sadly, from the day that my engagement to be married was publicly announced, the telephone went silent. I never heard from her again.

Other fans appeared on the way, a surprise one being the radio presenter, Joe Linnane. *More recently, I heard for the first time that the late Joe Linnane, the well-known Radio Eireann personality was a fan of mine. He revealed this on the air on 28 August 1981. In congratulating me on the occasion of my 80th birthday, he told how, as a young boy, he used to gaze in awe over the walls at Fitzwilliam. He could not-or would not! -pay the entrance fee to see me in action. It was probably more exciting to view the games from the top of the walls without paying in. Stolen apples can be sweeter.*

Maeve Flattery(Sligo) and partner (possibly Harry Thulier) enjoy this tennis dance (c. 1950)

Fitzwilliam Lawn Tennis Club (c. 1990)
All dressed up for the evening.

The tennis court side was always an opportunity to socialise, romance often followed. This photo was taken at Merville LTC (c. 1950). From left: Myra Nash(?), Sally Harte, Maria Boland, Patsy Nairn, Peter Coleman and Tommy Nairn.

The most beautiful thing I have ever seen is Helen Wills playing tennis. (Charlie Chaplin, on the American player who won the Irish Open in 1938).

Mixed doubles are always starting divorces. If you play with your wife, you fight with her. If you play with somebody else, she fights with you. (American Sidney Wood, the 1931 Wimbledon champion).

County Cavan LTC (c. 1895). Percy French (far right) met his wife Ettie Armytage Moore at a local tennis party.

The History of Irish Tennis

3.3.2   *Religion and Tennis*

Most of the members in those days belonged to the upper classes and were mainly of
one religious persuasion, a situation which prevailed until well into the 1930s
(Jim Duff, in Sutton LTC Centenary Booklet, 1982)

Ireland is not unique in that religion has, past and present, a bearing on social activity. Tennis had its place in an evolving cultural change and few lines on the subject are appropriate.

Just before the First World War, the relatively new Irish Lawn Tennis Association was developing quickly. The growth of tennis had slowed down a bit in the early part of the century but in Ireland it would flourish again. It became an organised sport on the national and international stage. The Irish Free State had not been established, but the Gaelic League had lead to a strengthening of indigenous Irish culture. This included the sports of Gaelic football, hurling and athletics. No one knows exactly, but the number of Catholics playing the game was low even though the game was strongly supported by some of the top Irish Catholic schools such as Clongowes Wood College in County Kildare. The Irish census in 1911 shows that there were 4.39 million people living on the island of whom 3.24 million were Roman Catholics (73.86%), 0.58 millions were Anglican (13.13%), 0.44 million (10.04%) were Presbyterian and 'Others' consisted of 0.13 million (2.97%).

There were 79 clubs affiliated to the ILTA in 1914. Twenty-eight of these had an average membership of 84. Based upon this figure, a guesstimated school playing population of 500, and perhaps another 1000 players playing in a few unaffiliated clubs and some local groups playing on private courts dotted throughout the country, the playing population was about 9,000 for the island.

The social distinctions between the well off, mainly non-Catholics, and sport were still strong. One would safely assume, therefore, that the number of Catholics playing the sport was less than 10%, and perhaps less than 5%. In the **Sutton LTC** centenary brochure of 1982, Jim Duff would make the following comment when referring to an 1884 photograph of club members: *A glance at the list of names would appear to confirm the opinion that most of the members in those days belonged to the upper classes and were mainly of one religious persuasion, a situation which prevailed until well into the 1930s.*

Interestingly, there were probably, in the 19th century, large numbers of Catholics playing cricket. At one time it was the primary sport at the Catholic school of St. Mel's Diocesan College, Longford. Soccer was equally popular in the many garrison towns throughout the island. These were affordable sports and 'team' sports. Lawn tennis on the other hand, derived much of its early players from 'big houses' where the earlier pastime of croquet was played on smooth lawns. Very few Catholics were to be found here, apart from the servants and gardeners.

Church Groups

Protestant communities would develop pastimes and sports through their church groups. This reflected society activity rather than sporting ones. Catholic society was, in the main, parish based, and would have its dual focus in both the Gaelic Athletic Association and the Gaelic League. Neither of these organisations was exclusively Catholic in membership. Charles Stewart Parnell (1844-1891) was a Protestant and was deemed to be *the most effective parliamentary leader of the Catholic people* (O'Brien & O'Brien, 1992). In response to a letter from Michael Cusack, when he was being asked to be a Patron of the newly form Gaelic Athletic Association, his reply included the comment *It gives me great pleasure to learn that a "Gaelic Association" has been established for the preservation of National Pastimes, with the objects of which I entirely concur.*

It was only natural that clubs that were established around a particular religious community would have members solely from that church group. These clubs included sports such as lawn tennis, croquet, badminton and table tennis. An occasional golf club would fit into this category also. At least twenty clubs at one stage had the word parish or a particular religion in their title. Some examples include **Ballynafeigh Methodist Church, Belfast Jewish Institution, Church of Ireland (Cork), Gilnahirk Presbyterian Church Recreational Club and Newry Catholic LTC.** In addition, there were over twenty other clubs called after a saint's name and likely to be associated with a religious community. It can be also pointed out that club's were linked to other social factors such as a club founded by the members of a particular work or educational organisation. Examples include the **Ulster College of Physical Education, Victoria Barracks LTC, Hospital TC (Letterkenny), CIE (Cork) LTC** and **Collins Barracks TC** (formerly the **Garrison TC**) in Cork City. The sports of boating, golf, rugby, Gaelic games, athletics, bowling, cricket, croquet, badminton, squash, pitch & putt and hockey are to be found as either the primary club with a tennis section or both on an equal footing. There are probably others. Clubs in other categories include the **H.M.S. Sea Eagle TC,** the **Aero LTC** (Coleraine), **Sion Mills Recreation Centre TC,** the **Irish Evergreens TC** and the **Greenisland War Memorial Committee Centre TC.**

Clubs have evolved in quite a number of ways. The religious element is linked. It has been thought that many clubs would not accept Catholics as members. A note in the history of **Glenageary LTC** centenary brochure seems to sum up the situation in many clubs. *Although-and contrary to an assumption that has sometimes been made in later years-membership* of the early twentieth century was never exclusively Protestant, it was predominantly so and seems also to have been strongly loyalist in support of the establishment of the day. Naturally clubs, which were exclusively church based, would often maintain that exclusivity. An interesting view of the religious connection to the sport can be found in the **Brookfield LTC** history, published in 1998, a club nearing its centenary year.

> *A steady decline set in during the 1960s and membership reached its lowest ebb in 1970 with 81 Seniors and 13 Juniors. Why did this happen? Possibly because of an increase in alternative attractions (golf, sailing, weekend cottages etc.) and also younger families were moving out to the suburbs. However, a major factor must have been the club's policy of restricting membership to members of the Protestant community. This was the policy of a number of other sports and social clubs, and was a reaction to the Catholic church's Ne Temere decree.*

Experience Abroad

Edward (McGuire) (1901-1992) was a success Irish Davis Cup in the 1920s and 1930s. He noted in his memoirs many aspects of the game, and related matters. He came in contact with many players of many nationalities. While in Austria for the Davis Cup in 1924 he noted the distinct social status of tennis. However, the following piece he recalls is a direct discrimination based upon religious persuasion.

While attending the Leipzig Trade Fair in 1932 I quickly realised that tennis was no exception to the rule of social disadvantage suffered by Germany's Jewish population on the eve of Hitler's rise to power. Jews wishing to play tennis in Leipzig had to form a club of their own. In Berlin, where the Blue Weiss Club practised discrimination, the Rot Weiss became a mainly Jewish club. In England, Ireland and all over the world, this kind of discrimination is not unknown and social and sporting clubs are slow to admit Jewish applications. Jews then come together to form their own clubs and societies and many of the world's finest tennis and golf clubs have been created as a result.

In the case of Kaufmann, the fur dealer with whom I stayed in Leipzig, I was asked to have him proposed for membership of Queen's Club, one of London's best tennis and social centres. A friend of mine in the club agreed to do so. Kaufmann received an application form from the secretary and his name was posted on the club notice board. He was duly elected a member. Another Jew who left Germany for London at that time was Daniel Press, a member of the famous Davis Cup team with Von Cramm and Henkel. Prenn made a great success in London's commercial world and became very rich. Godfried Von Cramm was no lover of the Nazis; indeed he was very much under the shadow of the Gestapo. He was even arrested (for alleged homosexuality) but was

later released and after the war he continued to play International tennis. Nazi thugs could count on no assistance or cooperation from a true gentleman such as Von Cramm.

Free State

An interesting series of changes took place when the Irish Free State formed. In the period 1920 to 1950, a freedom to have a separate identity in many areas of the republic would result in clubs arising from a Catholic base. In Boyle, for example, where the early **Boyle LTC** was formed in 1887, a second club was to be established. The original club had as its President the Right Honourable Colonel E. R. King-Harman, MP. It was a club built for the 'society' people of the region. The Boyle Catholic Club (founded in 1914) decided at a meeting in December 1934 that it might attract more members if tennis courts were built at the rear of the club premises. This church based club, using a loan financed by the church, built these new courts the following year. This was the foundation of the present club, now known as the **Boyle Community TC** and has no barriers to members from any religion. **Fitzwilliam LTC** was always at the forefront in terms of Irish tennis development, including the introduction of a women's event in the Irish Championships in 1879. It is noted, however, that until the 1990s that only men could become members. Similarly, it was a club where social standing was important. Military members were more than welcome, of the officer variety. Membership from 'trade' appeared to be have been first welcomed after the Second World War. However, back in 1912 and 1913 we see that Val Miley, a Catholic, was club champion. The right sex and social standing mattered, not what religion you were. Despite this, Edward McGuire, later a Davis Cup player and Senator (in the Irish Free State) and a Catholic had the following to say after a period of time in the club (he joined in 1921):

In my first year after leaving Clongowes, I joined Mount Temple and won a number of championships there. As a result, I received an invitation to join Fitzwilliam. There weren't many Catholics in the Club and I had the impression people in trade were frowned on. I didn't get off until five o'clock, so I was disheartened to find the door was always closed when I came along in the evening. It was considered, it seemed, at that time that Fitzwilliam catered only for those who were able to take the morning or the afternoon off to play. I resolved the problem by playing at lunchtime.

Sunday Play

This keenness to play the sport saw many new clubs formed in towns such as Mullingar, Athlone, Longford, Cavan, Belturbet etc. In Cavan town, the **County Cavan LTC** was joined by **The Pavilion LTC** about 50 years after the first club was formed. In Longford, the **County Longford LTC** was formed in the early 1896 but was probably seen as socially elite. Thus in 1934, under the chairmanship of a local Catholic priest, the **St. Mel's LTC** was formed. The club was named after the patron saint of the local

Catholic Church. The club president was the Catholic Church Administrator. Its honorary secretary was the sacristan at that church. Two factors clearly identify that club. Firstly, it was one many of the townspeople joined who would otherwise not have taken up the game. Secondly, Sunday tennis was allowed from the outset. Both clubs had members from Catholic and non-Catholic communities.

How important was tennis on Sunday? Christian religions believed Sunday to be a day of rest. This could be taken as being a day one should not work. Back in the 19th century the ascendancy could play sport on whatever day of the week they choose. The shopkeepers and industrial workers would work six days a week and it was only on Sunday that they could participate in sport. Many towns eventually introduced a half-day on either a Wednesday or Thursday. The shops would close and whoever chose could play a sport of their liking. For elite sports such as golf and lawn tennis, which could also be described up to the first world-war, at least, as being gentrified and socially exclusive, the ban on playing these sports on Sunday was prevalent if not total both in Ireland and England. Warrington Golf Club had a rule in 1904 that went even further. They *closed the links absolutely on Sundays both for play and promenading.*

Rosses Point, June 1984. Celebrity Tennis Challenge. From left: Robert Burnside (umpire), the late Father Jerry Crehan, Sister Dorothy, Tony McLoughlin (Mayor of Sligo) and Sister Gertrude.

Wigglesworth (1996) in his book, *The Evolution of English Sport,* had the following to say on the matter:

One particular difficulty encountered in church encouragement of recreation was the disapproval in some quarters of play on Sundays which dated back to the condemnation of unlawful sports in the sixteenth century and before. Much of this disapproval became apparent during the first half of the nineteenth century when more working people began to use Sundays for recreational purposes as the only day available to them after a six-day working week in the factories and workshops of the newly established conurbations. For the relatively leisured and church-going middle-class this smacked of unchristian behaviour and several organisation were established which sought to mitigate the harmful

effects such as licentiousness: the Temperance Movement in 1829, the Lord's Day Observance Society in 1831 and in the same year the Society for the Suppression of Vice which lambasted the 'shameful practice of races on Sunday'. We have already seen how the Lord Mayor of London prohibited boat hirers in the eighteenth century from letting out boats to apprentices on a Sunday and the gentrified sport of rowing continued to discriminate against rowing on Sunday, so much so that in Nottingham the working members of the local club were prevented from using the boats by its middle-class committee with the results that they formed the Nottingham Boat Club in 1894 which positively encouraged Sunday outings.

Sister Gertrude of the Ursuline Convent in full flight.

The situation was much the same in Ireland as in England at the end of the 19th century. However, there was a minor social revolution underway. It was the Celtic revival, the strong urge, among the majority, to come out from under the imperial influence and establish an identity of its own. The GAA was an important part of that revolution. It was formed in November 1884. In the following 14th March issue of United Ireland, Michael Cusack the honorary secretary of that organisation, wrote:

> *It has been urged that the GAA propose encouraging Sunday athletics, and that such a course would be an open violation of the Sabbath. The GAA is well aware that in clubs in Dublin frequented by Catholics and Protestants, skittles and rackets are played on Sundays. The skittle alley and the racket court are open to rich people, but the fields of Ireland are not to be opened to the people of Ireland the same day. This impudent absurdity will be removed by the GAA.*

Changing Attitudes

While the national sport of the Irish were to be held on Sundays, it would take many years for the phasing out of such a ban in a number of other sports such as lawn tennis. It could be said that there was a gradual freeing up of the Sunday ban between the wars and that this was further relaxed in the 1950s and 1960s. In 1906 a meeting of the Dublin Lawn Tennis Council was held on the 4th April in the Grosvenor Hotel and a report appeared in Lawn Tennis & Badminton on the 18th of that month.

The History of Irish Tennis

The hon. secretary, in his report, stated that more lawn tennis had been played last year than in previous years, but that paradoxically the fine summer had rather interfered with the matches, as some of the players had been tempted to desert their club to play in tournaments, and to take part in sports away from home on Saturdays. He regretted that no club except the Wilton had followed the good example set by golf clubs in being open for Sunday play, and reminded the Council that the Oxford Diocesan Conference saw no objection to lawn tennis and other sports being on Sunday.

seven days a week use of grass courts because they would be exposed to excessive wear and tear. By 1970, however, the former resistance was losing support, and it was felt that Sunday opening might be an attraction for younger members. But, even though the gates were finally unlocked on Sundays, it is perhaps worth noting that, particularly for the older members, the most active 'social tennis' continues to be pivoted around the traditional Club teas which are still held on Saturday (and Thursday) afternoons. (Centenary Brochure, 1987). Strong views on Sunday sports bans are still prevalent in small pockets, particularly in Ulster.

At the County Kildare Club (**Naas LTC**) in 1923 rugby was allowed to be played from 2 to 5 p.m. on Sundays. *It would take a further year before tennis was allowed. So, from June 18th, 1924, tennis could be played after 2p.m.* (Lyons, 1992). Another of our long established clubs, **Kilkenny County and City LTC**, agonised on the matter. *In 1929 at a Committee Meeting it was decided that play should not be allowed on Sunday except a general meeting be called specially for the purpose to sanction it. This was the case until 1930 when an Extraordinary General Meeting was held at which a resolution was passed allowing courts to be opened for play on Sunday afternoons provided that there should be no play before 3 o'clock. It was not until 1941 that the Committee were given the power to open on Sundays for American Tournaments and matches.*

Rule 14 of the **Donnybrook LTC,** which forbade tennis on Sundays, was relaxed in 1950. *The proposal mooted at the AGM in March 1950 was vigorously opposed and some prominent members resigned in protest. The majority, however, were enthusiastic for change, particularly because this could help to attract new members. In the same spirit juveniles (age 10-16) were allowed to play and members were granted the right to bring visitors every day.* (Henry Tierney in the 1993 Centenary Book).

It is not unexpected to hear that, where church trustees were responsible for a club, as in the case of many Protestant clubs, no play on Sundays was permitted for very many years. Often it was competition that was objected to – the possibility that one could win a £5 voucher was considered commercial and was definitely not allowed. Peter Jackson, that great Ulster player, recalls that one of the reasons he moved from **Cavehill LTC** to **Windsor LTC** was in order to be able to play the game on a Sunday.

By the mid-1960s the vast majority of tennis clubs in Ireland allowed Sunday play; many still had time restrictions still in force. Pragmatism, however, seems to have taken hold in most areas. The still *serene and quaint* **Glenageary LTC** of 1970 decided to open the club for Sunday play, the matter having been raised previously in 1944. .... *a decision had been long- postponed, partly because, it was claimed, there was no demand for such opening, and partly because there was a strong argument against the*

Priest is champ!

Dubliner, Father Paul Kelly, picked up his second provincial title in two weeks when he won the Leinster Championship—beating New Zealander Ben Cranwell, 6-3, 7-5, yesterday.

The Championships, sponsored by Finnegan Menton and run by the Leinster Club in Rathmines, had to be transferred to the indoor area in Fitzwilliam because of bad weather

Father Kelly, who has never previously won a title in Leinster, took the Connacht crown last week, and yesterday was far too steady for Cranwell, who is better known in this country as a squash player.

Father Kelly, accurate on service and consistent off the ground, was never in any real trouble, even in the second set which went to 12 games. He led Cranwell 5-3 and then dropped his service to be brought back to level terms at five-all but then won the next two games for the match.

Ann Keegan, the top seed in the ladies singles, duly confirmed her favouritism with an easy 6-3, 6-2 victory over Ann Moore. Miss Keegan, from Glasnevin, did not drop a set on her way to the title.

Details:

Men's Singles—Final—P. Kelly bt B. Cranwell, 6-3, 7-5.

Ladies Singles—Final — Miss A. Keegan bt Miss A. Moore, 6-3, 6-2.

Men's Doubles—Semi-finals — J. Casey and J. O'Shea bt R. O'Hanlon and H. Barniville, 6-4, 6-4; D. P. Foley and C. Smith bt B. Quinn and P. Kelly, 6-4, 9-7. **Final—**Casey and O'Shea bt Foley and Smith, 4-6, 6-3, 6-2.

LADIES' DOUBLES

Final—Miss A. Keegan and Miss H. Doody bt Miss M Mulvihill and Miss A. Moore, 6-3 6-3.

Irish Independent 5th August 1973

Some top players would not play on a Sunday. In one celebrated case an Irish player on the Davis Cup panel lost his chance to play in the reverse singles as it was to be played on the Lord's Day. England's Dorothy Round, who won Wimbledon in 1934 and 1937, would not play on a Sunday no matter how important the match. In the US Championships in 1933 the semi-final was scheduled for a Sunday afternoon. Fortunately the rains came down and saved her the need to scratch from the event.

The Angelus

One characteristic of the Irish is their sense of humour. Jokes about any sport or religion are usually taken in the spirit intended. One story related to this writer concerns lawn tennis in County Limerick in the 1950s. A tennis team from a 'Catholic' club played away in a league match against a team in a club recognised as being 'Protestant'. The visitors were being comfortably beaten. However the captain of the side was to be noted for his quick thinking. At 6pm, the local Catholic Church rang out its bells for the Angelus, the thrice daily Roman Catholic call to prayer. He immediately instructed his team to stop their matches and pray. His efforts might have been duly noted above, but the Lord chose to ignore them. A fairer referee one will not find. In the final analysis, the match was still lost.

In another situation help from above was called upon. The names are also to remain anonymous. It was the 1940s and the senior club championships were being played in a rural town. It was finals day and a large cup was being presented to the winner. The match was between two teenagers. The mother of one of the teenagers was to be seen looking out of their window which overlooked the club. She was praying with much gusto for her lad, rosary beads in hand defined her religious affiliation. It is not known who won the match.

Lastly, a small tennis story from the 1970s. Four ladies, part of a tennis team, crossed the border into Ulster to play a match. One was a Catholic. The latter's bags were alone thoroughly searched by the border security once the religion of the car's occupant's had been determined. Religion by its nature is good, as is sport. Society is increasingly becoming secularised and, while religion may have dictated when the game could be played, or who could join a club, this influence on the sport is passing rapidly. It is said that sport and politics don't mix. Can we be equally adamant about sport and religion? While the 'Angelus' did no work miracles in County Limerick, there is no doubt that many sports clubs (including tennis) would not have existed were it not for the efforts of a religious community in the first place.

True Story: The captain of the losing visiting Catholic team called his players to pray as the Angelus bells rang. (South of Ireland club-1950s)

3.4   *Eras of Change*

In each…epoch of human history, sports are integrally related to the
political and social structures dominant at the time. (William Baker,
1988)

In the context of a specific sport, once thought of as a pastime, now a life profession, the span of 125 years of *lawn tennis* has seen many changes and developments. While the basic rules of the sport have been fairly stable since Major Wingfield's time, the changes in equipment and fashions, let alone the way in which the game has been played, have been more than dramatic. We can look back over this interlude in time, a mere instant in man's overall evolution, and see changes throughout society running in parallel with those in the sport of lawn tennis. Since Ireland was one of the first countries to embrace the game, being part of a strong English influence, our records include a full range of changes. Latter day tennis nations have no such fund of history to examine. In 1610 there was an early version of *tennis* in vogue in Dublin (see map below). This sport was wide-spread on the continent, particularly in Italy and France, prior to the 1859 experiments on the lawn of Juan Batista Pereira's manor 'Fairlight', at Ampton Road, Edgbaston, Birmingham, England. The Spanish merchant and his friend, solicitor Harry Gem, were thus credited with starting the new game of *lawn tennis*. Initially they called it 'pelota'.

The changes in our society were not taking place in isolation. An island, once part of a world power, had to break off the shackles and exert its own independence. It had then to quickly develop its own identity in an increasingly integrated world society. A somewhat artificial class system has now virtually vanished. Education, once for the few, is now available to all. In close association with this the arts and sciences have brought forward talents from all corners. While this book is a history of a particular sport it is not unreasonable to compare the life and times of tennis players over the eras. There was once a time that just the leisured classes could devote time to excelling at sport. The clock has come full circle. Now, to excel and reach a peak, one must not just live for the sport but the sport must provide an adequate means of living.

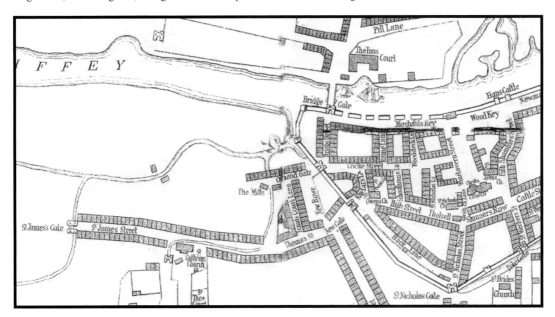

Central portion of John Speed's 1610 map of Dublin city (courtesy of Dublin City Library & Archive).Note Tennis Court Lane in the centre. The full map can be seen in Dublin airport. Tennis as we know it today began in the 1870s (see chapter 2). For several centuries previous to this various forms of racquet sports were played in Ireland and abroad. In an early era tennis was the indoor court game, now known as 'real', 'royal' or 'court' tennis and still played in England, the USA, Australia and France. The oldest recorded courts are those built for the gentlemen of Valencia in Spain in 1298. Each court was unique. The one in Earlsfort Terrace, Dublin, built in 1885, and now used for other purposes, is the only one in the world constructed of marble. A court was built for the students of Trinity College in 1741. The building on the west side of Tennis Court Lane above (built circa 1609) was large enough to have had two courts (north-south) and one along Thomas Street. It is not known if there was more than one court here. Though the streets have changed in the last 400 years it appears that Tennis Court Lane is now John Street West, a short distance SSW of the Liffey crossing at The Four Courts. Some recommended reads covering the topic of tennis include "Real Tennis" (Kathryn Nicoll, 2005), "Tennis: Origins and Mysteries" (Malcolm D. Whitman, 2004) and "Tennis: A Cultural History" (Heiner Gillmeister, 1997).

A country that saw large emigration before, during and after the famine of the 19th century, and further emigration in the 1950's, now sees the reverse being the case. We are now planning for an island of 6 million, in spite of smaller families. A country where cultural and religious controls were steadfast is now part of a more liberal movement, one found earlier in other societies. Our native language and sports were dying, then revived, but now must be looked at on a more global basis. We are truly part of a Western civilisation and no longer an isolated and controlled island.

There are further changes to come. While the *Ascendancy* has all but died out, the historical 'union' with Britain remains an important element in the lives of many. Ironically, what many see as a religious divide is not that at all. Many of the educated Ascendancy were Catholics and many of the poorer farmers were Protestant. People generalise. The burning of about 200 'big houses' during the early 1920's was thought to be an act of patriotism against the British Masters. In truth, most of the occupants had no political influence and were happier being Irish than being forced elsewhere. We should remember that Protestants, such as tennis playing Douglas Hyde, were part and parcel of our cultural revival. He only left the Gaelic League when it became used as a political tool. An interesting statistic can be found in the 1861 census. There were some nine teachers of Irish declared in that year in the whole island. Seven were non-Catholic. We can learn other interesting facts from the same census:

Occupation	R.C.	Other
Clergy	3014	3265
Officers in the Army	121	1076
Constabulary & Metropolitan Police	9426	4420
Ball-Court Keepers	5	0
Ball & Racquet Makers	20	6
Professional Racquet Players	2	1
Beggars	2405	181

An army officer was a profession that required financial backing. The comparison between the beggars listed probably reflects the welfare of both the Catholic and non-Catholic communities. One cannot disguise the historical facts relating to many large Catholic families - famine and smallholdings being among them. A job in the police force was possible. Perhaps a reason we hear of many Irish names today in the police forces of many American cities. It should be noted that lawn tennis was not invented in 1861, the year of the above census. Yet, from the table we can see that other racket sports were already here, a matter discussed in chapter 1 and 2.

The occupational categories listed in Donald Harman Akenson's book, *Small Differences* (1991), from where the above data was derived, are extensive.

Very few of those in high office on the island were in fact Catholic, despite the fact that this sector formed 78% of the population at the time. The Attorney General was one exception. After a long gestation period, Ireland as a whole is getting nearer to achieving a well-balanced society.

We can all see the benefits of sport. It too has a history from which we can learn. There are many countries today where tennis is a game for the few. That is not the case in Ireland, but it once was. Let us examine some aspects of sport development in Ireland. By definition sport is a game or pastime of an organised nature. In Ireland in 1169 the last of the official Aenach Tailteann Games took place. No infighting or the like were allowed for their duration. In 1527 the statutes of Galway forbade hurling and other sports "except alone football".

By 1609 we would find archery, horse riding and, a surprise, the first playing of "real tennis" in Thomas Street, Dublin. Trinity College was responsible for the instigation of many organised sports in Ireland- being the main venue for the meeting of young educated men with a penchant for games between their studies. In 1694 a "Fives" court was built there.

In the early 18th century (1720) poet Matthew Concannon recorded his native Swords beating Lusk at football. At that time there were many variations of the rules of village football as played throughout Europe. It was obviously much later that soccer, rugby and Gaelic football would be formalised. They all must be rooted in the same customs.

The 18th century would see 'elegant' Dublin as one of the more important cultural cities in Europe. Handel's most famous *Messiah* was first performed there on the 13th April 1742. We could say that today the popular U2 concerts at Slane Castle are a follow on from that time; certainly they are equally as popular. Back to sport. The educated, and those owners of land, saw cricket as an ideal sport to be played by gentlemen. The first recorded match in England was in 1744 and in Ireland in 1792. The latter was a match played in the Phoenix Park, Dublin, for a wager of 500 guineas between the Garrison and "All Ireland" side. By the 1840's cricket and fives (a form of handball, see Chapter 2) became a feature of British army life in Ireland under the sporting Duke of Wellington as commander in chief. Croquet 'parties', consisting of some sport and much social interchanging, took place at Castlebellingham (County Louth) as early as 1834. Two years later we would find a meeting of the Pembroke Boat Club taking place.

By the middle of the 19th century the leisure period in English society was underway while Ireland was suffering its serious famine. Leaving aside the sad element of the latter, we would, within a short number of years, see a thriving degree of sporting activity. The first Irish golf club, for example, was formed at the Curragh in 1852 by Scottish soldiers stationed there. Trinity College had its first athletic meeting for 'gentlemen' in 1857. Five years later the Board of the university agreed to the construction of a rackets court. The progression intensified over the remained of the 19th century. One could safely say that Ireland was part of the early development of many sports, many of which would subsequently become international ones.

With some logic, the remainder of the chapter will deal with, and compare, four appropriate time periods in Ireland. It will indicate the progress of the sport of tennis in parallel with society's progress. It is said that history repeats itself. A more practical saying is that we learn from our mistakes. Or do we? One sometimes wonders! Perhaps a better approach to sport, and all life, is to attempt to "understand the past and thus improve the future". Jay J. Coakley has published an excellent book on *Sport in Society: Issues and Controversies* (6th edition, 1998). Looking at the past he quotes some interesting references including the following:

Of the thousands of evils which exist in Greece there is no greater evil than the race of athletes.....Since they have not formed good habits, they face problems with difficulty. They glisten and gleam like statues of the city-state itself when they are in their prime, but when bitter old age comes upon them they are like tattered and threadbare rugs. (Euripides, Greek Dramatist, 5th century BC).

One may see signs of this degeneration of modern tennis players but today it is recommended that those in the veteran category play as often as they are able. They might not glisten with youth but they have an important perspective in what life should be about. His next quote is from historian William Baker (1988):

In each....epoch of human history, sports are integrally related to the political and social structures dominant at the time.

Time and again we see political intervention in sport. Note Hitler's phone message to Baron Gottfried von Cramm as he was about to play an important tennis match at Wimbledon. In Aix en Provence, France, in 1975, Rhodesia was barred from playing in the main draw of the Federation Cup for 'political reasons'. By some perverse logic they were allowed to play in the Plate Event.

The following few pages are a series of facts/issues based upon breaking up the time span of Irish lawn tennis into four time zones. The years selected are at the start of the early clubs followed by intervals of about forty years up to the present time. The facts are an eclectic gathering of information, sporting and otherwise. We could have picked other time periods of equal interest but as the oldest clubs are 125 years old it was decided to divide that time into roughly four quarters.

Time Zone1
1876 to 1880
The Early Lawn Tennis Clubs are formed.

A few events in **1876** do set up the reader for a look at the era of early tennis. The Chiricahua Indian Chief, Geronimo (real name Goyathlay), began a ten-year reign of terror when he leads his warriors into Mexico to avenge the killing of his family in 1858. On the 26th February, Japan recognises Korea's independence from China. In April the Royal Titles Act, passed by the British Parliament, makes Queen Victoria Empress of India. On the 25th June the Battle of the Big Horn in North America took place. The Sioux Indians angered by the slaughter of their buffalo by the advancing white settlers, kill a 264-strong Seventh Cavalry force under General Custer. On the 30th June Serbia declares war on Turkey. On the 2nd August the famed Wild Bill Hickock is shot from behind while sitting at a poker table in Deadwood, Dakota. He was 39 at the time.

This was also the year in which *The Adventures of Tom Sawyer* by Mark Twain is published and Thomas P. Westendorf writes the popular song *I'll Take You Home Again, Kathleen.* In **1877** Thomas Edison makes the first record player. On Thursday 19th July **1877**, Spencer William Gore became the first Wimbledon Champion when he beat William Marshall 6/1 6/2 6/4.

Locally, on a more mundane level, the Roscommon Stag Hunt Club, with their staghounds, ended up in the heart of Sligo town following their prey. *Although the streets were crowded with pedestrians no accident occurred, and the riders had such magnificent command that every obstacle was avoided. The oldest resident in Sligo has not seen a finer 'sight' than the stag-hunt through the Town on Thursday* (Sligo Chronicle 17th March **1877**).

In **1872** the Irish Champion Athletic Club was formed and, it reasonably to assumed, that tennis was played at the club (later called Lansdowne LTC) from 1875 onwards. In **1877** the clubs of Dublin University Lawn Tennis Club, Limerick Lawn Tennis Club, Monkstown Lawn Tennis Club and Fitzwilliam Lawn Tennis Club were all founded by keen followers of the new pastime – boxed in sets and sold from **1874** onwards. The Limerick Club held their first Open tournament, the 'original' South of Ireland, starting on 2nd August, shortly after the first Wimbledon championships. Monkstown had their own club tournament that summer, using the old 'racket' rules and described in detail, in poetic fashion, by a member (see chapter 3.7).

On the 12th April **1877** Britain annexes the South African Republic in breach of the 1852 Sand River Convention, which recognised the independence of the Transvaal. Twelve days later Russia declares war on Turkey. In November, US General Carleton orders Apache Indians in Arizona out of their Chiricahua reservation at Warm Springs. They were moved to San Carlos, which has summer temperatures of 40^0C (104^0F) and where there was no game or food supply. In this year Leo Tolstoy publishes *Anna Karenina* and Anna Sewell, *Black Beauty*. Peter Tchaikovski completes his music for *Swan Lake*.

The treaty of San Stefano (5th March **1878**) gives Romania, Montenegro and Serbia their independence. On July 22nd the Irishman, Sir Garnet Wolseley, arrives in Larnica, Cyprus, with 1500 British troops to a warm welcome from Bishop Kyriannos of Kitium. At the Berlin Congress in July the Ottoman Empire is divided up, leaving few nations involved satisfied. This year sees Gilbert and Sullivan write *HMS Pinafore*. The first major men's doubles lawn tennis championships were instituted at the Scottish Championships at Edinburgh. The second winner of the men's singles at Limerick was Vere Thomas St. Leger Gould. He would win the inaugural Irish Championships in **1879** and be the first Irishman to reach a Wimbledon final shortly afterwards.

In **1879** the Irish Championships were established and run by the members of **Fitzwilliam LTC**. They included the first major title for ladies singles and mixed doubles anywhere in the world. The first tournament was held in Australia-the Victorian Championships in Melbourne. In Sligo, the Harbour Board discussed the bathing during the summer months at the small Nett Island downstream from Ballast Quay ……. *not all of them observed the Victorian ideal of modesty in public places* (John McTiernan, 2000). According to a Mr. Crawford, Every day bathers might be seen without any bathing dresses, which was very objectionable, and particularly so to ladies travelling to and from Rosses Point by the steamer.

St. Stephen's Day, **1880** (Sligo Champion): Sligo Harriers Hunt held at Redgate and *was very large and representative of the gentry of the county. …The day was regarded as a holiday in the town, and the attendance of spectators on foot was rather numerous, and included all the farmers and labourers of the district, who appeared to take a keen interest in the sport. Among those mounted were Captain Campbell; Mr. Molony, R.M.; Robert Pettigrew, Esq.; Dr.Palmer, Alexander Lyons, Esq., and Major Wood-Martin.*

Sir William Orphen (1878-1931)
Born in Stillorgan, County Dublin, William Orphen, trained in London. He was one of the most successful artists of his generation. In 1924 he published "Stories of Old Ireland and Myself" in which he indicated his interest in tennis. He is known to have completed many self-portraits. The sketch here is a <u>detail</u> from a title "Letter with a self-portrait playing tennis at the Fitzwilliam Lawn Tennis Club, Dublin" (Courtesy of the National Gallery of Ireland).It is not known when the sketch was drafted.

Sligo Champion (27/3/**1880**): *For several miles around the town* (Ballymote) *–as far as the eye could see-bonfires blazed on every hill on Sunday 21ˢᵗ. in honour of Parnell's safe homecoming* (from America to Ireland). On St. Patrick's Day the temperance Band marched through the town. *Later, they set out to attend a Tenant Right Demonstration at Benada, accompanied by a large number of locals wearing sashes and carrying a large banner which on one side had a painting of St. Patrick and on the reverse a Celtic Cross, Round Tower and Wolf Dog* (John McTiernan, 2000).

In September **1880** there was an American Tennis Championships, open to all comers, held at the Staten Island Cricket & Baseball Club. The first official US Championships were held on the grass courts of Newport Casino, Rhode Island, in **1881**, following the formation of the US National LTA.

Time Zone 2
1919 to 1923
End of Great War-Changing Times

Since the early days of lawn tennis the world had undergone a complete revolution. Major advances in science and engineering were well advanced. The Davis Cup (1900) was off the ground as was the Irish Lawn Tennis Association (1908). The biggest mark on world history was the Great War in which nearly 10 million died. On the 11th November 1918, Germany signed an Armistice with the Allies at Compiegne. For the duration of the war, sport virtually closed down and many Irish clubs lost members. The Spanish Influenza in 1918, which originated in China, kills over 21 million people. After recovery from these disasters, the 1920's started off with a bang (the 'roaring 20's) but would end with a major stock market crash in 1929.

On the 3ʳᵈ January **1919** Rutherford first splits the atom. On the 23rd March Mussolini launches his Fascist party in Italy. On the 15ᵗʰ June Alcock and Brown completed the first non-stop flight across the Atlantic. The flight from Newfoundland and ending near Clifden, County Galway took 15 hours and 57 minutes (an average speed of 115 mph). Before the year ended John Alcock died in an aeroplane accident. On the 28ᵗʰ June the Treaty of Versailles was finally signed by Germany. The Treaty of Saint-Germain (10ᵗʰ September) obliges Austria to recognise the independence of Yugoslavia, Poland, Czechoslovakia and Hungary. The Treaty of Neuilly (27ᵗʰ November) obliges Bulgaria to also recognise the independence of Yugoslavia. On the 28th December women over thirty get vote for first time; of the 1600 candidates 17 were women. Sinn Fein candidate Countess Markievicz was the only female winner and would not take the oath of allegiance and thus could not attend Parliament. Of Ireland's 105 seats, Sinn Fein secures 73, Unionists 25, Home Rule Party 6 and Independent Unionist 1.

In sport, the first winner of the Irish ladies tennis championships not from these islands was Elizabeth Ryan of the USA. A flamboyant and fashion-conscious Frenchwoman, Suzanne Lenglen, took Wimbledon by storm and won the final 10/8 4/6 9/7 against Dorothea Lambert Chambers. The Sunday Times reports that Algernon Kingscote became the first foreign player to win the Australian Championships. This was an error, as Jim Parke from Clones had that distinction when he won it in 1912 in Hastings, New Zealand. Interestingly, up until 1925 it was called the Australasian Championships – the governing body was the Australasian LTA and incorporated New Zealand. The yellow jersey was first worm by the leader in cycling's 'Tour de France'. John Miley from Dublin wins the Ulster Tennis Championships.

On the 16ᵗʰ January **1920** prohibition was introduced in the USA. The manufacture and sale of alcohol was first banned in Maine in 1851. Due to pressure from the churches (who perceived drink as a sin) and women (who saw liquor saloons as a threat to the home) this now applied to all states. The League of Nations was inaugurated on the same day, without US representation, at the French Foreign Office in Paris. On the 20ᵗʰ March Tomas Mac Curtain was shot dead at his home. The coroner's jury finds that the 'murder was organised and carried out by the Royal Irish Constabulary officially directed by the British government'. On the 26ᵗʰ March the Black and Tans arrive in Ireland and on the 22ⁿᵈ June Greek forces move against Turkish Nationalist troops with support from Britain. The State of Lebanon was established by France on the first day of September. In this year the Baltic States of Lithuania, Latvia and Estonia are recognised as independent by Russia after attempts to make them part of the new Union of Soviet Socialist Republics fails. On the 10ᵗʰ December martial law is declared in Ireland after a wave of killings by the IRA.

D.H. Lawerence's *Women in Love* is published this year. Suzanne Lenglen wins all three Wimbledon titles without losing a set. Big Bill Tilden becomes the first American to win the men's singles at Wimbledon. In golf, spikes were fitted to shoes for the first time.

By June **1921,** some 2 million people were unemployed in Britain, the start of a slump. Death duties and the import of cheap foods led many landowners to sell their estates. Titles were also available for purchase; a knighthood for £10,000 or a peerage for £50,000. On the 4ᵗʰ August Lenin asks world to help with Russian famine. On the 3ʳᵈ September Albert Einstein was awarded the Nobel Prize. M.K. (*Mahatma*) Gandi started a campaign in India to boycott all things European on the 17ᵗʰ September. At 2.10am on the 6ᵗʰ December Articles of Agreement were signed (the 'Treaty') in London under threat from Lloyd George ('war within three days'). The Irish Free State (26 counties) was given dominion status and the six Ulster counties remained a province in the United Kingdom. Earlier in the year, at Wimbledon, Tilden and Lenglen retain their titles, as does Elizabeth Ryan in Dublin. Leinster beat Ulster 10/5 in the first interprovincial tennis match between these two provinces. In **1921** there were 75 clubs affiliated to the ILTA. This number would grow in the next few decades. Ireland was beaten by 8 matches to 7 by England in an international at Buxton.

On the 15th February **1922** the Permanent Court of International Justice was opened at The Hague. On the 28th October Benito Mussolini leads his black-shirted *Fascisti* in a 'March on Rome'. The following month Victor Emmanel III gives Mussolini a Ministry in the Government and dictatorial powers to restore order in Italy. On the 24th November Erskine Childers, writer (whose works included *Riddle of the Sands*) and member of the IRA, was executed by the Free State Authorities. The following day, in Egypt, Howard Carter opens the inner tomb of the celebrated Tutankhamun.

Published in **1922**, in Paris, was James Joyce's' *Ulysses. Owing to the unsettled state of the Country various Tournaments including the Championships were abandoned...The Close Championships were allotted to the Belfast Boat Club and duly played.* (The ILTA honorary secretary's report for 1922). At Wimbledon the Championships were played at the new grounds.

In **1923**, Ireland as a separate identity was entered in the Davis Cup competition for the first time. Having beaten India 3/2 in the first match we lost in the second round to France (1/4). Noteworthy was Cecil Campbell victory over Jean Borotra 6/1 7/5 6/0. The following year Borotra was to be Wimbledon champion. The Cork sponsored motion to remove the 'Ban' (on GAA members playing 'foreign' games) was rejected by 50 votes to 32. On the world stage matters were not good. Lenin established the first forced-labour camp in the Solovetsky islands and Mussolini dissolves all non-fascist parties. The earthquake in Japan on the 1st September, and the ensuing fires, killed 100,000 people. Sean O' Casey writes *The Shadow of a Gunman*. Adolf Hitler fails in his attempt to take over the city government of Munich; the Nazi party had been founded in 1919 by Anton Drexler. Unfortunately, Hitler's day would come.

In England, the Matrimonial Causes Act equalized the position of men and women seeking divorce, adultery by either party was just reason for seeking this divorce. In general, women's emancipation was truly underway in this decade....*women of all classes enjoyed greater personal independence than they or their predecessors had had before the war. That included the freedom to smoke, to wear cosmetics, to raise hemlines, and to go unchaperoned.* (Pamela Horn, 1995).

> ## Time Zone 3
> ## 1959 to 1963
> ## The Turning Tide-The 60s and
> ## Open tennis arrive

Following the second world-war emigration from Ireland continued at a high rate in the 1950's. In the 1960's major changes would take place in all aspects of Irish life. Open tennis would eventually arrive and incorporate both amateurs and professionals.

On the 3rd January **1959** Fidel Castro enters Havana and takes over as Head of State in Cuba. He would still be in power forty years later, a world war just being avoided when the Russians were forced to take out their missiles in the early sixties. On the 3rd June Singapore becomes independent. Alan Sillitoe's book, *The Loneliness of the Long Distance Runner,* is published. On the 25th June Eamon de Valera was installed as the 3rd President of Ireland. The 22-year old rock and roll singer, Buddy Holly, died in a plane crash on the 2nd February. Billy Wright of Wolves and England becomes the world's first soccer player to win a century of caps (leading England to a 1-0 victory over Scotland on the 4th April). Unseeded Rod Laver was beaten in his first Wimbledon singles final by Alex Olmedo, the Peruvian born son of a groundsman but now representing the USA. 19-year old Maria Bueno of Brazil wins her first Wimbledon and was thought to be the *most gracefully artistic of post-war women's champions.* (Barrett, 1999). She would win the Irish Championships in 1964 and 1965.

A revolutionary decade starts in **1960** with a major turning point in African history. Tonga, Cameroun, Malagasy Republic, Independent Congo, Somalia, Ghana, Dahomey, Upper Volta, Ivory Coast, Chad, Central African Republic, Gabon, Mali, Niger, Senegal, Nigeria and Mauritiana all gained independence. During this decade everyone could rent or buy a television set. They were black and white and warm weather, especially during Wimbledon, would cause waves to move down the screen. On the 13th February: France tests its first atom bomb over the Sahara while on the 21st March the infamous Sharpeville massacre took place in Johannesburg. Some 20,000 blacks protested against a law against blacks having to carry identification papers. 72 are killed by police. The law is suspended five days later.

In May, an earthquake near Concepcion, Chile, causes a tsunami, a series of long high tidal waves. They sped at 400 mph across the Pacific and even reach Japan. In 1960 the computer 'mouse' was invented. The words 'dropout', 'sit-in' and 'catsuit' were first used that year. The popular songs *Never on Sunday, The Twist* (also to be a dance craze) and *Itsy Bitsy Teenie Weenie Yellow Polka Dot Bikini* are first released. Italy beat the USA in the Davis Cup in Perth but then lost to Australia in the Challenge Round. The Olympic Games dominated the summer, starting in Rome on the 25th August. The Russians were delighted with their tally of 103 medals, 32 more than the USA. Cassius Clay won the light-heavyweight gold medal.

On the 3rd January **1961** the USA severs diplomatic links with Cuba. At the UN on the 15th the Cuban Foreign Minister claims the USA are to about invade. The Bay of Pigs invasion of the 17th is repelled. The last of the great transatlantic liners, the *France,* is launched. She is 315 meters long. At the end of May South Africa withdraws from the British Commonwealth. On the 13th August the border between East and West Berlin is closed and the *Berlin Wall* is constructed a few days later. It is to remain for nearly forty years. The UN Secretary General Dag Hammarskjold is killed in an air crash on the 18th September. During the year *Catch 22* (Joseph Heller) and *The Prime of Miss Jean Brody* (Muriel Spark) are published and Henry Mancini first plays *Moon River.* Football transfers are allowed in the English FA for the first time.

On the 20th May, George Davies set a pole vault world record with the new revolutionary fibreglass pole. Angela Mortimer and Christine Truman meet in the Wimbledon final, the first time, since 1914, that two home-based ladies would reach that stage. On July 13th, in stormy wet weather, Arnold Palmer beats Dai Rees of Wales by one stroke to taken the British Open Golf Championship for the first time. Peter Alliss halves his match with 'Arnie' in the Ryder Cup, but the USA wins by 13 matches to 8.

Tom Woulfe produced his famous 'thesis' on the GAA Ban, a monumental work that exploded many myths about the much-abused rule, (The ban being a smouldering issue from 1926 up to 1962 when it became a burning issue.) The **1962** Congress rejected Tom Woulfe's motion to appoint a committee to examine the Ban in depth by 180 to 40. On the 24th August the death occurred of Anew McMaster-the last touring actor to bring Shakespeare to rural Ireland. In October, the Russian leader Khrushchev moves his missiles out of Cuba. The term 'computer chip' comes into use for the first time.

The Beatles hit 'Love Me Do' broke into the UK top 20 on the 15th December and thus started one of the greatest musical phenomenon of all time. For nearly all of the next decade Wimbledon champions would abound the Irish Championships. Rod Laver wins the 1962 title when his opponent, Bobby Wilson of Great Britain scratches. It is the first time since 1902 that the same man wins both the All-England and Irish Championships in the same year. Margaret Du Pont (USA) wins the Wimbledon Mixed title at 44 years and 125 days old.

On the 29th August **1963** Martin Luther King makes his famous I have a dream speech at the Lincoln Memorial in Washington. The world's worst submarine disaster to date occurred on the 10th April when 129 lives were lost on board the USS Thresher. On the 26th June President John F Kennedy starts a 4-day tour of Ireland. Ten days earlier the first woman in space was Soviet Valentina Tereshkova. On the 8th August was the daring 'great Train Robbery' when

£2.5 million were stolen. The year's big film release was *Cleopatra* starring Richard Burton and Elizabeth Taylor. At $30 million it was the most expensive film ever made. Invented that year were the 'hover' mower and holograms using laser beams. Banned on the 17th June in the USA were reading the bible and saying prayers at school. One of the most shocking occurrences was the murder of John F. Kennedy, the American President. The 1950's fear of communism was still alive and many thought this might be the start of a world war. Unheralded left-hander, Bob Charles of New Zealand, wins the British Open Golf Championship. In September George Best made his League debut for Manchester United at the age of 17. The USA takes the Davis Cup away from the Australians for the first time in 9 years. At the first Federation Cup for women they also beat Australia (2/1). Ireland did not play in that inaugural tournament held at the Queen's Club, London. Billie Jean Moffitt (later King) wins the Irish Championships.

Time Zone 4
1999-2003
The Small World-New heroes instantly

In the previous forty year the world has changed radically. Apart from the space race, there have been many wars, the latest being the War in Iraq. The United States is now the 'policeman' of the world, many considering their world activity being one of self-interest. The United Nations is in need of a revival in order that its objectives are met. In Europe the Common Market has no become a political entity which is due to even get bigger in **2004**. Part of this latter union has been the introduction of the euro, Britain still holds on to its currency (perhaps the last vestige of Imperialism) but will eventually become Europeans.

Terrorism has been around for many years but *September 11* **2002** was a date which changed everything, the Twin Towers in New York being demolished by two jet airliners with the loss of thousands of lives but, more important, a sudden awareness that we are now on a small planet. The Israel-Palestine issue continues.

The environment has been an issue for some years with fears associated with global warming, the ozone layer, fluoridation of drinking water, flooding associated with *El Nino* and the rapid spread of disease (such as SARS). The continual fight against cancer and AIDS are daily issues. Even contamination in our modern hospitals has been a problem. Mobile phones have grown like mushrooms and even they are considered to have potential medical problems associated with them.

Communications have entered a new era. In this era the mobile phone technology has grown at an astounding rate. By 2003 most children have their own phones, never mind the adults. 'Texting' rapidly takes off as a new language of its own and within a few years these miniature phones would be able to take, and send, instant video signals to any part of the world. The internet is now well established and problems of plagiarism and illegal downloading of music and child pornography become serious issues to be resolved. Satellite television now makes available hundreds of channels straight into the living room. The cinema still survives and renting videos, with DVDs just about to take their place, are still popular. Newspapers each week-end attract purchasers by including a free music CD and possibly a novel. Film DVDs would shortly become a 'free' inclusion with the €1 or €1.50 newspaper.

In sport a number of new elements are now to be found. The emergence of the African nations in athletics has been astounding, the medal winners at World Championships in Paris in 2003 reflects this. Drugs testing is now the norm in most sports. Television, particularly the introduction of colour and, later, satellite channels, has revolutionised the contact between fans and their sport. Litigation has made the organisers of sport more careful in terms of their regulations and implementation, the protection of children being a major benefit. On the down side, we can see less people willing to make an effort in organising amateur clubs, coaching etc. The 'selfish' era has arrived and it is difficult to see it being reversed.

"Open" tennis is no longer an issue. Players now can earn a good living from the sport. Many more countries are now playing in the Davis and FED cup competitions. Even juniors can have a world ranking. For Ireland this, in part, has meant that the exciting days of the 1960's and earlier, when the world's tops players graced our courts, are no longer. On the positive side we do have players playing the game full-time and scholarships are available for the best of our youngsters.

In **2000,** one Dublin girl (Rachel Dillon) at the age of 12 or 13 moved to France for the very purpose of developing her tennis and later becoming a professional. Martina Navratilova, one of the eastern Europeans to move to the USA, has probably become the greatest female tennis player ever. She continues to play competitively, though well in to her 40s. Pete Sampras has set records too and officially retired in August **2003**. A new wave of players has now emerged with large numbers of Spaniards, Argentines and Russians beginning to dominate the game. The black Williams sisters are dominant, winning Wimbledon from 2000 to 2003. They have raised the bar and women's tennis is stronger than ever. Even the Swiss and Belgians are producing Grand Slam champions. The players are getting bigger, are fitter, faster and stronger, and the wooden racquet is now in the museum. Whither tennis?
[Footnote: Since drafting the above the American dominance has waned considerably. The ladies from Russia have arrived in large numbers. In the spring of 2006 Roger Federer of Switzerland and Amelie Mauresmo of France were world number ones. In August 2006 Federer won the US Open once again.

Russia's Maria Sharapova wins the singles. Martina Navratilova wins the mixed title at the age of 49 and Andre Agassi retires from the sport after a lengthy career at the top.]

3.5   *The Family Factor*

*The combined tennis talents of Harry and Geraldine Barniville
reaped impressive rewards in the Co. Wicklow Hard Court
Championships*
(Irish Independent 30th May 1966)

Undoubtedly, one of the most common reasons why players have taken up the game of tennis is linked to the fact that a member of their family played it before them. This linkage is a natural one and there are thousands of cases where this has occurred in Ireland. A few examples of well-known and lesser known sporting families tell their own stories. Some families span just two generation of association with racquet sports; others can be linked over a period of over 100 years. Some may be linked with different countries and exceeding average play in a range of activities. Yet others may have had minor peaks but are worth a reference.

Billy Burke and his sisters were among the best players in Connacht in the 1950s. However the next generations are also succeeding at the game too. This photograph was taken in 2003 shortly after Billy, his daughter Una (O'Halloran) and her daughter all won tournaments in the SAME week.

Why and how younger members of a family take to a sport is always a question asked of those that reach the pinnacle. The query is equally valid for those whose peaks of attainment are more likely to be linked to small hills in the valley of sport. Alan Haughton, the Munster Davis Cup player, can recall the years he played with his father and brother in competition. In the 1960s he would play with his own sons.

An annual challenge arose between Alan and either Hugh or Peter against Peter and Frank Mockler, two useful players of that time. Alan put up the "C Cup" for the event. This was the Crankshaw cup he had won for a 100-yard sprint while at school. The following are just a selection, if your family is not there then apologies.

The Arthurs

Wayne Arthurs, the Australian Davis Cup player is a good example where talent has been passed on through the genes. His mother, Angela Kidd, was an English County player and his father, Derek, a Davis Cup player from Ulster. Both father and son have had extremely good tennis records, detailed in chapter 6. What is interesting about the father and son Davis Cup players is a comment made about their serves. In 1958, Derek attended a coaching course given by John Horn for selected and promising young Irish players. His report on Derek included the comment that Derek had *Probably the best serve in Ireland*. Just over forty years later we find two of the best players in the world, Andy Roddick and Pete Sampras, saying that Wayne has one of the best serves in the world. Don't tell me that is just coincidence! We all know that there are people with the gift of a natural fluid service action that is difficult to return and impossible to read. Derek and Wayne Arthurs both have it in abundance. Further details later in chapters 5 and 6.

A family occasion at Clontarf LTC about 60 years ago. Did that young player cash in on his early promise as a tennis player?

The Barry's

Looking back over the Irish and Munster records we find many Barry names in the tennis annals. At least one has played at Wimbledon while others have been high achievers as administrators and/or players. At one point in time the name Harte-Barry came into the family. In latter decades there are two distinct families. However, Eric Harte-Barry is a Mallow man and there were Barry's in the **Mallow LTC** of the 19th century.

Mr. W. N. Barry of **Mallow LTC** was an entry in the Irish Championships in 1883 but was 'absent' and a walkover was given to Peter Aungier of Fitzwilliam Lawn Tennis Club. Mrs. Norton Barry won her first round at Wimbledon in 1901 when beating C.B. Bell of Great Britain 6/3 6/0. Unfortunately, in the second round she met lost another Irish lady, the great Louisa (Lou) Martin and lost in three sets (6/4 4/6 1/6). Remembering that Lou was one of the most successful of Irish lady players ever this was a respectable foray. (Lou won nine Irish Championships and was in the All-England All-Comer's singles final in 1898, 1900 and 1901).

A Mrs. D. R. Barry was winner of Irish Championships in 1911 and 1914, beating Miss A. Holder and Miss I. Clarke in the respective finals. Was this the same Mrs. Barry, or possibly a relative? One of male members of the Barry family was on the **Wilton LTC** 2nd team in 1910 when they played against Trinity College, Dublin.

Eric Harte Barry, with his wife Marjorie, at the Irish Close Championships at Sundays Well in 1959, the year he was President of the Munster Branch.

In 1927 we find a Mr. G. O. Barry playing the handicap mixed doubles at the Belfast Boat Club tournament. Was this too far north for a Munster Barry? A few weeks later, at the Irish Championships, we find that Dr. A.P. Barry played in the Open Mixed. He was a highly thought of Davis Cup Captain in the late 1920s and 1930s and died on the 2nd January 1938. 'A.P.' was a member of **Fitzwilliam LTC** and their honorary secretary from 1933 to 1935.

Many Harte-Barrys had significant influences in Munster tennis. Eric Harte-Barry, from Mallow, was a Munster interprovincial. Having served on the Munster Branch for a number of years and been elected their president in 1959. In 1964 he was elected president of the Irish Lawn Tennis Association.

In 1955 Mrs. W. Barry won the Open tournament run by **Collins Barracks LTC** when beating Mrs. M.

Lane 6/3 6/2. E.O. Barry was in the final of the men's doubles in that tournament. In 1960, Mrs. J. Barry won the same tournament. Was this the same lady? Also in 1960, Miss V. Barry wins the Irish Junior Close Championships at **Rushbrooke** (by the comfortable margin of 6/1 6/1 against Miss E. O'Rourke). Over at the **Sunday's Well** junior tournament that summer Don Harte-Barry reached the singles final while J. and V. Barry won the boys and girls events at **Youghal LTC**. In the junior girls, a young M. Barry lost a narrow final, 5/7 7/5 6/4 to T. Collins.

At the end of 1960 the Munster rankings show Mrs. W. J. Barry as number 2 while both J. Barry and Don Harte-Barry are ranked in the boys listing. By 1962 she is still competing for the province and Don is ranked among the top boys. If you are confused about the Barry's then so am I. Perhaps the full correct story can someday be told. More questions now arise than answers given. Let us move on.

The Blake's

Trying to get a family photograph can sometimes be difficult. Children 'flying' here and there, up to all sorts of useful activities. The Blake's is one such family, the photograph that follows was taken on 26th December 2002. At that point in time Aisling was due to return to France where she is studying and playing squash. Gareth ('Gary') was due to return to Vancouver and from there to San Francisco with South America shortly afterwards. Cian, the eldest of the four children, is due back in Cork where he works with an engineering consultancy firm (IDC) and Fintan is due to return to London where he currently plays in Middlesex Leagues and is looking for a new employment opportunity (he does have an excellent mathematics degree from TCD). Ed, the dad, an electrical engineer, is not long back from a stint in the Far East and Brid, keeping everything under tabs, is not long back from Malaysia where she was manager of the Irish under 18 squash team playing in the world championships. And that is not the half of it.

A modern young family, full of activity and ambition are the Blake's. Ed grew up in Cork where he attended CBC secondary school and then did his electrical engineering degree at University College, Cork. His sports included playing on the wing for one of the university rugby teams and athletic. The 100 yards was one of his events and years later he did the marathon in a respectable three hours and fifty-five minutes. His work took him to Dublin and then later to Sligo. By the end of the 1980s, like *all* the family he would have taken up all four racquet sports at Sligo Tennis club i.e. tennis, squash, badminton and table tennis. The whole family have skied too on winter holidays.

Brid (O' Hara) is originally from Dromahaire, County Leitrim and met Ed through her work at the ESB in Dublin. In 1983, while the children were small they moved to Sligo and took up the life membership family

The All-Rounder Blake Family. From left: Ed, Garrett, Aisling, Fintan, Cian and Brid.

The happy & determined Burke family. From left: Michael, Aisling, Niamh and Finnoula.

The sociable and talented Coleman family. From left: Sarah, Kevin, Hanna (front), Helen, Emily and Lucy.

offer that was to set up the present club facilities. In Dublin she too was a keen sportswoman, the 100m and swimming particularly. In Sligo it was the racquet sports and latterly golf. She and Ed have travelled more miles than most parents with their children in the cause of sport. It may have been to Scotland in the middle of winter for a squash tournament or to badminton and tennis events in many parts of Ireland.

The following pointers are a brief summary of the children's achievements. Cian (born 1976) has been on the Connacht u14 and u18 tennis team, the u17 badminton team and all age groups in squash. In the case of the latter he has an u14 cap for Ireland. He also had a Connacht u18 youths rugby trial, playing on the wing. When studying for his B. Eng at Queen's University, Belfast, he played in that position too. He has had a long list of squash titles, and won the senior club tennis championships a few years ago. Golf is one his recent activities. In 2002 he ran his first marathon with a time of about 4 hours 25 minutes. He is now (2004) married and working in Cork.

Fintan (born 1978) is the tallest of the family and uses his reach to great effect on the squash court. Growing up he was more than capable at all sports but concentrated on squash on was on all Connacht teams from under 12 to senior. He has three caps from his days playing in the U14 and U16 age groups. He was on the Summerhill secondary schools tennis and badminton teams. He captained the Trinity College team when studying for his mathematics degree.

Gareth (born 1980) is probably the most laid back of the family, has loads of talent but the family feel that he is the traveller and interested in environmental matters. At Summerhill College he played on the basketball team but also, like Fintan, played soccer for the local St. John's football club. He was on the local Cornageeha team that won the silver medal at the Mosney Community Games.

Aisling (born 1981) took like a duck to water when it came to sport. As recently as December 2002 she was in the Irish Senior Close Squash finals at **Fitzwilliam LTC** when beaten by full time professional Madeline Perry. She did beat the high rated Aisling McArdle of County Louth in the semi-finals. At the end of that week she was ranked number 2 in Ireland with Anna McGeever, another Sligo girl, at number 3. Aisling flew from Connacht events to being on the Irish side at the tender age of 15. In July 1999 she celebrated her eighteenth birthday while playing in the World Junior Championships in Brazil. While in secondary school, Aisling played on the Ursuline Convent's hockey team, on the wing, as one might have expected. She featured on the Connacht u14 and u18 tennis teams and was in Mosney for the Community Games badminton team. Having finished her studies in Brest, NW France, and her degree from TCD secured, Aisling became a full-time squash player (autumn 2004) period. Around that time Aisling, and fellow-Sligo girl Anna McGeever, formed two thirds of the Irish ladies' team that came 7th in world team championships. This included a win over the USA.

This family has an uncountable list of successes and, most importantly, while they take pride in each other's achievements, not one of their wins has gone to their heads. A real sports family if there ever was one.

The Burkes

Thomond College, Limerick and sport was where Michael and Finnoula Burke met in 1975. Today, over twenty years later, they have two teenage girls. Sport has become an important family activity. Michael is from Emly in County Tipperary and as a teenager played some tennis in the local club where there were about sixty members using two hard courts. He was also interested in athletics and ran the 100 and 200m but was best at the long jump, winning the Munster schools U17 title with a 20-foot plus distance. Like all Tipperary people hurling was important to Michael and he was delighted to represent that great hurling county on both minor and U21 teams. Later he played senior football for the county.

Michael was the first PE teacher in St. Muirdeachs College Ballina. He took up squash and played in the Hurst Hotel club, and then in the well-known Stephanites club. He moved to Sligo in 1980 (the year of his marriage) where he played in the Ballincar club and then joined the Sligo Tennis Club when the squash courts were built in 1985. The following year he was on the men's first team that was to win the Connacht Men's B team title. Today he potters around with a number of sports but can be seen most often playing either tennis or badminton with one or both of his two children. Michael works for the Sligo VEC. In the **Sligo Tennis Club** he has played a significant role in the club's management team, serving as honorary club secretary and also running the monthly 400-club draw.

Finnoula (Malony) is originally from Ennis. At the age of twelve she became a boarder in the Ursuline Convent here in Sligo. Her mother and six aunts all were boarders there as were Finnoula's six sisters. She is now a full-time teacher in the school with her PE and hockey skills being put to good use. While a student, she represented the school in the sports of tennis and hockey at both junior and senior levels. Additionally, she also won the schools senior table tennis title. Later she was to represent both Munster and Connacht at senior (club) interprovincial hockey.

At school Finnoula is well known for her hockey skills and motivation, the whistle being a potent weapon to any lethargic hockey player. She still plays tennis and, for fitness purposes, loves her swimming sessions three to four times a week. Finnoula was particularly good at squash playing initially in the Ballincar Hotel club and then in Sligo Tennis Club. In 1986 she was to be the first club champion at squash, a title she was to win on two other occasions. Her skills were noted at Connacht level and she represented the province twice on their senior ladies side. In the early 80s she played a lot of successful badminton for the local Presbyterian Hall Badminton Club.

The History of Irish Tennis

Aisling Burke, born in 1985, is the eldest of the two Burke daughters, and has attended the Ursuline College in Sligo. She has played several sports from a young age but badminton and tennis, are her favourites. She was good enough a few years ago to be selected on to the Irish U15 badminton panel. A few seasons ago she won the Connacht U14 singles, doubles (with Shauna Whelan) and mixed (with John O'Connor) titles and was runner-up in the Ulster U15 open doubles championships. 1997 was a good tennis year for Aisling when she won the U12 titles in Castlebar, the Connacht Open and Closed titles in Galway, in the Loughrea Open and in the Junior West of Ireland here in Sligo. Both Niamh, her younger sister, and herself have played for the Connacht tennis teams at under age level. In 2001 Aisling was the number 5 on a Connacht under age side, injuries prevented additional success. With a big smile she half-jokingly, half-serious, says that her dad "is my full time coach, manager and agent".

Niamh, by the age of eleven, had already climbed to great heights for one so young. She is also a player of exceptional standard in the sports of tennis and badminton. She likes both "equally". She was number 1 in Connacht and number 11 in the Irish under 12 rankings. In 1997, Niamh won the Connacht under 10 open and closed titles, the **Castlebar Open** and the West of Ireland Championships in **Sligo**. Her badminton is equally impressive winning the Connacht close and open titles at under 11 singles. She was also runner-up in the Ulster Open Singles championships. She has a string of doubles wins to augment her many singles results of note. By the end of 2001 she had beaten virtually all girls in her age group at one tournament or another, would be the number 1 under 14 in Connacht and number 6 in Ireland. If one was looking for an integrated sporting family, determined and successful, all with a pleasant demeanour and a great attitude to life, then one can look no further than the Burkes.

The Colemans

Sport is an important element in the Coleman household. Kevin, the dad, is originally from Roscommon where handball was his sport. When he came to work in Sligo he joined the St. Mary's GAA club, becoming keen on racquetball and, to a lesser extent, squash. Later he was to join the new **Sligo Tennis Club** where sport for himself and his growing family were inextricably linked. While playing a small amount of squash, badminton and table tennis, it was tennis that became his number one activity. He has become one of the few players that can play the game with the racquet in either hand. He only discovered this talent when the notorious 'tennis elbow' affected his primarily playing arm. New opponents were baffled and took a while to realise that he was constantly changing the racquet over from hand-to-hand during a match. This determination of Kevin's is a trait found in all the Coleman family. One event that many will recall was in the club tennis championships a few seasons ago. He managed to beat his opponent, Martin Holohan, with pure persistence. The match took three hours, the longest of the year. Kevin is a skilled card player and has

been a member of the Sligo Bridge Club for some years.

Helen is the mother in the Coleman household. From Sligo, she attended the Marist boarding school in Tubbercurry. There was little tennis played there. However, as goalie for the school's camogie team, she did make her name. Growing up in a large family with six sisters and four brothers, she had an ideal opportunity to play tennis at the **Merville Tennis Club** in Sligo and it became a game she would always enjoy. At an early stage she became a member of the tennis committee at Sligo Tennis Club and was honoured with the tennis captaincy for part of 1992 and all of the 1993 season. This duty she carried out with a great degree of enthusiasm and competence. It was, therefore, not in the least bit surprising that the Coleman children took to racquet sports from an early age. Like most modern families both parents share the taxi duties, willingly transporting the children to various events. Helen is fully occupied during the school year at the Carraroe national school and the family camping holidays in France have been a great way to relax away from work and committees.

There are four Coleman children, Sarah (25), Emily (24), Lucy (20) and Hanna (9). All are full of life and enthusiastic in what they do. While the youngest Hanna says Lucy is her 'best' sister one suspects that she herself is the favourite in the family. Despite this the Coleman's get on very well together as a family and will go places. Sarah was first off the blocks, born just a few months before the Sligo Tennis Club was formed. One of her initial interests was gymnastics and she was to become one of the most successful in the country in the under twelve category. Later Lucy was to enjoy the same sport in a Sligo club with plenty of talent.

At the Ursuline Convent the three eldest girls all played hockey with success. Sarah and Emily are now graduates and, while at Queen's and Dublin City University respectively, represented their university at the sport. They also represented their colleges in tennis. Growing up at the Sligo Tennis Club all have taken up tennis at about six years of age with Hanna just starting out with the short tennis game. This sport is suitable for young players being played with a sponge ball on a badminton court. By seven or eight they can progress to the full tennis court.

Sarah has represented Connacht at tennis (u14, u16, u18) badminton (u16) and hockey (u16) and Emily at tennis (u14, u18) and squash (u16, u19). The three eldest girls have a box full of trophies and medals earned from hard work and a gritty determination and skill. Sarah can remember one match in the West of Ireland Tennis championships (u14) when she came back from 5/1 down in the final set to beat the highly favoured Aisling Palmer. It took three and a half hours to do so. Sounds like Kevin's match. At 15, Sarah won the **Sligo TC** club badminton *senior* championships. She and Emily are qualified tennis coaches and have helped others with their game in their own club, in Strandhill and Mullaghmore. Emily has already obtained the bronze and silver stages of the *President's Award* and is heading for the gold award at present. This includes assisting with the teaching of mathematics in a school in Dublin. In 2002 Lucy was to be found moving into the coaching role at Strandhill with many new players taking up the game at the holiday village. Sarah has followed her dad into engineering and qualified with a mechanical engineering degree in Belfast. Currently (2005) she works in England and has become a playing member of **Leamington LTC**, the oldest lawn tennis club in the world. Emily studied computer applications. Sarah thinks that Lucy is the artistic one in the family, so she may yet diversify to other areas of endeavour. Based on the example set by her parents and sisters Hanna will undoubtedly be another successful Coleman. On and off the sports 'field' the family are a good example to all and will, justifiably, have many memories to look back on in the years ahead.

The Goodbodys

Due to the availability of records such as *Burke's Irish Family Records* and *The Landed Gentry of Ireland* we can trace a number of tennis playing families back to the early days of lawn tennis. Sometimes this can spring up surprises.

The Goodbody family is a good example. Excuse the unintended pun. Around 1660, John Goodbody, a Quaker, probably from County Cavan settled in King's County (present-day County Offaly). A descendent of his, Marcus Goodbody who lived at Inchmore, Clara (and Obelisk Park, Blackrock, County Dublin) married Hannah Woodcock Perry of Obelisk Park on the 13th December 1848. They had 13 children between 1850 and 1873. We know that at least three of these children played tennis. These were Margaret Elizabeth, Manliffe Francis and William Woodcock. Margaret married Corkman Benjamin Haughton on the 26th October 1880. They had several tennis-playing children including Benjamin who became a Davis Cup player. See the Haughton family and other chapters. Manliffe, the seventh eldest of the boys was to become the only Irishman to reach a US Open tennis final. He played soccer for Ireland too. Two years older was William Woodcock who married Caroline Harrison Spalding Dow, a New Yorker. He played the game but no details are available.

Two charts can be found in the following pages that highlight part of the family trees for the Goodbodys and Haughtons. Robert, of the family of 13 mentioned above, married Isabella Dora Pim of Dun Laoighre (called Kingstown at that time) on the 1st November 1872. They lived in New Jersey. Tennis player Marcus was born on the 20th November 1876- he was ranked 38th in the USA in 1897. Unfortunately Isabella died after their next child (Thomas Pim) in 1878. He married again in 1882. His second wife, Amy Sophia Urwick, died in May 1883, the month after the birth of their only child, Guy Urwick. In 1885 he married Margaret Jane Pim, the sister of

Isabella. It appears that they had four children, two boys and two girls. One of the boys, Maurice Frederick was known to have played tennis competitions in the mid-west. (Readers should note the highly significant Joshua Pim, a Wimbledon champion-details elsewhere).

One of Manliffe's brothers was James Perry (born 1853). His grandson, Harold Perry (1904-1972) was a Director of Ranks (Ireland) and of Irish Dunlop Ltd. and Admiral at the Royal Cork Yacht Club. He married Emma Margaret Newson of Cork in 1932. They had three daughters. The eldest was Margaret Perry. Her second sister was Penelope Elizabeth Perry (known as Penny) who was good enough to obtain a place on the Munster under 22 team in 1962. She married Cyril Eustace Hall, also a tennis player.

The third sister, Anthea Perry, would play for Munster for many years and earn her Irish colours in 1971. She was the number one lady in Munster for many years and had an Irish ranking of 3 in 1973. Back in 1962, the sisters played together in the Rushbrooke Open tournament. They reached the final only to meet the two finalists in the singles, Gene Hogan and Miss J. Midgley, and lose in two sets (8/10 1/6).

Through the Rushbrooke club, Anthea met Redmond O'Donoghue another useful tennis player. In fact Redmond's mother (Millicent, known at Mickie) and aunt (Moira) were exceptional players in their day. See elsewhere in book. They married in 1969 and now, living in Waterford, have two tennis-playing children in Christopher and Lynn. They have won much together including the Rushbrooke Open Mixed in the late 1970s. Playing together on the Irish veteran's team in recent years they have become the first husband and wife combination to achieve this standing.

There is no doubt that there are many other Goodbody tennis links that, in time, will be unearthed. One note of interest in this family is the fact that one of the Goodbody ladies became a Mrs. Fleming; their son Peter was to be one of the top American players in the 1980s. He was the tall partner to John McEnroe.

The Hacketts

Squash has been the main family sport since Padraig and Edel met for the first time over twenty years ago. They, and their children, all members of Sligo Tennis Club, are known throughout the four provinces for their keenness to play and promote the sport. On close examination we find that other sports also play an important role in the family. The children play their part. Teenagers, Cian and Aine have hours of enjoyment and success behind them and, no doubt, in their future.

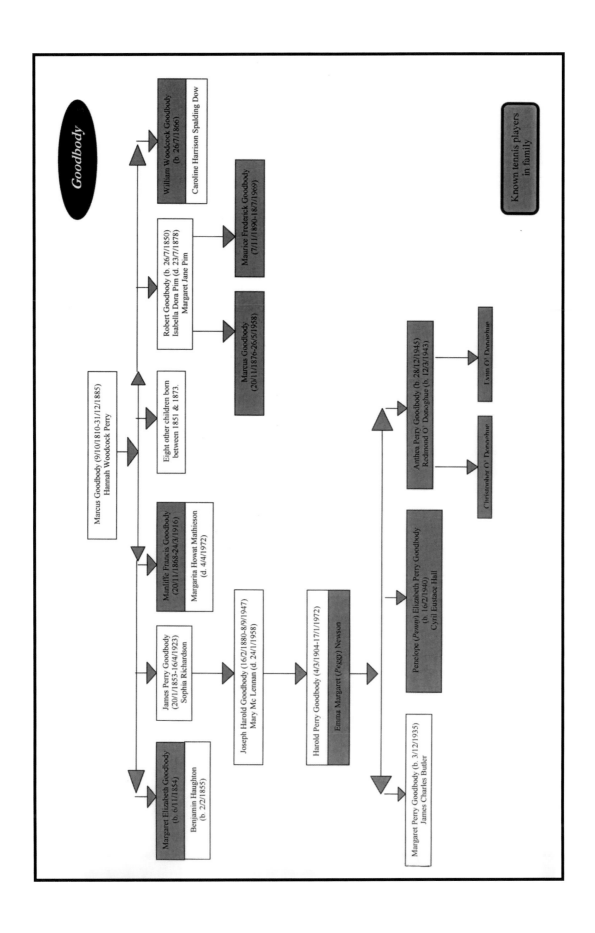

Goodbody

Known tennis players in family

Marcus Goodbody (9/10/1810–31/12/1885)
Hannah Woodcock Perry

William Woodcock Goodbody (b 22/7/1866)
Caroline Harrison Spalding Dow

Robert Goodbody (b. 26/7/1850)
Isabella Dora Pim (d. 23/7/1878)
Margaret Jane Pim

Maurice Frederick Goodbody (7/11/1890–18/7/1969)

Marcus Goodbody (20/11/1876–26/5/1958)

Eight other children born between 1851 & 1873.

Munliffe Francis Goodbody (20/11/1868–24/3/1916)
Margarita Howat Mathieson (d. 4/4/1972)

James Perry Goodbody (20/1/1853–16/4/1923)
Sophia Richardson

Margaret Elizabeth Goodbody (b. 6/11/1854)
Benjamin Haughton (b 2/2/1855)

Joseph Harold Goodbody (16/2/1880–8/9/1947)
Mary Mc Lennan (d. 24/1/1958)

Harold Perry Goodbody (4/3/1904–17/1/1972)
Emma Margaret (Peggy) Newson

Penelope (Penny) Elizabeth Perry Goodbody (b. 16/2/1940)
Cyril Eustace Hall

Margaret Perry Goodbody (b. 3/12/1935)
James Charles Butler

Anthea Perry Goodbody (b. 28/12/1945)
Redmond O' Donoghue (b. 12/3/1943)

Lynn O' Donoghue

Christopher O' Donoghue

The Hackett family of Sligo Tennis Club have had squash as their first sport but are equally competitive at other sports, including tennis. From left Aine Edel, Cian and Padraic. Aoife (front) was five when this photo and was just starting out on the sports trail.

The youngest, Aoife is just starting out on the sporting trail. Padraig is from Limerick city. There he attended the CBS secondary school. At that time hurling was his main interest. In addition, he played some soccer. In both, he modestly admits to being a non-achiever. He appears to have been introduced to squash by his father where they played at the Limerick Lawn Tennis Club. His father was a keen tennis player and, like most Limerick folk, was a keen rugby player, Shannon RFC being his club.

While studying in Sligo at the RTC, Padraig met Edel (Tully) and they were married a few years later. Edel, from Sligo had played a bit of hockey at school and some soccer with the Progression United Club. Both joined the Gillooly Hall Squash Club that had Sligo's only 'collapsible' court at the time. From there, they moved to the new Ballincar Hotel squash club where the game thrived in the early eighties. Both played for teams that did well in Connacht.

In 1985 the new facilities at the Sligo Tennis Club became the attraction and many squash players from Ballincar formed the nucleus of the new squash section there. Over the years this section was to see enormous success through the efforts of the better players. One loses count of the many junior interprovincial titles they contributed to, never mind the impressive representation at international level. Both Padraig and Edel have been firm supporters of this thriving section as players and organisers. Padraig became a qualified coach in 1986 and Edel was Squash Captain in 1988. She played an important part on the ladies team that won the Connacht A title in both the 1985 and 1987 seasons. Padraig has coached for many years, been a great organiser and could be found, in recent times, painting the squash courts keeping up his support for a game that has seen a recession in recent years. He has managed the interprovincial side in the past. The children have been very successful on the local courts, and at national level.

The Hackett family do have interests other than squash. Padraig took up tennis about seven years ago and he can be regularly seen with his children practicing on court. He has already won a 'B' section in the autumn league and, like many squash players before him, has a very strong backhand. He considers sport as a social outlet as much as anything else. He managed the Calry Community Games tennis side, they won bronze in 1998 and silver in 1999; Aine playing a large part in both teams and Cian in 1998. This is a good example where parents can be of benefit to a community as well as their own children. Aine's interests are broad as she plays Gaelic football as well as squash and tennis. When not studying she has also time for reading, modern dancing with Mary McDonagh and music (the tin whistle and the accordion). She has played on representative teams at u12 u13 u15 & u17. Cian is looking ahead and thinks he would like to study mechanical engineering. For the present squash, hurling and tennis are big interests. He admires the fighting spirit and tennis of Andre Agassi. On top of this he is a keen body boarder (a sport similar to surfing, we're told). His standard is such that he has in recent times been on the national under 17 squad. On the hurling side of things he has played on the successful Calry teams. As a goalkeeper he has also, at a young age, played on the County Senior team in that position. The Hackett family always seem cheerful. The balance between a competitive spirit on court and the enjoyment of the social side of sport is about perfect. May they long continue to play and be an example to others.

The Hamiltons

We can go back to the early 19th century to find the origins of one of the great racquet playing families of Ireland. On the 10th January 1849, Reverend Canon William Alfred Hamilton, Rector of Taney and Canon of Christ Church, Dublin, married Henrietta Katherine Cole of Annestown, County Waterford. They had six sons Henry Balfour (b. 18/12/1849), Alfred St. George (b. 5/12/1851), William Drummond (b. 4/8/1859), Willoughby James (b. 9/12/1864), Francis Cole Lowry (b. 26/4/1869) and Blaney (b. 13/6/1872). Willloughy was to have one of the most successful tennis records. His record includes winning six Irish Championships, three men's doubles (1886-1888), one mixed (1889) and two singles (1889 & 1890).

Willoughby is probably best remembered for the 1890 All-England Championships (Wimbledon) in which he beat another great Irishman Joshua Pim in the All-Comer's semi-finals. Having won this event he then faced the great Willie Renshaw in the Challenge round and came through to be the first Irishman to win Wimbledon (details elsewhere in book). Willoughby was also an international cricket player.

Willoughby James Hamilton was the first Irishman to win Wimbledon (1890). In the final he beat the great Willie Renshaw, seven times a winner. Willoughby also won the Irish Championships (1889), beating Willie's twin brother Ernest in the final.

The youngest of the Hamiltons was Blaney (born 13th June 1872). He lived at Dundrum Castle, Dublin and married Irene Kirkwood, daughter of General James Long Kirkwood. Two facts point to the possibility that she was from Boyle. Firstly there was a sizeable military barracks in the town and, secondly, there were several Kirkwood members at **Boyle LTC** at the time. Not much is known about Blaney's tennis playing career. He is confirmed as having had one international hockey cap and to have played 19 times on the Irish cricket team. He was the first winner of the Irish Open Badminton Championships in 1902. He also won the mixed at that event and, with Willoughby, took the men's doubles title. He would win the singles on two more occasions (1903, 1904), the men's doubles three times (1904, 1907, 1908) and the mixed a second time (1908).

Four of Blaney and Irene's children were to be prolific sportspeople. The second son, Arthur, born 29th January 1905, who lived at Churchtown, County Dublin, was an international badminton player but is most remembered for the fact that he won the first Irish Open Squash championships in 1932. At the time there was no Irish squash association and it would be several years before the first international would take place (against Scotland in 1937). He was a member of **Fitzwilliam LTC**, one of the few clubs to actually have squash courts at that time.

Willoughby (born 27th October 1907) was one of the best badminton players in the world in the late 1920s and early 1930s. According to Bernard Adams (1930) in *The Badminton Story* he was one of the best players in the world at that time. Mavis Henrietta Irene was born on the 14th September 1911. Mavis became Mrs. MacNaughton on 12th May 1934 and won titles under her married name. Both are said to have been international tennis and badminton players but Willoughby's son Hugh thought that they did not play any tennis of note. Hugh himself played several sports but none to the same high standard. He can remember being brought by Barbara Good (international tennis and badminton player) to a badminton club one evening. Initially he was put with the novices, and then when someone announced that he was the son of 'Rat' Hamilton (the name Willoughby signed his cheques with) he was put with advanced players. He was out of his depth he would admit. Hugh, however, has been a prominent member of **Fitzwilliam LTC** for many years and the club's honorary secretary in the late 1960s. In 1967, his claim to fame was the securing of Carroll's as sponsors of the Irish Open Tennis Championships.

Willoughby Hamilton-Irish open badminton champion.

Unfortunately, the tennis and cricket records are not complete but the Badminton Union of Ireland (BUI) in their 1981/1982 Yearbook published the full list of National and Open Champions since they began in 1911 and 1902, respectively.

Event	National*	Open
	Willoughby 1926, 1933, 1934	Blaney 1902, 1903, 1904
	Arthur 1931, 1932	Willoughby 1929, 1930, 1931, 1933
	Mavis 1931, 1932, 1933, 1934, 1935	Mavis 1939
	Willougby 1926, 1932, 1933	Willoughby James 1902
	Blaney 1931	Blaney 1902, 1904, 1907, 1908
	Arthur 1931	Willoughby 1934
Ladies Doubles	Mavis 1931, 1932, 1933, 1934, 1935	Mavis 1937, 1939,
	Willoughby 1926, 1932	Blaney 1902, 1908
	Mavis 1931, 1933	Mavis 1933
	Arthur 1931	

Irish Hamilton Badminton Champions

* Years refer to season starting in that year

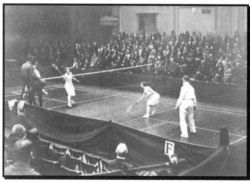

Mavis Hamilton (near side) playing an All-England mixed tie with Ireland's Jim Rankin against Donald Hume and Mrs. Betty Uber (of Uber Cup fame).

The Haughtons

The second family tennis tree, connected to the Goodbodys, is that of the Haughtons. They can be traced back to 1663, or earlier, in County Meath though the tennis branch of the family seems to have been in the south of Ireland. Many players over the age of 25 in Munster will know directly, or by reputation, of the skills and tennis talent of Alan Haughton. A gentleman, on and off the court, he has guided many players from the time he started playing tournaments in about 1930 up to the late 1980s.

It is only the true veterans in Munster that can recall his father and aunts. His father, Ben, was a Davis Cup player, followed by Alan in the same role, making them unique in Irish tennis. Ben's two

sisters were Margaret Wilhelmina (Marjorie) and Hannah Woodcock (Nancy), three and six years younger than Ben who was born in 1890. Their mother, Margaret Elizabeth Goodbody, born in 1854, was a tennis player. As we saw in the Goodbody family tree her sister was Manliffe Francis Goodbody who reached the final of the USA Championships in 1894. In the All-Comers Final he beat the great Bill Larned of the USA 4/6 6/1 3/6 7/5 6/2. In the Challenge round he was up against the holder Robert Wrenn. He did lose, 8/6 1/6 4/6 4/6, but Wrenn was one of the great American Davis Cup players, and US champion four times, so this was no disgrace. Among Manliffe's many achievements was an Irish Open Mixed title in 1893. It should not be forgotten that he was playing in that great 'golden' era of Irish tennis with Wimbledon champions such as Pim, Hamilton and Mahony at the top of the pile. Then there was Stoker, the doubles specialist. In the 1890s, Irishmen won four Wimbledon singles and two doubles with Lena Rice adding a ladies singles victory. More about these players later.

At Sunday's Well in August 1959, watching Alan Haughton win the Irish Close for the second time were his tennis-playing father, Ben, and aunts Marjorie (Margaret) and Nancy (Hannah). All four have won Open and/or Closed Irish championships.

Ben's father, also Ben (b. 1855), had a sister called Hannah Ridgway. She married a Goodbody too. This was Richard Goodbody from Tullamore who died in 1929. Ben (1890-1969) educated at Bootham school and then Trinity College, Dublin, married Marguerite Olive Beaulah (Daisy). The Haughton family were noted timber importers. He was one of four Davis Cup players from the Sundays Well Club in Cork. He featured on the team in 1926 while Alan did so in 1955. Ben's sisters, Marjorie and Nancy were excellent players.

It is noted that the eldest brother, Marcus (1888-1970), played some tennis too. In 1909, Marcus was 20 and Ben 19 years old when they played together in the handicap men's doubles at the **Blackrock** tournament. They appeared to have lost in the first round. Marjorie played singles at Wimbledon, with several wins, between 1920 and 1926. She and Ben were a very successful mixed combination. Their first senior tournament together was in 1908 at **Blackrock**, Cork. He was 18, she not quite 15. They won their first round 6/3 4/6 6/3 against J. Lyons and C. England but then lost to James Lyons and

Mrs. M. J. Daly 6/4 3/6 3/6. Their first tournament win was in 1911 when, off –3 again, they won the Open event at Tullamore beating Graham Trench and Miss Trench 6/4 3/6 6/2 in the final. Many mixed tournament **wins** would follow over the coming years including:

Year	Handicap	Tournament
1911	-15.1	Sunday's Well
1913	-40	Blackrock
1914	None	Blackrock
1914	-40	Blackrock
1915	-50	Club-Blackrock
1918	-40	Sunday's Well
1919	None	Blackrock
1919	-15	Fitzwilliam
1919	-40	Sunday's Well
1920	None	Blackrock
1920	-50	Sunday's Well
1920	None	Rushbrooke
1921	1/6 th	Roehampton
1921	None	Fitzwilliam-Irish Close
1923	None	Fitzwilliam-Irish Open
1923	None	Rushbrooke
1923	None	Blackrock
1924	None	Rushbrooke-Irish Close
1925	None	Sunday's Well-Irish Close
1925	None	Blackrock
1926	None	Rushbrooke
1926	None	Blackrock
1927	None	Blackrock
1934	None	Blackrock
1935	None	Blackrock

Probably some of their most significant wins were the Irish Close titles (1921, 1924 & 1925) and the Irish Open in 1923. In the latter they beat husband and wife combination of John and Una Miley in the final (6/2 6/3). At Wimbledon, in 1921, they beat G. Millard and the Honorary Mrs. Blanche Colston (6/4 6/4), Ernest Lamb and Mrs. Audrea Edgington (6/4 6/8 6/3) before losing, narrowly, to Alfred Beamish and Mrs. Ethel Larcombe (6/8 7/5 4/6). The latter reached the semi-finals that year. Mrs. Larcombe was a previous champion and won the mixed with Ireland's Jim Parke (1912 & 1914). Beamish was a Davis Cup player. He too partnered Jim Parke to two All-Comer's finals (1912 & 1913).

In the 1922 Wimbledon they had three wins. Two of their opposing men were Alfred Gore (Wimbledon Champion 1908 & 1909) and H. Roper Barrett, the men's doubles champion in 1912 & 1913. Mrs. Beamish, Gore's partner, was in the ladies doubles final in 1921. They beat that highly rated pair 9/7 6/1 in their third match but lost to Brian Gilbert and Mrs. Winifred McNair of Great Britain (2/6 3/6). Considering that Gilbert was a singles semi-finalist (1922) and Mrs McNair twice a quarter finalist

(1920 & 1921), this was no disgrace. The latter reached the semi-finals of the mixed that year. He also played in many club teams and in mixed matches with his second sister (Hannah/Nancy) and his wife (Marguerite/Daisy).

In the 1919 **Blackrock** Open tournament he played with Marjorie against Nancy and E. Harding in the final. In the **Rushbrooke** Open in 1921 he played with Nancy against J.F. Daly and Marjorie in the final. Guess who won? It was Ben and sister. With his wife Nancy, he won the **Nettleville** mixed in 1919, the Rushbrooke handicap mixed in 1920, the Waterford handicap in 1923, the **Tramore** handicap in 1924 and the **Glanmire** Open in 1926.

Ben Haughton in action at Fitzwilliam LTC in the mid 1920s.

Moving into the 1930s we see that Alan Haughton started to come into his own as a top player. In 1933, at the age of 16, he played with his older brother John (18 years) in the handicap men's doubles at **Rushbrooke**. They won their first match and lost the second in three sets against A.L. Moore and P. McCann. In the mixed, Alan played with his aunt Marjorie. They lost to C.J. Daly and Miss F. Daly. At Leighton Park School in 1934, it appears that Alan and F. Briathwaite won their doubles match against the old boys' pairing of Gammon and his brother John. The score suggests a tight struggle between the brothers (7/5 2/6 6/4).

In 1935 Alan won the handicap boys doubles at Rushbrooke. In the mixed he played with Pam Goodbody, a distant cousin. Despite the minus handicap they won this event losing only one set in four matches. At the Irish championships they had a handicap of –3 and won four before being stopped in the semi-final. Their conquerors were D. Jackson and R. Blair White (6/4 3/6 3/6).

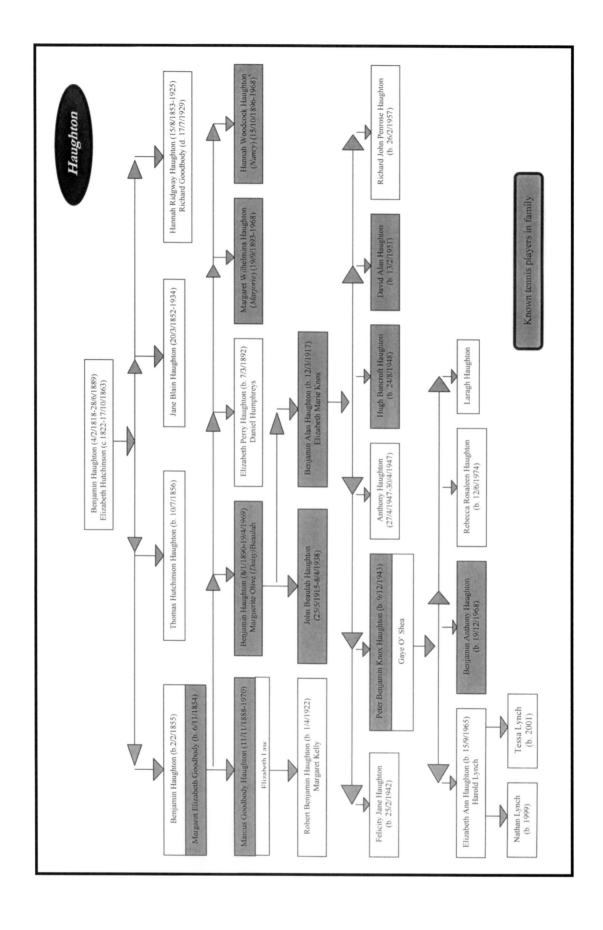

Haughton

Benjamin Haughton (4/2/1818-28/6/1889)
Elizabeth Hutchinson (c 1822-17/10/1863)

Hannah Ridgway Haughton (15/8/1853-1925)
Richard Goodbody (d. 17/7/1929)

Hannah Woodcock Haughton
(*Nancy*) (15/10/1896-1968)

Jane Blain Haughton (20/3/1852-1934)

Margaret Wilhelmina Haughton
(*Marjorie*) (19/9/1893-1968)

Richard John Penrose Haughton
(b. 26/2/1957)

Thomas Hutchinson Haughton (b. 10/7/1856)

Elizabeth Perry Haughton (b. 7/3/1892)
Daniel Humphreys

Benjamin Alan Haughton (b. 12/3/1917)
Elizabeth Marie Knox

David Alan Haughton (b. 13/2/1951)

Benjamin Haughton (b.2/2/1855)
Margaret Elizabeth Goodbody (b. 6/11/1854)

Benjamin Haughton (8/1/1890-19/4/1969)
Marguerite Olive (*Daisy*)/Beaulah

Hugh Bancroft Haughton
(b. 24/8/1948)

Laragh Haughton

John Beaulah Haughton
(25/5/1915-8/4/1938)

Anthony Haughton
(27/4/1947-30/4/1947)

Rebecca Rosaleen Haughton
(b. 12/6/1974)

Marcus Goodbody Haughton (11/11/1888-1970)
Elizabeth Law

Peter Benjamin Knox Haughton (b 9/12/1943)

Gaye O' Shea

Benjamin Anthony Haughton
(b. 19/12/1968)

Robert Benjamin Haughton (b. 1/4/1922)
Margaret Kelly

Felicity Jane Haughton
(b 25/2/1942)

Elizabeth Ann Haughton (b 15/9/1965)
Harold Lynch

Tessa Lynch
(b. 2001)

Nathan Lynch
(b 1999)

Known tennis players in family

Alan Haughton

In 1936, Alan played with his father Ben in the Open Men's doubles at the **Blackrock LTC** Open Tournament. He was 19 at the time and his father 46. It was to be an event that was long remembered by Alan and one of the best tennis moments in his long career. They beat P. J. Bromhead and J. E. Harding comfortably in the in the semi-final (6/2 6/1). The final was another matter. Their opponents were Captain Arthur Mahony, the Davis Cup player, and Ted Daly, the number 1 man in Cork at the time. They won the first set 6/3, and then lost the second agonizingly by five games to seven. They won the third set 6/3 and a most satisfying and proud title for both father and son. Ted Daly was the winner of the Open singles that year and Mahony on the winning side in the mixed. A newspaper report at the time said the following:

The best match on the programme on Saturday was the Open Men's Doubles, which heaped laurels on the head of the eighteen-year old Alan Haughton, who stood out in this battle as a player of amazing confidence and alert judgement. Patrnered by his father, who is always an impressive doubles player, he sent winning balls over the net time after time, picking out the best corners and eluding Daly and Mahoney who came up to the net to intercept. There was a good deal of close net play and clever volleying in all three sets, a feature that made the match extremely interesting for the spectators.

One suspects that this match was the changing of the guard and that dad, Ben, was proud of his young son. For the record Daly won that tournament (beating Freddie South in the final) and his partner Mahony was a Davis Cup player a few years earlier, no slouches. The same pairs met in the final at Blackrock a year later (1937). This time, Daly and Mahony won (7/5 4/6 6/4). Alan played again with his aunt Nancy while Marjorie played with Ben.

However, it was the young men (John and Alan) that came away with a title. They were off –15.3 in the men's doubles and went on to win the final 6/1 6/2 (against H. Robertson and H. Daly (-4)). This tournament was the last one recorded in the notebook of Ben Haughton, Alan's continued on until 1990.

At the back of the second book are the records of Alan's brother John from 1931 to 1937. In the handicap singles, at Blackrock (1937), he played off –3 and narrowly lost to Frank Mockler (-15.5) in the final 2/6 6/0 6/8.

Marjorie Haughton in her Wimbledon-playing days

Alan went on to great things on the tennis scene, details later. Three of his children and one grandson have taken up the game. In the early 1960s he played with son Peter in some tournaments. In 1965 he partnered his cousin, Anthea Goodbody, in a win for Munster over their Leinster rivals Harry Sheridan and Maureen O' Brien (4/6 6/2 6/2). The following year they won the mixed at Sunday's Well. In the final they beat Franks Furney and Ann Horgan 6/4 2/6 6/3. Further details on the life and times of tennis playing Haughtons can be found in other chapters.

The Jacksons

Families can be interlinked through tennis in many ways. Davis Cup player Peter Jackson of Belfast is a case in point. Many will not know that his older brother Billy (about 7 years of a difference) was a more than useful player too. They won a number of events playing together. In between was their sister Anne. She married another tennis player. He was Derek Noblett, a member of the **Cavehill LTC** in Belfast. Derek and Anne had a daughter, Susan, who was another player. She married Stephen Creber and, as modern day Ulster players will know, this husband

and wife combination have been associated with Belfast tennis administration for many years (Stephen being presented with the Torch Trophy Award by Princess Anne for his extensive efforts, in 1989). To complicate all this, Peter married Marjorie Jamison of Portadown. While the late Marjorie was a keen hockey player she was more a club tennis player rather than a serious competitor. She had a younger brother Lyn who has become a keen and useful player and was recently (2002-2003) the president of the Ulster Council. I think if we delved deeper we would find many more tennis connections. Has your club got such a network? I'd be surprised if the answer is no. The generations do pass on the love of the game in many ways.

Brothers Billy (left) and Peter Jackson in action.

The McGloins

From outside Ballyshannon, Kevin McGloin moved to England to seek employment in the early 60s. There he met Mary, his wife to be. She was originally from Ennistymon, County Clare and was studying nursing and then employed at the Old Church Hospital in Romford. While Kevin had played some handball in Donegal, he was to become interested in athletics and also become a Manchester United fan. Mary attended the Mercy Convent in Clare where camogie was her main sport. This was to change. From watching tennis it became something both could play and enjoy together on the many municipal courts available to them in England.

They returned to Ireland when job prospects in Sligo appeared and later joined Sligo Tennis Club. Tennis became a major interest as did badminton and keener members of a club would be hard to find. There has rarely been a competition in the last fifteen years without a member of the McGloin family participating. Both play regularly on badminton league teams in the winter months when the sport is most active. Tennis is now a twelve-month sport and Mary plays virtually every week. Kevin, who *had to be dragged out to play tennis* at one time, now sees the sport as his main interest. A number of years ago they build their own grass court at home. This has become a focal point for all the family, weather permitting. When Kevin took up badminton he added to his interests; he could not believe how enjoyable a sport it could be. In the club married couples annual tennis event they were delighted to win the 'C'

section a couple of years ago. What about the six McGloin children? They are all very successful in their studies, work and sport. There are a great variety of talents found in this happy household. Iona, the eldest, with a Masters degree in environmental science is employed as a pollution officer with a local authority in Kerry. She has an environmental diploma and a M.Sc. to her credit. A year younger is the twins, Caroline and Mark. Caroline is an analytical chemist and working in QA in the UK while Mark, with a primary degree from Limerick University, and a Masters degree in computing from Kent University, now works in the futures exchange in London. All are tennis players.

The eclectic McGloin family at their home court. From left: Atlanta, Kevin, Mary, Stephen and Caroline. Missing from photo are Iona, Mark and Naomi.

Atlanta was the first to be born in Sligo and subsequently attended the Mercy Convent. Hockey was her sport then. She has now diversified and, apart from some family tennis, is big into canoeing and has been secretary and/or PRO for a local club. She has also played some squash. She too has studied hard with a primary degree from UCD and a diploma from UCG. She is involved in sales, training and the teaching of computer technology. Naomi has always been a good badminton and tennis player and has a silver medal in the former from the community games a few years ago.

Naomi was voted by the family as the one with the *killer instinct*, in simple terms she likes to win at sport. On the academic front she looks like an achiever too having studied business studies and accountancy at Limerick University.

The youngest of the family Stephen took up softball, followed by badminton and tennis. Badminton has been his number one sport and he has been one of the best junior players at Sligo Tennis Club in recent years. Apart from club championships, he has won many open events over the last ten seasons. Now doing his Leaving Certificate at Summerhill College, Stephen would like to study computers in UCG next year. One suspects that there is a bit of the killer instinct in all the family. This is a compliment in the best possible way and it is augmented by a variety of characteristics but all personable in their own way. These features are used to best advantage in their studies, careers and in sport. The McGloins are a family setting a good example to all.

The O'Tooles

While Seamus learned his tennis in his hometown of Tinahely (County Wicklow) both he and his family are all keen and well-established members of the Sligo Tennis Club. Wife Lea (nee Tighe) is Sligo born and bred, first starting tennis in the Merville club and at the Ursuline Convent. All three daughters attended their mother's *alma mater* and have taken willingly to the sport with keenness.

While many kids learned their tennis by rallying against a wall or garage door Seamus had a 'net' at home. An old fishing net was used by the family in the backyard. He had a brother and sister who provided the opposition. A friend of the family, Helen Farrell, provided him with his first wooden racquet (metal/graphite racquets had not yet arrived). Qualifying as a civil engineer he joined Sligo County Council in 1979. With the new club now active he took up the game again (in 1983) and has been a committed member since.

Seamus is the current (2006) president of the club, having been tennis captain a couple of years ago. As keen a member as one could find. He has been involved in the tennis committee "for yonks" and was always a willing worker. He invariably finds humour in the running of the club and is always willing to contribute ideas on its operation. He has a keen interest in soccer. He also plays a little golf, particularly in the engineer's outings. When it comes to tennis he can be found winter and summer playing in the weekly doubles competitions, he particularly likes mixed doubles.

Seamus met Lea at the "Leinster CC" disco in Dublin in the early eighties. Tennis was a common denominator. However, she has other interests including camogie, having been a regular player during her time in the Ursuline. She also likes horse riding. Both can be found playing table tennis from time to time, and quite capably. Like Seamus, she is a keen weekly player and both would enter nearly every tournament in the club.

The O'Toole children were taxied and encouraged in sport from an early age. Olwyn took to gymnastics in the very good Sligo club with eagerness at the age of four. She was to become a junior and senior international. While Olwyn took up 'short' tennis at the age of six the gymnastics continued until two years ago. She has also played hockey, badminton, squash and table tennis. However, in the last few years, it is the tennis that has dominated her life. Undoubtedly, she is one of the best juniors to come from the Sligo club in its twenty-one years. In 1996 and 1997 she won the West of Ireland u16 singles titles and in 1998 the u18 title. She is probably one of the youngest qualified tennis coaches in Ireland and in 1999 was coaching up to 85 newcomers to the game. The club will be glad to hear that she thinks "the tennis practice wall is the best thing since sliced bread". In 2003 Olwyn was involved in the promotion of tennis among young people who would not normally have such an opportunity. Part of this was the organisation of celebrity matches in the city.

Among the participants was Mark Feehily of Sligo, now better known as a member of Westlife.

The keen and successful O'Toole family of Sligo. From left: Yvette, Karen, Lea, Seamus and Olwyn.

In a family of friendly clamour and banter ("Mum is a plugger at tennis" and Yvette "keeps rodents"), Karen and Yvette do get their say. Both took up short tennis (the game designed for beginners with a soft ball played on a badminton court) at the age of six. From the age of 8 Karen was a keen and successful gymnast for some six years. However, it is horse riding that is her favourite sport, working out at Island View and Mc Garry's. Her ambition in life is to be a veterinary surgeon. Yvette is also keen on animals, has a pet hamster and loves dogs and attending dog shows. She plays badminton 'on and off' and is a more than competent member of the schools U14 basketball team. Generous in praise of her older sister she says "she got better (at tennis) after coaching lessons from Olwyn". In any family this is a high accolade. The last word from Lea says much "they would be lost without Sligo Tennis Club".

Other Families

Above we have a scant profile of some well-known sports families complemented by some more local ones. They all have several things in common. Success has come through an interest in the sport, whether it is at club or international standard. Many sports, other than tennis, can be found among the younger and older members of a family. On top of this, the common interest in sport has proved to be a healthy bonding element. Sport has proved in each of these families to be a recipe for success in life.

In case the reader feels that other more significant families should be included then it is likely that they are included in detail later under the *Who's Who* chapter. For the present a few might be mentioned. The O'Shea family, members of **Monkstown LTC** are extremely talented. John, the father, is the former sports reporter and founder of GOAL, the international charity. In 2000, he was starting his 42nd consecutive season playing in the Dublin leagues. Mother, Judy (nee Gallagher) won the clubs Perpetual Challenge Cup for ladies six times in the 1960s. In 2000, she started her 38th year in the Dublin leagues. She was club honorary secretary from 1994 to 2001. Daughter Lisa was Irish number 8 in 1989 and

The Flattery sisters at "Aileach", their home court in Sligo in the 1940s. From left Finola, Eithne and Maeve.

number 7 for the year 2000. At the start of the leagues that year she was playing number one for the club and her brother, Stephen, number one on the men's side. Not too many families would make up such a talented quartet.

If we look around the country today, and in club's records, we will find hundreds, if not thousands, of tennis playing families. Many are dealt with in various ways later. In the 19th century, in the Dublin area we would find the Chaytor brothers and, as successful, the Langrishe sisters in Kilkenny. They also had a tennis-playing brother. As we move into the 20th century we find a number of Dublin Martin's, particularly Louisa.

The Scroope brothers, all three of them, were among the top in the 1910s and 1920s. The Miley dynasty started back in the 1910s, or earlier, and is still around (in a tennis sense) nearly 100 years later. The Blair-Whites, the Meldons and the Wallis's are three

families of note in the early part of the century. In the 1920s in Ulster we would find Jacksons, Pedlows, Corry and Gottos, all names that have come through to today.

Junior Close Finals

RESULTS of the finals of the Irish Junior Close Championships at Rushbrooke, Cork, on Saturday, were:—

SENIOR

Boys Singles—D. Mockler (Cork) bt M. Atkins (Cork) 6-3, 6-2.

Girls Singles—Miss F. Murphy (Rushbrooke) bt Miss L. Murphy (Rushbrooke) 4-6, 6-4, 7-5.

JUNIOR

Boys Singles—E. Smith (Cork) bt D. McCarthy (Cork) 6-2, 6-2.

Girls Singles — Miss M. O'Sullivan (Tralee) bt Miss M. Ronan (Rushbrooke) 6-4, 4-6, 6-4.

20th August 1950

Three generations of the tennis playing Bayliss family from the CIYMS club in Belfast. This was taken in 1983. The ILTA President (1979 and 1987) seen here with his mother Peggy and daughter Sarah.(Belfast Telegraph, 1983)

Michael & Orla Conlon from Ennis TC

Junior Close Finals

RESULTS of the finals of the Irish Junior Close Championships at Rushbrooke, Cork, on Saturday, were:—

SENIOR

Boys Singles—D. Mockler (Cork) bt M. Atkins (Cork) 6-3, 6-2.

Girls Singles—Miss F. Murphy (Rushbrooke) bt Miss L. Murphy (Rushbrooke) 4-6, 6-4, 7-5.

JUNIOR

Boys Singles—E. Smith (Cork) bt D. McCarthy (Cork) 6-2, 6-2.

Girls Singles — Miss M. O'Sullivan (Tralee) bt Miss M. Ronan (Rushbrooke) 6-4, 4-6, 6-4.

20th August 1950

Titles For Brother And Sister

G. D. FITZPATRICK, and his sister, Miss June Fitzpatrick, won the singles finals of the Co. Dublin Intermediate Tennis championships at Mount Temple yesterday.

The postponed men's singles was resumed with F. J. Horne leading Fitzpatrick 4-2, but his advantage soon vanished, the winner taking the first four games yesterday to win the set 6-4. The second opened brightly and it looked as if the match might run to three sets, but then Fitzpatrick returned to top form to win 6-3

After having been extended by Miss A. Morrin in the first set Miss Fitzpatrick ran out an easy winner of the second.

Men's Singles—G D Fitzpatrick bt. F. J. Horne, 6-4 6-3.

Ladies' Singles—Miss J Fitzpatrick bt Miss A Morrin 7-5 6-0

20th August 1951

In the middle of the 20th century names such as Kemp, Mockler, Peard, Egan and Hackett make regular appearances. In the latter half we find the great Fitzgibbons (Jim, Mary and Ken), the Beirne brothers, the Nugents, the Crowes, the Fearons, the Sheridans, the Doyles, all from the Dublin area, and the Tuffs in Belfast. The list goes on. The McArdles from County Louth are an interesting family and successful at badminton and squash as well as tennis. Jim senior was an Irish ranked player in 1952 while Jim junior was ranked from 1972 to 1984 (number 2 in 1976). At the Ardee Championships in 1965 Jim Junior beat his brother, Frank, in a three set final. Frank and Jim senior won the men's open doubles. Jim senior ten added to the family wins by taking the mixed with Miss Lewis.

Brothers Brendan (left) and Dermot Quinn followed their father Joseph into playing a major role in the success of Sutton Lawn Tennis Club for over four decades.

Two families connected to **Donnybrook LTC,** and other clubs such as **Fitzwilliam LTC**, and worth a mention, are the Davy's and the Sheehan's. Eugene was that great rugby player from the early par of the 20th century. His eight children all played tennis, a grass court at home was an added advantage to this development. Apart from the school teams of Mount

The History of Irish Tennis

Anville and Gonzaga, they featured right up to international standard. In order they were Miriam (b. 1944), Joseph (*Joe*) (under 19 champion at Gonzaga in 1961) (b. 1946), Alice, Charlie, Geraldine, Eugene (b. 1954), Bernadette (*Berni*) (Federation Cup player) (b. 1956) and Elizabeth (b. 1958). A cousin of these children, Brian Davy (b. circa 1941) was also school champion at Gonzaga, in 1960. Berni's children are now all fine young players making their mark at Donnybrook and elsewhere.

BROTHER AND SISTER WIN TENNIS TITLES

G. FITZPATRICK, the Belvedere College boy, added the Irish junior singles title to the Leinster and Irish close championship honours he had already gained this season, at Fitzwilliam club yesterday.

He beat T. Crooks of Ballymena in the final, but only after the match had gone to a final set.

The girls' championship final was also a three-setter, a marathon affair in which the holder, Miss Heather Cole, successfully resisted the challenge of Miss June Dwyer from whom she had captured the title last year.

Miss June Fitzpatrick, sister of the boy champion, made the occasion quite a family affair by retaining her under-fifteen title, and the boys' under-fifteen championship was taken by a very promising youngster in T. McNamara.

Details:—
CHAMPIONSHIPS

Senior Boys—G. Fitzpatrick (Belvedere Coll.) bt. T. Crooks (Ballymena Academy) —11-9, 4-6, 6-1.

Senior Girls—Miss Heather Cole (Alexandra Coll.) bt. Miss June Dwyer (Coombe House)—3-6, 6-4, 10-8.

Junior Boys—T. McNamara (St. Vincents C.B.S.) bt. B. Kilcoyne (C.B.S., North Brunswick Street, 8-2, 6-2.

Junior Girls — Miss June Fitzpatrick (Sacred Heart, Leeson St.) bt. Miss Tiffen Duggan (Sacred Heart, Mount Anville)—6-1, 6-0.

HANDICAPS

Boys' Singles—Class "A"—P. Molloy (15.2) bt. G. McNamara (—15)—6-3, 6-2. Class "B"—D. Mockler (—15.2) bt. J. Buckley (15.3)—6-2, 6-4

Girls' Singles—Class "A"—M. Ryan (15.3) bt. E. Colclough (—2)—10-8, 6-3. Class "B"—J. Morris (3) bt. L. Byrne (4)—6-4, 6-3.

Boys' Doubles—T. and G. McNamara (—2) bt. T. Cleary and J. Binchy (—15.5) —6-2, 6-3.

Girls' Doubles—Misses M. Mahon and R. Blair White (15) bt. Misses June and Joy Cairnduff (5)—14-12, 6-2.

Mixed Doubles—T. Cleary and Miss H. Cole (—5½) bt. J. Binchy and Miss S. Hannin (scr.)—6-4, 10-8.

29ᵗʰ August 1948

The Sheehan brothers were also prolific tennis players. In order of age they are James (*Joe*), Gareth (Gonzaga champion 1963 and 1964), Ronan (tennis writer among other things (b. 1953), Maurice (b. circa 1954) (good tennis and soccer player) and Jerry (b. 1957) (Gonzaga champion 1972-1975, Irish boy's champion 1975).

The Nilands from Limerick have made their note and are directly linked to the Ryan's who grew up in Galway. The Threadneedle Road club has provided many great players including the Dempsey's and Thornton's. Country areas have provided good tennis playing families among which we find the Houlihan's of Birr. Geraldine we know of but her father, uncle and aunt were more than useful. In Castlebar, there were the Milletts, Kilkellys and Goravans while at Merville (in Sligo) there were the Flattery sisters and the Burkes to contend with as competitive players. In the 1950s the three Burke sisters from Sligo (Margaret, Grace and Geraldine) all played together for the province. In a few years brother Billy did likewise.

Organising families included the Duffs and "The Mighty" Quinns of Sutton and the Crebers in Belfast. The Smiths and Scannels of Munster could be found

in playing and organising roles. The same could be said of the Brewsters of **Brookfield LTC** and the Spillanes and Blakeneys of **Glenageary LTC**. In Ulster, particularly in County Fermanagh, we find names such as Barnes, Cramsie, Semple, Winslow, Pollock and Taylor as players and some times organisers over a lengthy period of time.

Barnivilles take four titles

THE combined tennis talents of Harry and Geraldine Barniville reaped impressive rewards in the Co. Wicklow Hard Court Championships which ended at the Greystones Club yesterday.

Harry won the men's singles and doubles titles, and Geraldine captured the ladies' singles event and then joined her husband in a victorious mixed doubles partnership.

After Geraldine had ruthlessly applied the finishing touches to a brave but outclassed Ann Coghlan in the singles final, Harry, now watched by his wife, almost allowed Ronan Fearon to turn the tables on him.

Harry won the first set easily enough 6-3, but he lost his service when leading 5-3 in the second set, and eventually had to withstand a more than spirited challenge from the underdog before taking the second set.

Harry later teamed up with Jim Buckley, who was making his first appearance in a tournament this season, and beat Fearon and Harry Sheridan in a closely-fought doubles match. Despite the toll these two efforts must undoubtedly have taken on his stamina, Harry, playing with his wife, accounted for Danny Moroney and Valerie Barry in the mixed doubles.

Men's Singles Final—H. Barniville bt. R Fearon, 6-3, 8-6

Ladies' Singles Final — Mrs. H. Barniville bt. Miss A. Coghlan 6-1, 6-1.

Men's Doubles Final — H. Barniville and J. P. Buckley bt. R. Fearon and H. Sheridan, 6-3, 4-6, 6-3.

Ladies' Doubles Final — Misses A. O'Gorman and V. Barry bt. Mrs. J. P. Buckley and Mrs. M. Jackson, 6-3, 6-0.

Mixed Doubles Final — H. and Mrs Barniville bt. D. Moroney and Miss V Barry, 6-2, 6-2.

30ᵗʰ May 1966

The Gearty's of Longford have been useful players over the years but must be recommended for their organising roles over the last forty years plus. Lattin is a relatively new club (founded 1952) but has significant organisers in the Hourigan and Daly families. Being parochial for a moment, again, this writer would like to mention some further families who have been involved as players and organisers at **Sligo TC**. These include the McGarry's, Burke's (John), Walshe's (two), Butler's, Dolan's, Forkan's, Little's, O' Mahony's, McGee's and the Brennan's.

Twin Sisters In Junior Close Final

TWIN sisters, Flora and Laura Murphy, of Rushbrooke, will contest the final of the girls' senior singles in the Irish Junior Close Tennis Championships at Rushbrooke to-day.

David Mockler, last year's singles winner, meets Michael Atkins in an all-Cork Boys' Senior Singles final.

Senior Boys' Singles—Semi-finals—D Mockler beat J. D. Moore, 5-1, 6-0; M. Atkins beat M. Dorman, 6-2, 3-6, 10-8.

Junior Boys' Singles—Semi-finals—E. Smith (Cork) beat R. Sweetman, 6-2, 6-4; D. McCarthy (Cork) beat J. Leamy, 6-0, 6-4.

Senior Girls' Singles—Semi-finals—Miss F Murphy bt. Miss J. Ronan, 8-6, 6-4, 6-3; Miss L. Murphy bt. Miss P. O'Sullivan, 6-2, 6-0.

Junior Girls' Singles—Quarter finals—Miss S. Coffey w.o., Miss M. Goodbody scr.; Miss M. O'Sullivan bt. Miss I. Cussen, 6-2, 6-0; Miss G. McNamara bt. Miss D. Kelly, 6-3, 6-2. **Semi-finals**—Miss O'Sullivan bt Miss S. Coffey, 6-3, 7-5; Miss M. Ronan (Rushbrooke) bt. Miss McNamara, 6-4, 6-2.

19th August 1950

Often forgotten are tennis players who leave Ireland. However, to finish this brief, chapter a few notes on the Bowyer family. Brendan Bowyer was from Waterford, played tennis in his youth, but was best known as the professional showband singer. For many years now he has lived in Los Vegas, Nevada. He married Stella Brennan, a good tennis player at **Galway LTC**. Her brother John won the Irish Open under 15 title at **Fitzwilliam LTC** in 1960. In that final he beat Frank McArdle of Dundalk 4/6 6/2 6/4. Another brother Gerard and sister Joan also played representative tennis. Joan won the Connacht Open Singles championship in 1960. Brendan and Maeve had three success children. Brendan junior was the number 1 tennis player at high school in Las Vegas and ranked nationally. He won the Nevada State championships (junior?) four times and the Governor's Cup twice. In 1985, Brendan and his mother won their way through local, state and regional events before reaching the national mother and son final. They won this title. This was one event in the Family tournament, the finals being held during the US Open. In 1986 he came to Ireland and won the Open boy's title, as well as the doubles with Liam Croke. He was selected for the Irish junior side that year. He earned a tennis scholarship to the University

of Utah. Brendan is currently (2002) Director of tennis at the Cottonwood Country Club in Salt Lake City, Utah. Over the year Brendan has played against such tennis notables Andre Agassi, Pete Sampras and Jeff Terango. Stella has kept up her tennis and has represented her club, the Green Valley Athletic Club, for many years including national inter-club events.

Daughter Clodagh, like her brother, was ranked number 1 girl in Las Vegas for many seasons and won the Governor's Cup (State Championship) several times. She was a nationally ranked junior and was chosen by Mike Agassi for special training, over a six year period. She too has played many notables in junior tournaments. These included Linday Davenport, Lisa Raymond and Chanda Ruben. She also played with Andre Agassi, when home from his international engagements. At university, Clodagh also had a scholarship and was tennis team captain at the University of Utah. Clodagh trained as an actor in New York. While there she coached at places such as the Central Park Tennis Center and the tennis club at Grand Central. She has taught alongside John McEnroe and Monica Seles. She subsequently taught for a period in Dublin at Riverview and Castleknock. Today (2002) she continues to coach at Crosstown Tennis Center, 5th Avenue, New York, as well as being a professional actor on the stage and in television. The Pollack four brothers of **Omagh LTC** have been and still are, to varying degrees involved in the sport for about four decades. At their peak the twins Derek and Maurice were good enough to play in the Irish Open Championships. Another set of twins, Evie and Mimi Hallinan, played together on the Munster u18 team in 1942. Let us finish up here by noting that the tennis playing family is a wide and long living one. Also to be remembered is the fact that there are many in your club deserving recognition for long service. Finally may every parent give their children an opportunity to try the game and ensure their life does not pass without some memory of a perfectly timed and satisfying serve and volley, even though not necessarily in the same rally.

The 2001 husband and wife champions at Sutton Lawn Tennis Club were Joe and Gaye Walsh.

Limerick's International players Gina and Conor Niland started tennis at a young age.

The Brewsters at Brookfield LTC (l. to r.): Gerry, Patricia and Elizabeth. Family member James was the President of Tennis Ireland in 1993.

Cartoon illustration given to the husband and wife combination of Vincent & Agatha McGee when visiting their relations in Canada.

Sutton LTC 2002. From left: Joe Walsh (captain), Camillus Dooley (president), Peter & Collette Gillett, (husband and wife champions) & Mary Barry (lady captain).

The History of Irish Tennis

PROFILE — RAYMUND EGAN

At thirty-four years of age, Dublin wine-merchant Raymund Egan is still one of the leading tennis players in Ireland in spite of international experience dating back over twelve years. The second of a family of three boys and a girl, his father was a well-known amateur soccer player with the famous Freebooters Club, while his mother was a sister of Dr. J. D. McCormack, the international golfer, so the family has a good mixture of sporting blood.

At St. Gerard's School, Bray, Raymund divided his sporting activities between tennis and hockey, and while, subsequently he played the winter game for Three Rock Rovers for a few seasons, tennis gradually but surely absorbed all his spare time. He won the junior championship in 1933, and making steady progress from then onwards, he was chosen on the Davis Cup team and in the international against England in 1938. Further honours came to him in the following year when he played against Yugoslavia and England, and he was just about at his best when the war shut down on "big" tennis. He was Irish open champion in 1940 and 1941, and close champion in 1944.

He kept his place on the Davis Cup team when that competition was resumed in 1946, and in 1948 and 1949 figured in both matches against England. In all, he has secured thirteen "caps" so far, and as he keeps himself very fit, there should be more to come, for he is even more skilful now in doubles than in singles.

His younger brother, Bernard, has appeared with him on many successful Lansdowne teams in the Dublin inter-club competition, while his sister, Catherine, not only won the Irish girls' tennis title, but has since become the leading Irish woman table tennis player.

Raymund was only one of many successful members of the Egan family from Dublin. (The Irish Tatler & Sketch, May 1950)

Dublin star Michael Nugent with his parents.

Kevin, and father Sean, Sorensen both played Davis Cup for Ireland. In 2005 Louk earned this honour. Sean played between 1976 and 1987 while Kevin had his first match in 2004 and Louk in 2005. This is the first time that three members of the same family have played for Ireland in this competition. By July 2005 the winning score for the family is 36 wins to 29 losses.

1953- The Reeves-Smyth family were keen tennis players. This photograph was taken at their home court at Ashbrook. From left: Noni Plunkett-Dillon, Patrick Reeves-Smyth, Frank Plunkett-Dillon and Maeve Lanigan. Tom Cooper sits on swing awaiting his turn.

The Boden family enjoying family tennis on their Mediterranean holiday. From left: Ivar, Conor, Sheila (nee Hannon) and Dermot. Ivar captained the Belvedere College team fro three years (1939-1941) and then the UCD team that won the Dublin Class 1 league in 1946 and 1947. In 1955 he was Irish Close mens' doubles champion. Ivar and Sheila were lcub mixed doubles champions at the Queen's club in London in the 1960s. Dermot captined the English Public Schools' team that played against the All-England club. Conor reached the semi-finals of the Irish junior championships.

Brothers Gerry (on left) and Tom Cleary of Castleview Lawn Tennis Club (Carrick on Suir) before one of their many finals. In this match the younger Gerry won the Munster Championship, at Waterford. The photo was taken in the late 1950s. At the time Gerry was playing inter-varsity tennis for University College, Dublin. Tom won the South of Ireland title in 1953 at Limerick Lawn Tennis Club. Another brother, John, and Tom were on the Castleknock College, Dublin, senior team that won the Leinster School's Senior Cup for lawn tennis in 1948. Tom was captain of the school's successful senior rugby and table tennis teams that year. In 2005, Tom's niece, Ursula Kane Cafferty, wrote his very interesting life-story ("Suitcase Number Seven"). Tom played for the Munster senior team in 1957 and was a sub on the Irish rugby team for many years. In 1956 Gerry was the Irish boy's representative at Wimbledon. Another brother Michael, younger than Gerry & John and older than Gerry, added to the family tennis representation. He played on the same club team as Gerry & Tom in the 1950s. Tom's wife Maureen (nee O'Callaghan) was also on this team.

The Jackson family of Belfast (circa 1960). On left is Peter, one of the top Irish players in the 1950s and 1960s. Beside him is his brother Billy, a successful player on the Ulster scene. On the right are their parents.

Relaxing at the 1922 Sligo Open (now the West of Ireland) were (from left) Gundrede, Brigid and Gray Wynne. Gundrede won the title that year. In the 1921 final she was beaten by her sister Brigid in a closely contested final (3/6 7/5 5/7).

The Grier family at Elm Park attending the Dublin Lawn Tennis Council centenary dinner in 2001. From left: Stephen, Mary (Boden), Noel, Jenny, Gillian and David. A keen and successful tennis-playing family. Mary was hardcourt champion at the club in 1991, 2001, 2002, 2004 and 2005. She won the grasscourt championship in 2001 and 2004.

The History of Irish Tennis

3.6   *The Young Ones*

I never realised how appreciative young children could be.
(The Barniville Babes, 2002)

Ever since Lottie Dod first won Wimbledon (1887), at the tender age of 15 years and 10 months, there seems to have always been an interest in the up and coming tennis stars. It is part fascination and part curiosity when the spectator notices an immature boy or girl taking on the better adults and beating them. In international and local events this challenge becomes newsworthy, the bigger the player being knocked out the bigger the headlines. Recent memory can immediately go back to Wimbledon 1999 when 16-year-old Jelena Dokic upset number one seed Martina Hingis in the first round. The score line of 6/2 6/0 **was** news. In 1985, it was the 'wunderkid', Boris Becker who, at the age of 17, won Wimbledon. Not alone was he the youngest even men's champion but also the first unseeded player, and first German, to grab this most prestigious of titles.

A player closer to home who has done well is Limerick's Gina Niland. At 14 she was a senior interprovincial player. In 1988, as an under 16 player, she was number one in that age group and the under 18 category and number four in the Irish senior rankings. The following year she won the Maunsell Trophy and the Fergus O'Shee Memorial Award for her many successes. By 2001 she had represented Ireland on the Federation Cup team for an exceptional twelve years. Back in 1942 Joe Hackett was only sixteen when reaching the Irish Open final (losing to the distinguished Cyril Kemp in the final). Joe was subsequently to have an eleven-year stint as a Davis Cup player (1950 to 1961). There have been many other Irish juniors of note, some mentioned elsewhere in this book.

Attempts to keep young players in check, on and off the court, have been partly successful. Apart from burnout there are the etiquettes of the game (and of life) to consider. The former has to be prevented and the latter learned. It appears necessary, during the teenage years of development, to be wary of the needs of the younger players. Apart from the sports skills there are factors such as education, physical growth and an acquiring of social skills. Many will remember the blossoming of Treacy Austin, Andrea Jaeger and Jennifer Capriati. They all had problems. Richard Williams seems to have achieved the right balance as a parent and tennis coach. The better players have to learn the social skills fast as they are in the limelight on a regular basis. Many will have started out as under 10s and are good mixers. Others go on to court and their frustration and/or temper may bubble to the surface very quickly. John McEnroe took a long time to grown out of these phases. There are still signs of a volatile nature in his senior tour matches.

In an Irish context we have our better juniors attempting to be the big fish in a relatively small pool. From local tournaments, and a smattering of matches abroad, some may be asked to play in junior Wimbledon; others will play full time and progress further. In the not so distant past it was, for those

playing, a game to be enjoyed morning, afternoon and evening. Television had not arrived; tournament opportunities were limited and transport to tournament venues difficult. With increased mobility, in a rising 1960s economy, the junior game expanded. Those living in the metropolitan areas of Dublin, Belfast and Cork had a range of events near home. Juniors in the remainder of the country had to make more of an effort. Young players in Longford, for example, would get a bus to the Cavan Open week, perhaps a train to Mullingar or be driven by a parent to Galway. The more adventurous might challenge the Dubs in their own back yard. A week with an aunt in Dublin was acceptable; the tennis at a big venue such as **Lansdowne LTC** or **Fitzwilliam LTC** was the attraction.

Hadassah Robinson from Castlerock (near Coleraine) had to travel significant distances for competition. This effort was rewarded when she became the first Ulster girl to win the Junior Irish Open, at Fitzwilliam LTC in 1953.

Some time ago I heard a story of two youngsters from Longford drawn to Dublin in the 1930s and both reaching the quarterfinals. Yes, some more fancied players were beatable. Hadassah Lord (nee Robinson) had significantly further to travel in 1953. From Coleraine she was delighted to be the first Ulster girl to win the Irish under 18 Open championships. A disappointment was not making junior Wimbledon that year. Relative to Belfast, one gets the impression that Coleraine 'was in the sticks' at that time. However, determination can overcome these small hurdles, as it certainly did in her case.

The **Fergus LTC** in Ennis was prepared to travel with their juniors for many years. In 1946, under the guidance of Professor Tom Walsh, four young men travelled to the Irish Championships at Fitzwilliam. The players were Cyril Cuddy, Noel Cassidy, Tom Byrne and Larry Byrne. *All expenses were paid by the club. It was a wonderful week. We did well for four country boys (*recalls Noel Cassidy*).*

Junior at Ennis LTC (probably 1950s)

Irrespective of the era or country, city sportspeople naturally feel that they are superior. This is what one would expect. Numbers and past successes give that air of confidence, a confidence not always seen in their country cousins. A current example in Irish sport is the Limerick rugby players. For many years the selectors appear to have neglected many of the Munster clubs. The national leagues were an opportunity for the players from Shannon etc. to display their talent. Lessons have been learned.

Youngsters do well

IRISH COMPETITORS have done well in two Junior Open tournaments in England this week and, in fact, the Boys Under-12 Singles event at Surbiton in Surrey was played between two Irish boys. In Gilford, the Irish youngsters won both the boys' doubles and the mixed doubles.

At Surbiton — Boys' Singles Quarter-finals — G. Blake bt. D. Sapsford. Semi-finals — G. Blake bt J. Harbridge, 6-2, 6-1; E. Collins bt R. Clarke, 6-1, 6-1. Final — Collins bt Blake, 6-3, 6-1.

At Gilford — Mixed Doubles Final — S. Molloy and O. Ni Cuinneagain w.o.; A. Carlilse and H. Randle, scr. Girls Doubles Final — A. Knight and O. Ni Cuinneagain lost to H. Randle and K. Hunter, 6-1, 6-3. Boys Doubles Final — S. Molloy and M. French bt J. and R. Van den Broek (Holland) 6-2, 6-2. Boys Semi-final — S. Molloy lost to L. Matthews, 6-0, 6-2.

Irish Newspaper 31st July 1980

In junior tennis many of the better players have not been city bred. A few examples include Clodagh McMorrow (Tipperary), Maeve McCusker (Irvinestown), Elsa O'Riain (Kilcully), Maeve Flattery and Janine Walsh (Sligo), Nelson Boyle (Larne), Caitriona Ruane (Castlebar), Kate McNulty (Limavady), Franks Furney (Mallow), Heather Flinn (Kilkenny), Robin Gibney (Waterford) and the McArdle's from Dundalk. If we go back far enough we find Mrs. Barry from Mallow as one of that

dynasty of excellent players tennis-bred in that town. May Langrishe from Kilkenny and Florence Stanuell from Mallow were Irish Open Champions. The Irish Open Champion of 1903 was W. S. Drapes, believed to be from Carlow. One of the greatest of Irish players learned tennis as a junior in **Clones LTC**. This was, of course, James Cecil Parke. He was to be the hero of the 1912 Davis Cup win for the British Isles in Melbourne.

Clongowes Wood College 1955-Are the two juniors suggesting they take on the senior at tennis?

At the core of the successful junior section of Sutton LTC are keen adults. In recent years (from left) Willie Kinane, Aidan Bradshaw (professional coach) and John O'Shee have been in the midst of this activity.

Longford Open Week (1969). Two brothers act as ballyboys for a men's open singles match. The older, eleven year old, gets a Club Orange fro his troubles. The younger, extremely disappointed, nine year old doesn't even get a Mi-Wadi orange for what he sees as equal effort. He was not an 'official' ball boy.

The 1973 school results are interesting. In Munster, the Cork boys dominated the three schools categories. However, it was the Sacred Heart Convent, Roscrea, Dunmanway Convent and the Ursuline Convent, Waterford, who were winners of the senior, intermediate and junior girls titles. In Connacht, the Carmelite College (Moate) won the senior boys title while Taylor's Hill (Galway) took the girls equivalent. In Leinster and Ulster, Dublin and Belfast schools dominated. Galway and Limerick are in the city category and have produced many fine junior players.

Do the city players travel? They certainly do, and enjoy the experience. Ronan Sheehan's *Tennis Players* is a recommended read. Published in 1977 it tells the 'fictional' story of junior tournaments at Bettystown and Galway. Presumably, aided by his own experience, this Gonzaga educated player of note highlights the social goings on during open weeks. While picking up much of the sporting spoils, the social events are an experience for visitors and locals alike. A range of clubs and standards are the order of the day. While tennis is the main focus, equally memorable, and possibly more long lasting, are the late nights and the new liaisons. These are the wise city players.

Probably having a granny from the country helps to encourage parents to allow this freedom. It is all part of growing up and mixing with other lovers of the game. The tournament officials are delighted having many outsiders. A few top players from the city add to the glamour of the occasion.

Ballboys at the Irish Open Championships at Fitzwilliam in 1964 included Declan Carroll, Michael Dawson, Stuart Andrew, Terry O'Neill, Louis Lavelle, James Meenan and Ronan Collins (at front, second from right, the present-day television and radio personality).

Do the players of today have the same enjoyment as previous generations did? I think the answer is yes and no. Yes, because the serious players see travelling to a distant tournament as a proving ground in a low-key environment. The buzz is still there but probably in a much more informal way. There are now quality tournaments at many venues to choose from. Coaching, and an upsurge in standard, encourages this movement. A player who might be middle of the road

in a city event could be the star attraction at more distant venues. The girl or boy who was there the previous year, and caught the eye, just might be there again this year.

Despite appearances, Sligo boy Paddy Henry learned to love tennis, and became a useful player, as well as an excellent GP. (c.1930s)

No, because the lesser mortals, not realising the benefits, do not travel in the same numbers. They might see themselves being beaten in the first round. Why bother for just one match. The players of 100 years ago might raise an eyebrow at this. Irish players have travelled to the USA by ship, taking days to get there, and losing their one and only competitive match. Mind you the plate events do help. One would encourage all juniors to travel whenever and wherever they are permitted. Parent's consent and cost should be the only barriers. Games won, or narrowly lost, and new friends made will be memories to cherish.

Two people strike this writer in affirming this suggestion. The indomitable Michael Fleming is one. His quest to play, allied to a keen competitive nature,

Juniors at Glenanaar LTC in Cork in 1954.

could never be questioned. Whether it was badminton, tennis, golf or the other sports he has engaged in, he was always prepared to make an effort. In the 1930s, 40s, 50s and 60s he travelled far and wide in the pursuit of a game of tennis. In 1969, at the age of 53, he won the fairly competitive singles event at the Longford Senior Open Week. Today, as I write, at 84 years of age, he is as sporting as ever playing, golf at both Rosses Point and Carrick on Shannon. With a Roy Emerson type service he was able to outplay and outlast players half his age. Such was his enthusiasm.

Kate McNulty of Limavady is one of the excellent young players now moving towards the top.

Close to home I was all ears listening to my youngest brother. With a twelve-year age gap I would have missed most of his early tennis days. However, his enthusiasm must be commended. At the age of 11 or 12 he was determined to play in the County Cavan Open. Off on the Longford-Cavan bus. Keenness and excitement abounded. A tennis challenge to take on. It certainly was as, at that time, there was only an under 18 event. This did not deter him. Girls were not part of the equation but a mixed doubles entry meant more tennis. You can bet too that when he arrived home he would remember all the opponents and the scores. This story is not dissimilar to that of Harry Barniville's in the 1930s (as told in *The Barniville Babes, 2002)*.

> *While rugby was my first love, tennis was much easier to organise and being a competitive animal I soon looked for tournaments in which I could play. I found that Under 15 was the youngest available age group and some doubles events only existed at Under 18 level. However I entered everything and was continually thrashed by 'huge' 14 and 15 year olds. My very first effort was to enter the Irish Junior Championships at Fitzwilliam in 1938 when I was eleven. I persuaded my sister June, who was 10, to enter the mixed doubles-Under 18 but a handicap event. Despite a +40 handicap we lost 0/6, 1/6 in the first round to two 18 year olds but I still treasure that one game.*

Community games sport is a major success on the Irish scene. Apart from the usual sports one can find something for all, including art and draughts. The concept has spread to every parish in the Republic of Ireland. From Under 8 to Under 18 the enthusiasm

The History of Irish Tennis

abounds. The organisers and coaches must be complimented for their annual efforts. Somewhere, in the midst of the excitement, one finds lawn tennis. During the summer months the county, then provincial winners can be seen working towards what is probably a one off goal. In 2000, the Calry team picked up gold at Mosney with a team that might otherwise never feature at national level. These players (Sean Caheny, Fergal McFadden, Eoin Rooney, Katie Hennessy, Aine Hackett and Alex Potter) have had their thrills and a memory that cannot be erased. The local press are more than happy to record all the sports achievements and more than delighted if there is a selection of gold, silver and bronze medals returning to the fold. A modern army of kids bringing back the spoils. The mayor and/or the community games chairperson smiles as much as the kids in the compulsory photo shoot. Schools tennis got a shot in the arm in 1999 with the introduction of a national competition. This was the Ballygowan Senior Schools Tennis Cup. At eleven regional venues, teams fought it out to make the national finals. Approximately seventy schools participated.

Apart from the major junior titles there have been interprovincial events for many years in varying age groups. These are supplemented by regional inter-club under age titles. All are competitive. Within schools an interested PE teacher can have a dramatic bearing on the short-term and long-term successes. Top Ulster junior Hadassah Robinson was high in her praise of Miss Hermoine Chapman's guidance while at Coleraine High School and also of the coaching received from Bill Rainey of Ballymena. The evergreen Nora Taylor of Enniskillen and Omagh clubs was born in 1907 and was still playing tennis in 1999. *There were no coaches in my early years* she says. Unfortunately, talent may be lost if keen young players are not encouraged.

The same factors apply at club level. Maeve Jennings (nee Flattery) a very good player in her early years was directly responsible for a keen bunch of juniors in the Ballina club in the early 1970s. Three consecutive wins in the Connacht U18 Pitman Cup (for club teams) were the result. An interesting footnote is that at least two members of those teams (Maura Butler (nee Gilvarry) and Seamus Granahan have become excellent senior players and qualified coaches. Both have assisted with juniors in their respective clubs of Sligo and Castlebar. Throughout the country examples such as these abound.

Today there are coaches in every region and the opportunity to progress is available. Some small and relatively isolated clubs may not have sufficient keen adults or players of a high enough standard to make rapid progress. However, there are full-time and part-time qualified coaches prepared to travel. Tadgh Lambe and Jim Watt are two good examples. Funding should be the only obstacle. The Strategic Plan for Tennis (1999-2001), as published by Tennis Ireland, recognises the hurdles to be crossed and the importance of people in the promotion of the game. Parks Tennis is a useful mechanism for bringing it to the grass roots in many towns and cities such as Waterville, Letterkenny and Carrick on Suir.

Terenure College (Dublin) under 13 team in 1973. From left: B. O'Kelly, J. Menton, Conor O'Kelly, J. Pender, Francis Kinsella & Declan Kelly.

Irvinestown TC is an example to all. The old club died out many years ago and through a keen, fresh effort a new club thrived in this relatively small town. Large numbers of juniors abound and get maximum encouragement in quality facilities.

With the international profile for the sport no youngster is unaware of the skills and excitement associated with the game. A minimum amount of encouragement from the adult sector is all that is required. There are many veteran players who learned the game by practice and competition, never having being coached. They enjoyed it. Are we now at a stage that to maximise the numbers of juniors playing, and to improve standards, that facilities must be good, be available and be organised? I suspect so. With so many distractions, self-motivated juniors are significantly rarer than say thirty years ago. We must continue to encourage our people to play sport and make tennis as attractive an option as any other. If we don't then the overweight/unfit teenager will be a widespread health problem in the not too distant future.

Connact's number 1 Maeve Jennings (nee Flattery) passing on advice to Pauline Martin (left) and Mary Guy at Swinford Lawn Tennis Club in 1948.

Without doubt the tennis environment has changed. For the young player much remains the same. A sport with a massive spectator appeal is now available throughout the year, the cost is no longer prohibitive, the joy of a well-executed serve and volley has not altered and the social attractions are perpetual. If one were to advice juniors then the age-old truism applies. Talk to the older generations and be surprised. They enjoyed their sport without television heroes, they had poor equipment, bald tennis balls and travelled enthusiastically. In short, they loved the game. Some of it might rub off.

Junior Players at Birr in the 1930s

Juniors were not always welcome at tennis clubs. Decisions to include juniors have been the subject of many committee discussions. Children were to be seen and not heard. Acceptability varied and there is no exact pattern. At **Glenageary LTC,** the liberation of Ladies and the entry of juniors both occurred in the 1920s. Harry Maunsell, the noted honorary secretary of the ILTA for many years, proposed at **Glenageary LTC's** AGM in 1920 that 'children' of 14 to 16 years of age, on being elected, should be allowed to play up to 3 pm, except for Saturdays. With some change they were allowed to play between 11am and 3pm on court 5. They were not to be elected members and the committee could withdraw the privilege at any time. It was not surprising that no junior subscription was recorded for 1920 and 1921. The matter was reconsidered in 1922 but, apart from immediate relatives of existing members, the committee closed the 'list' after only six juniors had joined. It was to be the 1950's before significant numbers of juniors were members.

1950's junior tennis at Glenageary LTC. Patrick Varian and Bobby Anderson know their etiquette.

Dorothy Owens (nee Eaton) recalls in the club's centenary brochure her junior days in the 1930's:

My mother was a member of de Vesci Gardens, where she used to bring my brother and myself to play at a very early age while she sported the courts. There were underhand serves and a lot of hilarity, then on tea days we brought tins of cakes and goodies.

Going to G.L.T.C. where my father was a member, was a much more serious business. Play was of a much higher standard, and we were obliged to stay quiet. From an early age we were taught sideline etiquette: where and when we could move during play.

St. Mel's LTC formed in Longford in the 1930's had another angle on juniors. They would probably rightly claim to have the first 'crèche' at an Irish tennis club. They built a pen for the very young children, something similar to a chicken coupe. The mothers could enjoy their game and know that their young sons and daughters would not wander. (see chapter 8).

A 1930s junior is shown the correct grip (possibly at Glenageary Lawn Tennis Club)

Ballyfarnon LTC in about 1960. A junior final. At back, Andy O' Brien and Marie Flynn. To the front Michael and Dymphna Benson. Marie would later marry Tuam engineer Pat Forkan and raise a family of excellent tennis, squash and badminton players at Sligo TC. (Gavin, Cian & Laoise).

In 1995 14- year-old Jenny Timoney of Celbridge TC was giving her senior opponents a run for their money in open tournaments.

1959-Patrick Reeves Smyth, with daughter Anne helping, white lining the home court at Flemington. Patrick insisted the family dress in whites, even for social games at home.

The 2002 winner of the junior boy's club championship was Brendan Mulligan. In photograph with Mary Barry (lady captain) and Joe Walsh (captain).

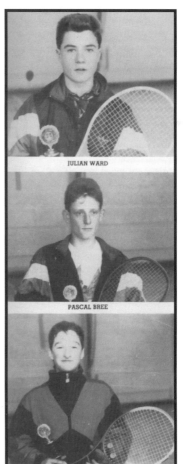

JULIAN WARD

PASCAL BREE

GAVIN FORKAN

Schools encouragement of tennis plays an important part in young people's interest in the sport.

At Summerhill College (Sligo) the 1989 boys to the left were winners of their year tennis titles. From the top:

JulianWard (first year), Pascal Bree (second year) and Gavin Forkan (third year).

Belfast Boat Club juniors (circa 1949). From left: Peter Jackson (who became a Davis Cup player in 1959), Miss Woods, Jim Getty, Ruth Abernathy, Peter Bayliss (who became president of the Irish Lawn Tennis Association in 1979, and again in 1987) and a. n. other.

Juniors who participated in the Junior-Senior match at Elm Park in July 2002. Front (l. to r.) David Loughnane, Brian O'Brolchain, Cormac O'Brolchain, Louise Boden, Sheena Warren, Claire Woods, Elaine Corcoran and Talma O'Sullivan. Middle (l. to r.) Simon Matthews, Conor Boden, Kevin Corcoran, Phelim O'Connor, Doireann O'Brolchain, Suzanne Lynch, Chloe Halpenny and Gillian Grier. Back (l. to r.) James Kelly and Aidan Claffey.

Starting young at Longford Lawn Tennis Club in 1968. From left sisters Jennifer and Columba Quinn with brothers Declan and Niall Higgins. The older and younger pairs won their respective mixed tournaments on the day the photograph was taken.

In 2001 Castleknock LTC won the under 14 Class I Girl's League. From left: Derbhle Gilroy, Niamh Duffy, Fiona O'Farrell, Sally Ann O'Connor (junior co-ordinator), Roisin MacDiarmede, Dorothy McGuinness and Aoibhin Garrihy.

*The Connacht Under 14
Team (c. 1982)*

*The Leinster Under 18
Team (c. 1982)*

*The Ulster Under 18
Team (late 1980s)*

The Munster Under 16 team at the interprovincial series at Sundays Well (Cork) in 1987. Back (l. to r.): G. Morris (NP captain), R. Callaghan (Douglas), D. Sheehan (Limerick Lawn), J. Barriscale (Douglas), C. Williams (Douglas) & C. Dolan (Rushbrooke). Front (l. to r.): J. O'Brien (Dungarvan), C. Hobbs (Douglas), E. Duane (Sundays Well) & S. Donovan (Douglas). The team won 10 out of 18 matches.

The Nescafe Under-21 Irish Championships were held at Sutton LTC in 1990. from left: Alain Pedersen (Nescafe), Gina Niland (LS champion), Jenny O'Brien (LD champion), Matt Byrne (President, Sutton LTC), Karen Fisher (Wales, LD champion), Mark Loosemore (Wales, MD champion), Ross Matheson (Scotland, MS & MD champion) and Gerry More-O'Ferrall (President, Tennis Ireland).

3.7   *Poetry and Other Writings*

The most reliable route to the origins of tennis is its language
(Heiner Gillmeister, 1997)

Tennis could be described as a clash of cannonballs, when two players with 120 mph serves face each other or moving art when a competitor with a great volley and delicate touch, such as John McEnroe, is on form. It might be a game for extreme effort when listening to grunters, such as Jimmy Connors, in action. It could be a thing of grace when Evonne Goolagong was at her best. Suzanne Lenglen brought fashion and a ballet like action into the game in the 1920s when winning all around her. Concentration was brought into focus by players such as Bjorn Borg and Chris Evert. Beautiful lady players on court are admired on court by both sexes. Everyone has his or her favourites. Maria Bueno (Brazil) was known not alone for her appearance on court but as one of the most gracefully artistic of women's champions. Sue Barker, the BBC commentator had her admirers. Gabriela Sabitini had many on her way to 27 singles titles. Today, there are many and the Russian, Anna Kournikvoa, must be at, or near the top, in most peoples list. She is the only one of the above-mentioned names yet to win a major singles championship.

Appealing was the quiet manner of Arthur Ashe on his way to winning Wimbledon in 1975. Ken Rosewall has been described as having a grace on court with an easy and economical style. The same could not be said for Andre Agassi whose grit determination has brought him success. In an earlier day, Ireland's Dr. Joshua Pim was described as being a robust competitor and one of the great geniuses of early tennis. He was in four Wimbledon singles finals, winning in 1893 and 1894. The charm and character of Ilie Nastase and Henri Laconte have drawn the crowds throughout the world. We could go on.

Defining the sport of tennis, and tennis courts, should be straightforward. Clarence Jones (1984) describes the game as follows: Tennis *is a game played on a court either by two people, one each side of a net which divides the court into two equal parts, or by four people, two each side of the net.* A simple description! This can be added to when detailing the rules, which include the net details and the court dimensions. All unnecessary ever since television became as important as electricity in a modern household. The game, however, does elicit the romantic side of our lives.

Court Asset

It can be part of our childhood memories. It can be a vivid element in describing the assets of a house being advertised for sale. *Donard*, for sale in Ballsbridge at a guide price of £2.65m, was described as a 1930s, six-bed roomed red brick building. *It has a sunny, often leafy, aspect and has a hard tennis court at the back* (Irish Times May 10th 2001). To some having a tennis court provides perhaps a social symbol. To a tennis playing family, it is a great asset. Des Traynor's £2m

Clontarf home included an all weather tennis court when it was offered for sale in April 2001. Many of the great homes of the 19th century had croquet and tennis lawns to entertain visitors. These included Lissadell House (the home of the Gore-Booths) and Ashford Castle (the home of Lord Ardilaun).

Helen Wills Moody won Wimbledon eight times, including 1938 when she accepted an invitation to play in the Irish Championships. Her interest in the writings of Oliver St. J. Gogarty was said to have made the difference. Here she is seen at Fitzwilliam Lawn Tennis Club with Gogarty and Willie Sandys (left) the tournament organiser.

Like a ballroom in a grand mansion, it was, in years gone by, a focus for social gatherings. Smaller clubs in the past had a tennis court or courts on which the game would proceed while the gathering, small or large, would engage in watching. Equally as important was having tea and sandwiches, evaluating the fresh cream cakes made for the event, and social intercourse. Subconsciously, the mating game was always being played, both on and off court.

Court in View

People remember the settings with fondness. In the opening chapter of Garret Fitzgerald's autobiography (1991) he sets the scene. His family moved to a house named Fairy Hill in 1928 when Garret was two:

Outside the kitchen was the vegetable-and-fruit garden, and beside it the stables with their lofts and mangers and numerous outbuildings, including a cow-shed and hen-house. Lawns broken by borders with rose bushes sloped down in front of the house to a tennis court, which served also as a croquet lawn, below which was a meadow and beyond that a small but mysterious wood. A gap in the trees revealed a dramatic view of the great houses of Sorrento terrace on the sea at Dalkey four miles away.

In 1932, Englishman David Thompson, arrived at *Woodbrook* as a tutor for Phoebe. He stayed for ten years and in 1974 published a book (*Woodbrook*) describing his life with the Kirkwoods. This Anglo-

Irish family had been playing tennis in nearby Boyle, and Sligo, back in the 19ᵗʰ century. The tennis court was still there. His early observations include that of the 'office', a room near the front hall when *Major Kirkwood used to store a vast heap of bills and letters……The room was also a repository for shoes, boots, fishing rods and a seldom used gun, tennis rackets, most of them with broken strings, golf clubs and old coats, croquet hoops and mallets, riding crops and walking-stick and several kinds of balls. I remember with nostalgia the faded colours of the croquet balls, blue, yellow, green and black, the feel of them, although I cannot remember any of us ever playing croquet.*

One of the windows of the dining-room opened on to a rough sloping garden with more shrubs in it than flowers, beyond which lay a tennis court and paddock, and beyond those the lake with the Leitrim mountains blue in the distance to the east.

Family conversations at the Kirkwoods often reverted to the times spend in India where comparisons between houses, servants etc. were made. In their memories of that time and place, nearly 100 years ago, the *gardens and tennis courts were beautifully kept.*

Sports readers of the Irish Times in the 1960s and 1970s would recognise the excellent coverage, particularly of tennis and hockey, by Vera McWeeney (nee Mahony). Vera (right) was the number 4 ranked lady in Ireland in 1937. Among her impressive tennis credentials were the East of Ireland and County Dublin singles championships. On the hockey pitch she captained the Irish ladies' team.

In his book *Teach Yourself Lawn Tennis* (1952), F. N. S. Creek describes the home of tennis, Wimbledon's Centre Court, as follows:

To the expert and to the beginner alike, everything is as can be imagined. Except for the mathematically accurate white lines and a slightly worn brown patch near each base-line, the whole court is a weedless stretch of green grass, with ample room at the ends and sides. At the south end is the Royal Box, and at the south-east and north-west corners are the two electrically operated score-boards.

Where a choice can be made the courts were aligned north south so that the setting sun would not cause a problem on a late summers evening. In one small club in Donegal, the owner of the court had it aligned in an east west direction in order that those sitting having their 'tea' at courtside could obtain the benefit of the evening sun.

California Welcome

The social nature of the sport was highlighted in poetry when the Irish Vets visited California in August 1988. One of their hostesses, Shirley Schieber, was enamoured of her visitors and penned the following as a tribute:

At the Veteran's Training Camp in Orange County were (from left) Ned Carmody, Niall O'Riordan, P. Uakiva (trainer), Roddy Feeley and P. Maguire (host).

The Ballad of the 405
(Shirley Schieber, 1988)

The Irish Folks
One lovely day
Came to this place
to play.

The Duber Cup, The Austria Cup
The Britannia Cup as well
We're Oh, so glad they came this far
We think they're mighty swell.

With lilting laughs and laughing eyes
And humour, oh, so subtle
And words we've never heard before
That threw us in a muddle.

Their picture of this area
Is very weird indeed
They think it's flat and paved and wide
And filled with cars and speed.

Divided into yellow stripes
With gravel on the side
That travels north and south so far
Is 8 to 10 lanes wide.

The History of Irish Tennis

From Racquet Club of Irvine
It extends to South Coast Westin
Then circles round, goes up and down
To Lindborg, North by Western.

So, they've never seen the cities
The villages, the ocean
They'll go back to Ireland
With a silly notion.

That we live on the freeways
At least within their sight
And when I think about it
They're very nearly right.
For if, indeed, they do come back
In a year or so,
They might find traffic at a stop
Instead of stop and go.

We'll be living in our cars, you see
Caught up in all this mess
If they invite us over
We'll surely holler, "Yes!"

Bring a helicopter, a hot air balloon
A kite,
And lift us out of gridlock
With all your main and might.

Oh Casey, Feely, Furney
O'Shaughnessey and Reid,
O'Riordan, O'Brien, Carmody
Hurry with God speed.

We'll need you lads to rescue us
From our follies and our fate
To get us off the freeways
Where we're doomed to wait.

We're, Oh, so pleased we've met you
We feel it as a thrill
Each time you roll an R you see
Or give a word a trill.

Please hurry back to see us
Bring your racquets and your brogue
We'll play tennis on the tops of cars
Or alongside the road.

We think you're clever, charming
Loveable and such
You can always tell an Irishman
But you can't tell him much.

The Irish Vets team who, on their visit to California in 1988, played in the Austria Cup. From left: Niall O'Riordan, Gerry O'Shaughnessey (captain), June Anne Byrne, Ned Carmody and Franks Furney.

Tennis Language

In Chapter 2 we dealt with the historical connections between the racquet sports. Here, long before Major Clopton was a twinkle in his mother's eye, writers would put pen to paper on many aspects of **tennis**. For those who are keen to delve into the background of the game, I would highly recommend *Tennis: A Cultural History* by Heiner Gillmeister. This was published in German in 1990 and then in English in 1997. He said that *The most reliable route to the origins of tennis is its language.* For this reason a few old quotations on the game are made here, thanks to the research and compilation of Gillmeister. They help to understand one reason why the modern sport still has its attraction. Some of the quotations are in French, the country where the main trust of the game originated. Battles, marriages, edicts from bishops, Shakespearian plays are all among the places where tennis can be found.

A man by the name of Geoffrey of Paris is said to have been the writer who blamed tennis for the death of Louis X of France in 1316, a not unimportant reason for inserting the following quotation:

En cel temps qu'estoit ceste chose,
Au rois Loys la vie esclose
Fu, droit au boys de Viciennes:
La perdi-il plums et pennes.
Disoit-on qu'en ceste maniere
Mourust de maladie ague,
Qui les saines genz souvent tue.
Li autres dient qu'il avoit
Joue a 1 gieu qu'il savoit,
A la paume, si s'eschaufa,
Et son conseil, qui le bifa,
L'en a mene en une cave
Froide; et a 1 hanap plein d'iave
Si but trop, et froit se bouta,
Et li sitost si se coucha
Qu'au lit acouchier le convint,
Ed de ce cele mort li vint.

At the time when this thing happened,
The life of King Louis was put to an end
Right in the middle of the Forest of Vincennes:
There he lost plumage and feathers.
It has been said that the kind of illness
From which he died was a stroke
Which often kills healthy people as well.
Others claim that he played a game
Which he knew well,
Namely tennis; he became so heated at it,
And his better judgement which betrayed him
Led him away to a cold cave,
And from a jug full of water
He drank too much, cold, he laid himself down,
And as soon as he had lain down,
He remained bound to the bed,
And of this jug death came to him.

In 1598, James I of England wrote *Basilicon Doron* for his four-year-old son, Prince Henry. Education and advice for young royals was always an important piece

The History of Irish Tennis

of work for educators. He took this role himself when he recommended exercises which included tennis:

Amang all unnecessaire things that are laufull & expedient I thinke exercises of the boddie maist commendable to be used be a young prince, in sicc honest games or pastymes as maye further habilitie & mainteine health, for albeit I graunt it be maist requisite for a king to exercise his engyne…………I uolde haue you to use (althoch but moderatlie not making a crafte of thaime) are rinning, leaping, urestling, fensing, dansing & playing at the cache [Cache was the Scottish word for tennis]

As Geillmeister says *our histories of tennis literally abound with tennis-mad kings, but are generally silent about the common people, who, throughout the Middle Ages, played and loved this game just as much as their royal masters did.* In a religious play, Secunda Pastorum, played in the town of Wakefield, the shepherds bring various gifts to the baby Jesus. The first cherries, the second a baby bird and the third a tennis ball:

Put forth thy dall!
I bryng the bot a ball:
Haue and play the withall.
And go to the tenys.

Stretch out your hand
I'm bringing you only a ball:
Take it and play with it
And go to the tennis.

In 1451, as a result of the organisation of a *kind of tennis league* within the precincts of the church, even in the burial grounds, in the parish of Ottery St Mary, the Bishop of Exeter, was so angered with the bad language, disputes etc that excommunication resulted for the offenders. He fully describes the goings on which includes the following (in Latin) (Dunstan, 1963-1967):

Nonulli tam clerici quam laici quorum nomina ignoramus pariter et personas, prout ex fidedignorum testimonio et fama publica accepimus, in cimiterio ecclesie beate Marie collegii predicti, pro sepultura christiana inibi consecrato….ad ludum pile vulgariter nuncupatum Tenys *diebus festivis sepissime et aliis tanquam in loco prophano seu theatro ludere quin verius illudere, atque vanis fedis et phophanis colloquiis et iuramentis inaniter et vanis et sepissime periuriis illicitis insistere, atque exinde sepius rixas, contenciones movere et conclamaciones erigere…*

Some members of the clergy, as well as of the laity, of whom we know neither name nor personality, about whom we are informed, however, by reliable witnesses vociferous complaints, apparently have no scruples about playing a game, or rather, an evil game called tennis *in the vernacular, in the churchyard of the above-mentioned collegiate church of St Mary, concentrated for Christian burials, and they play it on feast-days as well as on other days, and in a manner of a fair ground or theatre. In so doing they inveterately voice vain, heinous and blasphemous words and utter senseless curses, which, as a* consequence, *all too often give rise to squabbles, disputes, brawls and battles of words.*

As Heiner Gillmeister suggests the world was full of frocked John McEnroes even then. He also finds a tennis riddle written by Tharsia, the daughter of the *oldest tennis player we know, Appolonius of Tyre,* which goes as follows:

A grant plente ay de chevaulx
Autelz comme une vacque ou veaulx
Mais nulz ne les voit ilz sont dedens
De mains aux autres ce sachiez
Suis en lair boute et saciez
Et aussi tost court pres que vent.

Of hair have I plenty,
Such as a cow or calves;
But no one can see it, it is inside.
From hands to other hands, hear what I say,
Am I struck into the air and hustled
And almost as swiftly as the wind runs.

Apollonius knew that his daughter was talking about a tennis ball which was stuffed with hair. In the north of France the hair from cows and calves was used. Don't forget that before the use of bats, followed by strung racquets, the game of tennis was a handball game. The game was not welcomed by a parent who wrote *Ratis Raving,* in 1475, and *doled out a proper dressing down to young Scottish boys* (Gillmeister, 1997):

For resone than is yong and wak
And may nocht lat that eild to laik,
…now at the killis,
Now at the prop, and vthir-quhillis
Ryne at baris and at the ball
And at the caich play with-all,
Now at the tablis, now at the ches
Weill oft, and seldin at the mes
And mekile with playing at the dyce
That werk yhit hald I maist unwyB,
For thar is aithis set at nocht,
And infortunne to mekil socht.

Since reason is then immature and weak
And this age cannot refrain from playing
…[it is] now at skittles,
Then at the [archery] butts, another time
At running at the bars and at football
And especially at tennis;
Sometimes at backgammon, then very often
At chess, but only seldom at holy mass;
And much time at dice.
Such conduct I consider most foolish,
For their curses are considered a trifle,
And misfortune is virtually beckoned.

Tennis spread throughout Scotland. The second oldest known tennis court in the world, still intact, is that at Falklands Castle, Fife. It was built at the behest of James V between 1539 and 1541. In Sir David Lindsay's morality play, *Ane Pleasant Satyre of the Thrie Estaitis,* written in 1540, the Parson, in reply to the Scribe who asks him if he can preach he says:

Thocht I preich not I can play at the caiche:
I wait thair is nocht ane amang yow all,
Mair ferilie can play at the fut-ball:
And for the carts, the tabils and the dyse,
Aboue all persouns I may beir the pryse.

Although I do not preach, I can play tennis;
I know that there is not one among you all here
Who can play football better than I.
And as for cards, backgammon and dice
Before all parsons I would carry off the prize.

The Falklands Palace Real Tennis Court still in use.

From the fifteenth century onwards, tennis has exercised considerable influence on creative writers, especially on playwrights, and on poets writing in a didactic vein. ...The didactic poet's preferred method was one he had inherited from the Middle Ages: the allegorical....A poet may have been writing about a tennis match, but this was not what the poem was really about. (Gillmeister, 1997). Charles d'Orleans penned a poem on his forty-fifth birthday (24th November 1439) and compares life with a tennis match. The first verse is as follows; gnawing Worry *(Soussy)* is on the far side of the net:

J'ay tant joue averqcques Aage
A la paulme que maintenant
J'ay quarante cinq; sur bon gage
Nous jouons, non pas pour neant.
Assez me sens fort et puissant
De garder mon jeu jusqu'a cy.
Ne je ne crains riens que Soussy.

I have played at tennis with age
So long that now I am
At forty-five: for high stakes
We play, never for nothing.
I feel strong and vigorous
To determine the course of the game till now.
I fear nothing but Worry.

Charles was obviously aware of the counting system of tennis and its connection to his age. The Duke of Burgundy on his sixtieth birthday (1st August 1456) was said to have remarked: *I have played tennis. I've lost a game which I shall "write off". I lost yesterday, but to-day I will begin a new game.* For the following verse, penned by Theophile de Viau in 1622, he was banned from Paris. He compares female conquest with a game of tennis. Note that at that time forty five points came after thirty (whereas in England forty had become the norm):

Si vous le baises comptes quinze
Si vous touches le tetin trente
Si vous auees la motte prinse
Quarante cinq lors se presente
Mais si vous metes en la fente
Ce de quoy la dame a mestier
Notes bien ce que que ie vous chante
Vous ganges le Jeu tout entier.

If you kiss her, count fifteen,
If you touch the buds, thirty,
If you capture the hill,
Forty-five comes up.
But if you enter the breach
With what the lady needs,
Remember well what I sing to you,
You will win the game outright.

More relevant advice to the playing of the game came from Guillaume de la Periere in 1539. The tennis balls used at that time were not always perfectly round and it better to volley than let it bounce first; thus :

Qui pour le bond delaisse la vollee,
Ne fut iamais tenu ferme ioneur.

Whoever prefers the bounce to the volley
Has never been considered a good player.

God and Satan battle for man's soul in the poem of Francis Quarles in 1632. The tennis court becomes the battle-ground and is titled *On a Tenis-court.*

Man is a Tenniscourt: His Flesh, the Wall:
The Gamster's God, and Sathan: Th' heart's the Ball:
The higher and lower Hazzards are
Too bold presumption, and too base Despaire:
The Rackets, which our restlesse Balls make flye.
Adversity, and sweet Prosperity:
The Angels keepe the Court, and marke the place,
Where the Ball fals, and chaulks out ev'ry Chace:
The Line's a Civill life, we often crosse,
Ore which, the Ball not flying, makes a Losse:
Detractors are like Standers-by, that bett
With Charitable men: Our Life's the Sett:
Lord, in this Conflict, in these fierce Assaults,
Labourious Sathan makes a world of Faults;
Forgive them Lord, although he nere implore
For favour: They'l be set upon our score:
O, take the Ball, before it come to th' ground,
For this base Court has many a false Rebound:
Strike, and strike hard, but strike above the line:
Strike where thou please, so as the Sett be thine.

Described by Gillmeister as Germany's first physiotherapist, medical doctor Hippolytus Guarinonius was conscious of the value of exercise and health. He pointed out that tennis was played in more important towns and referred to it as "the chief game of all games". In his *The Atrocities of the Ruin of the Human Race* he noted the ballhouse in Prague and the five ballhouses in Padua, he had studied in both cities. The translated quote, from German, describes the physical merits of the sport as seen through the eyes of the good doctor. It could nearly be a description of modern day squash or handball:

The History of Irish Tennis

Suffice it to say that such a game is the best exercise for the whole man and all his limbs, since the head and neck as well as the eyes have to bend and turn into all corners and directions, after which the feet have to quickly carry the body to and fro after the flying ball. There you run, jump and swing up the masonry and the wall, bend low, rise again, turn back and to the fore, and to all directions, and, lifting the racket, you agitate the hand, and turning it, the fingers in all manners this way and that way, since at one time you have to receive and hit the ball overhead, then besides your feet, a third time straight, a fourth time without cut.

In 1810, a ten pence pamphlet, written by a Mr. Atkinson, in part or completely, was produced in Ireland. It consisted of a number of individual varied pieces on the philosophy of life, a religious theme being strong. Two letters of approval from clergymen are included. The primary heading caught this writer's attention in the National Library in Dublin: *A Sunday's Entertainment containing a Few Light Extracts from a work to be published next year under the title of ROLL OF A TENNIS BALL through the Religious and Social world.* It was published in 1810 and one of the first items in the pamphlet was the following:

The Tennis Ball
(Atkinson, 1810)

On earth's inclement shore was cast
Propelled by some mysterious blast,
A TENNIS BALL endued with powers
Of mind and mother like to ours;-
Trowen high in air and low in mire,
No force could stop its progress higher;
It flew to Earth's remotest bound,
Then took a circuit round and round,
Then stopp'd a while to pause and think,
Then stopp'd at Wisdom's well to drink,
And looking up with wondrous ken,
It saw the heads and hearts of men.
And now by virtue of its art,
It drew the face, the head, the heart,
The eyes, the brows, the tyrant's frown,
The coarser features of the clown,
And all the scenery within,
The source of virtue and of sin;
The motly pictures, readers see,
Some portrait' chance may answer thee.

You, the reader, can interpret the above in whatever way takes your fancy. Unfortunately, apart from this item, references to tennis in Ireland before lawn tennis are non-existent or waiting to be uncovered in some archives. We know that the students of Trinity College, Dublin were probably the first to try out most new sports. The university was to have a tennis court designed by the distinguished architect, Richard Cassels. (West, 1991) It was laid at the present Pearse Street boundary in 1741. One suspects that there are other references to the game during the 18th century, or perhaps earlier. It would be interesting to find out how the older game of tennis was viewed by both the 'gentlemen' of society, who undoubtedly played it at

TCD, and perhaps others who might have played on the court at Thomas Street, Dublin, when it was built in 1609.

From hereon we will leap into more modern times and where we can find scribes describing lawn tennis as we know it today. Perhaps, in fifty years time, the tennis observer may be lamenting the passing of lawn tennis. A campaign, similar to the recent one related to the Real tennis court at Earlsfort Terrace, Dublin, might be waged. That campaign might, but we hope not, be linked to the last remaining grass court in Ireland.

The following notice should not, however, be forgotten as it was the starting point of that specific branch of tennis. It appeared in the *Court Journal* of London on the 7th March 1874 and was written by Major Walter Clopton Wingfield himself who had, two weeks earlier, obtained a provisional patent on a *New and Improved Court for Playing the Ancient Game of Tennis.* Six months later the patent became valid.

We hear of a new and interesting game coming out, which is likely to attract public notice, now blasé with croquet and on the qui cire for novelty. It has been patented under the name of "Sphairistike or lawn tennis'. It has been tested at several country houses, and has been found full of healthy excitement, besides being capable of much scientific play. The game is in a box not much larger than a double gun case, and contains, besides bats and balls, a portable court, which can be erected on any ordinary lawn, and is ornamental as well as useful..

Major Wingfield gets most of the praise for introducing lawn tennis to a croquet weary society. His ideas, patent and marketing, lead to the sale of literally hundreds of lawn tennis sets in the first year. We must not forget Birmingham solicitor and his wealthy Spanish friend, businessman Jean Batista Augurio Perira. In 1859 they began experimenting with a version of lawn tennis on the croquet lawn of Perira's manor house on Ampton Road, Edgbaston. They would later refer to the sport as *pelota* (note the Spanish connection in Chapter 2).

In 1872, two years before Wingfield's patent, they, with Dr. Frederick Harry Haynes and Dr. Arthur Wellesley Tomkins, founded the world's first lawn tennis club, Leamington Lawn Tennis Club (Gibbons, 1987). From 1874 onwards they held annual tournaments. At the end of that season, Harry composed the following poem which, according to Gillmeister (1997), could be sung to the tune of the Irish song *The Wearing of the Green* (composed in 1798 as a political poem against the English laws preventing the growing and wearing of the Irish shamrock).:

The Manor House is moaning, there's a sigh in every breeze,
And the Leam is flowing sadly by the leaf-forsaken trees,
And the green grass that we've trodden now is darker in its woe,
As the tread of the Pelota boys it must no longer know.

As we tripped about the green,
As they slipped about the green,
As they fumbled, and they stumbled,
and they tumbled o'er the green.

Oh, remember, let's remember, we were merry when the sun
Shone o'er us bright and cheery in the days when we begun,
But the eyes that looked upon us were more bright and cheery still
And urged us on to desp'rate deeds of nimbleness and skill.

As we jumped about the green,
As we thumped about the green,
As we rattled, and we prattled,
and we battled o'er the green.

Let our deeds be written on the lasting roll of fame,
How Homer bet the shilling, and Tomkins won the game,
How Hayes' youthful vigour placed him high upon the list,
And battled all who hadn't got the Pereira twist.

As we stuck about the green,
As we struck about the green,
As we betted, and we sweated,
and we fretted o'er the green.

'Twas sad to see age vie with youth, it brought the heavy sigh,
To hear some old one saying, 'good bye, sweet youth, good bye'.
To see them limp, and hear them puff, and learn how idly vain,
It was to wish for eyes and limbs that won't come back again.

As they waddled o'er the green,
As they straddled o'er the green,
As they muffled it, and they puffed it,
and enough'd it o'er the green.

Farewell the turf, the bounding ball and nets are in the box,
The rackets on the shelf are laid to wait next season's knocks;
Then let us now pass round the wine, a brimming bumper fill,
And drink the great Pelota game, Lawn tennis if you will.

Yes! we'll toast it o'er the green,
And we'll boast it o'er the green,
And we'll chink it, and we'll clink it,
and we'll drink it o'er the green.

*****

Monkstown Marathon

While there have been words of wisdom, including rhymes, written on the subject of tennis in early days, probably the first Irish poem on lawn tennis can be associated with one of the oldest clubs, **Monkstown LTC.** Published in the centenary booklet on the club history (1977), the author, known only as A.R.F.E., had the following Preface seeking the indulgence and understanding of the club members.

The Author feels that some apology is necessary for the free use which he has made of the Members names; and trusts that, in the first place, a poet's license, and the exigencies of verse and rhyme will plead for him; and, in the second, that the Members will accept these lines in the spirit in which they were written. They were written originally without any definite object on the part of the author, save that of recording the first Tournament of the Club, to which he has the honour to belong, and are now only printed privately, at the request of others, who must, therefore, share the responsibility with the Author. In conclusion, the Author hopes, whatever liberties he

may have taken with the ladies' names in his efforts to amuse, that such liberties have not been taken in vain.

It might be noted that in understanding the following poem the modern player might not recognise the scoring system. At the first Wimbledon the 'modern' use of 15, 30 and 40 was adopted. The Monkstown tournament held that summer still used the old scoring system. This came from the sport of rackets i.e. a game comprised of 15 aces which could be won only by the server who remained 'hand in' until the loss of a rally. Many thanks to Caoimhin Kenna for passing on this complete, truly marathon, tennis poem. Perhaps it is of record length, surely for lawn tennis in any event!

The Lawn Tennis Tournament Monkstown
(A.R.F.E., 1877)

I
The members of the Monkstown Club,
By Jupiter they swore,
They'd have a tennis tournament
Before the year was o'er,
By Jupiter they swore it,
And fixed the opening day,
And bade the members all come there,
Tall and short, and dark and fair,
In suitable array.

II
Of course, as well you may suppose,
They offered a reward,
For those who proved their prowess best,
Upon the grassy sward.
They went and purchased at the great
Co-Operative store,
Two racquets, such a splendid pair
Were never seen before.

The History of Irish Tennis

III

The "Handicapper" wouldn't play,
(I dare not tell his name,)
For Why! He was intent upon
Another little game;
But how the players soon did prove,
He handicapped them well,
And how the fickle fortunes went,
Come here, Miss Muse, and tell.

IV

Well then, I'll now commence my theme,
The ladies, for I durst,
Ne'er look them in the face again,
Did I not place them first,
Were less than twelve in all by two,
Which makes just ten, you know,
Which were they! Well I'll try to tell
You in a line or so.

V

Cassandra, (name of classic lore!)
And Evelyn, both were there,
Orinda too, and Ada, you,
With sober matron's air.
And Fanny small, and Poppy tall,
And Lily fair as snow,
Besides Janetta, Georgie, Kate,
The Vances, famed trio!

VI

But here I hope the ladies will
Excuse me, if I dare
To leave them, and enumerate
The gents assembled there.
First then was a jolly wight,
Men called him "Monsieur Rat",
And Millar the left-hander,
Who later gained eclat.

VII

And Richard, of the self-same name,
(If A be changed to E),
And Robin, of Forensic fame,
And terrible A.B.
And Wolseley tall of stature, and
Lefroy and A.E.X.,
And now I think I'd best return
To the fair female sex.

VIII

But 'mongst so many "belles" 'tis hard
To choose which one to ring,
And I completely am perplexed,
Which contest first to sing.
So, t'other ladies will not deem
Me to their merits blind,
If I begin with number one,
(I would not be unkind.)

IX

Cassandra! Ah! It seemed as if,
Thy namesake's famed ill-luck
To thee, thro' all the lapse of years,
And centuries, had stuck.
For Poppy was thy bete-noire,
So well she played and keen,
That thou hadst little time to score,
E'er she was twice fifteen.

X

Next Georgie Vance and Fanny Holmes,
Are met, their game to play;
The big one and the little one,
In dresses black and grey.
Alas, fair Fanny fortune seemed
Thy merits to have missed,
For thou, frail fairy, could'st not beat
Thy great antagonist.

XI

Lily, to whom her sponsors gave
A name appropriate;
Nine aces got to equalise
Her fight with blue-eyed Kate,
Tho' well she played, and one good game
She to her credit placed,
Katie won two, and so her head
The victor's chaplet graced.

XII

Two games there were twixt Janette fair,
And Ada, Matron grave,
And Janette was the better player,
So aces nine she gave.
But although Ada in each bout,
To game-ball was ahead,
Janette soon made it game-ball all,
And won the games instead.

XIII

Now her first game Orinda lost
To Evelyn, I can find
For that no cause, except that cares,
Perplexed Orinda's mind.
But Evelyn strove to keep
The vantage she had gained,
For with Orinda after all
The victory remained.

XIV

Ah! Monsieur Rat! Ah Monsieur Rat!
Well pity thee I can,
'Twas thy hard fate to play against
The Able-Bodied man.
Ten aces could not make thee make,
Unto thyself a name,
For aces followed aces fast
Till Atty won the game.

XV

Next Millar the left-hander,
That was of stature small,
Was drawn to play against Wolseley,
That was of stature tall.
Full many a gallant tussle
They had the two games o'er,
For Wolseley's skilful volleying
Did puzzle Millar sore.

XVI

And very close their first game was,
'Twas warm work, both confessed,
But to the second soon they fell
With undiminished zest.
Alas! I have no space to tell,
How went that gallant fight,
How Millar with his left hand
Beat Wolseley with his right.

The History of Irish Tennis

XVII

"Robin and Richard" next did fight,
Weep inky tears, my pen,
They were unlike that loving pair,
That were such "pretty men."
They seldom smiled, when Robin won,
He didn't e'en look glad,
I'll pause not on the solemn theme,
For fear 'twould make me sad.

XVIII

And last in the first ties did play,
The poet and Lefroy,
Whose greeting pleasant meets your ear
With, "How are you old boy!"
But over their own actions,
All modest men are dumb,
So I'll be modest and in turn
Back to the ladies come.

XIX

Now next the second ties began,
Ah cruel, cruel fate!
Why should two sisters have to play,
Like Georgie versus Kate.
For Katie, thou wast overmatched,
Although so fair and deft,
And of the trio, once intact,
Georgie alone was left.

XX

But why! You'll ask, where's Janette, where,
I'm just about to tell,
(For she opposed to Poppy was,)
What fortune her befel.
These were the best contested games
Of all that yet were played,
And each in turn showed brilliant form,
And each to win essayed.

XXI

Janette got two aces start,
Enough to equal reckoned,
And game the first by her was won,
While Poppy won the second.
'Twas even betting which would win
The all important third,
And some in Janette placed their faith,
And Poppy some preferred.

XXII

But neck and neck they ran, and each
To head the other tried,
The score increased till "game-ball all,"
The watchful umpire cried;
To make the double-ace each served,
Twelve times without a doubt,
And twelve times each with crafty stroke,
Did put the other out.

XXIII

At last Miss Poppy scored an ace,
(She'd done it oft before),
And now she served a cunning serve
The other one to score,
It crossed the net, it touched the earth,
It never rose again,
And Janette, who fought so well
Was numbered with the slain.

XXIV

To tell how Millar beat the Bard,
Will not require much space,
How splendidly he played, and how
He won by many an ace.
For, hit he hard, or hit he soft,
The end was all the same,
His star in the ascendant was,
And so he won the game.

XXV

Ah Robin, sure thou foolish wert
Three aces to decline,
For thou wouldst only six accept,
Tho' A.B. offered nine;
For since with six one game you won,
I would be nothing loth
To say, that hadst thou taken all
Thou surely hadst won both.

XXVI

So in the final round remained,
Two gents and ladies three,
Orinda, Poppy, Georgie,
And Millar and A.B.
Orinda was 'gainst Poppy drawn,
While Georgie got a bye,
So how the various games were won,
To tell you now I'll try.

XXVII

Did I the marv'llous strokes relate,
Your feelings I'd appal,
How skilfully both played until
Poor Poppy got a fall.
That fall her nerves upset, and sent
A shock through all her frame,
At least, I fancied that was why
Orinda won the game.

XXVIII

But I was undeceived, for soon
I fain was to confess,
Orinda was the better player,
And well deserved success.
For though they both played very well
In game the second, still,
Poor Poppy lost that game, although
She didn't get a spill.

XXIX

But meet it is, and right, that I
Should render homage due
To ladies fair, so I will now
Description give to you,
Of how A.B. and Millar fought,
For I must end my song,
By telling you to which ladye
The victory did belong.

XXX

Well, then, the eager combatants,
Entered the grassy lists,
They did not, as prize fighters do,
Begin by shaking fists.
No, no, at once they fell to work,
Like heroes in their might,
And all spectators hoped to see,
A most exciting fight.

The History of Irish Tennis

XXXI

Nor were their expectations baulked,
And so the fight began,
'Twixt Millar, the left hander, and
The Able-Bodied man.
But Able-Body had to give
His foe four aces start,
And both were skilful, and first-rate
Professors in their art.

XXXII

No pen that contest can describe,
(You should the fight have seen),
How Millar but eleven scored,
While A.B. scored fourteen.
But Millar's left-hand still retained
Its wonted subtlety,
Five aces made he in one hand,
And won the victory.

XXXIII

In game the second, Millar seemed
At first to keep the fun
All to himself, till aces eight
He'd made to A.B.'s one;
But A.B. turned the tables soon,
And played so skilfully
That he had scored up aces twelve,
While Millar made but three.

XXXIV

"Eleven, thirteen, Millar in,"
Such was the Umpire's call,
And all impatient were to see,
Which first would reach game-ball.
So hand were in, and hands were out,
(both players were athirst),
But Millar scored most, and he reached
The wished for number first.

XXXV

And then he served a crafty serve,
And A.B. sent it back,
And swift and slow, and high and low,
The ball now made its track,
'Till Millar struck the ball so high,
That A.B. made quite sure
It would drop outside the court,
And him a hand procure.

XXXVI

And so he gazed, and upwards raised
Towards the ball his sight,
He marked it travel thro' the air,
He marked its lofty flight;
Downward it came, it reached the earth,
And with ill-fortune rare,
Fell just inside the outside line,
With just two lines to spare.

XXXVII

So Millar was the victor,
He won the racquet fine,
And though I am not envious,
I would it had been mine.
But no, 'tis his, and I must now
The final contest sing,
My pen is getting tired, and
Your patience on the wing.

XXXVIII

Would I Macaulay were, to write
An ancient Rome-ish lay,
Or George Lord Byron, to describe
That interesting fray;
But in this cold world wishes are,
Alas! Of no avail,
So, like Othello, I must tell
"A round unvarnished tale".

XXXIX

When Georgie and Orinda took
Their places on the ground,
All eyes were eager watching, and
Excitement reigned around.
But did I tell how each one scored,
My task would never end,
They played as well as any two
That ever did contend.

XL

This curious fact did happen, that,
When each had won a game,
The differences in aces was
In each one just the same.
Then having won a game apiece,
So sore were they distressed,
That to recruit their shattered strength
They needed two days rest.

XLI

So on the day appointed, each
Was at her proper post,
And Georgie did appear her strength
To have recruited most.
She got the side from which did blow
A strongly favouring gale,
And though Orinda struggled well,
'Twas all of no avail.

XLII

Though courts were changed at half the game,
And Georgie lost the wind
She played so well, that soon she left
Orinda far behind;
And soon she got to thirteen, while
But one Orinda made,
Whose score was seven, when Georgie won,
And so the games were stayed.

XLIII

So Georgie proved herself the best
Of all the ladies fair;
I wonder shall we see again
A tournament so rare.
Then friends, in bidding you farewell,
(For now my task is o'er,)
I've but to hope that I did not
Your kindly patience bore.

XLIV

My object being to amuse,
I pray you lenient be,
And trust that should I fail to please,
You still will pardon me.
And on the Archery Ground, I hope,
We all shall congregate,
And have another tournament
In 1878.

The History of Irish Tennis

*****

In 1883 the first issue of *Pastime* was published (Friday June 1st) at a cost of 2d. It was 'a weekly record of lawn tennis, tennis, rackets, lacrosse, cycling and athletic sports and recorded many of the activities of the mainly leisured classes in these islands. Lawn tennis was being played for less than ten years. Such was its rapid growth that the second issue (June 8th) included a list of some 35 Open tournaments as well as timetable for 150 other tennis matches. The majority of these were in England. The only other Irish events included are the starting dates for **Kilkenny County & City LTC** Open (June 18), **Limerick County C. & LTC**, Open Tournament and South of Ireland Championship (July 16, 23) and the **Waterford C. & LTC** Open (August 6). It is known that at this stage there were Irish tournaments being run by the **Downshire Archery & LTC** (Belfast), the **Armagh LTC** Open, the **County Kildare** Open, **Queenstown (Cobh) LTC** and **County Sligo LTC**. There were probably others. *Sport* was a particularly extensive weekly paper covering such events.

Percy French had a wide range of interests. Apart from his writings on tennis, he also managed to play in the Irish Championships. He said he preferred to be an average tennis player rather than a croquet king.

In these early days of lawn tennis it was not unusual to see poems published on the sport. In the July 20th issue (1883) the following poem appeared and written by the mysterious W…..m C….r. It was the first in an intended series of Recreation Rhymes (or *Presents from Past Times on Pastimes of the Present*). It is now quoted here as it reflects how lawn tennis was perceived in relation to other sports of the time. The English or British emphasis is strong as expected. Over the next twenty years the Germans and the Americans would consider the 'English' as the top tennis players in the world. The Irish tennis players were sometimes seen as a limb of that country, despite the fact that in the first full

international match between any two countries, Ireland were strong enough to beat England. It can be safely said that tennis life in Ireland was in the same mould as in England and many players regularly crossed the Irish Sea with racquets in hand, in both directions.

Lawn Tennis

I am monarch of all British Games,
My right there is none to contest,
For Britons all over the world
Acknowledge that I am the best.
Oh billiards! Say where are the charms,
That some people see in thy face;
Better have a good "rally" with me,
And endeavour "to keep up the pace."

Other Games I admit are at hand,
But conscience constrains me to own,
There are maidens and men by the score,
Who live but for Tennis alone.
There is Croquet, that once was the rage,
Folks now with indifference see,
And candour compels me to say,
Its tameness is shocking to me.

There is Cricket, an old English sport,
And a very good game in its way,
But its votaries all must admit,
It is most inconvenient to play.
For its players have nothing to do,
Half the time that they own is so dear,
And I've noticed, when once they are "out,"
They hurry to 'baccy and beer.

And Archery, Rinking, and Bowls,
Your charms are displayed but in vain;
No one cares the least atom for you,
Or desires to taste you again;
But with me folks their troubles assuage,
With me they are merry and gay;
Each game they enjoy more and more,
And are cheered by the "rallies" they play.

When driven with judgement and skill,
How swiftly my ball cleave the air,
And "topping the net" by an inch,
Call for no little caution and care;
How merrily too, sound my cries,
Though strangers can't make out their use;
My language is strange, I admit,
"Fifteen, love," "thirty", "forty," and "deuce."

When worn with the troubles of life,
Or harassed with business and care,
Cast your worries at once to the wind,
And straight to your Tennis repair.
In every "set" that you play,
There is pleasure and health to be got,
And I'm the best thing in the world,
To reconcile man to his lot.

The game itself has long been the subject of those with a poetic inclination. Percy French was a multi-talented engineer by qualification, but entertainer by profession. He put pen to paper on many occasions in the cause of tennis. The following short piece summarises his feeling for the game in a little booklet with rhymes and sketches he published in the late 1880s.

While at Trinity College he wrote the following about a tennis escapade in the late 1870s. It speaks for itself.

The Tennis Fiend
A tale of rapine and violence

Argument. Messrs. Milne and French having unlawfully taken possession of a tennis court in the "Provost's garden" (Trin.Coll.) are promptly evicted by Dr. Shaw, who having laid the matter before Mr. Tollett and the College Board causes the net to be removed and the garden to be left once more to its aboriginal inhabitant-the Provost's Cow!!
(Air- "An owl & a pussy cat went to sea")

I
Oh two little Engineers
Went to play
In a beautiful pea-green park
They set up a net
And they didn't forget
To keep it uncommonly dark
Said French: "I expect"
The Board may object"
And we may get into a row
This is but a surmise
So at present it lies
Between you and me and the cow.

II
But Shaw that owl
That elderly fowl
Whose soul is with rancour replete
Was awfully wroth
This vandal and Goth
Had invaded his silvan retreat
Men say his dark breast
Is never at rest
Unless he's engaged in some row
-It could not be endured
So he went to the 'Board'
With a grievance as big as the Cow.

III
"Oh Board are you willing"
"That French and that Milne"
"Should fill all our Park with their friends"
"This taking "French" leave"
"Is a course you perceive"
"Which to chaos and anarchy tends"
"Our locks they can pick"
"With a nail or a stick"
"Which is rather to cool you'll allow"
"It's an insult to Lloyd"
"I myself feel annoyed"
"And besides it's disturbing the cow"

Percy lived in that era of sporting development and played at **Boyle LTC**, at **Trinity College**, at the **Fitzwilliam** club and later having helping to found the **County Cavan LTC**. He did recognise his own limitations. While not as good as the world-beaters at the Irish Open Championships, he was able to capture the mood of the game in detail. However, we know the game inspired him and this love of the sport must be recorded, again! Worldwide the contribution of the **Fitzwilliam Lawn Tennis Club** to the sport is recognised and players should be reminded of this. In the second edition of the *Irish Cyclist & Athlete* there was a special Lawn Tennis Tournament Supplement published during the Irish Championships of 1887, priced 1/-. Ernest Renshaw was to beat the holder Herbert Lawford and repeat his winning form of 1883. Lottie Dod that young English girl was on her one and only visit and beat Maud Watson in the final. Percy sets the scene with the following piece dedicated to "King tennis":

In the Christmas edition of *The Irish Cyclist and Athlete (1887)* Percy strikes again. This time he includes praise for the Irish players, Tom Campion, a member of the **Dublin University LTC** (Trinity College), Grainger Chaytor, Willoughby J. Hamilton, Joshua Pim, Maxwell and M. J. Carpendale. He commences with an interesting explanation of the sport as seen by an outsider.

The Tennis Players

Then the noble hee-haw-watha,
Told them of another pastime,
Told them of the game of Tennis:-
How the young men and maidens,
How the old men and the children,
Played at Tennis all the summer;
How he tried to understand it,
Looking at them from a distance,
But he always failed to grasp it,

The History of Irish Tennis

Though a Frenchman kindly told him
That the way the game commences
Was to try and strike the netting
With the first ball of the service;
Then you get the next ball over,
Then you cry out, "Mine", or "leave it",
And again you bang the netting,
Crying "hard luck", "hit the tape line",
"Nuther inch an' I'd got it".
These, he told him, were expressions
He had heard among the players.
Then the noble Hee-haw-watha
Told them of the Tennis Champions,
Told then of the brothers Renshaw,
Told them of the lion Lawford,
Who for two years held the trophy
And the name of Irish Champion;
But that, this year, Ernest Renshaw
Wrested from his grasp the glory;
Told how Campion and Chaytor
Sailed across the Irish Channel
To the Northern Counties Meeting,
And returned again the Champions
Of the English Northern Counties;
Told them of the coming players,
Mentioned Hamilton the younger
As a player fit to follow
In his brother's phantom footsteps.
"Pim, I think", said Hee-haw-watha,
"Is a man that we will read of
In the future of Lawn Tennis;
Also Campion and Maxwell,
Carpendale, and D.G.Chaytor,
Are not names to be forgotten.
If you wish to read the glories
Of the great Fitzwilliam battle,
You should get the Extra Special
Tennis Number of the paper;
Copies of it may be ordered,
Post free, Sevenpence (Macreedi,
Office of this splendid Paper)".

The Tennis Tournament:
A Lay of Modern Dublin
[aka "Ye Tale of Ye Tournament-1884]
(1927 version as published in "Fitzwilliam's First
Fifty)

The great Fitzwilliam Tennis Club
Have met in High conclave,
The Jones and Browns and Robinson,
The beautiful and brave,
Now hold they solemn council,
(MaConchy in the chair),
In order to determine when
They'll hold their Tournament again,
In green Fitzwilliam Square.

There be seven bold committee men
With bows of brown and gold
Who ever in Fitzwilliam Square
Have made it their peculiar care
To keep it mown and rolled.
Morning and eve the seven
Have kept these courts full green,,
Traced out alright in line of white
With Elvery's machine.

Gay were the College Races,
The Lansdowne Sports were gay;
But the great Fitzwilliam Tournament
Is now our whitest day.
Now all the lofty hoardings
And walls which own his sway,
John Dillon fills with flaming bills
Anent the coming frawy.

An interesting note on the Northern Lawn Tennis Championships Tournament is the fact that it was in this tournament, held at the Lawn Tennis Grounds, Old Trafford, Manchester, that in 1882 the Langrishe sisters from Kilkenny won the first ladies doubles event in major competition anywhere. The Fitzwilliam Championships held their first ladies doubles in 1913 and Wimbledon in 1899.

The USA included ladies doubles in 1890, Ireland's Mabel Cahill was on the winning side in both 1891 and 1892; she was born in Ballyraggett, County Kilkenny. The West of England Championships at Bath were also advertised in the same newspaper which had a Tennis Tournament Supplement, encouraged by Percy French, one of their writers.

In the following lengthy piece, from 1884, further deeds of the court are recalled. The Elvery 'machine' used for the white lines on the courts get a plug. Visitors included those players from Birr, Castlerea, England, France and the USA. The term 'lay' was regularly used in referring to his works. It is a poem meant to be sung, a ballad (Oxford Dictionary, 1995).

The History of Irish Tennis

John Dillon and his myrmidons,
Have worked like one o'clock,
And soon, I ween, are posters seen,
At Booterstown-the Rock-
In Glenageary's wild ravines,
By Dalkey's lovely Bay,
Till ere the morn his bills adorn-
The sea-girt walls of Bray.

This week the only converse is
Of Ball, and Bat, and Net,
And men hold monster meetings
To determine what's a "Let".
The shopmen, too, have caught the craze,
And people rush to buy
The "Back-hand-volley bonnet",
Or the "Deuce and Vantage tie".

And now our haughty challenge
Has reached the Renshaw's home,
Swift, swift the great twin brethren
Come speeding o'er the foam;
And Horn and Montgomerie
Have crossed the self-same night,
And marched across the town to where,
All in the great Fitzwilliam Square,
Was fought the glorious fight.

Oh, brightly shone the sun upon
The nineteenth morn of May,
What time the mighty Renshaw rushed,
All eager, to the fray.
To meet him came the Richardson,
A Cheshire champion he-
From the green steeps where Mersey leaps
To join the Irish Sea.

It is not mine to chronicle
The details of the strife,
How Renshaw hit the ball a whack,
And Chester sent it flying back
Ere men could mutter "knife",
You'll find it in "The Freeman",
Or in the "Irish Times",
How Renshaw won the final set
And gallant Richardson was 'bet'
(Beaten's the proper word and yet-
A poet must have rhymes).

Sempronius Attratinus-
(His other name is Browne),
Is in the great Fitzwilliam Club
A star of some renown.
A man of mighty muscle,
A man of iron nerve,
And, when it happens to come off,
A very deadly serve.

But never had he met before,
A foe so cool and stern,
And never had he stood against
The Renshaw's swift return;
Back on the line he drives him,
And Dublin with dismay
Sees the stout knight in whom they trust
At length recumbent in the dust

And Renshaw wins the day.
But meanwhile in the "doubles"
Great deeds of arms were wrought,
Where Gould and Macnamara
And great Sir Victor fought.
Sir Victor of the long white coat-
And heather mixture hose,
The courts know well
The "long, stern swell",
Who wears such striking clothes.

From far and near the champions fly,
Undaunted men are they,
To beard the Lion Lawford,
To break the Renshaw's sway.
They come from lands far distant,
From countries far away-
A Rives arrives from Newport,
And a Coote from Castlerea.

J. Dwight, the small Bostonian,
Whose ardour never fades,
Garmendier the beautiful-
And loved of southern maids.
The gallant M. J. Carpendale,
The Monkstown men prefer;
The Garveys raise the standard high,
Of Parsonstown-(or Birr).

As sinks the stricken chimney,
When wind-blasts blow from far,
As falls the money-market,
When rumour speaks of War;
So sinks, so falls, the Renshaw,
Beneath the giant stroke
Of him who first was seen to burst
The great twin-breathern's yoke.

And now when poles are planted,
And stretched the tennis nets;
And men are serving lets,
With awe and admiration,
Still is the story told,
How Lawford won the champion cup
And belt of shining gold.

Percy French Relaxing. He was known to favour playing the banjo over his engineering studies.

The History of Irish Tennis

"Championship Meeting" Dublin 1883. Seated in centre were Herbert Lawford (with racquet) and Ernest Browne. Behind them were Ernest Renshaw (with racquet) and, immediately to his left, Eyre Chatterton, Vere St. Leger Goold and M. J. Carpendale. On the ground are Arthur Courtenay, Maconchy, Peter Aungier, Willie Renshaw and A. Graves.

"Championship Meeting" at Dublin in 1888. Back (l. to r.) Miss Exham, Louisa Martin, Miss Stanuell, ---, Maud Watson, Miss Beetham, Miss Steedman & May Langrishe. Sitting (from left) Blanch Hillyard, ---, Beatrice Langrishe, Miss B. Steedman.

A Fitzwilliam Square Tennis Tournament
(Percy French c. 1886)

Comrades, leave me here a little, leave me on this classic plain,
Let me in heroic stanzas fight the Tournament again.
'Tis the place and all around it as of old the cabmen swear,
When colliding at the corners leading to Fitzwilliam Square.
Let me hymn those mighty heroes, let me sing their deeds sublime,
Let me send their names resounding down the ringing grooves of time.
Here let me recall the combat in a mighty tide of song;
Leave me here, and when you want me, sound upon the dinner gong.

I myself have played at Tennis, looked upon myself as fair,
Till I saw the world-wide champions battling in Fitzwilliam Square.
Then I saw myself a duffer, saw that if I longed for fame,
I must choose another pastime, I must seek another game.
Far in some remoter region, where men play at Croquet still,
I will match me with the Curate, I will bend him to my will.
There, 'mid melancholy maidens, I would bear away the palm,
Pacing round each wiry crescent with meditative calm.

Fool! Again the dream, the fancy fancy 'tis I know full well,
For I hold the Tennis duffer higher than the croquet swell.
I who once have wielded a racquet, I to join that sorry group,
Pacing on yet slowly, slowly, moving on from hoop to hoop.
Not for me the milder pastime, Tennis is thye game I sing,
Better 'tis to fail at Tennis than to reign a Croquet king.
Here upon a bench I pondered, nourishing this truth sublime-
That good play is nought but practice and the long result of time.

Many a time I've seen the Renshaws rise triumphant from the fray,
Like a pair of mighty planets shining in the milky way.
Often to the white pavilion, where the sandwiches they munch,
Have I seen the lion Lawford slowly sloping to his lunch.
In the spring the maiden comes in latest fashions dressed,
In the spring the young man's fancy gets himself a brighter vest;
And my spirit leaps before me to behold the coming scene,
With the Nation's tennis players grappling in the central green.

There, methinks, would be enjoyment-more than city life entails-
Than the Tramways, than the loop-line, or accelerated mails.
For I dipped into the future, far as human eye might see,
Saw the vision of the players, and the Tennis that would be.
Saw the steamers filled with champion argosies of mighty males,
And the rapid might expresses shrinking down the coast of Wales;
Far along the Menai tunnel, glare of engine rushing fast,
And the funnels of the Connaught plunging through the thunderblast.

Till her engines throb no longer, gangways to the pier are hurled,
And along them pour the coming wonders of the Tennis world.
Scenting from afar the battle, comes each never-failing twin,
Comes the swarthy Lawford, smiling, ever a sardonic grin.
Daring Dwight, the "Boston Bantling", whom the "Dusky One" they dub,
Comes again to represent her-her the "Universal Hub".
See Hibernia's gloomy chieftain, on his brow the gathering frown,
Innisfallen's sons will cheer thee in combat, Ernest Browne.

Chatterton, the lengthy striding, through the medley of my dream,
Bears aloft the student-standard from the groves of Academe.
Chatterton's a lesser Renshaw, and although a champion bold,
Still his back strokes are to Renshaw's as a cough is to a cold.
In this paradise of pleasure, where the town and country meet,
Lying like a green Atlantis in the desert of the street;
Here the cautious poet pauses till the great event is o'er,
For it is not well foretelling what the future has in store:

Whether Renshaw wins or Lawford, or Hibernia's stalwart knight,
Or some unknown meteor flashes on the world's astonished sight.
Whosoe'er remains the victor, this the reader shall descry-
When the Tournament behind him as a foughten field shall lie.
....
Great Fitzwilliam Square, I leave thee, basking in the sunset's glow,
For a mighty thirst arises tending tea-ward, and-I go.

Some notes of explanation on the Fitzwilliam Square Tournament. Willie and Ernest Renshaw (born 3rd January 1861) were the talented Cheltenham twin brothers who won many Wimbledon and Irish Championships. Herbert Lawford broke their unbeaten runs during the 1880s. Eyre Chatterton was an Irish player of lesser standing whilst Ernest Browne was a member of the **Fitzwilliam LTC** and winner of the Irish Championship doubles in 1882. The Connaught was the name of the boat taking the players across the Irish Sea. It was also, later, the name of a Lawn Tennis Club. Daring Dwight was the father of American tennis, Dr. James Dwight, President of their association and the first American visitor to the All England and Irish Championships.

*****

Poetry in the Press

Scanning old newspapers in areas away from the capital one can always find interesting articles on all sorts of topics. Sports reports were not immune to a piece of poetry. The following piece, writer unidentified, was found at the start of the report on the County Sligo Open Tournament in July 1907:

> *There was a young man who possessed*
> *For the game of Lawn Tennis a zest;*
> *He asked "where shall I go?"*
> *They told him "to Sligo",*
> *For there you will sample the best.*

> *He took his relations advice*
> *And travelled to Sligo half-price,*
> *He found that the food*
> *Was remarkably good,*
> *The play was remarkably nice.*

> *Oh blithe was his heart as he donned*
> *The flannels, of which he was fond.*
> *(From the state of his clothes*
> *At the end, you'd suppose*
> *That he might have come out of a pond).*

> *But though his apparel was black*
> *He conquered the foes in his track,*
> *And with bank-notes and prizes*
> *Of various sizes*
> *Went cake-walking all the way back.*

Not classical poetry, but it does paint a picture of a tennis player who was able to take a bit of abuse and yet was more than useful at his chosen sport. The following poem is one penned by Hal Woodmartin, the long time secretary of **County Sligo LTC** and organiser of Sligo's Open tournament, first held in the 1880s; its descendant being the current West of Ireland Championship. His nephew, Dick, was later to be involved in running the tournament when the **YMCA Lawn Tennis Club** took over running the event in the late 1940s.

Hal Woodmartin (left) with G. Eccles at the 1922 County Sligo LTC Open Championships

Sligo Tennis Tournament, 1926
"Idle thoughts of an idle fellow"
With apologies to Shakespeare and any others.

All Sligo's at the Tournament,
And men and maidens many are keenly playing,
They show their faults and failings,
And the "umpire" rarely fails to "let" them.
They play their many "sets". First comes
The Novice, nervous and shaking on the service line,
And then the hardy annual, with quite new racket,
Slashing and lobbing like "Horatio" at the Bridge
Repelling all attacks. Then a "FOWLER" reappearing
After many rains-doughty as of yore with cross
Side shots and splendid smashes, winning his way,
To prizes and to cheers.
The a "Spinster", fairly fleet of foot and keen
Of eye-with back hand good and fore arm strong,
Finding the form of old, up to the Cup.
Hark to the Pibroch: A "Campbell" is coming;
With eye shade sprightly fixed, and full intent
To show "dear Terence" Sligigh Abu-
Driving and placing, as a "Champion" should.
The Umpires, stern and quick of eye to mark
And tell the "faults" and not afraid to call
Them, censorious, yet fair to all, who play
The game of Tennis true. Appreciating the shots
But dumb to shout-"Good Shot"-"Hard Luck";
And last, by no means least -The Secretary,
"Good Old Hal", Mahogany is the hue he wears,
Unruffled-but often tried, occasionally heard
To say "Mein Gott" I'm hot;
A noble company-men and maids-bon company;
Here's to you all, Vale, Good Luck
Last scene of all, they press around the stand,
Envious of Cups and Cheques-some to Dublin,
Mayo, Carlow, but Sligigh holds its own.
A gracious lady, giving to each and all,
What'er they've won-with words of kindly
Interest and thoughts of other days and
Older friends, who still look down and
Interest take in the struggles on the sward
in Sligo Town.

O TEMPORA O MORES; Times do change, but
Tennis friends do not.

The History of Irish Tennis

*****

Helen Wills Moody

Helen Wills Moody in action-A lady interested in poetry and art as well as tennis.

In 1938, Willie Sandys was determined to have the American Helen Wills Moody at the Irish Open. He knew that she admired the writings of Oliver St. John Gogarty, the poet surgeon and Gogarty, who was to see her in London about a visit to his country house in Renvyle.

It was Willie who contacted Dr. Gogarty and suggested he ask her to play at Fitzwilliam. *He, very kindly, accepted this idea and became most enthusiastic to help the club……..I did not receive the official entry until the Sunday morning before the tournament. Helen had to choose between playing in Dublin or Queen Mary's Garden Party on the Tuesday of our tournament. .....The weather was awful except on the last day when we earned two gates before and after lunch!...I hope it will not disillusion the young people when I say the hardest job I had was to sign the hundreds of autograph books which were sent to the club.*

Helen duly won the championship, beating England's Thelma Jarvis in the final. She stayed at the Shelbourne Hotel from where she was transported each day by Rolls Royce to the club. Immediately after the final she was presented with her prize by Jack McCann, the club President, and then *whisked off to Galway in Gogarty's Rolls which was waiting at the Club gates.*

As well as being the best lady lawn tennis player in the world at the time, she painted and had written novels. She had recently read *As I was going down Sackville Street* by Gogarty and much taken by the following poem thought to have been penned about her:

Though she guards it grace breaks through
Every blithe and careless movement
What shall I compare her to
When she takes the ball backhanded
Speed and sweetness are so blended
Nothing awkward can she do.

In the late 1930s an Irish *Badminton and Tennis Review* magazine was launched. It quickly included other sports. In the second edition, the Honorary Secretary of the ILTA, Harry Maunsell, wrote an article on the 'Golden Days' of the 1880s. He included the following: *In 1895 Messrs. Pim, Stoker and Mahony did not play in the English Championships, and the following verses appeared in "Lawn Tennis and Badminton", the official organ of the game in Scotland* (sic)*:-*

"Mr. Pim, Mr. Stoker, Mr. Mahony
Have you heard the sighs upon the classic green,
Have you heard what a sorry thing a week at
Wimbledon with you left out has been;
Are your triumphs so insipid that escaping
You forgo your English laurels for a whim;
Come back and set us all again agaping
Mr. Stoker, Mr. Mahony, Mr. Pim.

Mr. Pim, Mr.Stoker, Mr. Mahony
The play was very brilliant now and then
But frankly and without a bit of Blarney
'Twas not Wimbledon without the Irishmen;
Some there be who follow closely in your traces,
But the Champion of all England, what of him?
Come back and put them in their proper places
Mr. Stoker, Mr. Mahony, Mr. Pim

*****

Must Travel Nowadays

As you will read elsewhere in this book these three were among the best in their time, Pim (twice) and Mahony won the Wimbledon singles championships and Stoker, with Pim, the doubles twice. However, by 1938, those days seemed in the distant past and Harry Maunsell's article continued as follows:

It is perfectly true that nowadays it would be quite impossible for any player in this country, no matter what his talent was, to come to the top of the tree unless he could devote some years to the game and travel all round the world. Since 1897 Ireland has had some very distinguished players, such as J. C. Parke, The Hon. C. Campbell, J. F. Stokes, E. D. McCrea, C. F. Scroope, V. Miley, L. A. Meldon, E. A. Mc Guire, and others, all of whom learned a considerable amount of their tennis in this country. G.L. Rogers, who, with J.C. Parke and The Hon. C. Campbell, was the most outstanding of all players since the War, learned all his tennis abroad. Since 1896 we have never had six players at the one time comparable to the players in the early Nineties.

The magazine became the *Irish Sports Review* but appears to have disappeared as quickly as it arrived; the Second World War was perhaps its death knell.

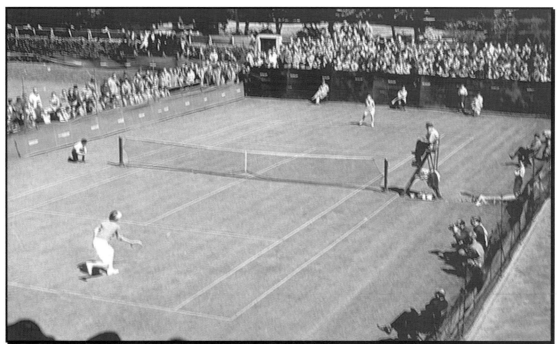

The 1938 Irish Championships at Fitzwilliam LTC. Helen Wills Moody (near side) beating Thelma Jarvis (England) in the final. Her grace on the tennis court is thought to have inspired St. J. Gogarty into verse.

*****

Wet Castlebar

The Connacht Hard Court Championships commenced after the Second World War. By the late 1950s the event was an attractive fixture, bringing a regular range of players from many parts of the country. In 1958, the duo of Jill Avaldi and Ann Mahony taking 'about twelve hours' arrived from **Glasnevin LTC** in Dublin. Ann was to meet local organiser John Garavan. They would marry in 1964 and, by 2003, Ann can proudly look at her 46th continuous entry into this event, now fixed at the August weekend. Socially the clubhouse was just not big enough and the town hall had to be used for the post-tennis activities. In the early 1960s. Geoff Oakley from Birr attended. It was a wet weekend. Alf Walsh, the Irish honorary secretary, had agreed to be the tournament referee while John Garavan, a local solicitor who became a District Justice, was the tournament secretary. John and Ann were engaged at this stage. During the showers Geoff put pen to paper.

If ever you see Alf Walsh go by,
You'll know for certain he's going to cry:
"On court, on court, what ails you all?
The weather is not too bad at all!
That court is not flooded-it's not even wet,
The top of the net is visible yet!"

"Our dresses will shrink", the ladies moan,
But ambling Alf has a heart of stone.
"What matter", he says, "if they shrink a bit-
As topless dresses they'll surely fit".

So the girls went out and hit winners all day,
For the men couldn't keep their eyes on the play.
The published results will surely puzzle the fans-
The Men's Singles cup went to one of the Anns!

But the cheers were cut short when the Guards made a raid,
And 'pinched' every blonde in the topless parade.
"To Court, to Court, we will fine them all,
For topless top-spinning a tennis ball".

Then at Castlebar Court, said a judge from the bench
"Give me every detail of each elegant wench".
Said Solicitor John, from eloquent lips,
"I've all the statistics at my finger tips".

So it ended at last with dismisses all round,
Save that in one case the learned Justice found
That Counsel one client must take as his wife,
And with countenance stern he pronounced sentence for life.

"On court, on court, what ails you all,
The weather is not bad at all".

David O'Donnell looking out from under the tent at the Castlebar tournament in about 1963.

*****
Scottish Praise

In 1960 the Irish tennis team travelled to play Scotland. The team of Joe Hackett, Peter Jackson, Eleanor O'Neill and Heather Flinn was a good one. Alf Walsh, the honorary secretary of the Irish Lawn Tennis Association at the time, was the effective manager of the team. The match was lost by 3 matches to 5. However, the team left an impression.

A local, only known as G.B.P., penned the following poem in tribute to the visitors on the 3rd September 1960.

Tribute to Ireland's Tennis Team

Of all the Teams that come to play
Against the Scottish L.T.A.
None have more pleasing looks and style
Than those who hail from Erin's Isle.

A hundred welcomes, J. D. Hackett,
Your game is in the topmost bracket,
We love the way you yield your racket,
As for the ball, oh how you whack it,
With volleys swift you do attack it:
Your play's A.1, dear Captain Hackett.

And then there's also P. H. Jackson:
We hail you, sir, with sounding Klaxon,
High tennis skill you do not lack, son,
In serve and smash you show great knack, son,
Its you the pretty colleens back, son:
Long life and cheers, dear Mr. Jackson.

And next----oh great is her appeal---
We sing the charms of Miss O'Neill:
Her graceful drive, her service deal
Rouse praise we simply can't conceal:
Fond adminiration, 'tis , all feel
For strokes like yours, dear Miss O'Neill.

No wonder you so often win
Your tennis matches, Mrs. Flinn:
Upon your shots you put such spin,
And place them where they are just in:
Your portrait on the wall we'll pin,
And long recall sweet Heather Flinn.

From Dublin Town to Kyle Lochalsh
All laud the name of A. H. Walsh,
A name that's held in high acclaim
Where e'er is played the tennis game;
Where e'er ther is an Irish team
He wins the uttermost esteem:
We welcome him to Scotland's shore,
And fain would see his presence more.

And now good health, each Irish friend,
To all, best wishes we extend,
But ere you leave our Scottish ken
Pray, say you'll soon come back again,
For if you do shall supply
A Day indubitably DRY.

*****
Sir Basil Goulding

Sir Basil Goulding was a long time member of **Fitzwilliam LTC**. As far as lawn tennis was concerned he was a true aficionado. Apart from being a more than competent tennis player, he was to be Irish squash champion in 1940 and played on the Irish team in 1948. He was to be made President of that well respected club for the years 1965 to 1968. During his term of high office the club was continuing to run the Irish Open and effectively putting the programme together. In those days there were many interesting articles on the game by professional journalists such as Vera McWeeney. Sir Basil added many of his thoughts on the sport and are worth recording.

Basil Goulding on Supporting Tennis
(Official Programme for The Lawn Tennis Championships of Ireland, 1966)

There is a distinct difference, first noticed by Mayow's mouse and thus by Mayow, between supporting life and living.
One meets in life all to many mice who are merely supporting it-under a glass bell and a whiff of oxygen provided by the office ceiling and the paycheck.

For others, though, there are chinks in the wainscotting, breaks in the tea, locks in the shotter. Through any such your spirited mouse can squeeze his form, bolt for Fitzwilliam, slip into his frilly beunos, and outfoam Ferrari's prancing horse.

What, then, serves him in the office of remorse? Why nothing at all, save maybe a pulled muscle, an' it nothing to speak of beside a pulled pint. For the rest, the reports from the old engine room are of the kind calculated to bring A1 gratification to Mr. Lloyd. The blood has coursed like superlube through the filing system; the nails there filed are hard as legs; and the break-horse power of one who has reached the end of this tether has now established animal superiority over man.

But hist,, we rhapsodize. This pourboire-the token coin which we fling to Fitzbill as tip (we call it subscription to save Bill embarrassment) will never support tennis, let alone the rhapsody of playing it.

Comes the annual opportunity, however. Comes the Open Championship. Come-why, yes, indeed-the great players of the world. You mean to Dublin? Yes, again, indeed.

Then (at that time) assuredly will be exposed the atavistic struggle between brute man and brute man from every tennis racket in Ireland to fight his way into Fitzwilliam by hook or, preferably crook, damn the cost?

No. Irishmen, we may prettily explain to our foreign visitors, are as dacent and reticent in their proposals to support tennis as they are in their proposals to support a wife (each).

The History of Irish Tennis

Comparison between bookings from all over Ireland for two months before the Open and those for two days previous to a performance of "Charlie's Aunt" have this point of interest; that there is nothing in it.

One could, it is true, aver with some assurance that the Aunt would be the clear winner, were it not, however, for the fact of Fitzwilliam's secret weapon, its Underground, resistance, in fact its Championship Committee.

Mysterious H, inscrutable chief of the whole nexus, with its fantastically organised cells of specialized activity, all precisely briefed to their complementary functions, each led by an anonymous fighter of many AGM's standing, is-where was I-thought to be, I said thought, one who covers his activities under the ingenious identity of an Idol of the Irish Courts; the one, they say, whom All England this year has honoured by adoption.

The purpose, and, ho, the achievement of this network is to weave the necessary foundation garment for the tournament. Now foundation garments have purposes to which we need not, in this happy issue, too precisely address ourselves; but their overall function is to present figures to best advantage. And so it is that the P. and L. account displayed by this tournament is at once the uplift of its popular appeal and the silhouette set by its foundation garment.

The essential weave of our garment has always been that the Programme and the advertisers in it: and again this year our chic girl-about-town look is to be ascribed to the gentle but firm means by which these good supporters of ours shape the P. and L. account.

But his year something splashy has also happened-two things.

Mysterious H. and his hushmen have penetrated certain warm corporate hearts hitherto jacketed. Here-within 10 business bosoms-they have sportive response; they have found; to lay romance aside, what it takes to pay for the travel and stabling of our pretty artist(e)s from foreign courts.

Here is that lost part, the part of The Patron, once again being rehearsed; and rehearsed, as is preferable, by several rather than by a single star.

Along with this development comes to Fitzwilliam Telefis Eireann, the archapostle of the popular, if not its sculptor.

So let us celebrate, or if it be too wet for play, celebrate the wonder of the day-the dawn of an Irish Wimbledon with its annual glamour and panache.

Give us but a year or so to reach to the delectably silly in couture, the scramble for debentures, the invidiations between sol y sombre, the essential sweetener of whispered impropriety of the week.

For the nonce, though, our excited plaudits go-never mind the players-to all those who are this year bringing things out into the Open.
Great ould s'ports.

*****

Funny Thing Happened Down the Club
(Sir Basil Goulding in the Official Programme for The Fitzwilliam Invitation Lawn Tennis Tournament, 1967)

I got kep' on as President.

Proper awkward then after that show-down. All me old Committee-pals took off like sparrers for Spain an' me left sittin' like I got stuck to an insulator.

You know about the show down? You followed the rallies to and fro? So you know who won? Good. More than I do.

But since it's the principle of the thing that didn't count I'll tell you what didn't happen. In a word Open is still Shut; but a blow has been struck for, I think, Irish motherhood and the Celtic carburettor. That or something.

Not too much levity, though, if you please. A sport is a sport is a vested interest. A player is a player is a bread-winner.
And ever the twain shall meet. Yes, an' if I ever met concurrence about anything it is that much as things are not what they used to be they are even more not what they should be. There are even dark whispers-mind you I heard nothing-whispers that some amateurs scarcely deserve that insult.

But tradition; now there's yer man, a man to rely on. There's nothing fly-by-night about tradition. Tradition will keep the decencies veiled long after the shorts of fact have been torn off in the scrum of life. Tradition is the O.K. aspect of history; it ensures that what you haven't learnt from experience won't be put into effect when experience changes.

Where was I? Ah, yes: the dear dead private tennis party with its brilliant youngsters, persevering elders, ludicrous partnerships, real lemonade, loaded tea-spread, and -remember? - amateur players.

Then the visited township tournament, with its doggy sniffing, soggy courts, pubescent gamesmanship, timeless pavilion squatting, and last-to-cancel-gets-the-cup. Still amateur, but precariously keener.

Later the badge on breast, picked to represent, foreign excursion, uphold the honour, expenses paid, great help expenses, dalliance on sidelines, great help dalliance; but alas no dalliance-expenses for amateurs.

Suddenly the limelight, blinking, glam: ambition akindle, selectors selecting, sideboard glittering, silvery; suggestions turn indelicate, financially, and perhaps...Career opens up, oblique attractions lode obliquity; what price amateurism, can't afford turn Pro.

But many and solid men say,
That this is a cynical way
Of treating tennis today
For even if one or two may

The History of Irish Tennis

Be as naughty as this, well, its they
Who alone put the balance astray,
While the majority stay
On the straight and narrow from pay.

All this, tell the chroniclers, was the stuff of which Fitzwilliam's 1967 tennis-quoits were made.

But how uncouth, dear boy, the way they were thrown! Mean to say, serve like that to poor Mr.Walsh, whom ILTA preserve (and vice versa). Somewhat Tabasco, eh? Mean to say, what could he but....?

And that fancy Club President where was he in all this ask a Bean Garda.

And so to the Club crisis, Manna, man. Respite, relief at last, after two long years of debilitating love-in-idleness. Spirits rise, their sale too. A real row on, members pour in from fir and mna. Laugh! Haven't had it so good since the last Committee got the ole' one two.

The meetings then, hushed from public view if not ear. The tepid tentative tones of the President weaving to escape violence. The flash of cunningly casual advocacy. Snap, crackle, pop! The fire buckets of simple sincerity in attempt to extinguish the blaze. The absence of a Club Rule upon all points arising. The confusatory detours by questioners.

Sir Basil Goulding, President of Fitzwilliam Lawn Tennis Club, with Princess Grace of Monaco, at the Irish Championships in 1965.

Then the division itself and the chaos of extempore voting papers. The reassembly, pregnant hush, throw-away verdict, inscrutable reception. The members gurgling out as bath water, in spirals. The pink-cheeked camaraderie in the bar, into the light.

Comes the dawn, the pale cold laminates of earth and air; and firewater. Comes the chagrin of the victors. Hurts me more, Barton, than you, Joe; come to think of it, hurts me much more, what with six weeks to no tournament.

But brisk bouncing boyos the new sparrers, able to land on live wires without falling on beaks. But live wire who? Who's for live wire? Where's that mine from Carrick?

Mine found, reluctant, keen, never mined, found. So.

Sparrers to work, now, much flutterin', no peckin'. Twigs ahunt, twigs everywhence, twigs against nesting time.

By such frenetic sequences, ladies and gentlemen, by such sequences - and I have been delicate as delph in omitting the post-natal sequence (as it turned out to be), the one in travail with Ashbrook and ILTA - by these we reach today an event which must, you suppose, be scarce recognisable from the classical events of which Fitzwilliam is the stately home. Even the new title - Invitation Tournament - tells you that all is changed utterly.

Well, sucks, it isn't. And that goes for the organisation, the aura, the sociality, even the players themselves.

Summer and tennis and Fitzwilliam: Johnston, Mooney & O'Brien; eat the best (memo: must get something out of Moloney for this). We shall witness again the usual swish and dash, the same strech and strife, the nicely so and the just not thus, the agility concentration and accomplishment, the sheer uncommon art of it. And we shall enjoy our own company as spectator in the special way that one does when one sits half-anaesthetized by the ambient relaxity, half-mesmerised by the prap-prap-prang of the rally-cycles. What splendid company one is, n'est-ce-pas, when one sheds one's responsibilities! How charming and amiable to watch with! What a percipient critic and how fascinatingly right, as it surely turns out!

Ladies and Gentlemen, we must present our apologies, for all this parochialism, to our flashing house-guests from without. It is truly sporting of them to come, apparently unruffled as to the perils of assassination by one side or other. When the board-of-honour in the Clubhouse come to terms, over the next year or two, with a perplexity or two of inscription we shall surely find some of our guests' names glowing there; followed perhaps by asterisks which will refer, not to their language on court, but to their special role as heralds of a new dawn. Will it be Open to doubt?

*****

On Knowing Nothing About Tennis
(Sir Basil Goulding in the Official Programme for The Lawn Tennis Championships of Ireland, 1968)

Asked could he play the piano, a good Kerryman replied that he didn't know, for he hadn't tried.

And it is surprising, indeed somewhat alarming, how far you can get-for example in matters of sex, business and Government-without much knowledge of your subject.

Thus, for two years past, before the Vice of my Presidency was recognised, I have written of tennis without saying a thing of it. I am well qualified to essay this year's essay.

Now, some things appear the more amazing if you know nothing about them, whilst others look less so. Personally, I put into the first category radio, all-in wrestling, cigarette advertising, trapeze acts and central banking.

In the other category, that of things which look as easy as falling off a log, I put falling of a log, television, ballroom dancing, political propaganda, ski-ing and, of course, cigarette advertising.

The fact that if you persuade me hard enough I will quietly agree to transfer any of these instances to the other category must, I see, have some significance; but it is not, I think, that the categories do not exist.

How then do you place tennis? Remember that the important thing is not to write and tell me.

Let us take a clue from something we all - all of us who just bashaballaboutabit - can agree. This is that watching good tennis convinces us that we are instantly improved, or that we have always been "naturals" and only just found out. We set out to play, after today, with much the same confidence as ordinary folk scorch home from a motor race.

Now, the fact that the consequence may well be similar is something of a knock to what was promising to be an attractive thesis-the thesis that you don't have to know about something to be good at it. Pity.

The nearest I ever got to polishing up this thesis was in the phase of life when I came, through the wooing of a then-hippophile wife-presumptive, to discover that the short-cut to success in the hunting field - where she would have me - was to send my horse to Dudgeon's riding school for a course of twelve lessons while I got on with the serious petting (no, you fool, not the horse).

Alas, for success in tennis you cannot just send your racquet to Fitzgibbon, even should you be well able to manage the other thing.

So here we are-thanks to some confusion on our part, but none at all on that of Carrolls, as to the change in our lives which open tennis is to make-in the fourth row and it looks like being a great battle.

It has already become clear, from the last match, that the determining factor is that of self-imposed exhaustion caused by serving; it being evident that the receiving player, who has but scant hope of returning, on the spur of something a good deal less than a moment, the rocket which an elabourate count-down and an unconscionable thrust has delivered, is well-placed to enjoy - never mind the few perfunctory waves of his

bat at the rocket - a well-earned respite after his own rocket-launching just completed.

What we have to watch out for now is not only the sublime figure in the second row across court but also the dastardly moment when the receiver so far forgets his role as a spent force as of a sudden to shoot his serving opponent through the braces with reflected few of very shafts that he, Jovelike, has been so imperiously launching.

One may be very fairly sure, of course, that when this happens the effort of it will cost the avenger his own vengeance in the next game; but at least we shall have felt a tingle like we just had a few shekels on David for the Goliath bout.

It would be satisfying, at around this point, to shout and wave a bit, and perhaps operate the rattle which, not knowing, we had brought. And we would expect, in the same vein, that one player might straff the other a bit and perhaps hack him on the shin as they change sides.

But it emerges, most disappointingly, that not only do no fouls occur in tennis - a foot-fault is to a foul no more unseemingly than a dribble is to an expectoration- and so no penalty shots are awarded.

Still more inexplicably it appears that the crowd has no palate for misbehaviour; and carries its gentility to such extremity that even the sort of mild expletive that Lady Chatterley's gamekeeper would have expected of her ladyship – and delivered, mind you, on the occasion of so wrong a line-decision as would send you or me home in a sulk - causes unanimous revulsion against its propagator.

It would be a rare treat to witness a couple of our stouter soccer players opposing each other in a tennis championship.

But if power seems to have emasculated in the matter of court behaviour and language, it seems, nonetheless, to have done its work of corruption in the matter of style. When we were lads, a fine flowing forearm, with plenty of graceful top-spin and flow-through, with the forward leg curtsied to the rising ball and the free hand dandled as a Princes', was what we liked to watch. Ane we were ready to hiss soul-so-dead who trod upon such poetry with blunt power.

Now you cannot see the smoke for the fire – no back-swing, no after-swing, just a muffled report like you were bringing down a stop in a mine.

And have you tried watching whether it is top spin or under cut that they use? Have you tried splitting the atom?

Some of the carry-on is not what we simpletons were expecting. For one thing there is none of that little talk-before-slaughter that the boxing referee gives the boys ("and let it be a good, clean fight and no holding"). Then there is that pathological phobia that they all have about an unauthorised ball watching the play; everything has to stop for its formal ejection under *caution. Perhaps they do not wish it to see what is going to happen to it next.*

Cautioning the ball, indeed, is pretty generally regarded as essential prior to serving. Some bounce it twice, others three times, with a withering imprecation to it on each bounce. The way it manages to bounce back for more would rejoice the heart of a politician.

And even if the wretched spheres behave as good children, still nanny comes to fetch them off to byes after only seven games.

Talking of children, though, what excellent training for later life it is to be a ballboy. It teaches a lad how to turn the other cheek to cheek, how to pick up a fleeting object at speed without tripping onto his beak and, above all, how to tell a woman from a man.

I am sure that all sport lovers will agree with me when I express the hope that the best man may win. But perhaps I should make it clear, in case you should think ill of me, that in the ladies' events I would like the best lady to win. And in the mixed doubles I would like either the best man playing with the best woman to win best: but if that may not be then either the best woman playing with the second best man, or else the best man playing with the second best bridesmaid – romance should always creep in before the end of a good tournament.

At any rate one may thankful that, since the ladies now dress in much the same way as lamb cutlets, it has become almost impractical for an imposter man to win the ladies' event. The chances for the imposteuse, however, are a good deal more sporting, by reasons of her rippling muscles, long hair, and shots like the kick of a mule.

If these few words of mine have been helpful in explaining some of the finer points of this great sport, guess what I shall be? Well rewarded.

At any rate, I hope that even if those who knew nothing about tennis have kept their ignorance unsullied then at least I have caused those who know everything some loss of confidence.

*****

Jimmy O'Dea, the well-known Irish entertainer for many decades used to include the following few lines as part of his stage show in which he teased the people of Rathgar (pronounced 'Raath Gaaar'). Much of his work was due to the skilful writings of Harry O'Donovan. The wording was passed on orally and may vary slightly from the original. However, the brief pen picture is clear.

And those fellows down in Fairview
Who play tennis in their braces.
Thank heavens we are living in Rathgar.

*****

The **Muckamore Cricket and Lawn Tennis Club** was founded in 1874. It had its first tennis courts in 1908. In their Centenary Booklet of 1974 we find the following poem. It was written in 1949 by Charles Witherspoon, a retired cricket-playing member of the club who had a love of the club and its setting. He did not forget tennis in his nostalgic expression.

Moylena's Banks

Oh, how I love to ramble,
Where the Six Mile River flows;
Down Moylena's lovely banks,
Where the water lily grows.

Thy wooded banks so fair to see,
The fir, the beech and chesnut tree;
And all around the blue bells bloom,
While thrushes chant their cheerful tune.

And past the old tall beetling mill,
The remains of other days;
Where the linen webs were finished,
In the good old ancient ways.

Down again here there may be seen,
The cloth spread out so white and clean;
To further bleach upon the green,
Up Fir grove way.
And here the lovely cricket field,
With tennis courts combined,
Made by the generous York Street firm,
Of long-standing and renown.

Where the young men and maidens fair,
In leisure time do all repair,
To spend some time in healthful sport,
In cricket field or tennis court.

Would I could live my life again,
To leave this place would give me pain;
The beauty spot that I adore,
Moylena's banks and Muckamore.

The Muckamore Cricket & Lawn Tennis Club League winners in 1973 were: Back (from left): D. Deery, Dr. R. Smith (Gent's Captain), D. Clement & N. Craig. Front (from left) Mrs. L. Ross (Ladies' Captain, Mrs. N.McKewon, Mrs. R. Sweetnam and Mrs. N. Craig.

*****

The following two poems gems of advice have no immediate known Irish connection but were published in the new format ILTA Yearbook in 1976. All have their relevant advice to the tennis player of all eras.

Win With a Grin

When people are unkind to you
It makes things ten times worse
If you hit back or sulk or fret,
Or weep a lot or curse.
But if you're big enough to grin,
Why, strangely, you're the one to win!

Motto of International Lawn Tennis Club of Great Britain

To set the Cause above renown,
To love the game beyond the prize,

To honour, when you strike him down,
The foe that comes with fearless eyes:

To count the life of battle good
And dear the land that gave you birth,

And dearer yet the brotherhood
That binds the brave of all the earth.

The following piece also relates to a tennis tournament of many moons past. The sentiments are well captured by Ellen Sheehan of the **Mallow LTC** (Published in the ILTA Yearbook in 1977):

The Tennis Tournament
(Ellen Sheehan, 1977)

All this happened
Upon my long ago
At the Annabella tournament
For the High Class (Not the low)
When the gentry came in parties
From Longueville and Waterloo
Bearforest and the Castle
All rated in Who's who,
Carriages, fine horses, Coachmen in profusion
Peel's force in action
Against traffic confusion
A band softly playing
Tea time inside the club
Seemed like Heaven on earth
The Society Hub-Hub.
We lived a stones throw
From cries of Love, then Game

The "At Home" day at Mallow LTC in 1913. The known persons in the photograph were Miss Davison(1), Miss B. Harold-Barry(2), Miss B. Smith(3), Mrs. Hume Kelly(4), Mrs. Locker(5), Miss G. O'Brien(6), Mrs. Wyatt(7), T. K. P. Williams(8), Miss N. Beecher(10), Mrs. Norton Barry(11), W. Harman(12), Mrs. Galwey(13), Miss M. Peirce(14), Rev. Leonard Swanzy(15), W. Peirce(16), J. A. Hardy R.M.(17), Miss O'Brien(210, "Willie" O'Brien(22), R.E. Tottenham(23), George Cooke(24) Captain Hume-Kelly(25), J. Daly(27), R. E. Smith(29), Victor Reeves(30), Rev. Allen French (31), Miss Lyons(32), Miss Haughton(32), "Tom" O'Brien(34), "Bob" O'Brien(35), Miss Kia Batwell(37), Miss Graves(38), Miss M. Graves(39), Miss Jones(41), Rev. Pierce Brown(42), Captain Umperville(43), E. Carroll-Leahy(44), Kingsmills B. Williams(45), T.H. Sarsfield(46), Miss Hardy(47), Major Wyatt(51), Mrs. Daly(53), Captain Sefton Findley(54), W. Norton-Barry(56) and Brazier Creag(57). The standard at Mallow Lawn Tennis Club was high and they produced many champions and players who featured at both the Irish and English (Wimbledon) Championships. Note the K.B. Williams in the second poem.

*Mallow Open Tournament (c.1946) Mrs. Sue(?)
Porter and Alan Haughton winners of the
singles with Kingsmills B. Williams (Club
President).(See K.B. in following poem)*

*Why couldn't we join the party
Wasn't it a shame
We sat there disconsolate
On the kitchen window sill
For Gran told me and Johnny
"You'll not be allowed in
Annabella's for the Elite
And not for folk like you"
But I wondered as I fell asleep
Could their blood be really blue*

A second offering from Mallow was probably penned in
the late forties or 1950s by Joan Williams and was
meant to be sung. Perhaps some of the locals can
identify with the days of croquet and the various
characters mentioned. Franks Furney who gets a
mention was one of the great players to arrive on the
scene in 1940s Mallow and still be playing six decades
later.

Mallow Tennis Club

*Oh! We'll sing a song to the Tennis Club
And its members in Mallow
To the games we've played, and the friends we've made
Way down in Duhallow.*
Chorus:
*It ain't gone to rain no more no more
It ain't gone to rain no more
Down with the brollies, up with the nets
It ain't gone to rain no more*

*Oh! Where would we be without K.B?
He and Tommy we must thank
But when we've repaid their L.s.d.
We still have to pay the bank.*
Chorus.

*Oh! What will we do for our land-ladies two
They've sold the tennis courts'es
And put the money at five to two
On their own racing horses.*
Chorus.

*Colonel Cregan won the Croquet prize
And for it a silver pot
And in it he put the pheasants and snipe
And the animals that he's shot.*
Chorus.

*Rosa's the Queen of the Tennis Club
My word, she is so smart
With her Erics and Dereks and Dermots too
Take care chaps she'll have your heart.*
Chorus.

*You can watch Frank Furney and the glamorous Cootes
And if you're a racing punster
Just have a dime on Caroline
For she's been picked for Munster.*
Chorus.

*The Tennis game, and the Croquet game,
And the Bridge game take their toll
But Colonel Sarsfield's thought up a newer game,
Climbing the old tent pole.*
Chorus

*The tennis-courts are soaked with rain,
The Croquet pitch is all mud,
And where in the world are the cakes for tea?
The Committee will have my blood.*
Chorus.

*To raise funds for the Tennis Club
We must all think up new ventures
Apart from this dance at Kilmacoom
There's always the old debentures.*
Chorus.

The History of Irish Tennis

Franks Furney and Meta Foley following their Open Championship victories at Mallow LTC in 1949.

*****

Dudley Georgeson was a well-known coach who ran a highly rated Tennis Academy in England for many years. Some Irish players went to receive his advice. He has also spent time in Ireland, invited over for coaching seminars and the like. Apparently a bit of a character, befitting of one prepared to put a poetic slant on the sport he loved. The following piece he penned and was published in the ILTA magazine. It contains much useful advice on the mental approach to the game.

The Winning Approach
Dudley Georgeson (English coach, 1970s)

If you think you are beaten, you are;
If you think you dare not, you don't;
If you like to win but think you can't
It is almost a cinch that you won't.

If you think you'll lose, you've lost;
For out in the world we find
Success begins with a fellow's will,
It is all in the state of the mind.

If you think you're outclassed, you are;
You've got to think high to rise.
You've got to be sure of yourself,
Before you can win a prize.

Life's battles don't always go
To the stronger or faster man;
But, sooner or later, the man who wins
Is the man who thinks he can.

*****

Sutton, one of the oldest clubs in the country, was founded in 1882. It has had many successes over the 1977. They were to win the Dublin Class I summer league for the third consecutive year. An unnamed member penned the following poem in tribute. Specifically mentioned is *Tadgh* Lambe who travelled many miles from Tullamore on a regular basis. Tadgh is now a well-known full-time tennis coach. Sutton were in fact to win this league for five consecutive years (1975-1979). Other players on the these teams were Brendan Minnock, Cliff Beirne, Kevin Menton, Paul Fitzsimons, Declan Heavey, Michael Smyth, Billy O'Boyle and John Dinan.

A Tribute to the History Makers

When '77 is past and gone,
One memory will forever linger on
'Twas that second Saturday in July
That Sutton's boys turned on the style.

For two years running Sutton were the champs
Despite the cunning of the opposition camps,
On Hardcourt the Double was won with class
And so was this year's hat trick proudly done on grass.

As a humble member of this mighty tennis crew
'Tis an honour to be one of the chosen few
My time is short so with no further adieu
The story of my mates I will unfold to you.

Mick, our captain, first deserves the noble call
For without him we would surely fall;
His non-stop action with racket and with tongue
Has left many an opponent completely numb.

When this year's final was threatened with ruin
And all our hopes and expectations seemed in gloom
The Kissinger of our side-Mick, of course,
Neatly settled one and all by slick resource.

Now it's time to meet our number one
Kevin is his name and our top gun
As he whips the ball from left to right
Friends and foes alike stare at this awesome sight.

For one so gifted he is extremely modest
To be blind to this I would be dishonest,
While his fame has spread far and wide
He never forgets his debt to the Sutton side.

A tribute now to Tadgh I must pay
For his heroic deeds on Final Day
With grit and power and dashing verve
He flattened his fancied opponent with his mighty serve.

The History Makers at Sutton were to win the Senior Dublin League for five consecutive years though the poem was written after three. The above team of (back, l. to r.) was Tadhg Lambe, Brendan Minnock & Paul Fitzsimons. Front (l. to r.) John Dinan, Michael Smyth and Kevin Menton. Others to feature were Cliff Beirne, BillyO'Boyle and Declan Heavey.

For years Tadgh has travelled many a weary mile,
His loyalty to the Sutton club has never been on trial.
Defeat or victory makes no difference to my mate,
'Cause like all of us he sportingly accepts his fate.

Paul is next in line and credit here is due
From the graceful and elegant way he makes his cue
On court he's strong and ruthless

To try to overcome him is quite fruitless.
As a boy he stood by the club through thick and thin
And as a man he duly paid his part in this exciting win,
His integrity on court is beyond reproach
And win or lose he's just as easy to approach.
Length makes strength, or so they say

The History of Irish Tennis

And with Brendan on our team it was our day.
They call him names, but he makes no fuss
Even when he is called the team octopus.

His court manoeuvring leaves us all in awe
And when he serves, outreaches the law,
He may be country, but we don't mind,
We need our Brendan, he is 'our' kind.

And so I come to Cliff, our youngest star.
His skill with racquet will surely bring him far,
But it's his positive commitment to the game
That will sell his name and bring him fame.

At number six Cliff was as steady as a rock,
The quality of his play made many of us take stock,
Sutton's long term goal is to remain on the top
And with his help we will not be caught on the hop.

*****

Wogan's Ways

Our beloved Terry may have left our shores many moons ago but never lost his sense of humour. With the kind permission of that Limerick-born broadcaster and entertainer, the following items on tennis are included. The first graphically discusses his game with an overweight doctor and takes off from there. It was first published in a Benson & Hedges Tournament in 1984 and then in a book compilation, *For the Love of Tennis*. The latter was a book edited by Ronald Atkin on behalf of the Lawn Tennis Writers' Association (1985). Terry wanders from his tennis match into the American sporting dream and then back to John McEnroe, via the Olympics. All in his own inimitable way. The second is from his book "Banjaxed" and is based on the Wimbledon time of year. Credit is to be given to his radio listener, Brenda Ray of Nottingham, for the poem on the late great New York tennis player, Vitas Gerulaitis, who died tragically at the age of 40.

The Way to Win
(Terry Wogan, 1984)

Nowadays, when I play tennis, there is usually a doctor in attendance. He's a cheerful, stocky man with powerful Welsh thews, that make him the fastest tennis player in the world over two metres. I've never seen a retriever like him, right down to his little damp nose. I don't know whether its Welsh 'hwyl', or sheer Celtic bloodymindedness, but this man is never beaten. No ball is ungettable, every forlorn chance is chased down. Jimbo Connors, nosediving into the crowds at Flushing Meadow, has nothing on this boy. A rally with this merry man of medicine is a scurryin, scrambling, heavy-breathing affair, and it's usually followed by a long thoughtful pause, because neither of us is exactly in the first flush of youth.

Our games together are characterised by fierce bursts of frenzied activity, freely interspersed by longer periods of airy badinage and manly joshing. Perhaps if old John and big Ivan could approach it in the same

way, we might all have a few more laughs, or at least, respite for our frazzled nerves.

Don't run away with the idea that the Doc and I are not competitive, that sensility has sapped either of our wills to win. Not likely. Why do you think he chases every ball as if it were his last? Why do you think I make him? It would be just as health-giving and a lot less exhausting to pat the ball back and forward over the net, with civil apologies every time you hit it out of your opponent's reach. No we're trying to kill each other, the Doc and me. Six-love, six-love, that's what we're shooting for. We sometimes lose track of the score, or what side of the court we're serving to next, but make no mistake, we're both going for the whitewash. It's the Corinthian ideal, you see. Play up and play the game...smile apologetically when you hit a screamer down the line, past your opponent's outstretched racket, murmur 'Bad luck!' at his double faults and shout 'Good shot!' when he leaves you for dead in the middle of the court. I tell you, Baron de Coubertin would be proud of the Doc and me.

Did you know that Terry Wogan played tennis, as well as rugby and golf? He can write amusingly about it too.

It's the way we were dragged up I suppose. You went out to win, bending every nerve and sinew, giving everything, but never, never showing it. No show of overt jubilation was encouraged for a good shot, still less for victory. That was accepted almost apologetically, and you covered your embarrassment with three cheers for the loser. Call it hypocrisy, self-delusion, suppression of our natural spirits. Do modern tennis stars seem to you to be better-balanced, sweeter-

tempered, more rounded human beings than those of yesteryear? Have all the tumult and the shouting, the obscene gestures, the arrogant postures, the flagrant abuses, produced happier players, a better game?

You'll be blaming the coloured element, of course. When the Founding Fathers of the two great continents landed on Plymouth Rock and Botany Bay, having flown, or been forced to flee, the tyranny of the Old World, they naturally rejected the old values, the cant, the hypocrisy, the two-facedness. Honestly and openness were the watchword, telling it like it was. Strive, work hard and everything and anything you want can be yours. Achievement became the goal, and over-achievement even more laudable. To win was what counted, and a loser was nowhere. Even second wasn't awfully good. If you're not a winner, thank you for taking part and good-night.

This glorification of the great God Win was never more evident than at the Olympics this year in Los Angeles. I was there, and saw an entire nation become obsessed with 'gold'. It couldn't have been more frantic in California during the Great Rush of a hundred years ago. The United States Women's Volleyball team won a silver medal, and it was as if they had failed to qualify! "What were those four years of training about?" carped the American pundits, forgetting the hundreds, perhaps thousands, of hopeful young women who had been training equally as hard for four years, perhaps more, and hadn't even got as far as Los Angeles, not to mind win a medal. The American swimmers, in the absence of the Soviet Bloc countries, particularly East Germany, swept all others aside in the pool, and the days seemed to be filled with the 'Star-Spangled Banner', crew-cuts, teeth and that peculiar American whoop that characterizes not only their sporting triumphs, but their politician conventions and TV quiz shows, as well.

However, there was one United States swimmer who was a grave disappointment. Not that he hadn't obliged with a gold medal. It was his manner, that, it was felt among the commentators, left something to be desired. "The bounder hadn't whooped." Not only that, but he hadn't jumped around, leapt into his team-mates' arms, waved to his mother in the stand, or burst into tears as the American flag was raised. There was even some question of whether he had his hand over his heart during the playing of 'The Star-Spangled Banner'! The nation was shocked. It wasn't exactly a clenched-fist Black Power salute, but such behaviour was flying in the face of all that was best in American life, including Disneyland and Mom's Apple Pie. The guy was obviously un-American, soft on Commies and probably didn't even chew gum. The poor unfortunate claimed in mitigation that although delighted to win for himself, the United States and President Reagan, he had been disappointed at not breaking a world record. It wasn't good enough. Somebody talked to him about his responsibility to The Flag, The American Dream, and his athletic scholarship, and the following day our hero made an abject apology to the entire American nation through television and the press for "letting everybody down by not being enthusiastic enough at my victory".... He won another gold medal a couple of days later, and you never in your life saw such whooping, jumping, bounding, waving, laughing and crying. It did

your heart good. The Prodigal had returned and repented the errors of his ways.

Not mine, though, I kept thinking of my old tennis coach, who doubled as the rugby trainer in the winter. He would probably have given the American swimmers a dressing-down and probably a thick ear, for 'showing off'. Boastful self-glorification at the moment of triumph is not a pretty sight, though an increasingly common one, these days.

But there, my little ones, I'm beginning to sound as old as I look. I'll just sit here a while and ponder over my pictures of that greatest of all Corinthians, C.B. Fry. Played for England at cricket and rugby, 'and' everything else, "treated triumph and disaster just the same", was a hero to every Englishman of his generation and never cursed an opponent or kissed a team-mate in his life. "Old-fashioned buffer", I hear you cry. Maybe, but do you think they'll ever offer the kingship of Albania to John McEnroe?

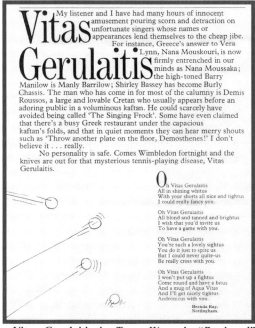

Vitas Gerulaitis in Terry Wogan's "Banjaxed" and the poem sent in by his radio listener Brenda Ray of Nottingham.

*****

Mary Briscoe

Celebrating a winning team's performance is just as valid a reason for poetry as watching the flight of a bird. Did not the kings of old have the resident bard prepare a piece to celebrate victory on the battlefield? Elm Park's Mary Briscoe sets the scene when their Ladies Class 2 Senior League Team (over 45) went to Sutton (31/10/1999) and beat Carrickmines in the final. Mary was tennis captain at Elm Park in 2002.

Mary Briscoe is photographed here (centre) with (from left) Yvonne Hagan, Mary Molloy, Gary Cahill (coach), Yvonne Ryan and Rita O'Reilly.

Game, Set and Match
(Mary Briscoe, 1999)

It was wild and windy, though the day was dry
Elm Park was committed to giving it a good try
To win the Senior Cup would be a coup, no doubt
That Elm Park would be proud about!

Supporters travelled from far and wide
Endeavouring to motivate the winning side
Thanks to them all we played our best
Promising ourselves a well earned rest

Proud to be sporting our red and yellow crests
Carrickmines certainly put us to the test
Lobbing and dropping the ball over the net
How difficult it was to win the set!

We waited patiently for this occasion to arise
Carrickmines always fielding a challenging side!
We had been in the finals several times before
But in recent years had been piped with the score

And so into the millennium with pride we go
With the Senior Cup now on show
The time was right we pulled all the stops out
Now it's time to celebrate and shout!

The Elm Park Class 2 Veteran Ladies Team of 1999 as lauded in verse. Back (l. to r.) Jennifer Blake, Kristine Lawlor, Breeda Claffey, Mary Grier and Antoinette Toole. Front (l. to r.) Helen McInerney, Maedbh McEvoy and Mary Briscoe.

***

A more recent offering greets the feats of Seamus O'Toole following his active year as club captain. Marina Swann the outgoing captain (**Sligo Tennis Club)** offered the following sentiments (December 1999), which might just apply in your club too.

Marina Swann: Tennis Player, Captain and Poet

Ode to Seamus O'Toole
(Marina Swann, 1999)

A great captain, he has been,
all throughout this year,
and now we take this chance to thank him,
in this season of good cheer.

The year started in January,
I'm sure he thought it would never end,
He kept the committee on the straight and narrow,
without driving us round the bend.

Watching the treasurer's purse strings,
sees Seamus at his best,
God help you if you try to play without paying,
during the Championships or the West.

The History of Irish Tennis

Also, a keen tennis player,
on Thursday nights he struts his stuff.
It's the only time you'll see Seamus,
acting mean and tough.

Although being Tennis Captain,
was probably a bit of a load,
If you pleaded with him long enough,
you could get the potholes filled on your road.

Selling raffle tickets for racquets,
his powers of persuasion are second to none,
Last year he convinced me to be Vice-Captain,
and I'm still wondering ,'what have I done?'.

A very special thanks to Lea,
Without whom he would be lost.
He may be captain in the tennis club,
But at home Lea's the boss.

Oh Lea you're a patient woman,
Retire? You thought he would.
But he's dying to get the treasurer's purse back,
as only Seamus could.

So, Seamus, we'd like to thank you,
for this year, and all you've done,
for the arguments, the discussions, the tennis,
but most of all the fun.

A small piece published by the Kiltoghert Parish Group and written by a former member of the Carrick on Shannon club. Greg Dunne echoes the changes that take place and the memories of tennis in a small rural club.

✶✶✶✶✶

Tennis As I Remember It
(Greg Dunne, Carrick on Shannon LTC, 2000)

It was a lovely summer's evening, a group of town's lads were sitting on the wall of Carrick Lawn Tennis Club looking through the iron railings at a Tennis Tournament being played by Carrick against Mohill or was it Boyle? It is difficult to remember, as the year was 1937. Mrs. Laird and her partner were in full swing winning easily on the well-manicured grass court nearest the Provincial Bank (The said Mrs. Laird was Head Teacher of the Church of Ireland Primary School on Main Street.) Occasionally a ball would be lobbed over the railings on to St. George's Terrace, and we took great delight in throwing back the ball. On other occasions a ball spun to the right and went through the railings separating the Tennis Grounds from the Provincial Bank basement.

These railings are still there but now in the middle of a concrete wall. Mid way through the tournament both teams and club officials retired to Victoria Hall for Afternoon tea. How we envied them as we sat with our noses through the railings. That is as far as we ever got to those tennis courts!

However, in those days the remainder of the grounds was covered in tall bushy laurel trees, brambles, long grass, ash trees and other trees including oak trees and other trees still standing.

Seamus O'Toole: His work is never done.

What happened the laurel trees, elderberry trees and brambles? A Mr. Steep, Manager of the Provincial Bank, and the writer, in later years cut down and cleared as much as they could. Eventually the members of that time cleared the whole area, making it the last green field area in Carrick.

But while it was still a wooded area, it was a great play area for the youngsters of Carrick, many a tree-house was built and games played under the canopy created by the oak trees. Occasionally we crossed the wall to the rowing club grounds and played "Relivio" using the large number of trees that grew there, now long gone. But we never ever set foot on the grass courts of the Tennis Club. To us, it was basically for Protestant families' use, yet it was left to the people of Carrick by the Whyte estate for one shilling a year, as long as it was used as a tennis club. There was no animosity against the large Protestant community of those days, as they were the people who played tennis at St. George's and badminton in Victoria Hall.

However, as time went by a new tennis club was formed and they played in the two courts, in the late John J. Flood's large garden at the back of "The One Price Warehouse" a very large drapery store and residence run by the Flood family.

23rd August 2003-the ideal setting of Carrick on Shannon Lawn Tennis Club.

The late John Dunne also transformed portion of his garden into a tennis court using his "Summer House" as dressing rooms, and many town's people played tennis there. Members of that new club were the late Paddy Boland, Alan Dunne, Patricia Dunne, all the Feely family boys and girls, Paddy Egan and his brother and others whom I can't recall.

In those far off days no attempt was made to train youngsters hot to play tennis. The adjacent Rowing Club was the only club, apart from the G.A.A., which attracted youngsters. Most youngsters learned to play tennis at the Marist Convent Boarding School and other Boarding Schools…but for some it was too late to start. However, the newly formed Tennis Club declined, but its members now joined St. George's Terrace Club and tennis was kept alive in Carrick with ups and downs or should one say with long and short volleys!

*****

The following article is one of a number put together in a great little booklet published in 2000. It was produced as part of the re-union of the members of the **Fergus LTC** in Ennis from the 1940s, 1950s and 1960s. Little gems are also recalled in other chapters of this book and reflect the relevant eras. Ghislaine now lives in the USA but was one of the prime movers in that re-union.

The Incidental Champion
(Ghislaine De Regge, 2000)

Now, almost half a century later, I feel it is time to describe my claim to fame as a tennis player.

It was 1958. Kilkee was officially opening its new tennis courts adjacent to the famed Hydro Hotel. An open tournament was organised for the occasion. As usual, our team from Ennis, with some of our best players, squeezed into Tom Mannion's- or was it Bobby O' Brien's –car on an exceptionally sunny Sunday morning: Mary Duggan, Liam Cahir, Jimmy Monahan, John Carroll, Johnny Quinlan and Joe Maloney. The Kilkee tennis facilities were magnificent – several pristine hard courts open to the ocean, and a large

white pavilion and club-house; picture perfect as I remember it.

We were to play mixed doubles. As luck would have it, I was paired with Joe Maloney with whom I had never played before. In fact, Joe and I had cool relations – if we had any at all. Naturally, Joe, a much better player, was less than thrilled to be teamed with me, and I was less than comfortable playing with him. Joe didn't do much to put me at ease; he was a man of few words. So, instead of the usual exchange of about who would serve first etc., Joe said in a low but distinct voice, "Just stay out of the way!"

Well, I did. Joe darted back and forth across the court scoring point after point. He smashed, lobbed and volleyed. He played the net and the baseline too. I did my part dodging the balls, which came at me from every direction like debris in a hurricane. Balls came straight for me, they whizzed past me, they fell from the sky, they looped over my head. I don't even remember serving, but I must have. For the rest, I just made myself scarce as Joe crisscrossed the court deflecting the projectiles.

We – or should I say, he – won game after game, set after set, match after match; it was truly awesome and yet terribly silent.

Still reeling from the tension, I found myself receiving a trophy – almost a spectator at my own moment of triumph. With that over, Joe and I sat as far apart from each other as possible when the photographer from the Clare Champion took the group photograph. I am seen seventh from right on the front row, Joe is sixth from right on the back row. A cold wind blew in from the ocean, and the sun began to set.

After all these years, I am ambivalent about the only trophy I have ever received; to proudly display it, or to leave it to tarnish as the reminder of a tournament I won by hardly playing at all? Or perhaps this really is the story of how Joe Maloney single-handed won the doubles tournament. Incidentally, the moment may have finally arrived for me to say, "Thanks Joe, I couldn't have done it without you."!

The History of Irish Tennis

The Veteran (over 35) Class 5 Ladies League Winning team from Elm Park in 2001 have been celebrated in poetry. Front (l. to r.): Rose Hough, Pam Wyse (captain) & Ann Nolan. Back (l. to r.): Mary Power, Virginia Costello and Mary Briscoe (tennis captain).

Elm Park's Mary Briscoe second poem relates to the over 35 ladies league team who beat Ashbrook 2 in the Division 5 final on the 21st October 2001 at **Templeogue LTC.** The excitement of victory brings out the poet in Mary, once again.

Match Point

In Templeogue on a sunny day
Elm Park and Ashbrook went out to play
The teams were enthusiastic and anxious to play
Against the opposition on finals day

Shot of the week and drill and till you drop
Were the ultimate tools in launching the plot
For the perfection of performance peak
Improving fitness and stamina week by week

Team spirit was alive and adrenaline flowing
The coaching and practice had set us a glowing
The head racquets were out in force
The search for a pennant was par for the course!

Navy skirts, white sweatshirts sporting the crest
White headbands, K-swiss and all the rest
Thanks to Seamus we looked the part
Now it was our turn to play our part

Backhands, volleys, serve and net
We were sometimes asked to play a let
Our supporters went that extra mile
To ensure the team won in style

Congratulations to the team, 'twas no small notion
The enthusiasm and fun was part of the devotion
Lets celebrate in style with bubbles
And continued success in the Senior Doubles.

*****

Tennis and Music

Music is allied to many occasions in life. One or two of the 'poems' above were meant to be sung. Before many international matches the pride of the players and the adrenalin rush is linked to their anthem. The same anthem can be used as medal ceremonies during flag raising. Of course, in many societies, Ireland being no exception, playing musical instruments and singing for their direct enjoyment may take place during the celebrations after a sporting fixture. If poems can be written about the game and it's people, then why not musical pieces and songs. The sport has always had a style to it and a rhythm. In the early days it was one of a pit-pat affair in many cases, rallies of one hundred strokes or more not being uncommon. In addition it was once impolite not to hit the ball towards ones opponent in what was essentially a social affair. Just as pop music has raised the decibels of life so has the noise of a racquets twang become clearer. Changing materials and more athletic players have altered the game. As with music there are now great heights to be achieved. A court can now be a place where one finds the combination of the echoes of racquet on ball intertwined with grunts. The day of the slow waltz of the 19th century tennis court was replaced by the quick step in the 1920s and the booms of the 1970s. Mind you we should mention the ballet-like tennis movement of Susan Lenglen in this foray into the arts. Evonne Goolagong was certainly among those whose tennis artistry could be set to music, never mind poetry.

Hugh Tinney, a top junior of the 1970s when at Gonzaga College, has become one of Ireland foremost pianists. He lived in London for a number of years and on returning to Dublin joined **Fitzwilliam LTC.** He has thoughts on the connection between tennis and the piano. These were published in the May 1999 issue of Fitz News, the club newsletter. The following are some of them; perhaps the next time you play or watch the game you might see a musical connection. Before we enter the thoughts of Hugh, a reminder that Count John McCormack of tenor fame, Des Keogh of *Lyric FM* fame and the young Mark Feehily of *Westlife* fame are among those of a musical bent that can be added to the tennis playing population of Ireland. (On the international stage one might add Cliff Richard, John McEnroe and Pat Cash)

Tennis and music, or specifically tennis and playing a classical music instrument don't go; or so people have been told for generations. Fortunately, I wasn't aware of this interdiction when, around the age of six and already learning piano, I took up a tennis racquet for the first time (very possibly inspired by the sight of the beautiful and elegant Maria Bueno competing at the Irish Open in the mid-sixties on the grass courts at the "old" Fitzwilliam Club; inspirations from that event would peak for me with the appearance of Rod Laver my tennis hero, whose autograph I managed to get there in 1970 and Evonne Goolagong, who enchanted this 12 year old in the summer of 1971.

I only gradually became aware of the unwritten canon I was breaking as, with music gradually playing an ever greater role in my life through my teens, more and more of the music fraternity looked askance at me as they asked me was I not concerned about breaking something. (I had broken three limbs in one 12 month period, but that had nothing to do with contact sports plus growing too fast had nothing at all to do with tennis), or about tennis elbow, or just stiffness in the muscles of an over-developed and asymmetric right forearm (although unlike the aforesaid hero Laver, I could not claim a forearm the size of Rocky Marciano).

That great pianist, Hugh Tinney, was once, and still is, an expert on the tennis court. Here, he 'conducts' with Gillian Magrane and Maria Donnelly at Donnybrook LTC in July 1976

One person who, fortunately for me, was extremely tolerant of the situation was my piano teacher. She did reflect somewhat wryly in later years about the post-summer "loosening-up" I required following non-stop tennis and only sporadic practice for two months but she also took a very positive view of the whole thing, sharing my admiration for the likes of Borg and

Connors in the mid-70s and we talked a lot about the elements in common, the performance psychology that is an unavoidable aspect of the challenge in both cases.

There was a period, in my mid-twenties, as the concert existence was becoming very busy and at the same time I was experiencing what I was told was "golfer's elbow" (which always mystifies people who know I'm no golfer), when I decided to "put music first" and I effectively gave up tennis for several years. Ironically, what drew me back to tennis after that was musicians-several professional musician friends of mine who were not "really" tennis players but were dead keen on the game. So bit by bit, I got back into it and having moved back to Ireland from London a few years ago, this year had my first experience of Winter League (playing for a Fitzwilliam team) since College days 20 years ago-which felt extremely odd but also great. The game is simply too enjoyable to stay away.

✶✶✶✶✶

The Dublin Lawn Tennis Council celebrated their Centenary with a function in June 2002. Mary Briscoe, the Lady Tennis Captain at **Elm Park**, put pen to paper once again. In the poem she refers to Tom Treacy (**Templeogue LTC**), the president, Michael Byrne (**Sutton LTC**) the honorary secretary and John Kenny, from her own club, the honorary treasurer.

The Dublin Lawn Tennis Council Centenary
(Mary Briscoe, 2002)

The DLTC is an institution
For which there is no substitution

League is the name of the game
Competition is our middle name

Teams have grown out of all proportion
Such is the interest to this devotion

Originally confined to the Dublin region
Has extended 30 miles in recent seasons

Winter, summer, mixed, senior and floodlit league
Competition continues without reprieve!

Lets not forget the juniors as well
Their league is testing; it's easy to tell

Class one to Class seven and all it entails
A great sense of fairness and competition prevails

With changes in format over the years
Accommodating more teams and delighting our peers

Fitness and technique are all that it takes
To keep the team in the winning stakes!

The league caters for young and old
It is never too late to reach for gold!

So say our President Tom, who recently won
He patiently waited and had great fun!

The History of Irish Tennis

Michael is the Secretary who organised it all
Thanks to him we've had a ball

John is our capable Treasurer too
Elm Park is truly proud of you

Hilary and Susan we cannot leave out
Their work is tremendous without a doubt

The Council holds meetings throughout the year
At venues in Dublin, far and near

The Berkeley Court was a wonderful convention
To celebrate the DLTC's invention

Thanks to tennis we have made great friends
Continued good luck and best wishes we send

John Fitzpatrick speaking at the Dublin Lawn Tennis Council centenary dinner in June 2002.

*****

Pat Boran who was born in Portlaoise in 1963 is an accomplished writer and has already published four collections of poetry as well as a number of books including "A Short History of Dublin" in 2000. The following story captures club tennis as he saw it in his younger days. To him it was a 'strange if strangely fascinating game'. Thanks to Pat and RTE's *Sunday Miscellany* who aired this story on the 15th January 2006, and brought back vivid memories to so many followers of the sport, that it was possible to reproduce his tennis tale here.

Love All

In the Portlaoise of the 1970s, where I grew up, there were two tennis clubs. One was owned and run by the ESB, as their staff social club, was just at the then outer limits of the town, and was open to the general public — the young boys of whom, like myself, gravitated to the pool tables in the club house, and watched their sisters and friends knock a handful of yellow tennis balls from the local tennis ball factory back and forth, desultorily, until the sun went down. The other tennis club, The Portlaoise Lawn Tennis Club, was a very different affair.

The Portlaoise Lawn Tennis Club was situated behind a small Protestant parish hall more or less in the centre of the town. The fact that it was right across from the wonderfully-named Dead Wall which, being the biggest wall I'd seen in my life, for at least the first 15 years of my life, gave it a kind of central authority. But if the Dead Wall had been built to hold up and back the weight of the thirty-foot railway embankment that runs through Portlaoise, the small lawn tennis club across the road from it was proof that gentler, more fragile things and activities could occupy the hearts and minds of the populace of the town.

In truth, I don't think I ever actually played what might be called a game of tennis, either in one of those clubs back then, or since. Despite the fact that my mother in her time had gone, and later both of my sisters often went out with tennis racquet in hand to play at one of the courts that was later built in the Presentation Convent grounds, tennis remained for me a strange if strangely fascinating game. It was true that, unlike any other I could think of, or saw anywhere around me, tennis alone broke the gender divide, which was a divide worth breaking, and couples could often be seen playing together, even around Portlaoise. And it was even true that the championships at Wimbledon, and maybe even at other tournaments, had a category called Mixed Doubles, which was exactly that — as if, despite its apparent tameness and a dress code that gave it an olde worlde feel, tennis was at the same time somehow, discretely, revolutionary. Yet the truth was that, in my age group at least, tennis was a girls' game, a game for girls, a game that us boys could watch, or pretend not to watch, but about which we were, as in so many other respects, in the dark. Surely there was more than meets the eye to a game in which the word 'love', not to mention 'match', was used over and over.

But boys simply did not play tennis. By which I suppose I mean Catholic boys. Where gaelic footballers, soccer or rugby players of my acquaintance seemed intent on mucking up their kit as quickly as possible after the initial throw-in or kick-off, tennis players at the end of a match would come off the court in the same virginal whites as they had gone out. It seemed to go against what games were all about, a kind of rough and tumble, a kind of letting go and giving in and going wild.

As it turned out, it took just a small incident one summer's night, in the late 1970s, to change my mind about tennis, and to see it less as some affected sports of the gods, stopping to sip their ambrosia, and more as just another, if more stylised, version of a much biger cosmic game.

Having spent the afternoon after school at a friend's house (where the main activities had been drinking Coca Cola and pillow-fighting in his elder brother's bedroom), this particular summer's evening I took a short cut back home up Railway Street, which meant I had to pass along the side of the Dead Wall (looming up over me like a cliff face), which meant I also had to pass by the Portlaoise Lawn Tennis Club. And as it happened, whatever evening of the week it was, a tennis club social was in full swing: some local tournament had concluded earlier in the day, and now disco music and the glow of flashing, coloured lights was spilling out of the high windows of the small hall. And it was then I noticed that the parked car beside which I was idly standing, half listening, half thinking of nothing at all, was moving from side to side, up and down. And, just as others had claimed, though I'd not

believed, it was then when I stepped back, startled, and glanced back again, through the steamed-up windscreen I could just about make out two shapes, two figures, one male, one female, both dressed in white, arms wrapped around each other, for all the world like two angels struggling to be human again.

✶✶✶✶✶

A chance meeting with fellow engineer Jim Fenwick at Lough Owel waterworks in May 2006 lead to an interesting e-mail two days later. Jim grew up in Cork where his tennis was limited to some mixed doubles. He was able, despite the passing of many decades, and in typical engineering fashion, to sketch the location of the clubs of Altona, Hillsboro' and Glenanaar, all adjacent to each other and 'vibrant' in the 1940s and 1950s. With help from his sister and brother-in-law he added:

The Fountainstown Club was formed in 1936 to cater for the people who came there on holidays (May-Sept.) and is still in existence with about 6 courts (4 hard and 2 grass) It is famous because it was the first club to make a "pitch and putt" course in 1937. It is not affiliated to ILTA. I can remember playing American tournaments there which were great fun.

I also remember the Tennis Club in Castlecomer, Co. Kilkenny which has long since disappeared. It was adjacent to the CI Church and I think was set up by the Wandesfordes - the local big house owner and land lord. It had at least 2 grass courts.

All the above is generally a 1930/40/50s scene and tennis of that era can be summed up in my mind by Sir John Betjeman's poem:"A Subaltern's Love Song"

Miss J. Hunter Dunn, Miss J. Hunter Dunn,
Furnish'd and burnish'd by Aldershot sun,
What strenuous singles we played after tea,
We in the tournament-you against me!

Love-thirty, love-forty, oh! weakness of joy
The speed of a swallow, the grace of a boy,
With carefullest carelessness, gaily you won,
I am weak from your loveliness, Joan Hunter Dunn.

It goes on and on but ends:
"And now I'm engaged to Miss Joan Hunter Dunn"

Many will empathize with Jim Fenwick's interest in mixed doubles and how his tennis memories turn to poetry, like Pat Boran turning to prose in the piece above. For the record, the lovely Betjeman poem extends for a total of eleven verses and can be found in John Murray's 'Collected Poems' (1978).

✶✶✶✶✶

Terry Browne of Sandycove had an interesting contribution to make. Taken by Sir John Lavery's tennis painting, *The Tennis Party* (1886), which is on view at the Aberdeen Art Gallery, he put together the following poem in its honour. Terry's father, also Terry, is still with us at 92 years-of-age, was one of the founding members of **Castleknock LTC** in 1927.

A Tennis Party

Oil on board
Eighteen eighty five
John Lavery plans a gentle painting
To test an image living in his heart
An impression
A sporting social moment
A commentary on the age
This single frame
Its poise
The echo of the ball
Still audible as a sweet soft noise

A tennis court
bordered with a white waist-high wooden rail
veiled in chicken wire
a high mesh at one end
to catch the wayward ball
the setting is a private park
the high broadleaf trees around
tell the time
early August

The oil on board draws
long dark shadows of evening
the grass is yellow and turf-brown
and in the light shade of the trees
a white five-bar gate is open
simply inviting

A mixed-doubles game
caught in a high tennis-moment
a beautiful flowing backhand plays the ball
receiver anticipating in flight
the narrow waist hinging such memorable delight
a man in athletic whites
runs crosscourt at full stretch

Around the wooden perimeter
a gallery of friends
some familiar challengers in waiting
a red post supports the net
an arched privet hedge marks
a gateway to a less playful world

This moving impression
an experiment on board
a practice match
caught at a precise time
the soft echo of the ball
hanging in the grassy air

In eighteen eight six
John Lavery stands back
casting his critical eye on the finished canvas
brush-in-hand fouled with oily greens
palette of opals brown and powdery white
the canvas brighter than the practice board
gone the shadowy eclipse of the trees
but it is the same moment of fulfilment

The gallery on the far side of the court is seated
matrons and patrons
uncles and aunts
a stylish pose reclining in the early August air
the grass in spots revealing summer's wear

Why did he paint this feminine moment
why did it mark his heart with such precision
and who are they and who is she
and who at this remove to say are we

She stirred his heart
won this moment
in the history of fine art
it still holds a precious thrill
her partner sidelined
her mother watches seated in a wicker chair
a niece queuing patiently with pony hair

A challenger a suitor
smoking waiting in the wings
racket at the ready to suggest his shrewd intent
added to the canvas
an addition since the practice game
to add balance to the painting

The extended family enjoys
the climax of a friendly game
a celebration of their civilised age
and for the heart
a white flamingo in an open cage

*****

From the religious message of Mr. Atkinson's 1810 booklet, to Hugh Tinney's piano lessons, to a century the Dublin Lawn Tennis Council, never mind Terry Wogan's doctor ("the fastest man in the world over two metres"), we can see that tennis is not just a sport, but an inspiration. Above all, it is worth enjoying and, therefore, recording.

If your days on the court are long past, then, no doubt, your volleys will have been sweeter as the years change ends. If you don't remember measuring the height at the centre of the net with your racquet, or tossing for service with "rough or smooth" then you **are** young. This does mean, however, there is time for you to live today's game today, to express your verbal skills in a style Percy French would not recognise, but would applaud, and wonder, perhaps in awe, about that sport those old codgers are talking about. It's definitely not tennis! Granddads of the future, you tell them! An amusing letter to finish off speaks for itself.

The History of Irish Tennis

6 The Oaks,
Grove House,
Milltown Road,
Dublin 6.

Mr Tom Higgins,
84 Cartron Bay,
Sligo.

10 September, 2003

Dear Tom,

Thank you for your letter dated 12 August, 2002 which came as a surprise. Regrettably, I have been away and have not had the opportunity to reply to your letter before now. Alas, I am not the Peter Clarke that represented Ireland in tennis and can only suppose that Tennis Ireland gave you my address in error.

I play Summer league class 3 and class 2 in the over 35 age category for Donnybrook Lawn Tennis Club. However, whatever skills I lack on court, is more than compensated by my enthusiasm and modestly!

As you requested on the form that I don't be shy, I am bound to proclaim that the younger Peter Clarke has never won an Irish Close Championship title, whilst I and my partner swept all aside in claiming the mixed doubles (class 4) event in the 1997 Irish Close Championships. Until he wins an Irish Open or Close Championship, I feel I can rightly claim that I am the real Peter Clarke and he is but an recent pretender!

I understand from your letter that the book will deal with the Who's Who in Irish Tennis. I shall not be offended if the pretender and I have to share a chapter, as I would not wish to hurt his feelings!

I regret I don't have a photograph for inclusion to the book that would do justice to myself and hope that sales will not be too adversely affected. Perhaps following release of the book and the expected publicity, I'll be able to set up a special website for my fans who have been remarkably mute to date!

On a serious note, good luck with the book which is a great idea.

Yours sincerely,

....
Peter Clarke

Chapter 4
The Organisation of Tennis in Ireland.

4.1 *The Tennis Clubs of Ireland*

In spite of the many hours of pleasure we got from playing at home, to be allowed to join the local club was a step forward towards pastures new. (Jim Duff, Sutton LTC)

Apart from the people who make up a sport, the most important element in most established sports are the clubs themselves. Each tennis club has its unique features, whether it be location, clubhouse, courts, success in competition, friendliness, the social scene, how it caters for juniors, its coaching schemes etc. They often reflect a certain age bracket. They can be exclusive in many ways, in terms of their player base, the cost of entry or, possibly, difficulty in entering in the first place. What is most important is that the majority, if not all, of the members are there because they love the game. It can be played from the age of five to ninety five. It transgresses social and national boundaries and, today it is a sport that can be found in virtually every corner of the globe. When we look at the list of over 700 clubs that have been founded in this island we see, with sadness, that many are no longer in existence. While sometimes it is a lack of sufficient interest, those that have demised have often done so for financial reasons. The practicality of keeping grass courts going, and the prohibitive cost of the alternatives in a small club, has resulted in untimely deaths. What about the successful clubs? They are many, despite the many distractions. In large urban areas survival should not be a problem. Some clubs have expanded their facilities to incorporate other sports, or upgraded their existing ones, thus maintaining their vitality. Fresh blood on committees is *always* necessary, not alone to keep up with the times but to ensure a healthy atmosphere.

In the mid 1940s **Sutton LTC** was just settling into their new premises (having moved from Howth) when club President E.C. Handcock (1944-1947) wrote to the members, pointing out how he saw the future for the club. The following extracts are worth noting as this key clubman (with honorary secretary, T. J. Geary) was to play an important part in the club's future. Such moments, and associated decisions, have been the turning points of many sports clubs.

There comes a time in every man's life.......That time is now in the life of tennis clubs as a whole. Tennis is a game for young people, many of whom are at school, are students or are starting in business, very few of whom are in a position to pay large subscriptions....The loss of grounds is already taking place and the obtaining of suitably placed new sites, making of new courts, etc. will require capital expenditure that may mean the disappearance of many clubs. This is not a pleasant picture but there is a solution.

He went on to indicate the merits of a social club with facilities for sports and other activities, all built around the tennis club. Apart from **Sutton LTC** there are many examples today of successful multi-purpose tennis clubs. These include **Galway LTC**, **Fitzwilliam LTC**, **Mount Pleasant LTC**, **County Sligo TC** and **Lisburn Racquets Club**. The latter, it might be noted, is probably best known for its success in the sport of

Mallow LTC in 1894. Known to be present were Leonard Swanzey (1), Mary Willis (3), Lucy Willis (5), Mr. F. Lyons (6), Eva Massey (7), Miss Norreys (9), Mrs. Massey (10), Miss Ormsby (11), Mrs. Hodges (12), Rev. Jones (Cecilstown) (13), Mrs. Willis (14), Mrs. Henry Longfield (14A), Miss L. Longfield (15), Miss Alice Harrison (16), Miss N. Becher (17), Bob Perry (19), Miss E. Jones (20), Mr. J. Bullen (24), Mrs. Webb (25), Miss S. Olden (26), Miss F. Massey (27), Miss Mary Davis (28), Col. Brown (29), Harry Longfield (30), Mrs. Lyons (31), Mr. E. Becher (33), Maud Smyth (34), Brazier-Creagh (35), Mrs. Tottenham (38), Miss Jones (41), Miss Annette Purcell (43) and Dora Olden (45).

badminton. Dubliner Ivar Boden is currently President of the Queen's Club in London. It hosts the televised "Stella Artois" tournament each year. What is not known is that this club has had many famous Irish members such as Joshua Pim and Willoughby Hamilton. In addition, it has been the home for *at least twenty-five different sports*. Back at Sutton, E. C. Handcock noted another aspect of a club's life. *Now for a very contentious point: a licence or not? The writer's upbringing says, no licence, but the tendency of recent years says definitely-yes. In the first place, many of the not so young will not play their part unless they get this amenity. Secondly, young people will go elsewhere (probably to places not so desirable) and get what they want, and it is better that it be provided openly and under some control. Thirdly it would help club finances.* One can imagine this debate has taken place in many clubs over the years. He added:

> *Social clubs as outlined are wanted throughout the whole country, and make no mistake about it, are coming. It is our responsibility to see that they take the form and shape that we know from experience is along the right lines, otherwise they will make their appearance in a very much more commercialised form to the detriment of that section of the community to which they belong. Under these circumstances lawn tennis would receive a new lease of life, the inter-club competitions and other tournaments would be of an interest and importance that only members and substantial finances can achieve.*

The President went on to say that if the readers thought it a good idea to have such a club, then they should *push it forward* and seek money and goodwill. *Don't forget, properly run, it is self supporting.* A listing of clubs that have functioned at one stage or another is compiled here. It was impossible to establish, in many cases, when in fact clubs first came into operation. The years are given which are either exact, approximate (c. for circa) or a date before which they were established (<). In the latter case it might have been a year or fifty.

In the 1980 edition of the ILTA Yearbook, there was an article entitled *WATERFORD: Apathy gets the cold shoulder.* In a brief manner it tells of a club, in fact two clubs, that amalgamated in 1954; both having had a long history, threading water. It should be an inspiration to all; the club today has the most modern facilities and a membership of about 1300, nearly half of them juniors.

> *Tennis in Waterford just seemed to be ambling along in a happy-go-lucky way. Players seemed happy with their lot and time, or rather the years went merrily on. We in St. Anne's-Waterford Tennis Club did not escape being caught up in this lethargy. For years we talked (and dreamed) of what our Club should be, but seemed to actually fight shy of the future. Time was running out and positive action was called for. Action there was, and on a bright and breezy January day in January 1979 that doyen of Waterford Tennis, Jack Shalloe, celebrated his 80th birthday by turning the first sod on the site of our new pavilion. Problems no doubt, there would be but something worthwhile was never achieved lightly……..Some clubs are fortunate enough to have within their ranks, members who by their dedication and unselfishness guarantee its very existence. We in St. Anne's-Waterford possess two such people-Jack Shalloe and Paddy Murphy. It would be utterly impossible in the space at our disposal to pay sufficient tribute to these devoted gentlemen for their unstinting services to our club and indeed to the game of tennis, over a long number of years.*

The "At Home" at Clontarf Lawn Tennis Club in 1938. This was the main social and playing day of the year, when club champions were decided. The custom is still maintained at very many clubs.

The Hawarden LTC Junior league winning team of 1949. Back (l. to r.) Sammy Tuff, G. Brown, E. Marshall, W. Andrews. Front (l. to r.) D. Patton, C. Timberlake, E. McKnight and I. Burton.

As to the demise of clubs, dates will nearly always be a mystery. Clubs die for practical reasons such as the number of players still playing or simple financial reasons such as the inability to meet an increased annual rent on the property. The wise clubs will have bought out their property as soon as they were in a position to do so.

One interesting story concerns the sudden death of a club. An exact date can be attributed to the end of the **Chichester LTC**, one that was only affiliated less than twenty years previously. Thanks to Derek Noblett of Belfast for the following anecdote:

Chichester Tennis Club was situated on Salisbury Avenue, Antrim Road, Belfast. It had six red En-Tout-Cas courts and a large clubhouse with a sprung maple floor renowned for its dancing qualities. In 1941 I qualified to become a senior member and forwarded my application together with the £2 entry fee. Unfortunately, I never got to play there as a senior member because the courts and clubhouse were destroyed in the German air raid of Easter Tuesday 15th April 1941. The enclosed photograph of the bomb crater at the tram depot on Salisbury Avenue pinpoints the site of the clubhouse, which was close to the wall of the depot. With a retrieved £2 supplemented with £1 and 3 shillings, i.e. 3 guineas in total, I became a member of Cavehill Tennis Club, North Circular Road, Belfast. After the war the site was re-developed as Salisbury Bowling Club.

In 1894 there was no national organisation. However, an Irish Lawn Tennis Handbook was produced for the first time and there were some 58 clubs identified. There were nineteen clubs in the Dublin area, one of which was **High School LTC**. In the rest of Leinster there were sixteen that included **Lucan LTC**, **Parsonstown LTC** (County Meath) and **Tullamore LTC**. The Birr and Banagher clubs were referred to as the **King's County and Ormonde LTC** and the **King's County West LTC**, respectively. In Ulster there were a total of ten clubs. These included **Cliftonville LTC.** That club organised the North of Ireland Championships in early June. **Ballyshannon LTC** ran the Championship of Donegal. In Munster there were ten clubs including a **County Clare LTC**. Connacht had only three clubs in this listing. These were the **County Sligo LTC** which had been around for over ten years and, perhaps surprisingly, a **Roscommon LTC** (possibly this was in fact **Castlerea LTC**, a reasonable assumption when we look at the early entries to the Irish Championships) and a **Queen's College LTC** i.e. University College, Galway.

The following paragraph, from the first handbook in 1894, gives the reader some idea of the way in which the sport of tennis had caught on in this country.

In concluding this sketch of the past season reference may fitly be made to two events that should have an important bearing upon the fortunes of the game in the metropolitan district. One of these, the formation, with a huge membership roll, of a new club at Donnybrook, is evidence of the fast hold lawn tennis has obtained upon the affections of the capital, already better supplied with tennis clubs than perhaps any city of its size in the Three Kingdoms; and the second was the evidence of a need for a late season handicap meeting in Dublin, afforded by the phenomenal success of the Mountjoy Square tournament, experimentally launched by some residents of the neighbourhood. The success of the venture is said to have quite astonished the promoters.

Lawn Tennis Clubs in 1894 Handbook

Dublin & Suburban

	Clones (Co. Cavan)
Blackrock	*County Clare*
Charleville	*County Kildare*
Civil Service	*County Sligo*
Clontarf	*County Tyrone (Omagh)*
Donnybrook	*County Wexford*
Drumcondra	*County Westmeath*
Dublin University	*Dundalk*
Fitzwilliam	*Dungannon*
Glenageary &	*Enniscorthy*
Kingstown	*Enniskillen*
Grosvenor	*Fermoy*
High School	*Glanmire*
Kenilworth	*Greystones*
Lansdowne	*Holywood (Co. Down)*
Mount Temple	*Howth*
Monkstown	*Kilkenny County & City*
Mountpleasant	*King's County West*
Sandycove	*King's County & Ormonde*
Wilton	*Limerick*
	Lucan
Country	*Mallow*
	Malahide
Armagh	*Mitchelstown*
Athboy (Co. Meath)	*Parsonstown (Co. Meath)*
Athy	*Queen's College (Galway)*
Banbridge	*Roscommon*
Ballyshannon	*Roscrea*
Castleblaney	*Rushbrooke*
Cliftonville (Belfast)	*Tullamore*
Carrick-on-Suir	*Waterford*

In the latter portion of the book the clubs in the northwest are dealt with in some detail. Here, for practical reasons, it is not possible to tell the story of each and every club. I have deliberately selected the older clubs and hope to identify, however briefly, their stories and how they have thrived. Details on a number of other clubs were available and are also included. Space and available information have mainly dictated the length of this chapter. In the 1982 Yearbook we find an attempt by the Leinster Branch to give the details of all the clubs affiliated through them. Of 88 clubs named, 59 had given their number of senior and junior members and all but two had specified their number and type of courts. The table below summarises this information. It is noted that Clongowes Wood College were an affiliated club at the time. This school has one of the longest records in terms of playing tennis in Ireland.

Leinster Branch Statistics 1982

Greatest number of courts	Clongowes Wood College (21); Fitzwilliam LTC (13), Elm Park (13)
Greatest number of grass courts	Clongowes Wood College (12), Elm Park (9)
Greatest number of hard courts	Sutton LTC (12)
Smallest number of courts	Kilmeade LTC (1) Ormonde LTC (1) Rathmore LTC (1)
Greatest number of members	Sutton LTC (1310)
Greatest number of adult members	Sutton LTC (650)
Greatest number of junior members	Sutton (660)
Smallest number of members	Balreask Old LTC (15)
Smallest number of adult members	Clongowes Wood College LTC (0), Rathmore LTC (10)
Smallest number of junior members	None: Ballyjamesduff LTC, Cherrymount LTC, E.S.B. LTC, Guinness LTC, Mount Pleasant LTC .

The Courts

Occasionally, courts are established for special events. For one of the GOAL charity ventures, the grass courts in Fitzwilliam Square were once again prepared after many years of disuse. The visiting players, and, one suspects, the home spectators would admire the setting and pity the day they were not in regular use. For the 1983 Davis Cup tie with the USA a large venue had to be secured to cater for the interest in the match. The multi-purpose Royal Dublin Society facilities were brought into use and were packed for the three days. That gentleman of tennis, the late Arthur Ashe, was the visiting captain. He would watch McEnroe do his stuff and the USA went away with the expected win. The house came down when Matt Doyle beat Elliott Teltscher on day one in what was to be our only winning rubber. In *Days of Grace (1993)* it was pointed out that Arthur Ashe was keen to see that McEnroe was focussed. This he was. His note of the venue for the match is somewhat amusing: *the Royal Dublin Society's Simmonscourt Pavilion- a fancy barn, really, where horse and cattle breeders showed their stock. The place had been cleaned out, fumigated, and a carpet set down for play. It was all a little odd. Still, during and after our victory, the Irish were ebullient, gracious hosts. And with his victories*

The old Belfast Boat Club clubhouse.

in Dublin, McEnroe broke my record of twenty-seven wins for the U.S. in singles matches. I did not begrudge him the record.

While Fitzwilliam Square has had its praise for its setting etc., and many clubs can proudly boast of all-weather courts of the highest quality, there may also be other unsatisfactory situations. The following is part of a report on a match between a larger club visiting a small struggling one for the first time. *.we received a friendly welcome....the courts were somewhat short, preventing any decent play behind the baseline....the playing surfaces are very poor, and with the wet day were really found to be dangerously slippy. The nets have no central fixed point, and were far too high.* Despite the *hospitality arrangements* being *first rate*, this small club of *dedicated people* obviously needed new courts and some financial support.

Relaxing at Elm Park tennis club. From left: Damien Hand, Mary Brady, Cleo Greene, Peter Murningham, Stell aShiels, Walter Rhatigan and Jean Maher.

There are very many small clubs throughout the country who would thrive if they were able to afford to

have in place the basics. The enthusiasm is often directed at raising funds for a new net while public or other support for new courts would bring about a major transformation. Funds for affiliation could then be the focus and, when the club is stronger, funds for changing rooms etc. We all know the link in this country between health and sport but will there ever be national policies to really do something substantial about it?

Clubs can be adjacent to one another, such as **Wilton LTC** and **Fitzwilliam LTC** were for many years. Des O'Brien the Triple Crown Rugby player and an exceptional hockey and tennis player lived at 13 Kenilworth Square in the 1930s and 1940s. In 2001 Des could remember the whole 'square', which in fact is not even an exact rectangle (and is about 275 metres long by an average width of about 150 metres). In that space there were four tennis clubs with pavilions (**Methodist LTC**, **Waverly LTC**, **Grosvenor LTC** and **Kenilworth LTC**) and the Kenilworth Ladies' Croquet Club. In total, he recalls, that there were 25 tennis courts. The solicitor representing the landowner put the square up for sale during or just after the war. The clubs could not afford the asking price (thought to be about £2000) and St. Mary's College bought it and, as Des said "all those beautiful courts were turned into two rugby pitches-a tragedy!"

Club Houses

Having a clubhouse is a naturally expected asset of all established clubs. While the land for one or two courts come first on the agenda, a club which has thrived for a period will seek it's own home. It will cost the members in time, effort and funds but has always been thought to be worth the effort. Today, large sums of money are required to provide what might be considered a clubhouse of minimum acceptability.

Not that long ago the members might have had a simple 'pavilion' with no electricity or running water. A few clubs have recalled details on early pavilions. Wooden structures with a galvanised roof were common. They might have had three main 'rooms'. The main room was the general area in the middle of the structure for tea making and occasional "dances". The two at the ends for ladies and men's changing areas. Off the main area might be an alcove for the gas cylinder where water was boiled for making tea-an important feature on Thursday or Saturday afternoons when a mixed tournament was interrupted, the lady members bringing along their sandwiches and cakes. In a small toilet off the men's and ladies' changing area would be a basic sanitary unit which included a toilet seat, cut up newspaper suspended by a large nail, and a bucket, regularly dosed with a disinfectant, and emptied at intervals by the caretaker.

Becoming a Member

Becoming a member of a club was often a dream for a young eight or ten year old and even for advanced teenagers. Today our children are generally so well served with televised sport and options to play in their local environment that much of that excitement no longer exists. Nearly all parents have transport, and acting as a taxi driver is the norm. Jim Duff, a member of **Sutton LTC**, when it was overlooking Howth Harbour and called **Howth LTC,** recalls tennis for him at that time.

I think my first memory goes back to the period 1935 or 1936, when I was first elected to junior membership of the club. This was a great thrill for me. We had a singles grass court on the front lawn at home and used it constantly for playing both singles and doubles. Playing doubles on a singles court, made your game very tight indeed, and you had to be exceedingly accurate. In spite of the many hours of pleasure we got from playing at home, to be allowed to join the local club was a step forward towards pastures new.

We juniors used to hunt in small packs, even in those days, and many is the joke and laugh we had together on the way to the club. On arrival, which took anything up to half an hour, if you caught the tram – straight out on to court, provided one was available. One of the seven grass courts was set aside for juniors. It had previously been ostensibly a croquet lawn. It had a slope on it-was very soft underfoot. The ball would barely hop. Needless to say, we made a dash for one of the better ones, but if it was required by seniors, we had to give it up.

I can also remember playing my first league match for Howth in Class IV against Clarinda (this club is now defunct) at Clarinda Park in Dun Laoghaire. The search for players was such that the club had to call on juniors and yours truly was put in at No. 6. I can well remember the indignation of my opponent at being beaten by a young whipper-snapper.

In 1896, the new **Longford Lawn Tennis Club** produced a Rules Book 4.2 inches by 2.7 inches in size. They were produced by local firm, Turners, a business that is still in operation today. The fifteen rules are concise and are worth recording here because it is probably one of the few examples of club rulebooks still extant from that era. Some of the rules could still apply today; others are showing their age.

1896
The Club Rules
At
Longford Lawn Tennis Club

1   The club shall be called "The Longford Lawn Tennis Club."

2   The rules of play shall be those of the All England Lawn Tennis Club.

3   The annual Subscription shall be 10s.6d. for Gentleman, and 5s for Ladies, but a member of the Cricket Club on being admitted a member of the Tennis Club shall pay on such admission a reduced Subscription of 7s.6d. only.

4   That the annual Subscription be due 1st January. Members not playing before the 1st May lose their rights of membership.

5   That the affairs of the Club be managed by a Committee of five (with Hon. Secretary and Treasurer as 'ex-officio'), and two form a quorum.

6   The Committee shall have power to co-opt a member to fill a vacancy should such arise in their number during their year of office.

7   The Committee shall have power unanimously to expel a member from the Club, his Subscription not to be returned; and his name struck off the list of members.

8   The Committee, Secretary, and Treasurer to be elected annually at a General Meeting to be held in January, the outgoing Secretary and Treasurer to furnish their accounts at the meeting.

9   Members to be admitted by ballot at a General Meeting, or at the Thursday club day, between the hours of 4 and 7 p.m., two black beans in five to exclude.

10   Names of Candidate, Proposer and Seconder to be furnished to the Hon. Secretary and posted on the board in the Pavilion seven days before. The Committee have power to admit Ladies without ballot, on being proposed and seconded.

11 The Proposer and Seconder of Candidates shall be responsible for the first year's subscription of those whom they propose.

12 Thursdays and Fridays shall be club days.

13 No parties shall play more than one set nor advantage games, if two or more members are waiting to play.

14 No dogs allowed on the ground

15 No person shall be allowed to play without proper tennis shoes, under a penalty of 10s.

No alteration of these rules shall be made, unless at the Annual General Meeting of the Club, or at an Extraordinary General Meeting called for the purpose, on the requisition of 5 members, when a majority of two-thirds of the members present shall be required to carry any alteration or addition. That these Rules be printed, and a copy supplied to each member.

The Groundsman

The groundsman, originally called ground man, was always a part of club life when grass courts needed much attention. These lowly paid, as a rule, workers, were part of the woodwork in very many clubs. They were generally characters, some amenable to players and juniors, others surly and treated with kid gloves by all the members. One noted keeper of the grounds was Danny Brennan of the **Kilkenny County and City LTC.** He was an all-Ireland Senior softball champion in 1929. He had also represented Ireland in the 1929 Tailteann Games. Before coming to the club in the early 1940s he had been in the army. He was to die in 1978, the year before the club's centenary celebrations. When times were financially difficult clubs would have to cut back on expenditure. Deflation affected poor Mr. Archibold of the same club. He was paid £1.10s.0.d in 1923, £1.5s.0d in 1935 and he was paired back to £1.0s.0d by 1939. These were not hourly rates, or even a daily payment but his weekly wage.

In 1944 it appears there was no caretaker at **Ballyfarnon LTC.** However, a Mr. T. Kerrigan cut the grass five times during that summer at 3/6 a go and was also paid £1 for the repair of the lawnmower. In April, the single court had been rolled at a cost of four shillings. Joe Coffey was the caretaker for a number of years catering for the five fine grass courts at the **County Longford LTC.** Typical of an outdoor worker, he always appeared to have been tanned, his mainly bald head shining on the fine summer evening of the 1960s. A dangling cigarette made up the image.

In the 1987 **Clontarf LTC** Centenary book we find the groundsman highly praised. *No history of Clontarf LTC would be complete without a special mention of Dave Fennelly. Dave came to our club in 1958 as groundsman and stayed with us in that capacity until 1963. During his period our courts were the envy of all grass court clubs. His expertise was apparent for all to see. Not only was he a groundsman but had a very special interest in the general welfare of the club. In 1963 he left us to go to Glasnevin and proceeded to accomplish there the same perfection of courts which he had produced here.* (n. b. He came back to the club as barman in 1969 and was to be a stalwart of the club for many years thereafter).

Many clubs had a family attached. In **Naas LTC,** Tom Legge was the caretaker with his wife involved in the catering; the cricket lunches and tea at 4 pm were part of the package. They served the club loyally from 1906 until 1931. At the **County Sligo LTC** the Chambers family were on board. The barefooted children acting as ballboys during the annual Open Tournament. It was not unusual for the ordinary member to assist the caretaker with court lining and even rolling the grass courts. Older teenagers, and adults, achieved some satisfaction at the beginning of the summer season assisting with such duties. There was a feeling that they were making their contribution, and at the same time speeding up the moment when the first serve and volley could be launched. The annual court weeding was meticulously carried out. Hard courts and clay courts demanded different maintenance. The tape that formed the lines of the courts had to be pinned down and possibly replaced.

The grounds man, "Diver Mac" poses with the members at the Fergus LTC in Ennis in the 1950s. Included are (front, l. to r.) Brian Maurer and Liam Cahir.; second row (l. to r.): Criona Wilson, Jerry Cahir, Alana Wilson, Mary Duggan & Olive Smythe.

The Professional

In 1925, Sir William Orphen, R.A. would publish his *Stories of Old Ireland & Myself*. In the 1890s he was a close friend of Percy French and was a close collaborator in producing the Jarvey. He would later become a painter of world acclaim. He lived through the growth of the Irish tennis scene into one of acclaim. In his book he reflects back to thirty years earlier. Tennis was well established and Irish players had been winners of several Wimbledon titles.

Lawn tennis was the great game in Ireland at that time, and proud we were; and why not? Wasn't George Kerr the professional at the Fitz-William Club, champion of the world, and wasn't Burke of the Lansdowne Club the greatest player in the world? Kerr would never play Burke level, but would always insist on owing him half fifteen, and was always beaten comfortably. But in those days professionals were not treated with that respect with which they are now. One summer evening of 1895 or '96, about eight o'clock, some nice Dublin gentleman walked into the club and sent for Burke to play him a game. Burke came along and played him; but he was not in his best form, as he had been spending the latter part of the evening with some friends, and had "had a few", thinking his day's work was over. The "gentleman" reported him and Burke was "sacked". He, the greatest player in the world at that time, and in receipt of 30s. a week pay, was "sacked"! That was why Burke left Ireland (and Irish lawn tennis declined). He was immediately taken up by Count X. (Count Voss of Germany, Chamberlain to the Great Duchess Anastasia), who installed him at Cannes, and from that day he had a most successful career, well known and respected all over France, North and South, from Cannes, and all over the Cote-d'Azur to Deauville, where he died in 1921. A very well-to-do gentleman, and his sons are carrying on in his stead. But I never heard of him ever going back to his native country. At that time we boys could have told you all about lawn tennis from that time of Lawford and Ernest Browne to Lewis, and from the Baddeleys, and Willoughby Hamilton, and the two great days when he first beat Ernest Renshaw, and then Willie Renshaw, and won the championship, and after the last stroke hit a ball over the houses that surround Fitz-William Square-a great "belt" to give a ball surely!

Other Staff

Apart from the groundsman's wife who multi-tasked, there are others whose work for clubs must be recognised. Bigger clubs could afford full-time staff. There might be one or several people involved. Club **managers** become experts at all sorts of duties. **Secretaries** may be paid employees but, more often than not, are honorary positions. A range of **administrators** and **secretarial assistants** can be found, again in the bigger clubs who need, and can afford, them. The titles can vary but all are involved in the operation of a 'business' as well as a club.

The caretaker may or may not have also been a **gardener**. On the social side the provision of teas for the weekly American tournament was a function of the ladies committee. Bigger clubs today have full-time **caterers** and **bar-staff**, others employing staff on an infrequent basis. The trick for a club is to ensure that the provision of food and drink is an economic one and, perhaps, be a profit-making element of the club.

Contract **cleaners** may be afforded in some cases, in others the members just rowed in to ensure dressing rooms are in order for the open week, and a brush up of the small dance area was undertaken with gusto. A lick of paint to the pavilion was demanded every 5 or 10 years.

Porters and **locker-room attendants** are a rare luxury. There is one story, involving a County Cavan lady, worth recalling and told in Roy McKelvie's 1986 history of the Queen's Club in London. While not an Irish club, it had strong connections to this country having had two Irishmen as chairmen, namely Dick Sandys and Ivar Boden. Roy's piece on Maggie Bird is worthy of inclusion here.

The end of the sixties was something of a watershed for the staff. The renowned Mrs. Tutt, having begun her association with the ladies' changing room back in the thirties, died in 1968. She was succeeded by Mrs. Maggie Bird who, now in her late sixties, remains in charge. It is a remarkable fact that these two ladies cover nearly sixty years of The Queen's Club history. Maggie Bird is Irish. She has seventeen children, ten girls and seven boys – 'No pill, no television in my young day' – and came to London from County Cavan near the end of the war. Working in the Shepherds Bush PO she replied to an advertisement for the job at the Club and was taken on by Dickie Ritchie, the secretary. 'It was a lucky day for us when you came through the gate,' remarked Ritchie one day. To which Maggie retorted 'I didn't. I came through a hole in the hedge.' The changing room in those days contained old furniture, including a settee and a large coal fire. Her co-worker – there were only two changing room attendants – was also Irish, Nora Pearce from Cork, who remained for some six years and now helps look after cancer patients at the Hammersmith Hospital while maintaining a long-time friendship with the Boden family.

Maggie's duties included taking in the court money and handing out the balls. "I used to have fights over the money. Some players pretended they had paid when they hadn't and I'd threaten to have them billed. Some people used to come and say 'I want this or I want that". I'd tell them not to talk like that but ask 'Can I have?' Virginia Wade and Chris Evert would always support me. They are real ladies, my favourites." During his brief reign as secretary Hassell sacked Maggie and this upset, among others, Clive Bernstein who had her reinstated.

She recalls, among other memories, O' Leary, the former head groundsman, arriving at the Club from hospital wearing only his pyjamas and a Miss Hutchings bitterly complaining that someone had stolen her tennis shoes which, she admitted, she had paid three shillings and six pence for eleven years previously! Maggie likes the Club as it is now – 'Much cleaner and more pleasant and with a much nicer management. That's my life down here in the changing room; my second home.'

Lady Members

In recent times many will recall the vote for lady members at our most prestigious of tennis clubs, **Fitzwilliam Lawn Tennis Clubs.** Due to the nature of the game ladies were involved from an early stage throughout the country. It was a suitable *pastime* for the gentler sex. Ireland, as we now know, was the first country to have an open Ladies Singles

The modern clubhouse at Waterford-St. Anne's Lawn Tennis Club.

Championship. The first Irish Championships in 1879 showed no discrimination, Miss May Langrishe beating Miss Meldon in the final. It was a club that ran that event, the very same **Fitzwilliam LTC**. It was to be five years later before the organising gentlemen's committee of the All England Croquet and Lawn Tennis Club introduced the ladies to their Championships. The South of Ireland Championships have their origins in 1877, two years before Fitzwilliam. The front page of the *Limerick Chronicle* on the 17th July 1877 speaks for itself.

George Hehir, in his booklet on the first decade of **Limerick Lawn Tennis Club,** has the following comment to make on the issue of ladies playing tennis. On one hand, it was a sport for all the leisured classes and, on the other hand, the efforts of lady players were the subject of some abuse by the occasional male onlooker. How times have changed!

By 1878 Lawn Tennis had almost completely supplanted Croquet as the summer game of the leisured classes and the fashionable thing was to hold a Tennis Party in the grounds of one's estate. Since we had more than our share of large estates in the neighbourhood, it is not surprising that the game caught on rapidly here. It seems that the young ladies took to the game with particular enthusiasm, and this inspires our earlier mentioned reporter to some male chauvinist outpourings.

Discussing lady players he says "looking at the thing impartially (?) one cannot help being forced to the conclusion that women's arms have not been made for much. In the mazy circlings of the dance, and in the shady nooks of conservatories, young bachelors will tell us that they have their uses. But, ye gods, have you ever seen the 'gaucherie' of a woman's first attempt to throw a stone, handle a billiard cue or make a stroke at Tennis?"

It appears that the first Open Ladies Singles event was the 1877 'first' South of Ireland Championship. It can, therefore, be of no surprise that Ireland's only lady singles winners of what are now known as the Grand Slams are from this part of the world. In 1890, Helena Rice from New Inn, County Tipperary won the 'All-England' title at Wimbledon. In the following two years, 1891 and 1892, it was Mabel Cahill from Ballyragget, County Tipperary, who put Ireland into the US Championship records. She won the singles, doubles and mixed in both years. These were exceptional ladies in their day and appeared to have learned their tennis on the 'home court' circuit. We should not forget that club tennis was as a result of the rapid expansion of the game on private courts, not vice versa.

The *Field* were great recorders of sport and their edition of Saturday June 7th, 1879 gave full details of the *Championship Meeting of Ireland.* Unlike the *Grand Lawn Tennis Tournament* at The Limerick Cricket Ground, we know that the ladies events were more discreet and not exposed to public gaze. Their singles event was *played on asphalte...in the private ground of the Fitzwilliam Club, when admittance will only be by a member's voucher.* In that first year of the Fitzwilliam event there was also a mixed event. It was held at Fitzwilliam Square.

It is noted in that early newspaper report, that the men who played represented the following clubs: **Fitzwilliam LTC, Dublin University LTC, County Carlow LTC, Monkstown LTC.** There were also a few representatives of the "82nd Regiment" and the "Grenadier Guards" The ladies were given no affiliation. In 1880, there were representatives from **Wilton LTC, Cheltenham LTC, Maida Vale LTC, Cork LTC, Waterford LTC, Hooton LTC, County Down LTC** as well as representatives of the "84th Regiment" and the "3rd Dragoons". Among the ladies we find, perhaps surprisingly, that both May Langrishe and Miss Butler were representing the **Fitzwilliam LTC.** Miss D. Meldon of the **Wilton LTC** won the singles. In 1881, E. de V. Tattersall of the "Queen's Bays" played and, in 1883, we find that a Mr. Percy Greene and Captain Spens were representing "The Buffs", the name used for a famous English military regiment. It is not known if the regiments had in fact clubs, but one can assume many of them had tennis courts available to them. One or two mystery names are difficult to decipher. Mr. A.W. Perry had after his name "A.M.D." in 1880, as did his doubles partner, W.S. Pratt. In 1881, Perry seemed to be playing for "Cork" while, in 1882, he had the name "Arduli" placed after his name in the reported results. Two complete mysteries are Captain Marshall with "R.H.A." and W.H. Darby with "R.A.". We will probably never know the full stories of these early exponents of the sport and where they played. The following, sometimes brief, stories can be told about our early clubs. In the lengthy table the known club names are given. Where it is confirmed that a club changed its name the original name is given in brackets. In some cases, due to the fact that the name could be found in more than one location in Ireland, the county is also recorded.

In terms of the oldest tennis-playing clubs in Ireland the date is linked to that when tennis became an organised sport. There are several examples when a club, rugby, golf and cricket, for example, added tennis in as a sport some time after the club was founded. **Monkstown LTC** (Dublin) had archery as its antecedent. Of course, many clubs evolved from the pastime/sport of croquet either at a club or in front of the 'big house'. I have attempted to make that distinction. A good example was that of **Muckamore Cricket & Lawn Tennis Club**. It was founded in 1874 but only had a tennis section from 1908. As there was no netting around their early grass courts a lot of ball retrieving was necessary...*but ball boys were not hard to find at 3d. for the afternoon, that being passing wealth for a youngster then.*

Club Numbers

A range of records has enabled the production of the list of clubs now compiled on the following pages. In the nineteenth century it is likely that on a *pro-rate* basis there were more tennis clubs in Ireland than in any other country. While the game of lawn tennis spread worldwide from England, the nature of Irish sporting and social life was such that it was readily assimilated into urban and rural areas here more quickly than elsewhere. An example of this enthusiasm for sport can be seen in the success of cricket. In a recent *Irishman's Diary* column (*The Irish Times, Monday January 10th 2005*) James Fitzgerald reviewed Patrick Bracken's book on cricket in County Tipperary. The sport had been introduced in

1834 and there were more cricket club in the county in 1850 than in the whole of Ulster. In 1876 there were at least 43 cricket teams in the county. "Cricket was widely played by Catholic and Protestant; landlord and tenant; clergyman and policeman; soldier and merchant". Lawn tennis was more of an individual pastime, and a step up from the game of croquet, rather than a serious sport. It could not compete with cricket as a team sport. Nevertheless, courts were laid in large numbers and, despite a lack of national co-ordination, there was a rapid growth in club tennis in the 1880s and 1890s. By 1900 there were over 100 tennis clubs in Ireland.

There was great difficulty in tabulating accurately the details of sports clubs. An attempt, though imperfect, is made here to do so. Information was secured from many sources but particularly from the 1894 and 1895 yearbooks, a limited number ILTA/Tennis Ireland yearbooks (especially from the mid-1970s onwards), ILTA minutes' books and yearbooks produced in Munster and Ulster.

Many clubs have changed their names while others amalgamated in order to survive. The information is far from complete. Many clubs never affiliated to the national organisation, or did do for only a short number of years. Clubs were allocated dates in one of three ways. Of the total of 749 clubs identified only 142 can be allocated "exact" years of formation. For another 106 clubs the approximate year of formation ('Circa') is known. For the remaining clubs, the majority, a prefix of < is allocated i.e. a year is given and it is known that a particularly club was formed before that year. It could be the previous year or twenty years earlier. This is the weakness in such as analysis. Despite this, patterns can be clearly seen when we group the clubs into the thirteen decades between 1875 and 2004. The last decade was converted to 11 years when recent information became available. Included, therefore, is a period of 131 years. The first two decades (1875-1884 and 1885-1894) and the period 1925 to 1934 are the periods when the **confirmed** new club formations were at their highest. These peaks hold true when the 'circa' years are added. The 'all' clubs listing in the 'Analysis' table is immediately weakened when we look at the decade 1955 to 1964. No doubt there were many clubs formed at this time, but as no yearbook could be found for the two decades prior to 1955, this figure is artificially high. Many of these clubs were probably formed in the previous few decades, or earlier.

The initial rapid growth of the game was predictable. Growth slowed down in the first two decades of the 20th century. Among the reasons for this were the formation of the Gaelic Athletic Association and the Gaelic League, the deliberate denigration of 'foreign' games, the Great War and the civil strife in Ireland. In Ireland, as elsewhere, there was a new excitement in the 1920s. Following the civil war, many new clubs were formed. While clubs who were reliant on 'gentry' membership found it difficult to survive, the new clubs, often chaired by a local Catholic clergyman, thrived. The game was no longer exclusive.

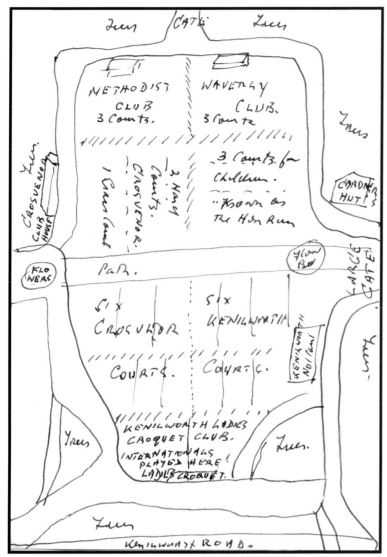

The sketch map shows handwritten labels including:

- Trees / GATE / Trees (top)
- METHODIST CLUB 3 Courts.
- WAVERLEY CLUB. 3 Courts
- CROSVENOR CLUB HOUSE
- 1 Grass Court
- 2 Hard Courts, CROSVENOR
- 3 Courts for Children.
- "Known as The Hen Run"
- GARDNER HUTS
- FLOWERS
- Path.
- SIX CROSVENOR COURTS.
- SIX KENILWORTH COURTS.
- KENILWORTH No 1 / Court
- LARGE GATE
- KENILWORTH LADIES CROQUET CLUB. INTERNATIONALS PLAYED HERE! LADIES CROQUET.
- Trees
- KENILWORTH ROAD.

Kenilworth Square Dublin in the 1930s

The late multi-talented sportsman Des O'Brien was generous with his efforts in recalling many aspects of tennis in Dublin in the years before the Second World War. He lived at 13 Kenilworth Square where from the roof it was possible to see all 25 courts in use as well as the two croquet lawns (for women only). His family lived here from 1914 to 1967. His copy photograph of the Square taken in 1936 from the roof has been mislaid but he was able, at 81 years of age, to sketch the layout (across) in detail. Each of the 90 Victorian houses around the Square paid £1 per annum for the key to gain access through gates on either side. There were two gardeners-called Pat and Tom-*we never knew their surnames. They were paid 30s weekly.*

He joined **Kenilworth LTC** at six years of age. Of the four clubs it was the only Catholic one *and it was the busiest both in tennis and social activities. Grosvenor was also busy tennis wise but not competitive in the Leagues.*

The clubs never mixed but were quite friendly. There was no wire netting between the six Grosvenor courts and the six Kenilworth ones. The main social difference was that the Grosvenor members being Protestant came to play straight from work and went home to dinner so that the courts could be empty by 7.30pm. The Kenilworth members had high tea and came out to play until the sun set and the dew started to fall. All courts were beautifully maintained by Tom-with no machinery-push rollers and lawn mowers. He was a lean cadaverous man, immensely strong. In the autumn, a group of women-the "Weeders" –came with sacking around their knees, and extracted every weed on every court, working on their knees and filling the holes with a mix of sand, earth and seed. The fringes of the square had been beautifully planted with a mixture of fine trees, and there were two well tended flower beds at the centre gates. Each club had its own club house, single stories wooden buildings. Grosvenor had a cold shower for the men but nothing for the ladies. Practically all the men would use the cold shower after playing. We seemed to have endless hot summers then!

Kenilworth committee laid on tea on Wednesdays, Saturdays and Sundays. Delicious cakes and sandwiches-I can remember Bewleys almond rings and barm brack, and sundry cream cakes and sandwiches-all provided by the ladies!

Des O'Brien (1919-2005)

We had a dance on most Saturdays which started at 10pm when the men were kicked out of Doherty's pub in Harold's Cross and would come back to the club with the Guinness bottles wrapped up in brown paper! We danced enthusiastically to a single pianist with occasionally a saxophone. The pianist Billy Withers was superb and had perfect rhythm-we all loved dancing (ballroom). Finals Day in July was a great occasion for which most of the members turned up. A marquee was erected on no. 1 court which covered the whole court, with a dance floor laid inside. We danced from 10 to 3 am and a huge supper was served at midnight. There was always complaints from the neighbours who had to endure the noise of an 8 to 10 piece band with ensuing revelry! We would quite often leave the square at 6am. Of course it was an ideal place for courting couples who would slip out of the marquee and wander hand in hand through the moonlit trees. On the Sunday we had a SCRAP party where the remains of the Saturday food was served and a small band provided the music! Once a year there was a picnic outing to Howth where we went by tram and train.

The other clubs were very respectable! Grosvenor Finals Day ended in tea at six p.m. We had very little to do with the other two clubs (i.e. the Waverly and Methodist clubs). Des also noted that the great James Cecil Parke lived on the Square. The Parke family had a foundry in Pearse Street. *My first bicycle was a "J. C. P.".* Further information on Des O'Brien and Jim Parke can be found in Chapter 6, among others.

Other Memories: In another one of his several communications he made notes on "Dancing" which included: *Most Catholic tennis clubs had dances through the season, some were monthly, some weekly..... Romance was always in the air and the Square was perfect for courting-there were seats in strategic places! On a warm summers night of which there seemed to be many, you could wander home at 4 or 5 am-or take your girl home on the crossbar of your bike-the ultimate thrill. Sex did not enter into the equation!*

Des O'Brien was an excellent tennis player and won many titles. His tennis 'style' was noteworthy, and it is not surprising that the players he most admired were the 'perfect stylists' Baron Gottfried Von Cramm (Germany) and Ko Sin Ko (Myanmar?). Another player he clearly recalled was Guy Jackson, a top Irish player in the late 1940s and 1950s, a Davis Cup player of note and Irish men's doubles champion in 1952 and 1953. *Guy Jackson was not a flamboyant character but very dedicated and single minded. I played a few friendly games with him when he came to the Guinness Brewery in London. He was M. D. of Guinness Dublin. He was steady in everything he did and played. He made very few mistakes on the tennis court and played mainly a baseline game. He was an outstanding sportsman and a perfect gentleman.* [While Des was most noted as an international rugby player, Guy and he both played on the Irish squash team together in the early 1950s. Both played hockey, Guy for Ireland and Des captained South Wales].

Gambling and tennis goes back to the time of Henry VIII, and beyond. He lost a lost of money on the game. It was common in Ireland too and is referred to in other parts of this book. The odd flutter was still taking place in the 1950s in Ireland. Des and Guy who have played many international squash matches together. Des recalled *After the war Ireland never won even one individual game against England-always 5-nil. There was a sweepstake (to be won by the first player to win a match against England!) that passed on and increased year by year in the Irish team, and it was eventually won by Guy who defeated his English opponent in a Fitzwilliam court in which the walls were dripping with condensation.*

****

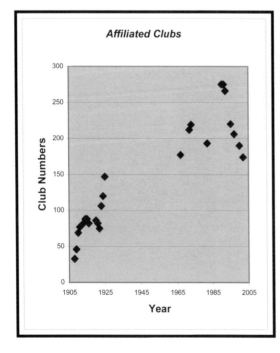

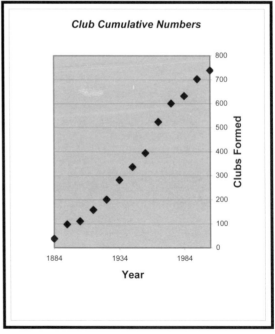

Decade	Years	"All" Clubs Recorded	% Clubs formed in each decade	Clubs recorded as "Exact or Circa"	% Clubs formed in each decade	Clubs recorded as "Exact" Year	% Clubs formed in each decade
1	1875-1884	38	5.1	34	13.7	17	12.0
2	1885-1894	60	8.0	57	23.0	18	12.7
3	1895-1904	12	1.6	12	4.8	10	7.0
4	1905-1914	48	6.4	19	7.7	12	8.5
5	1915-1924	43	5.7	15	6.0	7	4.9
6	1925-1934	82	10.9	25	10.1	18	12.7
7	1935-1944	57	7.6	22	8.9	15	10.6
8	1945-1954	61	8.1	16	6.5	9	6.3
9	1955-1964	131	17.5	6	2.4	4	2.8
10	1965-1974	77	10.3	10	4.0	7	4.9
11	1975-1984	31	4.1	5	2.0	4	2.8
12	1985-1994	70	9.3	16	6.5	14	9.8
13	1995-2005	39	5.2	12	4.8	7	4.9
Total	131	749	(100)	248	(100)	141	(100)

Analysis of Recorded Irish Tennis Clubs

Hawarden LTC 1959 Senior "B" League Winners.
Standing (l. to r.) Denis Young, Alan Smyth, Roy Hastings & Norman Penney.
Sitting (l. to r.) Elizabeth Ramsey, Audrey Roney, Olive Croskery & Ruth Abernethy.

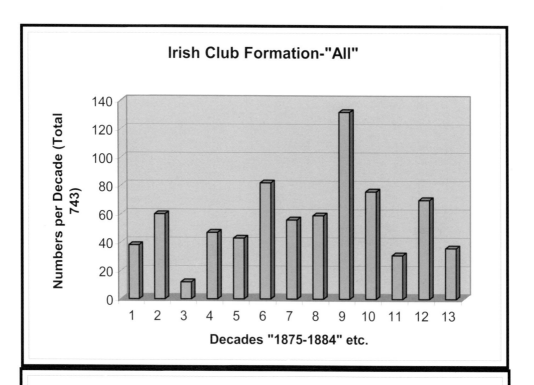

Irish Club Formation-"All"

Numbers per Decade (Total 743) vs Decades "1875-1884" etc.

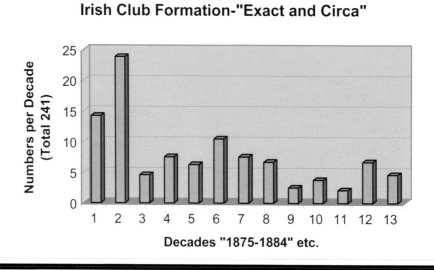

Irish Club Formation-"Exact and Circa"

Numbers per Decade (Total 241) vs Decades "1875-1884" etc.

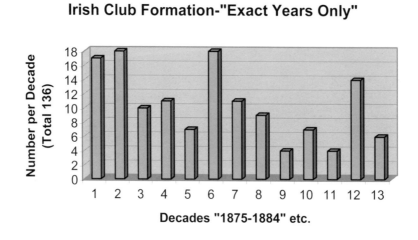

Irish Club Formation-"Exact Years Only"

Number per Decade (Total 136) vs Decades "1875-1884" etc.

1882	(c.)	Abbeyleix LTC
1956	(<)	Aer Lingus TC
1993	(<)	Ahare Park TC
1988	(<)	Aherlow LTC
1961	(<)	Ahoghill LTC
1993	(<)	AIB LTC
1956	(<)	Albert Foundry TC
1893	(<)	Alexandra College LTC
1935	(c.)	Alpha LTC
1949	(<)	Altona LTC
1925		Anglesea LTC
1923	(<)	Annadale LTC
1948	(<)	Annagh LTC
1936	(<)	Appletee LTC
1956	(<)	Ard na Greine LTC
1916		Ardee LTC
1927		Ardglass LTC
1936	(<)	Ardivere LTC
1973	(<)	Ardnacrusha LTC
1880	(c.)	Argideen Vale LT and Croquet Club
1921		Arklow LTC
1923	(<)	Armagh Archery and LTC
1880	(c.)	Armagh LTC
1927	(<)	Armagh Social TC
1973	(<)	Ashbourne TC
1922		Ashbrook LTC
1947	(<)	Ashley LTC
1973	(<)	Askeaton TC
1893	(c.)	Athboy LTC
1908	(<)	Athenry [County Galway] LTC
1885	(c.)	Athlone LT & Cricket Club
1895		Athlone LTC
1974	(<)	Athlone TC
1894		Athlone YMCA
1893	(c.)	Athy LTC
1956	(<)	Bagenalstown LTC
1993	(<)	Balbriggan TC
1934	(<)	Balinteer LTC
1951	(<)	Balla LTC
1976	(<)	Ballagh LTC
1943	(<)	Ballaghadeereen LTC
1938		Ballina LTC
1950	(<)	Ballinacarrigy LTC
1938		Ballinamore LTC
1938	(<)	Ballinasloe LTC
1952	(<)	Ballinasloe Mental Hospital LTC
1956	(<)	Ballindrait LTC
1953		Ballingaddy LTC
1955	(<)	Ballingarry LTC
1979	(c.)	Ballinlough LTC (Co.Cork)
1940	(<)	Ballinrobe TC
1999	(<)	Ballintubber & District TC
1960	(<)	Ballyarnett LTC
1955	(<)	Ballybay LTC

1928		Ballybofey-Stranorlar LTC
1906		Ballycastle LT [& Croquet] Club
1956	(<)	Ballyclare LTC
1980	(<)	Ballyconnell LTC
1973	(<)	Ballydehob TC
1938		Ballyfarnon LTC
1973	(<)	Ballygar LTC
2000	(<)	Ballygawley TC (County Tyrone)
2005	(<)	Ballyhooley TC
2000	(<)	Ballyhaunis TC
1960	(<)	Ballyjamesduff LTC
1955	(<)	Ballylanders LTC
1965	(c.)	Ballyleague-Lanesboro TC
1956	(<)	Ballylennon LTC
1920	(<)	Ballymena LTC
1922	(c.)	Ballymena Rugby Football Club-TS
1954	(<)	Ballymoe LTC
1900		Ballymote LTC
1961	(<)	Ballynafeigh Methodist Church LTC
1973	(<)	Ballypatrick Sports Centre-TS [BLTC]
1893	(c.)	Ballyshannon LTC (old)
1985		Ballyshannon TC (new)
1982	(<)	Balreask Old LTC
1976	(<)	Baltinglass LTC
1878		Banagher [King's County West] LTC
1890	(c.)	Banbridge LTC
1914	(<)	Bandon LTC
1927	(<)	Bangor Borough Council TC
1929	(<)	Bangor Cricket & Rugby Club-TS
1985	(c.)	Bangor Erris TC
1899		Bangor LTC
1954	(<)	Bansha LTC
1973	(<)	Bantry LTC
1991	(<)	Barna LTC
1921		Bective LTC [B. Rangers FC]
1923	(<)	Beechfield LTC
1924	(<)	Beechmount LTC
1927	(<)	Beechwood LTC
1898		Belfast Boat Club-TS
1936	(<)	Belfast Co-Op LTC
1947	(<)	Belfast High School LTC
1958	(<)	Belfast Insurance Offices LTC
1946	(<)	Belfast Jewish Institute LTC
1958	(<)	Belfast Royal Academy LTC
1927	(<)	Belfast YMCA LTC
1950	(<)	Belgrove LTC
1956	(<)	Bellaghy LTC
1999		Belleek TC
1976	(<)	Bellefield GAA Club-T.S.
1927	(<)	Belmont [B. Hockey & LTC] LTC
1946	(c.)	Belmullet LTC
1995		Belmullet TC
1960	(<)	Belturbet LTC
1908	(<)	Belvedere LTC

1956 (<)	Belvoir LTC	
1988 (<)	Bishopstown LTC	
1908 (<)	Blackrock LTC (Cork)	
1892 (c.)	Blackrock [Frascati] LTC (Dublin)	
1937	Blackrock LTC (Galway)	
1956 (<)	Bloomfield Presbyterian LTC	
1926 (<)	Bohemians LTC	
1934	Boyle Community Ass. TC [Boyle Catholic TC]	
1887	Boyle LTC	
1956 (<)	Braeside LTC	
1909 (c.)	Bray LTC	
1976 (<)	Bree LTC	
1995 (<)	Bridgeford LTC	
1894 (c.)	Brighton LTC [Brighton Square LTC]	
1992 (<)	Broadmills TC	
1956 (<)	Broadway Presbyterian LTC	
1906	Brookfield Recreation Club [Brookfield LTC]	
1909 (<)	Brooklyn LTC	
1920 (<)	Brownlow LTC	
1965 (<)	Brulla LTC	
1976 (<)	Bunclody LTC	
1961 (<)	Buncrana LTC	
1927 (<)	Buncrana Proprietary LTC	
1934	Burt LTC	
1956 (<)	Butt Hall [Ballybofey] TC	
1923 (<)	Cadogan Park LTC	
1950 (<)	Caherconlish LTC	
1890 (<)	Cahir LTC	
1934 (<)	Callan LTC	
1995 (<)	Canon Hayes Complex TC	
1993 (<)	Canovee LTC	
1973 (<)	Cappamore LTC	
1955 (<)	Cappawhite LTC	
1923 (<)	Carlisle LTC	
1878 (c.)	Carlow TC [Co. Carlow LTC] [Carlow Co. Cricket & LTC]	
1944 (<)	Carmel LTC	
1961	Carndonagh LTC	
1993 (<)	Carraig (Co.Dublin)	
1935 (c.)	Carrick on Shannon (Floods) TC	
1887	Carrick on Shannon LTC	
1892 (c.)	Carrick on Suir LTC	
1952 (<)	Carrickfergus Parish Church LTC	
1903	Carrickmines Croquet & LTC	
1988 (<)	Carrigaline LTC	
1956 (<)	Castle Espie LTC	
1923 (c.)	Castle LTC	
1893	Castle View LTC [Carrick on Suir LTC]	
1937	Castlebar TC	
1893 (c.)	Castleblaney LTC	
1973 (<)	Castleisland LTC	
1948 (<)	Castleknock College LTC	

1927	Castleknock LTC	
1906 (c.)	Castlepollard LTC	
1880 (c.)	Castlerea LTC [Clonalis LTC]	
1913 (c.)	Castlerock Golf Club-TS	
1909 (c.)	Catholic Institute (Limerick)	
1988 (<)	Causeway LTC (Co. Waterford)	
1923 (<)	Cavehill LTC [Cavehill Bowling & LTC]	
1962	Cavehill Methodist LTC	
1948 (<)	CBPPU LTC	
1925 (c.)	Celbridge & District LTC [Celbridge LTC]	
1963 (<)	Charleville LTC (County Cork)	
1894	Charleville LTC (Dublin)	
1996 (c.)	Cherryfield LTC	
1920 (<)	Cherrymount LTC	
1927 (<)	Chichester LTC	
1955 (<)	Church of Ireland (Cork) LTC	
1956 (<)	CIE LTC (Cork)	
1887	City of Belfast YMCA LTC	
1950 (<)	City of Derry LTC [Bayview LTC]	
1963 (<)	Civil Serv. (Imp.) Sports Ass. LTC	
1928 (<)	Civil Service LTC (Civil Service N.I.)	
1893 (c.)	Civil Service LTC (Dublin)	
1927 (<)	CIYMS LTC (Belfast)	
1972	Clane LTC	
1903 (<)	Claremont LTC	
1986	Claremont Railway Union & LT Club*	
1940 (<)	Claremorris LTC [St. Colman's LTC]	
1990	Claremorris TC (new)	
1973 (<)	Clareview LTC [Ballyclare LTC]	
1935 (<)	Clarinda LTC	
1956 (<)	Clarus LTC	
1927 (<)	Cliftonville Golf Club-TS	
1892 c.	Cliftonville LTC	
1955 (<)	Clogheen LTC	
1973 (<)	Clonakilty LTC	
1891 (c.)	Clones LTC	
1910 (<)	Clongowes Wood College	
1908 (<)	Clonmel LTC [South Tipperary LTC]	
1955 (<)	Clonmel Rowing Club	
1887	Clontarf LTC	
1935	Clontarf Parish Church LTC	
1929 (<)	Clooney LTC	
1993 (<)	Coachford (Co.Cork)	
1947	Coleraine LTC [The Aero Club]	
1986	Coleraine TC	
1973 (<)	Collen LTC (Co.Louth)	
1916 (<)	Collins Barracks TC [Cork Garrison LTC]	
1976 (<)	Colon LTC	
1956 (<)	Comber LTC	
1973 (<)	Constitution LTC	
1956 (<)	Convoy Presbyterian Church TC	
1985 (<)	Cootehill LTC	

1879 (c.)	Cork LTC		1920 (c.)	Drumcree LTC
1958 (<)	Corrib LTC		1938	Drumshanbo LTC
1956 (<)	County Borough of Belfast		1999 (<)	Drumsna TC
1883 c.	County Cavan LTC		1970 (<)	Du Pont LTC
1893 (c.)	County Clare LTC		1993 (<)	Dublin City University TC
1879 (c.)	County Down LTC		1914 (<)	Dublin Covered Courts Club
1877	County Limerick LTC		1927 (<)	Dublin Insurance LTC
1881	County Sligo LTC		1877	Dublin University (TCD) LTC
1892	County Westmeath LTC		1993 (<)	Duleek LTC
1893 (c.)	County Wexford LTC		1993 (<)	Dunboyne LTC
1880 (c.)	County Wicklow LTC		1956 (<)	Dundalk Rowing TC
	[Wicklow LTC]		1893 (c.)	Dundalk Tennis Bad. & Sq. C.
2002	Cratloe GAA Club-TS			[Dundalk LTC]
1956 (<)	Crawfordsburn County Club-TS		1890	Dundrum LTC
1923 (<)	Creag Athletic LTC		1910 (c.)	Dunedin LTC
1931 (<)	Cregagh Athletic Club-TS		1893 (c.)	Dungannon LTC
1973 (<)	Croagh (Limerick)		1923 (<)	Dungarvan LTC
1950 (<)	Croom LTC		1960 (<)	Dungloe LTC
1914 (<)	Crosshaven & Currabinny LTC		1976 (<)	Dunleer LTC
1948	Crossmolina TC		1961 (<)	Dunmanway LTC
	[St.Tiernan's L.T. & Croquet Club]		1993 (<)	Dunmore East TC
1908 (<)	Croydon LTC		1927 (<)	Dunmore LTC
1975 (<)	Culdaff LTC		1985 (<)	Dunmore LTC (County Galway)
1966 (<)	Cullybackey LTC		1923 (<)	Dunmurray LTC
1911 (<)	Curragh Camp LTC		1938 (<)	Dunranay LTC
1995 (<)	Curraha LTC		1973 (<)	Dunshaughlin LTC
1942 (<)	CYMS (Harrington Street) LTC		1928 (c.)	Easons LTC
1946 (<)	CYMS (Terenure) LTC		1909 (<)	Eaton Square LTC
1945 (<)	CYMS Recreation Club (L'kenny)		1962 (<)	Edenderry Golf Club
1924 (C.)	Dalkey LTC		1925	Edenderry LTC (Leinster)
1990	David Lloyd Riverview		1922	Edenderry LTC (Ulster)
	[Riverview Racq. & Fitness Club]		1956 (<)	Edenderry Mem. Rec. Guild LTC
1895	De Vesci LTC		1995 (<)	Edgeworthstown TC
1977	Deerpark LTC		1973 (<)	Eglinton LTC
1956 (<)	Derriaghy Cricket & TC		1925	Elm Park Golf & Sports Club Ltd.
1956 (<)	Doagh (DMRC) LTC		1973 (<)	Elphin LTC
1947 (<)	Donaghadee LTC		1972	Emly TC
1956 (<)	Donagheady Presby. Church TC		1892 (c.)	Ennis LT & Badminton Club*
1956 (<)	Donaghmore LTC		1893 (c.)	Enniscorthy
	[Donoughmore LTC]		1935 (c.)	Enniscrone LTC
1950 (<)	Donegal LTC [Donegal Town LTC]		1881	Enniskillen LTC
1947 (<)	Donegall Square LTC		1968	Erin's Isle TC
1893	Donnybrook LTC		1973	ESB LTC (Dublin)
1927	Douglas TC		1974 (c.)	ESB Social Club (Portlaoise)
	[Civil Service Hockey & TC]		2000 (<)	Esker (Clara) TC
1881 (<)	Downshire TC		1936 (<)	Ewart's LTC [Ewart's Recr. Ass.]
	[Downshire Archery & LTC]		1944 (<)	F.W. Woolworth LTC
1965 (<)	Downshire-Hillsborough TC		1934 (<)	Fairview CYMS TC
	[Downshire LTC]		1927 (<)	Falls [Falls Bowling & LTC] TC
1970 (<)	Drangan LTC		1929 (<)	Felix LTC
1936 (<)	Drimnagh LTC		1935 (c.)	Fergus LTC
1956 (<)	Drogheda LTC		1892 (c.)	Fermoy LTC [Straw Hall LTC]
1963 (<)	Dromahane LTC (Mallow)		1973 (<)	Ferns (Co.Wexford)
1893 (c.)	Drumcondra LTC		1928 (<)	Fernvale LTC

1973 (<)	Fethard LTC
2000 (c.)	Fintona TC
1961 (<)	First Dromore Presb. Ch. LTC
1877	Fitzwilliam LTC [Dublin LTC]
1931	Forth River TC
	[Forth River Bowling & LTC]
1927 (<)	Fortreda LTC
1936	Fountainstown LTC (Co.Cork)
1928 (c.)	Foxford LTC
1973 (<)	Foyle College LTC
1927 (<)	Foyle View LTC
1925 (<)	Gallery LTC
1936	Galway Commercial Boat Club-TS
1900	Galway LT [& Croquet] Club
1947 (<)	Garda TC [Brugh na Garda LTC]
1884	Garden Vale LT & Croquet Club
1990 (<)	Garryduff LTC (Co.Cork)
1956 (<)	Garvagh LTC (Co. Londonderry)
1921 (<)	Garville LTC
1956 (<)	Gilnahirk LTC [Giln. Pres. Ch. Rec. C.]
1892 (c.)	Glanmire LT [& Croquet] Club
1973 (<)	Glasheen LTC
1909	Glasnevin LTC
1887	Glenageary [& Kingstown] LTC
1971 (<)	Glenalbyn LTC
1954 (<)	Glenanaar LTC
1956 (<)	Glenanne LTC
1929 (<)	Glenarm LTC
1999 (<)	Glenarm LTC
1956 (<)	Glendermott TC
1973 (<)	Glin LTC
1921 (<)	Gorey LTC
1967	Gorey TC
1956 (<)	Gortmerron LTC
1958 (<)	Gortnessy LTC
1936 (<)	Graigavad LTC
1956 (<)	Greenisland War Memorial
	Community Centre TC
1893 (c.)	Greystones LT [& Croquet] Club
1893 (c.)	Grosvenor LTC
1959	Grove LTC (Malahide)
1963 (<)	Grove LTC (Tandragee)
1945 (<)	Guinness LTC
1939 (c.)	Hacketstown LTC
1961 (<)	H.M.S. Sea Eagle (L'derry) LTC
1927	Hawarden LTC
1962 (<)	Hazelbrook LTC
1973 (<)	Helens Bay LTC
1955 (<)	Herbert Park LTC
1893 (c.)	High School LTC
1973 (<)	Highfield LTC
1946 (<)	Hilden TC [Hilden Bowling & LTC]
1961 (<)	Hillbrook LTC (Enniscorthy)
1940 (<)	Hillsboro LTC (Cork)
1935	Hillview Sports Club [Clonmel LTC]

1928 (<)	Hinton LTC
1961 (<)	Hollerith [Hollerith Tabular] TC
1963 (<)	Hollymount LTC (Midleton)
1893 (c.)	Holywood LTC (County Down)
1976 (<)	Horeswood LTC
1927	Hospital LTC (Co.Limerick)
1978	Hospital TC (Letterkenny)
1955 (<)	ICICYMA (Cork)
1910 (<)	Ida LTC
1909	Ierne LTC
1963 (<)	Imperial Civil Service LTC
1934 (<)	Imperial Tobacco Company LTC
1942 (<)	Independent TC [Indep. News LTC]
1993 (<)	Inniscarra LTC (Co.Cork)
1894 (c.)	Innishannon LTC
1998	Institute of Technology (Sligo) TC
1923 (<)	Instonians LTC
1999 (<)	International LTC
1993 (<)	Irish Evergreens TC
1927 (<)	Irish Times LTC
1991	Irvinestown LTC (new)
1942	Irvinestown LTC (old)
1955 (<)	Islandbridge LTC
1927	Jewish Social & LTC
1973 (<)	Jordanstown LTC
1910 (<)	Kanturk LTC
1998 (<)	Kells LTC
1892 (c.)	Kenilworth LTC
1927 (<)	Kensington LTC
1927 (<)	Kensington LTC
1994 (<)	Kerry Pike TC (Co.Cork)
1956 (<)	Keshends LTC (Donegal)
1948 (<)	Killmessan LTC
1976 (<)	Kilbarry LTC
1993 (<)	Kilbeggan LTC
2000 (<)	Kilcormac LTC
1976 (<)	Kilcullen LTC
1976 (<)	Kildalkey LTC
1998 (<)	Kilfeacle (Co.Tipperary)
1973 (<)	Kilfinane LTC
1933 (<)	Kilkeel LTC
1879	Kilkenny [County & City] LTC
1929 (<)	Kilkenny CYMS LTC
1948 (<)	Killaloe/Ballina [Co.Clare] LTC
1993 (<)	Killarney LTC
1973 (<)	Killedy LTC
1955 (<)	Killenaule LTC
1923 (<)	Killiney LTC
1928	Kilmallock LTC
1982 (<)	Kilmeade LTC
1993 (<)	Kilrush TC
1940 (<)	Kilsheelan LTC (old)
1993 (<)	Kilsheelan TC
1975 (<)	Kiltane LTC
1990 (<)	Kilternan Country Club-TS

1993	(<)	Kilternan Parish TC
1957	(<)	Kiltimagh LTC [Streamstown LTC]
1992	(<)	Kiltonga (Bangor)
1973	(<)	Kilworth TC
1929	(<)	Kinedar LTC
1930		Kingscourt LTC
1963	(<)	Kingsland TC
1911	(<)	Kingstown Pavilion Committee LTC
1894	c.	Kingstown School LTC
1993	(<)	Kingswood TC (Co. Dublin)
1970	(<)	Kinnegad TC
1913	(<)	Kinsale LTC
1923	(<)	Knock LTC
1956	(<)	Knockbreda LTC
		[Knockbreda Youth Guild TC]
1988		Lakewood TC
1875		Lansdowne LTC
		[Irish Champion Athletic Club]
1973	(<)	Larkspur Park TC
1956	(<)	Larne Borough Council
1923	(<)	Larne Bowling and Tennis Club
1962	(<)	Larne Methodist LTC
1952		Lattin LTC
1907		Laytown & Bettystown LTC
1956	(<)	Leaslands LTC
1988		Lee LTC
1912	(<)	Leinster Cricket Club LTC
1950	(<)	Leinster-Stratford LTC
2000	(<)	Leixlip TC
1982	(<)	Leopardstown TC
1973	(<)	Letterkenny (High Road) LTC
1993		Letterkenny Tennis Centre
1955	(c.)	Letterkenny Town TC ["Tourist" TC]
		["High Road" TC][CYMS-TS]
1928	(<)	Limavady Recreation TC [Lim.LTC]
1950	(<)	Limerick Prot.Yng. Men's Ass. LTC
1970	(<)	Ling Physical Training College LTC
1911	(<)	Lismore LTC
1996		Lisnaskea LTC (new)
1959	(<)	Lisnaskea LTC (old)
1973	(<)	Listowel LTC
1894	(c.)	Londonderry LTC
1957	(<)	Londonderry RUC TC
1932	(<)	Longford Gardens LTC
1896		Longford TC
		[Co. Longford LTC][Longford LTC]
1973	(<)	Longwood LTC
1955	(<)	Loughrea LTC
1973	(<)	Lourdes LTC
1961	(<)	Lower Aghada LTC
1956	(<)	LPYMA
1891	(c.)	Lucan LTC
1938	(<)	Lucerne LTC
1881	(<)	Lurgan LTC

1936	(<)	Lynn Memorial TC
1929	(<)	Magee LTC
1980	(<)	Maghera
1931	(<)	Maine Wks. Am. Recr. Club-TS
1946	(c.)	Malahide Junior LTC
1879		Malahide LT & Croquet Club
1893	(c.)	Mallow LTC
		[Mallow LT & Croquet Club]
1993	(<)	Malone LTC
1929	(<)	Malone Presbyterian Church TC
1998	(<)	Manorhamilton LTC
1940	(<)	Marian Arts Society TC
1894	(c.)	Marmullane LTC
1956	(<)	Maryboro LTC
1956	(<)	May Street Church
1937	(<)	Mayfield LTC
1961	(<)	McQuiston LTC
		[McQuiston Presb.Church LTC]
1993	(<)	Meadowvale TC
1986		Melmount TC
1991	(<)	Merlin Park Hospital TC
1891	(<)	Merrion LTC
1907	(c.)	Merville LTC
1990	(<)	Midleton LTC
1973	(<)	Milford LTC (Cork)
1975	(<)	Milltown LTC
1973	(<)	Minnowburn LTC
1891	(c.)	Mitchelstown LTC
1893		Moate LTC
1889		Mohill LTC
1908	(<)	Monaghan LTC
1994		Monaleen GAA TC
1931	(<)	Monkstown Cricket Club
1880	(c.)	Monkstown LT and Croquet Club
1877		Monkstown LTC (Dublin)
1948	(<)	Mossley LTC
1893		Mount Crozier LTC
1893		Mount Pleasant LTC
1956		Mount Temple -Kenilworth LTC*
1893	(c.)	Mount Temple LTC
1893	(c.)	Mountjoy Square LTC
1908	(<)	Mountmellick LTC
1973	(<)	Moyglass LTC
1993	(<)	Moyle TC (Ballycastle)
1992	(<)	Moynalty LTC
1973	(<)	Muckamore Abbey LTC
1973	(<)	Muckamore Abbey LTC
1908		Muckamore Cricket & L T C
		[Muckamore Cricket Club]
1901		Mullingar Parocial Ass. LTC
1939		Mullingar Town LTC
1881	(<)	Muskerry LT [& Croquet] Club
1881		Naas [County Kildare] LTC
1912	(<)	Navan TC [County Meath LTC]

1880	(c.)	Nenagh LT [& Croquet] Club
1930	(c.)	Nenagh LTC (town)
1952		Nenagh LTC*
1993	(<)	Nethercross LTC
1912	(<)	Nettleville LTC
1955	(<)	New Inn LTC
1973	(<)	New Ross LTC
1973		New University of Ulster (Col.) TC
1956	(<)	Newbridge [St.Conleth's] LTC
1911	(c.)	Newcastle LTC
		[Newcastle LT & Croquet Club]
1956	(<)	Newcastle Urban District Council
1961	(<)	Newcastle West LTC
1992	(<)	Newline LTC
1962	(<)	Newport LTC (Co.Mayo)
1973	(<)	Newport LTC (Co.Tipperary)
1947	(<)	Newry Catholic LTC
1914	(<)	Newry LTC
1997	(<)	Newtown Park TC
1959	(<)	Newtowncunningham LTC
1931	(<)	Ninth Belfast Old Boys Ass. LTC
1947	(<)	North Kildare LTC
1882	(c.)	North of Ireland LTC
1929	(<)	Norwood LTC (Belfast)
1920	(<)	Norwood LTC (Dublin)
1952		O'Donnell Park LTC
1956	(<)	Old Bleach LTC [Old Bleach Soc. & Ath. Cl.]
1908	(<)	Olney LTC
1882		Omagh LTC [County Tyrone LTC]
1927	(<)	Ophir LTC
1927	(<)	Orangefield LTC
1879		Ormond LTC [King's County & Ormond LTC]
1973	(<)	Oughterard LTC
1929	(<)	Palmerston LTC
1929	(<)	Park LTC
1950	(<)	Passage West LTC
1908		Percy LTC
1956	(<)	Phoenix LTC (Derry)
1882	(<)	Phoenix LTC
		[Phoenix Cricket Club-TS]
1943	(<)	Pioneer LTC
2001		Portadown TC
1931	(<)	Portaferry LTC
1956	(<)	Portarlington LTC
1993	(<)	Portlaoise LTC
1931	(<)	Portrush LTC
1956	(<)	Portrush Urban District Council
1956	(<)	Portstewart Golf Club - TS
1943	(<)	Portumna LTC
1940	(<)	Presbyterian Association LTC
1976	(<)	Prosperous LTC
1993	(<)	PSLC LTC (Portmarnock)
2000	(<)	Puckaun TC
1973	(<)	QUB Staff LTC
1927	(<)	Queen's Island LTC
1947	(<)	Queen's University (Belfast) LTC
1912	(<)	Quoile [Quoile-Downpatrick] LTC
1959	(<)	RAF Aldergrove LTC
1959	(<)	RAF Ballykelly LTC
1995	(<)	Raheny LTC
1908	(<)	R'way [& Steam Packet] Un. LTC
1950		Ramelton LTC
1895	(c.)	Ranelagh School LTC (Athlone)
1950	(<)	Raphoe [Raphoe Royal] LTC
1956	(<)	Raphoe Close LTC
2004	(<)	Rathbane LTC
1999	(c.)	Rathdangan LTC
1956	(<)	Rathdowney LTC
1921	(<)	Rathgar LTC
1985		Rathgar LTC (new)
1993	(<)	Rathkeale LTC
1982	(<)	Rathmore LTC
1956	(<)	Ray LTC [Ray Presby. LTC]
		[Manorcunningham LTC]
1940		Rectory LTC (Letterkenny)
1958	(c.)	Rectory LTC (Birr)
1960	(<)	Rectory LTC (Dundalk)
1992	(<)	Rendezvous LTC
1969		Riversdale TC
1988	(<)	Rockfield LTC
1955	(<)	Rosanna LTC
1928	(<)	Rosario LTC
1950	(c.)	Roscommon Hospital LTC
1913		Roscommon LTC
		[Roscommon Town LTC]
1893	(c.)	Roscrea [Ashbury] LTC
1927	(<)	Royal Belfast Golf Club
1960	(<)	Royal Belfast LTC
1994	(<)	Royal College of Surgeons In Ireland LTC
1939	(<)	Royal North of Ireland Yacht Club
1973	(<)	Royal Victoria Hospital LTC
1923	(<)	Rugby Road LTC
1925	(<)	Rush LTC
1880	(c.)	Rushbrooke LT & Croquet Club [Queenstown LTC]
1935	(<)	Rutland LTC
1951	(<)	Saltz Ireland Ltd TC
1886		Sandycove Tennis & Squash Club [Sandycove LTC]
1956	(<)	Sandyford LTC
1894	(c.)	Sandymount LTC
1950	(c.)	Seagoe LTC
1982	(<)	Seneschalstown LTC (Navan)
1973	(<)	Shanakiel LTC
1994	(<)	Shanco LTC
1943	(<)	Shandon LTC (Dublin)
1986		Shankill LTC
1973	(<)	Shannon LTC
1930	(c.)	Shelbourne LTC

1970	(<) Sion Mills Recreation Centre TC
1924	(c.) Skerries LTC
1973	(<) Skibbereen LTC
1973	(<) Skryne LTC
1913	(c.) Slaney LTC
1978	Sligo [County Sligo] TC
1956	(<) South Tipperary LTC (Clonmel)
1991	(<) Spawell LTC
1925	(c.) St. Andrews LTC
1887	(c.) St. Anne's LTC
1955	(c.) St. Anne's Waterford LTC*
1920	St. Augustine's LTC
1976	(<) St. Brigid's LTC
1880	(c.) St. Columba's College
1976	(<) St. Conleth's LTC
1929	(<) St. Donard's LTC
	[St. Donard's Church LTC]
1973	(<) St. Finbarr's LTC
1953	(c.) St. Johnston LTC
1988	(<) St. Laurence's LTC (Dungarvan)
1935	(<) St. Luke's LTC
1950	(c.) St. Malachy's LTC (Coleraine)
1950	(<) St. Mary's Ch. of Irl. LTC (Athlone)
1948	(c.) St. Mary's College LTC
1973	(<) St. Mary's LTC (Co.Cork)
1961	(<) St. Mary's LTC (Kanturk)
1959	(<) St. Mary's LTC (Magherafelt)
1961	(<) St. Mary's LTC [Magerafelt LTC]
1934	St. Mel's LTC
1955	(<) St. Michael's LTC
1973	(<) St. Nicholas' LTC
1973	(<) St. Patrick's LTC (Lisburn)
1973	(<) St. Patrick's Racquets Club
	[St. Patrick's LTC]
1946	(<) St. Patrick's TC (Newtownabbey)
1956	(<) St. Polycarps TC
1986	(c.) St. Stephen's (Hospital) LTC
1951	Stackallen L T & Pitch & Putt C.
1956	(<) Strabane LTC
1990	Strandhill TC
1936	(<) Strandtown LTC
1963	(<) Stranmills College TC
1920	(<) Stranorlar LTC
1993	(<) Stratford LTC
1940	Strokestown LTC
1927	(<) Strollers LTC
1947	(<) Strugglers LTC
1993	(<) Summerhill LTC
1890	Sunday's Well Boating & LTC
1882	Sutton LTC [Howth LTC]
1945	Swinford LTC
1993	(<) Swords TC
1923	(<) Sydenham LTC
1973	(<) Tagmon LTC
1973	(<) Tallow LTC

1943	(<) Taney LTC
1993	(<) Taney Parish LTC
1993	(<) Tara LTC
1995	(<) Tara Mines TC
1995	(<) Teconnaught LTC
1995	(<) Temple Country Club-TS
1963	(<) Temple Hill LTC
1956	(<) Templecorran LTC
1977	(<) Templemore LTC
1906	Templeogue LTC
1973	(<) Templepatrick Presbyterian Church
1994	(<) The Bridge LTC
1993	(<) The Park LTC
1940	(<) The Pavilion LTC
1981	The Veterans' LTC of Ireland
1973	(<) Thomastown LTC
1922	(<) Thorndale LTC
1880	(c.) Tipperary County LTC
	[County Tipperary LTC]
1973	C. Toomevara LTC
1931	(<) Torca LTC
1995	(<) Tower Street LTC
1911	Trackside LTC
1911	(<) Tralee Green LTC
1956	(<) Tralee LTC**
1909	(<) Tralee Sports Field LTC
1921	Tramore LTC
1956	(<) Trim LTC
1912	(<) Tritonville LTC
1948	(<) Troy LTC
1938	(<) Tuam LTC
1947	(<) Tudor LTC
1880	Tullamore LTC
1956	(<) Tullow LTC
1962	(<) Ulster Coll. of Physical Education Tennis Club (Newtownabbey)
1956	(<) Ulster Transport Authority Bowling & Tennis Club
1893	(c.) Univ. Coll. Galway LTC [Queen's College LTC]
1956	(<) University College Cork LTC
1927	(<) University College Dublin LTC [National University LTC]
2001	(<) UCD Staff & Post-Graduates TC
1998	(c.) University of Limerick TC
1981	(<) Ursuline LTC (Cabinteely)
1922	(c.) Victoria Barracks LTC
1933	Victoria College (Belfast)
1954	(<) Virginia LTC
1938	(<) W.R. Jacob & Company LTC
1923	(c.) Ward Park LTC
1922	(c.) Warrenpoint LTC
1959	(<) Warrenpoint Parish Church LTC
2003	Waterford Institute of Technology TC
1879	(c.) Waterford LTC

	(<)	Weston LTC
1935	(c.)	Westport TC
1919	(<)	Westwood
		[St. Columba's [Squash &] LTC]
2000	(c.)	Westwood LTC -Fairview
1883		Wexford Harbour Boat and TC
1911		Wexford LTC
1998	(<)	Whitechurch LTC
1936	(<)	Whitehead LTC
		[Whitehead Presby. Ch.LTC
1956	(<)	Wicklow LTC
		[Wicklow Town LTC]
1928		Willowfield LTC
1956	(<)	Willowfield Parish Church TC
1930	(<)	Wilmer LTC [Birr LTC]
1879	c.	Wilton LTC
1946	(<)	Windro LTC
1901		Windsor LTC (Belfast)
1963	(<)	Windsor LTC (Lurgan)
1919	(<)	Woodbrook LTC
1973	(<)	Woodlands LTC
1947	(<)	Woodvale LTC
		[Woodvale Cricket & LTC]
1936		Woodville LTC
1910		YMCA LTC (Co.Dublin)
1934	(c.)	YMCA LTC (Sligo)
1893		Youghal LTC

[ ] **Alternative club name**

( ) **Location of club**

** **Resurrected club (probably)**

* **Amalgamated club**

(C.) **Approximate year of foundation**

(<) **Founded on or before the year specified**

TS **Tennis Section**

TC **Tennis Club**

LTC **Lawn Tennis Club**

Eileen Dundee, Mrs. Tess O'Connor and Peter Jackson at Galway Lawn Tennis Club during the interprovincial series in 1956.

Action during the Irish Open at Fitzwilliam LTC.

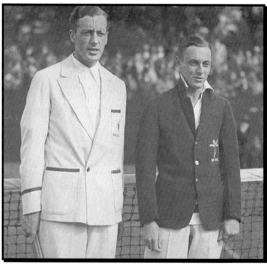

Ned McGuire (left) before his 1931 Davis Cup match against Vernon Kirby (South Africa) at Fitzwilliam LTC. Kirby won 4/6 6/3 7/5 7/5.

Lansdowne Lawn Tennis Club
[Irish Champion Athletic Club]
(Founded 1875)

It has been said that **Lansdowne LTC** was the oldest club in Ireland, being founded one year after the game was "invented". This would be, therefore, in 1875, two years before the other father figures of Dublin University, Limerick, Monkstown and Fitzwilliam. Assume, for a moment, some connection, perhaps incorrectly, with Lansdowne Rugby Football Club. This club was founded in 1872 as was also known as the "Irish Champion Athletic Club" and "Lansdowne Road". Would the 'pastime' of lawn tennis that came into being in 1874 be regarded by footballers as a suitable distraction at the time? Apparently yes. There was a connection with Dublin University, as in the case of many sports in Ireland at the time. Two books which identify the origins of this club are Trevor West' *The Bold Collegians* (1991) and *The Politics of Irish Athletics 1850-1990* by Padraig Griffin in 1990. Both excellent publications are worthy of a read.

The 'short' version of the story is as follows. A Trinity man called A.W. Dunlop in 1872 founded the Irish Champion Athletic Club (ICAC). The January 18th 1873 edition of *Irish Sportsman* declared that:

> *After a due period of incubation a new Athletic Club has burst into existence with the lofty title of the Irish Champion Athletic Club. The founding has all the appearance of vigorous life about it and the patronage under which it make's its appearance gives it every reasonable chance of a long and prosperous career.*

Eighteen patrons were named including Sir Arthur Guinness, Mr. H.W.D. Dunlop and 'representatives of the principal towns'. The first athletic meeting was held in July 1873 at College Park (i.e. in the grounds of Trinity College). It seems to have been well supported and Tom Davin had a high jump of 5 foot 10¼, *the best amateur jump to date.*

The club were hoping to have a 'running path' at College Park but in 1872, at a meeting of the University's Athletic Club, this proposal was defeated by 27 votes to 26, as it would interfere with other uses of the park. Trevor West takes up the story:

Although the club's officers (i.e. ICAC) *were mainly Trinity men, it had no formal connection with the college, and Dunlop was forced to look elsewhere. Regarding itself as "a National Club and not the product of mere rivalry", ICAC aimed to lease some land "of which the centre will be a cricket ground and the remainder used for the laying down of a proper 'cinder running path' now recognised as essential for really good athletic performances". Having investigated premises at Sydney Parade and Sandymount, Dunlop obtained a 69-year lease from the Earl of Pembroke of ground "near Lansdowne Road Station", and proceeded to develop a sporting complex with facilities for tennis, archery, cricket,* croquet and football, as well as a cinder track. Thus the Lansdowne Football Club (1872), initially composed principally of Trinity men, has athletic origins. ICAC was dissolved in 1881, it's last days marred by a financial dispute involving Michael Cusack. Since 1907 the Lansdowne Road ground has been the headquarters of the Irish Rugby Football Union.

In December 1873 the ICAC purchased 8¼ acres and a cinder track of 578 yards in circumference was laid down. The Viceroy officially opened it on May 23rd 1874. That same year Michael Cusack came from County Clare to live in Blackrock in County Dublin. He would be involved in athletics and later the founding of the Gaelic Athletics Association (GAA). At the new Lansdowne sports, in 1875, Maurice Davin won the hammer and the shot and George Kenny of Galway, a student at Clongowes Wood College, won the long jump with a leap of 22 feet 10 inches. He was six feet tall and fourteen stone in weight. Unfortunately, in 1876, while a student at Trinity College, he caught typhus and died prematurely.

One assumes that as part of the sports complex, tennis was introduced in a reasonably short time after Major Wingfield first patented the new sport in February 1874. By 1875 very large numbers of his sets (sold for 5 guineas) were distributed. The 5th edition of his booklet (which came with the boxed set of balls, racquets and net) would claim that they had been sold to 11 princes and princesses, 7 dukes, 14 marquesses, 3 marchionesses, 54 earls, 6 countesses, 105 viscounts, 41 barons, 44 ladies, 44 honourables, 5 right honourables, and 55 baronets and knights. Even in the first year a set had travelled to Hobart, Tasmania. Most likely, a set was purchased and in use at Lansdowne in 1875. While **Fitzwilliam LTC** held the premier position in the early days of tennis, **Limerick Lawn** would do so in the South of Ireland and **County Sligo LTC** in the West of Ireland. In Dublin, a club to grow and challenge the might of Fitzwilliam was **Lansdowne LTC**. With the evolvement of Lansdowne, through an athletics club in the beginning, it appears that there were a few years when not that much happened. However, by the sixth Irish Championships in 1884, the club was obviously active. In that year, H. K. McKay was the first representative of the club to play in this major event. He won his first match beating R. S. Templar of **Fitzwilliam LTC** 6/0 6/3 6/3. He then went and beat F. F. McClintock (**Fitzwilliam LTC**) when he *again showed really good form....winning his match easily* (6/2 6/1 6/3).

His next opponent, in a field of 39, was J. Dwight of the Longwood Cricket Club, Boston. The American club would, six years later, be the host for the first ever Davis Cup tie. He beat Dwight three sets to love. On investigation it appears that McKay's opponent was none other than Dr. James Dwight, the founding father of the US Lawn Tennis Association on the 21st May 1881. In August 1874, according to Lance Tingay's publication in 1983, Dr. Dwight played the first game of lawn tennis in the USA with F. R. Sears on a court at Nahant, Massachusetts.

'Clubs' at the Early Irish Championships	
First Year Entered	**Affiliation**
1880	3rd Dragoons
1879	82nd Regiment
1880	84th Regiment
1880	A.M.D.
1883	Abbeyleix LTC
1880	All-England LTC
1882	Arduli
1881	Armagh LTC
1883	Ayrshire LTC
1884	Biarritz LTC
1884	Cambridge University LTC
1883	Castlerea LTC
1883	Charterhouse LTC
1880	Cheltenham LTC
1884	Clifton LTC
1880	Co.Down LTC
1880	Cork LTC
1879	County Carlow LTC
1879	Dublin University LTC
1884	Edgbaston LTC
1879	Fitzwilliam LTC
1881	Frascati Club
1879	Grenadier Guards
1881	Hooton LTC
1883	Kilkenny LTC
1883	Kingstown LTC
1884	Lansdowne LTC
1884	Longwood CC (USA)
1880	Maida Vale LTC
1884	Mallow LTC
1884	Marylebone C.C.
1879	Monkstown LTC
1884	Newport (USA)
1883	North of Ireland LTC
1884	Old Carthusians LTC
1884	Parsonstown LTC
1882	Phoenix C.C.
1881	Prince's LTC
1881	Queen's Bays
1881	R.H.A.
1882	Roscommon Club
1884	Rushbrooke LTC
1881	St. Columba's College
1883	The Buffs
1881	Tullamore
1880	Waterford LTC
1881	West Middlesex
1881	Wicklow Club
1880	Wilton LTC
1883	Wimbledon Close LTC
1884	Worchester Park LTC

McKay went on to beat W. J. Hamilton of the **Phoenix Cricket Club** in the fourth round. This was *a long and extremely tedious match*, which McKay won by three sets to one. (6/2 7/5 6/8 6/4). His opponent was probably Willoughby James Hamilton who was 19 at time and would, six years later, be the first Irishman to win the Wimbledon championships. In the fifth round Mc Kay was no match for Eyre Chatterton of **Fitzwilliam LTC** losing 1/6 1/6 1/6. This was effectively the semi-final. Chatterton then lost the All-

Comer's final to Herbert Lawford, the latter beating Ernest Renshaw (the holder) in straight sets in the Challenge Round. In 1884 he played in the doubles with Tom Campion of the Lansdowne club. In their first match they beat a pair from the **Ayrshire LTC** (6/4 7/5), then a pair from **Wilton LTC** (6/2 5/7 6/0) before losing to Lawford and Browne (1/6 2/6) in the 'third round', effectively the semi-final. McKay set the pattern for the Lansdowne Club and with a few years they were to have many successful players. Two years later McKay and Hamilton played together in the Irish Championships and took the title. They beat Toler R. Garvey (**Parsonstown LTC**) and Eyre Chatterton (**Fitzwilliam LTC**). (4/6 7/5 6/2 6/2). Dr. Joshua Pim and Frank Stoker of **Lansdowne LTC** won many major titles over the next decade or so.

Some Early Club Champions at Lansdowne LTC	
1891	**Joshua Pim**
1892	**Frank Stoker**
1893	**Joshua Pim**

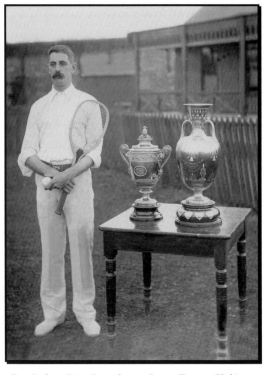

Dr. Joshua Pim (Lansdowne Lawn Tennis Club) was the greatest of Irish players. At his peak he was the undisputed number 1 player in the world of lawn tennis. He was in the Wimbledon singles final for four consecutive years, winning two. The above photograph was taken in 1893 or 1894 when he won the 'double', the Irish and All-England titles. Joshua and fellow club member, Frank Owen Stoker, were the best doubles pairing in the world. Between 1890 and 1895 they won five Irish and two 'English' Championships (i.e. Wimbledon). Frank played rugby for Wanderers R.F.C. and earned five Irish caps (1886 to 1891).

In the first Irish handbook of 1894, we see that Pim was club champion in 1893. Stoker would win the "County Dublin" championships at Lansdowne in 1894. He was a cousin of the well-known writer, Bram Stoker, the creator of 'Dracula'. The **Carrickmines Croquet & Lawn Tennis Club** having been running the County Dublin Championships since 1908. It appears, from their records, that it was first played at **Lucan LTC** in 1892 and then moved to Lansdowne, was abandoned in the early 1900s, due to lack of entries, and then revived by the south Dublin club.

The 1894 Championships at Lansdowne, held a week after the Irish Championships (starting on the 30th May) have been recorded and are as follows:

1894 County Dublin Championships

Event	First	Second
Championship Men's Singles	Frank Stoker	D. S. Chaytor
Men's H'cap S.	Harold Mahony	D. S. Chaytor
Men's H'cap S. (2nd class)	S. Fry	W. W. Goodbody
Men's H'cap D	O.R. McMullen/ S. H. Hughes	Joshua Pim/ P. C. Smyly
Ladies H'cap S.	Miss Snook	Miss Shaw
Mixed H'cap Doubles	W.H. Boyd/ Miss Boyd	O. R. McMullen/ Miss Shaw

The 1985 list of Open Tournaments did not include an event at Lansdowne.

Padraig Mulvihill President Lansdowne LTC 1998

Sir William Orphen recalled, in *Stories of Old Ireland & Myself* in 1925, travelling to Lansdowne, in the 1890s, to see some of the top players in the world in action. Joshua Pim was Wimbledon champion in 1893 and 1894 and, with Frank Stoker, won the doubles championship in 1890 and 1893. Pim won the Irish championships in 1893, 1894 and 1895 while the pair won the Irish doubles championships five times in the years 1890 to 1895.

Then, a little later, I used to get up early in the mornings and go and watch Jos. Pim, the amateur champion of the world, being trained by Burke at Lansdowne Road. People were real amateurs in those days, and Pim used to play with Burke at eight o'clock in the morning before his day's work began. That was the only time he could afford for tennis. Pim and Stoker, what a pair! Our little chests swelled out with pride when we mentioned them. Oh, it's true, young Ireland took its lawn tennis very seriously in those far-off days. We played every spare moment we had, till it was too dark for the eyes to follow the ball at all. Then we would retire to the little country club-house and talk "high" lawn tennis till the stars came out, and the corncrakes ceased their love-calls from the long grass of the fields round the courts. Then off to bed, to dream maybe of a back-hand drive with a top spin that was perfection. (Burke was the first man to hit the ball just before it reached the full height of its bounce, with a top spin and a "carry through").

Team Competition

Lansdowne have an exceptional record when it comes to team competition. In 1891 the Fitzwilliam club put up two trophies in the form of a Senior Cup and a Junior Cup. In 1892 Lansdowne won the Senior Cup, and the following year lost 5/4 to **Fitzwilliam LTC**. The winning team contained the three Chaytor brothers. The Lansdowne team included the Goodbody brothers, Joshua Pim and Frank Stoker in their team of six. Like many league matches, it went down to the wire. In the third men's doubles, there were six

Lansdowne LTC-Club Champions

	Men' Singles	Women's Singles		Men' Singles	Women's Singles
1900	R. M. Graham		1956	Harry Barniville	Heather Flinn
1902	William St. George Perrott		1957	Raymund Egan	Norah Conway
1903	R. M. Graham		1958	D. O'C. Miley	June Anne Fitzpatrick
1904	R. M. Graham		1959	Michael Hickey	Mary O'Sullivan
1905	R. M. Graham		1960	Michael Hickey	Joan Morton
1906	Shirley Dillon		1961	John O'Brien	June Anne Fitzpatrick
1907	G. H. Studdert		1962	John O'Brien	Margaret Burns
1908	H. H. Lawe		1963	John O'Brien	Joan Morton
1909	A. C. W. Posnett		1964	John O'Brien	Maureen O'Brien
1910	A. C. W. Posnett		1965	John O'Brien	Maureen O'Brien
1911	P. H. Stokes		1966	John O'Rourke	Maureen O'Brien
1912	R. M. Graham		1967	John O'Rourke	Ann Coughlan
1913	R. M. Graham		1968	Des Fox	Maureen O'Brien
1915	R. M. Graham		1969	John O'Rourke	Isobel Ryan
1920	A. K. Hodges		1970	J. De Collery	Maurethe Ruinn
1921	H. Tyrrell Smith		1971	Des Fox	
1922	H. Tyrrell Smith		1972	Des Fox	Betty Lombard
1925		Maud Price	1973	John O'Brien	Colette Egan
1926	D. Webb	Maud Price	1974	John O'Rourke	Joan Morton
1927	D. Webb	Una Miley	1975	John O'Rourke	Isobel Ryan
1928	R. M. Graham	Freda Pearson	1976	John O'Brien	Madeline Phillips
1929	R. M. Graham	Norma Stoker	1977	Brian Reid	Marie Gleeson
1930	R. M. Graham	Norma Stoker	1978	John O'Rourke	Joan Morton
1931	G. W. Kennedy	Norma Stoker	1979	John O'Rourke	Catherine Fitzgerald
1932	Eustace Fannin	Norma Stoker	1980	Tommy Burke	Alice Fawsitt
1933	G. W. Kennedy	Norma Stoker	1981	Tommy Burke	Alice Fawsitt
1934	Eustace Fannin	Norma Stoker	1982	Jim Pringle	Jean Tubridy
1935	Eustace Fannin	Barbara Flood	1983	Tommy Burke	Alice Fawsitt
1936	Eustace Fannin	Olive Poole	1984	Tommy Burke	Alice Fawsitt
1937	Eustace Fannin	Olive Poole	1985	Tommy Burke	Alice Fawsitt
1938	Raymund Egan	Olive Poole	1986	Tommy Burke	Alice Fawsitt
1939	Raymund Egan	Betty Lombard	1987	Tommy Burke	Suzanne Kelly
1940	Raymund Egan	Olive Poole	1988	Tommy Burke	Suzanne Kelly
1941	Raymund Egan	Olive Poole	1989	Neil Wilson	Alice Fawsitt
1942	Raymund Egan	Betty Lombard	1990	Neil Wilson	Gina O'Connor
1943	Raymund Egan	Betty Lombard	1991	Tommy Burke	Gina O'Connor
1944	Raymund Egan	Betty Lombard	1992	Glenn Beirne	Barbara Dillon
1945	Eustace Fannin	Mary Nichols	1993	J. Pringle	Eleanor Murphy
1946	Raymund Egan	Mary Nichols	1994	Bernard McCormack	Sheila Byrne
1947	Cyril Kemp	Betty Lombard	1995	David Mullins	Sheila Byrne
1948	Cyril Kemp	Betty Lombard	1996	Bernard McCormack	Sheila Byrne
1949	Guy Jackson	Betty Lombard	1997	Bernard McCormack	Eleanor Murphy
1950	Raymund Egan	Maeve Brennan	1998	Neil Wilson	Eleanor Murphy
1951	Guy Jackson	Betty Lombard	1999	Neil Wilson	F. Murphy
1952	Guy Jackson	Betty Lombard	2000	Neil Wilson	Lucy Jeffries
1953	Gerry Clarke	Joan Morton	2001	Mark Perry	Libby Lyons
1954	Raymund Egan	June Anne Fitzpatrick	2002	Bernard McCormack	Aoife O'Neill
1955	Raymund Egan	Heather Flinn	2003	Conor Darcy	Aoife O'Neill

The Lansdowne Lawn Tennis Club Class I Men's Team, winners of the Dublin Lawn Tennis Council League in 1949, 1950 and 1951. Back (l to r.) Frank Peard (1949), Tony Farrell (1950 & 1951), T.G. McDonald (1951), Cyril Odlum (1950), Dan O'Connell Miley (1949, 1950 & 1951). Front (l. to r.) Raymund Egan (1949, 1950 & 1951), R. W. Tunney (Captain, 1949, 1950 & 1951), Harry O' Donnell (Club President), Guy Jackson (1951), Eustace Fannin (1949 & 1950). Inset Cyril Kemp (1949).

singles, C. H. Chaytor and W. H. Boyd beat William and Manliffe Goodbody 10/8 0/6 6/2. It is worth noting here that, two years later, Manliffe, the younger of the two, would become the only Irishman to ever reach a US Open final.

Lansdowne's 2nd team won the Junior Cup in 1893. In the final they beat **Mount Temple LTC's** first team by 5 matches to 4. In 1894 in the Senior Cup Lansdowne beat Dublin University in the semi-final but, for some unknown reason, the final against **Fitzwilliam LTC** was never played. In 1895 they beat Mount Temple 5/4 in the semi-final while Fitzwilliam beat Dublin University 8/1. Despite the presence of Pim and Stoker, the Fitzwilliam team won the final 8/1. In 1894 Lansdowne's second team would have been promoted to the senior Cup and did not enter. Their third team scratched from the junior cup, which was won by **Mount Temple LTC**.

As many people know, the Dublin Leagues started for the men in 1902, and in 1910 for ladies. Their record in Class 1 is worth noting. Between 1902 and 2002 they won this competition on 26 occasions, the club nearest to this record is **Fitzwilliam LTC** with 14 wins. The Ladies Class 1 league record is even better. In the period 1910 to 2002 they won the title 36 times. Between 1936 and 1967 the event was held 32 times, the club won it 28 times in that period. This was a

dominance not recorded by any other club in the leagues' history.

In 1930 the club moved from the Rugby Union's grounds to those of the nearby Irish Hockey Union. In 1979 the club converted all of its grass courts into porous concrete ones. This ensured that the club would have play all year round. The front four grass courts were still in operation for a further period of time. Lights were officially launched with an exhibition match on Friday the 12th October 1979. A report in the 1980 Yearbook indicated that there were many international players on view in the challenge between the Club President's team (Kevin Sweeney) and that of the Captain's (Michael Boland). It ended in *a honourable, if confusing draw.* Today the club continues to have a high standard of play, draws in some great players, and fields a large number of teams in a range of leagues in which they compete. It has 10 all-weather surfaces, all floodlit. Each autumn, the Annual National Veterans' Championships are played here, in addition to the East of Ireland Championships in August and the Leinster Junior Championships in July. While David Roig, the club coach from Spain, has now returned to warmer Barcelona, Marie Harvey continues her years as club administrator and, with many members in roles as organisers and players, the future should be secure for the next century.

Limerick Lawn Tennis Club
(Founded 1877)

Ticking over for the last 126 years has been the jewel of a tennis club best known today as simply 'Limerick Lawn'. It is a club that has many claims to fame. In the first instance the South of Ireland Championships is the oldest event of its kind in Ireland. While **Fitzwilliam LTC** may have the first national ladies singles title to its credit, Limerick in 1877 appear to have been the first club 'in the world' to have had an open ladies singles event. The inaugural South of Ireland commenced on the 26th July 1877 with four events. These were the Gentleman's and Ladies Open Singles, the Gentleman's Handicap Singles and the Gentlemen's Open Doubles.

George Hehir compiled a lovely little booklet entitled *The First Decade: Limerick Lawn Tennis Club 1877-1886.* It mainly deals the 'South', the tennis event first held many years 'before' its golfing equivalent at Lahinch.

The club appears to have another distinct record (possibly a world one) in that the same event has been held at the same grounds, run by the same club, for over one and a quarter centuries. Historians will know that both the All-England and Fitzwilliam clubs have moved venue over the years. As the game first thrived in these islands, Limerick no doubt was among the leading lights. Here we relate a number of pieces on the club and its people.

The Limerick LTC team, winners of the Day Cup in 1976, were (from left) Claire Hayes, Marion O' Connor, Vera Shaw and Anne Condon.

George Hehir dedicated his booklet to Dickie Quinn a member of long ago who became President of the Munster Branch in 1957. So too did Lucy-Warner Ryan in 1989. Lucy, from Galway, has spent many years in the club both as a player and an administrator. She was the President in 2002, the year of the 125th South anniversary. We know that Edmund Bourke was the honorary secretary of the club 1877. He lived at Thornfields, Lisnagry, Limerick. His descendants still lived at Lisnagry until recent years. Perhaps they still do. The honorary secretary and treasurer in 1879 was Charles Armstrong who lived at 18, The Cresent. However, while there is no record of the full committee for 1877 the poster for 1879 does give a full listing (See Chapter 5). We can record that the Management Committee for 2002 as follows:

Management Committee 2002

Lucy Warner Ryan (President)
James Upton (Vice-President)
David O'Donnell (Honorary Treasurer)
Jennifer Wall (Honorary Secretary)
Mary Sherry (Membership Secretary)
Kevin Neville (Bar Secretary)
Brian McGann (Sponsorship/Coaching)
Claire McGuigan (Tennis Representative)
Eddie O' Toole (Junior Representative)
Kathleen Tierney (Social Representative)
Michael Barry (Squash Representative)

Ann O'Keeffe chaired the Social Committee while overlooking the smooth operations in the club is Manager Pat Casey. Tadhg Lambe has been appointed as club coach, being highly regarded in both the fields of squash and tennis. The Tournament Director for 2002 was Claire McNamara. As Claire pointed out the annual event *is an opportunity for tennis players and spectators to view some of the finest tennis available on the Irish scene and to renew old acquaintances.* The President, in the Programme added her words of welcome with a wise recommendation to all the participants that they should *enjoy the moment and remember winning isn't everything-wanting to win is!*

The club has seen it all. Wimbledon champion, Willoughby Hamilton, would take the South in 1885 and 1886. In the intervening years International matches and Davis Cup matches were played on the courts adjacent to the Ennis Road. It was also the scene of many interprovincials. The first year, when all four provinces were involved, was 1949. For many years it was nearly always Leinster's title with Ulster intervening the odd time. Limerick hosted the event in 1954 and 1962. However, in 1966, not alone did they host the event but the southern province took the Senior Interprovincial title for the first time. Munster had 13 points, Ulster 12, Leinster 5 and Connaught 1. That team includes Michael Hickey who was ranked in Ireland from 1960 to 1976, being the number 1 Irish player for several years. His Davis Cup record is equally impressive. He played in a total of 19 ties between 1962 and 1978. His record of playing in 15 years of competition is the best Irish record since Joshua Pim became the first Irishman to play in the event. That was in 1902. Details on this most successful of Limerick players are given elsewhere.

In more recent years the Niland family have set all sorts of records. How many families can say they have three tennis internationals on the team. Of course mother Pat, as well as her uncle and aunt all played for Connacht and her Foxford grandmother played in that Mayo club back in the 1940s. Gina, now playing out of **Fitzwilliam LTC** in Dublin, has played in a total of 42 Federation Cup ties between 1989 and 2001. She is the most prolific of all Irish women, the nearest being Lesley O'Halloran with 32 ties. Gina has had an exceptional 34 wins (22 singles, 12 doubles) in this international event for women, eleven more than the nearest Irish lady (Yvonne Doyle with 23 between

1971. The committee at Limerick Lawn Tennis Club. From left: Michael O'Farrell, Joe O'Connor, Nicholas Condon (president), Anne O'Connor, Frank Stafford, Mary Killeen (honorary secretary), Michael Greene (honorary treasurer) and Michael O'Malley. The club had recently opened two new squash courts with exhibition matches in which Donald Pratt (Irish number 1), Michael Hickey, Peter Ledbetter and Bernard O'Gorman took part. Within three weeks of the opening the club membership had to be closed at 450. A few years later the ILTA Yearbook (1977) reported that paractially all club members were interested in both sports. In addition, the club president, Vera Shaw, was also president of the irish Women's Squash Racikets Association.

1992 and 2005). Conor Niland has notched up seven Davis Cup caps (between 2000 and 2005) while Ross will always have the memory of beating Tim Henman in the final of the first Great Britain "Short Tennis" championships. That was in 1983. Liam Croke was another star developed in the club and has the distinction of being one of the few players ever to win the Irish Open Boys Championships in two consecutive years. This was in 1987 and 1988. In an earlier day, Limerick's John O' Brien was to be one of Ireland's top players. He played in the Davis Cup in 1977. John is now a trustee at **Lansdowne LTC**. Brian Lawlor is another player who thrived in Limerick. He took up the game at thirteen and was coached by Michael Hickey and Paul Douglas. In 1978 he would have an Irish ranking of four. Other players with Munster and Irish ratings included Fiona Long, Jo Sheridan, Aoife O'Neill, George McGill. Details on these and other Limerick players can be found in several chapters, particularly the Who's Who chapter.

Back in the 19th century the club had its first President in 1878. He was to be none other than as Baron, John Thomas William Massy. He lived at the Hermitage, Castleconnell. Perhaps another first for the Limerick club was the running of a veteran's tournament in conjunction with the Open Championships in 1879. It was a singles event and for Gentlemen over the age of 45. Much of the records were unearthed by George Hehir in the Limerick Chronicle. In the October 21st edition 1879, under the heading "The Querist", a few early thoughts on the game were posed. It should not be forgotten that at that time it was a strange and new fangled pastime, replacing the more sedate croquet. The principle queries are noted in the table across.

I think that reporter from the Chronicle was observant but as he didn't play tennis he can be forgiven when he suggests that the game might not survive. Did not the first winner at Wimbledon, just two years earlier (1877), Spencer Gore, say that he thought *The game is a bore* and *will never rank among the great sports of cricket and rackets.* How wrong he was. This was not the first regional paper to pen pictures of the early

game in 'rural' Ireland. A few others are quoted elsewhere.

It is noted by George that the game was played that summer in Kilkee, one of the favoured resorts for the wealthy in Limerick city. This reminds me of the Harris family, many of who played tennis in the Limerick club. However their deeds, with a tennis racquet, were noted in the special sport of Squash Racquets at Kilkee. See Chapter 2 and the winning Richard Harris among the Limerick visitors. Back in September 1979 the tennis tournament was held at Kilkee and the result for the event was that a Mr. Harris and a Miss De Montmorency beat Mr. de Ros Rose and Miss Mary Massy in the mixed final. More than likely this is the same Harris family.

LIMERICK LAWN TENNIS CLUB.
GRAND LAWN TENNIS TOURNAMENT,
To be Played on
THE LIMERICK CRICKET GROUND,
on
THURSDAY, FRIDAY, and SATURDAY,
JULY 26th, 27th, and 28th.

COMMITTEE:—

T. White
H. Considine
P. Gabbett
R. de R. Rose

E. H. M. Elliott, 82nd Regiment
C. Armstrong, Honorary Treasurer
E. BOURKE, Hon. Sec.

Events

1st.—Gentlemen's Open Singles. Second Prize if more than 2 enter. Entrance 5s.
2nd.—Ladies' Open Singles. Second Prize if more than 8 enter. Entrance 2s. 6d.
3rd.—Gentlemen's Handicap Singles. Entrance 5s. for 2s.
4th.—Gentlemen's Open Doubles, entering in pairs. Entrance 10s.

Entrances to be paid on or before Saturday, July 21st, to the Hon. Sec., L.T.C., Thornfields, Lisnagry, Limerick, to enable ties to be drawn. Name and address to be given. Entries and ties will be published. The size of court, weight of balls, &c., will be determined by the Marylebone rules.
For further information apply to
E. BOURKE, Hon. Sec., L.T.C.,
Thornfields, Lisnagry, Limerick.

July 10.

Limerick Chronicle-Saturday Evening July 14 1877

The History of Irish Tennis

> *Whether there ever was or ever will be a game so suddenly developed or pursued with such spontaneous mania as Lawn Tennis?*
>
> *Whether Lawn Tennis "shop" does not bid fair to rival weather "shop"?*
>
> *Whether Lawn Tennis conduces less to flirtation than Croquet?*
>
> *Whether many people have not played tennis almost in marshes, got thoroughly wet, and injured their health?*
>
> *Whether some gentlemen do not endeavour to make themselves agreeable by smoking when playing Tennis with the ladies, and that without the most distant apology?*
>
> *Whether if they were equally rude in a Railway carriage the guard would not order them out?*
>
> *Whether it is pleasant on missing a ball to hear it politely insinuated that you have a "hole in your racquet"?*
>
> *Whether it is perplexing no less than annoying if you happen to serve a ball into the net, to be reproached by your partner, while the opposite side blandly asks for "another of these"?*
>
> *Whether with a good many people, loss of a game does not involve a most unnecessary loss of temper?*
>
> *Whether it is possible for a really honourable man to cheat at lawn tennis?*
>
> *Whether in the year 1900 lawn tennis will be abolished in favour of lawn football?*
>
> *Whether a person who never plays and never will play tennis ought to make gratuitous animadversions on the game and the players?*

The 1881 South overran due to the large entry and had to be finished on Monday 22nd August of that year. On the Friday, as with most tournaments of that time, there was the grand Tournament Ball. That year it was held in the Athenaeum, which was *decorated with considerable taste and judgement*. The dancing started at 10 o'clock and went on into the early hours of the morning. The summer, which *was of a most 'recherché' character, was supplied by Mr. McMahon.* The term 'Championship of the South of Ireland' was first used in 1882 when a new cup had to be purchased. The Limerick Chronicle in 1883 had a leading article on the tournament.

While the site was bought on the Ennis Road in about 1869 it was not until about 1878 that it functioned as a Croquet Hockey and Tennis Club. Of course cricket was also played on this land. The first international rugby match played in the South of Ireland was played on the grounds in 1887. The Welsh rugby union had a disagreement with the Rugby Union and both Ireland and Scotland refused to play them in 1897. It was over

a proposal that never materialised, to give a 'house' to a retiring Welsh international called Arthur Gould. Wales rejoined the Union in February 1898 and, according to Van Esbeck (1999) *With cordial relations now resumed with the Welsh, the match was arranged for Limerick on 19 March.* For the record the Welsh won by 11 points to 3. Thanks to the IRFU for the following photograph of this unique event. Also, for the record, there were three Munster players on that team. These were T. McCarthy who played for the 'Cork' club and the Ryan brothers, Jack and Mick, whose affiliated 'club' was in fact Rockwell College. The same brothers were on the Irish team that beat Wales for the first time (in Cardiff in 1899) and at the same time winning Ireland's second triple crown.

Limerick's Michael Hickey
International tennis and squash player

It was all grass courts until 1939 when three hard courts of the 'en tout cas' variety were laid down. Two further hard courts were laid in 1979. By 1983 the club had three grass courts and seven hard courts. By 2000 there were 9 all-weather grass courts and three hard courts. Today there are 12 floodlit synthetic courts outside and three squash courts in the club building. Like many of the old clubs ladies were not on committees in the early days. However, in 1918, this hurdle was crossed and they have played an important role in the club ever since. In fact the following year 'County' member Doris Ballingal played in Wimbledon. She got a bye in the first round and then a walk over against Mrs. H.C. Hextall. In the round of 16 she was beaten by Mabel Parton of Great Britain 6/0 6/2 who, in turn was beaten by American player Elizabeth Ryan, the Irish champion that year as well as in 1920, 1921 and 1923.

Other prominent players in the early part of the 20th century were Arthur Bloodsmith, Maurice Goodbody, Bunty Westrop and Tom Cleary. Maurice was a nephew of Manliffe Goodbody, the US Open finalist in 1894. Manliffe, in turn, is a brother of Anthea Goodbody's great grandfather. She played for Munster and Ireland in the 1960s and 1970s. Just before we leave Limerick a couple of further words from George that leave one in no doubt about the club's pedigree.

The History of Irish Tennis

It was quite commonplace to have top players from both England and Ireland entering (the 'South'), so much so that in 1883 the committee introduced a rule which stated that, in future, winners of the Wimbledon or the Fitzwilliam tournaments would receive a –15 handicap. Perhaps the greatest player to have graced the Limerick tournament was William Renshaw, who entered and duly won the Gentlemen's Handicap Singles in 1881.

fast-growing game of Squash. The influx of a large number of Squash players who were being exposed to the game of Tennis for the first time was just the shot-in-the-arm which the sport needed. The last lingering vestiges of elitism were cast aside and a more egalitarian era was ushered in. Today the club has enthusiastic committees, professional coaching and an efficient full-time manager in Pat Casey. Like other clubs there will be ups and downs but it continues to strive forward and be a major sporting establishment in the south of Ireland. The club grounds were reduced in size in 1925 but once catered for hunting, hockey, croquet, cricket and even rugby. Ireland played Wales in the only full rugby international to be held in Munster. The date was 19th March 1898. Wales won 11/3. Some 15,000 attended.

In 2000 all three members of the Niland family played for Munster in the interprovincial series at Galway LTC. From left: Ross (2 wins out of 3), Conor (2 wins out of 3) and Gina (3 wins out of 3).

Brilliant Niland retains title

GINA Niland, the brilliant Limerick 16-year-old who represents Ireland at junior Wimbledon this day week, gave a superb performance at the Heineken South of Ireland championships when she retained her ladies singles title.

Twelve months ago Miss Niland made history when she became the youngest ever winner of the ladies title, and in yesterday's final she beat the Leinster senior intro-provential, Carmel O'Sullivan, 6-1, 6-3 in a repeat of the decider of 12 months ago.

Garry Henderson, the English international,

won the men's title despite dropping the first three games to Welch international Mark Loosemore.

Men's 'A' Singles—G. Henderson (England) bt M. Loosemore (Wales) 7-5, 6-3; Mens 'A' doubles—Henderson and S. Heron (both England) bt D. Roberts (Wales) and J. Lane (USA) 6-0, 7-6.

Ladies 'A' singles—G. Niland (Limerick) bt C. O'Sullivan (Dublin) 6-1, 6-3; Ladies 'A' doubles—C. O'Sullivan and S. Hunter (both Dublin) bt G. Niland and F. Long (both Limerick) 6-1, 3-6, 6-3.

Mixed 'A' doubles—D. Roberts and A. O'Sullivan bt G. Henderson and G. Niland 4-6, 6-4, 6-3.

Mens 'B' singles—P. Beary (Catholic Institute) bt S. Cleary (Catholic Instititue) 6-2, 7-5. Mens 'B' doubles—Messrs. Cleary and Beary bt T. & T. O'Shea, all Catholic Institute, 2-6, 6-0, 6-1.

Ladies 'B' singles—J. A. Mulholland (Limerick Lawn) bt G. O' Carroll (Catholic Institute) 6-1, 6-4. Ladies 'B' doubles—L. Ryan and P. Sheehan (Both Limerick LTC) bt P. Kerr and C. Power (Both Limerick LTC) 1-6, 6-2, 6-0. Mixed 'B' doubles—J. Reidy and S. Lane (both Limerick Lawn) bt N. O'Leary and N. O'Nolan, 7-, 6-2.

Mens 'C' singles—J. Hurley (Newcastle West) bt G. Ryan (Catholic Institute) 6-3, 7-6. Mens 'C' doubles—G. Ryan and B. Nolan (both Catholic Institute) bt Hurley and N. O'Connor (both Newcastle West) 6-2, 3-6, 8-6.

Ladies 'C' singles—N. Welderick (Limerick Lawn) bt J. O'Flynn (Catholic Institute) 6-2, 3-6, 6-4; Mixed 'C' doubles N. Murphy and B. Moroney (both Catholic Institute) bt P. and D. Casey 6-2, 6-0.

August 1989. The Limerick Leader reports on the second consecutive win by 16-year-old Gina Niland in the South of Ireland Championships.

Local papers like the Leader form an important part of the sports promotion. In 2000 (see photos following) the Leader (July 8th) recorded the story and results of the South as well as the full draws for the Limerick Open due to be held at the nearby Catholic Institute Club the following Saturday.

John O'Brien - Member of Limerick, Fitzwilliam and Lansdowne LTCs.

George noted the decline in tennis over four decades and that *were it not for the vision of a few members who in 1970 encouraged the club to embrace the then*

Kathleen Tierney and Ann Condon with the strawberries and cream for the 2000 South of Ireland Championships.

The 1954 senior interprovincial series at Limerick LTC. This was the second time they were hosted by the club. Leinster dominated the series. In 1966 "Limerick Lawn" hosted the event for the fourth time. Munster won the title for the first time with 13 points (to Ulster's 12, Leinster's 5 and Connacht's 1).John O'Brien and Michael Hickey were on that successful team.

Alison McHugh and Breda Hayes (right) beat Dianne Bennis and Edith O'Leary in the 'D' Doubles at the "South" in 2000. With them is Brendan McMorrow, club president.

The 2000 Men's A Doubles finalists with club vice-president, Pat Phelan. Winners Jack Quilligan and Ger Holliday(on left) beat Atilla Madarasz and Matt Mitchell 7/5 6/2

Pat Biggane and Tony Kelleher (right) beat Noel Rice and Gerry Kearns 6/3 3/6 6/4 in the "B" Mens' doubles finals at the South in 2000. Tony also won the "B" singles.

Club vice-president Pat Phelan poses with the "D" mixed finalists at the South in 2000. Eamonn and Deirdre Goode (left) beat Anne Marie and Denis McMahon 6/4 7/5.

LIMERICK COUNTY LAWN TENNIS CLUB,
1879.
GRAND LAWN TENNIS TOURNAMENT,
TO BE PLAYED ON THE
LIMERICK COUNTY CRICKET GROUND,
ON
Wednesday, Thursday, Friday & Saturday, Sept. 3rd, 4th, 5th, & 6th.

President:
LORD MASSY.

Committee:

CHARLES ARMSTRONG, Esq.	MAJOR MAUNSELL, R.A.
J. F. BANNATYNE, Esq.	WILLIAM MONSELL, Esq.
T. B. BROWNING, Esq.	R. D. O'BRIEN, Esq.
H. F. CONSIDINE, Esq.	R. V. O'BRIEN, Esq.
M. E. CONWAY, Esq.	R. DE ROS ROSE, Esq.
CAPT. DASHWOOD, 87th R. I. Fusiliers.	COL. STEVENSON, 87th R. I. Fusiliers.
WINDHAM GABBETT, Esq.	A. W. SHAW, Esq.
POOLE GABBETT, Esq.	CAPT. TODD, 87th R. I. Fusiliers.
W. LYSAGHT, Esq.	J. WHITE, Esq.
CAPTAIN R. M. MAUNSELL.	O. WALLACE, Esq.

C. ARMSTRONG, Esq., *Hon. Secretary and Treasurer*

EVENTS,
FOR WHICH HANDSOME PRIZES WILL BE GIVEN.

1ST. GENTLEMEN'S OPEN SINGLES. 2nd Prize if more than 12 Enter. Entrance 5/- ... — TO BE PLAYED OFF ON Wednesday, at 2 o'clock

2ND. GENTLEMEN'S HANDICAP SINGLES. Entrance 5/-. Half forfeit ... — Thursday, 11 o'clock

3RD. VETERAN OPEN SINGLES, for Gentlemen over 45. Entrance 5/- No Prize except 6 Enter ... — Friday, 11 o'clock

4TH. LADIES' OPEN SINGLES. 2nd Prize if more than 8 Enter. Entrance 2/6 — Friday, 2 o'clock

5TH. GENTLEMEN'S HANDICAP DOUBLES, Entering in Pairs. Entrance 10/-. Half forfeit ... — Saturday, 11 o'clock

6TH. LADIES' AND GENTLEMEN'S HANDICAP DOUBLES, Entering in Pairs. Entrance 5/-. Half forfeit. Prize only for Ladies ... — Saturday, 2 o'clock

All Final Ties to be played on Saturday.

Entries to be made on or before Two o'Clock, on Tuesday, the 2nd September, with the Honorary Secretary and Treasurer, 13, The Crescent, Limerick.

No Entry will be received without the Entrance Fee. Name and Address to be given, with name of Club belonging to. Entries and Ties will be published.

All Competitors to play in Tennis Shoes.

The above will be played under the New Rules.

Play to commence on Wednesday, First Day, at 2 o'Clock, and successive days, at 11 o'Clock sharp.

Any Player not being in attendance when called upon to play, will be disqualified.

The Committee reserve full power to modify the above Programme.

A MILITARY BAND WILL PERFORM EACH DAY.

CHARLES ARMSTRONG,
Hon. Secretary and Treasurer,
13, The Crescent,
Limerick.

4th August, 1879.

Guy & McQuakle, Printers, Limerick.

The 1879 poster detailing the committee and events to be held at the third open championships at Limerick Lawn Tennis Club. This was the predecessor of the present South of Ireland Championship and is historically significant for several reasons. It was the first important 'Open' in Ireland when it took place two years earlier, a matter of weeks before the first All-England championships at Wimbledon. In addition it included ladies' singles in 1877 and a veterans' singles in 1879. Probably unique too is the fact that the club has remained at the same grounds since its formation in 1877 (i.e. 129 years by 2006).

Some competitors in front of the Limerick Lawn Tennis Club clubhouse at the 2002 Junior South of Ireland Championships.

****

Trinity College L.T.C.
[Dublin University LTC]
(Founded 1877)

Without doubt, the Trinity College tennis club, also known as Dublin University tennis club, has been the source of some of the best players in the early days of the game. Many of the students will have played at 'tennis parties' in various parts of the country with the game becoming more competitive when at university. Some details are included in chapter on University and Schools tennis. Like other sports, the students took up the game with enthusiasm. They had links with their English counterparts at Oxford and Cambridge. It was mainly a male affair for many years. The players, having qualified, would join some of the top clubs in Dublin. **Fitzwilliam LTC**, **Lansdowne LTC**, **Wilton LTC** and **Mount Temple LTC** were among the clubs to have benefited on a regular basis. The President of the Dublin University Athletic Club, the governing body of sport at the University, in 1877 was the Right Honourable E. Gibson. Among the large committee were J. N. Gerrard, F. Smith, A. Stoker and J. J. D. La Touche. Interestingly, La Touche was, in November of 1877, on the first committee of the newly formed **Fitzwilliam LTC**. He was a barrister after university. Accordingly to the quote researched by Trevor West, and quoted in *The Bold Collegians*, J. J. Digges La Touche apparently a (rowing) cox who was a 'hardy,

wiry little chap and a strict and unmerciful task-master if over one (sic) in a boat. His tongue too was as long as his name! I don't suppose he weighed 7 stone'. Also in his excellent book on the University and its sports, we find the first reference to the club there. Trevor West's direct quote is from the College Register of the 19th May 1877:

The Lawn Tennis Club was founded in 1877, when permission was given to mark out courts in the New Square [now the headquarters of the Croquet Club], provided that "the committee of the club make themselves responsible for the orderly conduct of all persons using the grounds for this purpose". Two years later, with a college subvention of £100 and an input from the club of £150, asphalt courts were laid down in the vicinity of the Gymnasium. In that year the Tennis Club was sufficiently well established to enter a tug-of-war team in the Civil Service Sports!

In the first Irish Championships a Mr. Poole and Mr. Barter, representing **DULTC**, played together in the men's doubles. At the time both players in a pairing had to be from the same club. They beat H. Hodgson and R. Scovell from **Fitzwilliam LTC** 6/3 6/0. This was the inaugural Irish Championships. They lost in the next round to C. Barry and Peter Aungier also from Fitzwilliam 1/6 0/6, their opponents going on to reach the final. Barry was also in the singles final, and runner-up in the mixed, in those historic championships. In the singles, J. J. Sherrard (**DULTC**) beat Peter Aungier. The *Field* (Saturday June 7 1879) reported: *The match between Mr. Aungier and Mr. Sherrard was a very good one; the University man won the first set by six games to three, Mr. Aungier the second by six to four; but in the deciding set the latter seemed to tire very much, and, after winning the first two games, was beaten the next six straight off.* Sherrard lost in the next round, in a match which was also a *very good one,* to H. E. Tombe (**Fitzwilliam LTC**) 6/4 1/6 4/6. H. J. Daly of **DULTC** lost his first round singles to J. J. Cairnes of **Fitzwilliam LTC** 3/6 2/6.

Manliffe Goodbody-Club Champion 1887

In 1880, R. Hassard was the only Dublin University entry in the men's singles. He lost to Englishman Herbert Lawford 0/6 6/5 3/6 4/6. This was no disgrace considering Lawford would be Wimbledon champion a few years later. The *Field,* in their detailed reports of the Championships, mentioned that there were three new players of more than average strength coming into *public notice.* One of these was Hassard. He was described as *the strongest of the University players, has a remarkably good stroke, and played especially well in the doubles matches.* Playing with Miss Meldon, they reached the final of the mixed doubles. There they were beaten by S.D. Maul of the 84th Regiment and Miss Costello 4/6 5/7.

In the men's doubles there were 15 pairs, two from the university. Hassard, playing with F.W. Knox, beat the **Monkstown LTC** pair of A. Henry and J. Murray 6/4 6/3 before losing to Peter Aungier and J.J. Cairns. A most interesting pair, also from **DULTC**, was that of W. French and L. Milne. The former is in fact none other than William Percy French, widely known for many things other than tennis. His story is briefly related in chapter 8. However, in chapter 3 you may have already found some of his tennis poetry. One in particular is titled *The Tennis Fiend-a tale of rapine and violence.* It tells the story of two engineering students at Trinity College taking possession of a tennis court in the Provost's garden. His partner is none other than L. Milne. They were obviously training for the Irish Championships!! They duly departed the championships when beaten in the first round by a pair from Fitzwilliam. *Mr. E. de S. Browne and Mr. W. Hewitt rather easily scored the first set against Mr. W. French and Mr. L. Milne by six games to two, though four of these were called deuce; one on each side was a love game. It was a harder struggle for the second set, but it was finally won by the same players by six games to four; deuce was called in four of these, and Mr. Browne scored two love games. The best contested games were the fourth, sixth and ninth.*

The next noteworthy player representing the university appears in the championships in 1883. *Amongst the new players Mr.* (Eyre) *Chatterton showed by far the best game; his style was remarkably good, being characterised by a nice free action.* Against H. H. Wilson, a *fair-class player,* he won comfortably 6/1 6/1 6/0. Next came H. H. Berkeley of **Maida Vale LTC**. This was a *capital match* in which Chatterton lost the first set, but with a good-style, his backhand strokes and "lobbing" winning him many points, he came through. In the third round, Chatterton beat Peter Aungier of Fitzwilliam. *The match….proved wonderfully close and interesting, the latter winning by the odd set.* In the semi-final, the relatively inexperienced university player lost to the ultimate winner Ernest Renshaw 2/6 2/6 3/6. The Englishman would win two more Irish titles and a Wimbledon title. In July 1883 Chatterton went to Limerick and won, what we now call, the South of Ireland Championship. In the All-Comer's Final he beat A. Browning 4/6 6/1 6/1 6/1 followed by a comfortable win over E. Lysaght in the Challenge round (6/1 6/0 6/0). In 1884 Chatterton had moved on to the Fitzwilliam club and the sole university representative in the Irish Championships in May was Tom Campion. He beat Orlando R. Coote (**Castlerea LTC**) 6/2 6/3 7/5 followed by T. H. Griffiths of **Wilton LTC** (2/6 6/2 6/3 6/4). He exited the tournament in the third round against Willoughby Hamilton, a future champion, in four sets (2/6 6/4 2/6 0/6).

The club had a strong selection of players in 1890. These included Manliffe Frances Goodbody, W.H. Boyd, Grainger Chaytor, Harold Mahony and Herbert N. Craig. That year, Chaytor would win the *Fitzwilliam Purse*, a prize valued at £5 and open to all preliminary and first round losers in the Irish Championship. He lost the Wimbledon quarterfinals to Harry Barlow (England) in five sets, 10/8 4/6 6/2 1/6 1/6. Within six years Goodbody would be the only Irishman to ever reach the US Open finals and Mahony would have won the Wimbledon Championships.

Records on many clubs can be scanty. Trinity College is no different. One suspects that in the 1880s the club was one of the best in the country in terms of standards. However, by 1893, the other Dublin clubs were growing in strength and the university side were playing in the Fitzwilliam Cup, Second Class. Dublin University, as it was known then, were still strong and beat **Glenageary & Kingstown LTC** 9/0 in the first round. The score recorded also indicated that it was 18 sets to 3 and 122 games to 71. In the second round the **Lansdowne LTC** seconds team beat the students 6 matches to 3 (15 sets to 5 and 110 games to 74). Lansdowne went on to win the cup, beating **Mount**

A Dublin University versus Oxford University in about 1947. Trinity players included F.S.L. Lyons (back left), Franks Furney (back, 4th from left), J.C. Smyth (back, 2nd from right), W. J. Pasley (front left) and H. R. Browne (front, 2nd left). Guy Jackson (front, 2nd from right) played for Oxford Univeristy.

Club Championships

1st Prize	2nd Prize
Men's Singles	
1887 Manliffe Goodbody	Harold Mahony
1893 ?	A. H. Porter
1894 T. D. Good	
1907 A. M. Cave	
1977 Hugh Tinney	Davis Fitzgerald
Handicap Singles	
1893 A.E. Johnstone	A.H. Porter
Men's Doubles	
1893 R.Latham/C. Latham	O.Good/W. Good
1894 T.D. Good/W.I. Good	
1907 A.M. Cave/- Fleming	Harry Barton/-Scott
1952 A.D. Taylor/	Brian Ellis/
G. G. Moore	C. Zarb.
1953 A.D.Taylor/	Brian Ellis/
Peter Payne	C.Zarb
Ladies Singles	
1952 Miss B. Wallace	Miss M. Morris
1953 Miss G. Nichols	Miss M. Flavell
1977 Jean Tubridy	Livela Fenlon
Ladies' Doubles	
1952 M. Morris/	V. Browne/
S. Taylor	B. Duffy
1953 M. Morris/	M. Lodge/
S. Taylor	J. Ferguson

Temple LTC 5/4 in the final. In the limited list of early champions at Dublin University, worth noting is A.M. Cave. He became the Reverend A. M. Cave. From 1907 to 1909 he was Irish Open Badminton Champion. According to Adams (1980) in *The Badminton Story: An inter-club league was started in Dublin in 1904-several years before the London League. Very soon Irish players were challenging at the All England Championships and A.M. Cave came within a few points of winning the men's singles in*

1908. Dr. H. N. Marrett beat him in the final in what was (and still is) effectively the world championships. In the 1912-1913 badminton season, Cave, and another former Trinity tennis player, T.D. Good, won the second Irish National Badminton Doubles Championships. In a preview to the 1906 season, *Lawn Tennis & Badminton* had the following comment on the club: *Dublin University are an uncertain quality. The club membership is very large. They have lost Mr. Parke, and Mr. Dillon's services are doubtful.* James Cecil Parke had been Irish Champion in 1904 and 1905 and was obviously now qualified, he would be 25 on the 26th July. The Mr. Dillon is probably Shirley Dillon who was also a member of **Glenageary & Kingstown LTC** and reached the Irish Championship final in 1906. As far as numbers are concerned we only have a guide. In the listing of affiliated clubs for 1913, 1914, 1915 and 1920, the university was deemed to have 80 members. In 1913, this can be compared with **Clontarf LTC** (120), **Fitzwilliam LTC** (175), **Grosvenor LTC** (85), **Percy LTC** (60) and **Wilton LTC** (40).The University club gets a mention in a 1907 (June 12) report on Irish tennis in *Lawn Tennis & Badminton:In days gone by the Dublin University Club has turned out some right good men like Mahony, the Chaytors and Ball-Greene, besides men like T.D. Good, Parke and Dillon. For this reason this club's championships contests are always interesting. This year's champion is A. M. Cave, the Badminton player. Cave seems to be a good deal better than any of the others. He is a very useful player. The best sport was shown in the doubles, where Cave and Fleming only just beat Scott and Harry Barton after a 5-set match. Rain interfered with the game, and the counter attraction of an afternoon dance made the gallery a small one. All were sorry not to see Barton a winner, for he has been a plucky competitor for some years past, and his father is one of Trinity's warmest supporters. The average standard of play is better than for some years*

The History of Irish Tennis

past. The authorities might find the club a better ground.

In 1905, Parke presented a sterling silver, and ornate, cup to the **Dublin University LTC** for the annual championships. This suggests that he had won the existing cup outright for the year 1902 to 1904; this was the common practice at that time. The cup he himself presented is now in the hands of Peter Read, son of Harry, as he too won the cup for the three consecutive years 1910 to 1912. The names on that cup, donated by one of the most illustrious of Irish players ever, are as follows:

Dublin University LTC- Presented by J. C. Parke in 1905	
1905	H. V. S. Dillon
1906	H. V. S. Dillon
1907	A. M. Cave
1908	A. M. Cave
1909	C. F. Scroope
1910	H. M. Read
1911	H. M. Read
1912	H. M. Read

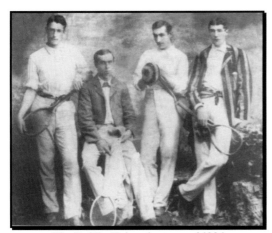

The Dublin University team of 1886

Each of these five players, as well as many before and since, were to become full international players. In 1913, Harry Read presented a Cup to the University for the Men's Annual Championships. He had previously won the James Cecil Parke Cup for three years and it became his property. His son Peter who lives in Roscrea now keeps it lovingly. Not alone was he an international tennis player but also an excellent rugby international. He was an international cricketer and, at the age of 74, played croquet for Ireland. A list of many of the winners is given in the table across.

This listing misses some years but does include many future international and a smattering of foreign players who studied at Trinity College Dublin. Thomas

Vincent Murphy was an internaitonal player as was his son-in-law, Jim Buckley many years later. The exploits of George McVeagh are dealt with elsewhere. His nephew was Donald Pratt who won many Irish Squash championships. Michael Kemp is son of the great Cyril, the Irish number one in the 1940s while E.J. Avory also has a famous father, Ted, the Vice President of the All-England Club. Michael Hannon, an Irish international, now lives in England and has been elected a member of that famous club. Details of other players are given in Chapter 6. In January 2005 Lady Annie Arnott presented Lady Captain Lorna Jennings with a Rose Bowl for the Lady Champion. The perpetual trophy was donated in honour of her late husband, Sir John Arnott.

Dublin University LTC- Challenge Cup Presented by H.M. Read in 1913	
1913,1914	H. R. Price
1919	E. D'Arcy McCrea
1920,1921	Gordon S. B. (*Curly*)Mack
1922	Thomas Vincent Murphy
1923	Dr. McKay
1924	G. W. Murray
1925	J. E. Wells
1926	A. de G. Gaudin
1927-1930	George McVeagh
1931,1932,1933,1936	Dick Sandys
1934,1935	Hector Ryan
1937,1938	D. Cameron MacNair
1939	G. S. Spiller
1940	M. Solomons
1941,1942	Paul I. Read
1944	W. F. Reid
1945,1946,1947	Norman Brown
1948	Franks Furney
1949	W. J. Pasley
1950,1951,1952	A. D. Taylor
1953	Peter R. Payne
1954	Brian D. Ellis
1955,1956	Donald Pratt
1957,1958,1959	R. Sweetman
1960	I. S. Steepe
1961,1963	E. J. Avory
1964,1965	J. A. Horsley
1966	Peter Ledbetter
1967	F. S. Graham
1968	T. K. Clapp
1969,1970	John Mulvey
1971	G. J. O' Herlihy
1973,1974	P. Quilligan
1975	P. Rungasamy
1976	D. J. Fitzgerald
1977,1979,1980	Peter Hannon
1978	Cliff Beirne
1982	Michael Kemp
1983	A. Dorman
1984	D. O' Loughlin
1985	Morgan Buckley
1986	Charles O'Brien

The Dublin University Lawn Tennis Team in 1911. Sitting in the middle front is the tennis captain, Harry Read. He was also captain of the Rugby and Cricket teams. He won the club championships (for the J. C. Parke Cup) in 1910, 1911 & 1912.

The Combined Trinity & Edinburgh University Ladies' Tennis teams in 1937. Extreme left is the late Winifred Matthews who worked in the University for many years and did much for Trinity Sportsmen and Sportswomen.

Monkstown Lawn Tennis Club
(Founded 1877)

We may never find out exactly which Irish club was the first to be established and run as a club. The 1979 ILTA Yearbook declared *Monkstown-the oldest club in the country,* in one of a number of articles on the club scene. We can be certain that its origin was amongst the members of the County Dublin (Monkstown) Archers Club founded in 1846. However, while several months older than **Fitzwilliam LTC**, this did not allow for the fact that Limerick Lawn Tennis Club was operational in July of 1877 and that at Trinity College Dublin lawn tennis courts were marked out at the University in the same year. There may be other claims. The club President Caoimhin Kenna who came into office in 1977 carried out much research on the club's history; a century after the club was founded.

To celebrate the first tournament held in the club a member composed an amusing poem. This is possibly the first poem on the sport of lawn tennis (see Chapter 3) and a noteworthy foundation to this veteran of the Irish club scene. While there is no evidence that dual membership of the archery and tennis clubs was available, it is noted that the last annual 'shoot' took place on the same grounds as the tennis courts in September of 1877. (It is noted that at Raglan and Mersey Bowmen there were two British clubs that did have archery and tennis combined in one club). At the early stages of the tennis club there were ten ladies and ten gentlemen as members, the Betham family previously having been archery exponents. Mr. M. C. J. Betham (1813-1880) was Irish champion eleven times and his daughter was lady champion twice and English champion three times. The earliest written record on members included the following names: H. G. Ward, L. E. Steel, E. Ward, A. Hamilton-Jones, G. W. Peacock, G. Murray, J. T. Peacock, E. Murray, S. B. Ward, J. G. A. Kane and N. S. Adeney. E. Archdale was the secretary of the club in 1894 according to one record of the 18 Irish clubs affiliated to the LTA in that year.

As Kenna indicated about the early days the club *It seems, however, to have had a fairly small, closely-knit membership. There was undoubtedly a definite link with the Establishment class.* The usual connection with the many British regiments was normal in early tennis clubs. For the "at home" in 1913 the programme indicated the list of music played on the day by the King's Own Scottish Borderers. The programme lists the various finals, eight in all, and the competitors. Six of the events were handicap and the name of D.C. Pim appears in the final of the gentlemen's singles, handicap B class. One can reasonably assume he was a relative of Joshua Pim, the south County Dublin player who won Wimbledon in 1893 and 1894.

For many years the club ran on a reasonably informal basis with committee meetings held as 'social venues' such as the Salthill Hotel, Ross's Hotel, the Royal Irish Yacht Club and Robert's Café (Suffolk Street, Dublin). The minute's books from 1930 are extant.

Christopher Preston, the President from 1954 to 1961, recalls *that it would have been unthinkable to have contemplated playing tennis without being able to partake of tea afterwards!* Sunday tennis was not permitted. Times were changing in many clubs in the 1920s and 1930s and a vote was taken in May 1933 on the issue. The status quo was maintained with a vote of 33 to 19. A further vote took place in 1941 and this time a change did take place by a vote of 20 for Sunday play and 16 against. However until about 1953 play was not allowed after 7pm.

Membership numbers were relatively small until the latter half of the 20th century. Between 30 and 40 members was typical for many years. Students *of Trinity College Dublin only* were encouraged to join. At the 1937 AGM a motion was passed allowing them membership *at a subscription of £1.1.0 without entrance fee.* Juniors got some little encouragement at that time. In 1936 the AGM agreed *that children might be allowed to play on (say) one afternoon each week on one court only during the whole season.* For many years there were seven courts, one of which was a single court. The latter was abandoned in about 1959. At the time of writing of the club history the President indicated that there were just over 240 members. In the 1979 ILTA Yearbook it was noted that the club had seven league teams and a membership of over 400. In that year three new hard courts were being constructed. By 1993 there were three artificial grass and 3 hard courts. By 1995 all six were converted to the artificial surface with three floodlit, a fourth being floodlit in the late 1990s.

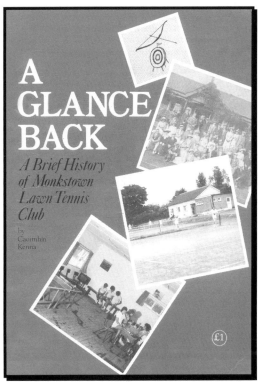

Monkstown LTC celebrated their centenary in 1977. Member Caoimhin Kenna compiled this booklet on the first 100 years of one of Ireland's oldest club. Caimhin was club president from 1977 to 1979. He now lives in Germany.

Club competition was always a regular feature and success in leagues was also to follow. The club have had some notable members such as Sean Redmond who kept the club going through his infectious enthusiasm when it might have collapsed in 1958. Earlier, an exceptional servant in the club could be found in Billy Marshall. He joined the club in 1926 and from 1937 he would remain as honorary secretary for over twenty years. Christopher Preston joined the club in 1931 when he was a student at TCD. His endeavours over the years were rewarded when he was elected an honorary life member in 1961. He was elected president for three years (1968 to 1971) and then made an honorary life member.

Bryan O' Neill is probably best known as a Treasurer at the Leinster Branch and at the ILTA. At Monkstown, not alone was he an organiser, but also a good tennis player. He won the President's Challenge Cup in 1976.

In 1962, a young Judy Gallagher won the first of eight 'At Home' Ladies Singles Championships. Seen here with J. Chapman (president) and G. Balfe (honorary secretary). Judy later became the club's honorary secretary.

Bryan O'Neill joined the club in 1960 and, as well as being a useful player, he was to prove to be a great administrator at club and national level. He has been a club trustee for many years. Alan Davy joined as a junior in 1956 and would be tennis captain twice and a secretary and committee member for many years. In 1973 he was elected as an honorary life member. Vincent Allman Smith was club champion nine times between 1925 and 1944 but became a club noteworthy when he was selected for the Davis Cup team in 1926, 1930 and 1932. He was also a member of **Fitzwilliam LTC.**

Mrs. Blair White was a superb tennis player in the 1920s and 1930s and won the Irish Open title in 1928 and 1931. Many other members of that family would distinguish themselves in the field of tennis. The following details on the Blair Whites membership at the club have been obtained from Caoimh Kenna:

The Blair-Whites

2 May 1914
C. Blair White and J.H. Blair White elected
8 May 1915
Miss Eileen Blair White and R. Blair White elected.
25 May 1916
Mrs. Blair White elected
10 May 1919
Cyril R. Blair White elected
15 May 1934
Mrs. A. Blair White resigns her membership
3 May 1947
Miss A. Blair White elected.

C. Blair White was the number 1 men's player for a number of years and club President from 1939 to 1942. His son, R.F. Blair, won the Men's Club Championships in 1945 and 1947.

Breeda Sheridan won many titles in the 1970s both at club level and elsewhere. She earned her place on the Federation Cup squad in 1977. That year she was number 3 in Leinster. She was also recognised as an extremely active club organiser. The O'Rourke family of Eleanor, John and Dermot graced the courts for a number of years; John won many titles in open competition. Dermot Whelan would reach the Irish Junior final in 1963 and win the club championships four times in the 1970s. The list of players could go on but one of special note is the O'Sheas. John and Judy (nee Gallagher) have won many club singles championships between them and their children have proved to be exceptional players too. Details on some of the successful and noteworthy Monkstown members are referred to elsewhere in this book.

No mention of the club grounds could be made without the mentioning of Mr. Gaskin. He was a famous grounds man for many years until he retired in 1930. At that time he was earning £2.50 per week. He was brought out of retirement and it was 1950 before he finally retired. *By all accounts, there was nothing that this dedicated man did not know about tennis courts. He spared no effort in maintaining them at the highest possible peak of perfection. And again, the evidence of this was reflected in lavish praise contained in the remarks section of the Visitors' Book. So successful was Mr. Gaskin in his work that the No 1 court became quite famous; and it became common for members of clubs from far and near to visit Monkstown for the privilege of playing on this court.* His last visit to the club was in the late 1950s for an "at home" day. He died in 1961.

The first clubhouse was built in about 1880. It was a wooden structure and was replaced in 1910. *At one time the veranda was adorned by climbing rose trees.* The minutes' book entry for the 23rd July 1938 indicates that the club was to be photographed for the periodical *Model Housekeeping.* The club was at a low in the late 1950s and just about survived. There was a renewed spirit thereafter. Unfortunately, a fire destroyed the club in 1973. A new building was constructed in two stages and completed in 1977, 100 years after the club came to life in the first place. One suspects that the club survived extinction and as a result became stronger and will have many years of success in the future.

Breeda Sheridan won the Ladies Perpetual Challenge Cup from 1973 to 1976. She receives the cup here in 1975 from club President, M. Greene.

Monkstown Lawn Tennis Club-The "At Home" in 1908.

The new Monkstown Lawn Tennis Club clubhouse was opened in 1978. At the ceremony were (from left): John O'Shea, Sean Sorensen, Caoimh Kenna (President), Professor Martin O'Donoghue (Minister for Economic Planning & Development), Councillor Tony Finnucane (Cathaoirleach, Dun Laoghaire Corporation), Harry Crowe and John Mulvey.

Monkstown Lawn Tennis Club
Ladies' Perpetual Challenge Cup

1932	Mrs. C. Blair White	1957	Kyra Wilson
1933	Mrs. C.R.E. Littledale	1958	Mrs. B. S. Malone
1934	Mrs. C.R.E. Littledale	1959	Mrs. M. O' Doherty
1935	Mrs. C.R.E. Littledale	1960	E. Kelleher
1936	Mrs. C.R.E. Littledale	1961	E. Kelleher
1937	Mrs. C.R.E. Littledale	1962	Judy Gallagher
1938	Mrs. C.R.E. Littledale	1963	Judy Gallagher
1939	Miss E.M. Dowse	1964	Judy Gallagher
1940	Mrs. J. Fitzgerald-Lombard	1964	Judy Gallagher
1941	Mrs. C.R.E. Littledale	1965	Judy Gallagher
1942	Mrs. B. Scroope	1966	Judy Gallagher
1943	Mrs. A.G. Quirke	1967	Miss R. Cantwell
1944	Mrs. A.G. Quirke	1968	Judy O' Shea
1945	Miss R. Mc Cormick	1969	Judy O' Shea
1946	Daphne Littledale	1970	Maria Lynch
1947	Daphne Littledale	1971	Maria Lynch
1948	Margaret Seale	1972	Jill Preston-Doyle
1949	Jean Kelly	1973	Breeda Sheridan
1950	Miss B. Tottenham	1974	Breeda Sheridan
1951	Jean Kelly	1975	Breeda Sheridan
1952	Jean Kelly	1976	Breeda Sheridan
1953	Jean Kelly	1977	Judy O' Shea
1954	Carmelia Fitzgerald	2002	Lisa O'Shea
1955	Mrs. J. P. Conroy	2003	C. Grace
1956	Mademoiselle Monique Brisson		

Monkstown Lawn Tennis Club-The "At Home" in 1954.

Monkstown Lawn Tennis Club
Gentlemen's Perpetual Challenge Cup

Year	Winner	Year	Winner
1902	W.B. Carson	1944	Vincent Allman Smith
1903	G.B. Pilkington	1945	R.F. Blair White
1904	C.T. Stewart	1946	Billy Marshall
1905	G.B. Pilkington	1947	R.F. Blair White
1906	C.T. Stewart	1948	G.P. Dempsey
1907	G.B. Pilkington	1949	N. St. J. McCarthy
1908	C.T. Stewart	1950	N. St. J. McCarthy
1909	C.T. Stewart	1951	R.D.G. Turbett
1910	G.B. Pilkington	1952	R.D.G. Turbett
1911	C.T. Stewart	1953	W.G. Hodnett
1912	C.T. Stewart	1954	R.D.G. Turbett
1913	C.T. Stewart	1955	W.G. Hodnett
1914	R. de C-Wheeler	1956	W.G. Hodnett
1919	C.T. Stewart	1957	P.J. Galligan
1920	C.T. Stewart	1958	P.J. Galligan
1921	C.T. Stewart	1959	E. Cahill
1922	C.T. Stewart	1960	J. O'Reilly
1923	I. Turbett	1961	E. Cahill
1924	C.T. Blair White	1962	J. O'Reilly
1925	Vincent Allman-Smith	1963	J. O'Reilly
1926	Vincent Allman-Smith	1964	John O'Shea
1927	A. St. J. Vaughan	1965	John O'Shea
1928	Vincent Allman-Smith	1966	John O'Shea
1929	Vincent Allman-Smith	1967	John O'Shea
1930	Vincent Allman-Smith	1968	John O'Shea
1931	Rev. Gordon Julian	1969	John O'Shea
1932	Vincent Allman-Smith	1970	D. Whelan
1933	S.C. Hutchinson	1971	D. Delaney
1934	S.C. Hutchinson	1972	D. Whelan
1935	W. P. Roper	1973	D. Whelan
1936	Vincent Allman Smith	1974	D. Whelan
1937	F. R. Longworth Damer	1975	Harry Crowe
1938	J. Nash	1976	D. Whelan
1939	Billy Marshall	1977	John O'Shea
1940	Billy Marshall	1985	Pat Crowe
1941	Vincent Allman Smith	2002	Stephen O'Shea
1942	Billy Marshall	2003	Stephen O'Shea
1943	Billy Marshall		

Presidents
at
Monkstown LTC

Period	Name	Period	Name
1877/1927	no record	1975/1977	Jack Hanlon
1928/1931	H. Dudgeon	1977/1979	Caoimhin D. Kenna
1931/1934	R.C. Peacocke	1979/1980	Edward Davis
1934/1937	Dr. R. de Courcy Wheeler	1980/1983	Stan Fox
1937/1939	H.J. Millar	1983/1985	Bryan O' Neill
1939/1942	C. Blair White	1985/1987	Ray McDonnell
1942/1945	E. Mitchell	1987/1988	Denis Fogarthy
1945/1949	Vincent Allman-Smith	1988/1990	Carmel Wyse
1949/1951	V. Drought	1990/1992	John Ahearne
1951/1954	J. R. C. Green	1992/1993	Michael O'Reilly
1954/1961	Christopher A. Preston	1993/1995	Tony Tallon
1961/1968	Jeremy Chapman	1995/1997	Hugh O'Neill
1968/1971	Sean M. Redmond	1997/1998	Edwin Hynes
1971/1973	Sean O'Meallain	1998/2000	Eric Cooney
1973/1975	Michael Greene	2000/2002	Micheline Grier

Captains
at
Monkstown Lawn Tennis Club

	Men's	Ladies'
Pre 1970	?	?
1970	Ronan Byrne	?
1971	Ronan Byrne	?
1972	Dermot Delaney	?
1973	Alan Davy	?
1974	Oliver Sheridan	Rosemary Ward
1975	Paul Kerr	Breeda Sheridan
1976	?	?
1977	Ray McDonnell	Nuala Galligan
1978	Brian Smyth	Nuala Galligan
1979	Eddie Davis	Anne Fox
1980	Michael O'Reilly	Hilary Walsh
1981	Sean Mallin	Kyra Thomas
1982	Sean Mallin	Kyra Thomas
1983	Sean Mallin	Martha Holland
1984	Norman Craig	Carmel Wyse
1985	John Ahearne	?
1986	Paul Swayne	Carol Beamish
1987	Gerry Halpenny	Brid Bunbury
1988	Dermot Delaney	Judy O'Shea
1989	Dermot Delaney	Annette Dunne O'Brien
1990	Edwin Hynes	Eileen Ryan
1991	Michael Kemp	Geraldine Coleman
1992	Bill Crowe	Geraldine Colgan
1993	John Mark Downey	Irene Scott
1994	Kein Polley	Pat Cowley
1995	Conor Browne	Susan Kennelly
1996	Brian McDaid	Betty O'Brien
1997	Michael Delahunty	Loreto O'Murchu
1998	Will McNabb	Anne D'Alton
1999	Kein Polley	Diane Ryan
2000	Frank Kane	Rosemary Ward
2001	Michael Walsh	Marie Louise Enderson
2002	Paddy McCarthy	Ailish Kelly

Monkstown Lawn Tennis Club-The "At Home" in 1961.

****

Fitzwilliam Lawn Tennis Club
[Dublin LTC]
(Founded 1877)

There are very few tennis players, anywhere, over the age of fifty, who have not heard of Fitzwilliam Lawn Tennis Club. If we limit that group to those who read even a little on tennis history, then we can be fairly sure of this assertion. Like all tennis players, this writer was aware of this great club from an early age. It was the club to which young players, from all over the country, would be drawn to at the end of August every year. 'Fitzwilliam Week' or 'Fitz Week' was the place where the Irish Boys and Girls Tennis Championships were held. The pinnacle of a young person's tennis life was to play there and, perhaps, win a match or two.

Of course, those that have followed the game over the years, will associate the club with even two more important events. These are the Irish Championships and the Davis Cup. The former was on a par with the All-England (Wimbledon) Championships for many years and might be said to have been better in many ways. It was first held in 1879. The Davis Cup took its first steps on Irish soil in 1923 when Ireland, for the first time on its own, played and beat India 3/2. This too was at the Fitzwilliam Club. Since that time the majority of home matches have been played at the club and provided many exciting contests.

Walk in to the present day club and just look in the trophy cabinet carefully. It will make the mouth water. The names on the trophies and the mementoes all are part of a club with a great pedigree. In nearly ever room and corridor there are the photographs of great players and events. They are of squash players too, the

club having been an important part of that sport's development too.

It is with a bit of trepidation that these next couple of pages are written. How can justice be done to such a club? With great difficulty. The stories, the great events, the facilities and the people add so much to the history. All demand, deserved, recognition. Help is at hand. J. J. Treacy, in 1927, compiled *Fitzwilliam's First Fifty*. This was followed, in the centenary year of 1977, by *The Fitzwilliam Story* written by Ulick O' Connor. We can add to this the many little stories to be found in Irish Yearbooks, but particularly in the programmes for the Irish Championships. The newspapers are always a good source. *The Field* wrote blow-by-blow accounts of the early Championships. In later years reporters such as Vera McWeeney, Colm Smith et al. kept the Irish public up to date on big competitions at the club. The club's own *Fitz News,* produced regularly for members since the mid-1990s, illustrates clearly that the club is still as vibrant as ever, has more activities than ever and has welcomed, even though late in the day, the weaker sex.

Most important of all are the people at the club. From the moment this book was broadened to an Irish History the assistance and co-operation in all sorts of ways has been exceptional. It would be correct, for fear of offence, to name no names. However, I will dare mention 'a couple'. General Manager, Terry Jermyn (General Manager), and others in administration such as Ros (Rosalind Dignam), Jenny & Michelle, as well as the Director of Tennis & Squash, Jimmy McDonagh, have been exceptionally courteous and obliging in very many ways. Several members, in random order, including David Fassbender, Barney Sherry, Frank Egan, Gina Niland, Gar Holohan, Eamon de Valera, Hugh Tinney, Joe Flood, Robin Gibney, Bernie Griffith, Albert Tee, Owen Casey and, not least, Harry & Geraldine

Barniville, are among those who have provided information on a broad range of Fitzwilliam and other Irish tennis items of interest. Lastly, not least of all, must go a special thanks to former (Centenary) president Joe Hackett, whose hands on advice and experience has been invaluable. These members have been a fund of information, wisdom and gave great encouragement.

Early Days

In November 1877 the **Dublin Lawn Tennis Club** was founded by the following gentlemen: F. W. Browne (solicitor), Arnold Graves (Secretary to the Irish Charity Commissioners), F. E. Greene (son of Rev. W.C. Green of St. John's Church, Stephens Green, Dublin), J. G. Kennedy, J. J. D. La Touche (barrister), C. D. La Touche, J. J. Stopford, G. McMurdo, J. L. Wingfield and Reginald Guinness (surveyor). These became the inaugural committee and were mainly professional, middle-class Protestants. The gentry would be members, in smaller numbers, but not in the same way as in the country clubs. At the time lawn tennis was moving slowly into gear, the Limerick and Monkstown clubs had tournaments the previous summer and the first Wimbledon Championships of that year established the rules of the game. This committee decided to have a limit of thirty members at an annual subscription of £3. Nearly 123 years later, in 2000 to be precise, the total membership (of all grades) would come to 2094, with the total subscription income coming to over £1 million. I think those founding members would be amazed. Not only at the growth of the club, but the huge achievements and the facilities now being provided.

The second club meeting, 23rd November 1877, decided to lease some ground in Upper Pembroke Street (near Fitzwilliam Square) on a ten-year lease of £25 per annum from Sir Francis Brady. By the third meeting (6th December) the club's name was to change and it was resolved:

> *That for the present to avoid confusion, the Club shall be called The Fitzwilliam Lawn Tennis Club.*

The way forward was a quick one. The committee were told, on the 15th December, that a Mr. Daly had agreed *to lay for the Club for the sum of 2s 4d a square yard such portion of the ground in Upper Pembroke Street that the Committee shall think fit, also including in this sum the laying of weeds and rubbish wherever the Committee shall decide: the asphalt to consist of a layer of tar concrete a half inch thick laid on ground properly prepared by him. Over this to lay a thin coating of boiled pitch.* Two courts were laid.

By 16th February 1878, Treacy (1927) later pointed out that: *In spite of all difficulties, the whole-hearted enthusiasm of that first committee enabled them to have four courts for play in less than three months.* The general meeting on that date were presented with the club rules and *the original committee retired, but*

was in the main re-elected. Colonel Arthur Henry Courtenay became a member at that meeting. Eight years later he would be the club's honorary secretary and the first president in 1896. One 'eminent' judge who was unanimously elected afterwards *wrote informing the club that he did not wish to join as his sons would not be admitted as well as himself on one subscription.* It appears, from the Treacy history, that the game was being compared with juvenile pastimes such as peg-top or tip-cat. The minutes of a subsequent committee meeting include "Resolved-That the eminent judge's letter having been considered, no answer be returned thereto".

Colonel Arthur Henry Courtenay of Fitzwilliam Lawn Tennis Club-One of the key men behind the early success of Irish tennis. He was club honorary secretary between 1886 and 1896 and president between 1896 and 1927.

The club was no doubt in the class of a 'men's club' right up to the latter end of the 20th century. One lady player noted that many of the early committee meetings were held in the Kildare Club. This I have not verified. Leaving out the issue of whether the club should have let ladies become members much sooner than they actually did, it is noted that ladies were part of the club's activities from an early date-albeit as invited guests.

In his 50-year history Treacy reported: *Provision had been made in the rules for the introduction of ladies by members; and certain hours had been set apart during which they were permitted to play. One of the first functions held by the Club was a Ladies' Tournament, during which tea and claret cup were provided. The cost of these refreshments were to be added to the general expenses, if given to the ladies; but to be paid for if partaken by members. A reminder of bygone manners is a minute to the effect that no member be permitted to smoke in the pavilion during ladies' hours.*

The Irish Championships at Fitzwilliam Square in 1897-the first international event to include ladies.

The Championships

The club made rapid progress in the early years and in 1879 held the first Irish Championships. In *The Field* of March 11th they inserted the following notice:

It is proposed to hold the Championships of Ireland open to all-comers under the auspices of the Fitzwilliam Lawn Tennis Club in Dublin on Monday, the 2nd June, and the following days.

That simple start was to commence a love affair over most of the next century. Many of the best players of the world would grace the courts of the club and, at the same time, enjoy the friendly welcome and atmosphere associated with this club. Up to 1990, the club would host and run the Irish Championships, every year it was held except for 1967. In the 36 years up to and including 1914, when the Great War was to stop play for four years, 20 of the Wimbledon Championship winners in the men's singles were also to win in Dublin. These were not twenty different individuals as there were players who won either or both championships more than once. These multiple winners were either English or Irish, the players moving back and forward across the Irish Sea. Percy French would observe this annual event, and even played in it himself. He would write in 1884:

And now our haughty challenge
Has reached the Renshaw's home,
Swift, swift the great twin brethren
Come seeding o'er the foam.

In about 1886 he would refer to *the steamers filled with champion argosies of mighty male......the Connaught plunging through the thunderblant. Till her*

engines throb no longer, gangways to the pier are hurled, And along them pour the coming wonders of the tennis world.

More picturesque words on the early game can be found in Chapter 3. There is no doubt that the Irish and English Championships were equally revered by the top players, they were to be the Adam and Eve of competitive tennis worldwide. While Wimbledon might be the Adam, having had the earlier start (in 1877), the attraction of Dublin and Fitzwilliam was irresistible to the players of the day. Any conqueror of both, in the same year, could be considered the champion of the world for that 'season'. Five gentlemen fitted this title. One was Doctor Joshua Pim in 1893 and 1894. The other four were in fact two sets of English brothers. Twins, Willie (1881, 1882) and Ernest (1888) Renshaw would win 7 Irish and 8 English titles between them. The Doherty brothers, Reggie (1899, 1900) and Laurie (1902), were to be part of a flagging tennis revival at the start of the 20th century. They would take away 4 Irish and 9 English titles between them.

We must not forget that in this early period Ireland's tennis strength was equal to any in the world. In Ireland the majority of the 'first class' players were members of the Fitzwilliam club. The first full-scale international anywhere in the world was held in Dublin in 1892. It was all doubles. Ireland beat England 5/4 in that match. The following table for the Men's Singles Championships in Ireland and England includes only those who have won at least two titles in that time period. The full Irish Championship listing, and a further discussion on this event, of winners is to be found in Chapter 5. The Irish players are indicated in **bold**. The first and last winning years are shown in

Irish Championship Men's doubles action at Fitzwilliam Square Dublin in 1898. The members of Fitzwilliam Lawn Tennis Club were responsible for the development and success of the Irish Championships.

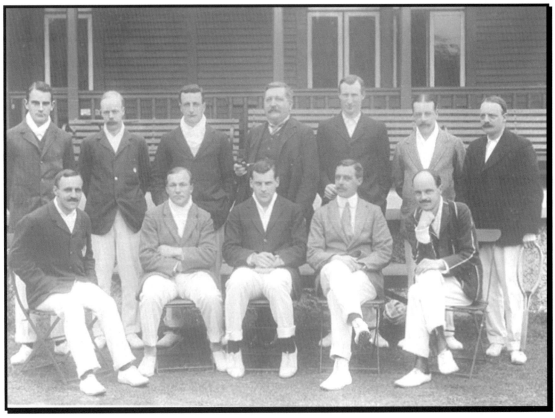

The 1908 match between Fitzwilliam Lawn Tennis Club and a visiting team from Yorkshire.

The History of Irish Tennis

In 1909 Ireland played their first international match outside these islands when they travelled to Berlin. The tie was lost by 11 matches to 4. In 1910 the return match (above) was hosted by Fitzwilliam Lawn Tennis Club in Dublin. This time Ireland won by 12 matches to 3. Most (if not all) of the Irish team were members of the host club. Details of this match are given in chapter 5.10.

brackets. Apart from New Zealander Tony Wilding, who does not appear to have played in the Irish Championships, the other multiple winners are from these islands. The first 'foreign' player to win at Wimbledon (the English Championships) was Australian Norman Brookes. That was in 1907. Were it not for the great War and the uprising in Ireland things just might have been different in Ireland in terms of international entries. We will never know. The first men's winner at Fitzwilliam from outside the home countries was in fact a Frenchman. This was Pierre Henri Landry.

Multiple Winners of Irish and English Singles Championships (Men) between 1877 and 1914.	Champs. Won		
	Ireland	England	Total
Willie Renshaw (1880-1889)	3	7	10
Jim Parke (1904-1913)	8	0	8
Reggie Doherty (1897-1901)	3	4	7
Laurie Doherty (1902-1906)	1	5	6
Ernest Renshaw (1887-1888)	4	1	5
Joshua Pim (1893-1895)	3	2	5
Herbert Lawford (1884-1887)	3	1	4
Wilfred Baddeley (1891-1896)	1	3	4
Tony Wilding (1910-1914)	0	4	4
Arthur Gore (1901-1909)	0	3	3
Ernest Lewis (1990-1991)	2	0	2
Willoughby Hamilton (1890-91)	1	1	2
Harold Mahony (1896-1898)	1	1	2
John Hartley (1879-1880)	0	2	2

A similar analysis of the ladies singles can be carried out but, from an Irish point of view, not an impressive one. We have had only one Irish lady winner of the Wimbledon Championships, namely Lena Rice of Newhill, County Tipperary. She did reach the Irish final in one year only. Then she was beaten by Louisa (*Lou*) Martin 7/5 6/0. Lou was perhaps the unluckiest of Irish ladies not to win Wimbledon. She won a total of nine Irish Championships between 1889 and 1903 and was runner-up at least three times. She appears to have played in the Wimbledon singles in only three years (1898, 1900 & 1901) and each time reached the All-Comer's final. The narrowest loss was to Chattie Cooper in 1900 (6/8 7/5 1/6). On the other hand, in Ireland she beat at least three Wimbledon Champions in Irish finals, namely Lena Rice, Blanche Hillyard and Chattie Cooper.

Mary Louisa (Lou) Martin, Winner of most Irish Championships (9) before the Great War.

Helena Rice from Newinn, County Tipperary is Ireland's only winner of the ladies' championship at Wimbledon. She won the Irish Mixed Championship in 1889 with Willoughby Hamilton in a best of five set match against England's H. S. Stone and Blanche Hillyard. In 1890 'Lena' reached the Irish singles final only to lose to Louisa Martin 9/7 6/4.

Another Irish lady to do well was May Langrishe. She won the Irish title three times (1879, 1883 & 1886). She was a member of the tennis-playing gentry family from Kilkenny. She appears to have played at Wimbledon only twice. In 1885 she lost to the winner Maud Watson in her first match (0/6 2/6) and in 1891 to Blanche Hillyard (4/6 1/6) having beaten M. Jacks (11/9 6/3) in her first round. Ruth Durlacher (nee Dyas) reached at least three Irish finals (1899, 1901 & 1902) each time losing to Lou Martin. She did well at Wimbledon reaching one All-Comer's final. This was in 1899 when she was beaten, by the eventual winner, Blanch Hillyard 7/5 6/8 6/1. Two years earlier, at the Queen's Covered Court Championships, she was beaten by Edith Austin in the final by the narrowest of margins 9/7 6/4 12/10. At the time no ladies match, anywhere, appears to have come near this total of 48 games. At Wimbledon it would be 1966 before this record was broken i.e. 52 games between Janine Lieffrig (France) and Helga Schultze (Germany). Unfortunately, the Irish records are not nearly as complete and no comparison can be made. For completeness the following table are the Englishwomen that won both Championships in that period of time.

We should not forget the doubles experts. There were a few players in the first fifty years of the club that won many titles. Not all of the best men, but most, were members of the club. Peter Aungier, Ernest

Browne, Eyre Chatterton, the Chaytor Brothers, George Ball-Greene, T.D. Good and J.F. Stokes were among them. Browne was in seven Irish doubles finals, winning one men's (1882) and two mixed (1882, and 1883). Stokes was the club's honorary secretary for a number of years and on the playing front Irish Doubles Champion no less than seven times (with four different partners between 1905 and 1921).

James (Jim) Cecil Parke was the winner of most Irish Championships (8) before the Great War.

Multiple Winners of Irish and English Singles Championships between 1877 and 1914.	Champs. Won		
	Ireland	England	Total
Blanche Hillyard (nee Bingley)	3	6	9
Charlotte Steery (nee Cooper)	2	5	7
Lottie Dod	1	5	6
Maud Watson	2	2	4
Muriel Robb	1	1	2
Ethyl Larcombe	1	1	2

Between the Wars

The club continued to grow in stature and in unison with the newly formed Irish Lawn Tennis Association in 1908. The standards were always high and players, provided they were of the right class, were invited to become members. Top players were particularly encouraged and, as Treacy said in 1927, Fitzwilliam was recognised as the leading club in Ireland. In 1926, some 49 years after the start of the club, Gordon

The History of Irish Tennis

Fitzwilliam Lawn Tennis Club has hosted many tennis events since their foundation in 1977. In 1890 they hosted the world professional title matches between Thomas Pettit of the USA and George Kerr of Fitzwilliam LTC. Kerr won the three-day series and a purse of £75. the photograph above was on the occasion of the next big professional encounter. This was between Fred Perry of England and Ellsworth Vines of the USA. Both had been Wimbledon champions before turning professional. "This was the last match of their European tour and was one of the first played by professionals at a club under the control of an amateur body" (O'Connor, 1977). Vines' cannonball service was not enough to stop the Englishman who had speed and magnificent footwork Perry won both matches (6/4 8/10 3/6 6/3 7/5 on day 1 and 6/4 6/4 6/4 on day 2). Back row (l. to r.) A. Robinson, Thomas Vincent Murphy, R. T. Cherry, Ellsworth Vines, Fred Perry, John Miley, R. H. Ryland & E. Tomlinson. Front (l. to r.) P. A. Ryan, J. McCann (president, Fitzwilliam LTC), Edward McGuire, J. B. Shortt & B. J. Monaghan.

Spectators at Fitzwilliam LTC in the mid 1920s.

The History of Irish Tennis

At the Irish Open Championships at Fitzwilliam LTC in 1965 Irish players Michael Hickey and Eleanor O'Neill (left) were beaten by world stars Tony Roche (Australia) and Maria Bueno (Brazil).

Lowe, a British Davis Cup player, wrote in his book *Lawn Tennis* that "The Fitzwilliam Lawn Tennis Club is known all over the world, and has produced more first-class players in the past than any other club." A statement to be proud of, and very true. As much of the details on the Irish Championships are in Chapter 5, we will move quickly from hereon. Between the wars the entry to Wimbledon rose dramatically with a very wide range of countries having players entered. In both the men's and women's game, the Americans and French dominated this period. Due to the 'troubles' there was no Irish Championships in 1922. A scattering of the top world players participated. These included Sidney Wood (USA) who won Wimbledon in 1931 and the Irish in 1932.

More women note appeared. These included Elizabeth Ryan who won the Irish for three consecutive years (1919-1921) and therefore the Cup became her property. Esna Boyd won in 1925. She won her own Australian Championships two years later. Hilde Krahwinkel of Germany won the Irish Championships in 1934. The French came next. She won their Championships (which only became open in 1925) three times (1935 to 1937). Another player to win the Irish and then a 'major' was Senorita Anita Lizana of Chile. She won the Irish in 1936 and then went on to win the USA Championships the following year. The great Helen Wills Moody of the USA won the Irish in 1938 followed by her countrywoman, Alice Marble. Further details added elsewhere in the book. We should not leave this period behind us without

mentioning some of the Irish notables at the Championships. Cecil Campbell was the son of Lord Glenavy (President 1928-1931) and had been 'entered in the books' at the age of six. He would prove to be an exceptional player with a great playing record, detailed elsewhere. The Miley brothers, the Scroope brothers, Ned Mc Guire and Thomas Vincent Murphy were notable members in this period. In the years before the Championships were suspended (in 1944 and 1945) three exceptional players evolved in the

Solicitor J. J. Shortt was the honorary secretary at Fitzwilliam LTC between 1923 and 1929 and oversaw the first Davis Cup matches played in this country.

Fitzwilliam LTC first hosted the Open Irish Boy's Championship in 1914. The first Girl's Open was in the 1920s. Each August the best Irish juniors, and many from abroad, congregate at Fitzwilliam LTC. The above photograph is that of the 1946 Championship of Ireland Girl's finalists. June Dwyer (right) from Cork beat Mary Roche (Sacred Heart Convent, Roscrea), 8/6 3/6 7/5. Mary later married Willie O'Neill who played on the Irish rugby team in the front row between 1952 and 1954.

mens' game. George Lyttleton Rogers, based at **Nice LTC**, and at one time ranked 4 in France, won the event in 1936 and 1937. In 1940 and 1943 it was Lansdowne's Raymund Egan. Cyril Kemp was to be the best player in the 1940s. He was the Fitzwilliam Club Champion from 1938 to 1949 and had a most distinguished tennis career. The multi-international George McVeagh was club champion in 1935 and 1950 and was not far behind. He did win the Irish Championship doubles in 1936.

The Australians

From the end of the war up to 1967, when Fitzwilliam did not run the championships, there was a great influx of international players. From India, South Africa, New Zealand, the USA and Australia came large numbers of the best. Such was the standard that in that 21-year period, that only one Irishman would claim the title in that period. This was Cyril Kemp in 1950. The most famous of our winners in that period was undoubtedly Australian Rod Laver. In this period, immediately before the advent of Open Tennis, the lady visitors were equally, if not more impressive in terms of world recognition. Among the winners were Louise Brough (1946), Maureen Connolly (1952, 1954) and Billie Jean Moffitt (1963) from the USA, Maria Bueno (1964) from Brazil and Margaret Smith (1966) from Australia. There were other Grand Slam champions too. In 1951, Ireland's Betty Lombard had a comfortable win over American Arvilla McGuire

6/2 6/3 in the final. The twenty-one titles went to the following nationalities:

Nationalities of Irish Singles Champions in the years 1946 to 1966.		
Countries of Winners	**Men**	**Ladies**
United States of America	7	8
Australia	5	3
Great Britain	3	4
South Africa	3	3
India	2	0
Ireland	1	1
Brazil	0	2

R. H. Ryland was a vice-president at Fitzwilliam LTC and between 1906 and 1926 the honorary treasurer.

Chattie Sterry (nee Cooper) won the Irish singles title in 1895 and 1898 and Wimbledon five times between 1895 and 1908. Her son Rex presented one of her Wimbledon trophies for the annual match between the All-England and Fitzwilliam clubs. The first challenge was in 1947. By 1976 the English club had won 13 ties and Fitzwilliam 12.

Internationals

From an early stage the club was to be the automatic venue for virtually all international tennis matches played on this island for many years. These started against England in conjunction with the Irish Championships. Matches with Germany followed. By the early 1920s Ireland was a single nation in the Davis Cup and the 'home' ties were Fitzwilliam based. Later, other competitions, including those in the sport of squash, would be organised with the able backing of the Fitzwilliam club.

This 1920s action shot is of a visiting player in one of Ireland's early Davis Cup matches. Fitzwilliam has been the venue for the majority of home matches since Ireland's first entry in 1923.

Controversy

The 1960s was to be a time of major change in world tennis. While more and more world-class players were travelling there was still a distinguishing mark between amateur and professional. However, the amateur could make ends meet when 'expenses' were adequate. These, however, were growing rapidly and the Fitzwilliam Committee decided that this 'shamateurism' should be eliminated and backed the principal of Open tennis. This matter had been 'on the table' since about 1960 when the International Lawn Tennis Federation set up a special committee on amateurism in 1960.

Lance Tingay, in *Lawn Tennis and Badminton* (Jan 1 1962), discussed the matter in detail. He quotes from the report:

> "The amount of time now given to the game by the leading amateurs is almost equal of the professional. There is quite a changed attitude to taking of money for the playing of games. The sports-loving public of the world now clamours to see the "artist" class of player in every sport, and appears quite willing to accept that the artist, say, in lawn tennis, who must devote the best part of his year to the maintenance and display of his high standard, should have-as with all other types of artists-some financial consideration for his artistry. It is equally obvious that the days have long since gone when any outstanding amateur lawn tennis player, without private means, could maintain his position in the game without looking to the game for financial assistance. Thus, over recent years, the leading amateurs inevitably have taken to themselves things that were regarded as belonging to the status of the professional."

He also mentions a sentence in the report by the great French player Jean Borotra "Amateurism is a state of mind, an ideal, which cannot be forced upon anyone." There was, at the time, no unanimity among the 'big' nations on the issue.

While the ILTA decided on the 7th April 1967 to oppose Open Tennis (see Chapter 4), Barton Kilcoyne, the honorary secretary at the **Fitzwilliam LTC** wrote to Alf Walsh, the honorary secretary of the ILTA, on the 12th April stating:

> *The Committee of Fitzwilliam are unanimously in favour of Open tennis. This Club has more experience of dealing with the expenses of players than any other body and the present position, always undesirable, has now become unworkable. The Committee have voted that the Fitzwilliam Lawn Tennis Club will not promote the Lawn Tennis Championships of Ireland this year if your Association oppose Open tennis.*

On the 23rd April the ILTA met and it was agreed unanimously:

That the General Council having met in Dublin on 23rd April in order to give consideration to a request from the Fitzwilliam Lawn Tennis Club hereby reaffirms its instructions to its representative to oppose "Open" Tournaments should that subject be raised at the International Federation meeting on 12th July next, and with great regret accepts the Club's decision not to promote the Irish Championships this year.

History will record that the Irish Open in 1967 was organised by the **Ashbrook LTC**, that the All-England club pushed the issue of Open Tennis, and that in December 1967 the ILTF decided, by a majority, to accept the principle of Open Tennis. On the world stage, and in the Fitzwilliam club, matters were not always unanimous. A special club meeting was called for the 7th May 1967 with a view to reversing the Committee decision and re-open negotiations with the ILTA. The proposal to do so was carried (54/51) and the Committee resigned as they said they would. The new Committee wrote to the ILTA and (a) offered their facilities for the Ashbrook Club (b) to jointly sponsor the event with Ashbrook or (c) to run the event as before. The original ILTA decision was to stand.

Ireland's Geraldine Houlihan was one of the more successful home-based players in the 1960s. In 1963 she reached the final of the Irish Open ladies' doubles with Ireland's Eleanor O'Neill. Geraldine won this title in 1966 when partnering Margaret Smith of Australia.

In 1968 Open tennis had arrived and the club was back on track. Carroll's came in as the big sponsor necessary to attract the top players. Right up to, and including, the 1973 Championships, there was always a current, or future Wimbledon Champion on finals day. The 1971 ladies final was one to relish. It was a repeat of the Wimbledon final from the previous week when Evonne Goolagong beat fellow Australian Margaret Court 6/4 6/1. At the Irish Championships Margaret Court won the tie. In the mixed, an all-Australian affair, Evonne and Fred Stolle beat Margaret and Owen Davidson. The two ladies from down under played together in the ladies doubles but were beaten by Betty Stove (Netherlands) and Lesley Turner (Australia).

In 1975, the 90th Lawn Tennis Championship Programme had a leading article by Vera McWeeney, the respected sports writer. It was titled "Some Tennis Changes" and contained many interesting points. She said:

There can be no doubt that the wind of change is blowing at full blast through the tennis world. Wherever one turns there are innovations as the money moguls seek more and more outre ways of stimulating more interest in the game and thus swelling their bank balances....That is great for the wealthy Tennis nations but not all the countries can pounce eagerly on departure from the traditional way of playing tennis for such things cost a great deal of money.

Due to the generous sponsorship of Carrolls for the last seven years the Irish Championships have given the Irish public a chance of seeing lots of the world top players. Alas, Carrolls understandably have ceased this subsidy and who can blame them for they suffered grievously from the rudeness and highhanded behaviour of some of the players. It is regrettable that this should have happened but let us not forget that in the days before there was any sponsorship, successive Fitzwilliam Committees brought us the cream of world players. A glance at the Championship Roll at the back of this programme will prove that these former Committees were pretty far sighted bodies for the list of winners in Dublin reads like the Wimbledon Championship roll.

Alf Walsh, the former ILTA honorary secretary, also had an article in the programme in which he said:

Those people who had contracted with P. J. Carroll & Co., the sponsors, to appear last year and did not turn up, thereby seriously injured the Tournament with the result that there is no sponsorship any longer. Let it be said here and now that Tennis supporters have every reason to be grateful to Carrolls for all they have done to help in the past few years.

Foreign players still came, but not of the same ranking as hitherto. **Fitzwilliam LTC** would continue with the event until 1991. Sponsors came back. Lombard & Ulster, Carlsberg and Bailey's were supporters of the event in the 1980s. In fact Carrolls were associated with the national club doubles events, a competition that was held in conjunction with the Irish Open in 1978.

The Open went to the Riverview club in 1991 and a few years later the event was split between the Ladies and Men's Irish Open, each having their own sponsors.

Competing in the Irish Open at Fitzwilliam LTC in 1946 were (from left) Jean Bostock (GB), Pat Todd (USA), Bea Carris (GB) & Doris Hart (USA)

The Club

There is a saying that everything that stands still will die. This is certainly not applicable to the membership at the **Fitzwilliam LTC**. Not alone were they at the forefront in terms of world tennis innovation, they also have continually moved with the times in the facilities provided for their members. This has been a path that has extended for some 125 years and continues to do so.

The facilities at the club were used for the inaugural Ladies Championships in 1879, the first of its kind in world tennis. May Langrishe beat Miss D. Meldon in the final, 6/2 0/6 8/6. It was described by Treacy as a *great adventure*. While the men played on the six grass courts in the splendour of Fitzwilliam Square, it *was considered too public* for the ladies. *To keep the matches as private as possible, admission was by members voucher only, which made people all the more anxious to witness the play.*

In 1880 the club moved to Wilton place to cater for the growing membership. A ground adjacent to Lad Lane was selected and No. 6 Wilton Place was purchased as the club premises. The grounds were to be those of the club for 92 years. The lease was ultimately purchased. The Championships would continue to be played in Fitzwilliam Square until 1903 and then at the club. In 1902, No. 6 was sold and a pavilion was built on the grounds and had a *hint of a Swedish summer house* about it.

The two-acre property was becoming more and more valuable and at the AGM on the 6th June 1969 it was decided to accept an offer. In 1972 the club moved to

Appian Way and has been there since. It did mean that the championships were to be on hard courts, maintaining of grass courts in our climate was no longer considered practical. The facilities included four grass courts however and 7 hard courts. In addition, there were to be two indoor courts, six squash courts, a heated swimming pool, a billiard room and fine dressing and social facilities. Additional indoor facilities are now available in the club and the outdoor court number is six. One of the best facilities one could find and certainly a long way forward from the old pavilion with its shaky stairs, wooden walls and floors and cramped locker rooms. In the year this book is being completed even further improvements are being made.

Sports Variety

Even at an early stage the club did not confine itself to tennis. Bicycle polo was played on the grounds and, at one time, the club hired a cricket professional for the members benefit. Cycling became one of the crazes at the end of the 19th century and the club organised cycle tours. As O' Connor pointed out: *An advantage of the cycling tour was that though Fitzwilliam was not open to women members, once you got the ladies in the countryside on their bicycles without chaperones, the severities of Victorian etiquette could be relaxed.*

A squash court was built at an early stage. It was not regulation size and was replaced in the 1930s. In about 1964 two courts, with a small gallery, were constructed. Many tennis players would play squash to keep fit but, for others squash became their premier sport. In either event, the club has probably produced more top class squash players in Ireland as well as tennis players. The first squash international was in 1937 when Ireland were beaten 4/1 by Scotland, in Edinburgh. All the team were from the club: George McVeagh, Willie Sandys, Paul McWeeney, Brendan Towers and Bruce Cairn-Duff. The club has in the intervening years hosted many international and Irish Championships with many of the top players in the world playing in their facilities. Between 1956 and 1972 Donald Pratt would be capped 52 times for Ireland, a world record at the time. He would also win 10 Irish Championships. Very many of the Irish Champions have been members of the club. A full listing of the Irish men's Open champions is given in Chapter 2.

In recent years the club produce a regular newsletter for their members. It is in fact a well produced magazine with up to date activities and results included. A glance at these magazines shows the expansion of interests. Committees are organised for these 'sports' and competition is high on the agenda. These include snooker, billiards, golf, bridge, swimming on top of tennis and squash. Added to this is an 'Intermediate Committee', organising events for younger members, a Wine Committee, a Gymnasium Committee and the well- established 'Fitzamblers', walks and picnics being the order of the day.

In the club is a photograph of the cyclists at Kilternan in 1897. To celebrate the centenary of that event,

A Munster-Leinster match at Fitzwilliam LTC (circa 1939). From left: Harry Cronin (M), Eustace Fannin (L), Hilda Wallis (L), Frances Daly (M), Teddy Daly (M), Binkie Harman (M) and Willie Sandys (L).

Club member Tom Phelan organised a cycle trip from the Golden Ball, Kilternan, back to the club. It was the 28th December and 12 hardy members did the 8-mile downhill cycle followed by mulled wine. Tom also composed a poem to celebrate the event. In issue 8 of Fitz News can be found the eight verses. The first two are:

> *Fitzwilliam Cycle Club, 1897*
> *Up there now, smiling from heaven*
> *On apostles honouring their picture on a wall*
> *On bikes, after Christmas, at the Golden Ball*
>
> *Their photo is now a hundred years old*
> *But we felt older and very cold*
> *'Twas a day for jackets, thermals and mitts*
> *Hell or high water, we were cycling to Fitz.*

The original cycle in 1897 was during the summer but Tom, in his last verse, pleads that their December 1997 efforts not to be forgotten by the cyclists of 2097.

> *So, two oh nine seven; look back if you like*
> *Have a drink for us, and on yer bike!*
> *We enjoyed our day, and we thought of you,*
> *And we think you'll enjoy that too.*

Competition

To detail the many tennis, and other successes, at Fitzwilliam Lawn Tennis Club, would nearly take a book in itself. The club has fielded teams in all ranges of competition from an early date. What many may not know is that the club was responsible for organising inter-club events in the days before the Dublin Leagues took off. At a *Meeting of Hon. Secs. of Lawn Tennis Clubs in Ireland*, held at Fitzwilliam on the 19th April 1888, Regulations for Inter-Club matches were discussed and agreed. These were adopted at a further meeting on the 23rd March 1889. A list of 18 regulations/rules were adopted. Interesting ones included :

[a] *The hour for cessation of play shall be fixed by mutual agreement before the commencement of play.*

[b] *The number of single-handed or four-handed (doubles) matches, or both, shall be settled by mutual agreement between the competing clubs.*

[c] *Players belonging to two competing Clubs shall play for the Club of which they have been members longest* and

[d] *Ayers' championship balls of the current season shall be used in every Inter-Club Match.*

Arthur H. Courtenay, the club's honorary secretary between 1886 and 1896, and later its first president, prepared a set of Rules (25 in number) for the *Fitzwilliam Inter-Club Challenge Cup Competitions.* The competitions were for the Fitzwilliam Cup (First Class) and the Fitzwilliam Cup (Second Class). The top event was for club teams having a 'first class' team. The latter for the second team of a club having a first class team of the first team of other clubs. A 3rd Class Challenge Cup was envisaged in the rules but in the Handbooks of 1894 and 1895 there is no mention of these events having taken place. This competition was for mixed team. The rules did say that *Unless there be at least five entries in this Class no Competition will take place.* The Rules were well thought out allowing for weather conditions, the safety of the Cups etc. Matters of dispute were referred *to the sole arbitration of the Committee of the Fitzwilliam Club, whose decision shall be final and binding upon the Clubs.*

The results for the first few years were as follows. The data comes from the 1894 and 1895 Handbooks. No result for Junior Cup is included for 1895 as the competition completion date in the Rules (30th June) was probably after publication while that of the Senior Cup was earlier (25th May in 1895).

	Senior Cup	Junior Cup
1891	Fitzwilliam	Mount Temple
1892	Lansdowne	Wilton
1893	Fitzwilliam	Lansdowne 2nds
1894	Not completed	Mount Temple
1895	Fitzwilliam	?

Due to the historic nature of this event the recorded details for 1893 and 1894 (in the first Handbooks on Irish Tennis) are summarised here.

Fitzwilliam Cup (First Class)
1893

Wilton (the winner of the Junior Cup in 1892) scratched to Fitzwilliam, leaving only two clubs in the event. **Fitzwilliam LTC** beat **Lansdowne LTC** 5/4 on the 19th May at the Fitzwilliam grounds.

Tom Chaytor lost to Joshua Pim 4/6 6/3 3/6
Grainger Chaytor beat Frank Stoker 6/4 6/4
George Ball-Greene lost to
                 Manliffe Goodbody 4/6 2/6
Ernest de S. Browne beat
                 R. J. Lonsdale 2/6 6/4 6/3
C. H. Chaytor lost to
                 W. W. Goodbody 6/1 3/6 6/8
Tom Chaytor/Ball-Green lost to
                 Pim/Stoker 2/6 7/5 6/8
G. Chaytor/Browne beat
                 Lonsdale/"St. George" 6/4 6/1
C. H. Chaytor/Boyd beat
                 Goodbody/Goodbody 10/8 0/6 6/2

1894

Three teams entered this years event, Fitzwilliam had a bye and Lansdowne beat Dublin University. The final was not played. No reason was given.

1895

Four teams entered. Fitzwilliam beat Dublin University 8/1 and Lansdowne beat Mount Temple 5/4. The final was played on the 25th May at

Fitzwilliam LTC. Fitzwilliam won the Cup by 8 matches to 1. The results were as follows:

Tom Chaytor beat Joshua Pim 6/2 6/2
Grainger Chaytor beat Frank Stoker 6/0 7/5
George Ball-Greene beat
                 William St. G. Perrott 6/1 6/1
H. Boyd beat W. W. Goodbody 6/3 6/2
C. H. Chaytor beat C. Orphen 6/0 6/1
J. T. Maxwell beat C.P. Brett 6/4 6/3
T. Chaytor/Ball-Greene lost to
                 Pim/Stoker 1/6 6/0 2/6
D. G. Chaytor/Boyd beat Perrott/Orphen 6/4 6/2
C. H. Chaytor/|Maxwell beat
                 Goodbody/Brett 6/1 8/6

Fitzwilliam Cup (Second Class)
1893

Seven teams competed for the Junior Cup this year. These were Wilton 2nd, Dublin University 2nds, Glenageary & Kingstown, Lansdowne 2nds, Clontarf, Mount Temple and Fitzwilliam 2nds. In the semi-finals Lansdowne beat DU 6/3 and Mount Temple beat Wilton 9/0. The final was played on the 8th July at **Mount Temple LTC**. **Lansdowne LTC** won this event by 5 matches to 4. The results were as follows (Lansdowne names first):

J. Head lost to W. Martin 9/7 1/6 3/6
Orphen lost to G. F. Carruthers 4/6 6/4 2/6
M'Cormick beat "Knight" 6/4 6/3
Knox beat S. L. Fry 15/13 3/6 6/4
"Alexander" beat E.P. Roe 6/3 7/5
Pim beat Rogerson 6/3 5/7 6/4
Head/M'Cormick beat Martin/"Knight" 6/3 6/2
Knox/Pim lost to Roe/Rogerson 7/5 5/7 7/5

1894

The seven teams entered were Clontarf 1sts, Dublin University 2nds, Fitzwilliam 2nds, Lansdowne 3rds (who subsequently scratched, their 2nd team were not eligible having won in 1893), Wilton, Glenageary & Kingstown, Mount Temples 1sts. In the semi-finals Fitzwilliams 2nds beat Clontarf 1sts 5/4 and Mount Templs 1sts beat Wilton by 8 matches to 1. The result in the final, played on the 14th July at **Fitzwilliam LTC**, was a 6/3 win for **Mount Temple LTC**. Details were as follows:

W. Martin lost to A.H. Porter 1/6 4/6
G. F. Carruthers beat J.T. Maxwell 10/8 2/6 6/3
S. L. Fry beat A.W. Rutherford 6/3 4/6 6/3
E. P. Rose beat A. Betham 6/2 6/3
W. Rogerson beat G. B. Pilkington 6/4 8/10 7/5
D. Rogerson beat E. Knox 6/2 6/2
Martin/Roe beat Porter/Betham 6/0 6/4
Carruthers/Fry lost to
                 Maxwell/Rutherford 12/14 4/6

The Sterry Cup in 1966 against the All-England Club. Back (l. to r.): AE member, Dr. Harry Barniville, P. Moys, Harry Trueman, Joe Hackett, Ivar Warwick, & Michael Hickey. Front (l. to r.) John O'Brien, N. Brown, Jim Buckley, AE member, Sir Basil Goulding & AE member.

Since these early days the club has won very many matches in leagues and in other events. The list of club champions, since first recorded in 1908, is one of players who were nearly all internationals. The ladies' competition, first played for in 1997, is equally impressive. An interesting event is the annual challenge between Fitzwilliam Lawn Tennis Club and the All-England Lawn Tennis Club. This first took place in 1948 in London. Dick Sandys who won the Irish Junior Championships in 1929, would subsequently study medicine and, as a member of Fitzwilliam won their club championships in 1936. He moved to England before the war and became a well-respected member of the Queen's Club and subsequently its Chairman for two terms. He was responsible for setting up this annual match. Fitzwilliam won this first match 6/3. The All-England Club team included Dr. Colin Gregory, the former English number 1 player. The results of this inaugural match were (Fitzwilliam names first):

> Robbie McCabe beat Derek Bull 6/3 11/9
> Roy Brown beat Eric Peters 13/15 6/2 6/0
> Joe MacHale lost to Claude Lister 1/6 4/6
> Cyril Kemp beat Eric Filby 6/2 6/1
> George McVeagh beat Colin Gregory 6/4 6/2
> Frank Kenny beat H.G. Cooper 6/4 7/9 6/0
> MacCabe/Brown lost to Bull/Cooper 3//6 2/6
> MacHale/Kenny lost to Peters/Gregory 3/6 6/8
> Mc Veagh/Kemp beat Lister/Filby 6/8 6/3 6/1

Dr. Dick Sandys, George McVeagh, Norman Brown, Ivar Boden, Guy Jackson and Dr. Harry Barniville are among those who have been elected members of the All-England Club. Temporary members have included Peter Hannon and Ross Niland. Honorary life members have included Jim Fitzgibbon and Joe Hackett. At **Fitzwilliam LTC** honorary Life members have included Pat Hughes that great supporter of Irish tennis, Raymund Egan, Willie Sandys, Guy Jackson, Cyril Kemp, Seamus Monaghan and Joe Hackett. Added to these are the All-England members Ted Avery, Neville Hooper, Buzzer Haddington, Peter Jackson, Robert Dolman and David Vaughan. In 1999 a special inaugural challenge match took place between the club and Belfast Boat Club. Two of Pat Hughes' trophies were presented by his sister in law, Sylvia Hughes, for the annual challenge. These had been won by Pat on a visit to Alexandria in Egypt in 1934. The winning team take home the larger trophy, the losers the smaller one. Nobody loses and the comradeship, through tennis, continues on.

ALL-ENGLAND RETAIN CUP

A VERY strong All-England Club team led by international **Ken Weatherley** retained the Sterry Cup on the grass-courts at Wimbleton on Saturday when they beat Fitzwilliam by 7½ matches to 1½ in their annual match.

All England Club 7½, Fitzwilliam 1½ (All England names first): K. Weatherley and C. McHugo bt T. Burke and K. Fitzgibbon 7-6, 3-6, 6-3; bt C. O'Reilly and J. Sheehan 6-4, 6-4; bt H. Lappin and H. Sheridan 7-5, 1-6, 6-3. R. Bennett and P. Moys divided tiwh T. Burke and K. Fitzgibbons 3-6, 7-6; bt C. O'Reilly and J. Sheehan 6-4, 6-4; bt H. Lappin and H. Sheridan 2-6, 6-1, 7-5; M. Carroll and M. Stokesbury lost to T. Burke adn K. Fitzgibbon 1-6, 6-7; bt C. O'Reilly and J. Shehan 6-4, 7-5; bt H. Lappin and H. Sheridan 7-6, 6-1.

Irish Independent 24th August 1981

The History of Irish Tennis

One could spend many pages on the members of this special club. These include not just the tennis and squash players, but also those intrepid organisers and committeemen. A few are mentioned here, others appear in the chapters dealing with the Irish Championships, the Davis Cup and in the Who's Who of Irish tennis. Colonel Arthur Courtenay is one of the earliest organisers who was not only the honorary secretary but the longest serving president. He was described as being 'far-seeing and meticulous'

The first 'professional' was George Kerr in 1883 who began life as a ballboy and ultimately became world champion. Solicitor J. B. Shortt was the honorary secretary from 1923 to 1929 and president from 1944 to 1946. He oversaw the first Irish Davis Cup matches in 1923 and was described as 'prudent and energetic'. John F. Stokes was not only the club's honorary secretary for many years but was an international and Irish men's doubles champion seven times. Harry Maunsell, whose name is to be always associated with the Maunsell trophies, was noted for his lengthy period as ILTA honorary secretary. He was club President from 1941 to 1943.

Other club presidents have gained international tennis honours. These include John Miley, Senator Edward McGuire, George McVeagh, Joe MacHale, Frank Kenny, Joe Hackett, Hector Ryan, Harry Barniville, Harry Crowe and John O'Rourke. Their honorary secretary Charles Chaytor (1896-1904) was one of the famous trio of tennis-playing brothers. Dr. A. P. Barry was a great ambassador as Davis Cup captain and was club honorary secretary from 1933 to 1935. Willie Sandys held that post and was responsible for bringing some of the best players to our shores in the 1950s and 1960s. Barton Kilcoyne was honorary secretary from 1964 to 1967 and president in the late 1980s. His specialty was squash and was Irish Open Champion in 1960. Were it not for the presence of the great Donald Pratt he would have won many more titles.

Sir Basil Goulding, a great observer of the game and whose writings are recorded in Chapter 3, was President from 1965 to 1968. He was Irish Open squash champion in 1939.

Lady Members

A modern issue has been that of lady members at the club. Fought off for many years, this has now changed and they play an integral role in the club. In 1997 Bernadette Griffith became the first modern lady club (tennis) champion. What is not realised is that in the 19th century there were other club champions of the female variety. In some way they were considered members as the highly credible Irish Handbook of 1895 included a ladies handicap singles and mixed handicap doubles for the 'club tournament' of 1894. The lists distinguish club tournaments from open tournaments. The ladies involved were no doubt members of other clubs in the Dublin area.

The 1894 Club Tournament at Fitzwilliam Lawn Tennis Club

Event	1st Prize	2nd Prize
MS	Tom Chaytor	George C. Ball-Greene
LHS	Miss Shaw	Miss Leet
MD	Tom Chaytor/ George Ball-Greene	Edward H. Browne/ "L. Tennis"
MxD h'cap	H. Wilson/ Miss I. Scott	E.E. Knox/ Miss M. Stokes

An idea of the range of friendly competition between the club and other teams can be found in the *Fitzwilliam News* (issue 19) celebrating the 125th year of the club in June 2002.

Nov 2001 Galway LTC (A) Lost 3/6
Feb 2002 Mackintosh (Cardiff) (H)Won 7/2
Feb 2002 Public Schools Old Boys LTA (London)(H) Loss 4/5
Mar 2002 Queen's Club Vets (A) Won 139/120
Mar 2002 Dungannon LTC (A) Draw
Apr 2002 International Club of GB (H) Won 8/1
Apr 2002 Queen's Club (H) Won 8/1

7 teams played in the Dublin Winter and Summer Leagues. In squash the club made history by winning both the All Ireland Club Premier Championships for men and ladies. Apart from fielding 12 league teams, a series of friendlies were played over the winter months as follows:

Nov 2001 Sunday's Well (H) Won 4/2
Feb 2002 UK Jesters (A) Lost ¼
Feb 2002 RAC Club (A) Lost 1/3
Mar 2002 Edinburgh Club (H) Won 4/2
Apr 2002 Queen's Club (H) Lost 2/3, 1 halved.

2002: Fitzwilliam's Premier Squash Teams-All-Ireland Club Champions. Back (l. to r.) Hugh Fitzsimons, Aisling McArdle, Sarah Berkeley, Nigel Peyton, David Corbet and Gar Holohan (President). Middle (l. to r.) Deirdre Hourihane, Clare O' Brien and Gina Menzies. Front: Captains Louise Finnegan and Darren Mylotte.

American Tennis Tournament at Fitzwilliam LTC on the 23rd May 1992.

Presidents

1896-1927	Coloney Arthur Henry Courtenay	1977-1978	Joseph D. Hackett
1928-1931	The Right Honorable Lord Glenavy	1979-1980	Seamus Monahan
1932-1940	J. McCann	1981-1982	Henry Hannon
1941-1943	Harry R. Maunsell	1983-1984	Niall McCarthy
1944-1946	J. B. Shortt	1985-1986	Hector Ryan
1947	John F. Miley	1987-1988	Barton Kilcoyne
1948-1950	The Honorable Mr. Justice Cahir Davitt	1989-1990	Maurice Davitt
1951-1953	Senator Edward A. McGuire	1991-1992	Dr. Harry Barniville
1954-1955	J. J. Murphy	1993-1994	Kevin McGilligan
1956-1958	Trevor George McVeagh	1994-1996	Harry Crowe
1959-1961	R.W.S. Greene	1996-1998	John M. O'Rourke
1962-1964	A. Robinson	1998-2000	David Fassbender
1965-1968	Sir Basil Goulding	2000-2002	Gar Holohan
1968-1971	Joseph P. MacHale	2002-2004-	Peter Gilligan
1971-1974	William A. Sandys	2004- 2006	Declan Heavey
1974-1976	Frank Kenny		

Fitzwilliam Lawn Tennis Club Tennis Committee 1991/1992

Back (l. to r.): Tom Phelan,
Paddy Donaghy, Bryan Smyth,
David Fassbender, Michael Cowhie,
Henry Lappin, Frank Egan
& Rod Ensor. Front (l. to r.):
Harry Crowe, John Coyle,
Dr. Harry Barniville (president),
Seamus Shelly & Jim Fitzgibbon

Honorary Secretaries

1877-1882	C. D. La Touche	1937-1940	Edward McGuire
1882-1883	Ernest de Sylly Hami Browne	1940-1964	William A. Sandys
1883-1886	A. Maconchy	1964-1967	Barton Kilcoyne
1886-1896	Colonel Arthur Henry Courtenay	1967-1970	Hugh Hamilton
1896-1904	Charles H. Chaytor	1970-1973	M.A.M. Stanistreet
1904-1905	A.H.C. Baker	1973-1977	Kevin McGilligan
1905-1910	John F. Stokes	1977-1983	A. K. Maytham
1910-1912	C. D. Harvey	1983-1984	J.B. Cairnduff
1912-1915	H. B. Pollack & H.C. Grenfell	1984-1989	Albert Tee
1915-1919	John F. Stokes & H.C. Grenfall	1989-1992	Liam Collins
1920-1923	H.A. Vernon	1992-1995	Gar Holohan
1923-1929	J.B. Shortt	1995-1999	Seamus A. Toomey
1929-1933	(?)	1999-2003	Bryan Smyth
1933-1935	Dr. Arthur P. Barry	2003-2005	Seamus Twomey
1936-1937	Hector Ryan		

Honorary Treasurers

Much of this data is not readily available. A few known names are included.

1879	J. J. D. La Touche	1927-1966	(?)
1880-1881	F. W. Browne	1967-1972	Julian Drury-Byrne
1882-1899	E. E. Knox	(?)	Declan Heavey
(?)	John F. Stokes	2001-2004	Willie Shannon
1906-1926	R.H. Ryland	2004-	Richard Belton

Notable members at Fitzwilliam LTC. From left: Frank Kenny (club president, 1974-1976), Bernadette Griffith (the club's first lady champion, in 1997) and Cyril Kemp (the most prolific of champions at the club). Cyril won the club singles title for twelve consecutive years (1938 to 1949)).

Club Tennis Champions at Fitzwilliam LTC

Year	Champion	Year	Champion	Year	Champion
1893	Tom Chaytor	1945	Cyril Kemp	1983	Tommy Burke
1894	Tom Chaytor	1946	Cyril Kemp	1984	Tommy Burke
1908	John F. Stokes	1947	Cyril Kemp	1985	Conor McCullough
1909	Boxell	1948	Cyril Kemp	1986	Conor McCullough
1910	Adamson	1949	Cyril Kemp	1987	David Miley
1911	Simon F. Scroope	1950	George McVeagh	1988	Michael Nugent
1912	Val Miles	1951	Guy Jackson	1989	Robbie Dolan
1913	Val Miley	1952	Joe MacHale	1990	Eoin Collins
1914	T. G. Good	1953	Jim Fitzgibbon	1991	Owen Casey
1919	Cecil Campbell	1954	Jim Fitzgibbon	1992	Michael Nugent
1920	Simon F. Scroope	1955	Ivar Boden	1993	Stewart Doyle
1921	W. G. Ireland	1956	Harry Barniville	1994	Garbhan O'Nuallain
1922	E. D. Mc Crea	1957	Joe Hackett	1995	Jerry Sheehan
1923	G. E. Mac Kay	1958	Guy Jackson	1996	James Pringle
1924	Louis A. Meldon	1959	Jim Buckley	1997	James Pringle
1925	Charles F. Scroope	1960	Harry Barniville	1998	James Pringle
1926	Edward A. McGuire	1961	Harry Barniville	1999	David O'Connell
1927	Edward A. McGuire	1962	Joe Hackett	2000	Owen Casey
1928	Edward A. McGuire	1963	Harry Barniville	2001	Owen Casey
1929	Edward A. McGuire	1964	Michael Hickey	2002	Nicholas Malone
1930	Edward A. McGuire	1965	Michael Hickey	2003	Timo Barry
1931	Edward A. McGuire	1966	Joe Hackett	2004	Nicholas Malone
1932	D. D. O'Sullivan	1967	W.P. Walsh	2005	Barry King
1933	Vincent Allman Smith	1971	Harry Sheridan		
1934	Hector J. Ryan	1972	Harry Sheridan		
1935	George McVeagh	1973	Harry Sheridan		

Lady Champions

1997	Bernadette Griffith
1998	Karen Lord
1999	Gina Niland
2000	Lisa O'Shea
2001	Gina Niland
2002	Lisa O'Shea
2003	Yvonne Doyle
2004	Lisa O'Shea
2005	Lisa O'Shea

1936	Richard (Dick) Sandys	1974	Harry Sheridan
1937	A. Eustace Fannin	1975	Harry Barniville
1938	Cyril Kemp	1976	Ken Fitzgibbon
1939	Cyril Kemp	1977	Robin Gibney
1940	Cyril Kemp	1978	Jim McArdle
1941	Cyril Kemp	1979	Tommy Burke
1942	Cyril Kemp	1980	Tommy Burke
1943	Cyril Kemp	1981	Robin Gibney
1944	Cyril Kemp	1982	Brian Lawlor

The minutes of the 23rd Annual General meeting were presented in an ornate scripted manner, no longer fashionable. The meeting was the first of the 20th century. The accounts presented detailed the year ended on the 31st December. At the time the club had 163 ordinary member (£3 p.a.), 29 country members (£1 p.a.) and unspecified temporary and military members. A more complete listing of incomes and expenditures are given in chapter 7. Today, this is an enormous multi-faceted club with about 2000 members (10 grades), a large range of sports and committees, a large financial turnover, extensive staff and a continual drive to upgrade and change with the times. It may have lost the feel it once had-a club with roots at the beginnings of lawn tennis. However, it has gained much more. Rather than die in nostalgia, which could easily have happened, it has always been at the cutting edge, prepared to take on board new ideas. It still fondly recalls the greats of Irish tennis and tennis competition. The club nature of Fitzwilliam Lawn Tennis Club has not been lost and never will. There is no question that when it celebrates its 200th

anniversary it will still be shining as a club, giving example and so much to the sport of tennis.

On the 22nd October 1977 the club held its Centenary Dinner and the respected President Joe Hackett invited Buzzer Hadingham (Chairman of the All England Lawn Tennis Club, 1984-1989) to be its guest speaker. He was elected an honorary life member of **Fitzwilliam LTC** at the AGM in December 1999. He presented the following verse at the dinner, an appropriate note to finish this short piece on a club Irish sportspeople will always revere.

Is that the sound of ball on gut
In old Fitzwilliam Square?
Do ancient rackets thrust and cut
Old champions reappear?
What sporting spectre do we see
Still playing with such force?
The answer? Surely it must be
"Ghost" Hamilton of course
or there now, look, another plays
A star who made his mark

To re-enact those golden days
When Dublin had her Parke!
And here's a fact to make you think
(You must admit it's fun)
For long before that well known drink
You'd proved: Pim's Number One!
Ah! Glorious names from Ireland's past
Let's give three rousing cheers
Fitzwilliam Club you're here at last
Proud of your hundred years
Who knows what triumphs lie ahead
To match your yesteryear?
Well time alone will tell instead
This hope we all can share
A future filled with tennis bliss
More years of court endeavour
So now your toast my friends is this
"The Fitzwilliam Club forever".

Joe Hackett, Fitzwilliam LTC (on left), with international stars Maria Bueno and Roy Emerson (mid 1960s).

Having a chat with Eamon deValera, President of Ireland, (centre) before the tennis action were (in 1962 (?)) from left: Kevin O'Brien-Kenney (hon. treasurer, ILTA), George McVeagh (Fitzwilliam LTC), J. B. Shortt (Fitzwilliam LTC) and Walter Nicholl (president, ILTA). In background is Robert Greene (club president, 1959-1961).

The 1947 final. Jean Bostock (left) beat Ireland's Betty Lombard 3/6 6/4 6/1 in the Irish Ladies' Championship final at Fitzwilliam Lawn Tennis Club.

Fitzwilliam Lawn Tennis Club has hosted an extensive array of events since first founded in 1877. For the first hundred years of the club's history most, if not all, of the top players in the world have played at the club.

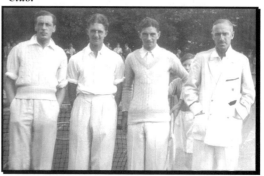

Ned McGuire (left) in a 1930s men's doubles at Fitzwilliam LTC. Senator McGuire was club president in the period 1951-1953.

The History of Irish Tennis

A selection of Fitzwilliam Lawn Tennis Club photographs

Carmel MacHale, wife of club President Joe MacHale, presents the mixed trophy to Marty Riessen (USA) and Pat Walkden (South Africa) after their victory over Bob Hewitt (South Africa) and Virginia Wade (GB) in the 1970 Irish Open final.

Rod Laver on the indoor facilities during the Open.

The History of Irish Tennis

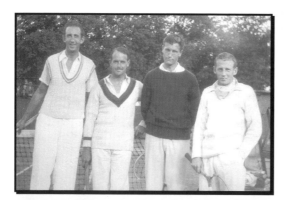

1960s Irish Open

Jorgen Ulrich playing for Denmark in the 3/0 victory over Ireland (30 April-2 May 1965). He beat Peter Jackson in three sets and with his brother Torben (below) beat Michael Hickey and Derek Arthurs in three sets. The Ulrich family, which includes their father Einer were involved in 80 Davis Cup 'ties' and 226 'rubbers' between 1924 and 1977. In 1948 the older brother Torben had beaten Cyril Kemp in the second round of the Davis Cup but lost to Guy Jackson and the Kemp/Jackson pairing in the doubles. Einer played against Ireland in 1932. This match in Copenhagen was won 3/2 by Ireland, Einer beating George McVeagh by losing to George Lyttleton Rogers in his two singles.

The stylish Andres Gimeno of Spain at the Irish Open at Fitzwilliam Lawn Tennis Club (circa 1963).

1926 visit of the Racing Club de Paris.

Irish Open 1970s

In 1960 Dennis Ralston (USA) won the Men's Championship when he Marty Mulligan (Australia) 6/3 6/4 7/5 in the final.

April 1996. The launch of the video "A Tribute to Joe Hackett and Cyril Kemp". From left: Harry Crowe (President, Fitzwilliam LTC), Cyril Kemp, Kevin McGilligan (past-President) and Joe Hackett.

Bobby Wilson (GB) won the Irish Championship Cup in 1963 and 1964.

Looks like sisters Thelma & Rita Jarvis (England) at the Irish Open in 1938 when they won the ladies' doubles title.

Enjoying the evening at the club

The History of Irish Tennis

2004: Andrea Maughan receiving her u16 trophy from Peter Gilligan club president.

Evonne Goolagong from Australia on her way to victory in the Irish Open in 1972.

Irish Open

Meeting the President of Ireland

1960s action

Christine Trueman (GB) (left) and Maria Bueno (Brazil)-Ladies' doubles champions at the 1965 Irish Open. In the ladies' singles final Maria beat Christine 10/8 6/4.

Action at Fitzwilliam LTC in 1920s.

Match over.

Ireland's June Anne Fitzpatrick (right) and Shirley Bloomer (GB) at the Irish Open (probably in the late 1950s). Miss Bloomer, later Mrs. Brasher, was winner of the Irish Championship in 1956 and runner-up in 1958.

The History of Irish Tennis

Shorts were the order of the day at the 1957 Irish Open. From left: Sandra Reynolds (South Africa) (ladies' champion), Sheila Armstrong (GB), Daphne & Trevor Fancutt (South Africa). Australian, Daphne (Seeney) had been playing as a single lady twelve months earlier. In 1956 she was in the mixed final with Hugh Stewart (USA) and in 1957 with husband Trevor. She won the ladies' doubles both years, in 1956 with Thea Hale (South Africa) and in 1957 with Sheila. The latter married an Irishman and came to live in Ireland.

Two of the great personalities at Fitzwilliam Lawn Tennis Club, Harry Barniville (left), and the late Jim Fitzgibbon, obviously enjoyed winning this veteran's title (circa 1970)

The History of Irish Tennis

Banagher Lawn Tennis Club
[King's County West LTC]
(Founded 1878)

Little is known about the early days of this rural club in County Offaly. In the County Library there are a series of photographs of groups of players, others playing tennis and a simple clubhouse. The dates shown are 1908 and 1914. A few of them are definitely early tournaments; all the ladies are wearing hats. The names that could be made out are Mrs. Burdette, H. K. (male), Artie, Muriel Waller, Tom Sherard, May, K. L. and Mrs. Landon. The club maintained its name right up until the 1940s. Either in 1947 or 1948, when open competitions were still being held, the name was changed to **Banagher LTC.** The annual tournament is one of the oldest in Ireland. In that year it was listed among the ILTA sanctioned events and the Challenge Cup was played for (presumably in men's singles). Some results of the open annual tournament are as follows:

Banagher LTC
Open Annual Tournament

	Men's Singles	Ladies' Singles
1893	Captain Foulerton	
1955	Gerry Clarke beat B. Keogh 6/3 6/2	M. O'Meara beat Gillian Kennedy 6/1 6/0
1956	Gerry Clarke	Norah Taylor
1957	Gerry Clarke beat Des Keogh 6/1 6/2	Geraldine Houlihan beat Ms G. Kennedy 6/3 6/2
1960	Harry Sheridan beat Gabriel Nolan 7/5 6/1	Gillian Kennedy beat Kathleen Galvin 6/0 6/1
1962	T. Francis beat D. O'Donnell 6/1 6/1	Gillian Kennedy beat Mrs. P.J. O'Connor 3/6 6/4 6/2

Banagher LTC
Pen Pictures of Old
(Courtesy Offaly County Library)

An interesting year for competition was 1957. Gerry Clarke (**Templeogue LTC**), known today for his work for veterans' tennis, won the event for the third successive year. In the final of the "Shannon Singles Championship" he beat Birr man Des Keogh, currently an entertainer, who was then a student at University College, Dublin.

In the ladies, a young 13 year old Geraldine Houlihan *crashed her way through to the final, beating the holder, Mrs. W. J. Taylor (Omagh), and the Irish badminton star, Miss Y. (Yvonne) Kelly (Glenageary), finally to dispose of Trinity student, Miss G. Kennedy, 6-3, 6-2.*

The records now show that this was the early winning days for a young lady who was to be one of our most prolific tennis and squash players ever. The then young Yvonne Kelly later concentrated on badminton, and became one of Ireland's foremost international players.

The club did not affiliate to the ILTA in 1967. No entry appears on the ILTA schedule for 1974 and the club was not on the affiliation listing. Both suggest the club had declined sometime in the previous ten years or so. The same applies in 1979 and later Yearbooks inspected.

＊＊＊＊

Military Lawn Tennis Clubs
(Late 1870s)

Evidence of clubs attached to military regiments has not been confirmed. However, as several officers did play in tournaments, from specified regiments, it has to be assumed that some courts were available to them. We know that there were players from the following playing in the Irish Open (no club was specified after their name):

82nd Regiment
Grenadier Guards
3rd Dragoons
84th Regiment
'The Buffs'

It is also well recorded that bands from various regiments were to be found playing a selection of music at tournaments and 'at homes'. Outside the Dublin area military personnel were members of clubs.

＊＊＊＊

Carlow Tennis Club
[County Carlow LTC]
[Carlow Co. Cricket & Tennis Club]
(Founded C. 1878)

This was one of the earliest clubs in the provinces. In 1879 at the first Irish Championships at **Fitzwilliam LTC** there were at least two entries from this club. In the singles Mr. E. Noble met the eventual winner "St. Leger" who would become famous for the wrong reason. Noble lost 6/1 6/1 and his opponent went on to win the inaugural championships. "St. Leger" of the home club and a Mr. B. "Phillips" of **County Carlow LTC**, two men in disguise, played together in the doubles. They won their first match beating H.F. Burke and S. Richards of Fitzwilliam in the first round (6/2 6/2)-*they were much too good for Mr. Burke and Mr. Richards.* It was a different matter in the second round. They played A. Graves and G. Hewson of Fitzwilliam. They lost the first set 4/6 *Playing in very fine form* they won the next set 6/0 and the last, in a *capitally-contested set* by 6 games to 4. In the third round, the semi-final, they were beaten by C. Barry and Peter Aungier of the home club again. It was a three-setter and they lost 6/4 2/6 2/6.

For the next few years there appears to have been no Carlow entrants. However, the club did make a name for itself in 1903. That year was the first when the event was not played in Fitzwilliam Square itself but at the club grounds in Wilton Place. There were few foreign entries and William Drapes, a banker from Carlow, beat James Cecil Parke in the final. Parke would prove a few years later to be one of the best players Ireland has ever produced. See chapter 6 for more on Drapes.

It is not known how the club name changed, or when. We do know that in 1917 the Club had the title which included cricket, perhaps it was always there but not included in early reference to lawn tennis in the town. The grounds were at Oak Park, Carlow. In 1917, during the Great War, a tennis tournament, including men's, ladies' and mixed doubles events, was held at the *County Carlow Cricket and Tennis Club Grounds* on the 8th and 9th August, play commencing at 1.30pm. The entrance fee for each event was 2/6 and to the grounds 6d. Under seventeen's would receive a handicap and players selected their own partners. Tea was served for 6d and would naturally have included fine baking by the local ladies (or their cooks). There was also a clock golf competition to raise funds. All was in aid of the Carlow Red Cross Society. A military band was in attendance.

In 1919 the 'joint honorary secretary' was a Mr. J. L. Kelleher. The AGM that year, held in the Town Hall on the 15th May, elected Mr. Kelleher again and Miss Gale. The honorary treasurer was a Mr. W. A. Lawler and the president Dr. Ryan. Interestingly, the newspaper report specifically noted that four lady members were admitted to the new committee. (A decision many clubs would not have made at that time). The joint secretaries in 1921 were J. S. McHugh and R. P. Gough, while in 1922 there appears

The 1959 Carlow team won the Crowley Cup in Clonmel that July. Back (l. to r.) Willie Purcell, Michael O'Dwyer, Noel Fannin & Emmet Shevlin. Front (l. to r.) Mai Hogan, Tess Delaney, Karina Haughey & Ann Bennett.

to have been only one (A. F. Dykes). In different years funds were raised for various charities such as the St. Vincent De Paul Society (1921) and the Carlow Mental Hospital (1922 and 1923).

It is known that the club was not affiliated to the ILTA in 1911 or 1920. This was not unusual at that time as many clubs were very much local affairs. However, having successful open tournaments did require sanction by the ILTA and most active clubs eventually joined the national body. By 1937, or earlier, the club was running the County Carlow Open Championships. That year the event started on the 28th June, the same day as the Irish Championships at **Fitzwilliam LTC.** The following year it started on the 4th July.

The club ran the County Carlow Open Championships for many years. A few of the results are as follows:

Championships of County Carlow
1949

MS W. Dawson beat N. L. Plewman
12/10 2/6 7/5 7/5
LS Miss A. McCabe beat Miss G. Jackson
6/0 4/6 6/2
MD Pat Reeves-Smith/W. Dawson
beat A. Telford/D. Gannon 6/8 6/4 6/4
LD Misses O'Dwyer/Murphy beat
Misses Lanigan/Jackson

1955

MS B. McCormack beat Willie Brown 6/3 6/2 6/2
LS Tess Delaney beat Mrs. M. Nairn 6/3 6/2

1961

MS Willie Browne beat Willie Purcell 6/3 6/3 6/1
LS Tess Delaney beat Paula Kerin 3/6 8/6 8/6
LD Tess Delaney/Ann Bennett
beat Paula Kerin/S. Purcell 6/8 7/5 8/6
MxD Willie Purcell/Tess Delaney beat
Willie Browne/Miss C. O'Connor 6/2 9/7

1962

MS Willie Purcell beat R. Quigley 6/1 6/4 6/1
LS Patricia O'Gorman beat
Miss M. O'Brien 8/6 6/2
MxD Willie Purcell/Ann Bennett beat
Willie Hosey/Tess Delaney 6/3 5/7 6/4

In the 1950s and early 1960s the Carlow club had some exceptional players in Willie Purcell, Tess Delaney, Willie Hosey and Ann Bennett. A member from that time recalls that there was a great interest in Tess Delaney who didn't come from a middle class background and who, today, might have made great strides if the opportunities had come her way. Willie Hosey junior some year later took up squash and became Ireland's number one in that sport. He apparently, was called in from the tennis court to fill in on a squash team and found his forte.

Carlow is noted for producing one of the best young players in Ireland in the 1960s. Des Early was Irish Boys' Champion in 1966, a year in which he also won the Connacht Junior Championships. In 1994 the Australian Ambassador to Ireland, Terence McCarthy, was made an honorary member by the club. The president at the time was Liam Quinn, and the occasion was the 25th annual Mona McGarry Cup Competition.

The following article discusses the July 1949 event and includes the activities of the noted Pat Reeves-Smith who was well known to rush off to horse races and back to the tennis again.

County Carlow Lawn Tennis Club 1922

The event was either the Open tournament or the "At Home". Both events were important social occasions during the year.

SUN SHONE FOR CARLOW TENNIS

After a rainstorm opening on Monday, the sun thought better of deserting Carlow Lawn Tennis Club's Open Week. For the remaining full and exciting five days the call was for cool breezes and soft drinks.

The entry -105- was an all-time record and competition for the Captain Douglas and Vice-President's Cups for ladies and men respectively, was exceptionally keen.

Perhaps the most interesting match of the series was the final of the Men's Singles which took 54 games to decide, W. Dawson and N.L. Plewman were two very evenly matched players. The first set was a real thriller and Dawson only won at 12-10. He lost the next 2-6, but went on to take the following two, 7-5 7-5.

A feature of the Finals' Day (Saturday) was provided by Mr. P. Reeves-Smith. He had reached the finals of both Men's and Mixed Doubles, due for play-off on Saturday evening-and he had also arranged to ride his own horse, Quai d'Orsay, in the 3.30 race at Tullamore.

He sped to Tullamore; rode his horse to third place; and returned to win the Men's Doubles and see the Mixed abandoned

Carlow Club and officials can be proud of their very successful meeting. Besides the large local entry, players came from Dublin, Athy, Enniscorthy, Wexford, Portlaoighise, Naas, Bagnalstown, Tullow and Kilkenny.

Des Early was one of the most successful of Carlow players. He was one of the few players to win the Irish Junior Open (u18) twice (1966 & 1967). In 1971 he won the County Dublin Championships at Carrickmines. He also played Davis Cup for Ireland. In the 1980s and 1990s Willie Hosey junior became Ireland's number 1 squash player. In his younger days he played a lot of tennis, just like his father before him.

****

Kilkenny County and City Lawn Tennis Club
(Founded 1879)

On Saturday the 25th October 1879 a local newspaper, "The Moderator", carried the following report:

On Wednesday evening last a meeting of gentlemen interested in the establishment of a lawn tennis club in this city was held at Archersfield, the tea house erected on the pretty pleasure grounds adjoining Mr. Arthur J. Boyd's garden being used for the occasion. The chair was occupied by Mr. J. S. Kelly, Manager of the Provincial Bank. The following were present- Edmund Smithwick, J.P., John Francis Smithwick, J. P., Thomas Kough, J. P., Simon Morris J. P., Dr. James, Dr. Hackett, L. J. Power, Richard Smithwick, D. Smithwick, Jnr., Adolphus Boyd, Arthur McMahon (City High Sheriff), T. J. Hogben S.I., R.I.C., Gladwell Boyd, T.S.B. Barton, John WadeJnr., W. B. Boyd, D. Doxey, E. J. Barry, Hugh Widenham, A. F. Towers, H. O'Sullivan.

Resolutions were adopted appointing the chairman as Honorary Treasurer and Messrs Barton and G. Boyd as Honorary Secretaries, and it was also agreed to make a concrete court, the ground being kindly given by Mr. Boyd, the popular solicitor.

This was the starting moment for one of Ireland's oldest clubs, thriving today with some eight all-weather courts. Back in October 1879 the Most Noble the Marquis of Ormonde was elected the first President, the post taken over by the Earl of Ossory in 1920. Today (2001) a more humbly titled, Mr. Steven Lanigan, holds the post. The first committee of the club consisted of A.J. Boyd, J. Empson, J.P., Dr. Johnson, R. Colles, A. Mc Mahon, J. Poe, L.J. Power, J. F. Smithwick, M. P., F. Sullivan J.P., J. Wade Jnr., R.C. Knox, Dr. Hackett, D. Smithwick Jnr. With ex-officio members in the form of Trustees being H. de Montmorency, J.P., T. Kough, J.P., E. Smithwick, J.P. and J. Sullivan.

The committee initially took out a twelve-year lease on the grounds in Archersfield. On 2nd December 1879 the committee agreed that the heads of families should be admitted on payment of one pound and be elected in the usual way (which was by ballot) and all members of the family would then be entitled to play. By the end of the following year there were 80 paid up members. And the club had one grass court and one asphalt court. Mr. R. Langrishe, a member of the family which became famous in tennis history, designed the first pavilion, which included dressing rooms for ladies and gentlemen. To-days more modern facility includes hot showers, a sauna etc., items not even considered at the end of the 19th century. The laying of the initial courts, and associated building work, was carried out by a Mr. Cleere at a cost of £91-4-0. Within a few years an extra grass court was installed as well as a four-foot bank around the courts. Entry to the club was by means of a pathway leading from the road through Mr. Boyd's field to a doorway at the end of the pavilion. A grounds man was employed to look after the courts for the princely sum of ten shillings a week (i.e. less than one euro in today's money).

1880 appears to have been the first Open Tournament at Kilkenny. The events run men's and ladies singles, men's doubles and mixed doubles. The entry fee for one event was 5 shillings and 10/6 for all events. Prizes came to a value of £40. Until 1889 all events were handicap. The club records listed below give the results for most years. *The Moderator* in its edition of Saturday 7th August 1880 reported the following:

The Open Tournament Presentation at the Kilkenny County and City LTC in 1913.

The opening tournament in connection with the Kilkenny Lawn Tennis Club commenced on Tuesday last on the grounds at Archersfield and the interest which evinced in the tournament by so many of the leading families of the county and city continues the club has a bright future before it. The club was established here last autumn and at once secured general support from the leading citizens and gentry of the county and the club has left nothing undone to make everything connected with the club in keeping with the important position it is destined to occupy.

Miss May Langrishe beat her sister Miss "B". (Maria Cecilia) Langrishe in the final by two sets to one. The former had won the inaugural Irish Championships (the first major ladies championships in the world of tennis) at **Fitzwilliam LTC** the previous year at the age of 14. The latter won second prize in Kilkenny by beating a Miss Hunt by two sets to nil. In the men's singles a Mr. Coote beat a Mr. Darby in the final by two sets to nil. Mr. Darby then played a Mr. Browne for second prize and won in the same manner. For the record O. R. Coote and F.W. Knox won the men's doubles when they beat C. Knox and Vans Agnew in the final. C. Knox and Miss Knox beat O. R. Coote and May Langrishe in the mixed final, the latter winning the second prize when defeating Mr. W. Pollack and Miss C. Connellan. The prizes were presented by Mrs. Bull of Newpark and a special tribute was paid to Lieutenant Colonel Sir James Langrishe for the invaluable services rendered by him during the tournament when *his intimate acquaintance with the intricate rules and regulations of tennis tournaments was constantly called upon.*

The Langrishe sisters went on to make a name for themselves in other years (see Chapter 6). They were both daughters of Sir James. There was also a third tennis playing sister, Adela Constance, the eldest. All three played in the Irish Championships in 1879. They had a brother Hercules. He was *a handsome and dashing young man known to everybody as Herky* and *won a tennis tournament on the same day as he won a famous bicycle race* (Mark Bence-Jones, 1987). Later in *Twilight of the Ascendancy*, Mark Bence-Jones would say the following about this hidden character: *Herky Langrishe, whose ancestral estate in County Kilkenny had been mortgaged seven times over, was able to support himself as a Master of Foxhounds, a yachtsman and a pioneer motorist by working his way through the £100,000 which his wife had been given by her father. As a first-class rider and shot, who was also highly intelligent and could be extremely entertaining, sometimes serious, sometimes playing the buffoon, he was one of the most popular men in Ireland; his popularity extended to England, where he knew everybody from King Edward VII downwards.*

In 1880, like many clubs of the time, tennis balls were hired by the players. The charge in Kilkenny was 3d "per rubber of three sets to provide for the wear and tear of balls". By 1913 the system had changed, players could then buy them from the grounds man for one shilling and sell them back to him for 6d. Used balls were purchased for 4d and sold back for 2d. (Note: One shilling became 10 pence following decimalisation; there were twelve old pence (d) in a shilling). The value of local military members was recognised in many clubs. Officers of the Army stationed in Kilkenny and certain regiments were admitted as honorary members whilst others paid a subscription of five shillings a quarter. At tournaments the local military band provided music. The refreshments were provided by the lady members at a charge of six pence per person. The price in the Kilkenny club remained unaffected by inflation and was only raised in 1941, to one shilling. During the First World War the committee of 1917 asked the ladies to confine the teas to one plain cake with bread and butter. Saturdays were the Club Days until 1930. The half- day in the bank changed to Thursday and the tournament day changed accordingly. The American tournament consisted of men's and ladies doubles and mixed doubles, all handicapped. The entry fee was 1/6 and one-day members, living outside a radius of two miles of Kilkenny, could play for the sum of 2/-.

In 1881, with Mr. Boyd giving the club permission to *take as much ground as was necessary for the club*, a second grass court was laid. Two further courts were laid in 1884 and the "No.5 court" was laid in 1914 i.e. the club now had five grass and a hard court. Mr. J. Woods, the grounds man in 1913 was given a raise from 10/- to 13/- and a new "Shanks" mowing machine was purchased by the club for £6.

Kilkenny City & County LTC Open Singles Winners

Year	Gentlemen	Ladies*
1880	Mr. Coote	May Langrishe
1881	R.Challoner Knox	May Langrishe
1883		B. Langrishe
1887		Miss Power
1889	D. Grainger Chayote	Miss Beresford
1891	A.G. Ash	Miss Burr
1892	V.G. Annealed	
1893	J.H. Head	
1895	C.J. Latham	
1896	K.A. Rind	Miss Languished
1897	R.O. Latham	Miss N. O' Sullivan
1898	J.L.N. Brown	Miss N. Sullivan*
1899		N. Brown*
1900	George Mercer	E.H. Boucher*
1901		F. Smith wick*
1902	C.K. Fowler	A. Sullivan*
1903		C. Cooper Chadwick*
1904		Miss Springfield*
1905		E.K. Fowler*
1906		L. Cuppage*
1907	W. O'Carroll	K. Allman Smith*
1908	E. Harper	M.H. Richardson*
1909	J.W. Crozier	E. Langrishe*
1910	G.C. Clery	Mrs. Clare*
1911	J.J. Carroll	E. Langrishe*
1912	W.H.T. Gahan	Mrs. Fleming*
1913	W.S. Caldwell	Mrs. Fleming*
1914	G.C. Clery	Mrs. Middleton*
1920	I.M. Fiennes	I. Marshall*
1921	G.C. Clery	D. Julian*
1923	H.A. Shore	M.E. Fudger
1924	W.E. Dudger	T.M. Maingay
1925	D.C.T. Lee Elliott	A. McClelland
1926	F. Boxwell	T.M. Maingay
1927	F.J. MacCabe	T.M. Maingay
1928	F.J. MacCabe	U.F. Foxall
1929	R. Hughes	B.E. Best
1930	R. Hughes	P.F. Lysaght
1931	R. Hughes	B.E. Best
1932	R. Hughes	Hope Furney
1933	A. Bradford	E.P. Priestly
1934	M. Henson	E.P. Priestly
1935	H.F. Sloan	E.P. Priestly
1936	R. Hughes	D. Hawkes-Corneck
1937	R. Hughes	Mrs. Kinahan
1938	P.E. Stewart	Miss Kearney
1939	P.E. Stewart	M. Harper
1940	J.A. Shalloe	W. Harper
1941		
1944	T. Ryan	K. Mitchell
1945	C.J. Davis	N. Sheehan
1946	T. J. Ryan beat D. Nolan 6/4 6/3 6/3	K. Mitchell beat A. McCabe 6/2 6/2
1947	Frazer Mc Mullen	Veronica Miley
1948	C. Cuddy	Heather Cole
1949	C. Cuddy	Heather Cole
1950	R.W. Tunny	Heather Cole
1951	Harry Crowe	Terrie Purcell
1952	Gerry Fitzpatrick	M. Meanan
1953	Harry Crowe	Heather Cole
1954	Barton Kilcoyne bt. H. Cummins 6/0 6/2 3/6 6/2	Rosemary Binchy bt. E. Dillon (Galway) 6/4 4/6 7/5
1955	P. Gargan	Rosemary Binchy
1956	T. F. McNamara	Rosemary Binchy
1957	P. Gargan beat P. Reynolds 6/1 5/7 6/4 6/4	Mrs. M.K. O'Dea bt. Miss J. Griffin 4/6 6/1 7/5
1958	P. Reynolds	J. Griffin
1959	D.K. Brown	Tess Delaney
1960		Tess Delaney
1961	J.C. Kelly	Mrs. D.B. O'Sullivan
1962	W. Purcell	Mai Hogan
1963	T. Byrne	Jean Kelly
1964		Sheila Purcell
1965		Sheila Purcell
1966	M. Whelan	L. O'Doherty
1967	A. O'Sullivan	Isabel Ryan
1968	M. Whelan	Ann O'Donovan
1969		Ann O'Donovan
1970	J.D. Lowry	Mary T. Walsh
1971	J.D. Lowry	Joan Byrne
1972	M. Whelan	Joan Byrne
1973	A. O'Sullivan	Dolores Dunbar
1974	Tagdh Lambe	Mary T. Walsh
1975	Noel Murphy	J. O'Connor
1976	Tagdh Lambe	Catherine O'Neill
1977	E.P. O'Neill	Jane Tyler
1978	P. Mullally	Jane Tyler
1981	D. McCarthy	Alice Fawsitt
1982	Liam Quinn	Alice Fawsitt
1983	K. Cashlin	Alice Fawsitt
1984	J. Fahy	Jean Tubridy
1985	Victor Drummy	Anita O' Neill
1986	Michael Daly	Eileen Ruddy
1987	Victor Drummy	Eileen Ruddy
1988	Victor Drummy	Emer Skelly
1989	Victor Drummy	Emer Skelly
1991	J. Conry	J. O'Brien
1992	D. Dillon	Fiona Long
1993	G. Harding	Fiona Long
1994	L. Carmody	I. McDonald
1995	L. Carmody	I. McDonald

*Only ladies handicap until 1923

By 1905 the club was in debt to the tune of £100 and guarantors had to be sought. This was reduced to £50 by 1911, the lowest since the club was founded some thirty-two years earlier. In the same year, the minutes book records that the annual tournament entries were down due to *the King's visit to Dublin and the Agricultural Show*. However, the club first showed a credit balance of £16.3s.6d in 1914, credit being given

The Open Week Committee at the Kilkenny County and City Lawn Tennis Club in 1945. Back (l. to r. F. Youell, R.Hughes, Walter Smithwick, J. Kirby, P.A. Healy, Reverend Purkis, G. F.Lwesi, R. Crotty, James Crotty, M. Deegan, Martin Crotty, P. O'Carroll, T.Stratham. Front (l. to. r) J. Crotty, E. Crotty, L. Phair, Mrs. Youell.

to the Reverend Mervyn Clare for his astute management. There were some financial difficulties during and after the war but by 1920 it was a very active club again. The subscription was raised to £1.10.s.0d for a member and his wife with an extra 10s.0d. for 'additional lady members'. Ladies joining independently paid 15s.0d per annum. County members were defined as those living more than five miles from Kilkenny and they were admitted at half price. The grounds man's wage was now £1 a week.

Times were to change. In 1930 an Extraordinary General Meeting agreed to allow play on Sundays, after 3pm. In 1941 play was allowed on Sundays for matches and American Tournaments, presumably at earlier starting times. The Open Tournament that started as a local tournament in 1879 has been continuous ever since, apart from two breaks. The first was during World War 1 and the second was in 1922 *owing to the inability of the outsiders to compete.* If we look down through the winners of this event over the years we see many players of note. Apart from the Langrishe sisters, we see winners who were international players, such as Heather Flinn (nee Cole) and Fiona Long. Among the men were internationals D. Grainger Chaytor and Gerry Fitzpatrick, as well as more recent notables in Tadhg Lambe of Tullamore and Connacht's Noel Murphy. One of the most sought-after trophies in Open Week is the Ladies Handicap Singles Cup. This was first presented for play by the Kilkenny Golf Club in 1889 and has been played ever since, even during the war years. Some results were published (See table).C. J. Shankley, father of the famous international athlete Maeve Kyle, was a committee member (as well as secretary) between 1918 and 1948. He was Headmaster at the local Kilkenny College. It provided the nursery for young tennis players in the area and a venue for club committee meetings. 1935 was noteworthy in that a bar licence was in operation in the club for the first time, during the last three days of the Open

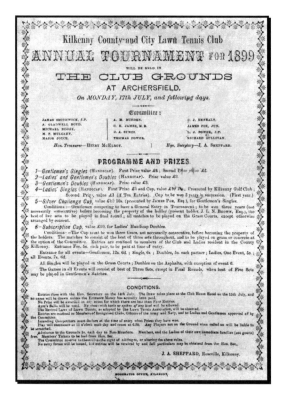

Tournament. During the Second World War there was a distinct lack of tennis balls and travel was difficult. For 1942 and 1943 the 'Open' was replaced by a tournament of a more local nature. Finances were difficult and the bank returned a cheque of £14, the amount of the annual rent. The committee changed banks and the following members became guarantors: James Poe, A.G. Davis, R. Reynolds, D. Scott, G. Kinahan, Mrs. Kinahan and W.A. Smithwick. *In Nov. of '43 another Extraordinary General Meeting was called to review the finances of the club as it was in*

the opinion of a section of the members that the club could not carry on.

The club survived and 1944 was to prove to be one of the best years the club ever had. An appeal for old tennis balls and adverts in both local papers and The Irish Times did the trick. Mr. Richard Hughes of Ballyrichard presented a solid silver cup to the winner of the men's open singles, Mr. T.J. Ryan of Dublin (who defeated M. O'Callaghan of Dublin 6/0 3/6 6/1 in the final). Despite the war, entries for the tournament were a record. It might be noted that Richard Hughes himself was one of the finest players ever to play in Kilkenny, winning the Open Singles a record six times between 1929 and 1937. He was also an active committee member and became President of the club in 1947.

Open Tournament
Kilkenny County & City LTC

Event	1st Prize	2nd Prize
	1893	
MS	J. H. Head	
MHS	Cecil Boyd	
LHD	Miss Smithwick/Miss Sullivan	
MHD	J. & D. Smithwick	
MxHD	J. & Miss Smithwick	
	1894	
MS	C. J. Latham	R. Packenham
MHS	C. J. Latham	K. A. Rynd
LHS		
MHD	W. S. Jeffares/ J. Sullivan	P. A. Browne/ D. Ross
LHD	Miss M. Sullivan/ Miss N. Sullivan	Miss N. Roe/ Miss B. Sullivan
MxHD	P.A. Browne/ Miss Sullivan	C. Latham/ Miss Dyas
	1896	
MS	K. A. Rynd beat C.J. Latham 6/2 6/4 1/6 6/1	
MHS	K. A. Rynd (-30) divided with D. Ross (-15)	
LS	Miss Langrishe beat Mrs. James 6/2 6/4	
MHD	K. A. Rynd/R. Sullivan (-15) beat D. &.G. Smithwick (Scratch) 6/3 3/6 6/3 6/3	

In 1944 the first juvenile tournament was held in the club, it being confined to club members. The winners of the boy's doubles were R. Furness and M. Crotty with Fracis Muldowney and P. Crotty runners-up. In the final of the girl's doubles Heather Cole and Maureen Knox beat Mary and Marjorie Aylward. Heather would win the Irish Open Junior Singles Championship at **Fitzwilliam LTC** in 1947, 1948 and 1949. Her subsequent Irish and International tennis as a senior are dealt with elsewhere in the book. Jack Kenealy and Kitty McGrath won the mixed title, their opponents in the final being Jimmy Manning and Susan Kinahan.

The junior competition was so successful it was decided to run a Junior Open Championship later in the season. It was to become one of the top junior

tournaments in Ireland. In the first year the entry included R. J. MacCabe (Irish Open Junior Champion in 1944), G. Rice (Irish Open Junior Champion the following year), N. P. Brown (ex Irish Junior Close Champion), D. Williams (Junior Ulster Champion and the winner in Kilkenny in that inaugural event in 1944), Harry Barniville (a subsequent Irish national player of note) and Arthur Fitzpatrick (Irish open under 15 champion in 1944 and Irish junior open champion in 1947). The girls included the 1943 Irish Open Junior Champion of 1943, M. Meehan. In the final she beat A. MacCabe, who would become the Irish Open Junior Champion in 1945.

In 1975 the club started a hardcourt league and a veterans' doubles competition. The following year the Molar Cup was presented to the club for a family competition and has also become an annual event. The club runs the Tuborg Cup, an annual team event for seniors and a Junior Day Cup, the latter presented by Dr. & Mrs. Tadhg to the club.

Outside Dublin the Provincial Towns Cup competition is the most competitive event, certainly in Leinster. In 1978 the club featured four teams, two in Class III. On the 27th August the club had a team in each of the Class finals held at Clongowes Wood College. The first team had beaten **Enniscorthy, Bray, Greystones, Carlow, Arklow** and, in the final, beat **Naas** 5/2. The thirds were in a competition of 46 teams and beat **Wicklow Town II, Wexford, Bunclody, Enniscorthy II, New Ross, Greystones III, Mullingar** and **Stackallen** in the final. The latter was sweet revenge as it was the County Meath club that knocked out the Kilkenny second side. Interestingly it was the **Kilkenny C.Y.M.S.** team who had won this event exactly forty-nine years earlier.

At the Centenary Exhibition Match in 1979 were (from left) Joe Wall (Captain), Jo Sheridan, Ron Girdham (Smithwick's),Bernadette Davy, Jim McArdle, Declan Heavey, Mary Mc Keogh (Club Secretary), Dr. Tadhg McKeogh (Club President) and Jim Murphy (Smithwick's)

The committee for the centenary year (1979) were as follows: president: Dr. Tadhg Keogh; honorary secretary: Mary Keogh; honorary treasurer: Nicholas Harte, tennis captain: Joe Wall; tennis vice-captain: Peter Fennelly; Committee: Rosemary Flanagan, Margot Hogan, John Lanigan, Jim Lowry, Catherine Mc Carthy, Harry McCarthy, Angela Moylan, P. J. O'Neill, Liam Reidy, Jane Tyler, Justin Wall, Dave

Glynn, John Mealy. The club vice-presidents at that time were: P. Coady, Mrs. M. Dore, Lieutenant Colonel F. Fahy, R. Girdham, B. Kenealy, J. Lanigan, J. Lowry (Snr.), W.R. McPhillips, V. Millett, J. D. Moylan, J. J. O'Callaghan, P. J. O'Neill, T. Phelan, P. G. Reynolds, Walter Smithwick and C. Bourke. The club has gone from strength to strength for well over the last century. It was one of the first to have

tournaments for ladies and progressed steadily. In the 19th century there were about 80 members. By the mid-1970s it had about 150 members but a new pavilion and improving courts over the years has brought it to where today it has about 700 members and 8 all weather floodlit courts and a future to look forward to.

Butler Cup winning team in 1976. Back (l. to r.): Roddy Cleere, Ger Molloy, Justin Wall, Michael Manning & Eamon O'Neill. Back (l. to r.): Liam Reidy, Margaret Walsh, Catriona Kelly, Margaret McPhillips, Brona Coughlan & Angela Moylan

1978 Kilkenny County & City Team. Class II runners-up. Back. (l. to r.): Jim Lowry, Joe Wall, T. K. McKeogh (president), Peter Fennelly & Harry McCarthy. Front (l. to r.): Anita O'Neill, Lily Lowry, Ann Greaney (Sheila Byrne (inset).

The Class 1 winners from Kilkenny County & City Lawn Tennis Club in 1978. Back (l. to r.) Joe Wall (captain), Eugene Daly, Paul Mullally, Tony Mitchell, Justin Wall & T. K. McKeogh (president). Front (l. to r.) Catherine McCarthy, Susan Reidy, Jane Tyler & Angela Moylan.

1978 Kilkenny County & City Class III winning team. Back (l. to r.): Joe Wall (captain), Liam Reidy, Jim Manning, John Lanigan & T. K. McKeogh (president). Front (l. to r.): Margaret Walsh, Margot Hogan, Catriona Kelly & Eilis Glynn. Missing: Noel Brennan.

The Kilkenny City & County LTC winning team in the 1966 Tuborg Cup competition. Back (l. to r.) Jim Lowry, Justin Wall, Frank Scott & Frank Lyons. Front (l. to r.) Ann O' Donovan, Angela Farrell, Joan Byrne & Barbara Kirwan.

To celebrate the Centenary year the club organised a Veteran's Competition on the 23rd June 1979 and included former international player. The winners were Jim Fitzgibbon with Con Denvir and Heather Flinn with June Anne Byrne.

Celebrating the opening of the new clubhouse in 1975 at Kilkenny County & City Lawn Tennis Club. Front (l. to r.): Mary Tobin, Pauline O'Donovan, Angela Moylan & Sheila Byrne. Back (l. to r.): Brian Kenealy, John Lanigan, Eilish Glynn, Ron Girdman, Liam Reidy, Nicky Harte, David Glynn, T. G. Lanigan, Tony Mitchell, J. D. Moylan & P. J. O'Neill.

Club Presidents	
1879-1919	Marquis of Ormonde
1920-1936	Earl of Ormonde
1937-1946	James Poe
1947	Richard Hughes
1948	Mrs. Day
1949-1952	Walter Smithwick
1953-1961	Mr. F.W. Cole
1962	J. O'Donnell
1963	Des O'Carroll
1964	D.B. O'Sullivan
1965-1966	R.J. Stevens
1967	W.A. Smithwick
1968-1971	J. D. Moylan
1972-1973	J. O'Callaghan
1974-1975	J. D. Moylan
1976-1978	Dr. Tadhg K. McKeogh
2001	Stephen Lanigan

****

Malahide Lawn Tennis & Croquet Club (Founded 1879)

This north County Dublin Club has been active for well over a century. It was originally based in the grounds of Malahide Castle, Lord Talbot was the first president. Like many early clubs the original surface was grass. Today, in a central location the club can boast of 9 floodlit all-weather courts. The site was known as "The Square".From early Irish handbooks we know that the honorary secretary was C. Dillon, J. P., The Lodge, Malahide, in 1894 and 1895. Today, Anne Hayes holds the position. A lady honorary secretary would not be contemplated in any club in the 19th century, never mind president. Times have long since changed. The club did not appear to have any early open tournaments. In 1913 there were 82 clubs affiliated to the ILTA, Malahide, like a lot of smaller clubs, did not join the fold until much later. There was no need to.

The Dublin Leagues are now over one hundred years old and the winning teams are a good indicator of activity. Over one hundred clubs in the Dublin region have been involved in the leagues. In 1963 **Malahide LTC** had a good ladies side and won their first title, the Class III competition. In terms of facilities the club built new hard courts in the late 1970s and by the middle of the 1980s they were regular winners in various grades. A summary of their 25 successes (with the first winning year included) is given in the following table. The Class 1 win by the Men in the Summer League of 1986 must rank among the club's greatest achievements.

Malahide's League Wins

League Category	Number of Wins	First Year to Win
Summer: Men's	7	1986
Summer: Ladies	3	1962
Winter: Men's	1	2002
Winter: Ladies	1	1998
Senior: Men's	1	1987
Senior: Ladies	4	1989
Floodlit: Men	5	1983
Floodlit: Ladies	1	1998
Boys U14: Class 1	1	1998
Boys U16: Class 1	1	2000

In 1977 the club staged the first County Dublin Junior Championships and had a staggering entry of 546 boys and girls. It was deemed to be a 'resounding success'. That year, for the second time in three years, the local team won the Community Games tennis gold and the Tom O' Loughlin Perpetual Trophy. The 1977 team was B. Cassidy, C. O' Flaherty, H. O' Loughlin, M. Donnelly, K. Harrold and A. O' Brien. In 1988 the club moved forward with a major development that involved 7 artificial grass courts and two hard courts. The town was continually growing as a suburb of Dublin and the club *had a major impact on the town of Malahide*. The town and club are inter-linked by so many members. In 1988 the town won, for the 5th consecutive year, the national Best Large Town Award in Bord Failte's Tidy Town Competition. The club did its part with extensive professional landscaping. Membership at that stage had reached 1,100.

Coaching programmes have helped develop such national players as Michael Nugent and Michael Cowhie. Coaches have included Roger Geraghty and Bernadette Rafferty. At a special EGM on the 26th November 1989 the members voted overwhelmingly to construct a new clubhouse, the existing prefabricated structure had served its purpose. The new building would be a two-storey affair with a plan area of 5,500 square feet and include a balcony. The club hosted the International Young Cup in 1992. This is for teams of Ladies (over 40). This was the first time such a competition was held in Ireland (see details in Chapter 5). For the record Ireland finished 8th out of 14 teams entered.

This club has truly moved into the modern era and we can expect only further successes in the years ahead.

Members make the club and one worth mentioning is Kieran Sheehan. He was the president and club leader for the period in the late 1980s and 1990s when the club took the great leap forward. The modern clubhouse and allied facilities were opened in 1992. The club is proud of its history and retains the croquet in the title. "Whites" must be worn during the summer months is another tradition still retained.

*****

Ormond Lawn Tennis Club
[King's County & Ormond LTC]
(Founded 1879)

In the records there is sometimes confusion on names and location. A club might be referred to as **Birr LTC** but in fact this name does not officially exist. Thanks to Geoff Oakley, a former member of both Birr clubs, and County Librarian, Anne Couglan, some details on tennis clubs in County Offaly have been unravelled.

International player, Geraldine Barniville (nee Houlihan), who grew up playing tennis in Birr, officially opens the new clubhouse in 1983. Member, David Taylor was the driving force behind this project, a necessity after the old clubhouse was destroyed by fire in 1977.

The old Ormond LTC clubhouse that was destroyed by fire on the 2nd April 1977.

The older 'Ormond' club, with a gentry background, has had grass courts since the 19th century. It thrived and produced some great players and held an attractive annual open tournament. Its origins can be pinpointed thanks to the following advertisement in the *King's County Chronicle* on the 18th December 1879.

KING'S COUNTY AND ORMOND LAWN TENNIS CLUB

At a Meeting of the Members of the above Club held at Parsonstown on the 10th inst., a letter from Toler R. Garvey, Esq., was read offering on the part of the Earl of Rosse, to let part of a field near Oxmantown Bridge on favourable Terms for the purpose of Laying down Courts etc. which field has been approved of by the Provisional Committee.

It was decided at the Meeting that the following should be the Terms of Entrance Fees and Annual Subscription to the Club: - An Entrance Fee of £1 for families or single individuals. In the case of families this Fee will cover the entrance of all members of the family, including those who might hereafter join. An Annual Subscription of 7s 6d from town residents, of 5s from Playing, and 2s6d from Non-playing Members, resident in the country, but not to amount to more than 15s from any one family; members of the family beyond that amount being admitted FREE.

It was also decided that a General Meeting of the present Members should be held at Dooly's Hotel, on Wednesday, 24th inst., at the hour of 3 p.m. for the purpose of Balloting for further Members, also to Elect a Permanent Committee, Secretary, and Treasurer, and approve of proposed Rules.

Ladies and Gentlemen wishing to be Balloted for will please send their names to the Hon. Secretary, Lieut.-Colonel Biddulph, John's Place, Parsonstown, or one of the members of the Provisional Committee.

In some tennis references in the 19th century, the club of **Parsonstown LTC** was mentioned. This was the club of the Garvey brothers and it was, incorrectly, referred to as being in County Meath. This confusion can now be sorted out. Two of the best players in the early days of Irish tennis were in fact the Garvey brothers from Parsonstown, Birr, County Offaly. Toler R. Garvey referred to in the cutting above as one of the founders of the **King's County and Ormond LTC** was in fact a very useful player. Present Birr tennis players will be delighted to know that the Garvey brothers were more than useful players, particularly Toler. Both played in the Irish Championships in 1884. In 1886, Toler reached the men's doubles and mixed doubles finals playing with Eyre Chatterton and one of the famous Langrishe sisters. Better still in the Wimbledon Championships that year, he reached the

All-Comer's semi-final before losing to Herbert Lawford (the champion in 1887). For the record, Toler Garvey beat Howard Pease (GB) 6/3 6/3 2/6 6/1, Edward Avory (GB) 6/4 1/6 6/4 6/3 and William Taylor (GB) 8/6 6/4 2/6 6/3 before meeting his match in one of the great players of that era. Lawford won in three sets (6/3 6/2 6/0). This appears to have been Toler's only visit to Wimbledon, in the singles event at least. The club progressed with obvious enthusiasm coming from the Garvey's. The club had six grass courts and, for many years, with a couple of short breaks, ran the Championships of the Midlands. This event goes back to 1893 or earlier. In 1893 and 1894, Toler won the singles championships. He apparently had a sister as a Miss Garvey was to share the ladies singles handicap prize with a Mrs. Kirkwood in 1893. In a 21 years lease, dating from 1st November 1912, the club was described as a Lawn Tennis and Croquet Club. The court used for croquet was subsequently reclaimed for the racquet game- but continued to be called "the croquet court". In the early years, one of the courts had an asphalt surface. The original wooden pavilion was destroyed by fire on the 2nd April 1977. It was replaced by a fine new structure with David Taylor as the driving force behind the venture.

The North Munster Junior Championships were staged at the Ormond grounds (*situated in Leinster!*) for two years before being replaced in 1956 by a new event, the Midland Counties Junior Championship. In the 1950s a Junior Open Tournament was added to the club's activities. The 1960 and 1962 results for the latter were as follows:

1960

U18 BS: A.J. Mulderrry beat J. Courteney 6/0 7/5
U18 GS: Penny Downes beat
                Kathleen Galvin 2/6 6/2 7/5
U15 BS: Gerry Waldron beat
                Brendan Minnock 6/3 6/1
U15 GS: Fidelma Hanly beat Joan Deegan 8/6 6/3

1962

U18 BS: Brendan Minnock beat
                Tadgh Lambe 6/8 6/2 9/7
U18 GS: Margaret Connolly beat
                Joan Deegan 6/4 6/2
U15 BS: John Kenny beat Tom Nugent 6/2 9/7
U15 GS: Susan Houlihan beat
                Doreen McKenna 6/2 6/1

Particularly of note were the Houlihan family. Des, Jack and sister Madeline were all good players. The boys were among the best in Leinster. Jack in fact beat Des in the final of the Irish boys under 15 championships in the 1930s. Geraldine and Susan, daughters to Des and Phyllis, became very good players. Susan won the Birr Junior Girls' Open title in 1962 when beating Doreen McKenna in the final (6/2 6/1). Geraldine was to become one of Ireland's most successful lady tennis players ever. Not alone has she had many international caps for tennis but, having taken up squash, she was equally as prolific in terms of titles won and international representation.

The 1956 Championship of the Midlands at Ormond LTC in Birr. From left: Des Keogh and Des Houlihan beat T. H. Kenny and Harry Read 6/2 6/4. The umpire was Alec Drought. Harry, a former international in the sports of tennis, rugby and cricket, was 67 at the time. Des Keogh is currently a well-known broadcaster and entertainer. Des Houlihan's daughter Geraldine later became the no. 1 player in Ireland.

A club member for three decades was Harry Read from Roscrea. He was an international played in the sports of tennis, rugby and cricket (see chapters 1.3 and 6). He was a veteran, at 67 years of age, in 1956 when he the final of the Men's Doubles Championship of the Midland. It was an all-Ormond final that year with Des Keogh and Des Houlihan beating Harry and T. H. Kenny, a member of another great tennis family. Des Keogh, today best known as a radio presenter and stage entertainer, was a very good player in his day. That year the local paper, The Midland Tribune, reported that he had completed "What sounds like a bookmaker's nightmare-a double, two trebles and an 'accumulator'". His singles win was the fourth in a row. He also won the doubles and mixed titles for the third year running. His mixed partner was Gillian Kennedy of Roscrea in 1955 and 1956. In the late 1950s Des acted as the referee for the Open Tournament. In the 1955 final of the open tournament at the club he beat Jack Dawson, another good local. Des's sister, Sally, married Jack and become a leading light at **Donnybrook LTC**. As recently as 1993-1995 she was the President of this prestigious Dublin club, having been treasurer and secretary for lengthy periods since the early 1970s. In the 1960s and 1970s, members of the Hanniffy family were to the fore on court and as tournament organisers. Particularly

prominent in both roles were Rita and her younger sister, Emer. Rita became wife of long serving Fine Gael T. D. Tom Enright and Olwyn, currently one of the rising stars of that party. Michael de Forge, Doreen McKenna, Gerry and David O'Donnell, Michael Grogan, Brendan and Declan Hanniffy, were others who helped build the club to a peak membership of 78 in 1969. As the new century came in Rory and Gary Hanniffy, sons of Declan and Geraldine (nee Kinsella) were making headlines on the County Offaly hurling team. With brothers Conor and Darren they won All-Ireland club hurling medals with Birr.

Tom Enright turns the sod for the new Ormond LTC clubhouse in 1983. Also in the photograph is Seamus Grennan, builder.

The gallery at The Midland Championships (organised by Ormond LTC) in the mid-1950s included Phyllis Houlihan, Mrs. Howe, Alicia Kenny, Dean Owen and Peggy Owen.

Miss Fitzpatrick's Tennis Victory At Birr

COMPETING for the first time in the Midland County Championship at Birr, Miss J. A. Fitzpatrick, Ireland's Wimbledon representative, won the ladies' singles.
Results:—
LADIES' SINGLES—Semi-final—Miss G. Hogan bt Mrs M. F. Twist, 6-2, 6-3; Miss J. A. Fitzpatrick bt. Miss O. Murray, 6-2, 6-0   Final—Miss Fitzpatrick bt Miss Hogan, 6-2, 6-0.
MEN'S SINGLES. - Semi-final — W. E. Dawson bt P. D. G. Reid, 12-10, 3-6, 6-4; D. J. Keogh (holder) bt. A. Wright, 6-1, 7-5.   Final—Keogh bt. Dawson, 6-0, 6-1, 7-5.   **Men's Doubles** Semi-finals – D. A. Houlihan and D. J. Keogh bt T. H. Kenny and W. Dalton 5-7, 6-0, 6-4; A. Wright and W. E. Dawson w.o. H. M. and P. D. G. Reid scr. Finals—Houlihan and Keogh bt. Wright and Dawson, 6-4, 6-3.

Irish Independent 2nd August 1957

1960s exhibition match at the Ormond club in Birr. Entertainer Des Keogh (left) and Geraldine Barniville (nee Houlihan, second left) grew up playing tennis in Birr.

At the time of the club's foundation and, for many years after, membership of the club was drawn largely from the local gentry and from the officers at the military barracks at Crinkle, outside Birr. This latter connection was to result in the provision of military band music for special occasion at the club. Membership was confined to what was regarded as "the upper classes". This ultimately led to the formation of a second club, The Wilmer Lawn Tennis Club, many years later. It had grounds on the other side of the Camcor River. It subsequently re-located to its present side at Burke's Hill and became a hard court club. Class distinctions faded over the years and anyone interested in playing the game could do so. In fact many people took up dual membership. Geoff Oakley, for example, was in the unique position of being the chairman in one club and, at the same time, the honorary secretary/treasurer in the other. He was a useful player and saw the benefit of the Wilmer membership as it had a table tennis team, a sport he was also good at.

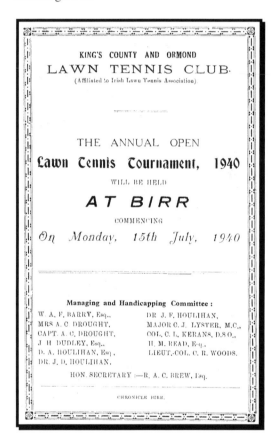

KING'S COUNTY AND ORMOND
LAWN TENNIS CLUB.
(Affiliated to Irish Lawn Tennis Association)

THE ANNUAL OPEN

Lawn Tennis Tournament, 1940

WILL BE HELD

AT BIRR

COMMENCING

On Monday, 15th July, 1940

Managing and Handicapping Committee:

W A. F. BARRY, Esq.,   DR J. F. HOULIHAN,
MRS A. C DROUGHT.   MAJOR C. J. LYSTER, M.C.,
CAPT. A. C. DROUGHT.   COL. C. L. KERANS, D.S.O.,
J. H. DUDLEY, Esq.,   H. M. READ, Esq.,
D. A. HOULIHAN, Esq.,   LIEUT.-COL. C. R. WOODS.
DR. J. D. HOULIHAN.

HON. SECRETARY :—R. A. C. BREW, Esq.

CHRONICLE BIRR.

The Wilmer club had a sand court at one time and then two hard courts. The late John Joe Sheerin was one of its leading lights in the 1970s. He was affectionately known as "Mr. Wilmer". This club decided to enter the Provincial Town's Cup in 1977. At the first attempt the club won the Class III title being promoted the following season to Class II. The Rectory Club was a more 'recent' tennis club in the town and a note on it is included later. In the late 1950s and 1960s the town of Birr with a population of less than 4,000 was therefore supporting three clubs. The Ormond club suffered as the Wilmer club steadily grew in strength.

The "Moorpark Sports Club"-an umbrella organisation under which Birr Rugby Football Club and the Ormond Tennis Club (the name it would have for many years, the King's County part of the title long gone out of use) shared use of a greatly extended premises and at the same time retaining their separate

Ladies' Doubles finalists at the Midland Championships organised by the Ormond LTC (probably 1956). From left: Susan Drought, Valerie Thrift, Monica O'Meara and Gillian Kennedy.

The 1973 Vintage Tournament at Birr

identities. The tennis-playing element was, however, in decline and, with Birr tennis being mainly at **Wilmer LTC**, the Ormond courts went into disuse and have not been played on since the late 1990s.

Open Tournament
Ormonde (Birr) LTC

Event	1st Prize	2nd Prize
1893		
MS	A. Wilson	
MHS	Toler R. Garvey	
LHS	Miss Garvey divided with Mrs. Kirkwood	
MHD	C. "Rowley"/H. Bennett	
LHD	Mrs. Kirkwood/Miss Paterson	
MxHD	J. Bennette/Mrs. Browne divided with H. Bennett & Mrs. Kirkwood	
1894		
MS	Toler R. Garvey	W.R. Clark
MHS	S.E. Smith	W.R. Clark
LHS	Miss Barff	Miss Robinson
MHD	S.E. Smith/-Powell	-Craig/-Stackpoole
LHD	Mrs. & Miss Waring	Mrs. Dykes/Miss Golding
MxHD	WRClark/Mrs.Waring	Rev. Craig/Mrs. Barff
1946		
MS	Championship of Midland Counties H. Kennedy beat Des Houlihan 6/2 6/1 6/1	
LS	Maeve Lanigan (Kilkenny) beat Miss W. O'Callaghan 6/1 6/2	
MxD	E. O. Barry/Miss W. O'Callaghan beat Des Houlihan/Maeve Lanigan 6/3 6/2	
1955		
MS	Des Keogh beat Jack Dawson 6/2 8/6	
LS	Norah Taylor beat Monica O' Meara 6/1 6/2	
MD	Des Houlihan/Des Keogh beat Jack Dawson/W. J. Dalton 6/3 6/2	
MxD	Des Keogh/Gillian Kennedy beat Des Houlihan/Monica O' Meara 6/4 3/6 11/9	
1960		
MS	Harry Sheridan beat Arnold Fanning 6/4 8/6	
LS	Miss G. Kennedy beat Mrs Norah Taylor 6/4 6/3	
MD	Harry Sheridan/Arnold Fanning beat Tom Egan/Des Egan(Athlone) 6/1 8/6	
MxD	Harry Sheridan/Miss Gillian Kennedy beat Tom Kenny/Mrs. Norah Taylor 6/1 6/4	
1961		
MS	Harry Sheridan beat Gordon Long 6/1 6/0	
LS	Monica O' Connor bt. Gillian Kennedy 6/4 6/3	
MD	Harry Sheridan (UCD)/Arnold Fanning (Birr) bt Gerry Nallen(Banag.)/G. Long(Clara) 2/6 6/1 6/1	
MxD	Harry Sheridan/Gillian Kennedy(Roscrea) beat Tom Dooley/Mrs.O'Connor (Roscrea) 4/6 6/1 6/1	
1963		
MS	Gerry Waldron beat Michael de Forge 6/3 6/2	
LS	Jean Russell beat S. Williams 7/5 6/1	
MD	D. O'Donnell/M. Grogan beat J. Hogan/B. Gilmartin 6/3 11/9	
MxD	A.Hudson/Jean Russell beat Gerry Waldron/Penney Downes 4/6 6/1 6/2	

Wilton Lawn Tennis Club
(Founded C. 1879)

While Wilton was one of the earliest clubs in the Dublin area, it never had the strength in depth that could be attributed to others such as **Fitzwilliam LTC** or **Lansdowne LTC.** It was set up and run as a propriety tennis facility by John Dowling. This meant that, while the **Wilton LTC** functioned within the facility, it was also a place where players could come in off the street, book courts and play on an hourly basis. Anna Kelly, a granddaughter of John Dowling was able to recall the club back in the 1930s.

At that time, membership included players from The Irish Times. Jack Murphy, Caity Fitzgerald and an Africa lady by the name of Miss Dutt are some of the names she recalls playing there. Schools such as Bertrand, Alexandra and Ling (PE College) used to rent out courts. The groundsman was a man named Ross who came every day from his room in Montague, Harcourt Street. While the very early days the courts were probably all grass courts, by the 1930s, she recalls, there were six hard courts and one grass court, the latter no longer being marked out for use. Annual membership fees were three guineas-'a lot of money in the thirties'. The club had its own emblem which was a circle divided down the middle showing two blue halves called Oxford and Cambridge blue. She remembers a 'charter' hanging on the clubhouse wall.

Further back, young John Dowling, who died at 21, used to coach and was employed as a 'tennis professional' at the then Vice-Regal Lodge. Michael and Molly Dowling used to coach too. In fact Molly (Mary) was, in the 1930s, the club coach, a popular teacher who used to make up a singles and doubles as required by visitors or members. This was on top of her role in stringing racquets. See Chapter 7.4. The club would see to function in the late 1940s.

Back in 1892 the club won the Fitzwilliam Junior Cup. This competition was for the clubs next in terms of strength behind the 'first class' clubs. They thus earned promotion to the top competition but felt that had not the strength to compete. In 1893, therefore, they scratched against **Fitzwilliam LTC** who then beat **Lansdowne LTC,** the only other team in this grade, 5/4 in the final. Wilton's second team were beaten by **Mount Temple LTC** 9/0 in the Junior Cup of 1893. Things were not much better in 1894. Having beaten **Glenageary & Kingstown LTC** in the first round of the Junior Cup (8 matches to 1) they went out tamely to the ultimate winners, **Mount Temple LTC,** by the same 8/1 margin.

The club did make a notable mark in a *Lawn Tennis and Badminton* report (April 18, 1906) on the affairs of the Dublin Lawn Tennis Council. The honorary secretary of the Council regretted that no club except the Wilton had followed the good example set by golf clubs in being open for Sunday play.

As reported in 1907 the "Wilton Sunday" was a great institution. It was obviously an open tournament day that those not concerned about Sunday play could attend. It *would still be there were enough visitors to patronise it. In the old days even greater fights were seen on this club's ground than in the Square itself. I am inclined to tell tales out of school. Wilton men always were and are still speculative, and Dowling is coaching one young player who will yet be seen on the centre court at Wimbledon. His name is Miley, and he is now at Oxford.* The writer was referring to Val Miley who was only 18 years of age at the time and had started his studies at Oxford the previous autumn. It was noted also that players from other clubs joined Wilton as it was open all year round and especially *for the asphalte play in winter.*

In the Irish championships of 1890 the only Wilton player in the field of 26 men was T.H. Griffiths. He was not to win but in Lansdowne tournament at the end of June he beat Tom Chaytor in the All-Comer's singles semi-final (6/1 6/3 6/1). In the final round he succumbed to Frank Stoker 4/6 6/4 1/6 1/6 who went on to meet Joshua Pim in the Challenge Round for the "Championship of the County Dublin". Wilton won three Dublin Summer Leagues. In 1912 and 1913 they won Class 2 in the Men's competition as well as Class 3 in 1913.

According to ILTA records the club had a total of about 40 members just before the Great War. The great Louis Meldon was a member of this club and was an elected member of the ILTA, representing Connacht. He was on the Council both before and after the war. Some details on his playing career are given in Chapter 6. He was Irish Close champion in 1921 and Irish Men's Doubles (Open) champion, with three different partners from 1923 to 1925. He played in 5 Davis Cup matches in the 1920s. In the 1920s, M.F. Linehan from the club was a Munster representative on the ILTA council. A few years later he represented Leinster in the same capacity.

It is not known when the club, a onetime neighbour of **Fitzwilliam LTC**, actually ceased to function. Its name does not appear in either the 1956 or 1960 ILTA Handbooks.

****

Cork Lawn Tennis Club
(C. 1879)

This was probably the first club in Cork City. No information is available on its history. By 1908, when the ILTA was formed, and had published listings of clubs, the Blackrock club was in operation. In 1893 the first Irish Yearbook showed just one club in the Cork City area i.e. **Glanmire LTC.** Perhaps the old **Cork LTC** changed its name in the interim.

In 1880 at the Irish Championships we find that M.G. McNamara was playing in the Gentleman's singles. He appears to be the first Munster man to play in this competition. He represented '**Cork LTC**'. In the first round he beat D. Sherlock of **Wilton LTC** (3 sets to love) then G. Hewson of **Fitzwilliam LTC** (3 sets to one). This was a *rather tedious affair, neither player*

attempting to keep the ball low in the their returns, and, as a consequence, some of the rallies were of tremendous length and the match was of long duration. He then got a bye but lost to the ultimate winner, the great Willie Renshaw in the semi-final ('fourth round') in an *extremely hollow affair,* 0/6 1/6 2/6. In 1881 he lost in the first round to Richard Richardson 2/6 0/6 0/6. His English opponent from **Hooton LTC** would reach the All-Comer's final here in Ireland and at the All-England Championships a few weeks later.

In the men's doubles, in 1881, he played with A.W. Perry (also from Cork it appears). They had a good win in the first round when beating "Mr. St. Leger" and W. Hewitt of **Fitzwilliam LTC.** (two sets to one). St. Leger was none other than the Irish champion of 1879 and in the Wimbledon All-Comer's final the same year. In round two they beat R.H. Henry and Sir Hercules Langrishe representing the **Fitzwilliam LTC** 6/0 6/3. 'Herky', as he was known, was a brother of the famous Langrishe sisters, the Langrishes being that famous Kilkenny family. They would lose in the semi-final to the Wilson brothers (J. & H.) from the Frascati club.

****

Argideen Vale Lawn Tennis and Croquet Club
(Founded C. 1880)

It is not known exactly when the Argideen Vale Lawn tennis club was founded. There was a tournament held there in 1892. It is likely that it was several years earlier when croquet was first played there. According to Bill Tayler's Munster History it originally started as a hockey and cycling club in about the middle of the 19th century, tennis badminton and croquet being added later. A the photograph in the history was assumed to be taken in the 1880s The cycling craze did not start until the end of the 19th century so perhaps dates and the order of the events will never be fully and accurately recorded. The activity of this club was in and around the village of Timoleague in County Cork. Timoleague Castle had two badminton courts, one on the second and one on the third floor. The badminton stopped in 1920 after the castle was blown up during the 'Troubles'. Various houses in the area had croquet lawns and tennis lawns and it is not surprising that a club would be formed to cater for the growing interest during the last quarter of the 19th century.

To this day the club is one welcoming to visitors for their Open Tournaments and many of today's members are in fact from overseas. During the summer the club only opens for a few days a week. In its earlier times there were some very good members. In 1903, William Drapes won the Irish Open, beating the famous James Cecil Parke in the final. This was the first time that the organisers, the **Fitzwilliam LTC,** ran the event at Wilton Place (having moved from Fitzwilliam Square). Bill Tayler (1990) records Drapes as a member of the Argideen Vale club. Earlier he had been a member of **County Carlow LTC.**

The 2003-2004 Naas LTC committee celebrate their second Eagle Star Club Award. Back (l. to r.): Denis McCudden (honorary treasurer), Orla O'Connell, Mary Sherlock (membership secretary), Kathleen O'Byrne, Lynda McLoughlin (junior co-ordinator) & Les Hogan (P.R.O.). Front (l. to r.): Shane Spring (club chairman) Joan Maher (ladies' captain), Michael Sherlock (men's captain) and Mary Rose Lyons (honorary secretary).

Blackrock College win the Leinster Boys' Senior cup once again.Holding the cup is team captain, Justin Purcell.

Managers of junior interprovincial teams in 2002 were (l. to r.): JimWatt (U), Gareth Barry (C), Ger Flynn (M) and Declan Donnellan (L).

Gents Singles

Gents Doubles

Ladies Doubles

Mixed Doubles

The Open at County Sligo Tennis Club in 1912
(Courtesy of The County Sligo Library (copyright))

The Irish Over 35 team that played in the Italia Cup in Florida and Berlin in 2002 and 2003 respectively. The team is unique in that all three members are from the same club, Lansdowne Lawn Tennis Club, Dublin. From left: Pat Guiry (captain), Bernard McCormack and Neil Wilson.

Sutton ladies 2004.

Sorcha McGinn /Eve Banahan Sutton LTC in 2002.

Fiona Long Limerick LTC & Ireland

Some of the tennis courts at Clongowes Wood College, County Kildare (Circa 1977).

In 2001 Mount Anville Convent in Dublin won the Leinster senior cup. Team (from left) was Jenny Lawlor, Alexia Tierney, Naomia McHale, Sarah Griffith, Rebecca Cox and Lisa Matthews.

Elm Park, Dublin

Queen's University Belfast Tennis Club
Team Photograph 2005

Bob English coaching at Sligo Tennis Club (circa 1985)

Mark Constant (Bishopstown Credit Union, sponsors) presents the primary school cup in 2001 to the captain of the winning team St. Catherine's Cork.

The Fitzwilliam Lawn Tennis Club team on their first visit to new York to play the West Side Tennis Club (at Forest Hills). The event took place in 1991 and the team were (from left): John O'Rourke, David Fassbender, Peter Gilligan, Albert Tee, Robin Quigley and Paddy Donaghy.

James Cecil Parke from Clones, County Monaghan, was one of the top players in the world in the 1910s. He was the first Irishman to publish a book on coaching (1920s).

Fiona Gallagher of Larne and Limavady won many junior titles and was awarded the Fergus O'Shee Trophy for the top girl (u18) in Ireland in 2005.

Hugo Flinn (son of international player Heather Cole) married Jo Sheridan on the 26th September 1980.

Maria O'Sullivan (Douglas LTC) President of Tennis Ireland in 2000.

The History of Irish Tennis

Tony O'Donoghue, Norman O'Leary, Ann Bradshaw (nee O'Connor) (South of Ireland winner in 1980) and Brendan Bradshaw at Limerick Lawn Tennis Club (circa 2003).

Maeve Jennings (nee Flattery), second from left, was an outstanding tennis, hockey and squash player. She took up golf in her 30's and reached a handicap of 14. Above with her fellow team members at Ballina GC in 1980. They brought the Connacht ladies' team title to the club for the first time

The senior girls' singles champion in 2000 at Sutton LTC was Della Kilduff. Photographed here with her dad Joe and grandmother Therese Kilduff.

Conor Carroll and H. Butler-Higgins winners of the Class 2 Open Mixed title at Mount Pleasant LTC ion the 25th June 2005.

Nora Taylor (Enniskillen LTC and Omagh LTC) passed away on the 19th April 2006 at the age of 99. She first took up the game in 1915. This photograph was taken at Val de Lobo in Portugal in 1999 where she received her first coaching lesson (from 'Pedro'). She was 92 at the time.

The 1975 Leinster senior cup winning team from the Holy Child Convent, Killiney. Back row (from left) Judy Sheridan, Grainne Duignan, Janet Finlay. Front row (from left); Sandra Drum, Kate Brown, Jo Sheridan.

Leigh Walsh (b. 6th June 1987) of Sutton Lawn Tennis Club. Currently, she is one of the top young ladies in Ireland. She has played on the Irish u14 side and, in 2004, was Irish Girl's (u18) Open Champion.

Elm Park members attending the Dublin Lawn Tennis Council Centenary dinner on the 21st June 2002. Front (l. to r.) Michael Wogan, John Fitzpatrick, Anne-Marie Ryan, Mary Briscoe (lady captain), Maureen Cassidy & Annette Sweeny. Middle (l. to r.): Helen O'Connor, Jean O'Byrne, Deirdre Fitzpatrick & Terence Sweeny. Back (l. to r.): Alan Haugh (honorary secretary), Myles Cassidy (captain), Dave Ryan & Eanna McHugh.

The reunion at the Fergus Lawn Tennis Club in Ennis in July 2000.

Carrickmines Croquet & Lawn Tennis Club
Open Week in 2003.

Marie Bevin (Credit Union representative, sponsor) presents the 2002 primary school girls cup to the captain of the winning Holy Cross "A" (Tramore) winning team. Also in the photograph is Peter Scott, president of the Munster branch.

Sunday's Well Boating & Lawn Tennis Club, Cork.

The History of Irish Tennis

Olwyn Raftery (Galway LTC)
President of Tennis Ireland in 1998 and 2002.

Yvonne Doyle
Irish Open Champion 2001.

Croquet at Rushbrooke Lawn Tennis and
Croquet Club, County Cork, in recent years.

The final days of the old clubhouse at Carrickmines Croquet
& Lawn Tennis Club (c. 1999)

Tournament play at Naas LTC in recent times

Junior at Rushbrooke (circa 2005)

Gary Cahill Coaching Clinic at Elm Park in August 2002. From Left: Yvonne Hagan, Mary Molloy, Gary Cahill (coach), Mary Briscoe (captain), Yvonne Ryan & Rita O'Reilly.

In 2001 St. Mary's Convent, Nenagh, won the Credit Union under 16 Munster cup. From left: Mary Ryan (St. Mary's school), Sarah Walsh, Claire McNamara (president, Munster branch), Mark Constant (Bishopstown Credit Union, sponsor), Helena Darcy, Katie Ryan, Ann Mare Darcy and Geraldine O'Meara (Munster branch).

The Holycross primary school in Tramore won the boys primary school shield in 2001. Mark Constant (Bishopstown Credit Union, sponsors) holds the shield with Claire McNamara (president, Munster branch).

Mark Channing and T. A. Walsh at Wexford Harbour Boat & Tennis Club (circa 1980)

Mixed Action at Rushbrooke (Circa 2003)

Kilkenny College Junior Tennis Team (1997/1998).
Back (l. to r.): Margaret Wall, Penny Huggard, Yseault McDonald & Heather Sharman (coach). Front (l. to r.): Shirley O'Donoghue, Clodagh Dorgan & Rachel Hendy.

Hawaiian night out
Mount Pleasant Lawn Tennis Club
9th May 2003.

The History of Irish Tennis

Committee & Trustees at Lattin LTC 2001-2002. Back (l. to r.): Pat Hourigan, Francis Breen, Michael Hourigan (President), Joan O'Dwyer, Margaret Breen & Alex Long. Second Row (l. to r.): Liam Ryan, Ann O'Dwyer, Pauline Finnan, Alice Ryan & Bernadette Ryan. Third Row (l. to r.): Shane Hourigan, Pauline Daly, Mary Hourigan, Nora Coleman, Mary Breen (Honorary Treasurer) & Bill Ryan (Chairman). Front (l. to r.): Evelyn Connery (Vice-Chairman), Mary Crowe, Helen Breen & Mary Long (Honorary Secretary). Missing : Noreen Long, John Kennedy & Cathy Breen.

Junior players with coach Pat Crowe (front left) and Roscoe Tanner (USA) at Carrickmines Croquet & LTC (Circa 2003)

August 2002 at Elm Park. From left: Brian O'Brolchain Catherine Haugh, Jennifer Bergin, Gary Cahill (coach), Gillian Grier, Cormac O'Brolchain, Emer Tunney & Darragh Jones.

The History of Irish Tennis

Lee LTC in Cork won the Mens' Division 1 Munster league in 2001. From left: Dave Hanam, Derek Smith, Peter Scott (Munster Branch), Terence McSweeney (AIB Bank), Claire McNamara (president, Munster Branch), Kevin Rea, Vincent Lawton & Stephen Daly (Munster Branch)

Mount Anville Convent won the senior Leinster Cup in 1974. Back (l. to r.) Bridget Nolan, Lisa Mullen & Grainne Magrane. Front (l. to r.) Sandra Egan, Bernadette Davy (captain) & Barbara Morris.

The sport of Real Tennis has many links to 'lawn' tennis (see chapter 2). Rob Fahey (left) from Australia whose grandfather was from County Mayo was many times world champion from 1994 onwards. Also in the photo at the Melbourne Tennis Club is Ben North of the Irish Real Tennis Association (IRTA). Note the racquet size and shape. One of the first world professional titles in the sport was held at the Earlsfort Terrace court, Dublin, in May 1890 between Tom Pettit (USA), the winner, and Charles Saunders (England). The following month, Pettit challenged George Kerr, the professional lawn tennis player for the 'Professional Championship of the World' (lawn tennis) at Kerr's club, Fitzwilliam LTC. Kerr won the title and £75.

May 2002.
Blackrock College win the Ballygowan All-Ireland Schools' Senior Championship, at Sutton LTC. From left: Adrian Crehan, Garett Doran, Robbie Kernan, Barbara Anne Richardson (Ballygowan), Olwyn Raftery (president, Tennis Ireland), Killian Pender & Andrew Hogan.

In 2002 Colaiste Mhuire, Ennis, won the Munster under 14 girl's schools title sponsored by the Credit Union. They were the first County Clare team to win any Munster club or school team title. From left: Michelle Barry, Emma Tierney (captain), Peter Scott (president, Munster branch), Marie Bevan (representing the Credit Unions, sponsors), Danny Comerford (coach), Darah Hoey and Rachel Comerford.

Brookfield Lawn Tennis Club members at Blackrock (2006).

Marie Bevin (Credit Union representative, sponsor) presents the 2002 primary school boys cup to the captain of the winning Holy Cross "A" (Tramore) winning team. Also in the photograph is Peter Scott, president of the Munster branch.

Sutton Lawn Tennis Club 2002. From left: John McGinn, Saoirse McGinn (grand-daughter), John Collin and Ciara Collins (daughter).

Men's doubles action at Brookfield LTC (c. 2004)

TSB Doubles Tournament at Bandon LTC in 2005

The Belfast Royal Academical Institution won the Ulster schools junior cup in 1983.

The successful 1987 Junior Cup team at Sligo TC. From left: Vincent McGee, Margaret Scallan, Morgan Walsh, Agatha McGee, Billy Mulvaney & Ann Christine Higgins.

Practice walls at Sligo TC (c. 2000)

2001:Bill Hyland presenting u14 winners Nestle Trophy to Conor GIbney (Elm Park).

Reliving tennis moments at Belfast Boat Club 2003 were (from left); Cecil Pedlow, Ken Reid, Peter Jackson and Lyn Jamison. All four have played significant roles in Irish sport, particularly tennis. Ken and Peter were ranked number 1 in Ireland. Cecil played rugby for the British Lions and Lyn was President of the Ulster Council of Tennis Ireland (2002-2004).

2002: Junior and senior members at Clane Tennis Club (County Kildare) celebrate their being awarded the Eagle Star Small Club of the Year and the Overall Club of the Year. In 2002 they once again won the Eagle Star Small Club of the year category.

Siobhan O'Sullivan receiving her Connacht Open Under 16 prize from James Ward (president, Connacht Branch). Keeping her eye on the results is Olwyn Raftery.(c. 2002)

Watching the proceedings at the 1995 Ireland Ghana Davis Cup match

Elm Park Class 2 DLTC Summer League winners 1976. Back (l. to r.): Michael Wogan D. O'Sullivan & P. Trundle. Front (l. to r.): V. Curtain, J. Fitzpatrick & R. Willis.

Junior West of Ireland 2001. Katie Hennessy (Sligo TC) beat Sarah Crilly (EnniskillenLTC) in the u12 final.

The winning Leinster under18 team at the Belfast Boat Club in 1986 with manager Gerry More O'Ferrall. Boys: Gavin Blake, Daryl Singh, Owen Casey, Niall Murphy and Julian Drury-Byrne. Girls: Jennifer O'Brien, Sandra Fearon, Anne Marie O'Grady, Anne Lydon & Sheila Byrne.

Junior West of Ireland 2001. Maura Butler presents the winners prize in the under 14 boys' singles to son Ross.

The Irish Davis Cup team and officials at the 1995 Davis Cup match in Accra. Ireland lost 3/2 to Ghana.

Junior West of Ireland 2001. Under 14 Boys' doubles Plate final. Cillian Woods and Jaser Farur (left) beat C. McHugh and Mark Brennan.

Junior West of Ireland 2001. Mary Ann Healy (Naas LTC) (left) beat Fiona Gallagher (Sligo TC) in the final

Junior team (A) 'international' event (c. 1990) at Sligo Tennis Club. Left to Right: Severina Degeneve (France), Fabio Fracassati (Italy), Shane Hayes, Igor Brandino (Italy), Franck Lapine (France), Gavin Forkan, Marcelline Gordon, Chicca Cerreto (Italy), Mel Bourke, Sonya Higgins, David Thullier (France) & Olga Higgins.

The History of Irish Tennis

Yvonne Doyle-One of Ireland's most successful ladies in the last decade. Note the Ellesse and Eagle Star logos, both sponsors of Irish tennis for several years.

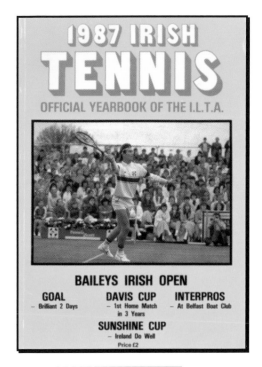

Junior West of Ireland 2001. Ross Butler and Roger Leahy (Sligo TC) (right) beat Sean Caheny (Sligo TC) and Michael Slowey (Enniskillen LTC) in the final of the under 14 doubles.

Junior West of Ireland 2001. Siobhan O'Sullivan (left) beat Aisling Burke (both Sligo TC) in the final of the under 16 girls' singles.

Practice in the heat of Accra when Ireland played Ghana in the Davis Cup (April 28-30th 1995).

The colourful young Laetitia Naufle from France playing at Sligo Tennis Club in a friendly match. (c. 1990)

A basket of new tennis balls is always welcome by both coach and player alike.

Patricia Karen and Aileen, the girls at Tennis Ireland (c. 2005)

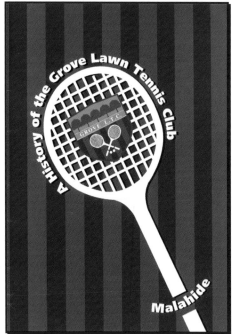

Mixed team at Sligo TC, August 1990. From left; Fintan Blake, Audrey Legras (France), Remi Gondron (France), Ariane Legras (France), Andrew Carrigy, Olga Higgins & Lorraine Devaney.

Mary Sawyer (Australia) on her way to winning the 1977 Irish Ladies' Open Championship at Fitzwilliam LTC. In 1879 the club were the first to host a national ladies championship, anywhere.

The Grove Lawn Tennis Club, Malahide, County Dublin, is one of the few in Ireland that have maintained grass courts for many years. It was founded in 1959 though it is linked to clubs in the area of much earlier vintage. This is the cover of the club history booklet, compiled by John Miley, Margaret Percival and Katy Swarbrigg.

Mats Willander (Sweden) at Trinity College Dublin for the GOAL charity matches in 1989.

International Claire Curran from Belfast (c. 2002)

Croquet lawns provided suitable surfaces for tennis when it first took off in 1874. Lawn tennis became the fashionable pastime in the years that followed. The above sketch illustrates the Irish Championships at The Casino, Marino, Dublin, in 1874. (Courtesy Clive Martin, Carrickmines Lawn Tennis & Croquet Club.)

Relaxing at Rushbrooke Lawn Tennis & Croquet Club (c. 2005)

Peter Jackson and Helen Lennon at Swansea in 1963.

Mary Rose Lyons has written two histories on Naas Lawn Tennis Club. Originally called the County Kildare Club, it was founded in 1881. Her first history covered the period 1881 to 1992.

Elm Park Charity Marathon (September 2001).From left: John Kenny, M. Rosemary Hough, Mary Briscoe & Hilary Hough.

Junior team (B) in 'international' event (c. 1990) at Sligo Tennis Club. Back (l. to r.): Ciaran Foley, Thierry Thullier (Paris), Audrey Legras (Paris), Ariane Legras (Paris), Suzanne Palmer & Deirdre Heaslip. Front (l. to r.): Laetitia Naufle (France), Deborah Czapnik (Belgium), Laurent Teissier (Paris), Cian Forkan & Ciara McManus.

The Leinster senior team that won the interprovincials held at the Belfast Boat Club in 1986. Back (l. to r.) Owen Collins, Jerry Sheehan, Michael Nugent, Michael Cowhie, Robbie Dolan and Jim McArdle (manager). Front (l. to r.): Aoife Wilson, Rhona Howett, Jennifer O'Brien, Sandra Fearon & Carmel O'Sullivan.

The Yoplait sponsored Junior Interprovincials that were held at Castleknock LTC in August 1992. That year Leinster was divided into three teams in each of the age groups (u18 u16 and u14). Teams: Ulster (u18) Geoffrey Hemphill, Zara Wolseley, Nevil Martin, L. Kane, Kirstie Henry, Claire Curran (u16) P. Flanagan, Helen Hunter, Andrew Curran, Brian McRandal, Anya Bowers, K. Hiles (u14) B. Cunningham, C. Curran, Stephen Watters, David Markey, Lynne Greenwood, Leonie McCabe, G. Traub. North Dublin: (u18) S. Harkin Yvonne Doyle, G. Glennon, Michael McMahon, Deirdre Walsh, O. Gallagher, (u16) Robert Collins, Emma Doyle, John Brennan, Cronan McNamara, Rachel Fagan, K. Doran, (u14) Joe Green, Sinead Walsh, John Doran, Conor Gallagher, E. Kiely, K. Ingoldsby. South Dublin: (u18) Justin Smyth, Catriona McCarthy, S. Duggan, F. Smyth, Jane Conan, Grainne O'Donoghue, (u16) T. White, R. McArdle, Marcus Purcell, Peter Rowell, L. Egan, C. Bollard, (u14) Barry Smith, Susan O'Neill, D. Mullins, A. Meagher, Alison O'Connor, Maria Scanlan. Rest of Leinster: (u18) Tom Hamilton, N. Berney, R. O'Shea, S. Vance, G. Mullns, T. Wickham (u16) James Pringle, Sheila Byrne, P. Quinn, R. Shanley, C. Daly, E. Leahy, (u14) David Nolan, A. Lennon, Nicky Malone, Sean Cooper, L. McCracken, M. White. Munster: (u18) Ray Niland, Louise Carmody, Mark Quinn, Danny Dolan, Jennifer Ann Mulholland, Kaithi O'Riain, (u16) George McGill, Caroline Flynn, Kevin Higgins, Tony O'Shea, Yvonne Flynn, Caroline O'Callaghan, (u14) Michael Moore, Derval Joyce, Peter Nolan, Brian O'Mahony, Aoife O'Neill, Aisling Palmer. Connacht: (u18) Enda Flynn, Orla McArdle, Mel Bourke, Patrick McGarry, Denise O'Gorman, Elaine Moore, (u16) Eamonn O'Floinn, Emma Kavanagh, David Kilroy, Keith Hopkins, Jenny Brennan, Janine Walsh, (u14) James McGarry, Sarah Coleman, Karl Gilligan, Darragh McCarthy, Ruth Mylotte, Laoise O'Shea. North Dublin won the u18 and u16 events and Ulster the u14 event.

Leinster

Leinster

Leinster-North Dublin u16

Munster-under 18

Connacht-under 14

Leinster-North Dublin u18

Ulster-under18

Leinster-u14

Leinster-Rest of Leinster u16

Munster-under 14

The History of Irish Tennis

Connacht-under 16

Leinster

Ulster-under16

Leinster-North Dublin u14

Leinster-u14

Munster-under 16

Connacht-under18

Ulster-under14

Elm Park (c. 2001): On left: Michael & Alice Wogan. On right: Angela & John Horn.

Elm Park Senior League team at Elm Park (2000). From left; Bobby Keogh, John Mulvey, Dave O'Donnell, Dave Ryan, Michael Wogan & Michael Dunne.

1985: Practicing for the GOAL matches at Elm Park. From left: Joachim Nystrom, Joe Tracy (club president), Mats Willander & John Claffey (captain).

Cake to celebrate opening of omni courts at Elm Park. (10 June 2001)

The O'Donnells at Elm Park. From left; Robert, Eileen & Richard.

The Connacht u16 team with Donal Dempsey (manager/Coach) in 1986.Boys: Eddie Moloney, David Thornton, Ciaran Foley & K. Burke. Girls: Ruth Glynn, N. Burke, M. Burke & F. Ryan.

The History of Irish Tennis

Elm Park: Class 2 Winter League Ladies' team. Back (l. to r.): Sandra Shaw, Kristine Lawlor, Laura Shilling, Louise Dunne & Breeda Claffey. Front (l. to r.) Ann Gibney, Karen Gobil and Mary Grier.

Elm Park Veterans' Invitation team winners (1994). From left: John Horn, Maedbh McEvoy, Breeda Claffey, David O'Donnell, Kristine Lawlor & Michael Wogan (captain).

Elm Park. Brian Claffey, 2001 hardcourt champion, with coach Breeda Claffey.

Attacking serve Sligo Tennis Club (c. 2002)

The Munster senior team in 1986. Men: Victor Drummy, Liam Croke, John Coulter & Conor O'Neill & P. Collins. Ladies: Rosemary Langford, E. O'Driscoll, Alice Fawsitt, Mairead Deegan & E. Ruddy.

Surprise defence Sligo Tennis Club (c. 1989)

In 2000 the Irish Open U16 girls' singles was won by Clodagh McMorrow (right, Tipperary County LTC). In the final she beat Rachel Halligan of Balbriggan.

Action at the Mount Pleasant LTC Open (c. 2005)

The St. Mary's LTC team that won the club invitation competition at Brookfield LTC (c. 2006)

Ladies' doubles at the West of Ireland (c. 2003)

Eoin Collins (c. 1986). In 1984, the 6'4" left-hander, at the age of 15, won the Irish Senior Close title.

Some of the top women's players competed at the RDS, Dublin, in the 1992 TSB Classic.

The History of Irish Tennis

2003: The match between Carrickmines Croquet & LTC and the All-England Croquet & LTC.

Sunday Tennis at Rushbrooke Croquet & Lawn Tennis Club (c.2004)

The 1998 junior interprovincials at Irvinestown Tennis Club.

Scenes at Naas Lawn Tennis Club (2004-2006)

Brookfield LTC Social (c. 2006)

Helen (left) claims that the cup is hers, not Ita's.
(Sligo Tennis Club, April 1996)

Tennis courts at Lisburn Racquets Club (Jan.1998)

Action at Naas LTC (c. 2005)

National Veteran Championships with Gerry Clarke
(right) in charge.(1998)

The successful over 35 ladies' team at Fitzwilliam
LTC (c. 2002)

August 1987
Sinead Walsh
beat
Sorcha Healy
in the final of
the under 14
championships
at
Sligo Tennis
Club.

Veteran doubles at Sundays Well Boating & Lawn Tennis Club (c. 2003).

July 1985: Junior Mixed tournament at Sligo TC.

Ballygowan Irish Schools Championship 2000. Boys' Winner: Gonzaga CollegeTeam: Barry King, Patrick Doran, Conor Fearon & George McMahon.

Ballygowan Irish Schools Championship 2000. Girls' Winner: Mount Anville team: Jenny Lawlor, Naomi MacHale, Sarah Griffith & Alexia Tierney.

Ballygowan Irish Schools Championship 2000. Girls' Runners Up: Santa Sabina team:Della Kilduff, Caroline McNulty, Lorraine Bracken & Sorcha Gillette.

Ballygowan Irish Schools Championship 2000. Boys' Runners Up: Belvedere College team: Robert Foley, Barry O'Driscoll, Kevin O'Dowd & Ciaran D'Arcy.

Ballygowan Irish Schools Championship 2000. Boys' Finalists: St. Gerard's College, Castlebar team:Donie O'Brien, Denis O'Brien, James O'Hara, Paul Moran, Warren Atkins & Richard Menton.

Ballygowan Irish Schools Championship 2000. Boys' Finalists: St. Flannan's College, Ennis team: Jason Comerford, David Hehir, Derek Flanagan & David Flanagan.

The Argideen Vale Lawn Tennis & Croquet Club back in 1892 during the first recorded holding of the West Cork Championships. Timoleague Castle is in the background.

Another member, Doris Ballingall, later Mrs. Eaton Travers, entered the Wimbledon Championships in 1919. She had a bye into the second round where she then had a walk-over against a Mrs. Hextall. At that stage she was beaten by Mrs. E.G. Parton (6/0, 6/2), the latter went out to the famous Mrs. Elizabeth Ryan of the USA in the next round, the quarter-finals. Doris was also a member of **Limerick LTC** at one stage. Miss Patience Conner (later Mrs. Fawsett) was winner of the Irish Junior Girls Open Championship in 1941. The club is primarily a social one with few internal competitions. However, individual players have travelled up to twenty miles on bicycles to play in open events, a number representing Munster in various categories. It did run the West Cork Championships as far back as 1892 and in recent years the club have entered teams in Munster competitions. The original site for the club was on the Travers land when four courts were laid out between Timoleague House (the Travers home) and the castle. When the ground was being laid out in the 1870s an old underground passage was discovered between the castle and the abbey. Henry Travers entered the passage with a canary, the latter died from the foul air and Henry's father had the passage immediately filled in.

The club moved to a site adjacent to the Hockey Club at Ummera in about 1901. There was also a racetrack there at the time. It was used for pony, cycling and athletic races. Eventually the hockey died out and the track had to go in order to make room for six tennis courts and two croquet lawns. The six grass courts are still in use to this day. During the Second World War the club closed for six years. There was a noble line of club secretaries, the most notable being Sampson Beamish who held the post for over thirty years. The present secretary (2001) is Diane Fawsitt who lives in Dunmanway.

Bill Travers (left) at Argideen Vale LTC in about 1976 with groundsman Dick Whelton. Bill has been the secretary and treasurer of the Munster Branch and was author of "A History of Munster Tennis" published in 1990.

Club Presidents

Robert Augustus Travers (Timoleague House)
Robert Travers (son of above)
Mrs. Edith Travers (widow of Robert)
Mrs. Rashley Lucas (Ummera House)
Mrs. Doris Travers (Wimbledon player)
Colonel Eaton Travers (widower of Doris)
Mr. E.B. Scott
Colonel A. Willington
Bill Tayler
Mrs. Phil Ryan
James O'Keeffe

Monkstown Lawn Tennis Club
(Founded C.1880)

According to the *Examiner* of the 10th September 1880 (?) the newly formed Cork club, Monkstown Lawn Tennis Club, had just held its first tournament. The winners of the men's singles was a Mr. T.H. Abrahall, he beat a Mr. W. Creag in the final. The club was known as Monkstown Lawn Tennis and Croquet Club, the croquet probably coming first. In its early days it had one grass court and one hard court. The latter was the first hard court in Cork and was made of rubble. Apparently it took a considerable time to dry out after wet weather. In a reverse of what was to happen all over the country, the hard court was converted into a grass court early in the 20th century. When the Irish Lawn Tennis Association was formed in 1908, Monkstown was one of the first clubs to affiliate and club member Mr. A.M. Cave was elected as one of the four Munster representatives to the new body. The others were M.J. Daly (Cork), S.E. Smith (Roscrea) and the Reverend W.H. Smith (Clonmel). Membership increased over the years with both senior and junior players entering inter-club competitions. In 1987 the club purchased some available land and laid down three new hard courts and a pavilion, the latter completed in 1989. Coaching was and is a feature of this club and some of the junior members were successful in open tournaments. According to the Tennis Ireland 2001 Handbook, the club currently has one of its courts flood lit.

✳✳✳✳

St. Anne's-Waterford Tennis Club
(Founded C.1879)

Thanks mainly to the efforts of Paddy Murphy, the mystery of this club in the south east is resolved. The LTA in their historical review (*Lawn Tennis & Badminton, February 5th, 1938)*) included the club at Waterford as one of four Irish clubs who had championships or tournaments which had been long established and still holding tournaments fifty or more years later. (The other clubs were **Limerick LTC**, **County Sligo LTC** and **Fitzwilliam LTC**). Paddy has confirmed that tennis was played on grass courts at the **Waterford Lawn Tennis Club** prior to 1880-an old engraved brass-silver plate, with the inscription "Waterford Annual Lawn Tennis Tournament 1880-Gentlemen's Singles Handicap-1st prize won by J.J. Hassard I.L.T.A." is still on display in the present club. The club ran very successful tournaments on the grass courts, attracting many top players. The following is a brief extract from *The Waterford Standard,* June 27th 1923:

> *Waterford Lawn Tennis Tournament was brought to a successful conclusion on Saturday afternoon. In the opinion of all concerned it was a wonderful week. There were many surprises in the finals, most of last years winners being defeated. Throughout the week the weather conditions were perfect, a fact that*

> *contributed to the remarkable success of the event. When the prizes were presented to the successful players on Saturday evening by Lady Goff, eulogistic references were made to the work of Mr. C. L. Fudger, the Hon. Tournament Secretary. The praise was well deserved, for the tournament was well organised with thoroughness that overlooked no detail. The catering department was also a model of efficiency.*

Paddy Murphy has been a member of Waterford LTC since 1946. For his tremendous services to the club he was made an honorary life member in 1977. In 2000 Paddy was winner of the J.P. O'Neill award for outstanding service to tennis in Munster.

The ladies singles, the Championship of the South of Ireland, was won by Mrs. Barry **Mallow LTC** one of the top ladies in Ireland at that time. The holder of the Gentleman's Singles Championship of County Waterford, held in 1921 and 1922 by Mr. M. H. Toppin, was met in the final by Ben Haughton, *surrounded by the largest crowd seen at a final in Waterford.* Ben, it appears, was a member of the home club, had played previously played for Waterford against Mallow in 1920. Ben won 6/1 6/3 3/6 6/2 and went on to win the men's handicap doubles with H.W.D. Gallwey (off –30.3) and the mixed handicap doubles with his wife, Daisy (Marguerite Olive), (off –30.2). In his thanks to the organisers he particularly mentioned the tournament secretary, Charlie Fudger. He had played in a large number of tournaments but had never met a better or keener honorary tournament secretary. Ben Haughton would go on to win the Irish Open Mixed title that year with his sister, Margaret Wilhelmina (Marjorie) beating John and Una Miley 6/2 6/3 in the final. He played in the Davis Cup team in 1926. Prior to 1954, two tennis clubs were operating in the John's Hill area of Waterford. The older club was **Waterford LTC**. It operated from the grounds currently occupied by **St. Anne's-Waterford Tennis Club**. The second club was called **St. Anne's LTC** and was in the grounds of St. Patrick's Hospital-the

Event	1st Prize	2nd Prize
Open Tournament at St. Anne's-Waterford LTC		
1880		
MHS	J.J. Hassard	
1893		
MS	H.R. Jones	
MHS	H.R. Jones	
LS	Miss Rice	
MHD	J.H. Head/S.L. Fry	
LD	Miss Bowers/Miss Brown	
MxHD	E.T. Chamberlain/Miss G. Roberts	
1894		
MS	R.F. Clifford	J.P. O'Shea
MHS	J.T. Hodgson	J. Butler
LHS	Miss M.H. Knox	Miss Yardley
MHD	J.T. Hodgson/ J. Congreve	J.P. O'Shea/ C.E. Denny
LHD	Miss Barrett Hamilton/ Miss Hardy	Miss S. J. Knox/ Miss M.H. Knox
MxHD	J. Butler/ Miss M.H. Knox	R.F. Clifford/ Miss Barrett Hamilton
1923		
MS	Ben Haughton beat M.H. Toppin 6/1 6/3 3/6 6/2	
MHS	W.E.Fudger (-15.1) w/o Hon. H.A. Shore (-5)	
LS	Mrs. Barry beat Miss M.E. Fudger 6/0 6/2	
LHS	Miss M.E. Fudger (-30) beat Miss A. McClelland (-15) 7/5 1/6 6/0	
MHD	Ben Haughton/H.W.D. Gallwey (-30.3) beat M.H. Toppin/C.L. Fudger (-30) 6/1 6/0	
LHD	Mrs. Byrne/Miss McClelland (-15) beat Mrs. Hall/Miss M. E. Fudger (-30) 6/3 6/2	
MxHD	Ben Haughton/Daisy Haughton (-30.2) beat C.L. Fudger/Miss M.E. Fudger (-30.3) 6/3 6/1	
1955		
MS	P. Reynolds beat D. Breen 8/6 8/6 0/6 1/6 9/7	
LS	Rosemary Binchy beat Beryl Umfreville 6/4 6/1	
MxD	Major Arthur Best/Beryl Umfreville beat P. Murphy/Miss B. Murphy 6/3 2/6 6/3	
1960		
MS	Gerry Cleary beat P. Reynolds 6/4 6/4 8/6	
LS	Mrs. M. Kenneally beat Miss B. Walton 6/2 6/0	
MxD	P. Reynolds/Mrs. M. Kenneally beat R. Willis/Miss A. O'Mailley 6/0 6/4	
1961		
Irish Close Championships (see Chapter 5)		
1962		
Irish Close Championships (see Chapter 5)		
1963		
South East of Ireland Championships		
MS	M. Hamid bt. Des Hardman 7/5 7/5 6/3	
LS	Ann Peppard bt. Mrs. M. Kennealy 6/1 6/4	
MD	P. Murphy/D.Gough bt G. Cheasty/N.Boyle 6/0 6/4	
MxD	M. Hamid/J.Ferguson bt D.Breen/B.Walton 6/4 6/3	

land on which the new Cheshire Homes are now in the process of being built. Tennis was played at this club from 1921.

Neither of the predecessor clubs owned their own premises- **Waterford LTC** rented land from the Waterford Protestant Cemetery Committee. The grounds originally had four grass courts *which through being meticulously maintained were amongst the finest in the country*. The St. Anne's club also rented their grounds from the County Hospital. The hospital authorities decided in 1954 to reclaim the tennis club land at the end of the season, supposedly for building extensions to the hospital-no building took place until the present homes in 2001.

At the opening of the new hard courts at Waterford-St. Anne's LTC in 1977 were (from left) Jack Shalloe (honorary life member), F. O' Mahony (president), Maureen Ryan (honorary secretary), P. Murphy (honorary treasurer) and D. Gough (vice-president).

With the **Waterford LTC** having a small membership at the time, it was decided by the committees of both clubs to amalgamate in the winter of 1954. The new name was to be **St. Anne's-Waterford Lawn Tennis Club.** The new club came into full operation in May 1955, still paying rental to the Cemetery Committee. Negotiations were then started with that committee for the outright purchase of the grounds, but were not finalised until 1963 due to difficulties with the deeds.

The original grounds were purchased for £500 and additional piece of land was purchased for £750. A fifth grass court and two hard courts (now called 6 and 7) were to be built here. The bank repayments to finance this purchase came from members' subscriptions and revenue from dances in an old Nissan Hut- the one dismantled and removed from the old St. Anne's club and re-erected in approximately the location of the present clubhouse.

It was found difficult to maintain the grass courts. The dry summers of 1975 and 1976 instigated action. All five grass courts were converted to tarmacadum and courts 6 and 7 were re-surfaced. The 'new' courts were officially opened on July 14th 1977, by Mr. Jack Shalloe, *the longest serving and most dedicated member of the club* (ILTA Yearbook, 1978). He had been made an honorary life member. In his day he was a player of exceptional ability, winning many singles and doubles titles in the south of Ireland and representing Munster at the interprovincials.

No one has done more to promote the game of tennis in Waterford, always encouraging young players and in his quiet and unobtrusive manner ensuring that the courts were always superbly maintained as well as single handily performing all repairs and extensions to the premises.

On the 15th July 1979, the new club building was first in use, appropriately on Heine Cup Day, the annual open team event. In January, on his 80th birthday, Jack Shalloe had turned the sod for this new club venture. That summer the club would enjoy considerable success on court and 'lift' many trophies. These included the Cleary Cup, the Sno Cup and the Ladies Day Cup.

IRISH LAWN TENNIS ASSOCIATION

President: REDMOND HOLLAND

Dinner

on the occasion of

THE IRELAND - ENGLAND
INTERNATIONAL

Saturday & Sunday,
16th - 17th August, 1980

*St. Annes-Waterford Tennis
Club*

The St. Anne's-Waterford LTC has been the scene for many important Irish tennis events over the years. Internationals were held at the club in 1958 (v Wales) and 1970 (v England). The 1980 celebration dinner was attended by Eddie Collins, TD, Redmond Holland (president, ILTA) and Mr. D. Doolin (president of the club).

In the 1980s the club erected flood lighting on the first four courts, thus extending the playing time considerably. 1990 was a critical year. Not alone were the other three courts flood lit but all seven courts were converted to all-weather artificial grass courts. *This turned out to be the catalyst that popularised tennis in Waterford, as within a few years, a waiting list for membership had to be established and is still in operation to this day* (Paddy Murphy). Further land was purchased and two more artificial grass courts were laid down. These would have special low-level

lighting *to prevent overspill of lighting into neighbours' property. The existing practice wall area was converted into two miniature (half-sized) courts- also artificial grass- for small children.*

The 1979/1980 committee at St.Anne's-Waterford Tennis Club, at a time when there were significant developments instigated. Front (from left): Maureen Ryan, Elaine Smyth, D.J. Doolin (President), Margaret Williams, Nora Kennedy, Mary Alward. Back (from left): Paddy Murphy (honorary treasurer), Richard Mc Carthy, Eddie O'Keeffe, Paul F. Nolan (chairman), David McCarthy, Donal Gough. Missing from photograph: Andrew Finn, Michael Flynn and Jerry Murphy.

In January 2000, the clubhouse was refurbished. The bar area enlarged to a capacity of 150 people. This extended over what was once a badminton hall. The kitchen, toilet and dressing room areas were improved. A noted feature was the upper floor balcony, enabling the viewing of all courts, from three sides of the building. Minister Martin Cullen officially opened this new clubhouse on the 3rd September 2000. The total expenditure on the club in recent years was about £0.5M.

The opening of the new clubhouse in 2000 at St. Anne's-Waterford LTC. From left: Dick McCarthy, Brendan Heylin, Mary Mountjoy (president, Munster Branch) and Des O'Shea.

All successful clubs rely on determined and dedicated people. The southeast has had its share. Apart from Jack Shalloe one must include Maureen Ryan, who fulfilled many roles in the club as well as being a player of international standing. She is a niece of another great tennis player, Des O'Brien (see chapter 6). Another member that should get special mention is Paddy Murphy, who has acted as both club secretary and treasurer. Notable members have included Willie Fanning, Frank Moriarty, Des O'Shea, F. O'Mahony,

Donal Gough, Dick Mc Carthy, Brendan Heylin, Martin Culen and Redmond O'Donoghue. The club has had many notable players over the years including Robin Gibney (Davis Cup player) and Anthea O'Donoghue (nee Goodbody) who played many times for Munster and had a full international cap in 1972. Anthea came from a long line of successful tennis players. She is married to Redmond, who, like herself, features on the veterans' scene these days. So too does Jean Russell. The late former international badminton and tennis player, Jim ("JJ") Fitzgibbon is a Waterford man and most likely played in the club back in the 1930s.

In 2000 the club officially opened their new clubhouse. From left: Mary Mountjoy (President, Munster Branch, Tennis Ireland), Redmond O' Donoghue, Mayor Davy Daniels, Minister Martin Cullen, Willie Fanning (Club President), Frank Moriarty (Club Chairperson) and Des O' Shea (Club Committee).

St. Anne's-Waterford were runners-up in the Munster Senior Cup in 2000. Front: (l. to r.): Grace Comerford, Mary Mountjoy, Jim O'Leary (Waterford Crystal), Niamh Kennedy (captain) and Aisling Palmer. Back (l. to r.): Dick McCarthy, Patrick mcgrath, Patrick O'Shea and Tim Conway (referee).

The club runs a series of well-supported annual events, open and closed. Among them is the Inter-firm event each May with up to 200 teams of four taking part. Each July is the Open Week with 20 events, including the South-East of Ireland championships. In August, the junior equivalent takes place. The club enters teams in many events throughout the Province. In 2000, the club won the Men's Riordan Cup, beating Limerick Lawn in the final. The team members were Men: Richard McCarthy, Robbie O'Keeffe, Alan Costine and Patrick O'Shea. The club currently caters for about 1300 members of whom nearly half are juniors, a recipe for the continued success of the club.

Open Tournament St. Anne's-Waterford LTC (SE of Ireland Championships for many years)		
Year	Men's Singles	Ladies Singles
1978	D. McCarthy	Maureen Ryan
1981	Ken Fitzgibbon	Maria Bolster
1982	Robin Gibney	Maria Bolster
1983	Tommy Burke	Diane Craig
1984	Willie Noteman	Diane Craig
1985	Tommy Burke	Jennifer Thornton
1986	Robbie Dolan	Margaret Redfern
1990	E. Grimson	
1991	J. Conroy	N. Kennedy
1992	Robin Gibney	L. Carmody
1993	D. Heffernan	L. Carmody
1994	D. Heffernan	L. Carmody
1998	Conor Darcy	L. Carmody
1999	Conor Darcy	Hilda Healy

St. Anne's Waterford Div IV winner of the Winter league in 2000. Front (l. to r.) Maria O'Sullivan (president, Tennis Ireland), Sheana Leslie, Amanda de Jough & Paddy Power. Back (l. to r.): Stephen Daly, Mick Kelliher (AIB), Colm Dunne & Mary Mountjoy (president, Munster branch).

St. Anne's Waterford Div V winner of the Winter league in 2000. Front (l. to r.) Maria O'Sullivan (president, Tennis Ireland), Wendy Coffey, Margaret Breen & Yuri Soickans. Back (l. to r.): Stepehn Daly (Munster branch), Mick Kelliher (AIB), Billy McCormack & Mary Mountjoy (president, Munster branch).

St. Anne's Waterford "A" winner of the Veteran Winter league in 2000. Front (l. to r.) Maria O'Sullivan (president, Tennis Ireland), Marie Duffy, Aylmer Barrett & Don Mullins. Back (l. to r.): Stephen Daly (Munster branch), Mick Kelliher (AIB), Alice Fawcett and Mary Mountjoy (president, Munster branch).

✶✶✶✶✶

Downshire Archery and Lawn Tennis Club
(Founded pre 1881)

On Wednesday the 10th August 1881 the Downshire Archery and Lawn Tennis Club had their second tournament of the season. The grounds, in the Botanic Gardens, Belfast, were in good order. It is not known when this club was formed, but it is surely one of the oldest in Ulster, along with **Enniskillen LTC** (1881), **County Cavan LTC** (C.1895), **Omagh LTC** (1892) and **Armagh LTC** (C.1881). Neither is it certain when this club died. Certainly by 1911, when the Irish Lawn Tennis Association (ILTA) was three years old, it was not an affiliated club. At that time there were 71 clubs affiliated including the following from Ulster: Ballycastle, Clones, County Cavan, Dungannon, Omagh, Monaghan and Cliftonville. Other clubs not affiliated at the time were Enniskillen, Belfast Boat Club, City of Belfast YMCA and Windsor. Many clubs in Ireland gradually became part of the governing body.

In 1881 local groups formed clubs which had tournaments of a confined nature. The following is part of the report in the popular paper of the time, *Sport (Saturday 13th August 1881):*

At the late meeting of the club the double matches were played, and the meeting on Wednesday was for the purpose of playing the single matches on the programme. The two meetings, both attended so largely, have been held with such a short internal, shows the popularity of the game and the interest taken in it by members of the club. Every requisite of comfort and convenience was provided. Precautions were taken against the weather, and the arrangements generally were efficiently carried out. Play commenced at 12 o'clock and concluded shortly after six. Amongst those present during the afternoon-Major Perceval Maxwell and the Misses Maxwell, Mr. J. Blackinston-Houston and the Misses Houston, Sir Charles and the Misses Lanyon and Party, Mr., Mrs.

and Miss McNeile; Mr. J. McNeile, Mrs. Lyons and the Misses Lyons, Mr. W. H. H. Lyons, Mr.J.B. Lyons, Mr. Mrs., and the Misses Graham and party; Captain and Mrs. Thompson, the Misses M'Clintock, Mr.F.G. Gordon and the Misses Gordon; Mr. F. St.John Gordon, Mr. W.R. and the Misses Young, Mr. F.L. Rawson, Dr. and the Misses Ferguson, Mr. and Mrs. Barklie, Mr. and Mrs. R.H. Reade, Dr.Tyner, Colonel and Mrs. Moorsom, Mr. and Mrs. F. Kinahan, Mr. S.D. Crommelin, Mrs. Allenson, Captain and Mrs. M'Cance, Mr. and Mrs. Dwyer, Captain Meynell, Colonel and Mrs. Bowles, Colonel and Mrs. Stothart, Mr.Stephen Maxwell.

It is interesting to note that the set only went to five games. This is perhaps surprising as the Irish and All England (Wimbledon) Championship rules were to six when the first championships were held three years earlier. Perhaps at the Down shire club there was a fall back to a time at Wimbledon when there was sudden death at 5 all i.e. a set could be won by 6 games to 5.

Tournament Singles Finals

Ladies Handicap Singles Miss M'Neilie (giving half 15) beat Miss Alicia Maxwell (giving 30) 5/1, 5/4.
Ladies Open Singles Miss Alicia Maxwell beat Miss M'Neile 4/5 5/3 5/3
Gentlemen's Handicap Singles Mr. F.L. Rawson (giving minus 40) beat Mr. J. M'Neile (giving 15) 5/4 5/2
Gentlemen's Open Singles Mr. F.L. Rawson beat Mr. F.G. Gordon 5/2 5/1

✶✶✶✶

Tullamore Lawn Tennis Club
(Founded 1880)

This midlands club does not appear to have any recorded history. The original club was located at Brookfield in the Charleville estate a couple of miles south west of the town. The Tullamore Golf Club was started here too-its official foundation date being 1906. The tennis club had moved to Spollanstown on or before 1901. Years later it would move again to Arden Vale (the Arden Road) in Tullamore town. The modern day coach/player Tadhg Lambe grew up playing here, as did his father before him. Ann Coughlan, the current County Librarian, is playing there for many years and can recall that the club had gone into disrepair, both the building and the courts. From a thriving club it dwindled down to about a dozen members. Potholes developed in the three courts, and the building was in such poor condition that the rats were to be seen gnawing away at the structure.

It was time to do something and in the 1980s a development committee got underway. Ann would eventually be the chairperson for this committee. Through sheer determination and a desire to bring the club to life again, a few people made it succeed. Membership is now back up to about 30 families or so with a total of about 100 players. More important, for future attraction to the sport, 3 new floodlit savannah courts are now in operation and a new building to replace the old one.

Taking a keen interest in proceedings is Geoff Oakley, a retired newspaperman, who played tennis for many years. In fact, he can go far enough back to say that he played the 'great' Harry Reid from Roscrea-that international player and all-rounder. Mind you Harry was at his peak in the 1910s before Geoff was born and when they met across the net he was well advanced in years. Geoff was a member of both the Wilmer and Ormond clubs in nearby Birr.

In the first Irish Handbooks (1894 and 1895) the club is mentioned but no secretary's name given. Around that time there were several tournaments being held in this midlands region namely in Birr, Banagher, Naas, Roscrea and Mulligar.

At the club grounds in Spollanstown in June 1901 were (from left) Reverend S. de Courcy Williams, Reverend Maxwell Coote, Isaacs Williams (bank manager) and Reverend Mr. Humphreys. (Courtesy Offaly County Library).

In 1881, Mr. O. R. Coote and Mr. R. Digby of 'Tullamore' were playing in the Irish Championships. Coote lost his singles to Mr. A. J. Holland, a useful player. The score was 6/4 0/6 3/6 2/6. The Tullamore pair (the designation LTC was not written after their names for some reason in the newspaper reports) won their first round men's doubles, beating Thomas and W. Rooke of **Wicklow LTC** with *very little difficulty* (6/1 6/3). In the second round they lost 2/6 2/6 to a useful pairing of Mr. S. D. Maul of the 84th Regiment and Peter Aungier of **Fitzwilliam LTC**. Aungier was the winner of this championship event in 1882 and 1883. The following year Coote was designated as being a Roscommon player and, in 1883, the **Castlerea LTC**.

Some results do exist for the 1911 open tournament at the club. Ben Haughton, who was 21 at the time and would later be a Davis Cup player, was in five finals. In the Open singles he beat a Lawerence Craig 6/3 6/2 in the second round. The full results are given for the mixed. With his sister, Marjorie (off-3), they won the final 6/3 6/3 against a Mr. Graham and Miss Trench (-

15). By 1913 **Tullamore LTC** was well established and had some forty members. By then the Reverend H.N. Craig from the club was on the Irish team. In 1907 he had reached the final of the Championship of Europe, held in Dublin for the first time. He was beaten by the Irish number one at the time, Jim Parke. In the 1920s, the Reverend Craig was a leading light in the town of Tullamore and a great promoter of library facilities for all.

In 1909, and possibly before, the club was running the Championships of Leinster, singles and doubles. Back in 1894 he won the Handicap Men's Doubles at the highly rated Beckenham tournament and was second in the Championship Singles there. In the 1920s there appears to have been no sanctioned event in Tullamore suggesting that playing activity was in low gear. In the 1920s, F. J. Egan of The Hall, Tullamore, was the club's honorary secretary. Some other club honorary secretaries are given below.

The annual 'cake fete' at Tullamore Lawn Tennis Club grounds in June 1901. From left Mr. Moore, Mrs. Moore, Miss Digby, Miss C. Armstrong and Vera......(?).(Photo courtesy Offaly County Library)

In 1951 when Ted Gallagher arrived at the club they had three courts at Arden, the location on the Kilbeggan Road. They were of a loose sand type material, possibly called whinstone, and took getting used to. There he could recall some good players like Bill Ennis, a local schoolteacher, Tom Keaney (owner of a drapery shop), Austin Cloonan and Bob English. The latter he would meet once again when they met up in Sligo. One lady of note, of Italian extraction, was Nat Luzzi. Apparently she, and her sisters, were excellent hockey players and of Leinster Provincial standing, playing out of the Loretto PPU hockey Club in Dublin. Tadhg Lambe was one of the best players to be developed at the Tullamore club. He won many titles at the club. In 1973 and 1974 he won the Open Singles Championships. In the 1974 final he beat Dermot Burke 7/5 6/3. Later that season he also beat Dermot in the final of the North Tipperary Championships at Nenagh (6/4 7/5). Tadhg won many events while a member of **Sutton LTC** in Dublin. He is now a full-time tennis and squash coach, based at **Limerick Lawn Tennis Club**. In 1983 the Tullamore club had four hard courts. These had been in place for many years. By the 1990s the club had three floodlit hardcourts in operation.

Some Longford LTC visitors to Tullamore LTC in 1968. From left: Ursula Broderick, Annette Donlon, Pat Higgins, Tom Higgins, Willie Higgins & Theresa McGough.

Some Honorary Secretary's at Tullamore LTC	
1956	*B. McCabe*
1964	*B. McEneaney*
1972-1974	*Sean Wrafter*
1977	*Cathal Coleman*
1978	*T.Clooney*
1979-1980	*P. Duffy*
1983-1985	*Maire Lambe*
1989-1997	*Louise Lennon*
1998-2000	*Dolores Rouse*

the Irish handbook, were for a club tournament; it was also open to temporary visitors. The 1894 event was recorded in the 1895 Handbook, with eleven other clubs, as being a "Club Tournament".

The secretary of the club in those early days was J. A. Lamphier, Ulster Bank, Blackrock. The club started off with grass courts, later hard courts and today has four all-weather floodlit courts.

Tournament at Blackrock Lawn Tennis		
Event	1st Prize	2nd Prize
	1893	
MHS	W. Posnett	
LHS	Miss M. Clover	
MHD	C. St. G. Orphen /W. Orphen	
MxHD	C. S. Giffard/Miss Barnard	
	1894	
MHS	C. St. G. Orphen	N. Staples
LHS	Miss Dunscombe	Miss Phelps
MHD	W. Posnett/	R.A. Andrews/
	T. Staples	H. Turner
LHD	Miss Place/	Miss Orphen/
	Miss Dunscombe	Miss Montfort
MxHD	J. Stokes/	T. Staples/
	Miss Phelps	Miss Place

****

St. Columba's College
(Founded C. 1880)

A Mr. C.F. Hyde from this club played in the Irish Championships in 1881. He beat R.C. Knox of **Fitzwilliam LTC** in round one (6/3 6/4 6/3). In the second round he was beaten by A. J. Mulholland representing the **Prince's LTC** and previously of the **Maida Vale LTC**. It is probable that Mr. Hyde was a teacher at the school. The school did have some notable pupils over the years. Probably one of the best known was Harry Read who was to be an international in the sports of cricket, tennis, rugby and croquet. The school at present has no active tennis. There is, however, a grass court in front of Hollypark House, which was probably the old court site in the 19th century. There are four other courts but as tennis is not a primary sport at the school they receive little use.

****

Blackrock Lawn Tennis Club
[Frascati LTC]
(Founded C. 1880)

The **Blackrock LTC** in Dublin appeared to have been called the Frascati club in 1881. That year, J. & H. Wilson from the club reached the semi-finals of the Irish Men's Doubles Championships at Fitzwilliam.

By 1893 the club was being referred to as **Blackrock LTC**. The results for the 1893 tournament, recorded in

****

Nenagh LT (& Croquet) Club
(Founded C. 1880)

What must be one of the most amusing stories in the history of Irish tennis relates to **Nenagh LTC.** It was reported in a small corner of the ILTA Yearbook in 1978. Terry Duncan who was the honorary secretary of the Ulster Branch for many years, and the president of the ILTA in 1954, was reputed as recalling the tale. Under the heading 'Developments in Munster' we find the following: *Elsewhere, we have written of developments at* **Nenagh** *but the plumbing there was not always as it is today and Terry Duncan tells of his visit to the Club in 1954 when on the Ladies' Room wall hung a row of "chamber pots" with the names of the various lady members painted on the undersides. Perhaps they were trophies.*

The local gentry on a magnificent setting of 3 acres and 2 roods started the club. Entry was strict as reported in the 1977 Yearbook of the ILTA. *The proposed member was subject to the most rigorous investigation and if he had all the attributes which would help to make him an excellent member and perhaps a player of distinction-yet on a ballot which was operated on a white and black "Bear" system-should the proposed new member receive three black bears his nomination for election was defeated.*

At one time the club had ten grass courts and two croquet lawns and it proved difficult to maintain them, particularly before the arrival of motorised mowers.

The History of Irish Tennis

By the late 1970s the club still had six grass courts but the croquet lawns were replaced by two hard courts. By the 1990s the club would have four operating hard courts, two of which were floodlit.

In about 1930 the Nenagh Town Tennis Club was founded. A second club started here, as in many other towns in that era, as there was a difficulty in entry to the old 'gentry' club. By 1952, the two clubs would merge, again a not unusual occurrence throughout the country; the older club losing numbers, the new one thriving. In the mid-1970s the grounds, *screened by magnificent beech trees,* would have an upgraded clubhouse. The Purcell family, in memory of their son Declan, donated equipment for a children's playground in the club. The club has been particularly keen on coaching and a number of their members have done well over the years. The club was one of the earliest to affiliate to the ILTA following its foundation in 1908. It has run tournaments for many years. Two early sets of results are as follows:

Some Nenagh LTC Open Results (Championships of North Tipperary)

1955

MS	J. K. D. Lacey beat R. Mahon 6/1 6/2
LS	M. O' Meara beat Mrs. Read 6/3 3/6 6/3
MD	J. K. D. Lacey/W.J. Fitzgerald beat Des A. Houlihan/T.Kenny 6/2 6/4
MxD	J. K. D. Lacey/N. Buchanan beat D.A. Houlihan/M. O' Meara 6/3 4/6 9/7

1963

MS	David Hurst beat Bruce Durow 6/4 4/6 6/1
LS	Sarah Williams beat Miss N. O'Hagan 6/3 7/5
MD	David Hurst/Bruce Durow beat F. O'Shea/T. O'Shea 6/1 6/3
MxD	T. O'Shea/Miss E. Kelly beat B. Hannify/Sarah Williams 6/2 6/4

1966

MS	Tadhg Lambe beat P. McDonagh 5/7 6/2 6/1
LS	Susan Houlihan beat Rita Haniffy 4/6 7/5 6/2
MD	Tadhg Lambe/P. McDonagh beat David O' Donnell/M. Grogan 6/1 6/1
MxD	F. Connolly/Susan Houlihan beat David O' Donnell/Rita Hannify 6/1 6/4

Nenagh LTC Clubhouse in 1976

Tipperary County LTC
[County Tipperary LTC]
(Founded C. 1880)

The club estimates that it was founded in about 1880. They do have confirmed records since 1896. The modern club came into full swing in the early 1920s when Colonel R. H. Holmes and Miss Bessie Harris (later Mrs. H. V. O' Brien) took charge of affairs. The pavilion still at the club in the late 1970s was the one they organised.

Some Munster H.C. Championship Winners

Year	Men's Singles	Ladies Singles
1926	Richard Hughes	Miss E. Preston
1928		Hilda Wallis
1938	Alan Haughton beat Paul McWeeney 6/3 6/4	
1939	Eustace Fannin beat Alan Haughton 6/3 3/6 6/4	
1955	D. B. Gloster beat Tom Cleary 6/0 6/1	Mrs. Umfreville beat Nan Conner 1/6 7/5 9/7
1956	Alan Haughton beat Gerry Clark 2/6 6/4 6/1	
1960	John de Courcy beat S. Clehane 6/1 6/4	Geraldine Houlihan bt. Mrs. N. Mansergh 6/4 6/3
1961	Gerry Cleary beat Gerry Clarke 6/3 6/1	Gene Hogan beat Mrs. J. H. Burgess 6/3 6/0
1962	Harry Sheridan beat C. Ryan 8/6 6/2	Bernie Burke bt Mrs. P. N Mansergh 6/2 6/2
1963	J. H. Burges beat W. Fennell 6/3 3/6 6/1	Gene Hogan beat Miss M. Delaney 6/1 6/2
1966	R. Stott beat Alan Denvir 6/2 6/4	Mrs. J. H. Burgess beat Miss I. Ryan 6/2 6/2
1977	Ronan Fearon	Jean Turbidy
1978	G. Morris	Alice Fawsitt
1981	Robin Gibney	Alice Fawsitt
1982	Tom Shelly	Alice Fawsitt
1983	Michael Daly	Alice Fawsitt
1984	P. Mangan	Jean Turbidy
1986	Pat Guiry	Jean Tubridy
1989	J. Heffernan	N. Ryan
1990	P. Staunton	Alice Fawsitt
1991	J. Conry	N. Kennedy
1992	Pat Guiry	J. Hyland
1993	P. Goebel	Fiona Long
1994	S. O' Sullivan	Fiona Long
1995	Robert Collins	M. L. Carmody
1996	P. Kelly	Fiona Long
1998	C. Darcy	
1999	W. Guiry	
2000	D. Dillon	

Some of the attendance at the 1929 Tipperary Lawn Tennis Club Open Tournament.

Tournaments started in 1924 and the first 'open tournament proper' was in 1926 when the winners of the singles were Richard Hughes and Miss E. Preston. This became the Hard Court Championships of Munster and has been more or less continuous until this day. In addition to the listed winners there have been many other notable Irish and foreign players on the winners rostrum. These have included John O'Brien, George McVeagh, Dick Sandys, Noel Callaghan (Australia) Nick Mansergh and Redmond O' Donoghue. Ladies of note who have played here have included Nora Conway, Binkie Harman, Patience Conner, Joyce Coyles (England) and Jill Knight (England). A junior tournament was introduced a number of years ago and proved very successful. Of all the members of note perhaps the one that must be mentioned is Charles Ogilvy Martin Southcote Mansergh. He was the honorary secretary of the club for many years, involved in the Munster Branch and then, in 1947, was made president of the Irish Lawn Tennis Association. Tipperary County and nearby Lattin are currently the only affiliated clubs in the country with clay courts. At Tipperary they were first laid down on three grass courts in 1940. At the time the war was in progress and tarmacadum was not available, red clay was the only hard surface that could be used. This proved a popular decision at the club. The club's honorary secretary said, in 1995, that there would be strong opposition to changing this situation. *Our members love the clay courts. They're ideal to play on, because the ball bounces quite high, and also because they're very easy on the limbs. The courts are also very popular with players from outside clubs who take part in our open competitions, and I know there would be a sharp decline in entries if we changed the surface.* Nora pointed out their need to be regularly swept and kept moist. On average, the club purchases clay from companies in England or France every

second year. Tipperary town is well off for tennis clubs. In addition to the long established Tipperary County club there is also the **Rosanna LTC** with three courts and the Cannon Hayes Complex club with two. Not bad for a town of 6000 people! May their successes long continue.

✳✳✳✳

County Wicklow LTC
[Wicklow LTC]
(Founded Circa 1880)

According to the 1988 ILTA Yearbook the club was formed in 1894 close to the base of beautiful Bray Head and under the patronage of Lord Meath, head of the Brabson family. No reference to a secretary for this club appears in the 1894 or 1895 handbooks. We do, however, find a Mr. T. Rooke of the 'Wicklow Club', played in the Irish Championships in 1881. A Captain G. Taylor with the same designation played in the singles in 1882. That year J. W. & R. P. Keogh played in the men's doubles. It is noted that Captain Taylor would play in the **Fitzwilliam LTC** colours in 1884. There is a suggestion that the club might have started in about 1880, but in a low key and that formally it only took off in 1894. In December 1972 the **County Wicklow LTC** building of over 70 years was burnt to the ground-*the molten eyes of a few could still see bright flickers of glory, disappointment, laughter and sorrow of times past in the eerie skeleton.* Certainly the club grew to be one of the finest in Ireland and run a Championship that was both respected and fought for by the best players of many eras. At one time it did have 10 grass courts to go with the elegant pavilion. It was the scene of the East of Ireland Championships and, in the 1940s, the Australian Davis Cup team

County Wicklow Lawn Tennis Club Championship Winners

Year	Men's Singles	Ladies Singles
1935	GeorgeMcVeagh bt L. Shaffi (London) 7/5 3/6 6/1 6/2	Norma Stoker beat Vera Mahony 6/2 6/4
1946	Raymund Egan bt. Cyril Kemp 8/6 6/8 6/3	Betty Lombard beat Norah Conway 6/1 6/4
1947	Cyril Kemp beat J. K. Drinkall (GB) 6/3 6/1	Betty Lombard beat Norah Conway 6/2 6/2
1948	Cyril Kemp beat Frank Kenny 6/1 6/1	Mary Fitzgibbon beat Betty Lombard 7/5 8/6
1949	Cyril Kemp beat Joe Hackett 6/1 6/2	Betty Lombard beat Mary Halford (GB) 6/0 7/5
1950	Joe Hackett beat Jim Fitzgibbon 4/6 6/3 7/5	Mary Fitzgibbon beat Betty Lombard 6/3 6/3
1951	Guy Jackson beat Cyril Kemp 6/3 6/2	Mary Fitzgibbon beat Maeve Downey 6/2 3/6 6/1
1953	Joe Hackett beat Cyril Kemp 5/7 6/1 6/4	Pat Ward (Eng.) beat Mary Fitzgibbon 6/3 6/4
1954	C. Bernstein beat Guy Jackson 6/3 1/6 6/4	Betty Lombard beat Angela Clarke 6/4 7/5
1955	Guy Jackson beat G. Oakley 6/2 6/4	Mary Fitzgibbon beat Mary O' Sullivan 6/2 3/6 6/0
1958	J. M. Ward (E.) bt. Joe Hackett 6/3 6/2	Eleanor O'Neill beat Betty Lombard 2/6 6/3 6/2
1959	Guy Jackson beat Joe Hackett 3/6 8/6 7/5	Betty Lombard beat Mrs. Joan Morton 8/6 6/3
1960	J. M. Ward (E.) bt. M. Braund 6/2 6/3	Eleanor O'Neill beat Heather Flinn 7/5 6/3
1961	Roger Mills (E.) bt. Joe Hackett 6/2 3/6 6/1	Eleanor O'Neill beat Mrs. Jill Mills (Eng.) 6/3 6/0
1962	Joe Hackett beat Harry Barniville 10/8 6/3	Eleanor O' Neill beat Lorna Cawthorn (GB) 6/4 3/6 6/3
1990	Eoin Collins	Carmel O'Sullivan
1991	Noel Murphy	Lesley O'Halloran
1992	Michael Nugent	
1993	Michael Nugent	
1994	Eoin Collins	Gina Niland
1995	Michael McMahon	L. Sheales
1996	John Doran	L. Lombardi
1997	Owen Casey	
1998	John Doran	Gina Niland
2004	Conor Niland beat David O'Connell	Yvonne Doyle beat Galina Misiurova

a knock on effect of the depressed 1950s. Three courts were lost to road development. In 1977 she was to have three new all-weather hard courts along with the four remaining grass ones. The 1978 ILTA article added: *if on your journey along the road from Bray to Greystones, you glimpse through the trees, a tall white double monopitch building, be heartened, for all is well with the County Wicklow Lawn Tennis Club.* In the 1988 Yearbook it is noted that a three-year development plan was approved and that the six, now all weather courts, are under lights. The **County Wicklow LTC** has played in leagues for many years. They have won a total of 22 titles since they first won the Ladies Class III Summer League in 1923. The ladies would win Class II in 1936 and 1940. The Men's first Summer League win was in the Class III event in 1969 followed by the Class II event in 1989. More recently, the men have won the Class 2 Winter League (1996), the Class 2 Floodlit League in 1989 and the Over 35 Class 2 in 1995 and 1997. The Senior Ladies have been busy too winning the over 35 Class 2 in 2000. Some past winners of the County Wicklow Championships, which go back, at least as far as 1913, when they were called the Championships of the South Eastern Counties, are in the table across (*In 1913 **Greystones LTC** ran these championships).

The remains of the County Wicklow LTC pavilion in 1972.This building had been in use for over seventy years. Below the 'new' clubhouse in1974.

The floodlit courts at County Wicklow LTC in the late 1980s.

played there. Alan Mills, the well-known Wimbledon referee, played and won the County Wicklow Championships. By the 1960s the club had dropped from one of the biggest in the land to a struggling one,

Armagh Lawn Tennis Club (Founded Circa 1880)

It is not certain if this northern club died out or survived under another name. We do know that in the early days of the Irish Championships at **Fitzwilliam LTC** there were players reported as being from the club. Mr. R. B. Templer played in the 1881 event, losing in the first round to Mr. R. Hassard of the home club in the first round in three straight sets. R.S. Templer, presumably a brother, from the same club was first on court and beat Mr. T. Rooke of the 'Wicklow Club' 6/2 7/5 6/1. In the second round he lost to Mr. O. E. Woodhouse of the **West Middlesex LTC** 2/6 3/6 0/6. Mr. C. Bourke from the club played in the 1882 event, losing in the first round to E. L. Coffey of the Phoenix Cricket Club. A Major G. Anson of the 'North of **Ireland LTC**' competed in 1883. Is this the same club under a different name? He was obviously a useful player beating the rated M. J. Carpendale of **Kingstown LTC** 6/4 6/4 7/5. In the second round he beat H.A. Robinson of **Fitzwilliam LTC** but lost to the great Ernest Renshaw in the third round (1/6 2/6 2/6). The latter went on to take the Championship. In the 1890s we find, in the first Irish Handbook, that an Armagh tennis tournament took place in 1893. The winners were:

Open Tournament Armagh LTC in 1893

Event	Winners
MHS	-Good
LHS	Miss Clarke
MHD	-Parkingson/B. Chadwick
LHD	Miss Buckley/Miss Clarke
MxHD	-Sinton/Miss Clarke

The Club Champion for 1893 was R. Chadwick and the honorary secretary for 1894 and 1895 was T. Gordon, The College, Armagh. The **Armagh LTC** continued to be active and was one of the early members of the Irish Lawn Tennis Association (formed in 1908). It was one of the first Ulster clubs to affiliate. This was either in 1912 or 1913. Certainly, in 1913 they were running officially sanctioned Ladies' and Gent's Challenge Cups. The event started on the 7th July. In the same week there were tournaments at **Mallow LTC**, **Kilkenny City & County LTC**, **Tullamore LTC** and at **Ballycastle LTC** (for the Championship of County Antrim). The club membership of 70 in 1913 was quite large (That year **Wilton LTC** in Dublin had 40 members and Sunday's Well in Cork 60). The tournament at Armagh was still being run in the 1930s but, based on a scan of several years in the 1940s and 1950s, seems to have died out. In the early 1920s the appearance of the name **Armagh Archery and Lawn Tennis Club** is recorded. This is perhaps the same club with a new name. It was affiliated up to 1963 at least, when a Mr. Douglas of Ivy Lodge, Armagh, was the honorary secretary. No Armagh club appears in the 1967, 1973 or 1974 handbooks suggesting the club had gone into decline.

Naas Lawn Tennis Club (County Kildare Club) (Founded 1881)

Formerly known as the **County Kildare Club** the tennis club at Naas has had a long and interesting history. Much of the information here has been gleaned from the history compiled by Mary Rose Lyons, an ardent member for many years and the Lady Tennis Captain in 1992 and 1993. She in turn recognises the assistance she had in preparing *History of Naas Lawn Tennis Club 1881-1993* from Hector Legge, Nora Murphy, Peter Brennan, Doris Whelehan, Joan Spring, Don Higgins, Timmy Conway, Major John de Burgh, Judge Patrick McKenzie, Elma Flanagan, the Greely Family, Rosario Fitzsimmons, Joan and Marjorie Gorry, Bridget Costello, Elizabeth Finnegan and Colin Sheridan.

Apart from the fact that the club is well over a century old, it has some features that are fairly unique. In August 1880, Colonel Thomas John de Burgh, the founder of the County Kildare Club, proposed in a letter to the existing members of the Naas and County Kildare Cricket Club and amalgamation with a new club. That new club came into existence on the 1st January 1881. Known initially as the **County Kildare Club**, it remained so until October 26th 1977 when the name **Naas Lawn Tennis Club** became the official title.

Over the years the club had an interesting range of sports. It became one of the outstanding sports centres in Ireland. Apart from cricket, one would find, at different times of the year, polo, soccer, croquet, table tennis, lacrosse, pitch & putt, rugby, hockey, pigeon shooting, trap & pea rifle shooting and, from time to time, the facilities were used by both cyclists and athletes. The De Burgh family at Oldtown were at the heart of this venture from the beginning. They have resided at Oldtown for about three hundred years and, apart from their generosity and interest, provided the club backbone through Colonel Thomas John de Burgh (1851-1931), Captain Hubert Henry de Burgh (1879-1960) and the present President, Major John Hubert de Burgh.

The rules of the club were framed at a General meeting held on the 18th February 1881 and provided for an annual subscription of £2. The first committee consisted of nine members, six shareholders (who had taken one or more shares of £5 each to help finance the Club in its infancy) and three "old" members (who had been members of the Cricket Club). Paul Brown, J. Blowney and J. Smyth were the cricketers and were joined on that committee by Sir John Kennedy, Baron de Robeck, T. Hendrick, G. Mansfield Jnr., Stephen Brown and Thomas John de Burgh. The latter acted as honorary secretary. It was not until 1935 that Club Captains were elected, prior to that time the secretary acted as Captain of the club. The sub-committee dealing with lawn tennis included G. Mansfield and G. De L. Willis. Another sub-committee dealt with cricket and football and a third with pigeon shooting. An interesting aside is the fact that Stephen Brown was a delegate to the inauguration of the GAA at

Thurles in 1884 and would become the vice-president of the Naas GAA club.

The first County Kildare Open Tennis Championships commenced on the 2nd August 1881. In 1891 an additional two tennis courts were laid to keep up with demand. In the period up to the First World War cricket was the dominant sport. The grounds were kept in magnificent order and the first clubhouse was built in 1906. The cost was £250 and the last instalment of £50 was paid in April 1909. The nearby military barracks and those at Naas, Kildare and at the Curragh provided a stream of cricketers and lawn tennis players. The latter was considered a sport suitable for young ladies who wished to meet suitable partners. The early outstanding tennis players included the Odlum family. The annual County Kildare Tennis Championships attracted players from all over Ireland and the eight grass courts were rated to be as good as any in Ireland. For the annual event nets and netting surrounds for the courts were hired from Elverys in Dublin. The ladies provided the catering, which included strawberries and cream in abundance. Money was raised by tournament fees and entrance charges to the grounds. Local boys and girls acted as ballboys and girls and were, apparently, happily rewarded.

During the Great War minutes were suspended and on the 20th June 1919 the club took off again. In that year it was decided that Wednesday be 'club day' for tennis with tea provided for 9d. Balls were provided by the players themselves and Claude Odlum bought six dozen balls at 12/- per dozen, the club selling them to members at 2/- for a new ball and 1/-3 for used ones. On the 23rd April, 1920, the following rule was passed: *Ladies can be admitted to membership of the Club by ballot at a subscription of 10/- per quarter or £1 per annum, payable in advance, but do not have the privilege of voting, except by payment of £2 per annum, as per Rule VII.* Further changes now were to come into operation.

The playing of rugby was allowed on Sundays in 1923 and tennis the following year. On March 24th, 1929, the extant minutes record that Mrs. Sargent was elected to the Committee, the first lady to break into this male domain of 48 years standing. Mrs. Molly Rooney, who ran a thriving news agency in the Main Street, Naas, was the first Lady Captain in 1935. She later recalled her days playing mixed doubles and, in particular, partnering Count John McCormack, a member of the club when he lived at Moore Abbey, Monasterevan.

The Club would regularly rent out their premises for some of the sports mentioned above. In fact, without being involved in club management, players could play tennis for 15/- per annum (men) and 7/-6 (ladies), players providing their own balls. Tom Legge, was the caretaker between 1906 and 1931. In 1920 his annual wage was raised from £75 to £104 but had to be reduced in 1926 *owing to the adverse balance of the Club.* His wife and family were fully involved in the Club and would provide catering facilities on a regular basis.

A rent reduction just before the Second World War, due to the generosity of the landlord, Captain de Burgh, enabled the club to survive. During the war itself members would have rotas to cut the grass. Shortages at that time reduced the amount of tennis that could be played and the associated socialising. Lack of transport prevented inter-club matches and the open tournament was suspended from 1939. In 1943 the opening club tournament of the season (9th May) was abandoned due to a hail storm. By the following evening the courts were under three inches of snow.

In 1948 a court marker was obtained at auction but, due to financial constraints, the purchase of a motorised mower for £100 in 1948 was rescinded. As few as twenty members were paying a capitation of £1 (to the I.L.T.A.) in the early fifties. Despite this the club played in the Provincial Towns Cup in 1952 and in various friendly matches, the latter were considered an important part of club life. Things were at a low ebb in 1958 when nets had to be borrowed for the annual August tournament. However, the Tennis Dance that week in Mrs. Lawlor's ballroom, made money and the overall profit of £141.50 for the tournament enabled a serious discussion on net purchase to take place. Around this time the Ladies' room in the clubhouse was refurbished with a jug, bowl and hangers. Present day tennis players might not know that for a club to have running water, showers etc. in days gone by was a luxury most clubs could not afford. In fact Naas, like other clubs, often found difficulty in collecting annual subscriptions.

Coaching was considered important at **Naas LTC** and John and Angela Horn were employed for that purpose. Their first visit was July 18th 1962. Another noted coach, Aidan Bradshaw, was also on hand in 1964. Members J. P. Greely and J. Spring went to coaching sessions at **Charleville LTC** and **Lansdowne LTC** in order that they could help with juniors back in their home club. Many others coached in the club over the years, including Davis Cup player Michael Hickey and Federation Cup player Helen Lennon.

Competition

Open tournament and club championships have been important elements in this successful club for many years. The first open tournament was held in 1881, one of the first in the country. The Men's Singles Challenge Cup was presented by Algernon Odlum a quality player in the early days of the club. The legendary George McVeagh won this cup in 1939. In 1983 the event was revived and the Odlum Group presented a fine replacement trophy. Hilda Wallis, the Irish Open Champion in 1924, 1926, 1930 and 1933, presented the Ladies Singles Challenge Cup in 1934. Before the tournament's revival in 1983, Ken Potterton found the cup in **Fitzwilliam LTC**, where presumably a former winner had deposited it. He, it might be noted, did much for club, Leinster and National tennis and was President of the ILTA in 1974. The **Naas LTC** was to make him an honorary life member along with J. Barry Brown, Joe Wheeler and Major John de Burgh.

Open Tournament County Kildare LTC	
1934	
LS	Miss Hope Furney beat Miss P. Spicer
1935	
MS	George McVeagh beat E. H. Porter
LS	Miss P. Spicer beat Miss M. Graham
Men's D	D. D. O'Sullivan/M. H. Toppin beat George McVeagh/Vincent Murphy 6/3 6/4
Ladies' D	Hilda Wallis/Norma Stoker beat Miss M. Craig/Miss D. Henry 6/0 6/3
Mixed D	George McVeagh/Miss M. Craig beat M. H. Toppin/Hilda Wallis 3/6 6/3 12/10

Over the years many top players would play in the championships organised by the club. In 1977, Mary Rose Lyons, was to be mainly responsible for the inauguration of the County Kildare Open Junior Championships. This was assisted by sponsorship from the Odlum Group. This event has become one of the top junior competitions in the country with regular entries now passing the 550 mark. An interesting, and pioneering, introduction in the senior open event was the "qualifying rounds" in singles and doubles. This system is used widely in European countries and the 'weaker' players not succeeding in this part of the event are entered in the Plate. The top standard players are automatically entered in the main draw.

Club Developments

After much discussion, and a long history of success, the club purchased the premises and grounds from Major John de Burgh in 1967. The cost was £2000 on a plot of 6.7444 acres. Following the final payment in 1972, the Major showed his true interest in the club by refunding a sum of £400, a most welcome gesture at the time. By 1977 the club owned 9.444 acres, a recreational area, pavilion, four grass courts and four hard courts. Further developments were required to meet the needs of a growing and thriving club. Courts 9, 10 and 11 were opened in May 1977. Permission for a new clubhouse was obtained, on appeal to An Bord Pleanala, in 1980. While the old building was renovated in 1978, the new one had to wait due to financial constraints. However, things did not stand still. A practice wall was built and tennis quick courts (4,5,6) with lighting were in operation in the autumn of 1982, a decision to abandon the grass courts having been already made. Recognised in the club's move forward was the help of AnCo and the accomplished grounds man, Len Taylor. Members in the middle of the developments were Mick Doyle, the rugby international, Mary Rose Lyons, Niall O'Neill, Sean McElligott, Eileen Power, Terry Mc Goff, David Brennan, Don Higgins and Gerry Laheen. The new clubhouse was finally ready for the club AGM on the

30th October 1990, at a cost of £375,000. By 1990 the club had 12 courts and a plan to build covered courts.

Some Tennis Highlights at Naas LTC	
1881	Open tournament
1934	Hilda Wallis presents Ladies Singles Challenge Cup
1939	George McVeagh wins Men's Singles Challenge Cup
1962	Intermediate Open Championships held.
1971	First two hard courts built, funded by life members, donations and a bank loan.
1973	Men and Ladies win Class IV Dublin Summer League. Dramatic increase in club competitions. Liam Flynn presents five cups to club for competitions.
1976	Ladies win Class II Dublin Winter League.
1977	First County Kildare Open Junior Championships first held. Men win Class III Dublin Summer League.
1978	Men win Class IV Dublin League.
1979	Claude Odlum presents cup to club.
1981	Men win Class II Dublin Winter League.
1982	Grass courts now replaced by three tennis quick courts with floodlighting.
1983	Junior Easter Championships inaugurated.
1984	First County Kildare Open Veteran's Doubles Championships.
1985	Qualifying round for Senior Open Championships introduced.
1986	First year of Graded Open Tournament.
1987	Juniors win McHugh Cup at **Templeogue LTC.** Men win Class V Dublin League.
1990	Frankie Boland secures veterans' interpro cap.
1991	First Naas Inter-Business tennis tournament held. Men win Class II and III Dublin Winter Leagues and Class III and V Dublin Summer Leagues.
1992	Launch of Mary Rose Lyons Club History.
1996	First County Kildare Senior Open Championships (Class 2 and under).
2005	A second club history (from 1992 to date) is prepared Mary Rose Lyons. The club copy all their many minutes' books on to CD covering 1881 to 2004.

As this club heads for a century and a quarter of play it can look back on a successful operation on both the playing and development front. It can boast of players of provincial and national standards and, in particular, has been successful with many open tournaments. It has been a businesslike club with members giving their professional expertise gladly. It has had the same firm of solicitors (Brown and McCann) to advise them since its foundation. It has some remarkable members such as the Odlums, the Mansfields, J. Barry Brown, Ken Potterton, Joe Wheeler and the significant backing of the de Burgh family. In more recent times there were many members of note as the club developed out of all recognition. One does not like leaving out the many who have contributed to a club's life but one that must be mentioned is Mary Rose Lyons, an all round player and administrator for over twenty years.

Naas LTC Tournament Committee 2003. From left: Peter Farrell (club coach), Lena Lenehan (tournament secretary), Mary Rose Lyons (tournament director), Aidan Morrison (director, trade relations, BWG), Helen Cosgrave (lady captain), Paddy Cassidy (men's captain) and Shane Spring (tournament referee)

The men's singles in the Spar sponsored open at Naas LTC in 2001 was Julian Morrison (Naas LTC). He beat M. Thomas (Navan TC) 6/4 4/6 6/4 in the final. In the ladies'singles Susan Campbell (Naas LTC) beat M. Kenneally (Castleknock LTC) 6/2 6/4 in her final.

The three clubhouse phases at Naas Lawn Tennis Club. From left: The pre-1881 building now used as a storage shed, the 1906 building now a Junior Clubhouse and the present clubhouse which was officially opened in 1992.

The County Kildare Junior Championships in 1978 at Naas LTC. From left: Barry O'Sullivan, Joe Spring, Mary Rose Lyons, Mick Doyle (the well-known rugby international who earned 20 caps between 1965 and 1968), Collette Ryan and Robert Lyons.

Club Singles Champions
Naas LTC

1963	William Couhlan	Kathleen Brown
1964	Donie Conway	
1965	Pat Glennon	
1966	Donie Conway	
1967	Donie Conway	
1968	Donie Conway	
1969	Donie Conway	
1970	William Coughlan	
1971	Donie Conway	Rosalie Sheehan
1972	Donie Conway	June Greely
1973	Peter Fulham	Antoinette Conway
1974	Donal Buckley	June Greely
1975	Peter Fullam	Collette Ryan
1976	Frankie Boland	Collette Ryan
1977	Frankie Boland	June Greely
1978	Ger Grehan	Geraldine Coleman
1979	Frankie Boland	Geraldine Coleman
1980	Frankie Boland	June Greely
1981	Gerry Kinnerk	Kay Conlon
1982	Gerry Kinnerk	Kay Conlon
1983	Morgan Buckley	Kay Conlon
1984	Gerry Kinnerk	Rose O'Reilly
1985	Morgan Buckley	Emma Allen
1986	Vinnie O'Reilly	Emma Allen
1987	Vinnie O'Reilly	Emma Allen
1988	Vinnie O'Reilly	Emma Allen
1989	Graham Harding	Nora Kelly
1990	Pat Coleman	Nora Kelly
1991	Graham Harding	Emma Allen
1992	Alan Donnelly	Nora Kelly
1993	G. Harding	Nora Kelly
1994	G. Harding	Nora Kelly
1995	G. Harding	Nora Kelly
1996	M. Finnegan	Nora Kelly
1997	G. Harding	Laura Gibson
1998	M. Finnegan	S. Campbell
1999	Adrian Conlon	S. Campbell
2000	Alan Donnelly	S. Campbell
2001	Alan Donnelly	Emma Allen
2002	Alan Donnelly	Monica O'Neill
2003	Alan Donnelly	Monica O'Neill

Naas Lawn Tennis Club (formerly County Kildare Club)

Year	President	Chairman	Honorary Secretary	Honorary Treasurer	Ladies Captain	Men's Captain
1881-1882	Thomas John de Burgh		Thomas John de Burgh	Thomas John de Burgh		
1883-1891	Thomas John de Burgh		George Mansfield	George Mansfield		
1892-1896	Thomas John de Burgh		Sir J. Kennedy	Mr. J. Brooke		
1897-1901	Thomas John de Burgh		Sir J. Kennedy			
1902-1907	Thomas John de Burgh		Sir J. Kennedy	R. Mansfield		
1908-1909	Thomas John de Burgh			H. Hendrick Aylmer		
1910-1913	Thomas John de Burgh		H. Hendrick Aylmer	H. Hendrick Aylmer		
1914	Colonel R. St. Leger Moore		F. Blacker	F. Blacker		
1915-1921	Colonel R. St. Leger Moore		E. de Vere Kennedy	E. de Vere Kennedy		
1922	George Mansfield		P. de Vere Kennedy	P. de Vere Kennedy		
1923-1925	George Mansfield		Major Mainguy	Major Mainguy		
1926-1928	George Mansfield		W.P. Flynn	J. Walsh		
1929-1932	A.M. Aylmer		W.P. Flynn	J. Wheeler		
1933	C. Pratt		Miss M. chell	J. Wheeler		
1934	C. Pratt		J. Cristland	J. Wheeler		
1935	C. Pratt		Miss M. chell	B. Coyle		
1936	C. Pratt		Miss M. chell	B. Coyle	Mrs. Rooney	
1937	C. Pratt		N. Byrne	R. J. Doyle	B. Hanna/B.Tyndall	
1938	C. Pratt		Miss M. chell	R. J. Doyle	I. Tyndall	W. Farrell
1939	C. Pratt		Miss M. Mitchell	R. J. Doyle	I. Tyndall	T. & M. Broe
1940	J. Barry Brown		A. W. Connor	F. J. Wright	I. Tyndall	P. Tynan
1941	J. Barry Brown		A. W. Connor	F. J. Wright	I. Tyndall	J. Brennan
1942	J. Barry Brown		A. W. Connor	F. J. Wright	M. Kelly	G. Grehan
1943	J. Barry Brown		G. Eason	J. Magee	M. Kelly	A. W. Connor
1944	J. Barry Brown		Jack Daly	Miss M. Tyrell	M. Gorry	J. Magee
1945	J.M. Wheeler		Colm elly/Denis Sheridan	G. F. Eason	M. Connolly	A. W. Connor
1946	J.M. Wheeler		Malcolm Payne	J. Daly	Stella Gorry	J. Magee
1947	J.M. Wheeler		J. zsimons	N. Doyle	Joan Gorry	Jack Daly
1948	J.M. Wheeler		J. zsimons	Martin Salmon	Fred Grehan	A. E. McMahon
1949	J.M. Wheeler		J. Fitzsimons	Martin Salmon	R. Brown	D. Sheridan
1950	J.M. Wheeler		J. zsimons	Noel Slattery	C. Whelan	James Maher
1951	J.M. Wheeler		J. Fitzsimons	Noel Slattery	M. Gorry	James Maher
1952	J.M. Wheeler		J. Fitzsimons	Noel Slattery	Fred Grehan	S. Higgins
1953	J.M. Wheeler		J. Fitzsimons	Noel Slattery	L. Doyle	James Maher
1954	J.M. Wheeler		Rev. L. Newman	V. Tomkins	R. Brown	Reverend L. Newman
1955	J.M. Wheeler		J. Spring	V. Tomkins	T. Mulvey	Reverend L. Newman
1956	J.M. Wheeler		D. Butler	Miss J. Davitt/Miss T. Mulvey	K. Brown	T. O'Connor
1957	J.M. Wheeler		Miss M. O'Connor	Miss B. Broe/Miss T. Mulvey	K. Brown	T. O'Connor
1958	J.M. Wheeler		Miss C. Wheeler	John Mc Myler/Miss T. Mulvey	K. Brown	Reverend L. Newman
1959	J.M. Wheeler		Miss C. Wheeler	Miss R. Browne	M. Dowling	P. Glennon
1960	J.M. Wheeler		Miss C. Wheeler	Miss R. Browne	K. Brown	J. Spring

Naas Lawn Tennis Club (formerly County Kildare Club)

Year	President	Chairman	Honorary Secretary	Honorary Treasurer	Ladies Captain	Men's Captain
1961	J.M. Wheeler		P. Dowling	Miss R. Browne	M. Dowling	D. Conway
1962	J.M. Wheeler		P. Dowling	J. Greely	A. Tynan	D. Conway
1963	L. Purcell		Miss R. Browne	J. Greely	A. Tynan	D. Conway
1964	L. Purcell		Miss R. Browne	J. Greely	A. Greely	J. Spring
1965	L. Purcell		Miss R. Browne	J. Greely	E. Tyndall	W. Glennon
1966	D. Conway		Miss T. Conway	R. Murphy	A. Tynan	W. Coughlan
1967	D. Conway		Miss A. Tynan	T. Conway	J. Daly	W. Coughlan
1968	D. Conway		P. Glennon	W. Coughlan	B. Langan	D. Brennan
1969	D. Conway		A. Fitzpatrick	W. Coughlan	D. Langan	D. Brennan
1970	P.W. Brennan		P. Glennon/C. Glennon	W. Coughlan	R. Sheehan	J. Greely
1971	Major John de Burgh	Malcolm Taylor, snr.	M. Carroll	D. Conway	M. Berney	G. Grehan
1972	Malcolm Taylor		A. Greely	D. Conway	A. Conway	J. Spring
1973	Malcolm Taylor		A. Greely	Robert Lyons	Mary Rose Lyons	J. Greely
1974	Malcolm Taylor			Robert Lyons	June Greely	J. Coughlan/D.Buckley
1975	Major John de Burgh		David Brennan	Brian O'Sullivan	C. Ryan	P. Dowling
1976	Major John de Burgh	J. Greely	David Brennan	Brian O'Sullivan	E. Taylor	D. Buckley
1977	Major John de Burgh	Mick Doyle	David Brennan	Brian O'Sullivan	L. Doyle	D. Conway
1978	Major John de Burgh	Mick Doyle	David Brennan	Brian O'Sullivan	L. Doyle	D. Conway
1979	Major John de Burgh	Mick Doyle	David Brennan	L. Doyle	U. Owens	B. Grehan
1980	Major John de Burgh	B. O'Sullivan	David Brennan	L. Doyle	M. Hayes	R. Lynch
1981	Major John de Burgh	Mary Rose Lyons	David Brennan	Brian O'Sullivan	E. Kilgallen	B. Farrell
1982	Major John de Burgh	Mary Rose Lyons	David Brennan	E. Kilgallen	N. Kelly	J. Nash
1983	Major John de Burgh	Mary Rose Lyons	O. O'Reilly	E. Kilgallen	O. Taffee	Brendan Conlon
1984	Major John de Burgh	Mary Rose Lyons	O. O'Reilly	E. Kilgallen	L. O'Beirne	Donal Buckley
1985	Major John de Burgh	Mary Rose Lyons	L. O'Beirne	E. Powell	O. Taffee	James Barrett
1986	Major John de Burgh	Mary Rose Lyons	Leo Powell	Gerry Laheen	Ann Downey	Brian O'Sullivan
1987	Major John de Burgh	David Brennan	D. Whelehan	Gerry Laheen	D. Whelehan	Brian O'Sullivan
1988	Major John de Burgh	David Brennan	D. Whelehan	Gerry Laheen	Ann Downey	Frank Flanagan
1989	Major John de Burgh	David Brennan	D. Whelehan	Don Higgins	Ann Downey	Maurice Stephens
1990	Major John de Burgh	David Brennan	D. Whelehan	Don Higgins	Jean Burke	Maurice Stephens
1991	Major John de Burgh	David Brennan	D. Whelehan	Don Higgins	Mary Rose Lyons	Brendan Conlon
1992	Major John de Burgh	David Brennan	D. Whelehan	Chris Conway	Mary Rose Lyons	E. Bergin
1993	Major John de Burgh	Don Higgins	Don Higgins	G. Grehan	Mary Sherlock	E. Bergin
1994	Major John de Burgh	Don Higgins	Don Higgins	G. Grehan	Katherine Mehigan	Henry Harding
1995	Major John de Burgh	Mary Rose Lyons	Mary Rose Lyons	G. Grehan	Katherine Mehigan	Finbar O'Sullivan
1996	Major John de Burgh	Finbar O'Sullivan	Finbar O'Sullivan	J. Brosnan	Katherine Mehigan	James Barrett
1997	Major John de Burgh	Katherine Mehigan	Katherine Mehigan	J. Brosnan	Lena Lenehan	Shane Spring
1998	Major John de Burgh	Katherine Mehigan	Katherine Mehigan	J. Brosnan	Lena Lenehan	Shane Spring
1999	Major John de Burgh	Katherine Mehigan	Katherine Mehigan	Charles Carri	Ann Cahill	Malcolm Taylor
2000	Major John de Burgh	Malcolm Taylor	David Brennan	Charles Carri	Lena Lenehan	Shane Spring
2001	Major John de Burgh	Shane Spring	Mary Rose Lyons	Charles Carri	Lena Lenehan	Patrick Cassidy
2002	Major John de Burgh	Shane Spring	Mary Rose Lyons	Denis McCudden	Helen Cosgrove	Patrick Cassidy
2003	Major John de Burgh	Shane Spring	Mary Rose Lyons	Denis McCudden	Helen Cosgrove	Michael Sherlock
2004	Major John de Burgh	Shane Spring	Mary Rose Lyons	Denis McCudden	Joan Maher	Julian Morrison
2005	Major John de Burgh	Breffni Carpenter	Ann Corrigan	Denis McCudden	Laura Gibson	Julian Morrison
2006	Major John de Burgh		Joan Maher		Valerie Waters	

Modern Times at Naas Lawn Tennis Club

The History of Irish Tennis

Sutton Lawn Tennis Club
[Howth LTC]
(Founded 1882)

In 1982 a seventy six page history was compiled to coincide with the centenary of this most successful of County Dublin clubs. Unfortunately, only a flavour of the club and its people can be included here. One of the earliest records of the club was taken in 1884 when it appears all 35 members were present in front of a large wooden pavilion. The mainstay of the club at the time was a man named E.V. Greer. The club was then called **Howth LTC.** It moved to Sutton as *recently* as 1941 and the name was changed to **Sutton LTC** in 1958 to avoid confusion to visitors. It was much more than a tennis club as we shall see.

According to Jim Duff's interesting article (in the commemorative brochure) the names of the original club members suggested that they all belonged to the upper classes and were mainly of one religious persuasion. This situation prevailed until well into the 1930s. According to a letter by Brigadier Stokes the original pavilion had a ballroom. This suggests that it was a centre for many social activities, possibly used by both the hockey and cricket fraternity. The ballroom was burnt down in the 1920s and a new, smaller, clubhouse was built. Old club records are lost. However, Mr. William Mc Sherry, club secretary in the 1930s, wrote in a local guidebook that the club *was delightfully situated in the lea of the Hill of Howth overlooking the harbour and commanding a beautiful panorama of the coastline northwards.*

In the last century (19th), *the game of lawn tennis was for the few, and a modern 'top-spin drive' or a 'cannon ball' service were simply unheard of. A five set tennis match nowadays demands as much, if not more, physical fitness from the modern athlete than say, a gruelling 'Rugger', soccer or Gaelic match.* (This point was also made by the great Cecil Parke who played twenty times for the Irish rugby team and virtually won the Davis Cup on his own in 1912). At the time the club had one men's and one ladies team in leagues. The annual subscriptions were £2, £1-10, 15/- and 10/- for gentlemen, ladies, juveniles and pavilion members respectively. Visitors to the area would pay on a weekly or monthly basis. The club had seven grass courts with good drainage. John Duff, father of Jim Duff, was club secretary in 1934 and William Mc Sherry the treasurer. Lady captains were already established and a Mrs. Griffith was the captain in that year.

For reasons unknown the men's single team dropped from Div II in the Dublin leagues to Div IV in the late 1930s and some of the juniors players had to be called in to make up the numbers. Sheila Guinan was an outstanding member at the time, winning the club championships in 1932, 1933 and 1934. She moved to **Clontarf LTC** at Oulton Road where she immediately made the first team. She would win their club championships five times. On the men's side G.J. Scally was the number one player, winning the club championships for four consecutive years. John Duff and Bill Mc Sherry were undefeated for many years as a doubles combination in inter-club competition and inter-club tournaments. While the club was to see visiting players of the calibre of Olive Poole and Betty Lombard, it was insufficient to keep the activity level up. There was a decline from the late 1930s onwards. It was suggested that possibly the growth of private courts in the area and associated tennis parties took from the club's vitality. Accessibility was also a problem. Jack Quinn, one of the stalwarts of the club, recalls that the objection to tennis on Sunday, by the mainly Protestant members, militated against success. A Mr. Scally persisted and, with many new Catholic members, had the decision reversed at an AGM. Many non-Catholic members resigned.

Jim Duff recalls that the club had only 14 members by 1938 and that the ground was required by the owners for other purposes.

> *One of the main reasons for the decline in membership, of course, was the inaccessibility of the grounds-there were no buses and very few cars in those days! The committee at that time were obliged to take a serious look at the situation. They reached a very far reaching decision after a lot of soul searching-and a little courage. Negotiations were entered into with T. J. Gaisford St. Lawerence and largely through his generosity, and others, it was decided, finally, to shut down the club on the hill and reopen it on new grounds at Sutton, which was obtained on a new long lease from the ground landlord.*

Jim Duff's father, J. J., was the honorary secretary at the time and the following letter to residents in the Howth and Sutton area summarises the thinking at the time.

Howth LTC in 1884. In May 1941 the club opened at its new location at Sutton. The names of those known in the 1884 photograph are 'Groundsman (1), Dawson Knox (2), E. Roper (3), Tharman Crawford (4), F. McClintock (6), M. O'Carroll (8), W. T. Griffith (9), Tharman Crawford (10), Arnold Graves (11) His Honour Judge Griffith (12), Francis Hall (13), Miss Emily Attwell (14), Miss F. Edge (16), Mrs. Watson (17), Miss Costello (18), E. V. Greer (19), R. McDougall (21), Mr. Lawrenson (22), Miss A. Roper (23), Miss Clare Hall (24), Miss Costello (25), Miss H. Hall (26), Miss M. E. Griffith (27), T. V. M. Knox (28), Master Joseph Watson (29), W. H. Griffith (30), Teck Hall (31), W. Roper (32), W. Knox (33), Miss Knox (34) and C. A. N. Knox (35). The mainspring of the club at that time was E. V. Greer, the man in the middle of the picture with a hat. In the first Irish Championships in 1879 a Miss Costello played with E. Elliott (82nd military regiment) and won the mixed title. She repeated this win in 1880 with S. D. Maul (84th military regiment) It is quite possible that she was one of the two Miss Costelloe's in this picture at Howth. F. W. Knox, played in the Irish championships of 1880. He was a Trinity College student at the time. The W. Knox above is perhaps the same person.

It appears that a member of the local council, Mr. T.J. Geary, knowing that the area in Sutton which was being offered to the club by Mr. Gaisford St. Lawerence, was earmarked as a green belt for sport and recreation, successfully opposed the suggestion it should be bought for development. This was the start of the Geary connection with the club and, on reflection, a most important day for the club. The membership had dwindled to 9. The deal was done and the playing surface, which had been used for hockey and rugby, was converted into seven grass and two hard courts (of the clay variety). This was 1941 and hard courts were comparatively rare at the time. Dr. Ward, his family, the grounds man and members, which included Jack Hart and Seamus Hayden, laid the two clay courts. The first Saturday in May 1941 saw them in action. At the time there was no pavilion but two wooden huts, each about 12 feet square, acted at the club premises for the next few years. Membership rose sharply and the club was on a distinct climb to new heights. Annual membership for seniors was £1-7-0.

The committee meetings were in Jack Hart's house on Greenfield Road. Here was hatched the new pavilion. It would be built at a cost of £543 in 1943. A decision to install an expensive maple floor suitable for dancing and other functions was made after much debate. The social side of club life was now on a firm footing. The building would act as a suitable location for various meetings, including the Aero Club and a debating society. During the office of Mr. Handcock a nine hole pitch and putt course was laid. It was opened by W. A. Collins, President of the Irish Pitch and Putt Union and within a short period of time was thriving with its own section and captains.

1945 was a year many would remember. A sports day was organised on a Sunday at the end of the season, the courts wire netting removed in order for the 100-yard race to take place. It was followed by a "hooly" and prizegiving. Oliver Campbell, father of Ollie the rugby international, was one of the participants. At the end of the 40s, and for much of the 50s, the club went through a serious decline in membership. It was suggested that the reasons included wet summers and the difficulty of keeping grass courts in a good condition, having good maintenance staff and the new boom in golf. Fortunately it was kept afloat and a rebirth took place in 1958. The name was changed to Sutton Lawn Tennis Club and the club colours changed from black and white to blue and orange. The courts were re-sodded. Jimmy Ennis, Bob Walsh and P. J. Henry were recognised for their services by being elected honorary vice-presidents. Then along came the Quinns. Joe Quinn was President in 1961. Dermot was to be secretary for eight years from 1959 and Brendan would be treasurer for twenty-three years, commencing in 1957.

Ambitious plans for the club were presented by the architect Michael Scott, a brother of Vice–President Bill, at the 80th anniversary dinner in the Country Club Hotel in Portmarnock. These were initially tapered back due to financial constraints. Things moved forward. On Easter Monday 1968 Alf Walsh, president of the Dublin Lawn Tennis Council officially opened four hard courts. Roadstone, who had laid the courts, sponsored the first open tournaments on these courts-the Harcourt Championships of Leinster. Membership was now a healthy 372, and would grow. Heather Flinn, the first Lady President of the Leinster Branch, opened further courts and a 'clubroom' on the 27th

June 1971. Under the Presidency of the notable Fergus O'Shee a Subscription Investment Scheme was launched, in effect members loans to the club. New plans were agreed at a meeting of members on the 28th February 1974. A new clubhouse with sauna and two squash courts was opened on the 21st December of that year. Ken Potterton, President of the I.L.T.A., and Brendan McKeown, President of the Leinster Squash Racquets Association, performed the ceremony. At that time membership had to be closed, there were 315 senior and 400 juniors in the club. On the 1st May 1976 Dr. Jim O'Neill, President of the I.L.T.A., officially opened three new Entous Cas courts. The next big date was the switching on of floodlights on the 14th July 1978, this time by a member, Charlie Brennan, who was also President of the I.L.T.A. 1981 was a busy year with court resurfacing and a further building development, including an additional, glass backed, squash court reflecting the expansion in that sports activity. (See chapter 6 for further details). By 1989 the club had a gym, offices, new function area and a snooker room In the early days success was limited. The move to the new home in 1941 was to bring an immediate change. The men's team of J. L. Duff, D. Duff, B.MacClancy, A.(Busty) Carragher,

A.D.A. (Gus) Browne and O'S (Sully) Roche won win the Class IV league final 8/1 against the **Railway Union** Club. The following year, the same team were now in Class III, reached the final and lost 5/4 to **Terenure C.Y.M.S.**, having match point in their favour in the last doubles. There was further promotion in 1943, and a league final (Class II) in 1944. This time it was a clearer 5/4 defeat, to **Sandycove LTC.**

In 1942 the committee invited Joe Hackett (a future Davis Cup player) and Catherine Egan (sister of Raymund Egan) to the club. They had just won the Irish Junior (under 18) Championships. In front of a large enthusiastic, and partial, audience, local club champions Jim Duff and Helen Dowdall won both singles and a mixed doubles challenge. While the 1950s were quiet, the 1960s was to see a rise in standard and associated success for the club. The men's first team was promoted to Class I in the 1964 leagues. The second team won Class III. Paul Fitzsimons won an Intermediate Cap for Leinster and in 1965 Eddie Flanagan was Irish Junior Open Champion. Kevin Menton (1970) and Declan Heavey (1973 and 1974) would also win this prestigious title.

In 2000 on the final day of the Dublin Leagues a special presentation was made to Ann Gallagher to honour her involvement in the leagues over six decades. From left: Brian Mulligan (captain), Brendan Quinn (honorary treasurer), Michael Byrne (honorary secretary of the Dublin Lawn Tennis Council), Camillus Dooley (president), Dermot Quinn (honorary secretary) and Neasa McCarthy (vice-president).

Some juniors at Sutton LTC in 2002. From left: Grainne O'Halloran, Sach Salveta, Tom Lawless, Daniel Harkin, Gary Scott, Andrew Hegarty, Eoin Considine, Conor Mahon, Mark Ryan and Lisa Killion.

May 1941. Dr. Con Ward (president) raises the club flag on the occasion of the opening of the new club at Sutton. Also in photograph are Bertie Bowen (vice-president), Donal Ward, Len Harvey, Breed Reynolds, Maura Barnwall, Mrs. Ward, Beatrice Bayley Butler, Rosaleen Ward, Josephine Reynolds, Don Duff, Brian Campbell and J. J. Duff.

In 1968 three Sutton members, Mick O'Neill, Paul Fitzsimons and Nuala Brett were selected for the Dublin team to play Belfast in the annual Duff Cup. This competition was named in honour of John Duff, a former member of Sutton and Secretary of the Dublin Leagues. His son was Jim Duff, a noted member of the club for many years. In 1969 the Ladies won Class II of the Dublin Winter League.

This club was to become one of the biggest and most successful in Ireland and below are some of the highlights of *recent* years.

The first men's team won Class I of the summer leagues for five consecutive years, 1975 to 1979. Only **Fitzwilliam LTC** has ever achieved this target. A poem elsewhere in this book was penned in honour of that team. In 1981 the Ladies team won Class I of the Dublin League, the first time in 99 years of the clubs history. The Ladies Captain at the time, Kate O' Neill, was justly proud of that side. The number one lady was Catherine O'Neill who could only look on as non-playing captain. However, the team of Annette Smith, Maeve Donnelly, Ann Keegan, Ruth Hackett, Jennifer Thornton and Moya Dunlop did the business against **Donnybrook LTC.** The ladies team pulled off a unique feat in 1989 winning Class 1,2,3 and 4 on the same day at their home club. In the same season they swept the boards in the inter-club competitions, adding the Winter League and Floodlit League titles, a landmark they again achieved in 2000.

Both men's and ladies team would win the over 45 Senior League Class I for five years running. The club has produced a long line of notable players at senior and junior level. Among the senior players are Davis Cuppers Kevin Menton and Eoin Collins with Jennifer Thornton and Carmel O' Sullivan.

For many years it has staged the Irish under 21 Championships and the East of Ireland Junior Championships, an attraction for players from Ireland and abroad. A notable winner in 1981 in the U18 'East' was none other than Mark McEnroe, younger brother of John. The senior interprovincials, triangular internationals and inter-league matches have all been played at this mature club. The biggest undertaking was probably the hosting of the Austria Cup between the 14th and 20th May 1995. This event is a world team championship for men over 55. Unfortunately, for the home side of Jim Buckley, Ronan Fearon, Tadhg Kennelly, Noel Lennon and Roddy Feely (non playing captain), we finished 19th of the twenty teams taking part. Of four matches played our only win was 2/1 against Argentina.

The organisers at Sutton have been second to none. The club has been fortunate in having many excellent administrators and coaches. Among the latter has been Aidan Bradshaw. Before arriving at Sutton as club coach he was with **Charleville LTC** in Glasnevin for some seventeen years. Administrators that must be mentioned (some of whom are discussed in Chapter 6) include John Duff (after whom the annual Belfast-Dublin inter-league Cup is named), Charlie Brennan (I.L.T.A. president in 1986), Brendan Quinn, Eugene O'Neill and Michael Byrne, all of them honorary secretaries of the Dublin Lawn Tennis Council. Fergus O'Shee was the honorary treasurer of the I.L.T.A. from 1978 to 1981. The Fergus O'Shee Trophy is named in his honour and is awarded to the outstanding Irish junior each year.

The club has featured prominently in the field of squash. and has links to other sports. Gail Hannagen became the first Sutton player to win a national squash title, winning the under 16 title in 1982. Club member and noted squash player Richie Power had prior to joining Sutton been a League of Ireland soccer player with Waterford. Kevin Menton's father was the well-known President of the F.A.I.. Robbie McGrath and Mick Fitzpatrick have graced the Irish rugby team and Frank McCraken won a gold medal at the Catholic Student Games in Rome (for tennis in 1981).

1975	Brendan O'Reilly
1976	Geoffrey Bourke
1977-1978	Peter Keane
1979	Jim Lillis
1980	Bernie Dillon
1981	Dan Mooney
1982	Tom Higgins
1983	Peter de Loughry
1984	Peter Leonard
1985-1987	Mick McGuinness
1988	Eamonn Ryan
1989-1991	Des McGoldrick
1992	John Proudfoot
1993	Colm Parsons
1994	Gary Donnelly
1995	Julie Jordan
1996	Kevin Kennedy
1999	Mark Meyler
2000	Ann Costello
2001	Feena Field
2002	Kevin Kennedy

Squash Chairpersons
Sutton Lawn Tennis Club

The annual presentations at the club include the following:

Hegarty Cup: Outstanding tennis playing lady. *Mr. Maurice Hegarty was very upset that only one lady had won the Flanagan Trophy. As a result he presented Hegarty Trophy for ladies only.*

Flanagan Cup: Outstanding tennis playing man. This was presented first in 1963 by Mrs. Flanagan for the outstanding player in the club. It became awarded for the outstanding man in the club when the Hegarty Cup was first presented.

Scott Cup: Outstanding League player (man or woman). This cup was presented in 1964 by Captain William Scott, the club president at the time.

Bradshaw Junior Tennis Trophy: Presented by club coach Aidan Bradsaw for the most improved junior. This is now for juniors in the 12 to 18 year old category.

Bradshaw Junior Squash Trophy: Presented by Aidan Bradshaw for the most improved junior during the year.

Balkhill Shield: *Ms. Beatrice Bailey-Butler, an old member from the Howth days, presented the Balkill Shield, for the most improved juvenile. This was to remember the Club's time in Balkill in Howth.* Juvenile was defined as under 12 player.

Fionnguala McKenna trophy: Oustanding volunteer.

Whelan Cup: This was presented by Jeff Whelan, in 1973, for the annual Husband and Wife competition. It is in the shape of a champagne bucket. In the first year for this event there was no trophy and the winners were Pat and Rita McLoughlin. Their names were subsequently added to the new cup.

Joe and Gaye Walsh with the Whelan Cup that they won at Sutton LTC in 2001.

Assero Cup: This was presented by Terry Donaghue for an over 50 years men's handicap event. It commemorates Terry's fathers birthplace in Donegal.

Lawless Cup: This was presented by the Lawless family in 1990 in memory of the late Terry Lawless. It is presented to the winners of a men's over 50 years doubles competition.

Kearns Cup: This was presented by the late Christy Kearns who lived to see his 100th birthday. Christy regularly attended this event which was played by the ladies (over 40 years).

President's Cup: This appears to be the oldest club cup. It was presented by Mr. Gainsford St. Lawerence of Howth Castle who originally owned the land on which the present club was built. It is the Men's Championship Singles Cup. It has been won by many notables including Davis Cup players Kevin Menton and Eoin Collins.

Larry Bogan (left) beat Fintan Hart in the 1959 Men's Singles Championship at Sutton LTC.

Vice-President's Cup: This is the Ladies Championship Singles Cup and was first won by Miss Sheila Guinan in 1932. It was presented by Dr. W. F. Aherne. Notable winners include Federation Cup player Jennifer Thornton.

Girl's under 18 Singles Championship Cup: This was presented by Mr. E. C. Handcock a past trustee and president of the club.

Boys under 18 Singles Championship Cup: This was presented in 1942 by H. D. Pearson. The first winner was T. Fitzpatrick.

Captain's Dinner 2002. From left: John Mooney, Collette Sheridan, Paddy Sheridan, Gay Walsh, Mary Barry, Tom Barry and Dermot Byrne.

Graham Smyth won the minor boys singles title in 2002. Seen here with captains Joe Walsh and Mary Barry.

Sutton LTC 2002. From left: Harry O'Reilly, Conor Lavin, Finola Barry and Alison Lavin.

Two of Sutton Lawn Tennis Club presidents, Maura Brown (1997-1999) and Eamonn Ryan (1994-1996).

The 1941 men's doubles club championship final at Sutton LTC. From left: Tom Quigley, J. L. (Jim) Duff, J. J. (John) Duff and Bill McSherry.

Brendan McKenna has been a long-time contributor to the life at Sutton LTC. Apart from his expertise behind the bar, he has made many useful contributions to club publications.

The Class III winning league team in 1964. Front (l. to r.) R. Murtagh, Jim Duff and T. Delaney. Back (l. to r.) R. Quigley, M. O'Neill (not on team), K. Bray and M. O'Dwyer (not on team). Absent Fintan Hart (captain).

Brendan Kernan (president, Sutton LTC 1979-1981) at the opening of centenary year.

Fergus O'Shee-One of Sutton LTC's most notable administrators. He was the honorary treasurer of the Irish Lawn Tennis Association from 1977 to 1981.

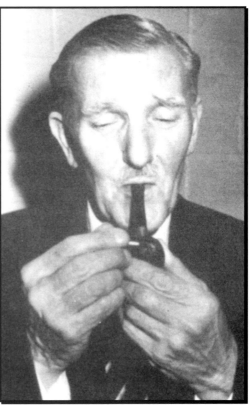

Robert W. (Bob) Walsh was a core club member at Sutton LTC from 1948 onwards. Although he didn't play tennis he contributed immensely to the club. He was honorary treasurer from 1950 to 1956 and club president in 1956.

Captain William J. Scott was club president at Sutton LTC from 1966 to 1968 after a five-year period as vice-president.

Junior team winners at Sutton LTC in Spring 2001. From left: Heather Barry, Laura Smyth, Stephen McDonald, Clodagh O'Gara (lady captain), David Gibbons, Catriona Loftus and Edward Valentine.

In 2000 the senior girls' singles champion was Della Kilduff. This was her eleventh junior title, the first being as an under 12 player. Catherine O'Neill makes a special presentation to her on behalf of the club.

Ann Gallagher was lady captain at Sutton LTC in 1952, 1953 and 1956, club champion in 1955. Previously she had been the girls (under 18) club championship twice. She is an honorary life-member at the club.

The summer of 2002: Graham Smyth, Conor McAvoy and Cathal Murray.

The editorial committee for the excellent tri-annual Sutton LTC yearbook in 2002 was (from left) Michael Dillon, Muiris Heron and Bernie Menton.

Joseph Quinn was one the inspirational leaders at Sutton LTC in the late 1950s and in the early 1960s. Joseph was the President from 1961 to 1965. His sons, Dermot and Brendan have carried on his enormous degree of dedication.

The History of Irish Tennis

The social side of life at Sutton LTC is important. In action on "ladies' night" in 2002 were (from left) Enda Annelynck, Catherine O'Neill, Linda Foley, Clodagh Whelan, Elizabeth Guinan, Collette Sheridan, Agnes Graham, Mary O'Donoghue and Margaret O'Donnell.

The 2002 Management Committee at Sutton LTC. Back (l. to r.) Darragh Griffin, Darrell Moore, Willie Kinane, Jean Banahan, Michael A. O'Neill, Ann Bracken, Eamonn Ryan, Bernie Menton, Kevin Kennedy, Eamonn McKiernan and Stephen Peppard. Front (l. to r.) Dermot Quinn, Joe Walsh, Mary Barry, Camillus Dooley, Neasa McCarthy and Brendan Quinn.

Brothers Brendan (left) and Dermot Quinn–Two of the great servants of Sutton LTC.

Captain's dinner 2002 at Sutton LTC. From left: Dympna Doherty, Ian Gleeson, Robert Turpin, Bryan McDermott, Barbara O'Neill, Lorraine Bracken and Caroline McNulty.

2002 Dublin senior league winners. From left: Camillus Dooley (president), Brendan Minnock, Denis Roawn, Billy Barrett (hiding), Tom Dwyer, Liam O'Dwyer and Joe Walsh (captain).

Sonya McGinn receives a specially inscribed tray to mark the fact that she was Ireland's first ever representative at the Olympics in the sport of badminton. Also in photo (from left): Neasa McCarthy (vice-president), Declan McGinn, Pauline McGinn and Dermot Quinn (honorary secretary).

Sutton LTC has a great record in producing high quality squash players. In the season 2000/2001 and 2001/2002 the club were Leinster Cup winners, Leinster league winners, All-Ireland club champions and came 6th in the European club championships held in France. Team (l. to r.): Mark Allen, Kevin O'Brien, Keith Murtagh, Eoin Ryan (captain) and Ronan Peyton. Absent: Brian O'Connor and Mark Meyler.

Sutton Lawn Tennis Club

Year	President	Vice President	Honorary Secretary	Honorary Treasurer
1940			J. J. (Jim)Duff	
'41-'42	Dr. Con Ward	Bertie Bowen	John Hart	W. (Bill) McSherry
1943	Dr. Con Ward	Bertie Bowen	John Hart	J. P. Spencer
1944	Bertie Bowen	E. C. Handcock	J. J. Geary	J. P. Spencer
1945	Bertie Bowen	E. C. Handcock	J. J. Geary	Miss Anna Duff
1946	E. C. Handcock	T. J. Geary	J. J. Geary	Miss Anna Duff
1947	E. C. Handcock	T. J. Geary	J. J. Geary	J. L. (Jim) Duff
1948	John Hart	-	Jimmy Ennis/Don Duff	-
1949	T. J. (Jim) Geary	John Hart	-	Don Duff
1950	R. Kenny	William J. Scott	G. N. Rafferty	R. W. (Bob) Walsh
1951	F. Gallagher	J. L. (Jim) Duff	Mrs. F. Griffin	R. W. (Bob) Walsh
1952	Bertie Bowen	John Hart	Mrs. N. Smythe	R. W. (Bob) Walsh
1953	Bertie Bowen	John Hart	S. Hart	R. W. (Bob) Walsh
1954	Bertie Bowen	John Hart	J. J. (Jimmy) Ennis	R. W. (Bob) Walsh
1955	J. J. (Jimmy) Ennis	S. Henry	S. Hart	R. W. (Bob) Walsh
1956	R. W. (Bob) Walsh	M. Brennan	L. J. Clarke	R. W. (Bob) Walsh
1957	L. J. Clarke	N. Barry	N. Geraghty	Brendan Quinn
1958	L. J. Clarke	Fintan Hart	B. Hearne	Brendan Quinn
1959	L. J. Clarke	B. Hearne	Dermot Quinn	Brendan Quinn
1960	L. J. Clarke	Fintan Hart	Dermot Quinn	Brendan Quinn
'61-'65	Joseph Quinn	William J. Scott	Dermot Quinn	Brendan Quinn
1966	William J. Scott	J. L. (Jim) Duff	Dermot Quinn	Brendan Quinn
1967	William J. Scott	J. L. (Jim) Duff	Eddie Flanagan	Brendan Quinn
1968	William J. Scott	J. L. (Jim) Duff	Miss F. Lyons	Brendan Quinn
1969	J. L. (Jim) Duff	J. J. (Jimmy) Ennis	Miss F. Lyons	Brendan Quinn
'70-'71	J. L. (Jim) Duff	Fergus O'Shee	Mrs. Anne Quinn	Brendan McKenna
'72-'74	Fergus O'Shee	J. J. (Jimmy) Ennis	Mrs. Anne Quinn	Brendan Quinn
'75-'77	J. J. (Jimmy) Ennis	Dermot Quinn	Aidan Hilliard	Brendan Quinn
1978	J. J. (Jimmy) Ennis	Brendan Kernan	Aidan Hilliard	Brendan Quinn
'79-'81	Brendan Kernan	Dermot Quinn	Aidan Hilliard	Brendan Quinn
'82-'84	Dermot Quinn	Mrs. Anne Quinn	Aidan Hilliard	Brendan Quinn
'85-'87	Mrs. Anne Quinn	Aidan Hilliard	Dermot Quinn	Brendan Quinn
'88-'90	M. Byrne	Jim Kelly	Dermot Quinn	Brendan Quinn
'91-'93	Jim Kelly	Eamonn Ryan	Dermot Quinn	Brendan Quinn
'94-'96	Eamonn Ryan	Mrs. Maura Brown	Dermot Quinn	Brendan Quinn
'97-'99	Mrs. Maura Brown	Camillus Dooley	Dermot Quinn	Brendan Quinn
'00-'02	Camillus Dooley	Ms Neasa McCarthy	Dermot Quinn	Brendan Quinn
2003	Ms Neasa McCarthy	Michael Byrne	Dermot Quinn	Brendan Quinn
2004	Ms Neasa McCarthy	Michael Byrne	J. Walsh	Brendan Quinn

The Sutton LTC Management Committee for Centenary Year (1982). Front (l. to r.) Brendan Quinn (honorary treasurer), Jim Kelly (captain), Anne Quinn (vice-president), Dermot Quinn (president), Carmel O'Shee (lady captain) and Aidan Hillard (honorary secretary). Back (l. to r.) Brendan McKenna, Kate O'Neill, Fionnguala McKenna, Paddy Bannon, Robert W. (Bob) Walsh, Mary Harte (lady vice-captain), James J. Ennis, Dorothy Byrne, Brendan Kernan, Frank Maguire, Eugene O'Neill (vice-captain), Luke Mahon and Tom Higgins. Inset: Geoffrey Bourke.

Sutton Lawn Tennis Club

	Captain	Lady Captain
1950	Bunny Carr	Miss P. Fogarty
1951	W. Campbell	Mrs. Florence Campbell
1952	J. J. (Jimmy) Ennis	none
1953	J. J. (Jimmy) Ennis	Miss Ann Gallagher
1954	J. McCaughey	Miss Ann Gallagher
1955	J. McCaughey	Miss R. Beddy
1956	J. McCaughey	Miss Ann Gallagher
1957	Fintan Hart	Miss M. McCaughey
1958	N. Barry	Miss E. Dillon
1959	N. Barry	Miss E. Dillon
1960	N. Barry	Miss Fionnguala Lyons
1961	Fintan Hart	Miss Fionnguala Lyons
1962	J. J. (Jimmy) Ennis	Miss N. Dillon
1963	J. J. (Jimmy) Ennis	Mrs. N. Brett
1964	J. J. (Jimmy) Ennis	Mrs. Elizabeth Egan
1965	J. J. (Jimmy) Ennis	Mrs. Elizabeth Egan
1966	E. Brett	Mrs. Elizabeth Egan
1967	M. O'Neill	Mrs. Elizabeth Egan
1968	Paul Fitzsimons	Mrs. Elizabeth Egan
1969	Paul Fitzsimons	Mrs. Anne Quinn
1970	Brendan Quinn	Miss M. Donovan
1971	Brendan Quinn	Miss M. Donovan
1972	J. L. (Jim) Duff	Mrs. P. Carroll
1973	Dermot Quinn	Mrs. M. Bourke
1974	Dermot Quinn	Mrs. M. Bourke
1975	J. B. Aston	Mrs. R. Kernan
1976	Jim Kelly	Mrs. J. Gallen
1977	Brendan Kernan	Mrs. Anne Quinn
1978	Geoffrey Bourke	Mrs. C. Jones
1979	J. Carey	Mrs. F. Henderson
1980	M. O'Neill	Mrs. Fionnguala McKenna
1981	M. O'Neill	Mrs. Kate O'Neill
1982	Jim Kelly	Mrs. Carmel O'Shee
1983	Eugene O'Neill	Mrs. M. Harte
1984	T. Donaghue	Mrs. N. Brett
1985	F. Motherway	Mrs. C. Walsh
1986	L. Murray	Mrs. A. Mortin
1987	G. Lawless	Miss A. Hayes
1988	S. O'Dwyer	Mrs. F. O'Callaghan
1989	R. Murray	Mrs. M. Brown
1990	B. Smyth	Mrs. M. Donaghue
1991	Aidan McNulty	Mrs. M. Lillis
1992	G. Cooke	Miss A. O'Gara
1993	P. Gillett	Mrs. B. Morgan
1994	T. Dwyer	Mrs. M. Donahue
1995	Tom Barry	Miss M. Ryan
1996	Willie Kinane	Mrs. Mary Murray
1997	Michael Byrne	Miss G. O'Dwyer
1998	P. Turpin	Miss E. Harte
1999	Pat Considine	Mrs. Catherine O'Neill
2000	Brian Mulligan	Mrs. Alice Duff Kenny
2001	Brendan Minnock	Miss Clodagh O'Gara
2002	Joe Walsh	Mrs. Mary Barry
2003	D. Moore	Mrs. Ann Bracken
2004	J. Collins	Miss B. O'Neill

Jimmy Ennis, "The Quiet Man", was club captain in 1952, 1953 and from 1962 to 1965. Jimmy was club president from 1975 to 1978. On the court he once shyly admitted his success was due to having a good partner in Jim Duff.

The 1999 captain's at Sutton LTC in 1999 were Pat Considine and Catherine O'Neill. Below are the 1996 captains, Willie Kinane and Mary Murray.

Sutton Lawn Tennis Club
Club Champions

	LADIES *Challenge Cup* *Presented by* *Dr. W. F. Aherne*	MEN *Challenge Cup* *Presented by* *T. J. Gainsford St.Lawerence*
'32-'35	Miss Sheila Guinan	
1935	Miss May Walsh	
1936	*no competition*	*No competition*
1937	Miss Flora McDonnell	J. J. (John) Duff
1938	Miss Greta Coyle	J. J. (John) Duff/O'S. Roche
1939	Miss Helen Dowdall	J. L. (Jim) Duff
1940	Miss Helen Dowdall	J. L. (Jim) Duff/Bill McSherry
'41-'42	Miss Helen Dowdall	J. L. (Jim) Duff
'43-'45	Miss Claire Fitzsimons	J. L. (Jim) Duff
'46-'47	Mrs. Sadie Greene	J. L. (Jim) Duff
1948	Mrs. Sadie Greene	Don Duff
1949	Mrs. Sadie Greene	J. L. (Jim) Duff
1950	*no competition*	J. L. (Jim) Duff
1951	Miss P. Wykes	Bunny Carry
'52-'53	Miss V. Saurin	J. McCarthy
1954	Miss M. McGrath	B. McHugh
1955	Miss Ann Gallagher	P. Shortall
1956	Miss Eithne Dillon	Fintan Hart
1957	Miss Eithne Dillon	J. McCaughey
1958	Miss Eithne Dillon	Fintan Hart
'59-'60	Miss Eithne Dillon	Larry Bogan
1961	Mrs. Elizabeth Egan	Paul Fitzsimons
'62-'63	Mrs. Eithne Quinn	Paul Fitzsimons
1964	Miss K. Dee	Paul Fitzsimons
1965	Mrs. Pat Donnelly	Paul Fitzsimons
1966	Miss M. Donovan	Eddie Flanagan
'67-'68	Miss M. Donovan	Paul Fitzsimons
1969	Miss M. Donovan	Michael Smyth
1970	Miss M. Donovan	Kevin Menton
1971	Miss M. Donovan	Paul Fitzsimons
'72-'73	Mrs. Moya Dunphy	Kevin Menton
1974	Miss V. Harris	Kevin Menton
1975	Mrs. Moya Dunphy	Kevin Menton
1976	Miss K. Cowhie	Tadhg Lambe
1977	Mrs. C. Foley	Michael Smyth
1978	Miss Una McEntee	Paul Fitzsimons
1979	Miss G. Flynn	Paul Fitzsimons
1980	Miss Ann Keegan	Frank McCracken
'81-'83	Miss Jennifer Thornton	Tadhg Lambe
'84-'85	Miss Jennifer Thornton	Frank McCracken
1986	Miss Susan Hunter	Glen Beirne
1987	Miss Una McEntee	Frank McCracken
1988	Miss Susan Hunter	Robert Collins
1989	Miss Deirdre Walsh	Robert Collins
1990	Miss Deirdre Walsh	P. Kilduff
1991	Miss Deirdre Walsh	Timo Barry
1992	Miss Deirdre Walsh	P. J. Lawless
1993	Mrs. Catherine O'Neill	Colm Collins
'94-'95	Mrs. Carmel O'Hare	Gary Kilduff
1996	Miss Una McEntee	Stephen Taylor
1997	Miss Della Kilduff	Gary Kilduff
1998	Miss Della Kilduff	Colm Collins
1999	Miss Caroline McNulty	Colm Collins
2000	Mrs. Carmel O'Hare	Darragh Griffin
2001	Miss Kate O'Flynn	Bryan McDermot
2002	Miss Leigh Walsh	Bryan McDermot
2003	Mrs. Carmel O'Hare	Bryan McDermot
2004	Miss Leigh Walsh	Darragh Griffin

The 1942 Ladies finalists were Helen Dowdall (winner) and Claire Fitzsimons.

The 2000 club champion was Carmel O'Hare. Also in photo (l. to r.) Brian Mulligan Men's captain, Camillus Dooley (president) and Alice Kenny (lady captain).Carmel won the title a second time in 2003.

The 2000 club champion was Daragh Griffin. Also in photo (l. to r.) Brian Mulligan Men's captain, Camillus Dooley (president) and Alice Kenny (lady captain).Darragh won the title again in 2004.

In 2002 Brendan Barry and Eamonn O'Reilly of Sutton LTC played on the Irish veteran's squash team.

Susie Baird-one of the backroom members who contribute to club life at Sutton LTC.

****

Rushbrooke Lawn Tennis & Croquet Club
[Queenstown Lawn Tennis Club]
(Founded C. 1880)

In the 6th August 1881 edition of *Sport* there is a report on the *annual* tournament at the **Queenstown LTC**, later to be called Rushbrooke Lawn Tennis and Croquet Club. The event started on Tuesday 2nd August and was resumed on that Thursday, the weather being more favourable. The nearby naval base no doubt contributed to the encouragement of the game. At this reported event there was a large attendance. The results appear to be incomplete. In the open men's singles the match between H. Maguire and Captain Hopwood *attracted much attention on account*

of the equality of the players and the closeness of the game. McGuire was the winner of their match but there is no indication that this was the final result.

There were also events for handicap men's singles, men's doubles and 'Ladies and Gentlemen's Doubles' (i.e. mixed). On Tuesday, Mr. Law and Miss Moore won first prize for the mixed but there was also a mixed event on the Thursday. Other male competitors were Mr. Curtis, H. Dawson, Mr. Benson, Mr. Mitchell, Mr. G. Clarke, Mr. Jenkins, Mr. Campbell, Mr. Box, Mr. E.B. Dawson, Mr. A.W. Allen, Dr. E. Townsend, Mr. Cronin, J. McGuire, Captain Baldock, Dr. W. Creagh, Mr. Thornton, Mr. Russell, Mr. Humphries, Mr. Hood, M. Kelly, Dr. H. R. Townsend, Mr. Staunton, Mr. Sherlock, Mr. Sandford, W. Morrogh and Mr. H. Davidson. Apart from Miss Moore there were a small number of other ladies mentioned as playing in the mixed doubles. These were Miss Curtis, Miss L. Townsend, Miss E. Boys, and Miss Boys.

A tournament was held at the club in 1893 with the winners as follows:

Open Tournament Rushbrooke Lawn Tennis & Croquet Club		
Event	**1st Prize**	**2nd Prize**
1893		
MS	William St. G. Perrott	M.G. McNamara
MHS	William St. G. Perrott	
LHS	Mrs. Waring	Miss Stokes
MHD	Lt.Galloway/ Lt. Puxley	Frank & Fred Lyons
LHD	Miss Athill/ Mrs. Waring	Miss Brasier/ -Creaghe
MxD (h'cp)	Lt.Puxley/ Miss Carpenter	Captain Parsons/ Miss M. Townsend
1894		
MS	William St. G. Perrott	Frank Lyons
MHS	Frank Lyons	Fred Lyons
LHS	Mrs. Waring	Miss White
MHD	Frank & Fred Lyons	G. Edwards/ L. Swanzy
LHD	Mrs. Waring/ Miss Atthill	The Misses Bretton
MxD (h'cp)	St. G.Killery/ Miss Atthill	WilliamSt. G. Perrott/ Mrs. Waring

The tournament was an open event and the winner of the "Men's' Championship Singles" was William St. G. Perrott. He was a member of the **Lansdowne LTC** and played tournaments throughout the country. He would become the first honorary treasurer of the ILTA in 1908 and later President for two terms. M. G. MacNamara, was runner-up to Perrott, and had played with success at the Wimbledon Championships between 1880 and 1888. He was obviously one of the best, if not the best player, in the Cork region at that time. The Irish Handbook (1894) indicated that the 1893 event *was also a record tournament, the increased interest taken in it by the public of the southern capital, as shown by a largely increased "gate", being particularly noticeable.*

Bill Tayler in his Munster History indicated that croquet was the original game played at the club. It was all grass courts until 1924 when the first hard courts were laid down and, by 1990, floodlighting was installed. In fact in 1975, few clubs had floodlighting and the club had erected them on the number 1 hard court providing a *facility unequalled in the south and in constant use throughout the winter.*

Club Members at Rushbrooke (circa 1900)

Today there are 9 floodlit all-weather Omni-courts, the last of grass courts being converted to 'hard' courts in July 1995. For a 'rural' club, though quite near Cork city, it has had a tremendous number of competitions of note over the years. These include the Munster and Cork Champions, interprovincials, Irish Junior and Senior Close championships and Davis Cup matches. It still has a preserved clubhouse giving it a quaint feel and many excellent photographs on its walls going back over many years of competition. Over the last 80 years there have been few, if any, top Irish players who have not played at the club at some time or another. It continues to thrive with many juniors playing the game.

In July 1982 Matt Doyle beat Sean Sorensen in the County Cork Championships at Rushbrooke. Maurice Dorney (Cantrell & Cochrane) presents the cup to Matt with acting Chairman, John Kelly, in attendance. Maria Bolster won the ladies singles that year.

There is nearly always a 'Rushbrooke' tournament reported in the Yearbooks. In some years it entailed running the Irish Close Championships. It appears that the first was held there in 1924. It was the year of the Haughton's. Ben and his sister Margaret (Marjorie) dominated this affair, either or both being on the winning side in all five championship events. Both

played at Wimbledon and Ben, and later his son Alan, were to play Davis Cup. Details are given in Chapter 5. Records are missing for a number of years but it does appear that they have been held at the club in 1938, 1955, 1958 and 1967. Most years the Championships of County Cork were to feature at this historic club. For many years the ILTA listing of events did not mention junior tournaments. These were likely in early days to be run in conjunction with the senior tournaments. Later, when they increased in popularity they would have a slot of their own. The Irish Close Junior Championships found a happy home at Rushbrooke.

In the 1952 Irish Boys' Close Championships, Derek Mockler (left) beat Eamonn Smith in the final. Mary O' Sullivan from Tralee won the Girls Senior Championship.

The following are extracts from a newspaper (possibly 'Sport') of Saturday the 19th July 1924, the 'Close' being completed the previous Saturday.

The managing committee deserve the greatest credit for having being able to play the finals on Saturday afternoon, considering the very adverse weather conditions.

It is true the courts were soft, so much so that some of the semi-finals were played on hard courts on the Saturday morning, but towards mid-day the sun came out and greatly improved the conditions and added to the pleasure of both the players and on onlookers....

The final of the open singles was a good match, and spectators were treated to as fine an exhibition of tennis as could be desired.....Meldon had to do quite a lot of chasing. Indeed at all times Meldon's tennis is greatly reinforced by his great speed in the court for not having a good backhand he has to run round many shots that would come more natural for him on this side.....Haughton demonstrated that although he may not be the most brilliant player in this country he is the most reliable and can generally be depended on to produce good form; he has not been beaten in the South of Ireland for many years....

Miss (Marjorie) *Haughton won the final 6/2 6/2 (beating Miss Miley). ..I should like very much to see Miss Haughton competing more in Dublin tournaments, as it is probable she is as good, if not better, than any Dublin lady, while she and her brother are, I would consider, easily the best mixed pair in Ireland; for although the Wallace'' might give them a close run, or even beat them, the latter play the more old fashioned game, with the lady at the back of the court, whereas the Haughtons both volley and volley well....*

The ladies' open doubles went to Mrs. Jackson and Miss Haughton, who beat Miss Allen and Miss Julian in the final, 6/2 6/0. It will be remembered that the latter pair won the Irish Open Championship Doubles.

Ben Haughton had two tennis-playing sisters, Margaret Wilhelmina (better known as Marjorie), Hannah Woodcock (better known as Nancy). His wife was Marguerite Olive (Beulah), better known as Daisy. Their two sons John and Alan both played tennis, the latter followed his father in gaining Davis Cup honours. John (18) and Alan (16) played together at the Rushbrooke senior tournament in 1933 off a +3 handicap. Having won their first match they then lost in three sets to A. L. Moore and P. McCann (-15.3) in 3 sets (6/4 2/6 1/6).

Rushbrooke Committee members in 1984. From left: Michael Granville, Regina McDonnell, Tony Murphy (chairman), Ella Verling, Seamus Mulherin, Michael Walley (honorary secretary) & Gerry Collins.

John played with his aunt Marjorie in the 1933 handicap mixed off –3. Having won two rounds, the second against Harry Cronin and Miss J. Creagh (-30.2) they lost in the third round to W. S. Harrington and Miss F. Kearney 3/6 5/7. Two years later, in the same event, John and Marjorie (scratch) reached the mixed handicap final. In that match they lost to R. F. Scovell and Miss Vera Mahony (-15.3) 2/6 4/6. John, unfortunately, was not to have that many more tournaments. He died at the young age of 22 (on the 8th April 1938). His younger brother Alan kept a record of many of John's competitive matches. The last entry in that listing was a handicap doubles win in the **Blackrock LTC** open tournament. This was in the summer of 1937. The young brothers off –15.3 reached the final winning four matches, and losing only one set. In the final itself they beat H. Robertson and H. Daly (-4) comfortably (6/1 6/2). Off –3, John worked his way into the handicap singles final. There he lost to Frank Mockler (-15.5) in three sets (2/6 6/0 6/8). At the same tournament, Alan played with their father Ben in the championships doubles and reached the final. They lost to Teddy Daly and Arthur St. J.

Mahony (5/7 6/4 4/6). In the championship mixed competition, Ben and Marjorie lost in an extremely length first-round match (6/4 2/6 15/17), to Freddie South and Miss J. Creag.

Ben Haughton regularly played at Rushbrooke in both open events and in inter-club matches. He kept thorough records of his matches. Some of the **finals** he played in were as follows:

Ben Haughton at Rushbrooke (Finals)

Singles
1919 Beat Lt. Com. Stowe 9/7 6/2 6/0
1923 Beat E.J. Mockler 6/2 6/2 6/4
1924 Beat Louis Meldon 3/6 6/4 6/1 6/4
1926 Beat Frank Crosbie 4/6 6/4 6/1 6/2
1927 Lost to D. M. Craig 7/9 6/4 4/6 3/6
1928 Lost to Charles Scroope 6/3 3/6 6/8 4/6

Doubles
1923 With J. F. Dwyer (-30.2) lost to
      James Daly/J. J. Barry (-15) 7/5 0/6 1/6
1924 With Frank Crosbie beat
      Simon and Garvase Scroope 6/3 6/4 6/3
1926 With D. C. Morrogh (-30) beat
      E. J. Mockler/E.R. Roche (-15.1) 6/2 6/4

Mixed
1920 With Nancy Haughton beat
      J. F. Daly/Marjorie Haughton 3/6 8/6 6/3
      With Daisy Haughton (-30.2) beat
      Lt. Com. Stowe/Miss N. Clarke (-30.2)
      6/3 8/6
1921 With Nancy Haughton beat
      J. F. Daly/Marjorie Haughton 6/2 6/4
1923 With Nancy Haughton beat
      J. C. Ronan/Miss Cummins 6/2 6/4
1924 With Marjorie Haughton beat
      Frank Crosbie/Miss S. Allen 6/3 7/5
1926 With Marjorie Haughton beat
      Frank Crosbie/Miss D. Julian 6/3 6/3
1927 With Marjorie Haughton lost to
      D. M. Craig/Mary French 6/4 4/6 2/6

Alan Haughton, has had a phenomenal record at Rushbrooke tournaments. His first was the 1931 under 15 events. His last was, sixty years later, the veterans' mixed doubles in 1990. Details are listed in Chapter 6. One final worth recording here took place in 1964. He and Des Scannell were playing against Julian Drury-Byrne and Roddy Feely. They won the first 6/3, lost the second 5/7 and were five games to love down in the third and the opponents had two match points at 40/15. In what must rank as one of the greatest of comebacks they won this game, the next six and the match.

Some fifteen members of Rushbrooke have gained major honours over the years. Anthea Goodbody, who was a Munster player for many years, would gain international honours in 1971. She met Redmond O' Donoghue at the club, he was no mean player either. They got married in the 1960s and now live, and play tennis, in Waterford. The following fifteen members have represented Ireland at varying levels:

Rushbrooke Lawn Tennis & Croquet Club International Members
Josephine 'Binkie' Harman
Alan Haughton
Mary McNamara
Charles Scroope
Millicent (*Mickie*) O'Donoghue (nee O'Keeffe)
Gerry Fitzpatrick
Diana Harrington
Freddie South
June Ann Fitzpatrick
Harry Cronin
Anthea Goodbody
Ben Haughton
June Barry
Frank McDonnell
Liam O'Brien

Christine Underwood a top junior in action at Rushbrooke in 1976 (courtesy Cork Examiner)

Harry Cronin was a member of the Munster Branch for many years. He would be honoured as President of the Irish Lawn Tennis Association in 1957. He, and his wife Moira, were on the Rushbrooke team as a pair in 1936. In a match against Blackrock they gave the Haughtons (Ben and Marjorie a run for their money, the score being 7/5 6/3. They had also played against the sister and brother combination in 1930, suggesting they were the club's top mixed pair at the time. They lost then 4/6 5/7. Harry was the number one singles player in 1930, losing 3/6 4/6 to Ben Haughton. They would play together that summer and win the Sunday's Well tournament beating E. J. Mockler and A. F. Toogood (7/5 3/6 6/4). They repeated the win over Toogood and a different partner the following year (1931). In the 1932 Munster Cup final in 1932, Ben Haughton beat Harry Cronin 6/1 6/3 in the singles and, with Miss P. O' Keeffe, beat Col. Mackenzie and

Miss M. French 1/6 6/0 6/2. One assumes that **Blackrock LTC** won this final, possibly incorrectly. Four years earlier Harry met Ben Haughton in the final of the Irish Close championships held at **Sunday's Well**. Ben won 6/3 5/7 6/3 6/3. Harry, with Ben, won the men's doubles at this Championships when they beat Simon Scroope and J.E. Harding 6/2 7/9 8/6 6/0. With Mary French of Rushbrooke too, they won the mixed title against Ben and Marjorie Haughton. It was a comfortable 6/3 6/1 scoreline.

Other team members at Rushbrooke in years gone by included Mr. F Lillis (1911), Mr. M. Lillis (1911, 1912), Miss Shee (1911), Mr. W. F. Cave (1912), Miss Carroll (1912), Mr. H. A. Davis (1917), Mr. O. Plunkett (1917), Mrs. Pike (1917), Captain Dobbie (1918), Miss Cooper (1918), Mr. J. V. M. Howe (1936), Mr. Tombs (1936), Don Harte Barry (1979), Redmond O' Donoghue (1979), Anthea O' Donoghue (1979), Deirdre Linehan (1979), Anne Weldon (1979) and Ronnie Daunt (1979).

Friendly doubles at Rushbrooke (circa 2001)

The Rushbrooke junior tournament goes back at least as far as 1931 and, I suspect earlier. An interesting set of matches was in 1932 in the boy's handicap doubles. John and Ben Haughton (17 and 15 years of age respectively) played off scratch and in their first match beat Willie Sandys and M. Ronayne (-2) 6/4 6/3. Sandys would later become President at **Fitzwilliam LTC** and his brother Dick, Irish Boys champion. In their second match they met none other than the Egan brothers from Dublin. The latter (-15) won the match 6/2 6/1. Raymund was about 18 at the time and his brother Bernard 16. Both would play for Lansdowne and Raymund become a Davis Cup player and Irish Number 1 only 8 years later.

The following are extracts from the *Cork Examiner* (August 19th 1933).

The Rushbrooke Juvenile Lawn Tennis Tournament was concluded yesterday, under glorious weather conditions, when four new junior Irish close champions emerged from the finals of the Junior Close Championship events on the programme....
Perhaps, one of the best matches ever witnessed in a juvenile tournament, was the boys' singles final, in

which Robertson was obliged to go all out for the title against B. Haughton, whose style was peculiarly reminiscent of his famous father-a well known figure in Irish tennis circles. (The match was won 10/8 by Roberston in the final set)...*It was anyone's title right up to the last service-a thrilling final, which might well have been-as far as the standard of tennis was concerned- a match between two senior champions...*

Miss (Frances) *Kearney, the new girl champion, was disappointing in her first set against Miss Robertson of Bandon. She allowed her opponent to take it to set point at 5-2, and it was only then that she returned to winning form, winning the next four games in a row, and eventually taking the set 9-7. Miss Roberston might easily have won this set, and taken the match to three for a decision, but in the second set she went down 6-3, although she fought pluckily and played lovely tennis. Miss Kearney, however, had the advantage of an excellent backhand, as against her opponents rather unconvincing one.*

There were 150 entries in the Irish Junior Close in 1952. Some heavy thundery showers marred play on the semi-finals day. On finals day, a Saturday in mid-July, the weather was 'favourable'. In the Boys Singles Derek Mockler 'annexed' the senior title from Eamon Smith and beat him 6/1 6/2. Mary O' Sullivan from Tralee had won the under 15 title in 1951 and now took the Senior Girls beating June McKenzie 6/1 6/3 in the final. Mary proved a 'very popular winner' and 'made a deep impression'. She had recently won the Leinster open girls championships and would later become a full senior tennis and badminton international.

There were over 500 entries for the 1953 event. There were some handicap events, as usual, but this did not help the younger players who had no option but to enter if they were to have adequate competition. The *Echo* (13th August 1953) put it like this: *It was ridiculous to see big boys playing very small boys not only here but in several other junior tournaments. Even with handicap adjustments it is nonsense to expect either to derive any benefit from the game. One of the bigger lads confided in me that he was afraid to hit the ball when playing a diminutive opponent. One wonders what might happen if the young David met a not-so-considerate Goliath.* (In a separate 1952 report, though there were no complaints whatsoever, an eight year old Peter Haughton (son of Alan) was entered, presumably in the under 15 events).

In the Senior Boys' singles Charles Callaghan of Limerick, the number 2 player at Blackrock College, Dublin, gave an impressive display but lost to R. Sweetman of Mallow in the 1953 final (2/6 6/2 1/6). In the Senior Girls' Singles final Margaret Ronan of Rushbrooke beat Sheila Coffey of St. Angela's College, Cork in two tight sets (6/4 7/5). *The outstanding final of the handicap events was the Senior Boys' Singles in which Eamonn Smith defeated Des Scannell, the winner owing 0.1.*This was for the Roche Cup, Eamon Smith was off –40 and Des Scannell off –30, the scores were 6/3 3/6 6/4. The Woodbourne Cup (Senior Girls' Handicap) was won by Aveen O' Reilly (off –30), the Dwyer Cup (Junior Boys' Handicap) was won by C. Morrisey (scratch) and the Wakenham Cup (Junior Girls' Handicap) by Katherine Moloney (-15).

Redmond O'Donoghue was on many successful Munster Cup teams with Rushbrooke Lawn tennis & Croquet Club between 1964 and 1982. Redmond brother Frank was also a member at the club at one stage. Frank became known as a top administrator and was elected president of the ILTA in 1972.Redmond's mother Millicent was an international player and ranked number 6 in Ireland in 1934.

In 1960 Anthea Goodbody won the junior Irish Close championships being held at her home club Rushbrooke. By 1968 she had won four Irish 'Close' senior titles and was picked for Ireland in 1971. She met Redmond O'Donoghue at the club where romance blossomed.

In 1954 it was a 6/0 6/3 win for Cork boy Sarsfield Smith beat Munster champion, Charles Callaghan from Limerick (6/4 10/8). The *Irish Press* (14th August 1954) said *Smith was always the stronger in a marathon match-it took almost three hours- and his strong back-hand drives from the baseline were the deciding factor.* In the other half of the draw, Ray Ward of Mallow beat Munster finalist Des Scannell (2/6 6/4 6/4). In the final, the winner, Sarsfield Smith, played 'effortless and steady tennis, winning many

The 1979 Rushbrooke team that won the Munster Cup for their club for the 17ᵗʰ time in 1979. From left: Anthea O' Donoghue, Redmond O' Donoghue, Jim Corr (Mayor of Cork), Bill Tayler (President, Munster Branch, ILTA), Don Harte Barry, Ronnie Daunt, Anne Weldon and Deirdre Limehan.

important points with brilliant cross-court drives'. He beat Ray Ward 6/0 6/3. The Senior Girls' final was a repeat of the Munster final. In the semi-finals Gillian Murphy beat Sheila Coffey 6/3 6/4 while Ann Delaney beat Terry O' Brien 7/5 6/3. The final between the two Cork girls was a reverse of the Munster final. Gillian Murphy beat Ann Delaney 6/4 6/1.

In the 1978 ILTA Yearbook a note is made of the vast improvements made at the club during the previous twelve months. These were particularly related to the pavilion, bar area and changing rooms. It noted that *One person missing from Rushbrooke tournament week this year will be Michael Dolan, for sadly Mr. Dolan passed away during the winter. Those who are regulars to Rushbrooke will remember him as the aged newspaper reporter who copiously 'phoned in his reports to the Cork Examiner and other newspapers or asked some of the travellers to Cork to take the report to the newspaper office on their way home....*In 1937 when Eamonn deValera was in Cork for the formal handling over of the port from the British, Michael stopped Dev's car *and asked the driver to take the report back with him to Dublin for delivery to the Dublin newspapers.*

Munster Cup

In 1907, Rushbrooke won the inaugural competition for the Munster Cup. By 1959 they had won the cup six times. In 1979 they were to win it for the seventeenth time. *In cool windy and wet conditions, Rushbrooke overcame a very strong Galway side which consisted almost entirely of the Connaught Senior Interprovincial team and also included the Irish Junior Triple Champion from the previous day, Caitriona Ruane.*

The six singles matches were played first, the men's matches at **Tipperary County LTC** *and the Ladies at* **Lattin LTC***, after which the result was 4/2 in favour of Galway. Rushbrooke then faced the task of winning the three remaining doubles matches.*

Don Harte Barry and Anthea O' Donoghue beat James Roche and Claire O' Brien in three sets, Anne Weldon and Deirdre Linehan beat Caitriona Ruane and Sheila Holland in three sets and finally Redmond O' Donoghue and Ronnie Daunt overcame Tony Poustie and Dave O' Donnell 6/2 in the third set having lost the first and been 4/4 in the second.

By 2005 the club had won the Munster Cup on at least 21 occasions. Apart from the Davis Cup match against Turkey in 1972 and the Federation Cup match against Mexico in 1973, the club has hosted very many Munster and Irish events. In **1932** the Irish Junior Close championships were hosted at the club and have remained there until this day. The inaugural winners were as follows:

Inaugural Irish Junior Close Winners
U14 Girls Singles: Josephine 'Binkie' Harman
U15 Girls Singles: Zelie Godfrey
U14 Boys Singles: D. E. Harmon
U15 Boys Singles: Roy Brown

The Clubhouse at Rushbrooke Lawn Tennis & Croquet Club (circa 2001). A new clubhouse plan was prepared in 2004.

Alan Haughton & Mickie O'Keeffe (later O'Donoghue) were both members of Rushbrooke LT & C Club and both international players. Alan's father Ben was another member, both played Davis Cup for Ireland.

"The Hibs" and the small membership was made up of sacristans of nearby churches. Another club was The County Tennis Club, otherwise known as Melrose. This club fizzled out about 1954. It was the old style 'gentry' club with social status being an important element among its members. At the Boat Club it appears that the first court was laid in 1883 and the first tournament took place the following year. In the following couple of decades another court was added.

Open Tournament Wexford LTC		
Event	**1st Prize**	**2nd Prize**
1893		
MS	A.H. Porter	
MHS	R. Latham	
LHS	Miss Hind	
MHD	W. Nunn/G. Bradish	
LHD	Miss Dyas/ Miss Ruth Dyas	
MxHD	R. Latham/Miss Dyas	
1894		
MS	A.H. Porter	C. Latham
MHS	A.H. Porter & H.R. Packenham divided	
LHS	Ruth Dyas	Miss Morrogh
MHD	C. & R. Latham	A.H. Porter/ H.R. Packenham
LHD	Misses Morrogh	Misses Wilson & Barrett
MxHD	C.Latham/ Miss Dyas	C. Warden/Mrs. Innes

Wexford Harbour Boat & Tennis Club (Founded Circa 1883)

Thanks to the excellent book *The Story of Wexford harbour Boat & Tennis Club 1873-2003* we can include here a synopsis of this club in the south east. Local Eithne Scallan (Maudlintown, Wexford), published this excellent volume as a result of her interest in local history. She spent much of her youth rowing at Dalkey and playing tennis as a club player at Sandycove. She moved to Wexford on marrying Sean Scallan and continued with these her many other interests. Any local with an interest in the club should have a copy. It is of broader interest to tennis enthusiasts in that the story of the club development is special.

Not very much is known about this original club in Wexford. However, the Dyas sisters should be noted as winners of the ladies doubles open event in 1893. It is thought that they were from the area. Ruth won the singles in 1894. She played several times in major championships. Ruth married tennis player Neville Durlacher. She reached the All-Comer's singles final at Wimbledon in 1899. H. Porter may also be from the Wexford area. He was, in 1893, studying at Trinity College, Dublin, and was their champion that year as well as winning many other titles (see Chapter 6).

There was at one time a club in Wexford known as the *Hibernian Tennis Club*. The members were known as

Wexford Harbour Tennis Club won Class II of the Provincial Towns Cup in 1975. Team (l. to r.) James O'Connor, Fionnoula Channing, Austin Channing (with cup), Julta Blitzner, Mick O'Leary, Joan O'Connor, Mary O'Neill and Jack Hancock.

According to Eithne Scallan's findings the *lady players were becoming distracted by the cat-calls from passers-by on the Redmond Road-sometimes not very complimentary.* Wiring was erected and up to 100 'macracarpa' hedge shrubs were thus laid. In June 1931 it was decided that the upper court be properly surfaced. It was levelled and tar and chips added, at a cost of £17. Concrete was laid on the lower court in 1934 at a cost of £45. Growth was slow but active. By 1937 the club was running tournaments and had affiliated to the ILTA. The membership numbers appear to include about twenty men and five ladies.

Tom Bolger (second from right) a key member of Wexford Harbour Boat & tennis Club in the successful promotion of the Open August tournament that has continued successfully since 1978. Also in photograph (from left) Tony O'Neill, Eileen Walker & Eileen Kennedy.

George Bridges was a keen player during the war years. His family had a shop in Selskar and he was able to obtain tennis balls at a time when there was a shortage. The Boat Club had the problem of balls lost out in the sea. It was normal for a skiff to be launched to recover these stray shots. When people became more affluent the balls were ignored but some young entrepreneur did quite well recovering them and the selling them at a reasonable price.

Keen players during the 30s 40s and 50s included Eugene McGrail (known as The Midnight Trader as he kept his shop open late), Larry Duggan, Ray Corish, Sean Kelly, Sandy Walsh, Jim Whelan, Frank Pettit, Paddy Kinsella, Dick Elgee, T. Pettigrew, William Cullen, Murth Joyce, Frank Keogh and P. J. O'Connor. One member was remembered as being called The Bear O'Leary.

Activity after the war was sporadic, and finances tight. In 1953 there was a decision taken to get "the tennis activities going". However, repairs to the boathouse roof were to taken precedence even though there were tree roots coming up through the tennis court surfaces. By 1956 tennis was taking up more discussion time than boating.

The club, more than most, had its colourful characters. Tennis and boating were common activities for the local postman who would lay down his bag during his daily round.

Tom McGuinness was though to be the main force behind the club's survival in the 1950s and 1960s. For the next three decades Austin Channing was a key member and the "Austin Channing" commemorative event is now played in his honour. His keen tennis-playing wife Fionnuala also has her name on an annual trophy. In 1978 the August Weekend Tournament was established, an event that now attracts players from all

quarters. Tom Bolger who had joined the club around 1974 became the primary motivator of this very successful competition, still played to this day.

*The 2003 Open Tournament
Wexford Harbour Boat & Tennis Club.*

Aidan and Matt Seaver getting ready for action at Wexford Harbour Boat & Tennis Club (circa 2003).

Through the 1980s membership gradually increased up to nearly 100. The annual tournament was more popular than ever and in 1990 a total of 42 courts in the area were being used for the large entry. Though continually being referred to as The Boat Club, the official change of title was ratified in 1994, becoming the Wexford Harbour Boat and Tennis Club. The 25th anniversary tournament in 2003 was 'another glorious spectacle'. The prize fund of €12,000 attracted many of the top local players as well as visitors Austria, France and Luxembourg.

Ciara Pender-Young member of Wexford Harbour Boat & Tennis Club (circa 2003)

As recently as February 2004 the tennis captain-Osnat Manning- reported that the club was in a very healthy state with 160 active adults and about 100 junior members. The club now has four flood-lit courts and an activity level and interest that should secure its future for many seasons to come.

✶✶✶✶✶

Sandycove Tennis & Squash Club
[Sandycove Lawn Tennis Club]
(Founded 1886)

At a general meeting held on Monday 15th February 1886 **Sandycove LTC** was founded. Some 42 people attended this meeting which was at 6 Elton Park, Sandycove, Dublin. The first honorary secretary was A. R. Darley. The first committee set about finding a site and eventually chose one at Elton Park, the site on which the present club stands. The club was continually active right up until 1917 when due to a loss of members to the First World War lead to its temporary closure. It re-opened in 1919.

Records are scanty but one player of note was Jimmy Casey. In 1956 he gave a great boost to the club by winning the Irish Open under 15 Championship at **Fitzwilliam LTC.** He would follow this with many senior tournament wins in the years to follow. During that period the club played in Class II of the Dublin Leagues, a quite respectable standard for a relatively small club. By 1959 the club *came close to extinction but survived.* Having been demoted from Class II they

sprang back into gear by winning Class III. This upsurge in interest was reflected in other ways in the club. Jim O'Shea, a key club organiser, was part of the organisation that took the club on three 'tours' abroad, surely an excellent idea for club spirit and exposure. In 1961 they visited Norway followed by Germany in 1963 and France in 1965. By 1981, the club had men's and ladies teams in Class II, III, IV and V of the Dublin Leagues.

Since the early 60s the club has been successful at all levels. Some players of note have been Robert Cherry, Robert Kernan, Helen Johnson, Margaret Ann Broderick, Brendan Henderson, Dick Willis, Philip Craig and David Mountjoy. The club have won a total of 26 league titles over the years. Some club successes in recent years are as follows:

1902	Winners Men's Class 3 League
1944	Winners Men's Class 2 League
1954	Winners Men's Class 3 League
1960	Winners Men's Class 3 League
1969	Winners Ladies Class 4 League
1970	Winners Men's Class 3 League
1982	Winners Ladies Class 3 League
1998	Runners-up Men's League Class 4
1990	Winners Ladies Class 2 League
1992	Winners Men's Over 45 Class I League
	Winners Ladies Over 40 Class I League
	Winners Class 2 Under 14 Boys League
1992	Winners Class 2 and 5 Men's Winter League
	Runners-up Class 2 Ladies Winter League
	Winners Men's Class 2 Over 50 League
	Winners Ladies Class I Over 45 League
1994	Winners Men's Class 2 League
1993	Winners Men's Class 2 League
1998	Winners Men's Floodlit Class 2 League
	Winners Men's Class 7 League
1999	Winners Men's Class I Winter League
2001	Winners Men's Over 35 Class I

January 22nd 1983 saw the opening of clubhouse extension. From left: Jim O' Shea (Chairman), Vincent Dunphy (Committee) and Conor O' Reilly (Club Captain)

In 1971 two excellent courts were constructed thanks to the excellent work of Aidan McCormack, Jimmy Casey, Michael Spellman, Frank McGovern and others. By 1978 the four grass courts were all converted to all-weather surfaces. This was followed by the completion of a new clubhouse in 1981. Permission for floodlighting was obtained in 1984.

Today, the club can be proud of facilities that include 6 omni-courts with floodlighting, 2 squash courts and a new bar. In tennis the club field teams in grades from I down to VII and in squash from division I to IV. Success for the future looks assured.

Discussing Centenary Tennis (Summer 1986) at the Sandycove tennis club were (from left): Conor O' Reilly, Bryan O' Neill, Rosemary Langford and Brian Cunningham.

*****

Clontarf Lawn Tennis Club (Founded 1887)

A club that had to be revived and then survive a fire, less than a year after extensive redecoration, has a spirit that will long continue. That fire was in 1982. In 1987, the club celebrated 100 years of life and published a lovely book of over 140 pages in length. In it are a most interesting selection of stories about the people and activities in the club. Particularly appropriate are the stories based upon the minutes recorded over the years. Let all secretaries take note. Your excellent and expansive notes will be appreciated in many years to come.

The Club was founded in 1887 with one court in a field at the rear of Number 45, St. Lawerence Road. There was a small clubhouse. In 1904 it moved to Beachfield, opposite the Clontarf Baths and, in 1932, the lease ran out and the club moved to its present site at Oulton Road. Today it has a thriving club and 9 floodlit all-weather surfaces. It had 120 members in 1913, one of the biggest in Ireland, 215 members in 1976 (75 men, 40 ladies and 100 juniors) and very many more today.

The club has been extensively involved in the Dublin Leagues. In total, it has won 28 titles over the various competitions, 13 of them were in the men's summer leagues. In 1936 the men's third team won Class 4 in the summer leagues. By 1940, the men's game was strong and the club won both the Class 1 and Class 2 titles that summer. They were the sixth club to achieve this double. The Class 2 title would be won again in 1942, 1949, 1950, 1951, 1954, 1965 and 2002. In 1984 the fourth men's team were the first winners of the Class 6 section when it was introduced. The Ladies won the Class 2 summer league in 1952 and 1980 and the Class 3 event in 1959. They have been particularly successful in the Floodlit leagues since they were first introduced in 1981. They have won Class 1 five times, the nearest rivals in that count is the Riverview club with three wins. In 1993, the club won the inaugural boys under 16 Class 1 title and added the Girls under 14 Class 1 title in 1990.

The club have had many key personnel in their ranks. In the early days it was the combined efforts of Henry Gibson (President 1887 to 1903) and James Moore (honorary secretary 1887 to 1894) that was the initial spark. The lists of officers and captains are included here. Space does not allow a full analysis of the club but a few might be noted. Maurice Farnan *lured the residents* to a meeting in 1969. This was to build the club up with a fresh impetus. Fergus Murray was a key fund-raiser at that time. Eoin O' Doherty was the key man behind building the club, once again, after the fire of 1982. Derek Mooney followed him into office as President. The *one-man committee* of Jack McElhinney will not be forgotten. (See chapter 6).

A few references to the club events over the years are worth noting here. They can only scratch the surface of a club's life. When James J. Moore retired as the honorary secretary in 1896 he was presented with a gold watch in appreciation. The first patrons of the club were Lord Ardilaun (formerly Sir Arthur Guinness, a great grandson of the founder of the St. James' Gate Brewery) and Colonel Vernon. As the one court wasn't enough for the club, a site was also leased on the 'Strand Road'. Here seven courts were laid out and there was a pavilion.

In the off-season period sheep grazing brought in some income. In 1893 the club entered the Fitzwilliam Junior Cup competition. They lost 6/3 to the Lansdowne second's. The historic team was K. S. Rynd, P. Leonard, J. Leonard, R. J. Hunt, E. Hunt and H. Hunt. There were a total of seven teams in that competition, the Lansdowne team beating Mount Temple 5/4 in the final. The following year Clontarf beat Dublin University 2nds by 5 matches to 4 but then lost to Fitzwilliam 2nds by the same margin, who in turn lost to Mount Temple in the final. The Clontarf Club Champion in 1893 was K. Rynd.

Clontarf LTC The 1894 Club Championships		
Event	1st Prize	2nd Prize
MCS	K. A.Rynd	R. G. Hunt
MHS	T. Stephens	J. P. Warren
MHD	R. G. & E. P. Hunt	W. C. M. Burland/ T. Thornhill
MxHD	T. Stephens/ Miss L. Stephens	R. G. Hunt/ Miss Kildahl
LCS	Miss L. Stephens	Miss H. Kildahl
LHS	Miss Kildahl	Miss H. Kildahl

In 1899 there were five vice-Presidents in the club, four of whom were Justices of the Peace. In 1907, following the proposal of S.F. Jackson and seconded by James Bullen, a ladies' committee of five were elected. That same year was to see the club's first entry into the leagues, men's team were included in the Class 2 and Class 3 competitions.

In 1908 the club was one of the first to apply to join the Irish Lawn Tennis Association. That year, an assistant was provided for the grounds man for a half day each week (costing 2/-) because of the extra work associated with the "Croquet court".

In 1988 Clontarf LTC was the host to an AIB sponsored tennis awareness day

In 1909 a tournament was organised for 'junior' players and a match arranged against Wesley College on the 10th June. Junior was referring not to under-age players but the 'class' of players in standard terms. 1909 was to see the first ladies team entering the newly formed ladies league. That team was Misses M. Cooke, Cooke, Hiase, Colvin, Lowers and Mrs. Woodcock, with Miss Symes and Mrs. Jordon as substitutes.

In May 1911, Bridget Nolan was hired at 5/- per week to provide afternoon teas from 4.30 to 7 pm each evening. The cost of teas, at that time were

Large Tea (with biscuits, bread & butter)	6d
Small tea (with 3 biscuits)	3d

After a trial period this was changed to ladies 4d and Gents 6d. There was a book supplied and you had to 'sign in' to reserve your tea. A letter came to the club that season from the Court Steam Laundry (Birmingham) offering to clean tennis balls at 1/-6 for 6. The Croquet competition was abandoned, as there were too few entries.

In 1914 a limited number of junior members were admitted at a subscription of 10/- and at the discretion of the committee. Pavilion membership (5/-) was also introduced that year. The following year members of the Clontarf Cricket and Golf clubs were admitted at a reduced subscription of 10/-6 with voting rights. About 20 members signed up for the Great War. Harry Greene, Walter Paul and former member Alfred Bailey were killed at the Dardanelles in 1915.

Some of the top players at Clontarf LTC in the late 1930s. Left to right: Roy Brown, Mai Finnegan, Frank Sweetman and Sheila Guinan.

In 1922, the club President, Charles Killingly died. The Killingly Cup for the Men's Club Championship was subsequently competed for in his memory. In 1928 **Easons LTC** were lent a donkey and roller by the club at an agreed rate of 2/-6 per day. In 1929, *Master Roy Brown was successful in reaching the final of the Junior Championship of the Free State.*

Five years later he would be selected to play on the Leinster team. At the beginning of 1934 Mr. Laurie loaned the club £100 which apparently saved it from ruin. He was subsequently presented a Grandfather Clock in thanks and the Laurie Challenge Cup for Ladies Handicap Singles was established in his honour.

In 1937 a new system of booking courts was introduced. From 7pm, onwards, each half-hour, a bell would be rung, the courts should be cleared and the next group would take over. In 1938, Roy Brown won the South of Ireland Championship and the following year was selected on the Irish team to play against Scotland. In 1947 he would secure his first of three caps on the Irish squash team.

One of the greatest achievements the club have made on the playing front was winning the Class 1 Dublin Leagues in 1942. The strength was emphasised when the second team won the Men's Class 2 league the following week. The ladies first team reached the semi-finals of the Class 2 league. The men's second

The historic Clontarf LTC's Men's Class 1 Summer League winners of 1942. Back (l. to r.) D. P. Mehigan, P. J. Kelly, George Pepper, W. M. Hopley, J. P. Mills, J. F. Donnelly & A. E. Timlin. Front (l. to r.) Roy Brown, J.R. Devlin, R.A. Morrison (President), Jack McElhinney (Captain), George Payne and Cecil Stephen.

team was D. P. Mehigan, K. McElhinney, Frank Mulligan, M. Murphy, Brendan McGoldrick and J. Lee. The first team are as in the photograph. In 1952 the club was in the classical dilemma. Their two top teams were in the Class I Summer League; the Class II side having won their title for three consecutive years (1949 to 1951) were promoted. The men's first team reached the finals where Bective beat them. The ladies 1st team won Class II for the first time. Brian McElhinney and Harry Morris would play for Leinster with Harry reaching an Irish ranking of 12 in 1952.

The club had eight teams in the summer leagues that summer in 1966. The club bought out their lease in 1967 with the assistance of monies from Paul Coyle and Ray Hughes. In 1964, Maurice Farnan after *a broken tennis engagement with a friend* coached some juniors. This was the beginning of a new era in the club. The junior numbers reached 180, the adult members were around the 40 mark. He ended up as club president; invited parents to a meeting (many of whom were not members) and a new boost to club activity took off. This was over a period of years when the lease purchase (£1500) had to be paid back.

At the A.G.M. in 1973 it was obvious that a new spirit was at work. The Bar was showing a healthy profit, the Ways & Means Committee were funding the developments. The Treasurer, Mantan Walshe was running a very tight rein on finances. Fund raising around that time included wine and cheese parties, Race nights, the Carnival, Fight the Flab, tea drinking competitions, Bonny Baby shows and Bingo. Three new hard courts came into play in 1974. In 1979

outgoing President Tommy Ryan switched on the floodlights on the 22nd March. 1982 saw the ladies winning the winter league, the club had five floodlit courts. However, at an emergency meeting on the 2nd June in Eoin O' Doherty's' house, it was reported that the clubhouse had been 'gutted by fire'. Some parts of the club were only partially destroyed and by 5th June

The Clontarf LTC Ladies team that won the Dublin Summer League (Class II) in 1980. Back (l. to r.) Gillian Chandler, Deirdre McClean, Helen Daly & Derek Mooney (Club Captain). Front (l. to r.) Frieda O' Brien, A. V. Moore (President), Emer Daly (Captain), Una Cripps and Chris O' Doherty (Ladies' Captain).

Clontarf LTC was founded in 1887. The photograph to left was taken fifty years later when celebrating the Golden Jubilee. The official jubilee day celebrations were held on Saturday the 24th July 1937.

Clontarf LTC. The men's team that Class II of the Dublin leagues in 1949, 1950 & 1951. Back (l. to r.) I. Finlay, T. G. Grey, J. Collins, W. M. Hopley, A. Hensey, Frazer McMullan, George Pepper, J. Gibbons, J. McElhinney (captain), D. P. Mehigan & J. F. Donnelly.

Clontarf LTC Ladies' Class II Dublin League winners in 1952. Back (l. to r.) N. Mullen, P.F. Brady (hon. treasurer), A. McCrum, J. G. Lyons (hon. secretary) & M. Monahan. Front (l. to r.) A. D. A. Browne (president), M. Todd-Johnson, M. P. Turvey (captain), Brid Byrne & B. P. McElhinney (captain).

Clontarf Lawn Tennis Club

Year	President	Hon.Secretary	Hon.Treasurer	Captain	Lady Capt.
'87-'91	Henry Gibson	James J. Moore			
1892	Henry Gibson	James J. Moore		E. O. Callaghan	
1893	Henry Gibson	James J. Moore	Charles Drury	W. C. M. Burland	
1894	Henry Gibson	James J. Moore	Charles Drury	W. C. M. Burland	
1895	Henry Gibson	G. D. Symes	Charles Drury	K. A. Rynd	
				R. G. Hunt	
1896	Henry Gibson	James J. Moore	Charles Drury	R. G. Hunt	
1897	Henry Gibson	George Tickell	J. K. Quail	R. G. Hunt	
1898	Henry Gibson	George Tickell	J. K. Quail	J. J. Moore	
1899	Henry Gibson	R. H. McFerran	C. Jacob	W. T. Crawford	
1900	Henry Gibson	R. H. McFerran	C. Jacob	W. T. Crawford	
1901	Henry Gibson	George W. Thornley	W. T. Crawford	Charles Killingly	
1902	Henry Gibson	George W. Thornley	W. T. Crawford	Charles Killingly	
1903	Henry Gibson	George W. Thornley	James Bullen	C. H. Jukes	
		S. F. Jackson		J. K. Quail	
1904	B. B. Jameson	R. N. Cashel	James Bullen	J. K. Quail	
1905	B. B. Jameson	R. N. Cashel	S. F. Jackson	J. K. Quail	
1906	B. B. Jameson	E. O. Hodges	S. F. Jackson	J. K. Quail	
		W. F. Scott			
1907	G. W. Thornley	W. F. Scott	S. F. Jackson	J. K. Quail	
1908	James H. Cooke	W. F. Scott	H. R. Polden	W. J. Dilworth	
1909	Matthew Adam	W. F. Scott	H. R. Polden	W. J. Dilworth	
1910	John Robb	W. F. Scott	H. R. Polden	W. J. Dilworth	
1911	E.S. Lowe	E. S. Lowe	H. R. Polden	W. J. Dilworth	
1912	Augustus Klingner	H. R. Polden	B. Hodges	W. J. Dilworth	
1913	Matthew Adam	G. E. Matthews	B. Hodges	G. E. Mitchell	
1914	George W. Thornley	G. E. Matthews	John McWade	G. E. Mitchell	
1915	George H. Bailey	S. E. Polden	John McWade	J. G. Greene	None
1916	George H. Bailey	S. E. Polden	John McWade	T. F. Bacon	
1917	George H. Bailey	S. E. Polden	Victor Dallas	Charles Killingly	
1918	George H. Bailey	S. E. Polden	Victor Dallas	Charles Killingly	
1919	G. D. Symes	S. E. Polden	Victor Dallas	Charles Killingly	
1920	G. D. Symes	S. E. Polden	Victor Dallas	H. R. Polden	
1921	Charles Killingly	R. H. Feary	Victor Dallas	A. E. Dallas	
1922	James H. Cooke	R. H. Feary	Victor Dallas	P. A. Ryan	
1923	R. H. McFerran	R. H. Feary	S. C. Percival	J. W. Parkes	
1924	John Foxall	R. H. Feary	S. C. Percival	P. A. Ryan	
1925	John Fisher	R. H. Feary	H. O. D. Foulkes	G. E. Matthews	
1926	John Sullivan	G. S. C. Russell	H. O. D. Foulkes	P. A. Ryan	
1927	Philip McNulty	G. S. C. Russell	R. A. Morrison	J. W. Parkes	
1928	Joseph Peters	G. S. C. Russell	W. A. Campbell	G. E. Matthews	
1929	S. E. Polden	G. S. C. Russell	E. A. Wheeler	R. A. Morrison	
1930	H. R. Polden	A. K. Wilhelmy	L. A. Steepe	G. S. C. Russell	
1931	J. D. Crozier	G. S. C. Russell	L. A. Steepe	A. K. Wilhelmy	
1932	T. F. Laurie	G. S. C. Russell	L. A. Steepe	J. F. Donnelly	
1933	T. F. Laurie	O. G. Giddings	J. K. Brown	E. A. Wheeler	
1934	T. F. Laurie	R. A. Morrison	H. O. D. Foulkes	G. S. C. Russell	
1935	T. F. Laurie	S. F. Sweetnam	George Pepper	Roy G. Brown	
1936	T. F. Laurie	S. F. Sweetnam	George Pepper	R. G. Richardson	
1937	T. F. Laurie	S. F. Sweetnam	George Pepper	A. D. A. Browne	
1938	T. F. Laurie	A. C. Will	A. J. Donnelly	S. F. Sweetnam	
1939	S. P.Mercier	A. C. Will	A. J. Donnelly	C. Armstrong	
1940	R. A. Morrison	B. Mc Goldrick	A. J. Donnelly	George Pepper	
1941	R. A. Morrison	B. Mc Goldrick	T. P. Murray	J. McElhinney	
1942	R. A. Morrison	B. Hensey	T. P. Murray	D. P. Mehigan	
1943	R. A. Morrison	B. Hensey	T. P. Murray	B. P. McGoldrick	

Clontarf Lawn Tennis Club

Year	President	Hon.Secretary	Hon.Treasurer	Captain	Lady Captain
1944	George Peppar	R. Hearne	T. P. Murray	D. Hurding	
'45-'46	George Peppar				
1947	George Peppar	I. Finlay	Jack McElhinney	H. J. Ryan	
1948	J. F. Donnelly	H. J. Ryan	Jack McElhinney	H. Morris	I. Furphy
1949	J. F. Donnelly	J. F. Donnelly	Jack McElhinney	J. Collins	Brid Byrne
1950	J. F. Donnelly	K. O'Brien	Jack McElhinney	I. Finlay	W. Mather
1951	J. F. Donnelly	J. G. Lyons	P. F. Brady	A. Hensey	Pat Turvey
1952	A. D. A. Browne	J. G. Lyons	P. F. Brady	BrianP. McElhinney	P. Hensey
1953	Roy G. Brown	W. Walshe	P. J. McDonagh	Brian P. McElhinney	E. Coughlan
1954	Roy G. Brown	W. Walshe	P. J. McDonagh	P.F. Brady	M. Todd Johnson
1955	Roy G. Brown	J. Joyce	D. Delaney	G. Jennings	M. Monahan
1956	Jack McElhinney	J. Joyce	D. Delaney	W. Brennan	T. Barry
1957	Jack McElhinney	Frank Mulligan	Jack McElhinney	Niall McMahon	A. McMullan
1958	Jack McElhinney	Frank Mulligan	Jack McElhinney	Ken Moriarty	Brid Byrne
1959	Jack McElhinney	J. B. Harkin	Jack McElhinney	W. Malone	
1960	Jack McElhinney	F. A. Kelly	Jack McElhinney	B. Shields	
1961	Jack McElhinney	F. A. Kelly	Jack McElhinney/ T. Cassidy		
1962	Jack McElhinney	F. A. Kelly	Jack McElhinney	Gerry Finnucane	
1963	C. Stephen	F. A. Kelly	Jack McElhinney		
1964	C. Stephen	F. A. Kelly	Jack McElhinney		
1965	E. P. Kinsella	Gerry Finnucane	Jack McElhinney	Terry Brennan	
1966	E. P. Kinsella	Gerry Finnucane	Jack McElhinney	Tony Walshe	
1967	Paddy Potts/ Jack McElhinney	Gerry Finnucane	T. Walshe	M. Shiel	
1968	Maurice Farnan	H. Mullen	Gerry Finnucane	Frank Cassidy	A. Walshe
1969	Maurice Farnan	B.Joyce	Gerry Finnucane	M. Shiel	A. Walshe
1970	Maurice Farnan	P.O'Neill	Oliver Fehily	M. Shiel	C. Walshe
1971	DouglasBeaddie	P.O'Neill	H. Daly	M. O'Brien	C. Walshe
1972	DouglasBeaddie	Tommy Ryan	Mantan Walshe	M. O'Brien	P. Cassidy
1973	DouglasBeaddie	Tommy Ryan	Mantan Walshe	M. O'Brien	I. Dobbs
1974	Fergus Murray	Tommy Ryan	Mantan Walshe	K. Byrne	Maeve Guirke
1975	Fergus Murray	E. O'Doherty	Mantan Walshe	K. Byrne	Maeve Guirke
1976	P. O' Neill	Maurice Brangan	Brendan Nicholl	Eoin O'Doherty	Maeve Guirke
1977	P. O' Neill	Maurice Brangan	Brendan Nicholl	E.oin O'Doherty	E. Daly
1978	Tommy Ryan	E. Palmer	Brendan Nicholl	D. Holmes/ K. O'Riordan	Deirdre McClean
1979	Tommy Ryan	E. Palmer	Brendan Nicholl	K. Byrne	Deirdre McClean
1980	A. Moore	D. McCarthy	M. Kelly	Derek Mooney	C. O'Doherty
1981	A. Moore	J. Clancy	M. Kelly	Derek Mooney	A. Haughey
1982	Eoin O' Doherty	Ivor Callelly	M. Kelly	Derek Mooney	H. Daly
1983	Eoin O' Doherty	Ivor Callelly	M. Frost/Pat Kenny	J. Brennan	H. Daly
1984	Eoin O' Doherty	T. O'Driscoll	Pat Kenny	J. Brennan	H. Daly
1985	Derek Mooney	T. O'Driscoll	Pat Kenny	J. Brennan	Chris O'Doherty
1986	Derek Mooney	T. O'Driscoll	Pat Kenny	Anto Kelly	Una Cripps
1987	Derek Mooney	A. Moore	M. Kelly	Anto Kelly	R. Brennan
1988		Christine Foran	A. Moore		
1989-2003		Christine Foran			

a bar 'of sorts' was in operation, an important social element in the club. A new building would be opened on Saturday 22nd December 1984 with a Christmas Carol Night. In

1985 Eileen Palmer was elected a life member for her tireless work for the club over a decade. Things were really advancing in 1987 when it was decided to install four new artificial grass courts and resurface the five old hard courts. The club now has nine artificial grass courts and is well into a new century of tennis.

Apart from the many organisers in the club there were to be many excellent players over the years. It would be difficult to pick out a full compliment. However we can include among the men Roy Browne, Frank Sweetman, Harry Morris, Jack McElhinney, Brian McElhinney, Paul McElhinney, J. J. McArdle, Frazer McMullen, Frank McArdle, Derek Mooney and John Fahy. Among the ladies we would find excellent players in Mai Finnegan, Sheila Guinan, Brid Byrne, Una McNulty, Pat Turvey, Emer Daly, Gillian Chandler and Deirdre McClean. There are many more.

The 1984 Class 6 Winning Team at Clontarf LTC. From left: John Beaddie, Maurice Griffin, Seamus Phelan, Pat Phelan, Ter Laughton & Paul Beaddie.

✱✱✱✱✱

City of Belfast Y.M.C.A. Lawn Tennis Club
(Founded. C. 1887)

Some clubs have a glorious period of activity but, for varied reasons, do not survive. Members of those clubs who have seen them at their best can reflect on many hours, days and year of enjoyment playing a sport that formed the focus of their valued leisure time. The 'Y.M' in Belfast is such a club. Thanks to the diligence and enthusiasm of a former keen member, Miss Doreen E. A. Muskett, the following history is recorded for posterity.

On Captain's Day, 18th June 1983, the Club recorded its 75th Anniversary as a formally constituted Club. However, it appears that while minutes were only available from 1908, it was thought that the club was in existence from around 1887. Tennis was first mentioned in the history of the City of Belfast

Y.M.C.A. alongside cycling, lacrosse and swimming as far back as that year.

It was probably played at YM's first recreation field called Prospect Park, Ormeau Road, near the Ormeau Bakery. Some time later ten acres were secured further down the road called Shaftsbury Grounds. This site was later to be vacated because of building developments, and in 1891 alternative grounds were secured on Crumlin Road near Carlisle Circus. Again building plans got priority and the Club moved to the Old Stranmillis Road on land around the present site at Richmond Park.

Eight acres at Bladon were acquired in 1922 and later additional land was bought. The complex covered some 19.5 acres with excellent facilities for soccer, cricket, squash, rugby, hockey, handball, table tennis, badminton and fencing. The situation was reputed to be the finest in Ireland in respect of drainage as it was located on a sand bank.

The first pavilion at Bladon was a Spartan structure, a place without frills. The members made it from motorcar crates and, because water and electricity were not available in the area, much of the atmosphere was captured with the use of paraffin lamps. Water was carried from a small spring at the bottom of a hill near Lester's Spring situated in the area now known as Lagan Meadows, grazing cows were the friendly neighbours.

The original club under construction in the early 1920s, the finished product used until the late 1960s and the modern clubhouse which was officially opened in 1968 at the City of Belfast YMCA LTC.

It was not until 1959 that a stand-pump first appeared on the red dust hard courts at Bladon, thanks to a private development by YM's first neighbour. From small beginnings the club went from strength to strength and in 1965 obtained its own proper pavilion with electricity, water and kitchen. The long-awaited showers were a welcome change from barrels of rainwater. In addition to the two red sand hard courts and eight grass courts, after much deliberation and fund-raising, two all-weather courts with floodlighting were opened in 1972. The club was renowned for its friendly membership of more than 100 and in 1955 a very important decision was made to form a Junior Section. This new venture proved a valuable asset and led to several YMCA players gaining Ulster Interprovincial caps. Indeed, on more than one occasion, so popular was the Junior Club that membership had to be closed at 200 and a waiting list formed. Coaching facilities were an added feature for both sections of the club and popular *tennis clinics* for juniors took place during the summer months. Annual club tournaments drew large entries from members for the handsome array of valuable silverware at stake.

YMCA LTC (Circa 1935)

YMCA LTC-Closing Day in 1940.
Mrs. Ireland presenting the Men's Singles Trophy-the McPherson Cup- to Charlie Savage

The History of Irish Tennis

Opening Day in April 1957

Closing Day in 1961. Front (l. to r.) R. Martin, Doreen Muskett, S. McKeown, J. Silcock, W. Harris, M. Sturgeon. Middle (l. to r.) A. Fowler, D. Dean, H. Johnston, A. McCullouch, A. Corry, O. Cassidy, D. Sheridan, N. Hill, Mr. & Mrs. E. Dornan, Mr. & Mrs. Casey, Walter Nicholl, D. Megaw. Back (l. to r.) C. Pearson, D. McMeekin, L. Johnston, Sammy Nelson, P. Marshall, H. Houston, A.N. Other, J.H. Ireland.

At the City of Belfast 75th Anniversary celebrations on the 18th June 1983 were (from left) Trevor Harrison, Patricia Rees, Walter Nicholl, W. E. Dornan (organising general secretary, YMCA), Ken Wallace and Doreen Muskett.

The History of Irish Tennis

Club Captains
City of Belfast YMCA Lawn Tennis Club

Year	Gentlemen	Ladies	Year	Gentlemen	Ladies
1924	D.W. Bullick	Miss S.Ervine	1959	Walter Nicholl	Mrs. W.G. Nicholl
1925	F.J.W.Shannon	Miss S.Ervine	1960	D.Dean	Miss S.H. Edgar
1926	J. Jordan	Miss K.Woods	1961	R.N.McMeekin	Miss S.M. McKeown
1927	C. Patterson	Miss E.Wren	1962	W.J.Silcock	Mrs. D.Megaw
1928	E.Thompson	Miss Q.Murphy	1963	W.N.D.Weir	Miss A.Fowler
1929	T.S.Montgomery	Miss D.Swann	1964	T.Fisher	Miss W.Pearson
1930	W.S.Patterson	Miss J.E.McFeeters	1965	M.Goodall	Miss L.McWatters
1931	H.D.Montgomery	Miss H.Bradley	1966	J.Neill	Miss M.McCall
1932	W.H.Crawford	Miss W.E.Logan	1967	L.J.Johnston	Mrs.A.H.McCullough
1933	A.H.Johnston	Miss R.Mc Vea	1968	L.J.Johnston	Mrs.A.H.McCullough
1934	N.Gray	Miss M.McDonald	1969	R.Baxter	Miss L.Gentleman
1935	H.D.Montgomery	Miss M.Martin	1970	W.E.Jackson	Miss J.McElwaine
1936	T.H.Boyle	Miss N.Storey	1971	W.E.Jackson	Miss J.McElwaine
1937	T.H.Boyle	Miss W.Sloan	1972	R.T.Hazelton	Miss H.Houston
1938	L.Richardson	Miss w.Sloan	1973	R.T.Hazelton	Mrs. E.M. McCrea
1939	T.H.Boyle	Miss M.Dawson	1974	P.M.Rees	Miss J.Harpur
1940	H.Savage	Miss F.Thomas	1975	E.M.Dobson	Mrs. L.Carson
1941	H.Savage	Miss M.Wallace	1976	A.K.Wallace	Mrs. F. Cunningham
1942	J.F.Hogg	Miss P.Rankin	1977	T.Goodall	Mrs. L. Carson
1943	J.Smyth	Miss E.Menary	1978	J.Toland	Mrs. C.A.Jackson
1944	W.J.Caldwell	Miss M. Wallace	1979	J.Toland	Mrs. S.H.Johnston
1945	G.E.McCullough	Miss K.Guiney	1980	R.M.H.Rudge	Mrs. S.H.Johnston
1946	D.W.McIllroy	Mrs.J.Walby	1981	R.H.French	Miss D.J.Orr
1947	W.McLaughlin	Miss K.Guiney	1982	T.J.Harrison	Mrs. M.P.Rees
1948	N.C.Linton	Miss F.Cooke	1983	C. R.Middleton	Miss E.Brown
1949	J.E.Howe	Miss M. Moffett	1984	T.J.Harrison	Mrs.J.Parke
1950	M.Simpson	Miss H.Johnston	1985	L.Carson	Ms. A. Clarke
1951	W.B.Watt	Miss H.Mc Dougall	1986	L.Carson	Miss A.Wright
1952	A.B.Talbot	Miss E.Winter	1987	E.M.Dobson	Miss A.Mawhinney
1953	J.M.Johnston	Miss M.Moffett	1988	E.M.Dobson	Miss R.McNiece
1954	A.H.McCullough	Miss N.McDougall	1989	N.Hall	Miss H.Rollins
1955	D.Jackson	Mrs.A.H.McCullough	1990	K.Dempsey	Miss H.Rollins
1956	L.J.Johnston	Miss D.P.N.Gracey	1991	K.Dempsey	Miss M.Wright
1957	J.Petticrew	Mrs. O.M. Power	1992	J.McClelland	Miss M.Wright
1958	R.C. Martin	Miss Doreen.Muskett			

The Invitation Club Doubles Championships were conceived and hosted during the years 1980-1991 and drew players from many parts of Ireland. Over the years many members have distinguished themselves by taking an active interest at administrative level. Walter Nicholl (1959,1964) and Gillian Carson (1984/1985) were to be honoured as Presidents of the Ulster Branch of the ILTA. See details in Chapter 6. Billy Jackson also served as a council member. Dorothy Cunningham and Elizabeth McCrea were members of the Belfast and District League for many years. Walter Nicholl was to be subsequently made a life member of the ILTA. He was very keen to encourage young players and, in association with Michael Dunne of the **Falls Tennis Club** was instrumental in structuring a Junior League Tennis competition in the Belfast and District region.

The 1983 anniversary was a day to remember. It was certainly a day of celebration with period costume, souvenir mugs, a nostalgic photograph display and lots of memories exchanged amongst the very large gathering, part of which overflowed onto the patio. The Ladies and Gents Captains of 1945 cut the suitably inscribed Anniversary Cake. An American Tournament was held with 60 participants, the less energetic played a game of croquet.

18th June 1983-Celebration Cake & Mugs

Some of the members who have been distinguished by playing at County or Provincial level were Lyle Carson, Adelaide Corry, Michael McCullough, Heather (Houston) McIvor, Robert Turnely, Robert Russell, Elizabeth (Dickie) McCrea, Diane (Craig) Maynes and Peter Little. Diane Craig was ranked number 6 in Ireland in 1981 and in both 1984 and 1985, was number 4. In 1984 she won the County Antrim Championship at Ballycastle and the championships at St. Anne's-Waterford. In 1985 she was South of Ireland Champion. On the Irish team to play England at Formby, she was the number one singles player (losing narrowly 7/5 6/4 to J. Davis) and was to win her doubles (6/3 6/3) with Jennifer Thornton.

The City of Belfast YMCA LTC league winning teams in 1970. Front (l. to r.): H. Houston, E. Dickie & J. Harpur. Middle (l. to r.): M. McCulloch, H. Thompson, A. Corry, L. Quinn & M. Simpson. Back (l. to r.): W. Jackson, R. Baxter, A. McCulloch, L. McClelland & T. Goodal..

Jill Elliott was one of ten Girl Guides chosen to play in a National Lawn Tennis Tournament at the Queen's Club in London on two occasions. Johnny Biscomb was to be honoured with Davis Cup selection (see chapter 6). Sammy Nelson was a keen junior member who was to distinguish himself as a soccer player for Arsenal and also Northern Ireland. The club was at a peak when it had four teams, including a Division one side, playing in the Belfast and District Leagues. Members were more than disappointed when, after some years of discussion, the YMCA decided to sell six acres for development. This included the hockey pitch, cricket square and tennis courts. Temporary facilities were sought but proved unsatisfactory and unpractical and, in 1992, it was *game, set and match* for the long-established Tennis Club at Bladon.

✶✶✶✶

Glenageary (and Kingstown) Lawn Tennis Club (Founded 1887)

Founded in March of 1887. The official opening of 7th July was attended by a *numerous and fashionable* company. Seven grass courts were in place as well as one asphalt. For about 100 years things remained

much the same. Now we have a thriving club that went through a few lows but has modern facilities with full participation of ladies and juniors. The May 9th 1906 issue of *Lawn Tennis and Badminton* indicated that the Kingstown Tournament has become the largest in Ireland, and is sure to be as successful as usual. (It is not clear whether the Kingstown club, later Glenageary, was solely, or in part, responsible for this state of affairs. It can be said with certainty that the club was a most active one for many years in the early part of the 20th century).

The old clubhouse at Glenageary LTC

The 1931 Mixed doubles club championships. From left: Colin Maidment, Tat Morrison, Hilda Hollwey & Fred Holman.

Club Mixed Doubles final in 1942. Pierce MacDermott and Norah Conway (right) beat Geoff & Eileen Trapnell.

By the 14th May 1887 a lease was agreed between Rosa Hanna and the club's new honorary secretary, Owen Wynne. The chairman at the time was F.G. Crofton. The following item in the Irish Times on the 16th May set the scene:

> *GLENAGEARY AND KINGSTOWN LAWN TENNIS CLUB has now been organised, and the admirably laid-out tennis courts, which are situated on Silchester Road, Glenageary, will soon be completed. The number of playing members is limited so as to avoid overcrowding on the courts and to ensure for each member a fair share of play in the sets. It is intended to have a club day on which members can introduce their friends, and thus a pleasant and social reunion will be provided for all, and fill a want, which has long been felt in Kingstown. The club will be managed by an influential committee.*

In March the subscription had been sets at £1 per annum with an entrance fee of 10/-. The official opening of the club on the 7th July was reported in the following days paper when *Mrs. Shapland M. Tandy, who, by throwing a ball across one of the nets of the courts, declared "the club open".* There were already about 100 playing members and about 50 non-playing ones whose subscription was *half a sovereign*. Mr. Anketell Jones gave a gift of wire netting to the club, which extended the whole length of the ground and prevented balls getting into the adjoining field.

Ladies 1st Team 1946 (Class2 Finalists). Back (l. to r.) Pat Acheson, Dorothy Eaton & Mrs. Dagg. Front (l. to r.) Mrs. K. Galloway, Mrs. Hilda Keenan & Eileen Trapnell.

The chairman was Captain the Hon. F.G. Crofton, the harbour master at Kingstown. The honorary secretary, Owen Wynne, was Chief Clerk at the harbour. Shapland Morris Tandy was a local solicitor. Other committee members were Colonel John Andrew Price, Major O'Brien Butler, James Dillon, M.I.C. E. described as an architect, Captain F. A. Symes, R.N., superintendent of the Irish Light Stores, Major Ternon, John Russell and Thomas W. Berry.

While the grass had not really grown in 1887 (*the green sod of Erin was nowhere to be seen*) due to the long drought of that year, things moved ahead in 1887. *During the non-playing season the committee one and all have worked with a will, not only completing seven grass courts, but also an asphalte one, which has been made by the contractor of the Fitzwilliam Club.* The centenary brochure (1987) indicates that in the 20th century the club had no more than five courts and suggested that these other three must have been abandoned quite early.

Glenageary LTC Men's team 1930s

The **first club tournament** was held during the week starting the **Monday 20th August 1888**. The weather was not great during the week but by the Saturday afternoon it was fine for the first "at home" and there was a *large and fashionable gathering* present. Throughout these early days of tennis the word 'fashionable' regularly occurs in many clubs, emphasising the social nature of the occasion. This ties in with the significant number of non-playing members found in many clubs. For the record, the scores in the finals of that inaugural tournament were as follows:

> **Gentlemen's Singles:**
> Mr. Arthur Ross (scr.) beat
> Captain Box (scr.) 6/3 6/4
> **Ladies Singles:**
> Miss Craig (-15) beat
> Miss Richardson (scr.) 6/2 4/6 6/2
> **Ladies' and Gentlemen's Doubles:**
> Mr. H. Bourchier and Miss Slaughter (-15) beat
> J. Swan Browne and Miss Atkins (+ half 15) 6/3 6/3
> **Gentlemen's Doubles:**
> H. Bourchier and A. Ross (-15 for one bisque) beat
> A. Samuel and H. French (3 bisques) 6/1 6/3

The club had croquet lawns and the game, which was extremely popular before lawn tennis took off, had an additional subscription attached. This was 2/6 per annum in 1894. The game continued to be a feature in the club until the early 1900s. The annual club income in 1894 came to £110. This was adequate for club outgoing. A noted minor expenditure was £1-10-0, the entry fee into the annual Fitzwilliam inter-club cup competition.

The History of Irish Tennis

Open Tournament at Glenageary & Kingstown LTC	
Event	1st Prize
	1893
MHS	W. D. Ross
LHS	The Hon. Miss M. Ffrench
LHD	Miss Price/Miss Ross
MxHD	W. D.Ross/Miss Wynne

The reporting on actual tennis played did not always match up to the social scene reports (see chapter 3). It might be noted, however, that the annual tournament did attract a large attendance. Well over 200 tickets for the finals day on Thursday 19th July 1894 were sold. By 1905 tennis membership had fallen to 43 and croquet had been 'abolished'. In a club letter to the landowner, Mrs. Harran, in the autumn of 1904, the state of affairs at that time were clearly defined:

Tennis in Ireland and particularly in Kingstown is on the decline and the Club at present has only 50 members with a subscription of £1 per annum which cannot be increased - that means an income of £50 per annum only, and the present rent £17/10/- out of same leaves a very small margin for working expenses.

Glenageary LTC won the Dublin Class II league in 1914. Back (l. to r.): W. S. Jeffares, C. H. Mitchell & R. W. Pim. Front (l. to r.): Paddy Coll, Noel Staples & Harry Maunsell.

Even with small numbers the club did prove successful on the playing front. In 1903 the club had two teams in Class II and one in Class III of the Dublin leagues. The club won Class II in 1909. On the team was none other than Harry Maunsell. He would become the honorary secretary of the ILTA from 1920 to 1948 and President of the **Fitzwilliam LTC** from 1941 to 1943. A lasting tribute to his service in the cause of Irish tennis was the introduction of the Maunsell Trophies in 1945. These are awarded annually to the Irish man and woman who are adjudged to have had the best record in Irish tennis during the previous playing year. Further details can be found in chapter 6. Another member of note was Paddy Coll who joined the club in

1899. He and Harry Maunsell had a great influence on the organisation of the club, and as players, for over thirty years. Paddy was a member of the committee for over three decades, honorary secretary (1915-1916), vice-President from 1933 and President from 1949 until his death in 1951. He was men's singles champion in 1912 and doubles champion for three years (1919,1920 & 1929).

Two of the excellent lady players at Glenageary LTC ladies (circa 1930): Norah Barton & Ena Robinson.

In 1910 the pavilion, situated behind courts two and three, consisted of gentlemen's, ladies', team and general 'rooms'. In that year a new *tea pavilion* was erected at a cost of £21-0-0 and other alterations including *conversion of the ladies' room into a shower bath.* In 1911 eight lockers were provided in the men's room and in 1912 a bicycle shed was erected. In 1929, the small and crowded facilities were replaced by a new pavilion, which was still in use in the Centenary Year 1987. This item took several years to sort out; the first step was the raising of over £100 in 1925 by a *stop-watch* competition. More money was brought in when member, Claude Exshaw, a member of an amateur drama group, produced a play, which ran for two nights in the Dalkey Town Hall. The old wooden tearoom became the tool shed and was eventually demolished in the 1970s and replaced by a concrete shed. In the winter of 1921-1922 the old asphalte court was replaced by a grass one.

After a period of decline the membership numbers rose and exceeded 80 in 1914. *The war posed severe, and sometimes harsh, issues for the Club (such as occasional assistance with the relief of wounded soldiers, and the death of at least one member on active service), but the events of Easter 1916 (referred* to in committee minutes as 'the troubles in Dublin') also had some impact. At its meeting on the 10th May the committee-which earlier in the year had been preoccupied by the trespass of sheep on the Club grounds-was told that the military had taken possession of the pavilion dressing rooms. The occupation lasted until 13th May and resulted in some damage, for which the Club claimed £5 against the O.C., 'A' Battery, 296th Brigade, Royal Field Artillery. As a result the Club did not open for play until 21st May.

The club's vintage playing years were from the end of the First World War until the early 1950s. This situation was helped by having a long serving honorary secretary (Colin Maidment from 1931 for 25 years) and, just as important, an excellent grounds man (Larry Brady from 1916 to 1953).

Glenageary LTC. The 3rd team in 1964 won the Class IV Dublin league. Back (l. to r.): Miss H. Waller, Miss G. McCullagh & Miss V. Hanna. Front (l. to r.): Sally Brewster, Miss H. Thorn & Mrs. I. Galloway.

At the 36th AGM held in April 1923 the club changed its name to **Glenageary Lawn Tennis Club.** This followed the 1920 decision of the local urban district council to abandon using the name Kingstown in favour of Dun Laoghaire. This latter change, and the dropping of the names Queen's County and King's County elsewhere, can be linked to a changing political climate and, ultimately, the signing of the Anglo-Irish Treaty on the 6th December 1921 and the formation of the Irish Free State.

The club had significant successes in league competition over the years. A noteworthy win was that of the ladies first team who won Class II of the Dublin Leagues in 1921. They were promoted in 1922 but, as the 1923 AGM indicated, this proved much too strenuous for them and they did not succeed very well. In 1923 they again would win Class II. The men were not to be outdone and won Class II in both 1922 and 1923. The 1922 victory was *celebrated by a very sumptuous dinner at Mr. Maunsell's and it may be*

recorded that only one of the party came to grief on his way home by falling into a quarry. A year later after another win it was recorded they duly celebrated at Mr. Maunsell's house, and the members of the team proved themselves to be excellent pedestrians-having to walk all the way home in the early hours of the morning.

Men's Doubles finalists 1955. Ken McComas, Leslie Green, Des Lacey & Des Legg.

Ladies were first elected onto the committee in 1923 and junior members were permitted from 1920. Both had their limitations and are mentioned elsewhere in this book. For the centenary brochure (1987) a number of the old hands were asked to pen their memories. The following are a few interesting extracts that might revive the readers memories or even wonder at how things have changed.

Gilbert Webb (Born C. 1902. He joined the club in 1918 and played on club teams in the early 1920s).

When I joined the club in 1918 it was at the end of the first world war and my recollections are of one strata of older members, and one of very young ones including myself. Presumably the middle strata was away at the war.

The courts were low lying with somewhat lush grass so that the ball tended to keep low. This caused difficulties when one encountered well drained courts as at the Bray tournament, where Glenageary members never seemed to get very far in the Competition.

I suppose it was due to the disparity of the two age groups but the older members seemed always to make up their fours among themselves so the younger group did likewise. A little more intermingling would have been helpful in bringing on the more promising younger players.

The best player in the club was Noel Staples. He was also a keen gardener and had often to be persuaded to leave his garden in order to make up a four. Among the ladies Norah Barton was the lady champion for several years. I believe she was the daughter of the Barton who presented the Barton Cup which is still competed for by golf clubs teams.

I left Ireland in 1926 to take up a job in England and later spent five years at Abadan in Iran where I found the tennis courts, composed of baked clay and crushed shell, a very different proposition to the lush green courts at Glenageary!

Tennis in those days was less competitive and more of a game than it is now. It wasn't quite the thing to serve one's hardest at a lady opponent and "poaching" at the net had to be restrained! One's racquet was strung with catgut and woe betide you if you played in the rain on a wet court. A broken string could be a minor tragedy as very few of us could rise to a reserve racquet.

Fred Homan Born in about 1897, he would join **Monkstown LTC** in 1917. T.F.O. ('Fred') Homan joined the club in 1921 and won the club championships seven times between 1925 and 1946. He was last in a final in 1962, at the age of 65. He has taken sets off Davis Cup players such as Eustace Fannin and Hector Ryan. He has been club secretary (1924-1927,1928-1965) treasurer (1928-1934,1939-1940) and President for much of the 1960s. His record of playing in the Dublin leagues for over forty years was honoured by the League Council in 1963 when he was a special guest of honour at the League finalists dinner and ball. He was recognised as the person most associated with the club for the greater part of the 20th century. At 85, when the tennis racquet was resting, he was on the Bank of Ireland team that won the I.B.O.A. competition in Belfast. That was in 1982. Some of his memories are as follows:

I joined the club in 1921. At the time there were four grass courts and one hard court, No.3, made of asphalt and showing signs of wear. Shortly after I became a member, it was decided to dig it up and a new grass court was sown. The new court always remained slightly harder than the adjoining courts.

On 'At Home' days a marquee was erected on Court 5. This day was a great social occasion and ices, when they were just coming into vogue, were provided by Mills the Caterers in big tubs packed with ice to keep them from melting.

Although the Club membership was small, the standard of play was high. As I was anxious for competitive play, I had the temerity to challenge a member of the 2nd team for his place. This match I duly won but was hardly off court before I was challenged in my turn, by, then university students, Gilbert Webb and George Robinson and finally A.H. Seale all in a matter of days. Having successfully held my place I was thereafter left in peace but this shows how keen members were to get on teams. I moved up to the first team in 1925, the year I won the Club Championship for the 1st time.

The **Conway sisters**, Norah and Phyllis, each won the club championships five times and were on the first ladies team that reached the Class I league finals in both 1936 and 1942. Phyllis was chosen to play for Leinster in 1936 and Norah a year later. Their championship successes included the Irish Close, both singles and doubles. Further details on their highly successful careers are given in chapter 6. 1964 was an interesting year. Norah, playing with Geoff Trapnell won the club mixed title. Phyllis, who was now Mrs. McFerran, was to see her daughter Ruth win the club singles. In the ladies doubles Norah and Phyllis now faced a much younger generation and beat Ruth and Leonora McFarran, Phyllis's daughters, in the final. Age and experienced counted and they were winning their fifth doubles title together in '29 years'. It might be pointed out that Ruth and Leonora were both useful players, having won this title in 1962. Norah would remember the 1930s clearly.

My chief recollection of playing in the League for Glenageary in the 1930s was that we started our matches at 2.30 or 3 o'clock at the latest, and that certain clubs would not play after 6 o'clock as their members were always giving dinner parties or going as guests to them. At least half the Glenageary team served underarm, and as a teenager when I first played for the Club I never used their Christian names. At least three times we were in the final of Class I.

Glenageary LTC ladies (Circa 1930)

Glenageary Lawn Tennis Club ladies' third team won Class IV of the Dublin leagues in 1949. Back (l. to r.): Mrs. C. H. Maidment, Mrs. S. Pringle & Mrs. Ina O'Farrell. Front (l. to r.): Mrs. S. Keady, Dr. K. Bayne & Mrs. Joyce Brewster. (Absent: Miss P. Carte).

Glenageary LTC 1920. Club's second team were runners-up in the Dublin leagues. Back (l. to r.): V. Price, G. T. Foley & T. C. Booth. Front (l. to r.): Freddie Gick, H. Exshaw & C. S. Collins (?)

Class III winners in the Dublin leagues in 1946 were the men's second team from Glenageary LTC. Back (l. to r.): Derek Snow, Kevin Keenan & B. C. Travers. Front (l. to r.): A. Orr, Jackie Brewster & N. Cardwell.

Richard Hamilton and Sally Fildes won the club mixed championships in 1979, 1981 & 1982

Men's First Team 1923 (Class 2 Winners). Back (l. to r.) G. Robinson, W.W. Woods & Claude Exshaw. Front (l. to. r.) Noel Staples, Charlie Mitchell & Freddie Gick.

The 1984 team winners at Wexford. From left: Douglas Burns, Lynn Spillane, Ollie Barry, Erica Dempsey, Jeneen Carter, Nicola Barr & David Spillane.

The History of Irish Tennis

Glenageary LTC
Ladies 1st team 1968
Class 2 Winners
Back (l. to r.)
Maeve O'Doherty,
Pat McIlwaine,
Sue Brewster.
Front (l. to. r.)
ZoePhilips,
Ruth McFerran
& Beryl Brady

Glenageary LTC Ladies'
3rd team 1985
Class IV Winners
Back (l. to r.):
Heather Burgess,
Catherine Healy
& Yvonne Brady.
Front (l. to r.):
Cherry Thompson,
Ann Ward &
Janeen Carter.

Glenageary Lawn Tennis Club Championships

Year	Men's Champion	Year	Ladies' Champion
1892	R. S. Dobbin		
1893	R. S. Dobbin		
1894	F. C. Newland		Sally Fildes
1896	A. H. Shea		(nee Falkner)
1897	A. H. Shea		Club Champion
1898	A. H. Shea		1967
1909	G. T. Foley		1970
1910	C. H. Mitchell		1971
1911	A. V. McCormick		1972
1912	Paddy Coll		1975
1913	Harry Maunsell		1976
1914	Noel Staples		1977
1919	Noel Staples		1980
1920	R. De Courcy Wheeler		1981
1921	A. V. McCormick		
1922	Noel Staples	1913, 1914	Mrs. H. Newton
1923	Noel Staples	1919, 1920, 1921	Miss Norah Barton
1924	A. V. Perrin	1922	Mrs. N. Fry
1925	Fred Homan	1923	Miss Norah Barton
1926	R. De Courcy Wheeler	1924, 1925	Miss Hilda Hollwey
1927	G. F. West	1926, 1927	Miss Norah Barton
1928	Seymour Webb	1928, 1929	Miss Hilda Hollwey
1929	O. A. M. Easton	1930	Miss Phyllis Conway
1930	L. C. Wilson	1931	Miss Norah Barton
1931	Pierse MacDermott	1932	Miss Norah Conway
1932	Fred Homan	1933, 1934	Miss Phyllis Conway
1933	Fred Homan	1935	Miss Norah Conway
1934, 1935, 1936	Pierse MacDermott	1936	Miss Phyllis Conway
1937	Fred Homan	1937, 1938	Miss Pat Acheson
1938	Colin Maidment	1939	Miss Norah Conway
1939	W. H. G. Robinson	1940	Miss Phyllis Conway
1940, 1941	Fred Homan	1941, 1942	Miss Norah Conway
1942	Pierse MacDermott	1943	Miss Evie McGlaughry
1943	Colin Maidment	1944, 1945, 1946, 1947, 1948	Mrs. Eileen Trapnell
1944, 1945	Pierse MacDermott	1949	Miss Cecily Draper
1946	Fred Homan	1950	Miss Pat Acheson
1947, 1948	Colin Maidment	1951	Phyllis McFerran (nee Conway)
1949	Dan O'Connell Miley	1952	Mrs. P. O'Brien
1950	N. Cardwell	1953	Phyllis McFerran (nee Conway)
1951	G. G. Moore	1954	Miss Cecily Draper
1952	Des Lacey	1955, 1956	Mrs. Eileen Trapnell
1953, 1954	G. G. Moore	1957	Miss Cecily Draper
1955, 1956, 1957, 1958	Des Lacey	1958	Mrs. Eileen Trapnell
1959	Ken McComas	1959	Mrs. O. E. Briggs
1960	Des Lacey	1960	Phyllis McFerran (nee Conway)
1961	R. Scott	1961, 1962, 1963	Mrs. Jean Marks
1962, 1963	Ken McComas	1964	Miss Ruth McFerran
1964	J. Henderson	1965	Mrs. Jean Marks
1965	D. V. McCowen	1966	Mrs. Maeve O'Doherty
1966	R. Anderson	1967	Miss Sally Falkner
1967, 1968, 1969, 1970	Bobby Blakeney	1968	Miss Ruth McFerran
1971	R. Widger	1969	Mrs. Pat Love
1972	Bobby Blakeney	1970, 1971, 1972	Sally Fildes (nee Falkner)
1973, 1974	Finbar Sheehan	1973, 1974	Mrs. Maeve O'Doherty
1975, 1976	Richard Hamilton	1975, 1976, 1977	Sally Fildes (nee Falkner)
1977	John Fleuury	1978, 1979	Mrs. Maeve O'Doherty
1978, 1979, 1980, 1981	Myles Downey	1980, 1981	Sally Fildes (nee Falkner)
1982, 1983	Paul Kirwan	1982	Mrs. Pat Love
1984	S. Lunt	1983	Miss Anne Hall
1985	David Rafferty	1984, 1985	Miss Elizabeth McKeever
1986	Bobby Hassett	1986	Mrs. Pat Love

The History of Irish Tennis

The husband and wife combination of **Geoff and Eileen Trapnell** were not alone excellent tennis players but both achieved interprovincial honours in badminton. They joined the club in 1939 and won the mixed championships in 1944. Eileen won the club singles championships eight times, and the ladies' doubles ten times, between 1943 and 1958. Between 1942 and 1950, Geoff won the men's doubles five times. He was a substitute on the Irish badminton team and became a top administrator in that sport (see chapter 6). His memories of the 1940s included the following:

The first four men, in varying order, were Fred Homan, Pierce MacDermott, Colin Maidment and Billy Robinson. The first three used to share the Club Championships and were very evenly matched. Freddie was a very canny base line (sic) player and woe betide you if you went to the net on a short shot. Pierce, a left hander was a clever and stylish all court player while Colin depended mainly on his good service and excellent net play. Billy Robinson...was rarely defeated in league play. The championship men's singles and doubles events were always the best of five sets. The top men played each other very regularly and on almost every day of the week except Fridays, the rest day. There was no Sunday play in those days.

A number of members played in the various local open tournaments such as the East of Ireland at Lansdowne, the Co. Wicklow at Bray and the Co. Dublin at Carrickmines. My favourite was the Bray tournament played on excellent firm grass courts in a beautiful scenic situation before house building spoilt the views. During the War and immediately after we would cycle to and from Bray.

It was rarely that the Club membership reached 100 and Junior play was almost non-existent. There was nothing like the great activity in the Club as there is now.

During the War years, tennis balls were hard to come by, but Dunlops took back old balls and sent them to their Cork factory for refurbishing. This consisted of reinflating them and putting new covers on them. Some of them were very lively which helped strong servers. However, it was a great service by Dunlops and helped to keep the game going.

One of my earliest memories was playing challenge matches with Max Falkner, Sally Fieldes' father. We always had three long sets and it was a toss up who would win. Several members of the Club were also good badminton players...and as a result our doubles play was often better than our singles.

Dorothy Owens (nee Eaton) was a member for many years as was her father, Oscar (from 1928). Her mother had been a member of the De Vesci Gardens club. She and her brother, Denis, played in the club events in the 1940s, winning the mixed club championship together in 1943. She won the same event in 1945 with J. S. Brewster. In the ladies doubles

she won the championships twice, with Eileen Trapnell. (1944 and 1945).

Table tennis was played in the pavilion during the 1940s. And of course the ubiquitous tea day was held-was it on a Thursday? There was elegant sartorial style on the day of the tournament finals. Cups and prizes were laid out on a black covered table at the rear end of No. 3 court.

Personalities came to mind: Dr. Maunsell, with his panama hat circled by a black petersham band, his trousers held up by a leather belt and his Pekinese waiting patiently on the back window of his car- a baby Austin. Freddie Homan, forever handicapped by some recent injury, but always winning in the end; his endless duels with Pierce Mc Dermott with ensuing post-mortems will not easily be forgotten.

Finbarr Sheehan was club champion in 1973 and 1974. However, his first memory of the club was back in the mid-1950s when he was playing for the **Longford Gardens LTC** against **Glenageary LTC** in a league match. The following speaks for itself.

The name of my rather elderly opponent escapes me but it was level pegging after two long gruelling sets (tie-breakers had not been invented). My opponent and I were resting on a garden seat before attempting the final joust when to my astonishment a lady club member appeared with some stately chinaware, a pot of tea and a plenitude of cucumber sandwiches and home-made sandwich cake. The game was over two and a half hours old at this point and with a potential extra hour in prospect, we demolished the repast with gay abandon. I will never know whether it was method within madness or not but I lost the final set 6-0 in about 9 minutes.

My first impression of Glenageary was one of a club with an ambience of seclusion and serenity; and it was not just my immaturity (or the whims of impressionable youth), because when I joined as a member at the beginning of the 1970s I found the atmosphere just the same. If anything it was somewhat a little more quaint as the era of the big modern club was coming on the scene.

The 1940;'s were a problem of cash and players for many clubs. Membership had fallen off and the club had a deficit of £25 when the 1943 AGM was held at the Mad Hatter Teashop on the Dun Laoghaire seafront. *..the minds of those present were focussed, not on the events of Stalingrad, Western Europe, the western desert of the Pacific.* An EGM followed and the subscription was raised by 5/- and the 'free teas' on Thursdays were abolished. Tennis balls and tea were in short supply. The Ministry of Supplies had refused to allow the club tea rations and what tea the members had put by was burgled from the clubhouse.

In 1953 the club lost the loved grounds man of 37 years, Larry Brady. Two years later, Colin Maidment died. He had been the honorary secretary at the club since 1931, and club champion in 1938, 1943, 1947 and 1948. In his annual report at the 1954 AGM he was aware of the need for change:

....new members are few and far between and even the ladies' membership, which had always been full over the last twenty five years, and for many years before that, is below the full number, whilst the men's membership has reached the perilously low figure of 24-The time has come when members must make an effort to recruit new members and to make the Club attractive to them, if we wish the Club to survive. We need young members, who will bring in other young people and so give the Club a future, which it will not have unless steps are taken to right the position. Empty courts, day after day, and enthusiasm confined to a few members, will not attract new members, and worse still, may even cause the few enthusiasts to seek their entertainment elsewhere. In 1939 the courts were so crowded that it was not possible to play more than a set at a time...those conditions...were better and healthier than the present state.

Ways of raising money were decided to not just make ends meet but to develop the club. An interesting one implemented was the showing, at monthly internals, film of the post-coronation royal tour, in the local St. Paul's parochial hall. A silver collection was taken up on each occasion. Don't forget that television was not available in Ireland at that time and the cinema was a thriving form of entertainment. In the 1960s a low point was reached when the men's second team had to be withdrawn from the league due to an inability to field this team. The club eventually turned to hard courts (1980-1983), which was to be an aid to an increasingly active junior group of players. The first

floodlights were installed during the winter of 1985-1986. In 1970 Sunday play had come into operation as it was felt that *Sunday opening might be an attraction for younger members.* The club made a major move in 1975 with a move to purchase the freehold for £1500, developments could then progress. By the centenary year, 1987, there had been a senior membership increase up to a limit of 274 and junior up to 140. A sign of changing times is a distinct emphasis on juniors and their development within the club. In 1986, Bobby Hassett, a junior at the time, won the club senior championships and juniors Jonathan Dodd and Glenn Kealy took the men's doubles title. The club could look forward to a new century with some satisfaction.

Pat Love (formerly McIlwaine) and Anne Hall (now MacBride) met in the Club Ladies Singles Final in 1983. Anne was the champion. Pat won the title in 1982 and 1986.

	Some Tennis Highlights at Glenageary Lawn Tennis Club.
1888	First annual club championships; first 'At Home' day.
	Early Men's Singles Winners: R.S. Dobbin (1892,1893,1895), F.C. Newland (1894), A.H. Shea (1896-1898)
1909	Men win Class II of Dublin leagues.
1911	Men win Class III of Dublin leagues.
1914	Men win Class II of Dublin leagues beating Wilton LTC 5/4 in the final
1906-14	Harry Maunsell wins 27 out of 38 league matches in this period.
1919	Ladies win Class II of Dublin leagues beating Lansdowne LTC in the final
1920	Ladies win Class II of Dublin leagues and are promoted to Class II for first time.
1922-23	Men win Class II of Dublin leagues for two successive years and are promoted to Class I.
1924	Former member, Shirley Dillon, plays for Ireland in Davis Cup match.
1936	Phyllis Conway first selected to play for Leinster and was ranked number 4 in Ireland in 1939.
1937	Norah Conway first selected to play for Leinster and was ranked number 4 in Ireland in 1949/1950.
1946	Men win Class II of Dublin leagues.
1949	Ladies win Class IV of Dublin leagues.
1964	Ladies win Class II and Class IV of the Dublin leagues. The Conway sisters win the ladies doubles club championships, first won by them in 1935.
1968	Ladies win Class II of Dublin leagues.
1975	Ladies win Class IV of Dublin leagues.
1988	Men's Over 45 team win Dublin league Class 2 beating Deerpark TC 2/1in the final.
1992	Men's Over 50 team win Dublin league Class 2 beating Clontarf in the final.
1997	Class 3 team win Dublin Winter league; Ladies Over 35 win Class 5 of Dublin league.
1998	Ladies Over 35 win Class 2 of Dublin league.
1999	Men's Over 35 win Class 3 of Dublin league; Boys Under 14 team win Class 2 of Junior league.

Glenageary LTC 1975. Ladies' third team won the Class IV Dublin league. Back (l. to r.): Mrs. B. McStay, Mrs. R. Horgan & Mrs. M. Fitzgerald. Front (l. to r.): Miss H. Mitchell, Miss G. Trapnell & Miss Anne Hall.

First team, Runners-Up Class I League in 1936. Back (l. to r.) Miss E. Robinson, NorahBarton, Pat Acheson. Front (l. to r.): Nora Conway, Phyllis Conway, Miss. J. Carroll.

Junior Club Winners in 1986. Back (l. to r.) Adrienne Fitzsimons, Julie Sheridan, Alison Clarke, Orla O' Doherty, Stephen Dunphy (hidden), Suzanne Fitzsimons, Pearse McDowell, Jonathan Dodd & Glenn Kealy. Front (l. to r.) Caragh McDowell, Barry Dunphy, Richard Donnelly, Conor Groarke & Stuart McGovern.

The History of Irish Tennis

Banbridge Lawn Tennis Club
(Founded Circa 1890)

This is one of the oldest clubs in Ulster. In 1891, the Ulster Lawn Tennis Association offered a cup for a knockout competition between clubs in the province. **Banbridge LTC** was the inaugural winner.

****

Mount Temple Lawn Tennis Club
(Founded Circa 1890)

It is only estimated that the club was founded in 1890. In 1891 they would win the Fitzwilliam Cup (Second Class) and be narrowly beaten in the same event (4/5) by **Lansdowne LTC** in 1893. In 1894, they met the Fitzwilliam second team in the final and won 6/3. They were promoted to the First Class (senior) Cup competition in 1895 and lost to **Lansdowne LTC** 5/4 in the semi-finals. There were only four teams in this class at the time. The other two were **Fitzwilliam LTC** and **Dublin University LTC**. The club champion in 1893 was W. Martin in 1893 and 1894. G. F. Carruthers was runner-up in both years. He was probably a relative of Louisa Martin the highly successful lady player of that era.

Club Championships 1894		
Event	1st Prize	2nd Prize
MS	W. Martin	G.F. Carruthers
MHS	W. Rogers	J.M. Thompson
LHS	Miss M. Johnson	Miss Bryan
MHD	G.F. Carruthers/ S.L. Fry	C. Ryan/ C. Piggott
LHD	Miss M. Johnson/ Miss D. Johnson	Miss Birmingham/ Miss B. Henshaw
MxHD	S. L.Fry/ Miss F. Henshaw	W.K. Rogerson/ Miss M. Johnson

Open Tournament Mount Temple Lawn Tennis Club		
Event	1st Prize	2nd Prize
	1894	
MHS	R.G. Hunt	William St. G. Perrott
LHS	Miss. M. Johnson	Miss Bryan
MHD	William St. G. Perrott/ W. Posnett	C. Carr/ A.B. Irwin
LHD	Miss M. Johnson/ Miss D. Johnson	Miss Birmingham/ Miss B. Henshaw
MxHD	William St. G. Perrott/Miss "Herbert" divided with S. L. Fry/Miss M. Henshaw	

Dundrum Lawn Tennis Club
(Founded pre 1891)

It is likely that the famous Hamilton sporting family played at this club in the 19th century. Blaney Hamilton, an *international Cricket and Tennis player,* lived here. He was born in 1872 and lived at Dundrum Castle, County Dublin. His brother Willoughby, born in 1864, who lived at Herbert Hill, Dundrum, was Wimbledon Champion in 1890. Other Hamilton people and stories are dealt with elsewhere in the book. The club was an affiliated one in 1911. It is not mentioned in the handbooks of 1894 and 1895 perhaps because, in the early days, it was a private court on which a local group of people played but was not an organised club as such.

****

Mitchelstown Lawn Tennis Club
(Founded Circa 1891)

The 1894 Irish handbook refers to the tournament at Mitchelstown as having had record entries in 1893. The club was one of the first to be affiliated to the ILTA in 1908 and was still holding sanctioned tournaments up to the early 1920s. Activity seemed to have dropped for a number of years thereafter. In the 1970s it was obvious that there was plenty of juniors playing at the club. Coaching in 1979 was in great demand with 65 juniors participating, and that was just in the under 12 category. Greg Morris was the popular visiting coach and this bore fruits when there were many wins throughout the province from under 10 to under 18. Particularly successful were Paul Holland (winner of the Munster and Irish Close under 14 titles) and Kieran Cotter who won the Irish Close under 12 title. Paul was the number 1 player on the Munster team in the interprovincials at Clongowes Wood College and Margaret Casey was selected on the under 16 side. Other juniors to feature during the year were Siobhan Hyland, David Holland, Kieran Cotter and Aidan Cotter.

Successful juniors Mitchelstown LTC in 1978. Back (l. to r.): Karen Herlihy, David Holland & Margaret Casey.Front (l. to r.): Kieran Cotter, Paul Holland, Claire Skinner & Catherine O'Keeffe.

Some of the successful juniors at Mitchelstown LTC in 1979

The 1980 ILTA Yearbook reported that *The adults also enjoyed the season albeit in a more leisurely fashion than the juniors! We had some very enjoyable Inter-Club Competitions and the season culminated with a very successful "Delaney Day" Open American Tournament in September. This attracted a large entry from clubs from the Counties Limerick, Cork and Tipperary and we hope to make it an annual event.*

Open Tournament Mitchelstown LTC		
Event	**1st Prize**	**2nd Prize**
1893		
MHS	S.W. Moore	
LHS	Miss Browne	
MHD	H. Scott/W. H.Bredir	
MxHD	J. D. Bredin/Miss Cooper-Chadwick	
1894		
MHS	W.E. O'Brien	S.W. Moore
LHS	Miss Bagley	Miss Browne
MHD	A.D. & S.W. Moore	H. Scott/J. Price

****

Lucan Lawn Tennis Club
[Founded Circa 1891]

It is not known for certain when this club was formed. However in the *Lawn Tennis* issue of September 16 1896 there is a report of the fifth annual open 'meeting' that took place in the first week of September. Perhaps this club is even older. A few notes from that report are appropriate. The grounds were described as being *picturesquely situated* and *adjoining the Lucan Hydropathic.* Hydropathy, being the use of water (internally and externally) in the treatment of disease and abnormal physical conditions, suggests the club was near some 'health springs' or baths.

The weather was most favourable during the week, and each day a large number of spectators from the Metropolis went to see the play. Although the entries were not quite as numerous as last year, the standard of play was much higher, and the committee appointed to frame the handicaps have every reason to feel proud of their efforts. Among the entries were players from **Fitzwilliam LTC, Lansdowne LTC, Donnybrook LTC, Dublin University LTC,**

Roscrea LTC, Carlow LTC and Middle Temple (presumably Mount Temple LTC).

****

Open Tournament
Lucan LTC

Event	1st Prize	2nd Prize
1893		
MHS	A.W. Posnett	
LHS	Mrs. Waskey	
MHD	H. Maguire/F. Egan	
MxHD	F.E. & Mrs. Bird	
1894		
MHS	P.A. Brown	S. Harrison
LHS	Miss M. Power	Mrs. Bird
MHD	P.A.Brown/D.Ross	F. &. F.L. O' Carroll
LHD	Miss Armstrong/ Miss "Elizabeth"	Mrs. Bird/ Miss Warren
MxHD	-O'Carroll/Mrs. Bird	

****

County Westmeath Lawn Tennis Club
(Founded 1892)

This midlands club, situated in the town of Mullingar, was quick to run regular open tournaments and, being on the railway line, was accessible. The honorary secretary in 1894 and 1895 was H. W. Lloyd.

The first handbook on Irish tennis was published in 1894 and gave the results for Irish tennis tournaments for 1893. In a surprisingly long list of events the following were the finalists at the County Westmeath club open tournaments in Mullingar in 1893 and 1894.

Open Tournament
County Westmeath LTC

Event	1st Prize	2nd Prize
1893		
MHS	W.R. Clark	- Bowen
MHD	W.R. Clark/ Count E.A.O'Byrne	-Kirkwood/ Captain Ritchie
MxHD	W.R.Featherson-H./ Miss Scott	R.H. Bond/ Mrs.Featherston-H.
1894		
MHS	A.S. Kirkwood	-Fetherston-H
MHD	A.S. Kirkwood/ P.O'Reilly	-Fetherston-H./ -Barton

This club was still functioning, with grass courts, until the 1960s. The nearby Mullingar Town Tennis Club was founded in 1939 and was in the ascendancy at that time while the old 'gentry' type club could not survive because of decreasing membership numbers.

****

Cliftonville Lawn Tennis Club
(Founded Circa 1892)

North of Ireland Championships
Cliftonville LTC

Event	1st Prize	2nd Prize
1893		
MS	Manliffe F. Goodbody	
MHS	A. H. Porter divided with	W.G. "St. George"
LS	Miss Shaw	
LHS	Miss M. Hamilton	
MD	Manliffe F. Goodbody/Ernest Renshaw	
LHD	Miss Shaw/Miss Corder	
MxHD	W. G. "St. George"/Miss Corder	
1894		
MS	A.H. Porter	D. Payn
MHS	W.R. Carson	H. Walker
LS	Miss Shaw	Miss F. Carr
LHS	Miss R. Carr	Miss F. Carr
MD	A.H. Porter/ W. "St. George"	D.R. Payn/ H. Tubber
MHD	O.R. M'Mullen/ S.H. Hughes	W.R. Carson/ H. Armytage Moore
LHD	Miss Nelson/ Miss E. Carr	Miss Platt-Higgins/ Mrs. Clarke
MxHD	D. R. Payn Miss Platt-Higgins	O. R. M'Mullen/ Miss E. Carr

While this club seems to have died out many years ago, it did have an early start. Interestingly, they were the first northern club to hold a 'major' championship. Whether this was deemed excessive or not at the time appears irrelevant. It did attract good support from various parts of the island. Note the winning pair in the Men's Championship Doubles (MD) of 1893 included none other than Englishman, Ernest Renshaw, the winner of many Irish and Wimbledon Championships. His partner was no slouch either. Manliffe Francis Goodbody would reach the final of the US Championships the following year. The only Irishman to achieve this distinction. One wonders did he beat Renshaw when winning the Championship Singles at this tournament? It was called the North of Ireland Championships, the predecessor to the Ulster Championships that were to take place, from 1919 onwards, at the Belfast Boat Club.

In 1893 the club were to be the third holders of the Ulster Inter-Club Cup competition. In the final they beat **Banbridge LTC**, the inaugural winners of the event organised by the Ulster Lawn Tennis Association in 1891. The winning club in 1892 was **Clones LTC**.

****

Ennis Lawn Tennis and Badminton Club
(Founded Circa 1892)

Situated by the Fergus River and near the town centre, the Ennis club has a history going further back than first thought. The present club is, in fact an amalgamation of three clubs. The original club was known as the **County Clare LTC.** This was a gentry type club of the 19th century and relied upon the well to do, and possibly professionals, for its membership base. According to one article the riverside location today was where the club established itself in 1917. Was this the original club or a new one, we might never know. Like many clubs of its ilk survival was a problem. Ultimately, in about 1950, the club invited the **Fergus LTC to** join or amalgamate with it. The latter had been successfully in operation on the Cusack Road since about 1935. It had four grass courts and a large timber pavilion, painted red and green. The amalgamated club thrived at the old 'County' site beside the Fergus River. It became commonly known at the **Ennis LTC.**

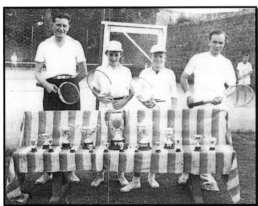

Ennis Open Tennis Championships in 1955. From left Sean Moriarty, John Breen, Liam Cahir and Michael Conlon.

One further change in title took place in 1982. The club had been going through a lean period in the 1970s. A former club champion, Father Sean Moriarty, held the club above water. The river regularly flooded the two clay courts and car park and membership was low. There were several attempts to buy out the valuable site. In 1982 he agreed that the club would amalgamate with the local badminton club – they had a large membership but no home of their own. This partnership led to a huge transformation. Two badminton courts were constructed in a new clubhouse. Three new tennis courts were constructed and floodlighting installed. Perimeter fencing was erected and the car park elevated to avoid further flooding. By 2000, the club had five tennis courts, three hard and two all-weather *Omni* courts. Future developments involve further lighting and all-weather surfaces on the remaining courts. For those that know their badminton the club has had a series of successes including the producing of players of international standing in the 1990s. Donie O' Halloran, now based in Dublin, became the first senior badminton international to learn his game in this County Clare

club. The club has become the HQ for the Clare Badminton Association and runs many open tournaments in this sport.

Early Days

In 1894 the first Handbook on Lawn Tennis in Ireland showed that the club was one of only ten in Munster at the time. There would have been a number of tennis playing centres but only a small number of organised clubs. This was a time before the ILTA was formed. Open tournaments held in Munster in 1894 were at Waterford, Glanmire, County Clare, Carrick on Suir, Rushbrooke, Mitchelstown, Mallow, Roscrea and Fermoy. These were the clubs. The missing one from the tournament list is Limerick Lawn TC. They in fact had held their first open tournament as early as 1877, a few weeks after the first Wimbledon. Perhaps they were going through a lean period in the 1890s. The County Clare open tournament winners in 1893 were:

Open Tournament County Clare LTC	
Event	**1st Prize**
1893	
Men's Handicap Singles	H. Crowe
Ladies Handicap Singles	Miss M. Simms
Men's Handicap Doubles	H. Crowe/G. Greer
Ladies Handicap Doubles	Misses A. & M. Simms
Mixed Handicap Doubles	H. Crowe/Miss Bomford

In August 1944 the Fergus LTC, under the guidance of Tom Walsh, sent four boys to 'Fitz Week'. These were, standing, Cyril Cuddy and Noel Cassidy (on right). Front (from left) brothers Tom and Larry Byrne.

Reunion

In July 2000, a large gathering of 'oldies' gathered in Ennis to recall the past, play some tennis and have a social and memorable trip down memory lane. Players and former members travelled from the USA, Great Britain, Hong Kong, The West Indies and Australia to Ennis They joined up with home based former members to have a reunion of the **Fergus LTC.** It was an idea hatched in a conversation between Jerry Cahir, Sean Donlon and Ghislaine de Regge. With Jerry at the lead, and *through Ghislaine's vision, enthusiasm and encouragement,* a fine booklet on the club's history was pieced together and former members were tracked down. While the majority of the players seemed to have been from the active 1950s and 1960s there was just as much enthusiasm from those of the 1940s. Many stories were written for the booklet on topics varying from 'hops' to visits to Fitzwilliam (when the members sponsored some juniors to travel to the August championships) to competitions to amalgamations. Contributors to the stories were Noel Cassidy, Jerry Cahir, D. Travers, Tom Mannion, Ghislaine de Regge, John Gallagher, Sinead Spellissey, Kevin Merry and Oliver Moylan. A few of the memories are quoted in various chapters in the book. Noel Cassidy would recall the time he with Tommy Byrne, Larry Byrne and Cyril Cuddy were sent to the Irish Junior Championships at **Fitzwilliam LTC.** *All expenses were paid by the club. It was a wonderful week. We did well for country boys.* While Mick Coleman was the number one player for a long time, others came along, these juniors being among them.

A good player, Fr. Sean Moriarty was a key club member in the survival of tennis in 1950s Ennis. From left: Fr. Sean Moriarty, Frankie Cassidy & Diver McNamara (grounds man).

Junior Tournament (Circa 1957) at Fergus LTC.

Getting the courts ready (mid 1950s)

Happy junior tennis players in Ennis (early 1950s. From left: Ann Marie Walsh, T. J. Cahir, Griffin brothers & Elizabeth Moylan.

Ennis 1950s. Note the wooden frames-a necessary clamp to prevent racquet warp. From left; Jimmy Monaghan, Mary Duggan, Bobby O'Brien, Joe Moloney, Elizabeth Moylan and Ann Mahon.

Overlooking the Fergus River to the present day tennis club in Ennis, County Clare.

Junior players at Fergus Lawn Tennis Club (1950s). Back (l. to r.): B. Quinlivan, Liam Cahir, Fiachra Duffy, Fergus Walsh, John Breen & John Blackwell. Middle (l. to r.): Ghislaine de Regge, Nesta McCarthy, Ann O'Donoghue, Alanna Wilson & Antoinette Nolan. Front (l. to r.): Ruth Wallace, John Carroll, Ann Marie Walsh, Michael Goucho (an annual French visitor), Mary Duggan & Joe Moloney.

The Fergus Lawn Tennis Clin (Circa 1938). Photograph taken on the 3rd court with Bank of Ireland Building in the background. Standing (l. to r.): unknown, Paddy Gallagher, unknown, Mick Coleman, Jack Quirke (hurled for County Clare and won a county hurling championship with Ennis in 1941), Larry O'Donoghue, Miss Kerins (the Copper Jung), Jerry Ryan, Mr. Cassidy (father of Noel) & Dinny O'Halloran. Sitting (l. to r.): Nellie McMahon, Frank O'Connell, unknown, Jack McCarthy, Mrs. McCarthy, unknown, Mai Murphy, Imelda Hickey (Clarecastle), Bill Bluett, unknown & Kathleen Kerins (the Copper Jung). Kneeling at front is Noel Cassidy who proved to be one of the best players in the region in the 1940s and 1950s, he won the club championships in 1946 and 1947.

22nd & 23rd July 2000. The Ennis Reunion. From left: John Duggan, Ghislaine de Regge, John Gallagher, Angela McCarthy, Brian Maurer and Jerry Cahir.

The History of Irish Tennis

A 1950s group of Winners at Ennis. Front (l. to r.) Christina Hurley, Mary McInerney, Fiacra Duffy, Tom Mannion Maire Rua McMahon and Antonette Nolan. Back (l. to r.) Noreen Smith, Mary Duggan, John Carroll, Frankie Cassidy, Liam Cahir and John Breen.

Championship presentation (circa 1950) at Ennis.

The 1945 Senior Club Championship Final at Fergus LTCl. From left: Noel Cassidy (16), Bill Bluett and Cyril Cuddy (18). Cyril won 7/5 7/5 6/4. Noel would take the title in 1946 and 1947.

Action at Ennis in 1997

****

Castle View Lawn Tennis Club
[Carrick on Suir LTC]
(Founded 1893)

The club was referred to as **Carrick on Suir LTC** in the inaugural Irish handbook of 1894.

Open Tournament Carrick-on-Suir LTC	
Event	1st Prize
	1893
Men's H'cap S	W.P. Black
Ladies H'cap S	Miss O. Whyte
Men's H'cap D	D.G. Ottley/H.S. Darley
Ladies H'cap D	Mrs.Kirkwood/Miss O. Whyte
Mixed H'cap D	H.T. Gordon/Mrs. Ottley

According to a 1980 article in the ILTA Yearbook tennis has been played at the same site in Carrick on Suir since 1893, in the shadow of the historic Ormonde Castle, the only Tudor Manor in Ireland. The club originally consisted of three grass courts and a small timber pavilion. It was also a croquet club. Initially it was used by British Army personnel and their friends. The first elected honorary secretary was Thomas Bunker and honorary treasurer Richard Dooley. The original gentry-class and military members gradually accepted professional and business people. In the 1920s with the formation of the Free State the latter began to dominate and run the club. It became generally open in the 1930s. The club closed in 1939 and reformed in 1945 after the war when the present club name was established. A fourth grass court was added and by 1968, when the grounds were bought outright, there had been a new pavilion constructed (in 1958) with water and electricity.

By 1979 the debts had been paid off and three hard courts were constructed. This was later increased to four with floodlighting added. The most noted

The History of Irish Tennis

The 1979 presentation to Mary Kelly who was honorary secretary at Castleview LTC for 33 years (1945 to 1978) by Dr. Paul O'Brien (vice-president). Also in photograph are Michael Lonergan (honorary treasurer), Patrick Burke (president), Noel Treacy (committee) and Gerard Cleary (captain).

Castleview Lawn Tennis Club (circa 1960)

Club team (late 1950s). Back (l. to r.): Dr. Paul O'Brien, Michael Clery, Gerry Cleary & Tom Cleary. Front: (l. to r.): Miss K. Phelan, Mrs. B. Dowley, Miss E. Murphy & Mrs. Maureen Cleary.

Jerry Moran (left) and Tom Cleary at Castleview LTC, Carrick-on-Suir in 1948. (In 1980, Jerry's widow Bernadette married Tom's widowed brother, Michael).

Castleview Lawn Tennis Club team photograph (Circa 1962). Back (l. to r.): Fred Nagle, brothers Gerry, Michael & Tom Cleary. Front (l. to r.): Joan Nagle, Maureen Cleary, Margaret Galvin & Eleanor Murphy.

member over the years was probably Gerry Cleary who played in Junior Wimbledon in 1957. However, it was his older brother Tom that first came to the fore as a very good player, reaching the Irish Junior Open final in 1948. Tom won the South of Ireland in 1953, beating the notable Dublin player Harry Crowe in a five-set final. Noel Treacy was a Munster Council delegate for fifteen years and became its president in 1968. Other representatives to the branch committee from the club included Tom Kennedy, Stephanie Cleary Keating and Michael Lonergan. The latter was editor of the Munster Tennis News for a period. In the 1990s Eileen Skelly was another member to achieve interprovincial status.

****

Roscrea Lawn Tennis Club
[Ashbury Lawn Tennis Club]
(Founded Circa 1893)

This Tipperary club was one of the oldest in Munster and seems to have died out some time ago. In 1896 at least one Roscrea player played at the **Lucan LTC** in County Dublin. Among the early players were the Read family, Harry becoming an international tennis player. He probably learned the game at the home court at Dungar House. He also played at St. Columba's College, Dublin and for Trinity College Dublin. Years later his son Peter played for the club and, with others, travelled all over Munster for tournaments.

Roscrea's Harry Read played in four sports for Ireland. Here, about 80 years ago he is serving at his home grass court at Dungar House.

Tennis at Roscrea in the early part of the 20th century.

In 1914, the club was affiliated to the ILTA and was running the Championships of Munster (Men's and Ladies Singles). They had about 80 members at the time. This event was still being held in the club in the 1920s, the Championships of Munster Men's Doubles being added to the programme. In 1939, the tournament, which started on the 24th July, was tied in with the Irish Close Championships. The Munster Mixed title was also part of that programme.

Secretary and that the club was still functioning. The club's name does not appear in the 1967 or 1974 yearbooks. The club's ground had been leased and it is known that there was some attempt to have a club operating by playing in the local school. Today the Roscrea tennis club is no more.

****

Moate Lawn Tennis Club
(Founded 1893)

A note on this club on the 13th March 1893 suggests that it was founded in that year. The grounds were situated near the Fair Green on the road to the railway station. It was being laid out and poled and there were some sixty members in that year. The committee included Stoppford Halpin as honorary treasurer-he was a banker- and William Clibborn as the honorary treasurer. The ordinary members of the committee were E.H. Winder (detective inspector, R.I.C.), F.W. Russell junior, Arthur C. Daly and Doctor H. Moorehead. According to the local newspaper report at the time the club *prided themselves on exclusivity.*

****

Donnybrook Lawn Tennis Club
(Founded 1893)

There are a number of clubs in Ireland that not alone have had a long history but one both successful in terms of social activity, on the playing 'field' and in the advancement of the sport among its younger members. Donnybrook fits this bill in every respect.

Open Tournament Roscrea LTC		
Event	**1st Prize**	**2nd Prize**
	1893	
MS	T. R. Garvey	
LHS	Miss Waring	
MHD	G.W. Powell/ S. E. Smith	
MxHD	S. E. Smith/Miss M. Waring divided with T. R. Garvey/Miss Davidson	
	1894	
MHS	T. R. Garvey	Captain Foulerton
LHS	Mrs. Waring	Miss Maude Golding
MHD	Count E.A. O' Byrne/ W. R. Clark	Rev. A. Sherrard/ William St.G. Perrott
MxHD	William St.G. Perrott/ Miss M. Golding	W. Clark/ Mrs. Waring

In 1947 and 1948 there is no tournament scheduled for the club. In fact it may have died somewhat at this stage since the Munster championships in 1947 were run by **County Tipperary LTC.** The 1955 and 1963 Yearbooks indicate that there was a **Roscrea LTC**

The Minutes book records the early meetings:

> *The first General Meeting of the Donnybrook Lawn Tennis Club was held in the Schoolhouse, Beaver's Row, Donnybrook, on Monday evening 10th of April 1893, Colonel Vesey Davoren, J.P. in the chair. There was a large attendance of members. The Chairman in his opening statement mentioned that some gentlemen residents in the district had met a few weeks ago to consider the desirability of forming a Lawn Tennis Club for Donnybrook district and in order to invite an expression of opinion on the subject they drew up a circular which was sent to a number of residents, and the response to said circular having been considered favourably a provisional Committee met and decided to accept terms offered by Mr. H. Bantry White for part of a field at the back of his residence Balliguile for three years (for which term Dr. Percival Wright had consented to let the said field to Mr. White) rent to be agreed upon at the same rate as he pays Dr. Wright for same. It was also agreed to accept Mr. John Morrisey's estimate for laying down three grass courts at £27, work to be finished within one month. The offer of the Merrion Lawn Tennis Club to sell their Pavilion, roller, lawn mower, marker, nets and posts, etc., on favourable terms was also accepted. The Chairman then called upon Mr. Perrott, the Hon. Sec. protem to read the Rules as drawn up by the provisional Committee for approval of the Meeting, when same were submitted and finally adopted. The following gentlemen were proposed to fill the offices of President and Vice-Presidents.*

> **President**
> **The Right Hon. Mr. Justice Madden**
> **Vice-Presidents**
> **Mr. Andrew Reid, Co. Vesey Davoren J. P., Mr. W. Jameson J. P.**
> **Honorary Secretary**
> **H. G. Knox Horner**
> **Honorary Treasurer**
> **W. St. George Perrott**
> **Committee**
> **Messrs. O. H. Braddell, H. Bantry White, Henry Plews, Frederick Isacke, Brabazon Bunker & Amos Vereker**

History will record that William St. George Perrott was to stay on as the honorary treasurer for eleven years and that he would hold the same post with the Irish Lawn Tennis Association from 1908, when first formed, until 1948. He would also be elected President of the ILTA for 1944 and 1945. A list of the club's officers since its early days are included here.

At that inaugural meeting it was decided that all the eighteen ladies and gentlemen that put forward their names would be accepted for membership without an entrance fee. The first membership 'ballot' would take place between 4 and 6 o'clock on Wednesday 26th April. The club history (published in centenary year 1993) indicates that the first Committee Meeting was on Friday the 21st April at 5.30pm on the Club ground. It was decided that a fourth court should be laid and Mr. Morrisey, who laid the courts, suggested he be caretaker for £1 per week. This was agreed. An account was open with the Ulster Bank, Lower Baggott Street and the club would still have the same bankers some 100 years later.

The club's boundary has remained virtually the same since the beginning and today the club has eight all-weather courts. The *Daily Express* (8th June 1893) reported:

> *On a part of the world famous Donnybrook Fair ground the members of the club will carry on their contests with the racket-the symbol of peace and pleasure.*
>
> *The ground is a remarkably neat one. Four good courts have been laid down and yesterday they played beautifully.*

By September of that first year the club had 147 members. Despite the theory that ladies were equal members form the start it would be 1948 before they were included on the committee. By the 31st December 1893 the efficient treasurer had completed accounts indicating an expenditure of £215 3s 2d. Income from subscriptions came to £133 3s 6d and income from 169 'visitors' came to a total of £8 9s 0d. The club's purchase of the Merrion club's pavilion was £7, it was erected for £20.

Typically, the grass court season started in early May and finished in mid to late September. Thursdays at the club were social occasions when the ladies served teas. This one assumes included providing the best of sandwiches and home cooked cakes, flans etC. At an early stage it was decided to improve the standard of play by securing the services of a professional player. Due to the demand on court time an early bye-law stated that *No member or Visitor shall play on any one court longer than for two consecutive sets unless no demand be made for the court.*

In 1897 the grounds man, a Mr. Feld, had to be warned by the committee and told that *unless he took the pledge at once he would be dismissed.* A year later the club advertised for a new grounds man. Several came and went but in 1937 they employed a gem. Gerard Collins stayed with the club for 40 years until his retirement in December 1977. In the early years sheep kept the grass under control. Some donkeys were allowed to graze in 1901 providing an income of 2/-6 per week. A horse was added *to the club's menagerie* as the grounds were used for hockey in the winter and the club pony pulled their roller. This club was wound up in 1907.

Even though a hard court was proposed as early as 1893, it was in 1926, with a loan of £130, that a hard court was laid. Proving successful another was laid in the autumn. The club now had six grass courts and two hard courts. The grounds committee resigned in 1926, their recommendation to buy a new push mower was overturned by the club committee who decide to buy a motorised version.

In October 1919 pavilion repairs included the necessity to make the following decisions:

1. *Alteration of position of window in Gents room through which drinks are handed in so that Members will not be on view to ladies getting out their bicycles or passing at the back of the pavilion.*

2. *A table to be put in the men's room and one or two strips of coconut matting leading from shower bath as Members complained that their feet got dirty before they could get their shoes and socks on.*

During the Great War club members, including some ladies on war duty, were deemed to be honorary members. Finances suffered. Possibly uniquely, the club agreed to share the cost of a grounds man in 1917 with Lansdowne Lawn Tennis Club.

At Home

The annual social/sporting day of the year was the "At Home " day. This started in 1894 and various trophies were presented. Many perpetual trophies, which were won by the champion, kept them on winning the event for three consecutive years. The 1895 'At Home' was attended by 600 people and a marquee, 50 feet by 30 feet, was erected for the occasion. Free tickets were sent to Fitzwilliam, Trinity, Lansdowne and Mount Temple tennis clubs. The press attended these social events and, as was the norm at that time, flowery

descriptions of those attending were nearly more common than details of the tennis events taking place. In 1894 the *Lady's Pictorial* would describe the supporting cast as follows:

The band of the Royal Irish Constabulary attended, and played a varied programme. Among the lady guests I noticed Lady Harrel, in dark grey striped silk; her daughters in black toilettes; Lady Jackson, in fawn and blue; Mrs. Plews and her pretty daughters, Mrs. Charles Lambert, Mrs. Herbert Manders, Mrs. And Miss Vesey-Davoren-the former looking assiduously after the tea-table-Mrs. And the Misses Vaughan, Mrs. And Miss Willard Jones, Mrs. Peyton, Mrs. William Fahie; Miss Horner, looking cool and nice in white frill and touches of blue in her hat; Mrs. Wakeley, Miss Inda Thompson and very many others. It was certainly the best dressed crowd I have seen at any rendezvous this Season.

Some of the interested audience at the 1955 "At Home" in 1955 at Donnybrook LTC.

By the 1920s the club was going well but, as in many clubs with the appropriate social standing, some things were slow to change with the times. Despite the fact that the 'Free State' was well established in 1928, the minutes point out that *F. C. V. Ireland was despatched to find a band that was willing to finish the programme with a rendition of 'God Save the King'.*

Competiton

The club was one of the first to enter the Dublin Lawn Tennis Council leagues. The competitions started in 1902 and the following year Donnybrook became the first club to win two titles in one season. Their first and second teams took the Class 2 and Class 3 summer leagues respectively. It would be many years before the winter leagues took off.

As a reflection of their attitude to the ladies play the game they were to be the first holders of the Ladies league in 1910 and by 1913 took both the Class 1 and Class 2 titles, again a first. This 'double' was followed by a special Committee invitation to the two teams to the new Mitchell & Sons restaurant in Grafton Street. *Irish Life* (October 24th) recorded the event…..*Mr. Plews made a short speech, in which he complimented the ladies on the honour done to the club, and hoped that the teams might have a similar success another year. Mrs. Blood, as captain of the 1st team, and Miss Hayes, as captain of the 2nd, in a few well-chosen words, thanked the Committee on behalf of their respective teams, for their great kindness and for all the trouble they had gone to in arranging such a pleasant evening for their benefit. Later, the party adjourned to the Theatre Royal, where everyone enjoyed themselves and appeared to be in the best of spirits.*

The clubs history records that "The ladies were to keep the club banner flying through the doldrums of the 1940s and 1950s." For the record the following is a summary of the Club's League wins as per the data supplied by the **Dublin LTC.** The summer leagues have now been augmented in more recent years by the winter, floodlit and junior leagues.

During the Second World War the 'At Home' was cancelled but the club played their Club Championships. During and after this period it was the ladies of this Dublin club that ensured the clubs survival. Among the members were international players in Mary Nichols (Mrs. Downey) and Maeve Brennan (Mrs. Downey) both of who were on the Irish team in the years after the war. To these can be added Mary Blaney (Mrs. Ensor), Alice Blaney (Mrs. Finlay), Miriam Meenan (Mrs. Healy), Dorothy Miley, Veronica Miley (Mrs. Tunney), Heather Boyd and Rita Rutherfoord.

July 1934: The "At Home at Donnybrook LTC.

Heather Boyd was not alone captain of the Class 1 winning team of 1953, but also the honorary treasurer between 1949 and 1964 and *one of the driving forces behind the club's recovery.* Heather was elected the club President for the 1971 and 1972 seasons. She was the first lady member in that capacity. Later, another lady would leave an equal impression. Sally Dawson was the honorary secretary from 1973 to 1977, the honorary treasurer for the period 1977 to 1992 and then president for 1993 and 1995. Other lady presidents over the years were Rita Ruterfoord (1979/1980), Valerie Clancy (1984/1985), Mary Gleeson (1989/1990), Elaine O' Brien (1997/1998) and Marguerite Murphy (1999/2001). Rita Ruterfoord was not alone a useful tennis player but represented Ireland at the highest level in the sports of lacrosse and hockey. In recent years, Marguerite Murphy having had many years on the committee, been lady captain and acted as the honorary secretary for four years, was elevated to the top post in the club. Elaine O'Brien has been involved with juniors for many years up to the time of her election to president in 1997.

Donnybrook LTC Winning League Teams

	Men	Ladies		
Summer Leagues				
Class 1	1982, 1984	1910,	1913,	1953,
		1982,	1984,	1985,
		1986,	1987,	1988,
		1993,	2001	
Class 2	1903, 1904	1912,	1913,	1914,
		1983,	1991	
Class 3	1903, 1974,	1938,	1963,	1974,
	1999	1978,	1999	
Class 4	1975	1978,	1982,	1993
Class 7		1995,	1997	
Winter Leagues				
Class 2	1995, 2002			
Class 3	1994			
Class 4		1996		
Class 5		1995		
Floodlit Leagues				
Class 1	1982, 1984,	1992,	1993	
	1991			
Class 2	1995	1984,	1997	
Class 3		1992		
Senior Leagues				
Over 35				
Class 1	1993, 1994,			
	1995, 1996,			
	2000			
Class 3	2000	1992,	1996	
Class 4		1992,	1997	
Over 45				
Class 1		2001		
Class 2	1997			
Junior				
	Boys	Girls		
Under 14				
Class 1	1990	1997		
Class 2	2002	1992,	2001,	2002
Under 16				
Class 1		1996,	1997	

Both Maeve Brennan (1943) and Mary Nichols (1939 and 1940) were Irish Open Girls Champions. Several members apart from these two ladies would grace the courts at Wimbledon. In a new generation in the 1980s we can find international ladies in the form of Bernie Griffith, Jenny O'Brien and Lesley O'Halloran. All three were Federation Cup players. Lesley O'Halloran would hold an Irish ranking for an incredible period of nearly 20 years. These ladies would form the backbone of the six Class 1 Dublin Summer league wins between the years 1982 and 1988. There have been many more ladies of note. A few of the many others that have done the club proud are Rhona Howett, Catherine Holohan, Lucy Kenny, Norah Meldon and Vivienne Lee.

The difficulty has been attracting top class men. If a club is playing in Class 1 in the men's leagues then good players will be attracted there, and vice versa. Despite this the club can claim to have its fair share of good players. These include Jim McArdle, John

Hackett, Conor McCullough, Jerry Sheehan, Declan Heavey, Conor Carroll and Brian Lawlor. Hugh Tinney, that Irish pianist of note, has been a member for many years. He was an excellent player when at his most active. Jim McArdle played some excellent Davis Cup matches but many of these men would also be on Irish teams. Jerry Sheehan was among those involved in coaching and would become president of the Leinster Branch for 1988 and 1989. Jim McArdle (1992/1993) and Henry Lappin (1984/1985) would also fill this role. All three, and others, would be involved in many aspects of the Irish Lawn Tennis Association and Tennis Ireland.

Heather Boyd (Team Captain) receiving the Class 1 League Cup for Donnybrook LTC in 1952. Heather was an important part of the club revival after the war. Among her roles included her time as honorary treasurer (1949-1965) and president (1971-1973).

In 1985 the club created the official posts of men and lady captain's. The first holders were Gerry McGrath and Liz Heavey. Others to hold the posts were Marguerite Murphy (1988, 1889, 1990), Sandra Banks (1990, 1991, 1993-) and Jerry Sheehan (1993-).

The club was balanced with players in 1984 when winning the All-Ireland Carroll's Doubles team event. The members of that team were Conor McCullough, Rhona Howett, Mandy Smith, Jennifer O' Brien, John Hackett, Lesley O'Halloran and Jim McArdle (captain). In the quarterfinals they beat Monkstown 25/10, in the semi-finals Templeogue 27/15 and in the final Elm Park 20/19. That year there was to be a repeat of their great year (1982) when they also took

the Class 1 Men's and Ladies League titles. Five of the men's team were international players: Jim McArdle (captain), Conor McCullough, John Hackett, Declan Heavey, Jerry Sheehan and Rod Ensor. The ladies side was no less glamorous with Mandy Smith (captain), Rhona Howett, Jennifer O'Brien, Vivienne Lee, Claire Kinnane and Rocky (Lesley, I presume) O' Halloran. The men beat Sutton 5/2 in the final and the ladies beat Carrickmines 5/1. There were great celebrations in the new clubhouse that year on the 18th August.

This club has had much success in the past, has continually improved its facilities over the years and can look forward to many more successful years as a thriving Dublin club. In 1978 the club hosted the Irish Close and Leinster Championships and, the following year, the interprovincials. From 1978 to 2002 the Close Championships have settled in at the club and are looked forward to each year at a club that is more than welcoming to players from all parts of Ireland. Here it is not possible to give the complete story and this writer would recommend a read of the club's Centenary book edited by Aisling Maguire in 1993. Today the club has eight floodlit *Omni* courts and an extensive programme, not least for the junior members, the seeds for a long and successful future.

1989 at Donnybrook LTC: From left: Jerry Sheehan, Kevin O'Brien, Conor Carroll & Conor Egan.

Jim McArdle (winner, on left) and Brian Lawlor at the Irish Close Championships in 1983. The event, first held in 1914, has become a permanent fixture at Donnybrook Lawn Tennis Club since 1978.

The Donnybrook LTC under17 team won the Dublin league in 1971. From left: Rod Ensor, Michael Dawson, Kevin O'Malley & Paul Monaghan.

In 1992 the Donnybrook LTC Class 4 Over 35 league winning team. Back (l. to r.): Marguerite Murphy, Michelle Linnane and Julie Gilligan. Front (l. to r.): Susan Ward, Audrey Loughran and Ann-Marie McMahon.

In 1978 the ladies' of Donnybrook were runners-up in the Class 2 Dublin league. Back (l. to r.): Elizabeth O'Hare, Grainne Magrane, Gillian Haslam & Deirdre Howett. Front (l. to r.): Rhona Howett, Niamh O'Carroll & Mandy Smyth.

The 1972 Boys' league winning team from Donnybrook LTC. From left: Geoffrey Dawson, Rod Ensor (captain), Jerry Sheehan & Brian Egan.

"The Six Pack" were photographed at the club in 1985. Back (l. to r.): Paul Coulson, Dennis Brennan & Paul Reddy. Front (l. to r.): Oisin O'Buachalla, Billy Gleeson & Michael Coughlan.

The 1971 girl's under 17 league winning team from Donnybrook LTC. From left: Eithne Tinney, Susan Coulson, Gillian Magrane and Lucy Kenny.

The Class 1 Summer League Winners of 1988. Back (left to right) Bernadette Griffith, Joanne O'Halloran, Liz Heavey. Front Row (left to right) Lesley O'Halloran, Jennifer O'Brien (captain) and Hazel Bowen.

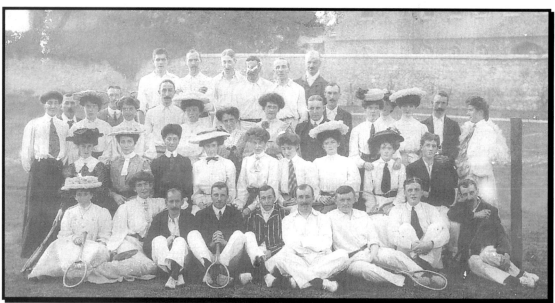

Donnybrook Lawn Tennis Club (Dublin) was founded in 1893 on its present site. By the following summer the club had 1000 members. The men's subscription at the time was 1 guinea and the ladies 10 shillings and 6 pence. The first three grass courts were laid for £24 and came into operation for the "Opening Day", 26th June 1893. The above club photograph was taken in 1905. The man in the front on the extreme right was a very notable member, William St. George Perrott. Apart from tennis success in the club he played in many parts of Ireland. He was also a reserve on both the Irish hockey and soccer team. He was the club's honorary treasurer from 1893 to 1903. When the ILTA was founded in 1908 he became its first honorary treasurer and remained in the post until 1948.

The 1989 Carlsberg Leinster Men's Challenge Cup winners. Back (left to right) Conor Egan, Jim McArdle, Jerry Sheehan (captain), Pat O'Keeffe. Front (left to right) Conor Carroll, Gerry McGrath and Stewart Doyle.

In July 1976 George McCaw, club president, officially opened the four new 'En-Tout-Cas' hard courts. These cost £20,000; much of the fund raising success was due to the efforts of the club's honorary treasurer, Paul Reddy. The club currently (2005) has eight flood-lit 'omnipro' tennis courts.

The 1974 Class 3 League winners were Back (left to right) Sally Dawson, Valerie Clancy & Rita Rutherfoord. Front (left to right) Mareth Jackson, Sandra Feehily & Eithne Tinney.

A young Class 2 League winning team in 1971 (from left) Paddy Ballagh, Paul Coulson, Michael Dawson, Kevin O' Malley, Paddy Quilligan and Ian McKenzie (captain).

Donnybrook LTC players. From left: John Hamill, Raymund, Egan, Cyril O'Sullivan & Hugh McDermott.

In 1990 the Donnybrook LTC U14 team won the DLTC Class 1 league. From left: Timothy White, Peter Rowell, Marcus Purcell (capt.), Michael Neary, Niall Dowling & Gavin Neary.

F.W. Dunlop, on left, the honorary treasurer 1933-1947 with Cameron McNair the honorary secretary 1923-1947.

The Donnybrook LTC ladies' team won Class 4 of the Dublin leagues in 1978. Back (l. to r.): Heather Boyd, Paddy Murphy (club president) & Rita Rutherfoord. Middle (l. to r.):June Keenan, Michael Gunne & Angela Moloney. Front (l. to r.): Breege O'Reilly, Sally Dawson & Carmel Noonan.

Henry Tierney (left) and Kenneth Downey at Donnybrook Lawn Tennis Club in 1955. Henry was club champion in 1947 and 1954, honorary secretary 1949-1954 and president 1957-1960. Kenneth was club champion in 1952 and 1953.

Ready for fancy dress tennis party in August 1981. Two years later the pavilion was replaced.

Donnybrook LTC Committee 2005

President	John Stewart
Deputy President	Anita O'Neill
Honorary Secretary	Peter Murphy
Honorary Treasurer	Charles Meehan
Honorary Secretary-Juniors	Valerie Clarke
House & Grounds	Bryan O'Rourke
Men's Captain	Ciaran O'Kelly
Ladies' Captain	Sheelagh Lyons
Committee	Claire O'Flynn
	Jennifer O'Brien
Club Manager	John Piggott
Club Administrator	John O'Donovan
Tennis-Co-ordinator	Claire Kirwan

Donnybrook ladies continue to prosper. Class 1 Summer League winners in 2001 were (back, l. to r.) Sandra Griffith, Jenny Lawlor, Sarah Griffith and Naomi MacHale. From (l. to r.) Catherine Holohan, Bernadette Griffith. Missing Jenny O'Brien and Clodagh McMorrow.

The centenary committee (1893-1894) at Donnybrook LTC. Back (l. to r.) Sabina Purcell, Jerry Sheehan (men's captain), Sandra Banks (ladies' captain), Donal O'S. Latchford, Elizabeth Governey, Tony Kearney & Deirdre Howett. Front (l. to r.): Marguerite Murphy (honorary secretary), Elaine O'Brien (honorary secretary for juniors), Hugh McDermott, Sally Dawson (president), David Horkan (honorary treasurer), Estelle Murray & Liz Heavey. Missing from photograph: John Hamill & Bill Pilkington.

In May 1893 Donnybrook LTC celebrated its centenary with an American Tournament in period costume. The club has had its account with Ulster Bank for the full century and were delighted to be part of the celebrations. From left: Marguerite Murphy (honorary secretary), Sally Dawson (president), Jerry Sheehan (men's captain), John McNally (Ulster Bank Director) & Lucia Leahy (committee member).

Donnybrook Lawn Tennis Club

Year	President	Honorary Secretary	Hon.Treasurer
1893-1901	Right Hon. Mr. Justice Madden	H.G.Knox Horner	William St. George Perrott
1902	Right Hon. The Earl of Pembroke	H. R. Edwards	William St. George Perrott
1903	Right Hon. The Earl of Pembroke	H. R. Edwards	Agustus Davoren
1904-1905	Right Hon. The Earl of Pembroke	H. R. Edwards	Agustus Davoren
1906-1917	Right Hon. The Earl of Pembroke	H. R. Edwards	Percy H. Stokes
1918	Right Hon. The Earl of Pembroke	E. K. Allander	Percy H. Stokes
1919	Right Hon. The Earl of Pembroke	E. K. Allander	Percy H. Stokes
1920-1922	Right Hon. The Earl of Pembroke	Norman N. Kennedy	Percy H. Stokes
1923-1926	Right Hon. The Earl of Pembroke	E. A. Cameron McNair	Percy H. Stokes
1927	Dr. Bantry White	E. A. Cameron McNair	Percy H. Stokes
1928	Dr. Bantry White	E. A. Cameron McNair	F. C. Ireland
1929	Mr. J. Dudley	E. A. Cameron McNair	F. C. Ireland
1930-1932	Mr. J. Dudley	E. A. Cameron McNair	Francis Klinger
1933-1934	Mr. J. Dudley	E. A. Cameron McNair	F. W. Dunlop
1935-1937	Mr. H. H. Murray	E. A. Cameron McNair	F. W. Dunlop
1938-1940	Major R. H. Plews	E. A. Cameron McNair	F. W. Dunlop
1941-1942	Mr. A. O. Fry	E. A. Cameron McNair	F. W. Dunlop
1943-1944	Mr. Manning Robertson	E. A. Cameron McNair	F. W. Dunlop
1945	Mr. F. W. Dunlop	E. A. Cameron McNair	F. W. Dunlop
1946	Mr. F. W. Dunlop	E. A. Cameron McNair	J. G. Mann
1947	Mr. F. W. Dunlop	Herbert R. McWilliam	J. G. Mann
1948	Mr. E. C. Bewley	Herbert R. McWilliam	J. G. Mann
1949	Mr. E. C. Bewley	Henry C. Tiernan	Heather Boyd
1950-1953	Mr. P. T. Brooks	Henry C. Tiernan	Heather Boyd
1954	Mr. P. T. Brooks	Cecil Curran	Heather Boyd
1955-1956	Mr. L. E. Werner	Cecil Curran	Heather Boyd
1957-1958	Henry C. Tierney	Cecil Curran	Heather Boyd
1959	Henry C. Tierney	Timothy J. Webb	Heather Boyd
1960-1962	Cecil A. Curran	George McCaw	Heather Boyd
1963-1964	Noel J. Purcell	George McCaw	Heather Boyd
1965-1967	Noel J. Purcell	George McCaw	Paddy Murphy
1967	Brian K. Overend	George McCaw	Paddy Murphy
1968	Brian K. Overend	Patrick Murray	Paddy Murphy
1969-1970	Jean-Pierre Eliet	Patrick Murray	Paddy Murphy
1971	Heather Boyd	Patrick Murray	Paddy Murphy
1972	Heather Boyd	Paul O' Higgins	Paddy Murphy
1973	George A. McCaw	Sally Dawson	Michael Gaffney
1974	George A. McCaw	Sally Dawson	John McGuigan
1975-1976	George A. McCaw	Sally Dawson	Paul Reddy
1977	Paddy J. Murphy	Sally Dawson	Sally Dawson
1978	Paddy J. Murphy	Mary Gleeson	Sally Dawson
1979-1980	Rita Rutherfoord	Mary Gleeson	Sally Dawson
1981-1982	Gerald McCracken	Mary Gleeson	Sally Dawson
1983	Gerald McCracken	Jane Dowling	Sally Dawson
1984	Valerie Clancy	Jane Dowling	Sally Dawson
1985	Valerie Clancy	Bernadette Griffith	Sally Dawson
1986	Kevin T. Feeney	Bernadette Griffith	Sally Dawson
1987	Kevin T. Feeney	Ruth Hackett	Sally Dawson
1988	Kevin T. Feeney	Owen Purcell	Sally Dawson
1989	Mary Gleeson	Owen Purcell	Sally Dawson
1990	Mary Gleeson	Marguerite Murphy	Sally Dawson
1991-1992	Henry Lappin	Marguerite Murphy	Sally Dawson
1993-1995	Sally Dawson	Hugh McDermott	David Horkan
1996	John Hamill	Hugh McDermott	David Horkan
1997	Elaine O' Brien	Robert Ryan	Billy Gleeson
1998	Elaine O' Brien	Robert Ryan	Billy Gleeson
1999-2000	Marguerite Murphy	Sue Ward	Shane Browne
2001-2002	Robert Ryan	John Stewart	Pat Hurley
2003-2004	Jack Fitzgerald	Charles Meenan	Paul Sullivan
2005	John Stewart	Charles Meenan	Peter Murphy

Donnybrook Lawn Tennis Club

Year	Men's Champions	Ladies' Champions	Year	Men's Champions	Ladies' Champions
1894	William St. George Perrott	Miss B. Barnard	1959	R. B. Fitzsimon	R. McGuire
1895-1901	?	?	1960	R. B. Fitzsimon	M. Healy
1902	H. Lowe	?	1961	R. B. Fitzsimon	Valerie Barry
1903	W. E. O'Brien	Miss L. Kennedy	1962-1963	John Blayney	Valerie Barry
1904	W. E. O'Brien	?	1964	Ian McKenzie	M. Healy
1905	Percy H. Stokes	?	1965	C. A. Curran	R. Comyn
1906-1911	?	?	1966	Ian McKenzie	Rita Rutherfoord
1912	?	Miss Lindsay	1967	H. Viani	M. Healy
1913	?	Miss Studley	1968	Paddy F. Ballagh	V. Murphy
1914	?	Mrs. Plews	1969	Denis Brennan	Valerie Clancy
1915-1917	?	?	1970	Paul Coulson	Valerie Clancy
1918	H. Bindon Blood	?	1971	Paddy Quilligan	Lucy Kenny
1919-1921	H. Bindon Blood	Mrs. Plews	1972	Michael Dawson	Lucy Kenny
1922	H. Bindon Blood	Mrs. Hogan	1973	Jerry Sheehan	Lucy Kenny
1923	H. Baker	Miss Kelly	1974	Michael Dawson	Frances Egan
1924	?	?	1975	Jerry Sheehan	Maurethe Jackson
1925	Rev. Dr. A. A. Luce	Mrs. Luce	1976	Jerry Sheehan	Claudia Tierney
1926	H. Bindon Blood	Mrs. Meade	1977	Kevin O' Malley	Barbara McQuillan
1927	E. Dunlop	Miss Cummins	1978	Jim McArdle	Barbara McQuillan
1928	R. B. Cairn Duff	Mrs. Meade	1979	Jerry Sheehan	Frances Egan
1929-1930	D. Plaistowe	?	1980	Jim Mc Ardle	Gillian Haslam
1931	D. Plaistowe	Mrs. Meade	1981	Jerry Sheehan	G. Flynn
1932	Francis Klinger	Mrs. Meade	1982	Jerry Sheehan	Vivienne Lee
1933	Francis Klinger	T. Nichols	1983	Declan Heavey	Claire Kinnane
1934	Francis Klinger	H. Banbury	1984	Jim Mc Ardle	Bernadette Griffith
1935	D.C. McNair	S. Henat	1985	Jerry Sheehan	Bernadette Griffith
1936	D.C. McNair	T. Nichols	1986	Conor McCullough	Jenny O' Brien
1937	E. Warren	H. H. Creswell	1987	Pat O' Keeffe	Bernadette Griffith
1938	E. Warren	Norah Meldon	1988	Jerry Sheehan	Mandy Smyth
1939	D.T. McWeeney	I. Nichols	1989	Jerry Sheehan	Jenny O' Brien
1940	Francis Klinger	Mary Nichols	1990	Conor Carroll	Jenny O' Brien
1941	J. A. Douglas	Mary Nichols	1991	Bobby Hassett	Jenny O' Brien
1942	P. T. Brooks	Mary Blayney	1992	Brian Lawlor	Jenny O' Brien
1943-1944	N. L. Peart	Mary Blayney	1993	Victor Drummy	Andrea Ryan
1945-1946	A. H. L. Archer	Mary Blayney	1994	Bobby Hassett	Jenny O' Brien
1947	Henry C. McTiernan	Dorothy Miley	1995	Peter Rowell	Bernadette Griffith
1948	D. C. McNair	Maeve Brennan	1996	Justin Purcell	Jenny O' Brien
1949	A. H. L. Archer	Maeve Brennan	1997	Cormac Jennings	Jenny O' Brien
1950	R. O. V. Lloyd	Maeve Brennan	1998	Peter Rowell	Caitriona Hannigan
1951	R. O. V. Lloyd	Rita Rutherfoord	1999	Cormac Jennings	Catherine Holohan
1952-1953	Kenneth Downey	Miriam Meenan	2000	Derek Fluskey	Caitriona Hannigan
1954	Henry C. McTiernan	Beth Lindsay	2001	Paul Morrisey	Catherine Holohan
1955	Ian McKenzie	Veronica Miley	2002	Paul Morrisey	Sandra Griffith
1956	Ian McKenzie	Joan Plews	2003	Eoin Heavey	Catherine Holohan
1957	Ian McKenzie	M. Healy	2004	Ciaran Dolan	Jenny Lawlor
1958	George McCaw	M. Healy	2005	Derek Boland	Lisa Lawlor

Mount Pleasant Lawn Tennis Club
(Founded 1893)

Mount Pleasant Lawn Tennis Club has a reputation for providing a good social environment. It results in the club's organised trips to many tournaments outside the Dublin area. The club also provides social and competitive membership in the sports of squash and badminton. The club started life as a tennis club in 1893, located in a beautifully preserved Georgian square of the same name, in Ranelagh, Dublin. The honorary secretary in 1894 and 1895 was N. Ormsby. He lived at 28 Mount Pleasant Square. The original wooden pavilion was in operation in the 1920s or earlier. In the late 1960s it was seriously damaged by fire. The club committee took action with a new development plan. The facility has been added to right up to 2000.

In the early days it was all grass courts. Some members (of the glass half-full variety) can recall sunny summer days with strawberries and cream as part of the afternoon tea. Others (of the glass half-empty camp) can recall the rainy days, the need to mow the grass, mark the lines and put up the poles, all before a ball could be struck. In the late sixties badminton and squash became part of the club's plan. The club includes table tennis among its sport and is the only club in Dublin to cater for all four racquet sports. Eventually, after much hot debate, a 'get rid of the grass courts' decision was carried. By the early 1990s the hard courts were converted to artificial grass.

2001: Mount Pleasant LTC president Yvonne Duffy being presented with the team award at the Wexford Open-the third year in row that the club won this prize.

The club has hosted many events over the years. In recent times these have included the 1988 Davis Cup (Ireland beating Greece 5/0) and a 'Futures' tour event in 2000. 'Local' inter-county finals were hosted by the club in 2002, 2003 and 2004. The ladies' Dublin winter league finals were held at the Ranelagh venue in 2003 and the senior league finals the following year.

Priegiving at Mount Pleasant LTC (Circa 1925)

Mount Pleasant LTC Class 2 league winning team 1938.

The club retains its social content and members are willing and enthusiastic to act on its many committees. The Open week each June is an annual highlight with all eleven courts fully utilized. Of the membership of about 1000, 700 are 'tennis' members, the remainder are divided between badminton and squash equally. The impressive facilities include 11 all-weather tennis courts, with floodlighting, 2 badminton courts, 3 squash courts, a gym, a sauna and a snooker room.

Large numbers of members take part in club tournaments, other events around Dublin (e.g. opens at Bective and Lansdowne) and further afield (e.g. Wexford, Sligo & Galway). The tennis players are particularly social conscious and prepared to travel. At the annual Wexford event, **Mount Peasant LTC** has won the 'club' prize virtually every year in the last decade.

The 2005 Management Committee at **Mount Pleasant LTC** for 2005/2006 is Colm O'Byrne (president), John Darby (honorary secretary), Siobhan Grehan (honorary secretary), Henry Gillanders (house & grounds), Caitriona Tiernan (social representative), Seamus Murphy (men's tennis captain), Cathal O'Connor (tennis committee representative), Tom Sexton (squash committee representative) & Douglas Wright (badminton committee representative). The ladies' captain for 2005/2006 is Sheila Kilduff. The other tennis committee members are Declan Byrne, Margaret Collins, Michael Ryan, Caitriona Tiernan,

Fionnuala Lawton, Joan Ward, Aoife O'Brien, Marie Galmiche & Morgan Pembroke.

Mount Pleasant LTC 'At Home' (Circa 1925)

Junior Squash players at Mount Pleasant LTC in April 2005.

The History of Irish Tennis

The Mount Pleasant LTC team were runners-up in the Class 3 summer league in 2001.

Open Week at Mount Pleasant LTC in June 2003

Conor Carroll-Club Champion 2005 at Mount Pleasant Lawn Tennis Club

December 2004-Christmas party for members of Mount Pleasant LTC.

May 2002: The Mount Pleasant LTC players enjoying the sunshine at the West of Ireland Championships in Sligo.

Halloween Fancy Dress at Mount Pleasant Lawn Tennis Club (1st November 2002)

Open Week 2003 at Mount Pleasant LTC

The club champion at Mount Pleasant LTC in 2004 was Caitriona Ryan.

The visit to La Manga-September 2005. One of the quotes of the holiday came from local coach Jorge when doing a video analysis of the missed smash of his Mount Pleasant pupil. "The most important thing about a contact point…is to have one". Another coach queried whether the footwork of one of his Irish pupils was a national dance?

Christmas party 2004 – Mount Pleasant LTC

7th December 2002-the Christmas party at Mount Pleasant Lawn Tennis Club.

Open Week at Mount Pleasant Lawn Tennis Club in 2005. F. Phillips and Marie Kinnane won the Class 2 ladies' doubles.

Recent Club Championship Winners at Mount Pleasant LTC

2001	MS	Conor Carroll
	LS	Claudia Muller
	MD	ConorCarroll/Tony Cannon
	LD	Leonora Mullet/Paula Mythen
	MxD	Conor Carroll/Paula Mythen
2002	MS	Conor O'Neill
	LS	Aideen Sheehan
	MD	Conor Burke/Justin Mahony
	LD	Yvonne Duffy/Dolores Nulty
	MxD	David Murphy/Aine McGrath
2003	MS	John Dunny
	LS	Pat McGoran
	MD	Terry Tew/Dermot Kearney
	LD	Mary O'Boyle/Laurie Flynn
	MxD	Jimmy Carroll/Andrea Sheridan
2005	MS	Conor Carroll
	LS	Marie Kinnane
	MD	Kevin Burke/Martin Hughes
	LD	Sheila Kilduff/Catriona Ryan
	MxD	Conor Carroll/Paula Mythen

Mount Pleasant LTC-2005 Club Championships

Mount Pleasant LTC were runners-up in the Class 7 winter league finals (at Sutton LTC) in March 2005. Team included Helen McNulty, Joan Ward, Gina O'Brien, Emer O'Sullivan, Niamh O'Sullivan & Aileen O'Meara.

Open Week 2003 at Mount Pleasant LTC.

President Colm O'Byrne and ladies' tennis captain Aoife O'Brien at the Mount Pleasant LTC club finals night (18th September 2004).

During Open Week (June 2004) the new club balcony was formerly opened by Government Minister Michael McDowell (third from left).

****

Mount Crozier Lawn Tennis Club
(Founded 1893)

This club is functioning but is not as active as in the past. The club had/has three clay courts and is located in Cobh County Cork, about two miles from the Rushbrooke club. In years long gone, the latter was the more exclusive with entry to the Mount Crozier club open to all. One of the best players at **Mount Crozier LTC** over the years was John Dominic Foster. He was a commerce teacher with the local vocational educational committee. He was playing at the club in the 1930s and later. He had a memorable win over Harry Cronin, the Munster and Irish player even though the latter was well past his best at the time. John travelled all over the province playing in tournaments. His niece Noreen Kelly, now living in Cobh, can recall the thrill in travelling to these events with her uncle. She herself enjoyed the game but was only a 'club' standard player. For work purposes John Foster moved to Mallow and became a member of **Leaselands LTC**. He died in the mid 1990s. The founding date for this club is given as 1893 above. This could not be confirmed and is assumed to be correct.

****

Youghal Lawn Tennis Club
(Founded 1893)

This small County Cork club is an active one with an extensive junior programme. The 2004 committee was as follows:

Chairperson	Dymphna Quill
Honorary Secretary	Betty Murphy
Honorary Treasurer	Deirdre O'Sullivan
Public Relations Officer	Paul Whyte
Tournaments	Cathy Dorrigan
Administration & tournaments	Mary Hogan
Membership Officer	Jan Power
Sponsorship	Alison O'Connor
Freehold coordinator	Patrick Corkery
Secretary/website maintenance	Kevin Callaghan
Junior development	Linda Donoghue
	Ita Treacy
	Peter McDermott

****

Athboy Lawn Tennis Club
(Founded Circa 1893)

This club was listed in the first Irish Lawn Tennis handbook in 1894. No honorary secretary was listed for this County Meath club. The club was not on the affiliated listing for the ILTA in 1914 or 1920.

1935	
MS	E. Stewart beat P.A. O'Reilly 4/6 6/4 6/3
LS	Miss G. Spicer beat Miss O'Reilly 6/3 7/5
MD	C. Chamney/S. McCollum beat S. J. Parr/P. A. O'Reilly 6/2 5/7 6/2
LD	Miss Stewart/Miss McCollum beat Miss J. Armstrong/Miss M. Armstrong 3/6 6/3 16/14
MxD	S. J. Parr/Miss O'Reilly beat W. G. Armstrong/Miss J. Armstrong 7/9 6/3 7/5

Athy Lawn Tennis Club
(Founded Circa 1893)

The honorary secretary for this Leinster club in 1894 and 1895 was J. A. Duncan. He lived at The Abbey, Athy.

****

Castleblaney Lawn Tennis Club
(Founded Circa 1893)

Little is known about this club. It appears in the first Irish handbook at **Castleblaney LTC** in 1894. No name for an honorary secretary was given in that year or the handbook in 1895 when the club gets a listing again. A random search indicates that it was not affiliated to the ILTA in 1911, 1956, 1963 or to Tennis Ireland in 1993.

****

Civil Service (Dublin) Lawn Tennis Club
(Founded Circa 1893)

The honorary secretary for this club in 1894 and 1895 was Mr. J. T. Hurford. He lived at 19 Montpelier Hill in Dublin.

****

Drumcondra Lawn Tennis Club
(Founded Circa 1893)

Very little information has been unearthed about this small Dublin club. Ann Garavan, the currently very active veteran player at **Castlebar TC**, and twin sister to another good player, Joan Brady of the Dundalk club, can recall hearing that her grandmother played at this club. The interesting thing about her was that, many decades ago, she was still playing tennis into her 70s and won a singles club tournament at the age of 75.

The honorary secretary of the **Drumcondra LTC** in 1894 and 1895 was Mr. A. M. Keogh. He lived at 17 Russell Place in Dublin at that time.

****

Dundalk Tennis Badminton & Squash Club
[Dundalk Lawn Tennis Club]
(Founded Circa 1893)

This club in a sizeable County town has had many interesting facets to its development. The original of the club today appears to have started on the 6th November 1913 at a public meeting held in the Town Hall. According to the article in the ILTA Yearbook it was *founded* by Dundalk solicitor Mr. P. McArdle who was also a director of the famous local brewery. Lands were leased from the brewery until 1922 when it bought the land outright for the sum of £100. That was in 1922.

The 1976 Dundalk players who won both the Provincial Towns Cup (Class 1) and Leinster Intercounty Cups. Back (l. to r.) Peter Hannon, John McArdle, Larry Stein, J. J. McArdle & Jim Pringle. Front (l. to r.) Joan Brady, Mary McCrystal, Stephanie Maguire and Pat McKinley.

The original club apparently had two grass courts which later became four and, in 1937, two *en tout cas* 'hard' courts were laid down. The cost of erecting the initial four courts and the pavilion was £313.

In 1965 the club amalgamated with the Phoenix Badminton Club. The 'complex' would contain two badminton courts, a bar, a table tennis table, a function room and a squash court. The driving committee behind this leap forward were J.J. McArdle, Miss Ide (*Twinkle*) Lewis, Mrs. Molly Nichols, Mr. P. Fitzgibbon (brother of J.J.), Mr. F. Matthews, and Mr. E. Henry among others. Two new squash courts were to be built in 1977. Today the club has 6 all-weather floodlit courts. In 1978 the club concentrated on juniors and there were about 100 playing in this category. The junior club champion in 1978 was Peter Hannon who would later become an international player. That year, among his many achievements, was to become the Irish Open Boys Champion.

In 1986 these under 11 Dundalk tennis club members were selected for special coaching. From left: Coghlan McKeane, Paul Pringle, Lee Colton & James Pringle.

The Dundalk LTC first team won the Senior section of the Provincial Town's Cup in 1946. Back (l. to r.): Miss Ide M. Lewis, Miss B. McArdle & Miss N. O'Reilly. Front (l. to r.): W. D. Willis, Laurence F. Steen (captain) & Dennis Williams.

The successful Louth team of 1978 were all from the Dundalk tennis club. Seated (l. to r.): Mary Johnson, Leenane Kiernan, Mary Pat McKinley, Brian McCoy, Ann Kiernan, Helen Kiernan, Joan Brady & Stephanie Maguire. Standing (l. to r.): Larry Steen, Peter Hannon, Paul Brady, J. J. McArdle, Jim Pringle, John Dwyer & Adrian Ledwith. Insert: Patrick McCann.

The club won the inter-county title in 1978 with an interesting mix of players. At one end of the scale was veteran J. J. McArdle and, at the other, 15 and 16 year old juniors. The team was: Adrian Ledwith, Jim Pringle, Larry Steen (jnr.), Peter Hannon, Brian McCoy, Patrick McCann, Stephanie Maguire, Helen Kiernan, Anne Kiernan, Leenane Kiernan, Joan Brady, Mary McKinley and Mary Johnston with John Dwyer and Paul Brady as substitutes.

The club has been very conscious of its multi-disciplinary nature. It included among its members international badminton player, John McArdle and Irish senior Squash Champion, Mahommed Ali. Today it uses the title Dundalk Lawn Tennis and Badminton Club while back in 1979 it was even longer (according to the ILTA Yearbook article) namely The Dundalk Lawn Tennis Badminton and Squash Club. Outside the club their members have been involved in branch and national administration. Mention should be made of Larry Steen who was Leinster Branch President in 1962. Jim McArdle (jnr.) playing in Dublin would honour this office in 1992 and 1993 (as well as captaining Davis cup team etc.). In 1966 Larry would become the President of the ILTA, the highest tennis post in the country. This was an interesting year with Irish tennis changing rapidly and the professional era moving in. J. J. McArdle, i.e. Jim senior, was involved in the preparation of the Irish Davis Cup team. The Dundalk open tournament was full of McArdles (see below). One member that is worth a mention is Molly Nichol. This lady not alone was a useful tennis player in her day but also exceptionally good at badminton. She became President of the Badminton Union of Ireland in 1978, the first lady President of the oldest national badminton organisation in the world. The following year she would be President of her home club.

One of the Dundalk Club's most promising young players, James Pringle, has won many titles from Irish Under 12 Singles upwards. In 1998, he won the County Louth Open Championships. In the photograph, Tennis Captain, Kevin Tynan (President in 2003), presents him with his prize.

Before we leave the past it is noted that in the first Irish Yearbook of 1894 there in fact was a club in Dundalk called **Dundalk LTC**. It appears to have been founded in about 1893 and the honorary secretary for 1894 and 1895 was a Mr. T. Callan of Clanbrassil Street, Dundalk. The 1894 Handbook recorded the tournament results at **Dundalk LTC** for 1893:

Dundalk LTC Tournament 1893		
Event	1st Prize	2nd Prize
Men's Handicap Singles	A. Rainsford	E.G. Rainsford
Mixed Handicap Doubles	E.G. Rainsford/ Miss E. Johnston	A.Rainsford/ Miss Garratt

This early club and the associated tournament might be a surprise to the present day members but there is no reason to think that this was not a predecessor to the present club. On the other hand it could well have been a low-key 'gentry' club of the time that subsequently died out. Nevertheless, it is confirmed, that the game was played in the town at least twenty years earlier than had been thought.

Competition

The club has thrived in all sorts of competitive ways. Because of geographical location the club is the only Leinster club that had played in the Mid-Ulster Leagues. They were regular participants until about 1969 when the 'troubles' flared up. It enjoyed the competitive challenges with some of the best northern clubs such as the Boat Club and Windsor. *It is hard to beat Northern hospitality and home made cakes* said one report.

The club has won many Provincial Towns Cup titles. Having won the Class 2 event in the late forties the teams got even stronger and in the 1950s and 1960s they were an exceptionally hard team to beat. There were McArdles all over the place. However, other notables appeared over the years, including Molly Nichol who won the junior Championships in Western Australia as far back as 1935. Larry Stein, Jim Pringle Paul Brady and Peter Hannon, Adrian Ledwith, Mary McCrystal and Joan Brady are some of the others to win many tournaments in various parts of the country. With a strong emphasis on juniors in the 1970s and 1980s, it was no surprise to see the Class 4 team of all juniors reaching the Leinster final in 1986. That year, for the first time, Miriam Ward became the first junior to be selected on the Leinster under 16 squad. That year we could see the rise of two young Pringle boys, Paul and James. The latter would represent Ireland at U12, U14, U16 and U18 and then senior. John McGahon is another talent and as the winner of the national Fergus O'Shee Trophy in 2000.

1940

The 1940 season was a good one for the club. In the Provincial Towns Cup the senior team beat **Kilkenny County & City LTC** 5/4 at **Fitzwilliam LTC**. The junior team (2nd seniors), on the same day, clinched their title when narrowly beating the same club at **Mount Temple LTC**. The latter team was Raymond

Williams, Paddy Finnegan (captain), Brian Rennison, Nora Whiting, Monica O' Brien and Maureen Lennon. The club president was none other than P. L. McArdle, father of the famous J. J. McArdle.

Paddy Finnegan was also a winner of Provincial Towns' Cup honours in badminton. Raymond Williams went on to become an international rugby referee. Maureen Lennon went on to marry Tommy Cradle, a man who would become President of Dundalk Golf Club.

Paddy Finnegan recalled later that the standard at the time was very high. *There was no such thing as coaching; we had to develop the skills ourselves. But competition was so intense, the standard automatically rose.*

In 1940 the courts were situated, as they remained so, on The Ramparts. There were four grass out of six courts, the number 1 court being the one with a carpet like surface. Everyone wanted to play on that court. Unfortunately, like the others, it would occasionally flood when the nearby ramparts rose.

Towns' Tennis Cup Retained By Dundalk

HEADED by international, J. McArdle. Dundalk proved too strong for Athy in the final of the Provincial Towns Tennis Cup, and won by 9 matches to 2.

This was Dundalk's third successive victory in the competition. Results:—
J. J. McArdle and L. F. Steen bt. H. Dawson and N. Plewman. 6-3, 4-6, 6-2; G. Crosbie and G. Corr bt. M. Minch and R. A. Wright. 8-6. 2-6. 7-5; M. Conlon and D. Williams bt. A. Telford and G. Clarke. 4-6. 6-3. 6-4; Miss I. M. Lewis and Miss P. O'Connell bt. Miss M. Fenlon and Mrs. Spiers. 6-4, 4-6, 8-6; Mrs. Hannon and Miss Lennon bt. Mrs. Plewman and Mrs. Lynch. 6-2, 6-1; Mrs Carroll and Miss M. Joyce bt. Misses R. and B. Fenelon. 6-3. 10-8; J. McArdle and Miss Lewis bt. W. Dawson and Miss Fenelon. 6-2. 6-2; L. Steen and Miss O'Connell bt. W. Plewman and Mrs Spiers. 6-3. 6-2; G. Crosbie and Mrs. Hannon lost to M. Minch and Mrs. Plewman. 5-7. 1-6; G. Corr and Miss M. Lennon bt. R. Wright and Mrs. Minch. 6-4. 6-4; M. Conlon and Mrs. Carroll lost to A. Telford and Miss R. Fenelon. 4-6. retired. G. Corr and Miss M. Lennon bt. R. A. Wright and Mrs. Minch. 6-4. 6-4.

Irish Independent 13th September 1954

1989

The 1989 season was a good one with more adults taking up the game and the top junior, James Pringle, winning the Irish boys under 12 title. The club was also involved in inter-schools competitions. The entry for the County Louth Junior Open was some 160 players in 14 competitions. Club champions that year were Adrian Ledwith and Grainne Mullins. The senior team did well in the Leinster Challenge Cup. The year

ended with a successful doubles team league won by the "Yops" team under the captaincy of Emmet Curran. Overall, the resurgence of both junior and senior tennis was a highlight of the year with much promise to come.

Dundalk Lawn Tennis & Badminton Club
Wins in Provincial Towns Competitions

Class	Years
Class 1	1950,1952,1953,1954, 1956,1959,1962,1963, 1964,1965,1975,1976, 1993
Class 2	1939,1947,1948,1984, 1986,1994
Class 3	1994, 2000
Class 4	1997,1999, 2000
Men's Class 1 League	1985
Ladies Class 1 League	1987

Championship of County Louth

Year	Men's Singles	Ladies Singles
1935	F.Henry beat P. H. Matthews 6/2 6/1	Miss P. Gill beat Miss G. Carty 6/2 6/1
1955	J.J. McArdle beat G. Crosbie 6/0 6/1	Mrs.D. Carroll beat Miss C. Dearey 6/1 6/4
1958		Ms Molly Nichol
1960	J.J. Mc Ardle beat J. Kelly 6/2 6/0	Miss R. Duffner beat Miss I. Lewis 6/4 6/3
1961	J.J. McArdle beat Frank Mc Ardle 6/3 6/4	Miss R. Daly beat] Miss D. Corcoran 6/4 6/2
1962	Frank McArdle beat J.J. McArdle 9/7 6/3	M. Gallagher beat Pat Mc Kinley 6/4 5/7 6/0
1967	Frank McArdle beat Jim McArdle 6/4 6/4	M. Gallagher beat Joan Brady 8/6 6/4
1982	Michael Ferguson	Gillian Chandler
1983	Peter Hannon	M. Wogan
1984	I. Schindler	Gillian Chandler
1985	Pat Mangan (USA)	Gillian Chandler
1986	Adrian Ledwith	
1991	J. Burke	N. Kelly
1992	Jim Pringle	S. Byrne
1993	Jim Pringle	S. Byrne
1998	James Pringle	
1999	Robert Collins	G. Eagleton
2002	John McGahon	

In 1983 the club were strong enough to enter a team in the Leinster Challenge Cup for men. This was a winning combination of Paul Brady, Peter Hannon, Adrian Ledwith, Jim McArdle, Jim Pringle, Frank McArdle, Adrian Ledwith and Larry Steen. An impressive line up! Details on some Dundalk players are given in the Who's Who chapter. The club has had its ups and downs but undoubtedly it has the basis of a club likely to thrive for many years to come.

In 1986 Dundalk Tennis Club won Class 2 of the Provincial Town's Cup competition. From left: Claire Ward, John O'Connor, Paul Brady and Miriam Ward.

****

Fermoy Lawn Tennis Club
(Founded Circa 1893)

This Waterford club has a long history. They set a mark in 1920 when, for the first time, they would win the Munster Cup for senior club teams in the province. The honorary secretary in 1894 and 1895 was a Miss Hendley. She lived at Mountrivers in Fermoy.

Open Tournament at Fermoy LTC	
Event	1st Prize
1893	
Men's H S	R.H. Bradford
Ladies H S	Miss G. Des Barres
Men's H D	G.C. Green/H.C. Hildyard
Ladies H D	Miss Briggs/Miss Harman
Mixed H D	A. McClintock/Miss K. Bond
1935	
MS	M. Bergl (Harrow) beat M.Lynch 6/2 6/0 6/0 (Victory Cup)
Men's H S	M. Bergl (owe 30) beat W. McCabe (owe 4.6) 6/0 6/2
Ladies' H S	Miss Carroll (owe 4.6) w/o Miss Roche (Scr.)
Men's H D	J. Holmes/Dr. Galvin (owe 3.0) beat General Bond/H. Ross (1.6) 6/4 2/6 6/3
Ladies'H D	Miss Priestly/Mrs. Conner (owe 15.3) beat Miss O'Sullivan/MissRoche (owe 3.6) 6/2 6/8 6/4
Mixed H D	Dr. Galvin/Miss Daly (owe 15.2) beat M. Bergl/Miss Zelie Godfrey (owe 30) 3/6 6/1 10/8

****

Glanmire Lawn Tennis (& Croquet) Club
(Founded Circa 1893)

Glanmire, the Cork club, won the Senior Munster Cup in both 1940 and 1941. The honorary secretary in 1894 and 1895 was Tristram Curry. He lived at North Eesk, Glanmire.

Open Tournament at Glanmire Lawn Tennis & Croquet Club		
Event	1st Prize	2nd Prize
1893		
MS	H. Noble	
MHS	-Lyons	
MHD	E. & F. Lyons	
LHD	Miss K. Skipworth/Miss White	
MxHD	W. St. George/Miss Atthill	
Open Tournament at Glanmire Lawn Tennis & Croquet Club		
Event	1st Prize	2nd Prize
1894		
MS	H. N. Craig	
MHS	T. Gresson	C.E. Murphy
All-C. MS	St. J. Killery	
LHS	Miss Baldwin	Miss C. Gregg
MHD	A. & C.E. Murphy	H.N. Craig/ W.C.L. Sullivan
MxHD	H.N. Craig/ Miss Baldwin	C. Fitzgerald/ Miss Jack

****

Dungannon Lawn Tennis Club
(Founded Circa 1893)

The **Dungannon LTC** was one of the oldest in Ulster. No record of the officers in that club could be found in the 1894 and 1895 Irish Lawn tennis Handbook. The club was one of the earliest to affiliate to the Irish Lawn Tennis Association when it was formed in 1908. In 1911 it was only one of 7 clubs in Ulster on the list of 71 affiliated clubs. The others were Ballycastle, Clones, County Cavan, Omagh, Monaghan, and Cliftonville.

****

Enniscorthy Lawn Tennis Club
(Founded Circa 1893)

In 1894 and 1895 the honorary secretary of the Enniscorthy club was Mr. A. G. Lamont who lived in Enniscorthy itself. It is not known whether this is the predecessor of the **Hillbrook Tennis Club** in Enniscorthy. The latter, in existence for at least four decades, has been particularly successful in recent years. In 2002 they won the very competitive Class A Leinster Summer league, beating the strong Mullingar team in the finals.

Greystones Lawn Tennis (& Croquet) Club
(Founded Circa 1893)

It is not known exactly what year this club was founded, but **Greystones LTC** (originally with croquet in the title) did run an open tournament in 1893 and 1894. This suggests perhaps an even earlier starting time. It was a sign of the times that in the initial Irish Handbooks the club was not listed in the Dublin & Suburban clubs but rather as a Country club. The honorary secretary in those two years was Mr. R. C. Dobbs, Knocklyon, Greystones, County Wicklow. The results given for 1893 specified that it was a club tournament but *open to Visitors joining the Club for a Month or other short period.*

Open Tournament Greystones Lawn Tennis & Croquet Club		
Event	**1st Prize**	**2nd Prize**
	1893	
MHS	D. Rogerson	
LHS	Miss B. Henshaw	
MHD	-Wilson/-Price	
LHD	Mrs. Fitzgibbon/Miss Lefroy	
MxHD	F.W. Forrest/Miss C. Scott	
	1894	
MHS	R.G. Hunt	W.S. Crawley
LHS	Miss I. Scott	Miss Leet
MHD	J. Corcoran/J. Mahony	-Mayne/-Roberts
LHD	Miss Bernard/ Miss M. Meldon	Miss Leet/ Miss C. Scott
MxHD	R.G. Hunt/ Miss I. Scott	A.C. M'Donnell/ Miss M. Scott

The 1975 committee at Greystones LTC. Back (l. to r.) Ronnie Fitzell (honorary treasurer), Maurice Neligan, Tom O' Meara & Martin Donoghue. Front (l. to r.) Berk Citron (vice-chairman), Paddy Dunne (chairman), Rosemarie Fawsitt and Jo Donnelly (honorary secretary). Missing from photograph: president: Major J. Kelly.

Being a County Wicklow club it was understandable that their first major entry to competition was to be in the Provincial Towns Cup in 1965. That year they reached the final of Class III, losing to Tullamore. They won Class II in 1967 and then Class I in 1968.

They would also have wins in 1974 (Class III) and 1977 (Class 1).

Their entry in the Dublin leagues seems to have first been in the late 1960s. Their men's team won Class 4 in 1969 and then Class 2 in 1986. The ladies, also in the summer leagues, won Class 3 in 1976 and then Class 2 in 1977, retaking the latter in 1999 and 2001. By 2002 they had won some 23 different leagues run by the Dublin Lawn Tennis Council. These include two boys' titles (1991, 2001), always a good portent for a club's future.

The club has had nine courts for many years. Today these are all weather and floodlit. This was not always the case. In the mid-1970s the number of members had passed out the 400 mark. Today it is considerably more. At that time the club had a small pavilion and three of their courts were badly broken up with age and use. Today, and for many years past, the work started at that time is bearing fruits. The club is situated on the Mill Road in Greystones.

Greystones Lawn Tennis Club Club Championships 2005		
Event	**Winner**	**Runner-Up**
MS	Gareth O'Nuallain	N. Fitzgerald
LS	Susie Perkins	S. Riordan
MS 'B'	D. O'Sullivan	K. O'Donnell
LS 'B'	S. Gogarty	M. Nolan
MS 'C'	D. Gilmore	A. Happonen
MD	G. O'Nuallain/ R. Stone	T. O'Connell/ C. Woods
LD	S. Riordan/ S. Perkins	L. Diggin/ J. Hayes
MxD	J. Perkins/ S. Perkins	S. Bourne/ R. Woods
MS Plate	N. Flynn	C. Harper
MS 'B' Plate	M. Flynn	B. Woods
MS 'C'Plate	P. Byrne	A. Gunning
LS Plate	E. Lendrum	E. McEntaggart

In 1966 the club first ran the Hard Court Championships of Wicklow. The winners of the men's and ladies singles titles were international players, the well-known husband and wife combination of Harry and Geraldine Barniville. The event became the South Leinster Hard Court Championships in about 1980 and with a high entry standard. Sam Smith, the winner of the ladies event in 1993, was one of the top ladies in England at that time and currently commentates on televised tennis worldwide.

In 2005 the club hosted a Junior Open and the Irish Veteran's Open. The club championship results for the year are in the table across. The club's trustees in 2005 were Dermot Devereaux, Art Grimes, Tim Hazelton,

Sam Smith the 1993 winner of the Carlsberg South Leinster Hard Court Championships being presented with her prize by Pat Barry (Guinness Group Sales) and (on right) Declan Power, president Greystones LTC. Currently, English girl Sam is currently a top television tennis commentator.

Pauline O'Reilly and Declan Power. The 2004/2005 executive committee at the club was Art Grimes (president), Brian Woods (chairman), David Kenny (treasurer), Doreen O'Reilly (membership secretary), John Rankin (club manager), Ailish Byrne (ladies' captain), Donal O'Sullivan (men's captain), Sarah Riordan (secretary) and general committee members, Billy Markham, Robert Mowett and Fergus Murphy.

South Leinster Hard Court Champions at Greystones LTC

Year	Men's Singles	Ladies Singles
1981	Jim McArdle	Bernadette Davy
1982	Tommy Burke	Rhona Howett
1983	Joe O'Dwyer	Lesley O' Halloran
1984	Robbie Dolan	Marie Bolster
1985	Joe O'Dwyer	Tami Lucero
1986	Michael Nugent	Sandra Fearon
1987	Eoin Collins	Jennifer Thornton
1988	Garbhain O'Nuallain	Janet Hazleton
1989	Peter Wright	Jennifer O'Brien
1990	Eoin Collins	Fiona Long
1991	Peter Wright	Deirdre Walsh
1992	K. Tomlin	C. Herbert
1993	S. Doyle	Sam Smith
1994	Eoin Collins	Claire Curran
1995	Eoin Collins	L. Sheales
1996	Owen Casey	S. Doyle
1997	Owen Casey	E. Knox
1998	Owen Casey	S. Sheppard
1999	L. Holland	Karen Nugent

****

Grosvenor Lawn Tennis Club (Founded Circa 1893)

The **Grosvenor LTC** was located in Rathmines and was one of about 18 clubs in Dublin when it was formed in the early 1890s. The honorary secretary in 1894 was F. W. Dunlop. He lived at Westminster, Grosvenor Road, Rathmines.

****

High School Lawn Tennis Club (Founded Circa 1893)

Over the years a few schools either affiliated to the national organisation as a 'school' or a club was formed utilizing the schools facilities and having staff, students and outsiders as members. The likelihood is that this mixed Protestant Dublin school organised such a club, at a time when there was no national organisation. When the ILTA was formed in 1908 it was not an affiliated member. The honorary secretary in 1894 was R. H. Moore, High School, 40 Harcourt Street, Dublin.

Holywood Lawn Tennis Club
(Founded Circa 1893)

This County Down club was one of the first to be formed in Ulster. The honorary secretary in 1894 and 1895 was Mr. R. A. Williams. He lived at Fernbank in Holywood. The club does not appear on the ILTA affiliation list in 1911, 1915 or 1921. It may have survived as a small club.

****

Kenilworth Lawn Tennis Club
(Founded Circa 1893)

Des O'Brien the noted rugby international, and also an excellent tennis player, lived overlooking Kenilworth Square in the 1930s. The square had twenty-five grass courts and two croquet lawns at that time. Four tennis clubs were in action on the courts in the square. They were **Methodist LTC**, **Waverly LTC**, **Grosvenor LTC** and **Kenilworth LTC**. It is reasonable to assume that the original club there was Kenilworth LTC. The honorary secretary in 1894 and 1895 was Mr. T. Butler who lived at 5 Grove Park, Rathmines.

****

Mallow Lawn Tennis (& Croquet) Club
(Founded Circa 1893)

It is well known that Mallow provided, over many years of Irish tennis, some fine exponents of the game. Apart from the Barry's, there was also K. B. Williams, Franks Furney, Ray Ward, and Meta Foley-Lane. Mrs. D. R. Barry was Irish Open Champion in 1911 and 1913. Previously, in 1901, a Mrs. Norton Barry played at Wimbledon. Perhaps this is the same lady as Mrs. D. R. Barry. Miss Stanuell was another Mallow member of note and was Irish Open Champion in 1893. It is not certain that this was the same lady. Meta Foley won her first tournament at Leaselands, Mallow in 1931 and her last at Rushbrooke in 1964. She was an exceptional character in every respect. In various parts of the book there are references to Mallow club members. A club history was not available anywhere. However, a few interesting pieces have been uncovered. Thanks to present honorary secretary, Philip Comyn, and Franks Furney that great player from the 1950s and 1960s, the Committee and Rules for 1914 were made available. Some of the interesting rules are included in the following page. There were about 90 members listed including 'Colonel De Falbe and Officers of the 1st North Stafford Regiment'. Other military tiles in the club were Major Bell, Colonel M. O'D. Braddell, Lieutenant-Colonel J. Brasier-Creagh, Colonel Brown, Major J. Creagh, Major Davidson, Major Farquhar,

The Committee of Mallow Lawn Tennis and Croquet Club in 1898. From left: R. E. Tottenham, Miss Norreys, Colonel Brown, Miss Ormsby, Harry Longfield, Mrs. James Hunt, J. F. (Jack) Smith, Mrs. Robert Webb, Robert (Bob) Perry (honorary secretary) and Miss K. Cotter.

Major the Hon. H.G. (D.S.O.) Heneage, Colonel Kirkpatrick, Colonel Longfield, Captain Nichols, General Paget and Colonel Williamson (Bruree). Among the clergy in the club were the Reverend G. S. Baker, Reverend R. Brougham, Reverend W. Cotter, Reverend F. H. Foley, Reverend S. H. P. Harman, Reverend J. A. Jegoe and Reverend L. Swanzy. Titled persons were fewer in number. The ones given were Lady E. Becher (suspect it may be Beecher as there was a Miss Beecher in the Irish Open Singles final in 1910), Lady Cotter and Lady Lisle. Two doctors are in the list and the names are perhaps linked to some successful Irish players at a later stage in Irish tennis. These were Dr. Homan and Dr. Montgomery.

tennis tournaments in the Munster region were held at Rushbrooke, Fermoy, Roscrea, Mitchelstown, Glanmire and Mallow. The **Mallow LTC** secretary at the time was a Mr. Finch Smith. The club was, perhaps, even a few years old at this stage. The following year, E. H. Montgomery of West End, Mallow took up the post. The results for those two years and some, many decades later, are given in table.

The club open tournament at Mallow LTC in 1936. Singles winners were Mrs. Carroll-Leahy and Major Grehan.

Quite a number of Mallow members were to feature on the Munster Branch and the ILTA. Of these the best known was probably Eric Harte-Barry who became President of the ILTA in 1964. In 1893, the

VI

Bone-fide Visitors staying with Members shall be admitted free for a fortnight and after that time to pay 2/6 per month and 2/- per month to Tea Fund. Visitors staying in the neighbourhood may be introduced by Members as Honorary members for 5/- per month (for not more than three months). Persons who reside more than 10 miles from Mallow may be introduced by Members as visitors, on payment of 6d. per diem. In all cases the names of visitors and Members introducing same must be entered in the book provided for that purpose.

VII

The grounds to be open for play from 11.30 a.m. to 1.30p.m., and from 3 to 7.30 p.m. Players must wear flat soled Lawn Tennis shoes. (A) Lawn Tennis-On Club days four balls, and on non-Club days three balls can be obtained for each court, and must be returned to the groundsman, or if lost paid for (1/-each). At the conclusion of a set, the court must be vacated for five minutes. No prize game to take precedence, except Tournaments sanctioned by Committee. (B) Croquet-On Club days no game must last more than one hour unless there is a vacant ground.

Extract from Rules for
Mallow Lawn Tennis Club (c. 1914)

Mallow LTC Presentation Night (Circa 1992)

The 1932 Open Championship at Mallow LTC. The men's singles winner was George Lyttleton Rogers the Irish number 1 while the ladies' singles winner was English visitor Vera Montgomery who reached the Irish Open final that year.

Note the men's singles final of 1950. It took 45 games, in the best of 3 sets, for Alan Haughton to beat Franks Furney. It was 48 games in 1956 when he was beaten by Harry Barniville, this time in a five set final. This increased to 65 games when the same players met in 1957. This time Alan won. In a number of years the Mallow tournament was in fact the Munster Championships.

There was a tournament scheduled for Mallow in 1974 (called the North Cork Championships). But records for tournaments since the 1960s are not apparent when perusing the ILTA Yearbooks. The club continues to function but the days when many of the top players in Ireland graced their courts have faded for the moment.

Mallow Lawn Tennis Club
Open Tournament

	Men's Championship Singles
1893	William St. George Perrott
1894	William St. George Perrott
1932	George Lyttleton Rogers
1937	Alan Haughton
1939	A. Haughton bt Donny Williams 6/2 6/2 2/6 6/4
1946	Alan Haughton beat Freddie South 1/6 6/1 6/2
1947	Franks Furney bt. Alan Haughton 6/4 3/6 7/5
1948	Alan Haughton beat Franks Furney 6/1 7/5 6/2
1949	Alan Haughton beat Freddie South 6/1 7/5 6/2
1950	Alan Haughton beat Franks Furney 6/3 10/12 8/6
1951	Alan Haughton beat D. Smythe 1/6 6/1 6/3 6/1
1953	Alan Haughton beat H. Mc Carthy 7/5 6/4
1954	Alan Haughton bt. Franks Furney 6/3 6/1 1/6 6/3
1955	Harry Barniville bt A. Haughton 1/6 6/2 7/5 6/3
1956	H. Barniville bt. A. Haughton 2/6 10/8 8/6 6/2
1957	Alan Haughton beat Harry Barniville 7/5 11/13 3/6 6/4 6/4
1960	Franks Furney beat H. Mc Carthy 6/1 6/2 8/6
1961	Franks Furney beat W. Nagle 7/5 6/2 6/2
1962	F. Furney beat Des Scannell 6/4 2/6 5/7 6/2 6/3
	Men's Handicap Singles
1894	--Smith beat W. St .G. Perrott
1937	Alan Haughton(-30) beat F. Stafford(15) 6/2 7/5
	Men's Doubles
1956	Alan Haughton/Franks Furney beat H. Barniville/H. McCarthy 6/3 6/1 4/6 2/6 6/4
1959	Alan Haughton/Franks Furney beat T. Seacy/H. McCarthy 11/9 6/2
1960	Franks Furney/E. Quinlan beat H. Mc Carthy/T. Seacy 8/6 6/1
1961	Alan Haughton/Franks Furney beat Sarsfield Smith/John O'Brien 6/1 6/2
1962	Franks Furney/Des Scannell beat Alan and Peter Haughton 6/3 8/6
	Men's Handicap Doubles
1893	C. Murphy/Fitz J.
1937	Alan Haughton/J. Dwyer (-15.5) beat J. Golden/J. Regan(2) 6/2 6/4
	Ladies Singles
1929	Marjorie Haughton
1930	Nancy Haughton
1931	Nancy Haughton
1932	Miss Vera Montgomery
1933	Mrs. Norton Barry
1934	Miss Moira O'Keeffe
1935	Miss Moira O'Keeffe
1937	Miss Patricia O'Keeffe
1938	Miss Frances M. Daly
1939	Miss Zelie Godfrey
1946	Meta P. L. Foley
1947	Meta P. L. Foley
1955	Meta Foley Lane beat Nan Conner 6/3 0/6 6/3
1960	Meta Foley Lane bt. Jill McAuliffe 4/6 6/1 6/1
1961	Meat Foley Lane beat Joan Barry 6/2 2/6 6/2
1962	Gene Horgan beat Meta Foley Lane 6/3 4/6 6/1

The championship winners at Mallow LTC in 1936 are a bit of a mystery. The man was a member of Herga LTC in England, according to the crest on his pullover.

Moate Lawn Tennis Club
(Founded 1893)

A note on this club on the 13th March 1893 suggests that it was founded in that year. The grounds were situated near the Fair Green on the road to the railway station. It was being laid out and poled and there were some sixty members in that year. The committee included Stoppford Halpin as honorary treasurer – he was a banker – and William Clibborn as the honorary treasurer. The ordinary members of the committee were E. H. Winder (detective inspector, R.I.C.), F. W. Russell junior, Arthur C. Daly and Doctor H. Moorehead. According to the local newspaper report at the time the club *prided themselves on exclusivity.*

*****

Mountjoy Square Lawn Tennis Club
(Founded Circa 1893)

It appears that in 1893 the residents of this square in Dublin came together, formed a club and ran a very successful tournament. In the first Irish Lawn Tennis Handbook, published in 1894, the writer made the following complimentary comment. He noted the success of the new **Donnybrook LTC** which was *evidence of the fast hold lawn tennis has obtained upon the affections of the capital, already better supplied with tennis clubs than perhaps any city of its size in the Three Kingdoms; and the second was the evidence of the need for a late season handicap meeting in Dublin, afforded byte phenomenal success of the Mountjoy Square tournament, experimentally launched by some residents of the neighbourhood. The success of the venture is said to have quite astonished the promoters.* The 'club' did not become an affiliated member of the ILTA in 1908 and is assumed to have died out in the previous few years.

*****

University College Galway (Queen's College) Lawn Tennis Club
(Founded Circa 1893)

The tennis club at the university in Galway was one of the first to be founded in Connacht. It is thought to initially have had grass courts. The club here has had its ups and downs with a relatively small membership. In the 1960s and 1970s there was a fairly active club with four hard courts in play in front of the old

Mallow Open-Results (Continued)	
Ladies Handicap Singles	
1893	Miss B. Beecher
1894	Miss A. Beecher beat Miss B. Beecher
Ladies Doubles	
1960	Ann Delaney/Jill McAuliffe beat Mrs. F. Furney/Miss M.P. Cronin 6/1 6/3
1961	Gene Horgan/Miss M. Delaney beat Joan Barry/Miss F. Murphy 6/4 7/5
1962	Gene Horgan/Miss Delaney beat Joan Barry/Miss F. Murphy 4/6 6/4 7/5
Ladies Handicap Doubles	
1894	Misses A. & B. Beecher
Mixed Doubles	
1950	Alan Haughton/Alice Fawcett beat Franks Furney/Miss R. Barry 12/10 3/6 6/3
1955	Dr. Young/Nan Conner beat Harry Barniville/Miss Baker 4/6 6/4 6/4
1956	Franks Furney/Betty Homan beat Alan Haughton/Miss Monaghan 6/2 6/1
1959	Alan Haughton/Miss Wood-Power beat T. Seacy/Mrs. Nagle 6/2 6/3
1960	P. Ahearne/Jill McAuliffe beat John O'Brien/Ann Delaney 6/3 6/4
1961	Alan Haughton/Mrs. D. Sarsfield beat John O'Brien/Gene Horgan 2/6 6/4 6/2
1962	Des Scannell/Gene Horgan beat Alan Haughton/Joan Barry 6/3 8/6
Mixed Handicap Doubles	
1893	W. St. G. Perrott/Miss Beecher
1894	W. St. G. Perrott/Miss A. Beecher

engineering building. In the 1990s the club was inactive for a period. It was revived in 2002 with Emer Clarke being one of the chief organisers.

*****

Charleville Lawn Tennis Club
(Founded 1894)

The first Irish Handbook indicates that this northside Dublin club was one of 18 in the Dublin area that was recognised. The honorary secretary for 1894 was E. V. Longworth of 2 Charleville Road, North Circular Road, Dublin. The following year's handbook indicates that the secretary for 1895 was J. G. M'Nab of 27 Charleville Road. The club is situated near Cross Guns Bridge on Whitworth Road. The club has five all-weather floodlit courts and a playing programme for all twelve months of the year. The current head coach is Hugh McDonagh.

1981 Open Singles Runner-Up at Charleville LTC was Tommy Burke

Peter Hannon was the 1981 winner of the Open at Charleville LTC.

The club won the Class III of the Men's Summer Leagues in Dublin in at least four years. 1967 was a particularly fruitful season when the club took both the both the Division II and III titles. They won Ladies Summer leagues in at least two seasons, the Class III title coming their way as far back as 1927. In the fairly recently started winter leagues they captured three men's titles namely, Class I in 1996, Class II in 1994 and Class III in 1995. They have also captured four veteran's titles (three by the men and one by the ladies). The Floodlit league, started in 1979, has been fruitful with Class I men's titles in 1995 and 1997 and a Class III title in 2002. Perhaps one of their best former players was Aidan Bradshaw, a full time coach, who was with the club for 17 years before moving to **Sutton LTC.**

Rhian Griffiths was the 1981 ladies' singles runner-up at Charleville LTC

In 1981 Eleanor Lightbody was the winner of the ladies' singles at Charleville LTC in 1981.

✲✲✲✲

Brighton (Brighton Square) Lawn Tennis Club
(Founded Circa 1894)

The Brighton Square club first appears in the Irish Lawn Tennis handbook in 1895. The honorary secretary lived at 44 Brighton Square, Rathgar but no name was included in the handbook. The club was affiliated to the ILTA in 1911, in 1915, when it had 60 members, but not in 1921. Seven handbooks produced between 1956 and 1974 had no listing for this club as affiliated at this time, the presumption being that activity level was very low over a long period of time.

In 1969 the Leinster Branch ran their inaugural hard court tournament at Brighton Square. In the men's singles 'veteran' Gerry Clarke, who had returned to Ireland that season after three years in Scotland, won the final in two sets. Ann Keegan had a notable three-set win over Geraldine Barniville in the ladies' final. The results were as follows:

> MS Gerry Clarke beat Ronan Fearon 6/4 7/5
>
> LS Ann Keegan beat Geraldine Barniville 5/7 8/6 6/2
>
> MxD Brendan Quinn/Ann Keegan beat
>   Gerry Clarke/Annette O'Gorman 4/6 6/4 6/3

The Irish Close championships were held for at least three years in the period up to 1977. Since 1978 the event has had a permanent home at **Donnybrook LTC.**

✲✲✲✲

Innishannon Lawn Tennis Club
(Founded Circa 1894)

The first appearance of **Innishannon LTC**, County Cork, is in the second Irish Handbook of 1895. As they held an open tournament that year a reasonable proposition is that the club was founded in about 1894. The winner of the men's championship singles is probably the same man who would become an Irish Open Doubles champion in 1903. J. Pim is likely to be Joshua Pim, Irish Open Champion in 1893, 1894 and 1895. The Innishannon club won the prestigious Munster Cup in 1910. This event started in 1907. The club honorary secretary in 1895 was G. Caulfield Browne.

In the 1913 list of affiliated Irish clubs we find that the club was an early affiliate. However, the tournament was not one of the 42 sanctioned events that year. In the County of Cork there were sanctioned events in Youghal, Blackrock, Mallow, Sunday's Well, Marmullane, Rushbrooke, Mitchelstown and Muskerry. But no Innishannon, perhaps a small local tournament was held that year. Interestingly, that year there was only one sanctioned event in County Dublin (i.e. the Irish Championships) and one in Belfast (at **Windsor LTC**). The club may have lasted longer than it first appears. It is not on the affiliated clubs list in 1921 nor was there a secretary for the club in the 1956 or 1974 handbooks.

Open Tournament at Innishannon Lawn Tennis Club in 1894		
Event	**1st Prize**	**2nd Prize**
	1893	
MS	H.N. Craig	St. K. Killery
MHS	J. Pim	A. Meade
LHS	Miss M.G. Baldwin divided with	
		Miss Donovan
MD	Fred Lyons/A.Craig	R. Meade/S. Payne
LHD	Miss M.G. Baldwin/	Miss R. Argles/
	Miss Donovan	Mrs. Hodson
MxHD	W. Sullivan/	F.J. Wright/
	Miss Baldwin	Miss Nash

✲✲✲✲

Sandymount Lawn Tennis Club
(Founded Circa 1894)

This club appears in the 1895 Irish tennis yearbook with not name given for the secretary. It had not been identified in the first yearbook, the previous year. It was listed among the 1915 and 1922 Irish Lawn Tennis Association affiliated clubs. It was not listed in the yearbooks published in 1956, 1963, 1967, 1983 or 1999. These facts suggest that either the club died out or later became known under another name.

****

Kingstown School Lawn Tennis Club
(Founded Circa 1894)

This school was not listed as a club in any of the early Irish yearbooks though apparently it did function for a period.

Open Tournament at Kingstown School LTC		
Event	1st Prize	2nd Prize
	1894	
MHS	H.F. Cotton	A.Rice M.H.D.
LHS	Miss B. M'Blaine	Miss Scott
MxH	K.A. Rynd/	J. "Porterfield"/
D	Miss B. M'Blaine	Miss Blaneken

****

De Vesci Lawn Tennis Club
(Founded 1895)

In 1895 a group of tennis enthusiasts, living in the locality, got together and, having obtained permission from the local residents of De Vesci Terrace to use an area of land within the De Vesci Gardens, formed a tennis club. So it was that the De Vesci Lawn Tennis Club was born, a location some 150m from the West Pier of Dun Laoghaire harbour. For the first 39 years the residents controlled the tennis club and in 1934 the club was granted a lease and became independent, free to manage and control its own operation. The first Annual General Meeting of the *new* club was held on the 15th March 1934 at the Kingstown Institute in Georges Street. The club colours were later selected as being purple and yellow, in deference to the Lilacs and Laburnums that were found around the grounds. Some of them are still there today.

In 1993 the team from DeVesci LTC won the O35 Class III section of the DLTC league.

Soon after formation a small red painted (possibly with some white) summerhouse was erected behind court number three. Interestingly, this acted as the changing room for the gentlemen of the club; the ladies were limited to the privacy provided by the

foliage of the surrounding trees and shrubs. A proper clubhouse was built in 1935 and served the club well until burnt down on Saturday the 25th January 1978. In their anniversary booklet the question was asked, where were you at 11.50pm on that night. At that exact moment in time *esteemed member, Peter Scales, was having a bath when he got a phone call from another member, Fergus Brady, to say that the Club house was on fire.* That year, with no clubhouse, the players were not permitted to field a team in the summer leagues. The teams were relegated the following year, the men's first team falling from a respectable Class II.

Like all of the older clubs, grass was the playing surface. From 1895 until 1982 this was the case at the south Dublin club. Maintenance was always a problem, invariably the baselines had to have new sods and reseeding was required. On one occasion the members were surprised *when daffodils grew along the baseline.* The competition from clubs with hard courts took its toll, membership dwindled and, with twenty pounds in the bank, drastic measures were required. In mid 1982 the committee put together a plan to finance replacing the grass with four tarmacadum ones. These were laid the following year and received a coating of red and green acrylic in 1984.

De Vesci Lawn Tennis Club
Centenary Celebration
1895 - 1995

By 1989 courts 1 and 2 were floodlit and in 1993 synthetic grass, in the form of *Savanna*, were laid. Courts 3 and 4 were to be floodlit. The club was now a vibrant one and plans for the centenary celebrations took shape. The centenary committee was Mary C. Rogan (President), Joan Mc Crum (honorary secretary), Roy Fitzell (honorary treasurer), Brian Cahill (men's captain), Helen Irwin (ladies captain), Ita Casey, Jenny Dalton and Jim Giles were committee members and Harry Nelson, Pat O'Keeffe and Peter Roughneen Club Trustees. The events included the amalgamation of the Open Day and Captain's Prize (May), a garden party (June), a first invitation tournament for about 20 outside clubs (July/August), *At Homes* (August and September), centenary dance at the Killiney Court Hotel (September) and a murder week-end at Renvyle House, Connemara (November). The juniors were catered for with a special event in late August. Walter Bernardini was thanked for his drawing and design of the centenary brochure cover, which included a sketch of the old clubhouse.

In 1990 the DeVesci LTC men's team above won the Class IV DLTC Winter league.

On the playing front a number of members have represented the Dublin Leagues over the years in the annual Belfast-Dublin Match. The following are some of the recent successes in the Dublin leagues. Over the years they have won some 10-league titles. The earliest wins were by the ladies. As far back as 1939 they won Class 4. This was repeated in 1952 when, on promotion, they went on to win Class 3 in 1953.

Some Recent Successes by De Vesci LTC				
1984	W	Men	Class 5	Summer L.
1993	M	Ladies	Class 3	O35
1993	M	Ladies	Class 5	O35
1997	RUp	Ladies	Class 2	O35
1998	W	Ladies	Class 2	Floodlit L.
1999	W	Ladies	Class 6	Winter L

****

Belfast Boat Club
(Founded 1898)

For over 100 years the tennis club at Belfast Boat Club has contributed much to the life of the sport in Belfast, Ulster and Ireland in general. As the name suggests, it was not a tennis club at the outset. In January 1876, representatives of the Lagan Amateur Boating Club (established in 1873) and the Ulster Rowing Club met to propose the amalgamation of the two clubs under the title of The Belfast Boat Club. The first meeting of this new club was held at the Linenhall Hotel, Belfast, on the 1st March 1876. Some of the boats were housed at the Lower Boathouse on Laganbank Road and some at the Upper Boathouse at the First Lock Stranmillis. In 1888, the Lower

Boathouse was demolished to make way for the Albert Bridge and, in 1895, the Club purchased its present site on Hay Island on the River Lagan at Stranmillis. On the 23rd May 1898 the New Boathouse, designed on the plan of the famous Stratford-on-Avon Club, was formally opened by the Mayor of Belfast, Lady Pirrie. Tennis and croquet were introduced; four grass courts being laid- "the committee are of the opinion that in order to utilise the tennis grounds to the fullest advantage, it may be desirable to admit ladies to limited membership"! The number of grass courts was extended to ten and, in 1921, three hard courts laid. The first Ulster Championships were held at the club in 1919. The three Championship titles were won by John Miley, Miss A.R. Taylor and the Miley brothers, John and Val, the men's doubles. In 1927 the ninth annual Open Lawn Tennis Tournament was held between Monday 13th June and Saturday 18th June. The following were the officers at the time:

Patron:	*His Grace the Duke of Abersorn, K.P.*
President:	*Edwin D. Hill*
Honorary Treasurer: *Herbert Quin, B.L., F.C.A.*
Honorary Referee:	*J. Gillespie*
Honorary Tournament Secretary: S.F. Jackson
Tournament Committee:
R.P. Corry, W.J. Johnston, J. Mathie, De. V. L. Crossley, A. MacKinnon, W.F. Scott, R.W. Harland F.C. MacNeice, W.N. McWilliam,

Modern followers of the game may recognise some of the following 'surnames' among the competitors in 1927. In the Men's Championship Singles J.T. Turner beat R. Pedlow 6/1 6/1 2/6 6/2 in the final. In the field of 32, competing were W. S. Corry, Rev. C. H. S. Craig, Harry Reid, J. D. M. McCallum and C. G. Gotto. Pedlow beat Gotto in the lower half of the draw (6/2 6/2) - did those surnames appear on the opposite half of the draw in Ulster events in the 1950s? There were 26 in the ladies draw with the Irish number one, Hilda Wallis of Dublin, winning the final comfortably (6/2 6/0). Her opponent was Miss F. Pearson. Others in the draw were Miss P. G. Corry, Mrs. A. S. Fairweather, Miss J. B. Ferguson and Mrs. R. L. Kemp. The Men's Championship Doubles (field of 16 pairs) was won by J. Mathie and J. T. Turner. They beat C. F. Montague and H. M. Read 6/2 6/2 4/6 6/3 in the final. The Ladies Championship Doubles had 22 pairs, Miss F. Pearson and Hilda Wallis winning the event comfortably. Her final opponents were Mrs. R. J. Horsley and Mrs. Norris, the score 6/1 6/2. R. Pedlow and Miss F.M. Fleming won the Championship Mixed, beating Read and Miss Pearson 6/4 7/5 in the final. 28 pairs took part in this event with 49 pairs in the mixed handicap. Other events, which were part of the week, were the handicap men's and ladies singles (A & B classes) and handicap men's and ladies doubles. An Open Boy's Championship of Ulster (under 18 on 1st June 1927) was won by L. Malcolmson. He beat H.C. Brown 6/3 7/9 6/0 in the final. Names in that field of 17 included J. Stevenson, A.C. Orr, R.E. Thompson and P. Jackson.

The old Belfast Boat Club Clubhouse

All the events were the best of three sets, apart from the final of the men's singles and doubles. Each day the ladies play commenced at 10 a.m. and the men's at 1 o'clock. The boy's singles competition did not start until Friday 17th at 3.30 p.m. Players were required to sign the attendance book on arriving at the club "Each day". On the opening day of the week's events there were Special Exhibition matches between top American and English players. The results for the two singles were: Bill Tilden (USA) beat Donald Greig (GB) 6/4 6/2 and Teddy Higgs (GB) beat Frank Hunter (USA) 8/6 6/3. The Americans won the doubles 6/2 6/3 6/2 and a few weeks later the Wimbledon title. (Tilden would win the Wimbledon singles three years later.) No doubt, these players were using these matches as practise for the Wimbledon championships that followed. The Belfast followers of the game no doubt enjoyed this exhibition and, perhaps, put some new shots into their own tennis during the rest of the week. The Annual Club Tournament, confined to members, was held that year between the 25th June and 2nd July. Over the years Belfast Boat Club hosted many interprovincial matches. The Leinster-Ulster series commenced in 1921 with a 10 –5 win for the visitors. These were teams just for men. The match was a regular feature of the 'tournament' week. The annual report of the honorary secretary of the ILTA for the 1922 season included the following paragraphs which tell their own story:

Owing to the unsettled state of the Country various Tournaments including the Championships were abandoned, but at a later date the Fitzwilliam Lawn Tennis Club held a very successful Tournament at which however the Championships were not played.

The Close Championships were allotted to the Belfast Boat Club and duly played. (They started on the 12th June and in conjunction with the Ulster Championships).

In the past, getting to the Boat Club involved a 'ferry' crossing for all, including international visitors at the Ulster Grasscourt Championships.

The L.T.A. refused to send a Team for the Annual Match between England and Ireland, but as the Championship meeting at which it was to have been played was subsequently abandoned this refusal did not prove of any importance. A strong Leinster Team together with six Substitutes were chosen to play the Annual Inter-Provincial match against Ulster during the progress of the Belfast Boat Club Tournament. Five of the Team and all the Substitutes stated their inability to travel and I was confronted with the greatest difficulty in securing the services of a Team. Messrs. W. Jackson, Patterson, W. B. Pollock, Purefoy, Webb and D. Kennedy finally constituted the team that was defeated by 8 matches to 1. In the intervening years ladies were included in interprovincials and all four provinces participated. An annual rotation followed. The Boat Club was still one of the favourite venues for such matches when the turn of Ulster came around. Under age 'interpros' gradually developed and the pattern of rotation followed. In 1986, for example, the club hosted the under 16, under 18, under 21 and senior interprovincals in the same week. A report at the time included the following:

Undeniably the setting for the Championships was outstanding. The Belfast Boat Club stands on the banks of the River Lagan; it has 10 grass courts, 4 hard porous concrete and had just completed the installation of one synthetic court in the centre court spot. …The Club is a tribute to the management and officials who have contributed to its development over the years. Efficient arrangements had been made for the catering. These centered on Margaret Bell, who ensured that players and officials were satisfied during the day, and in the evening a private catering firm provided the after-match dinner. On Tuesday morning a press reception was held to which officials, former Ulster Inter-provincials and all sections of the media were invited. Ulster Senior player, Peter Lowther, obviously because of his photographic qualities, was interviewed and filmed by the BBC. Futher details are included elsewhere in this book.

The History of Irish Tennis

The first 4-province interprovincial series were held at the Belfast Boat Club in 1949.

Summer 2002. Waiting for a game at the Boat Club

Despite the growth and interest of tennis at the club in the early half of the 20th century, rowing still held the interest of the more energetic members. In the 1930s the senior four carried off all the major trophies in Ireland. Competition ceased during the Second World War and *all the racing craft were disposed of, but many of the older members still look back with a feeling of nostalgia to the lazy afternoons spent on the upper reaches of the river in the pleasure craft.*

In addition to Bill Tilden and Frank Hunter, other top tennis players to play the club over the years included Pat Hughes (GB), Jaroslav Drobny (latterly GB), Donald Budge (USA), Bobby Riggs (USA), Bob Hewitt (South Africa), and Tom Okker (Netherlands).

As we know the club is also noted for the sport of squash. In 1967 two courts were built followed by two further courts in 1972. That sport has profited by the club's activities over the years. In 1989, the Northern Bank Services to Sport awards were presented at a Gala Banquet in Belfast. The club won the award in

the Voluntary Sports Organisation category. Pru Hamilton, a noted squash player and administrator, was president of the Club at the time and received the award on their behalf. In 1987, not for the first time, the club had hosted an international tennis match (Ireland versus England, followed by the second round Davis Cup match against Norway in 1988. *The match was of course the provinces first Davis Cup fixture and it was evident even before play commenced that the organisational committee had gone to great efforts to ensure everything would run smoothly.* The records show that the team of Matt Doyle and Peter Wright beat the visitors 3/2 and went on to win the Group II Zone final in Dublin when beating Greece 5/0. In the first round Ireland had beaten Cyprus 5/0 in Cork. On the 15th August of 1972 a terrorist bomb completely destroyed the Victorian edifice of the old clubhouse. A malicious fire also damaged their club facilities a few years later. To celebrate the 100th anniversary of the club a new clubhouse was constructed in 1977. Apart from squash and tennis the club has the usual function and changing facilities as well as a gym and snooker room. Over the years many players and officials from the club have contributed to the life of the game not alone in their own club, but in the province and at national level as well. In the early days of the ILTA R.W. Harland, S.F. Jackson and W.F. Scott were Ulster representatives on the ILTA, the club having first affiliated to the ILTA in 1914.

Lyn Jamison of the Ulster Council on a visit to the modern club facilities (2002).

****

Sunday's Well Boating & Tennis Club (Founded 1899)

A look at Richard Cooke's book *The Mardyke* will immediately put the Sunday's Well Boating and Tennis Club setting into its historical perspective. The modern traveller will normally fall in love with Cork, but finding this senior tennis club might be a little problem. One knows it is by the river. However, the entrance is so well hidden that the first time visitor should allow some extra time to discover its whereabouts. Having done so, one drives or walks down a laneway and is immediately hit by modern all-weather tennis courts of the highest quality. However it is the clubhouse that catches the eye. Its attractive clock placed centrally over the preserved building being special. Looking to the end of the courts we see another old building. It too has its history and adds to the glamour of the club. If anyone feels that this club is living in the past, this would be a wrong impression. It is continually improving.

In the clubhouse one finds well-documented photographs from many eras. A friendly manager, John Walsh, is proud to show you around the lounge and the latest improvements at the back. This is one of the cornerstones of the club facility. The name of the club is a giveaway. It backs on to the river and a more serene setting would be hard to find. There is now a glassed in conservatory with plenty of rooms for members and visitors to relax with post-match refreshment. When the weather is warmer this is complimented with an outdoor lounging area. It is just over one hundred years ago that this all took off.

In the late 19th century boating was one of the pursuits of the leisured classes. In July 1899 a "Sunday's Well Regatta and Water Carnival" was held. Some of that regatta committee leased a plot of ground off the Martine Walk. Boating on the River Lee had been a popular pastime of the local residents since about 1800. Regattas were a social affair held from early in that century. Apart from boat races there were other activities such as swimming, tub-races and water polo matches. Apart from the participants and the presence of large crowds, the upper crust as well as the ordinary city folk, a band played, there were Chinese lanterns lining the banks, illuminated boats were on the river in the evening and a fireworks display finished off the day. Many of the owners of riverside premises had built their own boat houses and piers in this lovely 'valley'. The first documented committee, in 1901, were T. McAuliffe as chairman (taking over from W.L. Cooke), W. L. Lyons as Captain of tennis and H. P. F. Donegan as captain of boating. The club might have started out on the river in 1899 but quickly the sports of lawn tennis and bowls were incorporated. Today one will also find squash and a long established billiards room.

Sunday's Well Ladies' Doubles 1931. From left: Eileen Fitzjames Murphy, Marjorie Haughton, Maureen Crosbie & Anita Lyons.

Over the year the Sunday's Well club contribute in a major way to holding of tournaments as well as interprovincials and international matches. The club organisers have included tennis captains who were also exceptional tennis players. These include Davis Cup player Alan Haughton and the Scannell brothers, Brian and Des. Brian was Munster Council secretary for a number of years starting in 1957. In 1970, Ken Stanton was tennis captain. His wife, Kay would become President of Tennis Ireland in 1996. In 1955, Frank Mockler became President of the Irish Lawn Tennis Association having been Munster Council President the previous year. Doctor Jim O'Neill was secretary of the Munster Branch in the mid-1970s and President in 1969 and 1984. He became President of the ILTA in 1976 and tennis captain at the Well for the following two season.

The 1988 Close championships at Sunday's Well LTC. From left: J. B. Murphy (captain), Marion Riordan (runner-up), Noel Howell (Carlsberg), Ger Flynn (title winner) and Matt Murphy (club chairman).

Dr. Jim Young playing with Billy O'Regan, is about to serve to Peter Mockler who was partnered by Peter Ahern (C. 1960 at Sunday's Well Boating & LTC, Cork).

The History of Irish Tennis

Sunday's Well Boating & Tennis Club

Year	Chairman	Tennis Captain	Year	Chairman	Tennis Captain
1900	W. L. Cooke	no information	1961	R. N. Cleary	Brian Scannell
1901	T. McAuliffe	W. F. Lyons	1962	R. N. Cleary	Alan Haughton
1902	D. E. Dunlea	W. F. Lyons	1963	J. J. Long	Alan Haughton
1903	E. Harding	J. Madden	1964	J. J. Long	Julian Drury-Byrne
1904	G. F. Bible	J. Madden	1965	Declan McSweeney	Julian Drury-Byrne
1905	M. T. Stapleton	J. Madden	1966	E. W. Heaslip	Des Scannell
1906	G. Crosbie	J. Madden	1967	E. W. Heaslip	John O'Brien
1907-1916	G. Crosbie	J. Lyons	1968	Walter Murphy	Peter J. Ahearne
1917	M. R. Boate	J. Lyons	1969	Walter Murphy	Greg O'Sullivan
1918-1919	C. Lane	J. Lyons	1970	Walter Murphy	Ken Stanton
1920	F. J. Marlow	J. Lyons	1971	Greg O'Sullivan	no information
1921	C. O. M. Williams	J. Lyons	1972	Greg O'Sullivan	Nicholas Cummins
1922	H. P. F. Donegan	J.C. Hart	1973-1974	Gordon T. Exshaw	Nicholas Cummins
1923	R. H. Patterson	J. Lyons	1975	Lionel O'Sullivan	Matt Murphy
1924	H. F. Donegan	W. A. Higgins	1976	Lionel O'Sullivan	John Kenneally
1925	C. O. M. Williams	W. A. Higgins	1977	Norman D. Henry	Dr. Jim O'Neill
1926-1927	C. O. M. Williams	D. C. Morrogh	1978	Jack Leahy	Dr. Jim O'Neill
1928	T. O' Donoghue	S. E. Skuce	1979	Jack Leahy	Anthony Steen
1929	C. L. Fitzgerald	S. E. Skuce	1980	Billy Williams	Anthony Steen
1930	C. T. F. Russell	E. V. Doyle	1981	James O' Donoghue	Niall P. Coffey
1931	F. H. Dale	E. V. Doyle	1982	James O' Donoghue	Michael Doody
1932	A. E. Hosford	R. A. May	1983	Tom Murray	Joseph Harvey
1933	Gordon Exshaw	D. F. Williams	1984	Tom Murray	Aylmer Barrett
1934	J. L. Blair	D. F. Williams	1985	Tom Murray	Declan Healy
1935	J. T. Foley	F. G. Heaslip	1986-1987	Declan Healy	Ken Buckley
1936	Stuart Musgrave	F. G. Heaslip	1988	Matt Murphy	J. B. Murphy
1937	C. L. Fitzgerald	W. J. Dwyer	1989	Matt Murphy	Tom Reidy
1938	F. H. Daly	W. J. Dwyer	1990	Aylmer Barrett	Ger Goggin
1939	J. Morrisey	Frank Mockler	1991	Aylmer Barrett	Norman Damery
1940	J. L. Lyons	W. J. Dwyer	1992	Aylmer Barrett	John Butler
1941-1942	J. L. Lyons	C. J. Daly	1993	Sean Durcan	Ger O'Callaghan
1943	J. McAuliffe	C. J. Daly	1994	Sean Durcan	James Foley
1944-1945	J. McAuliffe	H. J. Daly	1995	Norman Damery	
1946	Stuart Musgrave	H. J. Daly	1996	Norman Damery	John Quinn
1947	J. D. Blair	J. K. Carroll	1997	Jim O'Sullivan	Mary J. Kennefick
1948-1951	Declan McSweeney	J. K. Carroll	1998	Jim O'Sullivan	George O'Sullivan
1952-1953	J. D. Blair	J. K. Carroll	1999	Donal McCarthy	Marie Kirwan
1954	D. Coffey	J. K. Carroll	2000	Donal McCarthy	Marie Duffy
1955-1956	Declan McSweeney	Eddie Barry	2001	Fergus Daly	James Downey
1957-1958	Lionel O'Sullivan	Brian Scannell	2002	Fergus Daly	Sean Walsh
1959-1960	Gerry F.P. Guy	Brian Scannell			

Tournament at Sunday's Well in 1913. Included in photograph were: Charlie Blake, Florrie Lyons, Emma Beale, Percy Dale, Bessie Tivy, Fred Dale, Miss Dale, Charlie Scrooge, J. Ronan, F. Dwyer, W. Madden, J. Dwyer, J. Lyons, Bob Dwyer, E. Rowan, Tommy Wallace, Miss Di, Molly Ronan, Chris Lyons, Nellie Lyons, J. Waters, Mary Daly, Frank Daly, Captain Higgins, Mrs. Higgins, Cora England, Col. Purvis, Willie Cave, Mrs. Cave, Annie Madden, Agnes Harding, Nancy Harding, Miss Beecher, Muriel Daly, Miss Allen, Joe Daly, Tom Morrogh, Hilda Barry Smith, E. Morrogh, Mamie Harrington, Frank Daly, Captain Allen, Fred Lyons, Jim Daly, S. Fry, Nellie Tivy, Jim Lyons, Rev. Connolly & Billy Gregg.

The beautiful vista of the Sunday's Well Boating and Lawn Tennis Club adjacent to the river Lee, Cork (1963).

Some members at Sunday's Well Boating & LTC outside clubhouse in 1975.

Member, and Davis Cup player, Alan Haughton at Sunday's Well, the scene of many of his tennis triumphs (circa 2003)

Geraldine Cussen in action at Sunday's Well in the summer of 1977 (courtesy Cork Examiner)

✵✵✵✵
Carrickmines Croquet & Lawn Tennis Club
(Founded c.1900)

Carrickmines Croquet and Lawn Tennis Club was established around 1900, it was though that in fact there were two croquet lawns on the present site in 1898. In any event, the generosity of Mr. W.H. Wilson, a stockbroker of William Wilson & Son, Dublin and of Carrickmines House, was instrumental in its foundation. It was a proprietary club owned and run by the Wilson family with a Mr. A.E. Barrett as the honorary secretary and manager. Tennis was well established by 1903. In 2003 the club celebrated their centenary with the publication of a Centenary book. At the great exhibition of 1907 in Herbert Park the Wilsons purchased the ornate Norwegian pavilion, this was moved to the club and became the club pavilion. This was added to in 1912, when an old police hut was purchased from Foxrock Golf Club. This clubhouse, with minor adjustments, served the members right up

Carrickmines Croquet & LTC in 1909

until September 1999. After Mr. Wilson's death his son, Hugh, carried on the club organisation. In 1951 his godson and nephew, John Stokes, purchased it from him. A few years earlier the members took over the running and organisation and, in 1959, John Stokes made a generous offer to hand over Carrickmines to the members, selling them the freehold, buildings and all machinery. Since then the club constitution has remained essentially the same. Instrumental in the purchase was Mr. Thomas Vincent Murphy who later became club President.

The club has become famous for its tournament grass courts which double as croquet lawns. The Open Championship Tournament (the County Dublin Championships) has been held here for nearly a century (see Chapter 5). A 1998 article on the club highlighted the tournament and particular referred to the 1914 Open. On the organising committee were Willoughby Hamilton, Joshua Pim, John Stokes and Simon Scroope, some of the greats of Irish tennis who all lived locally. Play started each day at 10 am on the 12 grass courts. The entry fee for the men's singles was a 'staggering' 10 shillings; it was still the same some fifty years later. For visitors details on accommodation included the fact that accommodation at Bray hotels was available at an all inclusive charge of 7 shillings and 6 pence per day. A train from Bray took 13 minutes to Carrickmines. Entries were confined to *Members of recognised Clubs, Officers of the Army and Navy and the Ladies and Gentlemen approved by the Committee.* Y 1997 there were 8 grass courts in use for the tournament and a total of 600 competitors making it one of the most popular tournaments on the Irish calendar.

In the 1980s the excellent grass courts were used by John McEnroe, Yannick Noah, Mats Wilander,

Joachim Nystrom, Brad Gilbert and Carl Uwe Steeb in preparation for the fund raising GOAL challenges.

The first all-weather courts in Carrickmines were shale, followed by porous concrete (*Tennis Quick*) and, in 1989, all eight courts were replaced with sand filled carpet. The present outdoor courts are an upgraded version of this surface. The indoor surface, used for the first time in the Open in 2000, is an acrylic surface similar to that used at the Australian and US Opens.

Interestingly the Carrickmines ladies were playing in the Dublin Leagues since 1910 while the men only participated since the early 1920s. The ladies were to play in Class 1 for over forty years while the men's Class 1 participation has been for over 30 years. In the main summer leagues the club has fielded up to eleven teams. In the Dublin leagues, which started in 1902, the club have won a total of 80 titles, exceeded only by **Sutton LTC** (81) and **Lansdowne LTC** (107). More than half of them have been in the ladies summer leagues (42) while the men at the club have won only eleven.

The Carrickmines Ladies Team who were Winners of the Class 1 Dublin League in 1933. Back (L. to r.) Miss P. Wallis, Mrs. H. M. Hall & Miss P. McCann. Front (l. to r.) Vera Mahony, Miss N. Moore (captain) & Hilda Wallis.

The records supplied by the Dublin Lawn Tennis Council show that the first men's win in the summer leagues was Class II in 1969 followed by Class I in 1971. Since 1990 they have won Class I four times. The ladies record in the summer leagues is very impressive. Between 1910 and 1937 there were only three clubs winning the Class I event. Donnybrook took the title in 1910 and 1913, Lansdowne won eight but Carrickmines were on their own with 13 of the 23 titles in this category. In fact, in 1923, 1931 and 1933, they won both Class I and Class II. In 1973 they won

Hilda Wallis (left) was one of the many famous members of Carrickmines Croquet & Lawn Tennis Club. She was Irish Open Champions four times (1924, 1926,, 1930 & 1933) and won the County Dublin Championships at her own club in 1925, 1926, 1928 & 1932.Beside her is Vera McWeeney was also a member of Carrickmines and was one of the top women players in Ireland during the 1930s (see chapter 6). The tall man is Dr. Colin Gregory of England who won the County Dublin Championships in 1930 and 1933. On the right is the great George McVeagh one of Ireland's best all-rounder sportsmen ever. He won the singles title at these championships in 1932, 1934, 1935 and 1936.

Some past-presidents of Carrickmines Croquet & Lawn Tennis Club. From left: Harry Jackson, Finbar Costello, G. V. Byrne, Bernard Corbally, Richard Byrne, Joan McLaughlin, Sonja Buckley, John Moore, John Regan, Paul Horan, John Beatty and John McAuley. (Absent: Eddie French).

The modern (built circa 1999) clubhouse at Carrickmines Croquet & Lawn Tennis Club.

The future at Carrickmines Croquet and LTC. Back (l. to r.) are coaches Julie Regan, Alan Bradley jnr. and Pat Crowe. Middle (l. to r.): Harry Crowe, David O'Meara, Sean Conroy, Hugh Allen, Geoffrey Allen and Andrew Murphy. Front (l. to r.): Louise Madigan, Holly Ticson, Sally Crowe, Alexandra Spain and Katie Lyons. (circa 2002)

The 1946 Davis Cup in Sweden included that great Irish player Raymund Egan (background) from the Carrickmines club. On the left is the interesting King Gustav of Sweden (see chapter 5.12). Second from the left is George McVeagh (Lansdowne LTC) one of the best Irish players in the 1930s and 1940s.

Class I, II & III in the same year, a feat no other club seems to have achieved. The club had obviously a good team in the 1970s as they won Class I every single year, apart from 1975, between 1971 and 1979. Ladies such as June Ann Byrne, Jo Sheridan and Paula Ledbetter contributed towards many of these wins. In the floodlit leagues, started in 1981, they have had several wins but the first time they won Class I was in 2001. They repeated this success in 2002. The club won the inaugural Carroll's Doubles competition in 1977. Many Carrickmines players have had international honours, let alone provincial and championship successes. The men include Harry Cronin, Jim Buckley, Harry Barniville, Harry

Sheridan, Peter Ledbetter, Raymund Egan and, most successful of all, Joshua Pim. The lady players were equally impressive over the years and they included Hilda Wallis, Vera Mahony, Mary Bryan, June Ann Byrne, Geraldine Barniville and Sandra Fearon. Hilda Wallis was a multiple international, having played hockey and golf for Ireland, as well as tennis. Geraldine Barniville won the County Dublin Championships (Carrickmines) a record nine times as representing Ireland in very many tennis and squash matches. In recent years Ronan Fearon, Liam Nolan, Margaret Ann Broderick and Helen Johnstone have represented Ireland in various veteran categories.

Carrickmines member, Sonja Buckley, with Fred and Mrs. Perry in 1963.

In 1999 the old clubhouse was demolished and replaced by a more modern facility. The new facility was to include three indoor courts and a gym. The club is exceptionally active with a booming junior membership and up to 10 teams taking part in the Dublin Summer leagues.

Betty Pringle in action (circa 1930)

Elizabeth Ryan (USA) was one of greatest doubles players ever in world tennis. She won the County Dublin Singles Championship on her visits to Carrickmines in 1921, 1922 & 1923.

Brian Farrell-President at Carrickmines Croquet & Lawn Tennis Club in Centenary Year 2003.

Carrickmines Croquet & LTC (circa 1910)

The All-England and Carrickmines club teams.

The Carrickmines Men's team won the Class I summer league in 1973. Back (l. to r.): Jim Buckley, Ronan Fearon & J. Lavin. Front (l. to r.): Con Denvir, Julian Drury Byrne (captain) & Dr. Harry Barniville.

Ladies team at Carrickmines. Back (l. to r.) Kay Falkner, Jennifer Cronin & Sally Tierney. Front (l. to r.): Collette Egan, Jean Horan & Sonja Buckley. The year is likely to be 1970 (or 1962) when Carrickmines won the Class II Dublin Summer League.

The Men's Class 1 summer league winning team in 1997 was from Carrickmines Croquet & LTC. From left: Alan Doran, Pat Crowe, Michael Doran, Ronan Reid, Daryl Singh, John Sheridan, Julian Drury Byrne (captain) & Mark Buckley.

England's Sam Smith won the County Dublin Championship at Carrickmines in 1994.

In 1973 the Carrickmines Club won the Class 1, 2 & 3 Ladies' Summer Leagues (Dublin Lawn Tennis Council). No club, since there were first three classes for ladies in 1921, had ever achieved this feat.

Class 1

Back (l. to r.): Mary Pat Jackson, Mary Bryan & June Ann Byrne (captain). Front: Dr. Geraldine Barniville & Pam Egan. Insets: Paula Mullen (left) and June Keenan.

Class 2

Back (l. to r.) Kay Falkner, Sally Tierney, Cora Keaveney & Jeffy Cronin. Front (l. to r.): Collette Egan, Jean Horan (captain), Sonja Buckley & Elizabeth McCabe.

Class 3

Back (l. to r.): Barbara McNeill, Shirley Bewley, Suzanne Dahl & Sue Seagrave. Front (l. to r.): Sally McFerran, Gemma Byrne (captain) & Kate Brown.

In 2002 Carrickmines were the Class 1 Summer League ladies' champions. From left: Miriam O'Meara, Jane Conan, Emer Sloane & Laura McCarthy.

In 1993 the club were the first Dublin club to appoint a professional Director/Coach in Pat Crowe who looks after tennis affairs. The club expanded in 2000 with an enlarged clubhouse, a gym and three indoor courts to add to the seven outdoor ones.

****

Peter Jackson a great supporter of the Bangor tournament, had a great match with Australian, Arthur Marshall, in the 1955 final before going down 3/6 5/7.He, however, would win this title (the North Down Hard Court Championship) in many subsequent years.

Bangor Lawn Tennis Club
(Founded 1900)

The North Down Hard Court Championships have been played for many years at Ward Park, Bangor. They were always one of the more competitive of the Ulster championships. One of the biggest surprises,

possibly apart from the locals, themselves, was in 1959. Locals, Ian Archer and Val West created a stir. In the quarterfinals they beat Cecil Pedlow and Paul Sochor. They followed this up with a semi-final win over the very experienced Davis Cup players, Vivian Gotto and Cyril Kemp; another seeded pair. In the final they won the first set 6/4 against Peter Jackson

---

North Down Hard Court Championships at Bangor

Men's Singles

1955	Arthur Marshall beat Peter Jackson 6/3 7/5
1957	Peter Jackson beat Sam Cummings 6/1 8/6
1958	Peter Jackson
1959	Peter Jackson beat Tommy Crooks 6/2 4/6 6/2
1960	Peter Jackson beat Sammy Tuff
1961	Peter Jackson beat H. Mc Connell 6/4 3/6 7/5
1962	Peter Jackson beat Sammy Tuff 6/4 6/1

Ladies Singles

1955	Betty Lombard beat Heather Flinn 6/3 0/6 6/3
1957	Joan Wallace beat Audrey Roney 6/1 6/2
1959	Mary Lindsay beat Esther Young 6/0 7/5
1960	Mary Lindsay beat Eileen Logan
1961	Mary Lindsay beat Joan Wallace 6/3 6/2
1962	Hadassah Lord beat Joan Wallace 7/5 6/4

Men's Doubles

1955	Bruce Francis/A. Marshall beat Sammy Tuff/Roy Thornton 6/1 6/2
1957	Peter Jackson/Sammy Tuff beat Vivian Gotto/Cyril Kemp 6/1 6/3
1959	Peter Jackson/Sammy Tuff beat Ian Archer/Val West 4/6 6/0 6/0
1961	Peter Jackson/Sammy Tuff beat R. Clark/H. Mc Connell 6/3 6/3
1962	Peter Jackson/Sammy Tuff beat Ken Reid/B. Cowan 6/2 12/10

Ladies Doubles

1955	Betty Lombard/Heather Flinn beat Roguie Bain/Angela Clark 6/1 6/1
1957	Audrey Roney/J. Gilchrist beat Joan and Eileen Wallace 6/3 4/6 6/2
1959	Mary Lindsay/Esther Young beat Joan & Eileen Wallace 6/3 6/3
1961	Mary Lindsay/Esther Young beat Hadassah Lord/R. Abernathy 6/4 6/3
1962	Hadassah Lord/Joan Wallace beat Eileen Dundee Esther Young 6/3 6/1

Mixed Doubles

1955	H. Boyd/Miss D. Willis beat I. Cameron/Roguie Bain 6/3 7/5
1961	Peter Jackson/Mary Lindsay beat Ken Reid/Eileen Dundee 6/0 7/5
1962	R. Clark/Hadassah Lord beat Ken Reid/D. Byers 8/6 6/4

and Sammy Tuff but the dream finally ended for the youngsters, they lost the next two to love. It was, however, a week that the local pair will have remembered. In the same year, Mary Lindsay, the table tennis international, was a late entry and was unseeded. The Belfast schoolteacher achieved a *lifetime ambition*, winning her first championship when beating Esther Young of Belfast 6/0 7/5 in the final.

Ward Park Tennis Club in Bangor were Div. I winners in the Belfast & District Leagues in 1979

****

Athenry Lawn Tennis Club
(Founded pre 1908)

This was thought to have been called the County **Galway LTC** and perhaps considerably older than 1908.

****

Galway Lawn Tennis Club
[Galway Lawn Tennis & Croquet Club]
(Founded 1900)

It is a mystery who called what was to be the inaugural meeting of **Galway LTC**. This meeting took place in the Royal Hotel, Eyre Square on the 19th May 1900. William Persse acted as chairman when the 'exclusive' **Galway Lawn Tennis & Croquet Club** was founded. This club was the not by any means the first in the province but came to become the best known as the largest, and the club most likely to hold tennis events of importance in Connacht. Later it successfully expanded to include the sports of badminton and squash. Noted players include Dickie O'Connor who played for Connacht in the sports of tennis, badminton and rugby. Donal Dempsey was an all-rounder too, being somewhat an expert at tennis, squash, badminton and hockey. In addition, he has featured for many decades as a Connacht administrator and coach and was President of the Irish Lawn Tennis Association in 1973, 1977 and 1981. Another club member, Michael McCann held this high office in 1989. He was followed by Roy Thompson (1994) and Olwyn Raftery (1998 and 2004). Henry Blake became the second Connacht person to become president of the national association. This was in 1943. He also filled the post in 1948, 1952 and 1956. Terry McCarthy was in this important office for 1965.

In all, **Galway LTC** has had six Irish presidents covering 12 years of office. The club has provided the national association with more presidents than any other single club in the country.

1965-The laying of three hard courts in front of the old pavilion at Galway LTC.

The modern clubhouse at Galway LTC includes facilities for squash and badminton as well as modern bar etc. This photograph is of Chris Wilkinson (England) at the satellite International Tournament on Whit Weekend in 1991.

One of the founding members of the club was Sir Noel Galwey-Holmes. He was an active club member in its first decade. He became a Major in the British army. In 1922, 1923 and 1924 he won the Championship of the Rhine. He was one of nine Irish men to play at Wimbledon in 1927. Having got a walk-over, he lost in the second round to A. E. Browne in a long five-setter. In his one Davis Cup match he played in the doubles against Italy. With the Irish number 1, George Lyttleton Rogers as partner, they were no match for the combination of Hubert de Moorpurgo and A. del Bono. In 1928 he had two notable mixed victories, playing with Vera Marshall beating Leslie and Kitty Godfree (the 1926 Wimbledon mixed doubles champions) and with Mrs. Watson beating 'Muskateer' Jacques (*Toto*) Brugnon and Miss Rose.

The club had many successful players over the decades. Apart from Connacht interprovincial and Connacht Open champions, there was success further afield. In 1960 member John Brennan won the Irish Open under 15 singles championship at **Fitzwilliam LTC**. In the final he beat Dundalk's Frank McArdle (4/6 6/2 6/4). He was probably the first junior from Connacht to win an open junior tennis title. His sister Stella, another good player, married showband singer Brendan Bowyer. She still plays today, in their adopted Las Vegas. One of their children, Brendan junior, travelled to Ireland to play competition tennis and in 1986 beat Sean Molloy 6/2 6/4 in the Irish Open Boys' Championship (u18). In 1987 the young David Thornton won the Irish *Nestle* competition. He reached the international finals at Croydon, beating the best Welsh boy, Jonathan Lloyd, 6/4 6/2 in the semi-final. In 1989 he won the under 19 Pamela Scott singles championship. The following year David captured the Connacht Open title and, in 1991, the West of Ireland Championship. He entered the Irish senior rankings at number 8 in 1996.

Galway LTC
Club Captains-Tennis

1953	R. O'Connor
1954-1955	Michael Walsh
1956	G.Dodd/R. O'Connor
1957-1958	R. O'Connor
1959-1960	E. Cooke
1961	Des V. Kneafsey
1962-1964	Michael Walshe
1965-1967	Donal F. Dempsey
1968	G. Lannigan
1969-1970	S. Cullen
1971	Brendan Minnock
1972-1973	Noel Murphy
1974-1976	Michael McCann
1976	Aileen Kelly
1977	Eamonn Bradshaw
1978	Olwyn Raftery
1979-1981	Donal Geraghty
1982-1984	Frank Hayden
1985-1986	B. O'Boyle
1987	Roy Thompson
1988	D. McCarthy
1989	Peter Flanagan
1990	Charlie O'Connell
1991	Mike Geraghty
1992	M. Brennan
1993	Mike Weerakoon
1994	P. Flanagan
1995	Stan Mortimer
1996-1997	James Ward
1998-2000	Mike Geraghty
2000-2001	M. McNally
2001-2003	Mike Weerakoon

Recent club champions were the following:
2001 Sean Coughlan/Jenny Burrows
2002 Brian Plekker/Jenny Burrows
2003 Stan Mortimes/Jenny Burrows
2004 Brian Plekker/Jenny Burrows

The club has been involved in running many successful racquet sports championships. What was an open event of mainly local significance became the Connacht Championships from about 1939. Early local winners included Mrs. Braund and Walter Walshe. In the 1960s Galway's Maeve Lydon was nearly unbeatable in the ladies' singles championship. She won it for the seventh time in 1969. Dubliner Lesley O'Halloran won this event five times in the 1990s. In the men's doubles Fiachra Lennon was the

winner in the five consecutive years from 1999. The ladies' doubles has been a championship event for a limited period only. The mixed has long been a competitive event. One of the interesting pairs to win was the brother and sister combination of Tommy and Maeve Lydon. In the 1965 final they beat top Irish player Harry Sheridan (from Dublin) and local Pat Ryan. Maeve was a permanent member of the Connacht side during those years and, in 1965, was selected for an ILTA team to play against the Irish Universities in Belfast. Pat won the singles title in 1968 and was followed by her daughter Gina (Niland) taking the championship in 1994. Winners of Connacht Championships from abroad included visitors from England, New Zealand, South Africa and the USA.

ILTA Hand Book 1973

Donal Dempsey
President Irish Lawn Tennis Association
1973, 1977 & 1981

In 1935 the club hosted the intervarsity championships. In 1940 the club was well represented on the Connacht team that played against Munster at their home club. It was 1949 before the 4-province senior series first took place. Walter Walsh and Cecily McNally were on the Connacht team that year in Belfast. The club have had very many members on provincial teams since that time. It has hosted the event twelve times, the first being in 1952. It was/is an ideal venue for such an important annual fixture. There were only two years when it was not in Galway, when it was Connacht's turn to act as hosts. These were in 1992 (**Sligo TC**) and in 2004 (**Castlebar TC**). The club has hosted many junior and veteran tennis championships and interprovincial competitions and was always well represented on the provincial selections. In 1953 it hosted the Irish Close Championships. It has also hosted several international matches including fixtures against Wales (1969), England (1978) and Malta (1992 Davis Cup).

The Galway LTC men's tennis team that beat Fitzwilliam LTC 5/4 in 1997. From left: Philip Ryan, Donal Hegarty, Kevin Burke, James Ward, Kevin Rafferty & Gerry Brennan.

It would be remiss not to mention the many other activities that have taken place at the Galway club. These have included friendly tennis matches, socials of all types, the inclusion of a gym and table tennis etc. Others have been a car draw, a race night, a bowling night as well as participation in diverse sports such as golf, rock climbing and fishing. Of great importance in the last few decades have been the sports of badminton and squash. In both sections of the clubs there has been exceptional success on the playing front. In addition the club has acted as the venue for very many Connacht and international events of importance. In November 1999, the year the Badminton Unoin of Ireland celebrated its centenary, the club were the hosts for the match between Ireland and China.

In 1977 Galway LTC entered and won the Munster Senior Cup. Winning team (from left); Tony Poustie, Aileen Kelly, June Smith and Noel Murphy.

Fund raising and implementing various development programmes have taken up much time ever since the club took a leap forward in the 1960s. In 1974 the official title of the club company became Galway Lawn Tennis and Sports Club Limited to cater for the ever expanding sporting and legal requirements. The grass courts finally disappeared in about 1978 and modern lighting and all-weather courts are now in place. Today there are nine tennis courts, seven badminton courts and six squash courts making the club one of the most important of racquet sports venues in the country.

To honour Galway Lawn Tennis Club's centenary a team was invited to play at the All England LTC (Wimbledon) on the 4th August 2001. Back (l. to r.): Roy Thompson, Michael McCann, James Ward (team captain), Donal Geraghty, Eamon Bradshaw and Charlie O'Donnell. Front (l. to r.): Olwyn Raftery, Liz grogan, Pat Folan (president, Galway LTC0, Margaret McLoughlin and Maeve Brennan.

Two club members can claim a world record, submitted to the Guinness Book of Records. Mike Geraghty and Francis Power played continuous doubles against various club members for a period of 26 hours on the 20th and 21st June 2003. It is to be entered as "The Longest Competitive Doubles Match". *The intrepid duo did it again in August 2005, when they extended the record to 36 hours!* Over thirty years earlier students at University College held another world doubles event in Galway. This is noted elsewhere in this book.

The club has a long and successful history and many honours have been earned at home and on the intereational front. Many members featured over the years as Galway Sporting All-Stars. For services to the club a number of memers were given special thanks within the club itself. In 1983 Walter Walshe was made an honorary life president. Donal Dempsey was made an honorary life vice-president in 1986 the same year Tony Poustie departed for Australia. For services to the club Tony was made an honorary life member of the club before his departure.

In January 1991 Mike Geraghty and Michael McCann were made honorary life vice-presidents followed by Olwyn Raftery two years later. In 1999 long serving member Ita Dempsey was made an honorary life member. In 2004 the club were hosts to the British Special Olympic team. Member Eamon Bradshaw was subsequently awarded the MBE for his, and undoubtedly the club's, part in managing the hosting of the British athletes in Galway.

February 1999: Club president James Ward with a special presentation for Ita Dempsey who joined the club in 1936 and was being honoured with life membership of the club. Also in the photograph are Margaret McLoughlin and Donal Geraghty.

Two final quotes from Peadar O'Dowd's history. The first relates to the end of the last century (1999). *As the old waltz numbers whispered softly across the tennis courts, silent now beneath the winter sky, Michael 'Little Sport' Walsh sat at the bar and remembered when he and another young man, Donal Dempsey, first played tennis all these years ago on these hallowed grounds as the 1940s drew to a close.*

The club newsletter in February 2005 reported on the Irish u13 badminton title won by Jack Larkin and Ross Dempsey. Peader notes the importance of success by the young and upcoming racquet sports players. *Thankfully, the club's magnificent 'past' is ever present also, because as these two young players were reaching the pinnacle of their sport, back at Threadneedle Road, Ross's grandfather, Donal*

Dempsey, was ensuring his 80+ years service was still capable of dipping a tennis ball on the No. 1 court.Perhaps one might paraphrase the words of a famous song, "What's another hundred years....?", as one's pen finally runs out of ink.

Olwyn Raftery
President Tennis Ireland 1998 & 2002

A 1966 group photograph of the teams representing Galway LTC and the visiting Limerick Lawn Tennis Club.

The 1985 Management Committee at Galway LTC. Standing (l. to r.) Donal Dempsey, David Lillis, Brendan Maloney, Brendan O'Boyle, Noel Bolger, Eamon Bradshaw, Tony Kenny, Joe mcElwee & Garry O'Lochlainn. Seatred (l. to r.): Donal Geraghty, Rosemary Kent, Michael McCann (president), Patricia Buckley & Michael Walsh. [Michael McCann was President of the Irish Lawn Tennis Association in 1989. Gary O' Lochlainn is currently President of Galway Lawn Tennis Club]

The new Galway LTC complex was officially opened on the 25th September 1976 by Gerry Colgan, Mayor of Sligo. Also in photo (from left): Donal Dempsey, Ray Rooney, Michael Walsh & Michael McCann.

In October 1990 the new badminton courts were officially opened at galway LTC. From left: Father Kevin Donohue, Gerard Walshe (Honorary Club Treasurer),Olwyn Raftery (Club President), Michael Geraghty (Tennis Captain), Michael D. Higgins (Mayor of Galway), Gerry More O'Ferral (President, Tennis Ireland), Reverend Leslie Forest and Frank O'Reilly (President, Badminton Union of Ireland).

The History of Galway Lawn Tennis Club was launched in December 2005. Written by member Peadar O'Dowd, it contains a well scripted ramble through over a century of the club's life.

Galway Lawn Tennis Club Club Presidents*

Lord Killanin (1921)
Dr. J. Kinkead (to 1928)
P. J. Boland (to 1939)
Dr. W. A. Sandys (1939)
M. G. O'Malley (1953-1956)
Henry St. J. Blake (1957)
Ralph Ryan (1958-1963)
Dr. W. Sandys (1968)
Michael Walsh (1969-1981)
Donal Dempsey (1983)
Michael McCann (1985)
Tony Poustie (1986)
Eamon Bradshaw (1986-1987)
Olwyn Raftery (1989-1990)
Donal Geraghty (1992-1993)
Liz Grogan (1994-1995)
Charlie O'Connell (1998)
James Ward (1999)
Pat Folan (2002-2003)
Mike Geraghty (2003-2004)
Garry O'Lochlainn (2005)

*partial listing

Windsor Lawn Tennis & Squash Club (Founded 1901)

The **Windsor Lawn Tennis and Squash Club** is located in a Belfast suburb between the Lisburn and Malone roads. Mr. Robert (*Bob*) P. Corry and Mr. James McKeown founded it in 1901. Bob Corry was a man in his early thirties and was the main energy behind the club. He was a remarkable single-minded man with much energy and foresight. When the club's first constitution was written he was, by agreement, written in as a permanent member of the Club's Council. Early on he managed to secure a 10,000 year lease on the grounds for the club. At the club's fiftieth anniversary dinner he remarked "when the 10,000 years are up you will, of course, have to renegotiate. He lived until 1966 when he died at the age of ninety. This would probably make him a record holder as the longest serving member of any club's committee, anywhere!

The men's doubles finalists at the Ulster Championships at Windsor LTC in the early 1930s. From left: Mr. Grant, Mr. Fulton, Mr. Hill and R. P. Corry (the founder of Windsor LTC in 1901).

Not alone was he a great organiser but also a useful player. It is said that he won the Ulster Open Singles Championship in 1924 at the mature age of 48. As a perpetual chairman he guided the club's destiny for some 62 years. The club affiliated to the Irish Lawn Tennis Association in 1912. They, and Newcastle (County Down), were elected at the ILTA meeting on the 5th July of that year. In 1913 they were one of 82 clubs in that organisation (formed in 1908), twelve being from Ulster. That year the club had about 150 members, one of the biggest in the country. Bob Corry was elected President of the ILTA in 1930, the first Ulsterman to receive this honour.

The club started out with three grass courts to which four were added over the next twenty years as adjacent land became available. By 1930, all had been converted to hard, brick-dust surface and were thereafter tended with a mixture of loving care and ferocious threats by a splendid grounds man in Willie Turkington. Willie became the grounds man in 1920 after he had been demobbed. He too was a survivor, and devoted some 46 years of his life to the club. Today the club has five artificial grass courts, all floodlit. New carpets were laid in the autumn of 2002.

In the late 1960s a bar and a squash court were added and a second, glass-backed court followed a few years later. But more than a decade would pass before finances allowed the installation of new changing rooms. The original wooden pavilion lasted many years. It was built by the club's founders at a cost of £80. However, *the men's tiny shower cubicle, beloved by countless male players (and, be it whispered, the occasional adventurous female) had become functionally unpredictable, if not downright dangerous. One was only too likely to be either scalded or frozen within seconds by its still powerful cascade.*

The clay-courts had their life span too. The lack of numbers and borrowings eventually lead to the sale of some of the club land (i.e. three courts). This was the beginning of the five new all-weather carpet courts. In 1994 the final phase of the club's development was completed, the old wooden pavilion had lasted until 1980. The old Corry Hall had been transformed into a junior clubroom with table tennis, pool etc. The ground floor included a fitness suite. The new second floor would have a large function room, kitchen, new lounge bar and an intimate player's bar.

The club has always been a "player's club" and also hosted many events, including the Ulster Hard Court Championships for many years. No fewer than nine of Ulster's ten Davis Cup players were members here at one time or another. These are Tommy Crooks, Vivian Gotto, Peter Jackson, Robin Condy (who died in 2001), Ken Reid, Derek Arthurs (who lives in Australia and is father of the Australian Davis Cupper, Wayne), Johnny Biscombe (now living in South America), Peter Lowther and John Magrath.

The Irish Davis Cup team that played Great Britain at Eastbourne in 1969 had three Ulstermen and a Munsterman. The three are now, or were at one time, all members of Windsor LTC. From left: Ken Reid, Vivian Gotto, Peter Jackson and Michael Hickey (Munster).

Of the many women who graced their courts, perhaps Susan Minford is one of the most noteworthy. She did exceptionally well in the Wimbledon junior championships, was an Irish Federation Cup Player, British under 21 number 1 and Irish number 2 in 1970. Nuala McMordie, Victoria Reid, Jill Minford and Nicola McCormick can be added to this list. Ulster players also included Gerry Doherty, David Williams, Willie Noteman and Cecil Pedlow. The latter is a noted rugby and squash international. Squash would have other internationals in Dorothy Armstrong (former Ireland number 1), David Gotto (at one time the most capped player in the world), John Young, Yvonne Jackson, Tony Traub and Frank McKeever. The club would win the All-Ireland Club Championship in squash and be the only Ulster club to win the tennis club doubles championship. Ken Reid and David Williams are among the members who have excelled when representing **Windsor LTC** at both sports.

Perhaps the most successful lady to develop her game at Windsor LTC has been the Federation Cup player Susan Minford.

Over a period of time Windsor have had many distinguished guests on their tennis courts. These included four Wimbledon singles champions, the world famous harmonica player, Larry Adler, and the Sultan of Penang. The number of titles going their way has been extensive. In 2000, for example, in the Belfast and District Lawn Tennis Leagues, they would win Division I and II in the Floodlit Leagues, Ladies Division I Winter League, Ladies Division I Summer League, Division II of the Men's Knockout Cup and Div I of the Men's Evergreens League.

Considering the club now has 100 years behind it, it would be extremely difficult to catalogue a complete record. It can be said, however, that this has been one of the most successful clubs in Ireland, and can be expected to continue in this vein for many years to come. Former great, Ken Reid, not alone coached many of the current players but daughter Victoria became an Ulster player in several age categories. The

Gottos make up an equally impressive family of racquet players to emerge from the 'House of Windsor'. Between 1992 and 1995 Viv and David were, respectively, president and chairman of the club, a fairly unique piece of family contribution.

In the clubrooms a great collection of photographs can be found and a handwritten story of the club's first fifty years. This was the speech given by Bob Corry in the 50th season and at a function on the 30th October 1950, held in the Carlton. Some notes from that presentation include the following:

We rented a piece of ground in Windsor Avenue which originally been tennis courts of a kind, we took 2 evenings to get 40 men & 40 ladies explaining to the men that if they gave us their names at once each of them could nominate one Lady, -if we left without their names they would be too late.

An extraordinary meeting was called in Elmwood lecture hall as we expected a crowd, to consider the backing of this ground. Mr. McKeown, myself, and one other turned up owing to a snowstorm. We took the ground on a yearly basis, which was all we could get at the time & laid 3 grass courts. I hope some of you younger members will be able to refer in the year of the club's centenary that all the things I have mentioned have been completed & that the club is free from debt. Let me say in conclusion that we now have the best Hon. Sec. we ever had & long may Mrs. Spellman remain in office.

A distinguished visitor to Windsor LTC was the Sultan of Penang in 1957. In this friendly doubles he (foreground) played with Viv Gotto. A few years earlier Wimbledon singles champions from the USA, Vic Seixas (1953) and Tony Trabert (1955), played an exhibition match with Viv Gotto and Ireland's Cyril Kemp.

The History of Irish Tennis

Mrs. Barbara Spellman remained in office for another fifteen years and by 2001 the club certainly had progressed. Many of the other memories are included above in notes received from long time member, Vivian Gotto. The following few abbreviated stories from Viv (as he is known to his friends and colleagues) are those of a tennis player who has seen many sides to tennis and has a great turn of phrase in recalling them.

[a] *Of all the local tournaments, the one I remember best was Ballycastle. I played there before the war, and on returning 10 year later found that the entire scene had somehow become frozen in time. There were the same gentle old men in Panama hats still dishing out the wrong change for your tea: the same dear old ladies in flowered dresses presiding behind the same ancient kettle. There were even, I swear, the identical dead wasps embalmed in the very same jammy scones......*

[b] *The injection of big money into the game now makes one laugh at the contortions we went through as so-called amateurs. I was once invited to play an exhibition at Ballymena, with the whispered assurance That, if I accepted, no less than* **two pairs** *of new socks would appear miraculously in my tennis bag afterwards. I did better in Hungary on my last Davis Cup trip. Having refused to sign some patently cooked account-sheets presented by the opposition, I was taken quietly aside and offered £50 if I would append my autograph (Did I sign?-you'll just have to wonder...)*

[c] In an interprovincial match against Leinster in the late 1940s Viv was to meet the Irish number 1 Cyril Kemp, the latter having recently beaten Tom Brown of the USA, the Wimbledon finalist, (1947). The team captain instructed Viv to "Just stay on court for 20 minutes, Gotto". *In the event, Cyril won 6-3, 8-6-but I had at least fulfilled the time clause and was congratulated as if I had won.*

[d] The shower area in the old pavilion had *become the home of a large rat which, naturally resenting frequent soakings, would emerge at inconvenient moments. There was some talk of making it an honorary member in recognition of its role in putting off rival teams-a suggestion which failed to obtain Council approval.*

In 1988 Windsor LTC finally put to rest the red clay courts that had served the club since 1900. Some 29,000 square feet of carpet was laid on the five courts. At the opening were (from left): Ken Reid, Sir Robin Kinahan (club Trustee), Viv Gotto, Des Wylie and Chris Parsons.

The rodent at Windsor LTC got wet. This one has found a more comfortable home.

Ulster Tennis Season Opens

A THRILLING display during which the home side fought back from being 2-1 down to level 3-3 only to fade in spirited battles and lose 6-3 provided a grand curtain-raiser for the tennis season in the North yesterday.

The winners at the Windsor Club, Belfast, were an unofficial British Civil Service side led by former Davis Cup star, Geoff Paish. Their victims in an all-doubles tussle were Windsor selected, a team of Irish Davis Cup men and Ulster players.

Vivian Gotto and Cyril Kemp, the most experienced Irish pair, gave Paish and his partner, Kent county player Jack Deloford, a great match, in which Paish in particular, displayed his full range of strokes. It went to the visitors 6-3 6-2.

Results (Windsor names first):—
C. A. Kemp and R. V. Gotto bt. R. K. Kaley and J. W. B. Ireson—6-0, 6-3.

T. J. Crooks and S. C. Cummings lost to R. E. Carter and G. L. Emmett—7-5, 5-7, 3-6

S. Tuff and P. H. Jackson lost to G. L. Paish and I. L. Deloford—0-6, 4-6.

Kemp and Gotto lost to Paish and Deloford—6-3, 6-2

Crooks and Cummings bt. Kaley and Ireson—6-3, 6-4

Tuff and Jackson bt. Carter and Emmett—7-5, 6-4

Kemp and Gotto lost to Carter and Emmett—6-4, 8-6.

Crookes and Cummings lost to Paish and Deloford—6-4, 6-2..

Tuff and Jackson lost to Kaley and Ireson—7-5, 6-2.

7th April 1957

Full of star players, this friendly match between a British Civil Service team and a Windsor selection took place as a season's curtain raiser, at Windsor LTC, in the mid-1950s. The visiting team won by 6 matches to 3 (see report in column). Back (l. to r.): Geoff Emmet (CS), Sam Cummings, Peter Jackson, Tommy Crooks, Sammy Tuff, Viv Gotto, Cyril Kemp & Ronald Carter (CS). Seated (l. to r.): Jack Deleford (CS), Geoff Paish (CS), Reg Kaley & Jimmy Ireson (CS).

	President	Chairperson	Honorary Secretary	Honorary Treasurer
1928		R. P. (*Bob*) Corry	E. Steen	A. Blythe Jackson
1929-1930		R. P. (*Bob*) Corry	R. Stanley	W. H. Rosevere
1931-1940		R. P. (*Bob*) Corry	John (*Jack*) N. Colville	W. H. Rosevere
1941-1945		*club records not traceable*		
1946		R. P. (*Bob*) Corry	J. M. McBride	E. D. Hill
1947-1948		R. P. (*Bob*) Corry	J. M. McBride	J. M. Alexander
1949		R. P. (*Bob*) Corry	F. Coates	J. M. Alexander
1950-1963		R. P. (*Bob*) Corry	Mrs. Barbara Spelman	J. M. Alexander
1964-1966		J. Mc C Calvert	Mrs. Barbara Spelman	J. M. Alexander
1967-1969		J. Mc C Calvert	Paul Z. Socher	J. M. Alexander
1970-1971		J. Mc C Calvert	A. Young	C. G. Eyre
1972		J. Mc C Calvert	A. Young	C. G. Eyre
1973	J. Mc C Calvert	Paul Z. Socher	A. Young	W. Bothwell
1974	J. Mc C Calvert	Paul Z. Socher	A. Young	J. O. Swain
1975-1978	J. Mc C Calvert	R. Vivian (*Viv*) Gotto	E. Tuff	M. P. Alexander
1979	J. Mc C Calvert	D. Gilmore	E. Tuff/A. O. P. Norris	Chris Parsons
1980-1981	J. Mc C Calvert	D. Gilmore	Arthur Norris	Chris Parsons
1982-1983	J. Mc C Calvert	M. P. Alexander	Arthur Norris	Chris Parsons
1984	J. Mc C Calvert	Kenneth (*Ken*) C. Reid	Arthur Norris	Chris Parsons
1985-1987	J. Mc C Calvert	Kenneth (*Ken*) C. Reid	Arthur Norris	D. B. Cowan
1988	R. Vivian (*Viv*) Gotto	Chris Parsons	Arthur Norris	David R. Williams
1989	R. Vivian (*Viv*) Gotto	Chris Parsons	Arthur Norris	A. J. Payne
1990-1991	R. Vivian (*Viv*) Gotto	E. D. Omellas	Arthur Norris	A. J. Payne
1992-1994	R. Vivian (*Viv*) Gotto	David Gotto	Arthur Norris	S. Macartney
1995	R. Vivian (*Viv*) Gotto	David Gotto	Arthur Norris	G. McNamee
1996-1998	R. Vivian (*Viv*) Gotto	David R. Williams	Arthur Norris	G. McNamee
1999	R. Vivian (*Viv*) Gotto	R. Thompson/R. Ashe	Arthur Norris	Chris Parsons
2000-2001	R. Vivian (*Viv*) Gotto	Chris Parsons	David R. Williams	A. J. Payne
2002-2003	R. Vivian (*Viv*) Gotto	A. J. Payne	David R. Williams	Chris Parsons
2004	R. Vivian (*Viv*) Gotto	G. Rawe	David R. Williams	Chris Parsons
2005	R. Vivian (*Viv*) Gotto	G. Rawe	David R. Williams	Chris Parsons

Officers at Windsor Lawn Tennis Club

Vivian Gotto one of Windsor's some successful members. His son David became one of the top squash players on the world circuit. Vivian was president of the club from 1988 until his death in 2006.

Club trustee Sir Robin Kinahan launched the 29,000 square feet of new carpet on the tennis courts in 1988. Attending on the day was Virginia Wade who played an exhibition match and coached the club juniors. From 1979 onwards Chris Parson has played an important role in the club in 'steering the Club's finances into a sound position that any club would envy'. He has been the club's honorary treasurer for a total of 9 years (1979-1984, 1999 and 2002-2003). In 2001 and 2002 he was club chairman. A few words of summary (March 2004) from the current club secretary David Williams brings matters more or less up to date:

The nineties were very eventful with the carpet having to be replaced due to a defect and the sub surface repaired. One summer Saturday afternoon in 1994 a car bomb exploded in the Chapel Car Park adjacent to the courts. Fortunately no one was seriously injured including builders who were working at the time. However, flying bits of shrapnel ripped through areas of the relatively new carpet which had to be repaired.

Around the same time the Club had been successful in obtaining a grant from the Foundation for Sport and the Arts for £80,000. This was to build a second story above the existing Clubhouse – the total cost was estimated at £120,000 and after full consultation with the members it was decided to make up the shortfall by means of a levy. The project was completed in 1995 and improved the facilities for everyone and included the addition of a Fitness Suite. A Secretary/Manager was appointed to be responsible for the staff and managing the day-to- day running of the Club.

The Club thrived throughout the nineties when for the first time in the Club's history membership had to be closed due to court capacity being reached. In 1998

the Club appointed a Club Development Officer and introduced a very successful development programme for juniors which attracted almost 200 for the launch in one afternoon!

The Club celebrated its centenary year in style with a number of specially run events culminating in the highlight, which was the Centenary Dinner at the Wellington Park Hotel with guest speaker Dame Mary Peters.

What of the future? Windsor has just upgraded its playing facilities again and has recently appointed a Tennis Director to plan and run coaching schemes designed to appeal to all age groups. With many other club improvements also in the pipeline the new-look Windsor faces the coming years with confidence.

****

Claremont Lawn Tennis Club
(Founded pre 1903)

In 1938 a short article in *Irish Sports Review* discussed the early days of this club. Much of the following information comes from this source. By 1986, this club, and another long established one, **Railway Union LTC**, amalgamated and became **Claremont-Railway Union LTC.** It now thrives at Park Avenue, Dublin 4, with 6 all-weather and 6 grass courts. In the early days the club was one for many the local residents in Sandymount, Dublin. W.K. Laird and W.J. Young were among the early enthusiasts. After the Great War it grew and expanded with members from many parts of Dublin joining.

In the more recent period (i.e. 1930s), *Claremont has drawn a big proportion of its playing strength from former students of University College, and no less than eleven ex-champions of U.C.D. are among its members, covering a period of some twenty years, from the vintage of M.H. O'Connor and P.J. O'Brien down to D.O'Herlihy and F.C. Dwyer of the present era. In the past couple of years Trinity has also supplied its quota of good players to Claremont, as the names of R. J. Sandys, H. J. Ryan and T. B. Hannin testify.*

This happy association of both the Universities with Claremont has greatly influenced the development of the club, and should provide a guarantee of continuous playing strength in future years. Claremont has also drawn many of its members from the football fields, including "Green Caps" in P. E. Dunn and M. J. Dunne (Rugby) and J. J. White (Soccer), while such as the Davitts, the Hogans, J. L. McLoughlin, R. H. Ballagh and F. C. Dwyer are well-known to followers of football. (Gaelic, one presumes). [P.E. Dunn as a member of Bective RFC was capped against Scotland in 1923 while M.J. Dunne earned 16 caps between 1929 and 1934 as a member of Lansdowne RFC].

More Grounds

The eight grass courts at St. John's Road have always received expert attention and are in good condition this year. The Committee are contemplating the acquisition of some additional ground, so as to lay hard courts without seriously encroaching on their splendid grass courts. Claremont have been very successful in the Dublin Leagues, always fielding three strong teams in men's and women's classes. In 1936 both Class I and Class II trophies were captured by the Claremont men. The Class II Cup had previously been won in 1924, 1928 and 1932, while the Class I final was unsuccessfully contested in 1925 and 1931. Last year the club was runner-up in Class III. This year's first team is R. J. Sandys, R. H. Douglas, R. H. Ballagh, T. B. Hannin, B. R. Towers and J. W. Murphy, and they look to have a good chance of premier honours.

The Ladies' Teams

The ladies' teams in Claremont have not as yet succeeded in winning any of the Leagues, but this season they are stronger than ever before, and the first team with Mrs. N.V. Hogan (champion), Mrs. White, Miss M.P. Kelly and Miss D. Delaney of the old hands, and Miss G. Mc Auley and Miss V.A. Gillespie, new recruits of distinction, should go very far. They have already beaten a strong Co.Wicklow side. The Men's Championship of Claremont, singles and doubles, are strangely enough, the only events in this country, not excluding the National Championships, in which the best of five sets is played throughout. Recent winners of the Singles Championship have been B.R. Towers, R. H. Ballagh, T. B. Hannin and R. J. Sandys, the Irish International player. It is evidence of the high standard shown that H. J. Ryan, who played in the Davis Cup for Ireland this year, has not yet succeeded in winning the Claremont title.

Social Atmosphere

Apart from its successes in competitive tennis, Claremont has always been famous for its cheery social atmosphere. Its Handicap Mixed Doubles tournaments and dances have been most successful, and the At Home, held each year on the first Saturday in August, and providing first-class tennis, a talented concert party and a "don't-go-home-till-morning" dance, is regarded as one of the major events in the Dublin tennis season. The committee for 1938 was:

Captain:	G. P. S. Hogan BL
Honorary Secretary:	Kevin O'Brien-Kenney
Honorary Treasurer:	W. J. Young
Council:	Judge Davitt
	P.J. O'Brien, BDS
	T. D. McLoughlin
	J. M. Fay, BE
	T. B. Hannin BL
	P. E. Dunn LDS
	R. H. Douglas
	R. E. Davitt MB
	D. Llewellyn
	M. H. O'Connor MD

In 1985, both the **Claremont LTC** and the **Railway Union LTC** had about 100 members each, a quarter of whom were juniors. They decided to amalgamate and a new club, combining the names, was formed with Tony Hayes as the first honorary secretary in 1986. He was followed by Rosaleen O'Dwyer the following year when the club were now thriving with six grass and six hard courts. The future is now assured.

Over the years the club, and its antecedents, have been very successful in the Dublin Leagues winning a total of 33 titles. Of these 16 were in the men's summer leagues. Claremont won the Class II league in 1924, 1928 and 1932 and, in 1936 won both the Class I and Class II leagues. The combined club won class II and III in 1992. One of the more recent victories was the Class VI win in 1997. The ladies won both Class II and IV in 1938, the first of 8 wins recorded. The combined club has done particularly well in the senior leagues. In 1997 and 1998 they won the Over 35 Class I men's league.

****

Brookfield Lawn Tennis Club
(Founded 1906)

It is not certain, but appears that the club started by a group of friends who played regularly on a private court at a house called Brookfield on Richmond Avenue in Dublin. The club had originally played at Fortfield Terrace but had to move as the site was being sold for building purposes. It was thought that there were four grass courts there and, at the time the club had to move, two small pavilions that were sold for £15. The honorary secretary, C. G. Chute, wrote to the members in July 1927 informing them of the problem. The future of the club was then discussed at the AGM held on the 30th September at 17 Greenmount Road, Terenure. *Tea provided.* The club survived and today has six floodlit artificial grass courts and thrives. Back in 1927 the club made the decision to move to Palmerston Park. Five grass courts were laid in early 1928 at a cost of *£17 each.* Play commenced on the 12th May. A further court and a junior court were laid that autumn. In 1929, a croquet lawn was laid at a cost of £30 and a seventh tennis court the following year. A new pavilion was built for the sum of £228 in 1928. The layout of the club is shown on the next page and would remain essentially the same until 1975.

The old pavilion at Brookfield Lawn Tennis Club that was demolished in 1976 and replaced by a new clubhouse with modern facilities.

In 1935 a small extension was made to the pavilion for a kitchen. In 1972 a newly formed company, Squash Ireland, approached the club concerning the possibility of a development on the club grounds. Agreement was made but there were to be many planning problems and a fear that the club would lose out. In the final analysis the tennis club reached suitable agreements, a new club building was constructed and in use by May 1977. While the club lost some ground because of the development it gained in finances and in 1981/1982 built 6 *Tennisquick* hard courts. The wet summer of 1981, and also the need to play many home league matches at Alexandra College, helped in making this decision. In 1986 floodlights were possible for courts 1, 2 & 3. In 1992, all courts were to become 'artificial grass', courts 5 & 6 floodlit and a lounge extension built. In 1998, club member, a Mr. White, put together a *brief and personal history* of the club from which this potted version was abstracted.

Ladies' doubles at Brookfield Lawn Tennis Club. From left: Olga Wilson, Jean Burges, May Townsend & Elizabeth Brewster (circa 1970).

The unique entrance to Brookfield Lawn Tennis Club in Dublin. Note the absence of the word lawn, was this deliberate or accidental?

The grounds were leased in 1928 for the nominal sum of £40 per annum. The daughter of the original owner of the land, Richard Ganly, married Gerald Wilson and they lived in number 6 Palmerston Vilas, overlooking the club. In 1955, at a relatively nominal sum of £2000, the grounds were bought outright. The amount was well below the market value of the land due to the *Ganly/Wilson family's long association with the club*. Much fund-raising was required, including memorable jumble sales, until the club loan was

finally paid off in 1962. Club work parties were frequently used for painting the pavilion. *...during one notable spring the Pavilion was refelted. We even got the roller up on the roof to press the felt down- a great pity there are no photos of this. We lived with tar on our hands for two weeks. Work parties were one way that the lads and lassies got to know each other-as well as by playing round the (table tennis) table, or croquet under the glow from the street lights. Quite a number of Brookfield romances ensued from such activities.*

The White family outside the old clubhouse in 1971.

The Courts

Grass courts required a lot of work and were not playable during the winter. Like many clubs this would eventually lead to the change to hard courts and then artificial grass surfaces. Up to the late 1940s no suitable weed killers were available. At Brookfield the records show that in 1946 five men were employed for a week to hand weed the courts at 8/- per man per day.

The Brookfield LTC Men's first team in 1939. Back (l. to r.): Rex Barrett, Lesley Wills & L. A. White. Front (l. to r.): J. R. Bailey, Mervyn Fenelon & Cecil Morton.

The club were fortunate in having a dedicated grounds man for over fifty years. Ned Coleman, who died in 1968 at the age of 95, had the job of marking eight courts two or three times a week. The nets had to be looked after. Made of cord they had to be taken down

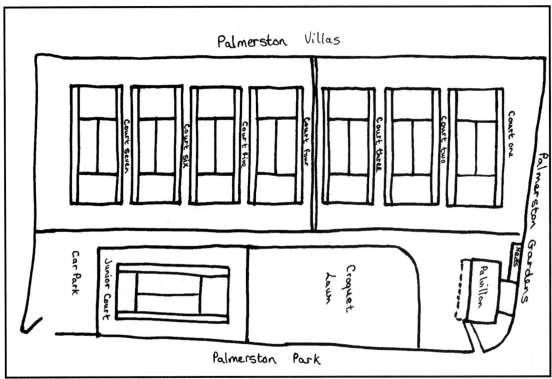

Layout of Brookfield Lawn Tennis Club 1928-1975.

each night by the committee member on duty and then erected the following day by Ned. During the war years the availability of petrol for the lawn mower was a problem. When Ned died he was followed by an able grounds man for the next ten years, Dick Synnott. After that time it was mainly short-term grounds men and grounds women. Re-sodding was by contract. The club is possibly one of the few that had its own borehole and an irrigation system installed for dry periods. This work was carried out in 1977.

The Game

The club held its own council from 1906 until 1929 when it first affiliated to the ILTA. At that time each club had to register 'club colours'. These were selected as being silver grey and red and are the club colours up to the present day (and enshrined in Rule 2). The membership number in 1929 was 160 and is now around 500, a maximum of 250 juniors included in this number. In 1929 the club *did quite well in the matches*, according to the honorary secretary's report. The club has not won that many trophies but is able to currently enter 4 men's and 4 ladies teams in the summer leagues.

Important as inter club matches are, most tennis is played within the club on a social basis. In times past the usual procedure was just turn up and play with whoever was there. Arranged games were unusual and singles were not allowed at popular times, unless they were challenge matches. After one set you had to come off and allow someone else on-and there were always people waiting at popular times. This was particularly so on Saturday afternoons-which was quite a social occasion, with afternoon tea being served. A (rapidly) diminishing number of members still adhere to the tradition. *Two outstanding players in the club have been Don Holloway and Jean Burges. Don would win the club championship fourteen times in seventeen years and Jean fifteen times over a twenty-two year period. The 'At Home' was always a popular day in the club and a* minor 'At Home' was added for the club handicap events.

Brian McConnell in Action (1970s?) at Brookfield LTC. Des Simpson does the line.

Brookfield LTC
The club won three titles in the Dublin winter leagues of 2004.The finals were at Templeogue LTC on the 21ˢᵗ March.

Men's winning team included Nap Keeling, Nicky Blake-Knox, Corne Mouton, Patrick Donaghy, Martin Murphy & Simon Hannigan.

Ladies first team included Carolyn Burges, Rachel McDonogh, Adrienne Taylor, Carol Fanagan, Betty Cronin & Sheila Chamberlain.

Ladies' second team included Judy O'Hanlon, Clodagh Veale, Joan Gillen, Jerry Schaffilitsky, Ruth Potterton & Sue Maxwell. In the final they beat Clane TC in a match interrupted by snow for one hour.

Brookfield Lawn Tennis Club

A brief and somewhat personal history

1998

The short history of Brookfield LTC was compiled by member Roger White in 1998.

As a reflection of the club's Protestant ethos, the grounds did not open on Sundays. This restriction was originally a clause in Mr. Ganly's lease for the grounds. In time the issue of Sunday play became less contentious. Full Sunday play was permitted from 1982 onwards when the hardcourts were laid.

At one time junior membership was provided *more as a facility to parents who were Senior members, and not so much as a breeding ground for the future.* This changed and there were large numbers joining the club after it went 'open' in 1974. *In 1985, egged on by James B., we started hosting a Junior Open in the Easter holidays. This was of great benefit in making the Club's name known more widely. It has also shown us the standard of play reached nation-wide in each of the age groups and a target for us to reach for.*

Roger White's history of the club is now on the web site (www.brookfieldtennis.com) and has many interesting anecdotes. A couple more are worth recording. Changing fashions has always been an issue wherever tennis is played. At Brookfield in 1935 it was not a matter of white or coloured clothing. *In 1935 a special committee meeting was held which decided to post the following notice in the ladies' changing room. "The committee request lady members not to wear shorts or divided skirts unless they reach the knee".* Now we argue whether Bermuda shorts are permitted or not.

The History of Irish Tennis

The 'At Home' was, and still is, the annual competition and social day ('Finals Day') in many clubs. A lot of committee time was spent organising this special day. *In the 1930s attendances in the afternoon were over 400, and there were often complaints that there were not enough ladies to serve tea-hardly surprising-and this in spite of engaging the services of five maids. Tickets for visitors had to be specially obtained beforehand from the committee. Mrs. Hording's five piece string orchestra played on the croquet lawn (at a fee of £5/5/0 in 1936). Hats were de-rigueur for the ladies and the umpires wore striped blazers and white flannels. I felt sorry for the poor umpire who had to call the score (without laughing) in a certain men's doubles final between Grey and Brown versus White and Darker.*

Brookfield LTC Club Championships 2004		
	Winners	**Runners-Up**
MS	Nap Keeling	Simon Blake-Knox
LS	Rachel McDonogh	Carol Fanagan
MD	Patrick Donaghy/ Corne Mouton	Simon Blake-Knox/ Simon Hannigan
LD	Rachel McDonogh/ Sandra Grey	Carol Fanagan/ Carolyn Burges
MxD	Simon Blake-Knox/ Carolyn Burges	Patrick Donaghy/ Rachel McDonogh
MSp	Keith Burns	Michael Butler

The Harris League Cup was won in 2005 by the team of Ben Gough, Carolyn Burges, George Hannigan (captain) and Siobhan Baird.

The 1995 Veterans' Dinner at Brookfield LTC. Back (l. to r.): Roger White (club historian), Jimmy Harris, Dick White & Cedric Bailey. Front (l. to r.): Eric Fenelon, Elizabeth Brewster & Alan Grey.

The club first entered open team competitions in 1929 when one men's' and one ladies' team were entered in the Dublin Lawn Tennis Council summer leagues. Some the wins over the years are as follows:

1933: Won Class 4 Men's Summer League
1949 & 1951: Won Class 2 Ladies' Summer League
1987: Won Class 4 Men's Summer League
1990: Won Class 4 & Class 6 Ladies' Summer League
1990: Won Class 3 Men's Floodlight League
1990: Won Under 14 Class 2 Girl's League
1992: Won Class 2 Ladies' Floodlight League
1996: Won Class 3 Ladies' Summer League
2000: Won Over 45 Class 2 Ladies' League
2001: Won Class 3 Ladies' Floodlight League

The men's singles final at Brookfield LTC in 1947-J. Briggs versus Alan Grey.

The modern omni-courts at Brookfield LTC.

An annual club prize giving in recent times.

The club continues to prosper and in 2006 celebrates a centenary of tennis at the club. Not to be forgotten are the many administrators at the club. One member of note that contributes to the games organisation outside the club is James Brewster, carrying on the tradition of his family in the life of the sport. Club coach Rachel McDonogh also plays a key role, she gaining her interest from her tennis playing dad and her mum, the latter being a squash international (brother Jimmy plays a similar role at Fitzwilliam Lawn Tennis Club. Historian Roger White is keen to keep the club history updated and welcomes any extra items for his web page, especially those that come under the section of "Social, Scandal & Gossip". Brookfield Lawn Tennis Club obviously appreciates all sides of the sport of tennis, and will undoubtedly thrive for another 100.

*****

Ballycastle Lawn Tennis & Croquet Club
(Founded 1906)

Ballycastle Golf Club was founded in 1890 and affiliated to the Golfing Union of Ireland in 1891. At a meeting in the club on the 31st December 1906 the Ballycastle Lawn Tennis and Croquet Club was founded. A committee of six was elected with Roger Casement as its first President cum chairman. He remained in this post for four years. It was thought that this man was the one subsequently hung for treason in Pentonville prison on the 3rd August, 1916. It appears, in fact, that it was his cousin with the same name.

The tennis club began on the grounds of the golf course, which was part of the sizeable Boyd family estate. For generations the family had lived in The Manor in Ballycastle. At the beginning of the 20th century the family owned most of the small seaside town of Ballycastle, nestling at the foot of Knocklayd Mountain in County Antrim. Miss Kathleen Boyd was one of the tennis club's founding members. A 3-year lease was obtained from Miss Boyd at an annual rent of £5. The club's first A.G.M. was held in the golf club on the 20th April 1907 and the rules of the club were passed. A tournament was to be held on the 20th July of that year with a prize fund totalling £34.5.0. The next A.G.M. was held on the 30th April 1908 and the family subscription was increased from £1 to £2. At a committee meeting on the 14th May the secretary read out a letter from the newly formed Irish Lawn Tennis Association. A copy of the rules of the I.L.T.A. was enclosed. The club decided to affiliate. The club must already have been in good standing as their tournament to be held that year, starting on the 19th July, was already sanctioned by the I.L.T.A. at their meeting on the 19th March. The event would include the singles Championship of County Antrim. At the A.G.M. of the 17th April 1913, the club recorded its first credit balance of £14.9.0. The Open tournament of 1912 had attracted some 254 entrants, the entry fees helping club finances considerably. The event had become a popular annual event.

At the A.G.M. meeting of the 29th June 1917 a letter was read from Kathleen Boyd of the Manor House and read as follows:

Dear Mr. Belford,
I hear the General Meeting of the Tennis Club takes place shortly. I should like to suggest that the tennis teas be dropped for this season on compliance of the Food Controller and also on account of the probable difficulty of obtaining supplies when the town fills up for the summer. As everyone who joins the club resides within five minutes walk of the ground I don't think it will be a hardship for them to have tea in their own houses. Please read this letter at the meeting.
Yours Truly,
K.J. Boyd.

The club had by now relocated from the original golf club location to the site of the former harbour. There were eleven grass courts in place making it one of the finest locations for lawn tennis in Ulster. At a committee meeting held on the 28th April 1933 efforts were being made to form a bowling club. A bowling green, controlled by the tennis club, had been in existence for a good number of years. The outcome of the meeting was to let the hotel ground to the bowling Club at 10 shillings per member and "to let" two grass courts to the Governors of the High School for use by pupils at a charge of £15 per annum. All tennis club members were eligible to play bowls. The committee also heard that a communication signed by Dr. Pedlow (president) and Mr. A. V. L. Johnstone (honorary secretary) of the Ulster Branch of the I.L.T.A. stating that at a special General meeting of the affiliated lawn tennis clubs of Ulster, held in the Grand Central Hotel, Belfast on the 6th April 1933, the following resolution was passed: "That the club be asked for a voluntary subscription of 10 shillings for each 50 members, or part thereof, the total subscription not to exceed £5.00".

At the A.G.M. of the 9th August 1935, the club's first lady President was elected. She was Mrs. Greer, wife of the late Senator T.M. Greer. The meeting agreed to sell the *Bowling Green* and two huts to the Bowling Club for £60-0-0. During the war years, 1939 to 1945, there were few meetings recorded. After the war there was a resurgence of interest in the game and the club reached its crowning glory in 1957. With a request from the Ulster Branch Secretary (Terence Duncan) and the approval of the I.L.T.A. the club had no hesitation in agreeing to stage an international match on Friday and Saturday the 23rd and 24th August.

Despite the poor weather, the Irish-English match was played with the visitors winning 9/2. The two teams were as follows:

Ireland: Joe Hackett (Leinster), Guy Jackson (Leinster), Peter Jackson (Ulster), Tommy Crooks (Ulster), Heather Flinn (Leinster), June Ann Fitzpatrick (Leinster).

Prize winners at the 1979 Senior Northern Bank Grass Court Championships held at Ballycastle.

Vivian Gotto playing at Ballycastle in the late 1950s

Juniors at Ballycastle in 1979 (the County Antrim Championships, sponsored by the Milk Marketing Board).

The History of Irish Tennis

England: Gerry Oakley (Surrey), Michael Hann (Surrey), Reg Bennett (Sussex), Jimmy Tattersall (Yorkshire), Mrs. Wheeler, Mrs. Shenton.

In the 1960s the club enjoyed success with a large crop of homegrown players, all pupils of the Ballycastle High School, (see section 4.7). Plans for a new clubhouse were drawn up in 1964, at an estimated cost of £6000. The saga of anew clubhouse was to continue over a number of years as the club sank further into financial difficulty. There was a proposal that the tennis and bowling clubs merge with the golf club.

The proposal came to nought. After meetings with the local Town Council, and the Ulster Council (I.L.T.A.) a club meeting on the 24th April 1975 agreed "the property belonging to Ballycastle Tennis Club should be handed over in its entirety to the Ballycastle Town Council". This included nets, posts, markers, mower, roller, benches, umpire chairs, tables and trophies. For the next eighteen years the courts were a council facility

Presidents of Ballycastle Lawn Tennis & Croquet Club

1906 to 1909	Roger Casement
1920 to 1927	Senator T. M. Greer
1928 to 1934	Mr. J. A. McCullagh
1935 to 1936	Mrs. T. M. Greer
1937	Colonel D. R. Coates
1938 to 1940	Captain S. J. Lyle
1941 to 1942	Mr. J. Chamney
1943 to 1947	Mr. E. R. Casement
1948	Mr. S. J. Gilmour
1949	Miss R. M. Wetherall
1950	Mr. W. J. Wilgar
1951	Miss Alison Casement
1952	Mr. J.W. McGaughan
1953	Captain G..........
1954	Mrs. D. Fullerton
1955 to 1957	Mr. A. G. German
1958	Mrs. Moriarty
1959 to 1960	Mr. H.A. Boyd
1962 to 1963	Mr. G. W. S......
1964	Lt. Col H.A......
1965	W. W. (Billy) Barnhill

In 1993 a new club was formed. Known as the **Moyle Tennis Club**, named after the Town Council, which was now known as the Moyle District Council. In 1998 the 10 natural grass and two hard courts were revamped. One court was lost but the club ended up with five of the original grass courts and six new polymeric rubber courts. During the 1980s, when the council were in charge, a clubhouse had been built. Raymond McCurdy, one of the best players to have been nurtured in the club, summarises the club's history as follows:

The tennis club throughout its history seems to have always been struggling with both a lack of money, *and too few members.....It has been extremely fortunate that the club has always had extremely enthusiastic and very capable honorary officials. Captain Arthur Green, in particular, was absolutely outstanding during his very lengthy association with the club over many years.*

In the 1950s and 1960s there were others of note such as Arhur Greene, W. W. (Billy) Barnhill and Colonel Harry Allen. One of the club's best-known characters was Theodore Barnes. He played virtually every day, well into his eighties. The following quotes are from an article written by Billy Barnhill (Club President in 1965) and published in The Coleraine Chronicle in the immediate period after the club's demise in April 1975.

My first visit to Ballycastle was in 1927 when I was home on leave from abroad. I borrowed the old family car and set out with a friend to take part in the August Tournament. Both of being impecunious, we decided to save money by sleeping in the car.

I remember one morning driving down to the old wooden pier (which no longer exists) to have a bathe. My friend was a hardy creature who used to bathe in the Isis all the year around, so I bade him take the plunge first. When he surfaced I shouted "What's it like?" and he replied "Just a pleasant nip". Thereupon I dived in, and I can still remember the icy shock! The waters around our Antrim coast are so clear and enticing to look at-but Oh so cold!

At intervals during the years that followed I visited Ballycastle and eventually, in 1961, my wife and I came there to live permanently. We rented a 1.5-acre plot and built a house. I planted about 600 (60?) trees, which are now about 25 ft. high. The view from our sitting room window is so lovely that I often sit there and do nothing but look.

To the north is the green expanse of the golf links, the sea and Rathlin. To the east our garden slopes down to the Glenshesk River, and above it one can see the top of Fair Head, the Mull and, on a clear day, the Paps of Jura.

It was tennis that first brought me to Ballycastle. There is something unique about the courts. They are built on what used to be an old harbour and, although sunk down below the road surface, they are very quick drying and never get waterlogged....Nearly everyone knows everyone else along 'the wall', and you must be very careful what you say about any of the play, particularly during children's events, because someone's aunt, or may times, removed cousin, is sure to be standing near you.....

Some years ago, two friends of mine, who had been visitors since their school days, were playing together in the doubles. They had been, and still were, useful players, but they were relegated to their proper place in the scheme of things by a remark of a youthful player watching from 'the wall'. 'Those two must have been good in their day'.

It is very pleasant to lean over 'the wall' on a summer evening, now watching the players, now looking over their heads to the shadows on Fair Head. All is peace until you see a bad stroke and give voice to some unfavourable criticism. Almost before the words have left your mouth you realise with horror that you have blundered! There is no need to turn around to see that there is indeed an aunt at your elbow………

In the last few years it became increasingly difficult to keep the club going due to two main causes-increasing labour costs and scant local support. This latter cause has a kind of historical origin in that, in the early years of the club, it acquired, not without justification, an image of exclusiveness, which barred many of the local people from membership.

This can best be illustrated in this way. Suppose you asked the man in the street 'Have you a golf club?' He would say 'Of course I have'. If the question were 'Have you a tennis club?' he might well say 'There is a tennis club but I don't know much about it'"

****

Templeogue Lawn Tennis Club
(Founded 1906)

The history of **Templeogue LTC** is intimately connected with the adjoining Templeogue Inn. Early in 1906 the licensee of the premises, a Mr. Faulkner, died and the executors, Messrs. Keating and Keating, solicitors, put up the property for sale. The reserve price of £600 was not reached and the property was bought by Ned Keating, a senior partner in the firm of solicitors. That summer he laid out a court on one of the level pieces of ground adjoining the inn. At the end of the year he sold the Inn to a Mr. Greer with a condition that he be permitted to continue using the tennis court.

Within two years, Keating and his friends had become extremely keen on the sport and laid out a second court on a level patch adjoining the river. They formed a semi-private club that continued up until 1914. The club then folded when the secretary, Paddy O'Byrne, joined the 16th Irish Division that participated in the Great War. Two years later he was invalided out of the British Army and in 1917 was approached by Mr. and Mrs. Raymond (*Ram*) Molloy who asked him if he could get the club re-started. He called a meeting in the Templeogue Inn on about the 20th May. The thirteen that attended were Pat Shortt, the last president of the old club, Chris Shortt, Margaret Shortt, Ned Keating, John Keating, the Molloys, Denis Nugent, David Riordan, Misses Linda and Lizzie Murphy as well as Paddy and Annie O'Byrne.

The club was officially born at this meeting when the following decisions were made (a) That there should be a completely new club founded to be known as **Templeogue Lawn Tennis Club** (b) That the members present at the initial meeting should form the committee of the new club for the first year (c) That all members of the old club should be entitled to rejoin without the formality of re-election (d) That the subscription should be ten shillings for men and seven and six for ladies and (e) That two courts should be laid out in the positions previously occupied by the two courts of the old club.

In this first year of the new club there were 16 men and 16 ladies in the club, the income was £14 and the expenditure £14-2-6. Within two years two more courts were necessary and were laid out on ground that was hilly and uneven i.e. the courts that today are occupied (albeit by newer courts) by the courts in front of the pavilion. For the princely sum of five shillings a week the part time grounds man, Denis Hayden, was employed. This ex British army soldier would mow and mark the courts each week during the summer months.

The Templeogue LTC Men's team won the Leinster Challenge Cup in 1984, beating Elm Park 4/1 in the final. Back (l. to r.) Der O' Sullivan, Ken Kelleher, Michael Smyth & Noel Murphy (captain). Front (l. to r.) Sean Molloy, Fergus Murphy & Michael Kenny. Four of this team (Des, Sean, Fergus & Michael (Kenny) won the Floodlit Class I league in 1985, previously won by the club in 1980, 1981 and 1983. Subsequently, the club's Class 1 team also won the floodlit league in 1988, 1992, 1993 and 2001. The ladies at the club won the 'floodlit' class 1 in 1994, Class 2 in 1989 and Class 4 in 1995.

At that time some shelter was obtained by using a large wooden box, the type used to import cars in. It was roughly converted into a 'kitchen' in which the ladies would boil water on a Primus stove for the Saturday Afternoon Teas. Sunday tennis was not, at that time, considered an option. In 1920 a Major Jackson was employed, and paid some £24, to re-sod the courts and a 'remarkable' job was done-they lasted for many years to come. Two years later there was further military involvement. Colonel Charlie Russell and technical officers of the new Free State erected a spacious wooden pavilion, which provided basic accommodation suitable for social gatherings such as club dances. That year, 1922, saw the club affiliating to the I.L.T.A. and entering a team in Class IV of the Dublin League. They were narrowly beaten in the semi-final and the following year entered Class III. The first club victory would not come until 1932. This win in Class III lead to celebrations in the village in which it joined in, and was long remembered.

Under the direction of one of the club's better players, Dick Sullivan, two more courts were laid. By 1934 there were dressing rooms for the men but in February of that year the premises was burnt to the ground on a windy night. The insurance of £250 was fully paid and an even better pavilion was built by January 1935 for the sum of £375. The night of the Ireland-England rugby international was chosen as the gala opening night. So many attended that the pavilion was full as were the front courts. Another night to remember with an estimated 1000 plus attending. With minor changes this pavilion lasted until 1985 when it was replaced.

In 1939 a lease for land was obtained from the Dublin Blessington Steam Tram Company. With the war over a contract was placed, with En Tout Cas, in 1946 for the provision of two hard courts costing £750. Messrs. Keenan supplied the wire fencing and a total expenditure of about £1000 was made. Ireland's leading players officially opened these in the spring of 1947 with a series of exhibition matches.

The 1976 Ladies Singles Final at Templeogue LTC. Ann Moore (right) was the winner over Enda Barry. Muriel Doyle, the ladies captain, was the umpire.

In 1976 three new En Tout Cas hardcourts were opened at the club, which meant the club then had six grass and five hard courts. In 1979 the last of the grass courts were converted to hard courts and, shortly afterwards, the word 'lawn' was dropped from the club's title. The old pavilion was closed down in 1984

and on the 22nd September 1985 the new clubhouse was officially opened. In 1991 the club bought several acres of land from Dublin Corporation for additional development. Today the club thrives with 12 floodlit all-weather *Omni Pro grass* courts.

Tessa Price (South Africa) on her way to the final of the 1987 Leinster Open at Templeogue LTC.

In the 1940s and 1950s the club was renowned for its Sunday Night Dances. Equally popular in the 1960s and 1970s were the Tennis Hops. Entertainers such as Phil Lynnott, Colm Wilkinson, Skid Row and Thin Lizzy were among those providing the entertainment. The club has run many major tournaments over the years not least the Open Hard Court Championships, starting in 1979. Visitors were always welcome. The Leinster Open has been played there for a number of years and a visitor described the club's hospitality in the late 1980s as "intense". The men's leg of the Irish Open Championships has been held at the club for the last number of years. The Tennis Ireland Magazine (December 1998) had the following compliment to pay.

Templeogue is famous for the quality of its tennis and the 1998 version proved again it's in the premier league for both venue and organisation.....Templeogue proved that if you keep believing, achievement will always wait with its reward.

Among the successful members at the club have been Ken Kelleher, Gerry Clarke, the Sparks brothers, Ann Egan, Ann Moore, Caitriona Ruane, Noel Murphy, Peter Hannon and Joanna Griffiths. The **Dublin LTC** leagues are a good indicator of success over the years. Templeogue have won a total of about 61 leagues covering a range from the men's summer leagues to senior to juniors. Only four clubs (Sutton (81), Lansdowne (107), Donnybrook (71) and Carrickmines (80)) have won more titles across the broad range of leagues which first started in 1902. The club's first win in the men's summer league was 1933 when taking the Class III event followed up by a Class II win in 1935. The club was really thriving when they won Class I in 1981.

Ken Kelleher one of the more successful players at Templeogue Lawn Tennis Club in the 1960s and 1970s.

The ladies won the Class 3 league in 1945 followed by Class II in 1946 and Class I as recently as 1991. In the winter leagues the ladies were the first holders of Class I in 1994. The men had won the Class I winter league in 1983. They followed this up by wins in 1986, 1990, 1995 and 2000 in this category. No other club has won this event five times. They must be hardy souls in this south Dublin club. The ladies won the first Class I league in 1994 as well as Class II (1999) and Class III (2000). The future of a club at any point in time is linked to the encouragement of the juniors. The club have won one boys title and four girls since these competitions started in the late 1980s. Interestingly, the under 14 Class 1 Girls League competition has only been won by four different clubs, Donnybrook (1), Clontarf (1), Castleknock (9) and Templeogue (4). Roll on the future.

★★★★★

Laytown-Bettystown LTC
(Founded 1907)

The Laytown/Bettystown Lawn Tennis Club was founded in 1907 with just one grass court. A Mr. Fitzpatrick was one of the leading lights in the early

years. During the Great War (1914-1918) tournaments were organised at the club to raise funds for the Red Cross. From the 1920s to the 1970s the annual fancy dress tournament was a great success, an end of year event eagerly awaited by members each summer.

Many keen players have passed through the club over the decades. Particularly important have been the administrators and coaches. For their exceptional efforts on behalf of the club honorary life membership was bestowed upon Joan Duffner and Maureen Gray. Roswitha Duffner, Ann Gray and Eleanor O'Neill are among the others to have left their mark on the club. Eleanor grew up in Bettystown and became one of Ireland's foremost players ever. In 1955 she won the Irish Girls' u15 open championship, and then from 1956 to 1958 the Irish senior girls' title. Her string of titles is exceptional (see chapter 6). She will remember appearing on the first Irish Federation Cup team with Geraldine Houlihan from Birr. As a pair these players, the top two in Ireland throughout the 1960s, complemented one another, Geraldine being the serve and volleyer and Eleanor the baseliner. Eleanor became a professional coach but never forgot the efforts of Patricia Gray and Joan Duffner in bringing along the juniors at the club.

Eleanor McFadden (nee O'Neill) learned her tennis at the Bettystown-Laytown LTC. She became one of the most successful players ever in Ireland.

For many years the North-East Junior Championships were organised by the club. Entries were extensive at this seaside club. Far from being a local event the players came from many parts of Ireland, as well as from such countries as France, Germany and the USA. As their club's centenary year approaches the junior events still continue each summer. Since the grass courts are long gone, the club, like many others, has now dropped the 'lawn' from its title. The current (2005) honorary secretary is Jackie Clarke.

The History of Irish Tennis

In 1977 Dermot Caffrey from Mullingar TC won the North East Leinster u14 title at Laytown Bettystown LTC.

The ladies' team from the Laytown & Bettystown LTC won their Dublin League in 1974. Back (l. to r.): Helen Curran, Mary Dwyer & Geraldine Farrell. Front (l. to r.): Dorothy Collins, Mary Curran & Anne Delaney.

⁎⁎⁎⁎⁎

Muckamore Cricket & Lawn Tennis Club
(Founded 1908)

Situated on the northern bank of the Sixmilewater River, the Muckamore club is in a most beautiful setting. It remains the only combined cricket and tennis club in Northern Ireland. John Joseph Robinson who came to live at the Muckamore School House in 1874 founded the club. Many cricket clubs were associated with linen firms; he was on the staff of the York Street Flax Spinning Company and played at Massereene in the late 1860s. The original grounds were at Boghead, and then it moved to a site opposite the school, then to the old racecourse at Oldstone and later to Harrigan's Hill where cricket has been played continuously for nearly 120 years. The club was always competitive and won many cricket plaudits over the years. It prided itself on its reputation for sportsmanship following the tradition set by John G. Entwistle, the cricket captain from 1899 to 1925. Perhaps a clue to this tradition was in the first page of their Centenary booklet of 1974. *In 1894 a local minister strongly disapproved of a barrel of beer being delivered to the ground each Saturday and finished on the \Sunday, so he formed the Greeenmount C.C. from our junior members and boys from his bible class. This club played on the opposite side of the Six Mile water from Harrigan's Hill. A few years later the clubs united.* Some of the "big" houses in the area already had courts. Cricket captain John G. Entwistle brought along a net and posts and the game took off. It was informal at first, the court being laid in the outfield of the cricket pitch. The numbers playing tennis grew and it was officially established in 1908. *There was no netting round the courts in those days but ball boys were not hard to find at 3d. for an afternoon, that being passing wealth for a youngster then.*

The Tennis Club soon became a social centre for the entire district, membership being a prized privilege and in one tournament confined to local players nine of the competitors had titles. Strawberry-fare was another inducement provided by a ladies committee whose teas were famous far and wide.

CURRAN SISTERS IMPRESS

Helen and Mary Curran gave a brilliant display in the ladies under 18 doubles in the North East Tennis Championship finals at Bettystown yesterday.

Boys under 18—Singles—M. Dawson (Donnybrook) bt. C. Brown (Bettystown), 6-2, 0-6, 6-4. **Doubles**—C. Brown & P. Houston bt. W. Kavanagh & D. O'Toole, 6-4, 6-3. **"Plate"**—O. O'Buachalla ceded a walk over to S. Gillian (Limerick).

Boys under 15—Singles—N. Coakley (Castleknock) bt. M. Rennix (Navan), 6-2, 6-4. **"Plate"** — F. McDowall (Ardee) bt. T. Farrell—best of one set—6-4.

Girls under 18—Singles — Miss B. Branigan (Donnybrook) bt. Miss R. McCabe (Bettystown), 6-4, 6-0. **Doubles** —Misses Helen & Mary Curran bt. Misses A. Flanagan and A. Begger, 7-5, 7-4. **Plate**—Miss M. Smyth bt. Miss G. McGrath, 6-1.

Girls under 15—Singles—Miss G. Farrell (Bettystown) bt. Miss A. Donnelly (Navan), 6-1, 6-2. **Plate**—Miss V. O'Kane (Drogheda) bt. Miss M. Conway (Dublin), 6-4.

19th July 1970

Muckamore Tennis Club League Winning Team 1973: Back (l. to r.) D. Deery, Dr. R. Smith (Gent's Captain), D. Clement, N. Craig. Front (l. to r.) Mrs. L. Ross (ladies' Captain), Mrs. M. McKeown, Mrs. R. Sweetman, Mrs. N. Craig.

Muckamore Cricket & Lawn Tennis Club. On the 1st May 1948 the hard courts were officially opened. From left to right (foreground) at the opening were C. Walker, J. Kirk, Mrs. J. Grainger, O. Merrifield, N. Kirk, GF. Grainger & J. Entwistle.

During 1908 the club had four grass courts and over sixty members, many of the early members were cricketers and their families. The Kirks from Antrim were among the better players, Martin being an outstanding player who sadly died in 1911. *Another player who helped to raise the standard of play was Captain Robert Thompson, the best player in the district who had gained a half blue for tennis at Cambridge University.*

Between the wars it is noted that it was tennis that helped to balance the books, it being more profitable than cricket. After the Second World War a rapid revival was attributed to people such as John Kirk and Joy Grainger and tennis membership rose to 150. Giving up the tennis courts to cricket on a Saturday was a bit of a problem. Eventually four hard courts and a car park were built in 1948. A tennis pavilion was built in 1950. The 1950s and 1960s were a golden age in the tennis section. Billy Crawford and Jim Tweed were at the fore and the latter was made an honorary life member for his efforts. A distinction between cricketers and tennis players was abolished in 1965 with a single membership. In 1973 the club won their league section, for the first time in many years.

In 1984 the club courts were replaces with asphalt surfaces and ten years later by four synthetic grass courts. *Along with most other clubs, Muckamore has no indoor tennis facilities, and modern youth is less inclined to play in wet, windy and cold conditions than those brought up in earlier times. The Club also suffers from what can only be described as the perception of elitism, although this is not what is wanted. Muckamore is part of the town of Antrim which has a large population of young people, but the Club has not yet succeeded in attracting more than a few of the less privileged members of society to its ranks.*

Muckamore Cricket & Lawn Tennis Club Presidents

1898-1900	R.H. Reade	1964-1966	E.B. Erskine
1901-1940	G.S. Reade	1967-1968	W.G. Henderson
1946-1947	J.S. Entwistle	1969-1970	N.C. Entwistle
1948-1961	Sir Mullholland	1971-1973	J. Ross
1962-1963	S. Henderson	1974	P. McCormick

Muckamore Cricket & Lawn Tennis Club Honorary Secretaries

1898-1900	R.M. Ferguson	1967-1969	S. Campbell
1901-1903	R.H. Coulter	1970	P. L.O'Hara/ G. Wallace
1904-1954	J. Entwistle	1971-1973	D.C. Clement
1954-1963	J. Ross	1974	H. Ruscoe
1964-1966	P.L. Campbell		

Muckamore Cricket & Lawn Tennis Club Honorary Secretaries

1898-1900	R. M. Ferguson
1901-1903	R. H. Coulter
1904-1954	J. Entwthistle
1954-1963	J. Ross
1964-1966	P. L. Campbell
1967-1969	S. Campbell
1970	P. L. O'Hara/G. Wallace
1971-1973	D. C. Clement
1974	H. Ruscoe
1976	N. Craig
1977- 1980	D. C. Clement
1982-1984	Mrs. V. Buckland
1985	Mrs. Maureen Harbison
1986-1997	Mrs. Margaret Clement
1998-2000	Mr. J. Mulholland
2002-2003	Pat Deerick

Muckamore Cricket & Lawn Tennis Club
Tennis Captains (1947-1974)

	Ladies	Gents
1947-1948	Mrs. J. Grainger	J. Kirk
1949-1950	Miss M. Reilly	W. Crawford
1951	Miss S. Gray	W. Crawford
1952	Miss S. Gray	D. W. Chadd
1953	Miss A Young	K. E. Petch
1954	Mrs. W. Jarden	W.A. Abercrombie
1955	Miss M. Wilson	E. Smyth
1956	Mrs. S. Cullen	B. Canavan
1957	Miss. J. Erskine	C. Blackbourne
1958	Mrs. S. Cullen	C. Blackbourne
1959	Miss R. Craig	N. Kane
1960	Mrs. S. Ball	R. Morrison
1961	Miss R. Craig	J. Bell
1962	Mrs. S. Ball	J. Bell
1963	Miss N. Clark	W. Honeyford
1964	Miss N. Clark	N. Craig
1965	Mrs. L. Ross	N. J. W. Hill
1966-1969	Mrs. R. Sweetmn	N. J. W. Hill
1970	Mrs. S. Sweetman	P. Scott
1971-1972	Mrs. N. Craig	N. Craig
1973-1974	Mrs. L. Ross	R. Smith

The club employed a tennis coach in the mid-1990s in order to bring along the youth in the area and *to teach short tennis in local schools.* The coach left to live in New Zealand. It currently, therefore, looks to the future with a need for some positive action to further the interest in the game and in the club. If John Entwistle's spirit is still alive then no doubt it will succeed.

****

Tralee LTC
(Founded <1909)

It is not known when the old club was founded in Tralee, for there were to be two clubs in the town for a number of years. However, the playing strength must have been reasonable. The Munster Cup for senior teams was started in 1907. The inaugural winners were **Rushbrooke Lawn Tennis & Croquet Club.** Two years later it was the Tralee club's turn to win.

It is known that **Tralee Sports Field LTC** was in action in 1909 and the **Tralee Green LTC** in 1911. Were these the same club? Years later a club would develop. A young Mary O'Sullivan went to Rushbrooke in the early 1950s and did exceptionally well. Years later she would be a senior tennis and badminton international, in the case of the latter sport one of the best in the world.

The game virtually disappeared in the town for many years. In 1979, the 'new' club was doing well in its second season, and the tennis section of the F.I.S.E.C. Games took place on the new hard courts of the Tralee Sports Centre. There were three age groups (under 18, 16 and 14) and entries were received from Austria, Great Britain, Italy and the Netherlands. In the team event Ireland won all three gold medals. According to the 1980 Yearbook *The local tennis players gave great assistance in umpiring matches, which in some cases were difficult on account of the various Nationalities and dialects.*

During 1979 friendly matches were held with neighbouring clubs in Listowel and Castleisland. The season ended with a *Grand Halloween Fancy Dress Party at the Earl of Desmond Hotel.* Trophies were presented to the Club Tournament finalists:

Event	Winners	Runners Up
MS	Pat Prenderville	Neil Kelly
LS	Margaret Davin	Mary Pat O' Sullivan
MS-Plate	Paudie Moriarty	
LS-Plate	Suzanne Kinch	

****

Glasnevin LTC
(Founded 1909)

On the north side of the Liffey in Dublin, the **Glasnevin LTC** was founded on the 22nd May 1909. The club initially had two grass courts, a croquet lawn and a small pavilion, on lands leased from a Colonel Lindsay. The club colours were navy blue and saxe blue.

Like other clubs during the 1920s the **Glasnevin LTC** was a very 'lively' one, a factor associated with the post-Great War era (the 'roaring' 20s is a term also associated with this era). The club membership grew and, with entry into league competition, there was a need for bigger premises. The club moved and now were to have six grass courts and a new, larger pavilion, built by the members themselves.

During the 1930s ladies were elected to the committee for the first time. During the Second World War (the 'emergency' period in the Republic of Ireland) one of the courts acted as a potato patch. Tennis, however, continued on the others. [In the 1940s, the Cleary family of Carrick-on-Suir had their own family court. Young Tom Cleary, who later won the South of Ireland, regretted the fact that the court was dug up in favour of a potato patch at that time].

In 1951 two hard courts were added to the club's facilities, thus extending the playing year. The Winter/Spring Hard-court championships were initiated and continue to this day. In the 1970s floodlights were added to the hard courts. In 1984 the grass courts were replaced by 5 flood-lit hardcourts, these in turn replaced by synthetic grass in the 1990s.

The club has eight all-weather courts and since 2005 access on one day a week to the nearby Tennis Ireland indoor facility. The indoor hall has a number of uses including the playing of badminton in the winter.

Glasnevin Lawn Tennis Club Committee 2005	
President	Eugene Bergin
Honorary Secretary	Gerry Bailey
Honorary Treasurer	Larry Shiel
Club Team Captain	Frank Moran
Club Team Vice-Captain	Anne Marie Mee
Membership Officer	Joan Gannon
Junior Development	Frank Moran
Committee Members	Tom Moore
	Coleen McManus
	Mick Finglas
	Denis O'Byrne
	Fintan Brennan
Club Stewart	Liam O'Byrne

Since 1987 the club has run a very successful open week. It has also hosted some large events such as the Ladies' Irish Open in 2001. Despite a rain interruption this proved to be an Irish triumph. Yvonne Doyle took the singles championships title, the first home-grown Irish winner of this prestigious event since Betty Lombard beat Arville McGuire (USA) 6/2 6/3. Yvonne beat Claudia Kuleszka of Germany 6/4 6/4 and with Karen Nugent won the doubles championship. It was an appropriate event for Irish tennis in that former **Glasnevin LTC** member David Nathan was President of Tennis Ireland at the time.

The clubs internal championships go back to 1913. In 1924 the Cecil Hunt Memorial Cups were first presented for the men's and ladies' champions each year. In the Dublin leagues, the following are some of the successes in various categories:

Glasnevin Lawn Tennis Club Some DLTC League Titles	
Men's Summer League	
Class 2	1957, 1974, 1979 & 1990
Class 3	1929 & 1966
Class 4	1954 & 1967
Class 5	2000
Ladies' Summer League	
Class 1	1968, 1969, 1970 & 1975
Class 2	1956
Class 3	1967
Ladies' Winter League	
Class 6	1995
Ladies' Senior League (035)	
Class 2	1996
Class 3	1991
Men's Senior League (055)	
Class 1	1990
Men's Floodlight League	
Class 2	2000

Dublin's Yvonne Doyle after her 2001 Irish Championship win at Glasnevin LTC.

David Nathan (left), President of Tennis Ireland, with Al Reid, the President of Glasnevin LTC, at the club during the Irish Ladies' Open Championships in August 2001.

****

Bandon Lawn Tennis Club
(Founded pre 1914)

Some junior spectators-the future at Bandon Lawn Tennis Club. Up to 100 juniors are now being coached at the club.

This County Cork club is small but very active. The club has three floodlit all-weather courts and a small functional clubhouse.

The committee for 2005 was as follows:

Bandon Lawn Tennis Club Committee 2005	
Chairperson	Niall Coonan
President	Eileen MacSweeney
Honorary Secretary	Catherine McCarthy
Honorary Treasurer	Catherine FitzMaurice
Club Team Captain	Maggie O'Toole
Club Team Vice-Captain	Niall Coonan
Children's Officer	Catherine McCarthy/ John O'Toole
PRO	Tish Canniffe
Committee Members	Sean Frank
	Paul Twomey
	Roger Pearson
	Therese Hurley

The clubhouse and spectators at the 2005 Bandon LTC championships

In the ladies' A championship final at Bandon LTC in 2005 Diana Fawsitt (left) beat Maggie O'Toole.

Winners at the Bandon Lawn Tennis Club championships in 1976 were (from left): D. Crowley (mixed), June Murphy (ladies' doubles), Paula Desmond (singles, doubles & mixed) and Tim Goggin (men's doubles).

The club is currently a very active one and, with the new courts in place, is looking forward to many successful years ahead. In the May 2005 newsletter it was pointed out that they had nearly 100 juniors being coached with Jack O'Toole, Katie Desmond and Kerry Desmond making it to Munster junior squads. On the coaching front the key members are Mike Lehane, Derek Stenson and Mark Cunningham. On the senior front Freda Roycroft was selected to play for the Munster veteran side for the second time in 2005. The club entered three teams in the Munster winter leagues in 2005. The Grade 3 side of Diana Fawsitt, Tish Canniffe, Freda Roycroft, Sean Frank and Stan Dvorsky reached the knock-out stages of the event, only to be beaten by the Douglas, the eventual winners of the title.

Some Men's Champions at Bandon LTC	
1963	T. Phelan
1964	E. Goggins
1968	T. Goggin
1970	J. Desmond
1971	M. Goggin
1972	P. Desmond
1973-1977	M. Goggin
1978	E. Goggin
1979	J. Desmond
1980-1981	M. Goggin
1983	M. O'Driscoll
1985	T. Goggin
1986	Martin O'Driscoll
1987	David Long
1988-1989	Alan O'Mahony
1990	Ed Brennan
1991	Tim Goggin
1992	Dave Sutton
1993	Terry Manopley
1994	Alan O'Mahony
1995	Dave Sutton
1996	Joe Nash
1997	Dave Sutton
1998-2002	Roger Pearson
2003	Stan Dvorsky
2004-2005	Sean Frank

Some Ladies' Champions at Bandon LTC	
1976	Paula Desmond
2004	Maggie O'Toole
2005	Diana Fawsitt

The 2005 men's doubles championships at Bandon LTC. Dave Sutton and Coman O'Sullivan (left) beat Barry Hurley and John O'Toole in the final.

Ann O'Mahony (left) beat Jo Callaghan in the ladies' B final at the Bandon LTC championships in 2005.

****

Ardee Tennis Club
[Ardee Lawn Tennis Club]
(Founded 1916)

One wonders would the present young tennis players at the County Louth club of Ardee have any idea of the high standard the sport reached many moons ago in their small club. Today, the club plays on four hard courts at the Ardee Community School. The original club closed in 1977 after a period of over sixty years in operation. In 1996 a new impetus was developed and the present club, with about 20 adults and 60/70 juniors, came into operation. The honorary secretaries for the first few years of the new clubs were Catherine Brennan and Marion Halpenny. The club is open winter and summer with regular competitions within the club. The school provides toilets and changing areas, as well as facilities for making tea during competitions. The school gym is also used during the summer holidays for indoor coaching when needed.

J. J. poised for 24th title

HAVING won the title for the past 23 years, J. J. McArdle of Dundalk reached the final of the Co. Louth Open Men's Singles Tennis Championship at Ardee yesterday.

Semi-final results were:

Men's Singles—J. J. McArdle bt. E. Barrett, 6-2, 6-3. T. Stein bt. P. McArdle, 6-4 6-0.

Ladies' Singles—Mrs. D. Reilly bt. Miss M. McCrystal, 6-3, 6-2. Miss A. Gray bt. Mrs. G. Kiernan, 6-4, 6-2.

Men's Doubles — J. J. and P. McArdle bt. L. P. Stein and N. McCann, 6-2, 6-1.

Ladies' Doubles—Miss P. Smith and Mrs. G. Kiernan bt. Miss McCrystal and Miss M. Clear, 6-2, 6-2. Miss I. Lewis and Miss N. McNicholl bt. Mrs. D. Reilly and Miss M. Curtis, 6-2, 6-1.

Mixed Doubles—T. Stein and Miss M. McCrystal bt. G. Kiernan and Mrs Kiernan 6-4, 6-3.

Ardee LTC Open
(Irish Independent, 27th July 1969)

Frank Aiken, an active member of the club, was a helpful source in sorting out the club's past. In 1916, the club started with two grass courts, this being increased to four in the 1930s. In the 1940s a fifth grass courts was developed. The club had a small clubhouse with a sloping galvanised roof, small dressing rooms, toilets and a general social area with a

The History of Irish Tennis

The Ardee LTC Open Tournament

Year	Men's Singles	Ladies Singles	Men's Doubles	Ladies Doubles	Mixed Doubles
				County Louth Championships (doubles)	
1955	J.J. McArdle beat Gerry Clarke 14/12 6/3	Mary O'Sullivan beat Heather Bretland 7/5 2/6 6/4	J. J. McArdle/LarryStei beat Gerry Clarke/ Pat Reeves-Smith 6/2 6/2	Mary O' Sullivan/ Heather Bretland beat W. Moore/P. O' Carroll 6/1 6/1	J.J. McArdle/H.Bretland beat Gerry Clarke/ Mary O'Sullivan 7/5 6/2
1960	Guy Jackson beat J.J. McArdle 7/5 6/3	Miss R. Duffner beat Miss I. Lewis 6/3 8/6	Guy Jackson/ Gerry Clarke beat J.J. & Frank McArdle 8/6 6/3	Miss I. Lewis/ Pat Mc Kinley beat R. Duffner/Mrs.Lindsay 7/5 6/3	Guy Jackson/ Mrs. Mary Lindsay beat Gerry Clarke/ R. Duffner 6/2 6/2
1961	J.J. McArdle beat Frank McArdle 6/4 6/2	Miss I. Lewis beat Miss M. Gallagher 6/0 6/0	J.J. & Frank McArdle beat J. & N. Ennis 6/4 4/6 6/1	Pat Mc Kinley/ Miss I. Lewis beat Miss Corcoran/ Miss Daly 6/3 6/4	J.J. McArdle/I. Lewis beat N & C. Ennis 6/0 6/1
1962	Gerry Clarke beat J.J. McArdle 2/6 6/2 6/2	Heather Bretland beat Miss A. Donnelly 6/4 6/0	J.J. McArdle/S. Eakin beat P. Goodman/ P. Fitzgibbon 6/2 6/4	Pat McKinley/ Miss Lewis beat Miss Moore/ Molly Nichol 6/4 6/2	Gerry Clarke/ Heather Bretland beat J.J. McArdle/ Miss J. Lewis 6/3 6/1
1966	J. McArdle beat Frank McArdle 6/3 6/8 6/3	Miss M. Gallagher beat Joan Brady 6/3 4/6 6/3	J.J. & Frank McArdle beat Larry and A. Stein 6/2 6/3	Miss I. Lewis/ Mrs. Molly Nichol beat Mrs. M. Gallagher/ Joan Brady 4/6 6/4 7/5	J.J. McArdle/ Miss I. Lewis beat S. Gillespie/Joan Brady 6/3 6/3

cubbyhole used for making tea. Some seats were to be found at the front under a small shelter and used for watching matches. Junior tennis was not part of the early club, as was the case in many clubs, but they were active members in the 1930s.

In the 1940s, under the presidency of Reverend J. M. (Monty) Jennings the club established the widely supported Open Tournament at which were held the Doubles Championships of County Louth, Men's, Ladies and Mixed. They are in abeyance at present but may well take off again. Many of the best players in Leinster and Ireland played here. These included Cyril Kemp, Raymund Egan, Guy Jackson, Mary O' Sullivan, Gerry Clarke and Dick Sandys. More local entries of a high standard came in the names of John Spicer, Louis Gibney (Navan) and J. J. McArdle (Dundalk). It was thought that the latter held the singles title at this championship for about 25 years.

Leinster clubs outside the Dublin area are well aware of the history and longevity of the Provincial Towns' Competitions. **Ardee LTC** was one of the best clubs in terms of standard of play in the 1920s and 1930s. Their first team won the Class 1 Provincial Town's Cup in 1926, 1928 and 1939. They also won the Class 2 title in 1934. Unfortunately, those days are past and perhaps someday will be researched and recalled as an encouragement to future generations.

Before we leave this club it might be noted that Reverend Jennings was not alone a great organiser locally but also on the Leinster Branch. He was elected President in 1943. The Stein family have had a long connection with the club, Larry Stein, a useful player, being President of the Branch in 1962 and of the ILTA in 1966. The following are some results that could be traced for the Open tournament. Perhaps someday they can be added to and with the very high standard that was once exhibited by both local and visiting players.

****

Wilmer Lawn Tennis Club
(Founded pre 1920)

The **Wilmer LTC** is the second club formed in Birr, the Ormond club being founded in 1879. The latter was originally known as the **King's County & Ormond LTC** while the Wilmer has been also known as **Birr LTC** and the **Birr Wilmer TC**. The original **Wilmer LTC** was in fact a grass court club and was formed in the early part of the 20th century. Its clubhouse was the original polo pavilion when that sport was active in the town. Apparently, in the 1940s the club moved to new grounds and constructed three sand based courts. In 1976 the committee under the leadership of JJ (John Joe) Sheerin, a long-time official at the club, one of these sand courts was converted into a tarmacadum one. In 1978 the club laid two more tarmacadum courts. Many years previously JJ Sheerin was on the clubs table tennis team (see photograph below). When he first took up tennis he had a loan of a racquet from Geoff Oakley, a keen racquets player, and organiser, in both clubs in the town.

The Wilmer Lawn Tennis Club in 1932. Back (l. to r.): Ernie Barber, Isobel Fanning, Harry Love, Brendan O'Riordan, Joe Murphy, Jim Gray, Tom Flynn, A. Telford, Tom Galbraith, Con O'Riordan, Mr. Ivory & D. Leake. Front (l. to r.): Hope Galbraith, Frances Leake, Ms Kelly, Eileen Walshe, Ms. K. Dillon. Mary Quigley, Ursula Clarke, Maureen O'Riordan, Vera Cowl, Biddy McLoughlin, Ms Ivory and Vera Hough.(Note: one name missing from front row).

The Wilmer Lawn tennis Club team that won the South West Leinster League in 1978 and Provincial Towns Class III Cup winners in 1977. Back (l. to r.): John Dunphy, Pat Hoctor, Michael Delaney, J. J. (John Joe) Sheerin (captain), Paul Barber (author of Birr: Pictures from the Past (1997)),Frankie Kenny and Steve Crofton. Front (l. to r.): Anne Kenny, Martina Butler, Marcella Grogan, Siobhan Tynan and Emer Hannify.

Wilmer Tennis Club (early 1950s). From left: G. O'Brien, A. Hennessy, P. O'Meara & W. Dillon.

Relaxing at Wilmer tennis club in the 1940s. Note the Birr hospital in the background. From left: I. Power, J. Kelly, N. Dooley, M. Leake & N. Kelly.

The Wilmer table tennis team that won the Laois/Offaly championship in the late 1950s. Back (l. to r.) David Howe, Noel Reedy, Gerry Oakley, Tony McLoughlin and J. J.(John Joe) Sheerin. Front (l. to r.) Rosaleen Howe, Marion Howe and Ada Cobbe.

In 1977 the club decided to enter the Provincial Towns Cup and the club won the Class III grade on its first attempt. The following season it had a good run in the Grade II event.

A number of Birr people joined both clubs. Even more interestingly is the fact that some dual members, such as Geoff Oakley, were on the committee of both simultaneously. The Wilmer club had table tennis as an additional sport and, while it started off with one sand court, its hard courts meant that it survived. Geoff was a member of the successful table tennis team of the late 1950s (see photograph). Also on that team were David Howe and his two sisters, Rosaleen and Marion.

****

Bective Lawn Tennis Club (Founded 1921)

In 1921 **Bective LTC** became a separate organisation to the long-established Bective Rugby Football Club. The club had seven grass courts but in recent years were converted to hardcourts with floodlighting. Back in 1963 the additional two hard courts were sacrificed for a new pavilion.

Over the year the club has had some notable members including internationals Jim Buckley and Joe Hackett. The clubs prides itself on its welcome to new members. Its web site declares "We have a reputation as a friendly, relaxed club with an enjoyable social scene providing lots of opportunities to meet new friends" and "We welcome all levels of tennis experience, from beginners to senior league players and all ages."

The club has entered teams in the Dublin Lawn Tennis Council leagues for many years. With so many clubs in these competitions it is difficult to win in any grade. Some of the titles won by the club are included in the following table:

Bective LTC DLTC league wins		
Men		
	1931	Class 3 & 4
	1932	Class 3 & 4
Summer League	1952, 1953, 1954, 1956, 1957, 1960, 1961, 1962	Class 1
	1970	Class 2
	1988	Class 3
	2005	Class 4
Winter League	1999	Class 3
	2005	Class 5
Floodlight League	2000	Class 4
Ladies		
Summer League	1943	Class3
	1983	Class 3
Senior League 035	1996	Class 4

Bective LTC grass courts in 1983. A few years later the club converted to hard courts-Hurricane Charlie doing much damage to the long-established grass surface.

Bective Lawn Tennis Club
A winner in the 2005 club championships.

Bective LTC (circa 1980). From left: Pat Hegarty, Rod Ensor & Simon Ensor.

Bective LTC Open Singles Championship Winners

Year	Men	Ladies
1974	M. D. Nelson	A. M. Ladley
1975	D. P. Foley	Breeda Sheridan
1976	D. M. Nelson	Breeda Sheridan
1977	Philip Crowe	Jean Tubridy
1978	D. P. Foley	Ann Egan
1979	D. O'Sullivan	Ann Egan
1980	J. H. Casey	Deirdre McClean
1981	F. McNamara	Barbara McQuillan
1982	D. P. Foley	Joanne O'Halloran
1983	J. Hackett	Norah Glynn
1984	M. Prendergast	Norah Glynn
1985		Helen O'Brien
1986	J. Hackett	Ciara Doheny
1987	Daryl Singh	Helen O'Brien
1988	Pat O'Keeffe	Anne Lydon
1989	Julian Morgan	Norah Glynn
1990		Vanessa McKay
1991		Karen Lord
1992		Norah Glynn
1993	Alan Butler	Norah Glynn
1994	Kevin Noble	Heidi Butler
1995	Mark Kavanagh	Heidi Butler
1996	Justin Purcell	C. Malone
1997	Conor Carroll	Heidi Butler
1998	Stephen O'Shea	Caitriona Hannigan
1999	Conor Carroll	Caitriona Hannigan
2000	Robert Nieland	Claudia Muller
2001	Stephen O'Shea	Heidi Butler
2002	Conor Casey	Susan McCarthy
2003	Conor Casey	Shionagh Morrissey
2004	N. Ted Ehirim	Suzy Perkins
2005	Conor Carroll	Heidi Higgins

The launch of the HOK sponsored 2005 Open Championships at Bective LTC. From left: Wade Wise (MD, HOK Residential), Ruth Quinn (captain) and Kevin Malone (president).

The Bective LTC men won the Class 5 Winter League competition in 2005.

Bective LTC
9th-16th July 2005
Finals

Event	Winners	Runners-up
MS Cl2	Conor Carroll	B. McDermott
LS Cl2	Heidi Higgins	S. Morrisey
MD Cl2	P. Hardy/ B. McDermott	A. Knox/ M. Papini
LD Cl2	Heidi Higgins/ L. Bagnal	S. Morrisey/ F. Morrisey
MxD Cl2	Conor Carroll/ Heidi Higgins	J. Goggin/ A. Neill
MS Cl4	P. Rybak	P. Gordon-Walker
LS Cl4	S. Cooper	H. O'Connell
MD Cl4	K. Purcell/ K. Malone	A. Norton/ S. Buckley
LD Cl4	H. O'Connell/ C. Maloney	L. Molloy/ B. Flynn Ryan
MxD Cl4	K. McGowan/ G. Bolger	K. Purcell/ F. Freeney
MS Cl6	M. Sweeney	D. Duff
LS Cl6	S. Cahill	J. Goode
MD Cl6	P. Roughneen/ A. Roughneen	P. Dunne/ S. Lalor
LD Cl6	M. Walker/ S. Kenny	J. Jennings/ C. Gillespie
MxD Cl6	D. Kavanagh/ J. Brady	M. Conway/ C. Tiernan

The 2005 committee at Bective LTC was:

President   Kevin Malone
Senior Vice President   Joe Donlon
Vice President   Jean Lane
Vice President   Sean Eustace
Honorary Secretary   Fiona McStay
Honorary Treasurer   Alan Morton
Captain   Ruth Quinn
Committee   Hilda Martin
                          Colm Holohan
                          Iarla Byrne

****

Tramore Tennis Club
(Founded 1921)

The seaside resort of Tramore has provided many facilities for holiday makers for over 100 years. In 1921 a tennis club was formally established. Today the club has an enviable club and location overlooking the sea. The club has promoted junior tennis and produced some of the best players in the province. The local schools have benefited with the Holy Cross convent team reaching the national school's girls final in 2000. the team included Sarah Arnold, Michelle Kirby, Orla Murray, Sarah & Catherine Darrer. The same year Erica Maughan won the Munster under 14 *Nestle* title and was runner-up in the Irish final. Andrea Maughan was a triple finalist at the Irish junior championships at **Fitzwilliam LTC** in 2000. She won the singles, and doubles, making her the top girl in this category in Ireland. Two years later she was Irish Open under 14 (junior) champion.

Cliff top court at Tramore Tennis Club (C. 2003)

Friendly Doubles at Tramore TC (C. 2003)

The History of Irish Tennis

The Irish Open Minor (u12) girl's doubles final in 2000. Andrea Maughan (extreme left) won the singles and the doubles with Sarah Crowley (Dublin. In the final they beat Emma Tierney (Ennis, extreme right) and Amy Hayes (Cork).

****

Edenderry LTC
(Founded 1922)

Clubs evolve; others rise from the ashes of a previously thriving club. Such is the case in Portadown where the **Edenderry LTC** thrived for many years and virtually died. While a new club (**Portadown Tennis Club**) has recently evolved, the Edenderry club still ticks over. In 1922, a few of the young men and ladies of the Edenderry Memorial Methodist Church obtained permission to build a tennis club at the rear of the Church. Initially the club consisted of three grass courts. By the late 1920s one was converted to clay, by the mid-1930s a second one followed and by the late 1940s the thriving club converted the last court to clay.

In the early days, like many others, the club fairly exclusive, membership being mainly professionals such as doctors, solicitors and teachers. It remained a thriving club from the 1940s to the 1970s with membership open to all denominations. Numbers dwindled in the 1980s and an added problem arose when the church required some development land and one of the courts had to be let go. In addition the **Edenderry LTC** lacked a proper clubhouse. By the mid-1990s, members were looking for a modern facility where a tennis club could once again thrive. This came to fruition with the formal opening of Portadown Tennis Club on the 12th June 2004. (See that club).

****

Ashbrook LTC
(Founded 1922)

In 1998 Dublin club Ashbrook Lawn Tennis Club celebrated its 75th anniversary. Soon afterwards the club set about upgrading their six courts to *Desso Grand Prix* with floodlighting. In addition the members have developed excellent club house facilities.

In August 1967 the club hosted the Irish Open Tennis Championships. This was the year when a diversity of opinion between **Fitzwilliam LTC** and the ILTA over 'Open' (i.e. tournaments open to amateurs and professionals) tennis came to a head. Over the years the club have run various tournaments, including the City of Dublin Open. In the DLTC leagues they have had some success. In 1958 their ladies' won Class 3 of the summer leagues followed by a win in Class 2 in 1963. In 1999 a ladies' team at the club won the Class 4 over 35 league.

****

Anglesea LTC
(Founded 1925)

Anglesea LTC after the flood-September 1931

Anglesea LTC-1930s. Joe MacHale as a boy with his trophy being congratulated by Ronald Davis. Joe won the Irish Junior Boys' title in 1934 and the Irish Senior Boys' title in 1939.

Charlie Davis with Catherine Egan (left) and Mary Nichols. Catherine won the Irish Junior title in 1944 and went on to become Ireland's number 1 lady table tennis player. Mary went on to become an Irish international tennis player and was the number one lady in Ireland in 1950 and 1956.

Elm Park Golf and Sports Club Limited
(Founded 1925)

This club owes its name to Elm Park House and lands, now the location of St. Vincent's Elm Park Hospital. The owner of the house in the early 1920s was a Dublin auctioneer who had a vision of a country club convenient to the city. This became a reality in 1925, tennis courts and badminton followed in 1926. From the beginning it was a multi-faceted club that catered for snooker, bridge, bowls, dances, whist tournaments etc. Two other properties were involved in the club's development, Nutley House and Bloomfield House; the former acts as the clubhouse with the tennis courts nearby. Golfers and tennis players from all over Ireland recognise the club as a major kingpin in the Dublin area.

At the present time the tennis membership is about three hundred and fifty, with about ten teams featuring in the Dublin leagues in any one season. In the early 1940s the club reached a new low in terms of members, twenty-seven to be precise. The war and associated shortages were a major cause of this decline. The club were to advertise for new members such was their plight. The club would spring to life and become not only the venue for many important tournaments but as a provider of high quality players and teams in all categories.

Originally the tennis courts (grass) occupied the site of the present St. Vincent's Hospital in its opening season in 1925. The hard courts followed in 1926. The Sisters of Charity bought the land in 1933 but Dick Kelly, a professional coach, continued to operate the courts on a private basis for some years. In 1936 the club was re-constituted on its present grounds with four hard courts and five grass courts. Leading figures at the time included Paddy Duffy, Joe Scannell and the Harte-Barry brothers, all survivors of the original club.

Ronald Davis of Anglesea LTC was a successful tennis player, his father Charlie being the key to this very active club in the years before the second world war.

****

An early 1940s photograph taken at Elm Park. On left are Raymund Egan and Mrs. Sally Lister with Barbara Good and Cyril Kemp. From 1937 to 1951 the Irish Hard-court Championships were hosted by the club. Raymund and Sally won the mixed Championship in 1944.

In the early days the club fielded two men's and two ladies teams in the Dublin leagues. It became a significant success with its annual organisation of the Irish Hard Court Championships each spring. In addition it was to run successful open and handicap events. The autumn tournaments attracted players from all four provinces. In the 1938 Open final Irishman Cyril Kemp had one of his first major wins beating New Zealand Davis Cup player, Dennis Coombes. The Open events continued during the war and one member, Cyril Boden, recalls staying up late each evening to prepare the draw for the following day and cycling into O'Connell Street so that it could be posted in the window in Elvery's shop window. Apart from his success as referee he has been credited as being a leader in reviving the clubs spirit and ambitions. Five extra grass courts (*the back courts)* were built following a decision in 1959 and were first used a few years later in the triangular series of matches with Wales and Scotland. *Both visiting Captains pronounced them the best courts outside Wimbledon, a wonderful tribute to the initiative and skills that brought them to that stage.* Green keeper Stephen Kane, with members such as Thomond Mockler and Harry Spain could take a well-deserved bow.

The club now had fourteen tennis courts and a new influx of members, Mount Temple and Longford Gardens being two clubs providing part of this flow. **Mount Temple LTC** was located at Dartry and closed in 1960; Davis Cup player Gerry Fitzpatrick (1954) took up membership and had an immediate impact winning the grass court club championships in 1961 and 1962 and the hard court championships in 1962 and 1963. In the Dublin leagues the club would win Class II, III and IV in 1961. In the next thirty years the club would win sixty-eight pennants.

The list of successful members is a lengthy one. Among the men are senior international players J. J. (James Joseph) Fitzgibbon, Gerry Fitzpatrick, Robin Gibney and Ken Fitzgibbon. Veteran internationals included John Horn, Michael Wogan, Gerry O'Shaughnessy, Niall O'Riordan, John Mulvey, John de Courcy, Maurice Fives, Meadbh McEvoy and Breeda Claffey. In 1937 the famous Raymond Egan won the men's singles championship. The noted international soccer player, Willie Browne won this event 11 times between 1963 and 1978. Later he would take up golf and get his handicap down to 9. Ken Fitzgibbon, a noted badminton player like his father before him, also won the title eleven times (the first in 1976).

The most notable of the lady players must have been Mary Fitzgibbon (nee Nichols). Not alone was she the first Irish girl to win the Open Junior Championships three times (1938-1940) but with JJ they won the Open Mixed Championship in 1951 and with Betty Lombard the Open Ladies doubles title in the same year. Both have played at Wimbledon. Mary won the Irish Open Ladies singles in 1941.She was ranked the number one Irish player for the year 1950. Notable among the ladies were Patricia O'Gorman and Helen

Tennis Captains at Elm Park

1954	Dudley Fisher	Muriel Kennedy
1955	Ozzie Dowling	Peg Tyrell
1956	Donal Murphy	Dorothy Murphy
1957	Don Cotter	Dorothy Murphy
1958	Don Cotter	Dorothy Murphy
1959	Don Cotter	Joyce Pender
1960	Don Cotter	Joyce Pender
1961	Thomond Mockler	Ann Peppard
1962	Brendan O'Sullivan	Ann Peppard
1963	Walter Rhatigan	Ann Peppard
1964	Walter Rhatigan	Veronica McDonald
1965	Walter Rhatigan	Stella Shields
1966	Walter Rhatigan	Veronica Mulcahy
1967	Walter Rhatigan	Doreen McNamara
1968	Paddy Duffy	Annette O'Gorman
1969	Paddy Duffy	Annette O'Gorman
1970	Shay O'Sullivan	Sheila Marlow
1971	Shay O'Sullivan	Sheila Marlow
1972	Shay O'Sullivan	Nuala Brady
1973	Harry Sullivan	Nuala Brady
1974	Harry Sullivan	Darina Boden
1975	John A. Fitzpatrick	Darina Boden
1976	John A. Fitzpatrick	Frances Shields
1977	Jim O'Loughlin	Frances Shields
1978	Jim O'Loughlin	Angela Phelan
1979	Fred Lewis	Angela Phelan
1980	Fred Lewis	Julie Russell
1981	Fred Lewis	Julie Russell
1982	Michael Wogan	Isin Kenny
1983	Michael Wogan	Geraldine Kilmurray
1984	Ray Doyle	Geraldine Kilmurray
1985	John Claffey	Daire Connell
1986	John Claffey	Margaret Towers
1987	Pat Lynch	Margaret Towers
1988	Pat Lynch	Sheila Smith
1989	Bill Scott	Sheila Smith
1990	John Kenny	Audrey McVey
1991	John Kenny	Helen McInerney
1992	Eanna McHugh	Jean O'Byrne
1993	Eanna Mc Hugh	Jean O'Byrne
1994	Hilary Hough	Helen O'Connor
1995	Hilary Hough	Anne O'Byrne
1996	Tony Bunbury	Anne O'Byrne
1997	Brian Hampson	Ann Marie Ryan
1998	Brian Hampson	Ann Marie Ryan
1999	Dave Ryan	Annette Sweeny
2000	Dave Ryan	Annette Sweeny
2001	Myles Cassidy	Mary Briscoe
2002	Myles Cassidy	Mary Briscoe
2003	Tom Dillon	Brenda McDonald
2004	Tom Dillon	Brenda McDonald
2005	Alan Haugh	Anne Nolan

Lennon; the latter gaining many caps and being captain of the Federation Cup for many years. Particularly notable was the ladies teams of 1965 and 1980 winners of the class one cup competition. Joyce Duffy (nee Pender) has a particular club record that will be difficult to break. She played on the first team in the class I leagues for a total of twenty-seven years

The History of Irish Tennis

(1957 to 1984) and was winner of seven singles club championships (1958, 1960 and 1973 on grass; 1959, 1960 and 1961 and 1973 on hard courts). The O'Gorman sisters, Patricia and Annette, were to feature at all levels of Irish tennis. Many other members would gain interprovincial status as well as winning a range of Open championships.

Brian Claffey-Winner of the under 18 boys' grasscourt championship singles in 2000 and 2001 also won the men's grasscourt and hardcourt championship singles in 2001 at Elm Park.

At the Dublin Lawn Tennis Council centenary dinner were (from left) Myles Cassidy (tennis captain), Mary Briscoe (lady captain), John Kenny (honorary treasurer, DLTC) and Anne-Marie Ryan.

The club is noted for its social happenings from dinner dances to fancy dress balls, from midnight swims at Killiney to a Mediterranean trip on the S.S. Devonia. Many a romance resulted. Visitors to the club have always been suitably impressed and come back annually. The present savannah courts were constructed in 1991. The following quote comes from the club history book published in 1993. It speaks for itself. *As time passes, one generation takes over from another on the tennis courts emulating and sometimes*

exceeding the achievements of their parents and elders. This brings to mind a story Harry O'Sullivan tells of meeting a youngster who ran him off his feet in a League match. In the general conversation afterwards it emerged that Harry was once a member of Norwood. "Oh" said the youngster, "did you know Jack so and so?" "Yes", said Harry, "I played a lot of tennis with him, don't tell me he is your father". "Oh no" said the teenager; "he is my grandfather".

Lisa Matthews won the junior girls under 18 championship singles at Elm Park in 1999, 2000 and 2001.

Mens' coaching at Elm Park, 17th August, 2002. From left: Cyril Maybury, Gus Warner, Conor Gibney, Roberto Arthurs, Brian Hagan, Gary Cahill (coach) and Jim Callan.

The History of Irish Tennis

Conor Gibney- onLeinster under 14 team in 2001.

The Gary Cahill Coaching Clinic at Elm Park (18th August 2002). From left: Brian Gibney, Simon Matthews, Stephen Byrne (junior captain), Gary Cahill, Deirdre Haugh (junior lady captain), Suzanne Lynch and Doireen O'Brolchain.

The Elm Park over 45 Class I team in 1987. From left: Richard Willis, Bobby Keogh, Michael Wogan (captain), Gerry O'Shaughnessy, Brendan Browne and Jim Lawlor.

Aidan, Mark, John Breeda and Brian Claffey, a family of tennis players at Elm Park.

Ladies at Elm Park being coached by Gary Cahill in 2002 were (from left): Sandra Shaw, Anne Gibney, Mary Grier, Virginia Costello, Lisa Matthews and Mary Briscoe (lady captain).

Jenny Claffey from Elm Park was the regional and provincial under 12 winner in recent years.

The 1992 over 50s league winners were the Elm Park team. From left: Gerry O'Shaughnessy, Richard Willis, Michael Wogan (captain), Bobby Keogh, John Horan and William Phelan.

The History of Irish Tennis

Friendly tennis at Elm Park. John Shorten (left) and Aidan Claffey.

Successful senior doubles Class 2 team at Elm Park in 1999. Back (l. to r.) Jennifer Blake, Kristine Lawlor, Breeda Claffey, Mary Grier and Antoinette Toole. Front (l. to r.) Helen McInerney, Maedbh McEvoy (captain) and Mary Briscoe. The team beat Carrickmines Croquet & LTC in the final.

The 2001 Class 4 Floodlit league winners from Elm Park. From left: Dave Ryan, Michael Wogan, Brian Claffey, John Shorten (captain) and Aidan Claffey.

The Elm Park Tennis Committee 2001. Back (l. to r.) Michael Wogan, Alan Haugh, Myles Cassidy (men's tennis captain), Leo Mangan and Tom Dillon. Front (l. to r.) Annette Sweeny, Rosemary Hough, Mary Briscoe (tennis captain), Mary Molloy, Rosalie Pettit and Mary Boden.

Captain's Day 1991-Winning team. Front (l. to r.): Beatrice Doran, Antoinette Toole, Jo Doherty & Rosalie Pettit. Back (l. to r.): Madeline McCormack, Tony Bunbury, Diarmuid Cunningham & Hilary Hough.

1980 Class I League Winning team from Elm Park. Back (l. to r.): Helen Lennon, K. Lawlor & Breeda Claffey. Front (l. to r.); Michelle Buckley, J. Russell (captain) & Meadbh McEvoy.

The History of Irish Tennis

Late 1950s at Elm Park. From left: Don Cotter, Eamon DeValera, Ken Murphy and Dudley Fisher.

The Elm Park Class II league finalists in 1980. Back (l. to r.): Paula Kerin, Rita Maguire & Joyce Pender (captain). Front (l. to r.): Annette Dunne, Rose Maher & Pauline O'Driscoll.

The Elm Park visit to Ballybunion in 1963 included Maurice Rafter, Myles Stanistreet, John Murnaghan, Jim Kerr, Damien Hand, Valerie O'Connor, Peter Murnaghan, Miriam O'Connor & Des Halley.

Eanna McHugh
Tennis Captain 1992-1993 at Elm Park

Jean O'Byrne-Lady tennis captain 1992/1993

In the 20-year period 1976 to 1997 Ken Fitzgibbon (on left) won 10 grass and 11 hardcourt club championship singles at Elm Park. Robin Gibney(on right) wins in that period included an impressive 7 grass and 9 hard court championships.

The History of Irish Tennis

Tennis Captains: Front Row (l. to r.) S. O'Connell, C. Kilroy, M. Cribbin, F. Shiels, D. McNamara & D. O'Hanlon. Second Row (l. to r.): P. Tyrrell, A. Phelan, G. Kilmurray, A. Dunne, S. Smith & D. O'Connell. Third row (l. to r.): S. O'Sullivan, J. Kenny, S. Marlow, N. Brady, J. Fitzpatrick, S. Nolan, H. Sullivan, W. Scott & P. Lynch. Back (l. to r.): J. Claffey, P. Duffy, W. Rhatigan, R. Doyle & T. Mockler.

The 1977 tennis committee at Elm Park. Back (l. to r.): P. Duffy, M. Maughan, G. Grehan, G. O'Sullivan, C. Normoyle & J. Fitzpatrick. Front (l. to r.): D. Weekes, F. Shields, J. O'Loughlin (captain), H. Rafter & K. Kelly.

Recent Mixed Doubles Champions Elm Park

	Grasscourt
2001	Brian Claffey/Breeda Claffey
2002	Diarmuid Cunningham/Laura Shilling
2003	Diarmuid Cunningham/Laura Shilling
2004	Mark McArdle/Carolyn McArdle
2005	David Ryan/Mary Grier

Recent Men's Doubles Champions Elm Park

	Grasscourt
2001	Joe Cummiskey/Richard O'Donnell
2002	Aidan Claffey/John Shorten
2003	Rory O'Connor/Diarmuid Cunningham
2004	John Shorten/Aidan Claffey
2005	Aidan Claffey/Morgan Dunne
	Hardcourt
2001	Michael Wogan/David Ryan
2002	Robin Gibney/Conor Gibney
2003	Roberto Cahiza/Brian Claffey
2004	John Broughan/Jack O'Keeffe
2005	Morgan Dunne/Aidan Claffey

Recent Ladies' Doubles Champions Elm Park

	Grasscourt
2001	Mary Grier/Sandra Shaw
2002	Virginia Costello/Jean Twohig
2003	Mary Grier/Sandra Shaw
2004	Kristine Lawlor/Mary Boden
2005	Sandra Shaw/Mary Grier
	Hardcourt
2001	Mary Grier/Laura Shilling
2002	Mary Grier/Sandra Shaw
2003	Jean Twohig/Virginia Costello
2004	Mary Boden/Annette Burke
2005	Annette Burke/Deirdre Howett

Lady champions at Elm Park (l. to r.); Breeda Claffey (1981, 1986), Maureen Smithwick (1974), Joyce Pender (1958, 1960 & 1973), Meadbh McEvoy (1975, 1976, 1977 & 1979) and Annette Dunne (1962, 1970, 1971 & 1972).

The 2002 gathering of the Tennis Captains at Elm Park. Back (l. to r.): Helen Chambers (nee McInerney) 1991, Michael Wogan 1982-83, Isin Kenny 1982, John Kenny 1990-91, Sheila Marlow 1970-71, Bill Scott 1989, Anne O'Byrne 1995-96, John Claffey 1985-86, Helen O'Connor 1994, Pat Lynch 1987-88 & Paddy Duffy 1968069. Middle (l. to r.): Jean O'Byrne 1992-93, Geraldine Kilmurray 1983-84, Sheila Smith 1988-89, Audrey McVey 1990, Frances Shields 1976-77, Darina O'Hanlon (nee Boden) 1974-75, Stella Nolan (nee Shields) 1965, Angela Phelan 1978-79, Margaret Towers 1986-87 & Eanna McHugh 1992-93. Front (l. to r.): Peg Tyrell 1955, Dave Ryan 1999-00, Annette Sweeny 1999-00, Myles Cassidy 2001-02, Mary Briscoe 2001-02, Brian Hampson 1997-98, Ann-Marie Ryan 1997-98 & John Fitzpatrick 19775-76.

The Class I Ladies' League team at Elm Park in 1965. Back (l. to r.): Paula Kerin, Joyce Duffy & Annette O'Gorman. Front: (l. to r.) Mary Rose Kearns, S. Nolan (captain) & Ann Peppard.

	Grasscourt	Hardcourt		Grasscourt	Hardcourt
1932	D. O'Connor	no competition	'75-'77	Meadbh McEvoy	Meadbh McEvoy
1933	no competition	no competition	1978	Helen Lennon	Meadbh McEvoy
1937	N. Delaney	no competition	1979	Meadbh McEvoy	Rhona Howett
1938	D. Hunt	no competition	1980	Helen Lennon	Rhona Howett
'39-'43	Maire Ely O'Carroll	no competition	1981	Breeda Claffey	Michelle Buckley
1944	P. Doran	no competition	1982	Maria Byrne	Breeda Claffey
1945	Mary Nichols	M. Brennan	1983	Isabel Roche	Isabel Roche
1946	Mary Nichols	D. Miley	1984	Michelle Buckley	Michelle Buckley
1947	Mary Nichols	M. Brennan	1985	Annmarie O'Grady	Michelle Buckley
1948		D. Miley	'86-'87	Breeda Claffey	Michelle Buckley
1951	D. Scally	June-Ann Fitzpatrick	1988	Rachel McDonogh	Maria Byrne
1952	Sheila Gorevan		1989	Rachel McDonogh	Joanne Murnaghan
1953	Sheila de Courcy		1990	Joanne Murnaghan	Antoinette Toole
'54-'55	Muriel Kennedy		1991	Sandra Shaw	Mary Boden
1956	June Counihan		'92-'93	Kristine Lawlor	Kristine Lawlor
1957	Maura O'Flaherty		'94-'95	Anne-Marie Hogan	Kristine Lawlor
1958	Joyce Duffy		1996	Anne-Marie Hogan	Orla Mc Carville
1959	Anne Peppard		'97-'98	Anne-Marie Hogan	Anne-Marie Hogan
1960	Joyce Duffy		1999	Laura Shilling	Anne-Marie Hogan
1961	Anne Peppard		2000	Sandra Shaw	Louise Dunne
1962	Annette O'Gorman		2001	Mary Boden	Mary Boden
'63-'65	Patricia O'Gorman	Patricia O'Gorman	2002	Virginia Costello	Mary Boden
'66-'69	Patricia O'Gorman	Annette O'Gorman	2003	Sandra Shaw	Virginia Costello
'70-'72	Annette O'Gorman	Annette O'Gorman	2004	Mary Boden	Mary Boden
1973	Joyce Pender	Joyce Pender	2005	Virginia Costello	Mary Boden
1974	Maureen Smithwick	Maureen Smithwick			

Singles Championship Winners at Elm Park

	Grasscourt	Hardcourt		Grasscourt	Hardcourt
1932	E.I. Harte Barry	no competition	1973	R.G. Ledbetter	Bobby Keogh
1933	E.O. Barry	no competition	'74-'75	Willie Browne	Willie Browne
1937	Raymond Egan	no competition	1976	Ken Fitzgibbon	Ken Fitzgibbon
1938	Eustace Fannin	no competition	1977	Ken Fitzgibbon	John Mulvey
1939	no competition	no competition	1978	Willie Browne	Ken Fitzgibbon
1940	R.H. Douglas	no competition	'79-'81	Ken Fitzgibbon	Ken Fitzgibbon
'41-'42	D.D. O'Sullivan	no competition	1982	Robin Gibney	Ken Fitzgibbon
1944	F. Ahern	no competition	'83-'84	Robin Gibney	Robin Gibney
1945	J.J. Fitzgibbon	J.C. Davis	1982	Robin Gibney	Ken Fitzgibbon
'46-'47	J.J. Fitzgibbon	Joe Hackett	'83-'84	Robin Gibney	Robin Gibney
1948	no competition	Joe Hackett	1985	B.T. Browne	Robin Gibney
1951	no competition	Gerry Fitzpatrick	1986	Ken Fitzgibbon	G. Blake
'52-'54	T.K. Megan	?	'87-'88	Ken Fitzgibbon	Ken Fitzgibbon
1955	Dudley Fisher	?	'89-'90	Jim McDonogh	Ken Fitzgibbon
1956	G. Walker	?	1991	Robin Gibney	Ken Fitzgibbon
'57-'59	Thomond Mockler	?	1992	Robin Gibney	Robin Gibney
1960	M. Carr	?	1993	Ken Fitzgibbon	Robin Gibney
1961	Gerry Fitzpatrick	?	1994	J. Cummiskey jnr.	Robin Gibney
1962	Gerry Fitzpatrick	?	1995	Ken Fitzgibbon	Robin Gibney
1963	Willie Browne	Gerry Fitzpatrick	1996	John Shorten	Robin Gibney
1964	H.E. Cummins	M. Hamid	1997	Ken Fitzgibbon	Robin Gibney
1965	Willie Browne	J. M. O' Rourke	1998	Robin Gibney	E. Barrett
1966	Willie Browne	Willie Browne	1999	Robin Gibney	D. Cunningham
1967	Willie Browne	J. Lawler	2000	D.Cunningham	D. Cunningham
1968	Bobby Keogh	P.Duffy	2001	Brian Claffey	Brian Claffey
1969	Willie Browne	Willie Browne	2002	John Shorten	Joe Cummiskey
1970	Willie Browne	John Mulvey	2003	John Shorten	Roberto Cahiza
1971	Willie Browne	P.Duffy	2004	Brian Claffey	John Shorten
1972	Willie Browne	Willie Browne	2005	Morgan Dunne	Morgan Dunne
1973	R.G. Ledbetter	Bobby Keogh			

****
Celbridge & District LTC
(Founded c. 1925)

The small County Kildare club at Celbridge was originally founded in the middle 1920s on Hazelhatch Road, the site of the present power station. Since 1940 it has been at its present location, also on the same road. The attractive clubhouse was built in 1992. As recently as 2001, with the help of lottery funds, synthetic grass courts were laid.

Apart from internal tournaments the club, plays in Leinster and Dublin LTC cup and league competitions. In 1998 the men's first team won the Dublin Class 3 summer league. In 1994 they won Class 2 of the over 45 men's league. This won this event again in 2005 with a team of Kevin O'Connor, Chris McCormac, Brendan Doyle, Fred Bradley, Brendan Kenny and Declan Keenan. The 2005 club senior singles champions were Michael Donaghy and Margo Delaney.

The clubhouse and courts at Celbridge & District Lawn Tennis Club in County Kildare.

Celbridge & District Lawn Tennis Club 2005 Committee

Chairperson	Fred Bradley
Vice-Chairperson	Marie Molloy
Honorary Treasurer	John Gleeson
Honorary Secretary	Michael O'Dwyer
Men's Captain	Alan Nohilly
Ladies' Captain	Brenda McNulty
Membership Secretary	Paul Deegan
Committee members	Collette Adanan
	Stephanie Timoney
	Anthony O'Connell
	Michelle Atkinson
	Mark Richardson
	Joe Moran
	Clair Murphy

Some juniors going through their paces at Celbridge & District LTC. In 2004 and 2005 the club was deemed to be among the best small clubs in Leinster and received an Eagle Star Award.

****

CIYMS Tennis Club
(Founded pre 1927)

This Belfast club has been an extremely active one since its foundation in the 1920s. It has been a multi-sports club for many years catering for rugby, badminton, cricket and squash, as well as tennis. The club started off with four grass courts and a small pavilion. The growth brought the numbers to over 200 in the 1980s, about half being juniors. The club have six courts with floodlighting.

The 1988 Junior Hard Court Championships played at the CIYMS club. Back (from left) Doreen Muskett (Northern Bank Sports & Social Secretary), Andrew Curran (U12), Eric Cameron (U18), Robin Mc Donough (Ulster Council). Front (l. to r.) Richard Beggs (U16), Bryn Cunningham (U10) & Neville Martin (U14)

The club have been involved in the Belfast and District leagues for many years. 1981 was a particularly good year winning both the Division 1 and Division 3 competitions in the Mixed Leagues, the

The 1977 CIYMS combined first and second teams. Back (l. to r.) Peter Bayliss, Olga Petticrew, Dennis Carlisle, David Owen, Frank Graham, Trevor Shanks, Stanley Russell, John Gaston and Gordon Watters. Front (l. to r.) Elizabeth McKeown, Margaret Neill, Patricia Brown, Kerry Mercier, Jean Shanks, and Alison Moore.(photo courtesy Belfast Telegraph).

The CIYMS Tennis Club, Circular Road, Belmont, Belfast, in 1946. In the front row (from second man on left) were J.A. Thompson, Doris Herd (Ladies Captain), Sir Milne Barbour (President), Gordon Thompson (Men's Captain), Captain Storey, Albert Smiley and a. n. other. At right (with bag) is Eileen Turner who was ladies captain during the late 1930s. Her husband Frank is at the other end with children Anne (6) and Frances (2). (Photo courtesy Eileen Turner and East Belfast Historical Society).

Men's Knock-Out Cup, the Junior Ladies Knock-Out Cup and the Ladies Autumn League. They have had many players of distinction in their ranks over the years.

The club have run many tournaments including the Ulster Junior Hard-Court Championships and the Belfast Hard Court Championships. They have been particularly noted for their work on the administration side of tennis. Dr. Elizabeth Hull was President of the Ulster Council for 1985 and 1986. However, the exceptional administrator must be Peter Bayliss. He was the branch honorary secretary from 1970 for five or six years, honorary treasurer for over twenty seasons right up to the present. Add to this the fact that he was President in 1968 and 1969. At national level he was President of the ILTA in 1979 and 1987. He has been on many tennis sub-committees including the Umpires Association. He and Elizabeth Hull acted as linesperson in the Davis Cup match versus the USA at the RDS, Dublin.

****

Douglas Lawn Tennis Club (Founded 1927)

Like many small clubs, **Douglas LTC** has had its ups and downs over the decades. The leading light in the early days of the club was a Mr. Lane. It was originally founded for Civil Servants and was called the **Civil Service LTC**. Members of that era referred to the 1930s as the 'halcyon days in the club. Members at that time included Leo Herde, Les Crowley, Jack Mahony, Christy Ronayne, Jack Brennan and Jimmy Whelan. The club played in the 'Junior' league until 1935. That year they won this title and were promoted to the senior league. It took until 1949 to win the senior league title. The Senior League trophy remained at Douglas for five consecutive years.

The club survived on a small pavilion and three courts that were at times considered 'sub-standard'. During the Second World War, and the decade afterwards, the club thrived. Like many clubs interest waned with increasing affluence and the ability for people to travel more outside their immediate neighbourhood. The club survived, much thanks being due to the efforts of Martin ('Busty'?) O'Keeffe. In the late 1960s the club employed coach and Davis Cup player Michael Hickey to look after the young players in the club. Within a few short years the fruits emerged. Junior success led to a greater interest among the adults and, in the late 1970s, an energetic committee set about seeking new premises. Within four years the club formally opened (4th July 1982) its new premises on a two acre site. The new club included a clubhouse and six hard courts. To mark the occasion an exhibition match was held between Davis Cup players Matt Doyle and Douglas-bred Sean Sorensen.

Among the important personnel to bring the club to its new status were Mr. Ned Quinlan (president, 1979), Mr. Liam Rigney (president, 1980), Mr. B. Boland (club captain, 1980-1981) and Mr. B. Wain (architect) as well as the committee of 1982:

President:	**Mr. H. Wilkins**
Vice-President:	**Mr. G. Dooley**
Honorary Secretary:	**Mrs. M. Boyle**
Honorary Treasurer:	**Mrs. M. Deegan**
Club Captain:	**Mr. G. Falvey**
Committee Members:	**Dr. P. Brett**
	Mrs. P. Britton
	Mrs. N. Roynane
	Mr. T. Desmond
	Mr. M. Rigney
	Mr. P. Rigney
	Mr. N. Farnan.

The old minutes' books in any club reveal much. Two people that must get mentioned are Donal O'Mahony and Frank Mockler. Donal was the club's landlord who in 1964, when the club was going through a lean patch, reduced the ground rent to 1 shilling per annum and gave £100 towards club improvements. About fifteen years later H. G. Wilkins wrote: *He has never demanded his 1/- and has always given us every help and co-operation. We thank him sincerely.*

Frank Mockler a prominent player and official is mentioned in a very good light too. He donated some eight tennis racquets for junior use and coached the club juniors free of any charge.

The 1976 Junior Hardcourt Championships of Cork City were hosted by Douglas LTC. Back (l. to r.): Liam Rigney (club vice-president), Eileen O'Driscoll (tournament committee), Billy Fennelly (tournament committee), Ger Lawlor (club treasurer), Billy Rigney (club secretary) and Margaret Fennelly (tournament committee). Front (l. to r.): Frances Hunt, Christine Bergano, Brian Fawsitt, Gail Maloney and Val Fennelly.

Douglas Lawn Tennis Club (circa 1982)

****
Hawarden Tennis Club
(Founded 1927)

Most clubs have a straightforward start to life. Hawarden's is a bit different. A Miss Walker was Headmistress at a school located at 163 Upper Newtownards Road. The house was named Hawarden after the country home of William Ewart Gladstone. It was also known as Miss Walker's School and later became Bloomfield Collegiate School. In 1923 or 1924 she acquired the use of four grass courts for her pupils at Sandown Park, the home of Sandown Football Club that is now the site of Strandtown School. Parents and their friends were encouraged to use these courts during the summer months.

Miss Walker and Mr. E. Burton, the first President of **Hawarden LTC**, acquired the lease of the club's present grounds (which was purchased outright on the 1st October 1953 for 8,900 years). Back in 1927 the club officially opened on the 1st May at 3 Clonlee Drive. The original landlord also happened to be a building contractor and a wooden pavilion was also constructed. As the grass courts at Sandown were limited in use due to rainfall, it was decided that the new club would have tarmacadum courts (3) at the Clonee Drive venue. Between thirty and forty members joined that first year and the club has grown since. Early on the members were involved in the Belfast & District tennis leagues.

In 1949, the tarmacadum courts were breaking up and three new En-Tout-Cas red dust courts were laid for the sum of £864. When payment for the courts and lease were finally completed the club decided to celebrate with a dinner dance. This was in 1959; the now traditional Hawarden Annual Dinner Dance had taken off. On the 18th June 1966 the building extension, which included showers and changing facilities, were completed. With a 50% grant aid from the Department of Education the club built a squash court to attract new members in 1977. The squash section quickly filled up. That year the Club became

'registered and could then offer bar facilities under the Registration of Clubs Act. In addition the courts were upgraded to all-weather ones with floodlighting. The present club honorary secretary, Ken Burbage joined at around that time, squash being his main interest then.

The new Roy Hastings Pavilion was opened in 1982 in honour of that great club stalwart for many years. The club keeps moving forward and six years later a further extension took place, existing changing facilities were upgraded and a viewing gallery constructed.

As recently as April 1998 three new polymeric courts were laid and the lighting upgraded and, in 2002, the heating and ventilation in the Clubhouse was also upgraded. Over the last few years, member Norman Penney, has added to the club's ambiance. He has carried out some exceptional landscaping that is appreciated by both members and visitors alike.

The club would not have succeeded without some great workers and *the number of far-sighted members who have formed the Council down the years.* It has also contributed extensively to the organising of tennis in the Belfast area, at the Ulster Council and on the Irish Lawn Tennis Association Council. In fact, three of its members, at one time or another were to be elected Presidents of the ILTA, the highest post in the sport in Ireland. Mavis Hogg was also the ILTA honorary secretary and was the first Irish person to receive a European Tennis Association Award for her services. (See Chapter 6). Between 1927 and the late 1977, the club's 50th anniversary, it had only three Presidents. Mr. E. Burton (1927-1956), Herbie Pepper (1956-1974) and Barton Quigley (1974 onwards).

On the playing front the club have done well in the league and have had players who represented Ulster at senior level. These included Georgie Brown, Dorothy Willis, Eileen Kirkpatrick, Lorna Croskery, Louise Tuff and Sammy Tuff. Further information on these players can be found in other chapters.

The Hawarden LTC Senior "B" League Winning team, 1933. Back (l. to r.) S.S. Bowden, J.R. Ralph, E.D. Burton (Captain), H.C. Ralph. Front (l. to r.) G. Fallon, E. M. Moore, P. Maxwell, M. McCulloch.

The Hawarden Lawn Tennis Club Intermediate League Winning team, 1960. Back (l. to r.) Tom Harbison, Bertie Walkington, Johnston Martin and Brian Neill. Front (l. to r.) Maureen Blakely, Olive Croskery, Honor Baraithwaite and Pamela Wilkinson.

View of the Hawarden LTC courts from the corner of the gallery, which was completed in 1988.

Based on the Tennis Ireland guidelines, the club produced a "Coaching & Development Plan" in 1999. By 2002 the number of juniors jumped from 20 to about 100 and associated success on the courts followed. The club coach is Carlos Miranda. Among the junior committee mention of the hard work of Jim Wilson and Margaret Harvey should be made. The club is relatively small but, in the autumn of 2002, the fruits of their work were recognised as they were one of the top nominations in Ireland for the Eagle Star Small Club category. This has been a morale boost for the members of a club that no doubt will continue to have a great future.

✶✶✶✶

Castleknock Lawn Tennis Club (Founded 1927)

In the modern era Castleknock Tennis Club built twelve flood lit championship tennis courts. These were officially opened by An Tanaiste, Brian Lenehan on the 14th July 1990. In December of the following year it was the turn of the President of Ireland to open the new clubhouse. This included rooms for junior, committee meetings, functions and snooker as well as the, now normal, function and changing room facilities. An enclosed practice wall was provided in 1999. In the late 1970s things were not so prosperous and the modern facility of today was a dream. At that time the club had four grass courts, an old wooden shed and a membership of about 100. However, the dream would be realised.

It all started in 1927, an era when Castleknock was considered as out in the country side. In fact it was considered a rural village. Thanks to the extensive memory of 90 year old Terence Browne, little details on its beginning are now known. This was a time in the 'south' when many clubs sprung up and the game had a new lease of life in Ireland. Four Catholic school boys from the village, who attended O' Connell Secondary School in Dublin, were wondering what to do during the summer holidays. They were made keen on tennis, used to attend any internationals and the Irish Championships at Fitzwilliam. They also lapped up the brief newsreel films on tennis at the cinema.

They decided, why not build a tennis court themselves? They got spades and, seeing a suitable field, started digging out a court. Initially they were ordered out but then it was discovered that the land was that of a farmer, Mr. Corcoran, father of one of the boys. They got a court laid and in operation fairly quickly. The boys were Terence Browne, Jack Cullen (later to work for Avery Scales), Gerry O'Driscoll (later to be an engineer with C.I.E., the national transport company) and Johnny Corcoran (later to become a doctor).

Around the same time the family who ran the Merville Dairies had a family court in the region. Among them was Mrs. Ellen Molloy. The boys had their own tennis games every day on their crude court and a 'few' other locals came to play there too. They were then invited to play on the Molloy court. (Mrs. Molloy was in fact an aunt of Terence's). This became a regular get together. Invited also along were some young ladies including a few who were employed by the Post Office on the North Circular Road who cycled the few miles to the court.

Gerry More O'Ferrall, a key member of the successful modern-day Castleknock LTC. He was the first president of Tennis Ireland. In 1990 the title was changed from the Irish Lawn Tennis Association.

The Sweeney brothers, James and Owen, were part of this evolving club. A tent was erected to accommodate the ladies for changing and a grass court was marked out. A pavilion was built by the members using materials not in use at the nearby Clonsilla aerodrome. In fact most of the work done was down to Joe Molloy who was in fact a carpenter by trade. This pavilion provided a place to make teas after Saturday afternoon tennis tournaments. On Sunday evenings, dances, with invitation tickets produced, were held in the pavilion. The law (influenced by the church) did not allow Saturday night dancing anywhere, as many older

Castleknock Lawn tennis Club in the 1930s.

generations well remember. Music was provided by
Kevin who played the piano and another lad played
the banjo. It was fairly simple fare by today's standard
but it provided a very definite social focus in a rural
village. In fact, some mothers would not let their
daughters near these dances in case they would be
scandalised in some fashion. Within a couple of
seasons the club thrived and entered 2 or 3 teams in
the Dublin leagues. The club affiliated to the ILTA in
1934 and the honorary secretary at the time was a Mr.
T.J. Brow. The club remained small and low key for
many years. However, over the latter portion of the
20th century, the population in area boomed, sports
activity was considerable and the club was to add
much to Leinster and Irish tennis on both the playing
and administration front.

Tennis in the late 1930s was very much a social affair
in the club though a league team was entered in the
Dublin leagues in 1939 and gave "credible
performances". In the 1940s the pavilion was
extended. A motorised mower was purchased form the
Dunsink Observatory and pushed to the club by Jim
Pemberton with help from Bearney and Paddy
Gilsenan.

In 1962 the membership fee was £1 and, when an
added pitch and putt facility was built, and opened by
the Minister for Social Welfare, Kevin Boland, the fee
for 'golf' and tennis was set at £2. By the end of the
1960s the club's first men's team was in the Class IV
division of the leagues. In the early 1970s, after a
considerable legal battle, a 100 year lease was
secured. The committee involved was chaired by Bill
Fitzgerald. The first junior Open tournament was held
in 1971.

Castleknock Tennis Club

	Chairmen/ Chairwomen	Honorary Secretaries
1934		Mr. T.J. Brow
1976	Aidan Prior	Mrs. K. Kettle
1977	Gerard McElligott	Mrs. K. Kettle
1978	Gerard Mc Elligott	Comdt. J. Costello
1979	Gerry More O'Ferrall	Comdt. J. Costello
1980	Gerry More O'Ferrall	Judy Glynn
1981	Gerry More O'Ferrall	Judy Glynn
1982	John McNamara	Judy Glynn
1983	John McNamara	Judy Glynn
1984	John McNamara	Ms B. Ross
1985	Christy Nolan	Deirdre O'Ferrall
1986	Christy Nolan	Mary McGrath
1987	Christy Nolan	Judy Glynn
1988	Christy Dorman	Ms K. Massey
1989	Christy Dorman	Niamh Doyle
1990	Paul O' Gorman	Niamh Doyle
1991	Paul O' Gorman	Aoife Wilson
1992	John Mac Donald	Rosemary Hayes
1993	John MacDonald	Maureen Black
1994	Tom Casey	Shelagh Manley
1995	Tom Casey	Shelagh Manley
1996	Ray Devlin	Shelagh Manley
1997	Ray Devlin	Shelagh Manley
1998	John Power	Clare Garrihy
1999	Geoffrey Ross	Clare Garrihy
2000	Geoffrey Ross	Clare Garrihy
2001	Bryan Barry	Eilish O'Sullivan
2002	Claire Garrihy	Eilish O' Sullivan

The finalists in the West Dublin Open Championships in 1982 were, from left, Ken Fitzgibbon, Michelle Buckley, Lesley O' Halloran and Dermot More O' Ferrall.

In 1974 the clubhouse was destroyed by fire and a new facility had to be built. Two hard courts were built in 1975 with four more added in 1978. Despite the decline during the 1970s the demand increased with an ever-growing suburban population. By 1983 there were over 1000 members. In 1983 it was fairly unique in that there were twice as many junior members as seniors. This would pay off in the quality of players produced in subsequent years.

Ladies' doubles finalists at the 1982 West Dublin Open championships at Castleknock TC. From left: Bernadette Davy, Jean Tubridy, Laura Roche and Gillian Chandler.

Gerry More O'Ferrall was to be one of a number of key personnel that ensured the club's ever-thriving nature. He was also a key member of Tennis Ireland for quite a number of years (see chapter 6). His son, Dermot, became a junior international. He was number 15 in Ireland in 1981, number 6 in 1982 and number 3 in 1983. His brother David was not far behind. He was number 24 in 1983, number 14 in 1984. The club has taken coaching of all its juniors to hand with many senior members getting involved. Currently, Declan Donnellan, son of former ILTA President Paddy, is virtually a full-time professional coach at the club. It might be noted too that Gerry More O' Ferrall not alone did he take over the Tennis Ireland handbook for many years, but was the President of Tennis Ireland in 1990.

Players come and go but the club can look back on many achievements. It has held many national junior and senior events and produced players to match. The club has hosted some very significant tournaments in recent years which included the West Dublin Senior and Junior Open events. In July of 2002 the club were

delighted to host the Ellesse Irish Women's Championships, the oldest major women's championship in world tennis. Yvonne Doyle, one of the clubs successful juniors and one of Ireland's current top ranked players, took up the game at **Castleknock LTC** at the age of seven. Up to the age of 15 she was coached by Shay Feely and, in more recent years, by Ronan Reid. Stewart Doyle, no relation, was Irish under 12 open champion in 1986, under 14 champion in 1988 and under 16 in 1990. He was ranked number 1 in 1990 and 1991. In 1993 and 1994 he was ranked 3 and 4 in the Irish Senior listing. Among many international matches he has played on the Davis Cup team in 1991 and 1994. His younger sister, Emma, was Irish open under 14 champion in 1990.

The 1982 West Dublin Championships at Castleknock TC. Men's doubles finalists. From left: Ken Fitzgibbon, Robin Gibney, Peter Hannon & Brian Lawlor.

The 1976 junior tournament at Castleknock LTC.

Laura Roche was the winner of the Crest West Dublin Open Championships at Castleknock TC in 1982. From left: Shay Feely (tournament referee), Wilma Fitzpatrick, Derek Kilpatrick (managing director, Crest Foods), Laura Roche, Peter Hannon (men's singles winner) & Gerry More O'Ferrall (acting president, Castleknock TC).

Other Irish open champions from the club also included Brian Kennedy (under 12 in 1995), Sarah McIntyre (under 12 in 1995), Aine Leonard (under 12 in 1997 and under 14 in 1999) and James McGee (under 16 in 2001). On the 25th November 2005 Castleknock Tennis Club deservedly received the Eagle Star Supreme Club of the year award.

senior side that season. That year club member Cyril Murphy won the Munster Open under 16 title and reached the Irish Open semi-final in the same category. Siobhan Sleator was also successful in junior events during the year. The club run an Open Senior Championships. Some results are as follows.

Club Champions at Castleknock Tennis Club

Year	Men	Ladies
1977	Mark Cooney	Patricia Lord
1978	Andy Kilfeather	Karen Lord
1979	Bud Moore	Patricia Lord
1980	Dermot More-O'Ferrall	Patricia Lord
1981	Dermot More-O'Ferrall	Aoife Wilson
1982	Dermot More-O'Ferrall	Aoife Wilson
1983	Dermot More-O'Ferrall	Aoife Wilson
1984	Dermot More-O'Ferrall	Karen Lord
1985	Dermot More-O'Ferrall	Niamh Doyle
1986	Jeremy Cleary	Niamh Doyle
1987	Dermot More-O'Ferrall	Niamh Doyle
1988	Dermot More-O'Ferrall	Yvonne Doyle
1989	Dermot More-O'Ferrall	Yvonne Doyle
1990	John Rendina	Yvonne Doyle
1991	David Collins	Yvonne Doyle
1992	Gary Cahill	Mary Pat Murphy
1993	Paul Quinn	Claire Bannon
1994	Leo MacCanna	Claire Bannon
1995	Christian Phelan	Laura Doyle
1996	Fiachra Lennon	Laura Doyle
1997	Philip O' Reilly	Barbara Black
1998	Fiachra Lennon	Sarah McIntyre
1999	Fiachra Lennon	Sarah McIntyre
2000	Brian Kennedy	Sarah McIntyre
2001	James Kirk	Alison Grehan
2002	James McGee	Sarah McIntyre

Hillview Open Tennis Championships of South Tipperary

Men's Singles	1999	
Premier	Des Dillon beat Willie Guiry	
	M. Murray beat J. O'Dwyer	
A	E. O'Brien beat Pat Coniry	
B	E. Kelly beat D. Desmond	
C	**2000**	
	Denis Heffernan beat Des Dillon	
Premier	Mark Lowry beat P J Hunt	
	Pat Coinry beat Patsy Hassett	
A	Jason Ryan beat Billy Kerton	
B		
D		
	1999	
Ladies' Singles	S. Greene beat M. Doody	
	M. O'Brien beat Y. Quigey	
B	**2000**	
C	Kay Cooney beat Kay Hickey	
C		

****

Hillview Sports Club [Clonmel LTC) (Founded 1935)

From 'humble' beginnings in the 1930s the Hillview club in Clonmel, County Tipperary, located at Mountain Road, became one of the most flourishing in Munster in 1970s. In the late 1970s the club could boast of over 500 members. The club had by that time some six tennis courts and an 18-hole pitch and putt course. The club was thriving and a new clubhouse had been built at that time. Responsibility for the boom was put down to a very active 'management committee'.

A successful Jean Tubridy was a member of this club (see Chapter 6) and won the Munster hardcourt singles title in 1977. She was also a member of the Munster

The open tournament at Hillview Tennis Club in 1972.

****

Appletee Tennis Club (pre-1936)

Appletee Tennis Club takes its names from a town land situated about four miles from Ballymena in County Antrim. The club was a small one but in 1977 they found that one court was insufficient and transferred to the six-court facility at Ballymena Academy Grammar School. Success was quick and by 1983 their first time was competing in the Division I of the Belfast & District leagues.

Junior interprovincial players at from the Appletee Lawn tennis Club in 1985 were (from left): Susie Kaytar, Charlotte Hamilton and Godfrey Gaston.

League prize presentations at Appletee LTC in 1985.

The men's singles 'B' team at Appletee LTC in 1985.

In 1984 they were delighted to beat Hawarden TC in the final of the knock-out cup competition. The players on that team were Jimmy Wilson, Brian Bailie, Patrick Taylor and Godfrey Gaston, players who had been the backbone of club teams for many years.

****

Hacketstown Tennis Club
(Founded c. 1939)

The County Carlow club at Hacketstown was founded in the late 1930s. A keen local man, Mr. Pat O'Toole, was the key figure in the clubs formation. He was the inaugural honorary secretary. In the first year a concrete hard court was laid down for the sum of £250. The lines on the court were in also concrete with a paint mixed into concrete. Traces of this court are still present today even though the club is no longer operational. It was intended to lay a grass court in year two. It is not known whether this ever functioned. Pat O'Toole and another young man Michael Fleming played on this new court every Sunday morning after Mass. On marriage in 1950 Pat moved some seven miles to Tinahely in County Wicklow. A son Seamus took up the game years later and became president of Sligo TC (see chapter 8).

In the first year of the Hacketstown club there were some 40 members, 18 of whom were ladies; a sizeable membership considering the size of the village. One member, Tessie McBride, was a very good player (*auburn haired and freckled*) who had played tennis during her secondary education at the Brigidine Convent in Tullow. Now, not long after leaving school, was the captain of the newly formed club.

The lady members of the Hacketstown Tennis Club (c. 1939). Front (l. to r.): Bridie Reardon, Joan Duggan, Maureen Darcy, Tessie McBride, Mrs. P. Byrne & May Darcy. Back (l. to r.): Maureen Boland, Sheila Deering, Rita Butler, Sheila Butler, Patty Weddick, Eileen Kerwin, Alice Byrne, Maude McBride, Mrs. M. Cullen, Kay Kennedy, Mary Doyle & Eileen Darcy.

Tessie McBride
The first tennis captain at Hacketstown
Tennis Club, County Carlow (c. 1939).

****

Mullingar Town Tennis Club
(Founded 1939)

In 1892 the County Westmeath club was founded in the town of Mullingar. It was rather exclusive in that it was social standing that dictated membership. This was not unusual in Ireland at that time. After the free State (26 counties) was formed in the early 1920s there was an increase in club formations in many regions. These new clubs developed from a different base. These were clubs with many shopkeepers and other non-professionals among their membership. In many cases, the local catholic clergy were involved, the older clubs having a mainly non-catholic club in their earlier years. By the end of the 1930s towns such as Cavan, Longford, Athlone, Boyle etc. had a second tennis club. The Mullingar 'Town' club was one of these. It was founded in 1939 on a derelict site, behind one of the main streets, and a short distance from the County club. The latter survived with a dwindling membership until the 1960s when it folded.

The initial members of the Mullingar Town Tennis Club had a lot of preparation to do in laying the seven grass courts, and later one hard court. Gertie Owens (nee McKenna) was the first honorary secretary and Garda Superintendent the first club captain. By the late 1950s the membership dwindled and the club was inactive into the early 1960s. The late Michael Creighton takes up the story:

The remaining members of the committee had a meeting with Fr. Joe Dermody Administrator in 1960 and subsequent years when water and sanitation was introduced and fences repaired. Juniors, without any formal committee, did great work in salvaging the clubhouse from near dereliction, ran hops, arranged friendlies.

Father Dermody and what remained of the committee asked those of us who ran a very successful Boys club during the winter to take on the organising of the Tennis club during the summer months. We took on the task in the mid-sixties. I had been President of the Boys club for six years and involved with Father Joe Dermody in the formation of the National Federation of Youth Clubs. Father Willie Cleary was spiritual Director of the Boys club and a keen tennis player. He had a sharp eye in spotting potential good young players-not unlike Dr. Barniville. And so it came to pass that Father Willie Cleary and myself were steeped in youth work and that the tennis club we entered in the mid-sixties was organised by juniors with few seniors. It was no wonder that for many years Mullingar Tennis Club thrived as a centre for top juniors.

Michael Creighton-at the core of the Mullingar Tennis Club success for over forty years.

By the middle of the 1970s the club was exceptionally active, particularly with juniors. When the club drew up a constitution in the early 1970s Father Cleary was elected President. He remained in this post until 1983 when he was appointed the Administrator of the Mullingar parish and time did not allow the same commitment. Michael Creighton who was single, a civil engineer with Westmeath County Council, was the honorary secretary for many years, and then honorary treasurer. These titles do not do justice to the man who spent so much of his spare time in the clubs promotion. This involved the club's physical development as well as the play itself.

Michael took junior players all over the country for tournaments. He also got involved in the Provincial Towns committee and was its treasurer for many years. While he was a player himself he felt that good coaches were important for the young players. Coaches Bernadette O'Rafferty and Peader O'Farrell *brought on our players a lot in the early years.* Bernadette introduced the Mullingar members to the "Barniville Babes" squad, the very successful Dublin-based group, led by Dr. Harry Barniville. The system promoted young players through squad coaching right throughout the year.

In 1978 Harry Barniville contacted the club with a few to giving promising juniors more than one years coaching. *John Conlon was the junior with the most potential to have ever joined Mullingar Tennis Club. He started playing at six, coming down to the club with his brother Michael. Our president, Father Willie Cleary quickly realised that he was someone special and he got every encouragement and coaching. ....John, still under 8, was among our entrants that year. He was one of the qualifiers! Doctor Barnivile and Father Cleary agreed that 4 years in the squads would be excessive and that the club would look after him for the year. He was on the squash under 9 and under 11, skipping under 10. He won the tournament in September 1981 and was unbeaten in Ireland under 11 or 12.*

Two of the top juniors at Mullingar Tennis Club in the 1970s were Brian McCormack and John Conlon. John (on right) started playing at six was said to been the player with the most potential to have ever joined the club. In 1982 he won the Irish Minor Championships at Fitzwilliam LTC.

Mary Waldron was one of the Mullingar players to participate in the Barniville squad. In 1979 she won the Irish Minor Girl's championship at **Fitzwilliam LTC**. In 1971 Aideen Dunne was part of the successful Loretto schools senior team. Although she was never coached she managed to win the under 15 junior titles at Mullingar and Moate. That was the year the club ran the first Junior Open Week, an event that was to be a tremendous success. The fact that Penn tennis ball factory was built in Mullingar in the 1970s was a great boost to the game. The company sponsored the junior open week annually. It became rated as one of the top four junior tournaments in Leinster. Aideen subsequently played against some of the top junior players from Dublin and put up such a performance that she was selected for the Leinster junior Inter-provincial team to play at **Sutton LTC** that year.

The club facilities were to develop in tandem with the great junior development. In 1972 the club pavilion was extended and by 1974 six hard courts were now constructed on the original grass surfaces. By 1976 there were updated dressing rooms, a canteen and a balcony. In the intervening years more and more adults became involved and a badminton hall was added to the club facilities. Members such as Jimmy

Lynch took over much of the work load which had hitherto fallen on the shoulders of Michael Creighton. If the spirit that promoted the club in 1939, and then resurrected it in the 1960s has rubbed off on the present membership at **Mullingar Town TC**, then the future decades should be successful.

Father Willie Cleary with two junior successes at Mullingar TC. Father Cleary and Michael Creighton were two of the few adults involved in the club in the 1960s. Primarily through their efforts the club prospered and produced some of the best juniors in Ireland during the 1970s and 1980s.

The St. Mary's College Junior tennis team won the Leinster College Cup in 1978. All were members of Mullingar Tennis Club. From left: Dermot Caffrey, Brian Smyth, Michael McNamee, David Smyth, Ray Smyth & John Hunt.

In July 1977 a party of young German players, sponsored by Penn the tennis ball manufacturer in Mullingar, were brought to Mullingar Tennis Club for tennis competition

Mr. Patrick Lawlor (financial controller, General Tires Ltd. (Penn), presenting Tom Shelly with the senior boy's trophy at the 1976 Open at Mullingar TC.

The 1979 senior boy's singles winner at Mullingar TC was Richard Blake. Presenting the trophy is Ken Potterton (Leinster Branch president). Also in photograph is the runner-up David Guest.

1976: As promising players at the club three Mullingar juniors were selected to travel to Dublin for special coaching. From left: Ray Smyth, Dermot Caffrey and Brian Smyth.

The History of Irish Tennis

In 1978 the Mullingar Tennis Club team won the Class II competition in the Leinster Provincial Towns Cup. Back (l. to r.): John Burke, Patrick McLoughlin, Brian McCormack and Jimmy Lynch. Front (l. to r.) Mandy Dunne, Aideen Dunne, Una Wallace and Rite Murphy.

In many towns there is a direct connection between tennis and schools and the activity at the local club. Mullingar is no exception and the Loretto Convent has been successful in schools tennis (see chapter 4.4). In 1981, the team above were the first to take the Leinster Junior Cup away from the Dublin area. From left: Helen Waldron, Mary Waldron, Ann Shaw, Sandra Shaw, Louise Andrews & Niamh Waldron. Mary Waldron won the Minor Irish Girls' Championship in 1979 and led the Junior Leinster team to interprovincial success in 1981.

Mullingar TC have had a very successful junior tennis programme. Local Jimmy Lynch presents the 1979 open intermediate boy's singles trophy to Conor McCullough.

In 1987 two members of Mullingar Tennis Club received the male and female Bank of Ireland Services to Sport Awards by Westmeath VEC. From left: Basil Clancy (Bank of Ireland), Nuala Higgins (award winner), Mary O'Rourke (Minister of Education) and Michael Creighton (award winner).

Brian Smyth
Under 14 Junior Champion of Westmeath in 1977.

Donaghadee Lawn Tennis Club
(Founded pre 1947)

One of the smallest tennis clubs in Ireland with membership numbers varying from 5 to 40, the **Donaghadee LTC** is sited at the top of the Ards peninsula. The club faces the Irish Sea and a short distance across to Portpatrick in Scotland. In *Ace* tennis magazine (April 2004) it was considered one of the most scenic clubs in the UK.

Donaghadee LTC Open Mixed Shield Winners	
Year	**Winners**
1977	E. McNamara/B. Savage
1978	N. Whittaker/P. Little
1979-1980	J. Elliott/P. Little
1981	S. Spearman/P. Little
1982	M. McGrehan/J. Beattie
1983-1985	I. Lyndsay/M. Hanna
1986	J. Scott/C. Smyth
1987-1988	S. Scott/A. Hutton
1989	D. Wilson/R. Wilson
1990	M. Wallace/A. Shields
1991	S. Brown/M. Hutchinson
1992	M. Hetherington/G. O'Rawe
1993	S. Scott/P. Ferguson
1994	Eric Browett/Anne Magee
1995	E. Kennedy/J. Curry
1996	D. Parke/K. Ross
1997	G. Allen/C. Preston
1998	Stephen McCausland/Margaret Jardine
1999	Not played
2000	E. Gould/A. Kirkwood
2001	Not Played
2002	No Result
2003	P. O'Neill/C. Duncan
2004	Alan Campbell/Carol Boyd

Donaghadee LTC Committee 2004	
President	Yvonne Mercer
Chairman	Kevin Copeland
Honorary Secretary	David Clegg
Honorary Treasurer	Sheila Speers
Match Secretary	Denise Smyth
Club Captain	Jonathan Rea
Committee	Gail Campbell
	Paddy Wylie
	Brian Mawhinney

The club plays in the Belfast and District leagues and prides itself on its courts, lighting and pavilion. In 2004 the club entered two teams in the Mixed Leagues, one team in the summer leagues and the men's singles team played in Division 2.

Each summer the club runs an open mixed pairs competition, often played in conjunction with the Donaghadee town festival. The Ards Borough Council presented a perpetual shield for the winning pair.

****

St. Mary's Lawn Tennis Club
(Founded c. 1948)

In the 1930s Kenilworth Square in Dublin had four tennis clubs within its boundary. The clubs could not afford to purchase the property and it was sold to St. Mary's College who used it for several sports, particularly rugby. Four past-pupils of the school, Matt Gilsenan, Bill Fagan, Dick Swan and Derek Corrigan, founded the **St. Mary's LTC**, playing in the square, after the Second World War.

At the club expanded, and the square was used more extensively by the school itself, they were forced to seek alternative premises. In 1952 and 1953 they were located at Mount Tallant, Harold's Cross, and in 1954 moved to their present home off Belmont Avenue, Donnybrook. The site was bought from the **Percy LTC** who had played there since 1908. It included six grass courts and a croquet lawn. The latter was not a success and the area was used for general recreation purposes, and was ideal for erecting marquees during the annual 'at home' days. In the mid 1960s the pavilion was extended and the first hard courts were laid. By the 1980s the courts were floodlit and upgraded with all-weather surfaces. Further clubhouse refurbishment also took place. In the 1990s the club secured a bar license and omni-pro surfaces were installed.

On the playing front the club have had mixed success. Of particular note has been the various league wins, particularly praiseworthy was the ladies' team who won three Class II summer leagues. Members Des Delaney, Jack Delaney, Frank Cinnamond and Simon Gordon have all had representative honours. The club has friendly home and away encounters with Grun-Weiss Tennis Club in Germany, an activity recommended for any club.

The pavilion at St. Mary's Lawn Tennis Club, Donnybrook, Dublin. The site was the home of the Percy Lawn Tennis Club in 1908.

The History of Irish Tennis

The Ballypatrick Sports Centre Committee (2ⁿᵈ September 2001) at their 50ᵗʰ anniversary celebration. Front (l. to r.): Mary O'Neill, Rosie Murphy (honorary secretary), Attracta O'Reilly (president), Claire McNamara (president, Munster Council, Tennis Ireland), and Joan O'Gorman (one of the club's founding members). Back (l. to r.): Jack O'Donnell, John Quinn, Peter Holt, Edmond O'Reilly, Eddie Holohan, John Tobin (honorary treasurer), Ebbie O'Reilly, Rose Holohan, John G. Purcell, Liam Tobin and Tom Flood.

Finally, a quote directly from the club's web site. *We are very proud of the spirit of sportsmanship and friendship that defines the club and we look forward with optimism to the future.*

****

Ballypatrick Tennis Club
(Founded 1951)

In September 2001 the South Tipperary tennis club at Ballypatrick celebrated its 50ᵗʰ anniversary. Local member John Tobin compiled a booklet to celebrate the club's history. In the area for a number of years was the Kilsheelan club. This ceased to function in 1943 and some of the members were still keen and were to be involved in forming the new club at Ballypatrick.

To quote the *Munster Tennis News* (December 2001): *A Friday Summer morning in June 1951 and Kitty (O'Neill) Cormac calls to her local creamery to collect the butter. A chat in the office with manager Michael J. Butler and Noreen Cooney and the talk came around to tennis. One thought borrowed another and the idea of a tennis club was born. They immediately went out to check the suitability of a local field.*

A lawn mower and a hedge clippers were immediately sought and by evening the court was almost ready. A net was secured and by Sunday they were playing tennis. The aforementioned Michael J. Butler was to be a huge influence, with others, in the development of the club over next number of years.

By the following summer the club had two enclosed courts and it began to flourish. By 1958 they had a third court and then a small pavilion in 1959. Throughout the 50s most of the tennis was local with friendlies against clubs such as Hillview, Castleview, New Inn, Callan, Killenaule, Ballingarry and Clonmel Rowing Club.

The club affiliated to the Irish Lawn Tennis Association in the late 1960s and by 1972 had a strong team that reached the semi-final of the Guinness Cup competition. The club moved to new premises in 1977 where it has remained ever since. The club improved over the years, reaching the 1982 final of the Michel Cup. In 1991 they won Division 5 of the Summer Mixed Cup competition.

In the club's anniversary year (2001) they beat **Douglas LTC** in the final of the Division III Munster Mixed Winter League. In that final they beat Kinsale TC 3/2. The Ballypatrick pairing for the final were Liam Tobin/Rosaleen Foley, Peter Holt/Rose Holohan, Liam Tobin/Peter Holt, Rosaleen Foley and Rose Holohan. Among the noted members at the 50ᵗʰ anniversary was Joan O'Gorman, a lady who was a founding member and, at one time, a member of the Munster Branch committee.

****

Stackallen Lawn Tennis and Pitch & Putt Club
(Founded 1951)

In 1951 a tennis club was founded at Stackallen in County Meath. Ground was rented from the Crinion family and the first captain was Pat Meade. In 1963 the club rented some 7 acres from the Land Commission to establish the pitch and putt course. This was bought out for £700 in 1976. The club has now six flood-lit all-weather tennis courts and a very active pitch and putt section. Some members have done well in both sports.

Over the years the club has had success in both team and individual tennis competitions. On the administration front Paddy Donnellan became president of the Leinster Council for 1975 and 1976 and then president of the Irish Lawn Tennis Association in 1982. Declan Donnellan was ranked number 3 on the Irish u18 listings in 1981. He later became a senior manager and tennis coach. Currently Joanie Macken, whose parents Paddy and Joanne are former club captains, has been a member for about 15 years is now one of the top young ladies in Ireland. She was number 7 on the Irish senior ranking list in 2004. That year she won an Irish under 18 singles title at Riverview. She has already travelled throughout Europe in pursuit of tennis and is likely to continue to progress in the immediate years ahead.

Stackallen is a progressive and social club and extends an invitation to all prospective members and visitors, private and corporate, to come, view and sample the Stackallen experience. (John Gilroy, chairman, 2005). The club has an overall executive committee looking after affairs. In 2005 the honorary president, honorary secretary and honorary treasurer were Michael grey, Tommy Finnegan and Tom Walsh respectively.

Stackallen Lawn Tennis and Pitch & Putt Club Tennis Committee 2005	
Ladies' Captain	Kathleen Devine
Gents' Captain	Pat Meade
Committee	Chris Nulty
	John McKenna
	Mary Morgan
	Frank Aiken
	Joanne Macken
	John Barrett
	Ann grey
	Peter Fleming
	Susie Weldon

****

Lattin Lawn Tennis Club
(Founded 1952)

In 2002 the Lattin Club of west Tipperary celebrated its 50 years with the production of a booklet to record their time in Irish tennis. It is not claimed as a definitive history but does record many "fond memories" that "bring the light of other days around me" (Thomas Moore). The compiler of the history was Pauline Daly, the President of the Irish Lawn Tennis Association in 1984 and 1985. A few snippets form the booklet are included here.

The Golden Jubilee is a defining moment in the history of any Club. Over the last 50 years the Club has played a central role in the recreational and social life of the parish.

Over the years Committees worked hard, players won trophies all over the country and dances and socials were held in towns and villages. Supporters enjoyed all the various functions hosted by Lattin LTC. In fact, they had a ball!

In 1952, a group of local residents got together and plotted the new club, on a site in the heart of the village. Known as Pat Carroll's plot, it was rented for the year for the sum of £3-10s. *The club in 1952 got off to a good start, as it was an exceptionally fine summer. There was a total of 70 paid up members that year.* The annual subscription was 5/- (about 20 cents in today's money). Two courts were put into operation that year. The first tournament was won by John Keane and Maggie Tucker. The runners-up were Taylor Condon and Teresa Hourigan.

In 1976 Lattin LTC were winners of the Plate competition in the Crowley Cup at Hillview LTC. Front (l. to r.): Maura Greene, Mary Paul Hourigan, Lochlan Nolan (president, Hillview LTC), Kathleen Greene & Lily Delaney. Back (l to r.): Philip Purcell, Brendan Walsh, Morgan Hayes & Davy Walsh.

Lattin Lawn Tennis Club		
Year	President	Chairman
1952-1953	Patrick Finnan	Michael Daly
1954	Patrick Finnan	Mossy Keane
1955	Edmond Hourigan	M. Keane/M. Daly
1956	Edmond Hourigan	Michael Daly
1957-1958	Edmond Hourigan	John F. Ryan
1959	Edmond Hourigan	Patrick Merrick
1960	Pauline Daly	Patrick Merrick
1961-1963	Pauline Daly	James Leahy
1964-1965	James Leahy	John Condon
1966-1967	James Leahy	George Ryan
1968	Liam Ryan	David Walsh
1969	Thomas Tucker	David Walsh
1970-1971	Thomas Tucker	Michael Howe
1972-1974	Michael Daly	Michael O'Halloran
1975	Gerald Hourigan	David Walsh
1976-1977	Gerald Hourigan	Seamus Hourigan
1978-1979	Thomas Tucker	Pauline Daly
1980	Thomas Tucker	Michael Howe
1981-1982	Michael	Patrick Hourigan
1983	O'Halloran	Patrick Hourigan
1984-1985	Michael Hourigan	James Power
1986	Michael Hourigan	John Daly
1987		Michael Hourigan
1988		Katie Vaughan
1989-1991	Pauline Daly	Patrick Hourigan
1992-1993	Liam Ryan	Patrick Hourigan
1994	Michael Hourigan	Denis Vaughan
1995-1997	Michael Hourigan	Mary Hourigan
1998-2001	Michael Hourigan	William Ryan

The officers on the committee in 1952 were Michael Daly (chairman), Patrick Merrick (honorary secretary) and Thomas Tucker (honorary treasurer). In 1954 the club looked for a secure permanent tennis grounds. On 19th July 1955 two new hard courts were first played upon on land purchased from Mr. Ned Hourigan. *A grass court and croquet lawn were laid out subsequently.* In 1956 a new pavilion was built at a cost of £680. Around this time the club ran an Open American tournament with 74 players from 12 different clubs participating.

In the 1960s the club would continue to have croquet and a fine billiard table to keep members active and happy. The Open Tournament in 1967 had 108 players participating in what was a social as well as an annual sporting occasion. In 1972 there were 145 members and some 50 benefited from an organised coaching programme. Davis Cup player, Michael Hickey from Limerick being the highly qualified coach involved. At that stage the number of courts had increased and there was a mix of 'en tout cas' and grass.

Lattin members would become involved at provincial and national level. Pauline Daly was elected President of the ILTA for the years 1984 and 1985. She had been President of the Munster Branch in 1976. In 1999 she was to receive the J. P. O' Neill award for outstanding service to Munster and Irish tennis. In 1975 two junior members, Finbarr and Stan Walsh would represent the club and Province at the Junior Interprovincial Championships. The children of members of old are now involved in the club and, if that spirit of enterprise that started the club remains, the future is a good one.

Lattin Lawn Tennis Clubs Officers over the Years	
Honorary Secretaries	Honorary Treasurers
Patrick Merrick	Tom Tucker
Jimmy Leahy	Pat Ryan
Thady Greene	Carmel Power
Lucy Hourigan	Pauline Daly
Maura English	Michael Howe
Mary Condon	Michael O'Halloran
Breda Kennedy	Nora Heffernan
Mary Barlow	George Ryan
Mairead Finnan	Bill Ryan
Eimear McGuire	Marie Columb
Joe Condon	Kay Dinne
Finbar Walsh	Eileen McGuire
Kathleen Howe	Helen Breen
Mary Hourigan	Mary Breen
Helen Breen	
Mary Long	
Alex Long	

Lattin Lawn Tennis Club-Silver Jubilee Dinner Dance in 1972 at the Galtee Hotel in Cahir. The club received the Munster Council's 'Club of the Year Award'. Front (l. to r.): Nora Greene, Anna Ryan, Joan Hourigan, Berna Barlow, Lucy Hourigan, Mary Hourigan, Pat Kelly, Mairead O'Halloran & Nora Moloney. Second row (l. to r.): Michael Barlow, Thady Greene, Seamus Hourigan, Michael Hourigan, Eamon Smith (president, Munster Council, ILTA), Michael O'Halloran (club chairman), Frank O'Donogue (president, ILTA), Mary Ellen O'Connor & Margaret Tucker. Back row (l. to r.): Gerald Hourigan, Pat Ryan, Philip Purcell, Jimmy Leahy, Johnny Condon, Kathleen O'Donoghue, Pat Hourigan, Teresa Breen, Francis Breen, Liam Ryan-Shronell, Claire Ryan, Liam Ryan-Lattin, George Ryan, Tom Tucker and Jim O'Neill (honorary secretary, Munster Council ILTA).

September 1978. The opening of the new hard courts at Lattin Lawn Tennis Club. From left: Paddy Connery, Liam Ryan, Maura Greene, Tom Tucker (president), Rev. Canon Ryan, Donal Duggan, Pauline Daly (chairperson), Maura English, Lucy Hourigan (honorary secretary), Gerald Hourigan, Carmel Power (honorary treasurer), Jimmy Power and Aisling Daly.

1960s team at Lattin LTC. Back (l. to r.): Philip Purcell, George Ryan, Phil Purcell & Davy Walsh. Front (l. to r): Maura Greene, Collette Greene, Claire Hourigan & Kay Finnan.

Juniors at Lattin LTC (1980s/1990s).

****

Ballingaddy Lawn Tennis Club (Founded 1953)

Thanks to tennis fan John Brazill the story of this small club has been recorded (in the "The Kilmallock Journal", November 2003). Near Kilmallock where there was a successful club since the 1920s, a few keen players developed a new club in 1953. As in many parts of Ireland, tennis was considered elitist and gradually from the 1920s to the 1950s this attitude changed. The result of this was that many new clubs were founded top cater for the very active interest in the sport.

The story of tennis at Ballingaddy started a few years prior to 1953. On their farm at Flemington, four young lady members of the O'Shea family set up a court on the lawn in front of their thatched farmhouse. When the family moved to The Cross of Black the front lawn of this house was again developed as a tennis court. Anne O'Shea had become Mrs. O'Grady. The tennis here gave Gay Clery and Seamus Sheedy the idea of establishing a club at Ballingaddy.

O'Grady field was used for hurling by the young boys of the area. During breaks in the hurling they took interest in the tennis being played by the girls and quickly there was a rush to play, naturally the chance to get closer to the girls was a major draw. As John Brazill says: *It was a measure of the forbearance and generosity of Mrs. O'Grady that she tolerated such a gathering on her front lawn, sitting on her window sills, damaging her shrubs and flowers and generally making a nuisance of themselves.*

Local farmers Michael Quinlan and Paddy Clery were among those to give enthusiastic support to the idea of a club and a plot in a field belonging to Willie Clery beside the local graveyard was secured at a nominal rent. Poles were bought at a forestry auction and 10 foot high wire netting at a local store. The ground was already level and with a little work the bumps were rolled smooth and two courts were laid. The court measurements were ascertained from an encyclopaedia by Mrs. Ann Clery and Mrs. O'Grady supplied her white-lining 'machine'. *Very few of us had racquets and money to buy them but Gay Clery came to our aid again by allowing us to buy them through his business at wholesale prices.*

The all-whites rule in most clubs at the time was not applied but the committee insisted on proper tennis shoes. Maurice "The Bard" Clery refused to wear them. *Down the road in Kilmallock our efforts were regarded in a slightly condescending manner and we were not taken seriously. The attitude did change somewhat within a year or two after they had invited us to play a match with them and they found that some of our members could play a reasonable game.* The club was a social centre for most of the local young people and over the next number of seasons matches were played with clubs in Kilfinane, Broadford, Ballylanders and Lattin. Members also enjoyed bus outings to Tramore and Galway where the beach, the races and local dances were enjoyed. At Tramore, John Brazill recalls a 10 shilling trip on a light plane taking off from the strand. *I had the personal experience of one of the ladies in the seat beside me grabbing me around the neck and screaming that we were all doomed as the light plane banked over the town of Tramore.*

In the early 1960s the membership dwindled and the club folded. Those still active and keen joined **Kilmallock LTC** where the sport still thrived. The casual homely atmosphere was no more but is fondly remembered by those such as John who built the club from scratch and saw it go through its full life cycle.

The County Limerick club of Ballingaddy LTC was formed in 1953 and survived for less than a decade. However, during that time the members enjoyed the experience of developing the club, socialising and playing to the full. This photograph of some of the members was taken in the mid-1950s. Back (l. to r.): Maurice Clery, John Brazill, James Leo, Jimmy Fleming, Clement McAuliffe, Charles O'Grady, George Fleming, Paddy O'Grady, Mick Murphy, Maurice "Bard" Clery & Seamus Sheedy. Front (l. to r.): John Casey, Patricia O'Grady (of Ballyporeen), Patsy O'Grady, Eileen McAuliffe, Marie Clery, Helen Casey, Marcus Clery, Peggy Fleming, Peggy O'Grady, Peggy Collins & Joan Murphy. When the club folded the remaining players joined the nearby Kilmallock LTC.

****

The Rectory Lawn Tennis Club
(Founded Circa 1958)

Thanks to the research of Geoff Oakley it has been established that, in the late 1950s, a third tennis club was founded in the town of Birr. Well established were the **The Ormond LTC** and **Wilmer LTC** in the town with a population at the time of less than 4000. The game was very popular at that time, and right throughout the 1960s. The 'club' was rather unique in that there was no membership fee! The club had the use of two grass courts in the grounds of the local rectory, thus the name. The rector at the time, Rev. Dr. F. Bourke, was keen to facilitate members of the YMCA Club who at the time played a considerable amount of badminton and table tennis during the winter months.

There was no formal structure of officers and committee but a Tournament was held annually on the occasion of the 'Parish Fete'. Friendly matches were played with the neighbouring Wilmer club-whose grounds were almost within serving distance-and with other local clubs. Activities reached a peak in the late 1960s, during the ministry in Birr of a Methodist clergyman, Rev. Trevor Kennedy, who developed a junior section. Like the Ormond club of earlier generations, the Rectory Club also engaged in the more leisurely game of croquet. It faded away in the 1970s.

****

Grove Lawn Tennis Club
(Founded 1959)

Located at Grove Avenue, Malahide, the **Grove LTC** came into being in 1959. It was linked to the **Castle LTC** (founded circa 1923) and the **Malahide Junior LTC** (founded circa 1946). All three clubs evolved directly or indirectly as a result of membership restrictions at the older **Malahide Lawn Tennis and Croquet Club**. The **Castle LTC** was located at the Malahide Cricket Club and had 95 members at one time. Lord and Lady Talbot were interested in the club and presented two perpetual trophies for the ladies' and gents' singles. The club moved to a new site behind Woodlawn in the early 1930s and closed completely before the decade was out.

The unusual **Malahide Junior LTC** was the brainchild of Mrs. Kitty de Carte Hodges. Kitty was club founder, manager, coach etc. It had its home on the cricket grounds too. Membership was restricted to those **under 18 years of age**. Mary Clarke (nee Burgess) recalls that when she joined there were only two courts, a third and fourth added later. Two 'crates' were donated by Mary's uncle for the club, one acted as a 'pavilion' and the other to house the club's tennis equipment. Kitty did have helpers but appears to have run the club virtually single-handed. *She is remembered as being strict but popular, but ruled the Club with and Iron Hand* (**Grove LTC** history). Michael Nugent (senior) and Bernadette Burke (later O'Rafferty) were among the best junior in the club and played in many events, including the Irish junior championships. Bernadette was to become one of the top full-time coaches in Ireland.

The championship singles winners at the Castle LTC, Malahide, County Dublin, in 1927 were Archie Bolton and Sheila O'Brien. This club was one of the predecessors of the Grove LTC.

Kitty Hodges with some of the 135 members at Malahide Junior Lawn Tennis Club in 1954. Kitty started this club so that juniors in Malahide would have a place to play tennis.

Malahide Junior LTC
Boys' Doubles Final in 1957.

In 1958 Kitty Hodges decided to retire from the Club. The club ceased to exist. She however approached Eoghan Kavanagh with a view to ensuring the children would have somewhere to play. A meeting took place in the local library on the 16th February 1959. Each person present contributed £1 towards initial expenses. Leo Fogarty was elected chairman. After a search for a suitable site, Pat Howard, who was planning the development of Grove Avenue, set aside a portion of the field for the club's use. New members (adult), including Eoghan Kavanagh, Tim Cremin, Jim Connolly, Archie Bolton and Tom French, commenced

the club development on the 8th April of that year. On the 13th of the month the old **Malahide Junior LTC** equipment and huts were moved to the new club. In its early days the new club badly needed funds and Luke McCabe of the Grand Hotel made his premises available for committee meetings and fund-raising activities. Mothers of junior players took it in turn to supervise the children. The courts were only open from 2pm to 6pm from June to September. In 1968 a major topic for discussion was a barbecue. After collecting enough wood, and people to police the grounds, it took off. The junior committee were complimented on a successful affair at which 20 chickens, 14 dozen rolls and 3 to 4 pounds of sausages were consumed.

In 1970 the club nearly would up. However, under the chairmanship of Bill O'Brien, and intense canvassing by himself and Geoff McAdam, some 54 new members were signed up. By 1972 the club has some 212 members and everything moved forward. A waiting list has to be instigated. The following year the club constitution was adopted and club trustees were appointed. These were Bill O'Brien, John Miley and Tom O'Flaherty. Three additional trustees were appointed in 1991. The club had affiliated to the ILTA and Bernadette O'Rafferty, now a professional coach, was very active. She was made an Honorary Life Member in 1972 in recognition of her contribution to the club; ("one of the proudest moments of my life"). The same honour was bestowed on Kitty Hodges two years later.

In 1975 the Malahide Sport and Recreation Association entered a team for the national Community Games. The team of Grove members won the gold medal. Under the management of Tom O'Loughlin it included John O'Farrell, Mark Harrold, Conor Geraghty, Pauline Pitcher, Una Miley and Una Kinahan. By 1977 the club had 435 members and a waiting list of 300. The club continued to expand on its activities. In October 1986, having negotiated the purchase of the property, Bill O'Brien retired as chairman after 17 years in this office. Michael Howard a nephew of the original landlord agreed the sale; included in the contract was that the children and grandchildren of Bertha Howard should be honorary life members. By the late 1980s the club finally had good kitchen and sanitation facilities and looked forward to further improvements.

The club has been responsible for the successful promotion of the game, with family and junior members a key. Apart from Bernadette O'Rafferty and Tom O'Loughlin, others contributed to Irish tennis in many ways. Michael Nugent junior became a Davis Cup player and David Miley one of the top administrators in the ITF (International Tennis Federation) organisation. Why has a club with grass courts continued to succeed in today's climate of all-weather courts for 12 months of the year. There appear to be several reasons. One is the club approach to its junior and senior members. Secondly, the committee member do not get 'tired' of running the club- the fact that each spring there is a freshness among the members to get back on court, adds to the love for the game and a willingness to make it work. Also must be included the fact that playing on grass is a great pleasure, being experienced by fewer and fewer. Looking at the club officers we can see people who are dedicated for lengthy periods. A few should be mentioned. Bill O'Brien remained as chairman from 1970 to 1986. The late John Miley was the treasurer from 1986 to 2003 and Margaret Percival the secretary from 1978 to 1986. Nuala Burke will posisbly pass all these, and others, out in terms of club service. She took over as secretary in 1987 and is still there today (2006) as 'fresh' and enthuastic about the club as she was on day one.

Malahide Junior LTC-Boys' Doubles Final in 1955. From left: Romilly McMahon, David Mahon, Brian Kearns, Jim Thompson & Terry McCabe.

Action at Grove Lawn Tennis Club Malahide.

The club with four grass courts continues to be in demand. At the present time, there is a membership of over 500 **and** a waiting list of several hundred. The club has alarge range of competitions played during their summer season with some 24 perpetual cups as part of the annual competition. These cups are from men's singles over 40 (Keating Cup) right down to under 8 girls singles (McCreadie Cup). Perhaps the most important annual award is the The "Merit Service" Plaque. This covers a broad range of club life and has been awarded for such efforts as painting/repairing the pavilion (Roger Percival and Robert Rooney in 1984) and designing the club logo (Nuala Burke, 1993). Last few words on this unique 'grass-court' club to Margaret Percival (Honorary Secretary (1978-1986) and Bill O'Brien (Chairman, 1970-1986) respectively.

> *.....the special Grove comradeship and sense of belonging is as strong as ever and this is highlighted by the number of teenagers who, voluntarily, appear each Friday to help run the Tournaments.*

Kitty Hodges outside the Malahide Junior LTC pavilion with two of her charges. This lady started and ran a great club for young players in Malahide, in the 1950s. Grove LTC took over in 1959.

> *I believe that the Grove has been (and is) a major force for good in the Malahide community and has been a factor (not necessarily recognised) in the development of tennis in our country. Long may it continue.*

Malahide Junior LTC 1956 semi-final. From left: Teresa Jones (Nugent), Romilly McMahon, Mary Clarke (Burgess), Jim Thompson & Michael Nugent (senior).Jim and Mary won the Dr. Harry Michael Cup (under 16 mixed doubles) that year.

The 1956 Mixed Final for the Doctor Harry Michael Cup (under 16 mixed doubles). Jim Thompson and Mary Clarke (Burgess) (on right) Rita Foley (Nugent) and Joe Connolly in the final. The umpire was Romilly McMahon.

1982 at Grove LTC. From left: Peggy Burke, Tom O'Flaherty, Davnet Moore & Joe McDonnell.

Grove Lawn Tennis Club
The Merit Service Plaque

1977	Don McGrane
1978	Bill Burke
1979	Betty Harrold
1980	John Miley
1981	Margaret Percival
1982	Bernadette O'Rafferty
1983	Tom O'Loughlin
1984	Roger Percival & Robert Rooney
1985	Malahide Lawn Tennis & Croquet Club
1986	Ray Donnelly
1987	Helene McCullen
1988	Miriam O'Brien
1989	Deirdre Smith
1990	Katy Swarbrigg
1991	Andrew McAllister
1992	Carol McAllister
1993	Nuala Burke
1994	Aidan McGuinness
1995	John Miley, Kathy Swarbrigg & Margaret Percival
1996	John Carroll
1997	Peter Mullock
1998	Rosemarie Mathews
1999	Barry Donaldson
2000	Jo O'Farrell
2001	Gerald Swarbrigg
2002	Mary Jones
2003	Dearbhla Kiernan & Sara Pollard
2004	Martine Murray
2005	Nicola O'Connor

John Miley and Miriam O'Brien perhaps discussing the entry fees at Grove LTC. John was part of the famous tennis-playing Miley family and contributed significantly to the life of the Grove LTC (see Chapter 6).The annual club's 'Merit Service Plaque' was presented to John in 1980 and to Miriam in 1988.

Debbie Mullock, Betty Harrold & Suzanne Fleury at Grove LTC (c. 1987).

At Grove LTC 1982. Left to right: Liam Burke, Kevin O'Flaherty, Richard Birchall & Stephen Quinn. This is probably the Robertson Cup (under 16 boy's doubles) final which was won that year by Richard and Stephen.

Preparing the 'teas' at Grove LTC. From left: Margaret Percival, Helene McCullen & Jo O'Mahony. (Photo probably taken in early 1990s).

Robbie Harrold with some of his trophies. Robbie won the McAdam Cup (under 13 mixed singles) in 1970, the Heeley Cup (under 16 boys) in 1971 and 1972 and the McCabe Cup (men's championship) in 1982, and 1988 at Grove LTC.

Kieran Leheny & Mark Harrold at Grove LTC. In 1984 Mark won the McCabe Cup for the Men's Singles championship at the club. Kieran had won it previously in 1978.

1982 at Grove LTC. From left: Kevin O'Flaherty, Tom O'Loughlin & Richard Birchall. That year Richard won the Kinahan Cup for boy's under 14 singles at the club. Tom O'Loughlin went on to be the premier promoter of Parks Tennis in Ireland.

Junior mixed match at Grove LTC includes Annette Johnson, Brendan O'Sullivan, G. V. Wright & Margaret McDonald. (early 1960s?)

Captain's Day at Grove LTC in 1995.

Grove Lawn Tennis Club

Year	Chairman	Honorary Secretary	Honorary Treasurer
1959	Leo Fogarty	Eoghan Kavanagh	
1961		Eoghan Kavanagh	
1962		Miss H. Carroll	
1963		Miss M. Wright	
1964		Miss A. Ingoldsby	
1967		Miss P. Dixon-Jackson	
1967	Mr. O'Reilly	Teresa McAdam	Kevin Mahon
1968	Mary O'Herlihy	Pauline Wright	Kevin Mahon
1969	Mary O'Herlihy	Peter Leonard	Kevin Mahon
1970	Bill O'Brien	Barry Pitcher	Arthur Brady
1971	Bill O'Brien	Dermot Pitcher	Arthur Brady
1972	Bill O'Brien	Dermot Pitcher	Arthur Brady
1973	Bill O'Brien	Pauline Pitcher	Arthur Brady
1974	Bill O'Brien	Mary Clarke	Tony Byrne
1975-1978	Bill O'Brien	Eleanor O'Flaherty	Tony Byrne
1979-1981	Bill O'Brien	Margaret Percival	Tony Byrne
1982	Bill O'Brien	Margaret Percival	Tony Byrne
1983	Bill O'Brien	Margaret Percival	Jim Collier
1984	Bill O'Brien	Margaret Percival	Jim Collier
1985	Bill O'Brien	Margaret Percival	Peter Mullock
1986	Peter Mullock	Margaret Percival	John Miley
1987-1988	Peter Mullock	Nuala Burke	John Miley
1989-1995	Peter Mullock	Nuala Burke	John Miley
1996-2003	Carol McAllister	Nuala Burke	John Miley
2004	Carol McAllister	Nuala Burke	Colman O'Keeffe
2005	Graham Cure	Nuala Burke	Colman O'Keeffe

1974   **Trustees** Appointed: John Miley, Bill O'Brien & Tom O'Flaherty
1991   Additional **Trustees** Appointed: Peter Mullock, Margaret Percival & Dave Smith.

About to prepare the way for the Grove LTC in 1959 were (l. to r.): Eoghan Kavanagh, Paid O'Keeffe, Dick Thompson, Tom French & Tony French.

Whether your prize at the end of the week is a valuable prize or a healthy thirst, tennis is a gloriously challenging game. It stretches your body mind and courage, bringing glowing health and tantalising mixtures of fulfilment and frustration. Strive always for the fulfilment, using the frustrations as lessons to hasten its achievement. In so doing so you will still be enjoying the game when you are into your seventies.

Grove Lawn Tennis Club Captains

1981	Ray Donnelly	Deirdre Nolan
1982	Tom Byrne	Eithne O'Loughlin
1983	Jim Kelly	Eithne O'Loughlin
1984	Tom O'Flaherty	Eithne O'Loughlin
1985	Ray Donnelly	Marian McDonagh
1986	John O'Mahony	Hazel Caird
1987	Ray Donnelly	Hazel Caird
1988-1989	Dave Smith	Hazel Caird
1990-1991	Dave Smith	Katy Swarbrigg
1992	Norman Boyle	Katy Swarbrigg
1993	Norman Boyle	Carol McAllister
1994	Billy Wallace	Carol McAllister
1995	Billy Wallace	Kathryn McGowan
1996	Barry Donaldson	Kathryn McGowan
1997	Barry Donaldson	Hilda Smyth
1998	Graham Cure	Hilda Smyth
1999	Graham Cure	Mary White
2000	John Carroll	Mary White
2001	John Carroll	Martine Murray
2002	Barry Donaldson	Martin Murray
2003	Barry Donaldson	Dorothy Moorehead
2004	Paul Murray	Dorothy Morehead
2005	Paul Murray	Chris Gilson

****

Gorey Tennis Club
(Founded 1967)

In 1967 a few tennis enthusiasts in Gorey formed a club and leased land from Gorey Badminton Club. They had two tennis courts. By 1973 they won their class in the Provincial Towns Cup and by 1977 were negotiating to purchase the land on which the courts were laid and to build a pavilion. The club continued to thrive into the 1980s with the two hard courts.

Interestingly, the committee members in the 1970s used the following quote from Angela Buxton as echoing the sentiments of their club:

Four of the founding members of Gorey Tennis Club. From left: Diarmuid Swords, Dean Nash, Dave Cullinane & George Willoughby.

****

Clane Lawn Tennis Club
(Founded 1972)

In October 2002, **Clane LTC** was declared the best club in the country. Consider it is just 30 years old and has only had its own premises since 1985, there was "astonishment and then huge cheer from the Clane table" when they were awarded the supreme prize at the Eagle Star awards held at **Fitzwilliam LTC** in Dublin. They had first won the category of best small club in Ireland and then the major award. At the ceremony from the club were the committee which included President (Billy Hopkins), Chairman (Mick Hennessy), Secretary (Mary O'Connor), Liam Burke (PRO), Ronan Ryle, Peter Duffy, Paddy Behan, Aine Woodhouse, Mary Skelly, Susan Ryle and Chris Lloyd Rogers. The club were delighted with the well deserved accolades, Des Allen doing the needful on behalf of Tennis Ireland. Congratulations were also made by Jean Kealy and Patrick Manley of Eagle Star.

Apart from the clubs great development, and programmes for adults and children, their outreach programme for the Kare Group- whereby local mentally handicapped children use the facilities-was especially lauded. The club, no doubt has, many years of tennis history to make. The first thirty are summarised as follows:

The 2002 Clane Lawn Tennis Club Committee with their Eagle Star National Awards. Back (l. to r.) Ronan Ryle, Peter Duffy, Jean Kealy (Eagle Star), Michael Hennessy, Paddy Behan and Liam Burke. Front (l. to r. r.) Aine Woodhouse, Mary Skelly, Susan Ryle, Mary O' Connor, Billy Hopkins and Chris Lloyd-Rogers.

In 1972 one of the Jesuit priests from Clongowes Wood College approached a number of young people in the village who were playing tennis just for fun in "home made" grass courts. He noted their enthusiasm for the game and explained that there were nine hard courts and six grass courts which could be made available to them during the College holiday period and at other times during the year. After a number of games and casual meetings, it was decided that Clane Lawn Tennis Club be founded.

There was immediate reaction from all interested and the first match was played against a Celbridge team in July 1972. The team captain was Bryan Sammon one of the founder members of the club. Bryan did tremendous work in those early days. It was in the back garden of Bryan's father's house that the first tennis court was developed in the late sixties. Chicken wire was used for the net but the courts were rolled and marked regularly, (we did purchase a proper net later).

The Club was very successful in Clongowes Wood College with over one hundred members. We participated in Provincial Towns Cup and Dublin Leagues. In 1979 the Club approached Fr. Hughes who was Parish priest of Clane with a view to purchasing the two acres of land behind the old boy's school. After a number of meetings it was sold to the club for £6,500. This was a lot of money at the time.

The Club raised it by offering life membership to 65 members at £100 each.

Some Clane LTC players at Fitzwilliam LTC in 1980s watching their team mates play in the Carroll's Club doubles event. In photo are Brid Higgins, Henry Wright, Seamus Manzor and Terry Fitzgerald.

The History of Irish Tennis

The Club got a loan of £25,000 and work began on the erection of five all weather courts. After thirteen very successful and happy years in Clongowes Wood College we moved to our new premises in 1985. Since then the club has gone from strength to strength with the erection of our new clubhouse and four savannah courts. We are now in the processing of re-surfacing the fifth court.

Successes at Clane Lawn Tennis Club

1972: Founding of Club
1979: Purchase of Two acres of land
1985: Court Clubs Opened
1994: Men's team win Class 5 Summer League
2001: Men's team r.-up in Class 4 Summer League
2001: Ladies' Team win Class 4 Floodlit League
2002: Ladies' Team win Class 5 Winter League
2002: Club Awarded *Eagle Star* Best Small Club and Best Overall Club in Ireland.
2003: Men's Team win Class 5 of Summer League.

Ladies' doubles final at Clane LTC (circa 1990). From left: Winners Geraldine Coleman, Marian Keane and runners-up Michelle Guest and Brid Higgins.

Tennis clubs are located over the world and prove to be a sporting target for visitors or new residents to an area. Clane TC is always welcome to new members. One of the most interesting new members in recent years is Dr. Subash Kohli. In 1956 he was Junior Champion in Nairobi, Kenya. While working as a medical doctor in Canada he started a junior tennis programme in New Brunswick. In 1975 he became vice-president of the Kenyan Lawn Tennis Association. He is now a welcome member at Clane TC.

****

ESB Lawn Tennis Club
(Founded 1970)

The Electricity Supply Board (ESB) is one of the biggest employers in the Republic of Ireland. In the early 1970s they had about 13,000 employees with about 5,000 of these working in the greater Dublin area. About sports clubs evolved among the employees. These eventually included the sports of tennis, table tennis, squash and badminton.

In 1970 a small group of keen tennis players formed a club and rented a single court at Merrion Square, Dublin. By 1973 the club was now more active and rented some three courts from the ILTA at Brighton Square. By 1979, Sportsco was established and a major new sporting facility at South Lotts Road was built. In 1972 the ESB agreed to £1 for £1 contribution towards this ambitious development. Some 3000 employees agreed to 15p weekly contributions. Four *En Tout Cas* courts were part of the initial development in 1979. Rory O'Donnell and Hoe Weir were the key personnel behind the venture, supported by the CEO P.J. Moriarty. It is noted that the ESB employees had an affiliated club operating at Portlaoise in the late 1970s.

The Dublin club under Sportsco thrived and eventually had floodlights included, thus ensuring the year-round use of the courts. By 1979 the club had won Division I of the Dublin Business Houses Tennis League for three consecutive years. These leagues were held at the club in 2001. Success has also been achieved in the Dublin leagues in many season.

ESB LTC
Honorary Secretaries

1980	Maura O'Carroll
1981-83	Mary Halligan
1984	Ms M. Towers
1985-88	Mary Halligan
1989	Ms P. Patchell
1990-93	Kevin Niall
1994	Anne O'Byrne
1995	Paula Thompson
1996-98	Rena Murphy
1999	Justin Mahony
2000-01	Gemma McCarthy
2003	Tony Barrett

****

Deerpark Tennis Club
(Founded 1976)

The Deerpark tennis club is a community based one in Mount Merrion, County Dublin. It has six all-weather tennis courts and floodlighting. It was founded in 1976 and has grown ever since. From a base of about 200 members there are currently 1100 members and a long waiting list. It has a new general-purpose and meeting rooms in the clubhouse. Swipe cards have been introduced to improve accessibility.

Its standards have gradually climbed and the top ladies team are now in Class 2 of the Dublin leagues while the men's top team are now in Class 3. An extensive junior programme has been introduced with Pete Lowther as the main coach, assisted by seven other coaches and assistants. The juniors are introduced to the game at the mini-midi stage and brought along to advanced or performance level.

Joe Flood has probably been one of the club's best known tennis people outside the club itself. He is currently the honorary secretary of the Leinster Branch and a member of the Council of Tennis Ireland. He was the President of the Leinster Branch in 1976 and has also been involved in veterans' tennis for many years and played on many international veterans' sides abroad. In 1976 the two people most involved in establishing the club were Joe and Dick Humphreys, the latter had many good ideas and was influential locally with the Residents Association etc.

Successful young players in the club during the late 1980s were Orla and Darina Ni Chuinneghain, Orla winning many events, a top ranked junior for several season and Runner up in the Irish under 18 championships.

In October 2002, **Deerpark LTC** was one of two 'medium' sized clubs to receive a National Eagle Star Award at the inaugural presentations. This obviously reflected the club's success in promoting the game and speaks for itself.

Deerpark Lawn Tennis Club

	Chairpersons	Hon. Secretaries
1976	Richard Humphreys	
1977	Richard Humphreys	
1978	Joe Flood	
1979	Joe Flood	
1980	Gladys Hamilton	
1981	Don Cockburn	
1982	Jerry Murray	
1983	Eithne Mc Donald	
1984	Joe Flood	
1985	Kay May	
1986	Michael Cahill	
1987	Michael McDonald	Ciaran O' Buachain
1988	Terence Sweeney	Ciaran O' Buachain
1987	Marie Flood	Ciaran O' Buachain
1990	Kevin O'Meara	Miss C. Sweeney
1991	Pat Brennan	Miss C. Sweeney
1992	Michael Cahill	Michele Prendiville
1993	Peter Burke	Michele Prendiville
1994	Ita Mangan	Geraldine Linehan
1995	Ita Mangan	Geraldine Lenehan
1996	Jim Callan	Geraldine Lenehan
1997	Jim Callan	Jim Callan
1998	Jim Malone	Ann Monaghan
1999	Jim Malone	Yvonne Wilde
2000	Cosmo Flood	Blanaid Farrell
2001	Cosmo Flood	Blanaid Farrell
2002	Liam Prendiville	Blanaid Farrell
2003	Liam Prendiville	Blanaid Farrell

****

Rathgar Tennis Club
(Founded 1985)

The Rathgar club is one of the newer clubs in the Dublin area. There had been a club in Rathgar over 80 years ago. It died out. Public courts provided tennis for the locals for several decades. However, a new life to the game in this Dublin suburb took place when the local residents association and the Dublin Corporation joined agreed to a new formula for its activation. The Rathgar Tennis and Bowling Club was formed in 1985. The club is known as a 'voluntary community club'.

The club has been very successful and has ten floodlit all-weather (savanna) courts. It has proved to be one of the most welcoming and friendly clubs anywhere in Ireland. Coaching, junior members and providing tennis for all grades has been the basis of the club's success to date.

On the playing front the club has had many moments to be proud of. These included the hosting of DLTC finals and, in 2005, their top men's' and ladies' teams moving up to Class 2 in the summer leagues. In recognition of the club's overall success in promoting the sport, and all this includes, they were awarded the Eagle Star Leinster Award as the top 'mid-sized' club in the province in 2005. The judges specifically cited *the success the club has had over the past year in recruiting new members through open days, and the large number of juvenile players that the club introduced to the game through several Summer activities.*

****

Shankill Tennis Club
(Founded 1986)

The relatively new club of Shankill was initially established on four Dublin County Council courts. An initially membership of 700 was outstanding. The portacabin clubhouse was burnt down in 1989 and, having spent one year in a B & I ship container the members, with the help and co-operation of the County Council, and the National Lottery, secured permanent clubhouse facilities.

Shankill Tennis Club
Executive Committee 2003-2004

Chairperson	June Murphy
Vice-Chairperson	Sean Cassidy
Honorary Secretary	Heather Maybury
Membership Secretary	Mary Kelly
Honorary Treasurer	Frank O'Neill
Vice-Treasurer	Susan Wilson
Ladies' Captain	Pauline Moore-Wiemann
Men's' Captain	Tim Eaton
Junior Co-ordinator	Rita Leonard
Clubhouse Manager	Peter Owen
Children's Officer	Paul Roche

The clubs facilities gradually improved through the efforts of members and it now includes seven fully lit omni-courts. Success on court quickly followed the club's growth and the club regularly fields 5 men's and 5 ladies' teams, as well as junior teams, in the Dublin leagues. In 1991 the club became the first 'county-Council' based club to be given a permit to run a junior open competition. The successful member to develop in the club to date has been David Mullins. He played at Junior Wimbledon in 1997. Between 2002 and 2004 he played in some five Davis Cup fixtures. He was number 3 in Ireland in 2002.

****

Monaleen GAA Tennis Club
(founded 1994)

It started off as a social outlet for a number of women in the Monaleen area of Limerick. Within two years the *Kilmurray Review*, a booklet reporting on all life in this region of the city, would report that there was a fully organised club catering for 180 people. This was the rapid success story of Monaleen GAA Tennis Club. Housewife Margaret Clarke was the initial spar. She was actively supported by the GAA club through the late Father Doran and Eamonn Cosgrave. Over 100 years earlier the activity of a GAA club and that of an exclusive tennis club were worlds apart, socially. Clubs were then associated with croquet and cricket, certainly not with the rough and tumble or parish Gaelic Games. How things have changed. At the GAA club facilities for babysitting and morning tennis became available. The initial idea was so successful that a tennis club was rapidly formed.

Over the initial two years of the club coaching, sponsored by *Kit Kat,* was provided for young players during the summer holidays. This was expanded to providing coaching for all members, young and old, Pat Molan organising the sessions and Frank O'Shea providing the initial tennis skills to many newcomers to the game. Doubles leagues for men and women were started and club championships, which included six separate events, were very successful. Allied to this on court success have been a number of successful club functions.

The highlight in 1996 was the provision of a second court. Officers of the GAA, John Stapleton and Noel Moynihan, in association with the determination of tennis club chairman Liz O'Sullivan, ensured that this court became a reality. *It is a perfect example of how two sporting organisations working together can provide a much needed addition to community facilities* said Michael Sheahan in the Kilmurray Review. No one knows what the future will bring in terms of tennis champions. What is most significant is that a hardworking tennis club, with a most supportive and forward thinking GAA club, have made a success of a new project from scratch. Perhaps the next item on the agenda will be the club affiliation to Tennis Ireland and the participation of the club in open tournaments and leagues.

****

Portadown Tennis Club
(Founded 2001)

On the 12th June 2004, the Directors of Portadown Tennis Limited welcomed many members, locals officials as well as the chief executive and management committee of Tennis Ireland, to the formal opening of an exciting public-private enterprise in the field of tennis.

The president of Tennis Ireland-James Foley gives an opening address at the new Portadown TC.

The local Council approached the club in 1996 with a view to rehousing the club and the town bowling club at Eden Villa Park. This was at a time many members were looking at the possibility of a move. The new grounds were nearby. In to the picture also came both the Portadown Golf Club and the Portadown Rugby Football Club. Both made proposals to take in the tennis club. Over a period of a year the tennis club had meetings with all three bodies. The club now had about 25 to 30 members and a vote decided that the club would move in with the rugby club at Chambers Park. A feasibility study was carried out by a leisure consultancy company in 1999. Their study showed there was a definite need for a modern tennis complex.

On the 28th February in 2001 a well attended public meeting endorsed the following objectives

[1]   Create the Portadown Tennis Club
[2]   Build 4 floodlit tennis courts
[3]   Develop cross-community tennis

A new constitution was drawn up on the 10th May 2001 and the first AGM of the new Portadown Tennis Club was held at Chambers Park was held on the same date. The committee who have undertaken the fund-raising and all matters connected to developing the new club was as follows:

Chairman	Lyn Jamison
Vice-Chairman	Colin Mathews
Honorary Secretary	Edith Jamison
Honorary Treasurer	Stanley Robinson
Development Team	David Binks
	Jim Cullen
	Sandra Davoust

The **Edenderry Tennis Club** continued to function and play in leagues etc. right up to the operation of the new club. Lyn Jamison was the obvious driving force behind the new club. He is a brother in law of the noted Ulster Davis Cup player, Peter Jackson. He is also a member of the Ulster Branch of Tennis Ireland and it's President in 2002. The new club has four floodlit synthetic grass courts. The future of tennis in Portadown is now secure.

Lyn & Edith Jamison-two of the key members of the Portadown club.

Letty Lucas enjoys her flowers

The brass band and marquee add to the occasion.

Tennis Ireland committee at the opening.

Working at good club PR.

Wheelchair tennis has all the skills.

Junior members of Portadown Tennis Club-Catherine Spence (left) and Rachael Mulligan

The History of Irish Tennis

At the new club's launch was Harry Martin, a man who started playing tennis at the Edenderry TC in Portadown in 1934 and has been a tennis administrator for about 40 years.

David Binks-A keen committee member and promoter of tennis in the region.

A tennis exhibition on the new courts at Portadown Tennis Club.From left Willie Noteman, Ken Rowe, David Binks (umpire), Conor O'Kane and Carlos Miranda (Spanish coach).

*****

More tennis moments

Ashbourne TC-Town's Cup Division II in 1975.

Rushbrooke Lawn Tennis & Croquet Club 2005. Winner of the 77th Niemals Aufgeben Cup was Kevin O'Donovan (left). Frank McDonnell (club chairman, on right) presents the cup. Also in photograph was Frank Walley who received a presentation for him many years as chairman of this special event.

Shannon Tennis Club
Championship Prize-winners in 1977

The History of Irish Tennis

Kilmallock Lawn Tennis Club-June 21ˢᵗ 1931. This County Limerick Club was founded primarily through the efforts of Joe Treacy in 1928. Prior to this Joe was 'courting' Mary O'Shea, one of the four sisters playing on the family court (see Ballingaddy LTC) at nearby Flemingstown. This court was built in the early years of the 20ᵗʰ century. Joe obviously took a great interest in the game and, following their marriage, they started the Kilmallock club in a field adjacent to their back garden. It developed a reputation for having excellent grass courts, six in all. All six Treacy children, including Dermot and Niall, proved to be keen and capable players during the 1940s and 1950s. Niall was involved in the club organisation when two of the courts were converted to 'en tous cas' 'hard courts' in about 1960. He unfortunately died a few years later. (Dermot kept up the game and became a life member of Sligo Tennis Club in the early 1980s. His own children then took to the sport.) Like most clubs at the time, Kilmallock invoked the 'all-whites' rule. The club was a small one, mainly social, with the American Tournaments at their own, and other clubs in the area, being the main competitive activity. The Limerick Echo put up a cup for inter-club competition and Dermot does recall Kilmallock having a team that won this cup on at least one occasion. The Kilmallock LTC died out in the1970s after a lifetime of about fifty years.

Tennis Captains at Trinity College for 2003- 2005.

Socialising at Rushbrooke bar (circa 2004).

December 2004. Ciaran McCabe (right) receives the Niemals Aufgeben ("we never give up") Cup from club chairman Frank McDonnell. The event is held every Sunday morning in the autumn.

2004- Rushbrooke L T & Croquet C. prizegiving

The History of Irish Tennis

Bowls as well as croquet and tennis are played at Rushbrooke, County Cork. (Circa 2004).

Paul Nolan (back right) the president of St. Anne's-Waterford LTC in 1985 with some of the prize winners at the Open Week.

The Hospital LTC in 1977. Back (l. to r.) Tom Bourke, Gerard Mitchell, Pat Leahy & Pat Farrell. Front (l. to r.): Lil Leahy, Aideen Coffey, Josephine Leahy & Liz Cooke.

Action at the Wexford Open Week in 2002.

Rita Bentick and Tom Durcan were the Mullingar Tennis Club lady and gent's captains in 1985.

County Kildare LTC (now Naas LTC) won the Class IV Men's and Ladies' Summer leagues in 1973. Back (l. to r.): Peter Fullam, Joe Spring, Monica O'Connor, Paddy O'Connor, John Coughlan, Denise Langan, Donal Buckley & David Brennan. Front (l. to r.): Rosaline Sheahan, June Greely, John Greely, Nary Rose Lyons, Antoinette Conway & Donal Conway.

Sandycove Tennis & Squash Club was founded in 1886 and originally had six grass courts. Squash was added in 1972. It was the first Irish club to tour abroad visiting Norway in 1961, Germany/Austria in 1963 and France in 1965. The above photograph of past champions was taken as the club prepared for their centenary year in 1986. From left: Father Robbie McCabe (1943), Jim Casey (13 times between 1962 and 1979), John O'Shea (1973, 1975 & 1976), Gerry O'Shaughnessy (1951, 1952, 1953 and 1955) and Conor O'Reilly (1981, 1982, 1983 and 1985).

Pauline Daly (president, Irish Lawn Tennis Association) in 1985 with some members of Lower Aghada Lawn tennis Club at the announcement of the Heineken sponsored South of Ireland Veterans' Championship.

Dundalk Lawn Tennis Club has been one of the most successful clubs in the Provincial Towns Competitions In 1948 they won both the senior and junior section of this Leinster event. This is the winning junior team that year. Back (l. to r.): F. Johnston, P. E. O'Connell, D. B. Green & W. D. Willis. Sitting (l. to r.): Miss N. Carroll, T. McArdle (captain) & Miss P. O'Connell. Absent: Mrs. W. D. Willis & Miss G. O'Reilly.

Glenageary LTC Juniors

Social gathering at Carlow tournament (c. 1922)

Peter Jackson of Belfast and Tommy Crooks of Ballymena met in many finals throughout Ulster. In 1959, Peter shakes hands with Tommy after their North Down H.C. Championship final. Peter won 6/2 4/6 6/2.

Mitchelstown LTC (1978) From left: Kieran Cotter, Karen Herlihy, Paul Holland, David Holland, Claire Skinner, Margaret Casey & Catherine O'Keeffe.

4.2 The Irish Lawn Tennis Association/Tennis Ireland

The Secretary told the meeting that he had received an anonymous sponsorship of £250 towards the cost of sending the [Federation Cup] *team to Naples.* (ILTA minutes Book, 3rd May 1974)

From 1877, when the first Irish clubs were formed, until 1908 when the I.L.T.A. came into being, the game in Ireland progressed steadily but was limited to a series of clubs sprouting up in varied locations. The game was limited to the gentry and, the encouraged military. One suspects it was the officer class of the latter that was made most welcome. There would be an expansion from the lawn courts of private dwelling, including castles, to the formation of clubs where common bonds were reinforced. Tennis parties became an acceptable, if not important, social dimension in society.

At the upper end of the game the best players would compete at tournaments held by clubs such as the **Kilkenny County & City LTC, County Sligo LTC, Sunday's Well LT & Boating Club, Monkstown LTC, Enniskillen LTC, the County Kildare Club, Armagh LTC, Limerick LTC, County Westmeath LTC** and the **Downshire Archery & LT Club**. By 1887, the Irish Lawn Tennis Championships were a well-established fixture, arguably on a par with Wimbledon, and ably organised by the members of the **Fitzwilliam LTC.** This and other important tournaments are dealt with elsewhere in this book. Without question the improved railway system, the constant flow of players back and forward across the Irish Sea and the competitive nature of some of our best exponents of the game would give the sport an ever-increasing status. As a summer sport it certainly challenged croquet and cricket. It had the advantage over cricket in that ladies could be fully involved.

In the 1887 special lawn tennis edition of the *Irish Cyclist and Athlete,* details of the ninth annual Irish Championships were included. Advertisements included such diverse items as Francis Falkner's Irish Whiskey, billiard and bagatelle tables, the Amateur Athletic Championships of All Ireland (to be held on the 30th May at Ball's Bridge Grounds) and the Quadrant Tricycle. Tennis items included Lawn Tennis Balls (*regulation size and weight* made by the East London Rubber Company), The "Pennsylvania" Lawn Mower (supplied by Dublin agents Robert G. Gatchell & Son, 7, Dawson Street, Dublin) and The "Never Slack" tennis bat (made by The Patent Racquet Company, London). Tennis tournaments mentioned, or advertised, were The Midland Counties Lawn Tennis Tournament (starting on the 27th June at the Edgbaston Cricket and L.T., Club, Birmingham), the Welsh Championships (to be held at Penarth on the 13th June), The **Cheltenham LTC** annual tournament (commencing on the 6th June), the Bath Lawn Tennis Week (starting May 31st) and the Northern Lawn Tennis Championship Tournament (starting on the 20th June at the Lawn Tennis Grounds, Old Trafford, Manchester).

In Ireland, the Church of Ireland Temperance Society held at a lawn tennis tournament from the 8th to the 10th June at the Earlsfort Rink, Earlsfort Terrace. This tournament, with three open and two confined events,

was run in parallel with an industrial exhibition; military bands playing each afternoon. A one-sentence notice mentioned that *A LAWN TENNIS CLUB had been started in Limerick, and Mr. Moore, 97, George Street, is the hon. sec.* (the club had, in fact, started play 10 years earlier). It might be noted that, by 1887, the Manchester event was one of the big tournaments of the time and it was there, five years earlier (1882), that *The first women's doubles champions were May Langrishe and her older sister Miss B. Langrishe* (Tingay, 1983).

On the 26th January 1888 a public meeting of players took place at the Freemasons' Tavern, London, at which it was decided to form a "National Lawn Tennis Association" to govern the rapidly expanding game. Over eighty were present. The L.T.A. was born. In the early years the Council had elected officers and *36 members who were representative of the six divisions into which the United Kingdom had been divided. These divisions were (1) North of England; (2) South of England; (3) Midlands; (4) Wales and Monmouthshire; (5) Scotland; (6) Ireland; and they returned respectively 8, 10, 6, 2, 4 and 6 representatives to the Council.* One can assume that these latter representations roughly reflected the number of clubs in each region.

By 1896 there were 28 tournaments sanctioned, some run by clubs, other by associations. The following year it would be recorded that 73 tournaments were sanctioned and the number of clubs had grown to 282 clubs (100 affiliated directly and the remainder through 15 associations). In 1938 *Lawn Tennis & Badminton* published a three-part article at the time of the LTA's Jubilee. The following is a direct quote from Part II (February 5th, 1938):

It would appear that the following fourteen championships or tournaments may claim to be the senior meetings in the British Isles:-

The Championships	*Northern (Manchester & L'pool)*
Eastbourne	*Northumberland and Durham*
Edgbaston	*(held as a combined meeting)*
Edinburgh	*Seaton*
Hull	*Teignmouth*
Leicester	*Tenby*
Limerick	*Waterford*

Other open tournaments established fifty or more years ago and still holding annual meetings are:

Bath	*Glasgow(Pollokshields)*
Beckenham	*Moseley (Birmingham)*
Caesarean(Jersey)	*Moffat*
Bournemouth	*Nottingham*
Budleigh Salterton	*Penarth*
Buxton	*Queen's Club (C.C.)*
Chiswick Park	*Scarborough*
Cheltenham	*Sunderland*
Clifton	*Torquay*

Cupar	*Westgate*
East Grinstead	*Fitzwilliam*
Galashields	*Sligo*
Ilkley	

For many, perhaps the surprising addition to many is the inclusion of the tournaments at Waterford and Sligo in the very early days of the sport. The Limerick tournament was held shortly after the first Wimbledon Championships in 1877. In the second listing the two Irish clubs seem to have been a belated addition (the others being alphabetical). The Irish Championships at **Fitzwilliam LTC** were first held in 1879 and the first tournament at the **County Sligo LTC** was held in 1882.

In 1892 Irishman, Dr. W. Stoker proposed an international match between Ireland and England. **This was to be the first full-scale team event between two countries in the game of lawn tennis.** The match was played at Ballsbridge, Dublin and Ireland won by five matches to four. Only doubles was played. (There was an international contest between the Clarke brothers (USA) and the Renshaw brothers (British Isles) in 1883; the Renshaws won both doubles contests held a week apart).

Handbook

Attempts to discover what Irish clubs were affiliated to the Lawn Tennis Association failed miserably. However, thanks to the astute collection of data by Harry Maunsell of the **Glenageary LTC** and honorary secretary of the Irish Lawn Tennis Association from 1920 to 1948, all was not lost. Among the collection of data he put together, now residing in the National Library, Kildare Street, Dublin, were some gems. Of particular interest were the two first handbooks on Irish tennis. In the front of the opening edition was a copy of a relevant letter from *Mr. Tennis* at **Fitzwilliam LTC**, Arthur H. Courtenay, the clubs honorary secretary at the time. Later 'Master' Courtenay would be Colonel and President of this most important of Irish clubs from 1896 to 1927.

Fitzwilliam Club,
6, Wilton Place,
April 30th, 1894.

Dear Mr. Abraham,
I am very pleased to learn that you intend bringing out a Lawn Tennis Hand-book for Ireland, and I feel sure that all members of this Club wish it success.
I shall, at all times, be very happy to give you any information likely to be of interest to the Readers of the Hand-book, which-from what I have heard of it-should provide for a want long felt by players in Ireland, for information as to the game in this country.

ARTHUR H. COURTENAY,
Hon. Sec
Fitzwilliam L.T.C.

According to the **Donnybrook LTC** centenary book of 1993, the formation of the ILTA had a 'fractious beginning'. Way back in 1896 a Mr. Keogh of **Drumcondra Lawn Tennis Club** began to drum up support for the idea of a national association. He got no encouragement from 'Master' Courtenay of **Fitzwilliam Lawn Tennis Club** who wrote on behalf of his club that it would not participate in any preliminary meeting and demanding to know what Mr. Keogh had done to promote such a meeting. The two sides to this historical incubation period might never be fully known. In any event, by 1908 there were about 45 clubs fully operational in Ireland, the game was thriving at club level, and things started to happen. For reasons of self-interest, the clubs at that time felt that a separate association would best serve the interest of Irish tennis. In March of that year the following notice appeared in a national paper:

LAWN TENNIS
PROPOSED IRISH ASSOCIATION

A meeting was held last night at the Grosvenor Hotel, in connection with the proposed formation of an Irish Lawn Tennis Association. The following were present – Messrs. W. St. G. Perrott (Donnybrook), Millner (Lansdowne), Vance (Grosvenor), Clery (Kenilworth), Phibbs (Dublin University), Henry (Mount Temple), P. Corbett (Drumcondra), Thornley (Clontarf), Tully (Sandycove).

Mr. W. St. G. Perrott occupied the chair, and Mr. Vance acted as hon. secretary to the meeting.

It was proposed by Mr. Henry, and seconded by Mr. Millner, and unanimously resolved – "That this meeting of hon. secretaries of clubs is in favour of forming an Irish Lawn Tennis Association, and that those present will communicate with their respective committees, with a view to their joining the proposed association".

The hon. secretary of the meeting was requested to forward a rough draft of rules, for information of committees, and the next meeting will be held on Friday 7th March, in the Grosvenor Hotel at 8 o'clock. Secretaries of clubs not receiving the above notice are requested to communicate with the hon. secretary (pro tem), Mr. James Vance, 18 York Road, Rathmines.

Minutes Books

Unless otherwise specified, the following dates and pages refer to items in the Minutes Books of the ILTA and Tennis Ireland. Des Allen and Tennis Ireland have kindly lent the author most of the books to hand and they have revealed much of the games history in the country. The italics are direct quotes.

At times the minutes are boring items that the Council had to deal with and for which the average player should be forever grateful. At other times, more interestingly, issues arose that have long been forgotten and required considerable debate at the time. These included such matters as the treatment of our Davis Cup team in Austria, the revolution in Hungary, play on Sunday's, Open tennis etc. etc. All are part of the evolution of the game and how we got to where we are today. Unfortunately, space does not allow all matters to be included here. Hopefully, no key matter is omitted. (n. b. For many years the minutes were handwritten and some words, particularly names, were difficult to read.)

The **first minutes book of the ILTA** records the following in its handwritten opening page:

The opening meeting of the Irish Lawn Tennis Association was held in the XL Café, Grafton Street, Dublin on Monday 27 April 1908 at 8pm.

Present:-

W.K.	*Mt Temple (Chairman)*
W.B. Pollock	*Mountpleasant*
H.E. Harris	*Glenageary*
J. Mone (?)	*Blackrock*
W.St.G. Perrott	*Lansdowne*
S. Hayes	*Blackrock*
J.F. Stokes	*Fitzwilliam*
J.D. Hughes	*Kenilworth*
T.S. Rorke	*Grosvenor*
H.R. Edward	*Donnybrook*
R. Yapp	*Wilton*
Rev.J.M. O'Connor	*Belvedere*
W.E. Cooke	*Clontarf*
Dr.Matus(?)	*King's Co. & Ormond*
A. Beckett	*Hon.Sec*

The Hon. Sec. read the resolution of the Dublin Lawn Tennis Council & the circulars covering the meeting.

Proposed J.F. Stokes
Seconded R.Yapp & passed unanimously
"That an Irish Lawn Tennis Assoct. be formed"

The proposed Rules was then considered, certain amendments made thereto and finally passed as follows:

It is apparent that, since the meeting of the Dublin secretaries in early March, a considerable number of meetings had been held and that the Rules were thoroughly investigated. No record of these meetings appears to have survived. One must assume that most, if not all, of those attending that first meeting were in fact secretaries of their clubs. J. F. Stokes, for example, was club secretary at **Fitzwilliam LTC** from 1905 to 1910. In addition, in 1908, he was club champion and won both the Irish Open Men's Doubles seven times between 1905 and 1921, the Open Ladies & Gentlemen's Doubles twice (1908 & 1911). W. Alfred Beckett was appointed as honorary secretary of the ILTA and, after a vote, William St. George Perrott as honorary treasurer. The former would stay in office until 1920 and the latter until 1948.

Rules of the Irish Lawn Tennis Association.

I.
The Association shall be called "THE IRISH LAWN TENNIS ASSOCIATION."

II.
The objects of the Association shall be to advance the interests of Lawn Tennis in Ireland, and to arrange Inter-National, Inter-Provincial, and other matches.

III.
The Association shall be formed of Irish Lawn Tennis Clubs.

IV.
The Association shall be managed by a Committee of eighteen Members, four from each province, to be elected at the Annual General Meeting, and an Honorary Secretary and Honorary Treasurer. No Club shall have more than one representative on the Committee at one time, unless it be either the Honorary Secretary or Honorary Treasurer. Five shall form a quorum. The Honorary Secretary shall have power to call a Committee Meeting whenever it is considered necessary, and shall give at least seven days' written notice of such Meeting to each Member of the Committee. The Committee Meetings shall be held in Dublin.

V.
The annual subscription for each Club shall be 5s., payable on the 1st January in each year, or on joining. Any Club whose subscription remains unpaid on the 15th April shall cease to be a Member of the Association.

VI.
The Committee shall have power to decide all questions referred to them by affiliated Clubs in Ireland ; and generally to decide upon all matters relating to the management of the Association. The Committee shall have power to refer questions for decision to the Council of the Lawn Tennis Association.

VII.
The Annual General Meeting of the Association shall be held in Dublin during the month of April in each year. Each affiliated Club shall be entitled to send one representative to every General Meeting.

VIII.
The Rules of the Association shall only be altered at the Annual General Meeting, or at an Extraordinary General Meeting, expressly called for the purpose, and by a majority of two-thirds of the representatives present at such Meeting.

IX.
The Honorary Secretary shall immediately call an Extraordinary General Meeting at the request of the Committee, or upon the receipt of a request in writing from six affiliated Clubs, stating the purpose for which the Meeting is to be called.

X.
At least fourteen days' notice of any General Meeting, mentioning the business to be considered, shall be sent to the Honorary Secretaries of all affiliated Clubs.

XI.
This Association shall be affiliated to the Lawn Tennis Association.

XII.
The Laws and Regulations of the Game, as revised at the Annual General Meeting of the Lawn Tennis Association, shall be adopted by this Association.

XIII.
To avoid clashing of dates, all Clubs and Committees wishing to hold a Tournament open to other than their own Members must make application to the Honorary Secretary of the Irish Lawn Tennis Association before 15th April in each year, specifying date on which such Tournament is to be held.

XIV.
The Champion of Ireland for the time being, playing in any Tournament sanctioned by the Irish L.T.A., shall owe 15 in any open singles event, except in the Irish Championship Meeting.

XV.
No Member of any Club affiliated to the Irish Lawn Tennis Association shall play in any Tournament in Ireland not sanctioned by this Association.

XVI.
The Association shall have power to appoint official handicappers.

XVII.
The Committee shall have power to suspend any Club or Player infringing the Rules, and shall also have power to deal with any question that may arise.

XVIII.
The Licensee Fee for Committees be £1 1s.

The early rules of the Irish Lawn Tennis Association

While a member of **Mount Temple LTC** chaired the first meeting, the next recorded meeting, a general meeting of the association, was held on the 25th May and chaired by the Reverend H. N. Craig of **Tullamore LTC.** He was followed by H. R. Edwards (**Donnybrook LTC**) at the meeting on the 7th October. At this point some 18 County Dublin clubs has signed up to the new association and 15 'provincial clubs'. In accordance with the rules, four representatives were nominated, and elected, for each province at the meeting of the 25th May. These were:

Leinster
> Rev. H. N. Craig (Tullamore LTC)
> S. L. Fry (Mount Temple LTC)
> H. R. Edwards (Donnybrook LTC)
> J. D. Hughes (Kenilworth LTC)

Connacht
> John M. Meldon (Galway LTC)
> A.G. Adamson (Athenry LTC)
> Joseph M. Meldon (Athenry LTC)
> W. E. Cooke (Clontarf LTC)

Munster
> M. J. Daly (Cork)
> S. E. Smith (Roscrea LTC)
> Rev. A.M. Cave (Monkstown LTC, Cork)
> Rev. W. H. Smith (Clonmel LTC)

Ulster
> H. E. Harris (Glenageary LTC)
> W. H. Belford (Ballycastle LTC)
> James C. Parke (Clones LTC)
> John F. Stokes (Fitzwilliam LTC)

By the October meeting the affiliated clubs were now numbered 46. Within five years this number was to nearly double. The clubs of Ireland are dealt with in detail in chapter 4.1. Ireland had an elected chairman in its association up until 1913. That year the first President was elected. A few years earlier, at the meeting on the 7th October 1908 Colonel Arthur Henry Courtney was nominated to serve as Vice-President of LTA with additional representatives in James Cecil Parke and S. L. Fry. Courtney became the first president of the ILTA. For the remainder of the chapter a short selection of interesting items are identified. The organisation of a national association of this longevity deserves a book in itself. Many items of relevance will be found in various chapters in the book.

19th March 1909

It was decided that the next meeting would select a team to compete in the English County Cup Competition (along with Wales Scotland and 5 English teams). The General Meeting of the ILTA to be on the 29th April, during Punchestown week *to facilitate delegates from Country Clubs.* The list of sanctioned tournaments was agreed at this meeting.

15th May 1909

Agreed to send a team to play Germany, in an international in Berlin, at Whitsuntide, provided the German club could guarantee £50 towards the cost of travel. Ireland lost this match 11/4 but on the return match in July 1910 Ireland won 12/3. Details in chapter 5.10. J. F. Stokes was playing captain for the first match.

18th June 1909

The **Clonmel LTC** tournament was sanctioned to start on the earlier date of 14th July.

14th April 1910

The AGM was held at XL Café, Grafton Street, Dublin. Fourteen attended. The accounts for 1909 were audited by W. E. Cooke and were as in table on the following page. How many clubs would love to have a simple annual account as that of the ILTA in 1909? A discussion took place at this meeting on the LTA's new rule to charge 10/-6 for all open tournaments, irrespective of the value of the prizes given. It was decided this rule was unfair to smaller tournaments where the players were mainly local. The honorary secretary was asked to write to the LTA on the matter.

The Swiss Lawn Tennis Association wrote to the ILTA concerning an account of irregularities by W. George K. Logue who won the Championship of Switzerland. The ILTA were asked to approve of the Swiss action in suspending the player from all future tournaments in that country. No further comment is made in the minutes book, making the issue a bit of an unsolved mystery.

For several years it appears the chairman of meetings was not an elected post. At the AGM of the 14th April 1910 it was T.O. Read of Birr who chaired the meeting. At the next ordinary meeting, on the 18th May 1910, it was Harry M. Read (**Roscrea LTC**), the noted player and rugby international, who chaired the meeting followed by the Reverend H. N. Craig (**Tullamore LTC**) on the 1st July 1910.

1st July 1910

Much discussion took place on team selection for the German match. The **Kilkenny LTC** was elected as a member. The honorary secretary was to write to the **County Kildare LTC** as they were advertising an open tournament and had not been affiliated to the ILTA. At the time the rules prevented any member of an affiliated club from playing in a tournament not sanctioned by the association. **Naas LTC** (County Kildare) would be affiliated at the December meeting.

4th October 1910

The joint meeting of the ILTA and **Fitzwilliam LTC** who organised the German match in July calculated that a profit of £5 – 10 – 4 was made and was to be distributed equally between the two organisations.

6th December 1910

The honorary secretary was instructed to open up negotiations with the LTA with a view to re-establishing the annual Ireland-England match. He was also to write to the LTA with a view to considering the

The Irish Lawn Tennis Association
Sanctioned Tournaments for 1909

Starting Date	Organising Club	Event Titles
21st June 1909	Rushbrooke LT & Croquet Club	Champ. of County Cork (singles)
22nd June 1909	King's County (West) (Banagher)	Challenge Cup
28th June 1909	Blackrock LTC (Cork)	
6th July 1909	County Limerick LTC	Champ. of South of Ireland (singles)
6th July 1909	Mallow LTC	
6th July 1909	County Cavan LTC	County Cavan Challenge Cup (singles)
12th July 1909	County Sligo LTC	
12th July 1909	Tullamore LTC	Champ. Of Leinster (singles & doubles)
12th July 1909	Sunday's Well LT & Boating Club	Champ. Of Cork (singles)
13th July 1909	Clones LTC	Challenge Cup
14th July 1909	Enniscorthy LTC	Enniscorthy Cup (singles)
19th July 1909	Carrickmines Croquet & LTC	Championships of County Dublin
19th July 1909	Ballycastle LTC	Champ. Of County Antrim (singles)
19th July 1909	King's County & Ormond LTC	Champ. Of Midland Counties (singles)
20th July 1909	Monaghan LTC	
20th July 1909	Inishannon LTC (Bandon)	Champ. Cup
26th July 1909	Fitzwilliam LTC	The Irish Championships
30th July 1909	Galway LTC	Champ. Of Connaught (singles)
2nd August 1909	Omagh LTC	Champ. Of County Tyrone (singles)
2nd August 1909	Mitchelstown LTC	
2nd August 1909	Roscrea LTC	
2nd August 1909	Greystones LTC	Champ. Of County Wicklow (singles)
6th August 1909	County Galway LTC (Athenry?)	Champ. Of West of Ireland (singles)
9th August 1909	Kingstown Pavilion LTC	Champ. Of East of Ireland (singles)
10th August 1909	Nenagh LTC	
17th August 1909	Muskerry LTC	
26th August 1909	Clonmel LTC	Champ. Of County Tipperary (singles)

Receipts		Expenditure	
Balance from 1908	£4 - 8 - 3	Travelling expenses to Berlin	£4 -12 - 3
Subscriptions, 54 clubs @ 5/	£13 - 10 - 0	Subscriptions to Lawn Tennis Association for 1909	£4 - 0 - 0
License fee	£ 1 - 1 - 0	Hire of room for meetings	12 - 0
		Postage printing & stationery	£5 - 0 - 3
		Balance in hands	£4 - 14 - 9
	£18 - 19 - 3		£18 -19 - 3

Irish Lawn Tennis Association>> ACCOUNTS-End of 1909

setting up of *an International Board (England, Scotland, Wales & Ireland) as in the case of Rugby Football.* This proposal immediately followed the discussion on fees payable to the LTA for "open" tournaments. The Irish suggestion was turned down by the LTA.

In July 1912, following the Davis Cup match in Folkestone, initial discussions took place at an informal meeting at which both teams and officials were present. This would ultimately lead to the inaugural meeting of the ILTF in Paris on the 1st March 1913. There were representatives of 13 nations present, not including the USA. The Americans refused to join the organisation when the LTA were given the exclusive rights to hold the world lawn tennis championships. They would join in 1923 when the word 'world' was removed from the All England Championship event.

Gillmeister (1997) points out that, in fact there were two other versions on the formation of the ILTF. Both

involve American Duane Williams, who lived in Geneva. The first suggests that he approached the secretary of the Swiss LTF, Charles Barde, who then brought the idea to Henry Wallet, a Frenchman on holidays in Geneva. The second suggests that Williams wrote to Wallet in October 1911 with an idea for a world championships on clay courts, and that this sparked the idea of setting up an international committee. *It was from this organising committee that the International Lawn Tennis Federation eventually evolved.*

2nd March 1911

The matter of the East of Ireland tournament at the **Kingstown Pavilion LTC** had been discussed for several years. Both the management of the tournament, and the state of the courts, had been criticised. W. Fry pointed out that the club would be resolving any problems for the coming tournament. A sub-committee was appointed to report on the matter by the General Meeting in April.

The matter of the England-Ireland match was left in abeyance until the Irish suggestion on an International Board was dealt with.

The honorary secretary was to write to the French association with a view to holding an international match between the two countries.

27th April 1911

The AGM was held at the XL Café. It was decided that clubs running tournaments who do not wish to pay additional fees to the LTA could do so by limiting entry to *Irish players or members of Irish Lawn Tennis Clubs*. The only disadvantage appeared to be that their tournament would not be on the *English Official List*. The honorary Secretary's report for 1910 indicated that *Ireland practically obtains no benefit from this expenditure to the parent body in England*.

5th May 1911

The committee agreed to establish a competition for boys and girls aged 13 and over but not for under 17. In November it would be reported that twelve boys entered and a successful competition was held. There were no girls for such an event. It was noted in correspondence that our representative to the LTA had withdrawn our motion (on establishing an International Board to govern the sport) *under pressure from the Council of the LTA, thus putting off the matter for another year.*

7th October 1911

The annual Ireland England match held at **Fitzwilliam LTC**, during the Irish Championships, had been renewed after a number of years. The match was won 10/5 by England and had a net profit of £104-14-5. It was unanimously agreed that the ILTA portion of the profit (50%) be allocated to a separate account called the *International Match Reserve Account and that it be invested in the Post Office Savings Bank*.

It was also decided that the same resolution be put forward as last year for the alteration of Rule IV in order to obtain, if possible, the formation of an International Board for the government of Lawn Tennis. The following was the resolution: "The Association shall be managed by an International Board consisting of 12 members, six to be elected from England, two from Scotland, two from Wales, and two from Ireland". The matter would be defeated at the AGM of the LTA held in London on the 9th December 1912.

3rd December 1912

The Davis Cup had just been held in Melbourne with James Cecil Parke on the British Isles team. His significant part in a win over Australia (see 5.12) had just occurred and the committee passed the following resolution (with a notice to be passed on to the Irish Times): *that the Irish L.T. Association congratulate Mr. J. C. Parke most heartily on the great success he has* achieved in the contest for the Davis Cup in Australia when fighting for the British Isles v Australia. A telegram had been received by the LTA on Parke's successes. The ILTA honorary secretary indicated that he had already sent a letter of congratulations to the LTA themselves. The meeting discussed the possibility of a "covered court" for lawn tennis in Dublin.

Clubs Affiliated to the ILTA in 1913

County Dublin [29]

Blackrock	Kenilworth
Brighton (60)	Kingstown Pavilion Committee
Brooklyn	Lansdowne
Carrickmines	Leinster
Charleville	Mountpleasant
Clontarf (120)	Mount Temple
Croydon	Olney (75)
Donnybrook	Percy (60)
Drumcondra (70)	Phoenix (60)
Dublin University (80)	Ry. & Steam Packet Union
Dundrum	Sandycove
Eaton Square	Sandymount
Fitzwilliam (175)	Tritonville
Glenageary	Wilton (40)
Grosvenor (85)	

Country [53]

Armagh (70)	King's Co. West (Banagher)
Athenry (Co. Galway)	Kinsale (40)
Ballycastle (75)	Lismore
Bangor (Co. Down)	Mallow (120)
Belfast Boat Club	Marmullane (Cork)
Blackrock (Co. Cork)	Merville (Sligo)
Bray (Co. Wicklow) (120)	Mitchelstown
Cliftonville (50)	Moate
Clonel	Monaghan
Clonmel	Monkstown (Cork)
Co. Cavan (60)	Muskerry (co. Cork)
Co. Kildare (Naas)	Nenagh
Co. Limerick (195)	Newcastle (Co. Down) (60)
Co. Meath (Navan)	Omagh (80)
Curragh Camp	Quoile (Downpatrick) (50)
Dungannon (80)	Roscrea (80)
Enniscorthy	Rushbrooke
Fermoy (230)	Sligo
Galway (80)	Sunday's Well (Cork) (60)
Garden Vale (Athlone)	Tipperary
Glanmire (Cork)	Tralee (Green) (30)
Greystones (220)	Tralee (Sports Field)
Ida (New Ross (30)	Tullamore (40)
Inishannon (Co. Cork)	Wexford (60)
Kanturk	Windsor (Belfast) (150)
Kilkenny County	Youghal
King's Co. & Ormond	

ILTA affiliated club listing April 1913. Playing membership numbers and club numbers in brackets.

24th April 1913

Twelve people attended the AGM held in the Grosvenor Hotel, Dublin. Rule IV was changed to include a President for the association. This was passed unanimously and Colonel Arthur Henry Courtenay, C.B., D.L., then became the first President of the ILTA.

He would also continue to be the Irish Vice-President of the LTA along with H. R. Edwards and Harold Murphy as representatives. The listing of the affiliated clubs as per the annual report of the honorary secretary included 29 in County Dublin and 53 others in the country. It might be noted that, of the clubs membership numbers given, that **Greystones LTC** was biggest with 220, followed by **County Limerick LTC** at 195. (See table, previous page).

20th November 1913

The matter of the Irish Close Championships was considered and it was decided to approach **Lansdowne LTC** with a view to their club being host for the event. The details were confirmed and adopted at a later meeting (6th March 1914) with the event scheduled for the following June. There were to be two open and two handicap singles events, a gent's doubles and a mixed doubles. Entries were from 3 to 5 shillings per event and the prizes were to have values from £1.5/- for the runners up in the ladies handicap singles to a cup and a prize of £5 value to the winner of the gents singles championship. The Challenge Cups to become the property of the players winning them three times, not necessarily in successive years.

The holders to play through in all events. The tournament committee would consist of the honorary secretary for the tournament, the honorary secretary of the ILTA and one representative from **Fitzwilliam LTC, Lansdowne LTC, Mount Temple LTC** and **Dublin University LTC.**

24th April 1914

At the annual general meeting the secretary's report included the following statement: *It is with great pleasure that I am able to report the change in the Rule of the LTA as to the payment of fees by Irish Clubs for the holding of Tournaments. After several years of agitation it has now been decided by the LTA that Irish Clubs holding Tournaments which are confined to Irish players need not be directly affiliated to the LTA under Rule 6 nor pay the Tournament Fee under Rule 30. The Irish LTA is to be heartily congratulated on achieving this result which will be a great boon to most Irish clubs.*

James Cecil Parke was congratulated for his magnificent performance in the Davis Cup once again. Even though the British Isles lost to the USA in the Challenge round (2/3) he would win both his singles matches once again. This time, against Maurice McLoughlin and Richard (*Dick*) Norris Williams II.

The 1914 English match would be played during the first two days of the Irish Championships.

For the purposes of the Irish Close Championships an Irish player was defined, and agreed unanimously, at this meeting as any person who *(a) was born in Ireland or (b) is a bona fide resident in Ireland at the date of the closing of the entries and is a member of a club affiliated to the ILTA. In case of dispute as to the eligibility of any player to complete, the decision of the Committee of the ILTA shall be final.* This definition would be reviewed in later years, for various reasons.

2nd July 1914

The selection committee of G. Pilkington (Chairman), H. B. Pollock, C. D. Harvey, Alfred Beckett and William St. G. Perrott met at 6 Ely place to pick an Irish team to play England on the 13th and 14th July and one, for the first time, against Scotland in Edinburgh on the 20th and 21st July. The team, Parke not being available, was Simon Scroope (captain), T. D. Good, J. F. Stokes, R. M. Graham, Harry M. Read and Louis Meldon. The substitutes were Charles Scroope, H. Craig, Cecil Campbell, H. Law and Frank Crosbie. By the time of the English match, Val Miley was selected and won his singles. Ireland won 12 matches to 4. Against Scotland it would also be a resounding victory 9/5 with one match unfinished.

29th October 1914

The question of colours for members of the International teams was discussed and it was agreed that *members of such teams playing for Ireland be authorised to wear a white flannel blazer with a shield of St. Patrick's blue.* The meeting agreed that those who played in either the English or Scottish match be presented with a blazer by the ILTA.

It was agreed to give a sum of £10 towards the National Relief Fund (following a letter from the LTA). The first Great War had started earlier that year. A letter from Major Jeffreys tendering his resignation was read to the committee- he had been appointed to Kitchener's army and was expected to be sent abroad soon.

29th April 1915

Following a resolution from the committee made in March the AGM (held at Mills Hall, Merrion Row, Dublin) agreed, unanimously, *That having regard to the existing state of affairs owing to the war............no Open Tournaments, International matches, or Inter-Club Cup Competitions should be held this year..*

The secretary's report for the year included a hope *that the clubs will endeavour to keep going with the members who from one cause or another are not able to take any active part in the military operations.* An additional motion passed recommended that no club championships be held that year.

13th April 1916

The AGM was held at Mills Hall, Merrion Row, Dublin. The President, Colonel Courtenay, sent his apologies- he was on military duty in England. The secretary's report for 1915 included the following comments: *The season of 1915 was unfortunately, owing to the War, a very barren one. ......play all over the country was more of less suspended owing to the large number of playing members in the different Clubs who were serving their country in the War.* At the meeting it was suggested that each club should make out a Roll of Honour of members, ladies and men, who are in active service at the front.

15th March 1917

This was the first meeting in a year and it was decided that no AGM would be held.

30ᵗʰ April 1918

The committee met for the first time in a year and recommended that *Clubs hold tournaments in aid of War Charities*. The question of play on Sunday arose. It was decided that this would be the decision of each club (a matter that would be debated in many clubs over many years to come).

The 1919 official ILTA Committee listing.

19ᵗʰ February 1919

With the Peace Conference opening at Versailles on the 18ᵗʰ January the ILTA agreed to recommence their activities for the 1919 season. A further meeting on the 2ⁿᵈ April arranged the AGM for the 17ᵗʰ of the month.

5ᵗʰ November 1919

The minutes book of the ILTA include a typed report prepared by the honorary secretary, Alfred Beckett, which was agreed by the meeting should be brought to the LTA secretaries meeting to be held in London on the 11ᵗʰ November. The issue of fees to the LTA was a main focus. It was pointed out that 99% of Irish Club Players were not open tournament players and that *to try to force the proposals on* Ireland *would either ruin the ILTA or would put them in direct opposition to the LTA-either course would be bad for lawn tennis in Ireland.* The report requested that *Ireland must ask to be treated in future as a Colonial or Foreign Association affiliated to the LTA as the parent legislating body for rules etc.*

8ᵗʰ December 1919

The committee meeting directed the honorary secretary to object to the fact that the LTA took it upon themselves to nominate W. Mewburn as a representative for Ireland in place of H. L. Murphy. An additional letter to be sent to Mr. Mewburn explaining the matter and indicating that the ILTA had no personal objection to him.

29ᵗʰ April 1920

The AGM at Mills Hall brought in alterations to six of the Associations rules. The honorary secretary and honorary treasurer *expressed their firm determination to retire at the end of 1920.* The former would retire but the treasurer stayed in office until 1948.

The Belfast Boat Club tournament was sanctioned for the middle of June and arrangements were to be made, if possible, for a match between Ulster and Leinster during the tournament. The Irish Close Championships would be held at Woodbrook in late June, *provided permission could be obtained from Sir Stanley Cochrane.*

12ᵗʰ May 1920

A letter was read from Alfred Beckett stating that he had been ill and would not be able to continue with his post as honorary secretary. H.R. Maunsell consented to act in that post for the remainder of the year. The records show that he would remain in that post until the late 1940s.

4ᵗʰ October 1920

The honorary secretary was directed to *ascertain from Mr. Edwards if the names of any Irish players were considered when the team for the Olympic Games was chosen.*

29ᵗʰ April 1921

The honorary secretary reported the loss of Alfred Beckett from the post but pointed out that he would be still on the committee as a representative for Leinster. The lengthy requests to the LTA to have part of the capitation fee returned for use by the ILTA was finally resolved when half of this amount was agreed would be returned.

1ˢᵗ June 1921

The bias at committee level appeared when it was found natural that on the 6ᵗʰ May the committee would propose players for an inaugural Leinster team to play Ulster. It should be noted, for practical reasons, the four representatives of each province were often, 1921 not being unusual, players who were member of Dublin clubs (presumably with a provincial connection). One Ulster, and all four representatives from Connacht and Munster, fitted this category. For the record, the Leinster team selected was (with some absences) as follows: Harry Read (Captain) (**Roscrea LTC**), Dr. D. P. Barry, Dr. W.E. Cooke (**Clontarf LTC**), Dr. R.E. Tottenham, Frank Devlin and E. S. Hornridge. T. Murphy subsequently replaced Dr. D. P. Barry, Leinster won the match 10 matches to 5. It was played during the Belfast Boat Club Tournament. (Frank Devlin became the best badminton player in the world in the 1920s.)

7th July 1921

An extraordinary General meeting defined the Rules and Regulations for all tournaments sanctioned by the ILTA, they were to come into operation on the 15th August of that year.

28th April 1922

The AGM agreed to the formation of the Belfast Lawn Tennis Council, the Dublin equivalent was already in operation for several years. In the report for 1921 it was stated that *Owing to the unsettled state of the Country the Lawn Tennis Association was unable to see its way to send a Team for an International Match* (i.e. the Irish-English match during the Irish Open Championships). *This was the more unfortunate as the Truce was declared shortly prior to the Tournament so the Match could have been played without any danger to the visitors.* Late in the season Ireland did play England at Buxton and lost 8/7, the committee had blamed the 11th hour inability of Mr. Ireland to travel.

17th May 1922

Some 14 clubs were newly affiliated to the association at this meeting. By the end of the year there would be over 100 clubs in the ILTA. A team of six and six substitutes was selected to represent Leinster in the second annual match against Ulster. Only one of the twelve travelled to Belfast and Ulster would win by 8 matches to 1.

6th December 1922

Considerable discussion took place as to the future of the ILTA owing to the creation of the Free State and it was decided to hold a Council meeting early in January and that meanwhile a circular should be issued to the Secretary of each of the Clubs in Northern Ireland stating that at the forthcoming meeting the following Resolution would be discussed and decided "The Council of the ILTA recommend that the ILTA be established on independent lines similar to those governing associations in the other Dominions". At the following meeting (15th January 1923) Mr. W.F. Scott (Belfast Boat Club) stated that subject to a slight alteration he believed the leading clubs in the six counties would be satisfied with the resolution but he was not so certain of the attitude of the junior clubs.

For many seasons, the organisers of international matches were Fitzwilliam LTC. They also provided the officials, including the referee. J. B. Shortt (back left) was the honorary secretary at the club in 1924 when Ireland played France in round 1 of the Davis Cup. Ireland's top player Cecil Campbell was not available and France comfortably won 5/0. Also in photograph at back (l. to r.) Rene Lacoste, Shirley Dillon, Dr. E. D'Arcy McCrea, Jacques ('Toto') Brugnon and Louis Meldon. Front (l. to r.) Edward Maguire, Max Decugis (French captain), Dr. Arthur Barry (Irish captain) and J. Couiteas. In 1923 McCrea had taken Borotra to five sets and Cochet to 11/13 in the third set. However in 1924, both McCrea and Dillon, despite taking Couiteas to five sets, lost comfortably to Lacoste. Dillon and Meldon lost to Lacoste and Brugnon 8/6 6/1 6/2. This was the era of the great French "Muskateers". Between 1924 and 1929 all six Wimbledon champions were French.

7th February 1923

An Extraordinary General Meeting took place in Mill's Hall, Dublin. Nineteen were present including Mr. S.F. Jackson and Mr. de Vere Crossley (both of the Boat Club, Belfast) and chaired by Mr. Sergeant Hanna (**Lansdowne LTC**). The following resolution was passed unanimously:

That the ILTA be established on independent lines similar to the Governing Associations in the Dominions and that the Council of the ILTA take the necessary steps to have the foregoing Resolution brought into operation.

16th February 1923

It was decided to enter an Irish team in the Davis Cup in it's own right. This first entry to this international competition is detailed in Chapter 5. The previous secretary, Alfred Beckett, who was also secretary of the Dublin Lawn Tennis Council for many years, was cordially thanked by all present- he was to depart the country shortly.

20th August 1923

Among a number of decisions made at this meeting were (a) *to take the steps necessary to have the Irish Championships deemed "National"* and (b) to enter Ireland for the Olympic Games in 1924. Both would come to fruition, the 1927 National Championship title being sanctioned by the International Tennis Federation in 1926.

29th November 1923

The committee decided to inform Colonel Courtney that they would like him to accept the life Vice-Presidency of the LTA that had been offered to him.

14th January 1924

Following a letter of request from Mr. J. B. Shortt, the honorary secretary of **Fitzwilliam LTC**, it was agreed that permission be given to hold the Hard Court Championships of Ireland starting on Easter Monday.

11th February 1924

After several requests it was agreed that the 1924 Irish Closed Championships would be allotted to the Rushbrooke club.

24th March 1924

Correspondence from Mr. Wallis Myers and Mr. Serjeant Hanna was read relative to Miss Ryan's eligibility to represent Ireland in the Olympic Games. (Elizabeth Ryan was born in the USA in 1892 and must have had some Irish connections. She was in the Wimbledon singles finals twice and won 19 doubles titles (12 ladies, 7 mixed) apart from USA, French and Irish doubles titles. She was well known in Dublin having won the Irish Singles Championship in 1919, 1920, 1921 and 1923 and was the first regular American competitor to our shores).

25th April 1924

At the well-attended AGM, the honorary secretary's report was an encouraging one. There were about 110 clubs now affiliated.....*owing to the difficulty in obtaining replies or subscriptions from some Hon. Secretaries it is rather difficult to be precise.*

The past season has been, I think I may say, the most momentous in the history of the game in Ireland since the first Irish Championships in 1878 were played. (actually 1879). *Owing to our recognition as a Lawn Tennis Country for the purposes of the Davis Cup we were enabled to provide Lawn Tennis enthusiasts with two splendid Matches against All-India and France. These Matches are, I am sure, present to the minds of every representative here and I need not refer to them at length, but since the palmiest days of the Irish Championships (now over thirty years ago) such crowds have never witnessed Lawn Tennis Matches in Ireland.* To add to this the Association had a net profit of nearly £500. It had been a busy year and the Committee *held no less than twenty-two meetings since the last Annual General Meeting......the Tailteann Games will take place at the Fitzwilliam grounds on the 11th August and following days and it is believed that various American Lawn Tennis Celebrities will put in an appearance.*

A new Constitution was approved. The format was changed and no longer would each province have four representatives. Rule 5 specified that the number of ordinary Members be nineteen (nine to represent Leinster, five to represent Ulster, four to represent Munster and one to represent Connacht). It is presumed that the numbers reflected the numbers of clubs affiliated in each province. Six Vice-Presidents were also elected, two nominated by Leinster, Ulster and Munster.

5th May 1924

Mr. J. F. Miley resigned from the Selection Committee *owing to the difficulties created by the fact that his brother was a possible candidate for the Davis Cup Team and in addition he felt himself in an awkward position owing to his duties as a newspaper Correspondent.*

27th August 1924

On the suggestion of Miss Haughton a ladies Inter-Provincial match was sanctioned. A Leinster team of Miss Wallis, Mrs. Blair White, Mrs. Miley, Mrs. Price, Miss Daly and Mrs. Tomlinson was selected to represent Leinster and travel to Munster.

29th September 1924

The matter of a covered court Club at Ballsbridge was mentioned and the chairman undertook to write to Mr. Bohane. At the following meeting it was pointed out that the Hall at Ballsbridge could not be used for such purposes at present *owing to the removal to Ballsbridge of the R.D.S.* [Royal Dublin Society].

29th January 1925

At the AGM it was pointed out that four members of the South African team and two Australians had played in the Tennis Section of the *Tailteann Games* the previous summer. Without the availability of the Honorary Cecil Campbell the Irish team were considerably weakened and lost the Davis Cup match against France 5/0.

The Closed Championships at Rushbrooke were successful. The honorary secretary gave an interesting report on the Olympic Games in Paris (see Chapter 5).

30th April 1925

The committee, nearly all Dublin based, still effectively acted as a Leinster Branch. They decided to send a team to play Munster in an Interprovincial match (men) and to have a visiting ladies team from Munster play a return match in Dublin.

1st May 1925

The committee of the ILTA had, for some time, looked into the possibility of the Association having its own grounds with suitable courts and a stand that would cater for international matches. In the final analysis an agreement was reached with the **Fitzwilliam LTC** on the matter. The club would erect a stand, *at their sole cost,* for not less than 900 people and costing not less than £1200. There were details on the ILTA use of the grounds as well as profits from matches. The agreement would be for ten years. The Extraordinary General Meeting passed the agreement. The initial stand proved too expensive and an amended agreement was passed at the next AGM.

29th January 1926

The AGM was held at 35 Dawson Street, Dublin. The affiliated clubs numbers for 1925 had gone up to 147. A postal voting system for provincial vice-presidents and ordinary members is tried for the first time. The record of attendance of various members of the committee is listed. In Leinster, Alf Walsh (**Norwood LTC**) topped this record while R.A.C. Barrett (**Skerries LTC**) and a representative for Munster missed only one of the 14 meetings. The Connacht representative, J. F. Stokes (**Fitzwilliam LTC**) attended only one meeting. The honorary secretary, H. R. Maunsell made a point of reporting that *the Leinster Vice-Presidents, Dr. A.P. Barry and Mr. G. Byrne, attended most regularly.* The number of attendances of the vice-presidents was listed in the annual report.

He also pointed out that *Whilst it is clear from the rapidly increasing number of Clubs in Ireland that the game is being extensively played I fear that the standard of play is still falling off.* The *unpleasant incidents* at the Davis Cup match were noted (see Chapter 5).

The advisability of Provincial Councils was to be considered by the incoming committee. A reference to the provincial secretaries was made at the meeting of the 9th February 1927.

21st June 1926

The Irish Field was appointed as the official organ of the ILTA.

22nd April 1927

This was the first meeting of the General Council under rules agreed at an Extraordinary General Meeting (24th January 1927) and as a result nominations were made from the Provincial Councils themselves for the first time. The President was the Right Honourable Lord Glenavy, the honorary treasurer, William St. George Perrott and the honorary treasurer, Henry R. Maunsell. The delegates, as listed in the Davis Cup programme in May, were as follows:

Leinster: G. Byrne, A. P. Barry, R. A. C. Barrett, J. F. Miley, T. O' Connor, W. W. S. Colquhoun, A. P. Dawson, M. F. Linehan, W. B. Pollock, S. E. Polden and A. H. Walsh.

Ulster: de Vere Crossley, A. Lane Joynt, E.S. Dashwood, T.B. Pedlow, R. P. Corrie and Major McCallum.

Munster: M.H. Toppin, S. L. Fry, W. McFettridge and J. B. Shortt.

It would be June 1933 before Connacht would have a separate Council.

20th February 1928

A discussion took place as to lawn tennis representation in the Olympic Games and it was decided that under no circumstances would a team be sent. The ILTF had been in dispute with the Olympic Council on control of the sport, and the tennis element of the Games in Paris in 1924 was far from satisfactory (see Irish experience in chapter 5). The upshot was that the ILTF themselves withdrew the game as an Olympic sport.

15th March 1928

A request for reinstatement as an amateur by Colonel M.J. Carpendale was considered and granted having regard to the fact that he had only turned professional with a view to earning money to support himself when his financial position was very bad.

24th June 1929

A discussion took place as to the expenses of Irish players playing in International Tournaments and it was decided to take no action in the matter until some competitor made a formal application. At this time Irish players would be found playing the South of France circuit as well as other events in Britain and Europe. After considerable discussion it was decided unanimously that the Men's Singles Championship Cup (Championship of County Dublin at Carrickmines) *should be competed for in future under the original terms which allowed it to become the absolute property of a player winning it three years in succession.* This matter and the cups for the Men's doubles had been an issue. On the 29th July the committee decided that the club could treat the cups for the men's doubles as perpetual. Like many minutes details are not specified.

29ᵗʰ July 1929

Two players nominated for Wimbledon would have to pay their own entry fees and expenses. A successful coaching scheme had taken place in Leinster and a lengthy discussion took place as to steps the ILTA took take to *further the progress of the game.* Among the suggestions were the possibility of inter-county matches, coaching schemes in the provinces and that clubs would be encouraged to provide at least one hard court for their members. It was decided that the 1930 Handbook would be published as early as possible and include the club secretaries names from the first handbook (in 1929) and that the 1930 list of secretaries would be circulated at a later date.

2ⁿᵈ June 1930

It was decided that in future years *the members of the Davis Cup and International match Committee should be invited to the dinner and dance.* The Entertainments Committee is regularly mentioned in the minutes, it being important that visiting players were well looked after. Following the Davis Cup match versus Monaco, it was pointed out that the tea arrangements were not satisfactory. It was suggested that the contract be given to a different firm in future.

20ᵗʰ June 1930

Every affiliated club must register its colours with the Hon. Secretary of its Provincial Council.

10ᵗʰ February 1931

The Hon. Secretary stated that he had nominated Colonel Leaden and his son as an Irish pair for the Butler Trophy. Following a letter from the South African Lawn Tennis Union it was decided to support their application (to the LTA) to have their Championships as an "Official Championships".

13ᵗʰ March 1931

The secretary reported that he found it impossible to get any club to take on the Close Championships for this year. It was agreed that he write to the Kilkenny and Birr clubs as two possibilities. At the next meeting the answer was to be a negative one and the secretary would then write to the Ballycastle, Portrush and Curragh clubs. By the 3ʳᵈ June the secretary indicated that he had finally allotted them to the **Curragh LTC.**

24ᵗʰ April 1931

Mr. E.A.M. Herd reinstated as an amateur, *he having given lessons in lawn tennis for some years but having ceased at the commencement of 1930.* Mr. F. Torkington was reinstated on the 3ʳᵈ June 1931.

24ᵗʰ August 1931

Following a suggestion from Mrs. Price the ILTA wrote to the LTA with a view to making the annual match with England a mixed one.

Harry Maunsell (Glenageary LTC & Fitzwilliam LTC) was one of the great administrators of Irish tennis. He was the honorary secretary of the Irish Lawn Tennis Association from 1920 to 1948.

19ᵗʰ January 1932

The committee was informed that the Leinster Council had passed a resolution that each member of an affiliated club in Leinster and Connacht, (which was under their umbrella at that time), paid a shilling to the Leinster Council. It was felt that this would avoid the Leinster Council having to apply to the ILTA for a coaching grant.

The honorary secretary reported the nominations from the three Provincial Councils. Leinster at this time had eleven nominees appointed. It was to be a significant change in that, for the first time that this writer is aware, a woman was elected to the ILTA. She was Miss Hilda Wallis the Irish Open Champion in 1924, 1926, 1930 and 1933 In addition, she was an international player in the sports of tennis, golf and hockey. Mrs. Price was to be a second female representative when the Leinster nominations for 1933 were submitted. It would be over fifty years later (1985) before the national association had a lady as its honorary secretary. This was that great Ulster organiser, Mavis Hogg. She took over from Charlie Brennan. She had already set a precedent in 1983 when becoming the first lady President. Since then the gates have opened and there have been seven other ladies to hold this highest of offices in Irish tennis.

2nd August 1932

Letters were received from the sports reporters of The Irish Times and the Irish Independent complaining that important official information was given to the Irish Press but not supplied to them. At that time, tennis was regarded as an important summer sport to be reported on. The honorary secretary pointed out that he supplied the three national papers with relevant information all at the same time. A circular had to be written to all members of the Council and Selection committees to indicate this approved procedure. There was no note mentioned of persons responsible for the leak. There was no mention of the Irish Field who had been appointed as the official organ of the ILTA six years earlier. Apparently, no information was supplied to the Belfast or Cork newspapers that would have a wide readership in their areas.

It appears that the **first mixed team** to represent Ireland was in the match versus England in 1932. The selected team was (in order of merit):

George Lyttleton Rogers
Edward McGuire
George McVeagh
H.F. Cronin
Hilda Wallis
Norma Stoker

19th August 1932

A letter was received from the ILTA enquiring about the views of the ILTA on the matter of whether lets should continue or, perhaps, should be allowed for all net cord shots.

18th October 1932

Two complaints were received about the County Cavan tournament. One related to a player who was permitted to play after being scratched. The other was the issue of players having to play on Sunday.

23rd January 1933

Kenny's Advertising Agency offered to supply the Association with 400/450 free Handbooks for the year provided they were allowed the sole advertising rights and the profits from sales. This offer was accepted.

The Kilkenny County & City club requested a ruling on a lady who was an agent for a firm of racquet manufacturers. The committee deemed that this lady's amateur status was not affected.

The committee decided not to support the South African proposal to make the Davis Cup a bi-annual event.

27th June 1933

Mr. K. West of the **County Sligo LTC** wrote to the Council indicating that at a special meeting of the affiliated clubs in Connaught there was a unanimous proposal to ask the ILTA to alter rules 5 and 12 thus permitting the establishment of an independent Connaught Provincial Council. The proposal was agreed with details to be worked out by a sub-committee. The final approval was made at the meeting held on the 16th January 1934. The sub-committee appointed to look at the amateur rules being re-defined by the ILTF suggested that an addition to Rule 22(b) should include: *A Gamesmaster in a School of College shall, with the written permission of his National Association, retain his amateur status.*

11th March 1935

It was decided that the age categories for the boys and girls Championships and interprovincials should be Under 18 for senior and Under 15 for Junior, the date being the previous 1st January.

29th May 1936

A letter was read from Mr. Lane Joynt stating that as a representative of Ulster he was unable to approve of a Davis Cup match being played on Sunday or of a wedding present being given to G.L. Rogers.......After considerable discussion it was proposed and seconded and carried unanimously that whilst a Davis Cup match should not be fixed for a Sunday it was to be at the discretion of the Committee of Management to play a postponed Match or Matches on a Sunday if in their opinion such a course was necessary.

At virtually all meetings during 1936 there were items related to the Davis Cup. Having obtained a bye in the first round European Zone, Ireland beat Sweden 4/1 in the second and Switzerland 3/2 in the third (both in Dublin). Unfortunately, they would lose 5/0 to Germany in the European semi-final in Berlin. (See Chapter 5).

28th September 1936

The Swedish LTA invited Ireland to participate in a competition for a Cup presented by the King of Sweden. It was decided not to compete this year due to the lack of a covered court in Ireland. At the same meeting a letter was read from the Australian LTA relative to an International event for women. The Council approved of the idea. However, it would be 1963 before the Federation Cup did take off.

A letter was received from **Fitzwilliam LTC** suggesting a change in the rules for tournaments in that *all entry fees must be paid by competitors prior to playing in any event.*

24th March 1937

It was decided that in future wives of players should not travel with the Teams (i.e. to Davis Cup ties).

Rules for the Close Championships were approved as follows:

(1) *All Cups shall be Perpetual Challenge Cups*
(2) *The Championships shall be played on grass courts.*
(3) *Persons entitled to play shall be (a) born in Ireland (b) had a parent born in Ireland or (c) had two years bona fide*
Residence in Ireland immediately prior to the date fixed for the commencement of the Championships.

31st March 1937

It was decided to amend sub-section (d) of Rule 25 so as to read:- *If four are to be seeded, Nos 1 and 2 as above No.4 shall be placed at the top of the second quarter, No. 3 shall be placed at the top of the fourth quarter.*

18th May 1937

A professional match between Fred Perry and Ellsworth Vines (both Wimbledon Champions in the 1930s) was agreed following an application by the **Fitzwilliam LTC**. On the 2nd May 1938 the committee agreed to the club's holding of exhibition matches by members of *W. T.Tilden's Troupe* on the 26th, 27th and 28th May.

A suggested match between our Davis Cup team and China was agreed.

A discussion took place in connection with the difficulty in obtaining racquets other than those made by Messrs. Gray Russell & Co., save under a very heavy import Duty and representations were made to the effect that the racquets turned out by Gray Russell & Co., were not sufficiently good for players in Davis Cup and International Matches. It was decided that the Hon. Secretary and Mr. Almond should draft a letter to Messrs. Gray Russell & Co., with a view to ascertaining if they could turn out a racquet which would be available for Davis Cup and International players.

16th October 1937

A sub-committee was set up to look into the matter of popularising winter tennis.

2nd May 1938

Agreed to a visit of the Tilden Troupe to the Fitzwilliam Club, for exhibition matches. It was considered to be to the advantage of lawn tennis in this country.

Mr. C.S. Almond reluctantly indicates he has to relinquish his offices on the ILTA and the ITF. His place is taken by Alfred H. Walsh. The matter of defaulters in the payment of annual subscriptions (to their clubs) was to arise again. The honorary secretary was to write to them and point out that the Council *prohibited each of them from playing in any open tournament or being a member of an affiliated club and directed that the affiliated clubs in Leinster should be circularised to that effect.*

30th May 1938

It was agreed to pay a sum of £2.14.3 to George McVeagh in payment for courts and balls when he was having practice in London with Tilden for the Davis Cup Match.

9th November 1938

The President of the association, Captain Willie Campbell had died in July and the secretary explained what had happened since. A vote of condolence with Mrs. Campbell and her daughter was passed. Miss Bradbury's application for reinstatement as an amateur was considered and on the proposal of Mr. McGuire was passed unanimously. A letter from Henry St. J. Blake, president of the Connacht Council, suggesting that the ILTA present a cup for competition among the Junior clubs in Connacht was passed. The cup to remain the property of the ILTA and returned if not competed for.

22nd March 1939

It was agreed, on the application of the Connaught Council, that they should have a second representative on the ILTA Council.

2nd August 1939

The Council was not in a position to assist George Lyttleton Rogers with expenses towards his trip to the USA. A series of letters were dealt with on the issue of expenses for players attending the Irish Championships. It started up with a latter from the LTA complaining that George McVeagh was inviting an English lady player to the tournament and offering to play her expenses and put her up in a hotel. The matter was eventually resolved insofar as it appeared that individual Fitzwilliam club members were prepared to *pay over the expenses of one or two players as they were unable to put them up.* and that there was no rule that forbade this.

4th April 1940

A letter was received from Dr. Pedlow of the Ulster Council indicating that at their AGM it was decided *not to take any active part in lawn tennis during the duration of the War.* A motion was also carried that the Open Championships should be held as usual.

15th July 1940

The Council was asked for a ruling on the matter of the Singles Challenge Cup at the **King's County LTC**. It had been won by Mr. G.A. Houlihan in 1937, 1939 and 1940, the 1938 being abandoned owing to wet weather. The Rule relative to the cup ran as follows; "Challenge Cup and prizes to be won three years in succession". *The Council decided that Mr. Houlihan was entitled to retain the Cup.*

16th October 1941

A series of four letters were dealt with on the matter of the final of the Waterford Open Singles Championship, which had been awarded to Mr. Peter O'Connor on the grounds that Mr. Shalloe had defaulted. Mr. J. A. Shalloe had claimed the match on the following grounds: "(1) The decision of the Umpire in granting a rest was wrong, and a breach of Rule 35, (2) The Umpire did not ask my consent before granting this rest, (3) The Referee having given his decision in favour of continuous play, I was not asked to resume play as should have been the procedure, (4) I was never informed of the Referee's ruling on the point, (5) The Umpire, on my initial objection, should have consulted with or referred the matter to the Referee for his decision before granting my opponent's request for a rest". *After full consideration,* it was agreed unanimously that the awarding of the match to Mr. O'Connor be confirmed.

24th April 1942

The death of the President, Mr. Frank Egan, was recorded and a vote of sympathy passed. The meeting was late due to the fact that the Connaught *Club* (sic) had only recently elected their representatives.

The Close championships would this year be held at the Blackrock Club in Cork. (In 1941 the Elm Park club hosted the singles and Sunday's Well the doubles). In junior tournaments, the practice of victors' (parents) treating the defeated players was to be discouraged.

4th March 1943

Tennis balls become an issue. Elvery's could supply 500 dozen and it was decided to allocate the Councils the following amounts: Leinster 285 dozen, Munster 155 dozen and Connaught 60 dozen.

10th June 1943

The **Galway LTC** had requested (through a letter from their honorary secretary, Mr. W. A. F. Sandys) that their tournament be allowed to start on a Sunday. The Chairman of the meeting, M.H. Toppin (Munster), proposed that permission be granted. The honorary secretary, Mr. H.R. Maunsell (Leinster), seconded the motion. Apart from Mr. W.A. Sandys (Leinster) there were no other supporters and the motion was defeated 8 to 3.

27th April 1944

As no fees had been paid by the Connaught Council for 1943 it was decided that Tournaments in that Province would not be sanctioned until the fees were paid.

After a long discussion it was decided that permission would not be given for the holding of Open Irish Championships this year.

14th December 1945

Decision taken to enter a team in the Davis Cup. After a long discussion it was decided that inter-provincial matches would be arranged between the provinces themselves. Raymund Egan noted that the honorary secretary, Mr. Maunsell, had completed 25 years in that office and the Council expressed its congratulations. On the 4th December a dinner had been held in his honour in the Hibernian Hotel. In his thanks Mr. Maunsell

referred to *the presentation to him by the Lawn Tennis Players of Ireland of two Cups, a Painting and an Illustrated Address and expressed his desire to donate the two Cups to the I.L.T.A. to be held by that body as perpetual trophies to be presented each year to the man and woman adjudged by a Committee (to be appointed each year by the General Council) to have the best national record in Irish Lawn Tennis.* For that first year the committee appointed was the President (William St. G. Perrott), Henry St. J. Blake, Charles Mansergh, Raymund Egan, Alf Walsh and a representative nominated by the Ulster Council.

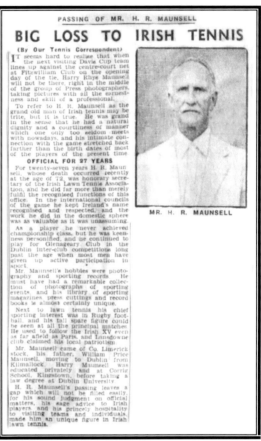

PASSING OF MR. H. R. MAUNSELL

BIG LOSS TO IRISH TENNIS

(By Our Tennis Correspondent)

IT seems hard to realise that when the next visiting Davis Cup team lines up against the centre-court net at Fitzwilliam Club on the opening day of the tie, Harry Rhys Maunsell will not be there, right in the middle of the group of Press photographers, taking pictures with all the earnestness and skill of a professional.

To refer to H. R. Maunsell as the grand old man of Irish tennis may be trite, but it is true. He was grand in the sense that he had a natural dignity and a courtliness of manner which one only too seldom meets with nowadays, and his intimate connection with the game stretched back farther than the birth dates of most of the players of the present time.

OFFICIAL FOR 27 YEARS

For twenty-seven years H. R. Maunsell, whose death occurred recently at the age of 72, was honorary secretary of the Irish Lawn Tennis Association, and he did far more than merely fulfil the recognised functions of this office. In the international councils of the game he kept Ireland's name recognised and respected, and the work he did in the domestic sphere was as valuable as it was unassuming.

As a player he never achieved championship class, but he was keenness personified, and he continued to play for Glenageary Club in the Dublin inter-club competitions long past the age when most men have given up active participation in sport.

Mr. Maunsell's hobbies were photography and sporting records. He must have had a remarkable collection of photographs of sporting events, and his library of sporting magazines, press cuttings and record books is almost certainly unique.

Next to lawn tennis his chief sporting interest was in Rugby football, and his tall spare figure could be seen at all the principal matches. He used to follow the Irish XV even as far afield as Paris, and Lansdowne club claimed his local patriotism.

Mr. Maunsell came of Co. Limerick stock, his father, William Price Maunsell, moving to Dublin from Kilmallock. Harry Maunsell was educated privately and at Corrig School, Kingstown, before taking a law degree at Dublin University.

H. R. Maunsell's passing leaves a gap which will not be filled easily, for his sound judgment on official matters, his sage advice to Irish players and his princely hospitality to visiting teams and individuals made him an unique figure in Irish lawn tennis.

MR. H. R. MAUNSELL

The 1948 Irish Independent obituary on the death of the long term honorary secretary of the ILTA.

5th June 1953

A meeting was called, between members representing the ILTA and **Fitzwilliam LTC**, to discuss the running of the Irish Championships.

20th January 1956

Due to the fact that a number of inferior tennis balls were appearing on the market, the Council felt it necessary to rule that only first-rate balls, approved by the LTA, would be accepted. At the time these were Dunlop Fort, Gray's Light Blue, A.W. Phillips Ltd., The Slazenger, Spalding LTA Official and Wisden.

9th November 1956

There had been ongoing correspondence, in relation to the application of re-instatement as an amateur by George Lyttleton Rogers, between the ILTA, the USLTA and the International Federation. To get over the impasse, after an amendment and a vote, it was agreed that Ireland re-instates him and advise the International Federation.

25th January 1957

In regard to the Irish Junior Championships a report a made to the Council on a Management Meeting for that event. .....*in future six Championship events should be run each year, viz:- Boys and Girls Singles under 18 and under 15 years, together with Boys Doubles and Girls Doubles. The entry to be limited to 64 competitors in each of the Singles events and 32 pairs in each of the Doubles. It was also agreed that due consideration shall be given to the qualifications of any entries which are put forward by any Provincial Council of the I.L.T.A. The mixed doubles event to remain a handicap one.*

The Hon. Secretary stated that the Fitzwilliam members of the Committee had been most sympathetic and co-operative in the whole matter and that whereas he personally would have liked to know that no entry would be turned down, nevertheless he reluctantly agreed that in the limited time available it was not possible to stage the Championships in conditions other than those set forth.

The Council felt that their representatives had been met by the Club in a very businesslike way and the Hon. Secretary was instructed to write to Fitzwilliam expressing the Council's appreciation.

8th March 1957

Extensive discussions took place on whether Ireland should send a team to an unsettled Hungary for the Davis Cup match in Budapest. On the 5th November 1956 Krushchev had ordered tanks to crush the democracy movement. A few weeks earlier there had been open defiance of the Soviet Union with hundreds of thousands of demonstrators on the streets shouting anti-Soviet slogans and demanding the departure of Soviet troops. The leader of the democracy movement, Imre Nagy disappeared, about 25, 000 were killed and 200,000 fled the country.

At the ILTA meeting the safety of the players was of major concern. A motion to send the team was ultimately defeated by 8 votes to 6. Among the comments was one from C. Boden who had talked to members of the Hungarian table tennis team who had said that the internal situation in their country was grim. A letter was to be sent to Hungary requesting an alternative venue. Several letters on the matter are included in the minutes book. The one from the Hungary association (dated 2nd February 1957) looked forward to the match. It has one or two interesting sentences included:

As to the place of the meetings we propose our People's Stadium, or a Tennis Count we shall build separately for the meetings, or the Tennis Stadium on the Maegaret Island, on red cinder court base.

Please indicate us your wishes regarding victuallings, lodgings, that we should make our utmost to satisfy all your wishes in this respect.

Belgium, who was due to play the winner, had also written and was interested to know our views on the matter.

29th March 1957

A special meeting of the Council was called due to deal with this matter. *A very full and lengthy discussion took ensued in which practically every Councillor present took part and finally the motion* (to travel) *was defeated by 13 votes to 8.*

Alf Walsh was the honorary secretary of the Irish Lawn Tennis Association from 1949 to 1971. He was the Irish representative for many years at international meetings. In 1963 and 1970 he was the president of the ILTA. He took over the role of running Irish tennis from Harry Maunsell and added his own touch of style and humour to this important honorary position.

31st May 1957

The Management Committee of the European Zone of the Davis Cup were requesting a fine of £25 for defaulting on our match with Hungary. It was agreed to send this fine but point out that the Clause in Rule 23 which *refers to a default being made "without sufficiently good cause"* and that Ireland should not be liable for this fine. [According to Alan Trengove (1991) in the 'Story of the Davis Cup' *They* (Ireland) *were unsuccessful in trying to get the tie transferred to Ireland or a neutral country. At the subsequent Davis Cup Nations meeting Ireland wanted the rules changed to cover such contingencies. A majority of delegates felt that politics should not interfere with sport and voted against the Irish motion. The episode foreshadowed the coming political problems over South Africa.*]

2nd May 1958

The International Federation report on Amateurism was discussed

20th February 1959

A rugby match (versus France on the 18th April) and play on Sunday (19th April) lead to lengthy discussions on dates for our match versus New Zealand in the Davis Cup. The agreed motion, proposed by T.S. Duncan, was that *In the exceptional circumstances the match be played in the week commencing Monday 13th April, and on Sunday the 19th April if the Match Committee so decided, such decision not to be taken as a precedent*
.

10th July 1959

A matter of concern to Provincial Councils was the number of guests being invited to inter-provincial functions and the cost associated with such numbers. A common policy was agreed. During July 1959 the ILTA was kept busy with the first visit of the International federation to Ireland. There was great support from sponsors for this event.

14th October 1960

A memorandum on Open tennis, prepared by the honorary secretary, Alf Walsh, was discussed in detail and passed. It was to be sent to the International Federation where the issue was to lead to a major overhaul during the 1960s. One key item in the Memorandum was that *It is the opinion of the Irish L.T. Association that no change should be made in the present definitions of Amateur and Professional players, and that any attempts to introduce a third category of player would reduce to ridicule the rules of the International Federation.* Apparently, a number of players had formed a group, not affiliated to any association or federation, for the purposes of playing exhibition tennis for profit.

9th December 1960

A new Inter-Provincial competition for players under 23 was suggested. The Guinness company, through Guy Jackson, have agreed to sponsor two young people for each of the next three years in order to gain playing experience abroad.

24th March 1961

Derek Arthurs and Michael Hickey received this sponsorship for the first year and arrangements had been made that they would play on the Riviera, Mr. V. Landan, an old Monagasque Davis Cup player, agreed to keep an eye on them.

4th May 1962

The President, Walter Nicholl, pointed out that the honorary secretary had been associated with the ILTA for 37 years and, on his suggestion, he be made President for 1963 *whilst he was in a position to enjoy the Presidency.* The proposal was passed by acclamation.

29th November 1963

During 1963, Alf Walsh uniquely held the office of President and honorary secretary of the ILTA. At this meeting, he thanked George Woods who acted as honorary secretary during the year, and suggested he be appointed as such in 1964. Alf himself was to be 73 in a few days and he thought it prudent that someone else become 'au fait' with the post of honorary secretary. This proposal was agreed.

30th January 1965

The Guinness Award scheme was discussed. The honorary secretary said that more publicity should be given to Guinness in thanks for their support for Irish tennis. The recipients of disbursements over the previous few years were Derek Arthurs (Belfast), Michael Rainey (Ballymena), Michael Hickey (Limerick), Lorna Croskery (Belfast), Eleanor O'Neill (Bettystown), Margaret Burns (Enniscorthy), Geraldine Houlihan (Birr), John O' Rourke (Dublin), Jim Buckley (Dublin) and Frank McArdle (Dundalk).

26th November 1965

This was the first Council meeting since April and a number of matters relating to the Irish Championships were brought up. Apparently, the televising of the last two days was cancelled by the *unilateral action of the Fitzwilliam Club.* This was obviously one of those niggly issues. Open tournaments also came into the discussion. The club had hosted this event since it's inception and yet the ILTA were there to represent Irish tennis. A long discussion ensued during which the Council unanimously agreed the following items:

(a) That *"Open Tournaments" should be entirely divorced from any discussion.*

(b) That *a similar position years ago had been resolved by a joint meeting and this should be repeated.*

(c) That *the granting of a Permit for the 1966 Championships should be conditional.*

(d) That *the Club should be told that a meeting was a necessity and that the Association represented the Country as a whole.*

(e) That *the Hon. Secretary should write to Mr. Kilcoyne* [the Hon. Sec. at **Fitzwilliam LTC**] *informing him of that fact and request an early agreement to a meeting.*

Betty Lombard announces her retirement from the Council and was thanked for her work for Irish tennis for so many years.

2nd September 1966

Since the previous December many meetings had taken place between the ILTA and **Fitzwilliam LTC** on the matter of the Championships, which included televising of same, loss of funds, the Championships committee etc. In the final analysis, the event was televised by RTE and the fee given to the club. The ILTA decided to take the matter into hand. A rule was agreed that *the*

I.L.T.A. reserves its right to negotiate any radio or television with the governing body (R.T.E.) and to accept and dispose of any fee payable. The meeting also *recommended that each Council should inform Club's in its Province that applications for the Irish Championships for 1967 were invited in the event that they were withheld from Fitzwilliam.*

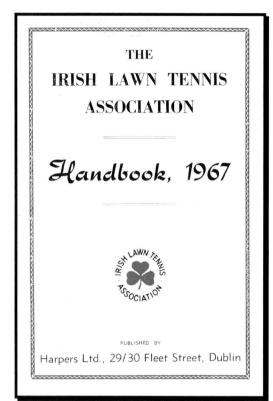

THE

IRISH LAWN TENNIS ASSOCIATION

Handbook, 1967

PUBLISHED BY

Harpers Ltd., 29/30 Fleet Street, Dublin

1967 Yearbook

Honorary Secretary: Alf Walsh:

Against England we went one better than last year being defeated by 8 matches to 3, with three matches so close that a little luck might have given us victory.

However, the Triangular Event was our biggest shock and one finds it difficult to relish our performance in being beaten by Scotland 8 events to nil and also by Wales by 5 events to 3....

Tennis is one of the games which can be played for most of one's life and provides health, exercise and enjoyment, all the more so if one is able to play fairly well. Tennis is a fascinating game, giving great scope for thought, and in addition develops both control and character.

3rd May 1968

The honorary secretary reported on the International Federation meeting held in Paris on the 30th March. "Open tennis" was agreed. It was noted at the ILTA meeting that Ireland's proposal in *establishing the legitimate status of an amateur, was incorporated in the decision.*

21st September 1968

The new Federation Rules were discussed. The category of players would be 'professional', 'registered player' and 'amateurs'. The registered player could not play in events for amateurs only and would not be eligible to make tennis his profession nor be paid for teaching the game. The 'professional' player could not play in the Davis or Federation Cup competitions. An 'amateur' could play in events with or against professionals without losing his/her status.

10th May 1969

Charlie Brennan reported on the Nestle Schools tournament. He noted that the number of schools entered this year was 137, as opposed to 115 in 1968.

30th January 1970

It was agreed that the eligibility date for under 18 events be changed from 1st January 1970 to 31st December 1969, in line with the ILTF rules.

22nd May 1970

The President said it was gratifying to see Fitzwilliam and ILTA working together in harmony at the Davis Cup Match today. The Council decided to appoint a Press Officer *with the responsibility of improving press relations.*

Dudley Magrath from Ulster was the Irish Lawn Tennis Association president in 1967 and 1971.

5th March 1971

The close championships were to be held at Rushbrooke and the honorary secretary asked that *some*

The History of Irish Tennis

attempt should be made to trace the present whereabouts of the trophies and perhaps Munster might try to do the needful.

4th June 1971

It was agreed that two cups be obtained for the veterans' championship being held in conjunction with the Irish Championships.

19th November 1971

Ted Parslow circulated an Interim report of the Coaching Committee. It was pointed out that during the previous year 55 centres were visited and some 3000 players received coaching.

25th February 1972

The Council considered the reports by the ILTA sub-committee that had been set up a year previously with a view to carrying out a self-analysis on the ILTA. The sub-committee included F.H. O' Donoghue (chairman), Mrs. June Ann Le C. Byrne, Robin Donovan, Ted Parslow and Samuel Tuff. Accepted, among the recommendations was that each Branch would elect its own Provincial Branch at a Provincial meeting. Rejected was the suggestion that the General Council should have a Vice-President who would be the President elect for the following year.

14th April 1972

It was agreed that teaching professionals would be eligible for ranking provided they played in two tournaments in Ireland sanctioned by the ILTA. They would, however, be ineligible for the Maunsell trophy awards.

On the proposal of Mrs. Flinn, and seconded by Mr. K. O' Brien, Mr. Alf Walsh was acclaimed as an honorary Life Member of the ILTA *in recognition of his service to tennis.*

1979 Yearbook
(President: Donal Dempsey)

We can play lawn tennis for relaxation or for competition........for most of us a leisurely, relaxing game in the evening in pleasant surroundings is our aim.

Forward thinking as evidence by our recent progress must not cease. We operate in a changing environment and at club level we must seek to promote this change, not to oppose it. Clubs which do not progress stagnate and die.....

2nd February 1974

The notice for this meeting, interestingly, due to start at 9.30 a.m. at **Fitzwilliam LTC**, allocates a time limit for each item. These varied from 5 minutes for the Minutes and 5 minutes for matters arising up to 40 minutes for the Election of Sub-Committees. For the record, these were [1] Coaching, [2] Davis Cup, [3] Emergency, [4] Finance, [5] Grounds and Development, [6] Junior Selection, [7] Presidential, [8] Representatives to Davis Cup and ILTF meetings, [9] Representatives to Committee of Irish Championships (Open, Junior and Hard Court) and [10] Senior Selection, Ranking and Maunsell Trophies.

3rd May 1974

The Secretary told the meeting that he had received an anonymous sponsorship of £250 towards the cost of sending the [Federation Cup] team to Naples. In addition to going to Naples the team had been invited to play in Rome....Mrs. Flinn had agreed to travel to Naples at her own expense to act as Captain for the team.

2nd June 1974

This meeting was held at O' Meara's Hotel, Nenagh. This tied in with the holding of the Senior Interprovincial Championships, which were won by Ulster. Apparently, a sponsor was prepared to cover the cost of holding the Federation Cup in Ireland. *After some discussion it was decided not to apply for the event.*

Ken Potterton was ILTA president in 1974.

30th November 1974

The revision of the rules of the ILTA, drafted by Walter Nicholl of Ulster, were again considered and agreed.

19th April 1975

A new under 14 interprovincial event was agreed and would be called the *Green Shield Juvenile Interprovincials*.

8th June 1975

It was agreed that unless the [hand]*book could be available within the next two weeks it would be useless.*

4th October 1975

It was reported that Ireland had beaten Wales 6/4 in a Junior International at Fitzwilliam on the 27th September. The team was Jerry Sheehan, John Biscomb, Jo Sheridan and Vivien Lee. David Miley and Tom Shelly had been sent to the international Student Games where they were runner-up in the doubles.

Dr. Jim O'Neill from Cork was the Irish Lawn Tennis Association president in 1971.

15th November 1975

The annual dinner was discussed. *The general opinion was that the dinner was no longer a great attraction.* It was agreed that it should be dropped.

Mr. Egan pointed out that it was not necessary that the [Maunsell] *trophies should be awarded to the No. 1 on the* [ranking] *list. Matters such as behaviour etc. should be taken into account.* Some details on the visit of the European Secretaries to Dublin were finalised. One of the issues of the time, to be brought to that body, was that of the anti-apartheid group.

20th June 1976

A press Reception to launch the new Yearbook had been held in Fitzwilliam on the 22nd June 1976. Those present had been very impressed by the Book. Mr. O' Donoghue was congratulated on the producing of such a fine first book.

16th June 1977

After trials, Louise Tuff and Peter Lawlor were selected as Ireland's representatives for Junior Wimbledon. While Peter was accepted, Louise was not as there had been 40 entries for 32 places and form at international tournaments, which Louise had not played in, was used for the selection.

1978 Yearbook
(No author given)

Ever since it was founded seventy years ago, the ILTA has been run on a purely voluntary basis with Honorary Officers. The feeling now prevailing is that if Irish tennis is to move ahead at a pace similar to the way in which the game has develop din other countries, the ILTA must have a full time paid Secretariat. A Committee under the Chairmanship of Trustee Terry Duncan has been sitting and most of the plans have been made.

7th October 1978

Father Winder reported on the Junior Interprovincials held at Clongowes Wood College. *Some difficulties had still to be overcome with regard to the running of this event in Clongowes and he recommended that a sub committee be set up to outline a policy on how to supervise the children and this policy should be sent to the participants.* It was decided that Henry Lappin, Mavis Hogg, Pauline Daly, Donal Dempsey and Father Winder be on this committee.

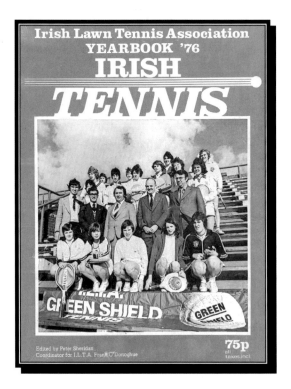

1979 Yearbook
(President Peter Bayliss)

I believe we are on the brink of a 'boom time' for tennis in Ireland. With the financial assistance available from Government sources both North and South of the border our coaches will be holding more and more courses designed firstly to improve the overall standard of play in clubs and schools and secondly to ensure that our better players are given every opportunity to reach the top.

1981/82 Yearbook
(President Paddy Donnellan)

This year, for the first time, our team successfully came through the Kings Cup Competition beating Spain, Portugal and Switzerland, to meet and beat Yugoslavia and Belgium in the final stages, thus qualifying for Division I tennis next year. With dreams of the past now becoming a reality, we can look forward to our tennis future with greater confidence and enthusiasm than ever before.

1983 Yearbook
(President: Mavis Hogg)

If you were to ask me what was the most important thing in tennis to me, I would have to answer, "my club".....Like so many other people, not only did "my club" as the centre of my sporting life, but also my social life.........

Why do I tell you this? Because I feel very strongly that most tennis players in Ireland feel as I do.........The provincial Councils and the Irish Association are only as strong as the administrators sent to them by their clubs.

1984 Yearbook
(President: Pauline Daly)

.......I salute the four Provincial Councils. Do the players realise how much work councillors do for the promotion of the game.

1st December 1984

During the year a sub-committee had prepared a set of rules for the awarding of The Raymund Egan Memorial Trophy. At this meeting, the recommendation of the first holder would be *Dr. J.P. O' Neill of Munster in consideration of his work on the Irish and Munster Councils and in particular his work with Juniors and for Coaching. This was unanimously approved. It was agreed that the President should present the Trophy to Dr. O'Neill in Cork.*

28th January 1984

After extensive discussion on the best way forward, to improve playing standards, and, in particular, coaching and training techniques, it was agreed to set up a 'working party' to consider the matter.

1985

At the meeting on the 25th May the President, Pauline Daly, had the following sad new to record. *The President referred to the recent death of Dr. Jim O' Neill who had been President of the Association, Convenor of the Coaching Committee and latterly a Trustee of the Association. His passing was a great loss to tennis in Ireland and particularly in Munster. The*

members observed two minutes silence as a mark of respect for Dr. O' Neill.

Two small items that arose in the proceedings of the Council of 1985 required letters of clarification from the honorary secretary. One involved a player who had applied to enter Junior Wimbledon directly. The player had to be informed that the proper etiquette was through the National Association. A senior player was informed that, despite the apparent information received by them from a councillor, there was no such ban imposed by the council on that player captaining teams....*Selection Committees were free to select any captain they wished, subject to the approval of the Council.*

1986-Charlie Brennan receiving his chain of office from outgoing President, Pauline Daly.

1986 Yearbook
(President: Charlie Brennan)

I was fortunate to be involved in the planning and development of the new ILTA Wright Indoor Tennis Centre at Kiltiernan opened during 1985 and it is my hope that it will continue to expand and prosper this year.

John Taylor, the former badminton international, was appointed during the year as the first Chief Executive. *The appointment of John Taylor will serve to go a long way towards achieving this aim.* (i.e. that of a full time executive to look after our affairs).

14th June 1986

John Taylor reported to the meeting on his first six months in the position of Chief Executive. While it thought initially he would devote half of his time to ILTA administration, and the other half to the new Tennis Foundation, he in fact found the administration and related duties took up more and more time and *highlighted the need for more back-up administration staff.*

He had many other useful comments to make. Some were as follows. *Many* (Council*) members were serving on too many committees and he felt that there was a need to involve more non-members to serve. ...working weekends should be held to motivate committees. Communication was a real problem and more* communication between the various committees would be helpful.

He intended to proceed with the investigation of a scheme for national registration and a national ranking system which he felt would help to rationalise the financial situation.

John Taylor closed by saying that friction in internal relations both in the General Council and at Provincial Council level was damaging to the image of tennis and could cause serious problems when seeking sponsorship. He appealed for an end to such friction in the interests of promoting the game.

1987 Yearbook
(President: Peter Bayliss)

While success at international level is most important if we are to capture the interest of young boys and girls in Ireland in this game, I hope we will never forget that good sportsmanship both on and off the court is the best possible advertisement for Irish tennis.

Chief Executive: John Taylor:

Our role in the Irish Lawn Tennis Association is to co-ordinate and promote tennis activity around the country, to run national and international events and to ensure that Irish tennis is properly represented at home and abroad.

This is not an easy task and it may appear at times that we are a little aloof from the average tennis players. One of our objectives for 1987 is to improve communications with the clubs and players generally......

1988 Yearbook
(President: Helen Clinton)

Coaching is a major priority with all the Councils. Squads have been set up in the Provinces together with a National Junior Squad. We were very pleased during 1987 to have the formal launching of the Irish Tennis Foundation. The aims of the foundation are to assist in the development of Irish Tennis by raising and then dispersing funds for special projects.

1989 Yearbook
(President: Michael McCann)

I am convinced that to ensure the development of tennis in this country the I.L.T.A. must concentrate its energies in two broad areas: (a) the promotion of the game among a wider population both geographically and socially and (b) the promotion of excellence among our top players.

1990 Yearbook
(President: Dr. Gerry More O'Ferrall)

In 1989 a three-year strategic plan for the development of Irish Tennis was approved by the General Council. The first step in the implementation of this plan was the appointment last July of Matt Doyle as National Coach and Marketing Director. Much of the work now being undertaken by Tennis Ireland could not have been

considered without the support of Cospoir and the increased funding from the national lottery. Many Clubs throughout the country have upgraded their facilities (social and playing) during the past decade so that many now have top class pavilions, while most now have all-weather courts, many of which are floodlit. This has made tennis a 12 month game which can be played 16 or 18 hours a day.

Dubliner John Taylor was appointed Chief Executive of the Irish Lawn Tennis Association in 1986. He was a former number 1 on the Irish badminton team.

1993 Yearbook
(President: James Brewster)

As part of the three-year plan, *Matt Doyle ran a talent search in all 4 provinces to try to identify athletic children to develop their skills. The data we collected will be invaluable for the future, and this scheme will be expanded in 1993.We held the first Level 2 coaches courses under the new syllabus develop here in Ireland. This gives a major extension to the Coaches training period but provides a much improved course.*

1994 Yearbook
(President: Roy Thompson)

During the year a "Market Audit" of Tennis Ireland and the game itself was undertaken by consultants to establish the status of the game, its public image, its potential and the role played by Tennis Ireland in its administration. The audit report highlighted several areas in need of improvement.

1998 Yearbook
(President: Olwyn Raftery)

This year we can look forward to the introduction of the TSB Grade Scheme whereby every tennis player in Ireland will be given a grading based on playing ability. All standards of play, from beginner to professional, will be accommodated in the system.

Tennis Ireland Magazine
(June/July Edition 1998)

Editor: Des Allen:
*As we go to press, we have just concluded the details of a substantial financial package which will allow us stage two weeks of Men's Professional Tennis at Riverview-**Men's Futures** from 1ˢᵗ-13ᵗʰ June 1998.This means we will have both Men's and Ladies ranking events in Ireland this year.*

Tennis Ireland Magazine
(Dec-Jan '99)

Editor: Des Allen:
Change is the only constant...Change is all around us.....Growth through change...sounds a bit like business conference babble but the concept is every bit as relevant in sport and in tennis as we reach the end of the century.....

Tennis Ireland will experiment with changes in the scoring of a game (N-Ad scoring) and also experiment with removing the "Let" in service from 1ˢᵗ January 1999..........let me know your reaction.

Tennis Ireland Magazine
(Winter Edition 1999)

Editor: Des Allen:
Our full-time players in the ladies game have reached unprecedented levels in world rankings-modest by the standards of the leading Tennis nations but reasonably comparable, for instance, with the standards in the U.K.....

On the down side, most of our problems relate to money or the lack of it. There is never enough.

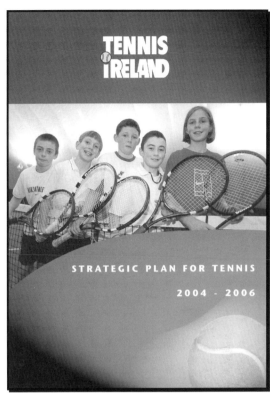

A recent Tennis Ireland professionally-prepared developed plan for tennis in this country.

The Tennis Ireland Council met in on the 12ᵗʰ June 2004 on the occasion of the opening of Portadown Tennis Club. From left: Seamus McCusker (president 2003-2004), Des Allen (chief executive), Tony Locke (honorary treasurer 2003-2006), Olwyn Raftery (president, 1998-1999 & 2002-2003), James Foley (president (2004-2005), Dee Jennings (president 2005-2006), Frank Goodman (honorary secretary 2001-2002) and George Stevenson (honorary secretary, 2002-2006)

Irish Lawn Tennis Association/Tennis Ireland-Presidents

1913-1923	Colonel Arthur Henry Courtenay [L]	Fitzwilliam LTC
1924-1929	The Right Honorable Lord Glenavy [L]	Fitzwilliam LTC
1930	Captain Robert (*Bob*) P. Corry [U]	Windsor LTC
1931	Dr. J. E. McCausland [M]	
1932	Dr. W.L. Murphy [L]	
1933	Dr. Thomas B. Pedlow [U]	Lurgan LTC
1934	Captain A.H.C.C. Home [M]	
1935	The Honorable Mr. Justice Henry Hanna [L]	Lansdowne LTC
1936	De Vere L. Crossley [U]	Belfast Boat Club
1937	Mr. Kingsmills B. Williams [M]	Mallow LT & Croquet Club
1938	Captain William Campbell [C]	County Sligo LTC
1939	Simon F. Scroope [L]	Fitzwilliam LTC
1940	Mr. Kingsmills B. Williams [M]	Mallow LT & Croquet Club
1941	Frank Egan [L]	Lansdowne LTC
1942	E.C. Harrington [M]	
1943	Henry St. J. Blake [C]	Galway LTC
1944-1945	William St. George Perrott [L]	Donnybrook LTC
1946	John (*Jack*) N. Colville [U]	Windsor LTC
	De Vere L. Crossley [U]	Belfast Boat Club
1947	Charles Ogilvy Mansergh [M]	Tipperary County LTC
1948	Henry St. J. Blake [C]	Galway LTC
1949	Senator Edward A. McGuire [L]	Fitzwilliam LTC
1950	A.S. Carse Burton [U]	Willowfield LTC/Hawarden LTC
1951	J. St. J. Riordan [M]	
1952	Henry St. J. Blake [C]	Galway LTC
1953	A. Percy Huet [L]	
1954	Terry S. Duncan [U]	Belfast Boat Club
1955	Frank J. Mockler [M]	Sunday's Well Boating & LTC
1956	Henry St. J. Blake [C]	Galway LTC
1957	Harry F. Cronin [M]	Rushbrooke LT & Croquet Club
1958	Dennis F. Wheeler [U]	Bangor LTC/Hawarden LTC
1959	Harry F. Cronin [M]	Rushbrooke LT & Croquet Club
1960	Michael J. Heverin [C]	Castlebar TC
1961	Raymond F. Egan [L]	Lansdowne LTC
1962	Walter G. Nicholl [U]	City of Belfast YMCA
1963	Alf Walsh [L]	Railway & Steam Packet Union LTC /NorwoodLTC
1964	Eric Harte-Barry [M]	Mallow LT & Croquet Club
1965	Terry McCarthy [C]	Galway LTC
1966	Larry F. Stein [L]	Dundalk LTC
1967	J. A. Dudley Magrath [U]	Annadale Grammar School
1968	Willie J. O'Regan [M]	Sundays Well Boating & LTC
1969	John Garavan [C]	Castlebar TC
1970	Alfred (*Alf*) H.Walsh [L]	Railway & Steam Packet Union LTC /Norwood LTC
1971	J. A. Dudley Magrath [U]	Annadale Grammar School
1972	Frank H. O'Donoghue [M]	St. Anne's Waterford LTC
1973	Donal F. Dempsey [C]	Galway LTC
1974	Kenneth W.E. Potterton [L]	Edenderry/Naas LTCs
1975	Douglas J.P. Ferguson [U]	Cavehill LTC
1976	Dr.James (*Jim*) P. O'Neill [M]	Sundays Well Boating & LTC
1977	Donal F.Dempsey [C]	Galway LTC

Presidents (continued)

1978	Charles (*Charlie*) J. Brennan [L]	Celbridge LTC/Marian Arts LTC/ Sutton LTC/Elm Park LTC
1978	Peter S.F. Bayliss [U]	CIYMS LTC
1979	Redmond Holland [M]	Collins LTC
1980	Donal Dempsey [C]	Galway LTC
1981	Patrick G.Donnellan [L]	Stackallen Tennis and P & P Club
1982	Mavis Hogg MBE [U]	Hawarden LTC
1984-1985	Pauline Daly [M]	Nenagh LTC/Lattin LTC
1986	Charles J. Brennan [L]	Marian Arts LTC/Sutton LTC
1987	Peter S.F.Bayliss [U]	CIYMS LTC
1988	Helen Clinton [M]	Hillview LTC
1989	Michael McCann [C]	Galway LTC
1990	Gerry More O'Ferrall [L]	Castleknock LTC
1991	Anne Taylor [U]	Queens University Staff LTC
1992	Rhoda McAuliffe [M]	St. Michael's LTC
1993	James Brewster [L]	Brookfield LTC
1994	Roy Thompson [C]	Galway LTC
1995	George Stevenson [U]	Bangor LTC
1996	Kay Stanton [M]	Sunday's Well Boating & LTC
1997	Ciaran O'Donovan [L]	Naas LTC/Templeogue LTC
1998	Olywn Raftery [C]	Galway LTC
1999	Walter Hall [U]	Belfast Boat Club
2000	Maria O'Sullivan [M]	Douglas LTC
2001	David Nathan [L]	Thorndale LTC/Glasnevin LTC/ Skerries LTC
2002	Olywn Raftery [C]	Galway LTC
2003	Seamus Mc Cusker [U]	Irvinestown TC
2004	James Foley [M]	Sunday's Well Boating & LTC
2005	Dee Jennings [L]	Kilkenny County & City LTC/ Donnybrook LTC
2006	Maria Kilkelly [C]	Castlebar TC

Irish Lawn Tennis Association/Tennis Ireland

At the 1998 launching of the TSB sponsored Grading Scheme were (from left) Olywn Raftery (president, Tennis Ireland), Dee Jennings (president, Leinster Branch), Elena Moore (Charleville LTC) & Joe Flood (Leinster Branch). Olwyn had a second term in office as president in 2002. In Connacht Olwyn has served as honorary secretary (2000, 2001, 2003 & 2004) and president (1996 & 1997). Joe was Leinster Branch president in 1996 and Dee in 2001.Dee was president of Tennis Ireland in 2005.

Irish Lawn Tennis Association/Tennis Ireland

Tony Locke (Charleville LTC) became the honorary treasurer of Tennis Ireland in 2003.

After many years as an administrator in Ulster, George Stevenson (Bangor LTC) became Tennis Ireland president in 1995, and its honorary secretary in 2002.

Honorary Secretaries

1908-1920	Alfred Beckett [L]	Dublin Univ. LTC/Fitzwilliam LTC/Gallery LTC
1920-1948	Harry R. Maunsell [L]	Glenageary LTC/Fitzwilliam LTC
1949-1971	Alfred H.Walsh [L]	Railway & Steam Packet Union LTC/Norwood LTC
1972 (acting)	G.W. Woods [L]	Leinster Stratford LTC
1973-1984	Charlie Brennan [L]	Celbridge LTC/Marian ArtsLTC/Sutton LTC/Elm Park
1985	Charlie Brennan [L] & Mavis Hogg [U]	Celbridge LTC/Marian ArtsLTC/Sutton LTC/Elm Park Hawarden LTC
1986-1992	Mavis Hogg [U]	Hawarden LTC
1993-1997	Frank Goodman [L]	Charleville LTC
1999-2000	Ciaran O'Donovan [L]	Naas LTC/Templeogue LTC
2001-2002	Frank Goodman [L]	Charleville LTC
2002-2005	George Stevenson [U]	Bangor LTC

Honorary Treasurers

1908-1948	William St. George Perrott [L]	Donnybrook LTC/Lansdowne LTC
1949-1972	Kevin O'Brien-Kenney [L]	Claremont LTC
1973-1976	Frank H. O'Donoghue [M]	St. Anne's Waterford LTC/Tramore LTC
1977-1981	Fergus O'Shee [L]	Sutton LTC
1981-1983	Reverend Percy Winder S. J. [L]	Clongowes Wood College
1984-1991	Bryan O'Neill [L]	Monkstown LTC (County Dublin)
1992-1993.01	Peter Kelly [L]	Lansdowne LTC
1994	James Brewster [L]	Brookfield LTC
1995-1996	Roy Thompson [C]	Galway LTC
1997-2001	Tony Locke [L]	Charleville LTC
2002	David Nathan [L]	Thorndale LTC/Glasnevin LTC/Skerries LTC
2003-2005	Tony Locke [L]	Charleville LTC

4.3 *Branch Organisation*

W. J. Poole was deemed to have resigned because of his failure to attend meetings and answer letters from HRM (nearly a hanging offence!). [A 1938 incidence relating to the Leinster branch, Harry Rhys Maunsell (HRM) was the honorary secretary at the time]

In terms of regional sport in Ireland the division of the country into four provincial branches is similar to many sports. This spreads the workload as well as securing a local interest. It has meant imbalances in many sports where Connacht, in many cases, would have a smaller number playing and poorer facilities than in other provinces. Exceptions might include the sports of golf and Gaelic Games. In tennis the game gradually had a provincial base despite the fact that as early 1908, the year the ILTA was founded, provision was made in Rule II *to arrange Inter-National, Inter-Provincial, and other matches.* In Rule IV we find that of eighteen Members of the Association's Committee, four were to be elected from each province.

Before the ILTA the Dublin Lawn Tennis Council functioned. At the AGM of the ILTA on the 24th April 1922 it was agreed that the Belfast Lawn Tennis Council be established. Four years later, at the ILTA AGM on the 26th January 1926 it was agreed that the incoming committee consider the setting up of branches in each province. At the Extraordinary General Meeting of the ILTA on the 24th January 1927 new rules agreed that these branches would form and elect their own representatives to the ILTA Council. The first meeting of the Council of the ILTA after the EGM was held on the 22nd April 1927. Nominations from Ulster, Munster and Leinster were taken at this meeting. Connacht would fall under the umbrella of the Leinster branch until 1933. For many years the terms *Council* and *Branch* have been used loosely. If we look at the Rules of the ILTA as printed in the 1967 Handbook it is clear that the Association is *formed of Irish Lawn Tennis Clubs* and that it is managed by the *General Council, with four Provincial Councils.* The word branch had no official rule in the rules. As is the case in many sports, the term is often used to refer to the sport's activity (or specifically its management committee) within a province. In the popular use of branch all players know exactly what is meant. If the branch decides on something or takes a specific action then it will be the council or one of its sub-committees that is being referred to. In the new format handbook in 1991 we find 'Branch' getting recognition side by side with the word council, council becoming a reference to the general committee of the branch. The official programme for the Ireland-South Africa Davis Cup match, held from the 6th to the 9th May 1927, summarises the thinking at the time. The small article included the following:

Owing to the number of affiliated Clubs having nearly doubled (since the ILTA was formed in 1908) it was found that the working of the Association was becoming difficult without the assistance of paid officials, and it was decided to frame a new

The Campbell Cup (Senior) Winners in 1939 and 1940 were Merville Lawn Tennis Club, Sligo. Back (l. to r.): Jimmy Hender, Bridie Dunne, Martin Mulligan (Club honorary secretary), Maureen Ruhan and Finola Flattery. Front (l. to r.) Gerry Westby (Captain, 1940), Maeve Flattery, Bill Jennings, Eithne Flattery, Charlie Cunningham and Nell Wilson.

Constitution consisting of three Provincial Councils one representing Leinster and Connacht, one representing Ulster and one representing Munster, the representation on the General Council being governed by the number of Clubs in each Provincial Council. This constitution is now formed, the representation of the Leinster, Ulster and Munster Provincial Councils on the General Council being 11, 6 and 4 respectively. Each Provincial Council arranges the Tournaments in its Province and collects the subscriptions from the affiliated Clubs in its Province. The arrangement for Inter-Provincial Matches is left to each Provincial Council.

Connacht

In 1938, the May-July edition of the new *Irish Sports Review* had an article reviewing sport in Connacht, penned by "Shuttle". The following is the brief piece dealing with tennis.

The unusual spell of fine weather experienced last month led players on an early move, and hard courts were made full use of; but the unfortunate thing was that so few first-class hard courts are to be found. This fact must have a bearing upon the standard of tennis not alone in Connacht but throughout Eire.

Quite a few clubs have officially opened their courts for the season-one of the first being Ballinasloe club. Tuam, too, were early in the field, while University College, Galway, have already played three friendly matches. The Galway Commercial Club has been hard at it for the past month, and their two hard courts have been in constant use. The Galway County and Blackrock Clubs have yet to open this season. The delay has been occasioned by the recent improvements carried out at the headquarters by way of putting down two first-class hard courts. The formation of a new club in Ballina with four splendid new courts will be welcomed, and the enthusiastic committee who are responsible for its formation are to be congratulated. The first captain is Mr. Matt O'Dowd, a well-known enthuastic of badminton and tennis.

The competition for the Campbell Cup, open to Connacht clubs, will this year be keener than ever, and the present holders-Galway County club-will be very hard to retain the trophy. Chief opposition will probably come from their immediate neighbour, the Blackrock club.

Sligo, possessing as it does some four first-class clubs, is a force always to be reckoned with, and will also have a very strong part in the competition. However, it is rather early yet to foretell; but as clubs begin to find their feet, there will be quite a few surprises.

The earliest available Minutes book for Connacht includes Minutes of the AGM held in the Imperial Hotel, Claremorris (County Mayo) on Saturday the 11th April 1942. Henry St. J. Blake was in the chair. Also at the meeting were T. Doyle (**Castlebar TC**), Andy Dolan (**Merville LTC**), P. McEllin (**Claremorris LTC**) and Martin Mulligan (**Merville**

LTC), all on the Council at the time, and Gerry Westby from the **Merville LTC**. Mr. M. Dwyer (**Clonalis LTC**), honorary secretary and honorary treasurer, *was not in attendance and failed to send a report to the meeting.* The following were elected for the coming season: Henry St. J. Blake (**Galway LTC**), J. J. McGettrick (**Ballymote LTC**), Henry Pitman (**Sligo YMCA**), T. Doyle (**Castlebar TC**), P. McEllin (**Claremorris LTC**), Andy Dolan (**Merville LTC**), R. H. Tilson (**Ballina LTC**), James McLoughlin (**Westport LTC**), Martin Mulligan (**Merville LTC**), W. A. F. Sandys (**Galway LTC**), J. Keane, M. Dwyer (**Clonalis LTC**), P. J. Brady and Gerry Westby (**Merville LTC**).

On the proposal of the chairman and seconded by A.J. Dolan, the following proposal was passed unanimously: *That owing to limitations on travelling due to existing conditions we deem it desirable that an Emergency Council be formed to transact all business of the Connaught Council until the first Annual Provincial Meeting after the cessation of the war. Such Emergency Council to have all the powers of a Provincial Council allowed by the Rules of the Irish Lawn Tennis Association, and all further powers as may be from time to time delegated to them by the General Council. Such Emergency Council to consist of seven members, the Officers to be the elected annual from the Councils. The President to be an ex – officio member of Council. The above resolution to be subject to the sanction of the General Council.*

The first Council meeting was held immediately after this AGM with the following elected, all unanimously: president: Henry St. J. Blake; Vice-President: A. J. Dolan (**Clonalis LTC**); honorary secretary & honorary treasurer: M. Mulligan (**Merville LTC**); Auditor: J.A. McFadden; Representatives to the General Council: Henry St. J. Blake and M. Mulligan.; Emergency Council: A. J. Dolan (**Clonalis LTC**), Gerry Westby, T. Doyle (**Castlebar TC**), R. H. Tieson (**Ballina LTC**), Henry Pittman (**Sligo YMCA LTC**), J. J. Mc Gettrick (**Ballymote LTC**). This meeting also decided instructed the honorary secretary to insure the "Campbell Cup" and "Connaught Junior Cup" for the sum of £25.

Despite the war and the difficulty in travel the Emergency Council subsequently were able to meet in May, June and July. The Council were in credit to an amount of £21.13.7 in May. However, fees to the ILTA had yet to be paid, request to clubs had to be made to re-issue cheques and some £13 in total was still due for the 1941 season from nine clubs. Here we have the nitty gritty of a provincal committee, trying to make ends meet. The clubs themselves, in many cases, had an equally frustrating task. The 1942 season was to have some promise with some 19 active clubs written to on the 16th of May requesting the following *(a) Affiliation fee for the season 1942 and Honorary Secretary's name and address, (b) Intention to play in the Campbell Cup (c) Intention to play in the Connaught Junior Cup and (d) To nominate 2 ladies and 2 gentlemen for inter-provincial honours.* Again we have the annual problem of secretary's everywhere. By the 30th May only **Boyle LTC**,

University College Galway LTC, **Claremorris LTC**, **Woodville LTC** (Ballisodare), **Sligo YMCA**, **Ballymote LTC** and **Merville LTC** replied.

Winner of the Connacht Junior Girl's Championship (circa 1941) organised by the Merville LTC in Sligo was Maeve Flattery (left) of Sligo. Her opponent was Ursula Byrne of John Street, Sligo.

The 30th May meeting sanctioned tournaments at Sligo YMCA (13th to 18th July), County Galway (Athenry?) (29th to 25th July) and **Merville LTC** (30th July to 1st August). By the middle of June the number of clubs affiliated for 1942 had risen to 13 but the 1941 accounts could not be finalised, some £5-10-0 was the balance due from five clubs. Expediency was the order of the day with travel being difficult during the 'emergency' years. The Campbell Cup teams were reduced to 2 men and 2 women and the competition was regionalised. In one region were the clubs of Sligo, Ballisodare, Ballymote and Boyle; in the second were those of Ballina, Castlebar and Claremorris and in the third those in Tuam and Galway. Like many minutes books, the draw and actual clubs competing in this or the Junior Cup were detailed, for 1942 at least. By the AGM on the 10th April 1943 (held in the Imperial Hotel, Sligo) the honorary treasurer was able to report a profit for the year (1942) of £4.16.1 and the honorary secretary (the same man M. Mulligan) was able to say that *pre-war activities were maintained and that these activities were splendidly supported by affiliated clubs*. He would also report that the entries for both cup competitions were up, the winners in both competitions were **Merville LTC**. The finals were held at the Castlebar club with County Galway runners up in the Campbell Cup and Tuam in the Junior Cup.

In tables for Campbell, Junior and Pittman Cups the number of entrants, where known, is given in brackets after the year of the competition.

In 1943, the hard working Henry St. J. Blake became the second president of the ILTA from Connaught. He had been president of the branch since 1938 when Captain Campbell (**County Sligo LTC**) died while in that office. The official minutes of the earliest years of the branch appear to be lost but a brief record was inserted in the book which commences with the 1942 season. It is noted here that Connaught applied to be a separate Province or Council at the ILTA meeting of the 27th June 1933. At that time, a special meeting of the affiliated clubs in Connaught had met and Mr. Kenny West (**County Sligo LTC**) had written to the ILTA seeking a change in Rules 5 and 12 of the ILTA. It was noted in the letter of request that *In any case the Connaught clubs will not continue to pay the capitation fee to the Leinster Council as no benefits are derived by the clubs from that source.* By the ILTA meeting of the 16th January 1934 full agreement, with the necessary rules changes, was made to this proposal.

Captain Willie Campbell (**County Sligo LTC**) became the first Connaught president (of the ILTA) that year and remained in this office until his death on the 17th July 1938. In the year of his death he was also president of the Irish Lawn Tennis Association. Mr. Kenny West (**Merville LTC**) was the first honorary secretary of the branch. In 1937 Captain Campbell presented a cup, the **Campbell Cup**, for play between the senior club teams in the province. **Galway Lawn Tennis Club** was the inaugural winner. In the third round Galway beat neighbouring club, **Blackrock LTC** by five matches to 3. In the final they beat **Sligo YMCA LTC** by 7 matches to 1.

Campbell Cup
(Connacht Senior Cup)
Inaugural Final 25th August 1937
Galway LTC 7 Sligo YMCA LTC 1

Dr. R. T. & W. A. F. Sandys beat
          Bob Hunter/R. Finlay 6/3 3/6 6/1
M. Coote/W. J. Blake beat
          F. Williamson/Joe Hogge 6/3 1/6 6/3
Mrs. Braund/Miss Boland beat
          Miss A. Kerr/Eva Stevenson 6/1 6/4
Misses C. & H. Symes beat
          Misses F. Buckley/M. Kilgallon 6/3 6/2
Dr. R. T. Sandys/Mrs. Braund beat
          Bob Hunter/Miss A. Kerr 6/2 6/2
W. A. F. Sandys/Miss Boland beat
          R. Findlay/Miss F. Buckley 6/4 3/6 7/5
M. Coote/Miss C. Symes beat
          F. Williamson/Eva Stevenson 6/4 9/7
W. J. Blake/Miss M. Symes lost to
  Joe Hogge/Miss M. Kilgallon 6/3 5/7 3-3 retired.

Ballina LTC won the Campbell Cup the second year when beating **Merville LTC** 5/3 in the final. The Sligo club (**Merville LTC**) took the title when beating **Galway LTC** in 1939. 1940 was a rematch in the final and was to be an extremely close affair and required a replay. Both matches were played at **Castlebar TC**. In the first match, despite a *breeze which was blowing rather strong at times, …the match lived up to expectations.* There were four mixed matches as well as two men's and two ladies' doubles. The result was 4/4. In the replay, **Merville LTC** won 6/1 but *nearly every match was a drawn out affair.* The results were as follows (Merville names first).

MD	Gerry Westby/Bill Jennings beat
	M. Walsh/Sandys 6/3 4/6 8/6
	Charlie Cunningham/Jimmy Hender lost to
	O'Malley/Molloy 8/6 3/6 4/6
LD	Eithne Flattery/Nan Wilson beat
	Mrs. Braund/Miss R. Blake 2/6 6/3 6/4
	Maeve Flattery/Finola Flattery beat
	Miss Symes/Miss Sandys 6/4 7/9 6/2
MxD	Bill Jennings/Eithne Flattery lost
	M. Walsh/Mrs. Braund 1/6 1/6
	Gerry Westby/Nan Wilson beat
	O'Malley/Miss R. Blake 6/4 6/1
	Jimmy Hender/Finola Flattery beat
	Molloy/Miss Sandys 6/3 6/2

In 1964 it was decided, by the Connacht branch one presumes, that the Campbell Cup would be played on an inter-county basis. There were only two entries, a team representing Galway county and another representing Galway town.

Campbell Cup*	
1937	Galway LTC
1938	Ballina LTC beat Merville LTC 5/3
1939	Merville LTC beat Galway LTC
1940	Merville LTC beat Galway LTC 6/1 in a replay after a 4/4 draw.
1942	Merville LTC beat Co. Galway LTC
1943	Galway LTC
1948	Merville LTC beat Castlebar TC
1949[6]	
1950	Merville LTC beat Galway LTC
1951	Merville LTC
1952	Merville LTC beat Galway LTC
1953[7]	Castlebar TC beat Merville LTC
1954[8]	Merville LTC
1955[6]	Merville LTC beat Galway LTC
1956[6]	Galway LTC beat Merville LTC
1957	Galway LTC beat Merville LTC
1958[7]	Galway LTC beat Merville LTC
1959	Merville LTC beat Galway LTC
1960	Galway LTC
1961	Galway w/o Merville LTC
1963	Galway LTC
1964	Galwy town v Galway county
1965	Galway LTC w/o Merville LTC
1966	Galway LTC v Merville LTC unplayed
1967	Galway LTC
1968	28th April :Competition deemed 'extinct'

(*Used for Under 15 Competition from 1972)

The Connacht Junior Cup (for second teams of stronger clubs or clubs with no team in the Senior Cup) was initially started in 1939. The inaugural winners were **Ballina TC**. In 1940, **Merville LTC's** "B" team beat **Clonalis LTC** (Castlerea) 7/1 in the semi-final and then beat **Castlebar TC** 4/2 in the final. This latter match was played at **Ballina LTC**. Due to heavy rain, two matches remained unfinished but the Sligo team had an unassailable set-advantage and were declared the winners. Thus, for the first time, the 'double', Connacht Senior and Junior Cups, went to the same club.

Connacht Junior Cup/ Connacht Inter-Club Cup*	
1939[22]	Ballina TC
1940	Merville LTC "B" beat Castlebar TC 4/2
1942	Merville LTC beat Tuam LTC
1943	Galway Commercial Boat Club
1948[14]	Carrick on Shannon LTC
1949[13]	
1950	Merville LTC
1951	Runners Up Athenry LTC
1952	Runners Up Athenry LTC
1953[24]	Castlebar TC beat Athenry LTC
1954[21]	Ballina TC beat Athenry LTC
1955[19]	Boyle Catholic TC beat Ballinasloe LTC
1956[18]	Galway LTC beat Boyle Catholic TC
1957	Boyle Catholic TC beat Castlebar TC
1958[16]	Galway LTC beat Ballymote LTC
1959	Galway LTC beat Merville LTC
1960	Boyle Catholic TC
1961	Boyle Catholic TC
1963	Castlebar TC
1964	Galway LTC beat Castlebar TC
1966	Galway LTC beat Mohill LTC
1967	Newport LTC & Galway LTC "A"
1968	Title now: Connacht Inter-Club Cup
1971	Mohill LTC
1972	Mohill LTC
1973	Mohill LTC
1974	Castlebar TC beat Strokestown LTC
1977[5]	Castlebar TC beat Galway LTC
1978[11]	Galway LTC beat Castlebar TC
1980	Castlebar TC beat Galway LTC

(*Called The Connacht Cup (from 1956) to avoid confusion with under age cups)

To add to competition within the province the branch played a North versus South match at Castlerea (**Clonalis LTC**) on the 8th September, 1940. The North team of Bill Jennings (**Merville LTC**), P.J. Hennigan (**Ballina LTC**), J. Martin (Sligo YMCA), A.J. Rogers (**Ballymote LTC**), Mrs. Newman (**Ballina LTC**), Eithne Flattery (**Merville LTC**), Maeve Flattery (**Merville LTC**) and Nan Wilson (**Merville LTC**) beat the South team of T.F. Doyle (**Castlebar TC**), J. McEllin (**Claremorris LTC**), J. Lowry, John Molloy, Mrs. Braund, Miss S. Blake (**Galway LTC**), Miss H. Thornton and Mrs. Flannery by 6 matches to 2. This was held prior to the AGM that year.

Connacht Open Championships

Year	Men's Singles	Ladies Singles
1938	R. J. Sandys	Mrs. K. Braund
1939	Domhnall McCullough bt. Walter Walshe 4/6 6/1 7/5	Mrs. K. Braund beat Miss F. Wren 6/3 3/6 6/4
1940	E.H. Porter	Miss S. Hogan
1941	Walter Walshe	Miss G. McAuley
1946	Stanley McElroy beat N. Robb 6/1 1/6 6/4	Maeve Flattery beat Miss M. Doran 6/0 6/1
1947	Joe Hackett beat H. O'Donoghue 6/4 6/2	Maeve Brennan beat Harry Sheridan 6/0 5/7 6/3
1954	Michael Walshe beat R. O'Connor 2/6 6/2 7/5 6/2	Mrs. R. Stone (Eng.)
1955	Dr. Des Kneafsey beat P. Gargan 3/6 3/6 7/5 7/5 6/4	Mrs. R. Stone (Eng.) beat Miss M. R. Ryan 6/1 6/1
1956	Gerry Clarke	Tess Delaney
1957	Gerry Clarke beat G. Walker 6/3 6/0 6/3	Tess Delaney beat Miss I. McDonnell 6/3 6/2
1958	I. Steepe	Clementine McGuinness
1959	R. Feely	Maeve Lydon
1960	J. M.Wilkington(NZ)	Joan Brennan
1961	John O'Brien beat P. Gilmore 7//5 6/3	Patricia O' Brien beat Joan Brennan 6/1 6/3
1962	Harry Barniville beat John O'Brien 7/9 6/2 3/6 6/4 6/3	Maeve Lydon beat Jean Russell 6/3 6/1
1963	Harry Sheridan beat John O'Brien 4/6 6/3 6/4 1/6 6/1	Maeve Lydon beat A. Folan 6/3 6/4
1964	Harry Barniville beat Harry Sheridan 6/0 5/7 6/3	Maeve Lydon beat Maureen O'Brien 0/6 6/0 6/3
1965		Maeve Lydon beat Jean Russell 6/0 6/2
1966	Jack Waltz (USA) beat Mike Brooks (USA) 5/7 10/8 6/4	Maeve Lydon beat Robin Shaw (South Africa) 6/2 6/2
1969	Tim Parke (England) beat Tony O'Shea 6/0 3/6 6/3	Maeve McEvoy beat Yvonne Menton 6/3 6/1
1972	Noel Murphy beat Brendan Minnock 6/4 0/6 6/4	J. A. Byrne beat Claire O'Brien 6/2 5/7 8/6
1978	Noel Murphy	Jean Turbridy
1981	Peter Hannon	Caitriona Ruane
1982	Brian Lawlor	Caitriona Ruane
1983	G. Beirne	Caitriona Ruane
1984	John Hackett	Carmel O'Sullivan
1985	Pat Mangan (USA)	Carmel O'Sullivan
1986	John Fahy	Carmel O'Sullivan
1988	Adrian Ledwith	Gina Niland
1990	David Thornton	Nicola Burke
1991	Noel Murphy	N. Wilson
1992	S. Singh	Lesley O'Halloran
1993	Paul Pounch	Lesley O'Halloran
1994	Gearoid O'Nuallain	Gina Niland
1995	T. Lek	Lesley O'Halloran
1996	S. Taylor	Fiona Long
1997	George McGill	Lesley O'Halloran
1998	J. Colhoun	M. Cosman
1999	Neil Fagan	Lesley O'Halloran
2000	Neil Fagan	Elana Moore
2001	Conor Taylor	Anna White
2002	Conor Casey	Suzie Perkins
2003	Fiachra Lennon	Niamh Burke
2005	K. Koik	Marion Hanley

Connacht Open Championships

Year	Men's Doubles	Ladies Doubles
1940	T.R. Martin/B.J. Sheehan (handicap)	Miss Burke/Miss Boudren (handicap)
1946	E. P. O'Kelly/Stanley McElroy beat T. Lynn/E. Lee 6/2 2/6 6/3	
1947	D. O'Keeffe/John Blaney beat Ivar Boden/Joe Hackett 6/2 6/2	
1954	R. W. Stone (England)/H.B. Clarke	
1955	R. W.Stone (England)/Gerry Clarke beat P. Gargan/F. Fennelly 6/3 6/3	
1956	Gerry Clarke/R. Donovan	
1957	Gerry Clarke/B. J. O'Driscoll beat G. Walker/Dr. Des Kneafsey 6/4 9/7	
1959	M. Vale/M. McMahon	
1961	D. Griffith/R. O' Connor beat J. C. Kelly/A. Denvir 6/4 6/3	
1962	Harry Barniville/John O'Brien beat D. McGoldrick/K. Fung 6/3 6/1	
1963	Harry Barniville/John O'Brien beat Harry Sheridan/C. Ryan 6/3 4/6 6/3	
1964	W. P. Walsh/Brendan Kelly beat Harry Sheridan/C. Ryan 6/4 0/6 7/5	
1966	D. R. Shaw/A. R. Horne (South Africa) beat Jack Waltz (USA)/J. Westcott (USA) 7/5 6/3	Martha Emerson/Ann Nally beat A. Folan/E. McGowan 6/3 6/2
1969	John de Courcy/T. Langan beat D. Dwyer (Eng.)/Tim Parke (Eng.) 8/6 9/7 6/3	
1972	Brendan Minnock/Donal Dempsey beat Gary O'Loughlin/Noel Murphy 6/0 6/2	June Anne Byrne/Claire O'Brien beat June Smith/Sue Emerson 6/4 6/3
1978	Ronan Fearon/P. O'Farrell	Jean Turbridy/Bernadette Davy
1981	Peter Hannon/Billy O' Boyle	Caitriona Ruane/F. Ruane
1982	Larry Steen/H. Ledwith	Caitriona Ruane/M. Cleary
1983	Glen Beirne/Peter Hannon	N. Murphy/J. Roche
1984	Paul Casey/M. Ferguson	D. Fearon/M. Smyth
1985	Pat Mangan/P. Reid	Carmel O'Sullivan/C. McGoldrick
1986	Noel Murphy/Jim Roche	M. Smith/Carmel O'Sullivan
1988	T. Connor/R. Bailey	S. Farrell/J. O' Halloran
1993	J. Burke/Paul Pounch	Lesley O'Halloran/D. Coll
1994	Enda Flynn/Eddie Moloney	N. Doyle/Gina Niland
1995	Conor Carroll/E. Mee	Lelsey O'Halloran//S. Walsh
1996	S. & C. Taylor	Fiona Long/D. Collins
1997	V. Lawton/T. Lek	M. O'Donovan/Lesley O'Halloran
1999	Fiachra Lennon/C. O'Brolchain	Lesley O'Halloran/Sandra Fearon
2000	Fiachra Lenon/Neil Fagan	Suzie Perkins/E. McLoughlin
2001	Fiachra Lennon/Neil Fagan	Anna White/Ann Marie Mee
2002	Fiachra Lennon/Neil Fagan	Aisling Sage/Laura Cuddy
2003	Fiachra Lennon/Timo Barry	Margaret McLoughlin/Marion Hanley

Connacht Open Championships
(Cross Cup)

Year	Mixed Doubles
1938	R. J. Sandys/Mrs. K. Braund
1939	T. MacLaughlin/Mrs. K. Braund beat P. Meenan/Miss M. O'Malley 6/1 6/2
1940	R. Hunter/Miss Campbell (handicap)
1946	E. P. O'Kelly/Miss V. Gillespie beat Stanley McElroy/Maeve Flattery 6/4 8/6
1947	Joe McCabe/MaeveBrennan
1948	Mr. & Mrs. R.W. Tunney
1951	H. O'Donoghue/H.V. Hanton
1952	Sam Cummings/Eileen Kirkpatrick
1953	Peter Jackson/Eileen Kirkpatrick
1954	Mr. & Mrs. R.W. Stone (Eng.)
1955	Mr. & Mrs. R.W. Stone (Eng.) beat D. Long/Miss M. Ryan 6/1 3/6 6/1
1956	J.G. Spicer/Miss M. Kelly
1957	Gerry Clarke/Miss I. McDonnell beat P. Sharkey/Maeve Lydon 6/2 6/2
1958	H. B. Clare/Miss L. Clare
1959	R. B. Feely/Mrs. B. Kneafsey
1960	W. Thorn (New Zealand)/Joan Brennan
1961	Dr. Des V. Kneafsey/Maeve Lydon beat D. Griffin/Mrs. D. Kneafsey 3/6 6/4 6/4
1962	Brendan O'Byrne/Joan Brennan beat D. McGoldrick/Sue Emerson 4/6 7/5 8/6
1963	Harry McConnell/June Emerson beat W. Cameron/Miss K. Connolly 6/3 8/6
1964	N. Mahon/Maureen O'Brien beat Harry Sheridan/Miss A. Nally 6/4 4/6 6/4
1965	Tommy & Maeve Lydon beat Harry Sheridan/Pat Ryan
1966	A. R. Horne/Mrs. Robin Shaw (S. Africa) beat Dave Benjamin (USA)/ Olga Sandys 6/4 7/5
1967	T. Langan/Pat Ryan
1968	T.Langan/Pat Ryan
1969	Tommy Lydon/Maeve McEvoy beat J. Kelly/Miss N. Corish 7/5 6/2
1971	J. De Courcey/Olga Sandys
1972	Donal Dempsey/Olga Sandys
1975	Noel Murphy/P.Byrne
1976	Noel Lennon/Louise Tuff
1977	Noel Murphy/Helen Lennon
1978	P. O' Farrell/Bernadette Davy
1979	Peter Hannon/Miss R. Lyons
1980	C. Beirne/Miss R. Lyons
1981	J. O' Dwyer/Caitriona Ruane
1982	Noel Murphy/Caitriona Ruanee
1984	Paul Casey/Carmel O'Sullivan
1985	Paul Casey/Carmel O' Sullivan
1987	G. Blake/Margaret Redfern
1989	A. Ashe/J. Hall
1990	Mr. & Mrs. M. Brennan
2000	Mario Woldt/Elana Moore
2001	Gerry Mannion/Jenny Burrows
2002	Conor Casey Suzie Perkins
2003	Conor Casey/Suzie Perkins

The Connacht Open Championships have been held at least as far back as 1939. **Galway LTC** has run this event at their Threadneedle Road location since that time. The 1939 event commenced on the 17th July and the Connacht Tribune noted:

Galway Tennis circles will welcome the revival of the annual Open Tennis Tournament...In order to encourage members of the other local clubs to compete special facilities are being arranged so that competitors who are busy in Galway until 5 or 6 o'clock can play their matches in the evening. Luncheons and teas are being provided by the Club. Known results are as in the following table.

Castlebar's Caitriona Ruane was a Federation Cup player in 1980 and 1981. She was Connacht Open champion in 1981, 1982 and 1983.

Under Age Club Team Cups

On the 12th April 1951, at the Annual General Meeting of the Y.M.C.A. Tennis Club, Mr. Ted Smith, the honorary secretary was delighted to report on the Connacht Council Meeting held in Castlebar on the 4th March. At that meeting *a beautiful trophy was presented by Mr.H. St. J.Blake, in memory of the late H.Pittman, much revered secretary of the Y.M.C.A. Club, for competition amongst the juvenile teams in Connacht* (Sligo Champion, April 28, 1954). This event, in honour of a devoted supporter of the game, was well received throughout the province, and played for since by club Under 18 teams.

By 1953 there were eleven teams playing in the event, **Castlebar TC** were the winners for the first three years. Fifteen teams competed in 1954, **Merville LTC** winning it for the first time. From 1955, the age limit was *amended to under 18 on the 1st January to bring it into line with other junior tournaments in Ireland.* Three boys and three girls on each team play two singles, two level doubles and three mixed matches. In

1958 Galway LTC won the Pittman, Senior and Junior cups. What was interesting about the event that year was that two of their young member, Sue and June Emerson, played in all three cup campaigns. They were only 14 and 15 years of age at the time.

CONNAUGHT COUNCIL.

At a meeting of the Connaught Council, held in Galway, Mr. W. A. F. Sandys (Hon. Sec., Galway L.T.C.) was co-opted a member of the Council in room of Mr. J. W. O'Callaghan.

The Council decided to accept the invitation of the Leinster Council to play an inter-provincial match in Dublin. Arrangements are proceeding in connection with a match with Munster, to be played at Galway.

It was decided to play a North v. South Connaught match at Castlerea before the end of the season.

Campbell Cup—The final of the Campbell Cup between Merville (the holders) and Galway will be played at Castlebar on Sunday next.

FINALS OF CONNAUGHT CHAMPIONSHIPS.

Finals at the Galway tournament were:—

Men's Singles (Championship of Connacht)—E. H. Porter beat B. J. Murphy—6-4, 6-8, -36, 6-1, 6-3.

Women's Singles—Miss S. Hogan beat Miss R. Blake—6-1, 6-3.

Mixed Doubles (Open)—T. Dunlop and Miss S. Hogan beat B. J. Murphy and Miss J. Mullaney—6-8, 6-1, 6-3.

Men's Singles Handicap—R. S. Lee beat J. Dowling—6-1, 6-2.

Women's Singles Handicap—Miss C. Fogarty beat Miss J. Ward—6-2, 5-7, 6-4.

Mixed Doubles Handicap—R. Hunter and Miss Campbell beat P. Scanlon and Miss M. Sheehan—6-3, 6-2.

Men's Doubles Handicap—T. R. Martin and B. J. Sheehan beat R. F. Jones and R. Buchanan—6-2, 0-6, 6-1.

Women's Doubles Handicap—Misses Burke and Boudren beat Miss Coy and Mrs. Elliz—77-5, 6-1.

Report on Connacht Championships in 1940.

Campbell Cup/Frawley Cup

In 1972, the Campbell Cup, which had been played for by senior teams since 1967, was allocated to an under 15 inter-club competition in 1972. The under 15 event was a new one in 1970, **Mohill LTC** winning it for the first two years. The Campbell Cup was presented for the winners of the under 16 inter-club team event from 1977 or earlier, until 1984. By 1986 it was the Frawley

Cup for the U16 team event. By 1997 there was no U16 team event and the Frawley Cup was used for an Under 12 team event. A junior championship of Connacht had been run for a number of years in the 1940s by the **Merville LTC** in Sligo. This was revived in 1954 when J. Ryan of **Castlebar TC** beat Tom Wrafter in the boy's final and Doreen Kilfeather beat Joan Gallagher in the girl's final, both from the home club. The following year Tom Wrafter won as did M. O'Beirne of Galway. The 1956 winners were A. Kilfeather and Miss D. Carroll. Brendan Kelly and Miss P. Begley were the 1957 winners. The event was postponed in 1958 and, in 1959, **Swinford LTC** applied for the event and ran it.

	Pittman Cup
1951	Castlebar TC
1952	Castlebar TC
1953[11]	Castlebar TC beat Galway LTC
1954[15]	Merville LTC beat Galway LTC
1955[14]	Clonalis LTC beat Merville LTC
1956[13]	Galway LTC beat Boyle Catholic TC
1957	Galway LTC beat Ballina LTC "A"
1958[13]	Galway LTC beat Sligo YMCA LTC
1959	Galway LTC beat Castlebar TC
1961	Galway LTC beat Mohill LTC
1962	Galway LTC beat Castlebar TC
1963	Mohill LTC
1964	Castlebar TC
1965	Galway LTC beat Castlebar TC
1966	Galway LTC beat Mohill LTC
1967	Galway LTC
1969	Mohill LTC
1970	Mohill LTC(under 16 event)
1971	Ballina TC
1972	Ballina TC
1973	Ballina TC beat Mohill LTC
1974	Ballina TC beat Strokestown LTC
1975	Strokestown LTC
1976	Castlebar TC
1977[6]	Swinford LTC beat Kiltullagh LTC
1978[7]	Castlebar TC beat Kiltullagh LTC
1979	Castlebar TC v Galway LTC
1983	Loughrea TC beat Sligo TC 4/3
1984	Castlebar TC beat Sligo TC 4/3
1986	Castlebar TC beat Galway TC
1987	Sligo TC w/o Castlebar TC
1988	Athenry LTC
1989	Galway TC beat Sligo TC
1990	Castlebar TC
1991	Castlebar TC v Galway LTC
1993	Sligo TC
1994	Sligo TC beat Galway LTC
1995	Sligo TC beat Roscommon TC
1996	Galway LTC beat Sligo TC
1997	Sligo TC beat Galway LTC
1998	Galway LTC beat Sligo TC
1999	Castlebar TC beat Galway LTC
2000	Castlebar TC

Poustie Cup (u14)

1977	Galway LTC beat Westport LTC
1978	Galway LTC beat Castlebar TC
1979	Castlebar TC beat Kiltullagh LTC
1983	Castlebar TC beat Galway LTC
1984	Galway LTC beat Loughrea TC
1988	Galway LTC beat Sligo TC
1987	Galway LTC beat Ballina TC
1988	Galway LTC
1989	Sligo TC beat Galway LTC
1995	No competition
1997	Galway LTC beat Castlebar TC
1998	Galway LTC beat Sligo TC

(Was played for the Bank of Ireland Cup in 1984)

Campbell Cup/Frawley Cup

1970	Mohill LTC
1971	Mohill LTC
1972	Ballina TC (Campbell Cup first allocated)
1973	Ballina TC
1974	Ballina TC beat Strokestown LTC
1977	Castlebar TC beat Galway LTC (new under 16 event. New Under 14 event started.)
1977	Castlebar TC beat Galway LTC
1978	Castlebar TC beat Kiltullagh LTC
1979	Castlebar TC beat Milltown LTC
1983	Castlebar TC beat Galway LTC
1984	Castlebar TC beat Galway LTC
1986	Sligo TC beat Athenry TC
1987	Sligo TC beat Loughrea LTC
1988	Galway LTC
1989	Barna TC beat Castlebar TC
1995	No competition
1997*	Sligo TC beat Westport TC
1998*	Castlebar TC beat Westport TC

(* U12 team event, no U16 event this year.)

Castlebar Tennis Club's Cup winning team in 1953. Back (l. to r.) Sam Ryan, Michael Heverin & Jim Ryan. Front (l. to r.): Peggy Flanagan, Gay McCormack & Bridie Herman.

James Ward of Galway LTC was president of the Connacht branch from 1998 to 2001.

Leinster

Even though there was a Dublin leagues committee for well over 25 years, and the ILTA minutes records vice-presidents in its minutes of 1926 (see previous chapter), it appears that the branch was formed on the 2nd March 1927. This meeting was held at the Engineers Hall, 35 Dawson Street (now the La Stampa Restaurant), Dublin and was to include Connacht Clubs. At that time, Connacht clubs were under the umbrella of Leinster and would not have their own Council for a number of years.

Under the chairmanship of John Miley (**Fitzwilliam LTC**), with Harry Maunsell (**Glenageary LTC**) as acting secretary, it was decided that fifteen members should constitute the Leinster Council, five being a quorum for meetings. It appears that a provisional council was elected on the 2nd March and that, a week later, Wednesday 9th March 1927, at 91 Merrion Square, Dublin, the first meeting proper of the Leinster Provincial Council was elected. The full compliment of elected persons was as follows:

President: Gerry Byrne (**Fitzwilliam LTC**)
Vice-President:
    D.W.S. Colquhoun (**County Wicklow LTC**)
Honorary Secretary:
    Harry Rhys Maunsell (**Glenageary LTC**)
Honorary Treasurer:
    Cecil S. Almond (**Norwood LTC**)

Representatives on General Council:
Gerry Byrne (**Fitzwilliam LTC**), Dr. A. P. Barry (**Fitzwilliam LTC**), R. A. C. Barrett (**Skerries LTC**), D. W. S. Colquhoun (**County Wicklow LTC**), A. P. Dawson (**Lansdowne LTC**), M. F. Linehan (**Mount Temple LTC**), John F. Miley (**Fitzwilliam LTC**), T. P. O' Connor (**Kenilworth LTC**), W. B. Pollock (**Mount Temple LTC**), S. E. Polden (**Clontarf LTC**) and Alfred H. Walsh (**Norwood LTC**).
Coaching Committee:
R. A. C. Barrett, A. P. Dawson, J. F. Miley, William St. George Perrott (**County Wicklow LTC**).

Selection Committee:
Dr. A. P. Barry, G. Byrne, M. F. Linehan, W. St. G. Perrott, A. H. Walsh.

The meeting granted permission for the Dublin Lawn Tennis Council and the *United* (sic*) Town's League* to carry on under their existing rules. The first AGM was held on the 31st October 1927 in Mills Hall, Merrion Row, Dublin 2. Council meetings were held at 91 Merrion Square, the offices of H. R. Maunsell's law firm, T. T. Macready. At that meeting were representatives of the following clubs: Norwood, Lansdowne, Mount Temple, Clontarf, Ardee, Skerries, Bective, Ashbrook, Beechwood, Dublin University, County Westmeath, Kenilworth, Irish Times LTC, National University, Mountjoy Square, County Wicklow and Fitzwilliam.

The Hon. Secretary's Report was adopted. The Hon. Treasurer's Report showing a balance in hands of £1.17.2 was passed subject to audit and Mr. Channing was asked to act as auditor of this Account as well as of the Account for the forthcoming Season.

Two interesting items arose at that meeting and worth a mention. The Lansdowne club received great praise for the successful running of a Juvenile tournament. As there were some complaints concerning the conduct of the schools cup competitions it was recommended that they be management by the Council in future. After the death of Harry Maunsell in 1948 both the Council meetings and AGM's were held at the Central Hotel.

Irish Tennis Rankings

THE Leinster Council have announced the following Lawn Tennis rankings over the 1954 season:—

MEN—1. G. P. Jackson; 2. J. D. Hackett; 3. G. D. Fitzpatrick; 4-5 (jointly); J. P. McHale and J. J. Fitzgibbon; 6. H. Barniville.

LADIES—1. Miss E. F. Lombard; 2. Miss J A. Fitzpatrick; 3. Mrs. M. Fitzgibbon; 4. Miss M. O'Sullivan; 5. Miss H. Bretland; 6. Mrs. J. M. Morton.

LEINSTER JUNIOR

Boys—J. P. Buckley, R. Davitt, P. Delaney, J. Drury-Byrne, R. Fearon, D. Jackson, J. O'Connell.

Girls—A Bannister, T. Delaney, P. Kerin, M. Lennon, R. Murray, M. O'Sullivan.

Leinster Council Officials—Pres., S. R. P. Harrison; Hon. Treas., K. O'B. Kenny; Hon. Sec., A. H. Walsh, 17 Leinster Rd., Rathmines, Dublin.

Leinster Rankings
Irish Independent-22nd November 1954.

That first meeting was in the headquarters of the Institution of Engineers of Ireland, as were the ILTA meetings around that time. That meeting elected George Byrne as the first president, a man who would stay in office for four years (1927 to 1930). Only Ken Potterton surpasses this total, being first in office as president in 1960 and the last time in 1979. Up to 2002 there have been 76 elections with 53 individuals heading up the branch activities. From 1930 onwards the office of ILTA (TI) president was on a rota between three provinces, with the first Connacht president coming into office (Captain Campbell of Sligo) in 1938. Therefore, twelve former Leinster branch presidents also became presidents of the national organisation. Interestingly, in 1940 the Leinster president was Raymund Egan of **Lansdowne LTC**, while his father, Frank, was president of the ILTA in 1941.

Harry Rhys Maunsell, in whose honour the Maunsell trophies are presented each year, was a member of the **Glenageary LTC**. He was the Leinster branch honorary secretary from 1927 to 1948 and held the same post in the ILTA from 1920 to 1948. He died in office, the Leinster branch AGM had to be postponed, but he will not be forgotten. Alf Walsh took over both posts in 1948. That year he was also president of the Branch. He handed over the Leinster branch post as honorary secretary to Charlie Brennan in 1970 who then held this office until 1982. Charlie also held the ILTA minutes book from 1973 to 1985. He too was president in Leinster (1964, 1977) and at the ILTA (1978, 1986).

Some branch treasurers had lengthy periods in office. Cecil Almond (1927 to 1937), William St. George Perrott (1938 to 1947), Kevin O' Brien Kenney (1948 to 1968) and Billy Meehan (1990 to 2002). An interesting comment from James Brewster-when kindly gathering data on the branch for this publication-related to the elected honorary treasurer of 1938: *W. J. Poole was deemed to have resigned because of his failure to attend meetings and answer letters from HRM (nearly a hanging offence!)*. HRM is the abbreviation for the honorary secretary, Henry Rhys Maunsell.

A few Leinster officials have had more than one position and many were also on various sub-committees. Examples include Gerry More O'Ferrall (**Castleknock LTC**) was branch treasurer (1980 to 1982), secretary (1983 to 1985) and president (1986 to 1987). On top of this he was the first president of the newly named Tennis Ireland (1990) and took on the responsibility of compiling the national handbook from 1991 to 2001. James Brewster (**Brookfield LTC**) has also been active in many areas. He was branch treasurer (1986 to 1989) and president (1990, 1991 & 2002) and, for Tennis Ireland, treasurer (1994) and president (1993). These, and many others, have also been extremely active in their own clubs as well. Sometimes, one wonders, do these administrators have any time for tennis! Do the ordinary players appreciate their efforts is another question that often arises!

This Kilkenny CYMS LTC were thought to have won the Provincial Town Cup in 1929. Back row (l. to r. Phil Mc Sweeney, Con Connolly, Milo Kennedy & Con Kennealy. Front Row (l. to r. Dorothy Healy, Grace Drea, Anne Barry & Kathleen Dunne.

Outside the 'Pale' there have been competitive tennis competitions taking place annually within Leinster from an early stage. The Provincial Towns Cup has been a continuing success since it first took place in 1925. It has its own committee. Two classes were required in 1933 and this was extended to three in 1967. The bigger clubs will have teams in several classes. Probably the most successful team in Class one has been **Dundalk LTC.** The late Muriel Bolton is one organiser that is not forgotten for her particular interest in this competition, one that is probably the only team competition that large numbers of the regional clubs are involved in each year. Even smaller clubs, such as **Ardee LTC** and **Rush LTC** had their days in the sun winning the main senior competition.

Connacht v Leinster in 1948

Above and below Lansdowne LTC league winning teams of the late 1940s and early 1950s.

Dee Jennings was the honorary secretary of the Leinster branch between 1992 and 1996 and president in both 1998 and 2001. In 2005 she became president of Tennis Ireland. She has been a member of Kilkenny City & County LTC and Donnybrook LTC.

In 1983, Dundalk Tennis Club won the Leinster Challenge Cup beating Templeogue LTC 4/1 in the final. Front (l. to r.) Frank Mc Ardle, Larry Steen & Peter Hannon. Back (l. to. r.) Jim McArdle, Adrian Ledwith & Jim Pringle. Inset, Paul Brady.

The Dundalk LTC Junior Provincial Towns' Cup winning team of 1948. Back (l. to r.) F. Johnston, P. E. O' Connell, D.B. Green & W.D. Willis. Front (l. to r.) Miss N. Carroll, Tommy McArdle (captain) & Miss P. O' Connell. Absent: Mrs. W. D. Willis and Miss G. O' Reilly.

Provincial Town's Competition-Leinster

1984	Kilkenny County & City LTC I	1984	Kells LTC I	1984	Wicklow LTC II	1984	Wexford Harbour BC LTC I
1985	Dundalk LTC	1985	Kilkenny County & City LTC	1985	Wexford Harbour BC LTC I	1985	Wexford Harbour BC LTC
1986	Kilkenny County & City LTC I	1986	Kilkenny County & City LTC I	1986	Kilkenny County & City LTC II	1986	Kilkenny County & City LTC II
1987	Kilkenny County & City LTC I	1987	Dundalk LTC I	1987	Wexford Harbour BC LTC I	1987	Wicklow Town LTC I
1988	Kilkenny County & City LTC I	1988	Kilkenny County & City LTC I	1988	Arklow LTC I	1988	Mullingar LTC I
1989	Mullingar LTC I	1989	Kilkenny County & City LTC I	1989		1989	Kilkenny County & City LTC II
1990		1990		1990		1990	
1991		1991		1991		1991	
1992	Mullingar LTC I	1992	Mullingar LTC I	1992	Mullingar LTC II	1992	Celbridge LTC I
1993	Kells LTC I	1993	Celbridge LTC I	1993	Trim LTC I	1993	County Cavan LTC I
1994	Mulliingar LTC I	1994	Mullingar LTC I	1994	Hillbrook LTC I	1994	Kilkenny County & City LTC I
1995		1995		1995		1995	
1996	Mullingar LTC I	1996		1996	Summerhill LTC I	1996	Stackallen T and P & P Club I

Class 3 Men's League		**Class 3 Ladies League**		**Class 4 Men's League**		**Class 4 Ladies League**	
1992	Mullingar LTC III	1992	Mullingar ITC III	1992	Tullamore LTC I	1992	Tullamore LTC II
1993	Kells LTC II	1993	Kells LTC I	1993	Summerhill LTC II	1993	Kells LTC II
1994	Kinnegad LTC	1994	Summerhill LTC I	1994	Kilkenny County & City LTC II	1994	Summerhill LTC II
1995		1995		1995		1995	
1996	Kells LTC I	1996	Summerhill LTC I	1996	Leixlip LTC I	1996	Bridgeford LTC I.

Class 1 League		**Class 2 League**		**Class 3 League**		**Class 4 League**	
1997	Mullingar LTC I	1997	Mullingar LTC II	1997	Stackallen T and P & P Club	1997	Kells LTC
1998		1998	Athy LTC	1998	Carlow LTC	1998	Kells LTC
1999	Kilkenny County & City LTC	1999	Mullingar LTC	1999	Athlone LTC	1999	Celbridge LTC
2000		2000	Kilkenny County & City LTC	2000	Kells LTC	2000	Celbridge LTC

In 1981 the ILTA president Paddy Donnellan (second right) made a special presentation to Ken Potterton on his retirement from tennis administration. Ken had been a member of the Irish, Leinster and Provincial Town's committees over many years. Also in photograph are Charlie Brennan (honorary secretary, ILTA) and Mrs. Potterton.

Provincial Town's Cup Competitions-Leinster

Class 1		Class 2		Class 3	
1925	Rush LTC	1933	Carlow LTC	1967	Tullamore LTC
1926	Ardee LTC	1934	Ardee LTC	1968	Stackallen T and P & P Club
1927	Rush LTC	1937	Carlow LTC	1970	Mullingar LTC
1928	Ardee LTC	1938	County Kildare LTC	1971	Stackallen T and P & P Club
1929	Navan LTC	1939	Dundallk LTC	1972	Stackallen T and P & P Club
1930	Skerries LTC	1938	County Kildare LTC	1973	Gorey LTC
1931	Carlow LTC	1939	Dundallk LTC	1974	Greystones LTC
1932	Navan LTC	1940	Dundalk LTC	1975	Arklow LTC
1933	Navan LTC	1947	Dundallk LTC	1976	Wicklow Town LTC
1934	Navan LTC	1948	Dundallk LTC	1977	Birr Wilmer LTC
1937	Carlow LTC	1955	Edenderry LTC	1978	Kilkenny County & City LTC III
1938	Navan LTC	1956	Laytown/Bettystown LTC	1981	County Cavan LTC I
1939	Ardee LTC	1957	North Kildare LTC	1984	Wexford LTC
1940	Dundalk LTC	1958	Laytown/Bettystown LTC	1986	Mullingar LTC II
1946	Dundalk LTC	1959	North Kildare LTC	1987	Wexford Harbour BC LTC II
1948	Dundalk LTC	1965	Tullamore LTC	1988	Naas LTC III
1950	Dundalk LTC	1966	County Kildare LTC	1989	Mullingar LTC II
1951	Athy LTC	1967	Greystones LTC	1992	Mullingar LTC III
1952	Dundalk LTC	1968	Navan LTC	1993	Hillbrook LTC II
1953	Dundalk LTC	1969	Hillbrook LTC	1994	Dundalk LTC III
1954	Dundalk LTC	1972	Lourdes LTC	1996	Dunboyle LTC I
1955	Athy LTC	1973	Mullingar LTC	1997	Stackallen T and P & P Club
1956	Dundalk LTC	1974	Stackallen T and P & P Club	1998	Wexford LTC
1957	Athy LTC	1975	Wexford Harbour BC LTC	1999	Stackallen T and P & P Club
1959	Dundalk LTC	1976	Arklow LTC	2000	Dundalk LTC
1961	Carlow LTC	1977	Mullingar LTC		
1962	Dundalk LTC	1978	Stackallen T and P & P Club II		
1963	Dundalk LTC	1981	Arklow LTC I		
1964	Dundalk LTC	1984	Dundalk LTC II		
1965	Dundalk LTC	1986	Dundalk LTC II		
1966	Tullamore LTC	1987	Carlow LTC II		
1967	Laytown/Bettystown LTC	1988	Mullingar LTC I		
1968	Greystones LTC	1989	Celbridge LTC II		
1969	Laytown/Bettystown LTC	1992	Navan LTC II		
1970	Navan LTC	1993	Stackallen T and P & P Club II		
1971	Hillbrook LTC	1994	Dundalk LTC II		
1972	Hillbrook LTC	1996	Mullingar LTC II		
1973	Hillbrook LTC	1997	Athy LTC		
1974	Stackallen T and P & P Club	1998	Stackallen T and P & P Club		
1975	Dundalk LTC	1999	Leixlip LTC		
1976	Dundalk LTC	2000	Wexford		
1977	Greystones LTC				

Class 1		Class 4	
1978	Kilkenny County & City LTC		
1981	Stackallen T and P & P Club I	1981	Rathoe LTC
1984	Stackallen T and P & P Club I	1984	Celbridge LTC
1986	Stackallen T and P & P Club I	1986	Carlow LTC III
1987	Kells LTC I	1987	North Kildare LTC II
1988	Stackallen T and P & P Club I	1988	Wexford Harbour BC LTC III
1989	Stackallen T and P & P Club I	1989	Navan LTC III
1992	Mullingar LTC I	1992	Hillbrook LTC II
1993	Dundalk LTC I	1993	Stackallen T and P & P Club III
1994	Kells LTC I	1994	Stackallen T and P & P Club V
1996	Stackallen T and P & P Club I	1996	Dunboyne LTC II
1997	Stackallen T and P & P Club I	1997	Dundalk LTC
1998	Kilkenny County & City LTC II	1998	Kells LTC
1999	Mullingar LTC	1999	Dundalk LTC
2000	Kilkenny County & City LTC	2000	Dundalk LTC

In 1979 Kilkenny County & City LTC celebrated their Centenary. The summer before the Club won the Class I competition in the Leinster Provincial Towns Cup. Back (l. to r.) Joe Wall (Club Captain), Eugene Daly, Paul Mullally, Tony Mitchell, Justin Wall and T.K. Mc Keogh (Club president). Front (l. to r.)Catherine Mc Carthy, Susan Reidy, Jane Tyler & Angela Moylan.

The Birr Wilmer Tennis Club, founded in the 1940s, first entered the Provincial Towns' Cup Competition in 1977. They were duly placed in Class III and won the title. The following year they won the South West Leinster League. Players from both teams are included here. Back (l. to r.) John Dunphy, Pat Hoctor, Michael Delaney, J. J. Sheeran (captain), Paul Barber, Frankie Kenny, Steve Crofton. Front (l. to r.) Anne Kenny, Martina Butler, Marcella Grogan, Siobhan Tynan and Emer Hannify.

1992 was a good year for Munster tennis. President of Tennis Ireland that year was Munster's Rhoda McAuliffe. In this photo she holds the all-Ireland inter-counties cup won by Tipperary. Also in photo (from left): Tim Conway (Munster branch), Deirdre McSherry (Tipperary team), Ann Fitzpatrick (Tipperary team) and Elaine Bermingham (president, Munster branch 1992).

The 1953 Hillsboro' Munster Junior League Cup winning team. Insets John Cremin (left) and N. Dilloughrey. Back (left to right): John Kenneally, Tim McNamee, D. McNally, B. Murray, Michael Hurley and John Cronin. Front (l. to r.): Kay O'Neill, M. Cantwell, Mary Hegarty, Mary O'Neill, Billy O'Regan (club captain), Mary Cronin, Eileen Crowley, Maura Harris and Mary Fenwick.

The History of Irish Tennis

The Munster Senior Cup competition dates back to 1907. That year Rushbrooke Lawn Tennis and Croquet Club were the winners. In 2003 Limerick Lawn Tennis Club won the Munster senior cup for the sixth year in a row. Three players who participated in all campaigns are seen above with the cup. From left: Fiona Long, Ger Holliday and Deirdre Collins.

Munster

Some of the oldest clubs in the country are in Munster. Limerick has the honour of having held the first 'open' tournament. That was in 1877. By 1938 when the Lawn Tennis Association were celebrating 50 years of play there were two Munster tournaments, out of five in Ireland, that were recognised as having had continual play for the previous 50 years (leaving aside the Great War). These were those events run by **Limerick LTC** and **Waterford LTC**.

According to Bill Tayler in his *A History of Munster Tennis,* the first mention of a private court in the province was in a letter from Miss O'E. Somerville to her sister Hildergard. This was in the early 1870's when she ordered that a court be laid at their home in Castletownshend in County Cork. Tennis grew throughout the province with Limerick, Waterford and Cork cities being particularly strong. By 1880 known clubs in the province included **Limerick LTC, Cork LTC, Waterford LTC, Argideen Vale LT & Croquet Club, Monkstown LT & Croquet Club** and **Rushbrooke LT & Croquet Club**. The latter appears to have been first known as **Queenstown LTC**, unless there was a second early club in Cobh (the port town previously called Queenstown). The club at **Muskerry** was formed around this time too. While the 'Open' tournament at Limerick in 1877 was held a few weeks after the first Wimbledon championships (see chapter 5.4), Bill pointed out that other clubs were also active in this regard. In particular he noted that the *Cork Examiner* of the 10th September 1880 reported a tournament run that week by the newly formed club at Monkstown. A Mr. T. H. Abrahall beat Mr. W. Creag

in the final of the men's singles. Before the end of the 19th century there were a number of open tournaments on the calendar including those at **Argideen Vale LT & Croquet Club** and at **Mallow LTC**. In the 1913 listing of ILTA tournaments there were a total of 42 to be played. There were 3 in Connacht, 10 in Ulster, 14 in Leinster and 15 in Munster. The first of the year were the open championship singles for the Glenbower Cups at **Youghal LTC**. This was a time when grass courts dominated and this event was scheduled as late as the 21st June. The other sanctioned tournaments in Munster were as follows:

Blackrock Lawn Tennis Club (1st July)
Mallow Lawn Tennis Club (7th July)
County Limerick Lawn Tennis Club (8th July)
      Championships of South of Ireland (singles)
Tralee Lawn Tennis Club (21st July)
Sunday's Well Boating & LTC (21st July)
         Championships of Cork (singles)
Rushbrooke Lawn Tennis & Croquet Club (28th July)
Roscrea LTC (29th July) C'ships of Munster (singles)
Fermoy Lawn Tennis Club (4th August)
Mitchelstown Lawn tennis Club (4th August)
Nenagh Lawn Tennis Club (5th August)
Lismore Lawn Tennis Club (5th August)
Marmullane Lawn Tennis Club (11th August)
Clonmel LTC (12th August) C'ships of Co. Tipperary
Muskerry Lawn Tennis & Croquet Club(18th August)

In the 1939 ILTA listing there were a total of 56 tournaments listed for the whole country, 20 of these were in Munster. No tournaments were sanctioned (as per the listing) for Marmullane, Tralee, Mitchelstown, Muskerry and Lismore in 1939. Additional events added were those in the clubs at Waterford, Stawhall, Glanmire, Tramore and County Clare. A noted change were the fact that there were second tournaments, for juniors, at Sunday's Well, Rushbrooke (Irish Junior Close), South Tipperary (Clonmel) and Tramore. The only other listed junior events in Ireland for juniors that year were those at Lansdowne (Leinster Open) and Merville (Junior Championships of Connacht). Often junior events were part of the senior tournaments. The Irish Junior Championships were held at Fitzwilliam. With many more hardcourts available from the 1930s onwards, not alone did tournaments start earlier in the year, but more junior and veteran events were instigated. If we fast forward to the Tennis Ireland Handbook of 1999 the tournament situation is as follows (not included are the interprovincial championships or international team events):

Irish Tournaments in 1999		
Events	Total	Munster
Senior	66	18
Junior	56	17
Veteran	19	6

By 1915 there were 88 clubs affiliated to the Irish Lawn Tennis Association (formed in 1908). Of the 56 affiliated from outside County Dublin there were 5 in Connacht, 13 in Leinster, 15 in Ulster and 23 in Munster. Though many clubs that existed at that time were not affiliated, this balance reflects a very active game in the province. These 23 clubs were as follows:

Munster Tennis Clubs Affiliated to the ILTA in 1915

Blackrock LTC
Clonmel LTC
Crosshaven & Currabinny LTC
Fermoy LTC
Glanmire LTC
Inishannon LTC
Kanturk LTC
Kinsale LTC
Limerick LTC
Lismore LTC
Mallow LTC
Marmullane LTC
Mitchelstown LTC
Monkstown LTC
Muskerry LT & Croquet Club
Nenagh LTC
Roscrea LTC
Rushbrooke LT & Croquet Club
Sunday's Well Boating & LTC
Tipperary LTC
Tralee (Green) LTC
Tralee (Sports Field) LTC
Youghal LTC

Munster continues to have a large range of clubs throughout the province. There were 43 affiliated clubs in the province in 1963, 40 in 1999 and 42 in 2006.

Munster players of note (circa 1960) (l. to r.): June-Ann Byrne (Cobh), Jim Fitzgibbon and Mary O'Sullivan. All three played at the Wimbledon championships. Both Jim (also known as JJ), from Waterford, and Mary, from Tralee, were also noted badminton international players.

Niall Coffey was president of the Munster Branch ILTA in 1987

Some members at the Catholic Institute club in Limerick (circa 1985)

The Munster team at Fitzwilliam LTC in 1942. From left: Mick Donnery, Evie Hallinan (later Magnier, mother of well-known Irish horse breeder John), Shane Jameson, Mimi Hallinan (twin sister to Evie), Jack Mackesy and Patience Conner (later Fawsitt, mother of Alice-Munster number 1 in 1979).The Hallinan twins won the Irish Close Ladies' Doubles title in 1943.

The province was always willing to compete and, at the suggestion of Marjorie Haughton, took on Leinster in the first ladies' interprovincial match. That was in 1924. In 1925, a Leinster mens' team travelled south and took on Munster for the first time. A mixed match between the provinces took place in 1927. One of the first junior interprovincial matches in Ireland was between Munster and Leinster. That was in 1942.

Today one of the more recent successes of the game at junior level are the national school competitions. These, and the Park's schemes, help to expose the sport to players who would otherwise might never hold a racquet in their lives.

One of the Provinces premier competitions is that of the Senior Inter-Club team event. It is known as the Munster Cup. Between 1908 and 1948 **Blackrock LTC** were one of the dominant clubs and won the title eighteen times. Among their noted members were the Haughton family. Freddie South was one of the stars of the successful Glanmire team in the 1940s. Up until 1959 **Rushbrooke Lawn Tennis & Croquet Club** only succeeded in winning this event on six occasions. By 1979, when they beat **Galway LTC** in the final, it was their seventeenth success. Some results are as follows are given below.

Some Munster Cup Winners	
1907	Rushbrooke Lawn Tennis & Croquet Club
1908	Blackrock LTC
1909	Tralee LTC
1910	Innishannon LTC
1911	Blackrock LTC
1920	Fermoy LTC
1925	Blackrock LTC
1928	Blackrock LTC
1932	Blackrock LTC
1940	Glanmire LTC
1941	Glanmire LTC
1946	Blackrock LTC
1972	Limerick LTC
1973	Rushbrooke LT & Croquet Club
1977	Galway LTC
1978	Rushbrooke LT & Croquet Club
1979	Rushbrooke LT & Croquet Club
1982	Rushbrooke LT & Croquet Club
1983	Rushbrooke LT & Croquet Club
1984	Sunday's Well Boating & LTC
1985	Sunday's Well Boating & LTC
1986	Sunday's Well Boating & LTC
1987	Sunday's Well Boating & LTC
1988	Sunday's Well Boating & LTC
1989	Rushbrooke LT & Croquet Club
1992	Sunday's Well Boating & LTC
1993	Limerick LTC

1994	Lower Aghada LTC
1995	Lower Aghada LTC
1996	Lower Aghada LTC
1997	Rushbrooke LT & Croquet Club
1998	Limerick LTC
1999	Limerick LTC
2000	Limerick LTC
2001	Limerick LTC
2002	Limerick LTC
2003	Limerick LTC

Players of note in recent times include juniors from Tramore, Waterford, Tipperary County as well as the more concentrated centres in Cork and Limerick. It was not that long ago that Sean Sorensen was making tennis news in events such as the King's Cup and Davis Cup. His two sons, German born, are now Irish internationals. In the 1960s Michael Hickey was the Irish number one for some time. Noted internationals over the years from the province include-the sometimes forgotten-Harry Read of Roscrea, Cork's Arthur Mahony and the Haughtons of the Blackrock club. Marjorie and Nancy Haughton and their brother Ben were all internationals. Ben's son Alan followed in their foot-steps. Also lost in time are the names of Binkie Harman, Alex McOstrich and Meta Foley.

Paul Nolan was the honorary treasurer of the Munster Branch ILTA between 1980 and 1982. He became president in 1983.

The organisation of tennis within a province relies in the first instance on the various clubs and their members. However, it is the provincial committees that co-ordinate competition, coaching and teams. Notable administrators over the years have included Brian Scannell (the honorary secretary from the late 1950s to the late 1960s). Dr. Jim O'Neill (**Sunday's Well Boating & LTC**), Pauline Daly (**Nenagh LTC & Lattin LTC**), Kay Stanton (**Sunday's Well Boating & LTC**) and Helen Clinton (**Hillview LTC**) at one stage or another filled the posts of Branch honorary secretary and president, and later president of the national association. Frank O'Donoghue from **St. Anne's Waterford LTC** was one of the few non-Leinster people to become the honorary treasurer of

the Irish Lawn Tennis Association. He was president of the Munster branch in 1971 and then the ILTA in 1972. While a few names of administrators are recalled here, there have been hundreds of volunteers that have played their part in promoting the game. Each deserves credit in what is still essentially an amateur game at club and provincial levels. In recent times-twice each year-an excellent Munster News magazine has been produced. One of the primary people responsible for this successful production is Tim Conway of Ballinaclough (branch president in 1997).

Ulster

It recognised that, in the 19th century, the **Fitzwilliam LTC** were the organisers of tennis in Dublin and, by virtue of their initiatives, the Irish game in general. What is not widely known, is that there was an Ulster Lawn Tennis Association at least as far back as 1891. The Irish Lawn Tennis Association was formed in 1908, about thirty years after the game of lawn tennis was first played in the country. The Ulster body, of whom we know little, offered a *handsome Inter-Club Challenge Cup for competition among the tennis clubs of Ulster.* The inaugural winner was **Banbridge LTC** thus setting a landmark for that club. The following year, at their first attempt, **Clones LTC** won the event. In 1893, **Cliftonville LTC** beat **Banbridge LTC** in the final. That year, and subsequently, if not earlier years too, the Cliftonville club ran the North of Ireland Championships. Manliffe Goodbody, the only Irishman to reach a US Open final, and Miss Shaw were the winners of the Singles Championships. Other details are included in Chapter 5.7 which deals with the Ulster Championships.

Thanks to the efforts of Lyn Jamison-former president (2002 & 2003) of the Ulster branch-much of the following information was unearthed. Two old minutes books for the periods 1927 to 1949 and 1958 to 1970 were found stored in the Public Record Office of Northern Ireland. Prior to 1927 there was a large active playing population in the province. Leagues were held in the Belfast area and in that year the **Belfast Boat Club** were holding their ninth Open tournament. This incorporated several Ulster championships. The first were held in 1919 when the Open singles titles went to John Miley and Miss A.R. Taylor.

Interprovincial matches had also been taking place. 1927 would mark the seventh consecutive year in which matches between Ulster and Leinster were held. Ulster had won the ties in 1922, 1923 and 1924, Leinster the other four.

In 1915 there were 15 clubs in Ulster affiliated to the ILTA. These were (with membership numbers in brackets):
Armagh (70)
Ballycastle (75)
Bangor
Belfast Boat Club

Castlerock Golf Club
Cliftonville (50)
Clones
County Cavan (60)
Dungannon (80)
Monaghan
Newcastle (60)
Newry
Omagh (80)
Quoile (50)
Windsor.

This number increased over the years and was probably at a peak in about 1961 when there were 92 affiliated clubs. Many died off in the 1960s and early 1970s but the numbers steadied and by 1999 there were 45.

The four Ulster representatives to the ILTA in 1909 were, according to the Minutes' book of the ILTA, S. J. Lyle (Ballycastle), J. C. Parke (Omagh), W. McWilliams (Monaghan) and J. F. Stokes (Fitzwilliam). Jim Parke was designated as a representative on the initial Council in 1908 but was recorded as being a member of the Clones club. Had he moved to Omagh or was the 1909 recording of that club an error?

Captain Robert (Bob) Corry (on right) was noted as a player and a very successful administrator at his club Windsor LTC. He was the honorary secretary of the Ulster Council (ILTA) in 1938 and 1938. In 1930 he became the first Ulster president of the Irish Lawn Tennis Association. The photo above was taken circa 1932 before the final of the mens' doubles at the Ulster Championship. From left: Messrs. Grant, Fulton and Hill.

In 1926, Ulster was represented by Dr. Tom Pedlow (**Lurgan LTC**), F.C. MacNeice (**Belfast Boat Club**), Captain E.S. Dashwood (**Windsor LTC**) and R. Mc Mullen (**Codogan Park LTC**) with Captain R.P. Corry and the Honorable Mr. Justice Hanna being Ulster vice-presidents of the organisation. A reviewed set of rules for the ILTA dictated that an Ulster Council be set up to organise and represent tennis in the province. The following is the opening minutes for the Ulster Provincial Council:

A meeting of representatives of Lawn Tennis Clubs in Ulster affiliated to the Irish Lawn Tennis Association, was held in the lounge of the Y.M.C.A. Belfast, on Wednesday 16th March 1927.

Under the altered rules of the I.L.T.A. it is now necessary to form an Ulster Provincial Council to manage Lawn Tennis affairs in that province and for this purpose the forementioned meeting was called.

Representatives of the following clubs were present. Ballymena, Ballycastle, Belfast Boat Club, Beechmount, Cavehill, Civil Service, Cliftonville, C.I.Y.M.S., Chichester, Enniskillen, Kensington, Lurgan, Newcastle, Newry, Ophir, Quoile, Sydenham, Queen's Island, Windsor, Warrenpoint, Ward Park and Belfast Y.M.C.A..

The chair was taken by Dr. T. B. Pedlow (Lurgan) on the proposal of Mr. Crossley (Boat Club) seconded by Mr. R. P. Corry (Windsor).

The chairman having explained the reasons for which the meeting had been called, Mr. W. S. Ritchie who was acting as secretary to the meeting on behalf of the Secretary of the I.L.T.A. read apologies from the following:

Miss Fleming	*Omagh Club*
Mr. J. Moore	*Armagh Club*
Mr. Lane Joynt	*Warrenpoint Club*

The Secretary having read the notice convening the meeting, a general discussion took place regarding the composition and numbers most suitable for carrying on the work of the Provincial Council.

Mr. Dobbyn (Newcastle) proposed and Major Mc Callum (Warrenpoint) seconded "That for the first year only, the Council should consist of 20 members, seven to form a quorum, and that thereafter the Council should consist of 15 members with a quorum of 5". This was passed unanimously.

The following were elected Council for 1927 on The Proposal of Capt. Creery (Newcastle) seconded by Mr. R. P. Corry (Windsor).

Major J. D. M. McCallum	*Warrenpoint*
Dr. T. B. Pedlow	*Lurgan*
Capt. S. J. Lyle	*Ballycastle*
Mr. A. M. R. Dobbyn	*Newcastle*
Mr.De.V. Crossley	*Belfast Boat Club*
Mr. R. P. Corry	*Windsor*
Mr.H. McCleery	*Cliftonville*
Mr. Claude Hamilton	*Omagh*
Mr. E. S. Corry	*Bangor*
Mr.H. E. Wynne	*Enniskillen*
Mr. J. Moore	*Armagh*
Mr. Thos. Wright	*Quoile*
Mr. A. Crang	*Larne*
Mr. Halpin	*Cavan*
Mr. H. Mc William	*Monaghan*
Major R. McCreevy	*Cavehill*
Mr. L. Waldron	*Ward Park, Bangor*
Mr. G. Leatham	*Beechmount*
Mr. T. Chase	*Queens Island*
Mr. H. D. Montgomery	*Belfast Y.M.C.A.*

Mr. W. S. Ritchie agreed to act as Hon. Secty to the council pro tem.

Major McCallum proposed and Mr. Dobbyn seconded "That the drawing up of the necessary rules be left to the Council". This was passed unanimously.

Mr. Wright proposed and Mr. Maze (Kensington) seconded "That the election of an Auditor for the General Council accounts be left to the Council", passed unanimously.

Mr. W. F. Scott (Boat Club) was unanimously elected Hon. Auditor for the Ulster Provincial Council on the proposal of Mr. R.P. Corry seconded by Mr. Crossley. It was unanimously agreed that the first meeting of the new council should be held on Thursday 24th March at 1-30pm.

Mr. R. P. Corry proposed and Mr. Dobbyn seconded "That the Hon Sec should write to the Secretary of the I.L.T.A. asking that for this season only the same dates as last year should be arranged for the various Open Tournaments". This was carried unanimously.

The meeting concluded with a hearty vote of thanks to the chairman proposed by Mr. W.F. Scott seconded by Mr. L. Waldron.

The first meeting of the Council was held in the British Empire Rooms, 20, Bedford St., Belfast, on Thursday 24th March 1927 and the following positions were filled.

Chairman (President):	Dr.Thomas B. Pedlow
Vice-President:	Mr. Robert P. Corry
Honorary Secretary:	Mr. W.S. Ritchie
Honorary Treasurer:	Mr. Thomas Wright
Representatives to ILTA:	Mr. De Vere Crossley
	Mr. Layne Joynt
	Mr. E.S. Dashwood
	Dr.Thomas B. Pedlow
	Mr. R.obert P. Corrry

Mr. Robert Pringle of Dublin was unanimously elected Ulster Auditor of the general ILTA accounts.

That first meeting appointed selection and emergency committees. An interesting resolution, which was passed, was that *the Council approves of the existing rules of the Belfast Lawn Tennis Tournament and agrees to accept the Executive of same as appointed by the clubs, as a sub-committee of the Council, and that the Belfast Lawn tennis Council shall submit a balance sheet to the Council each year, duly audited.* That summer matches were arranged with Leinster (at Belfast Boat Club), in Liverpool and against the Queen's Club (London) at Belfast Boat Club.

A Council meeting on 3rd January 1929 instructed the honorary secretary to apply to the ILTA to have the *name of the Ulster Provincial Council changed to the Ulster Council, a similar change to be made in the titles of the other Provincial Councils.* That same meeting also asked that Rule 27 of the Tournament Regulations be altered so that a player who was not a member of an affiliated club could play in open tournaments by paying a fee of 10/- in addition to the entry fees.

The 1929 AGM (21st November) brought up the issue of inter-county matches. A letter from the ILTA requested the council *to do everything possible to promote the construction of additional hard courts.* The secretary was instructed to reply pointing out that the Council had been promoting the construction of hard courts, and that there were already over 100 hard courts in the province. The secretary was also instructed to write to clubs and asking that they should send delegates to the AGM. Representatives of only seven clubs had attended that meeting. In January 1930 it was agreed that Mr. H. J. P. Aitken be engaged as a professional tennis player for four weeks from 16th April at £20 per week. The lessons were to be held in the Belfast Badminton Hall. A location for the Ulster Hard Court Championships was sought and it was decided to include a Veterans' (over 50) men's doubles event. Royal Belfast Golf Club was subsequently allocated the tournament as they were the only applicants. In May it was agreed to invite a Leinster team of 4 boys and 4 girls to play an interprovincial match on Saturday 9th August. Mr. Corry offered the Windsor Club facilities for the match. By 1931, apart from tournaments in the Belfast area, there had been reference to those in Omagh and Armagh among others. There had also been lawn tennis leagues for Derry & District and on the Ards Peninsula.

In 1933, a senior ladies interprovincial match with Leinster was mooted (11th May). In December 1933 the Council decided to have a central handicapping system and each club was to send in their best 6 men and 6 ladies, ranked in order, based upon the previous season of play. For some time it was attempted to raise money by a voluntary levy towards coaching and tennis promotion in the province. At the AGM in 1933 (20th November) it was decided against a levy of 1/- per member of an affiliated club but the proposal carried was 10/- per fifty members, or part thereof, 10/- for the second fifty or part thereof and an upper limit of £4 per club be made. The motion was passed at a Special General Meeting held on Tuesday 19th December. *Several representatives from the affiliated clubs expressed the view that the country clubs would not pay the levy as any return they were likely to receive would be very small.*

For a few years the ILTA allocated a sum of £40 or £50 towards the tennis promotion fund and in January 1934 congratulated the Council on their efforts. On the 11th February 1935 it was agreed that the five clubs who had not paid the levy and affiliation fees in 1934 would no longer be considered affiliated members. The Annual general Meeting for 1936 was held on Monday 27th January at the Grand Central Hotel. *At the outset Dr. Pedlow spoke of the severe loss the nation had sustained through the death of our beloved King George. Those present stood in silence as a token of respect.*

At the council meeting of the 4th February 1937 it was pointed out by the honorary secretary that there was *a movement in the city to try and form a Church Tennis League. He was instructed to attend a meeting being held on Wednesday 10th February and endeavour to get all the Clubs to affiliate to the Council.* The AGM held on the 9th December 1937 agreed that a paid secretary would be appropriate for the Ulster Council and that the *salary not to exceed £20 per annum.*

Inter-County

Rules for an inter-county competition were drawn up in 1938. It was to be on a league basis with 5 men and 5 ladies on each team. Players must currently be residing in the county for at least one year. Apart from the nine Ulster counties, the County Borough of Belfast was an additional eligible county. In the first year Monaghan and Donegal did not participate. Subsequently, a member of **Clones LTC**, Mr. G. E. Henderson, queried why Monaghan had no team. The honorary secretary was asked to write back explaining the steps taken by the Council to have all counties involved. A perpetual Cup, at a cost of £10 was purchased and the president, Dr. Thomas Pedlow, contributed £5 towards its cost. In 1939, after some discussion it was *decided to allot 18 balls to each match, this to be charged to the Council at 13/- and a rebate of 5/- to be allowed for those returned, those not returned to be paid for in full by the County.*

In 1973, the Derry Journal (20th October) reported on a successful inter-county competition at Portrush. In 1972 the County Donegal team were placed last of seven teams competing. This year (1973) they had moved up to fourth with a team including Dave Craig, John Allen, Jim McKane, Ian McArthur, Diana Craig, Ann McCafferty, Wendy Patterson and Mary McArthur. The other counties involved were Derry, Tyrone, Armagh, Antrim, Down and Belfast.

In July 1938 a letter was received from the Munster Council suggesting a mixed inter-provincial match be played on the 9th August. A ladies inter-pro team was to play a Leinster team on the 6th September.

The twelfth AGM was held on Thursday 6th October 1938 at 7pm in the Grand Central Hotel. The honorary treasurer had been Mr. Thomas H. Wright, a member of the Northern Bank, since 1927. He would continue in office and showed a bank balance of £83-18-7, up from £19-4-9 at the end of 1928. (By the end of 1966 the 'estimated' balance would be £830).

A schools cup competition was set up in 1939. Nine teams entered. After the war, Mrs. Winifred Templeton was the honorary secretary for schools tennis and some nineteen schools took part in a Girls' Schools Cup event. On the 3rd November of that year the last Council meeting for some time would take place. The honorary secretary of the ILTA had requested the ranking list of Ulster senior players for the 1940 Handbook. It was decided that *as the Council would not be meeting for the "duration" the ranking would not be necessary.* The duration would last over five years. The first meeting of the Ulster Council after the war was on the 7th January 1946. John (Jack) Colville was nominated at president of the ILTA on the request from the Irish secretary, Ulster's turn being

overdue. The ILTA minutes of their meeting on the 25th January confirms the appointment. Unfortunately, by their next meeting on the 22nd February his sudden death would be sadly recorded. He was to be replaced by Mr. De Vere Crossley. Dr. Thomas Pedlow, the President, having welcomed the delegates to the first AGM for some time (held on the 13th February 1946) *referred to the deaths of 2 old members of the Council, Captain Dashwood and Mr. Dobbyn & to all tennis players who had given their their lives in the great war. Those present then stood in silence.* At the meeting of the Council the following month another death would be recorded. At the age of 65, James Cecil Parke, probably the greatest tennis player ever to come from Ulster, had died on the 27th February. He was a relative of Dr. Pedlow's.

At the meeting of the 4th March the secretary would announce that a sum of £50 had been granted by the ILTA to assist in re-organising Ulster tennis. Junior tennis, coaching and tennis balls werr all immediate issues after the war as the following cuttings indicated. The efforts to get tennis going again were successful and in September the secretary reported that 55 clubs had affiliated (as opposed to 53 in 1939), the District leagues, the inter-county championships and the Girls' Schools Cup competition had all been completed. Monaghan, Donegal, Armagh and Derry had, unfortunately, not taken part in the inter-county event. Good news was that a District league had been formed in Londonderry and six clubs were taking part. A girls' under 17 team was selected to play against Leinster -Angela Clark (Ashleigh House), Jean Jones (Ashleigh House), Georgie Brown (Ballymena Academy), Valerie Nutt (Victoria College), Dorothy Willis (Methodist College) and Daphne Glass (Londonderry High School).

1946

At the AGM in 1946 a sensible rule was included in the Ulster Council. The new Rule 21 passed decided that the selection committee should have seven members, that no more than one from any club be included and no member of that committee be selected for a representative team. It is noted that of the 15 elected council members two were ladies of significant note in tennis circles. Miss F. M. Fleming from the **Omagh LTC** and Mrs. Winifred Templeton, the latter being the primary advocate for schools tennis in Ulster. Mr. de Vere L. Crossley retired from his post of honorary secretary after a period of 25 years of work promoting Ulster tennis. Mrs. Templeton reported on the Girls schools competition in which 19 teams took part. Ashleigh House beat Londonderry High School 5/0 in the final with one match unfinished. The final was held at **Windsor LTC.**

1947

In 1947 Mr. Vaughan Owen from Aberystwyth was appointed as coach to the Ulster Council from the 1st April to the 31st July. His salary was agreed at £250 for the period. The following *promising players* were to be coached without charge: Robin Condy, Vivian

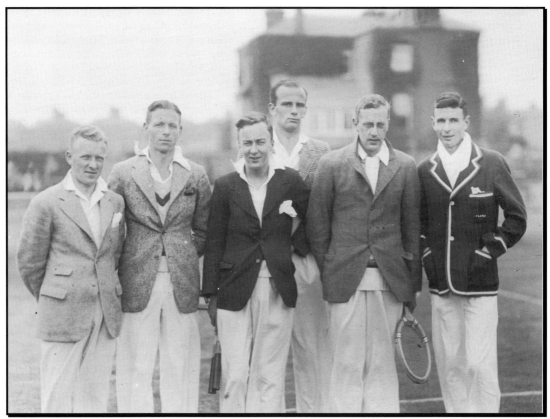

The Ulster team that played Leinster at Fitzwilliam LTC in 1934 were (from left): Tom Campbell, Jack O'
Keeffe, Jack O' Driscoll, Pierce Jackson, Eric Hill and Bertie Brown.

Gotto, H. B. Mercer, Brendan McGlade, M. Shortt, Ray C. Williams, Angela Clarke, Miss M. B. Clarke, Mrs. M. Lowry, Miss I. More and Miss M. Webb. Later in the year it was pointed out that during his four months the coach had visited twenty different clubs and coached over 300 individual players. Donegal were the only county (of ten) not to enter the 'knock-out' inter-county championships this year.

Due to heavy rain, an exhibition match between an Irish selection, playing against a Polish selection, had to be abandoned early on at the **Belfast Boat Club**. This was at the end of July (1947). A month later Belfast followers of the sport enjoyed exhibition tennis by American tennis professionals: Don Budge, Bobby Riggs, Pauline Betz and Sarah Palfrey Cooke. The first three were former Wimbledon singles champions.

The annual report on the Belfast & District Lawn Tennis League for 1947 was prepared by the honorary secretary, Carse Burton, and opens with the encouraging statement: *The end of the Second Post War Tennis Season has shown a recovery in Ulster Tennis, unsurpassed, proportionately by any other part of Great Britain.* The league had 27 clubs entering 53 teams in two divisions. The following were the winners for the year:

Senior 'A' Mens:	**Windsor LTC**
Senior 'A' Ladies:	**Windsor LTC**
Senior 'B'	**CIYMS**
Intermediate Section 1:	**Bangor LTC**
Intermediate Section 2:	**Ballymena**

(Ballymena win the final tie)

Junior Section 1:	**Willowfied LTC**
Junior Section 2:	**Malone Presby. Ch. LTC**

(Willowfied win the final tie)

1948

At the Council meeting of the 9th March 1948 it was agreed that a mixed inter-provincial match with Leinster, as proposed by Alf Walsh (honorary secretary of the Leinster Council), be arranged. An inter-league match, between the Dublin and Belfast leagues, was also agreed. The teams to exclude international and inter-provincial players.

The meeting of the 26th March 1948 noted the following: *The Honorary Secretary stated that it had recently come to his knowledge that two Clubs affiliated to the Irish Lawn Tennis Association had last year competed in a League-known as the 'Coast to Coast' League-in which non-affiliated Clubs had also taken part.*

Before the spreading of television, films were always welcome. Through the interest of Pat Hughes, the former British Davis Cup player, films on tennis were secured for showing in St. Mary's Hall Belfast on Friday 18th June 1948. Admission charge was 2/-. Efforts were made to answer the concern about tennis standards in the province (see coaching chapter) and an amended coaching scheme was agreed for 1949. At the AGM in 1948 (27th October) there was high tribute paid by the president, Dr. Pedlow, to Mr. Maunsell the ILTA honorary secretary who had died the previous week. This was followed by a minute's silence. The meeting agreed to the following proposals. Mrs.

Roguie Bain (**Windsor LTC**) proposed friendly matches between Belfast and Dublin clubs. Mr. J. R. Halpin (**County Cavan LTC**) proposed a new towns league, similar to that in Leinster. The press were thanked for their support for the game *despite the shortage of newsprint.* Though losing the senior inter-provincial match 18-0, the honorary secretary, Terry Duncan, would record a 9/1 victory in the Belfast-Dublin inter-league match and hoped that this event *will become a permanent feature in our annual Tennis calendar.* In 1948 County Tyrone won the provinces inter-county competition for the first time.

Winifred Templeton MBE was president of the Ulster Council ILTA in 1960 and honorary secretary from 1961 to 1962. She was noted for her development and organisation of schools' tennis. She was intensely involved with the sport of hockey and was president of the ILHU in three different decades.

1949

At the first meeting of the Council for 1949 (held on the 10th November 1948) a discussion took place on the possibility of a competition for the four provinces of Ireland, the honorary secretary being keen to promote this event. A sub-committee of Roguie Bain, Carse Burton and Terry Duncan drew up a set of rules for such an event. With one amendment, it was accepted by the other three provinces. The ILTA sanctioned the idea at their meeting on the 11th February and the event was scheduled to be played on the courts at Belfast Boat Club on Saturday 4th June 1949. The Ulster Council suggested that one of the four 'Downshire' Cups which were presented by Colonel Charley to them in 1946 be used for this event. (These cups had been used many years earlier by the **Downshire LTC** for competitions no longer being held).

In 1949, Ulster played a representative match against the West of Scotland. This was only the third time in the 75 year history of lawn tennis that sides representing Scotland and Ireland met. In 1914, a full

Irish side beat Scotland in Edinburgh 9/5. In 1946, the Scots visited Dublin and were beaten 6/2. The Ulster team played this third encounter at Glasgow and lost 7/4.

1950

In 1950 the Ulster team took on the West of Scotland team in an inter-association match in Belfast. The visitors won comfortably. The only consolation was the doubles win by Vivian Gotto and Ray Williams. They beat T. Boyd and A.B. Murray 6/4 6/4. That year G. Mc Coyle was the other top ranked man in Ulster. The top ladies were Roguie Bain, M. B. Clarke, Angela Clarke and Mrs. M. Lowry. The Ulster Hard Court Championships were a local affair. Number one seed, Vivian Gotto, beat William A. Rainey 6/3 6/1 in the final. In the ladies' singles final Angela Clarke beat M. B. Clarke 6/1 7/5. W. J. McFall and G. M. C. Coyle beat Tommy Crooks and I. Cameron 6/4 6/2 in the men's doubles. There does not appear to have been any ladies doubles title at stake. W. J. McFall and Mrs. A. Bland beat Vivian Gotto and Roguie Bain in an exceptionally close final. The winning score 7/5 7/9 6/4 tells its own story.

1951

In Spring 1951 the Ulster Official Rankings released were as follows:

	Men
1	Vivian Gotto
2	Ray Williams
3	Bill Rainey
4	Tommy Crooks
5	W. D. Smyth
6	G. M'Coyle
	Women
1	Roguie Bain
2	Miss M. B. Clarke
3	Angela Clarke
4	Eileen Kirkpatrick
5	Miss G. M. M'Coy
6	Miss G. Browne

The Ulster Closed Championships were held in Belfast early in the year. Vivian Gotto retained his title, saving six match-points and Robin Condy.

MS: Vivian Gotto beat Robin Condy 3/6 8/6 6/3
LS: Roguie Bain beat Miss M. D. McCoy 3/6 8/6 6/2
MD: Vivian Gotto/W. D. Muspratt beat
    Bill Rainey/Tommy Crooks 7/9 6/3 6/1
LD: Angela Clarke/Mrs. Bland beat
    Dorothy Willis/Eileen Kirkpatrick 2/6 6/1 6/3

1958

The minutes of the 27th May 1958 reiterated that friendly matches between affiliated clubs and non-affiliated clubs was excluded by virtue of Rule 19.

Affiliations to the Ulster Council ILTA-1957 to 1965

Organisations	1957	1958	1959	1960	1961	1962	1963	1964	1965
Clubs	91	89	88	84	90	86	78	78	71
Schools	46	46	47	46	43	47	43	50	53
Local Authorities	7	7	7	6	6	5	5	5	5
Other Bodies	1	1							
Totals	145	146	142	135	139	138	126	133	129

The winning teams in the four Ulster Leagues in 1958

League	Grade	Teams	Winning Club
Belfast & District	Senior A (Men)	10	Ballymena LTC
	Senior A (Women)	2	Cavehill LTC
	Senior B	14	Hawarden LTC
	Intermediate	27	Old Bleach LTC
	Junior	44	Comber LTC
	Juvenile	7	Windsor LTC
Derry & District	Mens	9	Limavady LTC "B"
	Mixed	9	Glendermott LTC
East Donegal	Senior	5	CYMS Letterkenny LTC
	Junior	8	Rectory LTC
Mid-Ulster		7	Joint Winners: Banbridge LTC & First Dromore Presbyterian Church TC

30th June 1958: Congratulations to Ulster team on their success in the Inter-provincials held at Rushbrooke, Cork. This was the first time the province won this event. The AGM later in the year would hear that *the issue was in doubt until almost the last stroke of the day.* The finals scores were Ulster 15, Leinster 14, Munster 5 and Connaught 0. *Each and every player contributed in large measure to the victory but perhaps special mention might be made of Mrs. Findlay's defeat of the Leinster No. 1 Miss June Fitzpatrick, thus giving her a triple victory over her inter-provincial rivals, a feat equalled by our Men's Doubles pair, R. S. Condy and R. V. Gotto.* June Fitzpatrick was in fact Irish number one in 1957.

8th July 1958: Donegal, in their first year in the Inter-county Championship win the South-West Zone.

August 1958: Cyril Kemp and I. Cameron resign from the selection committee in order that they would be available for selection for the remainder of the season. The October meeting records that Ulster beat the Civil Service Association 6/3 on September 6th and that Belfast (declared winners of the North-East) beat Donegal in the final of the Inter-County competition.

John O. Darbyshire presented a detailed typed annual report to the Ulster Council for their AGM held in the YMCA, Belfast on the 24th October 1958. Affiliated organisations were enumerated and included 5 new clubs in 1958. Data for years up to 1965 were also recorded at the Annual General Meetings. The figures show a slippage in affiliated organisations, the school number kept up and, in 1986, 48 schools played in the Ulster Schools competitions. There were fifty clubs affiliated that year. However, the numbers of clubs did drop dramatically over the period 1960 to 2000. The clubs affiliated in 2000 was 41, less than half the number (84) some forty years earlier.

The secretary noted that during the summer some leading players played an exhibition match on the new Warrenpoint UDC courts and hopes the interest of that local authority *will be followed by other Authorities in whose areas facilities for the game are sorely lacking.* It was noted that there were 71 members in the Patron Members' Association, six of whom were life members. (In 1959, it was out of the patron's account that Derek Arthurs received £25 towards playing in English tournaments during that summer). During the year (1958) there were 4615 affiliated club members and 814 persons entering tournaments. The coaching schemes cost £157-5-9 while the interprovincial match in Cork cost £91-16-10. In 1959 the Council had a profit on the professional exhibition, held at the King's Hall, Belfast. Over 6,500 attended the 'tournament'. The Kramer 'circus' brought Tony Trabert, Frank Sedgman, Ken Rosewall and Lew Hoad to Belfast. Ulster were pipped in 1959 in the Interprovincials held at **Elm Park**. Leinster 15 matches, Ulster 14, Munster 7, Connaught 0. While Ulster lost to the Leinster boys 6/3 and girls 8/1 respectively, they would beat the Munster boys (5/4) and girls (6/3).

Two boys were the subject of letters to and from the Council in August 1962. One player had been 25 minutes late for an under 18 final at **Cavehill LTC**. At one set all he withdrew. Another was granted a late entry to the Irish Junior Championships at **Fitzwilliam LTC**. A partner was also arranged for the boys' doubles. He had failed to appear at the event and had sent no notice of withdrawal. The Council decided that the *Fitzwilliam Club should be asked not to refund 15/- entrance fees in respect of this player.*

Ulster Cavaliers

The "Cavaliers" was a touring team selected by the Ulster Council, made up of players from a broad spectrum of background and ability. The purpose was to send a team to club or organisation or district to play a match against local opposition. The strength of the Cavaliers playing ability was selected to match as close as possible the strength of the local team.

Peter Bayliss was honorary secretary of the Ulster Council from 1970 to 1975. He took over the role of honorary secretary in 1976 and has held the post for 26 of the last 31 years. He served as president of the ILTA in 1979 and 1987.

Most of the Cavaliers would consist of a variety of players, young and old, ex representative players, administrators-trying to get an attractive balance between playing ability and personalities. The Cavaliers was the brainchild of John O. Darbyshire (the honorary secretary of the Ulster Council) who set it up in 1960 and he ran it for a number of years, then it was handed on to various others to run. The membership fee was fixed at 5/- and the match fee at 2/6. The Lord Mayor of Belfast, Alderman R.G.C. Kinahan, and the Lady Mayoress had agreed to become the first members of the Cavaliers. He would play for the club when civic duties allowed him. By the end of 1960 more than 10 matches had been played and others were already arranged. Erskine Willis was the secretary of the travelling team in the mid-1960.s. The touring team activity continued until the mid 1970s.

The first match was played in Carrickfergus at St. Nicholas Church and matches were then played throughout the province. In addition, here were tow occasions when the Cavaliers travelled to England. A ladies team played in Lancashire and a men's team played in Cheshire. The Cheshire team then visited Ulster for a return match.

A selection, at random, of some of those who played for the Cavaliers were: Viv Gotto, Walter Nicholl, Eileen Dundee, Sam Cummings, Jack Calvert, Ray Williams, Joy and Ken Dunbar, N.A. Palmer, Walter Little, Madeleine Calvert-Jones, Sir Robin and Lady Kinahan, Olive Melville and Doreen Muskett. There were many others from a range of clubs.

One former Cavalier recalls a match played at Thiepval Barracks, Lisburn. *The home team included the Brigadier and a Sergeant (it was a mixed team of military men and their wives, girl friends or other ladies) the order of the men was such that it went in order of rank, the Brigadier was the No. 1 and the Sergeant, No. 4. As the Sergeant was a better player than the Brigadier our team had to be shuffled around to get some sort of even competition! Ray Williams told the story of being on a Cavaliers team which he felt played an unofficial match which might not have been approved by the Council. It was against a team called the "Roundheads"!!* Play commenced in Ballymena but, for unspecified reason, concluded in Broughshane at around 4 a.m... *Bad light must have stopped play!*

No doubt there were many more untold stories of the Cavaliers. The purpose of this travelling team was to encourage the playing of tennis and to publicise the game. The warmth and generous hospitality received well repaid the effort of the travelling players.

North West Rovers
The North West branch of the Ulster Council also had a touring team called the "North West Rovers". Operated on similar lines as the Cavaliers, it functioned from 1965 to 1970. Those involved in running this team included Ian McPherson, Ernie Semple and Rosemary Templeton (Mc Dowell). Opposition included the club at Du Pont and the Coleraine Institute School.

1962
The annual report for 1962 noted that seven clubs were now defunct, the Dunedin club membership have been absorbed into the new **Cavehill Methodist LTC**. Nine clubs were to be suspended in the event of non-payment of affiliation fees. This seems to have been an annual headache in many branches.

The following item is a bit of a mystery and relates to the meeting of the 9th October 1962.: *TREATMENT FOR COURTS IN FROST: Mr.Darbyshire proposed that treatment with "HAR-COR-SAL" should be given free of cost to the following Club courts which are being used for Winter Coaching purposes- Belmont(3), Belfast Boat Club (1), Windsor (1), Limavady (1) and Larne (1), and it was agreed that this should be made available at once.*

The AGM in 1962 included a few interesting items. *Mr. H. Carson (Strandtown School), one of the Council's Professional Coaches, asked that in future, in giving the names of players in Junior Interprovincial teams and Ranking Lists, the name of the Club to which the player belonged should be stated, and not the School. He thought that the Schools did little to coach or encourage players to play tennis and that they should not receive all the credit.*

Mr. Ivan McCartney (Downshire), Hon. Secretary of the Mid-Ulster League, spoke of the lack of young players in his area, and mentioned the competition of golf.

Mavis Hogg MBE has acted as honorary secretary of the Ulster Council from 1979 to 1981 following a two year period as president. Her contribution to game was extensive at national level. She was honorary secretary of the ILTA/TI from 1985 to 1992 and president in 1983.

The annual report of the honorary secretary included the congratulations to the senior Ulster team, winning the Inter-provincials for the second time. They would win it again in 1963. The team in 1962 was R.C. Williams (non-playing captain), Peter Jackson, Tommy Crooks, Vivian Gotto, Cecil Pedlow, Hadassah Lord, Angela Findlay, Eileen Logan and Miss J. Wallace.

Special mention was made of "Notable Performances" during the year by Peter Jackson (Davis Cup), Derek Arthurs (Davis Cup), T.B. Barnes (veterans), Maureen Spelman (RAF team) and Michael Rainey (Irish Junior Champion). The report for the North West indicated

that there were now only 13 clubs affiliated, as opposed to 20 in 1961.

1963

In 1963 there was some concern about a *Wanderer's Club*. They were told that they would not be given permission to affiliate. They were also referred to as a *Nomads* club and a *Ramblers* Club, apparently on the line of the Ulster Cavaliers and the North-West Rovers. They functioned during 1963. The organiser was eventually suspended. The suspension was lifted in May 1964 when he signed an agreement to cease this activity.

In June 1963 the Trustees of the recently defunct Dunedin TC (due to the loss of their courts) offered the sum of £50 from their account to the Council, to be used in promoting junior tennis in the Province. Four trophies, to be called the "Dunedin Cup" were to be bought and to be played for in Under 15 and Under 18 Boys' and Girls' Singles Championships of Belfast. The Council conveyed their grateful thanks for this *most generous gesture.*

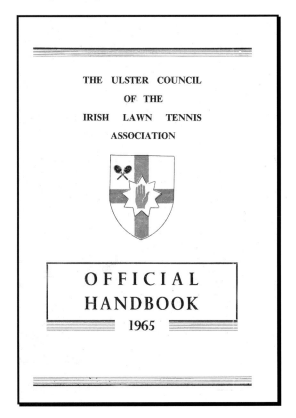

THE ULSTER COUNCIL
OF THE
IRISH LAWN TENNIS
ASSOCIATION

OFFICIAL
HANDBOOK
1965

The annual report for 1963 indicated that there was a marked expansion in the Province during the previous year. Standards were improving and coaching was extensive. The following comment from the honorary secretary's report may be familiar to committee members in present times or in the past. *Despite these advances the Council is aware of several weaknesses in the fabric of the Association in Ulster. The average age of tennis players is becoming younger every year, and while this may facilitate the development of higher playing standards, clubs are tending to become denuded of members with experience in organising the game. In addition, there had been a slight over-all falling off in the membership of clubs, and a number of small clubs have dropped out of affiliation.*

1964

The first indoor event in Ulster was held in March 1964 in the Palace Gardens, Holywood. The winner of the men's singles was Peter Jackson (beating Cecil Pedlow (**Windsor LTC**) in the final). In the ladies singles Lorna Croskery (**Hawarden LTC**) beating H. Braithwaite (**CIYMS**) in that final. Lorna had been the Irish representative in Junior Wimbledon the previous year. Sunday tennis came up as a subject on the meeting of the 6th October. *There was a long discussion on the merits and demerits of Sunday Tennis in Junior Tournaments. It was agreed that the Council should not legislate on the subject of Sunday tennis.*

Anne Taylor-Ulster Council
Honorary Secretary 1984-1986, 1989-1992
President 1987-1988

Recent Decades

In recent decades the game of tennis has undergone significant changes. Ulster went through its share, the difficulties of security and related matters not making matters easy for the promotion of any sport. However, a new period of promotion has evolved. Cross community and cross border initiatives have managed to use sport for good. Historically, tennis, cricket and rugby were associated strongly with the Protestant community while Gaelic Games were linked with the Catholic community. To complicate matters there is the fact that Ulster has six counties linked to the U.K. and three to the Republic of Ireland. Rising above this have been players and officials who have seen the value of sport as a means of linking people together. Mavis Hogg of **Hawarden LTC** was such an individual who contributed to the sport in the province and for many years as honorary secretary of the Irish association.

10th October 2003. George Stevenson receiving the Mavis Hogg Cup for his extensive services to the sport of tennis in Ulster. Also in photograph are Mavis Hogg and Lyn Jamison, president of the Ulster Branch in 2002 and 2003.

For over 30 years Peter Bayliss has made a major contribution as a player and administrator in Ulster, in particular as honorary treasurer for 26 years following a six year stint as honorary secretary. George Stevenson was a late comer to tennis-hockey had been his sport. Not alone was he a keen member of **Bangor LTC** but ultimately his interest expanded to the Ulster Council and Irish tennis. He has been president and honorary secretary of both bodies. Since 2002 he has acted as secretary to the Ulster Council and Tennis Ireland.

Downshire LTC and Ulster players John Canning and George Lucas were selected to play for Ireland's veteran's (over 55) team in the World Championships in Philadelphia in September 2004.

An interesting and important promoter of tennis is Seamus McCusker of **Irvinestown LTC**. Seamus saw tennis as a sport for bringing communities together in his own club. His keenness saw him get involved in the Ulster Council. He became its president in 1998 and 1999. In 2003 he was the Ulster president of Tennis Ireland. In the Tennis Ireland Yearbook for 2003 he said that he hoped to *visit as many clubs as possible during my year.* True to his word, this lover of all sports has apparently visited more clubs in Ireland as president than any previous holder of that office. We could continue through the listings of those within the Ulster game and find in each a person who has contributed, for a short of lengthy period, to the sport they love.

Vivienne Stewart
President Ulster Council 2006

The structure of the sport of tennis in Ulster is good. There continues to be people that are interested in the sport and are prepared to ensure that it thrives and develops. Long departed from their posts are those avid officers such as Thomas Pedlow (president 1927-1948), Thomas Wright (honorary treasurer 1927-1939), Terry Duncan (honorary secretary 1947 to 1957) and Walter Nicholl (honorary treasurer 1947-1975). Whether it is as a player, coach, schools' organiser or serving as branch officer, all tennis-loving people in the province should be very satisfied with how the game has blossomed and look forward to even better days ahead. This will not happen by itself, the juniors of today must be encouraged to participate

and become those leaders of tomorrow. To finish, a few words from Letty Lucas in 2004, the year she became president of the Ulster Branch. Letty has been a player and administrator for very many years and well aware of every aspect of the game in the province.

> *A major objective of the UBTI is the promotion of tennis as a healthy, enjoyable, social sport for life, open to all ages in the community.*
>
> *We are consulting clubs in order to formulate a new tennis development programme. The foundation of the plan is to assist hard working committee members in the development of their club.....We need to encourage many more young people to play tennis to ensure we don't miss that special person.*
>
> *Ulster Branch currently assist player development, leagues, tournaments, travel and teams coaching schemes, parks tennis and wheelchair tennis.*

She urged players to get involved in helping their club and the Ulster Branch in its endeavours. A sentiment that all presidents of sports' organisations would fully support.

On the 10th October 2003 the Ulster Branch (Tennis Ireland) held their 75th anniversary dinner. Past presidents attending are included here. At back (l. to r.): Erskine Willis (1974-1975), Lyn Jamison (2002-2003), Peter Bayliss (1968-1969), Sammy Tuff (1978) and George Stevenson (1989-1990).At front (l. to r.) Susan Creber (1991), Mavis Hogg (1976-1977), Seamus McCusker (1998-1999), Clem Shaw (1961), Gillian Carson (1983-1984) and Walter Hall (1994-1995).

Irish Lawn Tennis Association/Tennis Ireland Connacht Branch

YEAR	President	Honorary Secretary	Honorary Treasurer
1934	Captain Willie Campbell	Kenny West	Kenny West
1935	Captain Willie Campbell	Kenny West	Kenny West
1936	Captain Willie Campbell		
1937	Captain Willie Campbell		
1938	Henry St. J. Blake		
1939	Henry St. J. Blake		
1940	Henry St. J. Blake	Mr. M. J. Dyar	Mr. M. J. Dyar
1941	Henry St. J. Blake	Mr. M. J. Dyar	Mr. M. J. Dyar
1942-1945	Henry St. J. Blake	Martin Mulligan	Martin Mulligan
1946	Henry St. J. Blake	Martin Mulligan	Henry Pittman
1947	Henry St. J. Blake	Henry Pittman	Jack Cunningham
1948	Henry St. J. Blake	Mr. P. Henry	Tom Hannick
1949-1950	Henry St. J. Blake	Gerald Dodd	Gerald Dodd
1951-1957	Henry St. J. Blake	Dermot Kilgallon	Dermot Kilgallon
1958-1959	Ed. Ralph Ryan	Dermot Kilgallon	Dermot Kilgallon
1960	Ed. Ralph Ryan	John F. Garavan	Dermot Kilgallon
1961	Ed. Ralph Ryan	John F. Garavan	Dermot Kilgallon
1962-1963	Ed. Ralph Ryan	John F. Garavan	T. W. Hussey
1964	Ed. Ralph Ryan	John F. Garavan	T. W. Hussey
1965-1966	Terry Mc Carthy	Deirdre Coates	T. W. Hussey
1967	Terry Mc Carthy	Deirdre Coates	Deirdre Coates
1968	John F. Garavan	Deirdre Coates	Deirdre Coates
1969-1971	John F. Garavan	Vincent Frawley	Vincent Frawley
1972	Donal Dempsey	Vincent Frawley	Vincent Frawley
1973	Donal Dempsey	Vincent Frawley	Vincent Frawley
1974	Maeve Jennings	Donal Dempsey	Donal Dempsey
1975	Maeve Jennings	Declan Spring	Donal Dempsey
1976	Maeve Jennings	Pat Moore/Christina Millett	Donal Dempsey
1977-1980	Donal Dempsey	Christina Millett	Donal Dempsey
1981	Donal Dempsey	Christina Millett	Sheila Kilkelly
1982	Donal Dempsey	Christina Millett	Donal Dempsey
1983	Donal Dempsey	Christina Millett	Donal Dempsey
1984	Donal Dempsey	Christina Millett	Donal Dempsey
1985-1986	Vincent Frawley	Brigid Kilkelly	Donal Dempsey
1987	Vincent Frawley	Gary O' Lochlainn	Donal Dempsey
1988	Bob English	Gary O' Lochlainn	Donal Dempsey
1989-1990	Bob English	Roy Thompson	Donal Dempsey
1991	Bob English	Fionnghuala Kilkelly	Donal Dempsey
1992-1994	Michael Mc Cann	Fionnghuala Kilkelly	Donal Dempsey
1995	Roy Thompson	Fionnghuala Kilkelly	Donal Dempsey
1996	Olwyn Raftery	Fionnghuala Kilkelly	Donal Dempsey
1997	Olwyn Raftery	Gai Barry	Donal Dempsey
1998-1999	James Ward	Rosaleen O' Muircheartaigh	John Mc Hugh
2000	James Ward	Olwyn Raftery	John Mc Hugh
2001	James Ward	Olwyn Raftery	John Mc Hugh
2002	Maria Kilkelly	James Ward	John Mc Hugh
2003	Maria Kilkelly	Olwyn Raftery	John Mc Hugh
2004	Maria Kilkelly	Olwyn Raftery	John Mc Hugh
2005	Maria Kilkelly	Olwyn Raftery	John Mc Hugh
2006	Mary Loftus	Olwyn Raftery	John Mc Hugh

Irish Lawn Tennis Association/Tennis Ireland
Leinster Branch

YEAR	President	Honorary Secretary	Honorary Treasurer
1927-1930	George Byrne	Harry Rhys Maunsell	Cecil Almond
1931	Dr. Arthur P. Barry	Harry Rhys Maunsell	Cecil Almond
1932	William St. George Perrott	Harry Rhys Maunsell	Cecil Almond
1933	A. P. Dawson	Harry Rhys Maunsell	Cecil Almond
1934	James Ferguson	Harry Rhys Maunsell	Cecil Almond
1935	Alfred Walsh	Harry Rhys Maunsell	Cecil Almond
1936	R. A. C. Barrett	Harry Rhys Maunsell	Cecil Almond
1937	Cecil Almond	Harry Rhys Maunsell	Cecil Almond
1938	Maud Price	Harry Rhys Maunsell	W. J. Poole/C. S. Almond
1939	Captain C. J. Daly	Harry Rhys Maunsell	William St. George Perrott
1940	Raymund Egan	Harry Rhys Maunsell	William St. George Perrott
1941	Dr. Eustace Fannin	Harry Rhys Maunsell	William St. George Perrott
1942	Harry Harte-Barry	Harry Rhys Maunsell	William St. George Perrott
1943	Rev. J. M. Jennings	Harry Rhys Maunsell	William St. George Perrott
1944	Percy Huet	Harry Rhys Maunsell	William St. George Perrott
1945	Willie Sandys	Harry Rhys Maunsell	William St. George Perrott
1946	Terence H. K. Dunlop	Harry Rhys Maunsell	William St. George Perrott
1947	Kevin O' Brien-Kenney	Harry Rhys Maunsell	William St. George Perrott
1948	Alfred (*Alf*) Walsh	H. R. Maunsell/A. H. Walsh	Kevin O'Brien Kenney
1949	Percy Huet	Alfred (*Alf*) Walsh	Kevin O'Brien Kenney
1950	George McVeagh	Alfred (*Alf*) Walsh	Kevin O'Brien Kenney
1951	Brendan Read	Alfred (*Alf*) Walsh	Kevin O'Brien Kenney
1952	Harry Mc Guinness	Alfred (*Alf*) Walsh	Kevin O'Brien Kenney
1953	George Woods	Alfred (*Alf*) Walsh	Kevin O'Brien Kenney
1954	Henry Tierney	Alfred (*Alf*) Walsh	Kevin O'Brien Kenney
1955	Dick Harrison	Alfred (*Alf*) Walsh	Kevin O'Brien Kenney
1956	Guy Jackson	Alfred (*Alf*) Walsh	Kevin O'Brien Kenney
1957	Betty Lombard	Alfred (*Alf*) Walsh	Kevin O'Brien Kenney
1958-1959	Cyril Boden	Alfred (*Alf*) Walsh	Kevin O'Brien Kenney
1960	Ken Potterton	Alfred (*Alf*) Walsh	Kevin O'Brien Kenney
1961	Jim Roche	Alfred (*Alf*) Walsh	Kevin O'Brien Kenney
1962	Larry Steen	Alfred (*Alf*) Walsh	Kevin O'Brien Kenney
1963	Joe P. Murphy	Alfred (*Alf*) Walsh	Kevin O'Brien Kenney
1964	Charlie Brennan	Alfred (*Alf*) Walsh	Kevin O'Brien Kenney
1965	Fintan P. Clancy	Alfred (*Alf*) Walsh	Kevin O'Brien Kenney
1966	John (J. A.) Fitzpatrick	Alfred (*Alf*) Walsh	Kevin O'Brien Kenney
1967-1968	Danny Moroney	Alfred (*Alf*) Walsh	Kevin O'Brien Kenney
1969	Ken Potterton	Alfred (*Alf*) Walsh	Tom Hoare
1970	Ken Potterton	Charlie Brennan	Tom Hoare
1971	Heather Flinn	Charlie Brennan	Tom Hoare
1972	Heather Flinn	Charlie Brennan	B.M. Kennedy
1973	Robin Donovan	Charlie Brennan	B.M. Kennedy
1974	Gerry Clarke	Charlie Brennan	B.M. Kennedy
1975	Paddy Donnellan	Charlie Brennan	B.M. Kennedy
1976	Paddy Donnellan	Charlie Brennan	S. D. O' Sullivan
1977	Charlie Brennan	Charlie Brennan	Seamus Shelly
1978-1979	Ken Potterton	Charlie Brennan	Seamus Shelly
1980-1981	Willie Clayton	Charlie Brennan	Gerry More O' Ferrall
1982	Rev. Percy Winder	Charlie Brennan	Gerry More O' Ferrall
1983	Rev. Percy Winder	Gerry More O' Ferrall	Muriel Bolton
1984-1985	Henry Lappin	Gerry More O' Ferrall	Bryan O'Neill
1986-1987	Gerry More O' Ferrall	Henry Lappin	James Brewster
1988	Jerry Sheehan	Mary Goodman	James Brewster
1989	Jerry Sheehan	Mary Goodman	James Brewster
1990-1991	James Brewster	Denise Kelly	Billy Meehan
1992-1993	Jim McArdle	Deirdre (*Dee*) Jennings	Billy Meehan
1994-1995	Kieran Sheehan	Deirdre (*Dee*) Jennings	Billy Meehan
1996	Joe Flood	Deirdre (*Dee*) Jennings	Billy Meehan
1997	David Nathan	Ann O' Connor	Billy Meehan
1998	Deirdre (*Dee*) Jennings	Ann O' Connor	Billy Meehan
1999	Frank Goodman	Ann O' Connor	Billy Meehan
2000	Gerry Halpenny	Ann O' Connor	Billy Meehan
2001	Deirdre (*Dee*) Jennings	Ann O' Connor	Billy Meehan
2002	James Brewster	Joe Flood	Billy Meehan
2003	Tony Locke	Joe Flood	Billy Meehan
2004	Jimmy Cahill	Joe Flood	Billy Meehan
2005	Ann O'Connor	Joe Flood	Billy Meehan
2006	Rory Wilson	Joe Flood	Billy Meehan

Irish Lawn Tennis Association/Tennis Ireland
Munster Branch

YEAR	President	Honorary Secretary	Honorary Treasurer
1942		W.J. Dwyer	
1952			E.C. Harrington
1953	G.T. Eason	M. Donegan	E.C. Harrington
1954	Frank Mockler	M. Donegan	
1955	D. B. O'Sullivan	M. Donegan	N. Lucy
1956	P.S.Keating	M. Donegan	N. Lucy
1957	J. Richard (*Dicky*) Quin	Brian F. Scannell	D.J. Mc Carthy
1958	Willie J. O'Regan	Brian F. Scannell	Frank J. Mockler
1959	Eric I. Harte-Barry	Brian F. Scannell	
1960		Brian F. Scannell	
1961	M. O'Byrne	Brian F. Scannell	S. P. Hanan
1962	Comdt. J. Kenny	Brian F. Scannell	S. P. Hanan
1963	A. F. Kelly	Brian F. Scannell	S. P. Hanan
1964	Frank J. Mockler	Brian F. Scannell	S. P. Hanan
1965		Brian F. Scannell	S. P. Hanan
1966		Brian F. Scannell	S. P. Hanan
1967	Mrs. M. Lucas	Brian F. Scannell	S. P. Hanan
1968	Noel Treacy		
1969	Dr. Jim O' Neill		
1970	Kevin O' Brien		
1971	Frank H. O'Donoghue		
1972	Eamon Smith	Dr. Jim O'Neill	Bill Tayler
1973	Beryl Boyle	Dr. Jim O'Neill	Bill Tayler
1974	Martin O' Keeffe	Dr. Jim O'Neill	Bill Tayler
1975	Seamus Cleary		Bill Tayler
1976	Pauline Daly	Bill Tayler	Bill Tayler
1977	Redmond Holland	Bill Tayler	Bill Tayler
1978	Michael Ryan		Bill Tayler
1979	Bill Tayler	Pauline Daly	Brendan Bradshaw
1980	Peter Mc Carthy	Pauline Daly	Paul Nolan
1981	Maura Deegan	Pauline Daly	Paul Nolan
1982	Gerry Lawlor	Pauline Daly	Paul Nolan
1983	Paul Nolan	Pauline Daly	Gerry Lawlor
1984	Dr. Jim O' Neill	Pauline Daly	Gerry Lawlor
1985	John Madden	Pauline Daly	
1986	Helen Clinton	Kay Stanton	Clem Cusack
1987	Niall Coffey	Kay Stanton	Elaine Bermingham
1988	Pauline Daly	Kay Stanton	Elaine Bermingham
1989	Lucy Warner Ryan	Kay Stanton	Elaine Bermingham
1990	Rhoda Mc Auliffe	Kay Stanton	Elaine Bermingham
1991	Ruth Byrne	Kay Stanton	Pauline Daly
1992	Elaine Bermingham	Helen Clinton	Geraldine O' Meara
1993	Kay Stanton	Peter Scott	Geraldine O' Meara
1994	Maria O'Sullivan	Una Heffernan	Geraldine O' Meara
1995	Suzanne Dalton	Kay Stanton	Geraldine O' Meara
1996	Geraldine O' Meara	Maria O'Sullivan	Pat O' Doherty
1997	Tim Conway	Claire Mc Namara	Peter Scott
1998	James Foley	Claire Mc Namara	Peter Scott
1999	Una Heffernan	Claire Mc Namara	Peter Scott
2000	Mary Mountjoy	Marie Mc Mahon	Peter Scott
2001	Claire Mc Namara	Marie Mc Mahon	Peter Scott
2002	Peter Scott	Marie Mc Mahon	Aidan Foley
2003	Kay Stanton	Peter Scott	Aidan Foley
2004	Aidan Foley	Kay Stanton	John McLaughlin
2005	Eileen Mawe	Kay Stanton	John McLaughlin/Ger O'Meara
2006	Mary Long	Kay Stanton	John McLaughlin/Ger O'Meara

Irish Lawn Tennis Association/Tennis Ireland
Ulster Branch

YEAR	President	Honorary Secretary	Honorary Treasurer
1927	Thomas B. Pedlow	Mr. W.S. Ritchie	Thomas H. Wright
1928	Thomas B. Pedlow	Mr. W.S. Ritchie	Thomas H. Wright
1929	Thomas B. Pedlow	Mr. W.S. Ritchie	Thomas H. Wright
1930	Thomas B. Pedlow	Mr. W.S. Ritchie	Thomas H. Wright
1931	Thomas B. Pedlow	Mr. A.V. L. Johnstone	Thomas H. Wright
1932	Thomas B. Pedlow	Mr. A.V. L. Johnstone	Thomas H. Wright
1933	Thomas B. Pedlow	Mr. A.V. L. Johnstone	Thomas H. Wright
1934	Thomas B. Pedlow	Mr. A.V. L. Johnstone	Thomas H. Wright
1935	Thomas B. Pedlow	Mr. A.V. L. Johnstone	Thomas H. Wright
1936	Thomas B. Pedlow	Mr. J.R. Sterling	Thomas H. Wright
1937	Thomas B. Pedlow	Mr. J.R. Sterling	Thomas H. Wright
1938	Thomas B. Pedlow	Robert P. Corry	Thomas H. Wright
1939	Thomas B. Pedlow	Robert P. Corry/T.H. Boyle*	Thomas H. Wright
1940-1945		Ulster Council did not function during World War II	
1946	Thomas B. Pedlow	Eric D. Hill/Mr. De Vere Crossley***	Herbert Flood
1947	Thomas B. Pedlow	Terry S. Duncan	Herbert Flood
1948	Thomas B. Pedlow	Terry S. Duncan	Walter G. Nicholl
1949		Terry S. Duncan	Walter G. Nicholl
1950		Terry S. Duncan	Walter G. Nicholl
1951		Terry S. Duncan	Walter G. Nicholl
1952		Terry S. Duncan	Walter G. Nicholl
1953		Terry S. Duncan	Walter G. Nicholl
1954		Terry S. Duncan	Walter G. Nicholl
1955	Harry R. Bayliss	Terry S. Duncan	Walter G. Nicholl
1956	J.W. Moore	Terry S. Duncan	Walter G. Nicholl
1957	Freddie Rogan	Terry S. Duncan	Walter G. Nicholl
1958	Kenneth J. Dunbar	^Henry Wallace/John O. Darbyshire	Walter G. Nicholl
1959	Walter G. Nicholl	John O. Darbyshire	Walter G. Nicholl
1960	Winifred Templeton	John O. Darbyshire	Walter G. Nicholl
1961	Clem Shaw	Walter G. Nicholl/Winifred Templeton***	Walter G. Nicholl
1962	Douglas P.F. Ferguson	Winifred Templeton	Walter G. Nicholl
1963	Alastair Smyth	Winifred Templeton MBE	Walter G. Nicholl
1964	Walter G. Nicholl	John O. Darbyshire/Winifred Templeton MBE**	Walter G. Nicholl
1965	Mick J. Dunne	John O. Darbyshire/Winifred Templeton MBE**	Walter G. Nicholl
1966	Dudley Magrath	John O. Darbyshire/Barbara Coppel**	Walter G. Nicholl
1967	Dudley Magrath	Barbara Coppel	Walter G. Nicholl
1968	Peter S. F. Bayliss	Barbara Coppel	Walter G. Nicholl
1969	Peter S. F. Bayliss	Barbara Coppel	Walter G. Nicholl
1970	Sam E. Cummings	Peter S. F. Bayliss	Walter G. Nicholl
1971	Sam E. Cummings	Peter S. F. Bayliss	Walter G. Nicholl
1972	Jean Coote	Peter S. F. Bayliss	Walter G. Nicholl
1973	Jean Coote	Peter S. F. Bayliss	Walter G. Nicholl
1974	Erskine Willis	Peter S. F. Bayliss	Walter G. Nicholl
1975	Erskine Willis	Peter S. F. Bayliss	Walter G. Nicholl
1976	Mavis Hogg	John Canning	Peter S. F. Bayliss
1977	Mavis Hogg	John Canning	Peter S. F. Bayliss
1978	Sammy Tuff	John Canning	Peter S. F. Bayliss
1979	John Canning	Mavis Hogg	Peter S. F. Bayliss
1980	John Canning	Mavis Hogg	Peter S. F. Bayliss
1981	James Holland	Mavis Hogg	Peter S. F. Bayliss
1982	James Holland	John Canning	Peter S. F. Bayliss
1983	Gillian Carson	John Canning	Peter S. F. Bayliss
1984	Gillian Carson	Anne Taylor	Dorothy Armstrong
1985	Elizabeth Hull	Anne Taylor	Peter S. F. Bayliss
1986	Elizabeth Hull	Anne Taylor	Peter S. F. Bayliss
1987	Anne Taylor	George Stevenson	Elizabeth Hull
1988	Anne Taylor	George Stevenson	Ian Williams
1989	George Stevenson	Anne Taylor	Peter S. F. Bayliss
1990	George Stevenson	Anne Taylor	Peter S. F. Bayliss
1991	Susan Creber	Anne Taylor	Peter S. F. Bayliss
1992	Elaine Cuthbert	Anne Taylor	Susan Creber
1993	Elaine Cuthbert	Mavis Hogg	Susan Creber
1994	Walter Hall	Mavis Hogg	Peter S. F. Bayliss
1995	Walter Hall	Anne Taylor	Peter S. F. Bayliss
1996	George Stevenson	Walter Hall	Peter S. F. Bayliss
1997	George Stevenson	Walter Hall	Peter S. F. Bayliss
1998	Seamus Mc Cusker	George Stevenson	Peter S. F. Bayliss
1999	Seamus Mc Cusker	George Stevenson	Peter S. F. Bayliss
2000	Tom Wilson	George Stevenson	Peter S. F. Bayliss
2001	Tom Wilson	George Stevenson	Peter S. F. Bayliss
2002	Lyn Jamison	George Stevenson	Peter S. F. Bayliss
2003	Lyn Jamison	George Stevenson	Peter S. F. Bayliss
2004	Letty Lucas	George Stevenson	Peter S. F. Bayliss
2005	Letty Lucas	George Stevenson	Peter S. F. Bayliss
2006	Vivienne Stewart	George Stevenson	Peter S. F. Bayliss

^Acting Honorary Sec.   *Honorary Secretary/Secretary; ** Joint Honorary Secretaries; ***Honorary Assistant Secretary

4.4 *Tennis at School and University*

Properly and keenly played, Lawn Tennis is a game with few, if any, superiors.
(Val Miley, 1913)

Today, we see tennis everywhere. Not literally, but in the sense that it is widespread, gets its share of TV sports coverage, and has an image. At the top it is highly paid and, though few realise their dreams, every young person can aspire to such apparently elusive heights. There is a route. Professional tennis is here to stay. A young amateur golfer can win national 'majors' such as the West of Ireland, attend tour school and, if good enough, be launched into an enjoyable life career. Tennis is somewhat more open in the sense that there are qualifying tournaments that can be entered when wishing to compete at major tournaments such as Wimbledon. An initial target of passing through the qualifiers is the first target. Others follow, if one is good enough.

Perception and image are important words for young people. Tiger Woods, Serena Williams and Roger Federer are among the most celebrated of sportspeople anywhere. (Note it was not necessary to tell you, the reader, that Tiger is a golfer.) Not so long ago it was Seve Ballesteros, Martina Hingis and Pete Sampras that were in the sporting spotlight. These *stars* sit at the top table, albeit for a limited number of years. The young will see the skills exhibited as ones that can be copied. With a combination of determination, self-belief, coaching, effort and organisational backup, many rungs of the ladder can be climbed. The old dream of the past, and indulge themselves in their memories, sometimes flawed ones. They also dream of

what might have been. The young are open-ended; they dream of the future and the possible. In Ireland, I think most kids would know of Roy Keane, and recognise him straight away. If that youngster plays rugby he knows who Keith Wood and Brian O'Driscoll are, never mind Ronan O'Gara. If he is a hurler he will know of TJ Carey. All have national images. Until recently, Sonia O'Sullivan was regularly on the sports pages, all youngsters of the late 1990s will have heard of the girl from Cobh and her exploits in the world's athletic arenas. Do many know what famous sportsmen came from Clones, County Monaghan? The older ones probably do. One is Barry McGuigan, that world-champion boxer, now retired. In 1912, the name on the lips of sports followers was another man from the same town, James Cecil Parke. Who was he? Please read the chapters on All-rounders, the Davis Cup, the Irish Open and Wimbledon.

In the 17th century the Catholic population of Ireland were certainly deprived when it came to education. Under the Penal laws, enacted on the 7th September 1695, *No Catholic could employ a Catholic schoolmaster to educate his children* (Cusack, 1868). Mind you, at that time there were few Catholics who could afford any type of formal education. The better off did sent their children abroad but they were subject to a fine of £100 and *the child could not inherit any property either in England or Ireland.*

One of the earliest schools to promote tennis was Clongowes Wood College in County Kildare. This shot was of the 1930 schools final. Jack Houlihan a boarder from Birr won the final against Sean O'Sullivan. Jack's younger brother Des won the junior ('Lower Line') title that year.

For a long, time education abroad was necessary for those of all persuasions. With Catholic Emancipation, and a general opening up of education in the 19th century, things did change. Mind you, free education for all only became available towards the end of the 20th century. Boarding schools were for those that could afford it. Today, the most exclusive schools-even in a 'classless' Ireland-are expensive and a luxury. No one seriously objects to this, as education is provided from the age of four up to and including obtaining a university degree, without finance being the major barrier. Success is more linked to Leaving Certificate points or 'A' levels.

What about sport? We can blame the English for much, but their penchant for pastimes, games, and then organised sport, did have its benefits in Ireland as it did throughout the world. Ball games have had many origins such as a form of handball in America. Hurling, for example, can be claimed to be an Irish sport but then there was 'stick-fighting' in Cornwall in the early 1700s. Fathers 'encouraged their children thrash one another' (Methuen, 1939). The Scots may rightly claim to have started golf but *there is some evidence, that in fact it was the Dutch who first started swatting a ball with some sort of club* (Williams, 1985). Then there was ice hockey! One could go back and forward and yet not be exact on the origins of many sports. (Racquet sports are dealt with in chapter 2.) It is probably best to have a curious interest in the past but promote and enjoy sports as we find them today.

A youngster, during education, will be exposed to a range of sports. These he may keep with him for the remainder of his life. It is therefore important, for the long-term health of society, that sport be encouraged and supported from the first day at school. Not doing so is a disservice to our future generations. The fact that different schools have a varied range of primary sports should not be of concern. The basic nature of individual and team sports is such as to promote fitness, a healthy way of life and a valuable and unique asset in social development. In pre-Christian Ireland there were the Tailteann Games, possibly a similar meeting of people to that found in ancient Greece and Rome. According to Padraig Griffin (1990) *The Tailteann Aenach was an assembly of people of all kinds on the hill of Telltown, situated between Navan and Kells. It took place annually around the beginning of August and drew people from all over Ireland as well as Scotland. .....It appears from legend that the first four days were taken up with religious matters. There then followed athletics, gymnastics and equestrian events......Unlike the Olympic Games, women were allowed to be present. A universal truce operated during the time and fighting was forbidden.*

Schools would have followed society in a parallel sense. In early (expensive) secondary schools, sports were an organised form of recreation. The British 'Public' schools were the source of many sport developments such as rugby, rackets and tennis. Many young 19th century pupils crossed the Irish Sea for such education. Exposure to new pastimes would inevitably see their growth here. The Jesuit Fathers were among the religious orders that provided this type of education for the well-off Catholic population in Ireland. They were likely to encourage cricket, rugby and tennis. The diocesan schools were linked to the Gaelic Revival, in terms of cultural and sporting developments. Their pupils were linked to more rural catchments and few would have been in a position to pay expensive boarding school fees. The Grammar schools and more expensive Catholic schools were the schools most likely to encourage lawn tennis in Ireland. Team sports would virtually always have priority.

Clongowes Wood College, County Kildare, was educating young Catholic Irishmen as early as 1814. The school was one of the first in Ireland to install grass courts for tennis. In 1913, the *Clongownian* included an exceptionally interesting article on the subject of *Lawn Tennis as a Game for Schools.* A former pupil Val Miley wrote this article. He was one of the top Irish players of his time, a winner of the Irish Open Championship Singles and Doubles (with his brother) in 1920. The purpose of the article was to encourage schools to promote the game, giving reasons why the sport has much to offer. The peak of Irish tennis in 1890s had passed, a time when Irish men and women won Wimbledon and USA titles. One suspects that in the larger schools where sport was promoted that various forms of football were played during the winter and cricket was the primary summer game.

In Eugene McGee *St. Mel's of Longford* (1996) we see some revealing insights into a school that would be considered one of the great Gaelic Football schools. He quotes an editorial in the Longford Independent of 1890, which said that *When present middle-aged people were boys there was only one form of outdoor amusement-namely cricket. Football was known but it had fallen into disuse. Throughout society a dreary lack of physical amusement prevailed.* He pointed out that sport in St. Mel's College played little or no part in the life of the students for the first 50 years of the schools existence (it was opened in 1865). *Cricket was the main sport in St. Mel's, along with handball.* With the influence of the local military barracks, soccer became popular locally. *In 1915 there is a record of a soccer team from the college playing against Longford Town Juniors on October 9. The game ended in a 1-1 draw and when the replay took place two weeks later St. Mels won 2-0.*

While St. Mel's College was a Diocesan College it was not founded for the well to do but *If any pupils were favoured, it was the children of the less affluent.* Clongowes Wood College, on the other hand, catered for those who could afford education at a well catered for boarding school. St. Mel's followed the Gaelic revival and won the Leinster Schools football title at their first attempt in 1928, Clongowes had rugby football as their stable winter diet. These two schools perhaps represent two sides of Catholic Ireland. Matters are not always that simple. O'Connell Schools in Dublin who were active in Gaelic football before 1928, also promoted tennis and won the Leinster Schools' Cup for that sport in 1938.

Tennis was an individual sport and not a primary sport in any school. Back in 1913, Val Miley pointed out the recent success of James Cecil Parke in the 1912 Davis Cup. At the time the school had nine grass courts. By the early 1920s this had increased to twelve with some **twenty-three** in action in 1930. Val Miley's article is now reproduced in full and many of the points made are still valid nearly a century later.

Lawn Tennis as a Game for Schools

The question whether Lawn Tennis should receive official recognition at the great public schools as a school game is at present receiving some attention in England. The head masters are a conservative body, disinclined as a rule to encourage changes in the long-established customs of their schools. No doubt there are already some of the schools where Lawn Tennis does receive a somewhat half-hearted recognition. But the game is never really encouraged, and a few of the leading schools, at any rate in England, recognise it. An effort is now being made to induce these leading schools to take the game seriously. If the effort is successful, the other schools will follow and the movement will become a general one throughout the country. The immediate cause of this movement is the want in the United Kingdom of young players of the highest class.

In the present year, mainly through the brilliancy of that distinguished Irish player, J.C. Parke, the Davis Cup has been won back by the British Isles. One can therefore hardly complain of the decay of Lawn Tennis in Ireland or England. But is it a fact that its prestige is now being maintained by men who are considerably older than those representing other countries. On the Continent and in America, players are at their best between the ages of 18 and 30. Moreover, for every good young player in Great Britain there are ten in Australia, America, Germany or France. This state of affairs is, in the main, due to the fact that the game is not encouraged in the schools. Players in this country do not learn the game as boys, and thus great proficiency is made more difficult to attain, and is never or scarcely ever attained till many years after leaving school.

There is, of course, something to be said for the present attitude of the head masters. Lawn Tennis has come at school to be associated to some extent with "slacking"; and when played slackly or carelessly it is not good as a game for boys, nor indeed for anyone else. Thinking over the matter, however, one sees that this association is unjustifiable. There is nothing inherent in the game which tends to encourage slackness, although the conditions under which it is played are often responsible for such a tendency. No game would ever be played keenly, or as it should be played at school, if it were only on sufferance and unless there were some element of competition to stimulate the efforts of the players. If there were no out-matches, no Line-matches, and no school eleven or fifteen, is it likely that the average boy would be keen at either cricket or rugby? Of course there are some boys who would, just as there are some now who play keen Lawn Tennis.

Properly and keenly played, Lawn Tennis is a game with few, if any, superiors. It has been urged against it that it gives rise to a one-sided physical development. But anyone who has played seriously will know that the whole body is exercised with the possible exception of the left arm. So much cannot be said for Association Football which is universally praised as a form of exercise. Over almost every other game Lawn Tennis possesses some advantage. It requires less time than cricket and involves no waiting about, and, sharing as it does, the universal vogue of golf, it has this merit, that one has always an opportunity of playing it. Unlike football it can be played summer and winter and can be kept up till late in life. It excels rowing and athletics because it is a game as well as a sport. It is more strenuous, more of a battle than golf. More than any other ball game it demands accuracy and delicacy of touch as well as hard and vigorous striking.

The 1938 senior team (House VI") at Clongowes Wood College, County Kildare. Back (l. to r.) D. O'Meara, J. Clifford & P. O'Meara. Seated: C. Meehan (left) & R. Counihan. On Ground: Dan Miley.

The brain must work too if the tactics of the game are to be mastered and put into practice. Character is strengthened by this as by no other game. Only those who have played will appreciate how difficult it is to refrain from losing one's temper. The personal element is so strong and the opportunities for abusing one's partner, one's opponent, and one's luck are so numerous that it is the hardest of all games in which to keep a level mind; and nobody is ever a good player whose mind does not keep level. Finally, to be a good Lawn Tennis player it helps in many ways, when one has left school, to make life pleasant.

Admit then that if Lawn Tennis were given official recognition, and if the element of competition were introduced, the game would be keenly played: and that if keenly played, it is a fine game and one worth playing. It remains to consider whether such recognition is a practical possibility.

The two principal objections to summer play seem to be that it would interfere with cricket and that it would make the task of supervision a more difficult one. Of course there are many who will not admit that the latter is an objection, who will think that at any rate among the older boys the system of supervision might well give place to the more modern system of putting the boys on their honour and trusting them to do what is right. Still, whatever one may think as to that, ample opportunity for supervision will be assured if the courts are put on or adjoining the cricket grounds. This is, of course, the natural and usual place for them, and is where they are as a matter of fact in Clongowes. The first objection will be met by allowing Tennis only at certain times, such for instance, as the short recreations, or when one's own side is batting, or, as is done at Beaumont, for the last five or six weeks of term. It is merely a matter of organisation, and it might not be so difficult to devise a scheme that would suit the particular conditions and not interfere with cricket to any appreciable extent. In fact the encouragement of Lawn Tennis would in many cases be an actual benefit to cricket in that it would prevent boys tiring of cricket as they often do towards the end of the summer term.

As regards winter Tennis, there is an additional objection that most schools find it difficult to provide hard courts in anything like sufficient numbers to make the game in any sense a school game. Clongowes however does not suffer from this difficulty. Now that the old gravel football has been abandoned the grounds which were used for it could be made into satisfactory hard courts at no great expense, and enough courts could be laid out to give abundant opportunity for all to play. Such play would not be allowed to interfere with football matches. But the short winter recreations, during which there is at present a certain amount of desultory "kicking about", and little energy and less interest displayed, might be far more profitably employed playing Lawn Tennis on the hard courts.

The practical details of how the game should be encouraged are essentially a matter for those in authority in each individual case. As has already been suggested, Clongowes is in a peculiarly advantageous position to carry out a scheme. Hard courts could be laid out and facilities given for winter play. In the summer a greater number of courts could be prepared and marked out for each Line, many more than are provided at present. Tournaments could be arranged and carried through. Inter-Line competitions could be instituted and two or three out-matches could be fixed in the summer term: and all this could be done without interfering in any way with the established games. A system of booking courts could be introduced which would ensure everyone's having a chance to play and would prevent anything like a monopoly of the courts by a few players, such as often exists under the present conditions. The victory of Mr. Parke in the Davis Cup has directed the attention of the world's Lawn Tennis players to Irish Lawn Tennis. If these suggestions or something akin to them were adopted, Clongowes, besides making a substantial addition to its athletic life, would become in a very short time a nursery for players who would help Ireland to regain the proud position in the Lawn Tennis world that she held some twenty years ago.

One could spend much time analysing this unique article. He correctly points out the need to promote junior tennis and the fact that Ireland was already falling behind others countries. Tennis in Ireland seemed to have stood still while the game rapidly flew by us from about 1900 onwards. The need for hard courts and winter play has certainly proved correct throughout the country. Sligo Grammar School had an interesting solution. This mixed school had hockey as a winter sport. For the summer term a line of tennis nets would be positioned across the gravel pitch. The dark gravel would be white-lined. The big problem, of course, was than when a ball was served or smashed past a player it would keep going to the far end of the pitch.

Ned McGuire, Davis Cup player, playing an exhibition match at his old Alma Mater, Clongowes Wood College in 1930

It is noted that Ned McGuire, who attended Clongowes between 1915 and 1919, played in his first Davis Cup matches within five years of leaving school. A new breed of 'young' players came on stream in the 1920s. In 1942, a sixteen-year-old boy, Joe Hackett, attending Belvedere College, Dublin, reached the final of the Irish Open.

When we look at Tennis Ireland's 1999-2001 *Strategic Plan for Tennis* we see many strengths to the game mentioned, such as the fact that it is *a lifetime sport from aged eight to eighty*. Under *Weaknesses* we find item 5 as a key point worth noting: *The game is not always attractive to young athletes. The school sports structure does not generally encourage participation in tennis.* In its comprehensive set of goals and strategies there are some laudable elements applicable to schools tennis such as:

2 (k) Develop initiatives aimed at ensuring fewer top junior players leave the game in their mid-teens; 2(l) Develop a more systematic approach to introducing/promoting tennis at schools level which will be put in place by the development staff and 6(b) National Schools Cup: Seek a major national sponsor whose support would create a national second-level schools competition.

In the Tennis Ireland *Strategic Plan for Tennis 2004-2006* there is a six-phase plan in the 'long term player development model'. The stages are as follows:

[1] *Fundamental Phase* (boys 6-9, girls 6-8)
[2] *Learning to Train Phase* (boys 9-12, girls 8-11)
[3] *Training to Train Phase* (boys 12-16, girls 11-15)
[4] *Training to Compete Phase* (boys 16-18, girls 15-17)
[5] *Training to Win Phase* (male 18+, female 17+)
[6] *Retirement/Retention Phase*

This is a model that includes detailed expectations from the time a racquet is first held until the retired senior player is seen as being valuable as a coach, administrator etc. It is highly laudable and should be part of a long-term improvement in the sport. The role of schools should be complimentary to this, starting at primary level.

Secondary Schools

In many Ulster schools tennis was not a significant sport of interest. Campbell College, one of the great rugby schools, had virtually no tennis when Cecil Pedlow attended as a boarder nearly sixty years ago. He was mad keen but cricket was the main sport once the rugby season was over. Each Sunday, during the last few months of the academic year, his mother brought him to **Windsor Lawn Tennis Club**. There he played with his friend, and opponent, Czech boy, Paul Sochar. As early as 1939 a Miss B. Rodden wrote to the Ulster Council suggesting that a girls' league might be established for schools. The following month the minutes record that **Belfast Boat Club** offered a cup for a schools league. A cup competition was finally set up with two sections as follows:

Section A	Ballymena Academy
	Derry High School
	Cambridge House School (Ballymena)
	Manor House, Armagh

Section B	Victoria College
	Regent House, Newtownards
	Richmond Lodge
	Friend's School, Lisburn

Mrs. Winifred Templeton of Belfast High School was elected to the Ulster Council and took a particular interest in the schools event. In 1946, the first year of play after the war she was the honorary school's secretary and organised the Girls' Schools Tennis Cup for that year. Players had to be under 17 years on the 1st January. Nineteen teams took part. No competition for boy's schools seems to have been in place at that time. In 1948, twenty-one teams took part in the Ulster Schools' Cup competition, Ashleigh House School being the winners for the third successive year. In 1957 the Ulster Council inaugurated the Ulster Schools Lawn Tennis Association. The 1958 office bearers were: chairperson: Miss O. M. Pim; honorary secretary: Henry Wallace; honorary Competitions' secretary: Winifred Templeton and the honorary treasurer was Walter G. Nicholl. That year there were four separate Schools Cup competitions, with an entry of 82 teams. The winners were:

Senior Boys': Royal Belfast Academical Inst.
Senior Girls': Ashleigh House School
Junior Boys': St. Patrick's College, Armagh
Junior Girls': Strathearn School

The Belfast Royal Academy Senior Cup team that won the Ulster Schoolboys' Cup in 1952 were (from left): Jim Getty, Peter Jackson, Frank Daly and Alan White. Peter played for the Ulster senior team that season.

In 1960, the president of the Ulster Council was Winifred Templeton. She submitted a proposal to wind up the Schools Association and hand over the running of schools competition to the Council. She said that teachers in the summer term had little time to devote to this organisation and attendance at committee meetings was difficult. In practice it was branch members who did the work and, after a long discussion, the proposal was agreed.

A range of schools have done particularly well in tennis over the years. Royal Belfast Academical Institution (RBAI) is a regular finalist. In 1962 the Emergency Committee of the Ulster Council had to meet on the 21st June. The RBAI senior boys team had reached the finals of the cup and were hoping to win the competition for an unprecedented eight consecutive years. The problem was that Campbell College and Ballymena Academy had not played their semi-final on schedule. As it was the end of the school year, and it would not be possible for school teams to be available throughout the summer (without some team being at a disadvantage), the committee decided to suspend the competition.

In 1963 the age limit for the Schools' Senior Cup competitions was raised to under 19 on the 1st January of the year applicable. In 1977, in the three categories, senior intermediate and junior, Richmond Lodge became the first school ever to reach three finals in the same year. The senior team at the school's won the senior cup, the other two teams had to settle for the runners-up spot. First timers in the competitions were Cabin Hill, they excelled in winning the junior boys title. A total of 170 teams entered the six competitions. It is difficult to find out exactly the extent of tennis in schools in the early days. The Irish junior boys championships commenced at Fitzwilliam Lawn Tennis Club in 1914 with the first winner being C. H. D. O'Callaghan. The first girls competition was held in 1926, the winner being F. B. Bonner. If we look through the listing of winners through the years we can recognise many future interprovincial and international players. A few examples among the boys are Raymond Egan (Dublin) in 1933 and Munster's Alan Haughton in 1934. Joe Hackett was to win it twice in 1942 and 1943. He attended Belvedere College who had many notable tennis players, including that rugby Lion, Tony O'Reilly. Other double winners were Gerry Fitzpatrick (1948 and 1949), Derek Arthurs (1957 and 1958), Des Early (1966 and 1967) and Declan Heavey (1972 and 1973). It might be noted that today Derek Arthurs lives in Australia, still coaches, and his son Wayne, is one of the top players in that country and played in the Davis Cup final in 2001 and on the winning team in 2003.

The 1973 Gonzaga College Dublin that won the Leinster Schools Cup. Back (l. to r.) Hugh Tinney, Jerry Sheehan, Francois Eliet and Declan Meagher. Front (l. to r.) David Mulcahy, Rod Ensor and the late Father Edward Keane who organised tennis at the school for very many years.

There were several girls good enough to win the title for two consecutive years but, particularly impressive, were those who won it for three years. Munster's Josephine Harman, better known as *Binkie*, was exceptional. In 1928, at the age of thirteen, she won the under 15 title. She repeated this win in 1929 as well as winning the under 19 title. In 1931 and 1932 she won the girl's title for the second and third time. She had won the senior event three times and was still only 17. It is not known whether she played again in 1933. In 1934 she won the Irish Open mixed title, playing with American W. F. Breeze, and by 1936 she was the number one senior lady in the country. In the late 1930s Mary Nichols won the senior girls title for three consecutive years as did Hilary Cole (1947-1949), Eleanor O'Neill (1956-1958) and Niamh Glenn (1971-1973).

Team competition and inter-school rivalry is good for any sport. It appears that the Leinster boys' schools Senior Cup is the oldest tennis competition for schools in the country. It was first played for in 1922 and was won by the St. Stephen's Green School followed by the St. Columbas School the following year. C.U.S. first won this title in 1930 and became the most successful of schools winning the title twelve times by 1955. This included a six-year consecutive run from 1932.

The 1968 Leinster Senior Cup Winners Gonzaga College, Dublin. (Standing) Dennis Brennan, James Sheehan and Paul Coulson. (Sitting) B. Morris, Tony Ensor and Peter Murphy.

Gonzaga College, Dublin has been one of the strongholds of schools tennis for the last forty years. Their interest in the sport has been an exceptional one. Since 1960 there has been a schools championship with many players of note gracing the winners circle. The list of winners is given below. The Cup, which was missing for eleven years, is made of solid silver and bears the inscription: *The Gonzaga College Perpetual Challenge Trophy*. The winners have included the Davy brothers (whose young sister was to

be a Federation Cup player), Tony Ensor, a rugby international, and Jerry Sheehan, a highly accomplished player, coach and organiser. In fact Jerry older brothers Maurice and Garth won the schools cup before him. The Smith brothers, Connor and Barry, and the Doran brothers, Alan and Patrick, have added to the historical family continuity in the sport. Conor McCullough, one of several international players produced by the school, won the title four times, from 1979 to 1982. Declan Fassbender was the winner in 1992. He was obviously encouraged by his father, the president of **Fitzwilliam LTC** in 2000. Sean Molloy was one of the best and was on the Davis Cup panel during the Doyle/Sorenson era while still a schoolboy. In 1988 he played in his first Davis Cup match, with Peter Wright in the doubles in a 5/0 win over Cyprus in Cork. Success at schools level does not just happen. Father Edmund Keane S. J. was the driving force for many years and was responsible for building up the tennis standards there. In recent years, David Keenahan has taken over this mantle.

The Gonzaga Senior Cup
(Under 19 School Champion)

1960	**Brian Davy**
1961	**Joe Davy**
1962	**Brian Kirby**
1963,1964	**Gareth Sheehan**
1965, 1966, 1967 & 1968	**Tony Ensor**
1969	**Paul Coulson**
1970	**Paul Duffy**
1971	**Maurice Sheehan**
1972, 1973, 1974 & 1975	**Jerry Sheehan**
1976	**Hugh Tinney**
1977	**Richard Blake**
1978	**Peter Crowley**
1979, 1980, 1981 & 1982	**Conor McCullough**
1983	**Stephen Doherty**
1984	**Michael Carney**
1985 & 1986	**Sean Molloy**
1987	**Gavin Blake**
1988, 1990 & 1991	**Connor Smith**
1989	**Julian Morgan**
1992	**Declan Fassbender**
1993	**P. Smith**
1994,1995 & 1996	**B. Smith**
1998 & 1998	**Alan Doran**
1999	**Patrick Doran**
2000 & 2001	**Barry King**

Contacting a few schools we find the following facts that reflect the varied interest in the game:

Ursuline Convent, Waterford

Founded 1816.   Girls only

Four tarmacadam hard courts (two were previously grass). Coached by PE teacher. Davis Cup player Michael Hickey was a former part-time coach. Won numerous Munster Junior, Intermediate and Senior Titles. Former pupils of tennis note include **Valerie Fennelly and Aine Heglin.**

Mary Mountjoy (Munster Branch president) presents the Ursuline Convent Waterford team with the Munster Under 19 Cup in 2000.

Kilkenny College

Founded 1485   Mixed

The Senior' B' Kilkenny College team in 1978 were (back) Olive Walshe, Elizabeth Wellwood and (seated) Carol Carmody and Dorothy Dempsey.

Formerly 4 tarmacadum hardcourts. Now the school has 16 courts on an all-weather hockey pitch (*Astroturf*). The history of tennis at this Kilkenny school is sketchy. In 1973 there was an amalgamation with the Celbridge Collegiate girls school. Tennis had only a small part to play in the two predecessor schools. The school moved to a new site in 1985 and additional courts were added. Herbie Sharman at the school adds: *In the late '70s/early '80s there were some matches with Newtown School in Waterford but these petered out. It is hard for tennis to compete with rugby and hockey!!...Many of our local pupils play in the Kilkenny Tennis Club & some have done well through the club. Recently KCK has participated in a Kilkenny Schools tennis 1 day championship (junior & senior). Now an annual event & it takes place at the club.*

Mount Anville Secondary School, Dublin.

Founded 1853   Girls only

Formerly the school had nine tarmacadum hardcourts. It is now reduced to six with a further eight courts on the all-weather 'hockey' Astroturf. The school has an impressive tennis record and in 2001 held all six Leinster schools girls' titles, senior, intermediate and junior, A & B. Former pupil of tennis note include **Bernadette Davy, Jenny Lawlor, Sarah Griffith and Sandra Griffith.**

Blackrock College, Dublin

Founded 1854   Boys only

One of the larger schools in the country, it has always prided itself in its sporting achievement and provided a wide range of facilities for its students. The school won the Leinster Senior Cup as far back as 1940 (or perhaps earlier). It has had many wins in all age categories from the 1960s onwards. Unfortunately, a lot of the school trophies were stolen in the late 1980s. These included three tennis cups, but not the senior cup, which had been won by St. Michael's that year.

Former pupils of tennis note include **Pat Crowe, John Hackett, Tom Staunton, Michael McMahon and Tommy Hamilton.**

Mount Anville won the Leinster schools minor cup in 2001. Back (from left) Sandra Griffith, Sophie Carton, Hazel Bollard and Sarah Crowley. Front (from left) Naomi Barker (captain) and Louise Johnstone.

The 1946 Blackrock College junior team that won the Leinster Cup was (from left): P. Cregan, James Comerford, Tom Staunton (captain), Francis O'Connor, Niall Nolan and Pearse Nolan.

The 1965 junior team at Terenure College in were (from left) John Cronin, Colm Bannon, John Patrick Mahony, Maurice Greene, Conor Sparks, Pat Higgins and A. Isaac.

The senior '64 team at Terenure College. Back (l. to r.) Finian Lynch, Bosco Morrisey, Brian Harrington & John Stephens. Front: (l. to r.) Michael Mahony, Richard Kinsella, Paddy Donaghy and Pat Sparks.

Blackrock College, Dublin, 1989. Martin Byrne Philips Business Systems) sponsor the schools tennis teams. Also in photo (from left) John Sheridan, Michael McMahon and Tommy Hamilton.

Gonzaga College, Dublin

Founded 1950   Boys only

In the early days this school had three grass courts. Today there are five Omni-Court Pro courts. Many Leinster schools titles, and subsequently successful adult players, since the schools championships started just over forty years ago. There are many former pupils of tennis note as already identified in the school's championship listing.

Coleraine Academical Institution

Founded 1861   Boys only

The school has had five hard courts for many years. Coaching by both PE teachers and external coaches. Have been in many schools semi-finals and finals and won the Ulster senior boys title in 1977, beating RBAI in the final. Former pupils of tennis note include **Richard Beggs and William Noteman.**

Terenure College, Dublin

Founded 1860   Boys only

This school promotes many sports. Up to about 1950 there were five grass courts. By the summer of 1951 the old grass courts were re-laid and two new tarmacadum hard courts laid down. Some results of the senior (U18), junior (U15), juvenile (U13) and elementary (U11) school championships (see table across).

Former pupils of tennis note include **Gerry Clarke, Adrian Weakliam, Brendan Kelly, Bobby Keogh, Ken Kelleher, the Sparks brothers, the Mahony brothers and Michael Lynch.**

Some School Tennis Champions Terenure College (Dublin)

1951
Juvenile — T. O'Brien beat Ken Hanlon.
Elementary — J. Cahill beat Michael Hipwell.
1958
Senior — Bobby Keogh beat Brendan Kelly.
1962
Senior — Ken Kelleher beat Niall Sparks.
Junior — Richard Kinsella beat Declan Whitney.
Juvenile — Paddy Walsh beat Hugh O'Neill.
Elementary — Conor Sparks beat Maurice Greene.
1963
Senior — Ken Kelleher beat Niall Sparks.
Junior — Michael Mahony beat Pat Sparks.
Juvenile — Pat Higgins beat Maurice Greene.
Junior Sch. — Paul Meade beat Declan Herbert.
Elementary — Conor Sparks beat Pat Mahony.
1964
Senior — Richard Kinsella beat Pat Sparks.
Junior — Pat Higgins beat Roddy Walsh.
Juvenile — Conor Sparks beat Pat Mahony.
Elementary — John Cronin beat Brian Sparks.
1965
Senior — Pat Sparks beat Raymond Kinsella.
Junior — Pat Higgins beat Maurice Greene.
Juvenile — Conor Sparks beat John Cronin.
Junior Sch. — Austin Kinsella beat Gerry Morrissey.
Elementary — Ian Swanton beat Jimmy Menton.
1966
Senior — Pat Sparks beat Pat Higgins.
Junior — Conor Sparks beat Pat Mahony.
Juvenile — John Cronin beat Austin Kinsella.
Junior Sch. — M. Kinsella beat J. Kelly.
U12 — M. Kelly beat A. Neill.
1967
Senior — Pat Higgins beat Robin Constantine.
Junior — Conor Sparks beat Liam Bannon.
Juvenile — Jimmy Menton beat Martin Kinsella.
Elementary — Michael O'Kelly beat Raymond Kinsella.
1968
Senior — Conor Sparks beat Pat Mahony.
Junior — Johnnie Cronin beat Liam Bannon.
Juvenile — Raymond Kinsella beat P. MacMathuna.
Elementary — Niall O'Kelly beat Paul Joyce.
U12 — M. Barron beat I. McIver.
1969
Senior — Conor Sparks
Junior — Jimmy Menton
Juvenile — Raymond Kinsella
Elementary — Niall O'Kelly beat Paul Joyce
1970
Senior — John Cronin beat Patrick Mahony
Junior — Raymond Kinsella bt Padraig McMahon
Juvenile — Neil O'Kelly beat Martin Rogers
Elementary — Francis Kinsella beat Paul Greene

The five grass courts at Terenure College, Dublin (Circa 1950).

1937 St. Gerard's College versus Clongowes Wood College, County Kildare.

The 1967 Junior Leinster Cup winning team from Terenure College. From left: Brian Sparks, Jimmy Menton, Conor Sparks, Johnnie Cronin and Liam Bannon. Missing : Patrick Mahony.

Clongowes Wood College

Founded 1814   Boys only

Possibly the oldest school in Ireland to promote tennis. In 1912 there were 9 grass courts, by the 1920s this had increased to 12 and by 1930 there were no less than twenty three grass courts. They have had many tennis players of note. 1977 was a particularly good year with wins in the Leinster Senior, U16 Winter League and 2nd Senior Cups. Former pupils of tennis note: **Val Miley, John Miley, Ned McGuire, the Houlihan brothers and the Mocklers from Cork.**

The school champion at Terenure College in 1958 was Bobby Keogh (right). Tennis runner-up (left) Brendan Kelly was table tennis champion.

The 1932 'Lower Line' at Clongowes Wood College, County Kildare included J. Hooper, N. Devere & M. Dowling, N. Comyn, W. O'Dwyer, J. McMahon & W. Doolin.

Summerhill College, Sligo

Founded 19th Century   Boys only

Summerhill College is one of the biggest boys schools in the west of Ireland. It is a Catholic school that originally would have promoted Gaelic games but now is equally noted for its soccer teams. It has exposed its pupils to very many sports and has had three tennis

courts (tarmacadum) for many years. The 1990 annual had the following to add. *The College Tennis Court is at present being renovated and a League will be started as soon as possible, to give all those interested in playing tennis an opportunity to do so. So, get those racquets and tennis shoes out of the lockers! The College Tennis Club has got fantastic support from the Co. Sligo Tennis Club. We thank Mr. Bob English, Morgan Walsh (Captain), David Taylor, and the many Lady members for their interest and help. The school is very fortunate in having some very "useful" players on the staff: Mr. Kilcoyne, Mr. McGowan, Mr. McCormack (Newbridge Schoolboys champion), Miss Hynes (who was a key player on the Under 25 Badenndorf squad in the Hannoverian Bundesleague). Their expertise is invaluable to the club.* The interest generated in the school has lead to the winning of quite a number of Connacht titles over the last twenty years or so. Links with Sligo Tennis Club, the local club, has had a very definite influence.

Advances

Schools don't always get the recognition they deserve. In 1950, Father Kerr of C.U.S. proposed at the Leinster Schools Union AGM *that a competition be run among the schools during the winter.* Nothing happened for another twenty-five years.

George Hamilton went to Sligo Grammar School between 1933 and 1936. They had the use of only one court, *a few yards south of the Janitor's house.* It appears, also, that Doctor Mecredy, The Mall, had a court and would allow students to use it from time to time. He recalls that his first cousin, Harry Hamilton, had won the schools singles championship in 1930. The said Harry ended up as Chairman of Grimsby Football Club and brought them from the 5th to the 1st division. George still recalls a particular friendly match with the local Sligo YMCA club in about 1934.

Connacht Colleges Senior Tennis Champions in 1989 were Summerhill College, Sligo. From left: Robert Kelly, Alan Cummins, Donal O'Shea, Oisin Quirke, David Keane & Michael Kilcoyne (manager). (Missing: Gary Reynolds)

Daisy Bellew, Reception Committee, quickly realised we were more interested in food than tennis. We did her efforts justice. George played at the newly formed Ballisodare club, **Woodville LTC**, for several years before moving to England. He returned to Ireland after the war and became a member of the **Leinster Stratford LTC** in Rathmines. In the 1970s there was no sign of this single court at the Grammar School. However, there was a line of nets and courts marked out across the cinder hockey pitch. This was to be the home venue for the new **Sligo TC** for a couple of years after it were founded in 1978. The big problem was the lack of a backstop. Any passing shot, or smash, involved a long run back before the match could resume.

The tennis players in County Donegal had their own County Association in 1973 and introduced a schools' tennis tournament. Billy Watson (chairman), Mrs. W. Patterson (secretary) and Norman Watt (treasurer) were the key personnel pushing the effort which resulted in the following nine schools competing in what was probably their first competitive tennis outing: Convent of Mercy, Buncrana, Loreto Convent, Letterkenny, St. Eunan's College, Letterkenny, Loreto College, Milford, Royal and Prior Comprehensive, Raphoe, Glenties Comprehensive, Sacred Heart Secondary, Ballyshannon, St. Louis Convent, Bundoran and St. Columba's College, Stranorlar.

The Ulster Branch has, for a number of years, produced their own official handbook. In the 1965 issue there were some 55 schools and colleges affiliated. By 1973, there were 4 universities/colleges and an amazing 70 secondary schools. Locking in to this interest, even in the primary school sector, can only be good for the game throughout the island. Munster has been particularly good at promoting primary school tennis in recent years. This will no doubt provide many excellent players in the decades ahead.

Education through Games

Father Percy J. Winder, S.J., (ILTA honorary treasurer, 1981-1983) a long time promoter of the game at all levels, but particularly at schools, wrote the following interesting article for the 1976 edition of the ILTA Yearbook:

We live in the exam oriented society, a world in which education tends to be seen as preparation for examinations rather than preparation for life.

Most of us are aware of the pressures on pupils to compete for points. Even educators themselves can feel helpless. The whole emphasis in a school can be the preparation of pupils for successful Leaving Certificates. The pupil is treated as a computer, fed with data to be given out upon request to the examiner. If such a school has a tolerance for games it is because it sees games as a relaxation from study- 'Get them out for a while, let them have a run around, they'll study better for it.' As if study was the end of schooling, information rather than formation, and games a mere convenience.

Not so the true educationalist. He is concerned about the formation of the whole person, not just the information of minds. He knows the root meaning of the word 'educate'. So for him education is about helping to draw out all the potential and the talent locked within the young person. He sees it as his privilege, and his awesome responsibility, to help the young person to develop and form his character, to grow in humanity, in integrity, and in respect for others. Formation more than information.

Caught up in the present rat-race, in his moment of sanity, the perceptive educator is aware that, long after Algebra, Biology and Irish have been forgotten, the qualities of character and the virtues formed over the years of learning will be the things that count in a man's life. He will try to hold out against all the pressures because he believes that the development of the body, mind and character of his pupil is more important than the acquiring of 28 points and a place in Medical School. It is here that he will welcome games. Not as relaxation for study, not like the game of golf in the life of a busy executive, but as an important opportunity for learning and for development. Not peripheral, but central in education.

A few examples. A boy arrives in a school. On the tennis court and on the sportsfield he is undisciplined, bad tempered, not used to losing. He invariably acts up when the pressure's on. You as adult and coach will feel mad with him. You will be tempted to exclude him from teams and ban him from the game. But education isn't about banning, its about building, so you learn to be patient with him. You correct him, even suspend him for a match, but you encourage and counsel him. And slowly he learns and improves. In his final years you hardly remember the boy he was, so assured now, so disciplined. Through a game a remarkable educational process has taken place. The boy becomes the man, ready for life. Encouraged, you turn towards another newcomer and begin all over again.

Another example. Johnny is prone to cheat a wee bit. He's not adverse to an occasional bad call. Not much, just enough so he makes it easier for himself to win. Then comes the tight situation. A cup final, 3-4 down in the final set, 30-40 on his own service, fighting for his life, perhaps the hopes of his team mates resting on his tired shoulders. He serves a good service, but a better return, wide of his out-stretched racket, clipping the line. 'Out', he calls, and then, 'Sorry, that was in.' Around him he hears the spectators break into spontaneous applause, applause for his courage, the courage it took to change his mind, to be honest in such a situation. At that moment he has learnt, as he had never learnt before, that it is a manly thing, an admirable thing, to be honest and truthful. He is more ready for life now.

Then there's all the learning for life that comes in a game of Doubles. You find yourself stuck with a partner who 'couldn't hit an elephant if it were a foot away.' You will be tempted to get mad with him, maybe even walk out on him. But that'll solve nothing; that won't make you a winner.

The Tennis Players at the Marist Convent, Tubbercurry, County Sligo, circa 1960. Back (l. to r.) Moira Ryan, Bridie Reid, Maureen Durkin, Eileen Madden (RIP), Annie Mullarkey & Kathleen Gallagher. Front (l. to r.) Maureen Brennan, Rita Durkin, Sheila Kildunne, Sheila Mangan, Eilis O'Reilly and Maureen O' Connor.

So you suppress it. You find that, given a bit of encouragement, and understanding, he's not so bad and you begin to get along together. As a pair you may not be world-beaters but you can have fun together-even in a losing situation.

Father Percy J. Winter, S.J., one of the great workers for Irish tennis, particularly at schools level.

Or, another time, your partner is going through a bad patch. You can take it out on him and makes things worse for him. Or you can keep your cool, assume more responsibility for the match, try to take him away from the firing line for a while, and give him time to recover. Isolated in his problem, he can't cope;

supported by your awareness and undemonstrative help, he rides the storm and comes through undamaged. Isn't that what human relations is all about?

Or again, you can see the pair on the other side of the net as enemies, to be beaten at all costs, not excluding a bit of gamesmanship and cheating. Or you can see them as friendly rivals, there to make it a game. Through a game you can lose friends by showing yourself as a selfish person, or you can increase the circle of your friends by showing yourself as a sportsman. The game shows you up. Without it you could leave school and get away with not facing up to yourself- until adult life, much more cruelly, shows you up. Only then, it's too late to learn.

To end on a lighter note. Think of the opportunities for life to be had from Mixed Doubles. Beaten 'love and love,' you may still go on from there to engage in a more wonderful and exciting partnership.

Which reminds me of the joke: "What's the only game in which love counts for nothing?" I'd better be off before someone throws a racket at me.

Mullingar Example

Tennis has been in Mullingar town for over one hundred years. However, in the 1960s there was a significant revival with success at schools level occurring in the 1970s and 1980s. In 1971 the Mullingar Loretto Convent won the Loretto Shield, narrowly beating the Loretto Convent, Rathfarnham in the final. One of the stars of that team was Aideen Dunne. Although she was never coached she won the under 15 Junior titles at the Mullingar and Moate Opens that year as well as playing for her school. As a result of 'trials with other Leinster girls at Mullingar, she was selected to play for the interprovincial team at

The Loretto Convent, Mullingar won the Loretto League Minor Shield and the Leinster Minor Schools Cup in 1980. In 1981, with more or less the same team, went on to win the Leinster Schools Junior Cup by beating the Holy Child Convent, Killiney 2/1 in the final. This was the first time in the competitions 23-year history that a team from outside the Dublin area captured this cup. The team (above) was (from left) Helen Waldron, Mary Waldron, Ann Shaw, Sandra Shaw, Louise Andrews and Niamh Waldron.

Sutton. In 1980, the Loretta Convent team won the Leinster Minor College Cup beating Mount Anville 2/1 in the final. Two of the girls were to be part of the famous Barniville Babes, namely Sandra Shaw and Mary Waldron. With one change the team went on in 1981 to win the Leinster Junior Cup (under 15) in 1981. They beat the Holy Child Convent, Killiney in that final 2/1. This was the first time in the history of the event that the cup was won by a team outside the Dublin area. It reflected well on the club members at the Mullingar Town Tennis Club, Michael Creighton being a major part of that success.

Schools All-Ireland

In 2000 the all-Ireland competition for second level schools was organised by Tennis Ireland in conjunction with Ballygowan. Invitations were sent to 800 schools and a *very large entry* of 102 schools entered. There were qualifying rounds held at eight regional venues on the 10th March. The qualifying teams were:

St. Flannan's College, Ennis.
Summerhill College, Sligo.
St. Mary's Secondary School, Nenagh.
Ursuline College, Sligo.
Santa Sabina, Dublin.
Belvedere College, Dublin.
Mount Anville Secondary School, Dublin.
Gonzaga College, Dublin.
St.Angela's-Ursuline Convent, Waterford.
Colaiste Choilm, Cork.
St. Mary's College, Naas.

The play-offs and finals were held on the 24th March 2000 at Riverview Racquet and Fitness Club, Dublin. The results in the finals were as follows:

BOYS

Gonzaga College 25		**Belvedere College 14**
Barry King	bt.	R. Foley 9-4
Patrick Doran	bt.	B. O'Driscoll 7-6
Conor Fearon/		C. Darcy/
George McMahon	bt.	K. O'Dowd 9-4

GIRLS

Mount Anville 22		**Santa Sabina 17**
J. Lawlor	lost	D. Kilduff 5-8
N. Mc Hale	lost	Caroline McNulty 4-9
S.Griffith/		L. Bracken/
A. Tierney	bt.	S. Gillette 13-0

The winners of this Ballygowan sponsored event in 2001 and 2002 were as follows

Boys:	2001:	Gonzaga College, Dublin Beat Blackrock College 21/18
	2002:	Blackrock College, Dublin beat Gonzaga College 27-12
Girls:	2001:	Santa Sabina, Dublin beat Mount Anville, Dublin 28/11
	2002:	Mount Anville, Dublin beat Santa Sabina, Dublin 28-11

One of the consoling features of the 2002 event, which had reduced numbers, was the emergence of strong teams from Connacht. St. Gerard's, Castlebar in the boys came second to Blackrock in their round robin stage while the Ursuline College, Sligo, were just four points behind Mount Anville (81 to 77) in their section. A question that arises today is the extent of participation of children in sport. A recent survey (1994) in England of 4,000 children between the ages of 6 and 16 was revealing. Some 66% had taken part in tennis at least once in the previous year to the study and about a third (31%) had played the game frequently (at least 10 times). An interesting lesson for us is the fact that it was found that children were more likely to play the game outside school is they had played the game during school lessons. In the 'frequent' sports category they found that tennis was ranked equal sixth behind swimming, cycling, football, gym and athletics. It was also found that tennis was fourth among those children in the context of play in a sports club. In the Department of Education Report (Republic of Ireland) *Targeting Sporting Change in Ireland: Sport in Ireland 1997-2006 and beyond* specific analysis on participation is not included but rather some important aims such as: **To maximise co-operation and cohesion among the partners involved in the provision of sport for young people and optimise the structured linkages with physical education.**

The 1941 Junior Leinster Cup final (under 15). Terenure College (above),(from left) Hugh Gunn, Arthur Fitzpatrick, Frank Byrne, Gerry Clarke (currently Mr. Veterans Tennis in Ireland) including Gerry Clarke, Stanley McElroy and Tommy Moroney. They beat Belvedere College (from left) Joe Hackett, Vincent Coyne, Joe Doyle, Basil Collins, Brian Lemass and Willie Mulligan. The match was based on 3 singles and 3 doubles, after a tie, Terenure were declared winners by 8 sets to 6.

All will recognise these sentiments and the need to ensure that the trend for teenagers to move away from sport be reversed. Tennis can be a major asset in this approach to the future of our young. In a national study on Olympic Sports in 1999 it was found that national participation (again, Republic of Ireland) showed tennis to be third behind football and basketball. Can the same be said for young people? If not, a question for the future is to see in how the game

can best be expanded. This is already happening in many ways, such as the Parks Tennis scheme (see elsewhere in this book). It will only finally be achieved when expenditure on sports, and involvement at schools, is on a par with countries such as Holland.

The Summerhill College, Sligo, Junior team in 1989. Back (l. to r.) Michael Kilcoyne, Mel Bourke, Malcolm Walsh, Morgan Carroll & John Moran. Front (l. to r.) Gavin Forkan & Fergus Taylor.

The 1972 Belfast Royal Academy (BRA) Senior Girls A team who won the Ulster Inter-Schools Cup. From left: Ann Wallace, Linda Kennett, Pamela McIlhinney & Diana Kennett

The 1955 Munster Boys Schools final in which Christian Brothers Cork (CBC) beat Presentation Brothers Cork (PBC) 9-0.at Collins Barracks, Cork. In the semi-finals CBC had beaten Glenstal Abbey 7-1 and PBC had beaten Waterpark College 6-3. In photograph above (from left) Jim Kennifick (PBC), P. Aherne (CBC), J. Scannell (CBC), Des Fitzgerald (PBC), J. Leamy (CBC), M. Lucy (PBC), T. O'Riordan (CBC), M. Murphy (PBC), Billy Phelan (CBC), S. Smith (CBC), D. Murphy (PBC) and C. Drumm (PBC). (Cork Evening Echo Friday 10th June 1955).

The tennis players at Cistercian College, Roscrea in May 1960.Back Row (left to right): William Conway, Brian Jennings, Jimmy Lennon, Hilary Lawless, Tom Hainsworth, Donal Gallivan, Gordon Ballantyne, James McMahon, Bonnie Crosby, Tom Mulhearne. Middle Row (left to right): Liam Mc Niff, Emer Griffth, Dermot Rowan, John Sherry, David Brickley, Tom Higgins, Aidan McNulty, James Coffey. Front row (left to right): Sean Lane, Ned McMonigle, Sean Fitzgerald, Anthony Bennett, Damien Lane.

University

A university education in Ireland was, until recent times, something those of a middle class upbringing could aspire to. Even then, it was not necessary for success in life. For progress in life today, the perception is that it is it necessary to have a third level qualification. The points system in secondary schools has put pressure on the young, a pressure not found in the early days of third level education. Likewise, whether it is in one of the established universities, a new university or technical institute, sport seems to have lost much of its appeal. Life has become more serious and, unfortunately, serious social problems of drink, drugs, suicide etc. seem to have increased proportionally. The answer probably lies in the changes in society in general. There will always be sport at university and, one hopes, this element of education will become more significant once again.

Trinity College Dublin (Dublin University) was founded in 1592 on a site, then called Hogges-Green, *and the place was the "scite", ambit, and presinct"of the Augustinian Monastery of All Saints, which had been founded by Dermot Mac Murrough, King of Leinster, A.D. 1166"*. (Cusack, 1868). It first opened its gates to students in 1594. *Trinity designed to wean Gaelic Irish away from continental European establishments such as Louvain. Abel Walsh was the first student enrolled; James Ussher, later Church of Ireland Archbishop of Armagh, was second.* (Crealey, 1993). All those over the age of twenty-five will know that it was a Protestant University for many centuries. Integration, with religious persuasion no longer a factor, only came to this esteemed body in the latter half of the 20th century. The Catholic Church no longer banned their fold from its gates.

It is only natural that this university would be to the forefront of sport in Ireland with so many young people attending, particularly when sports had a distinct upsurge towards the end of the 19th century. In fact, by the middle of that century there were 1,500 students at Dublin University, as opposed to 1,300 at Oxford University (Reader, 1966). An estimated 1000 Irish students were also studying at English universities. What may be surprising was that *Games were prohibited by the college's early statutes, no doubt because of the violence, gambling and drinking that regularly accompanied them* (West, 1991).

The other Queen's Colleges at Belfast, Galway (1849) and Cork were founded much later. To the surprise of many people, the biggest University on the island, University College Dublin, was only founded in 1908 as the National University of Ireland. The origins of the latter are to be found under the Catholic University of Ireland (1851). Tennis is also played at other third level institutions not designated as universities. Ling Physical Training College, for example, had a tennis club over 30 years ago.

The Lawn Tennis Team at Dublin University in 1886 (Courtesy Trevor West, Trinity College, Dublin)

Back in Trinity, a 'fives' court was constructed in 1694 and a 'real tennis' court in 1741. In 1877 a Lawn Tennis Club was founded when permission was given to mark out courts in the New Square provided that *the committee of the club make themselves responsible for the orderly conduct of all persons using the ground for this purpose.* (College Register, 19 May 1877). Trevor West's *The Bold Collegians* (1991) is well worth a read in terms of the sports history of Trinity, it parallels the many sporting changes that have occurred in Ireland over the centuries. On the tennis front, many of the top players of the 19th and 20th centuries attended here. These included James Cecil Parke, George McVeagh and Harry M. Read. Read had been described by West as *one of Trinity's greatest sportsmen.* In the year 1911-1912 he was captain of the sports of rugby, cricket and tennis at the University and a senior Irish international in all three. Lesser tennis players who were educated here included Percy French and Douglas Hyde.

Details on early university tennis are slim. In *UCD Sport 2000-2001*, the origins of the intervarsity tennis trophies are discussed. The magazine reports: *The origins are disputed. One reliable source attributes the Cup to District Justice McCabe, a UCD graduate, who sat on the bench in Waterford. It was presented in 1931. Another source cites the Iveagh Cup, presented by the Earl of Iveagh in 1937.* The Gill Cup has been played for many years between the ladies' of trinity and UCD. One past graduate of UCD pointed out the fact that in and around 1950 the standard of the UCD team was such that most of the men on the first team were at or near international standard. He also pointed out that in today's professional era this was unlikely to be the case as a more full-time commitment to the game was required to reach the national standard. It could also be said that in the last 50 years a very distinct change applies to the number of sports played. To be at a high standard in tennis does require a winter commitment. Changing over from the football pitch in winter to the tennis court in spring is no longer sufficient for the highest grades.

In the first Handbook on Irish lawn tennis, published in 1894, **Dublin University LTC** and **High School LTC** (Dublin) are identified among the 18 clubs in the Dublin area. There were 39 "country clubs", three of which were in Connacht. These were the **County Sligo LTC**, the **Roscommon LTC** and **Queen's College (Galway) LTC**. No other school or university is mentioned as being in existence at that time, or in the listing provided for 1895.

The Galway college became University College, Galway and then at the end of the 20th century, NUI, Galway. No records of early tennis are readily available but the 1960s and early 1970s produced some excellent players. Among them were Pat, David and Siobhan Ryan, all members of the Salthill family, their mother being a prominent member of **Foxford LTC** many years earlier. Pat later married Sigerson player, Ray Niland, a medical student in the 1960s and their family would have many memorable moments on tennis courts throughout the world. The tennis numbers in Galway were not large but they were enthusiastic, most also being members of **Galway**

LTC. Jim Roche is one such player; he had won a significant under 15 title at Londonbridge Road and later represented UCG and Connacht. Noel Murphy was another to feature throughout the country during and after his student days. Further engineering students of note were Gary and Donal O'Lochlainn from Taylor's Hill, Galway, and sons of the long reigning Associate Professor of Engineering, Padraic. John Burke of Mullingar and Brendan Killoran of County Clare were highly thought of tennis players and were part of the university side around 1970. Non-engineers of note were Donal Geraghty and Barry Woods.

The marathon tennis match broke the world record of 32 hours of continuous play at the old tennis courts at University College, Galway in November 1971. From the left Donal O'Lochlainn, Gary O'Lochlainn, Barry Woods and John Burke.

In the distant days of the sixties many will remember Mao's little red book and the student riots in Paris. Study did get its place but so too did the social scene in what was a relatively small university at the time. Lucy Warner who lived across the road was noted for her hockey and tennis and became many years later the captain of the **Limerick Lawn Tennis Club**. Dave Ryan would hold the same position at **Elm Park LTC**. He was also one of the top table tennis players in Connacht, in fact Connacht champion if one's memory is in order. Margaret Brierly and Olwyn Ryder became prominent members of **Galway LTC**, Olwyn was honoured in the role of president of Tennis Ireland in 1998, and for a second term in 2002.

World Record

A notable event took place at the UCG courts, in front of the old Engineering Block in November 1971. It was rag week and starting at 8am on Monday morning four students took to the court to beat the Guinness Book of Records non-stop play for doubles tennis. It was all in aid of charity. The rules and regulations were followed to the letter with an allowed five-minute break each hour. Floodlights were erected for the occasion and, no doubt, Professor O'Lochlainn looked out of the engineering building disapprovingly, his two sons were on court and not studying. They paired together and played against John Burke and

Barry Woods. That Monday night there was a giant ballad session at Teach Furbo but the players played on through the night. Later in the week they could enjoy the all night progressive pop session and the Women's Lib Ball. The four players and many admiring onlookers will not forget the event. They played about sixty sets-all were competitive- in warm tracksuits and hats, Donal O'Loughlainn had one of the new steel shaft racquets, the others reliable Maxplys. By 8pm on Tuesday they had broken the world record by four hours. They ate sandwiches and glucose sweets as hunger dictated. During their official breaks they had their legs massaged. At the end of it all you would have expected them to collapse into bed. Not likely. Being typical students they headed off for hot whiskeys. Youth and fitness were certainly on their side. John Burke, after the best nights sleep he ever had played a mixed hockey match the next day.

Colours Matches

Unfortunately, like schools records, those in the university sector are pretty scant. We can count on Trinity College being the nursery for the some of the early greats, probably being able to field a team in the 19th century capable of beating the best of the rest of the country. The "colours" matches between TCD and UCD take place annually in many sports, a throw back to the challenges between Oxford and Cambridge in the sports of rugby, soccer, athletics, real tennis, rackets and lawn tennis. Rackets goes back to 1855 when played at The Queen's Club London. Lawn tennis between the universities was held at the same club in 1887. Irish sportsmen have been known to feature prominently on these English university sides.

In lawn tennis, one of our top players in the 1940s and 1950s was Guy Jackson. In the 1st March 1949 edition of *Lawn Tennis and Badminton* it was noted that: *G.P. Jackson, the Irish Davis Cup player, again represented Oxford University in their hockey victory over Cambridge at Beckenham, scoring one of the three Oxford goals.* That same summer he played a leading role when his side resoundingly beat Cambridge in the annual lawn tennis challenge by 14 matches to 1. The same magazine's report in June included the following comments:

This year's Oxford team was remarkable for its variety of style and its cosmopolitan character with N. D. Cox (England) as captain and G. P. Jackson (Ireland), F. H. Renouf (New Zealand), J. R. Frolik (USA), D. G. Wilson (Australia), F.R. Mott-Trille (Jamaica) and J. E. P. Halse (South Africa).

In singles Jackson and Frolik have been outstanding, both being undefeated this season. Jackson, the Irish Davis Cup player, is playing his third year for Oxford; his best performance being the 6-2, 6-3 win over H. F. Walton in the Edgbaston match.

Results (V Cambridge) included
G. P. Jackson (B.N.C.) bt. K. G. Isaacs (Queen's) 6-3, 6-1. Jackson & Frolik (O.U.) bt. Chandler and Khong 7-5, 5-7, 6-3; bt. Carter and R. H. Hack (Pembroke) 6-

2, 6-1; bt. Isaacs and S.P.O. Kumi (Queen's) 5-7, 9-7, 6-4.

The university played the International Club at Oxford that May with Dr. R. J. (Dick) Sandys on the visiting team. He had been club champion at **Fitzwilliam LTC** in 1936. He later (1963-1965; 1968-1971) became chairman of The Queen's Club, London. In this all doubles challenge the students won 5-4. The Irishmen faced each other in one of these challenges: Guy Jackson and I. Frolik beat Dick Sandys and H.E. Weatherall 6-3 6-4. Jackson and partner won two points for their side and retired in the third match.

The 1949 summer was a good one for Guy Jackson, beating some excellent players on his way to the final of the Wimbledon Plate. Later in the summer he featured on the combined Oxford and Cambridge side against the International Club. *For the 'Varsities G. P. Jackson was outstanding, beating C. Spychala, the present South of England Champion (6/3 6/4) and pushing G. L. Paish to a third set (6/1 3/6 6/1).* In 1950, now as a member of the International Club, he was on a winning team (5/4) against the visiting combined team of Harvard and Yale from the USA. Played at Hurlingham, he was paired with N. R. Lewis and won all three doubles matches. The tennis "colours" match in Dublin each year is a matter of pride to the teams involved. Full records do not exist but the information available does indicate teams with plenty of young Irish talent. One suspects that these matches did not take place until well into the 1920s, TCD having been in the sport since 1877 had a head start. Larger numbers, and a growth in the game on a broad base throughout the country, meant that by the 1940s and 1950s UCD would, theoretically at least, have the edge.

Letters to various third level tennis secretaries did not result in a flow of tennis data. However, the modern 'web' was helpful. Titled "Anyone for Tennis?" the Dublin University Lawn Tennis Club 'page' has been prepared by Robert P. Murphy-Junior Sophister. Apart from a brief history of the club he approaches the matter of membership of the club in a *light-hearted econometric approach* bringing his own knowledge of mathematics to the fore. One conclusion he makes is that *the weather does not affect a prospective member's 'propensity' to join.*

The UCD web site prepared by J. Sheehan, president of **UCD LTC**, summarises the last fifty years of the club in a detailed fashion and brings in a range of tennis people familiar to the reader. The following are some extracts:

*The late 1950s saw a group of players who were to leave their mark on the game, but not always in UCD colours. Ronan Fearon, Julian Drury-Byrne, Aidan McCarville, Robert Davitt, Roddy Feely and Kevin McGoran formed the backbone of the UCD men's team in this era. Later, many joined **Bective LTC** and won a hat trick of League titles in the years 1960-62. While winning the annual colour matches more often*

The Oxford and Cambridge teams in the 1949 Varsity match. The home team, Oxford, won 14-1. Standing (from left) J.R. Frolik (U.S.A.,O.U.), R.H. Hack (C.U.), D.G. Wilson (Australia, O.U.), B.R.O. Carter (C.U.), J.E.P. Halse (South Africa,O.U.) D.J. Warburg (C.U.), F.R. Mott-Trille (Jamaica, O.U.), S.P.O. Kumi (Gold Coast,C.U.), G. de Freitas (C.U.). Sitting (from left): Guy Jackson (O.U. & Ireland), K.S. Khong (C.U.), N.D. Cox (Oxford Captain), G. Chandler (Cambridge Captain), F.H. Renouf (New Zealand,O.U.), K.G. Isaacs (C.U.).

than not, they had stiff opposition from Trinity for whom Dick Sweetman and Donal Pratt were to the fore. Queen's also had a strong team boasting Cecil Pedlow, John Young, Ian Dick and Syd Miller in their squad.

The decade of the 60s was probably the most successful in the club's history, Annual Colours matches and Intervarsities were dominated. Excursions to the Hiney Cup in Waterford yielded more social success than that of the sporting variety. In the early years Harry Sheridan, Dan McDowell, Gerry Waldron, John Murray, Peter Delaney, Martin Kennedy and occasionally, John Mulvey, flew the flag. Mulvey is unique in being the only player to play successive Colours for UCD and Trinity (winning both).

In July 1962, the club was beaten comprehensively by a combined Harvard and Yale side but in August 1962 Harry Sheridan gave a commanding display to win the Men's Irish Close Championship. He was also successful in both the men's and mixed doubles. Sheridan and Geraldine Houlihan, at twenty years of age, caused a major surprise when they won the 1963 Irish hardcourt singles championships and both were selected on the Irish team against England.

The swinging sixties had arrived and Eamon de Valera, as secretary, steered the club from 1962 to 1968. The strength of the first team at the time was such that Class 1 of the Dublin Leagues presented the major challenge. Lansdowne took over the mantle of League champions in 1963 and 1964 but in '65 UCD recaptured the title. Lansdowne won again in '66, with UCD winning in '67, '68 and '70. In '69 and '71 we

were beaten finalists, losing to Elm Park and Carrickmines.

It is not without significance that Frank McArdle's span in the club was 1964 to 1969 inclusive. He was the outstanding talent of the time and during this period the UCD team either won, or was in the finals of the Leagues every year up to 1970. The other great players of the time were Terry Grant, Des Early, who became a professional coach in the USA, Paul Kelly, Eugene Daly, Frank O'Brien, Tony Ensor, who retired early from tennis to pursue a promising international rugby career and John Murray who gained international honours with the oval ball. Frank's lasting memory of UCD is a doubles match in which he partnered John Murray to victory over Michael Hickey and John O'Brien in a league match against Lansdowne. The match allegedly turned on a dubious service call. Don't they all?

In 1968, Frank's younger brother Jim arrived on the scene and continued the family tradition of a big serve and volley game so suited to the fast grass courts. Conor Sparks, another talented player also joined the team briefly, winning a league medal in 1970. He recalls victory in the Intervarsities held in Trinity in that year and a party in the Mews house of the legendary Hos Pizzell, a Trinity type of Iranian descent. Apart from an array of females which left the students (other than Hos) somewhat intimidated, Conor noted a young guitarist strumming strange tunes in the corner. He suggested to him that he play some Beatles numbers, to which he reluctantly agreed. Little did Conor know that he had interrupted the early career of none other than Chris de Burgh.

The Intervarsities were the most popular annual event. However, they invariably clashed with a League weekend. Not even de Valera's powers of persuasion could encourage the League Council to grant a postponement, thus leaving the College in the position of having to forfeit an entire fixture or otherwise field a seconds team.

On the ladies front, activity was not as hectic. In the late fifties Mary O'Sullivan was the dominant player and following victories by Hazel Irwin in 1961 and 1962 in the club championships, Geraldine Houlihan became not only the outstanding club player, but also Ireland's leading lady for many years. The mid-60s saw competition in Class 2 of the League and in 1966 came victory for the team led by Micheline Murphy, who still has a set of teaspoons as proof. Other players in this era were Sarah Williams, Marylyn Roantree and Liz Heffernan. In 1968 Paula Mullen enjoyed a successful, if brief, sojourn in UCD earning victory in Colours and Intervarsities. Geraldine Houlihan was still competing as was Jean Mathews and Miriam Walsh. Although the ladies did not have the strength in depth of the men, they generally fielded one, if not two, League team and enjoyed reasonable success in Colours and Intervarsities.

Moving into the 1970s, the available talent was distributed a little more evenly between UCD and Trinity. UCD won the Colours in 1972, however they lost out subsequently to a Trinity team lead by Kevin Menton, with Gavin O'Herlihy (son of Dan), Paul Coulson, Patrick Ballagh and Michael Coughlan. UCD still boasted Jim McArdle and Frank O'Brien in the early years, and subsequently Kevin O'Malley, Kevin Feeney (who was secretary of the club), Denis Brennan, Paul Duffy, Brian McGovern and Paul McArdle, another member of the Dundalk clan. To underline how fortunes had changed, Feeney recalls how the team had to leave the Intervarsities in Coleraine at 8am on a Saturday morning to field a team for a relegation play-off with CYM. In or about 1974 two brothers from Waterford, the Gibneys, Robin and Noel, together with Stephen Bowe were the mainstay of the team. They too had been on the losing side in the Colours match in '74. However, in 1975-76, a significant group of talented players came through the junior ranks to play for UCD. Some had full international honours while others were to be capped later in their careers. Throughout the years 1976-78, the Colours and the Intervarsities were won. In addition to Gibney, Tommy Burke, Declan Heavey, Brian Lawlor, Jerry Sheehan, Larry Steen, Tom Shelley, Robbie Harold and Noel Sheridan formed the platform for success on the domestic front. At Easter 1976 the men took on the might of Oxford and Cambridge-a trip which could have been jeopardised by a twenty first birthday party at Goggin's Pub in Monkstown which was conveniently located en route to the boat at Dun Laoghaire. Happily, the two "missing" players stepped on to the boat, as the gangway pulled up behind them. Oxford were defeated 5-4 while Cambridge stood no nonsense handing out a 9-0 trashing. A promising Class 1 campaign went all the way to the final that year only to lose out to a powerful Sutton team. Capturing the Winter League in the following year was some recompense.

Robin Gibney (UCD Captain) exchanges gifts with Mayor Allen Remley of Bloomsburg when the team played the Bloomsburg State College in September 1976. The UCD men's team won 5-3 and the Ladies 5-1. Photo (left to right) Barbara Morris, Sarianne Farrell. Local Police Chief Pat Haggerty, Mayor Allen Remley, Lucy Meehan, Jerry Sheehan, Collette Egan, Robin Gibney, Noel Sheridan, Tommy Burke, Larry Steen, Robbie Harrold, and Brian Lawlor. (The Morning Press, Thursday, September 30, 1976)

Later that year, the club hosted a match with a Harvard Yale selection, who numbered among their team a little known serve and volleyer by the name of Matt Doyle. Records do not confirm the match score, but Matt was later to become "Irish" and enjoy the most successful professional career of any Irish player in the modern era.

In 1976, the club made a little piece of history when a tour of the U.S.A. was arranged. The 1977 ILTA Yearbook recorded the following:

This golden opportunity arose when Mr. Tony O'Neill, secretary of the A.U.C. informed the club that two university soccer teams were planning a three weeks tour of the US and that several extra places were available should we wish to send a team.

We immediately accepted. It was a highly successful tour. On the competitive level our team performed creditably winning seven out of a total of nine matches. (The web history indicates the result was 5-4 in UCD's favour). *On the social side the tour was equally, if not more successful. The hospitality accorded us by our American hosts was really tremendous.*

With regard to the standard of tennis there we found that on the whole it was approximately equal to our own. A notable exception to this was U. of Penn. which had an appreciably higher standard. However, the facilities and the opponents were completely superior to that of our own. Most of the institutions, even the state colleges who had fewer students than our own, had indoor facilities and at least one full-time professional coach for their teams. Our opponents were quite amazed when they discovered we had no coach at all. As the seventies wore on Tom Shelly, David Miley, Joe Hackett (junior), Conor O'Reilly and others carried the UCD flag with more than reasonable success. They met stiff opposition from Trinity who regained the Colours through the efforts of Peter Hannon and Cliff Beirne.

More than one winter title was picked up in the '80s although our good relations with the League Council were put to the test when, having won the final, it emerged that one of the dreaded cards had gone missing. The rules laid down that the trophy could not be handed over. Students!

In 1985 the Winter League was won again as was the Intervarsity title. The team was Conor McCullough, Michael Carney, Michael Cowhie, Michael Kenny, Jimmy McDonagh, Gerry Kinnerk and Ronan Reid. By 1987 Cowhie was also an international. The mens and womens intervarsities were won in Limerick in 1991 under the captaincy of Eamon Mee. They were won again in 1992.

In the 1986 edition of *UCD Graduate* the sport was discussed in an article titled *Out of Court!* In it are explained a frustrating set of events at a time when tennis was particularly strong at the college.

The Lawn Tennis Club at UCD is one of the strongest clubs in the Country. Most tennis pundits would agree that with internationals like Conor McCullough and Michael Cowhie in the ranks, backed up by another half a dozen players of proven ability, College would be capable of doing extremely well in Class One of the Dublin Tennis Leagues, and probably capable of winning out.

The problem is that UCD cannot compete anywhere. The Council of the Dublin Tennis Leagues have slammed the door in their faces. In spite of the fact that all of UCD's leading players have signed a written commitment and have indicated that they will represent UCD in preference to their 'home' clubs, nobody seemingly wants to know them.

Last year's Captain, Ronan Reid tried to enter College in the 1985 Leagues. He was told that the entry was too late and that he should reapply in 1986. He did so, in plenty of time. Alas, early in May he received a communication saying that the closing date had expired and that there was no vacancy.

No doubt the Dublin Leagues Council will claim that UCD had to withdraw from the Summer Competitions a few years ago and they are afraid that the same situation would recur.

There were problems, too, in the Winter Leagues earlier this year. College were scheduled to play in the Intervarsity Championship in Portrush on Friday and Saturday of a particular week. On the Thursday night they were told that they would have to play the League Semi-Finals on the Sunday in Dublin. In spite of appeals to the Organising Committee, no change of date was allowed, and at 7.00 a.m. on the morning following the Intervarsities eighteen members of UCDLTC travelled from Portrush in a fourteen seater minibus to fulfil the fixture. Hardly the best preparation for an important semi-final (Again the view of officialdom in Tennis circles may be different).

There is little point in trying to identify the rights and wrongs of what appears to be a major issue. It is important, for the sake of Lawn Tennis at UCD that both parties are brought together so that the whole unfortunate episode can be resolved, and UCD can again take it's place in the premier competition of Irish tennis.

In the 1978 yearbook there is a rare report on tennis from UCG. There was a revived interest in the game in 1977 with the holding of the intervarsities, UCD winning both men's and ladies competitions. In the men's plate UCG would lose to UCC in a close match, the reverse having been the case in 1975. The report commented: *Tennis is alive and well in the West. Never before has there been such an interest in tennis and even in the sub zero temperatures of January there was a steady demand on all four courts.* Coaching had been provided by Michael McCann and Donal Geraghty and the university team played 'friendlies' with **UCC LTC, Galway LTC** and **Catholic Institute, Limerick.**

The 1981 Colours matches included many names of players who subsequently made the grade at national level. The teams and overall results were as follows:

TCD 1	UCD 6
Cathy Ryle	Gillian Chandler
Fiona Ruttle	Sandra Drum
Liz Bowden	Tina Meehan
Linda Fitzsimons	Gillian Haslam
Pamela Scott	Niamh O'Carroll
Orla Lyons	Aisling Cloonan

UCD 3	TCD 5
Joe Hackett	Peter Hannon
Conor O'Reilly	Cliff Beirne
Des O'Reilly	Kevin O'Connor
Paul Banks	Michael Kemp
Nicholas Kelly	John M. Downey
Jim O'Hanlon	Tony Dorman

The Intervarsities were held in Cork that year with UCD winning the men's (7 teams) and the ladies (6 teams) events. Their finals opponents were both TCD teams, the men reversing the colours match 5-4. University sides have always pushed out the boat. TCD had a successful visit to Paris in 1977.

In October 1981, under the management of ex-UCD player Tom Shelley, an Irish Universities side visited Russia. Some of the top players were missing for the trip. The team included Paul Banks, Conor O'Reilly and Jim O'Hanlon (UCD), John Downey and Michael Kemp (TCD), Peter Lowther (Queen's University) and M. Sullivan (UCC). The ILTA Yearbook report (by Jim O'Hanlon) continues:

The tour commenced with a visit to the Russian capital. After being given a whirlwind tour of the city's landmarks, the tennis started two days after arriving. It was interesting to note the lack of indoor facilities in Moscow, forcing the Irish team to play all their matches on one teraflex court, which hindered practice facilities.

The opposition comprised of the Soviet Universities tennis team or the Burevestnyk. However, while our team, which was made up of current students, the Burevestynk embraced any player who had been at University at any stage. Thus there were three 'students' of over 26 years of age on the Soviet team. One such student was Ahmerov, a full-time tennis player, who is ranked No. 5 in the Soviet Union.

Indeed, all the students, even those still at College, were full-time players who admitted to playing six days a week, five hours a day. Thus the Soviet opposition, including the Armenian No. 1 who brought Alex Metreveli to three sets, and three Galea Cup players, was the best the Soviets could muster. In this light, the results were a credit to the tenacity and application of the Irish players. Indeed it became apparent that while the full-time Soviets were miles ahead in technical ability, the Irish were far stronger competitors. This is doubtless due to the regularity of tennis competitions in Ireland and their sparsity in Russia. We learned from the Russian players that they rarely play foreign opposition, which accounts for the gratitude and respect they showed to the visiting team.

After Moscow, the team flew down to sunny Sochi on the Black Sea. Instead of a fast teraflex surface, the Irish were faced with clay courts in 80° of sunshine. The opposition was again of a high standard, including six Soviet 'Masters of Sport' and two of the country's leading juniors. Similarly their technical experience was not matched by their skills of concentration, which allowed Ireland to secure two commendable victories.

Michael Kemp was the Irish hero, winning his singles and partnering Peter Lowther to a doubles victory. Indeed, Ireland were unlucky not to notch up another victory, with Tom Shelley forced to retire after leading in the first set against the Sochi No. 1, and Jim O'Hanlon going down in a long three set match to the No. 3 in the Soviet Union Under-16.

PLAYER	COLLEGE	STATE
Maria Bolster (4)	Mississipi University for Women	Columbus, Mississippi
Michelle Buckley (1)	Indian River Community College	Fort Pierce, Florida
Paul Casey (1)	Gadsen State Junior College	East Gadsen, Alabama
Diane Craig (1)	Daytona Beach Community College	Daytona Beach, Florida
Robbie Dolan (3)	University of Hawaii	Honolulu, Hawaii
Maeve Donnelly (1)	Menlo College	Menlo Park, California
Denis Donovan (1)	Gadsen State Junior College	East Gadsen, Alabama
Tom Feehily (2)	Harry Hopmans	Florida
John Hackett (2)	Davidson County College	Lexington, North Carolina
Peter Lawlor (4)	Flagler College	Saint Augustine, Florida
Conor McCullough (1)	Cooke County College	Gainsville, Texas
Michael Nugent (2)	Nick Bolletieri Tennis Academy	Bradentown, Florida
Helen O'Brien (3)	High Point College	High Point, North Carolina
Joseph O'Dwyer (3)	North Kentucky University	Highland Heights, Kentucky
Joanne O'Halloran (4)	North Kentucky University	Highland Heights, Kentucky
Lesley O'Halloran (2)	North Texas State University	Denton, Texas
Rocky O'Halloran (2)	Columbus College	Columbus, Georgia
Harold Russell (3)	California State College	California, Pennsylvania
Jennifer Thornton (2)	University of Georgia	Athens, Georgia

Irish Students on Tennis Scholarships in the USA in 1982

After these two matches the team had a holiday in Leningrad before returning home.

All in all it was an invaluable trip not only in terms of tennis experience, but also in terms of cultural understanding.

Results:

| Burevestnyk 11 | Irish Universities 1 |
| Russian Republic 9 | Irish Universities 2 |

In the 1986 ILTA Yearbook, Conor McCullough penned an article on *Tennis in the Universities,* subtitled *Great Year for UCD!* A few brief notes from the report are worthwhile. *The year began inauspiciously for UCD Men's Team as their Captain, Ronan Reid, has his nose broken by his talented partner, Gerry Kinnerk, in Winter League. Amazingly, he played on; though it was quite obvious from the way he was playing that he was quite ill, but we did need the points! As for Ronan, he ended up in hospital.* They won the Winter League, bringing the trophy back to UCD for the first time in 10 years. *The victory was particularly satisfying, as in 1984, UCD were dismissed from the League in the final stages as a result of not posting a result. The player responsible was fined 12.5 pence and suspended for 24 hours.* UCD won the Intervarsities comfortably with two strong teams.

The 1985 UCD team won the Dublin Winter League as well as the Colours match with TCD and the Men's Inter-Varsities title. Captain Conor McCullough (left) with team of Michael Carney, Michael Cowhie, Michael Kenny, J. McDonogh and Gerry Kinnerk.

To foster tennis in the universities a new body was formed called *Irish Universities Lawn Tennis Union.* It was launched on the 9th April 1985 at **Fitzwilliam LTC** and, on the same evening, a team was announced to play the Rest of Ireland. The team of Conor McCullough, Michael Carney, Michael Cowhie, Michael Kenny (UCD), Peter Minnis (QUB), Glen Beirne, Richard Collins (TCD), Victor Drummy and John Coulter (UCC). They lost that match 1/3 (all doubles) and set off to England. First stop was a match against Cambridge and a narrow 5/4 loss. *Peter Minnis, an architect, used up two rolls of film, taking the roof of a 12th century chapel.* On the 13rd April, following arrangements with Peter Hannon, the team played and beat **Beckenham LTC** in London 8/3. *Yet again, the Universities were wined and dined splendidly by their hosts.*

A free day followed, most went to see Wimbledon, led by Michael Kenny they took the wrong tube and ended up in Wopping. Peter Minnis used up four more rolls of film walking around London. *Next stop was Oxford. Everyone got a great reception, where the very kind Capt. of the Oxford team, James Seddon- a nuclear physicist- went out of his way to welcome the team, putting all the visitors up in different Colleges around. The Irish Universities beat Oxford 10-4- in another close fixture.*

Tennis scholarships have enabled many Irish players of promise to blend education and sport, particularly in the USA. It has its disadvantages but the experience alone, never mind the tennis development, usually makes it worthwhile. Rhona Howett was one such student and started at Oklahoma State University in January 1984, later transferring to the Texas Christian University. The latter had 37 courts, including 6 indoor, for a student population of 7000. *Naturally, it is tough being away from home, but it certainly has made me more independent……People only come to know the American collegiate system by experiencing it. It is a very organised lifestyle and a lot of dedication is involved. …..I would highly recommend it, as it is a tremendous opportunity. But the desire to complete the four years must be innate.*

1993 Irish Universities Championships

Men		
Semi-Finals	UCD 'A' 5	UCC 'A' 1
	DCU 5	Dublin Univ. 1
Final	UCD 'A' 5	DCU 2
Plate Final	UCC 'C' 5	Cork IT 3
Women		
Semi-Finals	UCD 'A' 5	UCC 'A' 1
	Dublin Univ. 'A' 5	DCU 1
Final	UCD 'A' 5	Dublin Univ. 'A' 0
Plate Final	UCD 'B' 3	UCC 'B' 0

In 1982 there was an amazing 19 Irish students attending US academic/sporting institutions on scholarships. See table (previous page) with the year at college being in brackets. The game continues to be played in the Universities and most colleges probably now have better, all year round surfaces with floodlights, than they had in days gone by. In addition, there are now many third level colleges with improving facilities, some of which have tennis courts. One suspects that the game will gradually pick up at third level. Having an increasing number of continental students in the country adds a bit of colour too. In 2003, the tennis championships were hosted by NUI Galway, finishing on the 1st March. The fact that they were held at **Galway LTC** and not the university itself does indicate a need for some further expansion of tennis facilities at the university itself. It is hoped, in time, that this college, the second Irish university (to Trinity College) to have an organised club, back in the 19th century, will have the numbers and facilities to be a strength among the tennis playing clubs in Connacht.

Combined Team

One could say that in the early 1960s there was a renewed life in the country. Apart from leaving behind the 1950s, the young were positive, television became available throughout Ireland and, in general, all activity was on an upward curve. Guinness, through the efforts of international Guy Jackson, put up a significant amount of money towards developing junior tennis. Michael Hickey and Derek Arthurs were among those to benefit. Junior players were invited to Miami. Michael Rainey, from Ballymena, and Frank McArdle, from Dundalk, made this as part of a four-week tennis tour the USA. The universities were there too. At the ILTA Council meeting of the 4th December 1964, Eric Harte Barry, at his last meeting as president, requested consideration to be given to a match between the Universities and the Rest of Ireland. The matter was brought up at the next meeting when it was pointed out that the matter had been suggested at the last Intervarsity championships. By April, a letter had been received from Jeff Horsley of Trinity College, Dublin suggesting the match could be played on Sunday 20th June. The honorary secretary pointed out that ladies had not been mentioned. This would be considered at another time.

The match took place; only men involved, and proved a great success. The tie *produced the highest entertainment and excitement, with the students coming out narrowly on top by a margin 5-4. They only managed to get the verdict by winning the last of the three doubles. John Murray and F. McArdle, who have a number of commendable doubles successes to their credit over the past week, beat what was possibly their most difficult assignment yesterday when they accounted for the Ulster pair, Vivian Gotto and Kenneth Reid.*

The Universities tennis team prior to their departure on their 1981 Russian tour. They are photographed here with the Soviet Ambassador to Ireland, His Excellency, Mr. Nesterenko and staff. Front left is Tom Shelly the team manager.

The Combined Trinity College and Edinburgh University ladies' tennis teams in 1937

The full results from that match were as follows (University players names first): **Singles:** John Murray (UCD) beat John O'Brien, 6/2 2/6 6/3; Frank McArdle lost to Franks Furney, 7/9 10/8 2/6; Jeff Horsley (TCD) beat Julian Drury Byrne 3/6 6/3 6/2; Peter Ledbetter beat Vivian Gotto, 1/6 6/4 6/2; Harry Sheridan lost to Ken Reid, 1/6 5/7 and John Young lost to Ronan Fearon, 14/12 3/6 3/6. **Doubles:** Jeff Horsley and Peter Ledbetter lost to Ronan Fearon and Julian Drury Byrne, 6/3 2/6 2/6; Harry Sheridan and John Young beat Franks Furney and John O'Brien, 6/3 1/6 6/4 and John Murray and Frank McArdle beat Ken Reid and Vivian Gotto, 9/7 3/6 8/6.

This event ran for a few years, was revived in the 1970s by Gerry Clarke, but eventually died out, as university tennis 'appeared' to decline and other forms of competition was available for the top Irish players. Additional details on the game of lawn tennis at Trinity College, Dublin (Dublin University) can be found in Chapter 4.1. Today's serious and competitive students do not have the same leisure time to devote to sport, unless they happen to be on a sports scholarship with a light academic load. Nevertheless, during primary, secondary and third level education in this country there are opportunities to get involved in sport, and many do. Tennis is always an attractive option and it is in the hands of administrators and coaches to see that the sport thrives in the formative years.

Photo Gallery

The manager of the 1961 Munster boy's team Dr. Jim Young talks to his players at Sunday's Well. From left: Redmond O'Hanlon, W. Bolger, R. Thompson and Don Harte-Barry.

Bob English (Connacht Branch president) with the successful Ursuline Convent senior team (Sligo) in 1991.

The Terenure College junior cup team in 1969. From left: R. Kinsella, G. Kelly, J. Menton, D. Gahan, G. Flannery & M. Kinsella.

The junior tennis team at Terenure College in 1963. Back (l. to r.) David Joyce-Glynn, Willie Flynn, Tom Higgins & Pat Sparks. Front (l. to r.) Pat Higgins, Michael Mahony & Roddy Walshe.

The 1996 Castleknock College Junior Division2 team with coach Aidan Bradshaw.

The 1931 'Third Line' tennis team at Clongowes Wood College, County Kildare. J. Gannon, H. Dargan , C. Barrett., H. Seymour, William Doolin & J. Carrigan

Boarders Tom Staunton (left) from Castlerea and Paddy Henry from Sligo did not forget to bring their racquets when attending Blackrock College in the 1940s.

In 2001 the Ursuline College Sligo won the Connacht section of the senior girls' colleges. They then beat Loretto College, St. Stephen's Green, the Mercy College, Nenagh before losing out to the ultimate winners, Santa Sabina, Sutton. From left: Aoife Kerrin, Shauna Whelan, Aisling Burke and Fiona Gallagher. Missing are Siobhan O'Sullivan and Naoimh Burke.

The senior cup team at Terenure College in 1969. From left: Robin Constantine, A. Kinsella, Conor Sparks, Liam Bannon, Johnnie Cronin and Jimmy Menton.

The RBAI senior cup-winning team in 1985. From left: P. Palmer, P. Irvine, P. Kinnand, D. Irvine and A. Reid. At back The Principal (left) and Ronnie Maxwell, tennis organiser.

The 1970 Terenure College Junior team. From left: Raymond Kinsella, Padraig McMahon, Michael O'Kelly, T. Donaghy, A. Neil and C. O'Neill

The 1953 St. Columba's College, Dublin, senior team. Captain was Peter Reid (centre).

The winners of the Leinster schools senior cups in 1982 were Gonzaga College, Dublin, and Loreto Convent, Foxrock.

The 2000 PBC Munster cup-winning team with Mary Mountjoy (president, Munster Branch)

The Loretto Convent, Mullingar,Minor team in 1980 won the Loretto Minor League by beating Loretto Convent Rathfarnham 2/1 in the final and the Leinster Schoolgirls Minor Cup by beating Mount Anville 2/1 in the final. The team were (from left) Helen Waldron, Mary Waldron, Niamh Waldron, Sandra Shaw, Louise Andrews and Bernadette Freyne.

University Players in Cork

World Record Success for Continuous Doubles by University College Galway Students in 1971.

The 1960 tennis team at Prior School, Lifford, County Donegal. From left Alex Raffan (headmaster), Maureen Roulston, Wendy McCreary, Gloria Patterson, Edna Blackburn and Miss Marie O'Connor (teacher).

The Colaiste Mhuire, Cobh, school won the Munster Schoolgirls' Under 14 cup in 2001. Mark Constant (Bishopstown Credit Union) presents the cup. The referee was James Foley.

Colaiste Cholim, Cork, won the Munster Boys' Under 19 Cup in 2002. In photograph also were Peter Scott (president, Munster Branch) and Marie Bevan (Credit Union, sponsors).

The 1964 tennis team at Prior School, Lifford, County Donegal. F Back (l. to r.) Edith Roulston, Louise Ormsby, Joan McKean & Mary McKean. Front (l. to r.) Maureen Roulston, Alex Raffan (headmaster) and Noleen Craig.

The 1974 senior team at Terenure College, Dublin. Front (l. to r.): Paul Joyce, P. Moore & Niall O'Kelly. Back (l. to r.) David Pender, Enda Kelly, David Swanton and Victor Swanton.

The 1937 Catholic University School (CUS), Dublin, senior team included Paul Reid, J. D'Arcy and Frank Kenny (second left). Frank was Irish boy's champion in 1936 and 1937. Paul was the Irish Boys' table tennis champion in 1937.

The 1996 junior tennis team at Castleknock College, Dublin. From left: James Horan, Fiachra Lennon, Bruce McDevitt & Rory McEntee. Inset: James Smith (captain.)

The senior team at Terenure College in 1967. Back (l. to r.): P. Kelleher, Pat Higgins & Conor Sparks. Front (l. to r.): Robin Constantine, Liam Bannon and Johnnie Cronin.

The 1963 Munster schoolgirls' team.

The senior tennis team at Terenure College in 1963 reached the Leinster Schools' semi-final, captain Ken Kelleher was selected for Leinster. Back (l. to r.) Ray Flannery, P. Smith, Bosco Morrisey & Jack Stevenson. Front (l. to r.) Greg Doran, Ken Kelleher (captain) and Niall Sparks.

UCD Colours team in 1950. Back (l. to r.): Peter Morrin(6), Bob Towers(5), Harry Barniville(1) & Des Mulligan(2). Front (l. to r.): Vincent Browne(4) & Robin Donovan(3). TCD won the match 5/4.

The 1932 senior team at Clongowes Wood College, County Kildare, included T. Carragher, R. Gallagher, D. Dargan, Des Houlihan, W. O'Dwyer & M. Gallagher.

The 1970 senior cup team at Terenure College Dublin. From left: Liam Bannon, D. Barber, Brian Sparks, John Menton and Johnnie Cronin.

The 'house six' at Clongowes Wood College in 1929. Back (l. to r.) V. Moran, T. K. Murphy and B. Scally (honorary secretary). Middle (l. to r.) W. O'Driscoll, S. O'Sullivan & K. Dowling. Sitting: Jack Houlihan.

The 1964 junior tennis team at Terenure College, Dublin. Back (l. to r.) Pat Higgins (junior school champion), Hugh O'Neill & Roddy Walshe (school junior finalist). Front (l. to r.) Maurice Greene, Conor Sparks and Colm Bannon.

John Burke of Mullingar serving during the November 1971 world record by students at University College, Galway.

The 1930s cup winners were St. Gerard's College, Bray. Back left is Raymund Egan, later to become a Davis Cup player.

In 1935 Arthur Best (right) from Clonmel beat Frank Kenny (CUS, Dublin) in the final of the senior Irish boy's championships (3/6 7/5 6/0).

The winning Intermediate and Junior teams from RBAI in 1992. Front (l. to r.): Mark Sterlin, David Markey, Pat Ford & Stephen McQuitty. Back (l. to r.) Stephen Traub, Andrew Johnston & Stuary McQuitty.

The 'lower line' tennis team at Clongowes Wood College in 1932. In photograph J. Hooper, N. Devere, M. Dowling, N. Comyn, W. O'Dwyer, J. McMahon & W. Doolin.

Barbara Hamill and Julie Reid of the Ballymena Academy won the Coca Cola school girls championship at Campbell College in 1992.

*The 1965 senior team at Terenure College, Dublin.
From left: Pat Sparks (senior school champion),
David Joyce-Glynn, Michael Mahony, Gerard
O'Neill, Roddy Walshe, Richard Kinsella (senior
school finalist) & Pat Higgins (junior champion).*

*Regent House, Newtownards, won the 1992
intermediate Ulster school's title. From left: Kerry
Hiles, Lyne Greenwood, Anya Bowers & Liz
Anderson.*

*The 1996 Castleknock College senior team. From
left: Graham Jenkinson, Dupe Samuel, Kevin
Moore, Fiachra Lennon, Barry Connellan,
Alvard Martinez & Rory MacEntee.*

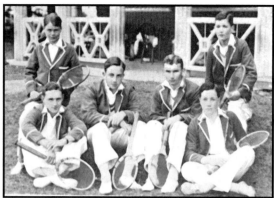

*The 1934 finalists at the school championships,
Clongowes Wood College, County Kildare.*

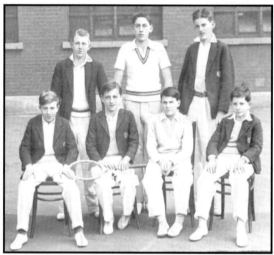

The 1937 junior tennis team at CUS, Dublin.

*Terenure College won the Leinster Junior Cup in
1941. Back (l. to r.): Hugh Gunn, Gerry Clarke and
Arthur (Archie) Fitzpatrick. Front (l. to r.) Tommy
Moroney, Frank Byrne and Stanley McElroy.*

The History of Irish Tennis

TENNIS/All-Ireland Cups

Sandra Griffith, from eventual winners Mount Anville, in action yesterday during the All-Ireland Schools' Cup finals at Sutton lawn tennis club, Dublin. – (Photograph: Brenda Fitzsimons).

Dublin dominate schools' finals

By Johnny Watterson

IN FINALS dominated by Dublin schools, Blackrock College boys and Mount Anville girls emerged as winners of the third Ballygowan All-Ireland Senior Schools' Cup at Sutton tennis club yesterday.

Over a long day during which the weather oscillated between cold downpours and warm sunshine, Blackrock College topped their four-team round-robin group by beating St Gerard's, Castlebar into second place before advancing to meet Gonzaga in the final.

Gonzaga, who won the trophy last year at the same venue and who nudged Belvedere College into second place in their group with 96 points to Belvedere's 90, finally lost out 27-12 in a one-sided final.

The most absorbing of the games was between Blackrock number one, Gareth Doran and Gonzaga's Irish under-18 number

one, Barry King.

In a game played largely from the baseline, the two players rasped a variety of shots on the balcony court in front of an appreciative audience.

Despite Gonzaga finally taking the match 8-5, it was Blackrock's number two Andrew Hogan and the doubles partnership of Robbie Kernan and Killian Pender who secured 10 and 12 points respectively for Blackrock's 27-point tally.

The girls' competition also produced two Dublin finalists, holders Santa Sabina facing Mount Anville. Both teams had emerged from their respective groups comfortably, although Ursulines Sligo came close to breaking the Dublin monopoly by finishing just four points behind Mount Anville's 81-point total.

The final was not without incident, although the 28-11 scoreline reflected a one-sided contest for the south Dublin school. That

scoreline was partly due to the Sutton school's number one Caroline McNulty pulling up injured with a damaged muscle when her match against Sandra Griffith had barely begun, Griffith leading 4-2.

After McNulty, despite some on-court attention, could not continue, the match and all of the remaining points were awarded to the Mount Anville player. As each match consisted of 13 games, Griffith was given an 11-2 scoreline.

The Mount Anville doubles team of Jenny Lawlor and Lisa Matthews, however, also stacked up the points in securing a 13-0 win over Leah Walsh and Kristina Lykkx, with Santa Sabina's Leigh Walsh beating Alexia Tierney 9-4 for an overall 28-point total.

FINALS: **Boys:** Blackrock College beat Gonzaga 27-12 (G Doran 5, B King 8; A Hogan 10, G King 3; R Kernan and K Pender 12, C Kane and C Tobin 1). **Girls:** Mount Anville beat Santa Sabina 28-11 (S Griffith 11, C McNulty 2; McNulty retired injured; A Tierney 4, L Walsh 9; J Lawlor and L Matthews 13, L Walsh and K Lynxx 0)

The Irish Times 2nd May 2002

JULIAN WARD

PASCAL BREE

GAVIN FORKAN

1980s junior players at Summerhill College, Sligo,

The 1989 senior team at Summerhill College. From left: a.n. other, Gary Reynolds, Donal O'Shea & Robert Kelly.

Scoil Mhuire were Munster Under 18 Girls' champions in 2001.

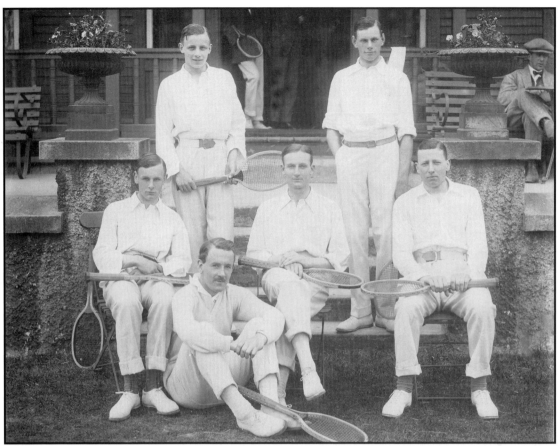

The strong Trinity College team in 1911 or 1912. Harry Read (centre) from Roscrea was captain of the university tennis, rugby and cricket teams in both these years. He played for the Irish teams in all three sports, as well as croquet and thus became one of Ireland's foremost all-rounders.

The Blackrock College Junior team in 1977. From left: D. Ryan, P. Kirwan, Willie O'Brien, David Fennelly, Gerard Kelly and M. Pilkington.

The senior team at Blackrock College, Dublin, 1976/1977. Left to right: Pat Crowe (no.4), Joe Hackett (no.1), Michael Benson (no.2), Denis Jackson (no.3), Willie O'Brien (no.5) and Gerard Kelly (no.6). In the 1977 Leinster Cup the team beat CUS and Gonzaga colleges. They were beaten in the final by Clongowes Wood College. Michael played in the Blackrock College final for third consecutive year only to be beaten by Joe Hackett

The Junior & Minor tennis teams at Terenure College, Dublin, in 1974. Back row (l. to r.) David Shortall, P. Greene, Conor O'Kelly, Edward Kelly, Kevin Donavan, Patrick Bolger & David Pender. Front row (l. to r.) Eugene Fitzgerald, Julian Clarke, F. Kinsella, John Menton, D. Kelly and Brian O'Kelly.

In 2000 The St. Mary's school, Nenagh, won the Munster Under 14 team Cup. Mary Mountjoy (president, Munster Branch presents the cup.

Anne Taylor (honorary secretary, Ulster Branch, Tennis Ireland) with the Strathern Grammar School team that won the 1992 Ulster junior schoolgirls title. From left: Lynn Gray, Kathryn Morrow, Caroline Calvert and Janet Bole.

St. Joseph's secondary school, Castelbar win the Connacht championship in 1978. Chris Millett (Connacht Branch) presents the Hynes Trophy to Caitriona Ruane (captain).

Mary Mountjoy (president, Munster Branch) presents Rockwell College, the winners of the 2000 Munster Under 16 Cup.

The Belfast Royal Academy won the Ulster Boy's and Girl's senior cups in 1952. From left: Alan White, Eileen Wallace, Jim Getty, a. n. other, Peter Jackson, Ann Harrison and Frank Daly.

In 2000 St. Mary's, Nenagh, girls' team won the Irish school's regional qualifier at Limerick Lawn TC. Kevin Herbert (Ballygowan) with team of Joanne Fitzpatrick, Cathleen Finn, Sarah Walshe & Katie Ryan.

In 2001, University College Cork ladies' team win the 3.1 divisional cup.

Mary Mountjoy (president, Munster Branch) presents PBC, the winners of the 2000 Munster Under 14 Cup.

Scoil Mhuire, Ballincollig
Munster Girl's Primary School winners (2000).

Scoil an Spioraid Naoimh
Munster Boy's Primary School winners (2000)

A challenge match between Sligo Grammar School and Prior School, Lifford in about 1966. The match was held in Sligo. The visiting team (front) included (l. to r.) Mary McKean, Joyce Rule, Joan McKean & Marion Reilly.

The 1968 Terenure College team won the Leinster schools cup. Front (from left): Brian Sparks, Martin Kinsella, John Cronin (captain & school champion) & John Menton. Back (from left) Liam Bannon & Austin Kinsella.

The Castleknock College, Dublin, minor team in 1996. Back (l. to r.) Mark Tobin, James Reid, Brian Macken, Andrew Rohan & Fearghaill Mulvihill. Front (l. to r.) Louis Greely, Aidan Bradshaw (coach), Barry McLaughlin & Joe McMahon.

Connacht Schools

Year	Senior Boys O' Donoghue Cup	Senior Girls Henderson Cup	Junior Boys Dempsey Cup	Junior Girls Pearse Cup
1971	Carmelite College, Moate	Dominican Convent, Galway		
1972	Carmelite College, Moate	Convent of Mercy, Moate		
1980	St. Gerard's, Castlebar w/o	Convent of Mercy, Moate beat Presentation Convent, Tuam		
1981	St. Gerard's, Castlebar beat St. Enda's, Galway	Convent of Mercy, Moate beat St. Joseph's, Castlebar		
1982	St. Gerard's, Castlebar beat St. Joseph's, Ballinasloe	Our Lady's, Athlone beat St. Joseph's, Castlebar.		
1983	St. Enda's, Galway	St. Joseph's, Castlebar beat Our Lady's, Athlone		
1984	St. Gerard's, Castlebar beat St. Joseph's, Galway	Convent of Mercy, Tuam beat St. Joseph's, Castlebar		
1985	St. Gerard's, Castlebar beat Colaiste Iognaid, Galway	Convent of Mercy, Tuam beat St. Joseph's, Castlebar	St. Gerard's, Castlebar beat Colaiste Iognaid, Galway	St. Enda's, Galway beat St. Gerard's, Castlebar
1986	St. Gerard's, Castlebar beat St. Enda's, Galway	Our Lady's, Athlone beat Presentation Convent, Tuam	Sligo Grammar School beat Presentation School, Athenry	Presentation College, Athenry beat Convent of Mercy, Castlebar
1987	Colaiste Iognaid, Galway beat Sligo Grammar School	Salerno Convent, Galway beat St. Joseph's, Castlebar	St. Joseph's, Galway beat Presentation School, Athenry	Salerno Convent, Galway beat St. Joseph's, Castlebar
1991	Summerhill College, Sligo	Salerno Convent, Galway	St. Enda's Coll., Galway	Salerno Convent, Galway
1994	Summerhill College, Sligo beat St. Joseph's, Galway	Ursuline Convent, Sligo beat Dominican Convent, Galway	St. Joseph's , Galway beat St. Raphael's, Loughrea	Dominican Convent, Galway beat Convent of Mercy, Claremorris
1995	St. Brigid's, Loughrea beat St. Enda's, Galway	Ursuline Convent, Sligo beat St. Brigid's Vocational School, Loughrea	Summerhill College, Sligo beat St. Joseph's, Galway	Ursuline Convent, Sligo beat Dominican Convent, Galway
1996	St. Brigid's, Loughrea beat Summerhill College, Sligo	Ursuline Convent, Sligo beat Dominican Convent, Galway	St. Gerard's, Castlebar beat Summerhill, College, Sligo	Salerno Convent, Galway beat Ursuline Convent, Sligo
1997	St. Gerard's, Castlebar beat St. Joseph's, Galway	Ursuline Convent, Sligo beat Dominican Convent, Galway	St. Joseph's, Galway beat Grange Vocational School, Sligo	Ursuline Convent, Sligo beat Convent of Mercy, Claremorris
1998	St. Gerard's, Castlebar beat Colaiste Iognaid, Galway	Dominican Conv., Galway bt St. Joseph's, Castlebar	St. Enda's, Galway beat Summerhill, College, Sligo	Dominican Convent, Galway beat Ursuline Convent, Sligo
1999	St. Gerard's, Castlebar beat Colaiste Iognaid, Galway	Our Lady's, Athlone beat Ursuline Convent, Sligo	Summerhill College, Sligo beat St. Enda's, Galway	St. Joseph's, Castlebar beat Dominican Convent, Galway
2000	St. Gerard's, Castlebar	St. Joseph's, Castlebar	St. Gerard's, Castlebar	Ursuline Convent, Sligo

Leinster Schools-Boys

Senior-Division 1 / Senior-Division 2

Year	Senior-Division 1	Senior-Division 2
1922	St. Stephen's Green, School	
1923	St. Columba's College	
1927	Belvedere College	
1929	Synge Street College	
1930	Catholic University School	
1931	St. Gerard's, Bray	
1932	Catholic University School	
1933	Catholic University School	
1934	Catholic University School	
1935	Catholic University School	
1936	Catholic University School	
1937	Catholic University School	
1938	O'Connell Schools	
1940	Blackrock College	
1944	Terenure College	
1947	Castleknock College	
1948	Castleknock College	
1952	Catholic University School	
1953	Catholic University School	
1954	Catholic University School	
1955	Catholic University School	
1956	Castleknock College	
1957	Castleknock College	
1958	Castleknock College	
1959	Castleknock College	
1960		
1961		
1962	Gormanstown College	
1963		
1964		
1965		
1966		
1967	Gonzaga College	
1968		
1969		
1970		
1971		
1972		
1973	Gonzaga College	
1974		
1975	Clongowes Wood College	
1976	Clongowes Wood College	
1977	Clongowes Wood College	Clongowes Wood College
1978		Clongowes Wood College
1979		Castleknock College
1980	Belvedere College	St. Michael's College
1981	Gonzaga College	Terenure College
1982	Gonzaga College	St. Benildas
1983	Belvedere College	Terenure College
1984	Gonzaga College	Pobalscoil Rosmini
1985	Gonzaga College	Gormanstown College
1986	Gonzaga College	Plunkett School
1987	Blackrock College	Newbridge College
1988	Blackrock College	
1989	St. Michael's College	Malahide Community School
1990		Terenure College
1991	Blackrock College	Newbridge College
1992	Blackrock College	St. Michael's College
1993	Blackrock College	Blackrock College
1994		Terenure College
1995	Blackrock College	Terenure College
1996	Blackrock College	Castleknock College
1997	Blackrock College	Wesley College
1998	Blackrock College	Gonzaga College
1999	Gonzaga College I	
2000		
2001	Blackrock College	Blackrock College
2002		

Minor-Division 1 / Minor-Division 2

Year	Minor-Division 1	Minor-Division 2
1973	Castleknock College	
1980	Gonzaga College	Gormanstown College
1981	Gonzaga College	Terenure College
1982	St. Michael's College	C.U.S.
1983	ClongowesWoodCollege	Terenure College
1984	Blackrock College	St. Conleth's College
1985	Blackrock College	C.U.S.
1986	Blackrock College	
1987	Blackrock College	Newbridge College
1988	Blackrock College	
1989	Terenure College	Clonkeen College
1992	Blackrock College	
1993	Blackrock College	
1995	Gonzaga College	
1996	Belvedere College	
1997	Blackrock College	
1998	Blackrock College	
1999	Belvedere College	

Junior-Division 1 / Junior-Division 2

Junior-Division 1	Junior-Division 2
Castleknock College	
Castleknock College	
Castleknock College	
Castleknock College	
Terenure College	
Castleknock College	
Gormanstown College	
Castleknock College	
Blackrock College	
Blackrock College	
Belvedere College	
Gonzaga College	
Blackrock College	
Terenure College	
Terenure College	
Gormanstown College	
Gonzaga College	
Castleknock College	
Castleknock College	
Gonzaga College	
Clongowes Wood College	
Clongowes Wood College	
Clongowes Wood College	
Castleknock College	
CBS Mullingar	
Gonzaga College	
Gonzaga College	Terenure College
Gonzaga College	Gormanstown College
Gonzaga College	St. Benildus College
Belvedere College	Gormanstown College
St. Michael's College	St. Conleth's College
St. Aidan's	Gormanstown College
Blackrock College	St. Conleth's College
Gonzaga College	Gormanstown College
Blackrock College	Newbridge College
Blackrock College	Newbridge College
Blackrock College	St. Mary's College
Blackrock College	Blackrock College
Blackrock College	Blackrock College
Blackrock College	
Blackrock College	
Belvedere College	
Gonzaga College	
Blackrock College	
Gonzaga College I	

Ulster Schools-Senior Boys

	Winners	Runners-Up
2002	Bangor Grammar School	C.A.I.
2001	Methodist College, Belfast	Bangor Grammar School
2000	Larne Grammar School	Royal Belfast Academical Institution
1999	Larne Grammar School	Royal Belfast Academical Institution
1998	Larne Grammar School	Royal Belfast Academical Institution
1997	Royal Belfast Academical Institution	Larne Grammar School
1996	Royal Belfast Academical Institution	B.R.A.
1995	Royal Belfast Academical Institution	Bangor Grammar School
1994	Royal Belfast Academical Institution	Bangor Grammar School
1993	Bangor Grammar School	Royal Belfast Academical Institution
1992	Methodist College, Belfast	Bangor Grammar School
1991	Methodist College, Belfast	C.A.I.
1990	Methodist College, Belfast	
1989	Methodist College, Belfast	Campbell College "A"
1988	Campbell College	
1987	Royal Belfast Academical Institution	B.R.A.
1986	Royal Belfast Academical Institution	Dalriada School, Ballymoney
1985	Royal Belfast Academical Institution	
1984	Royal Belfast Academical Institution	
1983	Campbell College	Ballymena Academy
1982	Ballymena Academy	Campbell College
1981	Campbell College	Banbridge Academy
1980	Royal Belfast Academical Institution	Bangor Grammar School
1979	Royal Belfast Academical Institution	
1978	Royal Belfast Academical Institution	
1977	C.A.I.	Royal Belfast Academical Institution
1976	Methodist College, Belfast	
1975	Methodist College, Belfast	
1974	Methodist College, Belfast	
1973	Methodist College, Belfast	
1972	Methodist College, Belfast	
1971	Friends' School	
1970	Ballymena Academy	
1969	Bangor Grammar School	
1968	Royal Belfast Academical Institution	
1967	St. Mary's CBS	
1966	St. Mary's CBS	
1965	Royal Belfast Academical Institution	
1964	Methodist College, Belfast	
1963	Methodist College, Belfast	
1962	withdrawn	
1961	Royal Belfast Academical Institution	
1960	Royal Belfast Academical Institution	
1959	Royal Belfast Academical Institution	
1958	Royal Belfast Academical Institution	
1957	Royal Belfast Academical Institution	
1956	Royal Belfast Academical Institution	
1955	Royal Belfast Academical Institution	
1954	Coleraine Academical Institution	
1953	Portora Royal School, Enniskillen	
1952	BRA	
1951	Ballymena Academy	
1950	Ballymena Academy	
1949	Portora Royal School, Enniskillen	

Ulster Schools-Senior Girls

	Winners	Runners-Up
2002	Assumption Grammar School	Methodist College Belfast
2001	Larne Grammar School	Methodist College Belfast
2000	Cambridge House	Victoria College, Belfast
1999	Glenlola Collegiate School	Banbold (?) SE Academy
1998	Victoria College, Belfast	Wallace High School
1997	Strathearn School	Wallace High School
1996	Strathearn School	Foyle & Londonderrry Academy
1995	Regent House	Victoria College, Belfast
1994	Regent House	Ballymena Academy
1993	Strathearn School	Victoria College, Belfast
1992	Ballymena Academy	Victoria College, Belfast
1991	Victoria College, Belfast	Ballymena Academy
1990	Strathearn School	Strabane Grammar School
1989	Strathearn School	Glenlola Collegiate School
1988		
1987	Strathearn School	Methodist College Belfast
1986	Methodist College, Belfast	Strathearn School
1985		
1984		
1983	BRA	Strathearn School
1982	Strathearn School	Banbridge Academy
1981	Victoria College, Belfast	Glenlola Collegiate School
1980	Victoria College, Belfast	Belfast Royal Academy
1979		
1978		
1977	Richmond Lodge	Strathearn School
1976	unknown	
1972-1975	Belfast Royal Academy	
1971	Princess Gardens	
1970	Ashley House	
1969	Ashley House	
1968	Ashley House	
1967	Strathearn School	
1966	St. Dominic's	
1965	Limavady Grammar School	
1964	Strathearn School	
1963	Strathearn School	
1962	Victoria College, Belfast	
1961	Ashley House	
1960	Strathearn School	
1959	Belfast Royal Academy	
1958	Ashley House	
1949-1957	unknown	
1948	Ashleigh House	Methodist College, Belfast
1947	Ashleigh House	Victoria College, Belfast
1946	Ashleigh House	Londonderry High School

Ulster Schools-Intermediate Boys

	Winners	Runners-Up
2002	Methodist College, Belfast	Campbell College
2001	St. Pat's College	C.A.I.
2000	Portora RS	Ballymena Academy
1999	Campbell College	Portora
1998	Methodist College, Belfast	Campbell College
1997	Royal Belfast Academical Institution	Campbell College
1996	Royal Belfast Academical Institution	Belfast High School
1995	Royal Belfast Academical Institution	Grosvenor Grammar School
1994	R.B.A.I./B.R.A. shared	
1993	Royal Belfast Academical Institution	Bangor Grammar School
1992	Royal Belfast Academical Institution	Bangor Grammar School
1991	Royal Belfast Academical Institution	Bangor Grammar School
1990		
1989	Sullivan Upper School	Ballymena Academy
1988	Sullivan Upper School	
1987	C.A.I.	Friends' School
1986	Campbell College	Cross & Passion College
1985	Royal Belfast Academical Institution	
1984	Royal Belfast Academical Institution	
1983	Campbell College	Royal Belfast Academical Institution
1982	Methodist College, Belfast	Royal Belfast Academical Institution
1981	Methodist College, Belfast	Sullivan
1980	Ballymena Academy	Campbell College
1979	Ballymena Academy	
1978	Sullivan Upper School	
1977	Royal Belfast Academical Institution	Portora
1976	Royal Belfast Academical Institution	
1975	Coleraine A.I.	
1974	Belfast H.S.	
1973	Orangefield Secondary School	
1972	Orangefield Secondary School	
1971	Carrickfergus Secondary School	
1970	Carrickfergus Secondary School	
1969	Somerdale Secondary School	
1968	Orangefield Secondary Intermediate	
1967	St. Augustine's, Belfast	

Ulster Schools-Intermediate Girls

	Winners	Runners-Up
2002	Loreto College	Hunterhouse College
2001	Loreto College	Sullivan Upper
2000	Strathearn Grammar School	Methodist College, Belfast
1999	Assumption Grammar School	Cambridge House
1998	Methodist College, Belfast	B.R.A.
1997	Victoria College, Belfast	Ballymena Academy
1996	Victoria College, Belfast	Enniskillen Collegiate
1995	Strathearn School	Regent House
1994	Strathearn School	Sullivan Upper
1993	Regent House	Cambridge House
1992	Regent House	Larne Grammar School
1991	Larne Grammar School	Friends' School
1990	Strathearn School	Larne Grammar School
1989	Glenlola Collegiate School	Victoria College, Belfast
1988		
1987	Strathearn School	Glenlola Collegiate School
1986	Cross & Passion College	Glenlola Collegiate School
1985		
1984		
1983	Strathearn School	BRA
1982	Strathearn School	Sullivan Upper
1981	Strathearn School	Cross & Passion College
1980	Strathearn School	Victoria College, Belfast
1979		
1978		
1977	Strathearn School	Richmond Lodge
1976		
1975		
1974		
1973		
1972	The Girls Model School, Belfast	
1971	The Girls Model School, Belfast	
1970	Orangefield Secondary Intermediate	
1969	Fivemiletown Secondary Intermediate	
1968	Fivemiletown Secondary Intermediate	
1967	The Girls Model School, Belfast	
1966	The Girls Model School, Belfast	

Ulster Schools-Junior Boys

	Winners	Runners-Up
2002	Larne Grammar School	Cambridge House
2001	Down High School	Sullivan Upper School
2000	Loreto College	Cabin HIll
1999	Methodist College, Belfast	Loreto College
1998	Methodist College, Belfast	Portora Royal School, Enniskillen
1997	Cabin HIll	Limavady Grammar School
1996	Royal Belfast Academical Institution	Larne Grammar School
1995	Sullivan Upper	Royal Belfast Academical Institution
1994	Royal Belfast Academical Institution	Sullivan Upper School
1993	Royal Belfast Academical Institution	B.R.A.
1992	Royal Belfast Academical Institution	Sullivan Upper School
1991	Royal Belfast Academical Institution	Sullivan Upper School
1990	Bangor Grammar School	
1989	Bangor Grammar School	Royal Belfast Academical Institution
1988	Methodist College, Belfast	
1987	Sullivan Upper	Methodist College Belfast
1986	CAI	Royal Belfast Academical Institution
1985	Cabin Hill	
1984	Bangor Grammar School	
1983	Royal Belfast Academical Institution	Belfast Royal Academy
1982	Royal Belfast Academical Institution	CAI
1981	Royal Belfast Academical Institution	Cabin Hill
1980	Methodist College, Belfast	Cabin Hill
1979	Ballymena Academy	
1978	Ballymena Academy	
1977	Cabin Hill	Ballymena Academy
1976	Bangor Grammar School	
1975	Royal Belfast Academical Institution	
1974	Friends' School	
1973	Belfast High School	
1972	Belfast High School	
1971	Carrickfergus Secondary	
1970	Methodist College, Belfast	
1969	Methodist College, Belfast	
1968	Friends School, Lisburn	
1967	Ballymena Academy	
1966	Friends School, Lisburn	
1965	Friends School, Lisburn	
1964	St.Mary's CBS	
1963	Royal Belfast Academical Institution	
1962	Methodist College	
1961	Limavady Grammar School	
1960	Campbell College	
1959	Royal Belfast Academical Institution	
1958	St. Patrick's College, Armagh	
1957	Royal Belfast Academical Institution	

Ulster Schools-Junior Girls

	Winners	Runners-Up
2002	Victoria College, Belfast	Methodist College, Belfast
2001	Strathearn School	R S Armagh
2000	Loreto College	Killicomaine
1999	Strathearn School	Loreto College
1998	Larne Grammar School	Methodist College, Belfast
1997	Larne Grammar School	Victoria College, Belfast
1996	Ballymena Aacdemy	Down High School
1995	Victoria College, Belfast	Enniskillen Collegiate
1994	Victoria College, Belfast	Down High School
1993	Strathearn School 'A'	Strathearn School 'B'
1992	Strathearn School	Methodist College, Belfast
1991	Regent House	Victoria College, Belfast
1990	Victoria College, Belfast	Dalriada School, Balleymoney
1989	Strathearn School	Hunterhouse College
1988	Strathearn School	
1987	Glenloa Collegiate School	Strathearn School
1986	Strathearn School	Dalriada School, Balleymoney
1985	Strathearn School	
1984	Glenloa Collegiate School	
1983	Glenloa Collegiate School	Strathearn School
1982	Cambridge House	Strathearn School
1981	Friends' School	Strathearn School
1980	Strathearn School	Methodist College
1979	Strathearn School	
1978	Victoria College, Belfast	
1977	Victoria College, Belfast	Richmond Lodge
1976	Victoria College, Belfast	
1975	Richmond Lodge School	
1974	Richmond Lodge School	
1973	Cambridge House School	
1972	Ashleigh House	
1971	Ashleigh House	
1970	Victoria College, Belfast	
1969	Princess Gardens	
1968	Ashleigh House	
1967	Ashleigh House	
1966	Strathearn School	
1965	Ashleigh House	
1964	Richmond Lodge School	
1963	Cambridge House School	
1962	Strathearn School	
1961	Richmond Lodge School	
1960	Strathearn Grammar School	
1959	Richmond Lodge School	
1958	Strathearn Grammar School	
1957	Ashleigh House	

4.5   *Coaching & Allied Developments*

Best tennis education was going to Wimbledon every day in 1951 (standing every second day). I learned more about strategy and tactics by watching than in the rest of my life!
(Gerry Clarke, Circa 2000)

Coaches, and their coaching, are now considered an essential part of any club interested in developing the play if its members. This was not always the case. Many of the older generations note the fact that they received no coaching whatsoever in their playing lives. Their process for advancing was twofold, watching good players in action and practicing what they had seen.

In 1940, *The Sligo Independent and West of Ireland Telegraph,* a local paper now long gone, declared in a sports page *BRILLIANT COACH FOR SLIGO.* The sub-heading was Y.M.C.A. Club's Initiative. The key word here was the initiative. A club had to go and seek out a coach, arrange for him to come, and be looked after. As it was a less than usual event to have a coach in the west of Ireland there was no problem in getting candidates to attend.

In 1948 the Ulster Council were to discuss the issue of standards at their meeting on the 21st June. The minutes recorded the following:

The Honorary Secretary reported that following the recent heavy defeat of the Ulster team by Leinster an unofficial meeting of the members of the Ulster Selection Committee, the Ulster and Leinster Teams and Mr. A. H. Walsh, the Assistant Honorary Secretary of the Leinster Council, had taken place at the Belfast Boat Club on Friday 11th June 1948.

The object of this meeting had been to endeavour to find out how the standard of tennis in the Province could be raised.

The Honorary Secretary read a report of the meeting in question which had been prepared by Mr. J. T. Turner the Non-Playing Captain of the Ulster Team.

The report was divided into two parts:

(A)   Obvious weaknesses in the play of members of the present Ulster Team:-

(i)   Service, with particular reference to second service.
(ii)   Ground strokes-failure to use angles.
(iii)   Smashing, Drop shots and the Lob.
(iv)   Ball control in the wind.
(v)   Doubles formation.
(vi)   Psychology.

(B)   The coaching and encouragement of promising junior players.

So far as (B) is concerned the Meeting generally agreed that the Council's existing coaching scheme whilst being undoubtedly of great value was not sufficiently concentrated.

Mr. Walsh gave details of the Leinster Coaching Scheme in which each affiliated Club is invited to forward to the Council the names of one boy and one girl under the age of twenty <u>who show definite promise</u>. These juniors are then coached for one week and at the end of that period the coach selects the most promising twenty who continue to receive coaching for a further period of about three weeks.

Mr. Walsh stated that the Leinster Council nominated a number of young players to play in several Open Tournaments during the season and pay their expenses; if finances permit Mr. Walsh said that he thought that the Ulster Council should give consideration to a similar scheme.

Mr. Walsh further indicated that increasing attention was being paid to Junior Tournaments in the South and he suggested that an effort should be made to induce a number of Ulster clubs to sponsor similar Tournaments.

Mr. Walsh said that he was so convinced as to the value of these Junior Tournaments that if the Ulster Council would nominate four Juniors to play in either the Fitzwilliam or Lansdowne Junior Tournaments this year he himself would be prepared to offer hospitality to two of them and he would make similar arrangements on his return to Dublin for the other two.

The Council unanimously agreed to accept this kind offer and that *the four players to travel to Dublin be selected from the following, each of whom it was arranged would receive free coaching on three afternoons during the month of July:- the Misses Georgina Browne, Angela Clarke, Sheila Harris, Eileen Kirkpatrick and Dorothy Willis.*

The October meeting recorded that *the hospitality indicated at the last meeting had not been forthcoming and as the result of which only two Ulster players, namely Mr. T. Crooks, Ballymena and Miss Angela Clarke, Windsor, had competed in the Irish Junior Championships at the Fitzwilliam Club, Dublin. Both of these young players had put up excellent performances- Mr. Crooks reaching the final and Miss Clark the semi-final of their respective singles event.*

In 1950 the Ulster Council of the ILTA initiated a coaching scheme for teachers in the province. They put a scheme into operation in conjunction with the Central Council for Physical Education. Nineteen players and PE teachers were the first to be involved under this scheme that started at the Exhibition Hall, Balmoral. Mr. Emlyn Jones was the visiting coach and he also attended a number of schools in the Belfast area.

A Miss P. M. T. Vernon submitted an interesting letter to Lawn Tennis & Badminton in the June 1 issue in 1950. Apparently a skit, during a Southdean

Professional Tennis Course, was made on the attempts of schoolmistresses to coach tennis. She took exception to this, pointing out that *It is ridiculous to expect a coaching standard equal to that of a professional, as we have to divide our time among so many other activities.* One imagines that all national organisations should take account of this problem, as teachers are not necessarily experienced tennis players, never mind coaches. She recommended that teacher training colleges might include professional coaches assisting with tennis methods as well as directly at the schools by *helping them in their almost impossible task, instead of jeering at them and deriding their efforts.*

Clem Higginbotham is a coach at Athlone TC. He is seen here, on right, with (left) Eugene Dooley (Men's Captain, 2003) and David Costello (Club Chairman).

In the 1930s minutes book of the Ulster Council it is noted that there was an annual effort, supported by the ILTA, to have a professional coach come over from England for about four weeks in April. The coaching was at one time in the Belfast Badminton Hall. In 1931 it was a Mr. H. Aiken. The minutes of the Council for the 13th February 1936 make the following comment: *The Secretary reported that he.....had booked it for four weeks from 6th April for the same terms as last season £3 per week. He had written to Lockyer (the coach) engaging him for this period at the same terms as previously £15 per week with 3rd class train and saloon boat Belfast London return.*

The Council decided at a later date that the visiting coach would attend Lurgan (11th April) Newcastle (18th April) and Limavady (25th April) and *that these clubs be asked to invite adjoining clubs to come and see him.* The coach for 1937 was a man called Collings (recommended by Davis Cup player Pat Hughes). He was to cost £12-12-0 per week plus travel from London and his expenses in travelling to three provincial centres.

Case Study

How does one climb up the coaching ladder? The routes are many and it does not necessarily follow that a good player makes a good coach. Certainly, a good player who has a good playing record is an asset not to be wasted. Some players, such as Davis Cup player Michael Hickey of Limerick, had a significant career travelling throughout the south of Ireland to schools and clubs passing on his know-how. The late John Horn, was junior Wimbledon champion in 1950. When he moved to Ireland in the mid-1950s he was a very accomplished player and added much to skills of Irish players over several decades.

The following is a summary of the coaching 'career' of Peter Lowther, a Belfast man who now resides in Dublin. His playing career has been extensive and is dealt with in chapter 6. Apart from club coaching, he has also acted as non-playing captain of both FED and Davis Cup teams. The selected C.V. speaks for itself.

Pete Lowther

1961	Born Belfast
1970	Took up tennis at Windsor LTC
1985	I.L.T.A. Elementary coaching certificate
1983-1987	Self-employed tennis professional at Belfast Boat Club
1985-1987	Ulster under 18 boys squad coach
1985-1986	Assist. Coach, nationwide tennis camp
1986-1991	Non-playing captain Ulster junior interprovincial teams
1987-1988	Chief Coach, Belfast Boat Club Easter tennis school
1987	S.L.T.A. Assistant Coaches Award
1987-1988	Scottish national under 16 boys squad coach
1987-1988	Post-graduate diploma in Professional studies (Sports Coaching)
1988	Scottish national junior squash coach, Surbiton LTC
1989	Irish national junior squad coach
1988-1991	Head Coach, Record Tennis Centre, Maidstone, England
1988-1991	Kent under 18 girls squad coach
1989	Attended World Coaches Conference.
1989-1992	Dale Farm School of Excellence, Ulster
1990	L.T.A. Professional Registration

1990,1993 & 2001	Non-playing captain, Irish senior team
1991	Attended World Coaches Conference.
1991-1993	Assistant Irish national coach
1991-1993	Non-playing captain, Men's European Team Championships
1992-2001	Non-playing captain, Women's European Team Championships
1995-2001	Non-playing captain, FED Cup team
2000	Non-playing captain, Davis Cup team
2002	Currently, Club coach, Templeogue LTC & in charge of coach education for Tennis Ireland

Peter is not the only coach with wide experience in Ireland. He is on the committee of the Tennis Ireland Coaches Association (TICA). A continuous professional development programme is in progress. In November 2001 Tennis Ireland acquired the services of Belgian coach, Ivo Van Aken, the man who guided Belgium to their first win in the FED Cup in Madrid that year. His efforts could only be temporary.

Roger Geraghty, another coach of note, has been in this career for about a quarter of a century. He makes some pertinent notes on the way things have changed. The preparation of coaches has certainly changed dramatically, only in a positive way to producing many quality players in all categories.

The old elementary focused mainly on technique and a little bit of tactics. The course nowadays incorporate the physical, mental, tactical and technique components of the game into programmes from the very first level.

Today on our first level, the candidates receive a course manual and annual training manuals for various age groups. ....our modern coaching system is a more co-operative approach as opposed to the old direct approach. This approach involves pupils in their own learning through guided discovery.

The 2001 Yearbook included a listing of 'coaches' at various grades as follows:

Tutors:	13
Registered Coaches	
Performance (Level 3)	23
Old Level 3	1
Advanced (Level 2)	31
Development (Level 1)	62
Assistant (level 0)	20

Some idea of the growth in coaching numbers can be obtained from the following graph which is based upon ILTA data.

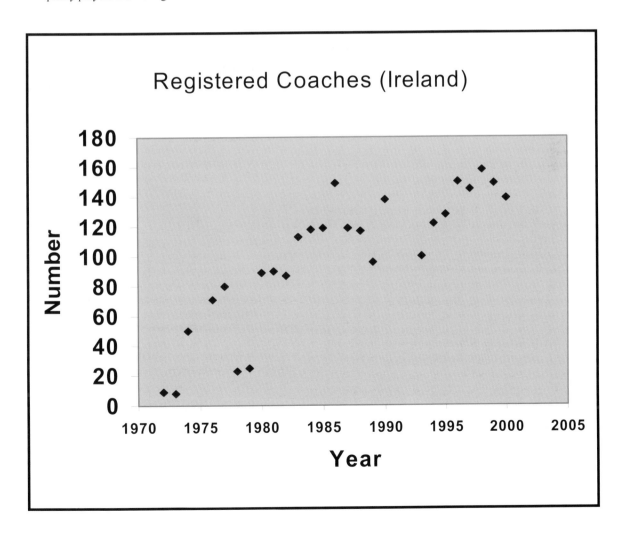

Castleknock College Junior II team with coach in 1996. Back (l. to r.) Mark Tobin, Aidan Bradshaw (coach) Simon Plunkett. Front (l. to r.) Brian MacCann, Barry McLoughlin & Ian McDevitt.

Coaches Remembered

Ask any experienced player who coached them and one of three answers, or combinations, are usual. Some players swear that they never received any coaching and their game was fully learned by observation and playing experience itself. This is probably true of many in past times when coaches were a rare entity on the ground. Nevertheless, these same players probably received 'tips' from their parents or other club members.

In the 1890s a number of 'professionals' were scattered throughout the tennis world. They may have been attached to a club, or their work may have been freelance in nature. Players too were involved in coaching on a more informal basis. Harold Mahony, the Irish (1898) and English (1896) Champion was one of these. He had the talent, the charm and the looks. One of his 'pupils' was Charlotte *(Chattie)* Cooper who would win the Irish and English (Wimbledon) titles. As a pair they won the Irish Mixed Championships (1895 & 1896). Chattie was quoted as saying the following:

Harold took me in hand. I used to ask him what was I doing wrong. He would show me and I would go home and try for hours in front of the looking glass to do what he told me. He was a wonderful teacher. He showed me all sorts of tactics; where to play a ball, using a little drop shot: "Always smash at a woman's feet", he would say.

According to O' Connor (1977), he also coached Anthony Wilding of New Zealand who attended Cambridge University in the early years of the 20th century. In 1904, they met in the second round at Wimbledon. Mahony was 37 at the time but was able to beat the 21-year-old in four sets (4/6 6/4 11/9 6/1). Just over a year later Mahony was killed when he fell of his bicycle in County Kerry. Wilding went on to win the Australian Open twice (1906 & 1909) and Wimbledon

four times (1910, 1911, 1912 & 1913). He too died young. At 31 years of age, he was killed in Belgium during the Great War.

An interesting fact about Mahony was that, despite being held in high regard as a teacher, he found it impossible to cure his own forehand, considered the 'worst' in first-class tennis. He would call up his friends saying that he had found the secret, and then the following day have a stroke *as ghastly as ever.* He was continually running around his forehand so that he could play it on the backhand side.

There is no doubt there are many cases where coaches have been the difference between a player sticking with the game, and possibly thriving on it later. John Pius Boland, the Dublin man, was one such case. For part of his education he attended the Oratory School in Birmingham. In an obituary for Father Edward Pereira in the 1939 school magazine Boland included this tribute: *But it was in lawn tennis that I was fortunate to have his coaching. It was my last year at school, reading for the London B.A. There was one half-hour in the week when I was given free time whilst the other boys were in class. Then it was that Eduard* (sic) *played singles with me, coached me, and laid down the foundation which was so useful for my game when, later, I played lawn tennis for Ireland in the first Olympic Games at Athens in 1896.*

Also in *The Oratory School Magazine* he discusses his brother Patrick's wedding to Norah O' Byrne. This took place in 1895 at St. Jean de Luz in the South of France. The town is on the Atlantic a few miles from the Spanish border. During their time there, they made many trips across the border to nearby San Sebastian. There they had *excellent practice* on the hard courts of the local club. The sessions included John Pius himself, Patrick, Eddie O' Byrne (brother of the bride), Ramon Olazabal and Jose Joachim Olazabal. That winter there was no tennis in Bonn where he was a student, it being a grass court game there. However, his preparation in the north of Spain did certainly help.

Some have received coaching perhaps 'once' or 'twice'. This was probably when a player was a teenager or young athlete and a coach visited the school or club. Gerry Clarke remembers being coached by a visiting American Hank Quinn who was in Dublin in 1948. *He claimed to have initiated group coaching and said that he was only the second best coach in the world! I got six lessons privately @ £1-10-0 during his 2 weeks post-Wimbledon visit to Dublin.* Gerry himself did pass the Intermediate Coaching Certificate programme but found himself too busy with playing and administration to put his skills into use. He makes an interesting comment that many will fully understand, and others might learn from watching. *Best tennis education was going to Wimbledon every day in 1951 (standing every second day). I learned more about strategy and tactics by watching than in the rest of my life!*

Angela Horn, coach and wife of the late John, was coached by Basil Bourne-Newton, the Sussex County coach. She herself became a qualified coach a few years later. John Horn was coached by Herbert Brown,

Specialised coaching for some top Irish juniors with top players/coaches (Circa 1996). From left Jeremy Bates, Colin O'Brien, James Colhoun, Catherine Lynch, Catherine Leonard & Jo Durie.

between 1941 and 1947, and then Dan Maskell. John and Angela Horn became Irish residents and coached many of our players to new heights. These included Jimmy McDonagh, the present coach at **Fitzwilliam LTC**, Bernie Griffith, the Federation Cup player, Mary Bryan (nee O' Sullivan) the international badminton and tennis player and Geraldine Barniville, one of Ireland's most successful players ever.

Others to come under the influence of John were Olwyn Raftery, twice President of Tennis Ireland, and Lucy Warner Ryan, President of Limerick Lawn Tennis Club. Both were Galway girls who received his expert tuition on his annual visit to Threadneedle Road (**Galway LTC**). Franklyn Connellan, not well known outside his native Longford, can recall John's visits to his school in the early 1960s. The lessons worked as Franklyn's team at Gormanstown College won four Leinster Schools titles during that period. Helen Lennon, one of our tops ladies in the 1970s, and now a full-time coach, can remember her lessons with Eleanor Mc Fadden (nee O' Neill). Eleanor was a committed tennis player and one of our first lady coaches. A Mr. Kelly was mentioned as coaching both Des Keogh (at **Elm Park**) and by Nan Conner (a Munster interprovincial player in the 1950s). Dick Kelly was coach to Jean Russell, a member of **St. Anne's Waterford LTC**, and a Munster Vets interprovincial in recent years. Were there several Mr. Kelly's around, or is this the same man?

> ### BRILLIANT COACH FOR SLIGO.
> #### Y.M.C.A. Club's Initiative.
> Mr. R. J. Kelly, the coach attached to Dublin's premier Tennis Club, Norwood, is at present fulfilling a week's engagement at the Sligo Y.M.C.A. Club, where his services are now available. Norwood are this season's winners of Class 1 and Class 2 inter-Club competitions and runners-up in Class 3 and their present high position is due in no small measure to the system of Mr. Kelly's tuition. He has just completed a series of engagements at Dundalk, Ballina, and Castlebar, and comes with the highest recommendations from these clubs. His services should be particularly useful to the members of the Juvenile and Junior Sections of the Club, of which there are now a large number. Members desiring to avail of Mr. Kelly's services should not delay in making arrangements with him or with the Hon. Secretary or Captain of the Club.

The Sligo Independent & West of Ireland Telegraph 20th July 1940

Fathers have influenced young players such as Geraldine Houlihan (now Barniville) at **Birr LTC** and Matt Murphy. The latter grew up in the USA and was coached by Howard Kinsey at the California Tennis Club in San Francisco. However, a stronger memory was probably the tennis played with his father and the promise of *five dollars for the first set I ever won from him (That was a lot of money in those days-late thirties, early forties).*

Mothers too played their part. Anthea O' Donoghue, a Munster player for many years, and an international in the early 1970s, remembered her mother's assistance. Peggy Goodbody was no mean player. Also to help Anthea was that great Davis Cup player, Alan Haughton. *He was a very helpful adviser to me in my early years.* Both Haughton and Goodbody families are steeped in the history of the game and connected through marriage (see chapter 3.5).

Another Englishman to coach in Ireland in the 1950s was Mitchell Currie. He coached a number of Munster people and Tim Scannell, one of the tennis-playing brothers, benefited making the Munster schools team in 1958 and the University College Cork team later. Billy Burke, a member of **Merville LTC** in 1950, remembers him *coming to town* (Sligo) and doing a few days.

Hadassah Lord (nee Robinson) reached the Irish Open Girls Championship final in 1952 and won the title in 1953. She remembers with fondness her school PE teacher at Coleraine High School. Hermoine Chapman was to give special interest to those keen on tennis and both would clear the courts of snow for training session during the winter. Hadassah also remembers the lessons of Bill Rainey of Ballymena and the exhibition/coaching visit of Dan Maskell and Fred Perry in the period after the war.

In reading Alice Marble's life story (*Courting Danger, 1991*) we see the influence of a coach in a dramatic fashion. From an early age Eleanor (*Teach*) Tennant take the young Alice on board. This was the 1930s. Alice became US champion four times and won Wimbledon in 1939. Alice's life story is an incredible read, from rape to car crashes, from singing to extreme ill health, and from coaching the top film stars to spying during the Second World War. Students of tennis history will know that Alice became the first serve and volleyer among lady players. In 1933 Teach brought Alice up to a mountaintop estate in Montecito, near Santa Barbara. There she received further coaching from Harwood "Beese" White. This man changed her game. *Beese made sure I was always overmatched by making me play with his male students, a lesson in humility as well as a stroke-builder. I soon preferred practicing with men, and later arranged to have male hitting partners at all my tournaments.* As Wimbledon champion, Alice arrived to play the Irish Championships in 1939 and sought out good male opposition. It was later thought that the top few players declined. However, Cyril Kemp, in his early 20s at the time, was ranked 3 in 1938 and 5 in 1939, did play with Alice, and had his hand's full. An American newspaper a couple of years earlier had accurately stated that "Marble's Playing a Man's Game". Practice with the American visitor did no harm to 24-year-old Kemp. He

went on to win the Irish Championships three times (1940, 1941 & 1950) and was the number one Irish player from 1941 to 1951.

Alice's coach Teach Tennant next brought the young Maureen Connolly to world fame in the early 1950s, a lady who would win many titles, including the Irish and All-England championships. In the mean time Alice herself became a professional (in 1941) player, and coached many top players over the years, including the great young Billie Jean King. There is one other minor Irish connection with Alice Marble. In 1933 Alice and Teach stayed at the 'castle' of William Randolph Heart, the multi-millionaire who lived near Monterey in California. There they played with and coached the stars, and enjoyed extreme luxury. Alice was about 20 at the time. At one special dinner party, George Bernard Shaw was the surprise dinner partner for Alice. Heart knew that Alice, a lady with a photograph memory, had written a thesis on Shaw at the University of California. Afterwards, Tech asked Alice what did they talk about? " I knew the names and characters of every one of his plays, so I talked about his work, and he talked about himself. He was a delightful old coot, but so egotistical" was her reply.

Coach Bradley

Gordon Bradley, visited Ulster in the later 1950s and spent a couple of months, based at **Cavehill LTC**. A press article at the time pointed out the benefits of having a full-time qualified LTA coach in the province. *Gordon, who is "stationed" once again at the Cavehill Club, Belfast, has added to the pleasure of many players....* and been *able to work wonders in a very short time.*

He's quick to spot the errors, no matter how elementary or complex-and, with equal speed, sorts them out. His visits to Ulster, he finds, are busy, a lover of tennis as well as a teacher of it, he doesn't mind whether the pupil is only a casual player anxious to improve his game, or one who counts himself a "duffer" of the lowest order. Or, indeed, one who appears to be on the way to the country's highest honours-an accomplished player, with few faults, with tactics rather than strokes to concentrate upon.

Ulster Davis Cup player, Peter Jackson, does remember receiving such coaching from Gordon. He, however, did not just consider the game as of benefit just to himself. In 1956, at the age of 21, he received his 'Proficiency Certificate' following a course for coaches. In *Ireland's Saturday Night* (4th May 1957), in an article with a heading "Peter Jackson Goes to Work", it was noted that Peter happily put his know-how to good use:

Salute in tennis this week goes to Peter Jackson, the young Cavehill and Ulster star. For Peter, interrupting his own training, has taken upon himself the task of coaching members of the club's newly formed Junior Section.

Mostly, the lengthy sessions are confined to Saturday mornings, with Peter, who is a qualified amateur coach, as "the boss".

It wasn't surprising to learn that the Juniors list had to be closed with the total at 74-and no shock either when Peter told me: "I'm swamped for practically every session".

To many people, coaching is a dull job. What does Peter think? "It's a lot more fun than I used to think it could possibly be," he said. "Naturally, I hope there'll be some promising future stars-I've several very promising young players-but even if we don't find any, then it's good to know that, with proper strokes, they'll enjoy their tennis a lot more in all the years ahead".

COACHING YOUNG PLAYERS

THE STANDARD OF TENNIS in the country has improved beyond measure in the last few years. Of particular importance is the increasing interest in the game among juniors in the North-West, where there are many promising young players.

These young players could not have better examples than Hadassah Robinson (Coleraine High School), who was Ulster and Irish girls' champion in 1953, Roy Thornton, Ulster boys' champion in 1953, Ian Wilson, Ulster boys' champion in 1954, and John Haldane, the present Ulster boys' champion.

That all the boys named came from Coleraine Academical Institution reflects great credit on the school, and also on Miss H. Chapman (Portrush), who coached both them and Miss Robinson.

It was mainly through the efforts of Miss Chapman and Roy Thornton that tennis was introduced at Coleraine Inst. in 1953.
Miss Chapman has a great interest in the progress of young players, and spends a great part of her time correcting their faults.

COULD MAKE GOOD

In the recent coaching courses organised by the Ulster Council of the I.L.T.A., Miss Chapman visited Derry and Bellaghy, and, in these areas, she says, there are many boys and girls who, if given a chance, could make good.

Besides these organised courses, Miss Chapman has her own pupils in Coleraine whom she coaches regularly.

She never boasts about her pupils, but prefers to let tournament results tell their own story.

And they do tell their story—four Ulster Junior champions in three seasons, and one of these also Irish Junior champion—an impressive record.

1955 Newspaper Article on Coaching

In a small newspaper item in 1953, Peter's own training was highlighted. This was the season after he had played for both the Ulster junior and senior sides in the interprovincials. *Eighteen year-old schoolboy Peter Jackson, ranked among the top six tennis players in Ulster, has worked out his own training plan for success this season-with the aid of two cardboard boxes. As soon as dusk falls, he takes a vacant court-his club is just at the back of his house-turns on the clubhouse lights and gets to work. And hard work it is. A box is planted in each service court and, with a dozen balls, he smashes down his services at these improvised targets.*

Some players never had any coaching. These include Leinster Joe Flood and Gerry More O' Farrell, both noted contributors to the administration of the Irish game. Willie Brown, a soccer international of note, played first class tennis for **Elm Park**. His own tennis regret, and that of many others, is of *not being coached early in life*. Mind you he did well and became an interprovicial player.

For quite a number of years Irish players have received coaching in the USA under student scholarships. An unusual recent case is that of the young Rachel Dillon of Donnybrook. In 2000 *I changed house, I changed school, I changed language, I changed tennis coach and I changed country in one week.* As followers of the game will know, Isabelle Demongeot, that famous tennis star from France, spotted Rachel's talent at eleven years of age. The family have given up much but Rachel now lives and is coached in France. In 2005, Rachel's success had elevated her into the top group of Irish senior players.

On the home front, coaching has become extensive and the standards are rising rapidly. In October 2002, the first National Coach of the Year was awarded. The recipient was Tagdh Lambe who is now associated with **Limerick Lawn Tennis Club**. A full time professional, who is also a qualified squash coach, is leaving his mark in many areas. There are many others and they too will be recognised in time. As long as the players receiving the coaching appreciate, enjoy and value the game, then it will all be worth the effort.

Owen Casey-International player manager and coach

The following are some of the full-time coaches currently employed by clubs in this country:

Brookfield LTC:	Rachel McDonogh
Carrickmines Croquet & LTC	Pat Crowe
Fitzwilliam LTC	Jimmy McDonogh
Limerick Lawn Tennis Club	Tadgh Lambe
Riverview David Lloyd Centre	Aled Jones
Templeogue LTC	Peter Lowther
Westwood-Clontarf	Larry Jurovich
Westwood-Leopardstown	Kevin Cochrane

Today a coach is more than just a good player with coaching skills. David Fassbender (**Fitzwilliam LTC**) said in 1998: *The right personality and organisational skills to increase tennis and squash activity would be the key features rather than being a top class player or coach.*

This is a far cry from the days of the professional player who went out and played with a club member on a one to one basis. The demands today are certainly more extensive.

David Miley has a family steeped in tennis history. Not alone did he become a top player but also a coach and administrator. In recent years he has been one of the chief coaching personnel at the International Tennis Federation, with many technical manuals to his name.

Publications

Today there are many books and manuals to read and use as a coaching aid for both players and the coaches themselves. James Cecil Parke, probably the best Irish player of the 20th century wrote one of the earliest books on the subject. It can be found in the Wimbledon Library.

Currently, Ireland's David Miley is the Executive Director of Tennis Development for the International Tennis Federation (ITF). Based in London, since 1991 he has travelled to some 120 countries on behalf of the ITF. He has co-authored many of the ITF's coach education publications including: the ITF Advanced Coaches Manual, the ITF School Tennis Initiative Teachers Manual, the ITF's "Being a Better Tennis Parent" and the ITF Competitions Formats Manual. In 1993 he established the ITF Coaching and Sports Science Review. This is a quarterly tennis specific sports science journal read by 17,000 coaches worldwide. He chaired the ITF's task force committee set up to develop a new world rating system. This was launched at the Australian Open in 2003.

The first Irish coaching manual. The author James Cecil Parke from Monaghan was the top Irish player before the Great War and ranked among the best in the world.

Jim Parke (Irish champion, 8 times in period 1904-1913) played tennis in the days when there were no one minute rest periods and once claimed that a long five set tennis match as tougher than a rugby match. He said:

I liked nothing better than chasing impossible balls, and there is an extraordinary satisfaction in making your point off a ball which your opponent is counting as a winner. It pays, too, for it rattles and worries him, and forces him into trying to accomplish more than he is able; but you need to be in tip-top physical condition if you are going to do it successfully.

He wrote the first Irish coaching manual in the 1920s and was, at that time, one of the most travelled, experienced and successful of Irish players. In the 1927 Fitzwilliam LTC history he had an article that included the following.

I have always regretted that my Tennis period came too late for me to see and meet those earlier giants of the game-Pim, Hamilton, Mahony, the Chaytors, and others who made Ireland famous in the nineteenth century. In one sense I was lucky in that I won the Irish Championship years before I could have hoped to do so if any of the players named had been to the fore; but, on the other hand, I lost infinitely more through not being able to watch and study their styles and improve my own game by playing against them.

For years I was in a rut, wanting the impetus of better players to practice against; and it was not until I had six weeks steady practice in Australia, in 1912, with the other members of the Davis Cup that I made any marked advance. In that short time my game improved by almost half thirty, and I believe that other players could make an equal advance under similar circumstances.

I am a strong advocate of practice in contrast to tournaments as a means of improvement, and I would even go to the length of saying that a continuous programme of tournaments is enough to benumb ['burnout'] anyone's game. If you take any of the present English players who indulge in a yearly round of tournament play you will see that they stick in the same dull old groove, certainly getting no better and probably growing steadily worse, whereas the French boys, who believe in practice, and study the why and wherefore of their shortcomings, have conquered the Tennis world at ages when our boys are only beginning to show signs of promise.

Past Lessons

Today, the game of tennis seems to be primarily originating at the base-line. Lovers of the grass court, and the serve-volley game, as this writer is, sometimes get bored of the lengthy rallies of marathon proportions, which is the nature of the game on slow courts. This issue was brought to the attention of the tennis followers in Ireland over 100 hundred years ago (below) The thoughts of the writer appear to indicate that, even then, when tennis was a baby, the matters were worthy of debate. If nothing else, the words of the writer are worth recording here. They may make us think and consider that there is always a valid opinion opposite to that of our own. The lessons of that time are equally valid over a century later. Let the coach and player ponder and decide their best options.

The Evolution of Tennis
(Irish Lawn Tennis Handbook, 1894)

Few games have undergone more frequent and sweeping changes in proportion to their years than the game which was originally introduced to the world under the classical but unattractive name of Spharistike. With the infancy of lawn tennis was associated neither the volley nor the smash, the former of which has twice since almost threatened to supersede the long low drive, itself the successor of an earlier form-the primitive lob of the late seventies. It is common knowledge that it is to Mr. W. Renshaw we owe the perfect development of the modern volley. Against such a brilliant forcing game as the ex-champion and hi brother, Ernest, played, the adherents of the older method found themselves at a considerable disadvantage. It seemed for a time, indeed, as if the ground stroke would become almost extinct in first-class tennis,

---

and it possibly to the wonderful skill and perseverance with which Mr. Lawford worked up this department of the game that (more even than to the lowering of the net, by which, alone, passing the volleyer with side line drives, was rendered feasible) the continued recognition of its good qualities is in the main due. By successive victories over masters of the game as E. Renshaw and E. de S. Browne-victories in several cases, if we remember alright, "achieved exclusively with ground strokes", if an occasional smash be excepted-Mr. Lawford showed that indiscriminate reliance upon the volley might prove fatal, when the man at the other side of the net was one who could unite consummate placing with severity and lowness of return. For a while even the ground stroke recovered its popularity so far as to take a slight lead of the volley, and then came the period when two distinct styles of play were tried in the same match-the defence, in which the player, if he did not rely chiefly upon back play, waited for a weak return before running into the net; and the forcing game, the prime feature of which consisted in following up the first serve on the chance of its being inefficiently returned by the stroker-out, when the server would have an opening for a smash or a volley placed beyond the reach of his adversary. Last season, however, the forcing game seemed, by consent, among nearly all the experts, to be regarded as the only one worth playing, and players no longer hesitated to run in even on a moderate second serve; in fact the object both server and striker-out seemed to have placed was in every case to get to the net at the earliest possible moment. It may easily be imagined that the consequences of this recklessness were in many cases disastrous to the players and disappointing to the spectators. Nevertheless, so far, apparently, were the players from recognising the defects of this policy that down to the last two days of the Wimbledon meeting it gained a steadily increasing esteem. On both these occasions, however, Mr. Pim, and, on the second, Mr. W. Baddeley, proved, to the satisfaction of the spectators at least, that the old reliable stroke from the base line was not only not played out, but that in the hands of a skilful pace and pace-maker it would oftener than not be found more serviceable, through the volleyer being "passed" at the net, and less fatiguing than the volley. It may be hoped that the proofs then afforded of the excellence of judicious alterations between the volley and the ground stroke will have rendered impossible the continued vogue of the new game, which, to its other drawbacks, has added a severe strain upon the physical powers of the contestants.

Sir William Orphen, the artist and writer, lived through the tennis scene in the late 19th century. He included pen pictures of life in Ireland at that time (*Stories of Old Ireland & Myself,* 1925), in which tennis got a few mentions. One relates to world champion professional from Fitzwilliam LTC (see chapters 5 and 6 for further details) and the other the professional at Lansdowne LTC. Don't forget that a professional/coach at that time was an employee and not probably not of social standing. He was a paid skilled racquet player and could receive the admonishment of club members.

> *Lawn tennis was the great game in Ireland at that time, and proud we were; and why not? Wasn't George Kerr the professional at the Fitz-William Club, champion of the world, and wasn't Burke of the Lansdowne Club the greatest player in the world? Kerr would never play Burke level, but would always insist on owing him half fifteen, and was always beaten comfortably. But in those days professionals were not treated with that respect with which they are now. One summer evening of 1895 or '96, about eight o'clock, some nice Dublin gentleman walked into the club and sent for Burke to play him a game. Burke came along and played him; but he was not in his best form, as he had been spending the latter part of the evening with some friends, and had "had a few," thinking his day's work was over. The "gentleman" reported him, and Burke was "sacked." He, the greatest player in the world at that time, and in receipt of 30s. a week pay, was "sacked"! That was why Burke left Ireland (and Irish lawn tennis declined). He was immediately taken up by Count X., who installed him at Cannes, and from that day he had a most successful career, well known and respected all over France, North and South, from Cannes, and all over the Cote-d'Azur to Deauville, where he died in 1921. A very well-to-do gentleman, and his sons are carrying on in his stead.*

Coaching is widespread today with very many players taking up coaching on a part-time or full-time basis. This is an essential step in ensuring that we put the skills of the sport on the right footing. We do have to be careful that all our players are not clones off an identical blueprint. It is unlikely as the Irish personality has thrived in its variety. We just hope that in the not too distant future some of our juniors players do make the grade in the bigger professional world. In that way the game will get its greatest boost ever. Keep up the work coaches, every player that learns the game has a skill for a lifetime, irrespective of whether the game becomes an interesting pastime or serious sport to them.

Junior coaching at Sligo Tennis Club (Circa 1985). In foreground (l. to r.): David Gilleece, Trudy Higgins and Enda Gallagher.

Michael Creighton was responsible for much of the junior success at Mullingar TC from the 1960s to the 1990s.

Tennis

PREPARATION OF IRISH TEAMS FAR FROM SATISFACTORY

IT SEEMS to be about time that a long hard look was taken at the Irish Lawn Tennis Association — its structure and the rather antiquated rules under which it continues to operate. It might well be asked how many copies of the rules are in circulation.

The structure of the I.L.T.A. is rather undemocratic in that the affairs of the Association are administered by delegates from the four provinces and the ordinary players — who in fact are the Association, cannot attend the rather mysterious meetings. Fair enough, say I, to exclude non delegates from Council meetings— but that there should not be an Annual General Meeting which any player could attend and see justice being oden seems odd.

— By —

VERA McWEENEY

The officials to whom I have spoken say that the Provinces have their own general meetings at which grievances may be aired and that such complaints may be debated at the Irish meeting if the Provincial delegates raise these matters. However — it is fairly stunning to hear that delegates usually are not given directives by their provincial councils on matters at issue but may vote as individuals.

It is not this aspect that concerns me at the moment but the manner in which Irish representative teams are chosen at present. Did many people know, I wonder, that the Irish Team for our ill fated foray into the 1974 Davis Cup competition was chosen (or at least some of the players were notified) on a Friday and the team left for Lisbon on the following Monday?

How much interest was taken in these trials? Were umpires and linesmen provided officially? Were Davis Cup match conditions stimulated at all? I must answer this with a colloquialism: "You must be joking!!"

The Federation Cup team preparation is faring no better. All the practice that has been done, and the players have really worked at their tennis, has been arranged by themselves. No trials were arranged until it was suggested by Mrs. Barniville that time was getting on and something should be done.

The Irish Times-1974

SPORTSMIX

By JOHN O'SHEA

12   EVENING PRESS, TUESDAY, APRIL 23, 1974

Whither Tennis?

WHITHER Irish Tennis? After yet another shattering, if predictable defeat at the hands of Portugal, it's imperative that those people who claim responsibility for the furtherance of the game in this country wake up to a few facts.

Firstly, there's no point in competing in a highly professional event such as the Davis Cup if we continue to adopt an ultra-amateurish approach. It's outlandish to think that the captain of the side was not appointed until a few days before the departure.

Secondly, and more important it must be clear by now to all who are even remotely interested in the game's development here, that we will NEVER have a chance of distinguishing ourselves in the Davis Cup, until we have players with 'circuit' experience.

It's a sad fact that we are one of the few nations who have no male player competing on the world's circuits. It's by playing on these circuits with and against the best players in the game, that a player gains the opportunity to fulfil his potential.

It's encouraging that in Sean Sorensen and Declan Heavey we have two players keen to make tennis their life. But they must get support.

This pair, along with Niamh Glenn, another promising player are seeking financial assistance to play on the European tour.

I'm convinced the ILTA should row in and allocate a portion of the Government grant to this trio.

Nothing is more sure, that until our top players get the chance to play 'in the big time,' we may as well throw our hat at competing in the Davis Cup and such competitions.

Federation Cup side

Despite the fact that the Irish Lawn Tennis Association have kept their plans a secret (at least from the Press), I gather (from some of the players) that the three-member Federation Cup side, will have a 'warm up' tournament in Florence from May 4-11.

Trials have been staged during the past few weeks and the team is likely to shape up something like this : Geraldine Barniville, Susan Minford and Helen Lennon or Niamh Glenn.

Susan Minford did not take part in the trials as she is at present competing on the U.S. circuit.

● Geraldine Barniville

Reporting by John O'Shea-No punches pulled.

Coaching For Young Tennis Talent

By a Special Correspondent

THE Ulster Council of the Irish L.T.A. will make every effort this season to find fresh talent. Every schoolboy and schoolgirl in the nine counties will have the chance of official coaching if they show promise.

It is hoped to thrash out all plans for the new season when the annual meeting of the Ulster Council takes place on Wednesday.

There will be difficulties in the way of a full return to pre-war conditions, but Mr. de V. Crossley, the secretary, tells me that, despite the late start, the Council will give all the aid in their power to clubs which show enterprise, and particularly in the matter of fostering the youngsters, from whom it is hoped to build up a team to hold its own with the southern counties.

Every effort has been made to find a first-class coach for this year, but so far without avail. Anyone who can help in this matter will be warmly welcomed.

The pre-war practice was to have a registered L.T.A. coach from England, but he had to be booked a year in advance, and the sudden end to hostilities left the Ulster Council without one for this year.

Post-War Coaching for Juniors in Ulster worked. In 1952 Cecil Pedlow won the Irish Boy's title and in 1953 Hazassah Robinson became the first Ulster girl to win the Irish Girl's title.

John Horn (left) and Donal Dempsey were sadly lost to tennis in recent years. They both left legacies behind them. John, junior Wimbledon champion in 1950, was a full-time professional and coached throughout Ireland from the 1950s to the 1990s. Donal was 'Mr. Tennis' in Connacht for nearly four decades. In 1996 (above) they won the Open veteran's doubles title at Galway LTC.

Mick Branagan and his coaching charges at Clontarf LTC over twenty years ago. Where are they now? Back row: M. McGreevy, C. O' Connor, M. McGreevy, Anne O'Gara, Cormac Kelly, Yvonne Leonard, Clodagh O'Gara, Anne Murray, Maurice & Anne Marie Farnan, Margaret Noonan, Pat Monaghan & Breda Noonan. Front: Aisling O'Gara, Lizzie Owens, Mary Palmer, Marion Ryan and Anna Palmer.

International star Roscoe Tanner (USA) in dark shirt with coach Pat Crowe (at Carrickmines Croquet and Lawn Tennis Club) and many promising juniors.